PROSPECT HANDBOOK

2002

Durham, N.C.

PUBLISHED BY
Baseball America Inc.

EDITORS
Jim Callis, Will Lingo

ASSOCIATE EDITORS
Allan Simpson, Josh Boyd

CONTRIBUTING WRITERS
Bill Ballew, Mike Berardino, Pat Caputo, Gerry Fraley,
Chris Haft, Tom Haudricourt, Jim Ingraham,
Michael Levesque, John Manuel, John Perrotto,
Tracy Ringolsby, Phil Rogers, Casey Tefertiller

EDITORIAL ASSISTANTS
Blair Lovern, Gary Martin, Matt Potter

PRODUCTION
Phillip Daquila, Matthew Eddy, Linwood Webb

STATISTICAL CONSULTANT
SportsTicker
Boston

COVER PHOTO
Josh Beckett by Ken Babbitt

BaseBall america

President: Catherine Silver
Publisher: Lee Folger
Editor: Allan Simpson
Managing Editor: Will Lingo
Executive Editor: Jim Callis
Design & Production Director: Phillip Daquila

baseballamerica.com

Contents

Foreword

None of us can explain why the future so fascinates us, why we want to know if Mark Prior really could be Roger Clemens or Wilson Betemit is the next great Braves prospect. We just do. And since before players like Prior or Betemit were born, Allan Simpson and Baseball America, which just celebrated its 20th Anniversary, have been the site to see if one cares about every floor of this high-rise complex of baseball.

What has made Baseball America so successful all these years is that it allows you to trace a player from his American Legion roots all the way to the major leagues. Scouting directors, crosscheckers and executives on all levels of the baseball business have long acknowledged that the publication's coverage of the amateur draft—taken to a new level by Baseball America's remarkable Website (baseballamerica.com)—is revered as an integral part of the draft itself. Executives, news services and fans have long waited with expectation for the late summer's minor league prospect lists, followed by the winter's organization Top 10 Prospects projections.

After creating the Super Register—far and away the more comprehensive register of professional talent ever assembled—Baseball America produced its first Prospect Handbook last year. It has already become a bible of its kind, for fans of a particular team who want to home in on what players to follow through the season, but also for those interested in those players who are mentioned in or actually traded in pennant race deals. You can survey organization overviews, get an in-depth look at their drafts, and look back on each team's top prospects of the last 10 years and wonder what would have happened had Frank Rodriguez played shortstop.

Others have attempted forms of minor league scouting publications. Now that Baseball America has established the Prospect Handbook, and in fact improved it already by adding more to each team's report, we realize that they're the only ones who could really get it right.

Peter Gammons
ESPN

Introduction

We didn't really understand the phrase "labor of love" until we started assembling the first Prospect Handbook last year. Baseball America is best known for two things: draft coverage and prospect analysis. So it was only natural that we would publish the ultimate prospect guide. We didn't want to do it, though, until we were sure we could produce the best one available.

We already had been assembling Top 10 Prospects lists since the magazine's beginnings in 1981. Allan Simpson, BA's editor and founder, started the magazine then because he couldn't find the kind of baseball information he wanted. And looking deep into the minor leagues for the best up-and-coming players was an essential part of that information.

But going from 10 players on 30 teams, spread over six issues of the magazine, to 30 players for 30 teams, all in one volume that needed to be out in time for spring training, ended up being more work than we thought. The sheer density of the information in the Prospect Handbook is hard to fathom. Just take a look at one of the prospect reports. You won't see a lot of fat there. And there are 900 of those. And two pages of in-depth information on each organization. And a page of draft analysis for every team. If we knew then what we know now . . . Well, of course we'd do it all again.

At the end of this project, as we proofread the final pages and add in those last little bits of information—we got So Taguchi's complete Japanese stats!—the excitement about how good the book has turned out again far outstrips the relief at the project being done. We have no doubt this is the best prospect book you can read. We know the work that went into it. We talked to the general managers, scouting directors, farm directors, scouts, managers, coaches, agents and anyone else we could find. We know we'll read excerpts from these reports in other media sources in the coming months, and we don't care. As long as you know where it came from (and you tell a friend), that's satisfaction enough for us.

And this is not the labor of just a few people. A large collection of fanatics put in hundreds of hours of work to make the book what it is. In addition to those of us on the editorial staff, our crack production team deserves special credit for continuing to make Baseball America look better than ever. And our correspondents have been the lifeblood of BA since the beginning. If you haven't already, take a moment to review the title page of the book and the names of all the people who worked so hard.

A couple of items of housekeeping: We define a prospect as anyone who is still rookie-eligible under Major League Baseball's guidelines (no more than 50 innings pitched or 130 at-bats), without regard to service time. And players are listed with the organizations they were with as of January 25. So Carlos Pena is the top prospect in Athletics system, not the Rangers. If you have any doubt how to find a player, just use the handy index.

So start turning the pages and enjoying the fruits of our labor. Again, we think it's the best, most complete book on prospects ever assembled. But we're already trying to come up with ways to make it even better for 2003.

Will Lingo
Managing Editor

TalentRanking

I n an effort to put this whole exercise of presenting top 30 players in every organization in perspective, first we bring you the top 30 organizations, in order. Among other things, we hope this shows that not all top 30 lists are created equal: the No. 23 player in the Cubs organization might be of better quality than the No. 23 player in another organization because he has more talent around him to compete with. The organization rankings are a blend of our judgment of the quality and quantity of talent in each system. We favor organizations that have a better share of high-ceiling prospects and/or a deep system, with the highest marks going to those that have both. Rankings are by the Baseball America staff, and the team capsules were written by Josh Boyd.

1. Chicago Cubs. The Cubs already were loaded a year ago when they came in a close second to their crosstown rivals on this list. They took the final step to the top after beefing up through the draft and the international market. Juan Cruz went to the majors and showed overpowering stuff, and he'd be the top prospect in most organizations, but 2001 first-rounder Mark Prior holds that distinction. The system has no glaring holes, and even injuries to six members of last year's Top 10 Prospects list couldn't dim the organization's outlook.

2. Seattle Mariners. Ichiro Suzuki exceeded expectations and led the Mariners to a major league-record 116 wins, overshadowing a farm system filled with impact prospects. Ryan Anderson and Antonio Perez spent the season battling injuries but should be back at full strength. The system had several pleasant surprises including Matt Thornton, who looked like a first-round bust before leading the California League in strikeouts last year. Seattle addressed a need for lefthanded pitching and lacks only a corner-infield prospect.

3. Houston Astros. Though the Astros have drawn Richard Hidalgo, Lance Berkman, Wade Miller and Roy Oswalt from their deep well of talent in recent years, the farm system still has such talents as Tim Redding, Carlos Hernandez and Jason Lane on the cusp. The steady success of the organization on a mid-level budget earned Houston Baseball America's Organization of the Year award for 2001. The Astros' .598 minor league winning percentage was by far the best in baseball, and their Venezuelan pipeline continues to serve them well.

4. San Diego. No system in baseball can match the premium prospects the Padres have at the top of their organization, led by Sean Burroughs. Burroughs, Xavier Nady and Jake Gautreau are three of the minors' best pure hitting prospects, and righthanders Dennis Tankersley and Jake Peavy are also blue-chip talents. The talent isn't concentrated at one position, either. Their Top 15 features at least one prospect at every position except catcher.

5. New York Yankees. An overlooked effect of the Yankees' seemingly unlimited budget is their ability to outbid other teams for top international free agents. They have little to show for the more than $12 million they invested in Hideki Irabu, Chien-Ming Wang and Jackson Melian but haven't shied away from spending on unproven talent, and that's the main reason their pool of talent hasn't dried up. They could have a homegrown infield soon, if first baseman Nick Johnson and third baseman Drew Henson join Alfonso Soriano and Derek Jeter.

6. Minnesota Twins. The Twins' low-budget operation features a small but efficient corps of scouts who have done a remarkable job bringing in talent. Plugging No. 1 overall pick Joe Mauer into a system with Justin Morneau, Michael Cuddyer and Michael Restovich gives the organization four budding sluggers. The Twins think their efforts in Australia will yield results soon. A lack of premium athletes has left the Twins short up the middle, however.

7. Atlanta Braves. The Braves have remained near the top of Baseball America's rankings since the organization was rebuilt in the late 1980s, finishing No. 1 in 1992, '93, '95 and '99. Atlanta is known for developing pitching but also has delivered position players like Rafael Furcal to the big leagues, and its top prospect is shortstop Wilson Betemit. The focus on the mound hasn't disappeared, though, as 11 of their top 15 prospects are pitchers.

8. Texas Rangers. The Rangers rarely have relied on their farm system for major league talent in recent years. New general manager John Hart is continuing that approach with an open checkbook from owner Tom Hicks and a win-now approach that reflects the pressure they feel to win, and not a thin farm system. Hank Blalock will compete for a job in spring training, and Mario Ramos was acquired from the Athletics to battle for a spot in the rotation this year. Giving up Carlos Pena for Ramos and three other prospects was a gamble, but Texas added another impact bat in Mark Teixeira in the 2001 draft.

9. Chicago White Sox. Last year's top-rated farm system continued to feed a young White Sox roster. Eight players from last year's top 30 list made it to the big leagues, and Chicago included prospects in several trades, leaving the system a bit thinned out but not bare. The next wave should be led by a healthy Jon Rauch, the 2000 Minor League Player of the Year who missed most of last year after shoulder surgery, Joe Borchard and Corwin Malone.

10. Florida Marlins. Righthander Josh Beckett was the 2001 Minor League Player of the Year, and his September performance in Florida was a prelude to what could be a special career. The Marlins leaned on a young nucleus to make a run in the National League East last year, but injuries and inexperience led to a late-season fade. Most of the organization's best prospects reside in the lower levels and can't be counted on for a couple of years.

11. Philadelphia Phillies. No rookie was more instrumental in the Phillies' surprising 2001 season than shortstop Jimmy Rollins, but several young arms contributed as well. Now rising prospects like Marlon Byrd and Brett Myers provide even more hope for the future. Led by farm and scouting director Mike Arbuckle, the Phillies have made significant gains in Latin America after ignoring the region for years.

12. San Francisco Giants. No organization has improved its talent more in recent years than the Giants. They have injected the system with a stable of power arms, led by Jerome Williams, while polished righthander Kurt Ainsworth is ready to break into the big league rotation. The Giants developed two starting shortstops—Royce Clayton and Rich Aurilia—in the 1990s, but the system now lacks overall athleticism up the middle.

13. Toronto Blue Jays. After several years of drafting on a budget, the Blue Jays got more money in 2001 to draft the best prospects on the board. Talented outfielders Gabe Gross and Tyrell Godwin came aboard as a result. New GM J.P. Ricciardi was hired away from Oakland in part for his approach to development, which is expected to resemble his previous organization. Toronto has plenty of catching depth, but the top power arms are a few years away.

14. Cincinnati Reds. The Reds' prospect chart took a hit when Drew Henson was dealt back to the Yankees and Adam Dunn graduated to the majors in the midst of a 51-homer season. Many of the newcomers who helped the Reds soar to the No. 3 slot a year ago were disappointing in 2001. Unproven prospects Wily Mo Pena, David Espinosa and Dane Sardinha are locked into major league contracts, which may not give them the proper time to develop.

15. Tampa Bay Devil Rays. Since a careless spending spree in 1999 that did little good for the franchise, the Devil Rays have relied on their farm to fill holes in the big leagues. Sixteen players have debuted in Tampa Bay in the last two years. It hasn't left the system devoid of prospects, but the upper-level depth has taken a hit. They can't afford to have potential franchise player Josh Hamilton miss any more time due to injuries. Money concerns are growing and almost cost the Rays Dewon Brazelton, the No. 3 overall pick in 2001.

16. Montreal Expos. This isn't the same Expos system that was the envy of baseball for much of the 1980s and '90s. Instability and financial woes have depleted talent in the front office and on the field. Top prospect Brandon Phillips is the kind of player the Expos have scored with in the past, and several projectable lefthanders provide another bright spot.

17. Anaheim Angels. Scouting director Donny Rowland's first two drafts infused high-ceiling prospects into an organization that perennially ranked in the bottom third in minor league talent. After finishing dead last in minor league winning percentage in 2000, the Anaheim improved to .499 last year. While Rowland targets high-upside (and at times high-risk) prospects, the Angels are working toward a balanced system.

18. Detroit Tigers. The Tigers continue to make progress since their well ran dry a few years ago. The influence of new president Dave Dombrowski should be felt throughout the system. Last year's draft was the best in the game. Detroit is accumulating speed, defense and pitching to play to the spacious dimensions of Comerica Park.

19. Oakland Athletics. Oakland GM Billy Beane has traded seven of his top prospects since losing to the Yankees in the playoffs last fall. He had to move four to acquire first baseman Carlos Pena, who should step in and produce immediately in Jason Giambi's absence. The Athletics also lost director of player personnel J.P. Ricciardi to Toronto and scouting director Grady Fuson to Texas. After dealing Mario Ramos, the A's best hopes for another homegrown starter are a few years away.

20. Cleveland Indians. Outside of C.C. Sabathia, Ryan Drese and Tim Drew, the 1997-99 drafts did little to bring new talent into the system. As the Indians enter a new era under GM Mark Shapiro, they'll have to rely more on scouting and player development as they adopt a more cost-conscious approach. Last June's draft, especially righthanders Dan Denham and J.D. Martin, and the Roberto Alomar trade provided a needed infusion of talent.

21. Kansas City Royals. The Royals' financial constraints have been more pronounced than ever, as they've unloaded two of their most productive bats in Johnny Damon and Jermaine Dye since the end of the 2000 season. They haven't brought enough talent back to the organization in return, which led to a gambling philosophy in the 2001 draft. While first-rounder Colt Griffin and second-rounder Roscoe Crosby have high ceilings, they also are two of the riskier players drafted in the first two rounds.

22. Pittsburgh Pirates. Since topping the organization talent rankings in 1997, the Pirates have been on a steady decline. The story of lackluster performances and injuries to top prospects has become all too familiar, as Pittsburgh continued to draft high-risk players with good tools who too often haven't panned out. GM Cam Bonifay was fired and replaced by Dave Littlefield, who hired Ed Creech to help him right the ship. Their résumés include experience with organizations successful in scouting and player development.

23. Arizona Diamondbacks. Mike Rizzo has done a good job of finding talent to restock a depleted farm system since he became scouting director in 2000, but the organization's depth chart still is littered with underachieving prospects. The Diamondbacks have been successful at going outside traditional talent hotbeds to mine for prospects, and continue to show interest in Latin America and Australia. Of course, winning the World Series tends to draw attention away from a mediocre farm system.

24. Colorado Rockies. With the ugly Matt Harrington saga behind them, the Rockies' development philosophy has started to swing in favor of more advanced prospects. In the meantime, top prospect Chin-Hui Tsao missed the entire season after Tommy John surgery and Choo Freeman, the organization's former top prospect, faded in his second straight year in the high Class A Carolina League. GM Dan O'Dowd has executed a few deals to try to boost the organization's minor league depth.

25. Los Angeles Dodgers. New Dodgers GM Dan Evans was with the White Sox in 1997 and was instrumental in putting together the then-maligned White Flag trade, which helped turn the organization around. In much the same way, Evans is tearing down what he found in Los Angeles to rebuild a franchise that was in disarray when he arrived. The new staff includes Terry Collins, Bill Bavasi, John Boles, Kim Ng and Logan White, and they'll emphasize scouting and player development. One of the focal points will have to be developing hitters.

26. Milwaukee Brewers. Even under new management, the Brewers haven't figured out how to remedy the injuries that have plagued their young arms for years. Talented young pitchers Ben Sheets and Nick Neugebauer were knocked out by shoulder problems. As the Brewers' feast-or-famine offense led to a major league-record 1,399 strikeouts, top position-player prospects like Bill Hall show the same propensity for the whiff.

27. New York Mets. The Mets sacrificed what little upper-level talent they had left to acquire Roberto Alomar from the Indians. Aaron Heilman went straight to the top of the prospect list, dethroning outfielder Alex Escobar, who was shipped to Cleveland. Escobar's struggles to fulfill his potential speak to one of the organization's inability to develop hitters. Shortstop Jose Reyes' emergence was a bright spot in an overall dismal season, which began with the death of prospect Brian Cole in an automobile accident at the end of spring training.

28. Boston Red Sox. New Red Sox ownership inherits a system almost devoid of upper-level prospects. Much of the hopes have been pinned on raw, live arms who light up radar guns but haven't been tested against advanced hitters. Boston has invested heavily in the Far East but still has little to show at the major league level. The Red Sox haven't drafted strongly in recent years, further hurting the system.

29. Baltimore Orioles. Owner Peter Angelos' impatient approach has left the Orioles without direction as they enter the post-Cal Ripken era. Angelos vetoed several trades that could have helped the rebuilding process, and GM Syd Thrift has failed to instill confidence in the rest of the organization. Scouting director Tony DeMacio has brought in a good group of southpaws, but they haven't been able to stay healthy.

30. St. Louis Cardinals. The Cardinals system has done its job in recent years, providing plenty of fodder for trades and sending such players as J.D. Drew, Rick Ankiel, Albert Pujols and Bud Smith to St. Louis. But few prospects of the same caliber are on the horizon. Injuries have decimated the pitching depth, with Tommy John surgery hitting at least six pitchers in the organization.

Top50Prospects

Well, at least there's one thing we can all agree on: Josh Beckett is the top prospect in the game. Beyond that, though, opinions start to diverge quickly. Talking about prospects is one of our favorite things at Baseball America, as is making a list. So you don't have to ask anyone here twice to jot down a list of favorite prospects. We present four lists here—the personal favorites of the four people who oversee BA's prospect rankings—to give you a peek into the process.

Each editor brings his own preferences to the table, something that becomes evident right away this year. Beyond Beckett and top hitters Hank Blalock and Sean Burroughs, differences are clear. Even Mark Prior, who we all agree is a premium player, goes straight to No. 2 for Jim Callis or Allan Simpson, while Josh Boyd and Will Lingo want to wait until he throws a professional pitch.

This list is a snapshot, so it likely would change the next time one of us puts it together. From lists like these, we build a consensus list and massage it, then get more opinions from people in the game. It all leads up to the release of our annual Top 100 Prospects in early March, what we consider the best compilation of up-and-coming players in the game.

Josh Beckett   rhp, Marlins

Allan Simpson

1. Josh Beckett, rhp, Marlins
2. Mark Prior, rhp, Cubs
3. Sean Burroughs, 3b, Padres
4. Hank Blalock, 3b, Rangers
5. Wilson Betemit, ss, Braves
6. Ryan Anderson, lhp, Mariners
7. Juan Cruz, rhp, Cubs
8. Josh Hamilton, of, Devil Rays
9. Mark Teixeira, 3b, Rangers
10. Carlos Pena, 1b, Athletics
11. Joe Borchard, of, White Sox
12. Dennis Tankersley, rhp, Padres
13. Drew Henson, 3b, Yankees
14. Joe Mauer, c, Twins
15. Jon Rauch, rhp, White Sox
16. Nick Neugebauer, rhp, Brewers
17. Brandon Phillips, ss, Expos
18. Nick Johnson, 1b, Yankees
19. Austin Kearns, of, Reds
20. Ty Howington, lhp, Reds
21. Marlon Byrd, of, Phillies
22. Corwin Malone, lhp, White Sox
23. Jerome Williams, rhp, Giants
24. Adam Wainwright, rhp, Braves
25. Justin Morneau, 1b, Twins
26. Carlos Hernandez, lhp, Astros
27. Rafael Soriano, rhp, Mariners
28. Boof Bonser, rhp, Giants
29. Michael Cuddyer, 3b/of, Twins
30. Angel Berroa, ss, Royals
31. Miguel Cabrera, ss, Marlins
32. Nate Cornejo, rhp, Tigers
33. Brandon Claussen, lhp, Yankees
34. Adrian Gonzalez, 1b, Marlins
35. Casey Kotchman, 1b, Angels
36. Jake Peavy, rhp, Padres
37. Juan Rivera, of, Yankees
38. John Buck, c, Astros
39. Gavin Floyd, rhp, Phillies
40. Jose Reyes, ss, Mets
41. Brett Myers, rhp, Phillies
42. Dewon Brazelton, rhp, Devil Rays
43. J.R. House, c, Pirates
44. Mario Ramos, lhp, Rangers
45. Mike Jones, rhp, Brewers
46. Chris Burke, ss, Astros
47. Josh Phelps, c, Blue Jays
48. Jimmy Gobble, lhp, Royals
49. Jimmy Journell, rhp, Cardinals
50. Chris Snelling, of, Mariners

Will Lingo

1. Josh Beckett, rhp, Marlins
2. Sean Burroughs, 3b, Padres
3. Joe Borchard, of, White Sox
4. Hank Blalock, 3b, Rangers
5. Mark Prior, rhp, Cubs
6. Drew Henson, 3b, Yankees
7. Wilson Betemit, ss, Braves
8. Jerome Williams, rhp, Giants
9. Joe Mauer, c, Twins
10. Austin Kearns, of, Reds
11. Brandon Phillips, ss, Expos
12. Carlos Pena, 1b, Athletics
13. Juan Cruz, rhp, Cubs
14. Dennis Tankersley, rhp, Padres
15. Nick Johnson, 1b, Yankees
16. Nick Neugebauer, rhp, Brewers
17. Mark Teixeira, 3b, Rangers
18. Josh Hamilton, of, Devil Rays
19. Ryan Anderson, lhp, Mariners
20. Michael Cuddyer, 3b/of, Twins
21. Jon Rauch, rhp, White Sox
22. Jake Peavy, rhp, Padres
23. Rafael Soriano, rhp, Mariners
24. Brett Myers, rhp, Phillies
25. Carlos Hernandez, lhp, Astros
26. Jimmy Journell, rhp, Cardinals
27. Brad Wilkerson, of, Expos
28. Angel Berroa, ss, Royals
29. Miguel Cabrera, ss, Marlins
30. Boof Bonser, rhp, Giants
31. Marlon Byrd, of, Phillies
32. Josh Phelps, c, Blue Jays
33. Ty Howington, lhp, Reds
34. J.R. House, c, Pirates
35. Carl Crawford, of, Devil Rays
36. Ricardo Rodriguez, rhp, Dodgers
37. Justin Morneau, 1b, Twins
38. Nate Cornejo, rhp, Tigers
39. Chris Snelling, of, Mariners
40. Hee Seop Choi, 1b, Cubs
41. Adrian Gonzalez, 1b, Marlins
42. Jason Lane, of, Astros
43. Xavier Nady, 1b, Padres
44. Casey Kotchman, 1b, Angels
45. Mario Ramos, lhp, Rangers
46. Jose Reyes, ss, Mets
47. Seung Song, rhp, Red Sox
48. David Kelton, 3b, Cubs
49. Gabe Gross, of, Blue Jays
50. Adam Wainwright, rhp, Braves

Sean Burroughs   3b, Padres

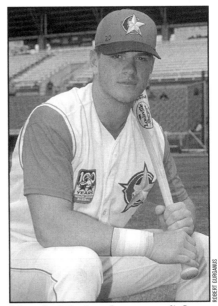

Hank Blalock   3b, Rangers

Jim Callis

Juan Cruz rhp, Cubs **Mark Prior** rhp, Cubs

1. Josh Beckett, rhp, Marlins
2. Mark Prior, rhp, Cubs
3. Hank Blalock, 3b, Rangers
4. Sean Burroughs, 3b, Padres
5. Carlos Pena, 1b, Athletics
6. Joe Mauer, c, Twins
7. Juan Cruz, rhp, Cubs
8. Ryan Anderson, lhp, Mariners
9. Mark Teixeira, 3b, Rangers
10. Angel Berroa, ss, Royals
11. Brandon Phillips, ss, Expos
12. Austin Kearns, of, Reds
13. Joe Borchard, of, White Sox
14. Drew Henson, 3b, Yankees
15. Wilson Betemit, ss, Braves
16. Dennis Tankersley, rhp, Padres
17. Jake Peavy, rhp, Padres
18. Josh Hamilton, of, Devil Rays
19. Nick Johnson, 1b, Yankees
20. Nick Neugebauer, rhp, Brewers
21. Rafael Soriano, rhp, Mariners
22. Hee Seop Choi, 1b, Cubs
23. Boof Bonser, rhp, Giants
24. Casey Kotchman, 1b, Angels
25. Justin Morneau, 1b, Twins
26. Ty Howington, lhp, Reds
27. Carlos Hernandez, lhp, Astros
28. J.R. House, c, Pirates
29. Adrian Gonzalez, 1b, Marlins
30. Jerome Williams, rhp, Giants
31. Jon Rauch, rhp, White Sox
32. Antonio Perez, ss, Mariners
33. Adam Wainwright, rhp, Braves
34. Brandon Claussen, lhp, Yankees
35. Chris Snelling, of, Mariners
36. Michael Cuddyer, 3b/of, Twins
37. Marlon Byrd, of, Phillies
38. Xavier Nady, 1b, Padres
39. Jose Reyes, ss, Mets
40. Kelly Johnson, ss, Braves
41. Jimmy Gobble, lhp, Royals
42. Corwin Malone, lhp, White Sox
43. John Buck, c, Astros
44. David Kelton, 3b, Cubs
45. Mark Phillips, lhp, Padres
46. Seung Song, rhp, Red Sox
47. Brett Myers, rhp, Phillies
48. Josh Phelps, c, Blue Jays
49. Dewon Brazelton, rhp, Devil Rays
50. Gabe Gross, of, Blue Jays

Josh Boyd

Drew Henson 3b, Yankees

Joe Mauer c, Twins

1. Josh Beckett, rhp, Marlins
2. Hank Blalock, 3b, Rangers
3. Sean Burroughs, 3b, Padres
4. Mark Prior, rhp, Cubs
5. Drew Henson, 3b, Yankees
6. Juan Cruz, rhp, Cubs
7. Carlos Pena, 1b, Athletics
8. Joe Mauer, c, Twins
9. Nick Johnson, 1b, Yankees
10. Austin Kearns, of, Reds
11. Nick Neugebauer, rhp, Brewers
12. Mark Teixeira, 3b, Rangers
13. Wilson Betemit, ss, Braves
14. Brandon Phillips, ss, Expos
15. Ryan Anderson, lhp, Mariners
16. Dennis Tankersley, rhp, Padres
17. Justin Morneau, 1b, Twins
18. Josh Hamilton, of, Devil Rays
19. Joe Borchard, of, White Sox
20. Jerome Williams, rhp, Giants
21. Rafael Soriano, rhp, Mariners
22. Jake Peavy, rhp, Padres
23. Marlon Byrd, of, Phillies
24. Adrian Gonzalez, 1b, Marlins
25. Angel Berroa, ss, Royals
26. Brett Myers, rhp, Phillies
27. Jon Rauch, rhp, White Sox
28. Xavier Nady, 1b, Padres
29. Carlos Hernandez, lhp, Astros
30. Mark Phillips, lhp, Padres
31. Chris Snelling, of, Mariners
32. Casey Kotchman, 1b, Angels
33. Boof Bonser, rhp, Giants
34. Josh Phelps, c, Blue Jays
35. Michael Cuddyer, 3b/of, Twins
36. Ty Howington, lhp, Reds
37. Antonio Perez, ss, Mariners
38. Hee Seop Choi, 1b, Cubs
39. Dave Kelton, 3b, Cubs
40. Miguel Cabrera, ss, Marlins
41. Jose Reyes, ss, Mets
42. Adam Wainwright, rhp, Braves
43. Jimmy Journell, rhp, Cardinals
44. Nate Cornejo, rhp, Tigers
45. John Buck, c, Astros
46. Jimmy Gobble, lhp, Royals
47. Chris Burke, ss, Astros
48. Gavin Floyd, rhp, Phillies
49. Denny Bautista, rhp, Marlins
50. Michael Restovich, of, Twins

ANAHEIM Angels

TOP 30 PROSPECTS

1. Casey Kotchman, 1b
2. Bobby Jenks, rhp
3. John Lackey, rhp
4. Chris Bootcheck, rhp
5. Joe Torres, lhp
6. Alfredo Amezaga, ss
7. Francisco Rodriguez, rhp
8. Nathan Haynes, of
9. Johan Santana, rhp
10. Jeff Mathis, c
11. Brian Specht, ss
12. Dallas McPherson, 3b
13. Derrick Turnbow, rhp
14. Rafael Rodriguez, rhp
15. Josh Gray, of
16. Phil Wilson, rhp
17. Steven Shell, rhp
18. David Wolensky, rhp
19. Jared Abruzzo, c
20. Steve Green, rhp
21. Bart Miadich, rhp
22. Scot Shields, rhp
23. Greg Porter, of
24. Dan Mozingo, lhp
25. Elpidio Guzman, of
26. Johnny Raburn, 2b
27. Joel Peralta, rhp
28. Rich Fischer, rhp
29. Jake Woods, lhp
30. Quan Cosby, of

By Josh Boyd

The Angels haven't been able to get everything working in the same season. In 2000, they ranked third in home runs and seventh in scoring in the American League. But their pitching staff sported a 5.00 ERA while every member of the regular rotation spent time on the disabled list, and Anaheim finished 82-80.

Last year, the Angels fixed their pitching staff, cutting their ERA to 4.20, the fifth-best mark in the AL. But with Darin Erstad and Tim Salmon leading the way, the offense imploded, hitting 78 fewer longballs while slipping to 12th in the league in scoring. Anaheim backtracked by seven games, going 75-87.

Will the Angels be able to compete with the still-strong Athletics and Mariners and the improved Rangers in the AL West this year? A better question might be how much longer Disney will hold onto the franchise. The sole owner of the club since March 1999, Disney hasn't been able to work its usual marketing magic and wants to get out of baseball.

Attendance has declined steadily each season, and Anaheim has been mentioned as a possible contraction candidate. Then-Marlins owner John Henry negotiated to buy the team this offseason before pulling out and becoming part of the group that purchased the Red Sox. Unable to divest itself of the Angels, Disney made changes at the top in January. Team president Tony Tavares resigned. Disney's head of parks and resorts and former Disneyland president Paul Pressler stepped in on a temporary basis to evaluate the corporation's sports holdings, which also include the NHL's Mighty Ducks of Anaheim.

"As long as we own these teams," Pressler said, "we have to do the best job we can at putting a competitive team on the field and the ice."

Part of that means focusing further on pitching. Aaron Sele was signed as a free agent, while free-agent bust Mo Vaughn was shipped to the Mets for Kevin Appier. General manager Bill Stoneman tried to trade Darin Erstad to the White Sox for more arms, but Tavares and Pressler vetoed the deal.

Mirroring the big league club, the system is stocked more with pitchers than hitters. In his two years with the Angels, scouting director Donny Rowland has built up the depth of talent, especially with high-ceiling arms. The farm department is under new leadership with former manager of baseball operations Tony Reagins taking over for Darrell Miller, who was fired in October.

Organization Overview

General manager: Bill Stoneman. **Farm director:** Tony Reagins. **Scouting director:** Donny Rowland.

2001 PERFORMANCE

Class	Farm Team	League	W	L	Pct.	Finish*	Manager
Majors	Anaheim	American	75	87	.463	8th (14)	Mike Scioscia
Triple-A	Salt Lake Stingers	Pacific Coast	79	64	.552	4th (16)	Garry Templeton
Double-A	Arkansas Travelers	Texas	66	70	.485	6th (8)	Mike Brumley
High A	Rancho Cucamonga Quakes	California	63	77	.450	7th (10)	Tim Wallach
Low A	Cedar Rapids Kernels	Midwest	60	77	.438	10th (14)	Tyrone Boykin
Rookie	Provo Angels	Pioneer	53	23	.697	1st (8)	Tom Kotchman
Rookie	AZL Angels	Arizona	22	34	.393	7th (7)	Brian Harper
OVERALL 2001 MINOR LEAGUE RECORD			343	345	.499	14th (30)	

*Finish in overall standings (No. of teams in league)

ORGANIZATION LEADERS

BATTING

*AVG	**Jose Fernandez**, Salt Lake	.338
R	**Jose Fernandez**, Salt Lake	99
H	**Jose Fernandez**, Salt Lake	153
TB	**Jose Fernandez**, Salt Lake	282
2B	Scott Morgan, Salt Lake	39
3B	Alfredo Amezaga, Salt Lake/Arkansas	9
HR	**Jose Fernandez**, Salt Lake	30
RBI	**Jose Fernandez**, Salt Lake	114
BB	Johnny Raburn, Cedar Rapids	63
	Scott Bikowski, Rancho Cucamonga	63
SO	Tommy Murphy, RC/Cedar Rapids	163
SB	Johnny Raburn, Cedar Rapids	37

PITCHING

W	**Brian Cooper**, Salt Lake	12
	John Lackey, Salt Lake/Arkansas	12
L	Dusty Bergman, Arkansas	13
#ERA	Pedro Liriano, Provo	2.78
G	Brendan Donnelly, Salt Lake/Arkansas	56
CG	Scot Shields, Salt Lake.	4
	John Lackey, Salt Lake/Arkansas	4
SV	Bart Miadich, Salt Lake	27
IP	John Lackey, Salt Lake/Arkansas	185
BB	Elvin Nina, Salt Lake	79
SO	Francisco Rodriguez, Rancho Cuca.	147

*Minimum 250 At-Bats #Minimum 75 Innings

Fernandez   **Cooper**

BEST TOOLS

Best Hitter for Average	Casey Kotchman
Best Power Hitter	Josh Gray
Fastest Baserunner	Quan Cosby
Best Fastball	Bobby Jenks
Best Breaking Ball	Joe Torres
Best Changeup	Tony Milo
Best Control	John Lackey
Best Defensive Catcher	Jeff Mathis
Best Defensive Infielder	Alfredo Amezaga
Best Infield Arm	Tommy Murphy
Best Defensive Outfielder	Nathan Haynes
Best Outfield Arm	Elpidio Guzman

TOP PROSPECTS OF THE DECADE

1992	Troy Percival, rhp
1993	Tim Salmon, of
1994	Brian Anderson, lhp
1995	Andrew Lorraine, lhp
1996	Darin Erstad, of
1997	Jarrod Washburn, lhp
1998	Troy Glaus, 3b
1999	Ramon Ortiz, rhp
2000	Ramon Ortiz, rhp
2001	Joe Torres, lhp

TOP DRAFT PICKS OF THE DECADE

1992	Pete Janicki, rhp
1993	Brian Anderson, lhp
1994	McKay Christensen, of
1995	Darin Erstad, of
1996	Chuck Abbott, ss (2)
1997	Troy Glaus, 3b
1998	Seth Etherton, rhp
1999	John Lackey, rhp (2)
2000	Joe Torres, lhp
2001	Casey Kotchman, 1b

PROJECTED 2005 LINEUP

Catcher	Jeff Mathis
First Base	Casey Kotchman
Second Base	Adam Kennedy
Third Base	Troy Glaus
Shortstop	Alfredo Amezaga
Left Field	Darin Erstad
Center Field	Nathan Haynes
Right Field	Garret Anderson
Designated Hitter	Tim Salmon
No. 1 Starter	Ramon Ortiz
No. 2 Starter	Bobby Jenks
No. 3 Starter	Jarrod Washburn
No. 4 Starter	Aaron Sele
No. 5 Starter	John Lackey
Closer	Troy Percival

ALL-TIME LARGEST BONUSES

Troy Glaus, 1997	$2,250,000
Joe Torres, 2000	$2,080,000
Casey Kotchman, 2001	$2,075,000
Chris Bootcheck, 2000	$1,800,000
Darin Erstad, 1995	$1,575,000

DraftAnalysis

2001 Draft

Best Pro Debut: 3B Dallas McPherson (2) batted .395-5-29 at Rookie-level Provo before breaking his arm on a tag play during a rare start at first base. LHP Jason Dennis (14), C Al Corbiel (16) and 2B Casey Smith (34) were Pioneer League all-stars.

Best Athlete: OF Quan Cosby (6), who signed for $850,000, excels at three sports and is better at football and track than he is at baseball to this point. He turned down a football scholarship from Texas to turn pro. 3B Greg Porter (45) played wide receiver and tight end at Texas A&M. C Jeff Mathis (1), a former high school quarterback, is athletic for his position and could play almost anywhere on the diamond, including shortstop.

Best Hitter: 1B **Casey Kotchman** (1) was the best high school hitter in the draft. He went 20-for-37 before straining his wrist.

Best Raw Power: Scouts often compare Kotchman to Rafael Palmeiro, for his ability to hit for average and power as well as his grace around the bag at first base. Kotchman has legitimate 40-homer potential.

Fastest Runner: Cosby was as fast as any player in the draft, with scouts likening his speed to that of Deion Sanders. He has been clocked from the left side of the plate to first base as quick as 3.7 seconds, which is almost unheard of. Cosby is raw but could be a terror at the top of an order if he hits.

Best Defensive Player: Mathis was another early pick whose debut was curtailed by an injury (broken hand). He's a premium receiver with an above-average arm, not to men-

tion plus hitting ability and average power.

Best Fastball: RHP Mark O'Sullivan (25), a converted outfielder, has touched 95 mph. He'll probably be passed by RHP Steven Shell (3), who already hits 94 mph with easy arm action. RHP Johnathon Shull (11), like Shell a high school product, also can reach 94.

Most Intriguing Background: Kotchman's father Tom is a longtime scout and minor league manager for the Angels. He also served as his son's agent, negotiating a $2.075 million bonus.

RICK BATTLE

Closest To The Majors: Kotchman could be the

Kotchman

first high school player from the 2001 draft to reach the majors, and should beat McPherson to Anaheim.

Best Late-Round Pick: Porter. He followed a strong yet brief Cape Cod League performance in the summer of 2000 with a disastrous .202-2-10 junior season at Texas A&M. Then he hit .331-10-34 at Provo.

The One Who Got Away: Sophomore-eligible Rich Hill (7) is a projectable 6-foot-5 left-hander who throws 86-89 mph and had a strong summer in the Cape League.

Assessment: Getting Kotchman with the 13th overall pick was a coup. The Angels also did their homework and gauged other teams' interest in Mathis and McPherson well enough to make sure they didn't lose them.

2000 Draft

Anaheim restocked its system with RHPs Bobby Jenks (5) and Chris Bootcheck (1), LHP Joe Torres (1), OF Josh Gray (13) and C Jared Abruzzo (2). They all need to get either more polished or more healthy, and if they do this grade will rise.   **Grade: C+**

1999 Draft

Despite not having a first-rounder, the Angels got RHP John Lackey (2) and SSs Alfredo Amezaga (13) and Brian Specht (9). RHP David Wolensky (42, draft-and-follow) just needs better command to take off.   **Grade: B**

1998 Draft

RHP Seth Etherton (1) reached the majors in a hurry, but he had a limited ceiling before getting traded to the Reds and hurting his shoulder. And he's easily the highlight of this group. Unsigned SS Bobby Crosby (34) became a first-round pick in 2001.   **Grade: D**

1997 Draft

3B Troy Glaus (1) has been everything Anaheim thought it was getting with the No. 3 overall pick. RHPs Matt Wise (6), Steve Green (10) and Scot Shields (38), as well as OF Mike Colangelo (21) all have seen time in the majors.   **Grade: B+**

Note: Draft analysis prepared by Jim Callis. Numbers in parentheses indicate draft rounds.

... Comparisons to sweet-swinging lefthanders abound, starting with Todd Helton and Rafael Palmeiro.

Kotchman **Casey** 1b

Born: Feb. 22, 1983.
Ht.: 6-3. **Wt.:** 210.
Bats: L. **Throws:** L.
School: Seminole (Fla.) HS.
Career Transactions: Selected by Angels in first round (13th overall) of 2001 draft; signed July 28, 2001.

The centerpiece of one of the most talented high school teams ever assembled, Kotchman led Seminole (Fla.) to a wire-to-wire No. 1 ranking in the Baseball America/ National High School Coaches Association poll. The Warhawks won the national title despite injuries and a transfer violation that caused them to forfeit 10 victories. Kotchman earned high school All-America honors by hitting .465-5-39 in 88 at-bats. Though his season wasn't a disappointment by any standards, Kotchman slid slightly in the draft because he got pitched around and didn't take good swings. Anaheim was surprised and delighted to find him available with the 13th overall pick in June, and his father Tom—an Angels scout and minor league manager—negotiated Casey's $2.075 million bonus. Casey has been around pro ball all his life, often accompanying his father during the summer, and they were reunited at Rookie-level Provo last August before a sprained wrist ended Casey's pro debut.

Kotchman had little difficulty leaving aluminum bats behind. He treated pro pitchers like high schoolers. Comparisons to sweet-swinging lefthanders abound, starting with Todd Helton and Rafael Palmeiro. Some scouts give Kotchman top grades on the hitting scale, and he's expected to develop well-above-average power because of his strong frame, bat speed and uncanny ability to put the barrel on the ball. He's an aggressive hitter, but he stays inside the ball well and uses the whole field. Kotchman's fielding and throwing also project as plus big league tools. He has all the makings of a future Gold Glover, playing a textbook first base with graceful actions, soft hands and solid footwork. The ball seems to disappear into his glove. Though Kotchman is a flexible athlete who excites scouts with his loose, limber body, he's a below-average runner. Any other perceived flaws are just nitpicking, however. After getting hurt at Provo and being limited by a back injury in 2000, he'll have to prove he's durable.

Kotchman missed instructional league with the wrist injury, but he was on schedule with his rehab and should be 100 percent for spring training. Most scouts can barely contain their enthusiasm when talking about him. Much like Joe Mauer, the No. 1 overall pick in 2001, Kotchman is quite refined for a teenager and ready to jump on the fast track. He should be the first high school player from last year's draft to reach the majors, perhaps in 2004.

Year	Club (League)	Class	AVG	G	AB	R	H	2B	3B	HR	RBI	BB	SO	SB
2001	Angels (AZL)	R	.600	4	15	5	9	1	0	1	5	3	2	0
	Provo (Pio)	R	.500	7	22	6	11	3	0	0	7	2	0	0
MINOR LEAGUE TOTALS			.541	11	37	11	20	4	0	1	12	5	2	0

2. Bobby Jenks, rhp

Born: March 14, 1981. **Ht.:** 6-3. **Wt.:** 225. **Bats:** R. **Throws:** R. **Career Transactions:** Selected by Angels in fifth round of 2000 draft; signed June 13, 2000.

Academically ineligible after his sophomore season at an Idaho high school, Jenks used a personal pitching coach, Mark Potoshnik, to gain recognition among scouts. His reputation grew after Jenks showed a plus fastball at private workouts, but his background scared some teams away. In his first full year as a pro, he earned a promotion to Double-A Arkansas for the postseason and led the Arizona Fall League in strikeouts. Jenks' first four pitches in a Texas League playoff game were clocked at 99 mph, and some reports had him touching 100 in the AFL. He consistently pumps his fastball into the mid-90s with an effortless delivery. His 80 mph curveball is a power breaker and ranks among the best in the system. Jenks still is learning how to pitch. He made strides in repeating his delivery and showing a feel for a changeup, but he finds himself behind in the count too often. He hasn't missed as many bats as he should with his stuff. His marriage helped focus him on his priorities while all but eliminating any questions about his makeup. Slated for Arkansas in 2002, Jenks has flashed dominance but not consistency. If he figures everything out, he has a chance to be special.

Year	Club (League)	Class	W	L	ERA	G	GS	CG	SV	IP	H	R	ER	BB	SO
2000	Butte (Pio)	R	1	7	7.86	14	12	0	0	53	61	57	46	44	42
2001	Cedar Rapids (Mid)	A	3	7	5.27	21	21	0	0	99	90	74	58	64	98
	Arkansas (TL)	AA	1	0	3.60	2	2	0	0	10	8	5	4	5	10
MINOR LEAGUE TOTALS			5	14	6.01	37	35	0	0	162	159	136	108	113	150

3. John Lackey, rhp

Born: Oct. 23, 1978. **Ht.:** 6-6. **Wt.:** 200. **Bats:** R. **Throws:** R. **School:** Grayson County (Texas) JC. **Career Transactions:** Selected by Angels in second round of 1999 draft; signed June 9, 1999.

Lackey has the look and build of a slugger, which he was in junior college, where he hit .440 with 16 homers as a sophomore two-way player and led Grayson County to the national juco title. Anaheim's top pick (second round) in 1999, he sped through the system with ease until getting roughed up in Triple-A Salt Lake last year. Despite his relative inexperience on the mound, Lackey has evolved into more than just a thrower. Arkansas pitching coach Mike Butcher taught him a true slider, which has opened up the plate for his 92 mph fastball, power curve and improving changeup. He goes right after hitters and has the control to hit his spots. His 6-foot-6 frame allows him to throw on an effective downward plane. Lackey's Triple-A performance in 2001 shows he still has to refine his repertoire before advancing to Anaheim. He's big and strong, but letting him pitch 450 innings in 2 1/2 years as a pro isn't the best way to keep him healthy. The Angels' offseason acquisitions of Kevin Appier and Aaron Sele made it that much easier to give Lackey more development time. He has the makeup of a workhorse middle-of-the-rotation starter or a potentially dominator at the back of the bullpen.

Year	Club (League)	Class	W	L	ERA	G	GS	CG	SV	IP	H	R	ER	BB	SO
1999	Boise (NWL)	A	6	2	4.98	15	15	1	0	81	81	59	45	50	77
2000	Cedar Rapids (Mid)	A	3	2	2.08	5	5	0	0	30	20	7	7	5	21
	Lake Elsinore (Cal)	A	6	6	3.40	15	15	2	0	101	94	56	38	42	74
	Erie (EL)	AA	6	1	3.30	8	8	2	0	57	58	23	21	9	43
2001	Arkansas (TL)	AA	9	7	3.46	18	18	3	0	127	106	55	49	29	94
	Salt Lake (PCL)	AAA	3	4	6.71	10	10	1	0	58	75	44	43	16	42
MINOR LEAGUE TOTALS			33	22	4.02	71	71	9	0	455	434	244	203	151	351

4. Chris Bootcheck, rhp

Born: Oct. 24, 1978. **Ht.:** 6-5. **Wt.:** 205. **Bats:** R. **Throws:** R. **School:** Auburn University. **Career Transactions:** Selected by Angels in first round (20th overall) of 2000 draft; signed Sept. 13, 2000.

More colleges recruited Bootcheck to play basketball out of high school, though the Devil Rays did draft him in the 17th round. He made steady progress throughout his Auburn career, prompting Tigers coach Hal Baird to say Bootcheck has the highest ceiling of any pitcher in the program's history, including former big league all-star Gregg Olson. His father Dan pitched in the Tigers system in the 1970s. Though Bootcheck has a long and loose body, he never has been an overpowering pitcher. He commands four pitches to both sides of the plate and induces groundballs with his sinking, 93-94 mph two-seam fastball. He always has relied on his darting 86-90 mph cutter, and his curveball and changeup are weapons hitters have to be aware of. His Double-A struggles show he still needs an out pitch. He has faced questions about his durability, and they won't stop after a sore shoulder stalled his pro debut last spring. He needs to add weight to his slender build. Bootcheck is headed back to Arkansas, where he finished his first pro season with seven shutout innings in the Texas League playoffs. He could reach Anaheim by the end of 2002.

Year	Club (League)	Class	W	L	ERA	G	GS	CG	SV	IP	H	R	ER	BB	SO
2001	Rancho Cucamonga (Cal)	A	8	4	3.93	15	14	1	0	87	84	45	38	23	86
	Arkansas (TL)	AA	3	3	5.45	6	6	1	0	36	39	25	22	11	22
MINOR LEAGUE TOTALS			11	7	4.38	21	20	2	0	123	123	70	60	34	108

5. Joe Torres, lhp

Born: Sept. 3, 1982. **Ht.:** 6-2. **Wt.:** 175. **Bats:** L. **Throws:** L. **School:** Gateway HS, Kissimmee, Fla. **Career Transactions:** Selected by Angels in first round (10th overall) of 2000 draft; signed June 21, 2000.

Torres went to the top of the list a year ago after being drafted 10th overall and dominating at short-season Boise. He started 2001 out on the wrong foot, though, reporting to camp out of shape and getting his mechanics to get out of whack. Torres studied hours of film before redis-covering his delivery. He didn't touch 96 mph as he did in his pro debut, but he was back up to 91-92 and flashing his power curveball by the end of instructional league. He has a fast, whip-like arm action from a low three-quarters slot, similar to Randy Johnson. His curve can be a devastating pitch. Last year served as a wake-up call for Torres, whose fastball dropped all the way to the mid-80s during the spring. He'll need to maintain his conditioning and prove himself in a full-season league. His changeup has potential but still lags behind his other two offerings. Some of his struggles can be attrib-uted to receiving too much advice. The Angels consider 2001 a learning experience for the teenager. Torres worked hard to get back into shape and should be primed to show his best stuff this year in low Class A Cedar Rapids.

Year	Club (League)	Class	W	L	ERA	G	GS	CG	SV	IP	H	R	ER	BB	SO
2000	Boise (NWL)	A	4	1	2.54	11	10	0	0	46	27	17	13	23	52
2001	Cedar Rapids (Mid)	A	0	3	5.82	4	4	0	0	17	16	12	11	14	14
	Provo (Pio)	R	2	2	4.02	9	8	0	0	31	32	20	14	15	39
MINOR LEAGUE TOTALS			6	6	3.63	24	22	0	0	94	75	49	38	52	105

6. Alfredo Amezaga, ss

Born: Jan. 16, 1978. **Ht.:** 5-10. **Wt.:** 165. **Bats:** B. **Throws:** R. **School:** St. Petersburg (Fla.) JC. **Career Transactions:** Selected by Angels in 13th round of 1999 draft; signed June 4, 1999.

Amezaga moved from Mexico to Miami for high school and first caught scouts' attention as a teenager at an inner-city baseball clinic. Brian Specht pushed him to second base in 2000, but last year Amezaga spent the entire season at shortstop. One scout said he saw a 15-year-old Amezaga turn the most amazing double play he's ever seen. He can make acrobatic plays with his quick actions, excellent instincts and first-step anticipation. His arm is average, but there's no longer any doubt that he can play shortstop in the majors. He's 70 runner on the 20-to-80 scouting scale and has good bunting ability. Amezaga makes a lot of things happen, but hitting for power isn't one of them. He usually slaps the ball the other way and occasionally can pull balls into the gap. Some scouts ques-tion if his slight build will allow him to hold up over a 162-game season. He doesn't walk enough to fully utilize his speed. The Angels haven't developed an everyday middle infield-er since Damion Easley, and they won't have to wait much longer for Amezaga. Their sta-tion-to-station lineup could use the energy his speed would provide.

Year	Club (League)	Class	AVG	G	AB	R	H	2B	3B	HR	RBI	BB	SO	SB
1999	Butte (Pio)	R	.294	8	34	11	10	2	0	0	5	5	5	6
	Boise (NWL)	A	.322	48	205	52	66	6	4	2	29	23	29	14
2000	Lake Elsinore (Cal)	A	.279	108	420	90	117	13	4	4	44	63	70	73
2001	Arkansas (TL)	AA	.312	70	285	50	89	10	5	4	21	22	55	24
	Salt Lake (PCL)	AAA	.250	49	200	28	50	5	4	1	16	14	45	9
MINOR LEAGUE TOTALS			.290	283	1144	231	332	36	17	11	115	127	204	126

7. Francisco Rodriguez, rhp

Born: Jan. 7, 1982. **Ht.:** 6-0. **Wt.:** 165. **Bats:** R. **Throws:** R. **Career Transactions:** Signed out of Venezuela by Angels, Sept. 24, 1998.

Rodriguez earned a $900,000 bonus with his live arm, but consecutive enigmatic seasons in high Class A have cast a shadow of doubt over his future. Shoulder and elbow tenderness have plagued him throughout his young career, and his elbow prevented him from pitching until May 20 last season. Capable of reaching 99 mph, Rodriguez' fastball generally sits around 93 mph with cutting action from a low three-quarters arm slot. Righties have little chance against his 80 mph curveball with hard, sweeping bite across the strike zone. Between the California and Arizona Fall leagues, he averaged 12 strikeouts per nine innings in 2001. Unfortunately, Rodriguez often has little idea where his pitches are going. He uncorked 17 wild pitches last year and struggled to command his fastball and curveball. He changes his arm speed on his changeup but needs to incorporate it into his repertoire to avoid a future as a reliever. His velocity fluctuated last season due to persistent arm troubles. Lefthanders batted .327 against him. His make-up also has been criticized. Rodriguez' promise was evident when he pitched in the AFL as a teenager last fall. He's finally ready for Double-A.

Year	Club (League)	Class	W	L	ERA	G	GS	CG	SV	IP	H	R	ER	BB	SO
1999	Butte (Pio)	R	1	1	3.31	12	9	1	0	52	33	21	19	21	69
	Boise (NWL)	A	1	0	5.40	1	1	0	0	5	3	4	3	1	6
2000	Lake Elsinore (Cal)	A	4	4	2.81	13	12	0	0	64	43	29	20	32	79
2001	Rancho Cucamonga (Cal)	A	5	7	5.38	20	20	1	0	114	127	72	68	55	147
MINOR LEAGUE TOTALS			11	12	4.22	46	42	2	0	234	206	126	110	109	301

8. Nathan Haynes, of

Born: Sept. 7, 1979. **Ht.:** 5-9. **Wt.:** 170. **Bats:** L. **Throws:** L. **School:** Pinole Valley HS, Pinole, Calif. **Career Transactions:** Selected by Athletics in first round (32nd overall) of 1997 draft; signed June 14, 1997 . . . Traded by Athletics with OF Jeff DaVanon and RHP Elvin Nina to Angels for RHP Omar Olivares and 2B Randy Velarde, July 29, 1999.

Haynes has kept team doctors busy. His medical file includes arthroscopic surgery on each of his knees, nagging wrist and shoulder injuries, and a career-threatening operation for a sports hernia. His resiliency is a testament to his work ethic and natural athleticism. After missing 61 games last season, Haynes hit .300 with nine steals in the Arizona Fall League. At a compact yet rock-solid 5-foot-9, he is starting to realize his limitations and stay within himself. Multiple knee surgeries haven't slowed him down, as he can still fly. He's a potential leadoff hitter with occasional power. A center fielder, he tracks down balls from gap to gap and has average arm strength. He is working on improving his selectivity, which will be critical in determining whether he hits at the top or bottom of the order down the road. He has just enough power to get him in trouble, because he tends to get long with his swing and tries to lift a lot of pitches. Despite being among the youngest players in his league every year and his injury-riddled past, Haynes hasn't had his development retarded. If he can get a healthy Triple-A season under his belt, he'll be on the verge of teaming with Amezaga in a speedy, new-look Angels lineup.

Year	Club (League)	Class	AVG	G	AB	R	H	2B	3B	HR	RBI	BB	SO	SB
1997	Athletics (AZL)	R	.278	17	54	8	15	1	0	0	6	7	9	5
	S. Oregon (NWL)	A	.280	24	82	18	23	1	1	0	9	26	21	19
1998	Modesto (Cal)	A	.252	125	507	89	128	13	7	1	41	54	139	42
1999	Visalia (Cal)	A	.310	35	145	28	45	7	1	1	14	17	27	12
	Lake Elsinore (Cal)	A	.327	26	110	19	36	5	5	1	15	12	19	10
	Erie (EL)	AA	.158	5	19	3	3	1	0	0	0	5	5	0
2000	Erie (EL)	AA	.254	118	457	56	116	16	4	6	43	33	107	37
2001	Arkansas (TL)	AA	.310	79	316	49	98	11	5	5	23	32	65	33
MINOR LEAGUE TOTALS			.275	429	1690	270	464	55	23	14	151	186	392	158

9. Johan Santana, rhp

Born: Nov. 28, 1983. **Ht.:** 6-2. **Wt.:** 150. **Bats:** R. **Throws:** R. **Career Transactions:** Signed out of Dominican Republic by Angels, Sept. 2, 2000.

After signing for $700,000 in 2000, Santana took his first step toward living up to lofty expectations. He earned a promotion to Provo after 10 starts, yet still led the Rookie-level Arizona League in strikeouts. Santana reminds the Angels of Ramon Ortiz and is more advanced at the same stage of his career. Santana has long fingers and a loose, lanky frame that oozes projectability. His mechanics were surprisingly polished and consistent. He blows 91-93 mph fastballs with an easy arm action and is capable of touching 95. He already is equipped with an advanced changeup. While Santana led the AZL in strikeouts, he also led the league in walks. He worked on his breaking ball in instructional league and needs to throw more strikes with it. Built along the lines of Ortiz and Pedro Martinez, Santana will face the same challenges they do in holding up over a full season. The Angels would like to see Santana vie for a spot in Cedar Rapids this year. They moved Ortiz rapidly and aren't afraid to do so with other precocious pitchers.

Year	Club (League)	Class	W	L	ERA	G	GS	CG	SV	IP	H	R	ER	BB	SO
2001	Angels (AZL)	R	3	2	3.22	10	9	1	0	59	40	27	21	35	69
	Provo (Pio)	R	2	1	7.71	4	4	0	0	19	19	17	16	12	22
MINOR LEAGUE TOTALS			5	3	4.31	14	13	1	0	77	59	44	37	47	91

10. Jeff Mathis, c

Born: March 31, 1983. **Ht.:** 6-0. **Wt.:** 180. **Bats:** R. **Throws:** R. **School:** Marianna (Fla.) HS. **Career Transactions:** Selected by Angels in first round (33rd overall) of 2001 draft; signed June 5, 2001.

Mathis was somewhat of a surprise as the No. 33 overall pick last June, but Angels scouts agreed he has first-round talent and wouldn't last until they picked again at No. 57. As a senior, he hit .506-10-31 as a shortstop/catcher and posted a 0.95 ERA and 108 strikeouts in 66 innings on the mound. Anaheim lured him away from Florida State with an $850,000 bonus. The Angels are intrigued with his' athleticism, which is off the charts for a catcher. Not only was he a talented two-way baseball player in high school, but he also starred at quarterback and safety for his football team. An advanced receiver, he got valuable experience catching quality pitching as the backstop for Indians first-round pick Alan Horne. With a quick, efficient stroke, Mathis projects to hit for average and some power. Mathis' pro debut ended after 29 games when he broke his hand when hit by a pitch. High school catchers drafted in the first round are always a risky proposition, but Mathis has the upside of Jason Kendall, a high school first-rounder who became an all-star. Mathis will go to low Class A, following the same path as 2000 second-rounder Jared Abruzzo, another prep catcher.

Year	Club (League)	Class	AVG	G	AB	R	H	2B	3B	HR	RBI	BB	SO	SB
2001	Angels (AZL)	R	.304	7	23	1	7	1	0	0	3	2	4	0
	Provo (Pio)	R	.299	22	77	14	23	6	3	0	18	11	13	1
MINOR LEAGUE TOTALS			.300	29	100	15	30	7	3	0	21	13	17	1

11. Brian Specht, ss

Born: Oct. 19, 1980. **Ht.:** 5-11. **Wt.:** 175. **Bats:** B. **Throws:** R. **School:** Doherty HS, Colorado Springs. **Career Transactions:** Selected by Angels in ninth round of 1999 draft; signed July 14, 1999.

It cost the Angels $600,000 to get Specht away from his commitment to Baylor in 1999. A stint in instructional league in 2000 went so well that he jumped all the way to high Class A to make his pro debut—a rare move for a teenager less than a year removed from high school. He held his own and ranked third on this list a year ago. Specht returned to the California League in 2001, when he had an up-and-down season interrupted when he suffered a minor shoulder injury diving back into first base in May. He was promoted to Double-A when Alfredo Amezaga went to Triple-A. Though Specht was among the youngest players in the Texas League, he reached base safely in 33 of his 45 games. He isn't flashy but has the potential for solid average tools in the future. His style evokes comparisons to workmanlike infielders such as Gary DiSarcina, Chris Gomez and Randy Velarde. Specht may not continue switch-hitting if he doesn't improve on his .188 average batting righthanders last year. He has a lot of movement in his swing and needs to shorten his stroke. With Amezaga stepping up as Anaheim's shortstop of the future, Specht won't have to be rushed and could end up in a utility role. He's scheduled to return to Arkansas.

Year	Club (League)	Class	AVG	G	AB	R	H	2B	3B	HR	RBI	BB	SO	SB
2000	Lake Elsinore (Cal)	A	.269	89	334	70	90	22	5	2	35	52	80	25
2001	Rancho Cuca. (Cal)	A	.242	65	264	45	64	13	6	7	31	24	78	17
	Arkansas (TL)	AA	.265	45	155	14	41	9	2	2	15	13	32	2
MINOR LEAGUE TOTALS			.259	199	753	129	195	44	13	11	81	89	190	44

12. Dallas McPherson, 3b

Born: July 23, 1980. **Ht.:** 6-4. **Wt.:** 210. **Bats:** L. **Throws:** R. **School:** The Citadel. **Career Transactions:** Selected by Angels in second round of 2001 draft; signed June 18, 2001.

Many teams favored McPherson as a pitcher entering 2001 because of his strong, durable build and power arm. He had looked good in the Cape Cod League the previous summer, touching the mid-90s and flashing a good slider. But he struggled on the mound as a junior at The Citadel, going 4-5, 6.65. Not only were the Angels scouting McPherson's bat, they also paid close attention to who else was watching him. He enhanced his draft profile by showcasing his lefthanded power for the Cubs in a predraft workout at Wrigley Field. After Anaheim took him in the second round, McPherson was flirting with .400 in his pro debut at Rookie-level Ogden. In order to let eighth-round pick Justin Turner play some third base, McPherson periodically moved to first base, where his inexperience showed when he broke his hand on a tag play. He returned in time to put his potent bat on display during the final week of instructional league. He has the look of a polished hitter, staying inside the ball and creating violent impact upon contact. He has launch power to left-center. Defensively, he moves well at the hot corner and has a strong arm. McPherson has a chance to move fast after he makes his full-season debut in Cedar Rapids this year.

Year	Club (League)	Class	AVG	G	AB	R	H	2B	3B	HR	RBI	BB	SO	SB
2001	Provo (Pio)	R	.395	31	124	30	49	11	0	5	29	12	22	1
MINOR LEAGUE TOTALS			.395	31	124	30	49	11	0	5	29	12	22	1

13. Derrick Turnbow, rhp

Born: Jan. 25, 1978. **Ht.:** 6-3. **Wt.:** 200. **Bats:** R. **Throws:** R. **School:** Franklin (Tenn.) HS. **Career Transactions:** Selected by Phillies in fifth round of 1997 draft; signed July 4, 1997 . . . Selected by Angels from Phillies in Rule 5 major league draft, Dec. 13, 1999.

The Phillies may yet regret losing Turnbow in the major league Rule 5 draft in December 1999, but his future is clouded by continuing arm problems. After serving as a mop-up man during his mandatory year in the majors in 2000, he broke the ulna in his right arm three starts into last season and spent the year rehabbing. Turnbow was firing 95-98 mph gas last spring before his injury. He made so much progress by instructional league that scouting director Donny Rowland says three coaches were speechless watching Turnbow throw in the bullpen—and he was only at 80 percent. Later in the offseason, however, doctors found his arm was not healing properly, and they inserted pins to stabilize it. When healthy, his arsenal features plus-plus boring action on his mid-90s fastball, and a hard biting curveball. He made progress with his delivery during his rehab, going from a drop-and-drive style to a more efficient, taller delivery that allows him to throw on more of a downward plane. Turnbow has logged just 52 innings in two years, and the latest setback leaves his future timetable in doubt. The Angels hope he can return to the mound sometime in 2002.

Year	Club (League)	Class	W	L	ERA	G	GS	CG	SV	IP	H	R	ER	BB	SO
1997	Martinsville (Appy)	R	1	3	7.40	7	7	0	0	24	34	29	20	16	7
1998	Martinsville (Appy)	R	2	6	5.01	13	13	1	0	70	66	44	39	26	45
1999	Piedmont (SAL)	A	12	8	3.35	26	26	4	0	161	130	67	60	53	149
2000	Anaheim (AL)	MAJ	0	0	4.74	24	1	0	0	38	36	21	20	36	25
2001	Arkansas (TL)	AA	0	0	2.57	3	3	0	0	14	12	4	4	5	11
MAJOR LEAGUE TOTALS			0	0	4.74	24	1	0	0	38	36	21	20	36	25
MINOR LEAGUE TOTALS			15	17	4.11	49	49	5	0	269	242	144	123	100	212

14. Rafael Rodriguez, rhp

Born: Sept. 24, 1984. **Ht.:** 6-1. **Wt.:** 170. **Bats:** R. **Throws:** R. **Career Transactions:** Signed out of Dominican Republic by Angels, July, 20, 2001.

The Disney Corp. has prevented general manager Bill Stoneman from doing some things he'd like to in terms of free agents and trades, but the scouting department has been given carte blanche in the international market. Rodriguez signed for $780,000 as a 16-year-old last summer. He first attracted the Angels when scouting director Donny Rowland and Latin American supervisor Clay Daniel saw him loosening up in the bullpen at a tryout camp in the Dominican Republic in 2000. Rodriguez has a lightning-quick arm action and reached 94-95 mph with his fastball in instructional league. He has the makings of a tight breaking ball and impresses Anaheim with his makeup. Like fellow Dominicans Ramon Ortiz and Johan Santana, he maintains consistent arm speed on his late-fading changeup. Rodriguez will travel the same path Santana did last year, and easily could skyrocket toward the top of this list following the 2002 season.

Year	Club (League)	Class	W	L	ERA	G	GS	CG	SV	IP	H	R	ER	BB	SO
					Has Not Played—Signed 2002 Contract										

15. Josh Gray, of

Born: Feb. 22, 1981. **Ht.:** 6-3. **Wt.:** 210. **Bats:** R. **Throws:** R. **School:** Rock Creek HS, Bokchito, Okla. **Career Transactions:** Selected by Angels in 13th round of 2000 draft; signed June 16, 2000.

A bum shoulder that required labrum surgery caused Gray to last until the 13th round in the 2000 draft. The lingering effects of the injury have relegated him to DH duty and kept him out of full-season ball as a pro. The Angels can't wait to see him at full health. Gray's power potential is a shade better than Casey Kotchman's. Thanks to quick hands, Gray can pull the head of the bat through the zone with explosive speed, and he's just learning to make adjustments and smack the ball the other way. An outfielder in high school, Gray may wind up at first base if his arm strength doesn't come back. He worked hard to get his body back into shape last year and finished with a bang in instructional league. That performance should propel him to low Class A in 2002.

Year	Club (League)	Class	AVG	G	AB	R	H	2B	3B	HR	RBI	BB	SO	SB
2000	Butte (Pio)	R	.327	40	147	31	48	11	3	8	36	19	41	1
2001	Provo (Pio)	R	.240	57	200	32	48	6	0	6	31	22	58	2
MINOR LEAGUE TOTALS			.277	97	347	63	96	17	3	14	67	41	99	3

16. Phil Wilson, rhp

Born: April 1, 1981. **Ht.:** 6-8. **Wt.:** 210. **Bats:** R. **Throws:** R. **School:** Poway (Calif.) HS. **Career Transactions:** Selected by Angels in third round of 1999 draft; signed Aug. 8, 1999.

On the heels of a successful debut in 2000, Wilson struggled to put together a run of consistent success last year in high Class A. Each time it looked like he was beginning to right himself, he followed with a disastrous start. Tall and lanky, he has grown four inches since the beginning of his senior year in high school, so he's still learning his body and developing consistent mechanics. His size creates a difficult downward plane for his pitches. Wilson's fastball runs in the low 90s with late life. He shows glimpses of being able to spin a tight slider and mixes in a fair changeup. He's intense and aggressive, and he isn't afraid to use the inner half of the plate. But his command is shaky, as his 15 hit batters and 19 wild pitches last year attest. The Angels are monitoring his delivery closely, and he started to make strides with his tempo in instructional league. A muscle strain in his right arm was discovered after he was drafted, but that hasn't hindered Wilson, who has averaged 168 innings in his first two seasons. In 2002, he's expected to be part of a prospect-studded Double-A rotation that also will include Bobby Jenks, Chris Bootcheck and Derrick Turnbow.

Year	Club (League)	Class	W	L	ERA	G	GS	CG	SV	IP	H	R	ER	BB	SO
2000	Cedar Rapids (Mid)	A	8	5	3.41	21	21	1	0	129	114	61	49	49	82
	Lake Elsinore (Cal)	A	3	0	1.96	6	6	0	0	41	32	9	9	10	33
2001	Rancho Cucamonga (Cal)	A	8	10	5.23	26	26	1	0	160	173	102	93	55	134
	Arkansas (TL)	AA	1	1	11.37	2	2	0	0	6	10	12	8	6	5
MINOR LEAGUE TOTALS			20	16	4.25	55	55	2	0	337	329	184	159	120	254

17. Steven Shell, rhp

Born: March 10, 1983. **Ht.:** 6-5. **Wt.:** 195. **Bats:** R. **Throws:** R. **School:** El Reno (Okla.) HS. **Career Transactions:** Selected by Angels in third round of 2001 draft; signed June 17, 2001.

As a sophomore, Shell was the MVP of an Oklahoma summer squad that went 110-6 en route to winning three state titles and the National Amateur Baseball Federation's Sophomore World Series. He fits the prototype of the righthanders the Angels have coveted under scouting director Donny Rowland. Like Phil Wilson, Shell is a lean, flat-chested pitcher who needs to bulk up to avoid running out of gas. Scouts said he had one of the easiest arm actions in the 2001 draft, and it creates deceptive 89-94 mph velocity and running life on his fastball. The ball exits his hand effortlessly and saws off a lot of bats. He also throws a good spike curveball and has the makings of a legitimate changeup. Though Shell looked overmatched in Provo, the Angels think his advanced mound presence will help him make adjustments this season. His instructional league performance may have helped earn him a spot in low Class A for 2002.

Year	Club (League)	Class	W	L	ERA	G	GS	CG	SV	IP	H	R	ER	BB	SO
2001	Angels (AZL)	R	1	0	0.00	3	0	0	0	4	1	0	0	2	3
	Provo (Pio)	R	0	3	7.17	14	4	0	1	38	52	31	30	15	33
MINOR LEAGUE TOTALS			1	3	6.48	17	4	0	1	42	53	31	30	17	36

18. David Wolensky, rhp

Born: Jan. 15, 1980. **Ht.:** 6-0. **Wt.:** 190. **Bats:** R. **Throws:** R. **School:** Chipola (Fla.) JC. **Career Transactions:** Selected by Angels in 42nd round of 1999 draft; signed May 3, 2000.

Signed as a draft-and-follow out of Chipola (Fla.) JC in 2000, Wolensky carved up the short-season Northwest League in his first pro summer. He picked up where he left off early last year in high Class A. But after dominating for two months, he was shut down with elbow pain and had bone chips removed in June. When he's healthy, his overpowering stuff rivals that of the system's top hurlers. He can crank his fastball up to 95-96 mph or pitch with heavy sink in the low 90s. Wolensky's diverse repertoire, which also features a late-diving splitter and occasional tight slider, has baffled pro hitters, who have batted .214 against him. His command still leaves something to be desired. Wolensky is on schedule to return at full speed in spring training and resume his career in high Class A.

Year	Club (League)	Class	W	L	ERA	G	GS	CG	SV	IP	H	R	ER	BB	SO
2000	Boise (NWL)	A	8	3	3.07	15	15	0	0	76	60	29	26	35	88
2001	Rancho Cucamonga (Cal)	A	2	0	3.34	8	7	0	0	32	24	13	12	14	26
MINOR LEAGUE TOTALS			10	3	3.15	23	22	0	0	109	84	42	38	49	114

19. Jared Abruzzo, c

Born: Nov. 15, 1981, in San Diego. Resides: La Mesa, Calif. **Ht.:** 6-3. **Wt.:** 225. **Bats:** B. **Throws:** R. **School:** El Capitan HS, Lakeside, Calif. **Career Transactions:** Selected by Angels in second round of 2000 draft; signed June 20, 2000.

Like the system's top-rated catching prospect, Jeff Mathis, Abruzzo is relatively inexperienced behind the plate. He split time between third base and the mound in high school. Anaheim challenged Abruzzo by sending him to low Class A as a teenager last year, then promoted him even though his performance didn't merit it. Despite his pronounced struggles at the plate in 2001, Abruzzo offers power potential from both sides of the plate. He displays a much more confident approach from the left side, while he's prone to chasing pitches from the right side. While he's making progress receiving, Abruzzo still is working on the fundamentals of catching. His arm strength is above average. He spent the offseason working out with good friend and fellow San Diego-area product Hank Blalock, the best hitting prospect in the game, and a personal trainer. He'll make a return visit to Rancho Cucamonga in 2002.

Year	Club (League)	Class	AVG	G	AB	R	H	2B	3B	HR	RBI	BB	SO	SB
2000	Butte (Pio)	R	.255	62	208	46	53	11	0	8	45	61	58	1
2001	Cedar Rapids (Mid)	A	.241	87	323	41	78	20	0	10	53	44	104	1
	Rancho Cuca. (Cal)	A	.208	28	101	13	21	1	0	2	13	9	30	1
MINOR LEAGUE TOTALS			.241	177	632	100	152	32	0	20	111	114	192	3

20. Steve Green, rhp

Born: Jan. 26, 1978. **Ht.:** 6-2. **Wt.:** 195. **Bats:** R. **Throws:** R. **School:** Fort Scott (Kan.) CC. **Career Transactions:** Selected by Angels in 10th round of 1997 draft; signed July 15, 1997.

After establishing himself as one Canada's top pitchers in the 1999 Pan American Games, Green was a sleeper on a beeline for Anaheim. Though he was anonymous outside of the organization, he stayed on course and made his major league debut last April with little fanfare. Upon returning to Triple-A, he won six of his first eight starts and looking primed for another shot at the big league rotation before he was shut down with a sore elbow. He had Tommy John surgery last June and isn't expected back until mid-2002. Green should be able to regain his 91-94 mph heater, 81-mph power curve and changeup. He relied almost exclusively on his sinking fastball before reaching Triple-A, where he started mixing in offspeed stuff more regularly.

Year	Club (League)	Class	W	L	ERA	G	GS	CG	SV	IP	H	R	ER	BB	SO
1998	Cedar Rapids (Mid)	A	2	6	4.54	18	10	1	0	83	86	49	42	25	61
1999	Lake Elsinore (Cal)	A	7	6	3.95	19	19	4	0	121	130	70	53	37	91
	Erie (EL)	AA	3	1	3.32	6	6	1	0	41	34	25	15	19	32
2000	Erie (EL)	AA	7	4	3.40	13	13	0	0	79	71	34	30	34	66
	Edmonton (PCL)	AAA	0	4	7.29	8	8	0	0	42	55	35	34	27	24
2001	Anaheim (AL)	MAJ	0	0	3.00	1	1	0	0	6	4	2	2	6	4
	Salt Lake (PCL)	AAA	6	2	3.66	10	10	1	0	59	59	30	24	13	40
MAJOR LEAGUE TOTALS			0	0	3.00	1	1	0	0	6	4	2	2	6	4
MINOR LEAGUE TOTALS			25	23	4.19	74	66	7	0	425	435	243	198	155	314

21. Bart Miadich, rhp

Born: Feb. 3, 1976. **Ht.:** 6-4. **Wt.:** 205. **Bats:** R. **Throws:** R. **School:** University of San Diego. **Career Transactions:** Signed as nondrafted free agent by Red Sox, Aug. 31, 1997 . . . Traded by Red Sox to Diamondbacks, Dec. 15, 1998, completing trade in which Diamondbacks sent RHP Bob Wolcott to Red Sox for a player to be named (Nov. 11, 1998) . . . Released by Diamondbacks, March 31, 2000 . . . Signed by Angels, May 23, 2000.

Miadich was undrafted out of the University of San Diego and had little success in the minors with the Red Sox, who traded him, and the Diamondbacks, who released him. Anaheim ignored his track record and signed him in May 2000 based on the recommendation of roving instructor Don Wakamatsu, who managed Miadich at Double-A El Paso the year before. Miadich worked his way onto the 40-man by the end of 2000 and reached the majors last season. His stuff has improved across the board and he now attacks hitters with a 92-94 mph fastball and an 83-85 mph slider with late, tight break. After making strides with his command, he regressed in the majors. Nevertheless, the Angels are counting on Miadich as a bridge to Troy Percival.

Year	Club (League)	Class	W	L	ERA	G	GS	CG	SV	IP	H	R	ER	BB	SO
1998	Sarasota (FSL)	A	3	2	3.14	22	0	0	7	49	40	20	17	15	64
	Trenton (EL)	AA	1	6	5.96	22	8	0	1	54	66	39	36	26	33
1999	El Paso (TL)	AA	0	2	8.10	12	0	0	1	20	37	22	18	7	16
	High Desert (Cal)	A	3	8	5.42	21	16	0	0	98	125	71	59	40	85
2000	Erie (EL)	AA	3	1	3.35	28	0	0	2	40	27	16	15	21	38
	Edmonton (PCL)	AAA	2	1	4.57	10	0	0	1	22	25	14	11	9	20
2001	Salt Lake (PCL)	AAA	4	4	2.44	55	0	0	27	59	40	20	16	29	73
	Anaheim (AL)	MAJ	0	0	4.50	11	0	0	0	10	6	5	5	8	11
MAJOR LEAGUE TOTALS			0	0	4.50	11	0	0	0	10	6	5	5	8	11
MINOR LEAGUE TOTALS			16	24	4.53	170	24	0	39	342	360	202	172	147	329

22. Scot Shields, rhp

Born: July 22, 1975. **Ht.:** 6-1. **Wt.:** 175. **Bats:** R. **Throws:** R. **School:** Lincoln Memorial (Tenn.) University. **Career Transactions:** Selected by Angels in 38th round of 1997 draft; signed June 9, 1997.

Like Steve Green and Bart Miadich, Shields was overlooked on his ascent to the major leagues, which culminated with a callup last May. Drafted in the 38th round out of tiny Lincoln Memorial (Tenn.) in 1997, he's not an imposing figure on the hill. But he continues to prove at every level that he can get hitters out. His fastball doesn't have overwhelming velocity at 88-92 mph, but Shields keeps hitters off balance by combining it with a darting slider, a changeup and a recently added curveball. Everything he throws moves, and his unorthodox, across-the-body release serves as another weapon. Shields learned to repeat his delivery last year, slashing his walk rate in half. After pitching 11 scoreless innings for Anaheim last summer, he heads into spring training as a viable option for the bullpen role vacated by Shigetoshi Hasegawa.

Year	Club (League)	Class	W	L	ERA	G	GS	CG	SV	IP	H	R	ER	BB	SO
1997	Boise (NWL)	A	7	2	2.94	30	0	0	2	52	45	20	17	24	61
1998	Cedar Rapids (Mid)	A	6	5	3.65	58	0	0	7	74	62	33	30	29	81
1999	Lake Elsinore (Cal)	A	10	3	2.52	24	9	2	1	107	91	37	30	39	113
	Erie (EL)	AA	4	4	2.89	10	10	1	0	75	57	26	24	26	81
2000	Edmonton (PCL)	AAA	7	13	5.41	27	27	4	0	163	158	114	98	82	156
2001	Salt Lake (PCL)	AAA	6	11	4.97	21	21	4	0	138	141	84	76	31	104
	Anaheim (AL)	MAJ	0	0	0.00	8	0	0	0	11	8	1	0	7	7
MAJOR LEAGUE TOTALS			0	0	0.00	8	0	0	0	11	8	1	0	7	7
MINOR LEAGUE TOTALS			40	38	4.07	170	67	11	10	609	554	314	275	231	596

23. Greg Porter, of

Born: Aug. 15, 1980. **Ht.:** 6-4. **Wt.:** 225. **Bats:** L. **Throws:** R. **School:** Texas A&M University. **Career Transactions:** Selected by Angels in 45th round of 2001 draft; signed June 9, 2001.

Porter was drafted by the Reds in the third round out of high school in 1998, but he elected to play football and baseball at Texas A&M. He spent part of his time with the Aggies catching passes from quarterback Mark Farris, a 1994 first-round pick of the Pirates. Porter never produced much at the plate for the Aggies, but some observers thought he was the best athlete to play in the Cape Cod League in 2000. Maybe he just needs to hit with wood, because he tore up the Rookie-level Pioneer League last summer after signing as a 45th-round pick, then returned for the latter part of his senior football season. He has good bloodlines, as his grandfather played football at Oklahoma State and his father was a linebacker at Mississippi State. That he could play wide receiver at his size gives the first clue about how athletic Porter is. He has good bat speed and power to all fields. A third baseman/DH in college, he took to right field quickly as a pro because of his agility and natural instincts. Like many two-sport athletes, Porter may never realize the potential he could have if he had focused solely on baseball. He'll have to prove he can hit on a consistent basis but is off to a good start. He'll get tested in Class A this season.

Year	Club (League)	Class	AVG	G	AB	R	H	2B	3B	HR	RBI	BB	SO	SB
2001	Provo (Pio)	R	.331	39	127	34	42	3	1	10	34	18	21	3
MINOR LEAGUE TOTALS			.331	39	127	34	42	3	1	10	34	18	21	3

24. Dan Mozingo, lhp

Born: June 3, 1980. **Ht.:** 6-2. **Wt.:** 210. **Bats:** L. **Throws:** L. **School:** Ashtabula Harbor HS, Ashtabula, Ohio. **Career Transactions:** Selected by White Sox in third round of 1998 draft; signed Aug. 20, 1998 . . . Traded by White Sox with RHP Jim Sweeney to Angels for SS Josh Shaffer and OF Scott Bikowski, Dec. 19, 2001.

The Angels bolstered their stable of promising young arms through a minor league deal with the White Sox in December. Lefthanders Mozingo and Jim Sweeney came to Anaheim for outfielder Scott Bikowski and infielder Josh Shaffer (Chicago senior scouting director Duane Shaffer's son). Drafted in the third round in 1998 based on his live arm, Mozingo looked like a bust with a career 7.02 ERA heading into 2001. He turned himself around after a trip to major league spring training showed him how much he had to learn. After rededicated himself to his career, he opened the season as a long man in low Class A and ended it as a starter in high Class A. Mozingo throws an 88-92 mph fastball, an average changeup and an improving curveball. He still has work to do on his conditioning as he ran out of gas at the end of last season. He'll likely debut for the Angels in high Class A, and he can earn a 40-man roster spot with a strong season.

Year	Club (League)	Class	W	L	ERA	G	GS	CG	SV	IP	H	R	ER	BB	SO
1999	Bristol (Appy)	R	4	7	6.04	13	13	1	0	67	79	59	45	32	68
2000	Burlington (Mid)	A	0	0	19.16	10	0	0	0	10	17	24	22	16	9
	Bristol (Appy)	R	0	0	3.00	9	0	0	1	15	13	5	5	6	16
2001	Kannapolis (SAL)	A	8	4	2.39	37	9	1	1	94	59	30	25	43	114
	Winston-Salem (Car)	A	0	3	11.91	3	3	0	0	11	21	19	15	6	17
MINOR LEAGUE TOTALS			12	14	5.10	72	25	2	2	198	189	137	112	103	224

25. Elpidio Guzman, of

Born: Feb. 24, 1979. **Ht.:** 6-2. **Wt.:** 165. **Bats:** L. **Throws:** L. **Career Transactions:** Signed as a non-drafted free agent by Angels, Oct. 15, 1995.

Guzman has been a constant on the Angels Top 10 list since 1999, when he peaked at No. 4. But last year his production went into a downward spiral as he endured career full-season lows in average, on-base percentage (.272), slugging percentage (.370), walks and steals. It was particularly disturbing because he made progress every year leading up to 2001. He's gifted with tremendous raw tools, including plus speed, defensive skills and arm strength. But he somehow completely lost his grasp of the strike zone, not drawing his first walk until his 24th game last year. He became easy prey for pitchers once they realized they didn't have to throw him strikes. Lefties gave him nightmares, as he hit just .208 with one homer against them. Guzman needs to repeat Double-A and regain the momentum he had prior to 2001. He could end up as a reserve outfielder.

Year	Club (League)	Class	AVG	G	AB	R	H	2B	3B	HR	RBI	BB	SO	SB
1996	Rays/Angels (DSL)	R	.233	42	116	11	27	6	0	0	13	19	17	11
1997	Butte (Pio)	R	.302	17	43	12	13	2	1	3	13	5	5	3
1998	Butte (Pio)	R	.331	69	299	70	99	16	5	9	61	24	44	40

1999	Cedar Rapids (Mid)	A	.274	130	526	74	144	26	13	4	48	41	84	52
2000	Lake Elsinore (Cal)	A	.282	135	532	96	150	20	16	9	72	61	116	53
2001	Arkansas (TL)	AA	.244	117	459	58	112	21	8	7	46	17	89	18
MINOR LEAGUE TOTALS			.276	510	1975	321	545	91	43	32	253	167	355	177

26. Johnny Raburn, 2b

Born: Feb. 16, 1979. **Ht.:** 6-1. **Wt.:** 165. **Bats:** B. **Throws:** R. **School:** University of South Florida. **Career Transactions:** Selected by Angels in 16th round of 2000 draft; signed June 13, 2000.

Raburn's brother Ryan was drafted in the fifth round last June by the Tigers and had a banner pro debut. Johnny doesn't possess the pop of his younger sibling, but that doesn't mean he doesn't have tools. In the midst of an all-star season in the low Class A Midwest League last year, he broke his arm sliding into second base in June. He'll never hit for power and needs to bulk up his wiry body. But he demonstrates a keen eye at the plate and has a knack for putting the ball in play on the ground. He's a quick and intelligent baserunner. A three-year starter at shortstop at South Florida, Raburn made the transition to second base last year. He's erratic in the field with a fringe average arm, though he does have solid instincts and quick feet. With a profile resembling David Eckstein's, Raburn's future could be as a utilityman. He had fully recovered by instructional league and should start 2002 in high Class A.

Year	Club (League)	Class	AVG	G	AB	R	H	2B	3B	HR	RBI	BB	SO	SB
2000	Boise (NWL)	A	.254	72	280	49	71	12	4	0	34	54	72	28
2001	Cedar Rapids (Mid)	A	.315	68	235	56	74	2	1	0	12	63	43	37
MINOR LEAGUE TOTALS			.282	140	515	105	145	14	5	0	46	117	115	65

27. Joel Peralta, rhp

Born: March 23, 1980. **Ht.:** 5-11. **Wt.:** 155. **Bats:** R. **Throws:** R. **Career Transactions:** Signed out of Dominican Republic by Athletics, July 4, 1996 . . . Released by Athletics, June 4, 1998 . . . Signed by Angels, Feb. 25, 1999.

Peralta was released by the Athletics after one season as an infielder in the Rookie-level Dominican Summer League. Scooped up by the Angels eight months later, his next stint in the DSL came as a pitcher and was more successful. He took a step back with a rough U.S. debut in 2000, then recovered and progressed all the way from low Class A to Double-A last year. The diminutive righty can run his fastball up to 95 mph. He also brings a hard slider and a changeup from a quick-armed, three-quarters delivery. His command tailed off during his brief stint in Arkansas but hadn't been a problem previously. Peralta's make-up is off the charts and he's determined to reach the majors. He worked on tightening the rotation of his slider in the Dominican this winter, which should help him when he returns to Double-A.

Year	Club (League)	Class	AVG	G	AB	R	H	2B	3B	HR	RBI	BB	SO	SB
1997	Athletics West (DSL)	R	.247	52	162	25	40	5	0	0	11	22	28	4
1998							Did Not Play							
MINOR LEAGUE TOTALS			.247	52	162	25	40	5	0	0	11	22	28	4

Year	Club (League)	Class	W	L	ERA	G	GS	CG	SV	IP	H	R	ER	BB	SO
1999	Angels (DSL)	R	2	3	2.50	24	0	0	12	36	27	14	10	16	35
2000	Butte (Pio)	R	2	1	6.63	10	1	0	1	19	24	15	14	10	17
	Boise (NWL)	A	0	0	6.48	4	0	0	0	8	12	6	6	5	9
2001	Cedar Rapids (Mid)	A	0	0	2.13	41	0	0	23	42	27	13	10	5	53
	Arkansas (TL)	AA	0	1	6.30	9	0	0	2	10	15	10	7	5	14
MINOR LEAGUE TOTALS			4	5	3.66	88	1	0	38	116	105	58	47	41	128

28. Rich Fischer, rhp

Born: Oct. 21, 1980. **Ht.:** 6-3. **Wt.:** 180. **Bats:** R. **Throws:** R. **School:** San Bernardino Valley (Calif.) JC. **Career Transactions:** Selected by Angels in 21st round of 2000 draft; signed June 9, 2000.

Though Fischer was a shortstop at San Bernardino Valley (Calif.) JC, scout Tim Corcoran coveted his arm strength and the Angels drafted him as a pitcher. Since leaving the bat behind, he has made encouraging progress on the mound. Fischer has an ideal pitcher's frame, a low-90s fastball and a good feel for a changeup. His breaking ball is usable and improved over the course of last year. Because he's so new to pitching, Fischer's delivery is a work in progress. He tends to push some of his pitches. While he had little trouble throwing strikes, Fischer needs to improve his offspeed stuff to fare better against left-handers, who ripped him for a .332 average in 2001. The Angels are excited about his potential and they know they'll have to be patient while waiting for him to mature. He'll move a step up to high Class A in 2002.

Year	Club (League)	Class	W	L	ERA	G	GS	CG	SV	IP	H	R	ER	BB	SO
2000	Butte (Pio)	R	3	5	5.91	18	13	1	1	70	103	63	46	26	45
2001	Cedar Rapids (Mid)	A	9	7	4.20	20	20	2	0	131	131	73	61	33	97
MINOR LEAGUE TOTALS			12	12	4.80	38	33	3	1	201	234	136	107	59	142

29. Jake Woods, lhp

Born: Sept. 3, 1981. **Ht.:** 6-1. **Wt.:** 195. **Bats:** R. **Throws:** R. **School:** Bakerfield (Calif.) JC. **Career Transactions:** Selected by Angels in third round of 2001 draft; signed June 13, 2001.

Bakersfield (Calif.) JC is getting a reputation for churning out pitching prospects. The Rangers made righthander Colby Lewis a supplemental first-round pick in 1999, and the Red Sox took lefty Phil Dumatrait in the first round in 2000. After Woods broke Dumatrait's single-season strikeout record, the Angels selected him in the third round last June. He's built like Mike Stanton, with a solid, stocky body and thick legs. Also similar to Stanton, Woods throws a power breaking ball with a tough three-quarters break toward the back foot of righthanders. He can command both sides of the plate with his fastball, which has increased from the low 80s in high school to 89-91 mph. Though he led the Pioneer League in strikeouts during his pro debut, Woods was inconsistent. He often got into trouble because he got too much of the plate with his fastball and didn't have the confidence to throw his changeup. By the end of instructional league, he had fallen in love with his change. He's anxious to make his full-season debut with confidence in three pitches.

Year	Club (League)	Class	W	L	ERA	G	GS	CG	SV	IP	H	R	ER	BB	SO
2001	Provo (Pio)	R	4	3	5.29	15	14	1	0	65	70	41	38	29	84
MINOR LEAGUE TOTALS			4	3	5.29	15	14	1	0	65	70	41	38	29	84

30. Quan Cosby, of

Born: Dec. 23, 1982. **Ht.:** 5-10. **Wt.:** 185. **Bats:** B. **Throws:** R. **School:** Mart (Texas) HS. **Career Transactions:** Selected by Angels in sixth round of 2001 draft; signed June 6, 2001.

Cosby was the fastest prospect in the 2001 draft. He won Texas state 2-A championships in the 100 meters (10.46 second) and 200 meters (21.31) and was even more accomplished on the gridiron. He led Mart High to a football title as a senior, scoring 48 touchdowns between quarterback, defensive back and kick returner. One of the nation's top football recruits, he turned down a scholarship from Texas—where he would have joined Dodgers 12th-rounder Cedric Benson—to sign for $850,000 as a sixth-round pick. He has a lot of work to do on the diamond, but unlike Benson he's committed to baseball full-time. The Angels project Cosby as a prototype leadoff hitter, and many scouts compare his explosive speed to Deion Sanders'. Cosby is a slap hitter from the left side but flashed some power from the right side with four homers in the final week of instructional league. He still has to develop a solid approach at the plate and learn to use his speed to get on base, then steal once he gets there. Cosby is a chiseled athlete who's starting to loosen up and get into baseball shape. His arm has improved more than a full grade since the spring. He's the best pure athlete the Angels have, but Cosby will be a long-term project.

Year	Club (League)	Class	AVG	G	AB	R	H	2B	3B	HR	RBI	BB	SO	SB
2001	Angels (AZL)	R	.243	41	148	21	36	4	1	0	8	9	40	8
MINOR LEAGUE TOTALS			.243	41	148	21	36	4	1	0	8	9	40	8

ARIZONA
Diamondbacks

TOP 30 PROSPECTS

1. Luis Terrero, of
2. Mike Gosling, lhp
3. Scott Hairston, 2b
4. Lyle Overbay, 1b
5. Jose Valverde, rhp
6. Jesus Cota, 1b
7. Lino Garcia, of
8. Jason Bulger, rhp
9. Brad Cresse, c
10. Beltran Perez, rhp
11. Josh Kroeger, of
12. Tim Olson, ss/3b
13. Oscar Villarreal, rhp
14. John Patterson, rhp
15. Jeremy Ward, rhp
16. Chris Capuano, lhp
17. Chad Tracy, 3b
18. Doug Devore, of
19. Brian Bruney, rhp
20. Bill White, lhp
21. Alex Cintron, ss
22. Jerry Gil, ss
23. Jay Belflower, rhp
24. P.J. Bevis, rhp
25. Corby Medlin, rhp
26. Brandon Webb, rhp
27. Brandon Medders, rhp
28. Victor Hall, of
29. Craig Ansman, c
30. Andy Green, 2b

By Josh Boyd

Not many organizations have executed a four-year plan more efficiently than the Diamondbacks. It actually started in 1995 when owner Jerry Colangelo, general manager Joe Garagiola Jr. and manager Buck Showalter laid out the framework for Arizona's first major league baseball team.

The Diamondbacks became the most successful expansion franchise in history by winning the World Series in their fourth year of existence. They beat the Yankees behind the dominance of Randy Johnson and Curt Schilling in a classic World Series.

Colangelo vows the Diamondbacks won't follow the path of the Marlins, who won a World Series in their fifth year before dismantling their roster. But Arizona's aging roster and financial situation do create concern. Colangelo got several players to defer salary and borrowed money from Major League Baseball in 2001. Following the World Series, he requested an additional $160 million from his ownership group to keep the team intact.

The Diamondbacks have relied on free agents since their inception, and their farm system still ranks near the bottom. The system has not produced a homegrown every-

day player or starter who has made a significant impact in Arizona. They have had success on the foreign market, landing such players as Byung-Hyun Kim and Erubiel Durazo. But spending freely on domestic talent hasn't paid off. After spending $16 million on loophole free agents Travis Lee and John Patterson in 1996, both players have been disappointments—though Lee was used in a trade for Schilling.

Arizona is trying to reverse the trend, and scouting director Mike Rizzo has two solid drafts under his belt. Continued efforts from Latin American coordinator Junior Noboa have helped bolster the system's depth.

A stockpile of powerful arms on the farm provides hope for the future of Arizona's shaky bullpen. Flamethrowing righthander Jose Valverde leads the way, while righthanders Brian Bruney and Corby Medlin flirt with triple digits on the radar gun.

With Durazo coming off the bench, Mark Grace locked up for another year and talent backed up in the system, a potential logjam existed at first base. But Jack Cust, the team's first-round draft pick in 1997 and top power prospect, was dealt to Colorado in January.

OrganizationOverview

General Manager: Joe Garagiola Jr. **Farm Director:** Tommy Jones. **Scouting director:** Mike Rizzo.

2001 PERFORMANCE

Class	Team	League	W	L	Pct.	Finish*	Manager
Majors	Arizona	National	92	70	.568	3rd (16)	Bob Brenly
Triple-A	Tucson Sidewinders	Pacific Coast	65	77	.458	12th (16)	Tom Spencer
Double-A	El Paso Diablos	Texas	57	83	.407	7th (8)	Al Pedrique
High A	Lancaster JetHawks	California	61	79	.436	t-8th (10)	Scott Coolbaugh
Low A	South Bend Silver Hawks	Midwest	70	66	.515	6th (14)	Steve Scarsone
Short-season	Yakima Bears	Northwest	33	42	.440	6th (8)	Greg Lonigro
Rookie	Missoula Osprey	Pioneer	52	24	.684	2nd (8)	Chip Hale
OVERALL 2001 MINOR LEAGUE RECORD			338	371	.477	21st (30)	

*Finish in overall standings (No. of teams in league)

ORGANIZATION LEADERS

BATTING
*AVG	Jesus Cota, Missoula	.368
R	Billy Martin, El Paso/Lancaster	101
H	Lyle Overbay, El Paso	187
TB	Lyle Overbay, El Paso	281
2B	Lyle Overbay, El Paso	49
3B	**Victor Hall**, South Bend	12
HR	Jack Cust, Tucson	27
RBI	Billy Martin, El Paso/Lancaster	107
BB	Jack Cust, Tucson	102
SO	Jack Cust, Tucson	160
SB	**Victor Hall**, South Bend	60

PITCHING
W	Beltran Perez, South Bend	12
L	Enrique Gonzalez, South Bend	12
#ERA	Ryan Holsten, Missoula	2.53
G	Jason Martines, Tucson/El Paso	63
CG	Three tied at	2
SV	Greg Belson, South Bend	16
IP	Kennie Steenstra, Tucson	170
BB	**Chris Capuano**, El Paso	75
SO	**Chris Capuano**, El Paso	167

*Minimum 250 At-Bats #Minimum 75 Innings

TOP PROSPECTS OF THE DECADE

1997	Travis Lee, 1b
1998	Travis Lee, 1b
1999	Brad Penny, rhp
2000	John Patterson, rhp
2001	Alex Cintron, ss

TOP DRAFT PICKS OF THE DECADE

1996	Nick Bierbrodt, lhp
1997	Jack Cust, 1b
1998	Darryl Conyer, of (3)
1999	Corey Myers, ss
2000	Mike Schultz, rhp (2)
2001	Jason Bulger, rhp

BEST TOOLS

Best Hitter for Average	Lyle Overbay
Best Power Hitter	Jesus Cota
Fastest Baserunner	Lino Garcia
Best Fastball	Jose Valverde

Hall   **Capuano**

Best Breaking Ball	Chris Capuano
Best Changeup	Mike Gosling
Best Control	Beltran Perez
Best Defensive Catcher	Mike DiRosa
Best Defensive Infielder	Jerry Gil
Best Infield Arm	Jerry Gil
Best Defensive Outfielder	Lino Garcia
Best Outfield Arm	Luis Terrero

PROJECTED 2005 LINEUP

Catcher	Brad Cresse
First Base	Lyle Overbay
Second Base	Scott Hairston
Third Base	Tim Olson
Shortstop	Alex Cintron
Left Field	Luis Gonzalez
Center Field	Luis Terrero
Right Field	Erubiel Durazo
No. 1 Starter	Curt Schilling
No. 2 Starter	Randy Johnson
No. 3 Starter	Mike Gosling
No. 4 Starter	Byung-Hyun Kim
No. 5 Starter	Rick Helling
Closer	Jose Valverde

ALL-TIME LARGEST BONUSES

Travis Lee, 1996	$10,000,000
John Patterson, 1996	$6,075,000
Byung-Hyun Kim, 1999	$2,000,000
Corey Myers, 1999	$2,000,000
Mike Gosling, 2001	$2,000,000

DraftAnalysis

2001 Draft

Best Pro Debut: 2B Scott Hairston (3) followed up his Arizona junior college triple crown by batting .347-14-65 and leading the Rookie-level Pioneer League with 81 runs. RHP Jay Belflower (17) survived the launching pad at high Class A Lancaster and even made one appearance in Triple-A, posting a 0.59 ERA with 11 saves.

Best Athlete: OF Jarred Ball (9) is a switch-hitter with exceptional speed. OF Richie Barrett (5) played guard for the NCAA Division III Ursinus (Pa.) basketball team, finishing as the all-time leading scorer in the Centennial Conference.

Best Hitter: The Diamondbacks believe so much in Hairston's hitting ability that they may jump him from Rookie ball to Double-A in 2002. 3B Chad Tracy (7) has a pretty left-handed swing and hit .340-4-36 in Class A.

Best Raw Power: Hairston's compact stroke allows him to hit for power and average.

Fastest Runner: Ball runs the 60-yard dash in 6.4-6.5 seconds. Barrett is a 6.6 runner.

Best Defensive Player: C Mike DiRosa (16) has standout catch-and-throw skills and erased 41 percent of basestealers in the short-season Northwest League. His .307-4-25 totals were a pleasant surprise.

Best Fastball: RHP **Jason Bulger** (1) was more of a third baseman in his first three years at Division II Valdosta State (Ga.), then threw 97 mph in the spring and summer. Mike Gosling (2) had one of the best arms among lefthanders in the draft and threw 94-95 mph in simulated games after signing.

RHPs Justin Wechsler (4), Brandon Medders (8) and Belflower all have strong arms.

Most Intriguing Background: Hairston's grandfather Sam, father Jerry, uncle John and brother Jerry Jr. all have played in the majors. Bulger's brothers Brian and Kevin were drafted by the Giants in June, while unsigned RHP Matt Fox' (6) brother Mike was taken by the Cardinals. Unsigned OF Seth Smith (48) was a reserve quarterback at Mississippi last fall.

Bulger

Closest To The Majors: Gosling didn't debut until the Arizona Fall League because he had shoulder tenderness, but he'll start 2002 in Double-A. He could be joined by Bulger, Hairston, Tracy, Medders and Belflower.

Best Late-Round Pick: Belflower's stock soared since he moved from the rotation to the bullpen at Florida last spring.

The One Who Got Away: RHP Brett Smith (21) was insurance in case Arizona couldn't sign Bulger or Gosling. A projected second- or third-rounder on talent, Smith joined UC Irvine's resuscitated baseball program.

Assessment: Arizona rated Gosling among the draft's top eight prospects, but gambled that he would slide to the second round. The Diamondbacks signed him for $2 million, which made it more difficult to sign Bulger. He eventually agreed to $936,000.

2000 Draft

Switching its focus toward college players, Arizona beefed up its offense with 1B Jesus Cota (14, draft-and-follow), C Brad Cresse (5), OF Josh Kroeger (4) and SS Tim Olson (7). LHP Bill White (3) may help as well. Not bad for a club without a first-rounder. **Grade: C+**

1999 Draft

The consensus was the Diamondbacks would take Ben Sheets fourth overall, but they blew the pick on 3B Corey Myers and then took RHP Casey Daigle. 1B Lyle Overbay (18), RHP Jeremy Ward (2) and LHP Chris Capuano (8) should salvage something. **Grade: C**

1998 Draft

Arizona didn't have a first- or second-rounder, and it might as well have not had a third-rounder. That became OF Darryl Conyer (3), who's now playing college football. RHP Bret Prinz (18) is all the club got out of this crop. **Grade: D**

1997 Draft

The Diamondbacks traded OF Jack Cust (1) this winter, deciding not to wait to find out whether he would be the next Jim Thome or the next Bob Hamelin. SS Alex Cintron's (36) star is fading fast. **Grade: C+**

Note: Draft analysis prepared by Jim Callis. Numbers in parentheses indicate draft rounds.

... He's an outstanding center fielder with the range to run down balls in the alleys and a plus arm.

Luis Terrero of

Born: May 18, 1980
Ht.: 6-2. **Wt.:** 183.
Bats: L. **Throws:** R.
Career Transactions: Signed out of Dominican Republic by Diamondbacks, Sept. 27, 1997.

Terrero is one of Latin American coordinator Junior Noboa's prized finds from the Dominican Republic. His development hasn't been without obstacles, but his tools are reminiscent of Vladimir Guerrero's. After getting off to a miserable start at low Class A South Bend last season, he went on the disabled list with a high left ankle sprain. He later found out it was a stress fracture and missed six weeks. Injuries are nothing new, as he missed six weeks with a broken right hamate bone in 2000. Terrero finally got on track and hit .349 between high Class A Lancaster and Double-A El Paso.

Scouts love players with Terrero's loose and easy actions, and his frame can handle more muscle as he fills out. His wiry strength and above-average bat speed give him power potential to all fields. He has the wheels to steal 30 bases a year if he doesn't bulk up too much. Despite his apparent lack of strike-zone judgment, he's under control and has good balance at the plate. He's an outstanding center fielder with the range to run down balls in the alleys and a plus arm capable of handling right field. The Diamondbacks say something clicked for Terrero at the end of the year, and his aptitude and work ethic will help him make adjustments. But he will struggle to get the most out of his five-tool potential until he takes a more disciplined approach. His poor strikeout-walk ratio illustrates how aggressive he is at the plate. Terrero likes to hack at the first close pitch he sees. He has enough strength and bat speed to make up for his long swing, but he has to shorten up with two strikes. He struggles with pitch recognition.

Noboa was encouraged with Terrero's progress in the Dominican League this winter, but he again was shelved after tearing cartilage in his left knee. He's still on schedule to play in Triple-A Tucson in 2002, and he'll provide insurance for Steve Finley. Terrero made up a lot of ground in a short time, but he needs to shake the injury bug and make key adjustments before comparisons to Guerrero become apt. A healthy year in Triple-A could make him Finley's successor in 2003.

Year	Club (League)	Class	AVG	G	AB	R	H	2B	3B	HR	RBI	BB	SO	SB
1998	Diamondbacks (DSL)	R	.231	56	169	19	39	7	1	2	15	13	44	9
1999	Missoula (Pio)	R	.287	71	272	74	78	13	7	8	40	32	91	27
2000	High Desert (Cal)	A	.190	19	79	10	15	3	1	0	1	3	16	5
	Missoula (Pio)	R	.261	68	276	48	72	10	0	8	44	10	75	23
2001	Yakima (NWL)	A	.317	11	41	7	13	2	1	0	0	2	8	0
	South Bend (Mid)	A	.157	24	89	4	14	2	0	1	8	0	29	3
	Lancaster (Cal)	A	.451	19	71	16	32	9	1	4	11	1	14	5
	El Paso (Tex)	AA	.299	34	147	29	44	13	3	3	8	4	45	9
MINOR LEAGUE TOTALS			.268	302	1144	207	307	59	14	26	127	65	322	81

RODGER WOOD

2. Mike Gosling, lhp

Born: Sept. 23, 1980. **Ht.:** 6-2. **Wt.:** 215. **Bats:** L. **Throws:** L. **School:** Stanford University. **Career Transactions:** Selected by Diamondbacks in second round of 2001 draft; signed Aug. 1, 2001.

After two years as a reliever at Stanford, Gosling overcame a tender elbow at the start of 2001 to excel as a starter, though Miami trounced him 12-1 in the College World Series championship game. The Diamondbacks gambled successfully they could get him in the second round. He signed for $2 million, the largest bonus outside the first round. Gosling is tough to hit, allowing a stingy .209 average as a collegian, but he didn't throw strikes consistently until ironing out his delivery as a junior. He has above-average velocity for a lefthander at 92-95 mph, and his fastball runs and tails. His array of breaking stuff is already among the best in the system. His curveball has late depth and his slider was sharp in the Arizona Fall League. He has an advanced feel for changing speeds. Gosling has a funky arm action, but most scouts say it works for him and adds to his deception. His velocity dipped to the mid-80s at the end of the spring, so he needs to build up his stamina. Gosling didn't join the AFL until midway through the six-week schedule, but he worked 29 innings. He's expected to jump right onto the fast track as a starter in Double-A.

Year	Club (League)	Class	W	L	ERA	G	GS	CG	SV	IP	H	R	ER	BB	SO
	Has Not Played—Signed 2002 Contract														

3. Scott Hairston, 2b

Born: May 25, 1980. **Ht.:** 6-0. **Wt.:** 190. **Bats:** R. **Throws:** R. **School:** Central Arizona JC. **Career Transactions:** Selected by Diamondbacks in third round of 2001 draft; signed June 15, 2001.

Four of Hairston's relatives have played in the majors: grandfather Sam, father Jerry, uncle John and brother Jerry Jr., who's Baltimore's second baseman. He won Arizona's junior college triple crown and was Baseball America's junior college player of the year after hitting .503-18-77 last spring. He recovered from a slow start to compete with teammate Jesus Cota for the Rookie-level Pioneer League triple crown. Hairston's deep baseball bloodlines are evident in his approach to the game. He positions himself well in the field and shows outstanding instincts on the bases. He has a chance to be a productive offensive player because he generates power with excellent bat speed, giving balls extra carry. Questions about Hairston's defense kept him from going higher in the draft. His arm is below-average and he's not polished with the glove. He could improve because like his brother he shows athleticism, soft hands and range to both sides. Hairston had one of the best debuts in the draft class of 2001. As a result, the Diamondbacks will jump him to high Class A and he could reach Double-A before the end of his first full season.

Year	Club (League)	Class	AVG	G	AB	R	H	2B	3B	HR	RBI	BB	SO	SB
2001	Missoula (Pio)	R	.347	74	291	81	101	16	6	14	65	38	50	2
MINOR LEAGUE TOTALS			.347	74	291	81	101	16	6	14	65	38	50	2

4. Lyle Overbay, 1b

Born: Jan. 28, 1977. **Ht.:** 6-2. **Wt.:** 215. **Bats:** L. **Throws:** L. **School:** University of Nevada. **Career Transactions:** Selected by Diamondbacks in 18th round of 1999 draft; signed June 8, 1999.

Overbay won the Big West Conference batting title as a senior at Nevada in 1999, then became the first player ever to drive in 100 runs in a short-season league. He was named the best batting prospect in the Double-A Texas League last year, leading the loop in hitting, doubles and on-base percentage (.423). Overbay is predominantly a line-drive, gap-to-gap hitter. Though he hasn't topped 14 homers in a pro season, some scouts say with his pure swing, he has a chance to develop 20-25 longball power. Overbay thinks contact first and gets good extension through the ball, spraying hits to all fields. The ball jumps off his bat, and he has shown the strength to drive the ball into the alleys with authority. Drafted as an outfielder, Overbay can be stiff and awkward around first base. He went to Mexico over the winter to work on his defense, and while he's no Mark Grace, he did show more fluid actions. With Grace locked up for another season and Erubiel Durazo waiting in the wings, Overbay will spend the year feasting on pitching in another hitter's league at Triple-A Tucson.

Year	Club (League)	Class	AVG	G	AB	R	H	2B	3B	HR	RBI	BB	SO	SB
1999	Missoula (Pio)	R	.343	75	306	66	105	25	7	12	101	40	53	10
2000	South Bend (Mid)	A	.332	71	259	47	86	19	3	6	47	27	36	9
	El Paso (TL)	AA	.352	62	244	43	86	16	2	8	49	28	39	3
2001	El Paso (TL)	AA	.352	138	532	82	187	49	3	13	100	67	92	5
	Arizona (NL)	MAJ	.500	2	2	0	1	0	0	0	0	0	1	0
MAJOR LEAGUE TOTALS			.500	2	2	0	1	0	0	0	0	0	1	0
MINOR LEAGUE TOTALS			.346	346	1341	238	464	109	15	39	297	162	220	27

5. Jose Valverde, rhp

JOHN SPEAR

Born: July 24, 1979. **Ht.:** 6-4. **Wt.:** 220. **Bats:** R. **Throws:** R. **Career Transactions:** Signed out of Dominican Republic by Diamondbacks, Jan. 31, 1997.

With injured closers Matt Mantei and Bret Prinz unavailable in the postseason, Diamondbacks manager Bob Brenly would have loved to call on Valverde's power arm when Byung-Hyun Kim imploded. To get there, Valverde has to prove his durability. A right shoulder strain limited him in 2000, and shoulder tendinitis cut short his 2001 campaign and precluded a trip to winter ball. Compared to Armando Benitez for his intimidating stature and overpowering repertoire, Valverde generates explosive late sink on his 94-96 mph fastball. He also throws a hard slider and operates from a deceptive maximum-effort delivery. Valverde is primarily a two-pitch pitcher, but he needs to develop a third pitch to combat lefthanders, who hit .348 against him last year. He's an animated pitcher who must curb his energy and emotions. He has yet to show the resiliency expected from a closer. Valverde is expected to be fully recovered in time to take Tucson's closer job. He'll be a tempting option should Arizona's bullpen falter again, though he must improve his control and stamina before becoming a dominant closer.

Year	Club (League)	Class	W	L	ERA	G	GS	CG	SV	IP	H	R	ER	BB	SO
1997	Diamondbacks (DSL)	R	0	0	5.30	14	0	0	0	19	20	12	11	13	19
1998	Diamondbacks (DSL)	R	1	3	1.75	23	4	0	7	51	31	14	10	22	56
1999	Diamondbacks (AZL)	R	1	2	4.08	20	0	0	8	29	34	21	13	10	47
	South Bend (Mid)	A	0	0	0.00	2	0	0	0	3	2	0	0	2	3
2000	South Bend (Mid)	A	0	5	5.40	31	0	0	14	32	31	20	19	25	39
	Missoula (Pio)	R	1	0	0.00	12	0	0	4	12	3	0	0	4	24
2001	El Paso (Tex)	AA	2	2	3.92	39	0	0	13	41	36	19	18	27	72
MINOR LEAGUE TOTALS			5	12	3.44	141	4	0	46	186	157	86	71	103	260

6. Jesus Cota, 1b

JOHN SPEAR

Born: Nov. 7, 1981. **Ht.:** 6-3. **Wt.:** 200. **Bats:** L. **Throws:** R. **School:** Pima (Ariz.) CC. **Career Transactions:** Selected by Diamondbacks in 14th round of 2000 draft; signed May 28, 2001.

A 14th-round draft pick in 2000, Cota improved his stock as a sophomore and signed for $60,000 a week before last year's draft. The last time the Diamondbacks signed a Mexican first baseman out of Pima Community College, they came away with Erubiel Durazo. Cota reached base safely in 68 of 75 games and won the Pioneer League triple crown. Beyond the obvious parallels that link Cota and Durazo, Cota's size and tools conjure further comparisons. The Diamondbacks project him to have 40-home run potential. He still needs to learn to generate more backspin and loft on the ball, but his quick, compact stroke has power written all over it. Cota is limited athletically and already is a big-bodied player who doesn't run well. He's learning to play first base after spending most of his amateur career in the outfield, and he needs work around the bag. First base is a crowded position throughout the organization. Cota's bat will have to carry him, and it can. He's a polished product at the plate and shouldn't have any trouble adjusting to low Class A Midwest League pitching in his full-season debut.

Year	Club (League)	Class	AVG	G	AB	R	H	2B	3B	HR	RBI	BB	SO	SB
2001	Missoula (Pio)	R	.368	75	272	74	100	22	0	16	71	56	52	2
MINOR LEAGUE TOTALS			.368	75	272	74	100	22	0	16	71	56	52	2

7. Lino Garcia, of

Born: Oct. 12, 1983. **Ht.:** 6-3. **Wt.:** 180. **Bats:** R. **Throws:** R. **Career Transactions:** Signed out of Venezuela by Diamondbacks, Feb. 22, 2001.

When Arizona scouts had Garcia at a private workout in Tampa, all they needed to see was him running the 60-yard dash in 6.4 seconds before they knew they weren't letting him leave without a contract. He signed for $65,000. His pro debut was interrupted when he broke a hand sliding into second base. A loose, natural athlete, Garcia has as much upside as anyone in the system. He's an 8 runner on the 2-to-8 scouting scale. He patrols center field with the ease of perennial Gold Glover Andruw Jones with a solid-average major league arm. Garcia projects to hit for more power because he generates plus bat speed and has leverage that propels the ball off the bat and creates backspin. Garcia went straight from extended spring training to the Pioneer League last season, skipping the Rookie-level Dominican Summer League. While he held his own, he was overmatched at times. His main needs right now are to add strength and gain experience. Garcia will make a big leap to South Bend, where he'll make his full-season debut before his 18th birthday. He has the tools to shoot up the depth chart in a hurry.

Year	Club (League)	Class	AVG	G	AB	R	H	2B	3B	HR	RBI	BB	SO	SB
2001	Missoula (Pio)	R	.243	46	140	34	34	6	2	4	22	14	32	8
MINOR LEAGUE TOTALS			.243	46	140	34	34	6	2	4	22	14	32	8

8. Jason Bulger, rhp

Born: Dec. 6, 1978. **Ht.:** 6-4. **Wt.:** 205. **Bats:** R. **Throws:** R. **School:** Valdosta State (Ga.) University. **Career Transactions:** Selected by Diamondbacks in first round (22nd overall) of 2001 draft; signed Sept. 18, 2001.

Bulger pitched little until his senior year at NCAA Division II Valdosta State, when he attracted attention with his fastball. He didn't project as a first-rounder but was considered an easy sign, then went in the first round and held out for the entire summer. He signed for $936,000, the second-lowest bonus in the first round. Brothers Brian and Kevin were selected later in the draft by the Giants. A converted third baseman, Bulger led Valdosta State in hitting, ERA and saves last season. He's capable of running his heater up to 97 mph, and it sits comfortably in the low 90s. He has an ideal pitcher's frame, similar to Kevin Brown's with broad shoulders and a loose arm. Bulger gives glimpses of a quality breaking ball, but until he hones his delivery it will be inconsistent. He rushes his delivery on his curveball and his arm has trouble catching up with his body. He has minimal mileage on his arm, but Bulger also lacks the savvy that comes with experience. His best chance to jump on the fast track will be in the bullpen. He'll debut as a starter in Double-A to build stamina.

Year	Club (League)	Class	AVG	G	AB	R	H	2B	3B	HR	RBI	BB	SO	SB
		Has Not Played—Signed 2002 Contract												

9. Brad Cresse, c

Born: July 31, 1978. **Ht.:** 6-4. **Wt.:** 215. **Bats:** R. **Throws:** R. **School:** Louisiana State University. **Career Transactions:** Selected by Diamondbacks in fifth round of 2000 draft; signed June 19, 2000.

Cresse hit 29 homers as a Louisiana State sophomore but wasn't drafted after a disappointing junior season. He rededicated himself and led NCAA Division I in homers as a senior, capped his career by driving in the championship-winning run in the 2000 College World Series and tore up pro pitching in his debut. Cresse's father Mark served as Dodgers bullpen coach, and Mark's godfather is Hall of Fame manager Tommy Lasorda. Cresse is a strong, durable slugger with tremendous raw power. He has a good idea at the plate and shows the ability to make adjustments. His bloodlines come across in his work ethic. He has plenty of arm strength and instills confidence in his pitching staff. At Cresse's size, mobility behind the plate will always present a challenge. While he has improved his footwork and overall receiving, he allowed 17 passed balls last year and threw out just 27 percent of basestealers. He gets too pull-conscious at times. The Diamondbacks have yet to develop an everyday catcher but think Cresse could be their first. He's a student of the game and could move quickly through Tucson to Arizona by the end of 2002.

Year	Club (League)	Class	AVG	G	AB	R	H	2B	3B	HR	RBI	BB	SO	SB
2000	High Desert (Cal)	A	.324	48	173	35	56	7	0	17	56	17	50	0
	El Paso (TL)	AA	.262	15	42	9	11	1	0	1	10	6	12	0
2001	El Paso (TL)	AA	.289	118	429	55	124	39	1	14	81	44	116	0
MINOR LEAGUE TOTALS			.297	181	644	99	191	47	1	32	147	67	178	0

10. Beltran Perez, rhp

Born: Oct. 24, 1981. **Ht.:** 6-2. **Wt.:** 160. **Bats:** R. **Throws:** R. **Career Transactions:** Signed out of Dominican Republic by Diamondbacks, Feb. 2, 1999.

Perez has pitched with poise that belies his youth since Junior Noboa signed him out of the Dominican Republic as a slightly built 17-year-old in 1999. Perez showcased his best stuff in a pair of emergency starts in the high Class A California League at the end of the 2000 season, which was more than enough to convince Arizona that he could handle South Bend in his first full season. His fastball is average at best, sitting in the 86-89 mph range and occasionally touching the low 90s, but his arm action suggests there is more velocity to come. Though he's not overpowering, he pitches on a tough downward plane and has outstanding finish on his fastball, making it seem quicker to hitters. His changeup is a major league pitch already because his arm works so free and easy, but his breaking ball needs work. Perez hits his spots and managers rated his control the best in the Midwest League last year. If he doesn't add a third pitch, he'll be destined for the bullpen, but he has plenty of time to develop it as a starter in the minors. He'll work on that this year in the Cal League.

Year	Club (League)	Class	W	L	ERA	G	GS	CG	SV	IP	H	R	ER	BB	SO
1999	Diamondbacks (DSL)	R	6	0	2.45	18	0	0	0	29	24	9	8	9	31
2000	Diamondbacks (AZL)	R	5	1	5.81	11	4	0	0	48	61	37	31	25	47
	High Desert (Cal)	A	0	1	3.60	2	2	0	0	10	8	4	4	5	11
2001	South Bend (Mid)	A	12	4	2.81	27	27	2	0	160	142	59	50	35	157
MINOR LEAGUE TOTALS			23	6	3.39	58	33	2	0	247	235	112	93	74	246

11. Josh Kroeger, of

Born: Aug. 31, 1982. **Ht.:** 6-2. **Wt.:** 190. **Bats:** L. **Throws:** L. **School:** Scripps Ranch HS, San Diego. **Career Transactions:** Selected by Diamondbacks in fourth round of 2000 draft; signed June 6, 2000.

Drafted as a 17-year-old, Kroeger had 497 at-bats before he turned 19. Recruited as a wide receiver out of high school, he combines strength, size and athleticism with a smooth left-handed stroke. He uses his upper-body strength to generate torque in his swing and the ball carries well upon impact, suggesting he'll develop power. Kroeger is a polished hitter for his age but still needs to learn which pitches he can and can't handle. He could also use some more patience at the plate. Kroeger will be limited to an outfield corner and may have just enough arm to play right field. His bat profiles well for that position. The Diamondbacks didn't operate an instructional league following the 2001 season and planned to send Kroeger to Australia so he could prepare for high Class A this year, but the league suspended operations this winter.

Year	Club (League)	Class	AVG	G	AB	R	H	2B	3B	HR	RBI	BB	SO	SB
2000	Diamondbacks (AZL)	R	.297	54	222	40	66	9	3	4	28	21	41	5
2001	South Bend (Mid)	A	.274	79	292	36	80	15	1	3	37	18	49	4
MINOR LEAGUE TOTALS			.284	133	514	76	146	24	4	7	65	39	90	9

12. Tim Olson, ss/3b

Born: Sept. 1, 1978. **Ht.:** 6-2. **Wt.:** 200. **Bats:** R. **Throws:** R. **School:** University of Florida. **Career Transactions:** Selected by Diamondbacks in seventh round of 2000 draft; signed June 14, 2000.

The versatile Olson is one of the organization's most athletic players. Before transferring to Florida from Hutchinson (Kan.) CC, Olson touched 93 mph as a pitcher. With the Gators, he earned third-team All-America honors and put together a school-record 27-game hitting streak as a junior outfielder. Since signing as a seventh-rounder in 2000, he hasn't settled at one position. After splitting duties between the outfield and third base in his debut season, Olson opened the 2001 season in Lancaster at the hot corner and finished as El Paso's everyday shortstop. A native of North Dakota, he's still relatively inexperienced and learning the game, so his success is a testament to his natural ability. He is a hard-nosed shortstop in the Mark Belanger/Dick Schofield mold, with more offensive upside. Some scouts don't view Olson as a prototypical shortstop because he doesn't possesses exceptionally quick feet. However, he runs well underway and owns plus arm strength. He committed 44 errors last season, so he'll have to get more reliable. It took him most of the year to settle on an approach at the plate, and he still needs to be more selective, but he has some raw power in his stroke. Olson could challenge Alex Cintron for the Triple-A shortstop job this year, and his versatility could make him an interesting option for the Diamondbacks by 2003.

Year	Club (League)	Class	AVG	G	AB	R	H	2B	3B	HR	RBI	BB	SO	SB
2000	South Bend (Mid)	A	.218	68	261	37	57	14	2	2	26	15	49	15
2001	Lancaster (Cal)	A	.289	61	239	36	69	12	4	6	32	14	49	13
	El Paso (TL)	AA	.317	46	167	29	53	13	0	2	24	11	36	4
MINOR LEAGUE TOTALS			.268	153	667	102	179	39	6	10	82	40	134	32

13. Oscar Villarreal, rhp

Born: Nov. 22, 1981. **Ht.:** 6-1. **Wt.:** 190. **Bats:** L. **Throws:** R. **Career Transactions:** Signed out of Mexico by Diamondbacks, Nov. 6, 1998.

As if it's not already challenging enough for pitching prospects to make their way to the big leagues, Diamondbacks farmhands are faced with the added burden of pitching in launching pads. Stats don't always tell the entire story, and Villarreal is a perfect example. With just 25 high Class A innings under his belt, he spent 2001 in the El Paso rotation and held his own as the second-younger pitcher in the Texas League. Villarreal succeeds by getting hitters to pound his sinker into the ground. He surrendered just 10 home runs while pitching his home games at Cohen Stadium, a notorious bandbox. He's not intimidating, but he works aggressively in all quadrants of the strike zone with a 91-94 mph fastball, a sharp slider and a deceptive changeup with late life. His 2001 workload was a career high, though he averaged just more than five innings per start—raising questions about his durability. Villarreal needs to settle on a consistent arm slot, which will improve his command. For the second winter in a row, he was one of the top pitchers in the Mexican Pacific League. Scouts say he pitches with more confidence and poise in his native country and think it's only a matter of time before he achieves the same success in the United States.

Year	Club (League)	Class	W	L	ERA	G	GS	CG	SV	IP	H	R	ER	BB	SO
1999	Diamondbacks (AZL)	R	1	5	3.78	14	11	0	0	64	64	39	27	25	51
2000	Tucson (PCL)	AAA	1	0	2.08	2	0	0	0	4	6	1	1	2	4
	South Bend (Mid)	A	1	3	4.41	13	5	0	0	33	37	19	16	17	30
	Diamondbacks (AZL)	R	0	0	9.00	1	0	0	0	1	2	1	1	0	1
	High Desert (Cal)	A	0	2	3.65	9	4	0	0	25	24	20	10	14	18
2001	El Paso (TL)	AA	6	9	4.41	27	27	0	0	141	154	96	69	63	108
MINOR LEAGUE TOTALS			9	19	4.16	66	47	0	0	268	287	176	124	121	212

14. John Patterson, rhp

Born: Jan. 30, 1978. **Ht.:** 6-6. **Wt.:** 200. **Bats:** R. **Throws:** R. **School:** West Orange-Stark HS, Orange, Texas. **Career Transactions:** Selected by Expos in first round (fifth overall) of 1996 draft . . . Granted free agency . . . Signed by Diamondbacks, Nov. 7, 1996.

Like the other draft loophole free agents from 1996, Patterson has yet to fulfill his potential. Injuries have posed roadblocks for Matt White and Bobby Seay in Tampa Bay, and Patterson will be entering his second year coming back from Tommy John surgery. The Diamondbacks' other loophole signee, Travis Lee, made the biggest splash before slumping with Arizona and getting traded to the Phillies in the deadline deal for Curt Schilling in July 2000. Prior to his injury, Patterson ranked among the very best prospects in the game and was on the verge of justifying his $6.075 million bonus. He had picture-perfect mechanics, mid-90s gas and an overhand 12-to-6 power curveball. He made his first start in more than a year last May in high Class A and climbed to Triple-A by season's end. His velocity was back in the 91-92 mph range, but he was inconsistent with the command of his curveball and a below-average changeup. The Diamondbacks have always babied Patterson, who never has surpassed 131 innings in a season, and he made it past the sixth inning in just three starts in 2001. They aren't sure what to expect out of Patterson in 2002, when he'll rejoin the Triple-A rotation. He worked hard in Tucson during the offseason to get ready for spring training.

Year	Club (League)	Class	W	L	ERA	G	GS	CG	SV	IP	H	R	ER	BB	SO
1997	South Bend (Mid)	A	1	9	3.23	18	18	0	0	78	63	32	28	34	95
1998	High Desert (Cal)	A	8	7	2.83	25	25	0	0	127	102	54	40	42	148
1999	El Paso (TL)	AA	8	6	4.77	18	18	2	0	100	98	61	53	42	117
	Tucson (PCL)	AAA	1	5	7.04	7	6	0	0	31	43	26	24	18	29
2000	Tucson (PCL)	AAA	0	2	7.80	3	2	0	0	15	21	14	13	9	10
2001	Lancaster (Cal)	A	0	0	5.79	2	2	0	0	9	9	6	6	3	9
	El Paso (TL)	AA	1	2	4.26	5	5	0	0	25	30	15	12	9	19
	Tucson (PCL)	AAA	2	7	5.85	13	12	0	0	68	82	50	44	31	40
MINOR LEAGUE TOTALS			21	38	4.06	91	88	2	0	453	448	258	220	188	467

15. Jeremy Ward, rhp

Born: Feb. 24, 1978. **Ht.:** 6-3. **Wt.:** 220. **Bats:** R. **Throws:** R. **School:** Long Beach State University.
Career Transactions: Selected by Diamondbacks in second round of 1999 draft; signed June 17, 1999.

As it did with John Patterson, Tommy John surgery knocked Ward off of the fast track. After signing out of Long Beach State as a second-rounder in 1999, he reached Triple-A in his first pro summer and posted a 1.62 ERA in the Arizona Fall League. He caught the attention of everyone in the organization in big league camp the following spring, when he nearly made the club. After that fast start, though, Ward missed almost all of 2000 and spent last year reestablishing his overpowering two-pitch arsenal. He experienced a minor setback in July with elbow discomfort, but bounced back and finished strong. After reaching the mid-90s in the past, Ward's fastball has settled in at 90-92 mph to go with a hard slider. He always has had an aggressive mentality and isn't afraid to challenge hitters. He joined fellow Diamondbacks farmhand Chris Capuano on Team USA's staff last fall at the World Cup in Taiwan, where he made three scoreless appearances as the U.S. won the silver medal. If Ward can stay healthy, he could be one of the first arms in line to help rebuild the Arizona bullpen.

Year	Club (League)	Class	W	L	ERA	G	GS	CG	SV	IP	H	R	ER	BB	SO
1999	High Desert (Cal)	A	0	0	2.08	4	4	0	0	9	5	2	2	3	12
	El Paso (TL)	AA	1	1	2.45	19	0	0	7	26	18	7	7	9	26
	Tucson (PCL)	AAA	0	0	0.00	1	0	0	0	2	2	0	0	2	1
2000	Tucson (PCL)	AAA	0	1	5.40	5	0	0	0	3	3	2	2	5	1
	Diamondbacks (AZL)	R	0	0	0.00	2	2	0	0	2	0	0	0	0	2
2001	El Paso (TL)	AA	0	0	1.13	6	0	0	0	8	2	2	1	1	6
	Tucson (PCL)	AAA	3	4	3.52	40	0	0	13	46	53	23	18	17	35
MINOR LEAGUE TOTALS			4	6	2.84	77	6	0	20	95	73	36	30	37	83

16. Chris Capuano, lhp

Born: Aug. 19, 1978. **Ht.:** 6-3. **Wt.:** 215. **Bats:** L. **Throws:** L. **School:** Duke University. **Career Transactions:** Selected by Diamondbacks in eighth round of 1999 draft; signed Aug. 24, 1999.

The Diamondbacks drafted Capuano in 1999 with the understanding he would not begin his professional career until he completed his degree at Duke. He made his debut in the summer of 2000 and overmatched low Class A hitters with his array of polished pitches. Last year, he jumped to Double-A, where the Texas League's smaller ballparks provided a challenge. He rebounded from a 2-7, 7.31 start with back-to-back shutouts as part of an 8-4, 4.21 finish. He finished second in the TL in strikeouts but also led the league in walks. Capuano throws an 89-92 fastball effectively to both sides of the plate. Managers rated his sharp, sweeping slider the best breaking pitch in the TL, and he also has an average changeup. Capuano hides his arm well in his delivery, providing deception that causes hitters to swing and miss frequently at pitches in and out of the zone. He needs to develop an effective pitch to combat righthanders, who hit .302 against him in 2001. He's inconsistent with his slider, though scouts say a simple adjustment would make it a strikeout pitch. As his hefty walk numbers illustrate, he also still needs work on his command. Capuano was generally more effective the first time through the lineup and was tough on lefties, leading some scouts to project him more as a middle reliever or swingman down the road. He's ticketed for Triple-A in 2002.

Year	Club (League)	Class	W	L	ERA	G	GS	CG	SV	IP	H	R	ER	BB	SO
2000	South Bend (Mid)	A	10	4	2.21	18	18	0	0	102	68	35	25	45	105
2001	El Paso (TL)	AA	10	11	5.31	28	28	2	0	159	184	109	94	75	167
MINOR LEAGUE TOTALS			20	15	4.10	46	46	2	0	261	252	144	119	120	272

17. Chad Tracy, 3b

Born: May 22, 1980. **Ht.:** 6-2. **Wt.:** 200. **Bats:** L. **Throws:** R. **School:** East Carolina University. **Career Transactions:** Selected by Diamondbacks in 7th round of 2001 draft; signed June 9, 2001.

Tracy capped his college career last June by hitting .435 with five homers in five NCAA playoff games for East Carolina, winning MVP honors as the Pirates defeated Winthrop in regional play before losing to Tennessee in the super regionals. His picturesque swing was regarded as one of the prettiest in the draft and even evoked memories of Robin Ventura's in his heyday at Oklahoma State. Tracy had been one of the best all-around hitters in the Cape Cod League in 2000 and looked good with wood bats again after signing. He hit .340 in low Class A, including a streak of seven consecutive multihit games, while walking as much as he struck out. At third base, he displays first-step quickness, soft and quick hands and a strong arm. In fact, before the draft his defensive tools even led some scouts to speculate that he could move to catcher. For now, the Diamondbacks will keep Tracy at the hot corner and challenge him with a move to Double-A. Given his pure hitting ability and disciplined approach, he could become an offensive menace when he adds upper-body strength.

Year	Club (League)	Class	AVG	G	AB	R	H	2B	3B	HR	RBI	BB	SO	SB
2001	Yakima (NWL)	A	.278	10	36	2	10	1	0	0	5	3	5	1
	South Bend (Mid)	A	.340	54	215	43	73	11	0	4	36	19	19	3
MINOR LEAGUE TOTALS			.331	64	251	45	83	12	0	4	41	22	24	4

18. Doug Devore, of

Born: Dec. 14, 1977. **Ht.:** 6-4. **Wt.:** 200. **Bats:** L. **Throws:** L. **School:** Indiana University. **Career Transactions:** Selected by Diamondbacks in 12th round of 1999 draft; signed June 3, 1999.

Scouts liken Devore's ability and frame to Paul O'Neill's. The key to achieving his ceiling could just be an issue of building confidence. He skipped the high Class A level and collected 58 extra-base hits with a .502 slugging percentage in Double-A last year, though he did hit 81 points higher at home than on the road and 11 of his 15 homers came in El Paso. Devore offers solid tools across the board, including an above-average arm suitable for right field. His swing is more of a line-drive stroke now, but he has the size and strength to lift more balls out of the park with experience. He'll need to be less pull-conscious and improve his selectivity as he makes the jump to Triple-A. He went to the Arizona Fall League, where wrist and hamstring injuries limited him to 38 at-bats. The Diamondbacks hope a spot on the 40-man roster and an invitation to big league spring training will spark Devore into a breakout campaign.

Year	Club (League)	Class	AVG	G	AB	R	H	2B	3B	HR	RBI	BB	SO	SB
1999	Missoula (Pio)	R	.235	32	115	22	27	4	4	3	22	14	36	2
2000	South Bend (Mid)	A	.292	127	452	64	132	27	4	15	60	47	101	9
2001	El Paso (TL)	AA	.294	128	476	67	140	32	11	15	74	46	118	11
MINOR LEAGUE TOTALS			.287	287	1043	153	299	63	19	33	156	107	255	22

19. Brian Bruney, rhp

Born: Feb. 17, 1982. **Ht.:** 6-3. **Wt.:** 220. **Bats:** R. **Throws:** R. **School:** Warrenton (Ore.) HS. **Career Transactions:** Selected by Diamondbacks in 12th round of 2000 draft; signed June 6, 2000.

In Mike Rizzo's two years as scouting director, Arizona has signed 32 pitchers out of the draft—with 31 of those coming out of college. The lone exception is Bruney, who threw three no-hitters and hit .505 during his career at Warrenton (Ore.) High, where he was also a basketball standout. After walking 29 in 25 innings in his pro debut in 2000, he wasn't the most likely candidate for a breakthrough. But the athletic righthander made outstanding progress towards harnessing his lively arsenal, which features one of the best heaters in the system. While he works consistently in the 91-95 mph range, Bruney's fastball has been clocked as high as 99. His high leg kick adds to a deceptive, powerful delivery. He shows the makings of an average breaking pitch with slurvy action, but he lacks an effective offspeed pitch to combat lefthanders. Bruney limited opponents to a .214 average and has a chance to move quickly if he continues to make strides with his command. Scouts have compared him to Kerry Ligtenberg.

Year	Club (League)	Class	W	L	ERA	G	GS	CG	SV	IP	H	R	ER	BB	SO
2000	Diamondbacks (AZL)	R	4	1	6.48	20	2	0	2	25	21	23	18	29	24
2001	South Bend (Mid)	A	1	4	4.13	26	0	0	8	33	24	19	15	19	40
	Yakima (NWL)	A	1	2	5.14	15	0	0	2	21	19	14	12	11	28
MINOR LEAGUE TOTALS			6	7	5.15	61	2	0	12	79	64	56	45	59	92

20. Bill White, lhp

Born: Nov. 20, 1978. **Ht.:** 6-3. **Wt.:** 210. **Bats:** L. **Throws:** L. **School:** Jacksonville State University. **Career Transactions:** Selected by Diamondbacks in third round of 2000 draft; signed June 28, 2000.

White led NCAA Division I with 16.0 strikeouts per nine innings at Jacksonville State in 2000 while also tying for fifth with 70 walks. The Diamondbacks drafted him in the third round not only because they were attracted to his live arm, but also because they liked his power curveball that was largely responsible for his gaudy strikeout rate. The scouting department felt comfortable turning White over to Rookie-level pitching coach Mark Davis, who won a Cy Young Award using a similar breaking ball. Work with pitching instructor John Denny, another former Cy Young winner, also helped White clean up his mechanics. White has an 88-93 mph fastball with natural tail to complement his plus curveball. His changeup slowly is developing into a reliable third option. White brings a confident attitude to the mound and he works at an aggressive pace. He still has command issues that need to be resolved, especially as he faces more advanced hitters. He was forced to leave the Arizona Fall League with shoulder soreness that required minor labrum surgery and was on schedule to resume throwing in January and join the Double-A rotation in the spring.

Year	Club (League)	Class	W	L	ERA	G	GS	CG	SV	IP	H	R	ER	BB	SO
2000	Diamondbacks (AZL)	R	0	1	6.00	4	1	0	0	6	3	4	4	5	9
	South Bend (Mid)	A	0	0	3.38	1	1	0	0	3	3	1	1	3	5
2001	South Bend (Mid)	A	9	3	3.80	19	19	0	0	111	90	53	47	53	103
	El Paso (TL)	AA	0	4	4.54	7	7	0	0	38	38	23	19	20	26
MINOR LEAGUE TOTALS			9	8	4.04	31	28	0	0	158	134	81	71	81	143

21. Alex Cintron, ss

Born: Dec. 17, 1978. **Ht.:** 6-2. **Wt.:** 180. **Bats:** B. **Throws:** R. **School:** Mech Tech HS, Caguas, P.R. **Career Transactions:** Selected by Diamondbacks in 36th round of 1997 draft; signed June 15, 1997.

After topping this list a year ago, Cintron hit .292 in Triple-A and even received a couple of major league callups. But he didn't convince scouts he was worthy of anywhere close to top billing again, as most now believe his skills are best suited for a utility role. He has proven to be a tough out with outstanding bat control, but otherwise his offensive profile is similar to that of the Dodgers' Alex Cora. Cintron has 13 homers and a .379 slugging percentage in 1,866 pro at-bats. He rarely walks and thus possesses mediocre on-base ability. He doesn't possess the actions of a natural shortstop and is outgrowing the position. As his legs get thicker, he's losing the quickness to make tough plays in the hole or up the middle. His arm is above-average but he has trouble reading hops. The Diamondbacks aren't strong in the middle of the diamond, though Cintron doesn't look like he'll be the answer. His ability to put the ball in play and experience at three positions give him a shot at a career as a utilityman.

Year	Club (League)	Class	AVG	G	AB	R	H	2B	3B	HR	RBI	BB	SO	SB
1997	Diamondbacks (AZL)	R	.197	43	152	23	30	6	1	0	20	21	32	1
	Lethbridge (Pio)	R	.333	1	3	0	1	0	0	0	0	0	1	0
1998	Lethbridge (Pio)	R	.264	67	258	41	68	11	4	3	34	20	32	8
1999	High Desert (Cal)	A	.307	128	499	78	153	25	4	3	64	19	65	15
2000	El Paso (TL)	AA	.301	125	522	83	157	30	6	4	59	29	56	9
2001	Tucson (PCL)	AAA	.292	107	425	53	124	24	3	3	35	15	48	9
	Arizona (NL)	MAJ	.286	8	7	0	2	0	1	0	0	0	0	0
MAJOR LEAGUE TOTALS			.286	8	7	0	2	0	1	0	0	0	0	0
MINOR LEAGUE TOTALS			.287	471	1859	278	533	96	18	13	212	104	234	42

22. Jerry Gil, ss

Born: Oct. 14, 1982. **Ht.:** 6-3. **Wt.:** 183. **Bats:** R. **Throws:** R. **Career Transactions:** Signed out of Dominican Republic by Diamondbacks, Nov. 5, 1999.

Gil is another shortstop who takes a tumble on this list after ranking fifth entering 2001. His tools remain raw and unproven after his first full season performance. Since signing out of the Dominican as a 17-year-old for a $767,500 bonus, he has drawn just 19 walks against 166 strikeouts. He was totally overmatched as the youngest everyday player in the Midwest League. His defensive tools stand out, though. Gil possesses soft hands and a plus-plus arm, but he lacks first-step explosiveness. He runs a notch below average now and won't get any quicker as he matures physically. The Diamonbacks are banking on him improving drastically at the plate as he fills out. Gil must improve his discipline and pitch recognition to get anything to happen offensively. He's easily fooled by breaking pitches and is occasionally off balance at the plate. Some scouts still project him to hit because he shows bat speed and continues to get stronger. He'll face a tough challenge of stepping to high Class A as a 19-year-old.

Year	Club (League)	Class	AVG	G	AB	R	H	2B	3B	HR	RBI	BB	SO	SB
2000	Missoula (Pio)	R	.225	58	227	24	51	10	2	0	20	11	63	7
2001	South Bend (Mid)	A	.215	105	363	40	78	14	5	2	31	8	103	19
MINOR LEAGUE TOTALS			.219	163	590	64	129	24	7	2	51	19	166	26

23. Jay Belflower, rhp

Born: Nov. 12, 1979. **Ht.:** 6-4. **Wt.:** 215. **Bats:** R. **Throws:** R. **School:** University of Florida. **Career Transactions:** Selected by Diamondbacks in 17th round of 2001 draft; signed June 20, 2001.

A move to the bullpen has served Belflower well. He struggled as a member of Florida's rotation early in the spring before changing roles, which boosted his confidence and his velocity. After signing in June, he carved up pro hitters with his three-pitch repertoire. He didn't permit an earned run in his first 24 appearances for Lancaster, which was all the more notable because he went straight to high Class A and pitched his home games in hitter-friendly Municipal Stadium. Belflower works down in the zone with a 92-93 mph sinking fastball that helps him keep the ball in the park. He complements his sinker with a slider and changeup and brings a closer's demeanor to the mound. He earned a taste of Triple-A after just 29 pro innings and he'll pitch for the opportunity to stay there in spring training.

Year	Club (League)	Class	W	L	ERA	G	GS	CG	SV	IP	H	R	ER	BB	SO
2001	Lancaster (Cal)	A	2	2	0.62	27	0	0	11	29	15	5	2	6	24
	Tucson (PCL)	AAA	0	0	0.00	1	0	0	0	2	2	0	0	1	2
MINOR LEAGUE TOTALS			2	2	0.59	28	0	0	11	31	17	5	2	7	26

24. P.J. Bevis, rhp

Born: July 28, 1980. **Ht.:** 6-3. **Wt.:** 175. **Bats:** R. **Throws:** R. **Career Transactions:** Signed out of Australia by Diamondbacks, May 17, 1998.

Signed as a 17-year-old out of Australia in 1998, Bevis spent three seasons in Rookie ball as a starter, doing little to attract attention as a prospect. The Diamondbacks dropped his arm slot to three-quarters last year and made him a reliever. The changes turned Bevis' career around, just as they had for Bret Prinz in 2000. Bevis also bulked up and watched his velocity soar from the high 80s to 92-94 mph, occasionally touching 95-96 mph. He mixes in a power curveball as well as a bigger, slower bender to keep hitters guessing. He still needs to refine his command. After starting 2001 in extended spring training, Bevis didn't surrender a run in his first 10 appearances at short-season Yakima and finished the season as the Double-A closer after Jose Valverde was shut down with a tender shoulder. He also earned a save against Canada at the World Cup in Taiwan. Bevis could return to El Paso to start 2002.

Year	Club (League)	Class	W	L	ERA	G	GS	CG	SV	IP	H	R	ER	BB	SO
1998	Diamondbacks (AZL)	R	3	3	5.96	14	9	0	0	45	55	39	30	10	48
1999	Missoula (Pio)	R	6	2	4.62	15	15	0	0	86	83	51	44	30	69
2000	Missoula (Pio)	R	3	6	3.33	14	14	0	0	84	92	50	31	22	63
2001	Yakima (NWL)	A	1	1	0.64	12	0	0	8	14	9	1	1	7	22
	El Paso (TL)	AA	0	0	2.16	14	0	0	6	17	11	4	4	6	19
MINOR LEAGUE TOTALS			13	12	4.04	69	38	0	14	245	250	145	110	75	221

25. Corby Medlin, rhp

Born: Aug. 4, 1981. **Ht.:** 6-3. **Wt.:** 185. **Bats:** R. **Throws:** R. **School:** San Jacinto (Texas) JC. **Career Transactions:** Selected by Diamondbacks in 22nd round of 2000 draft; signed May 17, 2001.

Medlin has improved significantly since the Diamondbacks drafted him in the 22nd round out of high school in 2000. He went to San Jacinto (Texas) JC, got his fastball up to 90-92 mph during the spring and was pumping gas at 94-96 mph by the end of the summer. His unorthodox delivery evoked some thoughts of Robb Nen and Rockies prospect Craig House, and that wasn't necessarily meant as a compliment. His mechanics could lead to control issues or injury problems down the road. Medlin complements his fastball with a true power slider that features late break and depth. He limited Pioneer League hitters to a .185 average. Arizona is anxious to see if he can continue to overpower hitters at one of its full-season Class A affiliates this season.

Year	Club (League)	Class	W	L	ERA	G	GS	CG	SV	IP	H	R	ER	BB	SO
2001	Missoula (Pio)	R	2	1	2.38	21	0	0	6	42	27	12	11	16	46
MINOR LEAGUE TOTALS			2	1	2.38	21	0	0	6	42	27	12	11	16	46

26. Brandon Webb, rhp

Born: May 9, 1979. **Ht.:** 6-2. **Wt.:** 200. **Bats:** R. **Throws:** R. **School:** University of Kentucky. **Career Transactions:** Selected by Diamondbacks in eighth round of 2000 draft; signed June 6, 2000.

Lancaster's Municipal Stadium is a tough place to pitch, though Webb posted an admirable 4.32 ERA there in 2001. He showed his true colors on the road, however, where he had a 3.57 ERA and held hitters to a .247 average. The highlight of his season was a 14-strikeout two-hitter at Modesto. It showed how much the Diamondbacks think of Webb that they sent him to high Class A after he pitched just 18 innings in his pro debut in 2000, when he was shut down with a sore arm. He established the single-season strikeout record in his final season at Kentucky and continues to prove himself as a strikeout artist. Webb has one of the best arms in the system, and projects to add more velocity to his 90-92 mph fastball. He has good command, works down in the zone and also offers an above-average curveball and a changeup. He relishes pitching inside and led the California League with 27 hit batters. Webb eventually could wind up in the bullpen and benefit from shorter outings, but he likely will join the Double-A rotation this season.

Year	Club (League)	Class	W	L	ERA	G	GS	CG	SV	IP	H	R	ER	BB	SO
2000	Diamondbacks (AZL)	R	0	0	9.00	1	1	0	0	1	2	1	1	0	3
	South Bend (Mid)	A	0	0	3.24	12	0	0	2	17	10	7	6	9	18
2001	Lancaster (Cal)	A	6	10	3.99	29	28	0	0	162	174	90	72	44	158
MINOR LEAGUE TOTALS			6	10	3.95	42	29	0	2	180	186	98	79	53	179

27. Brandon Medders, rhp

Born: Jan. 26, 1980. **Ht.:** 6-2. **Wt.:** 185. **Bats:** R. **Throws:** R. **School:** Mississippi State University. **Career Transactions:** Selected by Diamondbacks in eighth round of 2001 draft; signed June 11, 2001.

Medders has improved his stock each year. He was drafted in the 37th round by the Devil Rays out of high school in 1998, then in the 18th round by the Royals out of Shelton State (Tenn.) Community College a year later, but opted not to sign. He transferred to Mississippi State in 2000 and emerged as the Bulldogs' closer last spring before Arizona took him in the eighth round in June. The Diamondbacks think he could be a slightly bigger version of Tim Hudson. Medders gets a lot of sink on his 90-94 mph fastball and mixes it well with his slider and changeup. He had no problems going straight to high Class A after signing, as his 1.32 ERA, .184 opponent batting average and 11.4 strikeouts per nine innings attest. Some scouts were turned off by adjustments he made to his delivery as a junior but he hasn't had any difficulties to this point. Arizona hopes it can get the same production out of him next season as a Double-A starter.

Year	Club (League)	Class	W	L	ERA	G	GS	CG	SV	IP	H	R	ER	BB	SO
2001	Lancaster (Cal)	A	1	2	1.32	31	0	0	3	41	26	8	6	15	53
MINOR LEAGUE TOTALS			1	2	1.32	31	0	0	3	41	26	8	6	15	53

28. Victor Hall, of

Born: Sept. 16, 1980. **Ht.:** 6-0. **Wt.:** 170. **Bats:** L. **Throws:** L. **School:** Monroe HS, Sepulveda, Calif. **Career Transactions:** Selected by Diamondbacks in 12th round of 1998 draft; signed June 3, 1998.

After leading the Pioneer League in steals in 2000, Hall worked with Diamondbacks instructor Willie Wilson, a former American League stolen base champ, and further refined his technique. He swiped 60 more bases last year in low Class A, and even more impressive, he succeeded on 80 percent of his attempts. One of the fastest players in the organization, he has been compared to Lance Johnson. Hall has hit just five home runs in 1,172 pro at-bats, but he realizes his limitations and makes the most out of his blazing speed. He has grounded into just eight double plays in his career, an amazingly low total. He keeps the ball on the ground and demonstrates the patience befitting a leadoff hitter. Though it took him three years to get out of short-season ball, he's still young and held his own in low Class A last year. He'll move up a notch to high Class A in 2002.

Year	Club (League)	Class	AVG	G	AB	R	H	2B	3B	HR	RBI	BB	SO	SB
1998	Diamondbacks (AZL)	R	.188	28	101	10	19	1	1	0	10	10	29	14
1999	Diamondbacks (AZL)	R	.365	27	104	19	38	2	1	0	14	13	25	10
	Missoula (Pio)	R	.279	34	147	27	41	4	0	0	11	15	30	18
2000	South Bend (Mid)	A	.232	41	164	19	38	4	5	2	16	13	41	12
	Missoula (Pio)	R	.307	70	241	70	74	7	9	3	26	77	38	47
2001	South Bend (Mid)	A	.275	113	415	82	114	13	12	0	39	52	71	60
MINOR LEAGUE TOTALS			.276	313	1172	227	324	31	28	5	116	180	234	161

29. Craig Ansman, c

Born: March 10, 1978. **Ht.:** 6-4. **Wt.:** 225. **Bats:** R. **Throws:** R. **School:** Stony Brook University. **Career Transactions:** Signed as nondrafted free agent by Diamondbacks, June 8, 2000.

Ansman was the New England Collegiate Conference player of the year as a sophomore at Stony Brook, set the program's single-season homer mark with 20 as a junior, and hit .400 for the second straight season as a senior—yet he never got drafted. Signed as a free agent, he led the Midwest League with a .623 slugging percentage in his first full pro season last year. He's burly and strong, and power is his best tool. Offensively, he'll probably need more plate discipline as he moves up the ladder. Though opposing managers weren't crazy about his funky release, Ansman has a strong arm and led the MWL by erasing 42 percent of base-stealers. He still needs to improve his game-calling skills. At 23, he was old for low Class A, so a jump to Double-A isn't out of the question for 2002. He'll have to keep proving himself and profiles as a big league reserve.

Year	Club (League)	Class	AVG	G	AB	R	H	2B	3B	HR	RBI	BB	SO	SB
2000	Missoula (Pio)	R	.284	28	67	7	19	5	0	0	7	12	21	0
2001	South Bend (Mid)	A	.330	97	345	73	114	30	4	21	82	29	85	4
MINOR LEAGUE TOTALS			.323	125	412	80	133	35	4	21	89	41	106	4

30. Andy Green, 2b

Born: July 7, 1977. **Ht.:** 5-9. **Wt.:** 170. **Bats:** R. **Throws:** R. **School:** University of Kentucky. **Career Transactions:** Selected by Diamondbacks in 24th round of 2000 draft; signed June 14, 2000.

Green was an academic all-American at Kentucky who never missed a game during his four-year career. The Diamondbacks consider him their prospect version of Craig Counsell. He is a gritty, hard-nosed player with an excellent baseball IQ. Though he's not physically imposing, Green does have some tools. He is a plus runner with excellent baserunning skills. Like Counsell, he won't hit for power, but he is a throwback No. 2 hitter with the bat control to move runners. Managers also rated him the best defensive second baseman in the Midwest League last year. He's gifted with quick feet and good hands. The Diamondbacks think so highly of Green's makeup, they are considering a promotion all the way to Triple-A in 2002. He's already 24 and needs a sterner challenge than Class A.

Year	Club (League)	Class	AVG	G	AB	R	H	2B	3B	HR	RBI	BB	SO	SB
2000	South Bend (Mid)	A	.000	3	9	1	0	0	0	0	0	0	1	0
	Missoula (Pio)	R	.229	23	83	10	19	2	1	0	16	12	9	8
2001	South Bend (Mid)	A	.300	128	477	76	143	18	6	5	59	59	50	51
MINOR LEAGUE TOTALS				214	569	87	162	20	7	5	75	71	60	59

ATLANTA
Braves

Braves

TOP 30 PROSPECTS

1. Wilson Betemit, ss
2. Adam Wainwright, rhp
3. Kelly Johnson, ss
4. Brett Evert, rhp
5. Carlos Duran, of
6. Matt Belisle, rhp
7. Zach Miner, rhp
8. Gonzalo Lopez, rhp
9. Bubba Nelson, rhp
10. Jung Bong, lhp
11. Tim Spooneybarger, rhp
12. Bryan Digby, rhp
13. Ben Kozlowski, lhp
14. Richard Lewis, 2b
15. Kyle Davies, rhp
16. Billy Sylvester, rhp
17. Trey Hodges, rhp
18. Matt Wright, rhp
19. Ryan Langerhans, of
20. Matt McClendon, rhp
21. Macay McBride, lhp
22. Chris Waters, lhp
23. Andy Marte, 3b
24. Ramon Castro, ss
25. Josh Burrus, 3b
26. Adam Stern, of
27. Matt Merricks, lhp
28. Pat Manning, 3b
29. Cory Aldridge, of
30. Travis Wilson, of/2b

By Bill Ballew

The Braves not only extended the longest streak in professional sports history by winning their 10th consecutive division title during 2001, but they also continued a rebuilding program for the second straight season.

After watching shortstop Rafael Furcal earn Baseball America Rookie of the Year honors in 2000 and reloading with an emphasis on veterans during the offseason, general manager John Schuerholz dipped into his farm system again by calling up second baseman Marcus Giles in July. Mark DeRosa played well at short after Furcal was lost for the season, before Schuerholz shipped prospects Alejandro Machado and Brad Voyles to the Royals for veteran Rey Sanchez at the trading deadline. Other young players who contributed included pitchers Jason Marquis and Odalis Perez, both of whom appeared ready for full-time jobs in the rotation, particularly after John Smoltz moved to the bullpen and re-signed with the Braves. Perez and Brian Jordan were shipped to the Dodgers in January in a deal for Gary Sheffield, though, as Atlanta bolstered its outfield for 2002.

Two promising players who also could have an impact in Atlanta in 2002 received cups of coffee in September. Wilson Betemit could create some roster shuffling if he's deemed ready in spring training, while reliever Tim Spooneybarger could add depth to a veteran bullpen.

Those players represent the cream of a modest crop that has come through the upper levels of the system in recent years, but the Braves could be on the verge of developing another bonanza of prospects. Scouting director Roy Clark has put together strong drafts in his first two years.

Atlanta's seven minor league clubs had an overall .489 winning percentage in 2001, with short-season Jamestown the lone affiliate to reach postseason play. Rumors persist that Jamestown could be dropped from the system, which would leave a more typical six affiliates. The Braves don't feel the reduction would have a significant effect, as they have increased their presence in Latin America with a state-of-the-art complex in San Francisco de Macoris, Dominican Republic, and remain as committed to player development as any team in the game. That should lead to more turnover on an aging roster, as well as a strong chance at remaining one of the game's most successful franchises for seasons to come.

OrganizationOverview

General manager: John Schuerholz. **Farm director:** Dick Balderson. **Scouting director:** Roy Clark.

2001 PERFORMANCE

Class	Team	League	W	L	Pct.	Finish*	Manager
Majors	Atlanta	National	88	74	.543	t-5th (16)	Bobby Cox
Triple-A	Richmond Braves	International	68	76	.472	t-7th (14)	Carlos Tosca
Double-A	Greenville Braves	Southern	60	79	.432	8th (10)	Paul Runge
High A	Myrtle Beach Pelicans	Carolina	71	67	.514	3rd (8)	Brian Snitker
Low A	Macon Braves	South Atlantic	72	61	.541	5th (16)	Randy Ingle
Short-season	Jamestown Jammers	New York-Penn	39	36	.520	3rd (14)	Jim Saul
Rookie	Danville Braves	Appalachian	30	38	.441	9th (10)	Ralph Henriquez
Rookie	GCL Braves	Gulf Coast	30	30	.500	8th (13)	Rick Albert
OVERALL 2001 MINOR LEAGUE RECORD			370	387	.489	17th (30)	

*Finish in overall standings (No. of teams in league).

ORGANIZATION LEADERS

BATTING
*AVG	Marcus Giles, Richmond	.333
R	Alph Coleman, Macon	84
H	Wilson Betemit, Myrtle Beach/Greenville	153
TB	Wilson Betemit, Myrtle Beach/Greenville	225
2B	Wilson Betemit, Myrtle Beach/Greenville	34
3B	Alph Coleman, Macon	7
	Ramon Castro, Richmond/Greenville	7
HR	**Mike Hessman**, Greenville	26
RBI	**Mike Hessman**, Greenville	80
BB	Mike Forbes, Macon	72
SO	Cory Aldridge, Greenville	139
SB	Alph Coleman, Macon	38

PITCHING
W	Trey Hodges, Myrtle Beach	15
L	Marc Valdes, Richmond	11
ERA	Brett Evert, Macon/Myrtle Beach	1.74
G	Ray Beasley, Richmond	65
CG	Chris Waters, Macon	3
SV	Billy Sylvester, Richmond/Greenville	23
IP	Trey Hodges, Myrtle Beach	173
BB	Kenny Nelson, Macon	57
	Matt McClendon, Richmond/Greenville	57
SO	Adam Wainwright, Macon	184

*Minimum 250 At-Bats #Minimum 75 Innings

TOP PROSPECTS OF THE DECADE
1992	Chipper Jones, ss
1993	Chipper Jones, ss
1994	Chipper Jones, ss
1995	Chipper Jones, ss/3b
1996	Andruw Jones, of
1997	Andruw Jones, of
1998	Bruce Chen, lhp
1999	Bruce Chen, lhp
2000	Rafael Furcal, ss
2001	Wilson Betemit, ss

TOP DRAFT PICKS OF THE DECADE
1992	Jamie Arnold, rhp
1993	Andre King, of (2)
1994	Jacob Shumate, rhp
1995	*Chad Hutchinson, rhp
1996	A.J. Zapp, 1b
1997	Troy Cameron, ss
1998	Matt Belisle, rhp (2)
1999	Matt Butler, rhp (2)
2000	Adam Wainwright, rhp
2001	Macay McBride, lhp

*Did not sign.

TYLER BOLDEN

STEVE MOORE

Hessman   **McClendon**

BEST TOOLS
Best Hitter for Average	Wilson Betemit
Best Power Hitter	Michael Hessman
Fastest Baserunner	Carlos Duran
Best Fastball	Bryan Digby
Best Breaking Ball	Brett Evert
Best Changeup	Adam Wainwright
Best Control	Trey Hodges
Best Defensive Catcher	Steve Torrealba
Best Defensive Infielder	Tony Pena Jr.
Best Infield Arm	Wilson Betemit
Best Defensive Outfielder	Ryan Langerhans
Best Outfield Arm	Angelo Burrows

PROJECTED 2005 LINEUP
Catcher	Javy Lopez
First Base	Chipper Jones
Second Base	Marcus Giles
Third Base	Wilson Betemit
Shortstop	Rafael Furcal
Left Field	Gary Sheffield
Center Field	Andruw Jones
Right Field	Kelly Johnson
No. 1 Starter	Greg Maddux
No. 2 Starter	Tom Glavine
No. 3 Starter	Jason Marquis
No. 4 Starter	Kevin Millwood
No. 5 Starter	Adam Wainwright
Closer	Tim Spooneybarger

ALL-TIME LARGEST BONUSES
Matt Belisle, 1998	$1,750,000
Jung Bong, 1997	$1,700,000
Macay McBride, 2001	$1,340,000
Adam Wainwright, 2000	$1,250,000
Josh Burrus, 2001	$1,250,000

DraftAnalysis

2001 Draft

Best Pro Debut: RHP Kevin Barry (14) dominated the short-season New York-Penn League with 12 saves, a 0.86 ERA, 54 strikeouts in 31 innings and a .131 opponent batting average. RHP Kyle Davies (4) went 4-2, 2.25 with a 53-8 strikeout-walk ratio in the Rookie-level Gulf Coast League, then threw six scoreless innings at Class A Macon.

Best Athlete: The Braves signed two players away from major football programs. 3B Cole Barthel (2) was an Arkansas quarterback recruit, and his combination of size, power and speed has drawn comparisons to Matt Williams. OF Matt Esquivel (5) was going to walk on at Nebraska as a running back. OF Adam Stern (3) isn't as physically imposing as those two, but he's a Lenny Dykstra-type sparkplug without quite the same pop.

Best Hitter: SS Josh Burrus (1) hit just .193 in the GCL and 2B **Richard Lewis** (1) batted just .242 at short-season Jamestown, but the Braves have high hopes for both. Burrus has a very quick bat.

Best Raw Power: Burrus over Barthel. Though drafted as a shortstop, Burrus should outgrow the position and began playing third base in instructional league.

Fastest Runner: Stern has 6.4-6.5 second speed in the 60-yard dash.

Best Defensive Player: Lewis' quick hands help him at the plate as well as in the field. He played shortstop for Georgia Tech last spring and is smooth on the pivot.

Best Fastball: Despite being short and left-handed, Macay McBride (1) repeatedly has thrown as hard as 95 mph. The Braves had eight reports on him from high school, and each had him at 94 mph or better, with good life. He's not very projectable, but with that kind of stuff he doesn't have to be.

Most Intriguing Background: Burrus is a cousin of Jeffrey Hammonds. Atlanta drafted twins, SS Paco (42) and OF Danny Figueroa (48), but they opted for the University of Miami.

Closest To The Majors: Lewis or Stern should move quickly.

Lewis

Best Late-Round Pick: Barry showed a 91-93 mph fastball to go with a hard slider. The Braves also view C Travis Anderson (25), who has raw tools, as a sleeper.

The One Who Got Away: LHP J.P. Howell (2) has four big league pitches and allowed one earned run in 70 innings as a high school senior. The Braves weren't close to diverting him from the University of Southern California.

Assessment: Atlanta emphasized athletes and arms as usual, though it opted for more four-year college players than it has in the past. Having three first-round picks—all of which ended up coming from prospect-rich Georgia, incidentally—helped lessen the sting of not signing second-rounder Howell.

2000 Draft

RHP Adam Wainwright (1) and SS Kelly Johnson (1) rank 2-3 on Atlanta's prospect list. Two other first-rounders—3B Scott Thorman and 2B Aaron Herr—haven't fared as well, but RHPs Zach Miner (4), Bubba Nelson (2) and Brian Digby (2) all look good. **Grade: A**

1999 Draft

RHP Matt McClendon (5) looked like a steal until he backslid last season. Now RHP Brett Evert (7) and LHP Ben Kozlowski (12) are the best this crop has to offer. **Grade: C**

1998 Draft

Even without a first-round pick, the Braves did fine work. RHP Matt Belisle (2) can be a star if he recovers from back problems. RHPs Tim Spooneybarger (29) and Brad Voyles (45, draft-and-follow) were two late-round bullpen finds, though Voyles went to the Royals last summer for Rey Sanchez. **Grade: B**

1997 Draft

This was a rare disaster for Atlanta. 3B Troy Cameron (1) flopped and was traded to the Indians. LHP Joey Nation (2), dealt to the Cubs, had to retire because of a heart condition. The best prospect left is OF Cory Aldridge (4), a fringe prospect. **Grade: D**

Note: Draft analysis prepared by Jim Callis. Numbers in parentheses indicate draft rounds.

. . . Betemit is a natural baseball player and a budding five-tool talent who's still maturing.

Wilson
Betemit ss

Born: Nov. 2, 1981.
Ht.: 6-2. **Wt.:** 155.
Bats: B. **Throws:** R.
Career Transactions: Signed out of Dominican Republic by Braves, July 28, 1996.

In his first full season, Betemit reached the major leagues when rosters were expanded in September. Signed prior to his 16th birthday in violation of baseball rules, Betemit sued the Braves during the spring of 2000 before reaching a contract agreement shortly thereafter. He was the top prospect in the short-season New York-Penn League that year, then jumped to high Class A Myrtle Beach to start 2001. Promoted to Double-A Greenville in July after Rafael Furcal was lost for the season, Betemit rose to the occasion and improved in all phases of his game. Carolina League managers rated Betemit as their top prospect, while Southern League skippers ranked him third.

Betemit is a natural baseball player and a budding five-tool talent who's still maturing. His body will get stronger, which should enable him to hit for power from both sides of the plate. He hits to all fields with his line-drive stroke. He has outstanding athleticism, shown by the Ozzie Smith-style flip he sometimes makes when taking the field. Betemit also has slightly above-average speed that should allow him to steal 15 bases a year. Defensively, he has good range, a strong arm and soft hands. He thrives on challenges and raises his game to the level of the competition. He has lost his focus on occasion at shortstop, leading to careless mistakes. Some scouts say he will outgrow the position and will have to move to third base. He might be better there because it's a reaction position instead of one that requires concentration. His plate discipline is rudimentary and may be exploited by pitchers at higher levels.

The Braves showed with Furcal in 2000 they aren't afraid to let a middle infielder make a big jump to the major leagues. Betemit doesn't have an obvious job opportunity in Atlanta, but should he prove during spring training that he's ready to take over a starting job, the Braves are willing to create room. The Braves all but guaranteed he'll start the season at Triple-A Richmond by signing Vinny Castilla.

Year	Club (League)	Class	AVG	G	AB	R	H	2B	3B	HR	RBI	BB	SO	SB
1997	Braves (GCL)	R	.212	32	113	12	24	6	1	0	15	9	32	0
1998	Braves (GCL)	R	.220	51	173	23	38	8	4	5	16	20	49	6
1999	Danville (Appy)	R	.320	67	259	39	83	18	2	5	53	27	63	6
2000	Jamestown (NY-P)	A	.331	69	269	54	89	15	2	5	37	30	37	3
2001	Myrtle Beach (Car)	A	.277	84	318	38	88	20	1	7	43	23	71	8
	Greenville (SL)	AA	.355	47	183	22	65	14	0	5	19	12	36	6
	Atlanta (NL)	MAJ	.000	8	3	1	0	0	0	0	0	0	2	3	1
MAJOR LEAGUE TOTALS			.000	8	3	1	0	0	0	0	0	2	3	1
MINOR LEAGUE TOTALS			.294	350	1315	188	387	81	10	27	183	121	288	29

2. Adam Wainwright, rhp

STEVE MOORE

Born: Aug. 30, 1981. **Ht.:** 6-6. **Wt.:** 190. **Bats:** R. **Throws:** R. **School:** Glynn Academy, Brunswick, Ga. **Career Transactions:** Selected by Braves in first round (29th overall) of 2000 draft; signed June 12, 2000.

Wainwright learned valuable lessons in his first full season, getting off to a strong start before struggling for the first time in his career. He did break the Class A Macon single-season record for strikeouts, previously held by Bruce Chen. At 6-foot-6, Wainwright should develop into a strong pitcher with an intimidating presence on the mound. His low-90s fastball with good movement is his best pitch, and his curveball and changeup are close to being plus offerings. The Braves were encouraged about how he went from a thrower to a pitcher over the course of the year, learning about the art of getting hitters out even as the organization altered Wainwright's delivery and mechanics in 2001. Because he's still growing into his tall frame, he can become inconsistent with his release point, though his command has been solid to this point. He also needs to add stamina. Wainwright could use more experience, too, so that he becomes savvier in certain aspects of the game. Atlanta is in no hurry to push Wainwright. He'll open 2002 at Myrtle Beach and should spend most of the year making adjustments against Carolina League hitters.

Year	Club (League)	Class	W	L	ERA	G	GS	CG	SV	IP	H	R	ER	BB	SO
2000	Braves (GCL)	R	4	0	1.13	7	5	0	0	32	15	5	4	10	42
	Danville (Appy)	R	2	2	3.68	6	6	0	0	29	28	13	12	2	39
2001	Macon (SAL)	A	10	10	3.77	28	28	1	0	164	144	89	69	48	184
MINOR LEAGUE TOTALS			16	12	3.40	41	39	1	0	225	187	107	85	60	265

3. Kelly Johnson, ss

Born: Feb. 22, 1982. **Ht.:** 6-1. **Wt.:** 180. **Bats:** L. **Throws:** R. **School:** Westwood HS, Austin. **Career Transactions:** Selected by Braves in first round (38th overall) of 2000 draft; signed June 12, 2000.

Johnson made the Braves look brilliant in 2001. Little known as a supplemental first-round pick the year before, he blossomed into one of the most dangerous hitters in the South Atlantic League. After getting off to a 1-for-24 start, Johnson ended up second in the league with a .404 on-base percentage and fourth with a .513 slugging percentage. An excellent athlete with a potent stick, Johnson hits the ball hard and has as much raw power as anyone in the organization. He also has above-average speed that enabled him to steal 25 bases. Sally League managers tabbed him as the league's best prospect, best hitter, best power hitter and most exciting player. Johnson might not blossom, though, until he finds a comfortable defensive position. He struggled at shortstop in the season's first half, making numerous careless mistakes, before showing better concentration during the last two months. Johnson tends to ride the emotional roller coaster and can be hard on himself when he fails. Scouting director Roy Clark and scout Charlie Smith simply outworked the competition in evaluating Johnson. He'll move up to Myrtle Beach in 2002.

Year	Club (League)	Class	AVG	G	AB	R	H	2B	3B	HR	RBI	BB	SO	SB
2000	Braves (GCL))	R	.269	53	193	27	52	12	3	4	29	24	45	6
2001	Macon (SAL)	A	.289	124	415	75	120	22	1	23	66	71	111	25
MINOR LEAGUE TOTALS			.283	177	608	102	172	34	4	27	95	95	156	31

4. Brett Evert, rhp

Born: Oct. 23, 1980. **Ht.:** 6-6. **Wt.:** 200. **Bats:** L. **Throws:** R. **School:** North Salem HS, Salem, Ore. **Career Transactions:** Selected by Braves in seventh round of 1999 draft; signed June 9, 1999.

Evert struggled in his first shot at the South Atlantic League in 2000, but overpowered low Class A hitters in a brief return to the league in 2001 before receiving a promotion to Myrtle Beach. He was shut down with a minor shoulder problem in late July but looked strong again during instructional league. Evert is the total package: a big, strong righthander whose body has matured a lot since he signed. He's developing into a quintessential workhorse as well as a power pitcher with big-time stuff, featuring a 92-95 mph fastball, a plus curveball and workable changeup. Fearless on the mound, Evert also has a good feel for pitching and excellent command. As with any pitcher who has battled an injury, he needs to stay healthy and prove his shoulder is 100 percent. Otherwise, experience against better hitters should lead to natural improvements in his game. Spring training will determine if Evert needs more seasoning at Myrtle Beach or if he's ready to pitch at Double-A Greenville. No one in the organization would be surprised if he moved quickly.

Year	Club (League)	Class	W	L	ERA	G	GS	CG	SV	IP	H	R	ER	BB	SO
1999	Braves (GCL)	R	5	3	2.03	13	10	0	0	49	37	17	11	9	39
2000	Jamestown (NY-P)	A	8	3	3.38	15	15	0	0	77	92	52	29	19	64
	Macon (SAL)	A	1	4	4.64	7	7	0	0	43	53	27	22	9	29
2001	Macon (SAL)	A	1	0	0.74	6	6	0	0	36	25	5	3	3	34
	Myrtle Beach (Car)	A	7	2	2.24	13	13	1	0	72	63	25	18	15	75
MINOR LEAGUE TOTALS			22	12	2.70	54	51	1	0	277	270	126	83	55	241

5. Carlos Duran, of

Born: Dec. 27, 1982. **Ht.:** 6-1. **Wt.:** 165. **Bats:** L. **Throws:** L. **Career Transactions:** Signed out of Venezuela by Braves, signed July 29, 1999.

Duran debuted in the United States in 2001, after leading the Rookie-level Venezuelan Summer League with six triples while hitting .306-8-41 the previous year. He wound up leading Atlanta's Rookie-level Gulf Coast League club in batting, runs, hits, doubles and stolen bases as the league's fifth-best prospect. A potential five-tool player, Duran is making rapid progress in all phases of the game. He has great instincts and makes everything look easy. Duran has above-average speed with excellent range in center field, a good arm and the ability to make contact at the plate. His GCL manager Rick Albert said Duran won five games with his glove alone. Nothing in Duran's game needs the kind of improvement that experience won't solve. He's still making adjustments to playing in a different country and against top-flight competition, and he must consistently get the most of his tools. He needs to get stronger, which should come naturally, and show more patience at the plate. Duran's first two professional seasons have the Braves excited about his future. The organization expects him to prove in spring training that he's ready to make the jump to low Class A.

Year	Club (League)	Class	AVG	G	AB	R	H	2B	3B	HR	RBI	BB	SO	SB
2000	Chico Canonico (VSL)	R	.306	54	196	48	60	12	6	8	41	18	28	13
2001	Braves (GCL)	R	.304	54	204	35	62	10	3	2	17	12	30	16
MINOR LEAGUE TOTALS			.305	108	400	83	122	22	9	10	58	30	58	29

6. Matt Belisle, rhp

Born: June 6, 1980. **Ht.:** 6-3. **Wt.:** 195. **Bats:** R. **Throws:** R. **School:** McCallum HS, Austin. **Career Transactions:** Selected by Braves in second round of 1998 draft; signed Aug. 23, 1998.

Belisle made impressive progress in 2000 but ruptured a disc in his back during spring training that required surgery and forced him to miss all of 2001. He went through a rigorous rehab program and looked strong during instructional league, which led to an unexpected stint in the Arizona Fall League. Belisle isn't unlike righthander Brett Evert in that he has a strong, athletic body that could allow him to eat a lot of innings at higher levels. He's tenacious and won't give in to hitters in any situation. Belisle throws a low- to mid-90s fastball along with a changeup and breaking ball. He has excellent command of all three pitches. Anytime a player misses an entire season, there is reason for concern. The Braves believe Belisle made up for some lost time during the fall, but they will be looking for him to stay healthy for the entire 2002 season in order to get closer to the big leagues. Belisle had his sights set on Greenville before hurting his back. He'll have the opportunity to reach that destination once again this spring and appears ready to get back on the fast track to the majors.

Year	Club (League)	Class	W	L	ERA	G	GS	CG	SV	IP	H	R	ER	BB	SO
1999	Danville (Appy)	R	2	5	4.67	14	14	0	0	71	86	50	37	23	60
2000	Macon (SAL)	A	9	5	2.37	15	15	1	0	102	79	37	27	18	97
	Myrtle Beach (Car)	A	3	4	3.43	12	12	0	0	78	72	32	30	11	71
2001	Did Not Play—Injured														
MINOR LEAGUE TOTALS			14	14	3.35	41	41	1	0	252	237	119	94	52	228

7. Zach Miner, rhp

Born: March 12, 1982. **Ht.:** 6-3. **Wt.:** 190. **Bats:** R. **Throws:** R. **School:** Palm Beach Gardens (Fla.) HS. **Career Transactions:** Selected by Braves in fourth round of 2000 draft; signed Sept. 1, 2000.

A potential 2000 first-round pick who lasted until the fourth round because of signability questions, Miner signed for $1.2 million just before reporting to class at Miami. Making his pro debut in 2001, he led the New York-Penn League in innings and placed fifth in ERA. The Braves were thrilled with how well he performed against older and more experienced hitters. Atlanta officials are most impressed with Miner's knowledge of how to pitch despite his limited pro experience. A sinker-slider pitcher, he'll have better overall stuff as his body matures. His hard sinker clocks in the 89-91 mph range and he has command of all of his pitches. He's one of the fiercest competitors in the system. The Braves are looking for more consistency from Miner, particularly with his breaking ball. He tends to get lackadaisical at times and leave his pitches up in the strike zone. Otherwise, experience and fine-tuning should keep him on the right track. Miner looked so impressive with Jamestown that he could skip Macon and open 2002 at Myrtle Beach. Wherever he goes, he'll be looked upon as one of the leaders of the rotation.

Year	Club (League)	Class	W	L	ERA	G	GS	CG	SV	IP	H	R	ER	BB	SO
2001	Jamestown (NY-P)	A	3	4	1.89	15	15	0	0	91	76	26	19	16	68
MINOR LEAGUE TOTALS			3	4	1.89	15	15	0	0	91	76	26	19	16	68

8. Gonzalo Lopez, rhp

Born: Oct. 6, 1983. **Ht.:** 6-2. **Wt.:** 175. **Bats:** R. **Throws:** R. **Career Transactions:** Signed out of Nicaragua by Braves, July 8, 2000.

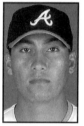

Few pitchers looked better in the Gulf Coast League than Lopez. The righthander skipped the Latin American summer leagues and made his pro debut by placing second in the GCL in strikeouts and fifth in innings. Managers ranked him the league's ninth-best prospect, one of three Braves tabbed among the league's top 20. Lopez' stuff is as good as that of any pitcher in the organization. Though still raw, he's a power pitcher with a developing 92-94 mph fastball that has outstanding movement. He also throws his curveball and changeup for strikes, and both have an excellent chance of becoming plus pitches. He shows good command for someone of his age and experience, though in many other ways Lopez shows that he is immature and has significant adjustments to make in all phases of his game. His stuff borders on major league quality right now, but he needs to learn how to put it together and have success every time he takes the mound. After showing steady progress in the GCL, Lopez is ready to take the next step into the full-season leagues. He is expected to open 2002 in the Macon rotation.

Year	Club (League)	Class	W	L	ERA	G	GS	CG	SV	IP	H	R	ER	BB	SO
2001	Braves (GCL)	R	5	4	2.45	12	11	0	0	59	44	17	16	10	69
MINOR LEAGUE TOTALS			5	4	2.45	12	11	0	0	59	44	17	16	10	69

9. Bubba Nelson, rhp

Born: Aug. 26, 1981. **Ht.:** 6-2. **Wt.:** 200. **Bats:** R. **Throws:** R. **School:** Robinson HS, Lorena, Texas. **Career Transactions:** Selected by Braves in second round of 2000 draft; signed June 23, 2000.

Along with Adam Wainwright and Zach Miner, Nelson is yet another top pitching prospect from Atlanta's 2000 draft class. He led the Gulf Coast League team with 54 strikeouts in 45 innings in 2000, so he already has 208 strikeouts in 195 professional innings. He showed more consistency as 2001 progressed and led the Macon staff in wins. Nelson impresses scouts with his heavy 93-95 mph fastball and competitive spirit. His changeup and curveball also should develop into plus pitches. Braves scouts thought he had the best breaking ball among the pitchers they scouted in 2000. No longer a raw thrower, Nelson has an excellent idea of how to pitch, and his progress appears to be on the verge of accelerating. He was a heavily scouted third baseman in high school, so he still is learning the nuances of pitching, particularly in working both sides of the plate. He tries to be too fine at times in spite of his stuff, often causing him to work from behind in the count. Nelson is expected to continue his steady climb by beginning 2002 at Myrtle Beach.

Year	Club (League)	Class	W	L	ERA	G	GS	CG	SV	IP	H	R	ER	BB	SO
2000	Braves (GCL)	R	3	2	4.23	12	6	1	0	45	40	24	21	13	54
2001	Macon (SAL)	A	12	8	3.93	25	24	2	0	151	144	76	66	57	154
MINOR LEAGUE TOTALS			15	10	4.00	37	30	3	0	196	184	100	87	70	208

10. Jung Bong, lhp

Born: July 15, 1980. **Ht.:** 6-3. **Wt.:** 175. **Bats:** L. **Throws:** L. **Career Transactions:** Signed out of Korea by Braves, Nov. 6, 1997.

After several years showing flashes of his talent, Bong finally became consistent and took the steps Atlanta officials had been hoping to see in 2001. He was the Braves' first significant sign out of the Far East, though the organization has been very active in other parts of the world. After a difficult April and May at Myrtle Beach, he went 9-4, 1.97 during the season's last three months. Bong succeeds by mixing his pitches and maintaining command of all his offerings. He uses both sides of the plate and throws strikes. His fastball registers in the high 80s and showed more movement in 2001. His changeup may be his best pitch, while his curveball developed a sharper break. Bong is an excellent athlete who fields his position well and swings the bat much better than the average hurler. The Braves want to see Bong become more confident with all of his pitches. As a starter, he needs to stay on top of his curveball in order to have an effective third pitch, which will make his fastball and changeup even better. Bong may not be a top-of-the-rotation pitcher, but he has the stuff and the ability to have success similar to Kirk Rueter's. Bong is expected to spend most of 2002 at Greenville.

Year	Club (League)	Class	W	L	ERA	G	GS	CG	SV	IP	H	R	ER	BB	SO
1998	Braves (GCL)	R	1	1	1.49	11	10	0	0	48	31	9	8	14	56
1999	Macon (SAL)	A	6	5	3.98	26	20	0	1	109	111	61	48	50	100
2000	Macon (SAL)	A	7	7	4.23	20	19	0	0	113	119	65	53	45	90
	Myrtle Beach (Car)	A	3	1	2.18	7	6	0	0	41	33	14	10	7	37
2001	Myrtle Beach (Car)	A	13	9	3.00	28	28	0	0	168	151	67	56	47	145
MINOR LEAGUE TOTALS			30	23	3.29	92	83	0	1	479	445	216	175	163	428

11. Tim Spooneybarger, rhp

Born: Oct. 21, 1979. **Ht.:** 6-3. **Wt.:** 190. **Bats:** R. **Throws:** R. **School:** Okaloosa-Walton (Fla.) JC. **Career Transactions:** Selected by Braves in 29th round of 1998 draft; signed May 19, 1999.

Spooneybarger placed himself in the running for a job in the Atlanta bullpen in 2002 with a dominating performance at Richmond last year. The Braves saw similar progress from him the year before at Myrtle Beach, and they were impressed with the adjustments he made against tougher competition after a slow start at Greenville last spring. After failing to look comfortable as a starter in the Carolina League two years ago, Spooneybarger has blossomed by showing a reliever's mindset. He also has the physical ability to succeed with regular use, as his stuff improves the more he takes the mound. Spooneybarger has a deceptive delivery that helped him hold opponents to a .205 batting average last year. His best pitch is an outstanding hard curveball. He also mixes in a two-seam fastball that acts like a splitter and a four-seam heater that consistently clocks at 93-95 mph. Confidence remains the key to his long-term success, though he has improved immensely in that area over the past two years. He was shut down in winter ball because of concerns he was overworking his arm while also on a weight-training regimen, but he is expected to be healthy and ready to compete for a big league job in spring training.

Year	Club (League)	Class	W	L	ERA	G	GS	CG	SV	IP	H	R	ER	BB	SO
1999	Danville (Appy)	R	3	0	2.22	12	0	0	0	24	15	11	6	14	36
	Macon (SAL)	A	0	1	3.60	7	0	0	0	10	7	4	4	10	17
2000	Myrtle Beach (Car)	A	3	0	0.91	19	6	0	0	50	18	7	5	19	57
2001	Greenville (SL)	AA	1	1	5.14	15	0	0	0	21	20	12	12	4	24
	Richmond (IL)	AAA	3	0	0.71	42	0	0	5	51	33	5	4	21	58
	Atlanta (NL)	MAJ	0	1	2.25	4	0	0	0	4	5	1	1	2	3
MAJOR LEAGUE TOTALS			0	1	2.25	4	0	0	0	4	5	1	1	2	3
MINOR LEAGUE TOTALS			10	2	1.79	95	6	0	5	156	93	39	31	68	192

12. Bryan Digby, rhp

Born: Dec. 31, 1981. **Ht.:** 6-2. **Wt.:** 190. **Bats:** R. **Throws:** R. **School:** McIntosh HS, Peachtree City, Ga. **Career Transactions:** Selected by Braves in second round of 2000 draft; signed June 9, 2000.

Digby joins several other Atlanta prospects as a budding power pitcher who has yet to emerge from the embryological stages of a thrower. His strength is a hard, sinking 94-mph fastball with excellent movement that he throws effortlessly and with a consistent arm slot. He's continuing to refine his secondary offerings, particularly his changeup, and lacks command of all his pitches. His 32 walks last year were the second-highest total in the Rookie-level Appalachian League. Nevertheless, Appy managers rated Digby as the fifth-best prospect in the league, noting his projectable body and raw stuff. With the Braves stocked with young pitchers throughout the bottom half of the organization, they'll be patient with Digby. He's expected to make the climb to the Macon starting rotation in 2002.

Year	Club (League)	Class	W	L	ERA	G	GS	CG	SV	IP	H	R	ER	BB	SO
2000	Braves (GCL)	R	1	3	7.33	10	3	0	0	27	28	28	22	21	34
2001	Danville (APPY)	R	3	5	3.38	12	12	1	0	61	52	33	32	32	49
	Macon (SAL)	A	1	0	1.13	3	1	0	0	8	3	1	1	7	6
MINOR LEAGUE TOTALS			5	8	5.16	25	16	1	0	96	83	62	55	60	89

13. Ben Kozlowski, lhp

Born: Aug. 16, 1980. **Ht.:** 6-6. **Wt.:** 220. **Bats:** L. **Throws:** L. **School:** Santa Fe (Fla.) CC. **Career Transactions:** Selected by Braves in 12th round of 1999 draft; signed June 12, 1999.

The Braves weren't shy about expressing their disappointment with Kozlowski following his efforts in 2000. Instead of pouting about his performance, Kozlowski showed more maturity, improved his dedication to his profession and emerged as a prospect. After going 3-8, 4.21 in 15 games at Macon in 2000 while battling tendinitis in his left shoulder, he returned to the South Atlantic League last year and ranked fifth in ERA. Kozlowski developed a stronger and firmer body with an offseason conditioning program. His work between starts also improved, thereby making him a smarter and more effective pitcher. Few scouts would be surprised if Kozlowski's body became even stronger in the next year or two, which should improve the quality of his pitches even more. He throws a 90-93 mph fastball, along with a good curveball and a changeup, and he isn't shy about throwing strikes or pitching inside. The Braves have been rewarded for their patience with Kozlowski and are hoping to see more progress and consistency this year at Myrtle Beach.

Year	Club (League)	Class	W	L	ERA	G	GS	CG	SV	IP	H	R	ER	BB	SO
1999	Braves (GCL)	R	1	1	1.87	15	0	0	3	34	28	9	7	6	29
2000	Macon (SAL)	A	3	8	4.21	15	14	0	0	77	76	53	36	39	67
2001	Macon (SAL)	A	10	7	2.48	26	23	1	0	145	134	60	40	27	147
	Myrtle Beach (Car)	A	0	2	3.77	2	2	0	0	14	15	7	6	3	13
MINOR LEAGUE TOTALS			14	18	2.97	58	39	1	3	270	253	129	89	75	256

14. Richard Lewis, 2b

Born: June 29, 1980. **Ht.:** 6-1. **Wt.:** 185. **Bats:** R. **Throws:** R. **School:** Georgia Tech. **Career Transactions:** Selected by Braves in first round (40th overall) of 2001 draft; signed June 14, 2001.

A supplemental first-rounder taken 40th overall last June, Lewis was the Braves' highest-drafted college player since they took Mike Kelly with the No. 2 overall pick in 1991. He was the starting second baseman on Team USA's college squad in 2000 and played three years at Georgia Tech, where he held the Yellow Jackets' offense together as a junior while superstar Mark Teixeira was injured. Lewis then held his own in the New York-Penn League before blossoming during instructional league, where his fielding and hitting discipline improved. He has excellent bat speed and quick hands at the plate and in the field. He saw extensive activity at shortstop in college last spring, has a good arm and shows above-average footwork, which allows him to make the double-play pivot with ease. Lewis is also considered a potential offensive contributor who could produce line drives while hitting second or in the bottom third of the batting order. He must make more contact and employ better strike-zone judgment. Atlanta believes his instructional league performance could enable Lewis to skip low Class A with a strong spring.

Year	Club (League)	Class	AVG	G	AB	R	H	2B	3B	HR	RBI	BB	SO	SB
2001	Jamestown (NY-P)	A	.242	71	285	37	69	7	1	4	27	20	50	16
MINOR LEAGUE TOTALS			.242	71	285	37	69	7	1	4	27	20	50	16

15. Kyle Davies, rhp

Born: Sept. 9, 1983. **Ht.:** 6-3. **Wt.:** 195. **Bats:** R. **Throws:** R. **School:** Stockbridge (Ga.) HS. **Career Transactions:** Selected by Braves in fourth round of 2001 draft; signed June 15, 2001.

Davies may have been the Braves' seventh pick (fourth round) last June, yet he may have the highest ceiling of any player in the team's draft class. While he developed as an amateur, Baseball America rated him the best 14- and 15-year-old player in the nation, and he received honorable mention at ages 16 and 17. He showed exceptional poise in the Gulf Coast League to earn a late-season callup to Macon, where he allowed two hits with seven strikeouts in a six-inning start. Davies is an excellent all-around athlete who could have been a catching prospect had he concentrated on that position. He's extremely competitive, and the Braves love his makeup and presence on the mound. Davies has the ability to command three major league pitches. His fastball was in the 88-90 mph range in the GCL after sitting on 92-93 mph during the spring. Atlanta thinks he had a tired arm after pitching for nearly two straight years and believes he'll start to make tremendous progress once he combines some rest with professional instruction. He didn't turn 18 until after signing with the Braves, making him one of the youngest and most promising pitchers in the organization.

Year	Club (League)	Class	W	L	ERA	G	GS	CG	SV	IP	H	R	ER	BB	SO
2001	Braves (GCL)	R	4	2	2.25	12	9	1	0	56	47	17	14	8	53
	Macon (SAL)	A	1	0	0.00	1	1	0	0	6	2	0	0	1	7
MINOR LEAGUE TOTALS			5	2	2.03	13	10	1	0	62	49	17	14	9	60

16. Billy Sylvester, rhp

Born: Oct. 1, 1976. **Ht.:** 6-5. **Wt.:** 218. **Bats:** R. **Throws:** R. **School:** Spartanburg Methodist (S.C.) JC. **Career Transactions:** Signed as nondrafted free agent by Braves, June 18, 1997.

Sylvester split the 2001 season between Greenville and Richmond, yet never found the consistency needed to succeed at the Triple-A level. He spent most of his time trying to improve his mechanics, which led to a lack of control. The Braves believe Sylvester can overcome his most recent hurdle and continue his development as one of the organization's top relief prospects. He owns a 93-95 mph fastball, along with a sharp-breaking curveball and a decent splitter. Sylvester has battled his confidence throughout his pro career and is faced with a similar challenge heading into 2002. Atlanta hopes he conquers this latest bout in Richmond to set the stage for a promotion to the majors when the need arises.

Year	Club (League)	Class	W	L	ERA	G	GS	CG	SV	IP	H	R	ER	BB	SO
1997	Braves (GCL)	R	3	4	3.91	12	9	0	0	53	45	25	23	28	58
1998	Eugene (NWL)	A	0	11	6.51	16	16	0	0	55	73	61	40	24	42
1999	Macon (SAL)	A	5	4	3.12	44	1	0	2	84	78	37	29	37	75
2000	Myrtle Beach (Car)	A	3	0	0.79	32	0	0	16	46	16	8	4	15	48
2001	Greenville (SL)	AA	1	0	2.37	26	0	0	12	30	18	8	8	24	41
	Richmond (IL)	AAA	0	4	5.11	36	0	0	11	37	28	21	21	27	41
MINOR LEAGUE TOTALS			12	23	3.69	166	26	0	41	305	258	160	125	155	305

17. Trey Hodges, rhp

Born: June 29, 1978. **Ht.:** 6-3. **Wt.:** 187. **Bats:** R. **Throws:** R. **School:** Louisiana State University. **Career Transactions:** Selected by Braves in 17th round of 2000 draft; signed June 21, 2000.

No pitcher in the Atlanta organization had greater success last year than Hodges, who shared Carolina League pitcher of the year honors with Cardinals prospect Jimmy Journell. He added that trophy to the College World Series MVP award he won in 2000, when he won the championship game in relief for Louisiana State. Fully recovered from 1999 shoulder surgery, he led the Braves system in wins and innings during his first pro season. He succeeds with a nasty slider that hitters find hard to lay off and harder to make contact against. Though not overpowering, Hodges also throws a sneaky fastball with good movement that does a good job of complementing his slider. After making minor adjustments to his mechanics last spring, Hodges was consistently ahead in the count and averaged 0.9 walks per nine innings. Unheralded prior to 2001, he'll try to make an even bigger name for himself this year at Greenville.

Year	Club (League)	Class	W	L	ERA	G	GS	CG	SV	IP	H	R	ER	BB	SO
2000	Jamestown (NY-P)	A	0	2	5.95	13	2	0	0	20	22	14	13	12	13
2001	Myrtle Beach (Car)	A	15	8	2.76	26	26	1	0	173	156	64	53	18	139
MINOR LEAGUE TOTALS			15	10	3.08	39	28	1	0	193	176	78	66	30	152

18. Matt Wright, rhp

Born: March 13, 1982. **Ht.:** 6-4. **Wt.:** 220. **Bats:** R. **Throws:** R. **School:** Robinson HS, Waco, Texas.
Career Transactions: Selected by Braves in 21st round of 2000 draft; signed June 21, 2000.

A 21st-round pick in 2000, Wright made incredible progress during the latter part of that Gulf Coast League season and in instructional league. He struggled last season in the Appalachian League before gaining a handle on his slider in early August, and went 2-2, 2.32 with 43 strikeouts in his final 31 innings. His efforts included a 13-strikeout performance at Kingsport. Wright is in the process of making the change from a thrower to a pitcher. He's a good competitor who is most effective when he stays within himself. His fastball is clocked in the 92-93 mph range and his changeup showed improvement last year. As with most hurlers who have yet to celebrate their 20th birthday, Wright needs to mature both physically and mentally, but he has a good idea of how to pitch and has shown to be a quick learner. He'll be expected to earn a job in Macon's rotation this spring.

Year	Club (League)	Class	W	L	ERA	G	GS	CG	SV	IP	H	R	ER	BB	SO
2000	Braves (GCL)	R	0	2	0.86	12	0	0	4	21	8	5	2	11	30
2001	Danville (Appy)	R	3	5	3.72	14	14	1	0	73	60	40	30	26	89
MINOR LEAGUE TOTALS			3	7	3.06	26	14	1	4	94	68	45	32	37	119

19. Ryan Langerhans, of

Born: Feb. 20, 1980. **Ht.:** 6-3. **Wt.:** 195. **Bats:** L. **Throws:** L. **School:** Round Rock (Texas) HS. **Career Transactions:** Selected by Braves in third round of 1998 draft; signed June 28, 1998.

Atlanta officials have differing opinions on Langerhans and his long-term potential. While some in the organization think he won't hit consistently enough to reach the majors, several others are convinced he's on track to be a major league right fielder. Langerhans has been the system's best defensive outfielder since he signed in 1998. He also has one of the strongest outfield arms and possesses the instincts to play any of the three outfield positions. His struggles have come at the plate, as Langerhans failed to hit above .268 in a full-season league prior to batting .287 last year during his second stint at Myrtle Beach. His bat showed signs of blossoming two winters ago in Australia, and he has enough power to hit 20-plus home runs in the major leagues. Langerhans also possesses above-average speed and is a good baserunner. In other words, all five tools of his tools have the potential to be average or better. The Braves are hoping he puts everything together in Double-A this year.

Year	Club (League)	Class	W	L	ERA	G	GS	CG	SV	IP	H	R	ER	BB	SO
1998	Braves (GCL)	R	.277	43	148	15	41	10	4	2	19	19	38	2	
1999	Macon (SAL)	A	.268	121	448	66	120	30	1	9	49	52	99	19	
2000	Myrtle Beach (Car)	A	.212	116	392	55	83	14	7	6	37	32	104	25	
2001	Myrtle Beach (Car)	A	.287	125	450	66	129	30	3	7	48	55	104	22	
MINOR LEAGUE TOTALS			.259	405	1438	202	373	84	15	24	153	158	345	68	

20. Matt McClendon, rhp

Born: Oct. 13, 1977. **Ht.:** 6-6. **Wt.:** 220. **Bats:** R. **Throws:** R. **School:** University of Florida. **Career Transactions:** Selected by Braves in fifth round of 1999 draft; signed June 18, 1999.

McClendon was a supplemental first-round pick of the Reds in 1996 who didn't sign and had a disappointing career at Florida, but he seemed to blossom after the Braves drafted him. So the organization isn't sure what went wrong with him last year. He had some minor injuries around the midpoint of the campaign, but those ailments fail to explain how miserable his command was for most of the season. Ranked as the organization's No. 2 prospect going into 2001, he couldn't find the strike zone after opening the season in Triple-A. He fared little better in two poor Double-A starts, then landed in high Class A in late July and continued to struggle in eight relief outings. After averaging 3.4 walks per nine innings during his first two years as a pro, he surrendered 7.0 per nine innings last season. When in a groove, McClendon has a low-90s fastball with good movement, a sharp curveball and a good knowledge of how to pitch. He was working on refining his mechanics last year but never could get back on track. After appearing on the verge of reaching the major leagues following the 2000 season, McClendon will try to regain his success in the upper reaches of the farm system this year.

Year	Club (League)	Class	W	L	ERA	G	GS	CG	SV	IP	H	R	ER	BB	SO
1999	Jamestown (NY-P)	A	1	1	3.91	7	7	0	0	23	18	11	10	11	24
2000	Myrtle Beach (Car)	A	3	1	1.59	6	6	0	0	40	24	7	7	8	43
	Greenville (SL)	AA	7	6	3.78	22	21	1	0	131	124	59	55	54	90
2001	Braves (GCL)	R	0	0	1.35	3	3	0	0	7	3	2	1	10	15
	Myrtle Beach (Car)	A	1	2	8.68	8	0	0	0	9	7	10	9	9	10
	Greenville (SL)	AA	0	1	5.91	2	2	0	0	11	10	7	7	7	9
	Richmond (IL)	AAA	0	6	8.16	10	10	0	0	46	50	45	42	31	31
MINOR LEAGUE TOTALS			12	17	4.42	58	49	1	0	267	236	141	131	130	222

21. Macay McBride, lhp

Born: Oct. 24, 1982. **Ht.:** 5-11. **Wt.:** 185. **Bats:** L. **Throws:** L. **School:** Screven County HS, Sylvania, Ga. **Career Transactions:** Selected by Braves in first round (24th overall) of 2001 draft; signed June 6, 2001.

The 24th overall pick in the 2001 draft, McBride showed an advanced ability to pitch for an 18-year-old in the Gulf Coast League. He threw his hard fastball consistently in the 94-95 range, averaging 11.0 strikeouts per nine innings and not allowing a homer. Unlike most of the top pitching prospects in the Atlanta organization, McBride isn't physically imposing and isn't very projectable. Still, when a left arm can produce as much gas as McBride's can, a pitcher tends to find his way to the top. He attracted comparisons prior to the draft to Houston closer Billy Wagner, who spoke with the young lefthander about his size (5-foot-10) and approach to the game. McBride has taken much of the advice to heart. His plans now call for refining his changeup and breaking ball and improving his overall command. He also needs to pitch inside more. A strong spring will land him in the Macon rotation.

Year	Club (League)	Class	W	L	ERA	G	GS	CG	SV	IP	H	R	ER	BB	SO
2001	Braves (GCL)	R	4	4	3.76	13	11	0	0	55	51	30	23	23	67
MINOR LEAGUE TOTALS			4	4	3.76	13	11	0	0	55	51	30	23	23	67

22. Chris Waters, lhp

Born: Aug. 17, 1980. **Ht.:** 6-0. **Wt.:** 170. **Bats:** L. **Throws:** L. **School:** South Florida CC. **Career Transactions:** Selected by Braves in fifth round of 2000 draft; signed June 7, 2000.

Overshadowed in the Macon rotation by Adam Wainwright, Bubba Nelson and Ben Kozlowski, Waters had a quietly successful 2001 season. Though his stuff isn't overwhelming, he gets results by competing well and throwing strikes. His 91-mph fastball isn't one of the best in the organization and his decent curveball never will be mistaken for Bert Blyleven's, but Waters knows what he wants to accomplish every time he takes the mound. As a result, he's making steady progress. He does a good job of setting up hitters and his easy, fluid delivery gives him good command of his three primary pitches. His curve and changeup could use some upgrading, but he still manages to prevent hitters from making solid contact. A promotion to Myrtle Beach appears to be imminent for Waters this spring.

Year	Club (League)	Class	W	L	ERA	G	GS	CG	SV	IP	H	R	ER	BB	SO
2000	Danville (Appy)	R	5	3	3.91	13	13	1	0	69	64	33	30	29	73
2001	Macon (SAL)	A	8	6	3.35	25	24	3	0	148	131	71	55	52	78
MINOR LEAGUE TOTALS			13	9	3.53	38	37	4	0	217	195	104	85	81	151

23. Andy Marte, 3b

Born: Oct. 21, 1983. **Ht.:** 6-1. **Wt.:** 185. **Bats:** R. **Throws:** R. **Career Transactions:** Signed out of Dominican Republic by Braves, Sept. 12, 2000.

A potential five-tool talent, Marte signed out of the Dominican Republic for $600,000 in September 2000, shortly after the end of the Braves' six-month ban on signing Dominicans, the result of grabbing Wilson Betemit before his 16th birthday. Scouts talk about the special sound a ball makes off the bat of premier players, and Marte's hits fall into that category. Marte has a smooth and easy swing, and balls jump off his bat. Atlanta officials believe he'll have plus power and will hit for average. He also possesses outstanding instincts in the infield with soft hands, excellent reflexes at the hot corner and a strong arm. Marte had a lackluster season at Rookie-level Danville and has considerable work to do with his plate coverage and strike-zone judgment. At the same time, he was 17. The Braves hope Marte will make the climb to Macon and be one of the youngest players in the South Atlantic League in 2001, but won't be disappointed if he plays at a lower level.

Year	Club (League)	Class	AVG	G	AB	R	H	2B	3B	HR	RBI	BB	SO	SB
2001	Danville (Appy)	R	.200	37	125	12	25	6	0	1	12	20	45	3
MINOR LEAGUE TOTALS			.200	37	125	12	25	6	0	1	12	20	45	3

24. Ramon Castro, ss

Born: Oct. 23, 1979. **Ht.:** 6-0. **Wt.:** 195. **Bats:** B. **Throws:** R. **Career Transactions:** Signed out of Venezuela by Braves, July 2, 1996.

When Castro reported to Greenville last year, he was considered an extra infielder. After Travis Wilson was promoted to Richmond in May, Castro took over at shortstop. He excelled, earning a starting job in both the Southern League and Double-A all-star games. The lone Greenville player selected to play in the Double-A event, he responded with a double and a home run in three at-bats, and was promoted to Triple-A shortly thereafter. Castro has to be evaluated over a period of five or six games to appreciate what he does. He's a steady defender who's capable of putting the bat on the ball, and he'll surprise some pitchers with his occasional pop. He also has an unmatched love for the game and works as hard as anyone in his preparation. A potential utilityman at the major league level, Castro is expected to return to Richmond after getting a look during spring training.

Year	Club (League)	Class	AVG	G	AB	R	H	2B	3B	HR	RBI	BB	SO	SB
1997	Eugene (NWL)	A	.199	71	226	20	45	8	3	1	23	24	56	7
1998	Eugene (NWL)	A	.260	74	296	33	77	10	1	3	33	22	49	8
1999	Macon (SAL)	A	.260	105	350	32	91	12	4	3	33	24	55	13
2000	Myrtle Beach (Car)	A	.252	108	385	52	97	20	3	5	44	44	76	13
2001	Greenville (SL)	AA	.307	76	261	35	80	19	5	6	31	25	56	5
	Richmond (IL)	AAA	.222	36	135	14	30	8	2	1	15	7	30	1
MINOR LEAGUE TOTALS			.254	470	1653	186	420	77	18	19	179	146	322	47

25. Josh Burrus, 3b

Born: Aug. 20, 1983. **Ht.:** 5-11. **Wt.:** 185. **Bats:** R. **Throws:** R. **School:** Wheeler HS, Marietta, Ga. **Career Transactions:** Selected by Braves in first round (29th overall) of 2001 draft; signed June 14, 2001.

Burrus struggled in his first taste of professional baseball after being drafted 29th overall last June. He had difficulty making adjustments at the plate in the Gulf Coast League, and his defense looked out of kilter for most of the summer. As a result, the Braves moved Burrus to third base during instructional league while giving him some time in left field. Atlanta officials believe he'll blossom now that he has gotten his feet wet as a pro and feels more comfortable on defense. He has an outstanding arm with plus speed and excellent all-around athleticism. Burrus also possess great bat speed that generates the best raw power of anyone in the Braves' 2001 draft class. An aggressive hitter, he showed a lack of patience in the GCL and tended to carry any difficulties at the plate to other aspects of his game. A cousin of the Brewers' Jeffrey Hammonds, Burrus will be expected to settle in this year at Macon and start to show why he was considered one of the top high school hitters available in the 2001 draft.

Year	Club (League)	Class	AVG	G	AB	R	H	2B	3B	HR	RBI	BB	SO	SB
2001	Braves (GCL)	R	.193	52	197	24	38	8	2	3	19	14	40	10
MINOR LEAGUE TOTALS			.193	52	197	24	38	8	2	3	19	14	40	10

26. Adam Stern, of

Born: Feb. 12, 1980. **Ht.:** 5-10. **Wt.:** 180. **Bats:** L. **Throws:** R. **School:** University of Nebraska. **Career Transactions:** Selected by Braves in third round of 2001 draft; signed June 12, 2001.

The Braves tried to help shore up center field, their weakest position in the minors, by drafting Stern in the third round in 2001. Rated the best draft prospect in Nebraska by Baseball America, he draws favorable comparisons to Lenny Dykstra with his all-out style of play and decent pop at the top of the order. Stern's greatest strength is his speed. He has been clocked between 6.4 and 6.5 seconds in the 60-year dash, covers center field from gap to gap and creates havoc on the basepaths with his aggressiveness. His arm is above average for a center fielder. Stern showed little difficulty in making the adjustment to wood bats and also had a good eye at the plate. A native of Canada, he hasn't played as much baseball as many of his American counterparts, but he has a chance to make an impact in an organization that has minimal talent in the outfield.

Year	Club (League)	Class	AVG	G	AB	R	H	2B	3B	HR	RBI	BB	SO	SB
2001	Jamestown (NY-P)	A	.307	21	75	20	23	4	2	0	11	15	11	9
MINOR LEAGUE TOTALS			.307	21	75	20	23	4	2	0	11	15	11	9

27. Matt Merricks, lhp

Born: Aug. 6, 1982. **Ht.:** 5-11. **Wt.:** 180. **Bats:** L. **Throws:** L. **School:** Oxnard (Calif.) HS. **Career Transactions:** Selected by Braves in sixth round of 2000 draft; signed June 26, 2000.

No Braves short-season pitcher was more consistent last year than Merricks, who succeeds without overpowering stuff. While Appy League teammates Bryan Digby and Blaine Boyer overpowered opponents, Merricks limited them to a .209 average while striking out 12.1 batters per nine innings. Not bad for his first taste of starting as a pro. He's a strike thrower with excellent command and a good feel for pitching. He gets ahead in the count by working off his high-80s fastball, which has good life. Merricks also throws a slider and changeup, both of which are workable but will need to be fine-tuned as he progresses through the organization. His next stop is scheduled to be the rotation at Macon, where he'll get his first taste of full-season ball.

Year	Club (League)	Class	W	L	ERA	G	GS	CG	SV	IP	H	R	ER	BB	SO
2000	Braves (GCL)	R	1	0	2.53	9	0	0	1	21	21	15	6	11	28
2001	Danville (Appy)	R	4	5	2.79	12	11	0	0	58	42	19	18	18	78
MINOR LEAGUE TOTALS			5	5	2.73	21	11	0	1	79	63	34	24	29	106

28. Pat Manning, 3b

Born: Feb. 27, 1980. **Ht.:** 6-1. **Wt.:** 185. **Bats:** R. **Throws:** R. **School:** Mater Dei HS, Santa Ana, Calif. **Career Transactions:** Selected by Braves in third round of 1999 draft; signed June 2, 1999.

Not unlike Brett Evert, Manning experienced somewhat of a comeback last year after an impressive debut in 1999 and a difficult campaign in 2000. He hit 23 home runs in Class A and made progress with his offensive game. While he made more consistent contact, Manning still has some holes in his big, uppercut swing and tries to do too much at the plate at times. The Braves would like for him to focus on hitting line drives in the gaps instead of home runs. Drafted as a shortstop and moved to second base during his first full pro season, Manning was shifted to third base in instructional league. His hands aren't particularly soft, and he needs more consistency with the leather as well as with his throws. He's scheduled to return to Myrtle Beach this year.

Year	Club (League)	Class	AVG	G	AB	R	H	2B	3B	HR	RBI	BB	SO	SB
1999	Braves (GCL)	R	.416	24	89	21	37	9	1	4	19	14	14	4
	Macon (SAL)	A	.259	43	170	25	44	11	2	4	19	14	42	3
2000	Macon (SAL)	A	.202	124	435	48	88	27	0	7	49	63	82	9
2001	Macon (SAL)	A	.284	62	211	40	60	13	1	13	29	37	46	6
	Myrtle Beach (Car)	A	.223	62	220	23	49	12	0	10	30	28	41	2
MINOR LEAGUE TOTALS			.247	315	1125	157	278	72	4	38	146	156	225	24

29. Cory Aldridge, of

Born: June 13, 1979. **Ht.:** 6-0. **Wt.:** 210. **Bats:** L. **Throws:** R. **School:** Cooper HS, Abilene, Texas. **Career Transactions:** Selected by Braves in fourth round of 1997 draft; signed June 8, 1997.

At times Aldridge will appear to be putting everything together and developing into a multitool prospect, only to look completely lost shortly thereafter. The former football standout looked to be taking his game to the next level last year in spring training, where he impressed Braves manager Bobby Cox by batting .333 and displayed both power and speed. He came back to earth at Greenville, where he hit .246 and continued to have problems with plate coverage and strike-zone discipline. A natural athlete, Aldridge's tools remain rough after five years in the organization. He could hit 20 home runs annually in the major leagues, and his defense and arm strength have improved over the past two years. If he can do a more consistent job at the plate, he might earn a shot as the Braves' fourth outfielder this season.

Year	Club (League)	Class	AVG	G	AB	R	H	2B	3B	HR	RBI	BB	SO	SB
1997	Braves (GCL)	R	.278	46	169	26	47	8	1	3	37	14	37	1
1998	Danville (Appy)	R	.294	60	214	37	63	16	1	3	33	29	48	16
1999	Macon (SAL)	A	.251	124	443	48	111	19	4	12	65	33	123	9
2000	Myrtle Beach (Car)	A	.249	109	401	51	100	18	5	15	64	33	118	10
2001	Greenville (SL)	AA	.246	131	452	57	111	19	2	19	56	48	139	12
	Atlanta (NL)	MAJ	.000	8	5	1	0	0	0	0	0	0	4	0
MAJOR LEAGUE TOTALS			.000	8	5	1	0	0	0	0	0	0	4	0
MINOR LEAGUE TOTALS			.257	470	1679	219	432	80	13	52	255	157	465	48

30. Travis Wilson, of/2b

Born: July 10, 1977. **Ht.:** 6-2. **Wt.:** 185. **Bats:** R. **Throws:** R. **Career Transactions:** Signed out of New Zealand by Braves, Aug. 31, 1996.

Wilson nearly made Atlanta's 2001 roster after hitting .415 in spring training. He continued to produce at an impressive rate during a one-month stint at Greenville before hitting the wall at Richmond. Wilson's greatest strength is his versatility, which allows him to play first, second and third base as well as the corner outfield positions. He also can be an aggressive hitter who makes the ball jump off his bat, resulting in line drives to all fields. A former fast-pitch softball player from New Zealand, Wilson possesses minimal patience and little idea of the strike zone. Triple-A pitchers took advantage of those weaknesses, which will cost him a shot in the big leagues if he doesn't improve. Another stint in Richmond is on Wilson's agenda for the 2002 campaign.

Year	Club (League)	Class	AVG	G	AB	R	H	2B	3B	HR	RBI	BB	SO	SB
1997	Danville (Appy)	R	.215	61	233	29	50	14	6	0	27	14	60	4
1998	Danville (Appy)	R	.323	65	269	48	87	25	5	9	48	17	54	16
	Macon (SAL)	A	.462	3	13	2	6	0	0	1	4	0	3	0
1999	Macon (SAL)	A	.309	90	363	65	112	20	4	11	63	9	66	14
2000	Myrtle Beach (Car)	A	.275	125	484	62	133	33	5	12	63	16	111	7
2001	Greenville (SL)	AA	.325	31	123	13	40	8	1	2	21	3	24	2
	Richmond (IL)	AAA	.243	103	383	34	93	22	3	3	38	7	81	4
MINOR LEAGUE TOTALS			.279	478	1868	253	521	122	24	38	264	66	399	47

BALTIMORE Orioles

By Will Lingo

As the Orioles continue to try to bring in and develop talent in the minor leagues, the misadventures in Baltimore leave fans wondering about the direction of a once-proud franchise. In Cal Ripken's final season, the Orioles moved ahead with their youth movement and finished 10 games worse than the year before, posting their worst record since 1988.

General manager Syd Thrift went into the offseason looking to make moves to retool the major league team, but several deals involving such players as Dustin Hermanson, Scott Rolen and Dmitri Young were vetoed by owner Peter Angelos. Rumors about Thrift and Angelos swirled throughout the Winter Meetings in Boston, prompting Angelos to issue the dreaded vote of confidence and explain that Thrift is making the baseball decisions, not him.

Perhaps Joe Strauss, who covers the Orioles for The Sun of Baltimore, summed it up best: "If there is indeed an organizational plan, it has been so bent, spindled and mutilated that it now resembles hieroglyphics not only to those outside the organization but to many who have committed themselves to a franchise that left Boston as an industry one-liner."

The organization's fractious structure trickles down to the farm system, best illustrated by the decision not to protect outfielder Keith Reed from the major league Rule 5 draft. The Orioles gambled that Reed, one of their best prospects, wouldn't get picked. They were correct, though several teams expressed interest in him before the draft and the decision was unpopular with some in the front office.

And while the Orioles are adding talent, the vacuum in Baltimore has prospects playing in the big leagues before they're ready or playing a level higher than they're suited for. Last season it added up to a .445 minor league winning percentage, the third-worst in the game. Just two affiliates had .500 records, and they combined to go one game over .500. Even longtime Triple-A affiliate Rochester has expressed interest in looking for a new major league partner when its current player-development contract expires.

If the organization has a strength now, it's in young pitching, especially lefthanders. Assuming the system's arms develop and stay healthy, they could provide a foundation for the Orioles to build on. But what the organization really needs is a blueprint.

OrganizationOverview

General Manager: Syd Thrift. **Farm director:** Don Buford. **Scouting director:** Tony DeMacio.

2001 PERFORMANCE

Class	Team	League	W	L	Pct.	Finish*	Manager
Majors	Baltimore	American	63	98	.391	13th (14)	Mike Hargrove
Triple-A	Rochester Red Wings	International	60	84	.417	14th (14)	Andy Etchebarren
Double-A	Bowie Baysox	Eastern	59	82	.418	11th (12)	Dave Machemer
High Class A	Frederick Keys	Carolina	70	69	.504	5th (8)	Dave Cash
Low Class A	Delmarva Shorebirds	South Atlantic	61	79	.436	13th (16)	Joe Ferguson
Rookie	Bluefield Orioles	Appalachian	33	33	.500	4th (10)	Joe Almaraz
Rookie	GCL Orioles	Gulf Coast	22	34	.393	t-11th (14)	Jesus Alfaro
OVERALL 2001 MINOR LEAGUE RECORD			305	381	.445	28th (30)	

*Finish in overall standings (No. of teams in league)

ORGANIZATION LEADERS

BATTING

*AVG	Willie Harris, Bowie	.305
R	B.J. Littleton, Delmarva	84
H	Franky Figueroa, Bowie	160
TB	Jose Leon, Rochester/Bowie	237
2B	Doug Gredvig, Frederick	40
3B	B.J. Littleton, Delmarva	18
HR	**Calvin Pickering**, Rochester	21
RBI	**Calvin Pickering**, Rochester	98
BB	**Calvin Pickering**, Rochester	64
SO	**Calvin Pickering**, Rochester	149
SB	Willie Harris., Bowie	54
	Tim Raines Jr., Rochester/Bowie	54

PITCHING

W	John Stephens, Rochester/Bowie	13
L	Mike Paradis, Bowie	13
#ERA	Erik Bedard, Frederick/GCL Orioles	2.20
G	Lesli Brea, Rochester	63
CG	Matt Schwager, Delmarva	4
SV	Jayme Sperring, Delmarva	26
IP	John Stephens, Rochester/Bowie	190
BB	**Mike Paradis**, Bowie	62
SO	John Stephens, Rochester/Bowie	191

*Minimum 250 At-Bats #Minimum 75 Innings

TOP PROSPECTS OF THE DECADE

1992	Arthur Rhodes, lhp
1993	Brad Pennington, lhp
1994	Jeffrey Hammonds, of
1995	Armando Benitez, rhp
1996	Rocky Coppinger, rhp
1997	Nerio Rodriguez, rhp
1998	Ryan Minor, 3b
1999	Matt Riley, lhp
2000	Matt Riley, lhp
2001	Keith Reed, of

TOP DRAFT PICKS OF THE DECADE

1992	Jeffrey Hammonds, of
1993	Jay Powell, rhp
1994	Tommy Davis, 1b (2)
1995	Alvie Shepherd, rhp
1996	Brian Falkenborg, rhp (2)
1997	Jayson Werth, c
1998	Rick Elder, of
1999	Mike Paradis, rhp
2000	Beau Hale, rhp
2001	Chris Smith, lhp

Pickering

Paradis

BEST TOOLS

Best Hitter for Average	Willie Harris
Best Power Hitter	Doug Gredvig
Fastest Baserunner	Tim Raines Jr.
Best Fastball	Richard Stahl
Best Breaking Ball	Matt Riley
Best Changeup	John Stephens
Best Control	John Stephens
Best Defensive Catcher	Octavio Martinez
Best Defensive Infielder	Ed Rogers
Best Infield Arm	Ed Rogers
Best Defensive Outfielder	Tim Raines Jr.
Best Outfield Arm	Keith Reed

PROJECTED 2005 LINEUP

Catcher	Eli Whiteside
First Base	Doug Gredvig
Second Base	Jerry Hairston
Third Base	Bryan Bass
Shortstop	Ed Rogers
Left Field	Luis Matos
Center Field	Tim Raines Jr.
Right Field	Keith Reed
Designated Hitter	Chris Richard
No. 1 Starter	Richard Stahl
No. 2 Starter	Erik Bedard
No. 3 Starter	Matt Riley
No. 4 Starter	Sidney Ponson
No. 5 Starter	Jason Johnson
Closer	Beau Hale

ALL-TIME LARGEST BONUSES

Beau Hale, 2000	$2,250,000
Chris Smith, 2001	$2,175,000
Darnell McDonald, 1997	$1,900,000
Richard Stahl, 1999	$1,795,000
Mike Paradis, 1999	$1,700,000

DraftAnalysis

2001 Draft

Best Pro Debut: Though he played just 10 high school games last spring before being suspended for a transfer snafu, SS Bryan Bass (1) hit .310-5-27 in Rookie ball.

Best Athlete: Alabama recruited Bass as a wide receiver. His worst tool is his power, which is still solid for his position. 2B Mike Fontenot (1) is another athletic middle infielder. LHP **Chris Smith** (1) and RHP Dave Crouthers (3) were two-way stars in college. Smith batted .375-14-66 as a Florida State sophomore, while Crouthers batted cleanup for Southern Illinois-Edwardsville's Division II College World Series club.

Best Hitter: Bass is a switch-hitter with gap power from both sides of the plate.

Best Raw Power: The Orioles didn't sign a masher, though C Eli Whiteside (6) has 20-homer potential. That would be a bonus, because defense is his strength.

Fastest Runner: Fontenot and Bass have both the speed and instincts to be threats on the bases.

Best Defensive Player: Baltimore likes the up-the-middle defenders it added. Fontenot is the most impressive.

Best Fastball: Crouthers and RHPs James Johnson (5) and Cory Morris (15) all have reached 95 mph, while Smith has hit 94. Johnson is the only high schooler in that group, so his fastball may have more upside.

Most Intriguing Background: RHP Joe Coppinger's (7) brother Rocky was once the Orioles' top prospect. Other draftees with big league connections include 1B Dustin

Yount (9), the son of Hall of Famer Robin, and unsigned OF Dustin Hahn (21), whose father Don was an original Expo. Unsigned SS John Hardy's (11) father Craig is a former tennis pro who played at Wimbledon, and John's cousin J.J. Hardy was Milwaukee's second-round pick in June. Bass' brothers Jayson and Kevin are outfielders in the Cubs system.

Smith

Closest To The Majors: Fontenot held out all summer while waiting in vain for Baltimore to increase its initial $1.3 million offer. He'll probably debut in high Class A this year, and his instincts and LSU experience should help him move quickly.

Best Late-Round Pick: Morris, who pitched his team into the 2001 NAIA World Series, threw 92-95 mph as a pro, harder than he did at Dallas Baptist. He also showed a good curveball and average changeup.

The One Who Got Away: Baltimore liked Hardy's defensive skills but couldn't sway him from the University of Arizona. The Wildcats also recruited J.J. Hardy but lost him to the Brewers.

Assessment: Besides outfielders, the Orioles system offers little in the way of position players. Baltimore addressed that shortcoming in this draft while adding one of the top southpaws in Smith.

2000 Draft

Injuries hampered RHP Beau Hale (1) and 3B Tripper Johnson (1) in their first full pro seasons. 1B Doug Gredvig (5) has power, while LHP Kurt Birkins (33) was one of the top draft-and-follows signed last year. **Grade: C**

1999 Draft

LHPs Richard Stahl (1) and Erik Bedard (6) and OF Keith Reed (1) rank 1-2-3 on Baltimore's prospect list. Two other first-rounders, OF Larry Bigbie and SS Brian Roberts, have reached the majors. But LHPs Josh Cenate and Scott Rice, have washed out, and RHP Mike Paradis, hasn't done much. That isn't much to show for seven first-round picks. **Grade: C+**

1998 Draft

This is another year in which multiple first-rounders, in this case OFs Rick Elder and Mamon Tucker, did the Orioles no good. OF Tim Raines Jr. (6) and RHP Steve Bechler (3) are the highlights of a mediocre crop. **Grade: C**

1997 Draft

Of three first-rounders, C Jayson Werth was traded to Toronto and OFs Darnell McDonald and Papy Ndungidi have been huge disappointments. But 2B Jerry Hairston Jr. (11), LHP Matt Riley (3, draft-and-follow) and RHP Sean Douglass (6) have been saving graces. **Grade: B+**

Note: Draft analysis prepared by Jim Callis. Numbers in parentheses indicate draft rounds.

... Stahl has all the attributes to become a No. 1 starter, including a mid-90s fastball that could improve as he fills out his frame.

Richard
Stahl lhp

Born: April 11, 1981.
Ht.: 6-7. **Wt.:** 185.
Bats: R. **Throws:** L.
School: Newton HS, Covington, Ga.
Career Transactions: Selected by Orioles in first round (18th overall) of 1999 draft; signed Aug. 31, 1999.

Stahl was part of the Orioles' 1999 draft class, which included seven first-round picks. He got the largest bonus of the bunch, $1.795 million, enough to pry him away from Georgia Tech on the day he was to begin classes there. He signed too late to pitch in 1999 and threw just 89 innings in 2000 because of back trouble. He started strong in 2001, earning a promotion from low Class A Delmarva to high Class A Frederick after just six starts. He looked even better there, but shoulder trouble sidelined him again after six. He was picked for the Futures Game but didn't pitch because of the injury, and he made just one rehab appearance in July before getting shut down for the rest of the season. Doctors performed arthroscopic surgery to remove a bone spur but otherwise found no structural problems.

Quite simply, no one else in the organization has a ceiling that matches Stahl's. He has all the attributes to become a No. 1 starter, including a mid-90s fastball that could improve as he fills out his 6-foot-7 frame and gets consistent with his mechanics. He has a smooth, easy delivery that should keep his arm healthy once he fully matures. He has the makings of a plus curveball and made progress with it last year, though it remains inconsistent. His changeup is average but also has potential. A basketball player in high school, he's a good athlete. The Orioles say Stahl's injuries have been the function of a growing body, not any chronic problems, but he still needs to prove he can stand up to the workload of a full season. What's more, he needs the innings to refine his secondary pitches and command, and to learn more about how to attack hitters. As with most tall pitchers, he also needs to find consistent mechanics, which should solve many of his other weaknesses.

With plenty of time to recover from his shoulder ailment, Stahl should be sound and ready to move in 2002. He'll probably return to Frederick to start the season, but a strong spring or fast start in the regular season could get him to Double-A Bowie quickly.

Year	Club (League)	Class	W	L	ERA	G	GS	CG	SV	IP	H	R	ER	BB	SO
2000	Delmarva (SAL)	A	5	6	3.34	20	20	0	0	89	97	47	33	51	83
2001	Delmarva (SAL)	A	2	3	2.67	6	6	0	0	34	24	15	10	15	31
	Frederick (Car)	A	1	1	1.95	6	6	1	0	32	26	13	7	15	24
	Orioles (GCL)	R	0	0	0.00	1	1	0	0	2	1	0	0	1	1
MINOR LEAGUE TOTALS			8	10	2.87	33	33	1	0	157	148	75	50	82	139

HAROLD WEST

2. Erik Bedard, lhp

Born: March 6, 1979. **Ht.:** 6-1. **Wt.:** 180. **Bats:** L. **Throws:** L. **School:** Norwalk (Conn.) CC. **Career Transactions:** Selected by Orioles in sixth round of 1999 draft; signed June 8, 1999.

Bedard has been one of the biggest surprises to come out of the Orioles' big 1999 draft class. Much of the credit goes to scout Jim Howard, who has a knack for finding cold-weather pitchers. An Ontario native whose high school didn't have a baseball team, Bedard walked on to his junior college team and steadily has improved. He continued his progress with a good Arizona Fall League. The velocity on Bedard's fastball has climbed from the 88-90 mph range when he signed to 90-92 now. He has a good curveball and changeup and good movement on all his pitches. The way he goes after hitters is outstanding, especially considering his limited experience. Opponents have batted just .214 against him for his career. Bedard's pitches have no real shortcomings, but he's inconsistent and must stay focused to avoid big innings. He was shut down with a sore arm for six weeks in 2001 and needs to get stronger. Added to the 40-man roster this winter, Bedard will get a look in major league camp. He should open the season in Double-A, but don't be surprised if he shows up in Baltimore sometime in 2002.

Year	Club (League)	Class	W	L	ERA	G	GS	CG	SV	IP	H	R	ER	BB	SO
1999	Orioles (GCL)	R	2	1	1.86	8	6	0	0	29	20	7	6	13	41
2000	Delmarva (SAL)	A	9	4	3.57	29	22	1	2	111	98	48	44	35	131
2001	Frederick (Car)	A	9	2	2.15	17	17	0	0	96	68	27	23	26	130
	Orioles (GCL)	R	0	1	3.00	2	2	0	0	6	4	2	2	3	7
MINOR LEAGUE TOTALS			20	8	2.79	56	47	1	2	242	190	84	75	77	309

3. Keith Reed, of

Born: Oct. 8, 1978. **Ht.:** 6-4. **Wt.:** 215. **Bats:** R. **Throws:** R. **School:** Providence College. **Career Transactions:** Selected by Orioles in first round (23rd overall) of 1999 draft; signed June 19, 1999.

Reed rose to the top of the Orioles' prospect list entering 2001, but was inexplicably exposed to the Rule 5 draft after getting bounced around the system. He was bothered by a leg injury at the beginning of the season and a hand injury at Bowie, but bounced back with solid three weeks at Triple-A Rochester. Regarded as one of the best athletes in the 1999 draft, Reed has done nothing to refute that. He's a pure tools player with good bat speed and the potential for a terrific power-speed combination. And his arm may be his strongest tool. Reed still is unrefined and needs lots of at-bats, which explains why he wasn't a Rule 5 pick. He still hasn't tapped into his power or speed. Pitch recognition is his biggest weakness at this point, and he needs to learn how to stay back on balls. Some in the organization also question his work habits. Reed's potential caused the Orioles to expect too much, too fast. He should return to Double-A and will develop into a good major league outfielder if the organization is patient.

Year	Club (League)	Class	AVG	G	AB	R	H	2B	3B	HR	RBI	BB	SO	SB
1999	Bluefield (Appy)	R	.188	4	16	2	3	0	0	0	0	1	3	0
	Delmarva (SAL)	A	.258	61	240	36	62	14	3	4	25	22	53	3
2000	Delmarva (SAL)	A	.290	70	269	43	78	16	1	11	59	25	56	20
	Frederick (Car)	A	.235	65	243	33	57	10	1	8	31	21	58	9
2001	Frederick (Car)	A	.270	72	267	28	72	14	0	7	29	13	57	8
	Bowie (EL)	AA	.254	18	67	7	17	3	0	1	8	6	10	2
	Rochester (IL)	AAA	.311	20	74	11	23	7	1	2	11	5	14	1
MINOR LEAGUE TOTALS			.265	310	1176	160	312	64	6	33	163	93	251	43

4. Matt Riley, lhp

Born: Aug. 2, 1979. **Ht.:** 6-1. **Wt.:** 205. **Bats:** L. **Throws:** L. **School:** Sacramento CC. **Career Transactions:** Selected by Orioles in third round of 1997 draft; signed May 28, 1998.

Following a disastrous 2000 season that began with immature behavior in major league camp and ended with Tommy John surgery, Riley spent all of 2001 rehabilitating his left elbow. He's expected to be ready for spring training in 2002, and by most accounts he has looked good in Florida workouts. When healthy, Riley throws a fastball that touches 97 mph, along with a curveball and changeup that also could be plus pitches in the major leagues. His delivery has looked more free and easy since the surgery, which bodes well for staying away from future injuries. Immaturity was Riley's biggest problem before he got hurt, and the injury may have helped him overcome that. He worked hard in rehab and should come to spring training in the best shape of his career. As with any injured pitcher, he'll have to prove his arm is sound and make up for two lost years. If Riley bounces back to pre-injury form, he gives the Orioles another premium lefty prospect. With the positive reports on his rehab, the organization is optimistic. Even so, he'll probably start off in Double-A unless he's overwhelming in spring training.

Year	Club (League)	Class	W	L	ERA	G	GS	CG	SV	IP	H	R	ER	BB	SO
1998	Delmarva (SAL)	A	5	4	1.19	16	14	0	0	83	42	19	11	44	136
1999	Frederick (Car)	A	3	2	2.61	8	8	0	0	52	34	19	15	14	58
	Bowie (EL)	AA	10	6	3.22	20	20	3	0	126	113	53	45	42	131
	Baltimore (AL)	MAJ	0	0	7.36	3	3	0	0	11	17	9	9	13	6
2000	Rochester (IL)	AAA	0	2	14.14	2	2	0	0	7	15	12	11	4	8
	Bowie (EL)	AA	5	7	6.08	19	14	2	1	74	74	56	50	49	66
2001								Did Not Play—Injured							
MAJOR LEAGUE TOTALS			0	0	7.36	3	3	0	0	11	17	9	9	13	6
MINOR LEAGUE TOTALS			23	21	3.48	65	58	5	1	341	278	159	132	153	399

5. Ed Rogers, ss

Born: Aug. 10, 1981. **Ht.:** 6-1. **Wt.:** 165. **Bats:** R. **Throws:** R. **Career Transactions:** Signed out of Dominican Republic by Orioles, Nov. 7, 1997.

Orioles officials and fans compared Rogers with the best shortstops in baseball after the 2000 season, and the organization jumped him to Bowie to start 2001. He was overmatched there but regained his footing at Frederick. His brother Omar is an infielder who played at Rookie-level Bluefield in 2001. Rogers has pure shortstop tools, with smooth, fluid actions, a great arm and outstanding range. He makes the infield smaller for those who play around him. He runs well and started to show a little pop in his bat last season. Double-A pitchers dominated Rogers, who has a long way to go to become a major leaguer at the plate. He has no real plate discipline and will need a couple of years of at-bats to improve his strike-zone judgment. Rogers has been taken off the fast track as the organization has tempered its expectations for him, at least in the short term. He still has a high ceiling if he can hit consistently. He'll probably return to high Class A this year to work on his hitting, and his bat will dictate how quickly he moves up.

Year	Club (League)	Class	AVG	G	AB	R	H	2B	3B	HR	RBI	BB	SO	SB
1998	Orioles (DSL)	R	.289	58	194	33	56	9	2	2	27	26	29	8
1999	Orioles (GCL)	R	.288	53	177	34	51	5	1	1	19	23	22	20
2000	Delmarva (SAL)	A	.274	80	332	46	91	14	5	5	42	22	63	27
	Bowie (EL)	AA	.286	13	49	4	14	3	0	1	8	3	15	1
2001	Bowie (EL)	AA	.199	53	191	11	38	10	1	0	13	6	40	10
	Frederick (Car)	A	.260	73	292	39	76	20	3	8	41	14	47	18
MINOR LEAGUE TOTALS			.264	330	1235	167	326	61	12	17	150	94	216	84

6. Sean Douglass, rhp

Born: April 28, 1979. **Ht.:** 6-6. **Wt.:** 200. **Bats:** R. **Throws:** R. **School:** Antelope Valley HS, Lancaster, Calif. **Career Transactions:** Selected by Orioles in second round of 1997 draft; signed July 9, 1997.

Douglass projected as a first-round pick before quitting his high school team midway through his senior year. He jump-started his pro career by beating the three first-round picks the Orioles took ahead of him—since-traded Jayson Werth, Darnell McDonald and Papy Ndungidi—to Baltimore. None of Douglass' pitches knock hitters out, but taken together they give him a quality repertoire. His fastball sits in the low 90s, and he also has a good slider and changeup. He has an effortless delivery, and the ball comes out of his hand easily and gets on hitters fast. His demeanor and presence on the mound are also positives. When Douglass struggles, it's because of problems with his command, which is very good when it's on. Because he lacks an out pitch, he has to be precise and keep the ball down to succeed. Douglass has the frame and ability to become a solid No. 3 starter in the big leagues, an innings-eater who takes the ball every five days. He should make the Baltimore staff this spring, possibly as a member of the rotation.

Year	Club (League)	Class	W	L	ERA	G	GS	CG	SV	IP	H	R	ER	BB	SO
1997	Orioles (GCL)	R	1	3	6.11	9	1	0	0	18	20	14	12	9	10
1998	Bluefield (Appy)	R	2	2	3.23	10	10	0	0	53	45	20	19	14	62
1999	Frederick (Car)	A	5	6	3.32	16	16	1	0	98	101	48	36	35	89
2000	Bowie (EL)	AA	9	8	4.03	27	27	1	0	161	155	79	72	55	118
2001	Rochester (IL)	AAA	8	9	3.49	27	27	0	0	162	160	79	63	61	156
	Baltimore (AL)	MAJ	2	1	5.31	4	4	0	0	20	21	12	12	11	17
MAJOR LEAGUE TOTALS			2	1	5.31	4	4	0	0	20	21	12	12	11	17
MINOR LEAGUE TOTALS			25	28	3.70	89	81	2	0	491	481	240	202	174	435

7. Tim Raines Jr., of

Born: Aug. 31, 1979. **Ht.:** 5-10. **Wt.:** 183. **Bats:** R. **Throws:** R. **School:** Seminole HS, Sanford, Fla. **Career Transactions:** Selected by Orioles in sixth round of 1998 draft; signed June 15, 1998.

Raines ran from Class A to the big leagues last year. On the way, he first played against his father (then with the Expos) in Triple-A. Then the Orioles traded for Tim Sr. and the two played together in the Baltimore outfield in October. Like his dad in his prime, Raines has outstanding speed that makes him a threat on both offense and defense. He projects as a leadoff man and started to figure things out at the plate in Double-A. He has surprising power potential for his size. He covers a lot of ground in the outfield and has a playable arm for center. A righthanded hitter growing up, Raines still is adjusting to batting from the left side. To be an effective leadoff man, he'll need to improve his plate discipline and make better use of his speed. The progress Raines showed in 2001 was exciting, but the Orioles rushed him a bit. He'll probably return to Double-A to begin this season and needs another full year in the minors.

Year	Club (League)	Class	AVG	G	AB	R	H	2B	3B	HR	RBI	BB	SO	SB
1998	Orioles (GCL)	R	.244	56	197	40	48	7	4	1	13	30	53	37
1999	Delmarva (SAL)	A	.248	117	415	80	103	24	8	2	49	71	130	49
2000	Frederick (Car)	A	.236	127	457	89	108	21	3	2	36	67	106	81
2001	Frederick (Car)	A	.250	23	84	15	21	3	1	3	13	13	23	14
	Bowie (EL)	AA	.291	65	254	46	74	14	1	4	30	34	60	29
	Rochester (IL)	AAA	.256	40	133	19	34	5	1	2	12	11	30	11
	Baltimore (AL)	MAJ	.174	7	23	6	4	2	0	0	0	3	8	3
MAJOR LEAGUE TOTALS			.174	7	23	6	4	2	0	0	0	3	8	3
MINOR LEAGUE TOTALS			.252	428	1540	289	388	74	18	14	153	226	402	221

8. Willie Harris 2b/of

Born: June 22, 1978. **Ht.:** 5-9. **Wt.:** 175. **Bats:** L. **Throws:** R. **School:** Kennesaw State (Ga.) University. **Career Transactions:** Selected by Orioles in 24th round of 1999 draft; signed June 7, 1999.

A late-round pick who has gone from an organizational player to legitimate prospect through strength of will, Harris is the nephew of former big leaguer Ernest Riles. He was born in Cairo, Ga., and became just the second big leaguer from the town—following Jackie Robinson. Harris' biggest strength is his drive, which allows him to play above his tools. He has solid skills and his makeup is off the charts. He's determined to be a major leaguer and doesn't get discouraged by setbacks. His speed is a tick above average, allowing him to play second base or center field, and his bat is his best tool. Harris has just enough pop in his bat to get himself in trouble when he starts swinging from his heels. Because his tools aren't overwhelming and he's just 5-foot-9, he'll have to prove himself every year and at every level. The Orioles started comparing Harris to Tony Phillips last year, and he continues to fulfill those expectations. He'll start 2002 in Triple-A and should be in Baltimore by the end of the year.

Year	Club (League)	Class	AVG	G	AB	R	H	2B	3B	HR	RBI	BB	SO	SB
1999	Bluefield (Appy)	R	.273	5	22	3	6	1	0	0	3	4	2	1
	Delmarva (SAL)	A	.265	66	272	42	72	13	3	2	32	20	41	17
2000	Delmarva (SAL)	A	.274	133	474	106	130	27	10	6	60	89	89	38
2001	Bowie (EL)	AA	.305	133	525	83	160	27	4	9	49	46	71	54
	Baltimore (AL)	MAJ	.125	9	24	3	3	1	0	0	0	0	7	0
MAJOR LEAGUE TOTALS			.125	9	24	3	3	1	0	0	0	0	7	0
MINOR LEAGUE TOTALS			.285	337	1293	234	368	68	17	17	144	159	203	110

9. John Stephens, rhp

Born: Nov. 15, 1979. **Ht.:** 6-1. **Wt.:** 200. **Bats:** R. **Throws:** R. **Career Transactions:** Signed out of Australia by Orioles, July 3, 1996.

RICH ABEL

The Eastern League's ERA champ in 2001, Stephens has proven himself at every level in spite of velocity that wouldn't get the attention of scouts at a high school game. His fastball slowed after nerve damage in his arm in 1998 at Delmarva, and it hasn't full returned. The comparison to Greg Maddux is an obvious one because Stephens is a surgeon on the mound. He gets hitters out by changing speeds and putting the ball exactly where he wants it with a deceptive delivery. He essentially has six different changeups, making his 82-86 mph fastball effective. His curveball is slow with a big break, making it look almost like a softball pitch. Though his velocity has come back a bit, Stephens is still a soft tosser with a small margin for error. He'll have to prove himself with every start. Stephens will return to Rochester, where he put up the highest ERA of his career last year. If he proves he can get Triple-A hitters out, he could get the improbable callup to Baltimore. The Orioles have given an opportunity to Josh Towers, who has a similar fastball.

Year	Club (League)	Class	W	L	ERA	G	GS	CG	SV	IP	H	R	ER	BB	SO
1997	Orioles (GCL)	R	3	0	0.82	9	3	0	1	33	15	3	3	9	43
	Bluefield (Appy)	R	2	0	2.25	4	4	0	0	24	17	6	6	5	34
1998	Delmarva (SAL)	A	1	2	2.60	6	6	1	0	35	25	11	10	13	40
1999	Delmarva (SAL)	A	10	8	3.22	28	27	4	0	170	148	75	61	36	217
2000	Frederick (Car)	A	7	6	3.05	20	20	0	0	118	119	45	40	22	121
2001	Bowie (EL)	AA	11	4	1.84	18	17	3	0	132	95	32	27	21	130
	Rochester (IL)	AAA	2	5	4.03	9	9	0	0	58	52	31	26	19	61
MINOR LEAGUE TOTALS			36	25	2.73	94	86	8	1	570	471	203	173	125	646

10. Bryan Bass, ss

Born: April 12, 1982. **Ht.:** 6-1. **Wt.:** 180. **Bats:** B. **Throws:** R. **School:** Seminole (Fla.) HS. **Career Transactions:** Selected by Orioles in first round (31st overall) of 2001 draft; signed July 13, 2001.

BILL SETLIFF

Bass moved from Alabama to Florida to get more exposure for the draft, but it didn't work out. He started out at Westminster Academy in Fort Lauderdale and transferred to Seminole (Fla.) High, but a snafu made him ineligible. He turned down a University of Alabama football scholarship to sign for $1.15 million. Scouting director Tony DeMacio remembers seeing Bass as a ninth grader while scouting his older brother Kevin for the Cubs. Even then, Bryan drew attention. He loves to play and makes big plays at the plate and in the field. His bat is his best tool, and he offers power from both sides of the plate. Despite good hands and a solid arm, Bass is a step short in terms of range and probably will end up at third base. Second base is another possibility. He comes off as arrogant to some people and is in a hurry to get to the big leagues. If he hits the way he did in his debut, he could move quickly. He should open his first full season in low Class A.

Year	Club (League)	Class	AVG	G	AB	R	H	2B	3B	HR	RBI	BB	SO	SB
2001	Orioles (GCL)	R	.297	21	74	12	22	3	6	0	7	5	25	4
	Bluefield (Appy)	R	.324	19	71	17	23	6	1	5	20	10	17	0
MINOR LEAGUE TOTALS			.310	40	145	29	45	9	7	5	27	15	42	4

11. Beau Hale, rhp

Born: Dec. 1, 1978. **Ht.:** 6-2. **Wt.:** 220. **Bats:** R. **Throws:** R. **School:** University of Texas. **Career Transactions:** Selected by Orioles in first round (14th overall) of 2000 draft; signed Aug. 18, 2000.

After leading Texas to the College World Series and going 14th overall in the draft in 2000, Hale looked great in his pro debut in 2001, making five strong starts at high Class A to earn a promotion to Double-A. He was less effective there because of a shoulder problem that kept him out for a month and reduced his velocity when he did pitch. The injury actually was in his left (non-throwing) shoulder, but it caused pain in his neck, which in turn slowed down his arm. His fastball, which is at 95-97 mph when he's healthy, was down to 89-92. Hale also throws a plus slider and added a curveball to his repertoire last season. He has developed a nice changeup and likes to throw it after coming into pro ball as a two-pitch pitcher. He's a quiet, determined workhorse with great work habits who just needs to learn more about the art of pitching. He has a tendency to leave pitches up. If he's healthy in 2002, Hale should continue a quick climb through the organization, arriving in Baltimore as soon as September. He profiles as a starter if his arm holds up and he continues to refine all of his pitches, but he also has the mentality to be a closer.

Year	Club (League)	Class	W	L	ERA	G	GS	CG	SV	IP	H	R	ER	BB	SO
2001	Frederick (Car)	A	1	2	1.32	5	5	1	0	34	30	8	5	4	30
	Bowie (EL)	AA	1	5	5.11	12	12	0	0	62	74	39	35	15	40
MINOR LEAGUE TOTALS			2	7	3.76	17	17	1	0	96	104	47	40	19	70

12. Chris Smith, lhp

Born: Dec. 10, 1979. **Ht.:** 5-11. **Wt.:** 190. **Bats:** L. **Throws:** L. **School:** Cumberland (Tenn.) University. **Career Transactions:** Selected by Orioles in first round (seventh overall) of 2001 draft; signed June 12, 2001.

Smith took a big risk after his sophomore season at Florida State in 2000. As the Seminoles' starting right fielder, he had hit .375-14-66. He also touched 93 mph in four relief appearances and asked for a spot in the rotation for 2001. Coach Mike Martin offered Smith only an opportunity to win a job, so Smith asked for his release to transfer. Martin declined, limiting Smith's options to NAIA schools. He chose Cumberland (Tenn.) and showed one of the best lefthanded arms in the college ranks, reaching 94 mph. He was projected as a mid-first-round pick, but the Orioles took him seventh overall because they liked him a lot and feared he'd be gone when they picked again at No. 19. He signed for $2.175 million just a week after the draft. He draws obvious comparisons to Mike Hampton, both for his bulldog approach and overall athleticism. He hit .414-17-67 at Cumberland and could have been drafted as an outfielder. His curveball and changeup show promise, but because he has pitched so little he will require a good deal of refinement. He could open 2002 in high Class A.

Year	Club (League)	Class	W	L	ERA	G	GS	CG	SV	IP	H	R	ER	BB	SO
2001	Orioles (GCL)	R	0	0	0.00	2	0	0	0	2	2	2	0	1	0
MINOR LEAGUE TOTALS			0	0	0.00	2	0	0	0	2	2	2	0	1	0

13. Doug Gredvig, 1b

Born: Aug. 25, 1979. **Ht.:** 6-3. **Wt.:** 225. **Bats:** R. **Throws:** R. **School:** Sacramento CC. **Career Transactions:** Selected by Orioles in fifth round of 2000 draft; signed June 9, 2000.

The Orioles were intrigued by Gredvig's power after his pro debut in 2000. Then he put up big numbers in high Class A last year, stamping himself as one of the organization's best prospects with the bat. He led the Carolina League in home runs and extra-base hits (57) and finished in the top five in runs, doubles and slugging percentage (.459). Then he spent the offseason in Baltimore going through a rigorous workout program designed to cut down on his body fat, make him faster and increase his already impressive strength. Gredvig has legitimate plus power potential and is a big, physical specimen with quick hands. He's not a hacker but can improve his control of the strike zone. He looked better than expected on defense last year and should be even better in 2002 now that he has dropped some weight. He'll move up to Double-A to start the season.

Year	Club (League)	Class	AVG	G	AB	R	H	2B	3B	HR	RBI	BB	SO	SB
2000	Orioles (GCL)	R	.444	2	9	0	4	0	0	0	1	0	1	0
	Delmarva (SAL)	A	.220	56	186	28	41	12	0	6	24	35	48	3
2001	Frederick (Car)	A	.254	129	484	71	123	35	2	20	62	37	125	2
MINOR LEAGUE TOTALS			.247	187	679	99	168	47	2	26	87	72	174	5

14. Mike Fontenot, 2b

Born: June 9, 1980. **Ht.:** 5-8. **Wt.:** 178. **Bats:** L. **Throws:** R. **School:** Louisiana State University. **Career Transactions:** Selected by Orioles in first round (19th overall) of 2001 draft; signed Sept. 5, 2001.

The Orioles went with Fontenot with the second of their first-round picks in 2001 because of his exceptional offensive potential. He was drafted by the Devil Rays in 1999 out of high school, but he turned down a six-figure bonus to attend Louisiana State. As a draft-eligible sophomore last year, he took most of the summer to negotiate a $1.3 million bonus. Fontenot might have gone higher if not for his size and injury problems with his wrist and hamstring during the 2001 college season, though he did hit .339-14-50 for the Tigers. He's healthy now and the Orioles see him as an offensive catalyst, the epitome of a baseball player, someone who knows how to play the game. He's solid in every phase of the game and is a plus runner with good defensive skills. Fontenot is as good a bet as anyone in the lower levels of the system to make it to the big leagues. He should debut in a full-season league this year, possibly as high as Double-A if he has a great spring.

Year	Club (League)	Class	AVG	G	AB	R	H	2B	3B	HR	RBI	BB	SO	SB
			Has Not Played—Signed 2002 Contract											

15. Steve Bechler, rhp

Born: Nov. 18, 1979. **Ht.:** 6-2. **Wt.:** 207. **Bats:** R. **Throws:** R. **School:** South Medford HS, Medford, Ore. **Career Transactions:** Selected by Orioles in third round of 1998 draft; signed June 5, 1998.

Bechler finally put together results to match his promise in 2001. After three decent seasons, he was sent back to high Class A to start the year and ended up in Triple-A. Coming from a cold climate, he figured to be a level-to-level player as he got the innings necessary for him to get the most out of his strong arm. Bechler throws 91-94 mph and occasionally touches higher speeds, and he has a knuckle-curve that's one of the better breaking balls in the organization. He's built like Curt Schilling with a big body, good mechanics and a clean delivery, and he should be a middle-of-the-rotation innings eater. His improved delivery has led to better command. Bechler still isn't a finished product, and he needs to work on his changeup and maintain consistency for longer stretches. He'll go back to Rochester and should get a full season there before receiving a big league opportunity in 2003.

Year	Club (League)	Class	W	L	ERA	G	GS	CG	SV	IP	H	R	ER	BB	SO
1998	Orioles (GCL)	R	2	4	2.72	9	9	0	0	50	51	22	15	8	39
1999	Delmarva (SAL)	A	8	12	3.54	26	26	1	0	152	137	69	60	58	139
2000	Frederick (Car)	A	8	12	4.83	27	27	2	0	162	179	98	87	57	137
2001	Frederick (Car)	A	5	2	2.27	13	13	1	0	83	73	24	21	22	71
	Rochester (IL)	AAA	1	1	15.95	2	2	0	0	7	14	14	13	5	6
	Bowie (EL)	AA	3	5	3.08	12	12	2	0	79	63	31	27	15	58
MINOR LEAGUE TOTALS			27	36	3.76	89	89	6	0	534	517	258	223	165	450

16. Jorge Julio, rhp

Born: March 3, 1979. **Ht.:** 6-1. **Wt.:** 190. **Bats:** R. **Throws:** R. **Career Transactions:** Signed out of Venezuela by Expos, Feb. 14, 1996 . . . Traded by Expos to Orioles for 3B Ryan Minor, Dec. 22, 2000.

Now that he has made a permanent conversion to the bullpen, Julio might be the most promising player the Orioles brought in during their housecleaning in 2000. Before trading him for failed Baltimore prospect Ryan Minor, the Expos had used Julio almost exclusively as a starter, moving him to the bullpen only after he failed in his second shot in the high Class A Florida State League. The Orioles made him a closer, and after not getting out of Class A in five years in the Montreal system, he made it all the way to the big leagues in 2001. Julio's power fastball reaches 97-98 mph and is well suited to a bullpen role. He also throws a hard slider as well that improved last season. He was much more effective when he didn't have to mess with his changeup. Julio's command also improved, though it still needs work. Julio should compete for a big league bullpen spot this spring.

Year	Club (League)	Class	W	L	ERA	G	GS	CG	SV	IP	H	R	ER	BB	SO
1996	Expos (DSL)	R	1	1	6.06	10	0	0	0	16	13	12	11	11	21
1997	Expos (GCL)	R	5	6	3.58	15	8	0	1	55	57	25	22	21	42
	W. Palm Beach (FSL)	A	0	0	0.00	1	0	0	0	0	2	1	1	0	0
1998	Vermont (NY-P)	A	3	1	2.57	7	7	0	0	42	30	12	12	15	52
	Cape Fear (SAL)	A	2	2	5.68	6	6	0	0	32	33	20	20	12	20
1999	Jupiter (FSL)	A	4	8	3.92	23	22	0	0	115	116	62	50	34	80
2000	Jupiter (FSL)	A	2	10	5.90	21	15	0	1	79	93	60	52	35	67
2001	Bowie (EL)	AA	0	0	0.73	12	0	0	7	12	5	1	1	2	14
	Baltimore (AL)	MAJ	1	1	3.80	18	0	0	0	21	25	13	9	9	22
	Rochester (IL)	AAA	1	2	3.74	34	0	0	12	43	39	27	18	19	48
MAJOR LEAGUE TOTALS			1	1	3.80	18	0	0	0	21	25	13	9	9	22
MINOR LEAGUE TOTALS			18	30	4.26	129	58	0	21	395	388	220	187	149	344

17. Rick Bauer, rhp

Born: Jan. 10, 1977. **Ht.:** 6-6. **Wt.:** 212. **Bats:** R. **Throws:** R. **School:** Treasure Valley (Ore.) CC. **Career Transactions:** Selected by Orioles in fifth round of 1997 draft; signed June 5, 1997.

After a strong professional debut in 1997, Bauer basically squandered his next three seasons and couldn't get past Double-A. He opened 2000 in the Bowie rotation before being sent to the bullpen and eventually down to high Class A. He bounced back with the best year of his career in 2001, making it all the way to Baltimore, and answered organizational questions about his work ethic. He held his own in six major league starts and will be expected to contribute in Baltimore in 2002. Bauer's stuff is good but not exceptional. He has a 91-92 mph fastball with good downward movement, and he made significant progress with his slider last year. His command has improved, but now he has to move the ball in the strike zone better and not leave his pitches up. He profiles as an end-of-the-rotation starter or long reliever, and will compete for those jobs in big league camp.

Year	Club (League)	Class	W	L	ERA	G	GS	CG	SV	IP	H	R	ER	BB	SO
1997	Bluefield (Appy)	R	8	3	2.86	13	13	0	0	72	58	31	23	20	67
	Delmarva (SAL)	A	0	0	0.00	1	0	0	1	2	0	0	0	1	2
1998	Delmarva (SAL)	A	5	8	4.73	22	22	1	0	118	127	69	62	44	81
1999	Frederick (Car)	A	10	9	4.56	26	26	4	0	152	159	85	77	54	123
2000	Bowie (EL)	AA	6	8	5.30	26	23	1	1	129	154	89	76	39	87
	Frederick (Car)	A	0	1	5.21	3	3	0	0	19	20	13	11	6	15
2001	Bowie (EL)	AA	2	6	3.54	9	9	2	0	61	52	27	24	10	34
	Rochester (IL)	AAA	10	4	3.89	19	18	1	0	113	119	63	49	28	89
	Baltimore (AL)	MAJ	0	5	4.64	6	6	0	0	33	35	22	17	9	16
MAJOR LEAGUE TOTALS			0	5	4.64	6	6	0	0	33	35	22	17	9	16
MINOR LEAGUE TOTALS			41	39	4.35	119	114	9	2	667	689	377	322	202	498

18. Kurt Birkins, lhp

Born: Aug. 11, 1980. **Ht.:** 6-2. **Wt.:** 175. **Bats:** L. **Throws:** L. **School:** Los Angeles Pierce JC. **Career Transactions:** Selected by Orioles in 33rd round of 2000 draft; signed May 25, 2001.

Birkins left UCLA after his freshman season and took a year off, coaching at his former high school in suburban Los Angeles and working out. He intended to return to UCLA but the Orioles drafted him in the 33rd round in 2000, so he went to Pierce JC instead. Birkins had an impressive fall and became one of the top juco prospects in the nation. His velocity slipped in the spring, but he still would have been a premium pick if Baltimore hadn't signed him for $400,000. He held hitters to a combined .192 average in his pro debut. Birkins showed a fringe average fastball and reached the low 90s last year, though the Orioles think he could add velocity. His curveball and command are both assets. Birkins' build and stuff remind Baltimore of Erik Bedard. The will send him to low Class A to start 2002.

Year	Club (League)	Class	W	L	ERA	G	GS	CG	SV	IP	H	R	ER	BB	SO
2001	Orioles (GCL)	R	2	1	2.05	5	4	0	0	22	13	5	5	3	24
	Bluefield (Appy)	R	4	1	2.92	6	6	0	0	37	28	14	12	5	42
MINOR LEAGUE TOTALS			6	2	2.59	11	10	0	0	59	41	19	17	8	66

19. Luis Rivera, rhp

Born: July 21, 1978. **Ht.:** 6-3. **Wt.:** 163. **Bats:** R. **Throws:** R. **Career Transactions:** Signed out of Mexico by Braves, Feb. 18, 1995 . . . Loaned by Braves to Mexico City Tigers (Mexican), May 4-Oct. 18, 1995 . . . Traded by Braves with OF Trenidad Hubbard and C Fernando Lunar to Orioles for OF B.J. Surhoff and RHP Gabe Molina, July 31, 2000.

When the Orioles got their rebuilding effort into full gear midway through the 2000 season, just about every prospect they brought in when they traded veterans came with significant question marks. With Rivera, whose live arm is unmistakable, the troublesome issue is his health. Doubts loom larger than ever after he missed the 2001 season with his most serious arm trouble to date. Blisters bothered him throughout his years with the Braves, and he was shut down after nine innings following the trade because of a tired arm. He worked in the mid-90s in the winter Mexican Pacific League after the 2000 season, but he wasn't able to throw with his usual fluid delivery in spring training, when an MRI revealed a torn labrum in his shoulder. If healthy, Rivera has one of the better fastballs in the minors, with plus velocity and good movement. Baltimore had positive reports on him from Mexico this winter, though he saw little game action. He has a hard breaking ball and an aggressive approach suited for a bullpen job. That's probably where he'll end up anyway, as he never has pitched more than 100 innings despite being a starter throughout his career. The Orioles just would like to see him pitch, as many in the organization still haven't seen him firsthand.

Year	Club (League)	Class	W	L	ERA	G	GS	CG	SV	IP	H	R	ER	BB	SO
1996	Braves (GCL)	R	1	1	2.59	8	6	0	0	24	18	9	7	7	26
1997	Danville (Appy)	R	3	1	2.41	9	9	0	0	41	28	15	11	17	57
	Macon (SAL)	A	2	0	1.29	4	4	0	0	21	13	4	3	7	27
1998	Macon (SAL)	A	5	5	3.98	20	20	0	0	93	78	53	41	41	118
1999	Myrtle Beach (Cal)	A	0	2	3.11	25	13	0	0	67	45	25	23	23	81
2000	Atlanta (NL)	MAJ	1	0	1.35	5	0	0	0	7	4	1	1	5	5
	Richmond (IL)	AAA	0	2	8.06	8	7	0	0	22	29	20	20	18	12
	Braves (GCL)	R	0	0	0.00	3	3	0	0	4	2	0	0	1	2
	Rochester (IL)	AAA	0	1	3.38	3	3	0	0	8	11	5	3	5	4
	Baltimore (AL)	AAA	0	0	0.00	1	0	0	0	1	1	0	0	1	0
2001						Did Not Play—Injured										
MAJOR LEAGUE TOTALS			1	0	1.23	6	0	0	0	7	5	1	1	6	5
MINOR LEAGUE TOTALS			11	12	3.47	80	65	0	0	280	224	131	108	119	327

20. John Bale, lhp

Born: May 22, 1974. **Ht.:** 6-4. **Wt.:** 205. **Bats:** L. **Throws:** L. **School:** University of Southern Mississippi. **Career Transactions:** Selected by Blue Jays in fifth round of 1996 draft; signed June 17, 1996 . . . Traded by Blue Jays to Orioles for C Jayson Werth, Dec. 11, 2000.

After coming over from the Blue Jays in a trade for Jayson Werth following the 2000 season, Bale played winter ball in Venezuela, where he and a teammate were held up on New Year's Eve. A man pointed a sawed-off shotgun at Bale's head but ran off when a car came around the corner. Even with the scare, Bale posted a 1.21 ERA in 22 innings of relief for Lara and had a good spring to win a spot in the Baltimore bullpen. He was sent down after three weeks, then battled elbow tendinitis, a strained forearm and a strained oblique muscle the rest of the season. Bale was impressive when he did pitch, mixing a fastball that sits in the low 90s and touches 94 with a changeup and a plus curveball. When healthy, he has good command and can pile up big strikeout numbers. He performed well in a September callup and should make the Baltimore staff in 2002 as at least a swingman.

Year	Club (League)	Class	W	L	ERA	G	GS	CG	SV	IP	H	R	ER	BB	SO
1996	St. Catharines (NY-P)	A	3	2	4.86	8	8	0	0	33	39	21	18	11	35
1997	Hagerstown (SAL)	A	7	7	4.30	25	25	0	0	140	130	83	67	63	155
1998	Dunedin (FSL)	A	4	5	4.64	24	9	0	4	66	68	39	34	23	78
	Knoxville (SL)	AA	0	0	6.75	3	0	0	0	1	1	1	1	0	0
1999	Knoxville (SL)	AA	2	2	3.75	33	4	0	1	62	64	32	26	16	91
	Syracuse (IL)	AAA	0	3	3.97	6	4	0	0	23	16	14	10	10	10
	Toronto (AL)	MAJ	0	0	13.50	1	0	0	0	2	2	3	3	2	4
2000	Syracuse (IL)	AAA	3	4	3.19	21	12	0	0	79	68	35	28	41	70
	Toronto (AL)	MAJ	0	0	14.73	2	0	0	0	4	5	7	6	3	6
2001	Rochester (IL)	AAA	1	1	2.05	9	7	0	0	31	31	8	7	5	41
	Baltimore (AL)	MAJ	1	0	3.04	14	0	0	0	27	18	14	9	17	21
	Orioles (GCL)	R	0	0	2.25	2	2	0	0	4	1	1	1	2	7
MAJOR LEAGUE TOTALS			1	0	5.01	17	0	0	0	32	25	24	18	22	31
MINOR LEAGUE TOTALS			20	24	3.93	131	71	0	5	440	418	234	192	171	487

21. Eli Whiteside, c

Born: Oct. 22, 1979. **Ht.:** 6-2. **Wt.:** 215. **Bats:** R. **Throws:** R. **School:** Delta State (Miss.) University. **Career Transactions:** Selected by Orioles in sixth round of 2001 draft; signed June 7, 2001.

Whiteside was one of the better backstop prospects in the 2001 draft after hitting .401-8-75 and throwing out 37 percent of basestealers during a Division II All-America season. He helped Delta State (Miss.) reach the semifinals of the Division II World Series. The Orioles sent Whiteside straight to low Class A, where he more than held his own. He was everything he was advertised to be on defense, with great catch-and-throw skills, a good catcher's body and a strong arm. He threw out 41 percent of basestealers at Delmarva, one of the best figures in the South Atlantic League. He also handled pitchers better than expected. He has promising power and good bat speed but will have to improve at the plate, especially with his grasp of the strike zone. He could skip a level and proceed to Double-A with a good spring.

Year	Club (League)	Class	AVG	G	AB	R	H	2B	3B	HR	RBI	BB	SO	SB
2001	Delmarva (SAL)	A	.250	61	212	30	53	11	0	7	28	9	45	1
MINOR LEAGUE TOTALS			.250	61	212	30	53	11	0	7	28	9	45	1

22. Napoleon Calzado, 3b

Born: Feb. 9, 1980. **Ht.:** 6-3. **Wt.:** 160. **Bats:** R. **Throws:** R. **Career Transactions:** Signed out of Dominican Republic by Orioles, Sept. 11, 1996.

Calzado followed up a South Atlantic League all-star season in 2000 with another in the Carolina League last year, as he led Frederick in hitting and stolen bases. He topped his year by playing for the Dominican Republic in the World Cup tournament in November in Taiwan, where he batted .306. Calzado is quite versatile. While the Orioles see him as a third baseman, he was the Carolina League's all-star shortstop and made the SAL team as a utilityman. He's a skinny guy but should add power as he fills out. The Orioles have him working out to try to add strength. He's a proven .280 hitter who doesn't strike out much, so if he adds some pop he could move up this list quite a bit. He combines good speed and savvy on the basepaths. Calzado could stand to be more selective at the plate, and he sometimes gets too emotional on the field. But he bears watching, especially if he matures mentally and physically.

Year	Club (League)	Class	AVG	G	AB	R	H	2B	3B	HR	RBI	BB	SO	SB
1997	Orioles (DSL)	R	.321	64	234	41	75	7	3	0	26	23	36	18
1998	Orioles (DSL)	R	.250	25	88	15	22	3	2	0	10	10	9	12

	Club (League)	Class	AVG	G	AB	R	H	2B	3B	HR	RBI	BB	SO	SB
	Orioles (GCL)	R	.230	31	113	15	26	6	4	1	18	10	17	1
1999	Bluefield (Appy)	R	.291	52	199	46	58	11	2	6	31	20	32	9
	Delmarva (SAL)	A	.278	6	18	2	5	1	0	0	1	0	4	0
2000	Delmarva (SAL)	A	.278	131	503	81	140	20	6	7	83	31	68	29
2001	Frederick (Car)	A	.287	121	464	50	133	20	2	5	41	16	52	34
MINOR LEAGUE TOTALS			.284	430	1619	250	459	68	19	19	210	110	218	103

23. Mike Paradis, rhp

Born: May 3, 1978. **Ht.:** 6-3. **Wt.:** 190. **Bats:** R. **Throws:** R. **School:** Clemson University. **Career Transactions:** Selected by Orioles in first round (13th overall) of 1999 draft; signed June 22, 1999.

Paradis put together a second straight healthy season in 2001, but he still hasn't made the kind of progress the Orioles were looking for when they made him the 13th overall pick two years earlier. His pro debut was ruined by a hyperextended elbow, and he didn't get his good stuff back until last season. When he's right, he has two plus pitches: a 92-93 mph fastball with great movement, and an 86-88 mph slider. Paradis just needs more confidence in his pitches. He's the classic case of a pitcher who just doesn't trust his stuff enough. He also must work on his changeup and command, and those improvements also are more mental than physical. Paradis will try to take the next step to Triple-A in 2002, where Baltimore hopes he'll finally put up dominating numbers.

Year	Club (League)	Class	W	L	ERA	G	GS	CG	SV	IP	H	R	ER	BB	SO
1999	Delmarva (SAL)	A	0	1	15.00	2	2	0	0	3	3	5	5	4	6
2000	Delmarva (SAL)	A	6	5	3.99	18	18	0	0	97	95	53	43	49	81
	Frederick (Car)	A	2	5	4.17	8	8	1	0	45	55	24	21	24	32
2001	Bowie (EL)	AA	8	13	4.71	27	26	1	0	138	157	98	72	62	108
MINOR LEAGUE TOTALS			16	24	4.48	55	54	2	0	283	310	180	141	139	227

24. Kris Foster, rhp

Born: Aug. 30, 1974. **Ht.:** 6-1. **Wt.:** 200. **Bats:** R. **Throws:** R. **School:** Edison (Fla.) CC. **Career Transactions:** Selected by Expos in 39th round of 1992 draft; signed May 26, 1993 . . . Traded by Expos to Dodgers for SS Rafael Bournigal, June 10, 1995 . . . Granted free agency, Oct. 15, 1999; re-signed by Dodgers, Oct. 22, 1999 . . . Traded by Dodgers with C Geronimo Gil to Orioles for RHP Mike Trombley, July 31, 2001.

Foster persevered through injuries to finally reach the big leagues last year after Baltimore obtained him from Los Angeles in a deadline deal for Mike Trombley. Foster hadn't even made it above Double-A until 2001, his ninth pro season, but his blazing fastball kept the Dodgers from giving up on him. He has endured every manner of arm trouble, including surgery in 2000 to remove a ligament in his right shoulder that was cutting into the muscle. He pulled a stomach muscle last season but should be fully healthy for 2002. Foster's calling card is his fastball, which sits in the high 90s and reportedly has been clocked in triple digits. He also throws a slider and has worked with a curveball, but he rarely uses the latter pitch because it has been blamed for some of his arm problems. Foster has simplified his delivery in the last couple of years, which should help resolve his long-term health issues as well as improve his command. If his power arm is 100 percent, he should make the Baltimore bullpen this year.

Year	Club (League)	Class	W	L	ERA	G	GS	CG	SV	IP	H	R	ER	BB	SO
1993	Expos (GCL)	R	1	6	3.43	17	3	0	1	45	44	26	17	16	30
1994	Expos (GCL)	R	4	2	1.55	18	5	0	4	52	34	21	9	32	65
1995	Yakima (NWL)	A	2	3	2.89	15	10	0	3	56	38	27	18	38	55
1996	San Bernardino (Cal)	A	3	5	3.86	30	8	0	2	82	66	46	35	54	78
1997	Vero Beach (FSL)	A	6	3	5.32	17	17	2	0	90	97	69	53	44	77
1998	Vero Beach (FSL)	A	3	5	6.79	24	6	0	1	53	59	45	40	27	52
1999	Vero Beach (FSL)	A	1	1	1.76	8	0	0	0	15	10	5	3	2	15
	San Antonio (TL)	AA	0	2	3.59	33	0	0	4	53	43	24	21	26	53
2000	San Bernardino (Cal)	A	0	0	0.77	10	1	0	2	12	7	2	1	1	19
2001	Jacksonville (SL)	AA	3	0	1.00	17	0	0	7	18	6	2	2	2	29
	Las Vegas (PCL)	AAA	0	1	3.86	21	0	0	12	21	25	13	9	4	17
	Baltimore (AL)	MAJ	0	0	2.70	7	0	0	0	10	9	4	3	8	8
	Rochester (IL)	AAA	0	1	5.40	9	0	0	6	10	11	8	6	6	11
MAJOR LEAGUE TOTALS			0	0	2.70	7	0	0	0	10	9	4	3	8	8
MINOR LEAGUE TOTALS			23	29	3.81	219	50	2	42	506	440	288	214	252	501

25. Sendy Rleal, rhp

Born: June 21, 1980. **Ht.:** 6-1. **Wt.:** 165. **Bats:** R. **Throws:** R. **Career Transactions:** Signed out of Dominican Republic by Orioles, June 30, 1999.

Rleal, who played mostly shortstop before he signed with the Orioles, has made steady progress while building arm strength and learning the nuances of pitching. Set to play his first full season in 2001, he was shut down in July with a strained elbow. Rleal has three solid pitches, with a fastball that sits at 92-93 mph and should get better as he matures. He maintains his velocity well. He also throws a slider and changeup that are good pitches when they're on but are still inconsistent. Rleal has moved on a slow patch because of his late conversion to pitching, so the Orioles would like for him to pick up the pace this season if his arm is sound. He'll open the season in high Class A.

Year	Club (League)	Class	W	L	ERA	G	GS	CG	SV	IP	H	R	ER	BB	SO
1999	Orioles (DSL)	R	4	3	3.47	9	9	0	0	47	43	24	18	20	43
2000	Bluefield (Appy)	R	6	2	3.39	13	12	0	0	61	61	26	23	25	55
	Delmarva (SAL)	A	0	1	10.80	1	1	0	0	3	3	5	4	3	4
2001	Delmarva (SAL)	A	3	6	3.57	20	20	1	0	103	79	50	41	27	83
MINOR LEAGUE TOTALS			13	12	3.61	43	42	1	0	214	186	105	86	75	185

26. Cory Morris, rhp

Born: June 2, 1979. **Ht.:** 6-2. **Wt.:** 185. **Bats:** R. **Throws:** R. **School:** Dallas Baptist University. **Career Transactions:** Selected by Orioles in 15th round of 2001 draft; signed June 7, 2001.

Morris was one of the biggest surprises to emerge from Baltimore's 2001 draft class, signing for $2,500 and holding his own after an emergency promotion to high Class A. He pitched well enough there to earn a spot in the rotation and stick there for the remainder of the summer. He also was impressive in instructional league. Thanks to his 92-95 mph fastball—which picked up velocity from the spring, when he helped lead Dallas Baptist to the NAIA World Series—and good curveball, he had only one bad start at Frederick and posted impressive strikeout numbers. His changeup also is a potentially above-average pitch. As he showed when he got thrown into the deep end in high Class A, Morris is a competitor with good mound presence and an understanding of how to pitch. He still needs to sharpen his command and get more consistent with his complementary pitches. But the Orioles see no reason not to send him to Frederick to start 2002.

Year	Club (League)	Class	W	L	ERA	G	GS	CG	SV	IP	H	R	ER	BB	SO
2001	Bluefield (Appy)	R	1	0	0.00	1	0	0	0	3	1	0	0	2	4
	Frederick (Car)	A	3	5	3.38	13	12	0	0	69	50	30	26	24	81
MINOR LEAGUE TOTALS			4	5	3.24	14	12	0	0	72	51	30	26	26	85

27. Octavio Martinez, c

Born: July 30, 1979. **Ht.:** 6-0. **Wt.:** 195. **Bats:** R. **Throws:** R. **School:** Bakersfield (Calif.) JC. **Career Transactions:** Selected by Orioles in 10th round of 1999 draft; signed June 4, 1999.

Martinez was regarded as a solid defensive catcher coming out of junior college, but the Orioles viewed him as something more after he was named Appalachian League MVP in 2000. His performance was so impressive that the organization considered him its top catching prospect and decided 1997 first-round pick Jayson Werth was expendable. Traded to the Blue Jays for lefthander John Bale, Werth responded with a strong 2001. Martinez, on the other hand, had a disastrous season that raises questions about whether 2000 was a fluke. In his defense, he did have a shoulder injury that bothered him much of the season. Martinez also lost control of the strike zone, raising doubts about his ability to bounce back against quality pitching. His defensive skills remain above-average. He has soft hands and a quick release, and he led the Carolina League last year by erasing 50 percent of basestealers. Martinez has a good mental approach and knows how to take charge of a game. He's a hard worker who will do everything he can to improve. He likely will return to high Class A this year.

Year	Club (League)	Class	AVG	G	AB	R	H	2B	3B	HR	RBI	BB	SO	SB
1999	Orioles (GCL)	R	.237	36	114	11	27	8	1	0	15	4	11	8
2000	Bluefield (Appy)	R	.387	49	181	45	70	14	1	7	46	19	21	0
	Frederick (Car)	A	.375	2	8	0	3	0	0	0	1	0	0	0
2001	Frederick (Car)	A	.217	98	336	23	73	14	0	1	29	10	47	3
MINOR LEAGUE TOTALS			.271	185	639	79	173	36	2	8	91	33	79	11

28. Leslie Brea, rhp

Born: Oct. 12, 1978. **Ht.:** 5-11. **Wt.:** 170. **Bats:** R. **Throws:** R. **Career Transactions:** Signed out of Dominican Republic by Mariners, Jan. 20, 1996 . . . Traded by Mariners to Mets for OF Butch Huskey, Dec. 14, 1998 . . . Traded by Mets with RHP Pat Gorman, SS Melvin Mora and 3B Mike Kinkade to Orioles for SS Mike Bordick, July 28, 2000.

While Brea's birthdate still is officially listed as 1978, most people outside the organization acknowledge that he's at least a few years older than that. Brea himself admitted to being born in 1973 after he joined the Orioles in 2000. Now used solely in relief, Brea got off to a bad start in Triple-A last season before righting himself and earning a September callup to Baltimore. He still has a mid-90s fastball and a hard slider, two pitches that can be overpowering. His efforts to develop a third pitch, which he never picked up, have ended with his move to the bullpen. The Orioles just want him to concentrate on throwing his fastball and slider for strikes consistently. After an encouraging winter performance in his native Dominican Republic, Brea will compete for a big league bullpen job.

Year	Club (League)	Class	W	L	ERA	G	GS	CG	SV	IP	H	R	ER	BB	SO
1996	Mariners (AZL)	R	1	0	5.06	7	0	0	0	11	7	10	6	6	12
1997	Lancaster (Cal)	A	0	0	13.50	1	0	0	0	2	5	5	3	1	1
	Everett (NWL)	A	2	4	7.99	23	0	0	3	33	34	29	29	29	49
1998	Wisconsin (Mid)	A	3	4	2.76	49	0	0	12	59	47	26	18	40	86
1999	St. Lucie (FSL)	A	1	7	3.73	32	18	0	3	121	95	64	50	68	136
2000	Binghamton (EL)	AA	5	8	4.24	19	18	0	0	93	85	53	44	61	86
	Norfolk (IL)	AAA	0	0	0.00	1	1	0	0	5	4	2	0	4	4
	Bowie (EL)	AA	1	1	4.26	2	2	0	0	13	12	6	6	9	3
	Baltimore (AL)	MAJ	0	1	11.00	6	1	0	0	9	12	11	11	10	5
	Rochester (IL)	AAA	1	2	6.05	4	4	0	0	19	27	18	13	8	13
2001	Rochester (IL)	AAA	2	6	3.83	63	0	0	1	82	80	44	35	35	98
	Baltimore (AL)	MAJ	0	0	18.00	2	0	0	0	2	6	4	4	3	0
MAJOR LEAGUE TOTALS			0	1	12.27	8	1	0	0	11	18	15	15	13	5
MINOR LEAGUE TOTALS			16	32	4.20	201	43	0	19	437	396	257	204	261	488

29. Tripper Johnson, 3b

Born: April 28, 1982. **Ht.:** 6-1. **Wt.:** 195. **Bats:** R. **Throws:** R. **School:** Newport HS, Bellevue, Wash.
Career Transactions: Selected by Orioles in first round (32nd overall) of 2000 draft; signed June 26, 2000.

The Orioles were high on Johnson after he showed athleticism and power potential in his pro debut. He was a three-sport star in high school and viewed as a prototypical third base-man, so the organization expected him to get on the fast track. It didn't work out that way as Johnson didn't even make his full-season debut last year. He got off to a terrible start with the bat at Bluefield before missing three weeks with a shoulder injury. Limited to DH when he returned, Johnson did salvage something with a strong finish. He should be healthy for 2002. He's a gamer who should develop above-average power. Both his strike-zone judgment and his glove need work, and he didn't get to address the latter while he was hurt. If he can bounce back this season, the Orioles will write off 2001 as a lost season due to injury.

Year	Club (League)	Class	AVG	G	AB	R	H	2B	3B	HR	RBI	BB	SO	SB
2000	Orioles (GCL)	R	.306	48	180	22	55	5	3	2	33	13	38	7
2001	Bluefield (Appy)	R	.261	43	157	24	41	6	1	2	26	11	37	4
MINOR LEAGUE TOTALS			.285	91	337	46	96	11	4	4	59	24	75	11

30. Eddy Garabito, 2b/ss

Born: Dec. 2, 1978. **Ht.:** 5-8. **Wt.:** 172. **Bats:** B. **Throws:** R. **Career Transactions:** Signed out of Dominican Republic by Orioles, March 30, 1996.

There's determination and then there's Garabito. As a child he left the Dominican Republic as a stowaway on a freight ship so he could live with his father in Puerto Rico and get more exposure. Baltimore scouts liked him and wanted to sign him, but had to make arrangements to get him back to the Dominican first. He has made steady progress but was left off the 40-man roster this offseason. Though he played well this winter in the Dominican, he escaped the major league Rule 5 draft. Garabito is undersized and doesn't have much in the way of tools, with the exception of his speed and glove. But he's heady and versatile. He's a switch-hitter who knows how to make contact. He played second base last year in Triple-A and short-stop in the Dominican, and the Orioles say he could probably play anywhere on the field. That makes him a strong candidate to be a big league utilityman in 2002.

Year	Club (League)	Class	AVG	G	AB	R	H	2B	3B	HR	RBI	BB	SO	SB
1996	Orioles (DSL)	R	.275	67	251	40	69	9	6	1	28	20	23	25
1997	Delmarva (SAL)	A	.000	2	4	0	0	0	0	0	0	0	0	0
	Bluefield (Appy)	R	.303	61	231	47	70	12	3	5	44	21	30	26
1998	Delmarva (SAL)	A	.247	135	481	81	119	20	8	9	66	44	93	25
	Frederick (Car)	A	.211	4	19	4	4	1	1	0	2	1	5	0
1999	Frederick (Car)	A	.256	132	539	76	138	24	4	6	77	52	68	38
2000	Bowie (EL)	AA	.251	116	482	72	121	21	3	6	52	27	55	22
	Rochester (IL)	AAA	.086	9	35	3	3	1	0	0	0	2	10	1
2001	Rochester (IL)	AAA	.267	127	517	65	138	29	6	3	34	31	76	24
MINOR LEAGUE TOTALS			.259	653	2559	388	662	117	31	30	303	198	360	161

BOSTON
Red Sox

TOP 30 PROSPECTS

1. Seung Song, rhp
2. Tony Blanco, 3b
3. Rene Miniel, rhp
4. Manny Delcarmen, rhp
5. Casey Fossum, lhp
6. Freddy Sanchez, ss
7. Phil Dumatrait, lhp
8. Josh Thigpen, rhp
9. Anastacio Martinez, rhp
10. Franklin Francisco, rhp
11. Mat Thompson, rhp
12. Juan Diaz, 1b/dh
13. Brad Baker, rhp
14. Mauricio Lara, lhp
15. Kevin Huang, rhp
16. Steve Lomasney, c
17. Luis Perez, lhp
18. Jorge de la Rosa, lhp
19. Dernell Stenson, of/1b
20. Kelly Shoppach, c
21. Juan Pena, rhp
22. Sun-Woo Kim, rhp
23. Ryo Kumagai, rhp
24. Greg Montalbano, lhp
25. Rolando Viera, lhp
26. Byeong An, lhp
27. Josh Hancock, rhp
28. Angel Santos, 2b
29. Kevin Youkilis, 3b
30. Jerome Gamble, rhp

By Jim Callis

For the first time since 1933, the Yawkey name won't be connected with ownership of the Red Sox. A group led by former Marlins owner John Henry and former Padres owner Tom Werner bought the club, as well as Fenway Park and 80 percent of the New England Sports Network, from the Yawkey Trust for $700 million on Dec. 21, 2001. Former Orioles and Padres president Larry Lucchino will assume the same role in Boston.

At an introductory press conference, Lucchino outlined his plan for the Red Sox: "We will invest both money and time in player development and scouting. Bringing in your own talent is the key to the long-term success of the franchise."

Lucchino also promised changes in the front office, though he declined to specifically address general manager Dan Duquette. After putting together a nine-figure payroll that didn't come close to making the playoffs, Duquette bounced back in the offseason, purging Carl Everett while adding John Burkett, Tony Clark, Johnny Damon and Dustin Hermanson.

When he arrived in Boston in 1994, Duquette also pledged to build through the farm system. Since drafting Nomar Garciaparra that year, the Red Sox have had little success growing their own players. The only other starter on the 2001 team signed and developed on Duquette's watch was Shea Hillenbrand.

Boston has concentrated heavily on the international market, with little to show for it so far. Righthander Seung Song is their top prospect, but the Red Sox also spent heavily on players such as Robinson Checo and Sang Lee, who fell far short of their fanfare. Such players have taken money out of the domestic budget, contributing to a string of failed first-round picks and unsigned draftees.

The result is a farm system that ranks among baseball's worst and is bereft of position players, the best of whom (Luis Garcia) was included in the December trade for Hermanson. Most of Boston's best prospects are pitchers who haven't played above low Class A, a demographic with a high rate of attrition.

Just three members of the top 15 have played in the upper minors: lefthander Casey Fossum and shortstop Freddy Sanchez, whose ceilings may be limited, and first baseman Juan Diaz, who spent 2001 in woeful shape.

Organization Overview

General manager: Dan Duquette. Farm director: Dave Jauss. Scouting director: Wayne Britton.

2001 PERFORMANCE

Class	Team	League	W	L	Pct.	Finish*	Manager(s)
Majors	Boston	American	82	79	.509	7th (14)	J. Williams/J. Kerrigan
Triple-A	Pawtucket Red Sox	International	60	82	.423	13th(14)	Gary Jones
Double-A	Trenton Thunder	Eastern	67	75	.472	8th (12)	Billy Gardner
High A	Sarasota Red Sox	Florida State	54	83	.394	14th(14)	Ron Johnson
Low A	Augusta GreenJackets	South Atlantic	74	65	.532	7th (16)	Mike Boulanger
Short-season	Lowell Spinners	New York-Penn	33	43	.434	10th (14)	Arnie Beyeler
Rookie	GCL Red Sox	Gulf Coast	37	22	.627	2nd (14)	John Sanders
OVERALL 2001 MINOR LEAGUE RECORD			325	370	.468	25th (30)	

*Finish in overall standings (No. of teams in league)

ORGANIZATION LEADERS

BATTING
*AVG	Freddy Sanchez, Trenton/Sarasota	.334
R	**Israel Alcantara**, Pawtucket	80
	Rontrez Johnson, Pawtucket/Trenton	80
H	Freddy Sanchez, Trenton/Sarasota	153
TB	**Israel Alcantara**, Pawtucket	270
2B	Freddy Sanchez, Trenton/Sarasota	39
3B	Three tied at	6
HR	**Israel Alcantara**, Pawtucket	36
RBI	**Israel Alcantara**, Pawtucket	90
BB	Kevin Youkilis, Augusta/Lowell	73
SO	Mark Fischer, Trenton	148
SB	Antron Seiber, Augusta	36

PITCHING
W	**Greg Montalbano**, Trenton/Sarasota	12
L	Anastacio Martinez, Sarasota	12
	Derrin Ebert, Pawtucket/Trenton	12
#ERA	Seung Song, Sarasota/Augusta	1.90
G	Corey Spencer, Trenton	55
CG	Carlos Castillo, Pawtucket	5
SVR	Rodney Dickinson, Sarasota/Augusta	22
IP	Carlos Castillo, Pawtucket	164
BB	Brad Baker, Sarasota	64
SO	Seung Song, Sarasota/Augusta	135

*Minimum 250 At-Bats #Minimum 75 Innings

TOP PROSPECTS OF THE DECADE

1992	Frank Rodriguez, rhp/ss
1993	Frank Rodriguez, rhp
1994	Trot Nixon, of
1995	Nomar Garciaparra, ss
1996	Donnie Sadler, ss
1997	Nomar Garciaparra, ss
1998	Brian Rose, rhp
1999	Dernell Stenson, of
2000	Steve Lomasney, c
2001	Dernell Stenson, 1b/of

TOP DRAFT PICKS OF THE DECADE

1992	Tony Sheffield, of (2)
1993	Trot Nixon, of
1994	Nomar Garciaparra, ss
1995	Andy Yount, rhp
1996	Josh Garrett, rhp
1997	John Curtice, lhp
1998	Adam Everett, ss
1999	Rick Asadoorian, of
2000	Phil Dumatrait, lhp
2001	Kelly Shoppach, c (2)

KEN BABBITT

Alcantara   **Montalbano**

BEST TOOLS

Best Hitter for Average	Freddy Sanchez
Best Power Hitter	Juan Diaz
Fastest Baserunner	Antron Seiber
Best Fastball	Manny Delcarmen
Best Breaking Ball	Casey Fossum
Best Changeup	Mat Thompson
Best Control	Seung Song
Best Defensive Catcher	Kelly Shoppach
Best Defensive Infielder	Kenny Perez
Best Infield Arm	Tony Blanco
Best Defensive Outfielder	Antron Seiber
Best Outfield Arm	Antron Seiber

PROJECTED 2005 LINEUP

Catcher	Jason Varitek
First Base	Tony Clark
Second Base	Freddy Sanchez
Third Base	Tony Blanco
Shortstop	Nomar Garciaparra
Left Field	Manny Ramirez
Center Field	Johnny Damon
Right Field	Trot Nixon
Designated Hitter	Juan Diaz
No. 1 Starter	Pedro Martinez
No. 2 Starter	Seung Song
No. 3 Starter	Rene Miniel
No. 4 Starter	Manny Delcarmen
No. 5 Starter	Dustin Hermanson
Closer	Ugueth Urbina

ALL-TIME LARGEST BONUSES

Adam Everett, 1998	$1,725,000
Rick Asadoorian, 1999	$1,725,000
Phil Dumatrait, 2000	$1,275,000
Robinson Checo, 1996	$1,150,000
Sang-Hoon Lee, 1999	$1,050,000

DraftAnalysis

2001 Draft

Best Pro Debut: 3B Kevin Youkilis (8) hit .317-3-28 and led the short-season New York-Penn League with 52 runs and a .512 on-base percentage.

Best Athlete: SS Eric West (5) has solid tools across the board. He has the hands, arm and range to stick at shortstop, as well as hitting ability and speed.

Best Hitter: Youkilis wasn't drafted as a junior in 2000, but starred in the Cape Cod League that summer and continued to shine as a senior. His 31-73 strikeout-walk ratio in his pro debut is a testament to his eye.

Best Raw Power: 1B Stefan Bailie (4) and OF Ryan Brunner (12) combined for just three homers last summer, but power will be their ticket. Brunner won the home run derby before the College World Series last year. C Jonathan DeVries (3) also should develop pop, though he went homerless in the Rookie-level Gulf Coast League.

Fastest Runner: OF Kris Coffey (25) is a 7 runner on the 2-to-8 scouting scale. West isn't as fast but has better instincts.

Best Defensive Player: C **Kelly Shoppach** (2) can deliver the ball to second base in 1.8-1.9 seconds. The 2001 Big 12 Conference player of the year, he was the best of a lean crop of college catchers in the draft. He's durable and also offers some opposite-field power, though some scouts think he has holes in his swing.

Best Fastball: Boston signed just two pitchers out of the first 10 rounds. RHP Billy Simon (9) is projectable at 6-foot-6 and already throws in the low 90s.

Most Intriguing Background: LHP Rolando Viera (7) defected from Cuba and went to court to avoid going into the draft, but lost his case and signed with the Red Sox for $175,000. His listed age of 27 made him the oldest player in the draft.

Shoppach

Closest To The Majors: Viera is a polished left-hander with an 87-89 mph fastball and command of several pitches. He pitched well in relief in the Arizona Fall League, and Boston has a glaring need for southpaw bullpen help.

Best Late-Round Pick: LHP Shane Rhodes (11) doesn't light up radar guns, but he knows how to pitch. He went 4-4, 2.89 with 58 strikeouts in 72 NY-P innings.

The One Who Got Away: The Red Sox were disappointed they couldn't sign LHP Matt Chico (2) and RHP Ben Crockett (10). Chico, who throws 91-93 mph, will play both ways at Southern California. Crockett, who has a similar fastball and has looked terrific in the Cape Cod League for two years, returned for his senior year at Harvard.

Assessment: Boston's attempt to add to its pitching depth was hampered by its failure to sign Chico, Crockett and RHP Justin James (6). The Red Sox' most intriguing signees may be their seventh- through ninth-rounders—Viera, Youkilis and Simon.

2000 Draft

The hopes of the Boston farm system rest on powerful if unproven arms such as RHPs Manny Delcarmen (2) and Josh Thigpen (16) and LHP Phil Dumatrait (1). SS Freddy Sanchez (11) has hit much better than expected. **Grade: B**

1999 Draft

The Red Sox stocked up on lefties with Casey Fossum (1), Rich Rundles (3) and Greg Montalbano (5, draft-and-follow), though Rundles was part of a package for Ugueth Urbina last summer. RHP Brad Baker (1) was the organization's best pitching prospect before taking a step back last year, when RHP Mat Thompson (2) made impressive strides. **Grade: C+**

1998 Draft

The Sox lost RHP Dennis Tankerlsey (38, draft-and-follow) in a trade for Ed Sprague, and may regret dealing SS Adam Everett (1) for Carl Everett. They didn't sign three premium 2001 picks in 3B Mark Teixeira (9), LHP Lenny DiNardo (10) and C Mike Rabelo (13). **Grade: B**

1997 Draft

Both first-round picks, LHP John Curtice and OF Mark Fischer, have failed. LHP Greg Miller (5) was traded, 2B David Eckstein (19) was waived and a future first-round pick in RHP Justin Wayne (9) wasn't signed. That leaves nothing for the Red Sox. **Grade: D**

Note: Draft analysis prepared by Jim Callis. Numbers in parentheses indicate draft rounds.

. . . Song pitches anywhere from 90-94 mph with his fastball, and he can put it anywhere he wants.

Song Seung
rhp

Born: June 29, 1980.
Ht.: 6-1. **Wt.:** 192.
Bats: R. **Throws:** R.
Career Transactions: Signed out of Korea by Red Sox, Feb. 2, 1999.

Song may not want the distinction of being Boston's No. 1 prospect, given his predecessors. Righthander Brian Rose (1998) has bounced around between four organizations in the last two years. First baseman/ outfielder Dernell Stenson (1999, 2001) has fallen out of the top 15 before reaching the majors, while catcher Steve Lomasney (2000) has missed as many games as he has played in since ranking No. 1. The Red Sox have poured a lot of money into the Asian market with little to show for it so far, and Song is their best chance at a contributing big lea- guer. He pitched Kyung Nam High to a Korean national title in 1998 before signing for $800,000 in February 1999. After leading the short-season New York-Penn League in strikeouts in 2000, Song finished second in the minors to Josh Beckett with a 1.90 ERA last season. He pitched a scoreless inning in the Futures Game in Seattle.

Song has succeeded at every step because of his intelligence and feel for pitching. It also helps to have good stuff. He pitches anywhere from 90-94 mph with his fastball, and he can put it anywhere he wants. Managers rated his control the best in the low Class A South Atlantic League in 2001. Song's curveball can overmatch hitters when it's at its best, and he improved his changeup last year to the point where it's an effective third pitch. He mixes his pitches and changes speeds well, and his corkscrew delivery makes him deceptive. Song has allowed just seven longballs in 261 pro innings and doesn't have any problems with lefthanders. He has sound mechanics and is durable. He does like to throw his fastball up in the strike zone and get batters to chase it. More advanced hitters may lay off the pitch or punish it. He comes straight over the top, which costs him some life on his pitches. Like any young pitcher, he needs to make his secondary pitches more consistent.

Having had no trouble in high Class A, Song probably will open 2002 in Double-A Trenton. If he continues his progress, he could reach Triple-A Pawtucket or perhaps even Boston by season's end. He projects as a No. 2 or 3 starter in the majors.

Year	Club (League)	Class	W	L	ERA	G	GS	CG	SV	IP	H	R	ER	BB	SO
1999	Red Sox (GCL)	R	5	5	2.30	13	9	0	0	55	47	29	14	20	61
2000	Lowell (NY-P)	A	5	2	2.60	13	13	0	0	73	63	26	21	20	93
2001	Augusta (SAL)	A	3	2	2.04	14	14	0	0	75	56	24	17	18	79
	Sarasota (FSL)	A	5	2	1.68	8	8	0	0	48	28	11	9	18	56
MINOR LEAGUE TOTALS			18	11	2.19	48	44	0	0	251	194	90	61	76	289

BILL SETLIFF

2. Tony Blanco, 3b

Born: Nov. 10, 1981. **Ht.:** 6-1. **Wt.:** 176. **Bats:** R. **Throws:** R. **Career Transactions:** Signed out of Dominican Republic by Red Sox, July 2, 1998.

Blanco set the Rookie-level Gulf Coast League home run record in his U.S. debut in 2000 and was rated the league's top prospect. He continued to show power last season despite bursitis in his right shoulder, which forced him to split time between third base and DH before he had arthroscopic surgery in August. The Red Sox named him their player of the year at low Class A Augusta. Blanco has a quick bat that makes him a threat to go deep at any time and allows him to hit for average. He held his own in the South Atlantic League as a teenager despite his shoulder problems. Defensively, he has a strong arm, good body control and some quickness. Overly aggressive at the plate, Blanco will have to show better discipline against more advanced pitchers. Though managers named him the best defensive third baseman in the SAL, he needs a quicker first step and smoother footwork. Blanco took things slowly in instructional league but should be healthy by spring training. Third base is the Red Sox' weakest offensive position, though they'll have to wait two or three years before Blanco is ready. He'll move up to high Class A in 2002.

Year	Club (League)	Class	AVG	G	AB	R	H	2B	3B	HR	RBI	BB	SO	SB
1999	Red Sox (DSL)	R	.277	67	249	36	69	12	5	8	41	29	65	12
2000	Red Sox (GCL)	R	.384	52	190	32	73	13	1	13	50	18	38	6
	Lowell (NY-P)	A	.143	9	28	1	4	1	0	0	0	2	12	1
2001	Augusta (SAL)	A	.265	96	370	44	98	23	2	17	69	17	78	1
MINOR LEAGUE TOTALS			.292	224	837	113	244	49	8	38	160	66	193	20

3. Rene Miniel, rhp

Born: April 26, 1981. **Ht.:** 6-2. **Wt.:** 175. **Bats:** R. **Throws:** R. **Career Transactions:** Signed out of Dominican Republic by Red Sox, Jan. 15, 1998.

Miniel had two nearly identical seasons as a reliever in the GCL before opening 2001 in Augusta's bullpen. When lefthander Mauricio Lara succumbed to back problems, Miniel moved to the rotation and struggled. Then he went 6-2, 1.48 in his last 15 starts, including seven no-hit innings in an Aug. 25 win against Charleston, S.C. Miniel's 91-96 mph fastball rivals Manny Delcarmen's as the best in the system, and he has good command of his heat. At times, he shows a hard curveball that gives him a second plus pitch. He gave up just one homer last year and held both lefties and righties to a .211 average. He held up well over his first season as a starter. Miniel is still a thrower at this point. He sometimes loses the tightness on his curve, which breaks out of the strike zone. His changeup is very much a work in progress. After being kept on a short leash with pitch counts, he'll have to prove he can work deeper into games. Because he's so raw as a pitcher, Miniel will move slowly through the system. He should spend 2002 in high Class A.

Year	Club (League)	Class	W	L	ERA	G	GS	CG	SV	IP	H	R	ER	BB	SO
1998	Red Sox (DSL)	R	4	5	1.85	13	11	1	0	73	58	34	15	27	38
1999	Red Sox (GCL)	R	1	2	4.06	21	0	0	1	38	40	28	17	16	37
2000	Red Sox (GCL)	R	2	4	4.00	21	1	0	7	36	37	21	16	21	31
2001	Augusta (SAL)	A	8	4	2.73	27	23	0	0	122	93	49	37	38	114
MINOR LEAGUE TOTALS			15	15	2.85	82	35	1	8	269	228	132	85	102	220

4. Manny Delcarmen, rhp

Born: Feb. 16, 1982. **Ht.:** 6-2. **Wt.:** 190. **Bats:** R. **Throws:** R. **School:** West Roxbury (Mass.) HS. **Career Transactions:** Selected by Red Sox in second round of 2000 draft; signed Aug. 22, 2000.

For obvious reasons, the Red Sox scout New England heavily. Their best local prospect is Delcarmen, a Dominican who was the first inner-city Boston player drafted in three decades. The Padres tried to get him when Boston was looking to foist Carl Everett on another club this winter, so the Red Sox swung a deal with the Rangers instead. Delcarmen has the potential for two plus pitches and a third that should be average. He has the best fastball in the system, regularly throwing 92-94 mph and reaching 95-96. He also has a hard breaking ball and a decent changeup. He shows poise and has an understanding of how to mix his pitches. Though he dominated GCL hitters, Delcarmen is still a long way from the major leagues. He'll have to throw more strikes as he makes the climb, and he'll also need to get more consistent with his breaking ball and changeup. Delcarmen has as high a ceiling as any pitcher in the system, including Seung Song and Rene Miniel, who rank ahead of him right now. He should head to low Class A in 2002.

Year	Club (League)	Class	W	L	ERA	G	GS	CG	SV	IP	H	R	ER	BB	SO
2001	Red Sox (GCL)	R	4	2	2.54	11	8	0	1	46	35	16	13	19	62
MINOR LEAGUE TOTALS			4	2	2.54	11	8	0	1	46	35	16	13	19	62

5. Casey Fossum, lhp

Born: Jan. 9, 1978. **Ht.:** 6-1. **Wt.:** 160. **Bats:** B. **Throws:** L. **School:** Texas A&M University. **Career Transactions:** Selected by Red Sox in first round (48th overall) of 1999 draft; signed July 19, 1999.

While fellow 1999 first-round picks Rick Asadoorian (since traded to the Cardinals) and Brad Baker regressed last season, Fossum finished the year in the Red Sox rotation. He allowed one earned run or less in 12 of his 20 Double-A starts, a far better indication of how he pitched than his 3-7 record. Fossum's 73-79 mph curveball is the top breaking pitch in the system; lefthanders can't touch it. He throws strikes and gets nice downward movement with his fastball, which rarely tops 90 mph. He's mentally tough. Because he has just one plus pitch, Fossum projects more as a reliever or swingman than a full-time starter. He had a good changeup in college but has gotten away from it as a pro. He's not durable, as he tires quickly and often starts leaving his pitches up in the strike zone by the fourth inning. Fossum had a 0.93 ERA as a big league reliever, compared to a 5.97 ERA as a starter. That performance, and Boston's offseason additions of John Burkett, Dustin Hermanson and Darren Oliver, means Fossum will compete for a bullpen job in spring training.

Year	Club (League)	Class	W	L	ERA	G	GS	CG	SV	IP	H	R	ER	BB	SO
1999	Lowell (NY-P)	A	0	1	1.26	5	5	0	0	14	6	2	2	5	16
2000	Sarasota (FSL)	A	9	10	3.44	27	27	3	0	149	147	71	57	36	143
2001	Trenton (EL)	AA	3	7	2.83	20	20	0	0	118	102	47	37	28	130
	Boston (AL)	MAJ	3	2	4.87	13	7	0	0	44	44	26	24	20	26
MAJOR LEAGUE TOTALS			3	2	4.87	13	7	0	0	44	44	26	24	20	26
MINOR LEAGUE TOTALS			12	18	3.07	52	52	3	0	281	255	120	96	69	289

6. Freddy Sanchez, ss

Born: Dec. 21, 1977. **Ht.:** 5-11. **Wt.:** 185. **Bats:** R. **Throws:** R. **School:** Oklahoma City University. **Career Transactions:** Selected by Red Sox in 11th round of 2000 draft; signed June 14, 2000.

Sanchez went to the NAIA World Series with Dallas Baptist in 1999, then earned NAIA all-America honors at Oklahoma City and short-season Lowell's MVP award the following year. But no one was prepared for his breakout performance last season. He led all minor league shortstops with a .334 average and made the Arizona Fall League all-prospect team after hitting .348. Sanchez has proven he can make contact, hit for average and drive balls into the gaps. He recognizes pitches well and has a sound stroke. He's a gritty player who has soft hands on defense. Most scouts don't think Sanchez can stay at shortstop. He lacks the range and agility for the position, and his average arm would fit better at second base. He spent most of his time in the AFL at third, but he lacks the power for the hot corner. Offensively, he could draw more walks. The Red Sox haven't give up on Sanchez as a shortstop. They might give him a look in spring training as a utilityman, but he'll probably wind up playing short in Triple-A this year.

Year	Club (League)	Class	AVG	G	AB	R	H	2B	3B	HR	RBI	BB	SO	SB
2000	Lowell (NY-P)	A	.288	34	132	24	38	13	2	1	14	9	16	2
	Augusta (SAL)	A	.303	30	109	17	33	7	0	0	15	11	19	4
2001	Sarasota (FSL)	A	.339	69	280	40	95	19	4	1	24	22	30	5
	Trenton (EL)	AA	.326	44	178	25	58	20	0	2	19	9	21	3
MINOR LEAGUE TOTALS			.320	177	699	106	224	59	6	4	72	51	86	14

7. Phil Dumatrait, lhp

Born: July 12, 1981. **Ht.:** 6-2. **Wt.:** 170. **Bats:** R. **Throws:** L. **School:** Bakersfield (Calif.) JC. **Career Transactions:** Selected by Red Sox in first round (22nd overall) of 2000 draft; signed July 10, 2000.

Because Dumatrait threw in the low 80s as a high school senior, he wasn't drafted in 1999. When his velocity soared in junior college, he became a first-round pick a year later. Signability played a part in his draft status, though he had a strong pro debut in 2001 after shoulder tendinitis sidelined him early in the season. Dumatrait's ceiling is considerably higher than Fossum's and is better than any Red Sox minor league lefty's. His curveball has a sharp 12-to-6 break and is a legitimate plus-plus pitch. He's not a soft-tossing southpaw, either, as he throws an 89-92 mph fastball that touches 94. He has good command of his pitches and emotions. Dumatrait's changeup shows promise but is still a ways from being an average pitch. As with Manny Delcarmen, any excitement about Dumatrait must be tempered by the fact that he has yet to pitch in full-season ball. Dumatrait and Delcarmen should team up again in low Class A. Because he's lefthanded, has more refined stuff and throws more strikes, Dumatrait is the favorite to win the race to Fenway Park.

Year	Club (League)	Class	W	L	ERA	G	GS	CG	SV	IP	H	R	ER	BB	SO
2000	Red Sox (GCL)	R	0	1	1.65	6	6	0	0	16	10	6	3	12	12
2001	Red Sox (GCL)	R	3	0	2.76	8	8	0	0	33	27	10	10	9	33
	Lowell (NY-P)	A	1	1	3.48	2	2	0	0	10	9	4	4	4	15
MINOR LEAGUE TOTALS			4	2	2.58	16	16	0	0	59	46	20	17	25	60

8. Josh Thigpen, rhp

Born: June 27, 1982. **Ht.:** 6-4. **Wt.:** 195. **Bats:** R. **Throws:** R. **School:** Rogers HS, Greenville, Ala. **Career Transactions:** Selected by Red Sox in 16th round of 2000 draft; signed July 11, 2000.

Scouting director Wayne Britton quickly identified Freddy Sanchez and Thigpen as the sleepers of his 2000 draft class, and both players made him look good last year. An all-Alabama performer in baseball, football and basketball in high school, Thigpen teamed with Manny Delcarmen and Phil Dumatrait to form an imposing front three in the GCL rotation. Thigpen has big-time velocity and plenty of projection. He already touches 96 mph with a nice, easy arm action, and he should reach that level more often once he fills out his 6-foot-4 frame. GCL hitters batted just .152 against him. Thigpen throws strikes and flashes an average curveball. The Red Sox praise his makeup as well. There's a lot to like about Thipgen, and there's also a lot he needs to work on. He needs to get more consistent with his curve, improve his changeup and fine-tune his command. With just 42 innings of pro experience, he still has much to learn. After two years in the GCL, Thigpen will be reunited with Delcarmen and Dumatrait in low Class A this season. It will be a good test for all three of them.

Year	Club (League)	Class	W	L	ERA	G	GS	CG	SV	IP	H	R	ER	BB	SO
2000	Red Sox (GCL)	R	0	1	15.00	2	0	0	0	3	3	5	5	6	2
2001	Red Sox (GCL)	R	4	2	2.52	10	6	0	0	39	20	15	11	14	44
MINOR LEAGUE TOTALS			4	3	3.40	12	6	0	1	42	23	20	16	20	46

9. Anastacio Martinez, rhp

Born: Nov. 3, 1980. **Ht.:** 6-2. **Wt.:** 180. **Bats:** R. **Throws:** R. **Career Transactions:** Signed out of Dominican Republic by Red Sox, Jan. 6, 1998.

Martinez had only sporadic success while pitching at Augusta in 1999 and 2000, but he handled the jump to Sarasota well last year. Though he led the Florida State League in losses, he did make 14 quality starts in 24 tries. Boston added him to its 40-man roster in November. His smooth arm action allows Martinez to throw in the low 90s with ease. He tops out in the mid-90s and has reached that level in the late innings. He throws strikes to both sides of the plate and locates his pitches well, getting lots of ground balls. Martinez is still a project, and some scouts see him as a middle reliever because he lacks a consistent offspeed offering. His slurvy breaking ball is a fringe pitch; his changeup is average at best. He'll need to improve one of them to succeed as a starter at the upper levels. The Red Sox will move Martinez to Double-A in 2002 and hope he can round out his repertoire. He has the fastball to be effective out of the bullpen, but they'd love for him to be able to stay in the rotation.

Year	Club (League)	Class	W	L	ERA	G	GS	CG	SV	IP	H	R	ER	BB	SO
1998	Red Sox (DSL)	R	0	1	13.50	2	2	0	0	7	13	11	10	7	8
	Red Sox (GCL)	R	2	3	3.18	12	10	0	0	51	45	28	18	12	50
1999	Augusta (SAL)	A	2	4	6.30	10	10	0	0	40	44	37	28	18	36
	Lowell (NY-P)	A	0	3	3.68	11	11	0	0	51	61	36	21	18	43
2000	Augusta (SAL)	A	9	6	4.64	23	23	0	0	120	130	69	62	50	107
	Red Sox (GCL)	R	0	1	9.45	2	1	0	0	7	15	9	7	3	1
2001	Sarasota (FSL)	A	9	12	3.35	25	24	1	0	145	130	69	54	39	123
MINOR LEAGUE TOTALS			22	30	4.28	85	81	1	0	421	438	259	200	147	368

10. Franklin Francisco, rhp

Born: June 11, 1980. **Ht.:** 6-2. **Wt.:** 180. **Bats:** R. **Throws:** R. **Career Transactions:** Signed out of Dominican Republic by Red Sox, Dec. 15, 1996.

Francisco is the fourth player in the top 10 signed out of the Dominican Republic by Levy Ochoa. He missed all of 1997 and most of 2000 with injuries, and he required elbow surgery before last season. He strained his shoulder in April but was dominant once he returned. Francisco is all about power, throwing a 92-95 mph fastball and a 78-80 mph curveball. Once he got both pitches working in tandem last year, it was all over for South Atlantic League hitters. In the final two months, he averaged 12.5 strikeouts per nine innings while opponents hit .124 against him. Repeated attempts to teach Francisco a changeup failed, which is why he's limited to the bullpen. He's probably 30 pounds heavier than his listed weight of 180 pounds. His body could go south in a hurry. He'll have to throw more strikes, though his command improved in July and August. Francisco will start 2002 in high Class A, where he may get his first regular opportunity as a closer, and could reach Double-A by the end of the season. He's two or three years away from Boston.

Year	Club (League)	Class	W	L	ERA	G	GS	CG	SV	IP	H	R	ER	BB	SO
1997	Did Not Play—Injured														
1998	Co-op (DSL)	R	0	5	10.31	16	13	0	0	48	44	66	55	76	53
1999	Red Sox (GCL)	R	2	4	4.56	12	7	0	0	53	58	39	27	35	48
2000	Red Sox (GCL)	R	0	0	18.00	1	0	0	0	1	2	3	2	2	1
2001	Augusta (SAL)	A	4	3	2.91	37	0	0	2	68	40	25	22	30	90
MINOR LEAGUE TOTALS			6	12	5.60	66	20	0	2	170	144	133	106	143	192

11. Mat Thompson, rhp

Born: Aug. 28, 1981. **Ht.:** 6-2. **Wt.:** 205. **Bats:** R. **Throws:** R. **School:** Timberline HS, Boise, Idaho. **Career Transactions:** Selected by Red Sox in second round of 1999 draft; signed July 3, 1999.

Thompson doesn't have the raw arm strength of the pitchers ahead of him on the list, but he has the stuff and intangibles to climb the ladder to Fenway Park. He never lost a game in high school and as a second-rounder in 1999 he was the highest Idaho draft pick since Boston took Mike Garman third overall in 1967. After two seasons in the Gulf Coast League, Thompson made a successful transition to low Class A in 2001. His best pitch is an 89-92 mph sinker that gets him grounders. He commands it very well, keeping it down in the strike zone. His changeup really improved last year, but his curveball still needs work. He slows down his arm action and changes his delivery when he throws the curve, tipping off hitters and also hurting its consistency. Thompson faded late in his first year in full-season ball and missed a start with a sore back, so he'll need to get stronger as he climbs to high Class A in 2002.

Year	Club (League)	Class	W	L	ERA	G	GS	CG	SV	IP	H	R	ER	BB	SO
1999	Red Sox (GCL)	R	0	0	1.20	5	2	0	0	15	7	3	2	4	12
2000	Red Sox (GCL)	R	4	2	3.65	12	11	0	0	57	65	33	23	18	54
2001	Augusta (SAL)	A	9	10	3.22	25	24	0	0	134	115	58	48	19	97
MINOR LEAGUE TOTALS			13	12	3.19	42	37	0	0	206	187	94	73	41	163

12. Juan Diaz, 1b/dh

Born: Feb. 19, 1976. **Ht.:** 6-2. **Wt.:** 225. **Bats:** R. **Throws:** R. **Career Transactions:** Signed out of Cuba by Dodgers, May 19, 1996 . . . Contract voided, June 25, 1999 . . . Signed by Red Sox, March 4, 2000.

Diaz is an enigma. Signed as a free agent in 2000, after Major League Baseball voided his contract because the Dodgers had illegally scouted him and outfielder Josue Perez in Cuba, Diaz was on the verge of getting called up to Boston when he dislocated his ankle on a bad slide. Since getting hurt, he hasn't made an effort to stay in shape and is at least 25 pounds heavier than his listed weight of 225. He was close to 300 pounds when he reported to camp last year, so the Red Sox kept him in extended spring training to work on conditioning for two months. In late July, he was suspended for a few days following an altercation with a Pawtucket trainer over Diaz' refusal to ride a stationary bike. The shame in all of this is that Diaz is one of the best power hitters in the minors, as scouts give him the maximum grade on their 20-to-80 scale. He can crush any fastball, though he struggles against breaking balls. He's a base clogger who isn't agile enough to inspire much confidence at first base. Boston could use his righthander power to complement Manny Ramirez and Nomar Garciaparra, but Diaz has to show he cares before he'll get an opportunity.

Year	Club (League)	Class	AVG	G	AB	R	H	2B	3B	HR	RBI	BB	SO	SB
1996	Dodgers (DSL)	R	.362	13	47	15	17	7	0	4	16	11	13	1
1997	Savannah (SAL)	A	.230	127	460	63	106	24	2	25	83	48	155	2
	Vero Beach (FSL)	A	.429	2	7	2	3	0	0	1	3	0	4	0
1998	Vero Beach (FSL)	A	.292	67	250	33	73	12	1	17	51	21	52	1
	San Antonio (TL)	AA	.266	56	188	26	50	13	0	13	30	15	45	0
1999	San Antonio (TL)	AA	.303	66	254	42	77	21	1	9	52	26	77	0
2000	Sarasota (FSL)	A	.275	14	51	7	14	2	1	4	12	4	15	0
	Trenton (EL)	AA	.313	50	198	36	62	14	1	17	53	10	56	0
	Pawtucket (IL)	AAA	.279	13	43	11	12	0	0	7	17	6	9	1
2001	Pawtucket (IL)	AAA	.269	74	279	45	75	17	1	20	51	17	85	0
MINOR LEAGUE TOTALS			.275	482	1777	280	489	110	7	117	368	158	511	5

13. Brad Baker, rhp

Born: Nov. 6, 1980. **Ht.:** 6-2. **Wt.:** 180. **Bats:** R. **Throws:** R. **School:** Pioneer Valley HS, Northfield, Mass. **Career Transactions:** Selected by Red Sox in first round (40th overall) of 1999 draft; signed July 26, 1999.

Boston's top-rated pitching prospect entering 2001, Baker was one of the organization's biggest disappointments last year. One of several New England products drafted by the Red Sox in recent years, his misguided attempts at weightlifting after the 2000 season left him bulky and tight. Baker still showed a quick arm action, but his fastball didn't sit in the low 90s or touch 95 mph like it had in the past. It also came in straighter than ever, making it all the more hittable. His overall control suffered as well, as he never looked comfortable with his body. His curveball was still a plus pitch at times, but his changeup continues to need refinement. Boston hoped Baker regained his flexibility this winter and returns to his previous form in 2002, when he'll probably return to high Class A.

Year	Club (League)	Class	W	L	ERA	G	GS	CG	SV	IP	H	R	ER	BB	SO
1999	Red Sox (GCL)	R	1	0	0.79	4	3	0	0	11	10	3	1	2	10
2000	Augusta (SAL)	A	12	7	3.07	27	27	0	0	138	125	58	47	55	126
2001	Sarasota (FSL)	A	7	9	4.73	24	23	0	0	120	132	77	63	64	103
MINOR LEAGUE TOTALS			20	16	3.71	55	53	0	0	269	267	138	111	121	239

14. Mauricio Lara, lhp

Born: April 2, 1979. **Ht.:** 5-11. **Wt.:** 185. **Bats:** B. **Throws:** L. **Career Transactions:** Signed out of Mexico by Red Sox, Sept. 14, 1998.

It doesn't say much about the Red Sox that two of the best pitchers in their system—Lara and Brad Baker—messed themselves up with offseason weightlifting programs during the 2000-01 offseason. If only Juan Diaz worked that hard. Lara made just four starts last year before back problems shut him down for nearly two months. When he returned, he wasn't the same guy who posted a 1.85 ERA in his first two pro seasons. Before he bulked up, Lara threw in the low 90s and topped out at 94 mph. His curveball gave him a second plus pitch, while his changeup was very much a work in progress. Boston still has high hopes for Lara, who was signed out of Mexico by Lee Sigman, the scout who helped land Teddy Higuera for the Brewers in the mid-1980s. He's on the same path as Baker, trying to rework his body so he can get back on track.

Year	Club (League)	Class	W	L	ERA	G	GS	CG	SV	IP	H	R	ER	BB	SO
1999	Cagua (VSL)	R	7	0	1.71	10	9	2	0	58	44	15	11	17	63
2000	Augusta (SAL)	A	1	0	1.41	16	0	0	0	32	25	11	5	13	33
	Lowell (NY-P)	A	4	3	2.12	15	14	1	0	85	70	22	20	21	83
2001	Augusta (SAL)	A	7	6	3.02	20	19	1	0	107	114	45	36	24	96
MINOR LEAGUE TOTALS			19	9	2.30	61	42	4	0	282	253	93	72	75	275

15. Kevin Huang, rhp

Born: April 25, 1982. **Ht.:** 6-0. **Wt.:** 172. **Bats:** R. **Throws:** R. **Career Transactions:** Signed out of Taiwan by Red Sox, July 24, 2000.

The Red Sox are as active in Asia as any organization, and Huang became their first Taiwanese signee in August 2000. He received a $60,000 bonus, which looks like a bargain after his first year in pro ball. He was more of a shortstop in high school, and Boston sent him to the Gulf Coast League as a reliever so he could get acclimated to pitching and the United States at a comfortable pace. When GM Dan Duquette saw him pitch a perfect inning while throwing 93 mph, he decided Huang should move up a level and begin starting. Huang was even better after the promotion and change of roles, striking out 12 over six shutout innings in his final start. He already has average to plus command of three pitches: a 90-91 mph fastball, a good breaking ball and a changeup. He needs more consistent velocity, but his broad shoulders give the Red Sox hope that he can fill out his compact frame and get stronger. Born Jun-Chung Huang, he has picked up the nickname "Kevin" since coming Stateside. A legitimate prospect by any name, he's destined for low Class A this year.

Year	Club (League)	Class	W	L	ERA	G	GS	CG	SV	IP	H	R	ER	BB	SO
2001	Red Sox (GCL)	R	0	2	3.65	10	0	0	3	12	14	5	5	10	15
	Lowell (NY-P)	A	5	2	2.25	10	8	0	0	48	41	16	12	12	55
MINOR LEAGUE TOTALS			5	4	2.54	20	8	0	3	60	55	21	17	22	70

16. Steve Lomasney, c

Born: Aug. 29, 1977. **Ht.:** 6-0. **Wt.:** 195. **Bats:** R. **Throws:** R. **School:** Peabody (Mass.) HS. **Career Transactions:** Selected by Red Sox in fifth round of 1995 draft; signed June 29, 1995 . . . Granted free agency, Dec. 20, 2001; re-signed by Red Sox, Dec. 20, 2001.

Little has gone right for Lomasney since he ranked as Boston's No. 1 prospect following the 1999 season. He started 2000 in an 0-for-19 slide and had his year end in mid-July with a hamstring injury. And that was good news compared to 2001, when he broke his right thumb in April and had the orbital bone around his right eye fracture when he was hit by a batting-practice liner in August. The Red Sox nontendered him in December but signed him a few days later. A former Boston College football recruit, Lomasney is a hard-nosed player with the mental toughness to come back from all that adversity. Less certain is his ability to hit for average. He sometimes overcompensates for his problems with breaking balls by looking for them exclusively, only to fall victim to fastballs. He does have some power against fastballs. Lomasney is more athletic than most catchers, but he relies more on guts than instincts behind the plate. His arm is average but his release is slow and his accuracy is inconsistent. After throwing out 33 percent of basestealers in Double-A last year, he went 0-for-21 in Double-A. With Jason Varitek establishing himself in Boston and top 2001 draft pick (second round) Kelly Shoppach about to begin his pro career, time is running out on Lomasney.

Year	Club (League)	Class	AVG	G	AB	R	H	2B	3B	HR	RBI	BB	SO	SB
1995	Red Sox (GCL)	R	.163	29	92	10	15	6	0	0	7	8	16	2
1996	Lowell (NY-P)	A	.139	59	173	26	24	10	0	4	21	42	63	2
1997	Michigan (Mid)	A	.275	102	324	50	89	27	3	12	51	32	98	3
1998	Sarasota (FSL)	A	.239	122	443	74	106	22	1	22	63	59	145	13
1999	Sarasota (FSL)	A	.270	55	189	35	51	10	0	8	28	26	57	5
	Trenton (EL)	AA	.245	47	151	24	37	6	0	12	31	31	44	7
	Boston (AL)	MAJ	.000	1	2	0	0	0	0	0	0	0	2	0
2000	Red Sox (GCL)	R	.267	6	15	2	4	2	0	0	1	4	6	0
	Trenton (EL)	AA	.245	66	233	30	57	16	1	8	27	24	81	4
2001	Trenton (EL)	AA	.249	58	209	24	52	14	2	10	29	23	76	0
	Pawtucket (IL)	AAA	.286	17	63	10	18	4	0	2	9	4	21	2
MAJOR LEAGUE TOTALS			.000	1	2	0	0	0	0	0	0	0	2	0
MINOR LEAGUE TOTALS			.239	561	1892	285	453	117	7	78	267	253	607	38

17. Luis Perez, lhp

Born: Feb. 10, 1981. **Ht.:** 6-0. **Wt.:** 150. **Bats:** R. **Throws:** L. **Career Transactions:** Signed out of Dominican Republic by Red Sox, Sept. 2, 1998.

Augusta used six regular starters in 2001, and all are legitimate prospects. Lefthander Rich Rundles was traded to the Expos during the season, but Seung Song, Rene Miniel, Mat Thompson, Mauricio Lara and Perez remain in Boston's plans for the future. After posting a 2.07 ERA and averaging 12.9 strikeouts per nine innings in two years of Rookie ball, Perez was successful if not dominant in low Class A. Perez has a quick arm action and sits around 90 mph with his fastball, which has a nice tail to it. He got away with pitching up in the strike zone in Rookie ball but learned that more advanced hitters will drive those pitches more often. Perez also uses a late-breaking curveball and a so-so changeup. He's not very big, so durability will be a concern, though he held up very well last year. His only physical setback was an April bout with tonsillitis. He'll graduate to high Class A in 2002.

Year	Club (League)	Class	W	L	ERA	G	GS	CG	SV	IP	H	R	ER	BB	SO
1999	Red Sox (DSL)	R	6	6	1.94	13	13	1	0	70	38	29	15	30	107
2000	Red Sox (GCL)	R	3	1	2.36	9	5	0	1	34	24	12	9	13	43
2001	Augusta (SAL)	A	8	8	3.58	26	25	0	0	126	118	69	50	42	113
MINOR LEAGUE TOTALS			17	15	2.90	48	43	1	1	230	180	110	74	85	263

18. Jorge de la Rosa, lhp

Born: April 5, 1981. **Ht.:** 6-1. **Wt.:** 192. **Bats:** L. **Throws:** L. **Career Transactions:** Signed out of Mexico by Diamondbacks, March 20, 1998 . . . Contract purchased by Monterrey (Mexican) from Diamondbacks, April 2, 2000 . . . Contract purchased by Red Sox from Monterrey, Feb. 22, 2001.

De la Rosa originally signed with Arizona in 1998. Two years later, the Diamondbacks transferred his contract to his hometown Monterrey Sultans, a Mexican League club with which they had a working agreement. When the agreement lapsed, the Sultans kept de la Rosa's rights, which suddenly became quite valuable when his velocity jumped 5 mph to 95-97 in the Mexican Pacific League that winter. After Boston landed him for $600,000, GM Dan Duquette dubbed de la Rosa "the Mexican John Rocker." He has the velocity to be an intimidating closer, but that's also the extent of his strengths. De la Rosa has inconsistent mechanics, which makes his command spotty, and he doesn't hide the ball well. He also lacks a second pitch he can trust. His 83-mph slider is better than his curveball, which he hangs too much, and he slows down his delivery when he throws his changeup. His arm action is a little too stiff for some scouts. He tore through high Class A in his Red Sox debut, then got hammered following a promotion to Double-A. Boston has been looking for a reliable lefty reliever for a few years, but de la Rosa will need to round out his game before he's the answer.

Year	Club (League)	Class	W	L	ERA	G	GS	CG	SV	IP	H	R	ER	BB	SO
1998	Diamondbacks (DSL)	R	1	0	4.50	13	0	0	1	14	8	7	7	8	21
1999	Diamondbacks (AZL)	R	0	0	3.21	8	0	0	2	14	12	5	5	3	17
	High Desert (Cal)	A	0	0	0.00	2	0	0	0	3	1	0	0	2	3
	Missoula (Pio)	R	0	1	7.98	13	0	0	2	15	22	17	13	9	14
2000	Monterrey (Mex)	AAA	3	2	6.28	37	0	0	1	39	38	27	27	32	50
2001	Sarasota (FSL)	A	0	1	1.21	12	0	0	2	30	13	7	4	12	27
	Trenton (EL)	AA	1	3	5.84	29	0	0	0	37	56	35	24	20	27
MINOR LEAGUE TOTALS			5	7	4.77	114	0	0	8	151	150	98	80	86	159

19. Dernell Stenson, of/1b

Born: June 17, 1978. **Ht.:** 6-1. **Wt.:** 230. **Bats:** L. **Throws:** L. **School:** La Grange (Ga.) HS. **Career Transactions:** Selected by Red Sox in third round of 1996 draft; signed July 10, 1996.

Stenson ranked No. 1 on this list year ago, but the Red Sox left him to rot during a third straight season in Triple-A. Managers rated him the best hitting prospect in the Double-A Eastern League in 1998 and in the Triple-A International League in 1999, but Boston never showed much inclination to include Stenson in its big league plans. Where he once was a promising young hitter, he now chases bad pitches, perhaps in an attempt to do too much. He still has some problems with breaking pitches. The bottom line is that he'll have to hit to play in the majors, because he can't do anything else. He's slow and a subpar defender in the outfield and at first base. He's not in the best of shape, though he's more toned than Juan Diaz or Calvin Pickering—not that that's saying much. One of five first baseman on the Red Sox' 40-man roster in January, Stenson's chances of reaching Fenway Park aren't getting any better. A change of scenery probably would be for the best.

Year	Club (League)	Class	AVG	G	AB	R	H	2B	3B	HR	RBI	BB	SO	SB
1996	Red Sox (GCL)	R	.216	32	97	16	21	3	1	2	15	16	26	4
1997	Michigan (Mid)	A	.291	131	471	79	137	35	2	15	80	72	105	6
1998	Trenton (EL)	AA	.257	138	505	90	130	21	1	24	71	84	135	5
1999	Pawtucket (IL)	AAA	.270	121	440	64	119	28	2	18	82	55	119	2
	Red Sox (GCL)	R	.217	6	23	2	5	0	0	2	7	3	5	0
2000	Pawtucket (IL)	AAA	.268	98	380	59	102	14	0	23	71	45	99	0
2001	Pawtucket (IL)	AAA	.237	122	464	53	110	18	1	16	69	43	116	0
MINOR LEAGUE TOTALS			.262	648	2380	363	624	119	7	100	395	318	605	17

20. Kelly Shoppach, c

Born: April 29, 1980. **Ht.:** 5-11. **Wt.:** 210. **Bats:** R. **Throws:** R. **School:** Baylor University. **Career Transactions:** Selected by Red Sox in second round of 2001 draft; signed Aug. 17, 2001.

Catching was an area of particular weakness in the system, but the Red Sox believe they addressed it last year. They spent their top pick (second round) on Shoppach, got offensive-minded Jonathan DeVries in the third round and signed Dustin Brown as a 35th-round draft-and-follow from 2000. Furthermore, Dominican Ivan Rodriguez batted .327 in his U.S. debut. The best of the group is Shoppach, who was the 2001 Big 12 Conference player of the year and also won the Johnny Bench Award as the top catcher in college baseball. He has tremendous catch-and-throw skills, taking just 1.8-1.9 seconds to deliver the ball from mitt to mitt on steal attempts. A football standout in high school, he brings that type of mentality and leadership skills to the mound. Shoppach offers opposite-field power but hasn't learned to turn on pitches and scouts are divided on his offensive potential. It took most of the summer to negotiate his $737,500 bonus. His only pro experience is instructional league, but he should be able to handle a Class A assignment in 2001.

Year	Club (League)	Class	AVG	G	AB	R	H	2B	3B	HR	RBI	BB	SO	SB
	Has Not Played—Signed 2002 Contract													

21. Juan Pena, rhp

Born: June 27, 1977. **Ht.:** 6-5. **Wt.:** 215. **Bats:** R. **Throws:** R. **School:** Miami-Dade CC Wolfson. **Career Transactions:** Selected by Red Sox in 27th round of 1995 draft; signed June 3, 1995.

Since winning his first two major league starts in May 1999, Pena has pitched just 56 innings. Shoulder tendinitis initially put him on the disabled list, and then he tore an elbow ligament and had Tommy John surgery in 2000. Though he was unable to pitch at the start of 2001, the Red Sox optioned him to Sarasota so they wouldn't have to pay him the major league minimum. He never felt comfortable and made just eight starts, when he would have been better off rehabbing his arm. He finally felt normal pitching in his native Dominican this winter. For Pena, that meant being able to spot his 89-91 mph sinker, curveball, slider and changeup for strikes. His best pitch is his curveball. He's not the most deceptive guy but he sure knows how to pitch. Boston doesn't have an obvious rotation spot open, so Pena probably will start 2002 in Triple-A, waiting for his second chance. His brother, also named Juan but lefthanded, pitches in the Athletics system.

Year	Club (League)	Class	W	L	ERA	G	GS	CG	SV	IP	H	R	ER	BB	SO
1995	Red Sox (GCL)	R	3	2	1.95	13	4	2	1	55	41	17	12	6	47
	Sarasota (FSL)	A	1	1	4.91	2	2	0	0	7	8	4	4	3	5
1996	Michigan (Mid)	A	12	10	2.97	26	26	4	0	188	149	70	62	34	156
1997	Sarasota (FSL)	A	4	6	2.96	13	13	3	0	91	67	39	30	23	88
	Trenton (EL)	AA	5	6	4.73	16	14	0	0	97	98	56	51	31	79
1998	Pawtucket (IL)	AAA	8	10	4.38	24	23	1	0	140	141	73	68	51	146
1999	Red Sox (GCL)	R	0	0	0.00	1	1	0	0	2	0	0	0	0	4
	Sarasota (FSL)	A	0	1	7.11	2	2	0	0	6	12	6	5	0	5
	Pawtucket (IL)	AAA	4	2	4.13	10	10	0	0	48	44	28	22	13	61
	Boston (AL)	MAJ	2	0	0.69	2	2	0	0	13	9	1	1	3	15
2000	Did Not Play—Injured														
2001	Sarasota (FSL)	A	0	3	5.19	8	8	0	0	26	29	15	15	11	31
MAJOR LEAGUE TOTALS			2	0	0.69	2	2	0	0	13	9	1	1	3	15
MINOR LEAGUE TOTALS			37	41	3.66	115	103	10	1	661	589	308	269	172	622

22. Sun-Woo Kim, rhp

Born: Sept. 4, 1977. **Ht.:** 6-2. **Wt.:** 180. **Bats:** R. **Throws:** R. **Career Transactions:** Signed out of Korea by Red Sox, Jan. 15, 1998.

Kim may have suffered from being placed on the fast track after signing out of Korea for $1 million in 1998. He went straight to high Class A at age 20 and kept getting promoted each year despite never posting an ERA below 4.82. Triple-A hitters have batted .295 against him over the last two seasons, while major league hitters have tagged him for a .312 average. Once projected as a possible frontline starter, Kim now figures to be more of a middle reliever. He'll reach 94-95 mph at times and his fastball has nice boring, riding action, but he uses it too high in the strike zone. His slider can be a plus pitch when he maintains his release point, but he gets under the pitch and flattens it out too much. He doesn't have command of his changeup and relies almost solely on hard stuff. Kim has yet to figure out how to get the ball inside on lefthanders. He likely will make a third trip to Pawtucket this year.

Year	Club (League)	Class	W	L	ERA	G	GS	CG	SV	IP	H	R	ER	BB	SO
1998	Sarasota (FSL)	A	12	8	4.82	26	24	5	0	153	159	88	82	40	132
1999	Trenton (EL)	AA	9	8	4.89	26	26	1	0	149	160	86	81	44	130
2000	Pawtucket (IL)	AAA	11	7	6.03	26	25	0	0	134	170	98	90	42	116
2001	Pawtucket (IL)	AAA	6	7	5.36	19	14	0	0	89	93	55	53	27	79
	Boston (AL)	MAJ	0	2	5.83	20	2	0	0	42	54	27	27	21	27
MAJOR LEAGUE TOTALS			0	2	5.83	20	2	0	0	42	54	27	27	21	27
MINOR LEAGUE TOTALS			38	30	5.24	97	89	6	0	525	582	327	306	153	457

23. Ryo Kumagai, rhp

Born: Aug. 22, 1979. **Ht.:** 6-1. **Wt.:** 180. **Bats:** R. **Throws:** R. **Career Transactions:** Signed ouf of Japan by Red Sox, January 15, 2002.

Even as the ownership of the club was changing hands, the Red Sox didn't stop working in the Far East. They signed Kumagai out of Tokyo's Tohoku Fukushi University for $450,000 in mid-January 2002. Kumagai pitched 9 1/3 scoreless innings and saved the title game as Tohoku Fukushi—also the alma mater of Kazuhiro Sasaki—won the Hawaii International Baseball Championship last August, and he had a shutout streak of 41 innings in college last fall. A potential 2004 Japanese Olympian before he signed with Boston, he's a submariner reminiscent of Byung-Hyun Kim. Kumagai throws 91-93 mph and also has a reverse slider that sinks and breaks in on righthanders. Hitters have a difficult time picking up his pitches, though he sometimes struggles to keep a consistent release point. Kumagai is very intelligent and figures to learn English quickly. He could make his pro debut as high as Double-A.

Year	Club (League)	Class	W	L	ERA	G	GS	CG	SV	IP	H	R	ER	BB	SO
	Has Not Played—Signed 2002 Contract														

24. Greg Montalbano, lhp

Born: Aug. 24, 1977. **Ht.:** 6-2. **Wt.:** 185. **Bats:** L. **Throws:** L. **School:** Northeastern University. **Career Transactions:** Selected by Red Sox in fifth round of 1999 draft; signed May 28, 2000.

Montalbano is a poor man's Casey Fossum, a lefthander who has succeeded as a pro but whose ultimate ceiling is in question. Boston's baseball writers voted Montalbano the organization's 2001 minor league player of the year. He led the system with 12 victories and threw nine no-hit innings in a high Class A Florida State League game in which he got no decision. Montalbano's best assets are his pitchability and his tenacity. He overcame testicular cancer while in college and shoulder problems in his first pro summer. His 86-92 mph fastball is a tick quicker and more lively than Fossum's, though his curveball isn't in the same class. Montalbano's curve has its moments but isn't consistent. He also throws a slider and changeup. He's much more of a fly-ball pitcher than Fossum, and thus more vulnerable to homers. While he has a deceptive delivery, scouts say Montalbano's stiff, stabbing arm action hinders him. He could return to Double-A to start 2002 but should reach Triple-A by the end of the year.

Year	Club (League)	Class	W	L	ERA	G	GS	CG	SV	IP	H	R	ER	BB	SO
2000	Red Sox (GCL)	R	0	2	3.75	4	4	0	0	12	13	6	5	3	14
	Lowell (NY-P)	A	0	1	1.74	2	2	0	0	10	4	3	2	4	15
2001	Sarasota (FSL)	A	9	3	2.96	17	15	0	0	91	66	36	30	25	77
	Trenton (EL)	AA	3	3	4.50	10	10	0	0	48	50	25	24	14	45
MINOR LEAGUE TOTALS			12	9	3.40	33	31	0	0	162	133	70	61	46	151

25. Rolando Viera, lhp

Born: Aug. 1, 1973. **Ht.:** 5-10. **Wt.:** 182. **Bats:** L. **Throws:** L. **Career Transactions:** Selected by Red Sox in seventh round of 2001 draft; signed Aug. 10, 2001.

Viera defected from Cuba and sued to avoid being made subject to the 2001 draft, but lost his case. Though he's lefthanded, Boston confused him with hard-throwing Cuban righthander Norge Luis Vera and drafted Viera in the seventh round. The Red Sox still may have something, however, after signing him for $175,000. Suspended in 2000 because he was branded as a potential defector, Viera had all his baseball equipment confiscated and had to resort to throwing lemons and oranges to stay in shape. While his fastball tops out at 87-89 mph and his arm action is a bit long, he thrives on using both his curveball and slider to get outs. Throw in Viera's splitter, changeup and knuckler, then add his varied arm angles and the possibilities are endless. After pitching just briefly in high Class A last summer, he impressed scouts in the Arizona Fall League. Viera is more polished than Jorge de la Rosa and could be the situational lefty that the Red Sox need.

Year	Club (League)	Class	W	L	ERA	G	GS	CG	SV	IP	H	R	ER	BB	SO
2001	Sarasota (FSL)	A	0	2	6.00	6	0	0	0	12	12	8	8	6	12
MINOR LEAGUE TOTALS			0	2	6.00	6	0	0	0	12	12	8	8	6	12

26. Byeong An, lhp

Born: July 1, 1980. **Ht.:** 6-2. **Wt.:** 190. **Bats:** L. **Throws:** L. **Career Transactions:** Signed out of Korea by Red Sox, Jan. 18, 2001.

The Red Sox forfeited their 2001 first-round pick to sign free agent Manny Ramirez, a move they didn't regret. They also felt like they got the equivalent of a first-rounder in An, whom they signed out of a Korean college for $750,000. Despite his relative inexperience and his inability to speak English, he went straight to high Class A and didn't permit more than one earned run in any of his first five outings. His fastball ranges anywhere from 83-92 mph at this point and his breaking ball usually looks like a slurve. Boston believes that once its coaches can communicate better with An, they'll be able to make his velocity more consistent and tighten his breaker into a true curveball. They also will be able to give him more help with his rudimentary changeup. He does a good job of throwing strikes and he varies his arm angle. An has a stocky frame with thick legs, and his weight could become a concern. He probably would benefit from some more time in the Florida State League so he could catch his breath.

Year	Club (League)	Class	W	L	ERA	G	GS	CG	SV	IP	H	R	ER	BB	SO
2001	Sarasota (FSL)	A	2	8	3.62	23	21	1	0	119	122	68	48	42	84
MINOR LEAGUE TOTALS			2	8	3.62	23	21	1	0	119	122	68	48	42	84

27. Josh Hancock, rhp

Born: April 11, 1978. **Ht.:** 6-3. **Wt.:** 217. **Bats:** R. **Throws:** R. **School:** Auburn University. **Career Transactions:** Selected by Red Sox in fifth round of 1998 draft; signed June 15, 1998.

In the 1998 draft, the Red Sox selected but failed to sign third baseman Mark Teixeira (the No. 5 overall pick by the Rangers last June), lefthander Lenny DiNardo (the Mets' 2001 third-rounder) and catcher Mike Rabelo (the Tigers' 2001 fourth-rounder). Boston's best hope for getting a homegrown player out of that draft crop is now Hancock, who was added to the 40-man roster for the first time in November. He has a big, strong build and a big, strong fastball that tops out at 94 mph. He challenges hitters and likes to bust righthanders inside. He throws across his body, which concerns scouts, and doesn't repeat his arm slot with his secondary pitches. His curveball is a solid average pitch at times but regresses to a slurve at others. His changeup is merely decent. He'll need to do a better job of missing bats and controlling his emotions. Hancock strained his groin in late August, which limited him to two innings in the Arizona Fall League. He'll move up to Triple-A at some point this year.

Year	Club (League)	Class	W	L	ERA	G	GS	CG	SV	IP	H	R	ER	BB	SO
1998	Red Sox (GCL)	R	1	1	3.38	5	1	0	0	13	9	5	5	3	21
	Lowell (NY-P)	A	0	1	2.25	1	1	0	0	4	5	2	1	4	4
1999	Augusta (SAL)	A	6	8	3.80	25	25	0	0	140	154	79	59	46	106
2000	Sarasota (FSL)	A	5	10	4.45	26	24	1	0	144	164	89	71	37	95
2001	Trenton (EL)	AA	8	6	3.65	24	24	0	0	131	138	60	53	37	119
MINOR LEAGUE TOTALS			20	26	3.94	81	75	1	0	431	470	235	189	127	345

28. Angel Santos, 2b

Born: Aug. 14, 1979. **Ht.:** 5-11. **Wt.:** 178. **Bats:** B. **Throws:** R. **School:** Miguel Melendez Munoz HS, Cayey, P.R. **Career Transactions:** Selected by Red Sox in fourth round of 1997 draft; signed July 26, 1997.

How thin are the Red Sox in terms of middle infielders? Santos and No. 6 prospect Freddy Sanchez are the only ones to crack the Top 30, and both look like they might be utilitymen rather than regulars in the majors. A switch-hitter, he makes more contact as a righty. From the left side he has a longer, more powerful swing that produced 13 of his 14 homers in 2001. He'll bunt to take advantage of his speed, which also allows him to steal bases. He strikes out too much, but at least he offsets his whiffs with some walks. He's an adequate second baseman who can get inconsistent on the double-play pivot. The biggest challenge for Santos is staying in the game mentally. He doesn't always give 100 percent, especially if he starts a game with a couple of bad at-bats. He and Sanchez likely will form the double-play combination in Triple-A this year.

Year	Club (League)	Class	AVG	G	AB	R	H	2B	3B	HR	RBI	BB	SO	SB
1997	Red Sox (GCL)	R	.183	17	60	8	11	1	0	0	7	7	11	8
1998	Red Sox (GCL)	R	.351	23	77	14	27	5	1	0	13	13	10	7
	Lowell (NY-P)	A	.245	28	102	19	25	4	1	1	12	9	12	2
1999	Augusta (SAL)	A	.270	130	466	83	126	30	2	15	55	62	88	25
2000	Trenton (EL)	AA	.258	80	275	32	71	17	2	3	32	32	60	18
2001	Trenton (EL)	AA	.271	129	510	75	138	32	0	14	52	54	106	26
	Pawtucket (IL)	AAA	.200	4	15	1	3	1	0	0	2	1	4	1
	Boston (AL)	MAJ	.125	9	16	2	2	1	0	0	1	2	7	0
MAJOR LEAGUE TOTALS			.125	9	16	2	2	1	0	0	1	2	7	0
MINOR LEAGUE TOTALS			.266	411	1505	232	401	90	6	33	173	178	291	87

29. Kevin Youkilis, 3b

Born: March 15, 1979. **Ht.:** 6-1. **Wt.:** 220. **Bats:** R. **Throws:** R. **School:** University of Cincinnati. **Career Transactions:** Selected by Red Sox in eighth round of 2001 draft; signed June 11, 2001.

Undrafted as a junior in 2000, Youkilis started attracting scouts with an all-star summer in the Cape Cod League. He followed up by leading Conference USA with a .405 batting average last spring before the Red Sox drafted him in the eighth round. He has a tremendous understanding of the strike zone, as evidenced by his New York-Penn League-leading 70 walks (in just 59 games) and .512 on-base percentage. He generates gap power out of a Jeff Bagwell-like crouch. Youkilis isn't blessed with a lot of physical tools, but he's athletic for his size. He doesn't clog the bases and he gets the job done at third base. Youkilis' advanced approach could land him in high Class A in 2002, when the Red Sox will begin to find out if he's for real.

Year	Club (League)	Class	AVG	G	AB	R	H	2B	3B	HR	RBI	BB	SO	SB
2001	Lowell (NY-P)	A	.317	59	183	52	58	14	2	3	28	70	28	4
	Augusta (SAL)	A	.167	5	12	0	2	0	0	0	0	3	3	0
MINOR LEAGUE TOTALS			.308	64	195	52	60	14	2	3	28	73	31	4

30. Jerome Gamble, rhp

Born: April 5, 1980. **Ht.:** 6-2. **Wt.:** 202. **Bats:** R. **Throws:** R. **School:** Benjamin Russell HS, Alexander City, Ala. **Career Transactions:** Selected by Red Sox in fourth round of 1998 draft; signed June 9, 1998.

Though elbow problems have limited him to 31 games in three pro seasons, Gamble is considered to have a raw arm as good as any in the system. His elbow flared up again last year, as he was shut down for 2 1/2 months after making two starts. He took the mound once again in late June before needing Tommy John surgery. The Red Sox hope he can take the mound again toward the end of spring training. When healthy, Gamble pumped 93-94 mph fastballs with plenty of movement. Very projectable, he figured to add velocity as he gained more strength. His curveball, changeup and command all have suffered from his lack of experience. He'll probably head back to high Class A whenever he's ready to pitch again.

Year	Club (League)	Class	W	L	ERA	G	GS	CG	SV	IP	H	R	ER	BB	SO
1998	Red Sox (GCL)	R	2	3	4.43	11	6	0	1	43	33	24	21	19	49
1999	Lowell (NY-P)	A	1	0	1.75	5	5	0	0	26	18	7	5	9	37
2000	Augusta (SAL)	A	5	3	2.52	15	15	0	0	79	69	26	22	32	71
2001	Sarasota (FSL)	A	0	0	7.88	3	2	0	1	8	11	8	7	4	7
MINOR LEAGUE TOTALS			8	6	3.19	34	28	0	2	155	131	65	55	64	164

CHICAGO
Cubs

By Jim Callis

The Cubs lost a combined 192 games in 1999-2000, edging the Royals, Expos and Devil Rays for the worst record in baseball. While those teams continued their last-place ways in 2001, Chicago rocketed back into contention with 88 wins. It was an affirmation of the talent rising through one of the top farm systems in the game.

Juan Cruz' stunning success in eight starts was a precursor of the pitching to come, while Courtney Duncan helped revitalize the bullpen and Scott Chiasson and Carlos Zambrano made late-season cameos. A wave of talented hitters also is on the way to Wrigley Field, and Corey Patterson probably arrived for good at age 21. Patterson, the No. 1 prospect on this list for three straight years, should be ready for stardom by 2003 or 2004—by which time the Cubs should have integrated their prospects into their major league club, leaving them poised to end a pennant drought that stands at 56 years.

Chicago has nice balance in its system with an even mix of position players and arms. Several of them have had success in the upper minors, while there also is plenty of talent percolating at the bottom rungs.

The Cubs have traded away several mid-level prospects in the past year, most notably Eric Hinske and Ruben Quevedo, without depleting their depth. The only major disappointment in 2001 was a run of injuries that struck current Top 15 Prospects Hee Seop Choi, David Kelton, Bobby Hill, Ben Christensen and Steve Smyth, among others. All five players should be healthy in 2002.

Assistant GM Jim Hendry was given the new title of vice president of player personnel in November, reiterating his status as GM Andy MacPhail's eventual successor. Hendry oversaw the rebirth of the system as farm and scouting director, and he scored big in his final draft in 2000. Seven of his first eight picks that year rank among Chicago's best 30 prospects, with Luis Montanez (first round), Hill (second) and Nic Jackson (third) all cracking the Top 10.

John Stockstill, the new scouting director, had a strong first effort last June. The Cubs landed Mark Prior, the consensus best prospect in the 2001 draft, and intriguing 6-foot-8 lefthander Andy Sisco in the first two rounds. Pacific Rim coordinator Leon Lee, who signed Choi in 1999, inked another top Korean in righthander Jae-Kuk Ryu.

OrganizationOverview

General manager: Andy MacPhail. **Farm director:** Oneri Fleita. **Scouting director:** John Stockstill.

2001 PERFORMANCE

Class	Farm Team	League	W	L	Pct.	Finish*	Manager
Majors	Chicago	National	88	74	.543	t-5th (16)	Don Baylor
Triple-A	Iowa Cubs	Pacific Coast	83	60	.580	3rd (16)	Bruce Kimm
Double-A	West Tenn Diamond Jaxx	Southern	59	80	.424	9th10)	Dave Bialas
High A	Daytona Cubs	Florida State	68	68	.500	6th (12)	Dave Trembley
Low A	Lansing Lugnuts	Midwest	65	75	.464	9th (14)	Julio Garcia
Short-season	Boise Hawks	Northwest	52	23	.693	1st (8)	Steve McFarland
Rookie	AZL Cubs	Arizona	26	30	.464	5th (7)	Carmelo Martinez
OVERALL 2001 MINOR LEAGUE RECORD			353	336	.512	11th (30)	

*Finish in overall standings (No. of teams in league)

ORGANIZATION LEADERS

BATTING

*AVG	Roosevelt Brown, Iowa	.346
R	Chad Meyers, Iowa	92
H	Blair Barbier, Lansing	153
TB	Jason Dubois, Lansing	249
2B	Blair Barbier, Lansing	38
	Ryan Gripp, West Tenn/Daytona	38
3B	Adam Morrissey, Lansing	11
HR	Chris Haas, West Tenn	25
RBI	**Ryan Gripp**, West Tenn/Daytona	94
BB	Adam Morrissey, Lansing	80
SO	Chris Haas, West Tenn	151
SB	Syketo Anderson, Lansing/Boise	29

PITCHING

W	Nate Teut, Iowa	13
	Todd Wellemeyer, Lansing	13
L	Matt Achilles, West Tenn/Daytona	12
#ERA	Tim Lavery, Lansing	2.43
G	Scott Chiasson, Iowa/West Tenn	63
CG	Steve Smyth, West Tenn	3
SV	Scott Chiasson, Iowa/West Tenn	34
IP	Nate Teut, Iowa	167
BB	Todd Wellemeyer, Lansing	74
SO	**Aaron Krawiec**, Lansing	170

*Minimum 250 At-Bats #Minimum 75 Innings

TOP PROSPECTS OF THE DECADE

1992	Lance Dickson, lhp
1993	Jessie Hollins, rhp
1994	Brooks Kieschnick, of
1995	Brooks Kieschnick, of
1996	Brooks Kieschnick, of
1997	Kerry Wood, rhp
1998	Kerry Wood, rhp
1999	Corey Patterson, of
2000	Corey Patterson, of
2001	Corey Patterson, of

TOP DRAFT PICKS OF THE DECADE

1992	Derek Wallace, rhp
1993	Brooks Kieschnick, of
1994	Jayson Peterson, rhp
1995	Kerry Wood, rhp
1996	Todd Noel, rhp
1997	Jon Garland, rhp
1998	Corey Patterson, of
1999	Ben Christensen, rhp
2000	Luis Montanez, ss
2001	Mark Prior, rhp

RICK BATTLE

DAN ARNOLD

Gripp   **Krawiec**

BEST TOOLS

Best Hitter for Average	David Kelton
Best Power Hitter	Hee Seop Choi
Fastest Baserunner	Dwaine Bacon
Best Fastball	Mark Prior
Best Breaking Ball	Juan Cruz
Best Changeup	Juan Cruz
Best Control	Mark Prior
Best Defensive Catcher	Ryan Jorgensen
Best Defensive Infielder	Bobby Hill
Best Infield Arm	Nate Frese
Best Defensive Outfielder	Mike Mallory
Best Outfield Arm	Mike Mallory

PROJECTED 2005 LINEUP

Catcher	Ryan Jorgensen
First Base	Hee Seop Choi
Second Base	Bobby Hill
Third Base	David Kelton
Shortstop	Luis Montanez
Left Field	Moises Alou
Center Field	Corey Patterson
Right Field	Sammy Sosa
No. 1 Starter	Mark Prior
No. 2 Starter	Kerry Wood
No. 3 Starter	Juan Cruz
No. 4 Starter	Jon Lieber
No. 5 Starter	Carlos Zambrano
Closer	Kyle Farnsworth

ALL-TIME LARGEST BONUSES

Mark Prior, 2001	$4,000,000
Corey Patterson, 1998	$3,700,000
Luis Montanez, 2000	$2,750,000
Jae-Kuk Ryu, 2001	$1,600,000
Bobby Hill, 2000	$1,425,000

DraftAnalysis

2001 Draft

Best Pro Debut: 1B Brad Bouras (21) was an all-star in the short-season Northwest League, where he hit .349-6-60, finishing first in doubles (25) and on-base percentage (.419) and second in average and RBIs. RHP Jeff Carlsen (22) still hasn't regained all of his velocity since shoulder surgery in 2000, but he had a 1.50 ERA and a 41-5 strikeout-walk ratio in 36 NWL innings.

Best Athlete: OF Dwaine Bacon (16) led NCAA Division I in steals per game in 2000 and ranked ninth in 2001. SS Ryan Theriot (3) isn't quite as gifted but is more polished.

Best Hitter: SS Brendan Harris (5) may wind up at second base or third base, but he'll hit. He went straight to full-season Class A and batted .274-4-22.

Best Raw Power: 3B Corey Slavik (10) made the NWL all-star team after batting .286-10-31. He may be able to move to second base, which would be a bonus.

Fastest Runner: A switch-hitter, Bacon has been clocked from home to first at 3.75 seconds from the left side of the plate.

Best Defensive Player: Theriot is a pure shortstop and handled the defense at high Class A with no problem. The Cubs will try to jump-start his bat after he hit .204, possibly by making him a switch-hitter.

Best Fastball: RHP Mark Prior (1) threw 94-97 mph all spring and was BA's 2001 College Player of the Year. Better yet, he's a complete pitcher who's as intelligent and driven as he is talented. **Andy Sisco** (2) is a raw, 6-foot-10 lefthander who can touch 96 mph.

Most Intriguing Background: RHP Dan Foli's (31) father Tim was the No. 1 pick in the 1968 draft. Unsigned C Matt Pagnozzi's (40) father Tom and unsigned RHP Jared Eichelberger's (44) dad Juan both played in the majors as well. RHP Ricky Nolasco's (4) brother David signed with the Brewers as a 23rd-rounder.

Sisco

Closest To The Majors: Some scouts said Prior, who didn't pitch last summer while negotiating a record $10.5 million contract, could have gone straight to the big leagues. Prior went to school rather than pitch in the Arizona Fall League, but will be in big league camp with a good chance to begin 2002 in Double-A.

Best Late-Round Pick: Bacon has an exciting ceiling. The question is whether he'll hit, and he batted just .193 in the NWL. SS Josh Arteaga (20) opened eyes by hitting .318-3-27 and playing steady defense at short-season Boise.

The One Who Got Away: RHP Marc Jecmen (42) threw as hard as 96 mph and would have been a high pick if not for his commitment to Stanford.

Assessment: Prior was the consensus best talent in the 2001 draft, and perhaps the top college pitching prospect ever. He alone should make this a memorable draft, and the Cubs added depth with Sisco, Nolasco, LHP Adam Wynegar (6) and RHP Sergio Mitre (7).

2000 Draft

2B Bobby Hill (2) and OF Nic Jackson (3) already are blue-chip prospects, and SS Luis Montanez (1) and OF J.J. Johnson (6) could be in time. Chicago also landed promising arms, led by RHP Todd Wellemeyer (4) and LHP Aaron Krawiec (3).   **Grade: A**

1999 Draft

RHPs Ben Christensen (1) and John Webb (19) and LHP Steve Smyth (4) all had promising futures before injuries struck them in 2001. They should be able to recover.   **Grade: B**

1998 Draft

The Cubs found three of the game's better young offensive talents in OF Corey Patterson (1) and 3Bs David Kelton (2) and Eric Hinske (17). Hinske was traded to Oakland for quality reliever Scott Chiasson.   **Grade: A**

1997 Draft

The grade doesn't penalize the Cubs for their egregious trade of RHP Jon Garland (1) for Matt Karchner. LHPs Scott Downs (3) and Nate Teut (4) were used in more sensible deals for Rondell White and Jesus Sanchez.   **Grade: C+**

Note: Draft analysis prepared by Jim Callis. Numbers in parentheses indicate draft rounds.

. . . Scouts say they've never seen a 20-year-old pitcher locate his fastball at will like Prior does.

Mark
Prior rhp

Born: Sept. 7, 1980.
Ht.: 6-5. **Wt.:** 225.
Bats: R. **Throws:** R.
School: University of Southern California.
Career Transactions: Selected by Cubs in first round (second overall) of 2001 draft; signed August 22, 2001.

Flirting with a no-hitter against Louisiana State at the 2000 College World Series and starring that summer with Team USA's college squad positioned Prior as the top pitching prospect for the 2001 draft. By the end of the season, several scouts called him the best college pitching prospect they had ever seen. After going 14-15 in his first two college seasons, Prior went 15-1, 1.69 with a Pacific-10 Conference-record 202 strikeouts and just 18 walks in 139 innings. Baseball America's College Player of the Year passed Georgia Tech third baseman Mark Teixeira as the consensus best player available. Drafting first overall, the Twins opted for Minnesota high school catcher Joe Mauer. Picking second, the Cubs had determined in March they'd take Prior if they got the chance. Negotiations began in earnest in August, when Prior signed a four-year major league contract with a guaranteed worth of at least $10.5 million, a draft record, including a $4 million bonus. In December, Prior won USA Baseball's Golden Spikes Award, the baseball equivalent of the Heisman Trophy.

Prior has everything scouts dream about in a pitcher. He throws his fastball at 94-97 mph, and his uncanny command of the pitch may be more impressive than its considerable velocity and life. Some scouts say they've never seen a 20-year-old pitcher locate his fastball at will like Prior does. He also can overmatch batters with his 12-to-6 curveball, another potential plus-plus pitch. Southern California coach Mike Gillespie insists Prior has a pretty good changeup, though he had little reason to give college hitters a fighting chance by throwing it. Prior has a classic pitcher's body at 6-foot-5 and 225 pounds; his mechanics are flawless. He's intelligent, poised and dedicated to his craft. His only real need is experience. The Cubs wish Prior had headed to instructional league or the Arizona Fall League after he signed, but he returned to college to finish his degree. He'll have to throw more changeups and get acclimated to throwing every fifth day as a pro.

Prior will be in big league camp and make his pro debut at Double-A West Tenn. A true No. 1 starter, he's an obvious candidate for a September callup if he hasn't reached Wrigley Field already by then. Scouts look at him and see the next Roger Clemens.

Year	Club (League)	Class	W	L	ERA	G	GS	CG	SV	IP	H	R	ER	BB	SO
Has Not Played—Signed 2002 Contract

2. Juan Cruz, rhp

Born: Oct. 15, 1978. **Ht.:** 6-2. **Wt.:** 155. **Bats:** R. **Throws:** R. **Career Transactions:** Signed out of Dominican Republic by Cubs, July 4, 1997.

Desperate for a starter in late August, the Cubs summoned Cruz to the majors. He made an impression on manager Don Baylor with his performance and courage. Cruz' stuff is just as exciting as Mark Prior's. Cruz also throws 94-97 mph, with more life but less command than Prior. He also has the best breaking ball (a darting slider) and changeup in the organization. He has been so overpowering since putting it all together in early 2000, the Cubs say they weren't surprised he was able to get the job done in the majors at age 20. Cruz just needs to put finishing touches on his command and pitching savvy. Lefties got to him in the majors, so he'll have to make some adjustments. Some opposing Southern League managers thought he was immature, but Chicago officials don't see that. Cruz will have a rotation spot awaiting him in spring training. He, Prior and Kerry Wood could form a nasty front three as early as 2003. In January, it came out that Cruz is two years older than his previously listed age, making him 23. That makes him less precocious but doesn't diminish the Cubs' enthusiasm about his special arm.

Year	Club (League)	Class	W	L	ERA	G	GS	CG	SV	IP	H	R	ER	BB	SO
1998	Cubs (AZL)	R	2	4	6.10	12	5	0	0	41	61	48	28	14	36
1999	Eugene (NWL)	A	5	6	5.94	15	15	0	0	80	97	59	53	33	65
2000	Lansing (Mid)	A	5	5	3.28	17	17	2	0	96	75	50	35	60	106
	Daytona (FSL)	A	3	0	3.25	8	7	1	0	44	30	22	16	18	54
2001	West Tenn (SL)	AA	9	6	4.01	23	23	0	0	121	107	56	54	60	137
	Chicago (NL)	MAJ	3	1	3.22	8	8	0	0	45	40	16	16	17	39
MAJOR LEAGUE TOTALS			3	1	3.22	8	8	0	0	45	40	16	16	17	39
MINOR LEAGUE TOTALS			24	21	4.37	75	67	3	0	383	370	235	186	185	398

3. Hee Seop Choi, 1b

Born: March 16, 1979. **Ht.:** 6-5. **Wt.:** 235. **Bats:** L. **Throws:** L. **Career Transactions:** Signed out of Korea by Cubs, March 4, 1999.

Signed to a $1.2 million bonus in 1999, Choi slugged his way through the minors in his first two years and led the Arizona Fall League in homers in 2000. Sent to Triple-A Iowa last spring to work on hitting left-handers, he lost much of the season to an injury in the back of his right hand. He had severe inflammation rather than a tear, but the hand was slow to heal. Choi is one of the top power hitters in the minors, and he still cranked out homers on a regular basis despite his painful hand problem. He drives the ball to all fields and is more than a slugger. He's an above-average first baseman who runs well for his size. In half a season Choi batted .286 with a .557 slugging percentage against lefties, so he may have solved that problem. His hand should be fine by spring training. His focus now is to watch his strikeouts and his weight. Chicago's trade for Fred McGriff pushed the timetable for making Choi the everyday first baseman back a year. He'll begin 2002 in Iowa and could be pushing for a promotion after the all-star break.

Year	Club (League)	Class	AVG	G	AB	R	H	2B	3B	HR	RBI	BB	SO	SB
1999	Lansing (Mid)	A	.321	79	290	71	93	18	6	18	70	50	68	2
2000	Daytona (FSL)	A	.296	96	345	60	102	25	6	15	70	37	78	4
	West Tenn (SL)	AA	.303	36	122	25	37	9	0	10	25	25	38	3
2001	Iowa (PCL)	AAA	.229	77	266	38	61	11	0	13	45	34	67	5
MINOR LEAGUE TOTALS			.286	288	1023	194	293	63	12	56	210	146	251	14

4. David Kelton, 3b/of

Born: Dec. 17, 1979. **Ht.:** 6-3. **Wt.:** 205. **Bats:** R. **Throws:** R. **School:** Troup County HS, La Grange, Ga. **Career Transactions:** Selected by Cubs in second round of 1998 draft; signed June 3, 1998.

Kelton seemed like Chicago's latest best hope to fill the void at third base that has existed since Ron Santo departed in 1973. After he made 15 errors in 54 games at West Tenn, he was set to move to the outfield before he popped something in his left hand on a checked swing, ending his season. He came back to play some outfield in the Arizona Fall League, where he batted .340. The best pure hitter in the system, Kelton was on pace to bat .300-30-100 in Double-A at age 21 when he got hurt. His swing is so pure the Cubs forbade their instructors from tinkering with it. He also has become more patient at the plate. Defensively, his speed and hands are fine. Kelton had shoulder surgery in high school, leaving him with modest arm strength. His release point got out of whack last year, resulting in throwing errors. He still needs work in the outfield, though the Cubs believe he can be at least an average defender. The initial plan for 2002 was to send Kelton to Triple-A and give him time at both third base and left field. But after the Cubs signed Moises Alou as a free agent, that closed off any opportunity in left field. They want to get Kelton's bat to Wrigley Field in the near future, so they'll hope he can handle the hot corner.

Year	Club (League)	Class	AVG	G	AB	R	H	2B	3B	HR	RBI	BB	SO	SB
1998	Cubs (AZL)	R	.265	50	181	39	48	7	5	6	29	23	58	16
1999	Lansing (Mid)	A	.269	124	509	75	137	17	4	13	68	39	121	22
2000	Daytona (FSL)	A	.268	132	523	75	140	30	7	18	84	38	120	7
2001	West Tenn (SL)	AA	.313	58	224	33	70	9	4	12	45	24	55	1
MINOR LEAGUE TOTALS			.275	364	1437	222	395	63	20	49	226	124	354	46

5. Bobby Hill, 2b

Born: April 3, 1978. **Ht.:** 5-10. **Wt.:** 180. **Bats:** B. **Throws:** R. **School:** University of Miami. **Career Transactions:** Signed by independent Newark (Atlantic), April 2000 . . . Selected by Cubs in second round of 2000 draft; signed Dec. 19, 2000.

After winning the College World Series with Miami in 1999, Hill turned down the White Sox as a second-round pick and spent a year in the independent Atlantic League. Signed by the Cubs for $1.425 million, Hill debuted in Double-A in 2001. The only downside was a slow-healing groin injury that limited him to 60 games and still bothered him in the Arizona Fall League. Hill is a quintessential leadoff man. He's a switch-hitter who hits for average and has decent pop from both sides, draws walks and steals bases. A college shortstop, he shows lots of range at second base and turns the double play well. Scouts questioned whether Hill had the arm to remain at shortstop, but he has plenty for second base. He struck out a bit more than desired for a No. 1 hitter in 2001. He hit .345 while playing at 85 percent in the AFL, and he might have been ready to take over at second base for Eric Young had he played a full season. Now Delino DeShields will likely keep second base warm while Hill gets at least a couple of months in Triple-A.

Year	Club (League)	Class	AVG	G	AB	R	H	2B	3B	HR	RBI	BB	SO	SB
2000	Newark (Atl)	IND	.326	132	481	109	157	22	9	13	82	101	57	81
2001	Cubs (AZL)	R	.222	3	9	1	2	0	0	0	1	2	3	1
	West Tenn (SL)	AA	.301	57	209	30	63	8	1	3	21	32	39	20
MINOR LEAGUE TOTALS			.298	60	218	31	65	8	1	3	22	34	42	21

6. Carlos Zambrano, rhp

Born: June 1, 1981. **Ht.:** 6-4. **Wt.:** 220. **Bats:** L. **Throws:** R. **Career Transactions:** Signed out of Venezuela by Cubs, July 12, 1997.

The Cubs called up Zambrano, another precocious Latin American pitcher, the day before they promoted Juan Cruz. Zambrano struggled in one start against the Brewers, returned to Triple-A and resurfaced as a reliever in September. He reached Triple-A at 18 in 2000 and moved from the rotation to the bullpen, then reversed course last year. Zambrano has a mid-90s fastball that has gone as high as 99 and maintains its velocity for nine innings. He likes to vary his arm angle with his fastball, giving batters two different looks and achieving plenty of sink when he lowers his slot. When it's on, his slider gives him two power pitches. Lowering his arm angle gives Zambrano problems, because it flattens out his slider and costs him command. Both his slider and control need more consistency. He must refine his changeup to give him a better weapon against lefthanders. The Cubs believe Zambrano either can be a power starter or a closer, though they have yet to determine what his role will be. He'll compete for a big league job in spring training.

Year	Club (League)	Class	W	L	ERA	G	GS	CG	SV	IP	H	R	ER	BB	SO
1998	Cubs (AZL)	R	0	1	3.15	14	2	0	1	40	39	17	14	25	36
1999	Lansing (Mid)	A	13	7	4.17	27	24	2	0	153	150	87	71	62	98

Year	Club (League)	Class	W	L	ERA	G	GS	CG	SV	IP	H	R	ER	BB	SO
2000	West Tenn (SL)	AA	3	1	1.34	9	9	0	0	60	39	14	9	21	43
	Iowa (PCL)	AAA	2	5	3.97	34	0	0	6	57	54	30	25	40	46
2001	Iowa (PCL)	AAA	10	5	3.88	26	25	1	0	151	124	73	65	68	155
	Chicago (NL)	MAJ	1	2	15.26	6	1	0	0	8	11	13	13	8	4
MAJOR LEAGUE TOTALS			1	2	15.26	6	1	0	0	8	11	13	13	8	4
MINOR LEAGUE TOTALS			28	19	3.59	110	60	3	7	461	406	221	184	216	378

7. Nic Jackson, of

Born: Sept. 25, 1979. **Ht.:** 6-3. **Wt.:** 205. **Bats:** L. **Throws:** R. **School:** University of Richmond. **Career Transactions:** Selected by Cubs in third round of 2000 draft; signed June 20, 2000.

Jackson slid in the 2000 draft because a ligament problem in the middle finger of his right hand cost him half the college season. The Cubs had an abundance of outfielders at low Class A Lansing in 2001, so they skipped Jackson to high Class A Daytona. Managers named him the Florida State League's most exciting player, and he led the league in hits. Jackson is an athletic outfielder in the mold of former Spiders product Brian Jordan. Daytona batting coach Richie Zisk showed him how to hit with backspin, and Jackson responded by driving balls all over the park. He has a quick bat and hits with authority against lefthanders. He runs well and could play center field, though he projects as a big league right fielder. Jackson's worst tool is his arm, which is average. He'll need to tighten his strike zone against more experienced pitchers. About two seasons away from the majors, Jackson is destined for Double-A in 2002. Corey Patterson and Sammy Sosa have two outfield spots nailed down for the long term in Chicago, so Jackson will eventually have to compete with David Kelton for left field if Kelton can't handle third base.

Year	Club (League)	Class	AVG	G	AB	R	H	2B	3B	HR	RBI	BB	SO	SB
2000	Eugene (NWL)	A	.255	74	294	39	75	12	7	6	47	22	64	25
2001	Daytona (FSL)	A	.296	131	503	87	149	30	6	19	85	39	96	24
MINOR LEAGUE TOTALS			.281	205	797	126	224	42	13	25	132	61	160	49

8. Ben Christensen, rhp

Born: Feb. 7, 1978. **Ht.:** 6-4. **Wt.:** 205. **Bats:** R. **Throws:** R. **School:** Wichita State University. **Career Transactions:** Selected by Cubs in first round (26th overall) of 1999 draft; signed June 25, 1999.

Christensen was one of the better arms in the 1999 draft, though he lasted until 26th overall after an incident in his junior season at Wichita State. He was suspended for throwing a pitch at Evansville's Anthony Molina and striking him in the eye while warming up. Christensen's ascent through the minors was progressing rapidly and probably would have taken him to the majors by now if not for shoulder problems. His 2000 season ended in early July because of tendinitis, and he made just three starts last year before needing surgery to tighten his capsule and repair some fraying. When healthy, Christensen shows command of four pitches. His two best are his 90-94 mph sinker and his slider. He has the long, loose body scouts like in a pitcher. But clearly his health has been the biggest cause for concern to this point. He has pitched just 176 innings in three years as pro and has made just 32 starts. He could have used more innings to work on his curveball and changeup, which aren't in the same class as his sinker and slider. The good news is that Christensen didn't have major shoulder damage and should be ready to go by spring training. If he's 100 percent, he should begin to move quickly again and should start the season at Iowa.

Year	Club (League)	Class	W	L	ERA	G	GS	CG	SV	IP	H	R	ER	BB	SO
1999	Cubs (AZL)	R	0	1	3.00	3	3	0	0	9	8	3	3	5	10
	Eugene (NWL)	A	0	2	5.91	5	5	0	0	21	21	14	14	14	21
	Daytona (FSL)	A	1	3	6.35	4	4	0	0	23	25	16	16	11	18
2000	Daytona (FSL)	A	4	2	2.10	10	10	0	0	64	43	18	15	15	63
	West Tenn (SL)	AA	3	1	2.76	7	7	0	0	42	36	18	13	15	42
2001	West Tenn (SL)	AA	2	1	6.48	3	3	0	0	17	20	12	12	9	9
MINOR LEAGUE TOTALS			10	10	3.73	32	32	1	0	176	153	81	73	69	163

9. Scott Chiasson, rhp

Born: Aug. 14, 1977. **Ht.:** 6-3. **Wt.:** 200. **Bats:** R. **Throws:** R. **School:** Eastern Connecticut State College. **Career Transactions:** Selected by Royals in fifth round of 1998 draft; signed June 2, 1998 . . . Traded by Royals to Athletics, June 10, 1999, completing trade in which Athletics sent RHP Jay Witasick to Royals for a player to be named and cash (March 30, 1999) . . . Selected by Cubs from Athletics in Rule 5 major league draft, Dec. 11, 2000.

The Athletics traded Jay Witasick for Chiasson in 1999. The Cubs plucked him with the No. 1 pick in the major league Rule 5 draft at the 2000 Winter Meetings, then dealt third baseman Eric Hinske to Oakland last spring to keep Chiasson. Southern League managers named Chiasson the best relief prospect in the league. West Tenn pitching coach Alan Dunn made adjustments to Chiasson's mechanics. Combined with a move from starting to relieving, his fastball went from 90-94 mph to 95-97. Chiasson uses a hard slider and has added a splitter. He pitches on a good downhill plane. Chiasson's slider is an effective pitch, but sometimes it flattens out when he drops his arm angle. He hasn't developed much of a changeup, though that isn't as crucial now that he's in the bullpen. Pitching well in six September appearances did Chiasson a lot of good in his bid to open 2002 with the Cubs. He'll compete for a middle-relief role in spring training.

Year	Club (League)	Class	W	L	ERA	G	GS	CG	SV	IP	H	R	ER	BB	SO
1998	Royals (GCL)	R	2	0	4.81	13	0	0	1	24	24	17	13	11	26
1999	S. Oregon (NWL)	A	2	2	5.22	15	13	0	0	69	80	52	40	39	51
2000	Visalia (Cal)	A	11	4	3.06	31	23	0	2	156	146	66	53	57	150
2001	West Tenn (SL)	AA	3	4	1.76	52	0	0	24	61	43	15	12	20	62
	Iowa (PCL)	AAA	0	0	2.25	11	0	0	10	12	11	3	3	0	14
	Chicago (NL)	MAJ	1	1	2.70	6	0	0	0	7	5	2	2	2	6
MAJOR LEAGUE TOTALS			1	1	2.70	6	0	0	0	7	5	2	2	2	6
MINOR LEAGUE TOTALS			18	10	3.38	122	36	0	37	323	304	153	121	127	303

10. Luis Montanez, ss

Born: Dec. 15, 1981. **Ht.:** 6-2. **Wt.:** 175. **Bats:** R. **Throws:** R. **School:** Coral Park HS, Miami. **Career Transactions:** Selected by Cubs in first round (third overall) of 2000 draft; signed June 6, 2000.

Though the Cubs struck a predraft deal worth $2.75 million with Montanez before taking him third overall in the 2000 draft, they say they valued his ability more than his price. Named MVP of the Rookie-level Arizona League in his pro debut, he got off to a rocky start at Lansing before adjusting as the season progressed. He hit .300 in the final month. Montanez has more offensive potential than the typical shortstop. He had 44 extra-base hits as a teenager in a full-season league, and he should add more power as he gets stronger and more experienced. He has solid hands and a strong arm at shortstop. Montanez isn't a bad runner, but he lacks the quickness associated with shortstops. His range is adequate, but some project him more as a second or third baseman. Many of his 32 errors last year came on errant throws, which can be addressed. He'll need to develop more plate discipline to develop offensively. The Cubs believe in Montanez as a shortstop, and think he'll be a good player if he hits as expected and plays average defense. He'll move up a notch to high Class A in 2002.

Year	Club (League)	Class	AVG	G	AB	R	H	2B	3B	HR	RBI	BB	SO	SB
2000	Cubs (AZL)	R	.344	50	192	50	66	16	7	2	37	25	42	11
	Lansing (Mid)	A	.138	8	29	2	4	1	0	0	0	3	6	0
2001	Lansing (Mid)	A	.255	124	499	70	127	33	6	5	54	34	121	20
MINOR LEAGUE TOTALS			.274	182	720	122	197	50	13	7	91	62	169	31

11. Steve Smyth, lhp

Born: June 3, 1978. **Ht.:** 6-0. **Wt.:** 195. **Bats:** B. **Throws:** L. **School:** University of Southern California. **Career Transactions:** Selected by Cubs in fourth round of 1999 draft; signed June 8, 1999.

The Cubs figured Smyth would make a decent lefthanded set-up man when they drafted him in 1999, and he didn't help his cause for the rotation by posting a 6.09 ERA in 15 starts in his pro debut. But in the last two years his velocity has jumped and he now projects as the lefty starter they've been looking for. He led the Southern League in ERA last year, and probably would have been called up when Chicago was desperate for starters in August if he hadn't had shoulder problems. He had surgery to tighten his capsule and clean up some fraying in his rotator cuff. Before he went down, Smyth was throwing 91-93 mph. Besides his fastball, he also has a slider, cutter and changeup, and all of his pitches are average or better. He's lagging a little behind in his rehabilitation and may not be ready to go at the start of spring training. As a result, the Cubs traded to get Jesus Sanchez from the Marlins in the offseason to make sure they have a southpaw starter. Once he's healthy, Smyth will go to Triple-A and shouldn't have any trouble elbowing Sanchez aside when he's ready.

Year	Club (League)	Class	W	L	ERA	G	GS	CG	SV	IP	H	R	ER	BB	SO
1999	Eugene (NWL)	A	1	1	4.38	5	5	0	0	25	29	17	12	7	14
	Lansing (Mid)	A	5	3	6.93	10	10	0	0	51	68	40	39	30	46
2000	Daytona (FSL)	A	8	8	3.25	24	23	1	0	138	134	62	50	57	100
2001	West Tenn (SL)	AA	9	3	2.54	18	18	3	0	120	110	38	34	40	93
MINOR LEAGUE TOTALS			23	15	3.64	57	56	4	0	334	341	157	135	134	253

12. Jae-Kuk Ryu, rhp

Born: May 30, 1983. **Ht.:** 6-3. **Wt.:** 175. **Bats:** R. **Throws:** R. **Career Transactions:** Signed out of Korea by Cubs, June 1, 2001.

Chicago struck prospect gold when it signed slugger Hee Seop Choi out of Korea for $1.2 million in March 1999, and eight months later they added potential backup catcher Yoon-Min Kweon from the same nation. Pacific Rim coordinator Leon Lee scored another blue-chipper last June when he signed Ryu for $1.6 million. Lee had followed him for a year and saw him strike out 20 in seven innings in one of his final high school games. The Cubs believe Ryu would have been a low first-round pick had he been eligible for the 2001 draft. Red tape prevented him from making his U.S. debut until August, when he allowed just one earned run in four Arizona League starts. He already throws 90-95 mph as a teenager, has a tight rotation on his curveball and the makings of a changeup. His breaking ball gets a little slurvy at times and his change still needs improvement, but all of the ingredients are there. Ryu's intelligence and feel for pitching are so advanced that a good spring will allow him to head to full-season ball before he turns 19.

Year	Club (League)	Class	W	L	ERA	G	GS	CG	SV	IP	H	R	ER	BB	SO
2001	Cubs (AZL)	R	1	0	0.61	4	3	0	0	15	11	2	1	5	20
MINOR LEAGUE TOTALS			1	0	0.61	4	3	0	0	15	11	2	1	5	20

13. J.J. Johnson, of

Born: Nov. 3, 1981. **Ht.:** 6-2. **Wt.:** 195. **Bats:** R. **Throws:** R. **School:** Greenbrier HS, Evans, Ga. **Career Transactions:** Selected by Cubs in sixth round of 2000 draft; signed June 10, 2000.

Vice president of player personnel Jim Hendry calls Johnson "a gut-feel guy" from the 2000 draft, over which Hendry presided as scouting director. Georgia area scout Sam Hughes loved Johnson's bat, so the Cubs took him in the sixth round. After a fine pro debut that year, he was even better in 2001, when he was named MVP and the No. 1 prospect in the short-season Northwest League, which he also led in RBIs. He has the stroke and bat speed to hit for power and average. Compared to Nic Jackson, Chicago's other top outfield prospect, Johnson has more power and less athleticism. But he's not a bad athlete, as his speed is average and he shows a strong arm in right field, where he moved last year after playing shortstop in high school and third base in the Arizona League. Though Johnson will need to tighten his strike zone as he moves up, he should be able to make the adjustments. He'll begin 2002 in low Class A.

Year	Club (League)	Class	AVG	G	AB	R	H	2B	3B	HR	RBI	BB	SO	SB
2000	Cubs (AZL)	R	.316	44	177	27	56	9	4	3	43	12	19	3
2001	Boise (NWL)	A	.317	70	287	55	91	15	5	7	61	20	50	18
MINOR LEAGUE TOTALS			.317	114	464	82	147	24	9	10	104	32	69	21

14. Angel Guzman, rhp

Born: Dec. 14, 1981. **Ht.:** 6-2. **Wt.:** 180. **Bats:** R. **Throws:** R. **Career Transactions:** Signed out of Venezuela by Royals, March 4, 1999 . . . Contract voided, June 24, 1999 . . . Signed by Cubs, Nov. 12, 1999.

The Cubs think they're sitting on two pitching prospects who will have breakthrough seasons in 2002: Guzman and Felix Sanchez, who ranks right behind him on this list. Guzman already made some noise in his U.S. debut last year, leading the Northwest League in wins and earning all-star recognition. He usually throws in the low 90s but can get his fastball up to 94-95 mph, something that should happen with more regularity as he gets stronger. Besides velocity, his fastball also has a lot of sink and life, and he throws it so effortlessly that it gets on hitters in a hurry. Guzman's curveball and changeup could give him three plus pitches by the time he reaches the majors. He has fine control and poise, having no trouble battling older hitters in the NWL and in Venezuela this winter. The Cubs believe all he'll need is continued health and more experience. He'll probably start 2002 in low Class A with a chance to earn a promotion before season's end.

Year	Club (League)	Class	W	L	ERA	G	GS	CG	SV	IP	H	R	ER	BB	SO
2000	La Pradera (VSL)	R	1	1	1.93	7	6	0	0	33	24	13	7	5	25
2001	Boise (NWL)	A	9	1	2.23	14	14	0	0	77	68	27	19	19	63
MINOR LEAGUE TOTALS			10	2	2.14	21	20	0	0	109	92	40	26	24	88

15. Felix Sanchez, lhp

Born: Aug. 3, 1982. **Ht.:** 6-3. **Wt.:** 165. **Bats:** L. **Throws:** L. **Career Transactions:** Signed out of Dominican Republic by Cubs, Sept. 15, 1998.

Sanchez spent his first two years as pro in the Rookie-level Dominican Summer League, and he didn't overwhelm Arizona League hitters when he made his U.S. debut last summer. But he looked tremendous after getting promoted to the Northwest League in August. His fastball reaches 95-96 mph, exceptional velocity for a lefthander, and he should throw harder as he fills out his 6-foot-3 frame. He also has a hard slider and is working on a changeup. He's not quite as advanced as Angel Guzman, as his secondary pitches and command need more refinement. But he could join him in Lansing this year and has the raw ability to move quickly through the system.

Year	Club (League)	Class	W	L	ERA	G	GS	CG	SV	IP	H	R	ER	BB	SO
1999	Cubs (DSL)	R	1	3	3.28	7	7	0	0	25	27	18	9	9	27
2000	Cubs (DSL)	R	4	2	3.15	13	13	0	0	54	45	26	19	15	61
2001	Cubs (AZL)	R	2	5	4.01	12	9	0	0	61	57	38	27	22	55
	Boise (NWL)	A	2	0	1.56	3	3	0	0	17	11	4	3	10	16
MINOR LEAGUE TOTALS			9	10	3.32	35	32	0	0	157	140	86	58	56	159

16. Jose Cueto, rhp

Born: Sept. 13, 1978. **Ht.:** 6-2. **Wt.:** 175. **Bats:** R. **Throws:** R. **Career Transactions:** Signed out of Dominican Republic by Rangers, April 20, 1996 . . . Released by Rangers, Jan. 8, 1997 . . . Signed by Cubs, Dec. 16, 1997.

Signed by the Rangers as an outfielder in 1996, Cueto was released after one season in the Dominican Summer League and spent a year out of baseball. The Cubs gave him a second chance as a pitcher, though he made little progress in his first three years in the organization. Cueto began 2001 in the Lansing bullpen and got knocked around in relief until a spot opened in the rotation in mid-May. He really hit his stride as a full-time starter, advancing two levels to Double-A by the end of the year. Cueto can hit 94-95 mph with his fastball, which may be more effective when he throws it in the low 90s and achieves more sink. He likes to pound hitters inside with his fastball, then go outside with his slider, which some scouts say is his best pitch. His changeup still requires more work, as does his command. Chicago still hasn't settled on his long-term role, but he'll return to Double-A as a starter in 2002.

Year	Club (League)	Class	AVG	G	AB	R	H	2B	3B	HR	RBI	BB	SO	SB
1996	Rangers (DSL)	R	.263	52	133	24	35	9	1	5	23	10	43	3
1997						Did Not Play								
MINOR LEAGUE TOTALS			.263	52	133	24	35	9	1	5	23	10	43	3

Year	Club (League)	Class	W	L	ERA	G	GS	CG	SV	IP	H	R	ER	BB	SO
1998	Cubs (DSL)	R	2	4	5.60	17	7	0	2	53	64	41	33	24	41
1999	Cubs (AZL)	R	3	4	2.86	11	9	0	0	57	49	32	18	22	66
	Eugene (NWL)	A	0	2	4.50	4	4	0	0	24	26	13	12	5	21
2000	Lansing (Mid)	A	0	4	5.74	16	1	0	0	27	26	19	17	25	35
	Eugene (NWL)	A	2	5	5.24	13	7	0	1	45	43	27	26	24	51
2001	Lansing (Mid)	A	4	4	3.79	22	14	2	0	95	71	50	40	44	105
	Daytona (FSL)	A	1	2	3.03	6	6	0	0	39	31	19	13	13	41
	West Tenn (SL)	AA	0	1	8.68	2	2	0	0	9	10	9	9	6	10
MINOR LEAGUE TOTALS			12	26	4.34	91	50	2	3	348	320	210	168	163	370

17. Ronny Cedeno, ss

Born: Feb. 2, 1983. **Ht.:** 6-0. **Wt.:** 170. **Bats:** R. **Throws:** R. **Career Transactions:** Signed out of Venezuela by Cubs, Aug. 27, 1999.

When the 2001 regular season ended, Cedeno had finished second in the Arizona

League batting race at .350. But when SportsTicker reviewed all of its statistics before declaring them official, it discovered that Cedeno actually had won the batting title. The Cubs thought Cedeno was special when they signed him out of Venezuela, likening him to a second-round pick, and they appear to be right. He obviously can hit for average and he also has good power for a middle infielder, not to mention above-average speed. He has plus tools on defense as well, as both his range and arm are assets. Cedeno just needs to add polish to his game. He'll have to control the strike zone better, improve his bases-tealing skills (he was caught 12 times in 29 attempts last year) and get more consistent defensively (his 22 errors tied for the AZL lead). He's ready for low Class A, where he might see some time at second base if 2001 third-round pick Ryan Theriot is assigned to Lansing as well.

Year	Club (League)	Class	AVG	G	AB	R	H	2B	3B	HR	RBI	BB	SO	SB
2000	La Pradera (VSL)	R	.287	51	167	35	48	8	3	3	14	19	37	13
2001	Lansing (Mid)	A	.196	17	56	9	11	4	1	1	2	2	18	0
	Cubs (AZL)	R	.350	52	206	36	72	13	4	1	17	13	32	17
MINOR LEAGUE TOTALS			.305	120	429	80	131	25	8	5	33	34	87	30

18. Todd Wellemeyer, rhp

Born: Aug. 30, 1978. **Ht.:** 6-3. **Wt.:** 195. **Bats:** R. **Throws:** R. **School:** Bellarmine (Ky.) University. **Career Transactions:** Selected by Cubs in fourth round of 2000 draft; signed June 10, 2000.

Wellemeyer received virtually no interest from big-time schools or major league organizations when he graduated from Louisville's Eastern High in 1997, so he planned on attending Kentucky as a full-time student. Then Bellarmine University, a local NAIA school, offered him a chance. Wellemeyer continue to fly under the radar of scouts until the summer of 1999, when he made the Coastal Plain League as an alternate, got to pitch and showed plenty of fastball. The Cubs expected Wellemeyer to struggle initially as a pro because of his small college background, and he did just that at the outset of 2001. He was working too much on his offspeed stuff and his fastball suffered, but he adjusted his approach and won his last 10 decisions. He has the tall, lanky body and loose arm that scouts love. Wellemeyer's 90-94 mph fastball explodes on hitters, and his changeup has so much life that many Midwest League opponents thought it was a splitter. His slider lags behind his other two pitches for now, though it flattened out much less often in the second half of 2001. He's still learning how to pitch and to throw strikes more consistently, but there's no question the package is there. He'll move up to high Class A this year.

Year	Club (League)	Class	W	L	ERA	G	GS	CG	SV	IP	H	R	ER	BB	SO
2000	Eugene (NWL)	A	4	4	3.67	15	15	0	0	76	62	35	31	33	85
2001	Lansing (Mid)	A	13	9	4.16	27	27	1	0	147	165	85	68	74	167
MINOR LEAGUE TOTALS			17	13	4.00	42	42	1	0	223	227	120	99	107	252

19. Frank Beltran, rhp

Born: July 25, 1980. **Ht.:** 6-5. **Wt.:** 220. **Bats:** R. **Throws:** R. **Career Transactions:** Signed out of Dominican Republic by Cubs, Nov. 15, 1996.

Beltran was the biggest surprise among the additions when Chicago filled out its 40-man roster in November. In his first four years in the organization, he surfaced in full-season ball for just 16 games, posting a 9.68 ERA. But when he was forced to sink or swim in high Class A in 2001, he struggled for six weeks and then survived. He went 4-1, 2.08 over a six-start span before he was hit by a bat and fractured a finger in June. Beltran missed six weeks and wasn't as dominant when he returned, but had shown enough to earn the Cubs' faith. His biggest assets are his intimidating size and his fastball, which hits 95 mph every time he takes the mound. His slider has its moments, though his changeup and control still have a ways to go. Chicago envisions him as a future set-up man or closer but will use him as a starter this year in Double-A to get him innings.

Year	Club (League)	Class	W	L	ERA	G	GS	CG	SV	IP	H	R	ER	BB	SO
1997	Cubs (AZL)	R	0	1	3.42	16	0	0	1	24	27	18	9	8	17
1998	Cubs (AZL)	R	1	1	5.55	12	5	0	0	36	49	23	22	14	26
1999	Cubs (AZL)	R	0	1	0.00	7	0	0	2	11	5	3	0	1	8
	Eugene (NWL)	A	0	2	8.36	16	0	0	0	28	41	32	26	14	28
2000	Lansing (Mid)	A	1	1	9.68	16	0	0	0	18	24	22	19	19	16
	Eugene (NWL)	A	2	2	2.68	25	0	0	8	44	28	16	13	20	52
2001	Daytona (FSL)	A	6	9	5.00	21	18	0	0	95	93	62	53	40	72
MINOR LEAGUE TOTALS			10	17	5.02	113	23	0	11	255	267	176	142	116	219

20. Aaron Krawiec, lhp

Born: March 17, 1979. **Ht.:** 6-6. **Wt.:** 210. **Bats:** L. **Throws:** L. **School:** Villanova University. **Career Transactions:** Selected by Cubs in third round of 2000 draft; signed June 19, 2000.

Outside of Felix Sanchez, Krawiec has the best arm among lefthanders in the system. What he doesn't have is consistent mechanics, which is why he went 12-10, 5.80 in three seasons at Villanova and had an up-and-down first full pro season in low Class A. Krawiec gets a lot of sink on his fastball, which usually arrives at the plate in the low 90s and gets as quick as 94 mph. His curveball gives him a second plus pitch and he also throws a change-up. At 6-foot-6, he throws his pitches on a tough downward plane. He offered a glimmer of his potential last April 29 against South Bend, when he worked eight innings and allowed two hits and no walks while striking out 17. Krawiec had five double-digit strikeout games in 2001, but too often he couldn't get his delivery in sync to throw enough strikes. He kept falling behind in the count, and while he didn't surrender an abundance of walks, he'd lay pitches over the plate. Midwest League hitters batted .297 against him, far better than his stuff should warrant. Krawiec will try to iron everything out this year in high Class A.

Year	Club (League)	Class	W	L	ERA	G	GS	CG	SV	IP	H	R	ER	BB	SO
2000	Eugene (NWL)	A	6	4	2.54	14	14	0	0	78	59	28	22	26	99
2001	Lansing (Mid)	A	7	11	4.58	27	26	1	0	153	183	108	78	51	170
MINOR LEAGUE TOTALS			13	15	3.89	41	40	1	0	231	242	136	100	77	269

21. Dontrelle Willis, lhp

Born: Jan. 12, 1982. **Ht.:** 6-4. **Wt.:** 200. **Bats:** L. **Throws:** L. **School:** Encinal HS, Alameda, Calif. **Career Transactions:** Selected by Cubs in eighth round of 2000 draft; signed July 6, 2000.

While the Cubs are looking for lefthanders for their big league rotation, they had no shortage of southpaw starters last year at short-season Boise, which had the best regular-season record in the Northwest League. Felix Sanchez came up at the end of the season, while Willis, Carmen Pignatiello and Adam Wynegar went a combined 19-7. Willis, a NWL all-star who led the league in innings, is the best prospect of the latter group. His curveball is his top pitch right now, and he already has an average fastball at 89-91 mph. Because he's big, lean and athletic, he projects to add velocity, which will give him a second plus pitch. While he's still working on his changeup, he already has command and an understanding of the importance of pitching aside, both well beyond his years. Willis will go to Lansing this year, where he could be part of a prospect-laden rotation with Jae-Kuk Ryu, Angel Guzman, Sanchez and possibly Sergio Mitre.

Year	Club (League)	Class	W	L	ERA	G	GS	CG	SV	IP	H	R	ER	BB	SO
2000	Cubs (AZL)	R	3	1	3.86	9	1	0	0	28	26	15	12	8	22
2001	Boise (NWL)	A	8	2	2.98	15	15	0	0	94	76	36	31	19	77
MINOR LEAGUE TOTALS			11	3	3.17	24	16	0	0	122	102	51	43	27	99

22. Ryan Jorgensen, c

Born: May 4, 1979. **Ht.:** 6-2. **Wt.:** 195. **Bats:** R. **Throws:** R. **School:** Louisiana State University. **Career Transactions:** Selected by Cubs in seventh round of 2000 draft; signed June 22, 2000.

The Cubs haven't signed an amateur catcher who developed into an all-star since drafting Joe Girardi in the fifth round in June 1986. At this point, they'd be happy if they could just come up with a regular. Their best hope now is Jorgensen, who was a backup catcher to Brad Cresse (now a top Diamondbacks prospect) on Louisiana State's 2000 College World Series champions. Jorgensen has lived up to his reputation as an outstanding catch-and-throw guy. In 2001, his first full season as a pro, managers rated him the best defensive catcher in the Florida State League and he threw out a combined 41 percent of basestealers at two stops. As a bonus, Jorgensen hit better than anticipated until his midseason promotion to Double-A, where he missed a month after straining his back in his third game. He still must prove he can hit in the upper minors, and adding some strength and making more contact definitely would help. Jorgensen batted just .225 in the Arizona Fall League, so Chicago may want to play it safe and let him begin this year back in the FSL.

Year	Club (League)	Class	AVG	G	AB	R	H	2B	3B	HR	RBI	BB	SO	SB
2000	Eugene (NWL)	A	.300	41	130	17	39	10	2	1	23	17	27	2
2001	Daytona (FSL)	A	.282	54	188	24	53	12	1	8	29	23	39	1
	West Tenn (SL)	AA	.119	32	109	8	13	4	0	2	7	11	38	0
MINOR LEAGUE TOTALS			.246	127	427	49	105	26	3	11	59	51	104	3

23. Andy Sisco, lhp

Born: Jan. 13, 1983. **Ht.:** 6-8. **Wt.:** 260. **Bats:** L. **Throws:** L. **School:** Eastlake HS, Sammamish, Wash. **Career Transactions:** Selected by Cubs in second round of 2001 draft, signed June 26, 2001.

The Cubs have used their second-round picks well, landing infielders of the future David Kelton (1998) and Bobby Hill (2000). They may have hit on another second-rounder last year when they signed Sisco, who's about as intimidating as a lefthander can get, for $1 million. He already stands 6-foot-8 and 260 pounds, plus he has a consistent 90-93 mph fastball that topped out at 96 in instructional league. If he can smooth out his mechanics, not the easiest task for a pitcher his size, he might approach triple digits in the future. Sisco impressed Arizona League managers with his splitter, which serves as his changeup. Among his three pitches, his slider needs the most work. He won't be a pitcher who blows through the minors in a hurry, but Sisco's ceiling is awfully high.

Year	Club (League)	Class	W	L	ERA	G	GS	CG	SV	IP	H	R	ER	BB	SO
2001	Cubs (AZL)	R	1	0	5.24	10	7	0	0	34	36	28	20	10	31
MINOR LEAGUE TOTALS			1	0	5.24	10	7	0	0	34	36	28	20	10	31

24. Ryan Theriot, ss

Born: Dec. 7, 1979. **Ht.:** 5-10. **Wt.:** 175. **Bats:** R. **Throws:** R. **School:** Louisiana State University. **Career Transactions:** Selected by Cubs in third round of 2001 draft, signed July 24, 2001.

Theriot was Ryan Jorgensen's teammate on Louisiana State's 2000 club, singling to lead off the bottom of the ninth and coming around with the title-winning run in the College World Series championship game. The Cubs had 2000 first-round pick Luis Montanez playing shortstop at Lansing and Theriot had played for college baseball's premier program, so the Cubs sent him to high Class A to make his pro debut after taking him in the third round last June. Theriot had been idle for two months and struggled offensively. There's still some hope for his offense, because he batted .299 with wood bats in the Cape Cod League in 2000 and he did walk more than he struck out in the Florida State League. But he'll have to get stronger if he's going to bat near the top of a batting order. He also may start switch-hitting in 2002. Regardless, defense will be Theriot's ticket to the majors. His instincts, arm and range all grade out as above average. Montanez is expected to move up to the FSL this year, so Theriot may go to Lansing to regroup.

Year	Club (League)	Class	AVG	G	AB	R	H	2B	3B	HR	RBI	BB	SO	SB
2001	Daytona (FSL)	A	.204	30	103	20	21	5	0	0	9	21	17	2
MINOR LEAGUE TOTALS			.204	30	103	20	21	5	0	0	9	21	17	2

25. Courtney Duncan, rhp

Born: Oct. 9, 1974. **Ht.:** 6-0. **Wt.:** 185. **Bats:** L. **Throws:** R. **School:** Grambling State University. **Career Transactions:** Selected by Cubs in 20th round of 1996 draft; signed June 20, 1996.

Duncan hit the wall as a starter in Double-A in 1998 but regrouped and made it to the majors last year as a reliever. He showed his resolve the previous offseason, when he headed to Puerto Rico for winter ball shortly after his brother murdered his wife (Courtney's sister-in-law) and then killed himself. Duncan led the league in saves and posted a 1.05 ERA, a springboard to making the Cubs out of spring training. He pitched well until a back strain and shoulder tendinitis weakened him during the summer. Before he ran out of gas, Duncan was throwing 90-94 mph consistently. He uses more pitches than most relievers, also employing a slider, cutter and changeup. He'll have to trust his stuff and throw more strikes. He also needs to find a way to battle big league lefthanders more effectively. Chicago lost free agents Todd Van Poppel and David Weathers this winter, so Duncan should play a prominent role in the big league bullpen.

Year	Club (League)	Class	W	L	ERA	G	GS	CG	SV	IP	H	R	ER	BB	SO
1996	Williamsport (NY-P)	A	11	1	2.19	15	15	1	0	90	58	28	22	34	91
1997	Daytona (FSL)	A	8	4	1.63	19	19	1	0	122	90	35	22	35	120
	Orlando (SL)	AA	2	2	3.40	8	8	0	0	45	37	28	17	29	45
1998	West Tenn (SL)	AA	7	9	4.26	29	29	0	0	163	141	89	77	108	157
1999	Daytona (FSL)	A	4	5	5.54	15	11	1	1	65	70	60	40	34	48
	West Tenn (SL)	AA	1	7	7.13	11	8	0	0	42	44	42	33	42	42
2000	West Tenn (SL)	AA	5	4	3.07	61	0	0	25	73	57	32	25	33	72
2001	Iowa (PCL)	AAA	1	0	3.24	7	0	0	0	8	7	3	3	5	15
	Chicago (NL)	MAJ	3	3	5.06	36	0	0	0	43	42	24	24	25	49
MAJOR LEAGUE TOTALS			3	3	5.06	36	0	0	0	43	42	24	24	25	49
MINOR LEAGUE TOTALS			39	32	3.54	165	90	3	26	608	504	317	239	320	590

26. John Webb, rhp

Born: May 23, 1979. **Ht.:** 6-3. **Wt.:** 190. **Bats:** R. **Throws:** R. **School:** Manatee (Fla.) CC. **Career Transactions:** Selected by Cubs in 19th round of 1999 draft; signed June 16, 1999.

Two of the Cubs' better pitching prospects succumbed to Tommy John surgery in 2001. Webb, who emerged in the shadows of Juan Cruz at Lansing the year before, missed all of April, made five appearances in May and then was done for the season. Fellow righthander Carlos Urrutia, who had a live arm but hadn't gotten past Rookie ball, didn't even take the mound last year. Ironically, Webb had very little mileage on his arm after playing mostly shortstop and occasionally working out of the bullpen as an amateur. Before going down, he had three effective pitches: a 90-92 mph sinker, a plus slider and a changeup. He kept the ball down in the strike zone and didn't hurt himself with walks, either. Chicago hopes he'll be back on the mound by June at the latest.

Year	Club (League)	Class	W	L	ERA	G	GS	CG	SV	IP	H	R	ER	BB	SO
1999	Cubs (AZL)	R	0	0	3.58	18	0	0	3	33	33	20	13	8	39
	Eugene (NWL)	A	1	0	0.00	2	0	0	1	4	1	0	0	1	3
2000	Lansing (Mid)	A	7	6	2.47	21	21	1	0	135	125	53	37	40	108
	Daytona (FSL)	A	1	1	4.76	4	2	0	1	17	17	11	9	3	18
MINOR LEAGUE TOTALS			9	7	2.82	45	23	1	5	188	176	84	59	52	168

27. Ryan Gripp, 3b

Born: April 20, 1978. **Ht.:** 6-1. **Wt.:** 210. **Bats:** R. **Throws:** R. **School:** Creighton University. **Career Transactions:** Selected by Cubs in third round of 1999 draft; signed June 9, 1999.

Gripp's stock took a huge hit in 2001. After winning the Midwest League batting title and leading all minor league third basemen with a .333 average the year before, he continued to hit for average and gap power in the Florida State League. But when he was promoted to Double-A to take over for an injured David Kelton, Gripp batted just .227. His plate discipline wasn't up to previous standards at either level last year, and he began pulling off of pitches in an attempt to hit for more power. His arm, range and mobility were all questionable to begin with, and he didn't play well defensively last year, making 31 errors. If he can stick at third base, he has a shot as a potential .280 hitter with 35 doubles and 15-20 homers. If he has to move to first base, that production won't be enough to unseat Hee Seop Choi. Headed back to Double-A, Gripp caught a break when FSL home run leader Jim Deschaine was traded to the Blue Jays in the offseason. Deschaine would have taken some playing time at third base, necessitating that Gripp play some first base, but now Gripp should have the hot corner to himself.

Year	Club (League)	Class	AVG	G	AB	R	H	2B	3B	HR	RBI	BB	SO	SB
1999	Eugene (NWL)	A	.308	73	266	40	82	18	1	12	48	27	65	2
2000	Lansing (Mid)	A	.333	135	498	87	166	36	0	20	92	68	86	4
2001	Daytona (FSL)	A	.295	67	241	35	71	19	0	5	49	27	57	6
	West Tenn (SL)	AA	.227	68	255	31	58	19	0	8	45	25	60	2
MINOR LEAGUE TOTALS			.299	343	1260	193	377	92	1	45	234	147	268	14

28. Mike Wuertz, rhp

Born: Dec. 15, 1978. **Ht.:** 6-3. **Wt.:** 180. **Bats:** R. **Throws:** R. **School:** Austin (Minn.) HS. **Career Transactions:** Selected by Cubs in 11th round of 1997 draft; signed Aug. 18, 1997.

Wuertz' won-loss record in Double-A was deceiving. His 27 outings included 15 quality starts—in which he went 4-0 with 11 no-decisions. However, a lack of run support wasn't the only reason for his disappointing season. His velocity was down for much of 2001, as he worked at 88-90 mph after throwing 90-93 while helping Daytona win the Florida State League championship the year before. His slider is a solid second pitch, but he needs to get the juice back on his fastball. He also must keep improving his changeup and his location within the strike zone. The Cubs praise his competitive nature and he's extremely durable, having made 97 straight starts in four years as a pro. Wuertz didn't make the 40-man roster this winter, and now projects as a fourth or fifth starter at best unless his fastball returns. He'll probably move up to Triple-A to start 2002.

Year	Club (League)	Class	W	L	ERA	G	GS	CG	SV	IP	H	R	ER	BB	SO
1998	Williamsport (NY-P)	A	7	5	3.44	14	14	1	0	86	79	36	33	19	59
1999	Lansing (Mid)	A	11	12	4.80	28	28	1	0	161	191	104	86	44	127
2000	Daytona (FSL)	A	12	7	3.78	28	28	3	0	171	166	79	72	64	142
2001	West Tenn (SL)	AA	4	9	3.99	27	27	1	0	160	160	80	71	58	135
MINOR LEAGUE TOTALS			34	33	4.07	97	97	6	0	579	596	299	262	185	463

29. Mike Meyers, rhp

Born: Oct. 18, 1977 **Ht.:** 6-2. **Wt.:** 210. **Bats:** R. **Throws:** R. **School:** Black Hawk (Ill.) JC. **Career Transactions:** Selected by Cubs in 26th round of 1997 draft; signed June 14, 1997.

Finesse righthanders like Meyers have to prove themselves at every step of the minors. Now that he's done that, the Cubs have accumulated so much pitching talent that he may not be able to find a role in Chicago. After succeeding in Triple-A last year, he has an outside shot at making the big league team but isn't in the running for the open spot in the rotation. Meyers led the minors with a 1.73 ERA in 1999, when he also pitched for Canada in the Pan American Games. His fastball operates at 88-90 mph, though it's effective enough because it has life and he's not afraid to pitch inside. His curveball is his best pitch and his changeup is average. Meyers has allowed just 37 homers in 534 pro innings, but he'll need to be stingier with walks in the majors because his margin for error is small. His ceiling is as a fourth or fifth starter, and his greatest value to the Cubs could come as part of a trade.

Year	Club (League)	Class	W	L	ERA	G	GS	CG	SV	IP	H	R	ER	BB	SO
1997	Cubs (AZL)	R	3	1	1.41	12	2	0	3	38	34	15	6	13	45
	Williamsport (NY-P)	A	0	0	0.00	1	1	0	0	4	3	0	0	1	2
1998	Rockford (Mid)	A	7	5	3.36	17	16	0	0	86	75	37	32	32	86
1999	Daytona (FSL)	A	10	3	1.93	19	17	2	0	107	68	30	23	40	122
	West Tenn (SL)	AA	4	0	1.09	5	5	0	0	33	21	5	4	10	51
2000	West Tenn (SL)	AA	5	2	2.44	9	9	3	0	59	41	18	16	26	51
	Iowa (PCL)	AAA	2	6	7.28	13	12	0	0	59	74	51	48	30	44
2001	Iowa (PCL)	AAA	7	4	3.23	25	25	0	0	148	129	58	53	64	124
MINOR LEAGUE TOTALS			38	21	3.07	101	87	5	3	534	445	214	182	216	525

30. Mike Mallory, of

Born: Dec. 8, 1980. **Ht.:** 6-4. **Wt.:** 220. **Bats:** R. **Throws:** R. **School:** Dinwiddie (Va.) HS. **Career Transactions:** Selected by Cubs in second round of 1999 draft; signed June 21, 1999.

Mallory has one of the best all-around packages of tools in the system but hasn't been able to do much with them yet. He has the body of a young Dave Winfield, oodles of raw power and speed, center-field range and a right-field arm. He also has a career average of .225 and has struck out almost five times as often as he has walked. He hasn't been able to do much against pro breaking balls and makes contact too infrequently. He is a high-percentage basestealer and the best defensive outfielder in that system, but that won't matter if Mallory can't hit. The Cubs like his makeup and dream that he'll be another Torii Hunter, who didn't become a viable big league hitter until his ninth year as a pro. Mallory will get a stern test from the pitcher-friendly Florida State League this year.

Year	Club (League)	Class	AVG	G	AB	R	H	2B	3B	HR	RBI	BB	SO	SB
1999	Cubs (AZL)	R	.242	42	149	20	36	6	0	4	15	12	48	2
2000	Eugene (NWL)	A	.210	70	262	39	55	12	3	6	30	16	98	9
2001	Lansing (Mid)	A	.228	127	434	51	99	17	3	12	47	28	132	17
MINOR LEAGUE TOTALS			.225	239	845	110	190	35	6	22	92	56	278	28

CHICAGO
White Sox

TOP 30 PROSPECTS

1. Joe Borchard, of
2. Jon Rauch, rhp
3. Corwin Malone, lhp
4. Matt Guerrier, rhp
5. Joe Crede, 3b
6. Tim Hummel, 2b
7. Kris Honel, rhp
8. Miguel Olivo, c
9. Dennis Ulacia, lhp
10. Aaron Rowand, of
11. Edwin Almonte, rhp
12. Matt Ginter, rhp
13. Brian West, rhp
14. Casey Rogowski, 1b
15. Wyatt Allen, rhp
16. Jason Stumm, rhp
17. Arnie Munoz, lhp
18. Andy Gonzalez, ss
19. Kyle Kane, rhp
20. Mitch Wylie, rhp
21. Delvis Lantigua, rhp
22. Anthony Webster, of
23. Guillermo Reyes, ss
24. Gary Majewski, rhp
25. Humberto Quintero, c
26. Mario Valenzuela, of
27. Heath Phillips, lhp
28. Charlie Lisk, c
29. Brian Sager, rhp
30. Aaron Kirkland, rhp

By Phil Rogers

For the White Sox, 2001 was a disappointing season. But, hey, it could have been a lot worse (see 1997, 1995, 1984 . . .).

With expectations higher than they had been since the strike in 1994, Chicago went out and laid an egg last April. But with their nucleus intact and one of baseball's most productive farm systems creating intense competition for spots on the 25-man roster, the White Sox could take consolation that a turnaround is right around the corner.

They have lots of talent on the way to join a team that rebounded from a 14-29 start to finish four games over .500, giving the team consecutive winning seasons for the first time since 1993-94. It's hard to accurately forecast this roller-coaster franchise, but it has the making of a run similar to the five consecutive winning seasons in the early 1990s.

Few organizations have amassed as many intriguing pitching prospects as the White Sox. In going 83-79 last season, they received 117 starts and 51 wins from Mark Buehrle, Jon Garland, Dan Wright and six other 25-and-under pitchers, most of whom were rated among the organization's top prospects in the last two seasons.

There's hardly a void behind those arms.

Jon Rauch, the 6-foot-11 righthander who was Baseball America's 2000 Minor League Player of the Year, and 1999 first-round pick Jason Stumm missed almost all of last season after surgeries. But the depth of the farm system was demonstrated by the rise of unheralded prospects such as Corwin Malone, Matt Guerrier, Dennis Ulacia and Edwin Almonte.

Much has been written about Chicago's stockpiling of arms, but the Sox also have done a great job developing talent, not just identifying it. Minor league pitching coordinator Don Cooper and coaches Kirk Champion, Curt Hasler, Juan Nieves and J.R. Perdew, among others, keep talent flowing up the pipeline toward Comiskey Park.

Though the organization is pitching-heavy by design, its talent doesn't stop there. Outfielder Joe Borchard put up impressive numbers in his first full season and should be a rookie-of-the-year candidate when he arrives in Chicago, perhaps as early as April. Joe Crede and Tim Hummel are likely to become fixtures.

No one doubts owner Jerry Reinsdorf's commitment to player development. Few organizations have kept their scouting and minor league staffs together as long as the Sox, and it shows.

Organization Overview

General manager: Ken Williams. **Farm director:** Bob Fontaine. **Scouting director:** Doug Laumann.

2001 PERFORMANCE

Class	Team	League	W	L	Pct.	Finish*	Manager
Majors	Chicago	American	83	79	.512	6th (14)	Jerry Manuel
Triple-A	Charlotte Knights	International	67	77	.465	10th (14)	Nick Leyva
Double-A	Birmingham Barons	Southern	80	60	.571	t-2nd (10)	Nick Capra
High A	Winston-Salem Warthogs	Carolina	54	86	.386	8th (8)	Wally Backman
Low A	Kannapolis Intimidators	South Atlantic	76	63	.547	4th (16)	Razor Shines
Rookie	Bristol Sox	Appalachian	38	26	.594	2nd (10)	John Orton
Rookie	AZL White Sox	Arizona	23	33	.411	6th (7)	Jerry Hairston
OVERALL 2001 MINOR LEAGUE RECORD			338	345	.495	16th (30)	

*Finish in overall standings (No. of teams in league)

ORGANIZATION LEADERS

BATTING

*AVG	Aaron Rowand, Charlotte	.295
	Joe Borchard, Birmingham	.295
R	Joe Borchard, Birmingham	95
H	Tim Hummel, Birmingham	152
TB	Joe Borchard, Birmingham	262
2B	Three tied at	34
3B	Three tied at	7
HR	Joe Borchard, Birmingham	27
RBI	Joe Borchard, Birmingham	98
BB	**Eric Battersby**, Birmingham	94
SO	Darron Ingram, Birmingham	188
SB	Chad Durham, Winston-Salem	50

PITCHING

W	Matt Guerrier, Charlotte/Birmingham	18
L	Eric Fischer, Winston-Salem	13
	Dario Ferrand, Kannapolis	13
#ERA	Joe Valentine, Win.-Salem/Kannapolis	1.79
G	Arnaldo Munoz, Kannapolis	60
CG	Dennis Ulacia, Char./Birm./W-S/Kann.	5
SV	**Edwin Almonte**, Birmingham	36
IP	Dennis Ulacia, Char./Birm./W-S/Kann.	180
BB	Eduardo Lantigua, Birm./Win-.Salem	76
SO	Corwin Malone, Birm./W-S/Kannapolis	177

*Minimum 250 At-Bats #Minimum 75 Innings

TOP PROSPECTS OF THE DECADE

1992	Roberto Hernandez, rhp
1993	Jason Bere, rhp
1994	James Baldwin, rhp
1995	Scott Ruffcorn, rhp
1996	Chris Snopek, 3b/ss
1997	Mike Cameron, of
1998	Mike Caruso, ss
1999	Carlos Lee, 3b
2000	Kip Wells, rhp
2001	Jon Rauch, rhp

TOP DRAFT PICKS OF THE DECADE

1992	Eddie Pearson, 1b
1993	Scott Christman, lhp
1994	Mark Johnson, c
1995	Jeff Liefer, 3b
1996	*Bobby Seay, lhp
1997	Jason Dellaero, ss
1998	Kip Wells, rhp
1999	Jason Stumm, rhp
2000	Joe Borchard, rhp
2001	Kris Honel, rhp

*Did not sign.

Battersby

Almonte

BEST TOOLS

Best Hitter for Average	Tim Hummel
Best Power Hitter	Joe Borchard
Fastest Baserunner	Chris Amador
Best Fastball	Kyle Kane
Best Breaking Ball	Corwin Malone
Best Changeup	Edwin Almonte
Best Control	Aaron Kirkland
Best Defensive Catcher	Humberto Quintero
Best Defensive Infielder	Jason Dellaero
Best Infield Arm	Jason Dellaero
Best Defensive Outfielder	Aaron Rowand
Best Outfield Arm	Joe Borchard

PROJECTED 2005 LINEUP

Catcher	Miguel Olivo
First Base	Paul Konerko
Second Base	Tim Hummel
Third Base	Joe Crede
Shortstop	Jose Valentin
Left Field	Aaron Rowand
Center Field	Joe Borchard
Right Field	Magglio Ordonez
Designated Hitter	Frank Thomas
No. 1 Starter	Jon Rauch
No. 2 Starter	Mark Buehrle
No. 3 Starter	Corwin Malone
No. 4 Starter	Dan Wright
No. 5 Starter	Matt Guerrier
Closer	Keith Foulke

ALL-TIME LARGEST BONUSES

Joe Borchard, 2000	$5,300,000
Jason Stumm, 1999	$1,750,000
Kris Honel, 2001	$1,500,000
Kip Wells, 1998	$1,495,000
Matt Ginter, 1999	$1,275,000

DraftAnalysis

2001 Draft

Best Pro Debut: SS Andy Gonzalez (5) and OF Anthony Webster (15) were Rookie-level Arizona League all-stars. Gonzalez hit .323-5-30, while Webster batted .307-0-30. LHP Tim Bittner (10) led the Rookie-level Appalachian League in victories, going 6-1, 1.10 with 53 strikeouts in 49 innings.

Best Athlete: Recruited by Southeastern Conference schools to play tailback, Webster has speed and gap power. Gonzalez, a high school basketball player, is more refined because he has more baseball experience. Some teams liked Gonzalez as a pitcher, and he threw in the low 90s last spring.

Best Hitter: Gonzalez. At 6-foot-3, he might outgrow shortstop, yet he lacks the power of a third baseman. The White Sox believe he'll hit and be able to stay at short.

Best Raw Power: C Charlie Lisk (24) hit five balls out of Atlanta's Turner Field during a predraft workout. He was a backup plan in case Chicago couldn't sign C Jonathan Zeringue (3), and that's what happened when Zeringue went to Louisiana State.

Fastest Runner: Webster runs the 60-yard dash in 6.55 seconds. He's a 4.2-second runner from the left side to first, which should improve as he cuts down his stroke.

Best Defensive Player: Lisk is an agile receiver with a strong arm. 2B Andrew Salvo (22) is the best defensive infielder.

Best Fastball: RHP **Wyatt Allen** (1) threw 97 mph in the Cape Cod League in the summer of 2000 and generally works at 93-94 mph. Junior college RHP Andrew Fryson (8) has a

91-95 mph fastball with terrific life, while high school RHPs Kris Honel (1) and Brian Miller (20) can touch 94-95 mph.

Most Intriguing Background: 3B Josh Crede (48), the brother of third-base prospect Joe, was in a car accident in the winter of 2000-01 that left him in a coma. He's still recovering and was able to play again as a senior. The Sox drafted Crede to give him a boost and to enhance his chances of getting a college offer. 3B Tim Huson's (11) uncle Jeff is a former big league utilityman.

Allen

Closest To The Majors: Allen. The White Sox have made a habit of turning around pitchers who struggled in college, and Allen reduced his ERA from 6.30 last spring at Tennessee to 3.16 in Class A.

Best Late-Round Pick: Webster, Lisk and Miller. Miller was also a contingency pick, and Chicago found the money to sign him when it couldn't get OF Jay Mattox (4).

The One Who Got Away: Zeringue and Mattox are at LSU. Zeringue is a four-tool catcher whose only weakness is receiving. Mattox is an athlete with speed.

Assessment: The White Sox stocked up on power arms again and addressed a shortage of southpaws with LHPs Ryan Wing (2), Jim Bullard (9) and Bittner. Drafting Miller and Lisk in the late rounds paid off.

2000 Draft

OF Joe Borchard (1) hasn't given any indication he won't live up to his record $5.3 million bonus. Borchard and 2B/SS Tim Hummel (2) are two offensive-minded players who should be Chicago regulars by 2003. **Grade: B+**

1999 Draft

Of their four first-rounders, the White Sox hit on three with RHPs Matt Ginter, Brian West and Jason Stumm and saw only RHP Rob Purvis tail off. And the first-rounders aren't the highlight of a crop that included RHPs Jon Rauch (3), Danny Wright (2) and Matt Guerrier (10); LHPs Corwin Malone (9) and Luis Ulacia (8); and 1B Casey Rogowski (13). **Grade: A**

1998 Draft

LHP Mark Buehrle (38, draft-and-follow) has been a revelation, exceeding the solid contributions of both first-rounders, RHP Kip Wells and OF Aaron Rowand. Wells and RHP Josh Fogg (3) were traded this winter for Todd Ritchie. **Grade: B+**

1997 Draft

LHP Jim Parque and RHPs Rocky Biddle and Aaron Myette (now with Texas) all spent time in big league rotations last year. RHP Kyle Kane re-emerged in the minors, leaving SS Jason Dellaero and OF Brett Caradonna as the only busts among the six first-rounders. **Grade: B**

Note: Draft analysis prepared by Jim Callis. Numbers in parentheses indicate draft rounds.

. . . He's a good bet for 30-plus homers as a rookie, with the better question being whether it happens now or in 2003.

Borchard **Joe** of

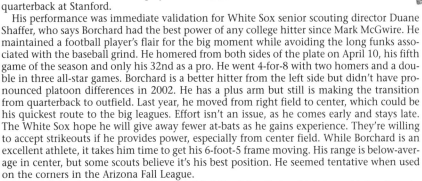

RON VESELY

Born: Nov. 25, 1978.
Ht.: 6-5. **Wt.:** 220.
Bats: B. **Throws:** R.
School: Stanford University.
Career Transactions: Selected by White Sox in first round (12th overall) of 2000 draft; signed Aug. 8, 2000.

There was no way Joe Borchard was going to be inconspicuous last season. The record $5.3 million bonus he got in 2000 blew his cover. But even if it hadn't, the switch-hitting Borchard would have stood out because of his tools and how well he used them in the first full season of baseball in his life. Despite being based in a pitcher's park, he led the Double-A Southern League in RBIs and finished second in homers and in the MVP voting. According to football scouting guru Mel Kiper, Borchard could have been one of the first players taken in the 2002 NFL draft had he continued to play quarterback at Stanford.

His performance was immediate validation for White Sox senior scouting director Duane Shaffer, who says Borchard had the best power of any college hitter since Mark McGwire. He maintained a football player's flair for the big moment while avoiding the long funks associated with the baseball grind. He homered from both sides of the plate on April 10, his fifth game of the season and only his 32nd as a pro. He went 4-for-8 with two homers and a double in three all-star games. Borchard is a better hitter from the left side but didn't have pronounced platoon differences in 2002. He has a plus arm but still is making the transition from quarterback to outfield. Last year, he moved from right field to center, which could be his quickest route to the big leagues. Effort isn't an issue, as he comes early and stays late. The White Sox hope he will give away fewer at-bats as he gains experience. They're willing to accept strikeouts if he provides power, especially from center field. While Borchard is an excellent athlete, it takes him time to get his 6-foot-5 frame moving. His range is below-average in center, but some scouts believe it's his best position. He seemed tentative when used on the corners in the Arizona Fall League.

Borchard should fit in well at the remodeled Comiskey Park, which turned into a launching pad after the fences were brought in. He's a good bet for 30-plus homers as a rookie, with the better question being whether it happens now or in 2003. Borchard's ability as a student will determine whether he can make better contact and get to more balls in the outfield, thus delivering on his all-star potential.

Year	Club (League)	Class	AVG	G	AB	R	H	2B	3B	HR	RBI	BB	SO	SB
2000	White Sox (AZL)	R	.414	7	29	3	12	4	0	0	8	4	4	0
	Winston-Salem (Car)	A	.288	14	52	7	15	3	0	2	7	6	9	0
	Birmingham (SL)	AA	.227	6	22	3	5	0	1	0	3	3	8	0
2001	Birmingham (SL)	AA	.295	133	515	95	152	27	1	27	98	67	158	5
MINOR LEAGUE TOTALS			.298	160	618	108	184	34	2	29	116	80	179	5

2. Jon Rauch, rhp

Born: Sept. 27, 1978. **Ht.:** 6-11. **Wt.:** 230. **Bats:** R. **Throws:** R. **School:** Morehead State University. **Career Transactions:** Selected by White Sox in third round of 1999 draft; signed June 9, 1999.

Shoulder problems cost Rauch, Baseball America's 2000 Minor League Player of the Year, a chance to establish himself with the White Sox last season. He made six starts with Triple-A Charlotte before having surgery to clean out his shoulder. Otherwise he may have made the same kind of leap as fellow 2000 U.S. Olympians Ben Sheets and Roy Oswalt. Rauch is an inch taller than Randy Johnson and has unusual command for such a tall pitcher. His mechanics are solid and he locates his pitches well. His fastball should return to the mid-90s. Rauch complements it with two above-average breaking pitches and has made progress with his changeup. His height gives him arm angles that are foreign to hitters. He's a good athlete who moves around well, but he figures to have more trouble with comebackers and bunts than other pitchers. He has yet to establish his durability. Rauch is viewed as a future No. 1 starter but could need at least one season in Triple-A, or perhaps even back in Double-A, before making the jump to Chicago. His health will be watched closely until he re-establishes himself.

Year	Club (League)	Class	W	L	ERA	G	GS	CG	SV	IP	H	R	ER	BB	SO
1999	Bristol (Appy)	R	4	4	4.45	14	9	0	2	57	65	44	28	16	66
	Winston-Salem (Car)	A	0	0	3.00	1	1	0	0	6	4	3	2	3	7
2000	Winston-Salem (Car)	A	11	3	2.86	18	18	1	0	110	102	49	35	33	124
	Birmingham (SL)	AA	5	1	2.25	8	8	2	0	56	36	18	14	16	63
2001	Charlotte (IL)	AAA	1	3	5.79	6	6	0	0	28	28	20	18	7	27
MINOR LEAGUE TOTALS			21	11	3.40	47	42	3	2	257	235	134	97	75	287

3. Corwin Malone, lhp

Born: July 3, 1980. **Ht.:** 6-3. **Wt.:** 200. **Bats:** R. **Throws:** L. **School:** Thomasville (Ala.) HS. **Career Transactions:** Selected by White Sox in ninth round of 1999 draft; signed June 7, 1999.

Everything came together in 2001 for the hard-working Malone, who planned to play linebacker at Alabama-Birmingham before the Sox drafted him. After relieving in the low minors, he soared when given the chance to start, beginning the year in the South Atlantic League and ending it with a victory in the Southern League playoffs. While Malone has great tools, he's also a top student. He has a 93-94 mph fastball, and hitters react as if it's in the high 90s. That helps his other pitches, the best of which is a snapping curveball. He gained confidence in his curve throughout last season, throwing it for strikes even when behind in the count. He averaged 7.9 walks per nine innings in his first two pro seasons but cut that figure to 3.6 in 2001. Now he needs to work on his command in the strike zone. He didn't throw many changeups as a reliever and still is developing the pitch. Pitching coordinator Don Cooper compares Malone's rise to that of Jason Bere, who helped the White Sox win a division title in 1993 after starting the previous season in low Class A. Malone could have that same kind of sudden impact, but his likely ETA is mid-2003.

Year	Club (League)	Class	W	L	ERA	G	GS	CG	SV	IP	H	R	ER	BB	SO
1999	White Sox (AZL)	R	0	2	8.00	10	0	0	0	18	16	19	16	16	24
2000	Burlington (Mid)	A	2	3	4.90	38	1	0	0	72	67	52	39	60	82
2001	Kannapolis (SAL)	A	11	4	2.00	18	18	2	0	112	83	30	25	44	119
	Winston-Salem (Car)	A	0	1	1.72	5	5	0	0	37	25	10	7	10	38
	Birmingham (SL)	AA	2	0	2.33	4	4	0	0	19	8	5	5	12	20
MINOR LEAGUE TOTALS			15	10	3.21	75	28	2	0	258	199	116	92	142	283

4. Matt Guerrier, rhp

Born: Aug. 2, 1978. **Ht.:** 6-3. **Wt.:** 190. **Bats:** R. **Throws:** R. **School:** Kent State University. **Career Transactions:** Selected by White Sox in 10th round of 1999 draft; signed June 17, 1999.

At first glance, it doesn't appear there's anything special about Guerrier. But don't be misled. He may not dominate but he wins, compiling a 26-8, 2.80 record in three pro seasons. He rang up 38 saves in his first 1 1/2 years in the system but pitched even better when given a chance to start, leading the minors with 18 wins in 2001. Guerrier is out of the Greg Maddux mold. His fastball averages only 88-89 mph but is one of four pitches he can throw at any time in the count. His curveball, slider and changeup are all plus pitches and he does a tremendous job of establishing, then following, a plan of attack. He holds runners well and fields his position. He shows signs of being a workhorse. With his velocity, Guerrier doesn't have much margin for error, though. The Sox will watch closely to see how he rebounds from pitching 200 innings (including 20 in the Arizona Fall League) last year. With the major league rotation uncertain beyond Mark Buehrle, Guerrier is a sleeper to watch in spring training. He could do what more heralded prospects like Kip Wells and Jon Garland could not, nailing down a spot in his first try.

Year	Club (League)	Class	W	L	ERA	G	GS	CG	SV	IP	H	R	ER	BB	SO
1999	Bristol (Appy)	R	5	0	1.05	21	0	0	10	26	18	9	3	14	37
	Winston-Salem (Car)	A	0	0	5.40	4	0	0	2	3	3	2	2	0	5
2000	Winston-Salem (Car)	A	0	3	1.30	30	0	0	19	35	25	13	5	12	35
	Birmingham (SL)	AA	3	1	2.70	23	0	0	7	23	17	9	7	12	19
2001	Birmingham (SL)	AA	11	3	3.10	15	15	1	0	99	85	42	34	32	75
	Charlotte (IL)	AAA	7	1	3.54	12	12	3	0	81	75	33	32	18	43
MINOR LEAGUE TOTALS			26	8	2.80	105	27	4	38	267	223	108	83	88	214

5. Joe Crede, 3b

Born: April 26, 1978. **Ht.:** 6-3. **Wt.:** 195. **Bats:** R. **Throws:** R. **School:** Fatima HS, Westphalia, Mo. **Career Transactions:** Selected by White Sox in fifth round of 1996 draft; signed June 5, 1996.

A two-time minor league MVP, Crede has become a staple on this list but almost certainly will graduate this time around. Many expected him to become the regular third baseman last season but he failed to break through, instead spending his first year in Triple-A. His offensive totals were down from previous seasons and his late-season showing in Chicago qualified as a disappointment. The White Sox drafted his brother Josh in the 48th round last June but didn't sign him. Crede is a productive hitter, especially when he trusts himself to drive the ball to the opposite field, and has shown the ability to come back from long slumps. He's a smooth fielder with good range and a plus arm. He could be part of a much-needed defensive improvement for the White Sox. Expectations have been high for Crede since he was the Carolina League MVP at age 20. He expects so much from himself that he's too critical at times. Despite playing in more than 600 games, he hasn't shown signs of cutting down his annual triple-digit strikeout totals. With Herbert Perry out of the picture, the Sox appear ready to give Crede 300-400 at-bats this season. He'll need to produce to play for a team with playoff aspirations.

Year	Club (League)	Class	AVG	G	AB	R	H	2B	3B	HR	RBI	BB	SO	SB
1996	White Sox (GCL)	R	.299	56	221	30	66	17	1	4	32	9	41	1
1997	Hickory (SAL)	A	.271	113	402	45	109	25	0	5	62	24	83	3
1998	Winston-Salem (Car)	A	.315	137	492	92	155	32	3	20	88	53	98	9
1999	Birmingham (SL)	AA	.251	74	291	37	73	14	1	4	42	22	47	2
2000	Birmingham (SL)	AA	.306	138	533	84	163	35	0	21	94	56	111	3
	Chicago (AL)	MAJ	.357	7	14	2	5	1	0	0	3	0	3	0
2001	Charlotte (IL)	AAA	.276	124	463	67	128	34	1	17	65	46	88	2
	Chicago (AL)	MAJ	.220	17	50	1	11	1	1	0	7	3	11	1
MAJOR LEAGUE TOTALS			.250	24	64	3	16	2	1	0	10	3	14	1
MINOR LEAGUE TOTALS			.289	642	2402	355	694	157	6	71	383	210	468	20

6. Tim Hummel, 2b

Born: Nov. 18, 1978. **Ht.:** 6-2. **Wt.:** 195. **Bats:** R. **Throws:** R. **School:** Old Dominion University. **Career Transactions:** Selected by White Sox in second round of 2000 draft; signed June 21, 2000.

Hummel was a polished hitter when the White Sox drafted him. He has moved all over the infield, settling in at second base in the second half of 2001. He spent his first full season as a pro in Double-A and then continued to be pushed in the Arizona Fall League. Hummel is an offensive player with lots of upside. He's a rare righthanded hitter described as having a stylish swing. He hits for average and is selective at the plate, traits that have given him a career .380 on-base percentage as a pro. Hummel uses the whole field. He showed emerging power last season but projects more as an ideal No. 2 hitter. He has a plus arm for second base but needs to work on his first step in the field. His range is limited, though he compensates with a good positioning. He isn't fluid on the pivot but makes up for it with solid throws. With Ray Durham in the last season of his contract, Hummel could be a 2003 regular. For that to be a successful transition for the White Sox, however, Hummel must improve enough defensively to be superior to Durham, a consistent liability through the years.

Year	Club (League)	Class	AVG	G	AB	R	H	2B	3B	HR	RBI	BB	SO	SB
2000	Burlington (Mid)	A	.326	39	144	22	47	9	1	1	21	21	20	8
	Winston-Salem (Car)	A	.327	27	98	15	32	7	0	1	9	13	12	1
2001	Birmingham (SL)	AA	.290	134	524	83	152	33	6	7	63	62	69	14
MINOR LEAGUE TOTALS			.302	200	766	120	231	49	7	9	93	96	101	23

7. Kris Honel, rhp

Born: Nov. 7, 1982. **Ht.:** 6-5. **Wt.:** 180. **Bats:** R. **Throws:** R. **School:** Providence Catholic HS, New Lenox, Ill. **Career Transactions:** Selected by White Sox in first round (16th overall) of 2001 draft; signed June 14, 2001.

Following in the footsteps of Oakland's Mark Mulder, Honel is the rare first-round pitcher who has survived an education in the batting cages around Chicago. He was projected as a possible top 10 pick before slipping to the 16th overall. That's the highest an Illinois high school pitcher has been selected since the Angels took Bob Kipper with the eighth pick in June 1982. Honel is big, strong and has excellent mechanics. He has hit 95 on guns and averages 91-92 with good movement. That's plenty of heat, considering he has two pitches better than his fastball—a knuckle-curve that acts like a slider, and a plus changeup. Like most kids just out of high school, Honel has some growing up to do. His emotions can get the better of him on the mound. He was bothered by minor elbow problems after signing, which caused his velocity to sink to the mid-80s at times. Scouting director Doug Laumann considers Honel to be from the Mark Prior starter kit. If he makes steady progress the next three years, he could become a homegrown star in his hometown.

Year	Club (League)	Class	W	L	ERA	G	GS	CG	SV	IP	H	R	ER	BB	SO
2001	White Sox (AZL)	R	2	0	1.80	3	1	0	0	10	9	3	2	3	8
	Bristol (Appy)	R	2	3	3.13	8	8	0	0	46	41	19	16	9	45
MINOR LEAGUE TOTALS			4	3	2.89	11	9	0	0	56	50	22	18	12	53

8. Miguel Olivo, c

Born: July 15, 1978. **Ht.:** 6-1. **Wt.:** 215. **Bats:** R. **Throws:** R. **Career Transactions:** Signed out of Dominican Republic by Athletics, Sept. 30, 1996 . . . Traded by Athletics to White Sox, Dec. 12, 2000, completing trade in which White Sox sent RHP Chad Bradford to Athletics for a player to be named (Dec. 7, 2000).

The White Sox' pitching surplus allowed them to trade Chad Bradford to Oakland for a potential long-term catcher. Olivo responded to the deal by turning in excellent seasons in Double-A and the Arizona Fall League, where managers voted him to the all-prospect team. After never playing more than 77 games in a season, he held together for 111 between the two stops. Arm strength always has been Olivo's calling card, but he has developed into a promising hitter, putting up on-base plus slugging percentages better than .800 in both Birmingham and the AFL. His total of 14 Double-A homers was impressive in a pitcher's park. Scouts still rave about Olivo's strong arm, with one saying it was the best he saw all season. He is prone to strikeouts. By all accounts, he still needs work on his receiving skills. His ability to call games and work with pitchers is the last hurdle between him and the big leagues. Olivo will open 2002 in Triple-A but could figure in Chicago's catching mix at some point this season. He's a strong candidate for regular duty in 2003 and is putting pressure on veteran Mark Johnson and second-year man Josh Paul.

Year	Club (League)	Class	AVG	G	AB	R	H	2B	3B	HR	RBI	BB	SO	SB
1997	Athletics East (DSL)	R	.271	63	221	37	60	11	4	6	57	34	36	6
1998	Athletics (AZL)	R	.311	46	164	30	51	11	3	2	23	8	43	2
1999	Modesto (Cal)	A	.305	73	243	46	74	13	6	9	42	21	60	4
2000	Modesto (Cal)	A	.282	58	227	40	64	11	5	5	35	16	53	5
	Midland (TL)	AA	.237	19	59	8	14	2	0	1	9	5	15	0
2001	Birmingham (SL)	AA	.259	93	316	45	82	23	1	14	55	37	62	6
MINOR LEAGUE TOTALS			.280	352	1230	206	345	71	19	37	221	121	269	23

9. Dennis Ulacia, lhp

Born: April 2, 1981. **Ht.:** 6-1. **Wt.:** 185. **Bats:** L. **Throws:** L. **School:** Monsignor Pace HS, Opa Locka, Fla. **Career Transactions:** Selected by White Sox in eighth round of 1999 draft; signed June 16, 1999.

Along with players like Corwin Malone, Edwin Almonte and Kyle Kane, Ulacia was one of the biggest success stories in the organization last season. The White Sox knew the potential was there, yet had to be amazed at how a 20-year-old could bounce back from a 4-14 season in low Class A to go a combined 15-5, 2.86, including a complete-game victory in a Triple-A emergency start. He ended a remarkable year by throwing a four-hit shutout in the Southern League playoffs. Nothing bothers Ulacia, whose mound presence belies his age. He has a complete selection of pitches, complementing a low-90s fastball with a plus breaking ball. He does a good job changing speeds. His change-up is a work in progress. His quick rise to the top of the system may have left him lacking in defensive fundamentals. Ulacia has made only four starts above Class A but is likely to come quickly. He has shown the White Sox that he's mentally tough, making him a candidate to pitch in the big leagues soon. He'll probably begin the year in Double-A.

Year	Club (League)	Class	W	L	ERA	G	GS	CG	SV	IP	H	R	ER	BB	SO
1999	White Sox (AZL)	R	3	2	3.79	8	8	0	0	38	36	19	16	11	52
2000	Burlington (Mid)	A	4	14	4.73	28	28	1	0	148	157	109	78	67	111
2001	Charlotte (IL)	AAA	1	0	2.57	1	1	1	0	7	6	2	2	1	3
	Birmingham (SL)	AA	1	1	2.25	3	3	0	0	20	11	7	5	5	18
	Winston-Salem (CL)	A	5	3	3.64	10	10	4	0	64	57	27	26	26	47
	Kannapolis (SAL)	A	8	1	2.43	15	15	0	0	89	68	25	24	36	93
MINOR LEAGUE TOTALS			22	21	3.71	65	65	6	0	366	335	189	151	146	324

10. Aaron Rowand, of

Born: Aug. 29, 1977. **Ht.:** 6-1. **Wt.:** 200. **Bats:** R. **Throws:** R. **School:** Cal State Fullerton. **Career Transactions:** Selected by White Sox in first round (35th overall) of 1998 draft; signed June 12, 1998.

Rowand spent more than half of last season with the White Sox, including 34 starts in the outfield, but still narrowly qualifies for this list. The most memorable moment of his rookie season came when he crashed into an outfield wall, taking away an extra-base hit to temporarily preserve a Mark Buehrle bid for a no-hitter. Rowand played with a sore shoulder afterward and watched his batting average slide from .316 on Sept. 1. He is a promising run producer who shortened his swing working with big league batting coach Gary Ward. Rowand also tightened his strike zone, chasing fewer pitches. He has hit at least 20 homers in each of the last three seasons but is more of a line-drive hitter. Rowand has spent most of his career playing the outfield corners but did a decent job in center for the White Sox. He has a strong arm but doesn't truly fit any of the outfield positions. Rowand runs OK but not as well as a typical center fielder. He also doesn't have quite the home-run power of a corner outfielder. Rowand could spend 2002 as Chicago's regular in left or center, depending on the status of Carlos Lee and Chris Singleton.

Year	Club (League)	Class	AVG	G	AB	R	H	2B	3B	HR	RBI	BB	SO	SB
1998	Hickory (SAL)	A	.342	61	222	42	76	13	3	5	32	21	36	7
1999	Winston-Salem (Car)	A	.279	133	512	96	143	37	3	24	88	33	94	15
2000	Birmingham (SL)	AA	.258	139	532	80	137	26	5	20	98	38	117	22
2001	Charlotte (IL)	AAA	.295	82	329	54	97	28	0	16	48	21	47	8
	Chicago (AL)	MAJ	.293	63	123	21	36	5	0	4	20	15	28	5
MAJOR LEAGUE TOTALS			.293	63	123	21	36	5	0	4	20	15	28	5
MINOR LEAGUE TOTALS			.284	415	1595	272	453	104	11	65	266	113	294	52

11. Edwin Almonte, rhp

Born: Dec. 17, 1976. **Ht.:** 6-3. **Wt.:** 200. **Bats:** R. **Throws:** R. **School:** St. Francis (N.Y.) College. **Career Transactions:** Selected by White Sox in 26th round of 1998 draft; signed June 6, 1998.

After three solid but nondescript seasons in the White Sox system, Almonte made his presence known with 36 saves in Double-A. Not only did he break Jerry Spradlin's Southern League record, but he also totaled the most saves ever by a Sox minor leaguer. He has a career ratio of 3.5 strikeouts for every walk while compiling a 2.90 ERA, which he lowered considerably last season. Almonte is considered a younger version of Keith Foulke. His out pitch is an excellent changeup, which he sets up by locating a fastball that occasionally hits 90 mph but is generally in the upper 80s. Growing up on the streets of New York gave him the mental toughness needed to work late innings. Plus Almonte knows how to pitch. He won't overpower hitters. His slider is a solid pitch but he must work to be able to locate it when he's behind in the count, keeping hitters from sitting on his fastball. With Foulke's salary rising, Almonte is well positioned as a closer-in-waiting. If the Sox are convinced he can do the job, they'll be tempted to listen to offers for Foulke, who is two seasons away from free agency.

Year	Club (League)	Class	W	L	ERA	G	GS	CG	SV	IP	H	R	ER	BB	SO
1998	White Sox (AZL)	R	0	0	0.93	5	0	0	0	10	6	5	1	1	8
	Bristol (Appy)	R	3	0	3.38	8	3	0	0	27	29	14	10	4	26
1999	Burlington (Mid)	A	9	12	3.03	37	5	2	5	116	107	48	39	28	85
2000	Winston-Salem (Car)	A	3	1	3.16	33	7	0	2	77	66	32	27	20	73
	Birmingham (SL)	AA	1	3	4.54	7	6	0	0	40	45	22	20	9	21
2001	Birmingham (SL)	AA	1	4	1.49	54	0	0	36	66	58	16	11	16	62
MINOR LEAGUE TOTALS			17	20	2.90	144	21	2	43	335	311	137	108	78	275

12. Matt Ginter, rhp

Born: Dec. 24, 1977. **Ht.:** 6-1. **Wt.:** 215. **Bats:** R. **Throws:** R. **School:** Mississippi State University. **Career Transactions:** Selected by White Sox in first round (22nd overall) of 1999 draft; signed June 24, 1999.

While aggressive advancement has created mixed results with many of their young pitchers, Ginter is the White Sox' biggest tease. The 1999 first-round pick has been successful in the minors, posting a 2.60 ERA while doing most of his work at the upper levels, but he frequently has fallen apart when promoted to the big leagues. The difference lies in his ability to throw strikes. Major league hitters aren't as quick to chase Ginter's hard slider, leaving him too often working behind in the count. The slider is a dynamite pitch that he combines with a low-90s fastball to overmatch righthanders. He has developed a decent changeup but he needs to command his fastball better. Ginter has pitched well as a starter in the minors but his future appears to be in the bullpen. He once was viewed as a future closer or middle-of-the-rotation starter, but the Sox will be tickled if he establishes himself in any role. Ginter will go to camp this spring with a chance to win a job as a long man.

Year	Club (League)	Class	W	L	ERA	G	GS	CG	SV	IP	H	R	ER	BB	SO
1999	White Sox (AZL)	R	1	0	3.24	3	0	0	1	8	5	4	3	3	10
	Burlington (Mid)	A	4	2	4.05	9	9	0	0	40	38	20	18	19	29
2000	Birmingham (SL)	AA	11	8	2.25	27	26	0	0	180	153	72	45	60	126
	Chicago (AL)	MAJ	1	0	13.50	7	0	0	0	9	18	14	14	7	6
2001	Charlotte (IL)	AAA	2	3	2.59	22	10	0	0	76	62	26	22	24	67
	Chicago (AL)	MAJ	1	0	5.22	20	0	0	0	40	34	23	23	14	24
MAJOR LEAGUE TOTALS			2	0	6.80	27	0	0	0	49	52	37	37	21	30
MINOR LEAGUE TOTALS			18	13	2.60	61	45	0	1	304	258	122	88	106	232

13. Brian West, rhp

Born: Aug. 4, 1980. **Ht.:** 6-4. **Wt.:** 230. **Bats:** R. **Throws:** R. **School:** West Monroe (La.) HS. **Career Transactions:** Selected by White Sox in first round (35th overall) of 1999 draft; signed July 1, 1999.

Another product of a rich 1999 draft in which the White Sox selected pitchers with 14 of their first 15 picks, West continues a textbook, step-at-a-time climb up the system. The former Texas A&M football recruit pitched at age 20 in the high Class A Carolina League last year and figures to get a year in Double-A at age 21. He's strong, throws hard and is developing a good idea about pitching. West has a two-seam fastball that hits the low 90s. He made a major step forward in 2001 by developing a dynamite changeup to go with his slider. He's working on a curveball to use as his fourth pitch. He's also a good athlete who fields his position well. Given the arms ahead of him, it's hard to see West jumping to the big leagues from Birmingham, but a strong season there will put him on the threshold of what should be a long major league career.

Year	Club (League)	Class	W	L	ERA	G	GS	CG	SV	IP	H	R	ER	BB	SO
1999	White Sox (AZL)	R	0	1	13.50	2	0	0	0	5	10	7	7	2	3
	Bristol (Appy)	R	1	2	10.50	8	1	0	2	18	26	25	21	14	17
2000	Burlington (Mid)	A	8	9	3.78	24	24	0	0	148	146	81	62	73	90
	Winston-Salem (Car)	A	0	1	11.37	2	2	0	0	6	10	12	8	6	3
2001	Winston-Salem (Car)	A	7	12	3.46	28	28	3	0	169	179	75	65	70	130
MINOR LEAGUE TOTALS			16	25	4.24	64	55	3	2	346	371	200	163	165	243

14. Casey Rogowski, 1b

Born: May 1, 1981. **Ht.:** 6-3. **Wt.:** 230. **Bats:** L. **Throws:** L. **School:** Catholic Central HS, Redford, Mich. **Career Transactions:** Selected by White Sox in 13th round of 1999 draft; signed June 22, 1999.

If prospects were measured on neck size alone, Rogowski would be among baseball's elite. The powerfully built heavyweight wrestling champ from Michigan is a brute but not an oaf. His athleticism allowed him to be a high school standout in football as well as baseball and wrestling. Unranked on this list a year ago, he's No. 14 with a bullet. While the White Sox love his potential as a power hitter—he homered into the upper deck at Tiger Stadium while still in high school—managers also rated him the best defensive first baseman in the South Atlantic League last season. Rogowski improved as a hitter in 2001, chasing fewer pitches and driving the ball in hitter's counts. He's a long way away from Comiskey Park but will get every opportunity to get there if he continues to show 30-plus homer potential.

Year	Club (League)	Class	AVG	G	AB	R	H	2B	3B	HR	RBI	BB	SO	SB
1999	White Sox (AZL)	R	.288	52	160	23	46	7	2	0	27	26	34	2
2000	Burlington (Mid)	A	.231	122	412	62	95	19	1	6	41	47	89	11
2001	Kannapolis (SAL)	A	.287	130	439	66	126	18	3	14	69	62	95	16
MINOR LEAGUE TOTALS			.264	304	1011	151	267	44	6	20	137	135	218	29

15. Wyatt Allen, rhp

Born: April 12, 1980. **Ht.:** 6-4. **Wt.:** 205. **Bats:** R. **Throws:** R. **School:** University of Tennessee. **Career Transactions:** Selected by White Sox in first round (39th overall) of 2001 draft; signed June 26, 2001.

This guy has come to the right place. With tremendous arm strength and an erratic delivery, Allen fits the mold of raw pitchers such as Dan Wright and Corwin Malone, who harnessed their talent in a hurry after joining the White Sox system. Allen opened scouts' eyes by beating Middle Tennessee State's Dewon Brazelton (the No. 3 overall pick in the 2001 draft) in an NCAA regional showdown. He was running on fumes after Chicago selected him with a supplemental first-round pick it received after losing Charles Johnson to free agency. He still reduced his ERA from 6.30 as a Tennessee junior to 3.16 with low Class A Kannapolis. He was clocked at 97 mph in the Cape Cod League during the summer of 2000, but generally works at 93-94 with two- and four-seam fastballs he throws to both sides of the plate. His curveball needs improvement and the Sox are working to give him a changeup. Allen may not have as much upside as Wright, but he could come to the big leagues just as quickly.

Year	Club (League)	Class	W	L	ERA	G	GS	CG	SV	IP	H	R	ER	BB	SO
2001	Kannapolis (SAL)	A	4	5	3.16	12	11	2	0	63	60	29	22	16	45
MINOR LEAGUE TOTALS			4	5	3.16	12	11	2	0	63	60	29	22	16	45

16. Jason Stumm, rhp

Born: April 13, 1981. **Ht.:** 6-2. **Wt.:** 215. **Bats:** R. **Throws:** R. **School:** Centralia (Wash.) HS. **Career Transactions:** Selected by White Sox in first round (15th overall) of 1999 draft; signed June 21, 1999.

Mr. Everything as a high school star in the Pacific Northwest, Stumm was the most highly regarded of the truckload of talented pitchers the White Sox collected in the 1999 draft. Now he has become the organization's Concern No. 1. Elbow reconstruction cost him most of the last two years and he hasn't had as smooth a recovery as many Tommy John surgery survivors. Stumm returned in a little more than a year to make four outings in the Rookie-level Arizona League last August, but he suffered a setback that may keep his comeback from beginning in earnest this spring. When he was healthy, Stumm could hit 96-97 mph with his fastball. His slider and changeup are works in progress that have been delayed by his pitching just 133 innings in his first 2 1/2 seasons as a pro. Stumm, a league MVP in football and basketball in high school, gets high marks for leadership and character. If he can get back on track, the early adversity could make him a hardened competitor.

Year	Club (League)	Class	W	L	ERA	G	GS	CG	SV	IP	H	R	ER	BB	SO
1999	White Sox (AZL)	R	0	0	3.27	3	2	0	0	11	13	8	4	3	9
	Burlington (Mid)	A	3	3	5.32	10	10	0	0	44	47	31	26	27	33
2000	Burlington (Mid)	A	2	7	4.61	13	13	2	0	66	66	46	34	30	62
2001	White Sox (AZL)	R	0	2	2.25	4	4	0	0	12	6	4	3	5	12
MINOR LEAGUE TOTALS			5	12	4.52	30	29	2	0	133	132	89	67	65	116

17. Arnie Munoz, lhp

Born: June 21, 1982. **Ht.:** 5-9. **Wt.:** 170. **Bats:** L. **Throws:** L. **Career Transactions:** Signed out of Dominican Republic by White Sox, Dec. 20, 1998.

Don't judge this book by its cover. The little Dominican may have been standing on a telephone book when he was measured at 5-foot-9, but he's a fighter with lots of heart. Munoz had enough talent for the White Sox to sign him at age 16, and he needed only one season at their Dominican academy to earn a coveted visa. Last year he held hitters to a .161 average and averaged 13.0 strikeouts per nine innings in the South Atlantic League, which he led with 60 appearances. Munoz has an eye-popping, Barry Zito-style curveball that makes him essentially unhittable for lefthanders. He complements it with another effective curveball that breaks down. His fastball is sneaky fast, reaching the low 90s at times. Opponents almost never try to run against Munoz, whose move to first base is a true weapon. He needs to work on getting ahead of hitters, as he has walked 5.2 per nine innings in his short career. He won't turn 20 until the middle of this season, which means his velocity could increase in coming years. He has all the makings of a feared situational lefty.

Year	Club (League)	Class	W	L	ERA	G	GS	CG	SV	IP	H	R	ER	BB	SO
1999	White Sox (AZL)	R	0	2	5.25	14	0	0	1	12	13	10	7	8	12
2000	Burlington (Mid)	A	2	3	6.81	22	0	0	0	38	45	34	29	25	44
2001	Kannapolis (SAL)	A	6	3	2.49	60	0	0	12	80	41	24	22	42	115
MINOR LEAGUE TOTALS			8	8	4.02	96	0	0	13	130	99	68	58	75	171

18. Andy Gonzalez, ss

Born: Dec. 15, 1981. **Ht.:** 6-2. **Wt.:** 175. **Bats:** R. **Throws:** R. **School:** Florida Air Academy, Melbourne, Fla. **Career Transactions:** Selected by White Sox in fifth round of 2001 draft; signed June 16, 2001.

It has been 26 seasons since the White Sox had a homegrown regular at shortstop. They've spent several high draft picks trying to end that drought, including a first-rounder on Jason Dellaero in 1997. Since trading Bucky Dent after 1976, they've gone outside the organization for their last 11 primary shortstops, with only Ozzie Guillen having staying power. Gonzalez, a fifth-round pick in the 2001 draft, played well enough in the Arizona League to establish himself as a strong candidate to end the trend. He's a big kid in the mold of Alex Rodriguez and shows the potential to develop into a run-producing hitter as well as a solid fielder. The ball jumps off his bat with 25-homer potential. Gonzalez moves well at short but piled up errors in his pro debut, which was to be expected. His arm is above average. Some teams, in fact, considered drafting him as a pitcher after he threw in the low 90s following his move from Puerto Rico to a Florida high school for his senior year. His few critics question how he will hold up to a full-season grind. The only other question is how Gonzalez lasted until the fifth round of the draft.

Year	Club (League)	Class	AVG	G	AB	R	H	2B	3B	HR	RBI	BB	SO	SB
2001	White Sox (AZL)	R	.323	48	189	33	61	18	1	5	30	15	36	13
MINOR LEAGUE TOTALS			.323	48	189	33	61	18	1	5	30	15	36	13

19. Kyle Kane, rhp

Born: Feb. 4, 1976. **Ht.:** 6-3. **Wt.:** 215. **Bats:** L. **Throws:** R. **School:** Saddleback (Calif.) CC. **Career Transactions:** Selected by White Sox in first round (33rd overall) of 1997 draft; signed Aug. 24, 1997.

This guy is an example of better late than never. Kane, whose strong arm prompted the White Sox to select him ahead of Jim Parque and Rocky Biddle in the 1997 draft, entered last season as a candidate to be released and finished it as one of the more upwardly mobile pitchers in the organization. He handled every challenge thrown his way, compiling a 2.15 ERA with 75 strikeouts in 59 innings over 40 appearances as he rose from high Class A to Triple-A. He followed up on that by winning the ERA title (1.80) and a spot on the manager's all-prospect team in the Arizona Fall League. It's hard to believe this was the same guy who had been overweight and seemingly indifferent in his first three pro seasons. Knee injuries and a lack of experience on the mound contributed to Kane's early difficulties but his talent is obvious. He throws 95 mph with a slider that longtime major leaguer Bob Stanley says might be the hardest he's ever seen. Kane was added to the 40-man roster and has a chance to open eyes in spring training. His advancement depends on him getting a little more command on his fastball and doing a better job slowing runners. If his head is right, he's got a chance.

Year	Club (League)	Class	W	L	ERA	G	GS	CG	SV	IP	H	R	ER	BB	SO
1998	Bristol (Appy)	R	1	0	5.32	13	0	0	0	24	34	21	14	8	17
1999	Bristol (Appy)	R	2	0	2.57	5	5	0	0	28	19	8	8	11	23
	Burlington (Mid)	A	1	0	13.50	12	0	0	1	18	28	29	27	12	17
2000	Winston-Salem (Car)	A	1	2	5.86	32	0	0	0	51	57	39	33	31	47
2001	Winston-Salem (Car)	A	1	0	2.08	14	0	0	1	22	10	5	5	8	32
	Charlotte (IL)	AAA	0	0	6.00	1	1	0	0	3	4	2	2	1	0
	Birmingham (SL)	AA	2	1	1.85	26	0	0	3	34	20	9	7	6	43
MINOR LEAGUE TOTALS			8	3	4.83	103	6	0	5	179	172	113	96	77	179

20. Mitch Wylie, rhp

Born: Jan. 14, 1977. **Ht.:** 6-3. **Wt.:** 190. **Bats:** R. **Throws:** R. **School:** St. Ambrose (Iowa) University. **Career Transactions:** Selected by White Sox in eighth round of 1998 draft; signed June 7, 1998.

Two years removed from Tommy John surgery, Wylie made huge leaps in 2001. He tied for the Southern League lead with 15 wins, earning a spot on the 40-man roster. He helped Birmingham to a second-half title with a nine-game winning streak in which his ERA was 1.89. Wylie's work ethic during his rehab has allowed him to come back throwing harder than he did before surgery. His fastball has been clocked at 95 mph and generally parks in the 91-93 range. He takes charge on the mound and isn't afraid to knock batters off the plate, hitting 12 last season. His changeup is his second-best pitch but he needs to improve his slider. He also must work on holding runners and cutting down his time to the plate. Wylie will be challenged by a move to Triple-A, where he will be based in a hitter's park. While he's behind the cast of usual suspects, there are openings in the major league rotation. Wylie could put himself into the picture at some point this season if he finds the groove he was in last July and August.

Year	Club (League)	Class	W	L	ERA	G	GS	CG	SV	IP	H	R	ER	BB	SO
1998	Bristol (Appy)	R	0	2	3.30	20	0	0	6	30	34	12	11	11	32
1999	Burlington (Mid)	A	1	0	1.97	6	6	0	0	32	28	11	7	11	27
2000	Winston-Salem (Car)	A	3	7	4.34	17	17	0	0	95	112	59	46	34	57
2001	Winston-Salem (Car)	A	0	1	3.60	1	1	0	0	5	7	2	2	1	4
	Birmingham (SL)	AA	15	4	4.21	24	24	0	0	141	138	70	66	46	123
MINOR LEAGUE TOTALS			19	14	3.92	68	48	0	6	303	319	154	132	103	243

21. Delvis Lantigua, rhp

Born: Jan. 5, 1980. **Ht.:** 6-0. **Wt.:** 176. **Bats:** R. **Throws:** R. **Career Transactions:** Signed out of Dominican Republic by Dodgers, May 8, 1998 . . . Released by Dodgers, July 13, 1999 . . . Signed by White Sox, July 16, 1999.

Lantigua has a chance to end the White Sox' drought in the Dominican Republic. He emerged from deep in the ranks of the organization's pitchers, pitching well enough in spring training to earn a spot in high Class A and ending the 2001 season with an unbeaten run in Double-A. Lantigua has a live arm and gets lots of movement on his fastball. His slider is also a good pitch. Both of those help him set up a devastating changeup that has become his best pitch. Lantigua needs work commanding his fastball. He also must improve his mound presence, as he sometimes lets his emotions get the better of him. He can be nasty when everything's working, as it did in two shutouts and a combined no-hitter in 2001. He'll return to Double-A in 2002, when a solid season could put him in the crowd of pitchers competing for spots on the Chicago staff.

Year	Club (League)	Class	W	L	ERA	G	GS	CG	SV	IP	H	R	ER	BB	SO
1998	Dodgers (DSL)	R	1	0	3.57	8	3	0	0	23	17	12	9	15	19
1999	Dodgers (DSL)	R	5	2	3.91	9	8	1	0	48	44	33	21	12	60
	White Sox (DSL)	R	1	0	9.53	5	0	0	0	6	5	7	6	8	3
2000	Bristol (Appy)	R	2	7	5.31	12	12	1	0	59	63	42	35	30	59
2001	Winston-Salem (Car)	A	8	6	3.06	22	19	1	0	121	92	46	41	58	113
	Birmingham (SL)	AA	4	0	3.71	7	7	2	0	44	40	19	18	18	34
MINOR LEAGUE TOTALS			21	15	3.90	63	49	5	0	300	261	159	130	141	288

22. Anthony Webster, of

Born: April 10, 1983. **Ht.:** 6-0. **Wt.:** 190. **Bats:** L. **Throws:** R. **School:** Riverside HS, Parsons, Tenn. **Career Transactions:** Selected by White Sox in 15th round of 2001 draft; signed June 16, 2001.

This guy was as raw as they come beginning his pro career but wasted no time putting his athleticism on display. Webster wasn't drafted until the 15th round in 2001 but impressed managers enough to be rated the No. 7 prospect in the Rookie-level Arizona League. Skippers liked his hard-nosed approach as much as his ability. He finished second in the AZL in stolen bases and fourth in hits. An outstanding high school tailback recruited by Southeastern Conference schools, Webster has intrigued the Sox with his combination of quickness and strength. He shows power to the gaps and uses his speed to get extra-base hits. He covers lots of ground in center but time will tell whether he stays there or moves to a corner. The Sox will know more about Webster after he plays a full season, but it appears all the pieces are there.

Year	Club (League)	Class	AVG	G	AB	R	H	2B	3B	HR	RBI	BB	SO	SB
2001	White Sox (AZL)	R	.307	55	225	38	69	9	7	0	30	9	33	18
MINOR LEAGUE TOTALS			.307	55	225	38	69	9	7	0	30	9	33	18

23. Guillermo Reyes, ss

Born: Dec. 29, 1981. **Ht.:** 5-9. **Wt.:** 160. **Bats:** B. **Throws:** R. **Career Transactions:** Signed out of Dominican Republic by White Sox, Dec. 25, 1998.

A strong first half in 2001 got Reyes promoted to high Class A at age 19. While the under-sized Dominican struggled at the plate against tougher pitching, he did nothing to cool enthusiasm over his long-term potential. He has moved between second base and shortstop in three seasons in the organization but settled in at shortstop last year, where he stood out in the South Atlantic League. He's a smooth fielder with soft hands and enough arm strength to play short. His range is excellent at second but only average at shortstop. Reyes isn't a burner but is a good basestealer. A switch-hitter, he's tough to strike out but not strong enough to do much damage. The key for Reyes is to continue improving as a hitter, especially his on-base ability. The Sox believe he'll play in the major leagues, and his bat will determine if it's as a regular or a reserve.

Year	Club (League)	Class	AVG	G	AB	R	H	2B	3B	HR	RBI	BB	SO	SB
1999	White Sox (AZL)	R	.250	54	200	27	50	5	3	0	15	20	25	18
2000	Bristol (Appy)	R	.296	66	257	45	76	10	2	3	31	22	24	21
2001	Kannapolis (SAL)	A	.279	71	280	49	78	8	5	0	26	27	30	29
	Winston-Salem (Car)	A	.208	59	216	24	45	4	1	0	24	14	33	16
MINOR LEAGUE TOTALS			.261	250	953	145	249	27	11	3	96	83	112	84

24. Gary Majewski, rhp

Born: Feb. 26, 1980. **Ht.:** 6-2. **Wt.:** 200. **Bats:** R. **Throws:** R. **School:** St. Pius X HS, Houston. **Career Transactions:** Selected by White Sox in second round of 1998 draft; signed Sept. 2, 1998 . . . Traded by White Sox with RHP Andre Simpson and LHP Orlando Rodriguez to Dodgers for RHP Antonio Osuna and LHP Carlos Ortega, March 22, 2001 . . . Traded by Dodgers with LHP Onan Masaoka and OF Jeff Barry to White Sox for RHP James Baldwin, July 26, 2001.

It was a tale of two seasons for this Texan, who ranked No. 11 on this list a year ago. Majewski came unglued after going to the Dodgers in the Antonio Osuna trade at the end of spring training, but reasserted himself after Chicago reacquired him in the James Baldwin deal. These developments don't say much for his ability to adjust but the White Sox are happy to have him back. He throws 92-93 mph with late movement, prompting batters to hit the ball on the ground while returning to the dugout mumbling about his "heavy" ball. Majewski has yet to polish the other pitches to complement his natural sinker, but his slider is showing improvement. He looks unassuming but has a headhunter's mindset. After two years in Class A, he'll be tested in Double-A in 2002.

Year	Club (League)	Class	W	L	ERA	G	GS	CG	SV	IP	H	R	ER	BB	SO
1999	Bristol (Appy)	R	7	1	3.05	13	13	1	0	77	67	34	26	37	91
	Burlington (Mid)	A	0	0	37.80	2	0	0	0	3	11	14	14	4	1
2000	Burlington (Mid)	A	6	7	3.07	22	22	3	0	135	83	53	46	68	137
	Winston-Salem (Car)	A	2	4	5.11	6	6	0	0	37	32	21	21	17	24
2001	Vero Beach (FSL)	A	4	5	6.24	23	13	0	1	75	103	57	52	36	41
	Winston-Salem (Car)	A	4	2	2.93	9	6	1	0	43	42	15	14	10	31
MINOR LEAGUE TOTALS			23	19	4.21	75	60	5	1	370	338	194	173	172	325

25. Humberto Quintero, c

Born: Aug. 2, 1979. **Ht.:** 5-10. **Wt.:** 190. **Bats:** R. **Throws:** R. **Career Transactions:** Signed out of Venezuela by White Sox, Jan. 16, 1997.

Few catchers get the ball to second as quickly as Quintero. He possesses both a cannon for an arm and quick feet, allowing him to consistently get the ball to the bag in 1.8 seconds. That's Pudge Rodriguez territory. Quintero threw out 49 percent of runners last season between the South Atlantic League, where he was a midseason all-star, and the Carolina League. But his bat continues to lag far behind his defensive skills. He's likely to be promoted to Double-A in 2002 but has not yet shown he can hit even high Class A pitching. Quintero can make contact but rarely drives the ball or draws a walk. The White Sox hope he'll be a late-blooming hitter as he gets stronger. He played in his native Venezuela this winter, which could help him make the jump to Birmingham.

Year	Club (League)	Class	AVG	G	AB	R	H	2B	3B	HR	RBI	BB	SO	SB
1997	Guacara 1 (VSL)	R	.262	24	42	4	11	2	0	0	0	5	9	1
1998	Miranda (VSL)	R	.205	30	73	6	15	1	0	0	1	3	12	0
1999	Bristol (Appy)	R	.277	48	155	30	43	5	2	0	15	9	19	11
2000	Burlington (Mid)	A	.238	75	248	23	59	12	2	0	24	15	31	10
	White Sox (AZL)	R	.393	15	56	13	22	2	2	0	8	0	3	1
2001	Kannapolis (SAL)	A	.269	60	197	32	53	7	1	1	20	8	20	7
	Winston-Salem (Car)	A	.240	43	154	15	37	6	0	0	12	5	19	9
	Birmingham (SL)	AA	.211	5	19	0	4	0	0	0	2	0	2	0
MINOR LEAGUE TOTALS			.258	300	944	123	244	35	7	1	82	45	115	39

26. Mario Valenzuela, of

Born: March 10, 1977. **Ht.:** 6-2. **Wt.:** 190. **Bats:** R. **Throws:** R. **Career Transactions:** Signed out of Mexico by White Sox, June 19, 1996 . . . Loaned by White Sox to Saltillo (Mexican), 1997.

Valenzuela is a sleeper. He played well enough in a season split between Double-A and Triple-A to earn a job in the Arizona Fall League and consideration for a 40-man roster spot. Though he finished second in the AFL with eight homers, the White Sox left him off their roster but were happy nobody pounced on him in the major league Rule 5 draft. Valenzuela is a poor man's Magglio Ordonez without quite as much bat speed. His tools are average across the board but he has become a consistent run producer. His power has emerged over the last two seasons. He's not flashy, but he makes all the plays in right field and has enough arm for the position. With Ordonez, Carlos Lee, Jeff Liefer, Joe Borchard and Aaron Rowand on hand, Valenzuela faces steep odds to break through with the White Sox. But he's the kind of player another organization might want in a trade.

Year	Club (League)	Class	AVG	G	AB	R	H	2B	3B	HR	RBI	BB	SO	SB
1996	White Sox (GCL)	R	.260	21	73	6	19	3	2	1	8	4	20	0
1997	Saltillo (Mex)	AAA	.250	19	40	7	10	2	2	0	4	3	9	1
1998	Bristol (Appy)	R	.330	61	233	44	77	13	1	10	46	24	49	6
1999	Burlington (Mid)	A	.323	122	477	89	154	31	6	10	70	44	77	13
2000	Winston-Salem (Car)	A	.261	138	524	87	137	31	2	21	85	59	110	11
2001	Charlotte (IL)	AAA	.291	49	176	19	46	7	1	10	26	8	34	2
	Birmingham (SL)	AA	.290	88	341	50	99	17	3	12	53	21	61	4
MINOR LEAGUE TOTALS			.291	498	1864	302	542	104	17	64	292	163	360	37

27. Heath Phillips, lhp

Born: March 24, 1982. **Ht.:** 6-3. **Wt.:** 205. **Bats:** L. **Throws:** L. **School:** Lake City (Fla.) CC. **Career Transactions:** Selected by White Sox in 10th round of 2000 draft; signed May 12, 2001.

Mark Buehrle and Corwin Malone weren't hyped when they came into the White Sox organization but appear destined to excel. Phillips, who like Buehrle pitched well immediately as a draft-and-follow, is positioned to follow in their footsteps. He was one of the top hitters and pitchers in the Florida junior colleges last spring in his lone season at Lake City (Fla.) CC. The organization's coaches say it's eerie how much Phillips reminds them of Buehrle. He arrived with surprising poise and polish, requiring only some fine-tuning to keep him from rushing his delivery. In his half-season in low Class A, Phillips had a 3-1 strikeout-walk ratio and a lower ERA than Buehrle had in his pro debut. Phillips' best pitches are a fastball that dances and a slider. Though the White Sox probably won't push him as quickly as they did Buehrle, who arrived in the majors in his second pro season, they won't be surprised if Phillips moves fast.

Year	Club (League)	Class	W	L	ERA	G	GS	CG	SV	IP	H	R	ER	BB	SO
2001	Kannapolis (SAL)	A	2	7	3.64	14	12	1	0	72	74	36	29	18	54
MINOR LEAGUE TOTALS			2	7	3.64	14	12	1	0	72	74	36	29	18	54

28. Charlie Lisk, c

Born: Jan. 3, 1983. **Ht.:** 6-3. **Wt.:** 200. **Bats:** R. **Throws:** R. **School:** Fort Mill (S.C.) HS. **Career Transactions:** Selected by White Sox in 24th round of 2001 draft; signed July 29, 2001.

After failing to sign high school All-America catchers in the last two drafts, the Sox invested $390,000 in a kid who they got to know because he hung out around their ballpark at Triple-A Charlotte. He may not have come with the resumes of Jonathan Zeringue (a 2001 third-rounder who opted to play at Louisiana State) and Tony Richie (a 2000 fifth-rounder now at Florida State), but the Sox think as highly of Lisk, who slid to the 24th round because he seemed intent on playing for the University of South Carolina. He's an advanced prospect for his age, showing soft hands, a good arm behind the plate and the potential to hit with power. Lisk got high marks in a brief audition in the Rookie-level Appalachian League. He's part of a striking upgrade in the organization's catching depth over the last two years, which also includes trades for Miguel Olivo and Lee Evans, plus the draft-and-follow signing of bilingual Wally Rosa.

Year	Club (League)	Class	AVG	G	AB	R	H	2B	3B	HR	RBI	BB	SO	SB
2001	Bristol (Appy)	R	.289	13	38	8	11	1	0	0	6	7	14	3
MINOR LEAGUE TOTALS			.289	13	38	8	11	1	0	0	6	7	14	3

29. Brian Sager, rhp

Born: Oct. 30, 1979. **Ht.:** 6-5. **Wt.:** 230. **Bats:** R. **Throws:** R. **School:** Georgia Tech. **Career Transactions:** Selected by White Sox in 13th round of 2001 draft; signed Jan. 14, 2002.

Twice Sager seemed destined to be a first-round pick, but he lasted until the 13th round last June after an injury-plagued junior season at Georgia Tech. He was drafted in the same round out of high school, but only slid that far because he was set on attending Stanford, and the Diamondbacks' $1 million bonus offer couldn't dissuade him. Sager spent two years at Stanford before transferring to Georgia Tech for 2001, when he pitched just 26 innings because of forearm problems. After drafting him, the White Sox took a wait-and-see approach. Sager had October surgery to repair a decompressed nerve in his forearm, then impressed Chicago in two bullpen sessions in Arizona before signing for $385,000. He has classic pitcher's size and his fastball and slider are big league pitches when he's healthy, though that has been rare in the last two years. He also had shoulder problems at Stanford in 2000. The Sox will take a good look at him in spring training before deciding where Sager will debut.

Year	Club (League)	Class	W	L	ERA	G	GS	CG	SV	IP	H	R	ER	BB	SO
					Has Not Played—Signed 2002 Contract										

30. Aaron Kirkland, rhp

Born: March 1, 1979. **Ht.:** 6-5. **Wt.:** 195. **Bats:** R. **Throws:** R. **School:** Troy State University. **Career Transactions:** Signed as nondrafted free agent by White Sox, June 15, 2001.

It's hard not to notice a pitcher who begins his pro career with 62 strikeouts and zero unintentional walks. That's what the lanky Kirkland did in the Rookie-level Arizona League after signing with the Sox as an undrafted college senior. This strike-throwing machine had dropped only a few hints of his potential at Troy State, where he went 5-5, 5.70 as a senior. He used an unusually funky splitter to come into his own when the Sox tried him as a closer. He led the AZL in ERA, saves and opponent batting average (.158). Kirkland throws a darting slider and a two-seam fastball that hits 91 mph with movement. The Sox believe he'll gain velocity from their weight-training program. He was old for Rookie ball at 22, so the Sox will hold off on hyperbole until he passes the tests they plan for him at higher levels in 2002.

Year	Club (League)	Class	W	L	ERA	G	GS	CG	SV	IP	H	R	ER	BB	SO
2001	White Sox (AZL)	R	0	2	0.40	29	0	0	13	45	25	5	2	4	62
MINOR LEAGUE TOTALS			0	2	0.40	29	0	0	13	45	25	5	2	4	62

CINCINNATI
Reds

By Chris Haft

Adam Dunn loomed over the entire organization in 2001, and not just because he's 6-foot-6. Dunn's development and success symbolized the franchise's hopes of rebounding from the injuries and controversies that have blunted progress.

Though Dunn's no longer part of Cincinnati's farm system, his image is integral to holding it together. Emboldened by the rookie outfielder's production, which included 51 homers (19 in the majors) in 2001, the Reds believe they're poised to mint similarly talented performers. As a smaller-revenue franchise, it's more important for them to perpetuate this assembly line.

"We want to try to have a tremendous impact guy every year," farm director Tim Naehring said. "We're very confident that in 2002 we'll be able to do the same type of thing."

Five of the Reds' six affiliates reached the postseason in 2001, including champions in the International League and Pioneer League. The Rookie-level Gulf Coast League club was the only one to miss the playoffs, yet it posted an organization-best .621 winning percentage.

Replenishing the stock of prospects was the first step in recovering from Marge Schott's years of neglect. The success of the farm system in 2001 marked another step. It's also an extension of Naehring's emphasis on a focused approach throughout the organization. Uniform and grooming codes went hand-in-hand with instruction.

"I think players were surprised at first, but in the end they received it very well," Naehring said. "With good discipline, demands on work ethic and an overall philosophy of respecting the game and the organization, eventually the talent will surface."

Another encouraging sign was the continued rise of players such as righthander Jose Acevedo from the Dominican Republic and shortstop Ranier Olmedo from Venezuela. This reflected the Reds' continued efforts to revitalize their previously dormant programs in Latin America.

By contrast, the failure to sign first-round draft pick Jeremy Sowers was both forgettable and regrettable. The Reds selected Sowers, a high school lefthander from Louisville, though it was obvious from the start they wouldn't be able to meet Sowers' bonus demands.

Organization Overview

General manager: Jim Bowden. **Farm director:** Tim Naehring. **Scouting director:** Kasey McKeon.

2001 PERFORMANCE

Class	Farm Team	League	W	L	Pct.	Finish*	Manager
Majors	Cincinnati	National	66	96	.407	15th (16)	Bob Boone
Triple-A	Louisville RiverBats	International	84	60	.583	3rd (14)	Dave Miley
Double-A	Chattanooga Lookouts	Southern	72	67	.518	5th (10)	Phillip Wellman
High A	Mudville Nine	California	74	66	.529	4th (10)	Dave Oliver
Low A	Dayton Dragons	Midwest	82	57	.590	4th (14)	Donnie Scott
Rookie	Billings Mustangs	Pioneer	46	29	.613	3rd (8)	Rick Burleson
Rookie	GCL Reds	Gulf Coast	36	22	.621	3rd (14)	Edgar Caceres
OVERALL 2001 MINOR LEAGUE STANDINGS			394	301	.567	2nd (30)	

*Finish in overall standings (No. of teams in league)

ORGANIZATION LEADERS

BATTING
*AVG	Gary Varner, Billings	.351
R	Ben Broussard, Chattanooga/Mudville	95
H	Raul Gonzalez, Louisville	161
TB	Ben Broussard, Chattanooga/Mudville	254
2B	Steve Smitherman, Dayton	45
3B	Elvin Andujar, Dayton/GCL Reds	9
HR	**Adam Dunn**, Louisville/Chattanooga	32
RBI	Wily Mo Pena, Dayton	113
BB	Mark Burnett, Mudville	84
SO	Wily Mo Pena, Dayton	177
SB	Ranier Olmedo, Mudville	38

PITCHING
W	Ryan Mottl, Dayton	15
L	Three tied at	10
#ERA	Ty Howington, Chatt./Mudville/Dayton	2.30
G	Michael Neu, Mudville	53
CG	**Jared Fernandez**, Louisville	4
SV	Frank Bludau, Dayton	21
	Michael Neu, Mudville	21
IP	**Jared Fernandez**, Louisville	196
BB	Scott Dunn, Chattanooga/Mudville	102
SO	Scott Dunn, Chattanooga/Mudville	160

*Minimum 250 At-Bats #Minimum 75 Innings

TOP PROSPECTS OF THE DECADE

1992	Reggie Sanders, of
1993	Willie Greene, 3b
1994	Pokey Reese, ss
1995	Pokey Reese, ss
1996	Pokey Reese, ss
1997	Aaron Boone, 3b
1998	Damian Jackson, ss/2b
1999	Rob Bell, rhp
2000	Gookie Dawkins, ss
2001	Austin Kearns, of

TOP DRAFT PICKS OF THE DECADE

1992	Chad Mottola, of
1993	Pat Watkins, of
1994	C.J. Nitkowski, lhp
1995	Brett Tomko, rhp (2)
1996	John Oliver, of
1997	Brandon Larson, ss/3b
1998	Austin Kearns, of
1999	Ty Howington, lhp
2000	David Espinosa, ss
2001	*Jeremy Sowers, lhp

*Did not sign.

Dunn

Fernandez

BEST TOOLS

Best Hitter for Average	Ben Broussard
Best Power Hitter	Wily Mo Pena
Fastest Baserunner	Gookie Dawkins
Best Fastball	Chris Booker
Best Breaking Ball	Ryan Snare
Best Changeup	Ricardo Aramboles
Best Control	Dustin Moseley
Best Defensive Catcher	Dane Sardinha
Best Defensive Infielder	Ranier Olmedo
Best Infield Arm	Edwin Encarnacion
Best Defensive Outfielder	Alejandro Diaz
Best Outfield Arm	Austin Kearns

PROJECTED 2005 LINEUP

Catcher	Dane Sardinha
First Base	Sean Casey
Second Base	David Espinosa
Third Base	Aaron Boone
Shortstop	Gookie Dawkins
Left Field	Adam Dunn
Center Field	Ken Griffey Jr.
Right Field	Austin Kearns
No. 1 Starter	Ty Howington
No. 2 Starter	Chris Reitsma
No. 3 Starter	Ricardo Aramboles
No. 4 Starter	Dustin Moseley
No. 5 Starter	Ryan Snare
Closer	John Riedling

ALL-TIME LARGEST BONUSES

Austin Kearns, 1998	$1,950,000
Ty Howington, 1999	$1,750,000
Brandon Larson, 1997	$1,330,000
Alejandro Diaz, 1999	$1,175,000
Dustin Moseley, 2000	$930,000

DraftAnalysis

2001 Draft

Best Pro Debut: 1B Jesse Gutierrez (20) batted .294-16-61 at Billings, tying for the Rookie-level Pioneer League home run crown. RHP Justin Gillman (2) went 4-2, 1.75 with 38 strikeouts in 36 innings in the Rookie-level Gulf Coast League.

Best Athlete: OF Alan Moye (3) is built like Mike Cameron and offers similar power and speed. He was considered a tough sign because his parents are teachers and he was committed to Baylor, but the Reds got him under contract quickly.

Best Hitter: Gutierrez or Moye. Moye had been a switch-hitter, though he'll focus on batting from the right side for now.

Best Raw Power: Gutierrez led NCAA Division I with an .855 slugging percentage in 2000 at Texas-Pan American and Division II with 28 homers in 2001. He hit two homers in his final college game, helping St. Mary's (Texas) win the Division II College World Series and earning MVP honors. Gutierrez caught some in college and the Reds will use him there in the future.

Fastest Runner: Moye gets from the right side of the plate to first base in a consistent 4.1-4.2 seconds. 2B Domonique Lewis (34) has similar speed.

Best Defensive Player: SS Jeff Bannon (18) is a solid glove man.

Best Fastball: RHP Joe Powers (23) had an 8.42 ERA as a Wright State junior, so he didn't get a lot of attention. But he throws 93-94 mph, and with mechanical adjustments he might get as high as 97. RHP Scott Light

(6) tops out at 96 mph, and RHP Bobby Basham (7) is right behind at 95.

Most Intriguing Background: Basham was a backup quarterback at Richmond. Unsigned RHP John Palmer's (21) father David pitched in the majors.

Closest To The Majors: RHP Steve Kelly (4) has an 88-92 mph fastball and plus curveball. He's polished and comes from a big-time program at Georgia Tech. Gillman is advanced for a high school pitcher and reminiscent of 2000 Reds first-rounder Dustin Moseley.

Sowers

Best Late-Round Pick: Gutierrez or Powers. Another to watch is 3B Ryan Fry (22), who's converting to catcher. He has above-average arm strength and power potential.

The One Who Got Away: LHP **Jeremy Sowers** (1) has a lot going for him—great command, great curveball and a 90-91 mph fastball. He also had a $3 million price tag, and the Reds offered him less than half that to sign. He decided to attend Vanderbilt instead.

Assessment: Not signing Sowers allowed Cincinnati to stop borrowing from next year's signing budget, ending a cycle that dates back to 1999. Some clubs believe that was the logic behind taking him, though the Reds say they were interested in signing him. His loss meant Cincinnati didn't land an obvious impact player.

2000 Draft

Cincinnati got creative, signing SS David Espinosa (1) and C Dane Sardinha (2) to big league deals with no bonuses and RHP Dustin Moseley (1) to a 2001 contract. So far the trio has been outperformed by LHP Ryan Snare (2), RHP David Gil (3) and OF Steve Smitherman (23). **Grade: C+**

1999 Draft

LHP Ty Howington (1) and OF Ben Broussard (2) don't get all the credit and attention they deserve. We'll give it to them here. **Grade: B+**

1998 Draft

By the end of the second round, the Reds had two potential superstar OFs in Adam Dunn (2) and Austin Kearns (1). LHP B.J. Ryan (17) reached the majors quickly but was traded to Baltimore. **Grade: A**

1997 Draft

RHP Scott Williamson (9) was the National League's top rookie two years later. 3B Brandon Larson (1) is leveling off, but SS Gookie Dawkins (2) still could be Barry Larkin's successor. **Grade: B**

Note: Draft analysis prepared by Jim Callis. Numbers in parentheses indicate draft rounds.

. . . Kearns ranked ahead of Adam Dunn as a prospect entering the 2001 season.

Austin Kearns of

Born: May 20, 1980.
Ht.: 6-3. **Wt.:** 220.
Bats: R. **Throws:** R.
School: Lafayette HS, Lexington, Ky.
Career Transactions: Selected by Reds in first round (seventh overall) of 1998 draft; signed July 30, 1998

Kearns ranked ahead of Adam Dunn as a prospect entering the 2001 season, but Dunn left him in his dust when Kearns tore a ligament in his right thumb. A strong finish at Double-A Chattanooga (.346-3-17 in his final 15 games) and a torrid Arizona Fall League performance (.371-4-31 in 33 contests) renewed the Reds' faith in him. Before the season, Kearns asserted his presence in the organization by improving his power numbers annually while maturing overall at the same impressive rate.

Though Kearns' injury affected his performance, it didn't spoil his approach—which is why he's the organization's top prospect for the second year in a row. Other Reds who earned the No. 1 distinction in consecutive years were Reggie Sanders (1991-92) and Pokey Reese (1994-96). His ability to hit to all fields and maintain command of the strike zone long has impressed the organization. He is also a precise outfielder who takes good routes on fly balls and has an above-average arm. If anything, Kearns' injury bolstered his status in the organization. His speedy recovery, along with the determination he showed, announced he could handle the adversity that ultimately strikes even the game's biggest stars. While no one would label Kearns lazy, because success has come easily to him, some in the Reds' inner sanctum fear he won't always apply himself as diligently as they might hope. Establishing a daily routine involving on- and off-field preparation—something the Reds try to stress throughout the organization—remains essential to Kearns' improvement. Like other hitters rising through the minors, he needs the savvy that comes with facing more experienced pitchers. His AFL stint should help in that regard.

Kearns just might find himself in a Cincinnati uniform on Opening Day as a member of the starting lineup. The Reds' insistence on trying to win now on their limited budget forced them to trade Reese and Dmitri Young for pitching help. Unless he regresses, Kearns' arrival in Cincinnati probably will occur no later than midseason.

Yr	Club (League)	Class	AVG	G	AB	R	H	2B	3B	HR	RBI	BB	SO	SB
1998	Billings (Pio)	R	.315	30	108	17	34	9	0	1	14	23	22	1
1999	Rockford (Mid)	A	.258	124	426	72	110	36	5	13	48	50	120	21
2000	Dayton (Mid)	A	.306	136	484	110	148	37	2	27	104	90	93	18
2001	Chattanooga (SL)	AA	.268	59	205	30	55	11	2	6	36	26	43	7
	Reds (GCL)	R	.176	6	17	2	3	2	0	0	4	2	7	0
MINOR LEAGUE TOTALS			.282	355	1240	231	350	95	9	47	206	191	285	47

2. Ty Howington, lhp

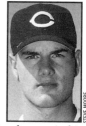

Born: Nov. 4. **Ht.:** 6-5. **Wt.:** 220. **Bats:** B. **Throws:** L. **School:** Hudson's Bay HS, Vancouver, Wash. **Career Transactions:** Selected by Reds in first round (14th overall) of 1999 draft; signed Nov. 1, 1999.

Arthroscopic elbow surgery in late March delayed the start of Howington's 2001 season, but he recovered smoothly to excel at both Class A levels and perform respectably in Double-A. That followed a 5-15, 5.27 pro debut in 2000 at Class A Dayton, during which the Reds were pleased that he gained experience and showed durability by making every start. Howington aroused concern at the start of his pro career with his complicated delivery, but he has streamlined his mechanics. Proof comes in his fastball, which regularly travels at 92-93 mph. Howington's curveball and changeup are both effective when he finishes his delivery, giving them late life. He still needs the sheer repetition of performing a fundamentally sound delivery. Not only will that increase the effectiveness of his pitches, but it also will help him avoid future arm trouble. He must devote attention to his pickoff move. Howington is tentatively slated to open 2002 at Double-A Chattanooga. He's almost certain to reach Triple-A at some point.

Yr	Club (League)	Class	W	L	ERA	G	GS	CG	SV	IP	H	R	ER	BB	SO
2000	Dayton (Mid)	A	5	15	5.27	27	26	0	0	142	150	91	83	86	119
2001	Dayton (Mid)	A	4	0	1.15	6	6	1	0	39	15	7	5	9	47
	Mudville (Cal)	A	3	2	2.43	7	7	0	0	37	33	18	10	20	44
	Chattanooga (SL)	AA	1	3	3.27	7	7	0	0	41	36	18	15	24	38
MINOR LEAGUE TOTALS			13	20	3.93	47	46	1	0	259	234	134	113	139	248

3. Wily Mo Pena, of

Born: Jan. 23, 1982. **Ht.:** 6-3. **Wt.:** 215. **Bats:** R. **Throws:** R. **Career Transactions:** Signed out of Dominican Republic by Yankees, July 15, 1998 . . . Traded by Yankees to Reds for 3B Drew Henson and OF Michael Coleman, March 20, 2001.

The Reds longed for Pena as far back as the spring of 1999, when he signed a $3.7 million major league contract with the Yankees. They weren't heartbroken to part with third-base prospect Drew Henson, whom they knew they couldn't keep away from a potential NFL career, because Pena came in return. Cincinnati figured Pena could flourish if they left him in one place for an entire season and allowed him to settle in. His impressive build, which prompts comparisons to Sammy Sosa, magnifies his five-tool skills. So did Pena's performance, which made him one of three minor leaguers with 25 home runs and 25 stolen bases. Pena's work ethic and enthusiasm are almost as impressive as his physical gifts. Pena needs to stop swinging at everything, especially breaking pitches off the plate. Defensively, he still needs work on reading the angles of batted balls, which should come once he learns to get better jumps. Pena's contract requires him to open 2003 in the majors or be exposed to waivers. The Reds must hope he accelerates his development, aware that he's doomed to be rushed to the bigs.

Yr	Club (League)	Class	AVG	G	AB	R	H	2B	3B	HR	RBI	BB	SO	SB
1999	Yankees (GCL)	R	.247	45	166	21	41	10	1	7	26	12	54	3
2000	Greensboro (SAL)	A	.205	67	249	41	51	7	1	10	28	18	91	6
	Staten Island (NY-P)	A	.301	20	73	7	22	1	2	0	10	2	23	2
2001	Dayton (Mid)	A	.264	135	511	87	135	25	5	26	113	33	177	26
MINOR LEAGUE TOTALS			.249	267	999	156	249	43	9	43	177	65	345	37

4. Ricardo Aramboles, rhp

Born: Dec. 4, 1981. **Ht.:** 6-2. **Wt.:** 170. **Bats:** R. **Throws:** R. **Career Transactions:** Signed out of Dominican Republic by Marlins, July 2, 1996; contract voided, Dec. 3, 1997 . . . Signed by Yankees Feb. 26, 1998 . . . Traded by Yankees to Reds for RHP Mark Wohlers, June 30, 2001.

Aware they couldn't afford to retain reliever Mark Wohlers in 2002, the Reds sent him to the Yankees for Aramboles, who has recovered from Tommy John surgery in 1999, though he was shut down with a strained elbow shortly after the trade. Aramboles thrilled the Reds because they've recently had so few pitchers like him. He has an uncanny ability to adjust to changes in game situations, with a fastball that regularly travels at 93-94 mph, an excellent changeup and a decent curveball. He was the club's top pitcher in instructional league. Aramboles must stay on top of all of his pitches and resist the temptation to push off the rubber too quickly so he can drive down off the mound more forcefully. His results aren't as overpowering as his stuff because he trusts his changeup too much. After bouncing around with four teams in 2001, Aramboles could benefit from some stability in Double-A.

Yr	Club (League)	Class	W	L	ERA	G	GS	CG	SV	IP	H	R	ER	BB	SO
1997	Marlins (DSL)	R	1	1	1.71	8	2	0	0	21	15	7	4	7	14
1998	Yankees (GCL)	R	2	1	2.93	10	9	0	0	40	33	14	13	13	44
	Oneonta (NY-P)	A	1	0	1.50	1	1	0	0	6	4	2	1	1	8
1999	Yankees (GCL)	R	2	3	3.89	9	7	0	0	35	35	18	15	14	42
	Greensboro (SAL)	A	1	2	2.34	6	6	1	0	35	25	9	9	12	34
2000	Greensboro (SAL)	A	5	13	4.31	25	25	2	0	138	150	81	66	47	150
2001	Tampa (FSL)	A	7	2	4.06	12	11	0	0	69	72	37	31	19	59
	Columbus (IL)	AAA	1	3	3.04	4	4	0	0	24	26	11	8	4	14
	Chattanooga (SL)	AA	0	2	8.00	2	1	0	0	9	12	8	8	0	5
	Dayton (Mid)	A	1	2	3.66	4	4	0	0	20	23	8	8	4	9
MINOR LEAGUE TOTALS			21	29	3.71	81	70	3	0	395	395	195	163	121	379

5. Dustin Moseley, rhp

Born: Dec. 26, 1981. **Ht.:** 6-3. **Wt.:** 190. **Bats:** R. **Throws:** R. **School:** Arkansas HS, Texarkana, Ark. **Career Transactions:** Selected by Reds in first round (34th overall) of 2000 draft; signed Nov. 21, 2000.

The Reds didn't have money for Moseley in their 2000 signing budget, so he signed that November after their 2001 fiscal year began. They figured he was mature enough to begin his professional career in low Class A in 2001, and his performance justified the decision. Invited to big league camp in 2001, Moseley endured volleys of good-natured razzing from veterans who asked if he had his driver's license. He demonstrated an excellent feel for pitching, despite his youth, guiding his pitches through the strike zone and past hitters. Moseley's fastball can hit 92 mph, which isn't overpowering but is hard enough when he hits his spots with late movement. His curveball and changeup were effective more often than not. With his beanpole build, Moseley must gain the strength that will enable him to reach the 200-inning level in coming years. Polished as he is, he can tweak his delivery by staying over the rubber a little longer, which will help him maintain better balance. The Reds don't need to rush Moseley. They know he'll progress quite nicely on his own. For now, moving up to high Class A Stockton will suffice, though he could finish the season in Double-A.

Yr	Club (League)	Class	W	L	ERA	G	GS	CG	SV	IP	H	R	ER	BB	SO
2001	Dayton (Mid)	A	10	8	4.20	25	25	0	0	148	158	83	69	42	108
MINOR LEAGUE TOTALS			10	8	4.20	25	25	0	0	148	158	83	69	42	108

6. Ben Broussard, 1b

Born: Sept. 24, 1976. **Ht.:** 6-2. **Wt.:** 220. **Bats:** L. **Throws:** L. **School:** McNeese State University. **Career Transactions:** Selected by Reds in second round of 1999 draft; signed June 2, 1999.

Adam Dunn deservedly got most of the headlines, but Broussard also had a productive 2001 season. He led the Southern League in hitting and slugging percentage (.592), while ranking second in on-base percentage (.428) and fifth in home runs. Broussard's performance erased the disappointment of a 2000 season that was marred by a wrist injury. The Reds' hopes that Broussard would cut down on his strikeouts were fulfilled. Like Sean Casey, Broussard hasn't yet developed overwhelming power but compensates by using the entire ballpark. Broussard uses nice quick hands in his swing, the key to his versatility as a hitter. Broussard played primarily first base in 2001 after drifting between there and left field the previous two seasons. He's barely adequate at both spots. The focus on Broussard will intensify now that he's on the 40-man roster. The Reds' emphasis on employing young, inexpensive talent could afford him the opportunity to reach the majors soon, though he'll also have to deal with a logjam at his positions.

Yr	Club (League)	Class	AVG	G	AB	R	H	2B	3B	HR	RBI	BB	SO	SB
1999	Billings (Pio)	R	.407	38	145	39	59	11	2	14	48	34	30	1
	Clinton (Mid)	A	.550	5	20	8	11	4	1	2	6	3	4	0

Yr	Club (League)	Class	AVG	G	AB	R	H	2B	3B	HR	RBI	BB	SO	SB
	Chattanooga (SL)	AA	.213	35	127	26	27	5	0	8	21	11	41	1
2000	Chattanooga (SL)	AA	.255	87	286	64	73	8	4	14	51	72	78	15
2001	Mudville (Cal)	A	.245	30	102	14	25	5	0	5	21	16	31	0
	Chattanooga (SL)	AA	.320	100	353	81	113	27	0	23	69	61	69	10
MINOR LEAGUE TOTALS			.298	295	1033	232	308	60	7	66	216	197	253	27

7. David Espinosa, ss

Born: Dec. 16, 1981. **Ht.:** 6-2. **Wt.:** 175. **Bats:** B. **Throws:** R. **School:** Gulliver Prep, Miami. **Career Transactions:** Selected by Reds in first round (23rd overall) of 2000 draft; signed Sept. 1, 2000.

Like Dustin Moseley, Espinosa spent the summer of 2000 negotiating and made his debut in full-season Class A in 2001. The cash-strapped Reds signed him to an unusual eight-year major league contract worth a guaranteed $2.75 million, but no bonus. He started shakily at Dayton before righting himself. Espinosa is a switch-hitter with some pop, and he has the speed to be a threat on the bases. He also draws walks, so he could fit at the top of a lineup. Despite committing 48 errors, Espinosa actually improved markedly on defense as the 2001 season progressed. He moved back to shortstop after trying second base briefly. Though Espinosa has slightly more pop in his bat as a lefthanded hitter, he maintains the same aggressive approach from both sides. He often is too aggressive, as his strikeout total indicates. He struggled at times with his throwing because he lacked a consistent arm angle and polished footwork. Some Midwest League observers project Espinosa as a second baseman and center fielder. The Reds will keep him at shortstop in 2002, which he'll open in high Class A.

Yr	Club (League)	Class	AVG	G	AB	R	H	2B	3B	HR	RBI	BB	SO	SB
2001	Dayton (Mid)	A	.262	122	493	88	129	29	8	7	37	55	120	15
MINOR LEAGUE TOTALS			.262	122	493	88	129	29	8	7	37	55	120	15

8. Gookie Dawkins, ss

Born: May 12, 1979. **Ht.:** 6-1. **Wt.:** 180. **Bats:** R. **Throws:** R. **School:** Newberry (S.C.) HS. **Career Transactions:** Selected by Reds in second round of 1997 draft; signed June 8, 1997.

Having spent part of the last three years in Double-A, Dawkins appears stuck in neutral. Yet the Reds maintain faith in his ability. Bothered by a right knee injury at the end of 2000, Dawkins had barely recovered when he sprained a ligament in the same knee rounding third base in April. His 2001 season essentially didn't begin until mid-May. As a veteran of the 1999 Pan American Games and the 2000 Olympics, Dawkins has a well-rounded understanding of the game. His knee injuries haven't ruined his speed and quickness, which he uses in the field and on the basepaths. His range and strong arm help him make difficult plays look routine. The Reds aren't sure what has kept Dawkins in a two-year offensive funk, which he started to come out of in the Arizona Fall League. He tends to drift into pitches, resulting in a lot of awkward swings and the sense that pitchers can knock the bat out of his hands. Dawkins is a strong candidate to open 2002 in Triple-A, though a return to Double-A isn't out of the question. He has experience at second base, but shortstop is Dawkins' natural position. Obviously, as a result of the Pokey Reese trade, he's got a much better chance of seeing time there when the chance comes.

Yr	Club (League)	Class	AVG	G	AB	R	H	2B	3B	HR	RBI	BB	SO	SB
1997	Billings (Pio)	R	.241	70	253	47	61	5	0	4	37	30	38	16
1998	Burlington (Mid)	A	.264	102	367	52	97	7	6	1	30	37	60	37
1999	Rockford (Mid)	A	.272	76	305	56	83	10	6	8	32	35	38	38
	Chattanooga (SL)	AA	.364	32	129	24	47	7	0	2	13	14	17	15
	Cincinnati (NL)	MAJ	.143	7	7	1	1	0	0	0	0	0	4	0
2000	Chattanooga (SL)	AA	.231	95	368	54	85	20	6	6	31	40	71	22
	Cincinnati (NL)	MAJ	.220	14	41	5	9	2	0	0	3	2	7	0
2001	Chattanooga (SL)	AA	.226	104	394	59	89	16	3	8	40	32	88	14
MAJOR LEAGUE TOTALS			.208	21	48	6	10	2	0	0	3	2	11	0
MINOR LEAGUE TOTALS			.254	479	1816	292	462	65	21	29	183	188	312	142

9. Dane Sardinha, c

Born: April 8, 1979. **Ht.:** 6-0. **Wt.:** 210. **Bats:** R. **Throws:** R. **School:** Pepperdine University. **Career Transactions:** Selected by Reds in second round of 2000 draft; signed Sept. 1, 2000.

Sardinha signed a deal similar to David Espinosa's, getting no bonus but a six-year big league contract worth at least $1.75 million. In his pro debut at high Class A, he gave the Reds about what they expected. He sparkled defensively and continued to need help offensively. The Reds believe Sardinha could survive defensively in the majors right now. He gets rid of the ball quickly and with plenty on his throws, finishing second in the California League by nabbing 38 percent of basestealers in 2001. While his offense wasn't overwhelming, he does have power to the gaps. To avoid becoming branded as a defensive specialist, Sardinha must keep refining his offensive approach, particularly by getting himself in decent hitting position as he uncorks his swing. He also has to refine his strike zone. Quiet by nature, he needs to assume more of a take-charge attitude behind the plate. With Jason LaRue establishing himself in the majors, veteran Kelly Stinnett serving as his backup and Corky Miller becoming a factor, Sardinha should be allowed to progress at a comfortable pace. He'll move up to Double-A in 2002.

Yr	Club (League)	Class	AVG	G	AB	R	H	2B	3B	HR	RBI	BB	SO	SB
2001	Mudville (Cal)	A	.235	109	422	45	99	24	2	9	55	12	97	0
MINOR LEAGUE TOTALS			.235	109	422	45	99	24	2	9	55	12	97	0

10. Ranier Olmedo, ss

Born: May 31, 1981. **Ht.:** 5-11. **Wt.:** 155. **Bats:** B. **Throws:** R. **Career Transactions:** Signed out of Venezuela by Reds, Jan. 21, 1999.

Olmedo plays the most exciting infield defense the organization has seen since Pokey Reese was ascending through the system in the mid-1990s. In Olmedo's native Venezuela, the comparisons he draws are to that nation's other great shortstops. He has the quickness, deft footwork, arm strength and range of an elite shortstop. With those gifts, his flashiness is no surprise. Asked to try switch-hitting in 2001, Olmedo accepted the task and held his own when he batted lefthanded for the first time. He used his speed to lead the organization in stolen bases. Olmedo occasionally is too slick for his own good and needs to make routine plays more routinely. He has work to do offensively, because he doesn't walk or make contact often enough for the singles hitter that he is. He also needs to refine his basestealing technique after getting caught 17 times. The Reds are confident Olmedo, who has an unquenchable work ethic, can hone his game while receiving a promotion to Double-A. Though Cincinnati has a glut of middle infielders, Olmedo may force the organization to make room for him.

Yr	Club (League)	Class	AVG	G	AB	R	H	2B	3B	HR	RBI	BB	SO	SB
1999	Reds (GCL)	R	.236	54	195	30	46	12	1	1	19	12	28	13
2000	Dayton (Mid)	A	.255	111	369	50	94	19	1	4	41	30	70	17
2001	Mudville (Cal)	A	.244	129	536	57	131	23	4	0	28	24	121	38
MINOR LEAGUE TOTALS			.246	294	1100	137	271	54	6	5	88	66	219	68

11. Ryan Snare, lhp

Born: Feb. 8, 1979. **Ht.:** 6-0. **Wt.:** 190. **Bats:** L. **Throws:** L. **School:** University of North Carolina. **Career Transactions:** Selected by Reds in second round of 2000 draft; signed Aug. 11, 2000.

Like most of Cincinnati's top 2000 draft picks, Snare signed too late to play professionally that year. This didn't bother the Reds, who knew that his college experience had given him the polish many other pitchers lacked. His stuff isn't overpowering, but he makes it work with impressive command. He's especially adept at spotting his fastball, which ranges from 88-91 mph. Snare complements it with a sharp-breaking curveball that's major league-caliber. His changeup is decent and he has a good pickoff move. Snare has no glaring flaws. He struggled with his consistency at times last season, the only reason he wasn't promoted to high Class A. He probably will bypass that level and begin this year in Double-A. He could make his major league debut sometime in 2003.

Year	Club (League)	Class	W	L	ERA	G	GS	CG	SV	IP	H	R	ER	BB	SO
2001	Dayton (Mid)	A	9	5	3.05	21	20	0	0	115	101	45	39	37	118
MINOR LEAGUE TOTALS			9	5	3.05	21	20	0	0	115	101	45	39	37	118

12. Justin Gillman, rhp

Born: June 27, 1983. **Ht.:** 6-2. **Wt.:** 185. **Bats:** R. **Throws:** R. **School:** Mosley HS, Panama City, Fla. **Career Transactions:** Selected by Reds in second round of 2001 draft; signed June 26, 2001.

As the highest-ranked 2001 draftee on this list, Gillman made an immediate impression. The Reds were astounded that such a young pitcher could have as much command and poise as he displayed. He thrived with his fastball, which hovers from 89-93 mph. He also has an above-average curveball and an average changeup. The Reds believe that Gillman can ultimately be a No. 2 or 3 starter in their rotation, though he obviously needs plenty of seasoning. Gifted with a pitcher's frame, Gillman still needs to work on his strength and conditioning to realize his full potential. With a little more beef behind his pitches, he could develop into a bona fide power pitcher. The Reds don't want to rush Gillman, but they're not averse to challenging him. He could open 2002 in high Class A.

Year	Club (League)	Class	W	L	ERA	G	GS	CG	SV	IP	H	R	ER	BB	SO
2001	Reds (GCL)	R	4	2	1.75	9	7	0	0	36	19	10	7	11	38
	Billings (Pio)	R	1	0	0.00	1	1	0	0	6	0	1	0	5	2
MINOR LEAGUE TOTALS			5	2	1.50	10	8	0	0	42	19	11	7	16	40

13. Brian Reith, rhp

Born: Feb. 28, 1978. **Ht.:** 6-5. **Wt.:** 190. **Bats:** R. **Throws:** R. **School:** Concordia Lutheran HS, Fort Wayne, Ind. **Career Transactions:** Selected by Yankees in sixth round of 1996 draft; signed June 22, 1996 . . . Traded by Yankees with 3B Drew Henson, OF Jackson Melian and LHP Ed Yarnall to Reds for LHP Denny Neagle and OF Mike Frank, July 12, 2000.

Reith and outfielder Jackson Melian are the only two players remaining in the organization of the four the Yankees gave up for lefthander Denny Neagle in July 2000. Last spring, third baseman Drew Henson was traded back to New York and lefthander Ed Yarnall was sold to Japan's Orix BlueWave. Some Reds officials wonder if Reith might as well be gone too. Nobody doubts his ability. But being rushed to Cincinnati in 2001 to shore up a starting rotation riddled with injuries and ineffectiveness may have scarred him. He got shelled once he returned to Double-A, which wasn't a good sign. Reith gave up 13 homers in 40 big league innings, a tipoff that hitters knew what was coming. He still has plenty of stuff: a lively fastball that ranges between 90-93 mph, a crackling slider and a changeup that he didn't use enough in the big leagues. He just needs to gain savvy and regain his confidence. Reith probably will open 2002 a step away from the majors in Triple-A Indianapolis.

Year	Club (League)	Class	W	L	ERA	G	GS	CG	SV	IP	H	R	ER	BB	SO
1996	Yankees (GCL)	R	2	3	4.13	10	4	0	0	33	31	16	15	16	21
1997	Yankees (GCL)	R	4	2	2.86	12	11	1	0	63	70	28	20	14	40
1998	Greensboro (SAL)	A	6	7	2.28	20	20	3	0	118	86	42	30	32	116
1999	Tampa (FSL)	A	9	9	4.70	26	23	0	0	140	174	87	73	35	101
2000	Tampa (FSL)	A	9	4	2.18	18	18	1	0	120	101	39	29	33	100
	Dayton (Mid)	A	2	1	2.88	5	5	0	0	34	33	12	11	8	30
	Chattanooga (SL)	AA	1	3	3.90	5	5	0	0	30	31	14	13	11	29
2001	Chattanooga (SL)	AA	6	4	3.97	18	18	1	0	104	103	63	46	42	89
	Louisville (IL)	AAA	0	0	3.60	1	1	0	0	5	7	2	2	1	6
	Cincinnati (NL)	MAJ	0	7	7.81	9	8	0	0	40	56	37	35	16	22
MAJOR LEAGUE TOTALS			0	7	7.81	9	8	0	0	40	56	37	35	16	22
MINOR LEAGUE TOTALS			39	33	3.32	115	105	6	0	647	636	303	239	192	532

14. Edwin Encarnacion, 3b

Born: Jan. 7, 1983. **Ht.:** 6-1. **Wt.:** 175. **Bats:** R. **Throws:** R. **School:** Manuela Toro HS, Caguas, P.R. **Career Transactions:** Selected by Rangers in ninth round of 2000 draft; signed June 12, 2000 . . . Traded by Rangers with OF Ruben Mateo to Reds for RHP Rob Bell, June 15, 2001.

Encarnacion initially attracted attention before the 2000 draft, when he was considered one of the top prospects in Puerto Rico. The Reds wouldn't have traded righthander Rob Bell to the Rangers unless he was included in the return package along with outfielder Ruben Mateo. The Cincinnati brass loves his Encarnacion's athleticism, which essentially makes him a shortstop playing third base. He has the organization's strongest infield arm, plus good range to either side as well as soft hands. He's still learning to hit—more patience at the plate would help—though the Reds were encouraged that he began to display a little bit of power in 2001. He must fill out physically to withstand the rigors of professional ball. Complaints also linger about Encarnacion's intensity. Though he's hardly a malingerer, some observers believe he doesn't play as hard as he should every day. Diligence often comes with maturity, which the Reds hope Encarnacion will gain with a full season in low Class A this year.

Year	Club (League)	Class	AVG	G	AB	R	H	2B	3B	HR	RBI	BB	SO	SB
2000	Rangers (GCL)	R	.311	51	177	31	55	6	3	0	36	21	27	3
2001	Savannah (SAL)	A	.306	45	170	23	52	9	2	4	25	12	34	3
	Billings (Pio)	R	.261	52	211	27	55	8	2	5	26	15	29	8
	Dayton (Mid)	A	.162	9	37	2	6	2	0	1	6	1	5	0
MINOR LEAGUE TOTALS			.282	157	595	83	168	25	7	10	93	49	95	14

15. Brandon Larson, 3b

Born: May 24, 1976. **Ht.:** 6-0. **Wt.:** 210. **Bats:** R. **Throws:** R. **School:** Louisiana State University. **Career Transactions:** Selected by Reds in first round (14th overall) of 1997 draft; signed July 22, 1997.

The Reds' first-round pick in 1997, when he set an NCAA record for homers by a short-stop with 40, Larson finally made his big league debut last season. However, there's plenty of internal debate as to whether he can prosper in the majors over the long haul. Having built his reputation with offense as an amateur, Larson has proven to be a solid third baseman as a pro. He charges balls and makes off-balance throws expertly, and he shows a well above-average arm on more routine plays. At the plate, Larson's power is beyond question. When he hits a ball solidly, it stays hit. But his lack of consistency concerns the Reds, who think he might benefit from trying to hit to the opposite field more often. The club also began to wonder about his conditioning as 2001 progressed and are curious to see if he eliminates the perceived flab by spring training this year. Larson is likely to begin 2002 in Triple-A.

Year	Club (League)	Class	AVG	G	AB	R	H	2B	3B	HR	RBI	BB	SO	SB
1997	Chattanooga (SL)	AA	.268	11	41	4	11	5	1	0	6	1	10	0
1998	Burlington (Mid)	A	.221	18	68	5	15	3	0	2	9	4	16	2
1999	Rockford (Mid)	A	.300	69	250	38	75	18	1	13	52	25	67	12
	Chattanooga (SL)	AA	.285	43	172	28	49	10	0	12	42	10	51	4
2000	Chattanooga (SL)	AA	.272	111	427	61	116	26	0	20	64	31	122	15
	Louisville (IL)	AAA	.286	17	63	11	18	7	1	2	4	4	16	0
2001	Louisville (IL)	AAA	.255	115	424	61	108	22	2	14	55	24	123	5
	Cincinnati (NL)	MAJ	.121	14	33	2	4	2	0	0	1	2	10	0
MAJOR LEAGUE TOTALS			.121	14	33	2	4	2	0	0	1	2	10	0
MINOR LEAGUE TOTALS			.271	384	1445	208	392	91	5	63	232	99	405	38

16. Alan Moye, of

Born: Oct. 8, 1982. **Ht.:** 6-2. **Wt.:** 185. **Bats:** R. **Throws:** R. **School:** Pine Tree HS, Longview, Texas. **Career Transactions:** Selected by Reds in third round of 2001 draft, signed June 9, 2001.

Moye's potential to combine power with speed thrills the Reds. As is the case with many young players, he didn't show much of the former immediately, though he displayed plenty of the latter. He has inspired comparisons within the organization to Wily Mo Pena for being so richly gifted yet raw. Moye needs extensive work on his outfield play. He has a fair arm, but his faulty footwork prevents him from uncorking good throws when he comes in on balls. He nullifies his quickness by getting bad jumps and taking indirect routes to fly balls. The Reds are convinced that Moye will hit for average, so if he develops his power he could advance quickly. They'll probably start Moye this season at Dayton, where outfield prospects Adam Dunn, Austin Kearns and Pena have flowered in the last two years.

Year	Club (League)	Class	AVG	G	AB	R	H	2B	3B	HR	RBI	BB	SO	SB
2001	Reds (GCL)	R	.287	48	171	24	49	9	2	2	18	8	34	12
MINOR LEAGUE TOTALS			.287	48	171	24	49	9	2	2	18	8	34	12

17. Jackson Melian, of

Born: Jan. 7, 1980. **Ht.:** 6-2. **Wt.:** 190. **Bats:** R. **Throws:** R. **Career Transactions:** Signed out of Venezuela by Yankees, July 2, 1996 . . . Traded by Yankees with 3B Drew Henson, LHP Ed Yarnall and RHP Brian Reith to Reds for LHP Denny Neagle and OF Mike Frank, July 12, 2000.

Melian's stock has slipped since he joined the organization in the Denny Neagle trade with the Yankees in July 2000. He's impressively built and looks like a big leaguer. Of course, looks aren't everything, as his batting average reflects. He did show promise in 2001, nearly doubling his previous career high for homers as he began displaying the power everybody knew he had. Better yet, Melian can hit the ball out to all fields. He again showed off a strong throwing arm, legitimizing his reputation as a solid defender. But he remained erratic overall and prone to impatience at the plate. He managed to avoid serious hamstring injuries, a problem for him in previous seasons, and the Reds want him to continue to improve his flexibility. Though overenthusiastic club officials lumped Melian with Adam Dunn and Austin Kearns a year ago, he unquestionably has been left in their wake. Melian probably will spend more time at Double-A until he develops consistency, and he'll have a hard time cracking a potential big league outfield of Ken Griffey Jr. flanked by Dunn and Kearns.

Year	Club (League)	Class	AVG	G	AB	R	H	2B	3B	HR	RBI	BB	SO	SB
1997	Yankees (GCL)	R	.263	57	213	32	56	11	2	3	36	20	52	9
1998	Greensboro (SAL)	A	.255	135	467	66	119	18	2	8	45	41	120	15
1999	Tampa (FSL)	A	.283	128	467	65	132	17	13	6	61	49	98	11
2000	Norwich (EL)	AA	.252	81	290	34	73	8	4	9	38	18	69	17
	Chattanooga (SL)	AA	.167	2	6	0	1	0	0	0	0	0	0	0
2001	Chattanooga (SL)	AA	.237	120	426	64	101	22	0	16	52	36	95	10
MINOR LEAGUE TOTALS				523	1869	261	482	76	21	42	232	164	434	62

18. Alejandro Diaz, of

Born: July 9, 1978. **Ht.:** 5-9. **Wt.:** 190. **Bats:** R. **Throws:** R. **Career Transactions:** Signed out of Dominican Republic by Hiroshima (Japan), 1998 . . . Signed by Reds, March 2, 1999.

Be careful before labeling Diaz a bust. Most of the Reds' inner sanctum remains sensitive about Diaz and the inexplicable $1.175 million bonus he received when Cincinnati purchased him from Japan's Hiroshima Carp in 1999. But he might be on the brink of blossoming, though a shoulder injury prevented him from doing so last season. He played this winter in the Dominican League in an attempt to make up for lost time. The Reds particularly like Diaz' vast fielding range and, when healthy, his imposing throwing arm. Though his injury robbed him of his timing at the plate, he looked pretty good before his season ended. He still has to tighten his strike zone, but Cincinnati continues to believe he just needs repeated opportunities to play. The club's growing glut of outfield prospects may eventually make him an afterthought. The Reds believe that a return to Chattanooga and full health will help Diaz the most right now.

Year	Club (League)	Class	AVG	G	AB	R	H	2B	3B	HR	RBI	BB	SO	SB
1998	Hiroshima (CL)	JPN	.311	—	61	8	19	1	0	3	9	—	—	0
1999	Clinton (Mid)	A	.285	55	221	39	63	14	3	6	41	12	35	28
	Chattanooga (SL)	AA	.264	55	220	27	58	9	8	7	35	8	31	6
2000	Chattanooga (SL)	AA	.267	122	491	69	131	19	8	13	66	14	77	18
2001	Chattanooga (SL)	AA	.299	25	87	13	26	2	0	3	10	2	12	0
MINOR LEAGUE TOTALS			.273	257	1019	148	278	44	19	29	152	36	155	52

19. Luke Hudson, rhp

Born: May 2, 1977. **Ht.:** 6-3. **Wt.:** 195. **Bats:** R. **Throws:** R. **School:** University of Tennessee. **Career Transactions:** Selected by Rockies in fourth round of 1998 draft; signed June 5, 1998 . . . Traded by Rockies with LHP Gabe White to Reds for LHP Dennys Reyes and 2B Pokey Reese, Dec. 18, 2001.

Because they didn't want to tender a contract to Pokey Reese, whom they didn't want to go to arbitration with, the Reds traded him to the Rockies in December. The transaction was essentially a salary dump plus a swap of lefthanded relievers (Dennys Reyes for Gabe White), but Cincinnati also got Hudson. He could amount to more than a throw-in. Hudson had a lot of success as an amateur—winning national titles in Pony Baseball's Pony (13-14) and Colt (15-16) programs, plus two California state championships in high school—but hasn't translated it to the professional level. Despite having a losing record in three of his four pro seasons, Hudson has the physical ability. Scouts love his body and his arm, but he lacks command of his fastball. Hitters seem to pick it up easily though he throws in the low 90s. He does have a good curveball with depth and a decent changeup. The Reds will take a good look at Hudson in spring training before deciding whether to send him to Triple-A or back to Double-A.

Year	Club (League)	Class	W	L	ERA	G	GS	CG	SV	IP	H	R	ER	BB	SO
1998	Portland (NWL)	A	3	6	4.74	15	15	0	0	80	68	46	42	51	82
1999	Asheville (SAL)	A	6	5	4.30	21	20	1	0	88	89	47	42	24	96
2000	Salem (Car)	A	5	8	3.27	19	19	2	0	110	101	47	40	34	80
2001	Carolina (SL)	AA	7	12	4.20	29	28	1	0	165	159	90	77	68	145
MINOR LEAGUE TOTALS			21	31	4.09	84	82	4	0	443	417	230	201	177	403

20. David Gil, rhp

Born: Oct. 1, 1978. **Ht.:** 6-4. **Wt.:** 215. **Bats:** R. **Throws:** R. **School:** University of Miami. **Career Transactions:** Selected by Reds in third round of 2000 draft; signed June 29, 2000.

Were it not for a minor arm injury and a pulled groin muscle, Gil might have joined the procession of minor league pitchers who found their way to Cincinnati in 2001. That would have been quite an accomplishment, considering it was his first full pro season. He reached Double-A the year before, shortly after signing out of the University of Miami, where he went 31-5 and was part of one national championship in four seasons. Gil throws his fastball in the low 90s and sharpened its consistency last year. He also has the standard complement of secondary pitches, including an effective slider. His control got out of whack at times in 2001, though that may be attributable to his physical problems. Gil will compete in the spring for a spot in the Triple-A starting rotation, though it wouldn't be a shock to see him back at Chattanooga.

Year	Club (League)	Class	W	L	ERA	G	GS	CG	SV	IP	H	R	ER	BB	SO
2000	Dayton (Mid)	A	1	1	2.70	4	4	0	0	27	20	13	8	11	15
	Chattanooga (SL)	AA	2	0	2.16	6	3	0	1	25	15	7	6	13	25
2001	Chattanooga (SL)	AA	6	1	3.10	11	10	0	1	61	65	23	21	30	55
	Reds (GCL)	R	0	2	7.36	4	4	0	0	11	19	15	9	6	14
	Dayton (Mid)	A	1	0	0.77	2	2	0	0	12	11	1	1	3	15
MINOR LEAGUE TOTALS			10	4	2.99	27	23	0	2	135	130	59	45	63	124

21. Luis Pineda, rhp

Born: June 10, 1978. **Ht.:** 6-1. **Wt.:** 160. **Bats:** R. **Throws:** R. **Career Transactions:** Signed out of Dominican Republic by Rangers, June 14, 1995 . . . Released by Rangers, May 22, 1997 . . . Signed by Diamondbacks, June 25, 1997 . . . Released by Diamondbacks, July 4, 1998 . . . Signed by Tigers, July 30, 1998 . . . Granted free agency, Oct. 16, 1998; re-signed by Tigers, Dec. 29, 1998 . . . Traded by Tigers with OF Juan Encarnacion for IF/OF Dmitri Young, Dec. 11, 2001.

Like Luke Hudson, Pinieda joined the Reds this winter in a trade designed to keep the club out of arbitration. Juan Encarnacion was the bigger-name player acquired from Detroit for Dmitri Young, but Pineda could make the Cincinnati bullpen in 2002. After never having pitched above high Class A going into last season, he finished the year in the majors. Pineda has a power arm capable of delivering 92-95 mph fastballs with regularity while occasionally touching 98. On a given day, his curveball can be anything from a very good to a below-average pitch. He's not closer material but he can be a useful middle reliever. Control of his pitches and of himself have been his biggest problems. Both the Rangers and Diamondbacks released Pineda before he made his climb through the Tigers system. He missed much of 2000 with an elbow strain but held up throughout last season.

Year	Club (League)	Class	W	L	ERA	G	GS	CG	SV	IP	H	R	ER	BB	SO
1995	Rangers (DSL)	R	6	1	3.00	12	5	0	0	39	36	17	13	31	19
1996	Rangers (GCL)	R	6	3	3.52	11	11	1	0	72	67	31	28	25	66
1997					Did Not Play—Injured										
1998	Tigers (DSL)	R	2	0	0.89	12	0	0	5	20	7	3	2	14	43
1999	West Michigan (Mid)	A	0	2	3.57	24	3	0	7	40	30	18	16	26	55
	Lakeland (FSL)	A	0	1	1.04	8	0	0	0	9	6	2	1	7	8
2000	Lakeland (FSL)	A	1	3	3.38	18	0	0	4	27	23	13	10	19	42
2001	Erie (EL)	AA	6	2	3.05	16	12	2	0	86	68	33	29	28	92
	Toledo (IL)	AAA	1	0	0.00	2	0	0	0	8	3	0	0	0	6
	Detroit (AL)	MAJ	0	1	4.91	16	0	0	0	18	16	10	10	14	13
MAJOR LEAGUE TOTALS			0	1	4.91	16	0	0	0	18	16	10	10	14	13
MINOR LEAGUE TOTALS			22	12	2.96	103	31	3	16	301	240	117	99	150	331

22. Chris Piersoll, rhp

Born: Sept. 25, 1977. **Ht.:** 6-4. **Wt.:** 195. **Bats:** R. **Throws:** R. **School:** Fullerton (Calif.) JC. **Career Transactions:** Selected by Cubs in 19th round of 1997 draft; signed June 10, 1997 . . . Selected by Reds from Cubs in Rule 5 minor league draft, Dec. 11, 2000.

After spending four years in the Cubs system as a middle reliever, Piersoll joined the Reds as a Triple-A Rule 5 draft pick and quickly found a cozier niche as the Double-A closer. He isn't overpowering, as his fastball ranges from 90-92 mph, but he neutralizes hitters with his sterling command and movement on his pitches. He induces plenty of ground balls with his sinking two-seam fastball, which he'll throw to either side of the plate. Piersoll predictably suffers when he elevates his pitches, a pitfall for pitchers lacking tremendous stuff. He needs to improve his command so he can pitch down in the strike zone and cut down on his walks. Piersoll will get the chance to win a middle-relief role in the majors this year. If he fails, he'll secure a prominent role in the Triple-A bullpen.

Year	Club (League)	Class	W	L	ERA	G	GS	CG	SV	IP	H	R	ER	BB	SO
1997	Cubs (AZL)	R	4	0	2.08	15	0	0	2	35	26	12	8	9	41
1998	Rockford (Mid)	A	2	0	3.92	27	4	1	2	60	52	28	26	20	55
1999	Daytona (FSL)	A	7	3	3.72	33	0	0	5	68	68	30	28	24	74
	West Tenn (SL)	AA	0	0	0.63	8	1	0	1	14	12	1	1	3	14
2000	West Tenn (SL)	AA	3	3	2.08	47	0	0	2	61	51	17	14	28	54
2001	Chattanooga (SL)	AA	1	4	3.38	50	0	0	19	56	48	24	21	30	78
	Cincinnati (NL)	MAJ	0	0	2.38	11	0	0	0	11	12	4	3	6	7
MAJOR LEAGUE TOTALS			0	0	2.38	11	0	0	0	11	12	4	3	6	7
MINOR LEAGUE TOTALS			17	10	3.01	180	5	1	31	293	257	112	98	114	316

23. Luis Valera, rhp

Born: Jan. 30, 1982. **Ht.:** 5-11. **Wt.:** 180. **Bats:** R. **Throws:** R. **Career Transactions:** Signed out of Venezuela by Reds, March 10, 1999.

It's rare but not unprecedented for a successful reliever to begin his career as a position player. Cincinnati believes Valera could join the company of Trevor Hoffman, Troy Percival and Felix Rodriguez. He hit .210 in two years of Rookie ball and didn't look like he'd ever hit enough to hold down an everyday job. Moreover, he lacked the fluid footwork and hands required of a catcher. The Reds didn't want to waste Valera's valuable arm strength, so they converted him to pitching last summer—ironically, the day after he hit a grand slam. Despite never having pitched before, Valera immediately warmed up to the role. His fastball ranges from 90-94 mph and he garnishes it with a wicked 84-mph slider. He continued to progress after the season, earning most-improved-pitcher honors in Cincinnati's instructional league camp. As expected, he needs work on his command and on such subtleties as holding runners on base and developing a changeup. He's likely to spend his first full year as a pitcher in low Class A.

Year	Club (League)	Class	AVG	G	AB	R	H	2B	3B	HR	RBI	BB	SO	SB
1999	Cagua (VSL)	R	.225	48	129	14	29	3	0	3	14	17	20	2
2000	Reds (GCL)	R	.193	33	114	8	22	3	0	1	11	8	21	1
MINOR LEAGUE TOTALS			.210	81	243	22	51	6	0	4	25	25	41	3

Year	Club (League)	Class	W	L	ERA	G	GS	CG	SV	IP	H	R	ER	BB	SO
2001	Reds (GCL)	R	1	0	2.40	10	0	0	3	15	7	4	4	6	16
MINOR LEAGUE TOTALS			1	0	2.40	10	0	0	3	15	7	4	4	6	16

24. Gary Varner, of/3b

Born: Dec. 7, 1980. **Ht.:** 6-0. **Wt.:** 185. **Bats:** R. **Throws:** R. **School:** St. Catharine (Ky.) JC. **Career Transactions:** Selected by Reds in 10th round of 2000 draft; signed Aug. 11, 2000.

Primarily known by his nickname "Noochie," Varner has done more than add to the Reds' collection of players with odd monikers. He blossomed at the plate in 2001, leading the Rookie-level Pioneer League in hits and finishing fourth in the batting race. A supremely confident hitter, he uses the entire field. He may have too much faith in himself, because there's some thought he might resist making adjustments at the upper levels. He also strikes out too much. Varner's biggest flaws come with his glove. He played his way off third base to left field last season, and he still needs to get better defensively. He's ticketed for low Class A to start 2002, but he could earn a midseason promotion if he continues his torrid hitting.

Year	Club (League)	Class	AVG	G	AB	R	H	2B	3B	HR	RBI	BB	SO	SB
2000	Billings (Pio)	R	.257	11	35	4	9	1	1	0	3	2	10	0
2001	Billings (Pio)	R	.351	72	291	55	102	20	5	8	55	29	64	7
MINOR LEAGUE TOTALS			.340	83	326	59	111	21	6	8	58	31	74	7

25. William Bergolla, 2b

Born: Feb. 4, 1983. **Ht.:** 6-0. **Wt.:** 150. **Bats:** R. **Throws:** R. **Career Transactions:** Signed out of Venezuela by Reds, Nov. 15, 1999.

Signed out of the Reds' Venezuelan camp, Bergolla represents another mini-triumph in the organization's continuing efforts to upgrade its Latin American scouting. As impressive as his batting average was in 2001, his intangibles may have been more admirable. Displaying an excellent feel for the game, he proved adept at bunting, moving runners over and using the entire field. Though he showed signs of developing some power, he'll probably need to keep playing the little game on offense. His basestealing skills and ability to make contact should allow him to do so. He moved from shortstop to second base last year and must continue making the adjustment. Routine plays still give him trouble. As with many teenage professionals, Bergolla also has a long way to go in developing himself physically. He'll probably start 2002 in low Class A.

Year	Club (League)	Class	AVG	G	AB	R	H	2B	3B	HR	RBI	BB	SO	SB
2000	Cagua (VSL)	R	.372	13	43	6	16	3	2	0	5	8	3	1
	Reds (GCL)	R	.182	8	22	2	4	0	0	0	0	4	2	3
2001	Billings (Pio)	R	.323	57	232	47	75	5	3	4	24	24	21	22
MINOR LEAGUE TOTALS			.320	78	297	55	95	8	5	4	29	36	26	26

26. Steve Smitherman, of

Born: Sept. 1, 1978. **Ht.:** 6-4. **Wt.:** 230. **Bats:** R. **Throws:** R. **School:** University of Arkansas-Little Rock. **Career Transactions:** Selected by Reds in 23rd round of 2000 draft; signed June 7, 2000.

Older than most of Cincinnati's outfield prospects, Smitherman is trying his best to make up for lost time. Fortunately for him, he's pretty good at hurrying. His speed, which is impressive for a man of his size, helped him lead the low Class A Midwest League in doubles in 2001. Displaying the aptitude to refine his game, Smitherman began using more of the field with Dayton, hitting balls to the gaps. He continued his development in the off-season by being named MVP in the Reds' instructional league program. Among the skills he tried to refine there was recognizing curveballs. He also could use more plate discipline. Defensively, Smitherman has a decent throwing arm but must work on taking better routes to balls. At 23, he'll probably be exposed to Double-A at some point this year.

Year	Club (League)	Class	AVG	G	AB	R	H	2B	3B	HR	RBI	BB	SO	SB
2000	Billings (Pio)	R	.316	70	301	61	95	16	5	15	65	23	67	14
2001	Dayton (Mid)	A	.280	134	497	89	139	45	2	20	73	43	113	16
MINOR LEAGUE TOTALS			.293	204	798	150	234	61	7	35	138	66	180	30

27. Danny Mateo, ss

Born: Oct. 27, 1982. **Ht.:** 6-0. **Wt.:** 150. **Bats:** B. **Throws:** R. **Career Transactions:** Signed out of Dominican Republic by Reds, Oct. 15, 1999.

Gookie Dawkins, Ranier Olmedo and Edwin Encarnacion give the Reds an abundance of surehanded infield prospects. Some observers believe Mateo may have better defensive tools than any of them. His soft hands are rivaled by his nimble feet. He puts the latter to good use on offense, relying on his speed to leg out infield hits and steal bases. He led Cincinnati's Rookie-level Gulf Coast League club in swipes last year. He's still adjusting to switch-hitting and needs to solidify his approach from both sides of the plate. He also could stand to add about 25 pounds to his lightweight frame. Mateo will remain in Rookie ball at Billings, where he received a brief trial in 2001.

Year	Club (League)	Class	AVG	G	AB	R	H	2B	3B	HR	RBI	BB	SO	SB
2001	Reds (GCL)	R	.244	53	180	29	44	6	0	1	14	15	48	27
	Billings (Pio)	R	.556	4	9	1	5	0	0	0	2	0	3	0
MINOR LEAGUE TOTALS			.259	57	189	30	49	6	0	1	16	15	51	27

28. Casey DeHart, lhp

Born: Nov. 1, 1977. **Ht.:** 6-1. **Wt.:** 180. **Bats:** L. **Throws:** L. **School:** Texarkana (Texas) JC. **Career Transactions:** Selected by Reds in 11th round of 1998 draft; signed June 3, 1998.

As DeHart has risen through the organization, so have expectations surrounding his projected role with Cincinnati. He's now regarded as a potential situational lefty. His makeup certainly fits the job description. He's hard-nosed and ultra-aggressive, challenging hitters with a 90-mph fastball that he doesn't mind throwing inside. He's a master at getting ground balls when needed. DeHart also has command of a nice assortment of breaking pitches that should give him an edge against lefthanders. Oddly enough, he was better against righties in 2001, as they hit .203 compared to .266 by lefties. He still needs more command, consistency and seasoning. He'll start the year in Double-A and could start to move quickly.

Year	Club (League)	Class	W	L	ERA	G	GS	CG	SV	IP	H	R	ER	BB	SO
1998	Billings (Pio)	R	3	1	5.79	15	0	0	3	23	26	20	15	22	18
1999	Reds (GCL)	R	0	1	7.71	2	2	0	0	5	7	4	4	2	6
	Clinton (Mid)	A	2	0	3.38	24	0	0	0	21	16	10	8	16	17
2000	Dayton (Mid)	A	6	3	4.26	50	0	0	2	63	67	39	30	38	52
2001	Mudville (Cal)	A	4	3	2.23	49	0	0	4	69	54	20	17	36	64
MINOR LEAGUE TOTALS			15	8	3.67	140	2	0	9	181	170	93	74	114	157

29. Paul Darnell, lhp

Born: June 4, 1976. **Ht.:** 6-5. **Wt.:** 190. **Bats:** R. **Throws:** L. **School:** Tarleton State (Texas) University. **Career Transactions:** Selected by Reds in 11th round of 1999 draft; signed June 9, 1999.

Darnell is another lefty who lacks overwhelming stuff but compensates with command. He likes to use his curveball and slider to get strikeouts. His fastball, clocked at 88-90 mph, is adequate. He helps himself with a deceptive delivery, subjecting hitters to a dazzling vision of moving limbs, elbows and knees before the ball suddenly comes toward the plate. The higher Darnell climbed in 2001, the more he was used in relief after having pitched almost exclusively as a starter in his pro career. Though the Reds project him as a reliever, his experience in the rotation enhances his value. His late-season success at Triple-A virtually assures him of returning there to open 2002.

Year	Club (League)	Class	W	L	ERA	G	GS	CG	SV	IP	H	R	ER	BB	SO
1999	Billings (Pio)	R	3	3	5.21	9	9	0	0	48	55	37	28	22	39
	Clinton (Mid)	A	3	2	3.06	6	6	0	0	35	35	19	12	13	23
2000	Clinton (Mid)	A	9	10	3.51	26	25	3	0	162	131	81	63	67	164
2001	Mudville (Cal)	A	2	1	3.38	5	5	0	0	32	27	13	12	8	33
	Chattanooga (SL)	AA	3	1	2.58	21	4	0	0	38	39	13	11	13	43
	Louisville (IL)	AAA	2	0	2.57	21	0	0	0	21	15	6	6	11	32
MINOR LEAGUE TOTALS			22	17	3.53	88	49	3	0	337	302	169	132	134	334

30. Chris Booker, rhp

Born: Dec. 9, 1976. **Ht.:** 6-3. **Wt.:** 230. **Bats:** R. **Throws:** R. **School:** Monroe County HS, Monroeville, Ala. **Career Transactions:** Selected by Cubs in 20th round of 1995 draft; signed June 15, 1995 . . . Traded by Cubs with RHP Ben Shaffar to Reds for OF Michael Tucker, July 20, 2001.

Anyone who sees Booker's fastball might fantasize about John Wetteland, Robb Nen or another smoke-throwing closer. It's the main reason the Reds asked for him in the trade that sent Michael Tucker to the Cubs last summer. But you won't get any Cincinnati officials to project Booker as a closer just yet, because he's so raw. He's still a thrower, not a pitcher. He can reach 97-98 mph but velocity is essentially his lone asset on the mound. He also throws a slider and a splitter, neither of which is major league-ready. He must develop one of those two pitches to complement his fastball. If Booker can do that, he'll reach the majors in a hurry. He's likely to begin 2002 in Double-A to work on his command.

Year	Club (League)	Class	W	L	ERA	G	GS	CG	SV	IP	H	R	ER	BB	SO
1995	Cubs (GCL)	R	3	2	2.76	13	7	0	1	42	36	22	13	16	43
1996	Daytona (FSL)	A	0	0	0.00	1	1	0	0	2	1	1	0	3	2
	Williamsport (NY-P)	A	4	6	5.31	14	14	0	0	61	57	51	36	51	52
1997	Williamsport (NY-P)	A	1	5	3.35	24	3	0	1	46	39	20	17	25	60
1998	Rockford (Mid)	A	1	2	3.36	44	1	0	4	64	47	32	24	53	78
1999	Daytona (FSL)	A	2	5	3.95	42	0	0	6	73	72	45	32	37	68
2000	Daytona (FSL)	A	0	2	2.28	31	0	0	10	28	25	12	7	14	34
	West Tenn (SL)	AA	1	0	3.68	12	0	0	0	15	10	8	6	12	21
2001	West Tenn (SL)	AA	2	6	4.33	45	0	0	1	52	39	29	25	36	76
	Chattanooga (SL)	AA	2	0	3.94	16	0	0	1	16	13	7	7	11	25
MINOR LEAGUE TOTALS			16	28	3.77	242	26	0	24	399	339	227	167	258	459

CLEVELAND
Indians

By Jim Ingraham

For much of the 1990s, the Indians were the blueprint many teams used to rebuild a franchise. Cleveland officials now hope they can provide the blueprint for how to reload what has been rebuilt. Adding to the challenge is that the club will attempt to do so with a brand-new front office.

New general manager Mark Shapiro, who replaced John Hart at the end of the 2001 season, has a tough act to follow. Hart, who left of his own accord and quickly resurfaced with the Rangers, orchestrated the longest run of sustained excellence in franchise history. Shapiro inherited an aging major league roster and a depleted farm system lacking in prospects at the upper levels, as well as a mandate to trim the big league payroll by approximately $15 million.

All that made for some difficult moves in Shapiro's first few months at Cleveland's helm. Longtime contributors Dave Burba and Kenny Lofton weren't asked back as free agents, nor were Marty Cordova and Juan Gonzalez, who helped power one of the game's best offenses in 2001. Most significant, future Hall of Fame second baseman Roberto Alomar was traded to the Mets for Matt Lawton and four prospects.

That deal may have been the most unpopular in Cleveland since Rocky Colavito was shipped to Detroit in 1960, and it represented a huge gamble. But it also capped a year in which the Indians did have an influx of minor league talent. Outfielder Alex Escobar, lefthander Billy Traber and righthanded reliever Jerrod Riggan all have the ability to help the big league club in the very near future.

Last season in Cleveland, C.C. Sabathia made a seamless jump from Double-A, won 17 games and would have been the American League rookie of the year if Ichiro Suzuki had stayed in Japan. Cuban defector Danys Baez finally started living up to his $14.5 million contract and established himself in the bullpen. Two other pitchers, Ryan Drese and David Riske, also showed exceptional promise in brief major league trials last year. The Indians also addressed their lack of position prospects in the upper minors by trading righthander Zach Day to the Expos for Milton Bradley, who should replace Lofton in center field.

While there's little else in the way of immediate help, Cleveland did restock at the lower levels thanks to a surplus of four first-round picks. In what has the potential to be one of their best drafts ever, the Indians collected a group of intriguing young arms led by first-rounders Dan Denham and J.D. Martin.

Organization Overview

General manager: Mark Shapiro. **Farm director:** John Farrell. **Scouting director:** John Mirabelli.

2001 PERFORMANCE

Class	Team	League	W	L	Pct.	Finish*	Manager
Majors	Cleveland	American	91	71	.562	4th(14)	Charlie Manuel
Triple-A	Buffalo Bisons	International	91	51	.641	1st (14)	Eric Wedge
Double-A	Akron Aeros	Eastern	68	74	.479	7th (12)	Chris Bando
High A	Kinston Indians	Carolina	89	51	.636	1st (8)	Brad Komminsk
Low A	Columbus RedStixx	South Atlantic	77	59	.566	3rd (16)	Ted Kubiak
Short-season	Mahoning Valley Scrappers	New York-Penn	26	49	.347	14th (14)	Dave Turgeon
Rookie	Burlington Indians	Appalachian	31	37	.456	t-7th (10)	Rouglas Odor
OVERALL 2001 MINOR LEAGUE RECORD			382	321	.543	4th (30)	

*Finish in overall standings (No. of teams in league)

ORGANIZATION LEADERS

BATTING
*AVG Victor Martinez, Kinston .... .329
R **Ryan Church**, Kinston/Columbus 80
H Nate Grindell, Akron/ Kinston 140
TB Karim Garcia, Buffalo 239
2B Simon Pond, Akron/Kinston 37
3B J.J. Sherrill, Columbus 11
HR Karim Garcia, Buffalo 31
RBI **Ryan Church**, Kinston/Columbus 91
BB **Ryan Church**, Kinston/Columbus 72
SO Corey Smith, Columbus 149
SB Alex Requena, Kinston/Columbus 47

PITCHING
W Jason Davis, Columbus 14
L Jason Stanford, Buffalo/Akron 11
#ERA **Ryan Larson**, Kinston/Columbus 0.88
G Martin Vargas, Buffalo/Akron 54
CG Mike Bacsik, Buffalo/Akron 3
SV Brian Jackson, Kinston 25
IP Brian Tallet, Kinston 160
  Jason Davis, Columbus 160
BB Matt White, Akron 60
SO Brian Tallet, Kinston 164

*Minimum 250 At-Bats #Minimum 75 Innings

TOP PROSPECTS OF THE DECADE

1992 .... Kenny Lofton, of
1993 .... Manny Ramirez, of
1994 .... Manny Ramirez, of
1995 .... Jaret Wright, rhp
1996 .... Bartolo Colon, rhp
1997 .... Bartolo Colon, rhp
1998 .... Sean Casey, 1b
1999 .... Russell Branyan, 3b
2000 .... C.C. Sabathia, lhp
2001 .... C.C. Sabathia, lhp

TOP DRAFT PICKS OF THE DECADE

1992 .... Paul Shuey, rhp
1993 .... Daron Kirkreit, rhp
1994 .... Jaret Wright, rhp
1995 .... David Miller, 1b/of
1996 .... Danny Peoples, 1b/of
1997 .... Tim Drew, rhp
1998 .... C.C. Sabathia, lhp
1999 .... Will Hartley, c (2)
2000 .... Corey Smith, 3b
2001 .... Dan Denham, rhp

Church

Larson

BEST TOOLS

Best Hitter for Average .... Victor Martinez
Best Power Hitter .... Corey Smith
Fastest Baserunner .... Alex Requena
Best Fastball .... Dan Denham
Best Breaking Ball .... Ryan Larson
Best Changeup .... Jason Stanford
Best Control .... Kyle Denney
Best Defensive Catcher .... Victor Martinez
Best Defensive Infielder .... John McDonald
Best Infield Arm .... Corey Smith
Best Defensive Outfielder .... Alex Escobar
Best Outfield Arm .... Alex Escobar

PROJECTED 2005 LINEUP

Catcher .... Victor Martinez
First Base .... Russell Branyan
Second Base .... Ricky Gutierrez
Third Base .... Corey Smith
Shortstop .... John McDonald
Left Field .... Matt Lawton
Center Field .... Milton Bradley
Right Field .... Alex Escobar
Designated Hitter .... Jim Thome
No. 1 Starter .... C.C. Sabathia
No. 2 Starter .... Bartolo Colon
No. 3 Starter .... Ryan Drese
No. 4 Starter .... Dan Denham
No. 5 Starter .... J.D. Martin
Closer .... Danys Baez

ALL-TIME LARGEST BONUSES

Danys Baez, 1999 .... $4,500,000
Dan Denham, 2001 .... $1,860,000
Tim Drew, 1997 .... $1,600,000
Corey Smith, 2000 .... $1,375,000
C.C. Sabathia, 1998 .... $1,300,000

DraftAnalysis

2001 Draft

Best Pro Debut: RHP J.D. Martin (1) put up the best numbers of any 2001 draftee, going 5-1, 1.38 with a 72-11 strikeout-walk ratio at Rookie-level Burlington. His teammate, RHP **Dan Denham** (1), was the Appalachian League's top pitching prospect. 1B Andy Baxter (32) led the Appy League with 46 RBIs and 31 extra-base hits. He finished second in homers, as did 1B Rickie Morton (25) in the short-season New York-Penn League, where he batted .282-12-40.

Best Athlete: OF Jonathan Van Every, a draft-and-follow from 2000, was the best athlete signed by the Indians in 2001. From the draft, OF Jose Cruz (36) gets the nod.

Best Hitter: OF Mike Conroy (1) hit .244-2-23 in the Appy League, but the Indians aren't worried. They like his tools and don't think his performance is out of line for a New England high school player.

Best Raw Power: Morton broke Greg Vaughn's season home run record at Sacramento City College before going to Pacific.

Fastest Runner: A switch-hitter, Cruz can get to first base in 4.0 seconds from the left side of the plate and in 4.2 seconds from the right.

Best Defensive Player: Van Every is the best pure center fielder in the system. Among the 2001 draftees, SS Bryce Uegawachi (26) is a plus defender.

Best Fastball: Denham had a 94-95 mph fastball in the Appy League and instructional league. RHP Travis Foley (4), another quality high school arm, throws 93-94 mph.

Most Intriguing Background: Martin and

his older brother Kevin, a nondrafted free agent from Southern Colorado, were signed as a package deal, one of three instances when a first-round pick was signed with an older brother by the same organization.

Closest To The Majors: LHP Marcos Mendoza (5) has a plus slider that could hurry his ascent as a middle reliever. Mendoza and RHP Nick Moran (3), whose best pitch is a curveball, will start this season at high Class A Kinston.

BILL SETLUFF

Denham

Best Late-Round Pick: RHP T.J. Burton's (18) instructional league had Cleveland thinking of a young Bret Saberhagen. He's projectable at 6-foot-3 and 170 pounds, throws strikes and shows a fringe-average fastball and an average slider. The Indians signed Burton, Cruz and RHP Jimmy Schultz (22) after missing out on . . .

The One Who Got Away: RHP Alan Horne (1), their second of four first-round picks. Horne was part of an exceptionally deep crop of high school righthanders, and Cleveland settled for Denham and Martin.

Assessment: Denham and Martin make nice compensation for the loss of Manny Ramirez, especially after Juan Gonzalez replaced Ramirez, even temporarily. The Indians' biggest need is pitching, and they tried to fill it with this draft.

2000 Draft

Cleveland considers 3B Corey Smith (1) its best prospect, and LHP Brian Tallet (2) could move quickly. OFs Ryan Church (14) and Jonathan Van Every (29) were nice late-round finds. **Grade: C**

1999 Draft

The Indians had no first-round pick and spent their next two choices on C Will Hartley (2) and OF Eric Johnson (3), who were out of baseball two years later. The next pick, SS Jeff Baker (4), didn't sign and will become a first-rounder this June. LHP Shane Wallace (6) has shown promise but needed Tommy John surgery last summer. **Grade: F**

1998 Draft

LHP C.C. Sabathia (1) led Cleveland with 17 wins as a 20-year old in 2001. He and RHP Ryan Drese (5) could form 40 percent of the Tribe's future rotation. **Grade: A**

1997 Draft

The Indians overspent on RHP Tim Drew (1), then compounded the situation by rushing him. He still has a brighter future than the other first-rounder, OF Jason Fitzgerald. OF Dustan Mohr (9) made it to the majors with Minnesota after being released. **Grade: D**

Note: Draft analysis prepared by Jim Callis. Numbers in parentheses indicate draft rounds.

. . . Smith gets rave reviews for his makeup and work ethic. He is, plain and simple, a baseball player.

Smith Corey 3b

Born: April 15, 1982.
Ht.: 6-1. **Wt.:** 205.
Bats: R. **Throws:** R.
School: Piscataway (N.J.) HS.
Career Transactions: Selected by Indians in first round (26th overall) of 2000 draft; signed June 15, 2000.

The Indians traditionally have avoided drafting high school infielders in the first round, doing so just twice in the last 20 years. They took Mark Lewis in 1988 and Smith in 2000. The muscular Smith was a shortstop in high school, but the Indians wasted no time in moving him to third base, where they feel his size and power potential make him a more natural fit. In Smith's two years as a pro, the transition to third base has gone much better offensively than defensively. Club officials downplay his stuggles with the glove, partly because his upside with the bat is so vast.

Smith gets rave reviews for his makeup and work ethic. He is, plain and simple, a baseball player. A throwback. He loves the game and works hard to improve his weaknesses. He's intelligent and has tremendous athletic ability as well as an aptitude for learning. He has excellent bat speed that should produce even more power than he already has shown. Smith has yet to hit for a high average but that may come as well. He seems to rise to the occasion offensively and is a very tough out with men on base. Despite his obvious physical gifts, his biggest strength may be his passion. He's a potential franchise cornerstone once he reaches the big leagues. Smith needs to work on his strike-zone discipline, but the most obvious flaw in his game is his defense. In 187 games as a pro, he has made 77 errors—45 at low Class A Columbus in 2001—most of them on poor throws. Smith has arm strength but lacks consistent mechanics. He made major strides in that area during instructional leagues. Smith tends to try to do too much defensively, which also has contributed to his third-base difficulties. Except for the errors, the position switch has gone better than expected. His speed is below-average but he's not a baseclogger.

Until Cleveland got Alex Escobar in the Roberto Alomar trade, Smith was by far the organization's best position-player prospect and he still ranks as No. 1. He won't be rushed despite the lack of bats ahead of him. At age 20, he'll start this season at high Class A Kinston. He probably won't arrive in the big leagues before late 2004.

BILL SETLIFF

Year	Club (League)	Class	AVG	G	AB	R	H	2B	3B	HR	RBI	BB	SO	SB
2000	Burlington (Appy)	R	.256	57	207	21	53	8	2	4	39	27	50	8
2001	Columbus (SAL)	A	.260	130	500	59	130	26	5	18	85	37	149	10
MINOR LEAGUE TOTALS			.259	187	707	80	183	34	7	22	124	64	199	18

2. Alex Escobar, of

Born: Sept. 6, 1978. **Ht.:** 6-1. **Wt.:** 180. **Bats:** R. **Throws:** R. **Career Transactions:** Signed out of Venezuela by Mets, July 1, 1995 . . . Traded by Mets with OF Matt Lawton, RHP Jerrod Riggan and two players to be named to Indians for 2B Roberto Alomar, LHP Mike Bacsik and 1B Danny Peoples, Dec. 11, 2001; Indians acquired LHP Billy Traber and 1B Earl Snyder to complete trade (Dec. 13, 2001).

RICH ABEL

Escobar had been the bright light of the Mets system since a breakout season in 1998 in the low Class A South Atlantic League, but New York grew impatient waiting for him to make the final steps in becoming a major league regular. Faced with the prospect of getting Roberto Alomar in a December trade, the Mets included Escobar in the five-player package they sent to Cleveland. Escobar has exciting tools across the board. When he's right offensively, he generates line drives and above-average power while utilizing the entire field. He also has speed, and if he puts everything together he could be a 30-30 player. A standout center fielder, he offers the best outfield defense and arm in the system. Escobar struggled in Triple-A and the majors last season as his plate discipline deteriorated. He was befuddled by conflicting advice from a variety of Mets coaches before reverting to an open stance with his legs spread wide and his hands held high. While his arm is strong, it isn't always accurate. The Indians aren't as desperate for outfielders as the Mets were, so Escobar could spend most of 2002 at Triple-A Buffalo trying to polish his game. If he can't, the whispers that he could be the second coming of failed prospect Ruben Rivera only are going to get louder.

Year	Club (League)	Class	AVG	G	AB	R	H	2B	3B	HR	RBI	BB	SO	SB
1996	Mets (GCL)	R	.360	24	75	15	27	4	0	0	10	4	9	7
1997	Kingsport (Appy)	R	.194	10	36	6	7	3	0	0	3	3	8	1
	Mets (GCL)	R	.247	26	73	12	18	4	1	1	11	10	17	0
1998	Capital City (SAL)	A	.310	112	416	90	129	23	5	27	91	54	133	49
1999	Mets (GCL)	R	.375	2	8	1	3	2	0	0	1	1	2	0
	St. Lucie (FSL)	A	.667	1	3	1	2	0	0	1	3	1	1	1
2000	Binghamton (EL)	AA	.288	122	437	79	126	25	7	16	67	57	114	24
2001	Norfolk (IL)	AAA	.267	111	397	55	106	21	4	12	52	35	146	18
	New York (NL)	MAJ	.200	18	50	3	10	1	0	3	8	3	19	1
MAJOR LEAGUE TOTALS			.200	18	50	3	10	1	0	3	8	3	19	1
MINOR LEAGUE TOTALS			.289	408	1445	259	418	82	17	57	238	165	430	100

3. Ryan Drese, rhp

Born: April 5, 1976. **Ht.:** 6-3. **Wt.:** 220. **Bats:** R. **Throws:** R. **School:** University of California. **Career Transactions:** Selected by Indians in fifth round of 1998 draft; signed June 25, 1998.

DIAMOND IMAGES

Projected as an early first-round pick and in line to be the No. 1 starter on the 1996 U.S. Olympic team, Drese was derailed by elbow surgery in college. He pitched a total of just 90 innings over his final three college seasons and has had problems staying healthy as a pro, missing almost all of 2000 following reconstructive knee surgery. Drese pitches with a mean streak and supreme confidence that borders on cockiness. He has four major league average to above-average pitches—a fastball that touches the mid-90s, a slider, a changeup and a curveball. He can throw all four for strikes and has a great feel for pitching. In part because he doesn't repeat his delivery consistently, Drese still hasn't mastered command of his fastball within the strike zone. Once he does that and is able to throw more first-pitch strikes with his fastball, the sky is the limit. Based on his history, his durability remains a question. Drese was so impressive in a late-season trial with Cleveland in 2001 that he earned a chance to win a spot in the major league rotation. He did show the ability to pitch out of the bullpen last year as well, so he could make the club as a swingman.

Year	Club (League)	Class	W	L	ERA	G	GS	CG	SV	IP	H	R	ER	BB	SO
1998	Watertown (NY-P)	A	2	5	4.07	9	9	0	0	42	40	21	19	14	40
1999	Kinston (Car)	A	5	4	4.93	15	15	1	0	69	46	47	38	52	81
	Mahoning Valley (NY-P)	A	0	2	2.65	5	5	0	0	17	8	6	5	7	26
	Columbus (SAL)	A	0	2	4.50	2	2	0	0	12	9	6	6	4	15
2000	Kinston (Car)	A	0	1	3.86	1	1	0	0	2	2	1	1	1	4
2001	Akron (EL)	AA	5	7	3.35	14	13	1	0	86	64	34	32	29	73
	Buffalo (IL)	AAA	5	1	4.01	11	10	0	0	61	60	28	27	17	52
	Cleveland (AL)	MAJ	1	2	3.44	9	4	0	0	37	32	15	14	15	24
MAJOR LEAGUE TOTALS			1	2	3.44	9	4	0	0	37	32	15	14	15	24
MINOR LEAGUE TOTALS			17	22	3.98	57	55	2	0	289	229	143	128	124	291

4. Dan Denham, rhp

Born: Dec. 24, 1982. **Ht.:** 6-2. **Wt.:** 195. **Bats:** R. **Throws:** R. **School:** Deer Valley HS, Antioch, Calif. **Career Transactions:** Selected by Indians in first round (17th overall) of 2001 draft; signed July 7, 2001.

Denham was the first of five high school pitchers the Indians selected in the first four rounds of the 2001 draft. He signed in time to make eight starts at Rookie-level Burlington, and while his numbers there weren't great, he still impressed managers enough to be rated the Appalachian League's best pitching prospect. He has great natural ability and arm strength. He threw 95 mph in high school, with plus life and sink on his fastball, and showed a power breaking ball. He's also developing a changeup. All three of his pitches have a chance to be well above average. He's very athletic and has shown a lot of intensity plus the ability to make adjustments. Denham has no major shortcomings. He lacks experience, but that will take care of itself. He's also a little inconsistent with his delivery, which is normal for a pitcher his age. He'll follow a similar course to the one the Indians used with the last California high school pitcher they drafted in the first round: C.C. Sabathia. In his second year, Sabathia started six games at short-season Mahoning Valley before moving to Columbus. Denham likely will head straight to low Class A.

Year	Club (League)	Class	W	L	ERA	G	GS	CG	SV	IP	H	R	ER	BB	SO
2001	Burlington (Appy)	R	0	4	4.40	8	8	0	0	31	30	21	15	26	31
MINOR LEAGUE TOTALS			0	4	4.40	8	8	0	0	31	30	21	15	26	31

5. J.D. Martin, rhp

Born: Jan. 2, 1983. **Ht.:** 6-4. **Wt.:** 170. **Bats:** R. **Throws:** R. **School:** Burroughs HS, Ridgecrest, Calif. **Career Transactions:** Selected by Indians in first round (35th overall) of 2001 draft; signed June 20, 2001.

It didn't take long for the Indians to realize they had something special in Martin. In his fourth pro start, Martin pitched five hitless innings, striking out 14 of the 16 batters he faced. "That's a line you don't ever see," former Tribe GM John Hart said. "That's like something out of Bruno's Groceries, in Little League." Some scouts say they've never seen an 18-year-old command both sides of the plate with his fastball the way Martin does. The pitch also has tremendous sink. He also has the ability to throw a changeup for strikes on three-ball counts that also leaves observers shaking their heads. His slider has a late, hard break. He has a tremendous feel for pitching. Martin needs to get a lot stronger, but he has a very projectable frame and should be able to do so as his body naturally matures. The velocity on his fastball is slightly below average at 87-89 mph, but it should pick up as he physically develops. Because of their status as high school first-round picks from the same draft, Martin and Dan Denham likely will climb the minor league ladder together. This year they could comprise a devastating one-two punch in low Class A.

Year	Club (League)	Class	W	L	ERA	G	GS	CG	SV	IP	H	R	ER	BB	SO
2001	Burlington (Appy)	R	5	1	1.38	10	10	0	0	46	26	9	7	11	72
MINOR LEAGUE TOTALS			5	1	1.38	10	10	0	0	46	26	9	7	11	72

6. Victor Martinez, c

Born: Dec. 23, 1978. **Ht.:** 6-2. **Wt.:** 170. **Bats:** B. **Throws:** R. **Career Transactions:** Signed out of Venezuela by Indians, July 15, 1996.

Catchers don't normally win batting titles, so when Martinez led the high Class A Carolina League in hitting in 2001, it propelled him onto this list for the first time. Martinez, the most improved player in the organization, made gigantic strides after missing two months in 2000 season with shoulder problems. He has hit .305 in five years a pro. He's a switch-hitter who can produce for average, and he should hit for more power as he matures. There aren't too many catchers who can do that. But it doesn't end there. He also has tremendous poise, presence and leadership. He has unbelievably soft hands and calls a great game. Managers rated him the CL's best defensive catcher. His arm is a little weak, so he has to rely on a quick release to throw runners out. He erased just 29 percent of basestealers in 2001, compared to the CL average of 39 percent. He'll have to work hard on his throwing mechanics in order to control a running game. With Einar Diaz established on the big league club, there's no need to rush Martinez. He'll open the 2002 season at Double-A Akron.

Year	Club (League)	Class	AVG	G	AB	R	H	2B	3B	HR	RBI	BB	SO	SB
1997	Maracay 1 (VSL)	R	.344	53	122	21	42	12	0	0	26	32	11	6
1998	Guacara 2 (VSL)	R	.269	55	160	28	43	13	0	1	27	32	14	8
1999	Mahoning Valley (NY-P)	A	.277	64	235	37	65	9	0	4	36	27	31	0
2000	Kinston (Car)	A	.217	26	83	9	18	7	0	0	8	11	5	1
	Columbus (SAL)	A	.371	21	70	11	26	9	1	2	12	11	6	0
2001	Kinston (Car)	A	.329	114	420	59	138	33	2	10	57	39	60	3
MINOR LEAGUE TOTALS			.305	333	1090	165	332	83	3	17	166	152	127	18

7. David Riske, rhp

Born: Oct. 23, 1976. **Ht.:** 6-2. **Wt.:** 180. **Bats:** R. **Throws:** R. **School:** Green River (Wash.) CC. **Career Transactions:** Selected by Indians in 56th round of 1996 draft; signed Oct. 21, 1996.

Riske is the lowest Indians draft pick ever to reach the big leagues. He has staggering numbers in five minor league seasons, including 295 strikeouts and just 175 hits allowed in 240 innings. He also has grit, rebounding from back and shoulder surgeries in 2000 to emerge as one of Cleveland's most consistent relievers last year. Riske has great makeup and is unflappable on the mound. He's essentially a one-pitch pitcher, relying almost exclusively on a deceptive, explosive fastball that plays bigger than its low- to mid-90s velocity. The pitch takes off on hitters, who can't catch up to it as it rides up out of the zone. He needs a reliable secondary pitch to keep hitters off his fastball. Attempts to develop a breaking ball have led to a change in his arm angle, which adversely affects his heater. Though major league hitters didn't make him pay last year when he gave up walks, he'll have to fine-tune his control. A closer in the minors, Riske is evolving into a valuable middle reliever and potential set-up man in the big leagues. He'll spend 2002 two or three chairs down from closer Bob Wickman in the Cleveland bullpen.

Year	Club (League)	Class	W	L	ERA	G	GS	CG	SV	IP	H	R	ER	BB	SO
1997	Kinston (Car)	A	4	4	2.25	39	0	0	2	72	58	22	18	33	90
1998	Kinston (Car)	A	1	1	2.33	53	0	0	33	54	48	15	14	15	67
	Akron (EL)	AA	0	0	0.00	2	0	0	1	3	1	0	0	1	5
1999	Akron (EL)	AA	0	0	1.90	23	0	0	12	24	5	6	5	13	33
	Buffalo (IL)	AAA	3	0	0.65	23	0	0	6	28	14	3	2	7	22
	Cleveland (AL)	MAJ	1	1	8.36	12	0	0	0	14	20	15	13	6	16
2000	Akron (EL)	AA	0	0	0.00	3	1	0	1	4	2	0	0	0	4
	Buffalo (IL)	AAA	0	0	3.00	2	0	0	0	3	2	1	1	2	2
2001	Buffalo (IL)	AAA	1	2	2.36	38	0	0	15	53	45	16	14	17	72
	Cleveland (AL)	MAJ	2	0	1.98	26	0	0	1	27	20	7	6	18	29
MAJOR LEAGUE TOTALS			3	1	4.14	38	0	0	1	41	40	22	19	24	45
MINOR LEAGUE TOTALS			9	7	2.02	183	1	0	70	241	175	63	54	88	295

8. Brian Tallet, lhp

Born: Sept. 21, 1977. **Ht.:** 6-7. **Wt.:** 208. **Bats:** L. **Throws:** L. **School:** Louisiana State University. **Career Transactions:** Selected by Indians in second round of 2000 draft; signed Aug. 1, 2000.

Pitching for college baseball's premier program (Louisiana State) in pressure situations (he started the 2000 College World Series championship game) has helped Tallet in his development as a pro. He dominated at Mahoning Valley in his pro debut in 2000, and last year he led the Carolina League as well as Indians minor leaguers in strikeouts. Tallet reminds some scouts of a young Chuck Finley. Tall and rangy, he has three solid pitches in his low-90s fastball, his slider and his changeup. He's aggressive and has a good feel for pitching. He pitches with confidence and shows a knack for changing speeds. His size is an asset, especially for a lefthander. His main concerns are repeating his delivery more consistently and refining his changeup. Tallet also will have to throw more strikes with his secondary pitches in order to get hitters out at the upper levels. When the Indians drafted him, they projected him as a reliever. He since has pitched so well as a starter that those plans have changed. He'll begin this year in the Double-A rotation.

Year	Club (League)	Class	W	L	ERA	G	GS	CG	SV	IP	H	R	ER	BB	SO
2000	Mahoning Valley (NY-P)	A	0	0	1.15	6	6	0	0	16	10	2	2	3	20
2001	Kinston (Car)	A	9	7	3.04	27	27	2	0	160	134	62	54	38	164
MINOR LEAGUE TOTALS			9	7	2.86	33	33	2	0	176	144	64	56	41	184

Cleveland Indians

9. Billy Traber, lhp

Born: July 18, 1979. **Ht.:** 6-5. **Wt.:** 205. **Bats:** L. **Throws:** L. **School:** Loyola Marymount University. **Career Transactions:** Selected by Mets in first round (16th overall) of 2000 draft; signed Sept. 5, 2000 . . . Traded by Mets with 1B Earl Snyder to Indians, Dec. 13, 2001, completing trade in which Indians sent 2B Roberto Alomar, LHP Mike Bacsik and 1B Danny Peoples to Mets for OF Matt Lawton, OF Alex Escobar, RHP Jerrod Riggan and two players to be named (Dec. 11, 2001).

While Alex Escobar was the biggest name among the prospects Cleveland received in the Roberto Alomar trade, Traber may be a safer bet to succeed. The 16th overall draft pick in 2000, he agreed to a $1.7 million bonus before a routine physical revealed ligament damage in his elbow. Forced to settle for $400,000, he was healthy throughout his pro debut last year and reached Triple-A. Traber has three pitches that can get hitters out—an 89-91 mph fastball, a plus curveball and a splitter that he saves to escape jams. His command makes those pitches even better, as he keeps hitters off balance by mixing his pitches and locations. He also throws on a nice downward plane. His fourth pitch right now is a changeup, and it needs the most work. He did make some strides with it and learned to trust it more last year. Though Traber logged 152 innings and did not miss a start in 2001, there's still concern abut his elbow. The Indians don't have the stockpile of lefty starters that the Mets have, so Traber may find it easier to reach the big leagues in his new organization. He'll be a phone call away this year in Triple-A.

Year	Club (League)	Class	W	L	ERA	G	GS	CG	SV	IP	H	R	ER	BB	SO
2001	Norfolk (IL)	AAA	0	1	1.29	1	1	0	0	7	5	3	1	0	0
	Binghamton (EL)	AA	4	3	4.43	8	8	0	0	43	50	25	21	13	45
	St. Lucie (FSL)	A	6	5	2.66	18	18	0	0	102	85	36	30	23	79
MINOR LEAGUE TOTALS			10	9	3.09	27	27	0	0	151	140	64	52	36	124

10. Alex Herrera, lhp

Born: Nov. 5, 1979. **Ht.:** 5-11. **Wt.:** 175. **Bats:** L. **Throws:** L. **Career Transactions:** Signed out of Venezuela by Indians, July 4, 1997.

Herrera had escaped notice until last year, when he was untouchable in high Class A. He limited Carolina League hitters to a .171 average while striking out 12.5 batters per nine innings, and Double-A batters didn't find him much easier to solve. He lacks size but he doesn't lack heat. He has a lively 92-96 mph fastball, which hitters aren't accustomed to seeing from a lefty. His slider is inconsistent, but it's also a plus pitch at times. When he has both pitches working, he's in charge. Herrera's delivery varies, so his command and stuff do as well. He also throws a changeup, but like his slider it's far from a finished product. At 5-foot-11, it's not easy for him to leverage the ball down in the strike zone. If he can add one or two secondary pitches and firm up his mechanics, Herrera has back-of-the-bullpen potential. He had a strong winter pitching in his native Venezuela, which could springboard him to Triple-A at the start of this season. His name has started to come up in trade inquiries, but so far the Indians have resisted.

Year	Club (League)	Class	W	L	ERA	G	GS	CG	SV	IP	H	R	ER	BB	SO
1998	Guacara 2 (VSL)	R	7	4	2.30	18	11	0	3	74	70	34	19	17	68
1999	San Felipe (VSL)	R	3	2	1.28	16	9	0	5	56	42	19	8	20	74
2000	Columbus (SAL)	A	4	3	3.43	20	0	0	0	42	41	25	16	21	41
	Kinston (Car)	A	0	1	2.32	17	0	0	1	31	28	11	8	19	40
	Akron (EL)	AA	0	0	0.00	2	0	0	0	1	2	1	0	1	1
2001	Kinston (Car)	A	4	0	0.60	28	0	0	3	60	36	6	4	18	83
	Akron (EL)	AA	3	0	2.83	15	0	0	2	29	24	9	9	9	22
MINOR LEAGUE TOTALS			21	10	1.96	116	20	0	14	293	243	105	64	105	329

11. Willy Taveras, of

Born: Dec. 25, 1981. **Ht.:** 6-0. **Wt.:** 160. **Bats:** R. **Throws:** R. **Career Transactions:** Signed out of Dominican Republic by Indians, May 27, 1999.

The Indians think highly enough of Taveras that they turned him loose in low Class A as a 19-year-old. A graduate of the club's increasingly productive program in the Dominican Republic, he has tremendous athleticism, game-changing speed and fearlessness on the bases. He has some pop for a center fielder, though he'll hit more for average than for power. He already steals bases at a high percentage, but he doesn't reach base as often as someone with his wheels should. Taveras is a free swinger who managed just a .317 on-base percentage last season. Offspeed pitches still baffle him at times. He must realize his job is to get on base however possible. Taveras covers a lot of ground in center field and has a plus arm. He could start 2002 back at Columbus or in high Class A.

Year	Club (League)	Class	AVG	G	AB	R	H	2B	3B	HR	RBI	BB	SO	SB
1999	Indians (DSL)	R	.354	68	277	57	98	19	6	3	44	32	32	26
2000	Burlington (Appy)	R	.263	50	190	46	50	4	3	1	16	23	44	36
2001	Columbus (SAL)	A	.271	97	395	55	107	15	7	3	32	22	73	29
MINOR LEAGUE TOTALS			.296	215	862	158	255	38	16	7	92	77	149	91

12. Tim Drew, rhp

Born: Aug. 31, 1978. **Ht.:** 6-1. **Wt.:** 195. **Bats:** R. **Throws:** R. **School:** Lowndes HS, Valdosta, Ga. **Career Transactions:** Selected by Indians in first round (28th overall) of 1997 draft; signed July 27, 1997.

Drew exemplifies the perils of rushing a young pitcher to the big leagues. When their rotation was riddled by injuries in 2000, the Indians summoned an unprepared Drew, and he hasn't been the same since. The younger brother of J.D. Drew—they're the only siblings to go in the first round of the same draft—Tim pitched his way onto the Opening Day roster last year, then quickly pitched his way back to Triple-A. He's a tremendous athlete and a hard worker, plus he has good stuff. For some reason, it just hasn't translated yet at the big league level. Drew's fastball is average but there's enough there that he should be getting more out of it than he does. His best pitch is a changeup and he also throws a slider. Drew must learn to trust his stuff more in the strike zone. He tends to be a nibbler, then can't recover once he falls behind in the count. Drew will be given a chance to win a spot in the major league rotation in training camp. As a contender, Cleveland can't afford to give him on-the-job training, so he could wind up in Buffalo again.

Year	Club (League)	Class	W	L	ERA	G	GS	CG	SV	IP	H	R	ER	BB	SO
1997	Burlington (Appy)	R	0	1	6.17	4	4	0	0	12	16	15	8	4	14
	Watertown (NY-P)	A	0	0	1.93	1	1	0	0	5	4	1	1	3	9
1998	Columbus (SAL)	A	4	3	3.79	13	13	0	0	71	68	43	30	26	64
	Kinston (Car)	A	3	8	5.20	15	15	0	0	90	105	58	52	31	67
1999	Kinston (Car)	A	13	5	3.73	28	28	2	0	169	154	79	70	60	125
2000	Akron (EL)	AA	3	2	2.42	9	9	0	0	52	41	19	14	15	22
	Cleveland (AL)	MAJ	1	0	10.00	3	3	0	0	9	17	12	10	8	5
	Buffalo (IL)	AAA	7	8	5.87	16	16	2	0	95	122	69	62	31	53
2001	Cleveland (AL)	MAJ	0	2	7.97	8	6	0	0	35	51	39	31	16	15
	Buffalo (IL)	AAA	8	6	3.92	18	18	1	0	108	115	54	47	27	75
MAJOR LEAGUE TOTALS			1	2	8.39	11	9	0	0	44	68	51	41	24	20
MINOR LEAGUE TOTALS			38	33	4.25	104	104	5	0	602	625	338	284	197	429

13. Jerrod Riggan, rhp

Born: May 16, 1974. **Ht.:** 6-3. **Wt.:** 197. **Bats:** R. **Throws:** R. **School:** San Diego State University. **Career Transactions:** Selected by Angels in eighth round of 1996 draft; signed June 10, 1996 . . . Released by Angels, April 17, 1998 . . . Signed by Mets, July 9, 1998 . . . Traded by Mets with OF Matt Lawton, OF Alex Escobar and two players to be named to Indians for 2B Roberto Alomar, LHP Mike Bacsik and 1B Danny Peoples, Dec. 11, 2001; Indians acquired LHP Billy Traber and 1B Earl Snyder to complete trade (Dec. 13, 2001).

Riggan should make the most immediate impact of the four prospects the Indians acquired in the Roberto Alomar trade with the Mets. He no longer qualifies as a rookie, but he's eligible for this list despite pitching in 36 big league games because he hasn't exceeded 50 innings. New York promoted Riggan from Triple-A five times last year, and he settled in with a 2.36 ERA after the all-star break. Released by the Angels after two years as a starter, he has flourished in relief. He throws strikes with an 88-92 mph fastball, a slider and a splitter. Unlike some control pitchers, he's not hittable because he won't just lay the ball over the plate for the sake of throwing a strike. Riggan needs to get tougher on lefthanders and basestealers, but he should make the Opening Day roster.

Year	Club (League)	Class	W	L	ERA	G	GS	CG	SV	IP	H	R	ER	BB	SO
1996	Boise (NWL)	A	3	5	4.63	15	15	1	0	89	90	62	46	38	80
1997	Cedar Rapids (Mid)	A	9	8	4.89	19	19	3	0	116	132	70	63	36	65
	Lake Elsinore (Cal)	A	2	5	6.07	8	8	0	0	43	60	36	29	16	31
1998	Capital City (SAL)	A	4	1	3.70	14	0	0	1	41	38	21	17	14	40
1999	St. Lucie (FSL)	A	5	5	3.33	44	0	0	12	73	69	33	27	24	66
2000	Binghamton (EL)	AA	2	0	1.11	52	0	0	28	65	43	9	8	18	79
	New York (NL)	MAJ	0	0	0.00	1	0	0	0	2	3	2	0	0	1
2001	Norfolk (IL)	AAA	2	0	1.95	28	0	0	13	32	26	7	7	4	37
	New York (NL)	MAJ	3	3	3.40	35	0	0	0	48	42	19	18	24	41
MAJOR LEAGUE TOTALS			3	3	3.26	36	0	0	0	50	45	21	18	24	42
MINOR LEAGUE TOTALS			27	24	3.85	180	42	4	54	460	458	238	197	150	398

14. John McDonald, ss

Born: Sept. 24, 1974. **Ht.:** 5-11. **Wt.:** 175. **Bats:** R. **Throws:** R. **School:** Providence College. **Career Transactions:** Selected by Indians in 12th round of 1996 draft; signed June 5, 1996.

McDonald was born about three or four decades too late. He's a vintage 1960s or 1970s good-field, no-hit shortstop stuck in an era of high-octane offense. He's a state-of-the-art defender with borderline Vizquelian gifts. But his path has been blocked by Omar Vizquel himself, and McDonald's Mark Belanger-like bat hasn't helped. Given the chance to play every day, McDonald would be a "SportsCenter" regular for his defense, which is Gold Glove-caliber. He's not as acrobatic as Vizquel, but McDonald has more range and a better arm. He has great hands, quickness in the field and wonderful instincts. All that won't matter unless he can hit, however. McDonald batted a combined .236 between Triple-A in the majors last year, has just six homers in the last four seasons and rarely hits for extra bases. He makes reasonable contact but doesn't draw walks and isn't much of a basestealing threat with his average speed. McDonald will compete for a spot as a backup middle infielder on the big league club this year. Trade rumors continue to swirl around Vizquel, and a deal would make McDonald the starter.

Year	Club (League)	Class	AVG	G	AB	R	H	2B	3B	HR	RBI	BB	SO	SB
1996	Watertown (NY-P)	A	.270	75	278	48	75	11	0	2	26	32	49	11
1997	Kinston (Car)	A	.259	130	541	77	140	27	3	5	53	51	75	6
1998	Akron (EL)	AA	.230	132	514	68	118	18	2	2	43	43	61	17
1999	Akron (EL)	AA	.296	55	226	31	67	12	0	1	26	19	26	7
	Buffalo (IL)	AAA	.316	66	237	30	75	12	1	0	25	11	23	6
	Cleveland (AL)	MAJ	.333	18	21	2	7	0	0	0	0	0	3	0
2000	Buffalo (IL)	AAA	.269	75	286	37	77	17	2	1	36	21	29	4
	Mahoning Valley (NY-P)	A	.118	5	17	0	2	1	0	0	1	2	3	0
	Cleveland (AL)	MAJ	.444	9	9	0	4	0	0	0	0	0	1	0
	Kinston (Car)	A	.333	1	3	0	1	0	0	0	0	0	0	0
2001	Buffalo (IL)	AAA	.244	116	410	52	100	17	1	2	33	33	72	17
	Cleveland (AL)	MAJ	.091	17	22	1	2	1	0	0	0	1	7	0
MAJOR LEAGUE TOTALS			.250	44	52	3	13	1	0	0	0	1	11	0
MINOR LEAGUE TOTALS			.261	655	2512	343	655	115	9	13	243	212	338	68

15. Ryan Church, of

Born: Oct. 14, 1978. **Ht.:** 6-1. **Wt.:** 190. **Bats:** L. **Throws:** L. **School:** University of Nevada. **Career Transactions:** Selected by Indians in 14th round of 2000 draft; signed June 7, 2000.

Church began his college career as a pitcher, but hurt his arm at Nevada, turned to the outfield and has become one of Cleveland's better position-player prospects since signing in 2000. He was named MVP of the short-season New York-Penn League in his pro debut and had a strong performance in Class A last year. Church doesn't have an overwhelming tool but he's solid across the board. He has the chance to hit for average and power in the majors. He's an average runner. Defensively, Church gets good jumps on balls and has enough arm for right field. At times his swing tends to get a bit long as he tries to force his power. But he's as good an all-around outfielder as the Indians have in their system. A good spring could position Church to open the season in Double-A.

Year	Club (League)	Class	AVG	G	AB	R	H	2B	3B	HR	RBI	BB	SO	SB
2000	Mahoning Valley (NY-P)	A	.298	73	272	51	81	16	5	10	65	38	49	11
2001	Columbus (SAL)	A	.287	101	363	64	104	23	3	17	76	54	79	4
	Kinston (Car)	A	.241	24	83	16	20	7	0	5	15	18	23	1
MINOR LEAGUE TOTALS			.286	198	718	131	205	46	8	32	156	110	151	16

16. Alex Requena, of

Born: Aug. 13, 1980. **Ht.:** 5-11. **Wt.:** 155. **Bats:** B. **Throws:** R. **Career Transactions:** Signed out of Venezuela by Indians, July 25, 1998.

Requena has sensational speed. He's the fastest runner in the organization and perhaps in all the minors. He led the South Atlantic League with 87 stolen bases in 2000 and swiped 47 in 95 games last year. His speed shrinks the field. He covers tremendous ground in center field and is very aggressive on the bases. He also has a solid arm. Requena has a long way to go as a hitter, however. He hit .227 in Class A in 2001 and never has topped .259 in three minor league seasons. He has shown very little plate discipline, consistent contact or the ability to make adjustments. Like Willy Taveras but even more so, Requena has to figure out how to play to his strengths. Though the Indians would like to develop Requena as a leadoff hitter, he has yet to show the requisite on-base ability. He may give high Class A another try in 2002.

Year	Club (League)	Class	AVG	G	AB	R	H	2B	3B	HR	RBI	BB	SO	SB
1999	Mahoning Valley (NY-P)	A	.234	61	214	44	50	6	3	0	18	36	64	44
2000	Columbus (SAL)	A	.259	126	482	90	125	6	6	1	24	66	137	87
2001	Columbus (SAL)	A	.255	33	137	22	35	6	0	2	13	9	40	15
	Kinston (Car)	A	.212	62	259	30	55	7	4	2	13	19	80	32
MINOR LEAGUE TOTALS			.243	282	1092	186	265	25	13	5	68	130	321	178

17. Jim Ed Warden, rhp

Born: may 7, 1979. **Ht.:** 6-7. **Wt.:** 195. **Bats:** R. **Throws:** R. **School:** Tennessee Tech. **Career Transactions:** Selected by Indians in sixth round of 2001 draft; signed June 12, 2001.

A big, strong righthander, Warden is yet another product of the Indians' promising 2001 draft class. In February, the Major League Scouting Bureau gave him an overall future potential grade of 57 grade on the 20-to-80 scale, two points higher than fellow Tennessee collegian Dewon Brazelton, who went No. 3 overall to the Devil Rays. Warden isn't really in Brazelton's class, but he's a legitimate prospect who made quite an impression in Rookie ball and instructional league. The Indians love his makeup, arm strength and ability to both spin a breaking ball and repeat his delivery. His size allows him to create a good downhill angle for his low-90s fastball. The next step for Warden will be to continue to work on his change-up, which could make his fastball even more effective. He's scheduled to start 2002 in the low Class A rotation.

Year	Club (League)	Class	W	L	ERA	G	GS	CG	SV	IP	H	R	ER	BB	SO
2001	Burlington (Appy)	R	4	5	4.27	12	12	0	0	53	56	32	25	13	52
MINOR LEAGUE TOTALS			4	5	4.27	12	12	0	0	53	56	32	25	13	52

18. Shane Wallace, lhp

Born: Dec. 29, 1980. **Ht.:** 6-2. **Wt.:** 200. **Bats:** L. **Throws:** L. **School:** Newman Smith HS, Carrollton, Texas. **Career Transactions:** Selected by Indians in sixth round of 1999 draft; signed June 24, 1999.

Wallace was on his way to a possible 20-win season in 2001 when he was derailed by elbow problems that eventually led to Tommy John surgery. His tremendous makeup will help him in his comeback. Wallace has a good feel for pitching, operating with a low-90s sinker and an effective curveball and changeup. He cuts his fastball at times, making it look almost like a slider. The cutter and changeup are his best pitches against righthanded hitters. The changeup could use some further refinement, but the biggest concern about Wallace is just keeping him healthy. It may take a full year to regain his form following the surgery. When healthy, he's one of the top two or three lefties in the organization. When he's ready, he'll start back in high Class A.

Year	Club (League)	Class	W	L	ERA	G	GS	CG	SV	IP	H	R	ER	BB	SO
1999	Burlington (Appy)	R	1	5	5.25	12	12	0	0	48	58	35	28	15	38
2000	Columbus (SAL)	A	2	2	2.82	13	8	1	1	54	53	27	17	14	40
2001	Kinston (CL)	A	10	2	1.61	13	13	1	0	84	65	22	15	16	60
MINOR LEAGUE TOTALS			13	9	2.90	38	33	2	1	186	176	84	60	45	138

19. John Peralta, ss

Born: May 28, 1982. **Ht.:** 6-1. **Wt.:** 185. **Bats:** R. **Throws:** R. **Career Transactions:** Signed out of Dominican Republic by Indians, April 14, 1999.

One Indians official says Peralta has the best hands he has ever seen on a 19-year-old. Those soft hands, and Peralta's over-the-top throwing motion, have led to defensive comparisons to former Gold Glover Alan Trammell. Peralta has a strong, accurate arm, and plenty of range. Defensively, there's no question he could play shortstop in the major leagues. But like John McDonald, Peralta still has a ways to go offensively. He strikes out way too often and doesn't produce much in the way of extra-base hits or stolen bases. Peralta will draw walks, but he still needs a better approach and concept of the strike zone. He's young, so he still has plenty of time to make adjustments. He could return to high Class A or move up to Double-A to begin 2002.

Year	Club (League)	Class	AVG	G	AB	R	H	2B	3B	HR	RBI	BB	SO	SB
1999	Indians (DSL)	R	.303	62	208	48	63	14	6	6	43	33	49	14
2000	Columbus (SAL)	A	.241	106	349	52	84	13	1	3	34	59	102	7
2001	Kinston (Car)	A	.240	125	441	57	106	24	2	7	47	58	148	4
MINOR LEAGUE TOTALS			.254	293	998	157	253	51	9	16	124	150	299	25

20. Martin Vargas, rhp

Born: Feb. 22, 1978. **Ht.:** 6-0. **Wt.:** 160. **Bats:** R. **Throws:** R. **Career Transactions:** Signed out of Dominican Republic by Indians, July 5, 1995.

A converted catcher originally known as Martin Bautista, Vargas still is learning how to pitch, as evidenced by his up-and-down performances in Double-A the last two years. He has a great arm and owns a power sinker, but that alone isn't enough to guaranteee success. His slider and splitter shows flashes of being at least average pitches, but not on a consistent basis. After five years on the mound, Vargas still lacks pitching instincts and command. He's wild both in and out of the strike zone. He did pitch better after a promotion to Triple-A, where he'll head to start 2002. Once he figures out what he's doing, he'll be a candidate to pitch in Cleveland.

Year	Club (League)	Class	AVG	G	AB	R	H	2B	3B	HR	RBI	BB	SO	SB
1996	Co-op (DSL)	R	.223	39	103	7	23	6	1	0	12	12	25	1
MINOR LEAGUE TOTALS			.223	39	103	7	23	6	1	0	12	12	25	1

Year	Club (League)	Class	W	L	ERA	G	GS	CG	SV	IP	H	R	ER	BB	SO
1997	Indians (DSL)	R	3	5	2.45	14	14	0	0	70	52	33	19	39	43
1998	Columbus (SAL)	A	1	4	10.01	7	7	0	0	30	42	36	33	24	25
	Burlington (Appy)	R	3	7	4.76	13	13	1	0	74	78	49	39	35	64
1999	Columbus (SAL)	A	6	3	4.95	15	12	0	0	67	80	46	37	20	51
	Kinston (Car)	A	6	1	2.76	20	0	0	2	42	31	16	13	20	44
2000	Akron (EL)	AA	10	8	5.42	53	0	0	7	81	96	52	30	58	
2001	Buffalo (IL)	AAA	0	3	2.93	22	0	0	4	28	20	11	9	17	22
	Akron (EL)	AA	1	5	5.63	32	0	0	9	40	52	29	25	23	35
MINOR LEAGUE TOTALS			30	36	4.67	176	46	1	22	432	547	272	224	208	342

21. Josh Bard, c

Born: March 30, 1978. **Ht.:** 6-3. **Wt.:** 205. **Bats:** B. **Throws:** R. **School:** Texas Tech. **Career Transactions:** Selected by Rockies in third round of 1999 draft; signed Aug. 12, 1999 . . . Traded by Rockies with OF Jody Gerut to Indians for OF Jacob Cruz, June 2, 2001.

After designating Jacob Cruz for assignment last May, the Indians traded him to the Rockies for Bard and outfielder Jody Gerut. While Gerut didn't play last year following knee surgery, Bard was everything he was advertised to be in his half-season with Akron. He has size and strength, leadership abilities and catch-and-throw skills. He probably could handle game-calling duties in the major leagues right now. He did a nice job of working with an unfamiliar pitching staff after changing organizations. Offensively, Bard is a switch-hitter who fares better from the left side. He has shown some power potential but lacks a solid approach to hitting. His defense clearly is ahead of his offense at this point, and how much he hits will dictate his future. Despite the questions about his bat, Bard has no glaring weaknesses. He'll be the starting catcher in Triple-A this year.

Year	Club (League)	Class	AVG	G	AB	R	H	2B	3B	HR	RBI	BB	SO	SB
2000	Salem (Car)	A	.285	93	309	40	88	17	0	2	25	32	33	3
	Colo. Spr. (PCL)	AAA	.235	4	17	0	4	0	0	0	1	0	2	0
2001	Carolina (SL)	AA	.258	35	124	14	32	13	0	1	24	19	23	0
	Akron (EL)	AA	.278	51	194	26	54	11	0	4	25	16	27	0
	Mahoning Valley (NY-P)	A	.273	13	44	7	12	4	0	2	8	6	2	0
	Buffalo (IL)	AAA	.000	1	4	0	0	0	0	0	0	0	1	0
MINOR LEAGUE TOTALS			.275	197	692	87	190	45	0	9	83	73	88	3

22. Maicer Izturis, 2b

Born: Sept. 12, 1980. **Ht.:** 5-8. **Wt.:** 155. **Bats:** B. **Throws:** R. **Career Transactions:** Signed out of Venezuela by Indians, April 1, 1998.

After spending the previous three seasons as the top shortstop in the Indians system, Izturis was moved to second base last year because of repeated injuries to his throwing arm. He had shoulder surgery in 1999 and elbow problems in 2000. Like his brother Cesar, a Dodgers shortstop, Izturis is a standout with the glove who makes defense look easy. He has great hands and fielding mechanics, plus good speed. But Izturis missed so much time with injuries that he's just starting to catch up in his development. Last year was the first time in his four years in the organization that he was injury-free. Izturis runs well enough to steal bases, but that's the extent of his offensive contributions. He lacks power, strength and patience. He needs to have another healthy year in 2002 to get his career back on track. He'll be the starting second baseman in high Class A or Double-A.

Year	Club (League)	Class	AVG	G	AB	R	H	2B	3B	HR	RBI	BB	SO	SB
1998	Burlington (Appy)	R	.290	55	217	33	63	8	2	2	33	17	32	16
1999	Columbus (SAL)	A	.300	57	220	46	66	5	3	4	23	20	28	14
2000	Columbus (SAL)	A	.276	10	29	4	8	1	0	0	1	3	3	0
2001	Kinston (Car)	A	.240	114	433	47	104	16	6	1	39	31	81	32
MINOR LEAGUE TOTALS			.268	236	899	130	241	30	11	7	96	71	144	62

23. Hector Luna, ss

Born: Feb. 1, 1982. **Ht.:** 6-1. **Wt.:** 170. **Bats:** R. **Throws:** R. **Career Transactions:** Signed out of Dominican Republic by Indians, Feb. 2, 1999.

Luna is another talented Indians middle infielder who's still trying to prove he'll hit enough to one day be a big league regular. He has some offensive upside with a strong frame, quick bat, good pop for a shortstop and some semblance of plate discipline. Now he has to turn those tools into performance. He has average speed that's enhanced by his instincts, which make him a threat to steal an occasional base. Luna is quick and athletic at shortstop, with the hands, range and arm to play the position. His upside is as a five-tool shortstop, though there's some concern that he may eventually outgrow the position. Where John Peralta winds up to start the season will determine whether Luna goes to Kinston or Columbus.

Year	Club (League)	Class	AVG	G	AB	R	H	2B	3B	HR	RBI	BB	SO	SB
1999	Indians (DSL)	R	.256	61	234	44	60	13	2	1	24	27	36	29
2000	Burlington (Appy)	R	.204	55	201	25	41	5	0	1	15	27	35	19
	Mahoning Valley (NY-P)	A	.316	5	19	2	6	2	0	0	4	1	3	0
2001	Columbus (SAL)	A	.266	66	241	36	64	8	3	3	23	23	48	15
MINOR LEAGUE TOTALS			.246	187	695	107	171	28	5	5	66	78	122	63

24. Jason Stanford, lhp

Born: Jan. 23, 1977. **Ht.:** 6-2. **Wt.:** 200. **Bats:** L. **Throws:** L. **School:** UNC Charlotte. **Career Transactions:** Signed as nondrafted free agent by Indians, Nov. 16, 1999.

A nondrafted free agent in 1999, Stanford was the organization's minor league pitcher of the year in 2000. He kept opening eyes last year. He spent most of 2001 in Double-A, and spun a three-hit shutout with 10 strikeouts and no walks in his Triple-A debut. After the regular season, he posted a 1.42 ERA in the Arizona Fall League and went 2-0, 0.75 for Team USA at the World Cup. Stanford's stuff is solid across the board. He commands his fastball to both sides of the plate, throws his breaking ball for strikes and has an effective change-up. His makeup, mental toughness and pitchability are also assets. If he has a weakness it's that he lacks an out pitch, though his changeup has the potential to become one. He likely will open 2002 in the Triple-A rotation.

Year	Club (League)	Class	W	L	ERA	G	GS	CG	SV	IP	H	R	ER	BB	SO
2000	Columbus (SAL)	A	7	4	2.73	14	14	0	0	79	82	32	24	20	72
	Kinston (Car)	A	4	3	2.57	11	11	1	0	70	68	22	20	17	58
	Akron (EL)	AA	1	0	1.59	1	1	0	0	6	5	1	1	1	5
2001	Akron (EL)	AA	6	11	4.07	24	24	1	0	142	152	71	64	32	108
	Buffalo (IL)	AAA	1	0	0.00	1	1	1	0	9	3	0	0	0	10
MINOR LEAGUE TOTALS			19	18	3.21	51	51	3	0	305	310	126	109	70	253

25. Zach Sorensen, ss

Born: Jan. 3, 1977. **Ht.:** 6-0. **Wt.:** 190. **Bats:** B. **Throws:** R. **School:** Wichita State University. **Career Transactions:** Selected by Indians in second round of 1998 draft; signed July 1, 1998.

Sorensen missed much of the 2001 season with shoulder problems, but he rebounded to hit .371 in the Arizona Fall League, where he was named to the all-prospect team. He's a solid gamer who plays with a lot of passion, and those qualities have endeared him to the Indians since they drafted him in 1998. A switch-hitter, he has shown a decent bat that, based on his play in Arizona, may still be improving. He has a good idea on what he wants to do at the plate. Sorensen also has some speed, though he really lacks a single above-average tool. He does everything well, nothing great. There still are some questions about his arm strength at shortstop—his shoulder woes didn't help his cause—and some thought that he might be better suited for second base. Sorensen projects as a backup middle infielder in the big leagues and will be on call in Triple-A this year.

Year	Club (League)	Class	AVG	G	AB	R	H	2B	3B	HR	RBI	BB	SO	SB
1998	Watertown (NY-P)	A	.300	53	200	38	60	7	8	4	26	35	35	14
1999	Kinston (Car)	A	.238	130	508	79	121	16	7	7	59	62	126	24

2000	Akron (EL)	AA	.259	96	382	62	99	17	4	6	38	42	62	16
	Buffalo (IL)	AAA	.263	12	38	5	10	1	1	0	2	3	9	1
2001	Akron (EL)	AA	.232	46	194	24	45	6	1	5	16	11	30	10
	Mahoning Valley (NY-P)	A	.245	14	53	10	13	0	1	1	11	2	8	2
	Buffalo (IL)	AAA	.286	2	7	2	2	0	0	0	1	0	0	0
MINOR LEAGUE TOTALS			.253	353	1382	220	350	47	22	23	153	155	270	67

26. Jason Davis, rhp

Born: May 8, 1980. **Ht.:** 6-6. **Wt.:** 195. **Bats:** R. **Throws:** R. **School:** Cleveland State (Tenn.) CC. **Career Transactions:** Selected by Indians in 21st round of 1999 draft; signed May 18, 2000.

A basketball player in junior college, Davis signed as a draft-and-follow in 2000 with little fanfare. He proved to be better than expected in his first full season. He shows plenty of arm strength with a sinking fastball that clocks in at 93-94 mph. The next step will be developing his offspeed pitches. Davis is working on a breaking ball and changeup, but still is a long way from having command of both. His size makes him an intimidating presence on the mound and allows him to throw his pitches on a tough downward plane. His athletic ability and aptitude for learning should help him make adjustments and polish his repertoire. He'll begin this year in the rotation at high Class A.

Year	Club (League)	Class	W	L	ERA	G	GS	CG	SV	IP	H	R	ER	BB	SO
2000	Burlington (Appy)	R	4	4	4.40	10	10	0	0	45	48	27	22	16	35
2001	Columbus (SAL)	A	14	6	2.70	27	27	1	0	160	147	72	48	51	115
MINOR LEAGUE TOTALS			18	10	3.07	37	37	1	0	205	195	99	70	67	150

27. Kyle Evans, rhp

Born: Oct. 10, 1978. **Ht.:** 6-3. **Wt.:** 190. **Bats:** R. **Throws:** R. **School:** Baylor University. **Career Transactions:** Selected by Indians in sixth round of 2000 draft; signed June 15, 2000.

Like Kinston teammate Shane Wallace, Evans got off to a quick start in the Carolina League last year before succumbing to elbow problems that required Tommy John surgery. Evans played some shortstop at Baylor before making a quick and smooth transition to pitching. He does a nice job of mixing his fastball, slider and changeup to keep hitters from getting comfortable. His feel for pitching and his deceptive delivery allow his stuff to work better than it looks on radar guns. Evans is a good athlete who throws strikes and isn't rattled easily. While may pitchers bounce back from Tommy John surgery better than ever these days, the operation still raises concerns about Evans' future. He has worked a total of just 93 innings in two years as a pro and won't get a full workload this year in high Class A.

Year	Club (League)	Class	W	L	ERA	G	GS	CG	SV	IP	H	R	ER	BB	SO
2000	Mahoning Valley (NY-P)	A	5	2	3.14	12	11	0	0	63	56	29	22	22	53
2001	Kinston (Car)	A	2	1	2.70	7	7	0	0	30	35	9	9	9	16
MINOR LEAGUE TOTALS			7	3	3.00	19	18	0	0	93	91	38	31	31	69

28. Earl Snyder, 1b

Born: May 6, 1976. **Ht.:** 6-0. **Wt.:** 207. **Bats:** R. **Throws:** R. **School:** University of Hartford. **Career Transactions:** Selected by Mets in 36th round of 1998 draft; signed June 5, 1998 . . . Traded by Mets with LHP Billy Traber to Indians, Dec. 13, 2001, completing trade in which Indians sent 2B Roberto Alomar, LHP Mike Bacsik and 1B Danny Peoples to Mets for OF Matt Lawton, OF Alex Escobar, RHP Jerrod Riggan and two players to be named (Dec. 11, 2001).

Snyder was named Mets minor league player of the year in 2001 before joining the Indians as part of the Roberto Alomar trade. A 36th-round pick out of the University of Hartford—which also produced another first baseman named Jeff Bagwell—Snyder is a classic overachiever who has succeeded at every level. He has hit at least 20 homers in each of the last three seasons, and last year he improved his strike-zone judgment. He's not an exceptional first baseman, but he's not bad either. He also has seen time at third base and in the corner outfield positions. Before trading him, New York officials compared Snyder to Benny Agbayani in the way he exceeded expectations. Snyder should spend most of this season in Triple-A.

Year	Club (League)	Class	AVG	G	AB	R	H	2B	3B	HR	RBI	BB	SO	SB
1998	Pittsfield (NY-P)	A	.252	71	262	39	66	8	1	11	40	23	60	0
1999	Capital City (SAL)	A	.267	136	486	73	130	25	4	28	97	55	117	2
2000	St. Lucie (FSL)	A	.282	134	514	84	145	36	0	25	93	57	127	4
2001	Binghamton (EL)	AA	.281	114	405	69	114	35	2	20	75	58	111	4
	Norfolk (IL)	AAA	.474	6	19	5	9	3	0	0	3	3	1	0
MINOR LEAGUE TOTALS			.275	461	1686	270	464	107	7	84	308	196	416	10

29. Fernando Cabrera, rhp

Born: Nov. 16, 1981. **Ht.:** 6-4. **Wt.:** 175. **Bats:** R. **Throws:** R. **School:** Disciples of Christ Academy, Bayamon, P.R. **Career Transactions:** Selected by Indians in 10th round of 1999 draft; signed Aug. 23, 1999.

Cabrera followed an unimpressive pro debut in 2000 with an attention-getting performance in low Class A last year, averaging more than a strikeout per inning and holding opponents to a .241 average. He has a long, lanky body and plenty of arm strength. He throws a heavy, dominating fastball that tops out at 97 mph. Cabrera also can spin a breaking ball, though not consistently. He still needs work on his mechanics, as his long arms make it difficult for him to repeat his delivery. His secondary pitches, command and durability all require improvement as well. But pitchers with arms like Cabrera's always get plenty of chances. He'll move up to high Class A in 2002.

Year	Club (League)	Class	W	L	ERA	G	GS	CG	SV	IP	H	R	ER	BB	SO
2000	Burlington (Appy)	R	3	7	4.61	13	13	0	0	68	64	42	35	20	50
2001	Columbus (SAL)	A	5	6	3.61	20	20	0	0	95	89	49	38	37	96
MINOR LEAGUE TOTALS			8	13	4.03	33	33	0	0	163	153	91	73	57	146

30. Mike Conroy, of

Born: Oct. 3, 1982. **Ht.:** 6-3. **Wt.:** 190. **Bats:** L. **Throws:** L. **School:** Boston College HS, Dorchester, Mass. **Career Transactions:** Selected by Indians in first round (43rd overall) of 2001 draft; signed July 5, 2001.

Conroy was the only hitter the Indians selected with their first nine picks in the 2001 draft. His $870,000 bonus was the second-highest in club history for an amateur hitter, trailing only the $1.375 million that fellow first-round pick Corey Smith got the year before. Conroy draws some Paul O'Neill comparisons because of his lefthanded swing, power potential and solid defensive skills. He had a humbling season in Rookie ball and had a difficult time adjusting to failure. Cleveland officials praise his makeup, though he tends to be hard on himself—another O'Neill trait. As a high school player coming from the Northeast, Conroy may take a while to develop. The Indians are willing to wait and will send him to low Class A this year.

Year	Club (League)	Class	AVG	G	AB	R	H	2B	3B	HR	RBI	BB	SO	SB
2001	Burlington (Appy)	R	.244	43	156	19	38	7	1	2	23	13	49	5
MINOR LEAGUE TOTALS			.244	43	156	19	38	7	1	2	23	13	49	5

COLORADO
Rockies

By Tracy Ringolsby

Finally, the Rockies see hope for the future when they evaluate their farm system. After concentrating more on signability than ability when drafting under original general manager Bob Gebhard, and emphasizing pitchers over hitters, Colorado is beginning to develop some balance.

For the first time in the franchise's 10-year history, the Rockies will field a Double-A affiliate filled with prospects instead of castoffs from other organizations. At least five hitters and four pitchers among the team's 30 best prospects—led by starters Aaron Cook, Ryan Kibler and Jason Young, plus outfielder Rene Reyes—figure to open the season at Carolina. That's a far cry from 2001, when the April promotion of shortstop Juan Uribe and the June trade of catcher Josh Bard to the Indians left the Mudcats without a legitimate position prospect.

"Almost every player on Carolina should be a homegrown position player," GM Dan O'Dowd said. "That's a big step for us. And out of that at the end of next season, what we have to pray and hope for is we can look at two or three or maybe four of those position players and say they're going to help us here in Colorado within the next 12 to 18 months."

The Rockies found out in 2001 that the jump from Double-A isn't that far. Uribe and righthander Jason Jennings, who finished the season as regulars in Colorado, both opened with Carolina.

Colorado's six farm teams finished a combined 31 games below .500 in 2001, but the Rockies were encouraged that three of their lowest four affiliates—Class A Salem and Asheville, plus Rookie-level Casper—made the playoffs, and Salem won the Carolina League championship.

O'Dowd says that sets a good foundation for the future.

"I think the biggest thing that happened for us in Cleveland is we won so much in the minor leagues that when the players got to the big league level, winning was part of their daily activity. It wasn't a surprise," said O'Dowd, a former farm director and assistant GM with the Indians. "I think you develop players better in a winning atmosphere.

"The excitement of coming to the ballpark, competing and challenging for something, makes for more of a winning situation. I think we made strides in that area, but we have a long way to go."

OrganizationOverview

General manager: Dan O'Dowd. **Farm director:** Michael Hill. **Scouting director:** Bill Schmidt.

2001 PERFORMANCE

Class	Team	League	W	L	Pct.	Finish*	Manager
Majors	Colorado	National	73	89	.451	12th (16)	Buddy Bell
Triple-A	Colorado Springs Sky Sox	Pacific Coast	62	79	.440	14th (16)	Chris Cron
Double-A	Carolina Mudcats	Southern	62	76	.449	7th (10)	Ron Gideon
High A	Salem Avalanche	Carolina	70	68	.507	4th (8)	Dave Collins
Low A	Asheville Tourists	South Atlantic	68	71	.489	9th (16)	Joe Mikulik
Short-season	Tri-City Dust Devils	Northwest	39	36	.520	3rd (8)	Stu Cole
Rookie	Casper Rockies	Pioneer	37	39	.487	t-4th (8)	P.J. Carey
OVERALL 2001 MINOR LEAGUE RECORD			338	369	.478	19th(30)	

*Finish in overall standings (No. of teams in league)

ORGANIZATION LEADERS

BATTING
*AVG	**Brent Butler**, Colorado Springs	.335
R	Brad Hawpe, Asheville	78
H	Rene Reyes, Asheville	156
TB	Butch Huskey, Colorado Springs	236
2B	Garrett Atkins, Salem	43
3B	Three tied at	7
HR	Brad Hawpe, Asheville	22
RBI	Butch Huskey, Colorado Springs	87
BB	Garrett Atkins, Salem	74
SO	Justin Lincoln, Salem/Asheville	160
SB	Rene Reyes, Asheville	53

PITCHING
W	Ryan Kibler, Carolina/Salem/Asheville	14
L	Robert Averette, Colorado Springs	14
#ERA	Ryan Kibler, Carolina/Salem/Asheville	2.15
G	Justin Huisman, Asheville	55
CG	**Jason Jennings**, Colo. Springs/Carolina	4
SV	Justin Huisman, Asheville	30
IP	Ryan Kibler, Carolina/Salem/Asheville	184
BB	Ryan Price, Salem	85
SO	Ryan Kibler, Carolina/Salem/Asheville	161

*Minimum 250 At-Bats #Minimum 75 Innings

TOP PROSPECTS OF THE DECADE

1993	David Nied, rhp
1994	John Burke, rhp
1995	Doug Million, lhp
1996	Derrick Gibson, of
1997	Todd Helton, 1b
1998	Todd Helton, 1b
1999	Choo Freeman, of
2000	Choo Freeman, of
2001	Chin-Hui Tsao, rhp

TOP DRAFT PICKS OF THE DECADE

1992	John Burke, rhp
1993	Jamey Wright, rhp
1994	Doug Million, lhp
1995	Todd Helton, 1b
1996	Jake Westbrook, rhp
1997	Mark Mangum, rhp
1998	Choo Freeman, of
1999	Jason Jennings, rhp
2000	*Matt Harrington, rhp
2001	Jayson Nix, ss

*Did not sign.

Butler   **Jennings**

BEST TOOLS

Best Hitter for Average	Garrett Atkins
Best Power Hitter	Jack Cust
Fastest Baserunner	Tony Miller
Best Fastball	Aaron Cook
Best Breaking Ball	Chin-Hui Tsao
Best Changeup	Ryan Kibler
Best Control	Ryan Kibler
Best Defensive Catcher	Dan Conway
Best Defensive Infielder	Clint Barmes
Best Infield Arm	Hector Tena
Best Defensive Outfielder	Dan Phillips
Best Outfield Arm	Dan Phillips

PROJETCED 2005 LINEUP

Catcher	Ben Petrick
First Base	Todd Helton
Second Base	Jose Ortiz
Third Base	Garrett Atkins
Shortstop	Juan Uribe
Left Field	Jack Cust
Center Field	Juan Pierre
Right Field	Larry Walker
No. 1 Starter	Mike Hampton
No. 2 Starter	Chin-Hui Tsao
No. 3 Starter	Aaron Cook
No. 4 Starter	Ryan Kibler
No. 5 Starter	Jason Young
Closer	Cam Esslinger

ALL-TIME LARGEST BONUSES

Jason Young, 2000	$2,750,000
Chin-Hui Tsao, 1999	$2,200,000
Jason Jennings, 1999	$1,675,000
Choo Freeman, 1998	$1,400,000
Ching-Lung Lo, 2001	$1,400,000

DraftAnalysis

2001 Draft

Best Pro Debut: OF Tony Miller (10) was a Rookie-level Pioneer League all-star, hitting .306-10-34 with 28 stolen bases. RHP Kip Bouknight (13) went 3-5, 2.78 with an 86-18 strikeout-walk ratio at short-season Tri-City.

Best Athlete: A former Toledo defensive back, Miller has foot speed, bat speed and center-field skills. OF Jason Frome (3) has speed and power potential. RHP Jay Mitchell (4) was an all-state basketball player at his Georgia high school.

Best Hitter: SS **Jayson Nix** (1) has a quick swing that should allow him to hit for average with decent power. After batting .294-5-24 in Rookie ball, he moved to second base in instructional league.

Best Raw Power: 1B David Burkholder (15), whose pro debut was abbreviated when he broke a foot running the bases. OF Trey George (22) has a short power stroke.

Fastest Runner: Miller has 65 speed on the 20-to-80 scouting scale.

Best Defensive Player: Cory Sullivan (7) has speed and outstanding center-field instincts. He also has a solid average arm and threw 87-89 mph as a pitcher at Wake Forest. His game calls to mind a young Steve Finley. C James Sweeney (9) has solid catch-and-throw skills.

Best Fastball: RHP Gerrit Simpson (5) was clocked at 94-95 mph last summer, though the book on him at Texas was that he was more effective when he threw in the low 90s. Mitchell (4) could pass Simpson in time, because he's a 6-foot-7 teenager who already can reach 94 mph. RHP Jamie

Tricoglou (6) started throwing 93-94 mph last spring and could be a closer.

Most Intriguing Background: Bouknight won the Golden Spikes Award and Burkholder was the NAIA player of the year in 2000. RHP John Toffey (47), who opted to play hockey and baseball at Ohio State, is the son of agent Jack Toffey. Nix' brother Laynce plays in the Rangers system. Unsigned SS Eric Patterson (23) is the brother of Corey, while unsigned 3B Duke Sardinha (41) has brothers in the Reds (Dane) and Yankees (Bronson, a 2001 first-rounder) chains.

RODGER WOOD

Nix

Closest To The Majors: Because the Rockies are always in search of pitching, Simpson should beat Sullivan to Coors Field.

Best Late-Round Pick: George would have been a much higher pick if not for a commitment to Tulane. He's an offensive player who has all of the tools except speed.

The One Who Got Away: Colorado found the money to sign George when it couldn't get LHP Trey Taylor (2). He took his 92-93 mph fastball to Baylor.

Assessment: In their early drafts the Rockies loaded up on pitchers, yet their biggest success came with 1995 first-rounder Todd Helton. Now they're taking a more balanced approach and getting better results.

2000 Draft

3B/1B Garrett Atkins (5) is the system's best hitter, and RHP Jason Young (2) could emerge as the top pitcher. Those two, plus LHP Cory Vance (4) and 1B/OF Brad Hawpe (11), erase the bad taste left by the RHP Matt Harrington (1) fiasco. Also keep an eye on LHP Zach Parker (21, draft-and-follow). **Grade: C+**

1999 Draft

RHPs Ryan Kibler (2) and Jason Jennings (1) have exactly the type of sinkers needed to survive at Coors Field. But they're not nearly as good as unsigned RHP Bobby Brownlie (26), who projects as the possible No. 1 overall pick in the 2002 draft. **Grade: C+**

1998 Draft

All three first-round choices—RHP Matt Roney, OF Choo Freeman and C Jeff Winchester—have fallen short of expectations, while OF Juan Pierre (13) has surpassed them. OF Matt Holliday's (7) bat still has promise. **Grade: C+**

1997 Draft

The Rockies always believed RHP Aaron Cook (2) was better than RHP Mark Mangum (1), a signability pick, and they were right. RHP Justin Miller (5) blossomed after being traded to Oakland. **Grade: C**

Note: Draft analysis prepared by Jim Callis. Numbers in parentheses indicate draft rounds.

. . . He is a dominant power pitcher with a legitimate mid-90s fastball and excellent slider.

Chin-Hui
Tsao rhp

Born: June 2, 1981.
Ht.: 6-1. **Wt.:** 180.
Bats: R. **Throws:** R.
Career Transactions: Signed out of Taiwan by Rockies, Oct. 7, 1999.

Tsao was the Rockies' first significant international signing, receiving what was then a franchise-record $2.2 million signing bonus in October 1999. He had just gone 3-0 with 23 shutout innings for Taiwan in the World Junior Championship, then pitched a one-hitter with 15 strikeouts against China as the lone amateur in the Asia Cup. After making a stunning debut in 2000, he showed up for spring training last year unable to pitch because he hadn't throw during the offseason. After just four starts at high Class A Salem, Tsao was shut down with torn ligaments in his elbow and required Tommy John surgery. With the strong comebacks made by others who have undergone the operation in recent years—including the Cardinals' Matt Morris, who tied for the National League lead with 22 victories in 2001—Colorado is confident Tsao will regain his previous form.

Tsao has the makings of a dominant power pitcher. He has a legitimate mid-90s fastball and an excellent slider he can throw anytime in the count. He has a good feel for pitching, particularly at such a young age. Tsao also has shown an ability to throw strikes and is a quick study. Obviously, missing the bulk of last season and not being expected to be ready at the start of 2001 will rob Tsao of what he needs most: experience. He was so dominant in his native Taiwan that he is still learning about the demands of success in the big leagues. The work required to come back from Tommy John surgery should give him an idea of the effort involved. There's a strong feeling that his lack of an offseason throwing program set the stage for his elbow problem. Tsao has such a good slider that at times he'll forget to use his fastball. He did begin throwing a two-seam fastball early last year to give hitters a different look.

Tsao's rehab work had him ahead of schedule in his return from surgery, yet he still isn't expected to be ready to pitch until late May at the earliest. A potential No. 1 starter, Tsao figures to return to Salem when he's ready. As soon as he shows he's healthy, he'll return to the fast track to Coors Field.

Year	Club (League)	Class	W	L	ERA	G	GS	CG	SV	IP	H	R	ER	BB	SO
2000	Asheville (SAL)	A	11	8	2.73	24	24	0	0	145	119	54	44	40	187
2001	Salem (Car)	A	0	4	4.67	4	4	0	0	17	23	11	9	5	18
MINOR LEAGUE TOTALS			11	12	2.94	28	28	0	0	162	142	65	53	45	205

ROBERT GURGANUS

2. Aaron Cook, rhp

Born: Feb. 8, 1979. **Ht.:** 6-3. **Wt.:** 175. **Bats:** R. **Throws:** R. **School:** Hamilton (Ohio) HS. **Career Transactions:** Selected by Rockies in second round of 1997 draft; signed July 13, 1997.

Cook hasn't had a winning record in five pro seasons, but he showed signs he was ready to emerge last season when he followed up an 11-11 regular season by dominating in the high Class A Carolina League play-offs. He threw 17 shutout innings in helping Salem win the league title, including a four-hit, one-walk win against Wilmington in the finals. He was considered the Rockies' best player from the 1997 draft class despite being chosen behind first-rounder Mark Mangum, a signability pick. Cook has the best fastball in the system. He consistently shows mid-90s velocity and is durable, having been clocked at 98 mph in the eighth and ninth innings. He also has a quality slider with the action of a forkball. Instead of relying on his fastball 90 percent of the time, Cook is learning to mix his pitches. He has started to develop an offspeed pitch that is a variation of a splitter, and he can turn it into a legitimate split as he matures. Cook will open 2002 at Double-A Carolina, and it's not out of the question that he could be in the big leagues by season's end.

Year	Club (League)	Class	W	L	ERA	G	GS	CG	SV	IP	H	R	ER	BB	SO
1997	Rockies (AZL)	R	1	3	3.13	9	8	0	0	46	48	27	16	17	35
1998	Portland (NWL)	A	5	8	4.88	15	15	1	0	79	87	50	43	39	38
1999	Asheville (SAL)	A	4	12	6.44	25	25	2	0	122	157	99	87	42	73
2000	Asheville (SAL)	A	10	7	2.96	21	21	4	0	143	130	54	47	23	118
	Salem (Car)	A	1	6	5.44	7	7	1	0	43	52	33	26	12	37
2001	Salem (Car)	A	11	11	3.08	27	27	0	0	155	157	73	53	38	122
MINOR LEAGUE TOTALS			32	47	4.17	104	103	8	0	588	631	336	272	171	423

3. Garrett Atkins, 3b/1b

Born: Dec. 12, 1979. **Ht.:** 6-3. **Wt.:** 210. **Bats:** R. **Throws:** R. **School:** UCLA. **Career Transactions:** Selected by Rockies in fifth round of 2000 draft; signed June 22, 2000.

The MVP in the short-season Northwest League in his pro debut, Atkins made the jump to high Class A for his first full pro season and earned Carolina League all-star honors as a first baseman. With Todd Helton entrenched at that position in Colorado, Atkins is working on moving across the infield to third base, where he played occasionally at UCLA. Atkins has mastered the most difficult part of hitting: driving the ball the opposite way. He stays inside the ball well and has a compact swing, bringing up comparisons to a young Helton or Don Mattingly because of his potential to hit for power once he gets a better feel for how pitchers approach him. Atkins tends to glide when hitting and hits off a firm front leg. He'll have to work on his defense at third base. His initial work there was slowed because of shoulder tendinitis, and he spent the off-season in Denver in a conditioning program to strengthen his shoulder. Atkins will move to Double-A Carolina to start 2002. The trade of Jeff Cirillo removed a roadblock, and Atkins should reach the majors by the end of 2003. He could hasten his timetable if he adapts quickly to third base.

Year	Club (League)	Class	AVG	G	AB	R	H	2B	3B	HR	RBI	BB	SO	SB
2000	Portland (NWL)	A	.303	69	251	34	76	12	0	7	47	45	48	2
2001	Salem (Car)	A	.325	135	465	70	151	43	5	5	67	74	98	6
MINOR LEAGUE TOTALS			.317	204	716	104	227	55	5	12	114	119	146	8

4. Ryan Kibler, rhp

Born: Sept. 17, 1980. **Ht.:** 6-2. **Wt.:** 185. **Bats:** R. **Throws:** R. **School:** King HS, Tampa. **Career Transactions:** Selected by Rockies in second round of 1999 draft; signed June 17, 1999.

After returning to low Class A Asheville to open last season, Kibler forced his way into the Rockies' plans, moving up and dominating at both Salem and Carolina. He led the organization with 14 wins and a 2.15 ERA, and went a combined 11-1 in 19 starts at the two higher classifications. One American League scout describes Kibler as a Brad Radke type with better stuff. Kibler has a lively sinker, and he can vary its velocity from 87-92 mph during a single at-bat. He also has a quality changeup, but most of all he has a determination to succeed. He watches hitters, even when he's not pitching, and develops a game plan. He likes to pitch inside. Kibler needs to develop more consistent location with his slider. He drops his elbow at times, causing his pitches to go flat. The safe move would be for Kibler to open the season in Double-A, but he pitched so well there last year he could force himself into the Triple-A Colorado Springs rotation with a strong spring. If that happens, he could surface in the majors after midseason.

Year	Club (League)	Class	W	L	ERA	G	GS	CG	SV	IP	H	R	ER	BB	SO
1999	Rockies (AZL)	R	6	2	2.55	14	14	2	0	81	77	35	23	14	55
	Portland (NWL)	A	0	0	21.60	1	1	0	0	3	8	8	8	4	4
2000	Asheville (SAL)	A	10	14	4.41	26	26	0	0	155	173	107	76	67	110
2001	Asheville (SAL)	A	3	5	2.93	10	10	1	0	61	50	26	20	27	59
	Salem (Car)	A	7	0	1.55	11	11	0	0	76	53	19	13	16	61
	Carolina (SL)	AA	4	1	2.11	8	8	1	0	47	38	17	11	19	41
MINOR LEAGUE TOTALS			30	22	3.21	70	70	4	0	424	399	212	151	147	330

5. Jason Young, rhp

Born: Sept. 28, 1979. **Ht.:** 6-5. **Wt.:** 205. **Bats:** R. **Throws:** R. **School:** Stanford University. **Career Transactions:** Selected by Rockies in second round of 2000 draft; signed Sept. 26, 2000.

Elated to get Young with the 47th overall pick in 2000, the Rockies handed him a club-record $2.75 million bonus. Making his pro debut last season, he was selected for the Futures Game. His season ended on July 12, when a tender right elbow caused him to be shut down, though he did return in time to make four starts in the Arizona Fall League. Young has three quality pitches with movement: a fastball with sinking action, a slurve that has good action when he keeps his elbow up, and a changeup. When he's healthy, his fastball tops out at 94 mph. He has a good feel for using his changeup. He's competitive and intelligent. A knee problem that has bothered him since college limits Young's conditioning to riding a stationary bike, which keeps him from developing the stamina to carry a game into the late innings. He had a tight shoulder in 2000 at Stanford before his elbow woes last year, and needs to stay healthy to get some needed pro innings. Young has the ability and savvy to be a front-of-the-rotation starter and move quickly. He figures to open the season at Double-A but could pitch his way to the big leagues before the end of 2002.

Year	Club (League)	Class	W	L	ERA	G	GS	CG	SV	IP	H	R	ER	BB	SO
2001	Salem (Car)	A	6	7	3.44	17	17	2	0	105	104	47	40	28	91
MINOR LEAGUE TOTALS			6	7	3.44	17	17	2	0	105	104	47	40	28	91

6. Jack Cust, of

Born: Jan. 16, 1979. **Ht.:** 6-1. **Wt.:** 205. **Bats:** L. **Throws:** R. **School:** Immaculata HS, Flemington, N.J. **Career Transactions:** Selected by Diamondbacks in first round (30th overall) of 1997 draft; signed July 14, 1997 . . . Traded by Diamondbacks with C J.D. Closser to Rockies for LHP Mike Myers, Jan. 7, 2002.

Though Cust established himself as one of the few legitimate cleanup-hitting prospects in the minors, Arizona parted with him and catcher J.D. Closser in a curious January trade for lefty specialist Mike Myers. Cust's inability to make progress defensively frustrated the Diamondbacks, who concluded they'd never be able to use him in a DH-less lineup. His younger brother Kevin was drafted in the 11th round in 2000 and made his pro debut in 2001, while another brother, Michael, turned down the Cardinals as a 35th-rounder last year and will attend Seton Hall. Cust is a batting-cage rat who wants to hit around the clock. He has uncommon strike-zone judgment for a young hitter and has topped 100 walks in each of the last two seasons. He rarely chases bad pitches, especially early in the count. He looks for pitches to drive and displays well above-average power to all fields. His power comes from his compact, muscular frame and a natural lefthanded uppercut stroke, a la Jim Thome. He also often swings from his heels trying to hit every ball out of sight, leading to his lofty strikeout totals. He has been labeled a DH since he was drafted. He has proven incapable of handling first base or right field, and he has made little progress in left field. His lack of speed or defensive prowess would be magnified by the spacious outfield at Coors Field, leading to talk that Colorado might trade Cust to an American League team. If he stays put, he's slated for another year as a Triple-A outfielder.

Year	Club (League)	Class	AVG	G	AB	R	H	2B	3B	HR	RBI	BB	SO	SB
1997	Diamondbacks (AZL)	R	.306	35	121	26	37	11	1	3	33	31	39	2
1998	South Bend (Mid)	A	.242	16	62	5	15	3	0	0	4	5	20	0
	Lethbridge (Pio)	R	.345	73	223	75	77	20	2	11	56	86	71	15
1999	High Desert (Cal)	A	.334	125	455	107	152	42	3	32	112	96	145	1
2000	El Paso (TL)	AA	.293	129	447	100	131	32	6	20	75	117	150	12
2001	Tucson (PCL)	AAA	.278	135	442	81	123	24	2	27	79	102	160	6
	Arizona (NL)	MAJ	.500	3	2	0	1	0	0	0	0	1	0	0
MAJOR LEAGUE TOTALS			.500	3	2	0	1	0	0	0	0	1	0	0
MINOR LEAGUE TOTALS			.306	513	1750	394	535	132	14	93	359	437	585	36

7. Rene Reyes, of

SPORTS ON FILM

Born: Feb. 21, 1978. **Ht.:** 5-11. **Wt.:** 202. **Bats:** B. **Throws:** R. **Career Transactions:** Signed out of Venezuela by Rockies, Aug. 29, 1996 . . . On disabled list, April 6-Sept. 29, 2000.

Reyes won the batting title and MVP award in the Rookie-level Arizona League in 1998, then followed up with two injury-plagued seasons. Arthroscopic surgery on his right shoulder limited him to 62 games in 1999, and he missed all of 2000 after surgery on his right knee. He bounced back last year, with another batting crown/MVP double in the low Class A South Atlantic League while moving from first base to the outfield. A natural hitter, Reyes holds his bat high, like Manny Ramirez, from the right side and has a quieter approach as a lefty. He has quick hands and power potential. Right now, he's more of a home run threat from the left side. Reyes runs well despite his bulky frame, and he has an above-average arm. He needs a challenge to produce. Injuries have kept him from fine-tuning his talent, but he's finally healthy. He also stayed in Denver during the winter for a conditioning program and will be expected to jump past high Class A and go to Double-A in 2002. If a need arises in the big league outfield, he could get an audition.

Year	Club (League)	Class	AVG	G	AB	R	H	2B	3B	HR	RBI	BB	SO	SB
1997	Guacara 1 (VSL)	R	.220	38	82	8	18	2	2	1	9	7	14	1
1998	Rockies (AZL)	R	.429	49	177	40	76	9	4	5	39	8	15	16
1999	Rockies (AZL)	R	.361	22	97	21	35	4	4	1	20	4	14	6
	Asheville (SAL)	A	.350	40	160	26	56	6	1	3	19	6	22	1
2000						Did Not Play—Injured									
2001	Asheville (SAL)	A	.322	128	484	71	156	27	2	11	61	28	80	53
MINOR LEAGUE TOTALS			.341	277	1000	166	341	48	13	21	148	53	145	77

8. Jason Jennings, rhp

JOHN SPEAR

Born: July 17, 1978. **Ht.:** 6-2. **Wt.:** 230. **Bats:** L. **Throws:** R. **School:** Baylor University. **Career Transactions:** Selected by Rockies in first round (16th overall) of 1999 draft; signed June 9, 1999.

Baseball America's 1999 College Player of the Year, Jennings was a two-way star at Baylor. He showed off those skills last August at Shea Stadium, where he became the first player in major league history to both homer and throw a shutout in his debut. His father Jim played in the Rangers system, and his grandfather James is a longtime stadium announcer for the Dallas Cowboys and the Mesquite Championship Rodeo. Jennings has three quality pitches, including a lively 92 mph sinker that's the perfect pitch for Coors Field. He has a hard slider and understands the importance of using his changeup. He has a thick lower body, but he's a quality athlete who fields his position exceptionally well and can hit. He sometimes overuses his slider and has to learn to pitch off his fastball, which is a big league pitch. A catcher in high school, he's still learning the art of pitching. Jennings will get a prime shot at Colorado's rotation this spring.

Year	Club (League)	Class	W	L	ERA	G	GS	CG	SV	IP	H	R	ER	BB	SO
1999	Portland (NWL)	A	1	0	1.00	2	2	0	0	9	5	1	1	2	11
	Asheville (SAL)	A	2	2	3.70	12	12	0	0	58	55	27	24	8	69
2000	Salem (Car)	A	7	10	3.47	22	22	3	0	150	136	66	58	42	133
	Carolina (SL)	AA	1	3	3.44	6	6	0	0	37	32	19	14	11	33
2001	Carolina (SL)	AA	2	0	2.88	4	4	0	0	25	25	9	8	8	24
	Colo. Spr. (PCL)	AAA	7	8	4.72	22	22	4	0	132	145	80	69	41	110
	Colorado (NL)	MAJ	4	1	4.58	7	7	1	0	39	42	21	20	19	26
MAJOR LEAGUE TOTALS			4	1	4.58	7	7	1	0	39	42	21	20	19	26
MINOR LEAGUE TOTALS			20	23	3.81	68	68	7	0	411	398	202	174	112	380

9. Ching-Lung Lo, rhp

Born: Aug. 20, 1985. **Ht.:** 6-4. **Wt.:** 165. **Bats:** R. **Throws:** R. **Career Transactions:** Signed out of Taiwan by Rockies, Oct. 20, 2001.

Lo is Colorado's second major signing out of Taiwan, after No. 1 prospect Chin-Hui Tsao, and an indication of its growing efforts on the international front. The Rockies beat out the Braves, Dodgers, Mariners, Red Sox and Yankees to get Lo under contract, surprising the competition to sign Lo for $1.4 million. He attended Koio Yuan High, which is also Tsao's alma mater, and helped Taiwan win the junior Asia Cup tournament in September. Lo beat Australia 14-4 in the semifinals, working five innings and giving up two hits with eight strikeouts. Taiwan beat Japan 2-0 later in the day to win the title. Lo goes by the nickname Dragon. Lo has a full assortment of pitches, including a 93 mph fastball. He also has a slider and a splitter. Despite his youth, he has fluid mechanics. Lo is young and inexperienced. He has dominated in Taiwan but will have work ahead to make the adjustments to professional baseball, which will be as much cultural as physical. He is still growing and filling out his large frame and he needs to get stronger, which will happen once he gets started on a regular conditioning program. Lo will report to extended spring training before spending his first pro season with Rookie-level Casper. Much like they did with Tsao, the Rockies will be reluctant to move him quickly, wanting to give Lo a chance to adapt to the United States without any more distractions than necessary.

Year	Club (League)	Class	W	L	ERA	G	GS	CG	SV	IP	H	R	ER	BB	SO
Has Not Played—Signed 2002 Contract															

10. Jayson Nix, 2b

Born: Aug. 26, 1982. **Ht.:** 5-11. **Wt.:** 180. **Bats:** R. **Throws:** R. **School:** Midland (Texas) HS. **Career Transactions:** Selected by Rockies in first round (44th overall) of 2001 draft; signed July 14, 2001.

JOHN SPEAR

Nix led Midland High to the Texas state 5-A title, earning tournament MVP honors when he saved the semifinal game and pitched a complete game in the final. He missed the first few weeks at Casper and struggled to hit .200 in his first month, but finished strong and went 15-for-29 in his final eight games. He turned down a scholarship from Texas A&M, following in the footsteps of his brother Laynce, who passed on Louisiana State to sign with the Rangers as a fourth-round pick in 2000. Nix is an offensive player and will have plus power for a middle infielder. He's prepared for every at-bat and uses the entire field. He eagerly accepted the suggestion that he needed to move from shortstop, where he played in high school and for Casper, to second base. Nix' swing is a little long, but it will get shorter as he adjusts to pro pitching. He's so intense he can create problems for himself because of his expectations of excellence. Nix will make the move to the full-season level at Asheville in 2002. With his youth and a position change, the Rockies figure to give him the whole season there to adjust.

Year	Club (League)	Class	AVG	G	AB	R	H	2B	3B	HR	RBI	BB	SO	SB
2001	Casper (Pio)	R	.294	42	153	28	45	10	1	5	24	21	43	1
MINOR LEAGUE TOTALS			.294	42	153	28	45	10	1	5	24	21	43	1

11. Matt Holliday, of

Born: Jan. 10, 1980. **Ht.:** 6-4. **Wt.:** 215. **Bats:** R. **Throws:** R. **School:** Stillwater (Okla.) HS. **Career Transactions:** Selected by Rockies in seventh round of 1998 draft; signed July 24, 1998.

One of the nation's top high school quarterbacks in 1998, Holliday got an $840,000 bonus to pass on a football scholarship to Oklahoma State, where his father Tom is the baseball coach. When Florida and Tennessee tried to lure him to college football last summer, Holliday signed a six-year deal that guarantees him a minimum of $700,000. Initially a third baseman, Holliday is moving to the outfield, but his transition has been slowed by foot surgery two winters ago and reconstructive elbow surgery last July. Holliday is a legitimate power source and was emerging as a force when his 2001 season ended. He has good plate coverage and a solid idea of the strike zone. He has the leadership ability of a quarterback, and the athleticism that comes with being a multisport athlete. The consistency hasn't been there. He has spurts when he reinforces the scouting reports that he's going to be an impact hitter, but has yet to sustain those hot streaks. He has accepted the idea of moving to left field but needs time to get comfortable there. Holliday is headed to Double-A. The Rockies need righthanded power and hope he can provide help soon.

Year	Club (League)	Class	AVG	G	AB	R	H	2B	3B	HR	RBI	BB	SO	SB
1998	Rockies (AZL)	R	.342	32	117	20	40	4	1	5	23	15	21	2
1999	Asheville (SAL)	A	.264	121	444	76	117	28	0	16	64	53	116	10
2000	Salem (Car)	A	.274	123	460	64	126	28	2	7	72	43	74	11
2001	Salem (Car)	A	.275	72	255	36	70	16	1	11	52	33	42	11
MINOR LEAGUE TOTALS			.277	348	1276	196	353	76	4	39	211	144	253	34

12. Denny Stark, rhp

Born: Oct. 27, 1974. **Ht.:** 6-2. **Wt.:** 210. **Bats:** R. **Throws:** R. **School:** University of Toledo. **Career Transactions:** Selected by Mariners in fourth round of 1996 draft; signed June 19, 1996 . . . Traded by Mariners with RHP Jose Paniagua and LHP Brian Fuentes to Rockies for 3B Jeff Cirillo, Dec. 15, 2001.

For the Rockies, Stark was the key player among the three they received when they traded Jeff Cirillo to the Mariners in December. Stark's 2001 season was the best of his six as a pro, as he was the Triple-A Pacific Coast League's pitcher of the year and led the league in wins and ERA. It also marked just the second time in five full seasons that he was able to stay healthy for the entire year. Stark throws two-seam and four-seam fastballs, achieving sink with the former and touching 94 mph with the latter. He also throws a hard breaking ball and a changeup, and is at his best when he mixes his pitches. His control was markedly improved in 2001, another key to his success. Stark's health has been in question for much of his career. He had a stress fracture in his arm in 1998 and a torn labrum in 2000. Those problems appear behind him, but he still hasn't established himself in the majors at age 27. His biggest need now is to refine his changeup. Stark will compete for a rotation spot in spring training. His upside is as a third or fourth starter.

Year	Club (League)	Class	W	L	ERA	G	GS	CG	SV	IP	H	R	ER	BB	SO
1996	Everett (NWL)	A	1	3	4.45	12	4	0	0	30	25	19	15	17	49
1997	Wisconsin (Mid)	A	6	3	1.97	16	15	1	0	91	52	27	20	33	105
	Lancaster (Cal)	A	1	1	3.24	3	3	0	0	17	13	7	6	10	17
1998	Lancaster (Cal)	A	1	2	4.29	5	5	0	0	21	18	12	10	17	21
	Mariners (AZL)	R	0	0	2.16	3	1	0	0	8	9	2	2	2	13
1999	New Haven (EL)	AA	9	11	4.40	26	26	2	0	147	151	82	72	62	103
	Seattle (AL)	MAJ	0	0	9.95	5	0	0	0	6	10	8	7	4	4
2000	New Haven (EL)	AA	4	3	2.19	8	8	1	0	49	31	13	12	17	42
2001	Tacoma (PCL)	AAA	14	2	2.37	24	24	0	0	152	124	64	57	25	117
	Seattle (AL)	MAJ	1	1	9.20	4	3	0	0	15	21	15	15	4	12
MAJOR LEAGUE TOTALS			0	0	9.95	5	0	0	0	6	10	8	7	4	4
MINOR LEAGUE TOTALS			22	23	3.38	73	62	4	0	364	299	162	137	158	350

13. Cam Esslinger, rhp

Born: Dec. 28, 1976. **Ht.:** 6-0. **Wt.:** 180. **Bats:** R. **Throws:** R. **School:** Seton Hall University. **Career Transactions:** Selected by Rockies in 16th round of 1999 draft; signed June 9, 1999.

A starter in college and in his first year of pro ball, Esslinger has blossomed in two seasons as a reliever. He has been selected to play in his league's all-star game in two of his three pro seasons, including in the Double-A Southern League last year. He'll hit 96 mph with his fastball, but pitches best in the 91-93 range. Esslinger also has a hard slider that ranges from 82-88 mph. Hitters don't get a good look at him because he uses a violent delivery and a high leg kick, plus he hides the ball well in his delivery. Esslinger has to gain more consistent command of his fastball. If he's going to evolve into a closer, he'll need to use a changeup to get lefthanders out. After a strong Arizona Fall League performance, he's ticketed for Triple-A in 2002.

Year	Club (League)	Class	W	L	ERA	G	GS	CG	SV	IP	H	R	ER	BB	SO
1999	Portland (NWL)	A	6	3	3.83	14	14	0	0	80	76	37	34	35	68
2000	Asheville (SAL)	A	4	2	3.06	47	2	0	24	65	55	23	22	23	84
2001	Carolina (SL)	AA	1	1	4.93	40	0	0	16	42	32	26	23	31	51
MINOR LEAGUE TOTALS			11	6	3.81	101	16	0	40	187	163	86	79	89	203

14. Josh Kalinowski, lhp

Born: Dec. 12, 1976. **Ht.:** 6-2. **Wt.:** 190. **Bats:** L. **Throws:** L. **School:** Indian Hills (Iowa) CC. **Career Transactions:** Selected by Rockies in 33rd round of 1996 draft; signed May 28, 1997.

Kalinowski was drafted twice by the Rockies before signing as a draft-and-follow after a year at Indian Hills (Iowa) Community College. He's also a product of Casper (Wyo.) Natrona County High, which also produced big leaguers Tom Browning, Mike Devereaux and Mike Lansing. Since being named Carolina League pitcher of the year and winning his second consecutive league strikeout title in 1999, Kalinowski has battled an assortment of ailments the last two seasons. He had arthroscopic elbow surgery in 2000 and an esophagus virus that put him in the hospital in 2001. He finally regained his full strength during the Arizona Fall League. Kalinowski has three-pitch potential. His curveball is his calling card, but he has to learn to use his fastball more to set up the curve. He showed progress with his changeup in the AFL, using it as many as 15 times in a game. A high school quarterback, Kalinowski is a competitor but sometimes can't control his emotions. He most likely will return to Double-A to open 2002 but could surface in the big leagues as a left-handed reliever later this season.

Year	Club (League)	Class	W	L	ERA	G	GS	CG	SV	IP	H	R	ER	BB	SO
1997	Portland (NWL)	A	0	1	2.41	6	6	0	0	19	15	6	5	10	27
1998	Asheville (SAL)	A	12	10	3.92	28	28	3	0	172	159	93	75	65	215
1999	Salem (Car)	A	11	6	2.11	27	27	1	0	162	119	47	38	71	176
2000	Carolina (SL)	AA	1	3	6.23	6	6	0	0	26	30	22	18	12	27
2001	Carolina (SL)	AA	7	8	4.06	25	25	0	0	137	151	76	62	65	116
MINOR LEAGUE TOTALS			31	28	3.45	92	92	4	0	517	474	244	198	223	561

15. Cory Vance, lhp

Born: June 20, 1979. **Ht.:** 6-1. **Wt.:** 195. **Bats:** L. **Throws:** L. **School:** Georgia Tech. **Career Transactions:** Selected by Rockies in fourth round of 2000 draft; signed July 17, 2000.

After leading the Atlantic Coast Conference with 13 victories in 2000, Vance put together a solid first full pro season in high Class A before a pulled groin affected him in the playoffs. Though he said he felt fine, he failed to get past the third inning in either of his postseason outings after going 4-1, 1.30 in his last eight regulars-season starts. Vance has a big-time curveball and changeup. His fastball varies between 86-92 mph and is most effective at 88-89. Lefthanders couldn't touch him in 2001, hitting .173 with no homers in 81 at-bats. Vance has decent command but doesn't put hitters away, which keeps him from getting deeper in games. A good athlete, he fields his position well and holds runners. He'll move to Double-A in 2002.

Year	Club (League)	Class	W	L	ERA	G	GS	CG	SV	IP	H	R	ER	BB	SO
2000	Portland (NWL)	A	0	2	1.11	7	3	0	0	24	11	5	3	8	26
2001	Salem (Car)	A	10	8	3.10	26	26	1	0	154	129	65	53	65	142
MINOR LEAGUE TOTALS			10	10	2.83	33	29	1	0	178	140	70	56	73	168

16. Choo Freeman, of

Born: Oct. 20, 1979. **Ht.:** 6-2. **Wt.:** 200. **Bats:** R. **Throws:** R. **School:** Dallas Christian HS, Mesquite, Texas. **Career Transactions:** Selected by Rockies in first round (36th overall) of 1998 draft; signed July 13, 1998.

A three-sport star in high school and a Connie Mack League teammate of Blue Jays outfielder Vernon Wells, Freeman turned down a scholarship to play wide receiver at Texas A&M to sign with the Rockies. A pure athlete, he has been slow to develop. He repeated high Class A last year and performed worse than he had in 2000, batting just .240 with three homers in the final two months. He did open some eyes during instructional league, when he began to develop a rhythm in his swing. Freeman benefited from the defensive expertise of Salem manager Dave Collins and began trusting his athletic abilities, which allowed him to play a shallower center field. He has the physical strength and speed to be a multitalented offensive threat, reminding scouts of a young Ellis Burks. But he'll have to learn the strike zone and improve at the plate to live up to that potential. He'll get his first chance at Double-A this year.

Year	Club (League)	Class	AVG	G	AB	R	H	2B	3B	HR	RBI	BB	SO	SB
1998	Rockies (AZL)	R	.320	40	147	35	47	3	6	1	24	15	25	14
1999	Asheville (SAL)	A	.274	131	485	82	133	22	4	14	66	39	132	16
2000	Salem (Car)	A	.266	127	429	73	114	18	7	5	54	37	104	16
2001	Salem (Car)	A	.240	132	517	63	124	16	5	8	42	31	108	19
MINOR LEAGUE TOTALS			.265	430	1578	253	418	59	22	28	186	122	369	65

17. Garett Gentry, c

Born: June 27, 1981. **Ht.:** 5-10. **Wt.:** 210. **Bats:** L. **Throws:** R. **School:** Victor Valley HS, Victorville, Calif. **Career Transactions:** Selected by Astros in 13th round of 1999 draft; signed June 11, 1999 . . . Traded by Astros to Rockies, Sept. 27, 2001, completing trade in which Rockies sent RHP Pedro Astacio to Astros for RHP Scott Elarton and a player to be named (July 31, 2001).

The player to be named from the Astros in last summer's Pedro Astacio trade, Gentry's development was put on hold when he had surgery to repair a torn right labrum. He had played through the shoulder pain and averaged more than an RBI per game in low Class A, where several managers thought he deserved to be the Midwest League's MVP. Gentry is an offensive player with home run potential. He has a solid understanding of the strike zone and his present gap power should increase as he matures physically. He needs to refine his catching skills, but as a lefthanded hitter with pop he'll get the benefit of the doubt. He blocks balls well and has carry on his throws, but needs to improve his footwork and quicken his release. MWL managers were divided on Gentry's chances to remain behind the plate. He figures to DH until he rebuilds his arm strength. He most likely will begin his Rockies career in high Class A and could move to Double-A once he's 100 percent.

Year	Club (League)	Class	AVG	G	AB	R	H	2B	3B	HR	RBI	BB	SO	SB
1999	Martinsville (Appy)	R	.239	33	117	16	28	4	2	2	14	9	26	4
2000	Auburn (NY-P)	A	.286	62	231	38	66	15	3	4	34	26	27	5
2001	Michigan (Mid)	A	.299	98	358	62	107	18	3	24	103	39	45	5
MINOR LEAGUE TOTALS			.285	193	706	116	201	37	8	30	151	74	98	14

18. Brian Fuentes, lhp

Born: Aug. 9, 1975. **Ht.:** 6-4. **Wt.:** 220. **Bats:** L. **Throws:** L. **School:** Merced (Calif.) JC. **Career Transactions:** Selected by Mariners in 25th round of 1995 draft; signed May 26, 1996 . . . Traded by Mariners with RHP Jose Paniagua and RHP Denny Stark to Rockies for 3B Jeff Cirillo, Dec. 15, 2001.

While Denny Stark was the most important player the Rockies received from the Mariners for Jeff Cirillo, veteran Jose Paniagua and Fuentes should bolster the Colorado bullpen. Fuentes stalled in the Seattle system when he had shoulder problems at Double-A in 1999, but a switch to a low three-quarters delivery the following season got him going again. His best pitch is his changeup, and his fastball and slider qualify as average. He mixes the three pitches well, though he's going to have to throw more strikes and work ahead in the count more often in the majors, especially in Coors Field. Lefthanders batted just .188 with 26 strikeouts in 64 at-bats against Fuentes in 2001, and righties didn't do much better at .206 and 54 whiffs in 141 at-bats. Adding Fuentes allowed the Rockies to trade Mike Myers to the Diamondbacks for prospects Jack Cust and J.D. Closser. Adding Fuentes allowed the Rockies to trade Mike Myers to the Diamondbacks for prospects Jack Cust and J.D. Closser. Fuentes should replace Myers as Colorado's lefty specialist this year.

Year	Club (League)	Class	W	L	ERA	G	GS	CG	SV	IP	H	R	ER	BB	SO
1996	Everett (NWL)	A	0	1	4.39	13	2	0	0	27	23	14	13	13	26
1997	Wisconsin (Mid)	A	6	7	3.56	22	22	0	0	119	84	52	47	59	153
1998	Lancaster (Cal)	A	7	7	4.17	24	22	0	0	119	121	73	55	81	137
1999	New Haven (EL)	AA	3	3	4.95	15	14	0	0	60	53	36	33	46	66
2000	New Haven (EL)	AA	7	12	4.51	26	26	1	0	140	127	80	70	70	152
2001	Tacoma (PCL)	AAA	3	2	2.94	35	0	0	6	52	35	19	17	25	70
	Seattle (AL)	MAJ	1	1	4.63	10	0	0	0	12	6	6	6	8	10
MAJOR LEAGUE TOTALS			1	1	4.63	10	0	0	0	12	6	6	6	8	10
MINOR LEAGUE TOTALS			26	32	4.10	135	86	1	6	516	443	274	235	294	604

19. Jose Vasquez, of

Born: Dec. 28, 1982. **Ht.:** 6-3. **Wt.:** 220. **Bats:** L. **Throws:** L. **School:** Booker HS, Sarasota, Fla. **Career Transactions:** Selected by Rockies in 16th round of 2000 draft; signed June 7, 2000.

Vasquez has big league power right now. He just doesn't make big league contact. He hit .402 when he put the ball in play at Casper in 2001, and his home runs were monster shots. The problem is that he struck out 96 times in 228 at-bats and had a streak of 23 consecutive games with at least one whiff. Vasquez does draw some walks, so he just needs to tone down his all-or-nothing swing and find a happy medium. To his credit, he wants to learn. Vasquez is working to become a decent left fielder but has a ways to go, particularly with his throwing. He does have some arm strength but isn't particularly accurate. He did cut his errors from 11 in 29 games in 2000 to two in 30 contests last year. Vasquez most likely will return to extended spring training in 2002 before heading to short-season Tri-City. He's not ready for full-season ball yet.

Year	Club (League)	Class	AVG	G	AB	R	H	2B	3B	HR	RBI	BB	SO	SB
2000	Rockies (AZL)	R	.311	46	177	37	55	12	5	5	38	27	73	10
2001	Casper (Pio)	R	.232	64	228	40	53	6	3	14	39	27	96	1
MINOR LEAGUE TOTALS			.267	110	405	77	108	18	8	19	77	54	169	11

20. Trey George, of

Born: Jan. 26, 1983. **Ht.:** 6-0. **Wt.:** 200. **Bats:** R. **Throws:** R. **School:** Bellaire (Texas) HS. **Career Transactions:** Selected by Rockies in 22nd round of 2001 draft; signed Aug. 26, 2001.

Scouting director Bill Schmidt decided to take a couple of longshots on the second day of the 2001 draft, figuring if he had trouble signing one of his top selections he could make a run at a player who slid because of signability questions. When second-rounder Trey Taylor decided to attend Baylor, Schmidt used a portion of the money to sign George, a projected third- to fifth-rounder who scared teams off with his commitment to Tulane. He played with Rockies ninth-rounder James Sweeney at Houston's powerful Bellaire High, which finished 2001 ranked sixth in the nation. George didn't sign in time to play last summer but made quite an impression in instructional league. Scouts are impressed with his approach to hitting, and his compact stroke reminds some of former National League MVP Kevin Mitchell. He has a quiet body at the plate with good balance, plus bat speed and an aggressive approach. He's primarily an offensive player who's a marginal runner and outfielder. He does have some arm strength, having thrown 91 mph while going 6-0 on the mound as a senior at Bellaire. George will begin 2002 in extended spring training.

Year	Club (League)	Class	AVG	G	AB	R	H	2B	3B	HR	RBI	BB	SO	SB
			Has Not Played—Signed 2002 Contract											

21. Javier Colina, 2b

Born: Feb. 15, 1979. **Ht.:** 6-1. **Wt.:** 180. **Bats:** R. **Throws:** R. **Career Transactions:** Signed out of Dominican Republic by Rockies, June 5, 1997.

Colina rebounded from a dismal Double-A performance in 2000, getting back on track offensively while batting everywhere from first through sixth in high Class A last year. What perks the interest of scouts is watching him in batting practice, where he relaxes and gives a hint of what could be. Colina has the ability to have legitimate gap power and be an above-average defensive player. The problem so far has been what happens when the game starts. Colina doesn't let his ability take over. He tries to do too much and gets pull-conscious when he should be using the entire field. He's ready to return to Double-A on a full-time basis, though he went just 1-for-24 with 10 strikeouts in seven games at Carolina in 2001.

Year	Club (League)	Class	AVG	G	AB	R	H	2B	3B	HR	RBI	BB	SO	SB
1997	Guacara 1 (VSL)	R	.246	26	65	4	16	2	1	0	8	5	14	3
1998	Rockies (AZL)	R	.320	44	169	28	54	6	2	6	39	18	30	9
1999	Asheville (SAL)	A	.302	124	516	70	156	37	3	6	81	26	101	12
2000	Carolina (SL)	AA	.217	130	429	34	93	12	1	2	35	44	81	5
2001	Carolina (SL)	AA	.042	7	24	0	1	0	0	0	2	0	10	0
	Salem (Car)	A	.285	113	439	67	125	33	7	9	58	22	61	9
MINOR LEAGUE TOTALS			.271	444	1642	203	445	90	14	23	223	115	297	38

22. John Barnes, of

Born: April 24, 1976. **Ht.:** 6-2. **Wt.:** 205. **Bats:** R. **Throws:** R. **School:** Grossmont (Calif.) JC. **Career Transactions:** Selected by Red Sox in fourth round of 1996 draft; signed July 22, 1996 . . . Traded by Red Sox with RHP Matt Kinney and LHP Joe Thomas to Twins for LHP Greg Swindell and 1B Orlando Merced, July 31, 1998 . . . Claimed on waivers by Rockies from Twins, Sept. 18, 2001.

The Rockies scour the waiver wire, always on the lookout for upper level minor leaguers who can add depth to their system. That's how they found Barnes last September, claiming him from the Twins, who had gotten him from the Red Sox in a 1998 trade. He missed the first seven weeks of 2001 with torn cartilage in his left knee but is fully healthy now. Barnes led the minors with a .365 batting average in 2000 and has gap power. He makes consistent contact, draws a few walks and has enough speed to be a threat to steal bases. Defensively, he has solid instincts that allow him to play all three outfield positions, as well as an accurate arm. Though Barnes projects more as an extra outfielder than as a starter, he can be useful in that role. He'll get a look in big league camp but seems destined for a third tour of duty in Triple-A.

Year	Club (League)	Class	AVG	G	AB	R	H	2B	3B	HR	RBI	BB	SO	SB
1996	Red Sox (GCL)	R	.277	30	101	9	28	4	0	1	17	5	17	4
1997	Michigan (Mid)	A	.304	130	490	80	149	19	5	6	73	65	42	19
1998	Trenton (EL)	AA	.274	100	380	53	104	18	0	14	36	40	47	3
	New Britain (EL)	AA	.268	20	71	9	19	4	1	0	8	9	9	1

1999	New Britain (EL)	AA	.263	129	452	62	119	21	1	13	58	49	40	10
2000	Salt Lake (PCL)	AAA	.365	119	441	107	161	37	6	13	87	57	48	7
	Minnesota (AL)	MAJ	.351	11	37	5	13	4	0	0	2	2	6	0
2001	Edmonton (PCL)	AAA	.293	81	311	42	91	21	2	8	42	27	28	3
	Minnesota (AL)	MAJ	.048	9	21	1	1	0	0	0	0	1	3	0
MAJOR LEAGUE TOTALS			.241	20	58	6	14	4	0	0	2	3	9	0
MINOR LEAGUE TOTALS			.299	609	2246	362	671	124	15	55	321	252	231	47

23. Gerrit Simpson, rhp

Born: Dec. 18, 1979. **Ht.:** 6-3. **Wt.:** 200. **Bats:** R. **Throws:** R. **School:** University of Texas. **Career Transactions:** Selected by Rockies in fifth round of 2001 draft; signed June 19, 2001.

The Reds drafted Simpson twice out of Connors State (Okla.) Junior College but couldn't sign him either time. Their loss was the Rockies' gain after he spent a year at Texas. Because he worked 122 innings for the Longhorns, Colorado monitored his pro debut closely. He initially worked in relief and then pitched 12 innings over three starts before being shut down for the summer. Simpson has a mid-90s fastball but is better off throwing in the low 90s with a less stressful delivery. He can pinpoint the pitch within the strike zone, making his late-breaking slider even more effective. Simpson returned for instructional league, where he made progress with his changeup. He's penciled in for low Class A this year.

Year	Club (League)	Class	W	L	ERA	G	GS	CG	SV	IP	H	R	ER	BB	SO
2001	Tri-City (NWL)	A	2	1	1.11	8	3	1	1	24	14	5	3	3	40
MINOR LEAGUE TOTALS			2	1	1.11	8	3	1	1	24	14	5	3	3	40

24. Zach Parker, lhp

Born: Aug. 19, 1981. **Ht.:** 6-2. **Wt.:** 205. **Bats:** R. **Throws:** L. **School:** San Jacinto (Texas) JC. **Career Transactions:** Selected by Rockies in 21st round of 2000 draft; signed May 27, 2001.

Sean Henn, who signed for $1.7 million with the Yankees out of McLennan Junior College, was the hot lefthander on the Texas juco draft-and-follow market last May. But rival San Jacinto had another in Parker, who like Henn was recruited by Louisiana State but never made it to Baton Rouge. San Jacinto has a strong pitching tradition led by alumni such as Roger Clemens and Andy Pettitte, and Parker has the stuff to follow them to the majors. He has a solid fastball that ranges from 89-93 mph, and he has a good feel for both a curveball and a changeup. Parker is athletic and has an easy arm action, but he needs to get stronger to develop into a big league starter. He got rocked in Rookie ball, showing his need to improve his command and secondary pitchers, but he rebounded in instructional league. Though he had elbow surgery while at San Jacinto, he made a full recovery and hasn't had any problems since. Parker most likely will pitch at Tri-City in 2002, but he could force his way into the picture at Asheville with a strong spring.

Year	Club (League)	Class	W	L	ERA	G	GS	CG	SV	IP	H	R	ER	BB	SO
2001	Casper (Pio)	R	1	2	7.52	8	8	0	0	26	42	26	22	12	19
MINOR LEAGUE TOTALS			1	2	7.52	8	8	0	0	26	42	26	22	12	19

25. Jay Mitchell, rhp

Born: Jan. 5, 1983. **Ht.:** 6-7. **Wt.:** 205. **Bats:** R. **Throws:** R. **School:** La Grange (Ga.) HS. **Career Transactions:** Selected by Rockies in fourth round of 2001 draft; signed June 9, 2001.

Scouting director Bill Schmidt once again showed his penchant for multisport athletes in the 2002 draft. Mitchell, a fourth-rounder, was an all-Georgia basketballer who turned down a chance to play hoops at Georgia Tech. Tony Miller, a 10th-rounder, was more known as a defensive back than as an outfielder at Toledo. Mitchell has a chance to be a true power pitcher. Despite his gangly build, he's a fluid athlete who figures to get stronger with off-season workouts. He has the potential for a mid-90s fastball and also throws a short, heavy curveball. Like many young pitchers, Mitchell tends to overthrow at times and gets out of sync with his command. Once he develops consistency and a changeup, he could move quickly through the system. He'll probably pitch this year at Tri-City.

Year	Club (League)	Class	W	L	ERA	G	GS	CG	SV	IP	H	R	ER	BB	SO
2001	Casper (Pio)	R	4	5	6.34	14	14	0	0	55	54	47	39	38	35
MINOR LEAGUE TOTALS			4	5	6.34	14	14	0	0	55	54	47	39	38	35

26. James Sweeney, c

Born: June 13, 1983. **Ht.:** 6-1. **Wt.:** 197. **Bats:** R. **Throws:** R. **School:** Bellaire (Texas) HS. **Career Transactions:** Selected by Rockies in ninth round of 2001 draft; signed June 5, 2001.

Trey George's teammate at Houston's Bellaire High, Sweeney had a scholarship from Texas but told the Rockies he'd sign no matter what round he was drafted in as long as he was the first catcher they picked. He kept his word, agreeing to terms the day after he was selected. Scouts were impressed with how quickly he adapted to pro ball. Sweeney shows the potential to be a quality defensive catcher with run production ability. He has a quick swing and understands how to work counts in his favor. He already shows an average arm that projects to be well above average. Most impressive, he has a good feel for handling a game. He took charge with the inexperienced staff at Casper, making the pitchers follow his intelligent gameplan. As mature as he is, Sweeney easily could wind up in full-season ball at Asheville this year.

Year	Club (League)	Class	AVG	G	AB	R	H	2B	3B	HR	RBI	BB	SO	SB
2001	Casper (Pio)	A	.278	26	90	19	25	4	1	3	12	8	32	1
MINOR LEAGUE TOTALS			.278	26	90	19	25	4	1	3	12	8	32	1

27. Brad Hawpe, 1b/of

Born: June 22, 1979. **Ht.:** 6-2. **Wt.:** 200. **Bats:** L. **Throws:** L. **School:** Louisiana State University. **Career Transactions:** Selected by Rockies in 11th round of 2000 draft; signed June 21, 2000.

Hawpe led the system with 22 home runs in his first full pro season. A second-team All-America first baseman who played on Louisiana State's College World Series championship team in 2000, he initially moved to the outfield as pro. When Rene Reyes moved into the Asheville outfield at midseason last year, Hawpe returned to first base and was more comfortable. The Rockies wanted to see more power out of him, and he became enamored with Asheville's short right-field porch and got pull-conscious. When it became apparent he wasn't going to get back to his old style of using the entire field, roving hitting instructor Alan Cockrell and Asheville coach Billy White decided to adapt to Hawpe's new approach. They got him to move up on the plate and open his stance. To everyone's surprise, instead of accentuating his tendency to pull, the adjustment wound up getting Hawpe to use all fields. He's very patient at the plate but will have to reduce his strikeouts. He'll go to high Class A in 2002.

Year	Club (League)	Class	AVG	G	AB	R	H	2B	3B	HR	RBI	BB	SO	SB
2000	Portland (NWL)	A	.288	62	205	38	59	19	2	7	29	40	51	2
2001	Asheville (SAL)	A	.267	111	393	78	105	22	3	22	72	59	113	7
MINOR LEAGUE TOTALS			.274	173	598	116	164	41	5	29	101	99	164	9

28. Mario Encarnacion, of

Born: Sept. 24, 1977. **Ht.:** 6-2. **Wt.:** 210. **Bats:** R. **Throws:** R. **Career Transactions:** Signed out of Dominican Republic by Athletics, July 2, 1994 . . . Traded by Athletics with 2B Jose Ortiz and LHP Todd Belitz to Rockies as part of three-way trade in which Royals sent OF Jermaine Dye to Athletics and Rockies sent SS Neifi Perez to Royals, July 25, 2001.

Encarnacion teased the Athletics with his tools for years, but they finally got tired of waiting and sent him to Colorado in a three-team deal that landed Jermaine Dye in Oakland and Neifi Perez in Kansas City last summer. There's no question about Encarnacion's physical skills. He covers a lot of ground in center field and has a strong arm. Offensively, he offers plenty of raw power and speed. But he hasn't produced much because he lacks instincts and plate discipline. He also makes mistakes on the bases and in the outfield. Before handing him a big league job, the Rockies want him to prove he can make the necessary adjustments, so he's ticketed for Triple-A. He didn't make much progress playing in his native Dominican Republic this winter.

Year	Club (League)	Class	AVG	G	AB	R	H	2B	3B	HR	RBI	BB	SO	SB
1995	Athletics (DSL)	R	.345	64	229	56	79	11	5	8	44	40	36	17
1996	West Michigan (Mid)	A	.229	118	401	55	92	14	3	7	43	49	131	23
1997	Modesto (Cal)	A	.297	111	364	70	108	17	9	18	78	42	121	14
1998	Huntsville (SL)	AA	.272	110	357	70	97	15	2	15	61	60	123	11
1999	Midland (TL)	AA	.309	94	353	69	109	21	4	18	71	47	86	9
	Vancouver (PCL)	AAA	.241	39	145	18	35	5	0	3	17	6	44	5
2000	Sacramento (PCL)	AAA	.269	81	301	51	81	16	3	13	61	36	95	15
	Modesto (Cal)	A	.200	5	15	1	3	0	0	0	1	1	4	0
2001	Sacramento (PCL)	AAA	.285	51	186	29	53	8	2	12	33	17	61	4

Colo. Spr. (PCL)	AAA	.378	16	45	8	17	5	0	2	10	4	8	0
Colorado (NL)	MAJ	.226	20	62	3	14	1	0	0	3	5	14	2
MAJOR LEAGUE TOTALS		.226	20	62	3	14	1	0	0	3	5	14	2
MINOR LEAGUE TOTALS		.281	689	2396	427	674	112	28	96	419	302	709	98

29. Chris Buglovsky, rhp

Born: Nov. 22, 1979. **Ht.:** 6-1. **Wt.:** 170. **Bats:** L. **Throws:** R. **School:** College of New Jersey. **Career Transactions:** Selected by Rockies in third round of 2000 draft; signed June 14, 2000.

An all-New Jersey selection in baseball and soccer in high school, Buglovsky set several school records at NCAA Division III College of New Jersey. Coming from a small school, he has had to make significant adjustments to pro ball. He rebounded from a 1-7, 6.36 start in 2001 to go 7-3, 2.53 over his final 14 outings. He could move quickly now if he begins to trust his ability. Buglovsky has a hard sinking fastball that sometimes reaches the mid-90s, as well as a cutter that he calls a slider. It doesn't have much tilt but it does have velocity. He also has the makings of a changeup, which still requires considerable work. He also needs to fill out physically, which should give him added velocity and stamina. Buglovsky will pitch in high Class A this year.

Year	Club (League)	Class	W	L	ERA	G	GS	CG	SV	IP	H	R	ER	BB	SO
2000	Portland (NWL)	A	5	5	2.63	14	12	0	0	65	50	30	19	32	50
2001	Asheville (SAL)	A	8	10	4.08	26	26	0	0	143	158	83	65	32	119
MINOR LEAGUE TOTALS			13	15	3.63	40	38	0	0	208	208	113	84	64	169

30. Tony Miller, of

Born: Aug. 18, 1980. **Ht.:** 5-9. **Wt.:** 180. **Bats:** R. **Throws:** R. **School:** University of Toledo. **Career Transactions:** Selected by Rockies in 10th round of 2001 draft; signed June 7, 2001.

Miller was a defensive back at Toledo, but he knew his size dictated that his professional athletic career would be in baseball. He's a tools player who's still raw because he didn't focus on baseball in college. Miller's raw speed and willingness to draw walks make him a potential leadoff hitter, though he still needs to work on his offensive approach. He needs to smooth out the mechanics of his batting stroke and make more contact. He set the Toledo single-season record for steals with 29 last spring and can be an exciting player on the basepaths. He's still learning the nuances of stealing bases, such as how to get good leads. His mistakes come from aggressiveness. Miller has excellent range in center field and throws adequately. At his age, he needs to be challenged and should play this year in low Class A.

Year	Club (League)	Class	AVG	G	AB	R	H	2B	3B	HR	RBI	BB	SO	SB
2001	Casper (Pio)	R	.306	70	268	68	82	17	3	10	34	41	63	28
MINOR LEAGUE TOTALS			.306	70	268	68	82	17	3	10	34	41	63	28

DETROIT Tigers

TOP 30 PROSPECTS

1. Nate Cornjeo, rhp
2. Omar Infante, ss
3. Eric Munson, 1b
4. Kenny Baugh, rhp
5. Ramon Santiago, ss
6. Andres Torres, of
7. Nook Logan, of
8. Andy Van Hekken, lhp
9. Cody Ross, of
10. Jack Hannahan, 3b
11. Preston Larrison, rhp
12. Matt Wheatland, rhp
13. Mike Rivera, c
14. Michael Woods, 2b
15. Chad Petty, lhp
16. Fernando Rodney, rhp
17. Tim Kalita, lhp
18. Ryan Raburn, 3b
19. Neil Jenkins, of
20. Shane Loux, rhp
21. Mike Rabelo, c
22. Matt Coenen, lhp
23. Ronnie Merrill, 2b/ss
24. Joe Valentine, rhp
25. Mark Woodyard, rhp
26. Tommy Marx, lhp
27. Jeff Farnsworth, rhp
28. Kris Keller, rhp
29. Eric Eckenstahler, lhp
30. Anderson Hernandez, ss

By Pat Caputo

Not since the late 1970s, when the nucleus of their 1984 World Series championship team was in the minor leagues, has the Tigers system been this deep. After annually ranking among the worst organizations for most of the 1990s, Detroit has made significant progress.

The Tigers have drafted well since Randy Smith became general manager prior to the 1996 season. He brought in Greg Smith as scouting director starting with the 1997 draft, and the club has been productive ever since. Closer Matt Anderson and starter Jeff Weaver, first-round selections in 1997 and 1998, respectively, already have established themselves in the big leagues. First baseman Eric Munson, a 1999 first-rounder, likely will reach the majors to stay this season.

Detroit's 2001 draft—rated the best in the game by Baseball America—was particularly promising. Righthander Kenny Baugh ended the season in Double-A. The Tigers got second baseman Michael Woods, projected for the middle of the first round, with a supplemental first-round pick. They also got hard-throwing righthander Preston Larrison in the second round after he figured to go late in the first. All three rank among the club's top 15 prospects, as does third-rounder Jack Hannahan, a third baseman.

The Tigers are in a position where they can build from the middle of the diamond out. Catcher Brandon Inge, their No. 1 prospect entering 2001, may have struggled offensively during his rookie season but already is an above-average defender by big league standards. Weaver and Nate Cornejo—this year's No. 1 prospect after winning a combined 20 games at Double-A, Triple-A and the majors—will anchor the rotation. Anderson converted 22 straight games last year as the closer. Omar Infante and Ramon Santiago are Detroit's best middle-infield prospects since Alan Trammell and Lou Whitaker. Speedy Andres Torres has a chance to be an everyday center fielder.

Besides quality, the Tigers also have quantity. They had a dozen or so pitchers in Double-A or Triple-A last year who have pitched in the majors or will in the future. Their strength in numbers increases their odds of finding some arms who can make a significant impact.

The key is patience, which is in short supply among the fan base in Detroit. Comerica Park was built with the idea it would house a contender, not a rebuilding project, but the Tigers have suffered through eight consecutive losing seasons.

OrganizationOverview

General manager: Randy Smith. **Farm/scouting director:** Greg Smith.

2001 PERFORMANCE

Class	Team	League	W	L	Pct.	Finish*	Manager
Majors	Detroit	American	66	96	.407	11th(14)	Phil Garner
Triple-A	Toledo Mud Hens	International	65	79	.451	12th (14)	Bruce Fields
Double-A	Erie Sea Wolves	Eastern	84	58	.592	2nd (12)	Luis Pujols
High A	Lakeland Tigers	Florida State	67	69	.493	9th (12)	Kevin Bradshaw
Low A	West Michigan Whitecaps	Midwest	65	72	.474	8th (14)	Brent Gates
Short-season	Oneonta Tigers	New York-Penn	37	37	.500	7th (14)	Gary Green
Rookie	GCL Tigers	Gulf Coast	34	26	.567	5th (14)	Howard Bushong
OVERALL 2001 MINOR LEAGUE RECORD			352	341	.508	12th (30)	

*Finish in overall standings (No. of teams in league)

ORGANIZATION LEADERS

BATTING
*AVG	Brian Rios, Toledo	.325
R	Eric Munson, Erie	88
H	Omar Infante, Erie	163
TB	Chris Wakeland, Toledo	263
2B	Eric Munson, Erie	35
3B	Anderson Hernandez, Lakeland/GCL	12
HR	**Mike Rivera**, Erie	33
RBI	Eric Munson, Erie	102
BB	Eric Munson, Erie	84
SO	Eric Munson, Erie	141
SB	Nook Logan, West Michigan	67

PITCHING
W	Nate Cornejo, Toledo/Erie	16
L	Mark Woodyard, West Michigan	12
#ERA	Michael Howell, W. Michigan/Oneota	1.79
G	Terry Pearson, Erie	59
CG	**Tim Kalita**, Erie	5
SV	Terry Pearson, Erie	23
	Mike Steele, Lakeland/West Michigan	23
IP	**Tim Kalita**, Erie	200
BB	Calvin Chipperfield, Lakeland	81
SO	Lee Rodney, West Michigan	149

*Minimum 250 At-Bats #Minimum 75 Innings

TOP PROSPECTS OF THE DECADE

1992	Greg Gohr, rhp
1993	Greg Gohr, rhp
1994	Justin Thompson, lhp
1995	Tony Clark, 1b
1996	Mike Drumright, rhp
1997	Mike Drumright, rhp
1998	Juan Encarnacion, of
1999	Gabe Kapler, of
2000	Eric Munson, 1b/c
2001	Brandon Inge, c

TOP DRAFT PICKS OF THE DECADE

1992	Rick Greene, rhp
1993	Matt Brunson, ss
1994	Cade Gaspar, rhp
1995	Mike Drumright, rhp
1996	Seth Greisinger, rhp
1997	Matt Anderson, rhp
1998	Jeff Weaver, rhp
1999	Eric Munson, c/1b
2000	Matt Wheatland, rhp
2001	Kenny Baugh, rhp

Rivera   **Kalita**

BEST TOOLS

Best Hitter for Average	Omar Infante
Best Power Hitter	Eric Munson
Fastest Baserunner	Andres Torres
Best Fastball	Fernando Rodney
Best Breaking Ball	Tim Kalita
Best Changeup	Kenny Baugh
Best Control	Nate Cornejo
Best Defensive Catcher	Mike Rivera
Best Defensive Infielder	Omar Infante
Best Infield Arm	Omar Infante
Best Defensive Outfielder	Nook Logan
Best Outfield Arm	Cody Ross

PROJECTED 2005 LINEUP

Catcher	Brandon Inge
First Base	Eric Munson
Second Base	Ramon Santiago
Third Base	Jack Hannahan
Shortstop	Omar Infante
Left Field	Bobby Higginson
Center Field	Andres Torres
Right Field	Dmitri Young
Designated Hitter	Robert Fick
No. 1 Starter	Nate Cornejo
No. 2 Starter	Jeff Weaver
No. 3 Starter	Kenny Baugh
No. 4 Starter	Andy Van Hekken
No. 5 Starter	Preston Larrison
Closer	Matt Anderson

ALL-TIME LARGEST BONUSES

Eric Munson, 1999	$3,500,000
Matt Anderson, 1997	$2,505,000
Matt Wheatland, 2000	$2,150,000
Kenny Baugh, 2001	$1,800,000
Jeff Weaver, 1998	$1,750,000

DraftAnalysis

2001 Draft

Best Pro Debut: Following an All-America season at Rice, RHP Kenny Baugh (1) over-matched Class A Midwest League hitters and posted a 2.97 ERA in five Double-A starts before being shut down with a tired arm. 3B Jack Hannahan (3) not only hit .318-1-27 in the MWL, but his defense also drew raves.

Best Athlete: Michael Woods (1) is athletic as it gets for a second baseman. He didn't face major college competition on a regular basis at Southern, but he does have strong instincts and leadership skills.

Best Hitter: Hannahan and C Mike Rabelo (4) have sweet swings and good approaches at the plate. Rabelo, who hit .325-0-32 at Oneonta, is a switch-hitter who was considered more of a catch-and-throw guy at the University of Tampa.

Best Raw Power: At 6 feet and 185 pounds, Raburn isn't huge, but he takes a big swing and balls jump off his bat.

Fastest Runner: OF Vincent Blue (10) leads the way at 6.6 seconds in the 60-yard dash.

Best Defensive Player: Hannahan is agile and has a strong arm. He makes highlight plays as well as the routine ones. He committed just 10 errors in 57 pro games.

Best Fastball: RHP **Preston Larrison** (2), Evansville's best prospect since Andy Benes, can touch 97 mph. When he's on, Baugh can reach 95. RHP Jason Moates (20) topped out at 96 mph before Tommy John surgery in 2000, but he hasn't regained his velocity yet.

Most Intriguing Background: LHP Joe Connolly (28) pitched for Oneonta (N.Y.) High

in the spring and the Oneonta Tigers in the summer. RHP Tom Farmer (7) started and won the College World Series championship game for Miami in June. Another Hurricanes RHP, Dan Smith (17), also played tight end for Miami's football team. LHP Kevin Mc-Dowell (15) is the son of former all-star Sam Mc-Dowell. OF Jason Knoedler's (6) twin Justin went one round earlier to the Giants.

ROBERT GURGANUS

Larrison

Closest To The Majors: At worst, Baugh will open 2002 in Double-A, with Triple-A a possibility. He should be one of the first players from this draft to reach the big leagues.

Best Late-Round Pick: Moates, if he can stay healthy and recapture his pre-surgery form. LHP Ian Ostlund (34) doesn't have outstanding stuff, but his finesse and command give him a chance.

The One Who Got Away: 3B Joey Metropoulos (16) has power, but he'll show-case it at Southern California. He projects as a first-rounder in 2004.

Assessment: The Tigers need help, and this draft should provide some—and soon. In the first five rounds, the Tigers got Baugh, Woods, Larrison, LHP Matt Coenen (2), Hannahan, Rabelo and Raburn. All are proven performers who made smooth transitions to the pros.

2000 Draft

OF Nook Logan (3), RHP Matt Wheatland (1) and LHP Chad Petty (2) all rank among Detroit's second tier of prospects. RHP Mark Woodyard (4) has raw arm strength, while 2B Ronnie Merrill (7) already has reached Double-A. **Grade: C**

1999 Draft

1B Eric Munson (1) has made steady progress, but the Tigers were expecting the spectacular when they gave him a $6.75 million big league contract. Munson and OFs Cody Ross (4) and Neil Jenkins (3) have the power Detroit needs. **Grade: C**

1998 Draft

RHP Jeff Weaver (1) quickly became Detroit's best pitcher, and RHP Nate Cornejo (1) joined him in the rotation last summer. C Brandon Inge (2) has Gold Gloves in his future. OF Andres Torres (4) and LHP Tommy Marx (3) have good tools. **Grade: B+**

1997 Draft

RHP Matt Anderson, the No. 1 overall pick, became Detroit's closer in 2001. Unless RHP Shane Loux (2) turns himself around, he might be the only contributor from this crop. LHP Bud Smith (9) didn't sign in 1997 or as a draft-and-follow in 1998. **Grade: B**

Note: Draft analysis prepared by Jim Callis. Numbers in parentheses indicate draft rounds.

. . . Scouts compare him to Kevin Brown because of the velocity and sink on his fastball.

Nate
Cornjeo rhp

Born: Sept. 24, 1979.
Ht.: 6-5. **Wt.:** 200.
Bats: R. **Throws:** R.
School: Wellington (Kan.) HS.
Career Transactions: Selected by Tigers in second round of 1998 draft; signed Aug. 6, 1998.

There were few doubts about Cornjeo's arm strength as the 1998 draft arrived. It was considered first-round all the way, perhaps the best in the high school ranks that year. The questions about him centered on his knees. He blew both of them out during a high school career in which he also starred in football and basketball. Those concerns have been unfounded because Cornjeo has proven to be durable to this point. Considered one of the Tigers' top prospects since signing, he took a dramatic leap forward last season, winning 20 games in the upper minors and the majors. He dominated Double-A hitters and was even better in Triple-A before his promotion to the big leagues in August. With Detroit, Cornejo ran the gamut from very good to very bad. He comes from a baseball family, as his father Mardie pitched for the Mets and his brother Jesse pitches in the Devil Rays system.

Both Cornjeo's fastball and breaking ball are excellent pitches. His fastball has exceptional movement, breaking down and in on righthanders. During his first three pro seasons, he consistently threw his fastball at 90-91 mph. Last year, his velocity rose to 93-94 and he didn't lose any life on the pitch. Cornejo also has an outstanding breaking ball, which is a cross between a slider and a curveball. He has good command of it. Despite his height, his mechanics are consistent, and he is athletic for his size. After throwing a lot of innings in the minor leagues, Cornejo didn't flash quite the same stuff once he reached the majors. His fastball didn't have quite the same zip and his breaking ball suffered after the big league staff ill-advisedly told him to change his grip. His changeup is not nearly as good as his other two pitches. Command of his fastball could be a problem because his ball moves so much.

Unless he doesn't pitch well during spring training, Cornejo will start 2002 in the major leagues. Scouts compare him to Kevin Brown because of the velocity and sink on his fastball. Though it would be a stretch to expect it this season, Cornejo could become a No.1 starter in the future.

Year	Club (League)	Class	W	L	ERA	G	GS	CG	SV	IP	H	R	ER	BB	SO
1998	Tigers (GCL)	R	1	0	1.26	5	0	0	1	14	12	2	2	2	9
1999	West Michigan (Mid)	A	9	11	3.71	28	28	4	0	175	173	87	72	67	125
2000	Lakeland (FSL)	A	5	5	3.04	12	12	1	0	77	67	37	26	31	60
	Jacksonville (SL)	AA	5	7	4.61	16	16	0	0	92	91	52	47	43	60
2001	Erie (EL)	AA	12	3	2.68	19	19	3	0	124	107	47	37	41	105
	Toledo (IL)	AAA	4	0	2.12	4	4	0	0	30	24	8	7	7	22
	Detroit (AL)	MAJ	4	4	7.38	10	10	0	0	43	63	38	35	28	22
MAJOR LEAGUE TOTALS			4	4	7.38	10	10	0	0	43	63	38	·35	28	22
MINOR LEAGUE TOTALS			36	26	3.36	84	79	8	1	512	474	233	191	191	381

2. Omar Infante, ss

Born: Dec. 26, 1981. **Ht.:** 6-0. **Wt.:** 150. **Bats:** R. **Throws:** R. **Career Transactions:** Signed out of Venezuela by Tigers, April 28, 1999.

Driven by the shooting death of his brother Asdrubal, a pitcher in the Tigers organization, Infante has taken big steps the last two seasons. In 2000, he came out of nowhere to hold his own as an 18-year at high Class A Lakeland and became the youngest player ever in the Arizona Fall League. Managers rated him the best defensive shortstop in the Eastern League. Infante has excellent hands and smooth actions at shortstop. He was bothered by a sore throwing shoulder for most of 2001 but still threw accurately. He has a quick initial step and good range. As a hitter, he punches the ball into right field with authority and at times will turn on pitches. He's an exceptionally intense and focused player. His speed is just average for a middle infielder. At this stage of his career, he might struggle if pounded inside with good fastballs. He doesn't walk enough and strikes out too much for the type of hitter he needs to be at the major league level. Less than three years after the Tigers signed him, Infante could be their starting shortstop on Opening Day. He'd provide more defense than Deivi Cruz, who was designated for assignment in December.

Year	Club (League)	Class	AVG	G	AB	R	H	2B	3B	HR	RBI	BB	SO	SB
1999	Tigers (GCL)	R	.268	25	97	11	26	4	0	0	7	4	11	4
2000	Lakeland (FSL)	A	.274	79	259	35	71	11	0	2	24	20	29	11
	West Michigan (Mid)	A	.229	12	48	7	11	0	0	0	5	5	7	1
2001	Erie (EL)	AA	.302	132	540	86	163	21	4	2	62	46	87	27
MINOR LEAGUE TOTALS			.287	248	944	139	271	36	4	4	98	75	134	43

3. Eric Munson, 1b

Born: Oct. 3, 1977. **Ht.:** 6-3. **Wt.:** 220. **Bats:** L. **Throws:** R. **School:** University of Southern California. **Career Transactions:** Selected by Tigers in first round (third overall) of 1999 draft; signed June 24, 1999.

A catcher at Southern California, Munson was converted into a first baseman after signing a $6.75 million big league contract as the No. 3 overall pick in the 1999 draft. He missed most of the second half of the 2000 season with a back ailment, which also kept him from playing in the Arizona Fall League. In 2001, Munson played every day and got better as the season went on. He showed much more power during the second half of the season, hitting 21 homers in his final 72 games. Quick hands are Munson's forte. As far as he's concerned, the harder a pitcher throws, the better. He'll center the ball on his live bat regardless. When he makes contact, the ball jumps off his bat with extraordinary velocity. Like a lot of hitters with fast hands, Munson is prone to trying to pull everything. He strikes out too much even for a power hitter. At best, he's an average defender. He is the Tigers' first baseman of the future, but there has been a logjam at his position that was only partially relieved when Tony Clark was waived in November. Whether Munson opens the season in the major leagues or at Triple-A Toledo could depend on the numbers game.

Year	Club (League)	Class	AVG	G	AB	R	H	2B	3B	HR	RBI	BB	SO	SB
1999	Lakeland (FSL)	A	.333	2	6	0	2	0	0	0	1	1	1	0
	West Michigan (Mid)	A	.266	67	252	42	67	16	1	14	44	37	47	3
2000	Jacksonville (SL)	AA	.252	98	365	52	92	21	4	15	68	39	96	5
	Detroit (AL)	MAJ	.000	3	5	0	0	0	0	0	1	0	1	0
2001	Erie (EL)	AA	.260	142	519	88	135	35	1	26	102	84	141	0
	Detroit (AL)	MAJ	.152	17	66	4	10	3	1	1	6	3	21	0
MAJOR LEAGUE TOTALS			.141	20	71	4	10	3	1	1	7	3	22	0
MINOR LEAGUE TOTALS			.259	309	1142	182	296	72	6	55	215	161	285	8

4. Kenny Baugh, rhp

Born: Feb. 5, 1979. **Ht.:** 6-4. **Wt.:** 185. **Bats:** R. **Throws:** R. **School:** Rice University. **Career Transactions:** Selected by Tigers in first round (11th overall) of 2001 draft; signed June 5, 2001.

It was viewed as something of a reach and a signability pick when the Tigers drafted Baugh 11th overall last June. A fifth-round pick by Oakland in 2000, he opted to return for his senior season and was named Western Athletic Conference pitcher of the year. After signing for $1.8 million, he justified Detroit's faith by pitching well and reaching Double-A Erie before being shut down with a tired arm. His changeup already is an above-average pitch. His fastball, which occasionally reaches 94 mph, has good sink and he commands it well. He's an excellent athlete, which helps him repeat his delivery and throw strikes with ease. Most pitchers drafted in the upper half of the first round consistently throw harder than Baugh. While he tops out at 95 mph, he more often works at 88-91. His curveball is far from ready for the major leagues at this time. Baugh will begin this season in Double-A or Triple-A. If he performs reasonably well, he likely will make his big league debut at some point in 2002. He's the frontrunner to be the first player from the 2001 draft to reach the majors.

Year	Club (League)	Class	W	L	ERA	G	GS	CG	SV	IP	H	R	ER	BB	SO
2001	West Michigan (Mid)	A	2	1	1.59	6	6	0	0	34	31	14	6	10	39
	Erie (EL)	AA	1	3	2.97	5	5	1	0	30	23	16	10	6	30
MINOR LEAGUE TOTALS			3	4	2.24	11	11	1	0	64	54	30	16	16	69

5. Ramon Santiago, ss

Born: Aug. 31, 1981. **Ht.:** 5-11. **Wt.:** 150. **Bats:** B. **Throws:** R. **Career Transactions:** Signed out of Dominican Republic by Tigers, July 29, 1998.

Santiago starred defensively during his first two years as a pro, but he tore his labrum in 2000. The injury cut short that season, and shoulder surgery relegated him to DH duties last year. He got off to a slow start in high Class A as a teenager in 2001, before closing strong and putting respectable numbers. Santiago made great strides as a hitter last season by shortening his stroke and making more consistent contact. He's more quick than fast, but he's a smart baserunner who can steal bases. Before his arm injury, he was a brilliant fielder with good range, excellent hands and exceptional arm strength. He needs to get stronger. He hits too many fly balls and doesn't walk enough to suit the style of player he is. His arm has regained its strength since the surgery, but he has struggled to relearn his throwing mechanics. With Omar Infante also on hand, Santiago may be moved to second base at some point. He and Infante figure to be Detroit's double-play combination of the future. Santiago will start this season in Double-A.

Year	Club (League)	Class	AVG	G	AB	R	H	2B	3B	HR	RBI	BB	SO	SB
1999	Tigers (GCL)	R	.321	35	134	25	43	9	2	0	11	9	17	20
	Oneonta (NY-P)	A	.340	12	50	9	17	1	2	1	8	2	12	5
2000	West Michigan (Mid)	A	.272	98	379	69	103	15	1	1	42	34	60	39
2001	Lakeland (FSL)	A	.268	120	429	64	115	15	3	2	46	54	60	34
MINOR LEAGUE TOTALS			.280	265	992	167	278	40	8	4	107	99	149	98

6. Andres Torres, of

Born: Jan. 26, 1978. **Ht.:** 5-10. **Wt.:** 175. **Bats:** B. **Throws:** R. **School:** Miami-Dade CC North. **Career Transactions:** Selected by Tigers in fourth round of 1998 draft; signed June 23, 1998.

Torres ran a lot of track and played little baseball during his youth in Puerto Rico. He didn't begin switch-hitting until he was at Miami-Dade Community College North. Following a breakout season in high Class A in 2000, he had an up-and-down year in Double-A in 2001 that was cut short by surgery on his sore throwing shoulder. Torres has excellent speed. He's consistently timed at 4.0 seconds from the right side of home to first base and has plenty of range in center field. He has improved as a hitter, particularly from the left side. His arm injury shouldn't cause long-term problems, and he makes accurate throws. To take full advantage of his speed, he needs to make more consistent contact. He needs better basestealing technique because he gets thrown out too often. Though he can cover vast amounts of ground, Torres often gets turned around or takes poor angles on balls hit directly over his head. At times, he has shown a lack of maturity. The Tigers desperately need a center fielder at the major league level and Torres is the prime candidate coming through the system. He likely will start 2002 at Triple-A Toledo and will get a chance in the majors as soon as his performance warrants.

Year	Club (League)	Class	AVG	G	AB	R	H	2B	3B	HR	RBI	BB	SO	SB
1998	Jamestown (NY-P)	A	.234	48	192	28	45	2	6	1	21	25	50	13
1999	West Michigan (Mid)	A	.236	117	407	72	96	20	5	2	34	92	116	39
2000	Lakeland (FSL)	A	.296	108	398	82	118	11	11	3	33	63	82	65
	Jacksonville (SL)	AA	.148	14	54	3	8	0	0	0	0	5	14	2
2001	Erie (EL)	AA	.294	64	252	54	74	16	3	1	23	36	50	19
MINOR LEAGUE TOTALS			.262	351	1303	239	341	49	25	7	111	221	312	138

7. Nook Logan, of

Born: Nov. 28, 1979. **Ht.:** 6-2. **Wt.:** 180. **Bats:** B. **Throws:** R. **School:** Copiah-Lincoln (Miss.) CC. **Career Transactions:** Selected by Tigers in third round of 2000 draft; signed July 8, 2000.

Logan's first full season of pro ball went about as expected. He had moments where he looked like a future star and others in which his rawness was evident. Drafted as a shortstop in 2000, he was moved to center field during instructional league that fall. The Tigers also turned him into a switch-hitter. Logan is long, lean and exceptionally fast. He stole 67 bases in 86 attempts last year and is capable of being more prolific in the future. He took to center field well. Considering his lack of experience at the position, he misplayed few balls. He needs to get stronger and continue to develop as a switch-hitter. A natural righthander, he hit just .254 from the left side in 2001. He strikes out way too much for a player with his speed, and though he draws walks he will need to get on base more often. He seemed to wear down toward the end of last season. Logan is slated to spend all of this season in high Class A. If Torres eventually can't handle the center-field job, Logan could get the next opportunity.

Year	Club (League)	Class	AVG	G	AB	R	H	2B	3B	HR	RBI	BB	SO	SB
2000	Tigers (GCL)	R	.279	43	136	29	38	2	2	0	14	31	36	20
	Lakeland (FSL)	A	.333	11	42	4	14	1	0	0	3	2	13	2
2001	West Michigan (Mid)	A	.262	128	522	82	137	19	8	1	27	53	129	67
MINOR LEAGUE TOTALS			.270	182	700	115	189	22	10	1	44	86	178	89

8. Andy Van Hekken, lhp

Born: July 31, 1979, in Holland, Mich. Resides: Holland, Mich. **Ht.:** 6-3. **Wt.:** 175. **Bats:** R. **Throws:** L. **School:** Holland (Mich.) HS. **Career Transactions:** Selected by Mariners in third round of 1998 draft; signed June 26, 1998 . . . Traded by Mariners to Tigers, June 26, 1999, completing trade in which Tigers sent OF Brian Hunter to Mariners for two players to be named (April 21, 1999); Tigers also acquired OF Jerry Amador (Aug. 26, 1999).

A year after drafting him in the third round, the Mariners traded Van Hekken to the Tigers for outfielder Brian Hunter. Van Hekken has done nothing but win games, going 41-15 as a pro and 35-12 in the Detroit system. His 31 victories over the last two years are the most among minor league pitchers. Van Hekken has excellent command of his fastball and works the outside half of the plate exceptionally well. His fastball tails in on lefthanders and away from righthanders, making it difficult to hit with authority. His curveball is sharp and he also can spot it where he wants. He doesn't throw hard, pitching in the high 80s most nights, and doesn't appear to have enough pop on his fastball to challenge big league hitters near the heart of the plate. His changeup isn't a quality pitch yet. To start 2002, Van Hekken will return to Double-A, where he went 5-0 last year but didn't pitch particularly well. He could reach Detroit quickly if he continues to experience success.

Year	Club (League)	Class	W	L	ERA	G	GS	CG	SV	IP	H	R	ER	BB	SO
1998	Mariners (AZL)	R	6	3	4.43	11	8	0	0	41	34	23	20	18	55
1999	Oneonta (NY-P)	A	4	2	2.15	11	10	0	0	50	44	17	12	16	50
2000	West Michigan (Mid)	A	16	6	2.45	26	25	3	1	158	139	48	43	37	126
2001	Erie (NYP)	A	5	0	4.69	8	8	0	0	48	63	29	25	8	29
	Lakeland (FSL)	A	10	4	3.17	19	19	2	0	111	105	43	39	33	82
MINOR LEAGUE TOTALS			41	15	2.71	75	70	5	1	408	385	160	139	112	342

9. Cody Ross, of

Born: Dec. 23, 1980. **Ht.:** 5-11. **Wt.:** 180. **Bats:** R. **Throws:** L. **School:** Carlsbad (N.M.) HS. **Career Transactions:** Selected by Tigers in fourth round of 1999 draft; signed June 12, 1999.

Some scouts liked Ross better as a lefthanded pitcher coming out of high school, but the Tigers zeroed in on him as an outfielder. He started to display power in 2001, hitting 15 home runs in the spacious stadiums of the high Class A Florida State League. Twelve of those 15 longballs came in the second half of the season. A competitive player, Ross never takes at-bats off, runs the bases hard and hustles as a corner outfielder. His bat is surprisingly live and he consistently drives the ball. Ross doesn't strike out as much as most power hitters. His arm is both strong and accurate. His size is a concern, especially given that he has only average speed. His power is good but not great, and he doesn't have one tool which stands out. He'll need to show a little more patience at the plate as he advances. Ross could be in for a big Double-A season in 2002. Erie's Jerry Uht Park is friendly to righthanded hitters and could magnify his numbers.

Year	Club (League)	Class	AVG	G	AB	R	H	2B	3B	HR	RBI	BB	SO	SB
1999	Tigers (GCL)	R	.218	42	142	19	31	8	3	4	18	16	28	3
2000	West Michigan (Mid)	A	.267	122	434	71	116	17	9	7	68	55	83	11
2001	Lakeland (FSL)	A	.276	127	482	84	133	34	5	15	80	44	96	28
MINOR LEAGUE TOTALS			.265	291	1058	174	280	59	17	26	166	115	207	42

10. Jack Hannahan, 3b

Born: March 4, 1980. **Ht.:** 6-2. **Wt.:** 205. **Bats:** L. **Throws:** R. **School:** University of Minnesota. **Career Transactions:** Selected by Tigers in third round of 2001 draft; signed June 20, 2001.

Like Joe Mauer, the No. 1 overall pick in last June's draft, Hannahan starred in baseball and football at St. Paul's Cretin-Derham Hall. The 2001 Big Ten Conference player of the year, Hannahan also had a huge pro debut like Mauer did. Hannahan spent most of his summer at low Class A West Michigan, impressing Midwest League managers with his all-around game. He has good bat control and looks capable of hitting for a high average. He stays behind the ball well and can lace line drives into the gap. He's also an above-average third baseman, showing steady hands, an accurate arm and solid instincts. He was considered the University of Minnesota's best defensive third baseman since Terry Steinbach, who became an all-star catcher with the Athletics. Hannahan will have to hit for a high average if he is going to be an effective major league player because he doesn't have much home run power. His other shortcoming is that he doesn't run well. Some scouts think he could follow Steinbach's path to the majors as a catcher, but third base is a position of need for the Tigers. He could move fast at the hot corner, possibly reaching Double-A quickly in 2002.

Year	Club (League)	Class	AVG	G	AB	R	H	2B	3B	HR	RBI	BB	SO	SB
2001	Oneonta (NY-P)	A	.291	14	55	11	16	4	1	0	8	5	7	2
	West Michigan (Mid)	A	.318	46	170	24	54	11	0	1	27	26	39	4
MINOR LEAGUE TOTALS			.311	60	225	35	70	15	1	1	35	31	46	6

11. Preston Larrison, rhp

Born: Nov. 19, 1980. **Ht.:** 6-4. **Wt.:** 215. **Bats:** R. **Throws:** R. **School:** University of Evansville. **Career Transactions:** Selected by Tigers in second round of 2001 draft; signed July 13, 2001.

The Tigers felt fortunate to get Larrison in the second round of last June's draft with the 55th overall selection. Coming off an impressive summer in the Cape Cod League, Larrison seemed like a certain first-round pick entering his junior year at Evansville. When he didn't dominate during the spring, his stock fell to a degree. After signing, Larrison pitched well at short-season Oneonta and displayed a live arm. His fastball usually works in the 92-94 mph range and has good sinking action, plus he throws it for strikes. The makings are there for Larrison to have a good breaking ball and changeup as well. Some scouts questioned his demeanor before the draft, feeling he's too passive on the mound. Detroit hasn't found that to be a problem, instead praising his work ethic and intensity. He'll probably open 2002 in low Class A.

Year	Club (League)	Class	W	L	ERA	G	GS	CG	SV	IP	H	R	ER	BB	SO
2001	Oneonta (NY-P)	A	1	3	2.47	10	8	0	0	47	37	22	13	21	50
MINOR LEAGUE TOTALS			1	3	2.47	10	8	0	0	47	37	22	13	21	50

12. Matt Wheatland, rhp

Born: Oct. 18, 1981. **Ht.:** 6-5. **Wt.:** 215. **Bats:** R. **Throws:** R. **School:** Rancho Bernardo HS, San Diego. **Career Transactions:** Selected by Tigers in first round (eighth overall) of 2000 draft; signed June 12, 2000.

Wheatland has pitched just 69 innings since signing as the eighth overall selection in the 2000 draft, as injuries have held him back. During his first summer in pro ball, he developed circulation problems in his right hand. His index finger would go numb, apparently caused by the grip on his breaking ball. In 2001, his throwing shoulder became loose and he missed most of the season. When Wheatland has thrown, he has been impressive. He works consistently in the low 90s with his fastball and has an outstanding breaking ball, considering his experience level. He has a good changeup as well, and his command and feel for pitching are strengths. It's just a matter of whether he'll get healthy or be a pitcher who consistently breaks down. Detroit will see what Wheatland looks like in spring training before determining his 2002 assignment.

Year	Club (League)	Class	W	L	ERA	G	GS	CG	SV	IP	H	R	ER	BB	SO
2000	Tigers (GCL)	R	2	1	1.25	5	4	0	0	22	14	4	3	1	21
	Oneonta (NY-P)	A	1	2	5.55	5	5	0	0	24	30	18	15	4	25
2001	West Michigan (Mid)	A	0	2	10.93	3	3	0	0	14	21	18	17	4	17
	Tigers (GCL)	R	0	0	0.00	3	3	0	0	9	3	0	0	3	5
MINOR LEAGUE TOTALS			3	5	4.57	16	15	0	0	69	68	40	35	12	68

13. Mike Rivera, c

Born: Sept. 8, 1976. **Ht.:** 6-0. **Wt.:** 190. **Bats:** R. **Throws:** R. **School:** Dr. Agustin Stahl HS, Bayamon, P.R. **Career Transactions:** Signed as nondrafted free agent by Tigers, Jan. 20, 1997.

During the 2001 season, Rivera took a major step forward in three significant areas. He improved his power to the point where he became one of the most feared hitters in the Eastern League. Defensively, he got much better at receiving and throwing. And he also was more consistent, both in terms of his performance and makeup, than he had been in the past. Rivera isn't the second coming of Ivan Rodriguez defensively, but he has progressed to the point where he's capable of being a bona fide everyday catcher in the major leagues. The biggest question in regard to his future probably involves his bat. He's a dead-pull hitter who benefited greatly from Erie's bandbox Uht Park, where 23 of his 33 homers came last year. He also tailed off his second time around the Eastern League, hitting just six longballs in his final 42 games. Comerica Park is probably the least forgiving place in the big leagues for a righthanded pull hitter.

Year	Club (League)	Class	AVG	G	AB	R	H	2B	3B	HR	RBI	BB	SO	SB
1997	Tigers (GCL)	R	.286	47	154	34	44	9	2	10	36	18	25	0
1998	West Michigan (Mid)	A	.275	108	403	40	111	34	3	9	67	15	68	0
1999	Lakeland (FSL)	A	.278	104	370	44	103	20	2	14	72	20	59	1
	Jacksonville (SL)	AA	.174	7	23	3	4	1	0	2	6	2	5	0
2000	Lakeland (FSL)	A	.292	64	243	30	71	19	4	11	53	16	45	2
	Toledo (IL)	AAA	.231	4	13	0	3	3	0	0	1	0	2	0
	Jacksonville (SL)	AA	.193	39	150	10	29	8	1	2	9	7	30	0
2001	Erie (EL)	AA	.289	112	415	76	120	19	1	33	101	44	96	2
	Detroit (AL)	MAJ	.333	4	12	2	4	2	0	0	1	0	2	0
MAJOR LEAGUE TOTALS			.333	4	12	2	4	2	0	0	1	0	2	0
MINOR LEAGUE TOTALS			.274	485	1771	237	485	113	13	81	345	122	330	5

14. Michael Woods, 2b

Born: Sept. 11, 1980. **Ht.:** 6-1. **Wt.:** 200. **Bats:** R. **Throws:** R. **School:** Southern University. **Career Transactions:** Selected by Tigers in second round of 2001 draft; signed June 29, 2001.

As with Preston Larrison, the Tigers were pleased to land Woods on draft day 2001, when he slid from a projected mid-first-round pick to 32nd overall. He finished third in NCAA Division I with a .453 average last spring and stole 32 bases in 35 attempts despite hamstring problems. While he held his own in full-season ball, he's still a raw talent in need of refinement in most areas of his game. Woods hit the ball hard in his pro debut, but not with much consistency. He struck out too often, though he showed good ability to draw walks and get on base. The Tigers expected Woods would have hit with more power, but he doesn't lift the ball much at this point and went homerless in 200 pro at-bats. His speed is average for a middle infielder and his arm strength is adequate for second base. His movements in the field aren't fluid and he needs work on the double-play pivot, but he doesn't make many errors. Woods will begin 2002 at one of Detroit's Class A affiliates.

Year	Club (League)	Class	AVG	G	AB	R	H	2B	3B	HR	RBI	BB	SO	SB
2001	Oneonta (NY-P)	A	.270	9	37	6	10	2	0	0	3	4	5	5
	West Michigan (Mid)	A	.270	44	163	30	44	8	4	0	17	32	44	13
MINOR LEAGUE TOTALS			.270	53	200	36	54	10	4	0	20	36	49	18

15. Chad Petty, lhp

Born: Feb. 17, 1982. **Ht.:** 6-4. **Wt.:** 200. **Bats:** L. **Throws:** L. **School:** Chalker HS, Southington, Ohio. **Career Transactions:** Selected by Tigers in second round of 2000 draft; signed June 12, 2000.

Petty learned a valuable lesson last season about being prepared. He came to spring training out of shape and paid for it with a sore arm. His stock fell in the eyes of team officials, who were surprised because they expected more from Petty based on his pro debut in 2000. After recovering and putting in the necessary work, Petty returned for his second year in the Rookie-level Gulf Coast League, where managers rated him the No. 1 prospect. He's a tall, athletic left-hander. He isn't overpowering at this point, usually throwing in the high 80s, but he's very projectable. He easily could develop more pop to his fastball as he matures physically and his pitching mechanics become more consistent. Petty does spot his fastball well, but struggles to command his breaking ball and changeup. He'll probably start this season in low Class A.

Year	Club (League)	Class	W	L	ERA	G	GS	CG	SV	IP	H	R	ER	BB	SO
2000	Tigers (GCL)	R	2	3	3.00	9	7	1	0	39	31	18	13	20	38
2001	Tigers (GCL)	R	6	0	1.11	12	10	2	0	57	35	11	7	13	52
	Oneonta (NY-P)	A	0	1	2.84	1	1	0	0	6	6	5	2	2	0
MINOR LEAGUE TOTALS			8	4	1.93	22	18	3	0	102	72	34	22	35	90

16. Fernando Rodney, rhp

Born: March 17, 1981. **Ht.:** 5-11. **Wt.:** 170. **Bats:** R. **Throws:** R. **Career Transactions:** Signed as Dominican Republic by Tigers, Nov. 1, 1997.

The hardest thrower in the organization, Rodney joined the 40-man roster in November after reaching Double-A during the regular season. Though he made 10 starts last year, the Tigers project him as a closer or setup man down the road. His calling card is his fastball, which sometimes lights up radar guns at 98 mph. There's not much deception to his delivery, though, and his fastball is as straight as an arrow. He's going to have to spot the pitch to be effective as he moves up the ladder. Rodney has a good changeup, though he doesn't throw it often while working in short relief. He has yet to develop a third pitch, struggling mightily to throw his breaking ball over the plate. He also hasn't been especially durable, never pitching more than 83 innings in a pro season. He'll return to Double-A this year.

Year	Club (League)	Class	W	L	ERA	G	GS	CG	SV	IP	H	R	ER	BB	SO
1998	Tigers (DSL)	R	1	3	3.38	11	5	0	1	32	25	16	12	19	37
1999	Tigers (GCL)	R	3	3	2.40	22	0	0	9	30	20	8	8	21	39
	Lakeland (FSL)	A	1	0	1.42	4	0	0	2	6	7	1	1	1	5
2000	West Michigan (Mid)	A	6	4	2.94	22	10	0	0	83	74	34	27	35	56
2001	Lakeland (FSL)	A	4	2	3.42	16	9	0	0	55	53	26	21	19	44
	Tigers (GCL)	R	0	0	0.00	1	1	0	0	1	0	0	0	1	1
	Erie (EL)	AA	0	0	4.26	4	0	0	1	6	7	3	3	3	8
MINOR LEAGUE TOTALS			15	12	3.03	80	25	0	13	214	186	88	72	99	190

17. Tim Kalita, lhp

Born: Nov. 21, 1978. **Ht.:** 6-2. **Wt.:** 220. **Bats:** R. **Throws:** L. **School:** University of Notre Dame. **Career Transactions:** Selected by Tigers in seventh round of 1999 draft; signed June 11, 1999.

Kalita's promise wasn't all that evident during 2000, when he struggled in high Class A. The problem was his lack of command, as he simply didn't throw strikes early in the count. It seemed like every hitter took him to a full count, with the payoff either a fat pitch down the heart of the plate or ball four. Kalita got himself together last year in Double-A. He led the Eastern League in wins, starts, complete games and innings. Though there still are times when he falls into a rut, he did a much better job of getting ahead of hitters in 2001. There's no need for Kalita to nibble. His fastball is consistently in the 90 mph range, which is above average for a lefthander, and his delivery is somewhat deceptive. His breaking ball should be his out pitch when he reaches the major leagues, but only if he develops it to the point where he throws it over the plate more consistently. Kalita did allow 25 homers last year, tied for the most in the EL, reinforcing the fact that he can't put himself in hitter's counts. He'll move up to Triple-A in 2002.

Year	Club (League)	Class	W	L	ERA	G	GS	CG	SV	IP	H	R	ER	BB	SO
1999	Oneonta (NY-P)	A	0	0	0.00	3	3	0	0	12	3	1	0	5	15
	West Michigan (Mid)	A	4	1	4.18	9	9	0	0	47	46	26	22	27	35
2000	Lakeland (FSL)	A	7	12	4.57	27	25	1	0	150	146	93	76	73	107
2001	Erie (EL)	AA	15	9	3.83	30	29	5	0	200	190	98	85	49	147
MINOR LEAGUE TOTALS			26	22	4.02	69	66	6	0	409	385	218	183	154	304

18. Ryan Raburn, 3b

Born: April 17, 1981. **Ht.:** 6-0. **Wt.:** 185. **Bats:** R. **Throws:** R. **School:** South Florida CC. **Career Transactions:** Selected by Tigers in fifth round of 2001 draft; signed June 20, 2001.

Another member of Detroit's banner 2001 draft class, Raburn wasn't drafted in 2000 because he was at the University of Florida but went in the fifth round last June. His brother Johnny is an infield prospect in the Angels organization. A fundamentally sound hitter, he drove in 42 runs in 44 games in the short-season New York-Penn League. His stroke is compact and quick, while his pitch recognition is excellent. He's strong and has good power potential. A shortstop in high school and an outfielder at Florida, he moved to third base at South Florida CC. He made 23 errors at Oneonta because he struggles with his footwork, both when he fields grounders and when he sets to throw. He does have a good arm and is relatively athletic. Raburn will start this season in low Class A, where he'll be watched closely for his defensive progress. If he still struggles at third base, a return to the outfield could be in order.

Year	Club (League)	Class	AVG	G	AB	R	H	2B	3B	HR	RBI	BB	SO	SB
2001	Tigers (GCL)	R	.155	19	58	4	9	2	0	1	5	9	19	2
	Oneonta (NY-P)	A	.363	44	171	25	62	17	8	8	42	17	42	1
MINOR LEAGUE TOTALS			.310	63	229	29	71	19	8	9	47	26	61	3

19. Neil Jenkins, of

Born: July 17, 1980. **Ht.:** 6-5. **Wt.:** 205. **Bats:** R. **Throws:** R. **School:** Dwyer HS, West Palm Beach, Fla. **Career Transactions:** Selected by Tigers in third round of 1999 draft; signed July 7, 1999.

Jenkins was considered the best power hitter coming out of the high school ranks in 1999, but he dropped down to the third round in part because of concerns about his diabetic condition. While that hasn't been a problem, a back injury shut him down after 23 games in high Class A last year. He didn't require surgery, but he has endured a long process of rest and rehabilitation. It was a key year for Jenkins, too, because it was his first as an outfielder after struggling defensively at third base. What he does best is hit the ball hard and far. He has a very live bat and enormous power potential. What he does worst is make contact. Jenkins has fanned 213 times in 608 professional at bats. He was a poor fielder at third base but had displayed signs of becoming an adequate outfielder, despite his lack of speed, before his back injury. He's destined to return to Lakeland in 2002.

Year	Club (League)	Class	AVG	G	AB	R	H	2B	3B	HR	RBI	BB	SO	SB
1999	Tigers (GCL)	R	.297	33	111	18	33	13	3	2	15	16	37	2
2000	West Michigan (Mid)	A	.253	112	411	56	104	16	5	13	65	38	151	0
2001	Lakeland (FSL)	A	.302	23	86	14	26	8	1	1	6	2	25	0
MINOR LEAGUE TOTALS			.268	168	608	88	163	37	9	16	86	56	213	2

20. Shane Loux, rhp

Born: Aug. 13, 1979. **Ht.:** 6-2. **Wt.:** 205. **Bats:** R. **Throws:** R. **School:** Highland HS, Gilbert, Ariz. **Career Transactions:** Selected by Tigers in second round of 1997 draft; signed June 14, 1997.

Loux underwent surgery to clean out loose deposits in his elbow following the 2000 season. When he came back last year, his sinking fastball had dipped from its usual 92 mph to 88. The Tigers expected as much and believe he'll regain his velocity in 2002. In the meantime, Loux proved that he could pitch effectively at less than his best. He won 10 games in Triple-A while showing more maturity than in the past. Intensity had never been a problem, but channeling it properly had been. Loux' curveball and changeup are both effective, and he has a good feel for pitching. He didn't throw as many strikes last year as he had in the past, but that was another byproduct of the surgery that should be overcome with time. He'll be back at Toledo to start this season.

Year	Club (League)	Class	W	L	ERA	G	GS	CG	SV	IP	H	R	ER	BB	SO
1997	Tigers (GCL)	R	4	1	0.84	10	9	1	0	43	19	7	4	10	33
1998	West Michigan (Mid)	A	7	13	4.64	28	28	2	0	157	184	96	81	52	88
1999	West Michigan (Mid)	A	1	3	6.27	8	8	0	0	47	55	39	33	16	43
	Lakeland (FSL)	A	6	5	4.05	17	17	0	0	91	92	48	41	47	52
2000	Lakeland (FSL)	A	0	1	1.80	1	1	0	0	5	2	1	1	3	6
	Jacksonville (SL)	AA	12	9	3.82	26	26	2	0	158	150	78	67	55	130
2001	Toledo (IL)	AAA	10	11	5.78	28	27	2	0	151	203	111	97	73	72
MINOR LEAGUE TOTALS			40	43	4.47	118	116	7	0	652	705	380	324	256	424

21. Mike Rabelo, c

Born: Jan. 17, 1980. **Ht.:** 6-1. **Wt.:** 195. **Bats:** B. **Throws:** R. **School:** University of Tampa. **Career Transactions:** Selected by Tigers in fourth round of 2001 draft; signed June 20, 2001.

Rabelo was arguably as good as any college catching prospect in the 2001 draft. He blossomed offensively last spring after learning to switch-hit in college. He continued to hit in his pro debut. Rabelo hits the ball hard and uses the entire field, but he doesn't have much power at this stage. He does have good balance in his stance from both sides of the plate. His key will be cutting down on his strikeouts, increasing his walks and developing more strength so the line drives he hits now for singles find their way into the gaps for doubles and triples. A pitcher in high school, Rabelo didn't catch until college and still is smoothing out his defensive game. His arm isn't overly strong and he threw out just 26 percent of basestealers in the New York-Penn League. If he makes it to the big leagues, it will be his bat that gets him there.

Year	Club (League)	Class	AVG	G	AB	R	H	2B	3B	HR	RBI	BB	SO	SB
2001	Oneonta (NY-P)	A	.325	53	194	27	63	4	2	0	32	23	45	1
MINOR LEAGUE TOTALS			.325	53	194	27	63	4	2	0	32	23	45	1

22. Matt Coenen, lhp

Born: March 13, 1980. **Ht.:** 6-6. **Wt.:** 230. **Bats:** L. **Throws:** L. **School:** Charleston Southern University. **Career Transactions:** Selected by Tigers in second round of 2001 draft; signed July 12, 2001.

It's not so much what Coenen does now which makes him an intriguing prospect. It's what he might do in the future. He's a 6-foot-5 lefthander whose fastball was clocked as high as 93 mph by Detroit's scouts before the draft. Like Preston Larrison, he was more impressive in the Cape Cod League during the summer of 2000 than he was during his final season of college. After turning pro, Coenen generally pitched at 88 mph. The Tigers aren't concerned because they expect he'll throw harder as he matures physically and hones his mechanics. He has a three-quarters delivery that causes his fastball to tail in on lefthanders and away from righthanders. His breaking ball, a cross between a slider and curve that he can throw for strikes, is a better pitch than his changeup at this point. Coenen's change likely will have to be revamped, something he'll work on this year in low Class A.

Year	Club (League)	Class	W	L	ERA	G	GS	CG	SV	IP	H	R	ER	BB	SO
2001	Oneonta (NY-P)	A	2	2	3.04	10	9	1	1	47	44	26	16	16	37
MINOR LEAGUE TOTALS			2	2	3.04	10	9	1	1	47	44	26	16	16	37

23. Ronnie Merrill, 2b/ss

Born: Nov. 13, 1978. **Ht.:** 6-1. **Wt.:** 185. **Bats:** B. **Throws:** R. **School:** University of Tampa. **Career Transactions:** Selected by Tigers in seventh round of 2000 draft; signed June 12, 2000.

The knock against Merrill, a former teammate of Mike Rabelo's at the University of Tampa, is that he doesn't have a particular tool that stands out. He doesn't run well and isn't a threat to steal. He doesn't have good range or an overpowering arm. Drafted as a shortstop, he has mostly played second base in the minors. What Merrill does well, however, is produce. He's a pesky hitter who consistently has hit around .300. His value in the long run is as a utility player. Merrill can play adequately at second base, shortstop or third base. In order to become an everyday player in the major leagues, his bat will have to be considered a plus tool, which is probably a reach. He could be Ramon Santiago's double-play partner in Double-A this season.

Yr	Club (League)	Class	AVG	G	AB	R	H	2B	3B	HR	RBI	BB	SO	SB
2000	Oneonta (NY-P)	A	.311	33	135	21	42	5	2	1	21	12	23	6
2001	West Michigan (Mid)	A	.317	83	309	53	98	11	3	8	53	36	47	15
	Erie (EL)	AA	.293	37	147	22	43	14	0	4	18	12	27	0
MINOR LEAGUE TOTALS			.310	153	591	96	183	30	5	13	92	60	97	21

24. Joe Valentine, rhp

Born: Dec. 24, 1979. **Ht.:** 6-2. **Wt.:** 195. **Bats:** R. **Throws:** R. **School:** Jefferson Davis (Ala.) JC. **Career Transactions:** Selected by White Sox in 26th round of 1999 draft; signed June 26, 1999 . . . Selected by Expos in Rule 5 major league draft, December 13, 2001; sold to Tigers.

Valentine's mid-90s fastball was the reason the Tigers wanted to pick up Valentine from the Expos in a straight cash deal, after Montreal took him fourth overall in the major league Rule 5 draft at the Winter Meetings. He'll have to stick on Detroit's 25-man roster all season, or else be exposed to waivers and then offered back to Chicago for half of the $50,000 draft price. A closer who posted 22 saves and a 1.79 ERA in Class A last year, Valentine will have to skip two levels to the big leagues, but he might have the stuff to do it. He has a good slider to go with his fastball. He lacks command at times, and he's going to have to do a better job of getting ahead of hitters in the majors. The jury is out on Valentine's makeup. He carries himself in a manner that some find cocky, while others just see him as confident.

Year	Club (League)	Class	W	L	ERA	G	GS	CG	SV	IP	H	R	ER	BB	SO
1999	White Sox (AZL)	R	0	0	0.00	3	0	0	0	4	2	0	0	1	2
	Bristol (Appy)	R	0	0	7.02	11	0	0	0	17	27	17	13	9	14
2000	Bristol (Appy)	R	2	1	2.88	19	0	0	7	25	14	10	8	12	30
2001	Winston-Salem (CL)	A	5	1	1.01	27	0	0	8	45	18	7	5	27	50
	Kannapolis (SAL)	A	2	2	2.93	30	0	0	14	31	21	10	10	10	33
MINOR LEAGUE TOTALS			9	4	2.66	90	0	0	29	122	82	44	36	59	129

25. Mark Woodyard, rhp

Born: Dec. 19, 1978. **Ht.:** 6-2. **Wt.:** 185. **Bats:** R. **Throws:** R. **School:** Bethune-Cookman College. **Career Transactions:** Selected by Tigers in fourth round of 2000 draft; signed June 29, 2000.

The Tigers rolled the dice on the intriguing Woodyard, taking him in the 2000 draft's fourth round—far ahead of where he was expected to go. Detroit figured the product of tiny Bethune-Cookman might be a diamond in the rough, and to this point he has been neither a shining light nor a disappointment. He has merely held his own. Woodyard is raw and has gone just 8-17 as a pro, but he has shown flashes of potential. His fastball regularly reaches 90 mph or better, hitting 94 mph at times. His curveball is either very good or not good at all. There seems to be no in-between in that regard, especially when it comes to commanding his curve. Woodyard has struggled to find a consistent release point, which hurts his control, or a changeup. Yet he's athletic—he also played first base in college—and his work ethic has been good. He'll begin this season in high Class A.

Year	Club (League)	Class	W	L	ERA	G	GS	CG	SV	IP	H	R	ER	BB	SO
2000	Oneonta (NY-P)	A	1	5	4.59	11	9	0	0	51	48	32	26	39	38
2001	West Michigan (Mid)	A	7	12	4.51	25	25	2	0	144	147	81	72	69	84
MINOR LEAGUE TOTALS			8	17	4.53	36	34	2	0	195	195	113	98	108	122

26. Tommy Marx, lhp

Born: Sept. 5, 1979. **Ht.:** 6-7. **Wt.:** 200. **Bats:** R. **Throws:** L. **School:** Brother Rice HS, Bloomfield Hills, Mich. **Career Transactions:** Selected by Tigers in third round of 1998 draft; signed June 9, 1998.

Marx's greatest strength, his size, is also his biggest weakness. On one hand, he's an intimidating presence on the mound with a 90-mph fastball. On the other hand, like a lot of taller pitchers, he struggles to maintain his mechanics. Last season was a good one for Marx in the sense that he managed to start 27 games in high Class A and fight his way through adversity. It wasn't a good season in that his curveball and changeup, pitches he was starting to develop in 2000, both vanished. If Marx manages to get his offspeed pitches back on track, he'll have enough ability to pitch in the major leagues someday. Another question mark surrounding him is his durability. He was shut down after 18 starts in 2000 and wore down again last year. He'd probably be best served by returning to Lakeland in 2002.

Year	Club (League)	Class	W	L	ERA	G	GS	CG	SV	IP	H	R	ER	BB	SO
1998	Tigers (GCL)	R	1	3	4.29	12	12	0	0	42	33	27	20	39	38
1999	Tigers (GCL)	R	3	2	3.43	8	8	0	0	42	35	24	16	32	39
	Oneonta (NY-P)	A	2	1	3.22	6	4	0	0	22	20	14	8	13	19
2000	West Michigan (Mid)	A	7	6	2.74	18	18	1	0	99	74	35	30	51	83
2001	Lakeland (FSL)	A	8	11	4.91	28	27	1	0	150	160	92	82	78	97
MINOR LEAGUE TOTALS			21	23	3.95	72	69	2	0	355	322	192	156	213	276

27. Jeff Farnsworth, rhp

Born: Oct. 6, 1975. **Ht.:** 6-2. **Wt.:** 190. **Bats:** R. **Throws:** R. **School:** Okaloosa-Walton (Fla.) CC. **Career Transactions:** Selected by Mariners in second round of 1996 draft; signed June 5, 1996 . . . Selected by Tigers from Mariners in Rule 5 major league draft, Dec. 13, 2001.

Farnsworth joins Joe Valentine as major league Rule 5 draft picks who could make Detroit's pitching staff this year. A second-round pick in 1996, Farnsworth's career was put on hold as an elbow injury sidelined him for most of the next two years. He became a starter and dropped his arm slot down to a low three-quarters angle last season, showing significant progress in the second half of the season. He earned more notice by setting a Venezuela League record with 53⅓ straight innings without a walk and leading the league in ERA this winter. The Tigers took him on the recommendation of Phil Regan, the former big league manager and pitching coach who managed in Venezuela this winter and will be the skipper at West Michigan in 2002. Farnsworth's fastball is in the low 90s and his breaking ball is serviceable. He may have an easier time sticking with Detroit out of the bullpen but also could get a look as a starter.

Year	Club (League)	Class	W	L	ERA	G	GS	CG	SV	IP	H	R	ER	BB	SO
1996	Everett (NWL)	A	3	3	4.12	10	7	0	0	39	33	19	18	13	42
1997	Lancaster (Cal)	A	1	1	6.97	5	5	0	0	21	24	20	16	8	18
1998	Did Not Play—Injured														
1999	Lancaster (Cal)	A	3	6	6.50	26	9	0	3	72	91	61	52	43	43
2000	New Haven (EL)	AA	9	3	3.46	39	8	0	2	101	91	40	39	25	70
2001	San Antonio (TL)	AA	11	10	4.35	27	27	0	0	155	182	92	75	47	113
MINOR LEAGUE TOTALS			27	23	4.63	107	56	0	5	389	421	232	200	136	286

28. Kris Keller, rhp

Born: March 1, 1978. **Ht.:** 6-2. **Wt.:** 225. **Bats:** R. **Throws:** R. **School:** Fletcher HS, Neptune Beach, Fla. **Career Transactions:** Selected by Tigers in fourth round of 1996 draft; signed June 29, 1996.

There are times when Keller lights up the radar gun at 97 mph. There are other times when he doesn't throw 90 mph. How hard he throws depends directly on his command. On the nights when Keller comes out throwing strikes, his fastball seems to get quicker with each pitch. When he can't find the plate, he starts guiding the ball and isn't nearly as effective. Keller's fastball is straight, so he needs the added velocity. He throws both a curveball and a slider, and the slider is the better of the two breaking balls. He threw a circle change regularly for the first time last season and got some outs with it. He has also flirted with the idea of developing a splitter. Until he can maintain his fastball from outing to outing, he won't be ready for Detroit. Keller will return to Triple-A in 2002.

Year	Club (League)	Class	W	L	ERA	G	GS	CG	SV	IP	H	R	ER	BB	SO
1996	Tigers (GCL)	R	1	1	2.38	8	6	0	0	34	23	12	9	21	23
1997	Jamestown (NY-P)	A	0	2	8.67	16	0	0	0	27	37	33	26	20	18
1998	Jamestown (NY-P)	A	1	3	3.27	27	0	0	8	33	29	12	12	16	41
1999	West Michigan (Mid)	A	5	3	2.92	49	0	0	8	77	63	28	25	36	87
2000	Jacksonville (SL)	AA	2	3	2.91	62	0	0	26	68	58	24	22	44	60
2001	Toledo (IL)	AAA	5	2	4.48	52	0	0	4	68	64	42	34	38	60
MINOR LEAGUE TOTALS			14	14	3.75	214	6	0	46	307	274	151	128	175	289

29. Eric Eckenstahler, lhp

Born: Dec. 17, 1976. **Ht.:** 6-7. **Wt.:** 210. **Bats:** L. **Throws:** L. **School:** Illinois State University. **Career Transactions:** Selected by Tigers in 32nd round of 1999 draft; signed May 25, 2000.

After a decidedly underwhelming first pro season in 2000 after signing before that year's draft as a fifth-year senior, Eckenstahler dazzled the organization's coaches with the way he threw last spring training. He was consistently at 90-92 mph and maintained that velocity throughout the season, most of which he spent in Double-A. His breaking ball was also much improved, as he was able to throw it for strikes. Because he's a tall lefthander, Eckenstahler often is compared to Graeme Lloyd. He still needs to fine-tune his command and is projected as a middle or situational reliever, not as a closer. He's already 25, so he doesn't offer much more upside. He'll move up one step to Triple-A this season.

Year	Club (League)	Class	W	L	ERA	G	GS	CG	SV	IP	H	R	ER	BB	SO
2000	West Michigan (Mid)	A	0	2	5.79	10	3	0	1	19	21	15	12	11	22
	Oneonta (NY-P)	A	0	0	1.64	8	0	0	0	11	7	3	2	3	13
2001	Lakeland (FSL)	A	1	0	1.50	4	0	0	1	6	3	1	1	2	7
	Erie (EL)	AA	4	2	3.90	46	0	0	4	65	65	32	28	31	73
MINOR LEAGUE TOTALS			5	4	3.86	68	3	0	6	100	96	51	43	47	115

30. Anderson Hernandez, ss

Born: Oct. 30, 1982. **Ht.:** 5-9. **Wt.:** 150. **Bats:** B. **Throws:** R. **Career Transactions:** Signed out of Dominican Republic by Tigers, April 23, 2001.

The Tigers are high on many of their middle-infield prospects. New York-Penn League batting champ Juan Francia and Juan Gonzalez, who finished second in the Gulf Coast League batting race, couldn't quite crack this list. Hernandez, whom managers rated as the No. 2 prospect in the GCL behind Chad Petty, just barely made it. Signed out of the Dominican Republic in April, Hernandez led the GCL in triples and steals in his pro debut. An athletic switch-hitter, he's not very big and will have to get stronger and more disciplined to be much of a threat at the plate. His speed and defense are his strengths. He has more than enough range and arm to stay at shortstop. Hernandez could start 2002 in extended spring before heading to short-season ball in June, or he could open the year in low Class A if the Tigers decide to be more aggressive with him.

Year	Club (League)	Class	AVG	G	AB	R	H	2B	3B	HR	RBI	BB	SO	SB
2001	Tigers (GCL)	R	.264	55	216	37	57	5	11	0	18	13	38	34
	Lakeland (FSL)	A	.190	7	21	2	4	0	1	0	1	0	8	0
MINOR LEAGUE TOTALS			.257	62	237	39	61	5	12	0	19	13	46	34

FLORIDA
Marlins

TOP 30 PROSPECTS

1. Josh Beckett, rhp
2. Miguel Cabrera, ss
3. Denny Bautista, rhp
4. Adrian Gonzalez, 1b
5. Allen Baxter, rhp
6. Abraham Nunez, of
7. Claudio Vargas, rhp
8. Blaine Neal, rhp
9. Josh Wilson, 2b/ss
10. Rob Henkel, lhp
11. Jason Stokes, of
12. Pablo Ozuna, 2b
13. Chip Ambres, of
14. Kevin Olsen, rhp
15. Hansel Izquierdo, rhp
16. Will Smith, of
17. Ramon Castillo, rhp
18. Ronald Belizario, rhp
19. Wes Anderson, rhp
20. Geoff Goetz, lhp
21. Jose Soto, of
22. Jim Kavourias, of
23. Nate Rolison, 1b
24. Gary Knotts, rhp
25. Jason Grilli, rhp
26. Jon Asahina, rhp/dh
27. Jesus Medrano, 2b/ss
28. Brett Roneberg, of
29. Kevin Hooper, 2b
30. Derek Wathan, ss

By Mike Berardino

Shortly after marking his 10-year anniversary as the architect of the Marlins, a franchise he joined 18 months before it played its first game, general manager Dave Dombrowski jumped ship, becoming Tigers team president. Some took this as a sign the Marlins had degenerated into a mess of Titanic proportions, but that remains to be seen after the most tumultuous year in club history.

Rumors of contraction and relocation hover over the franchise. Owner John Henry, frustrated with the dormant push for a new stadium, led a group that bought the Red Sox and planned to sell the Marlins to Expos owner Jeffrey Loria. Major League Baseball will run the Expos, and most of the Montreal front office is expected to move to South Florida.

Most of the Marlins' key front-office officials got two-year contract extensions after Dombrowski left, but his club presidency and GM roles remained vacant, as did the manager's post. In an unusual arrangement, the Marlins committed to a three-headed GM in which Al Avila, Scott Reid and John Westhoff shared power, but that fell apart when Avila joined former Marlins assistant GM Dave Littlefield with the Pirates. He was

one of several club officials who jumped ship as it became clear many Marlins employees would be forced out by former Expos coming south.

Avila began the year as scouting director, presiding over his third straight solid draft. When Littlefield was hired as Pirates GM in mid-July, Avila was promoted and national crosschecker David Chadd became scouting director. Dombrowski had set a 2002 payroll goal of $45 million to keep the club's nucleus intact. It was uncertain if new management would come close to that figure, leaving open the possibility of a second dismantling in four years.

A year that began with tough talk of the team's first division title ended with an 86-loss whimper and a fourth-place finish. Even more shocking than Dombrowski's departure, in some ways, was the May 28 firing of manager John Boles, who couldn't overcome a 22-26 start or the public criticism of reliever Dan Miceli. Boles, who spent two stints as farm director and managed parts of four seasons, chose to leave the organization he had helped found and joined the Dodgers. Former Devil Rays pitching coach Rick Williams, in his first full year as farm director, oversaw a system that finished 55 games over .500.

Organization Overview

General manager: Open. **Farm director:** Rick Williams. **Scouting director:** David Chadd.

2001 PERFORMANCE

Class	Team	League	W	L	Pct.	Finish*	Manager(s)
Majors	Florida Marlins	National	76	86	.469	11th (16)	J. Boles/T. Perez
Triple-A	Calgary Cannons	Pacific Coast	72	71	.503	7th (16)	Chris Chambliss
Double-A	Portland Sea Dogs	Eastern	77	65	.542	t-4th (12)	Rick Renteria
High A	Brevard County Manatees	Florida State	80	55	.593	1st (14)	Dave Huppert
Low A	Kane County Cougars	Midwest	88	50	.638	1st (14)	Russ Morman
Short-season	Utica Blue Sox	New York-Penn	27	47	.365	13th (14)	Kevin Boles
Rookie	GCL Marlins	Gulf Coast	29	31	.483	9th (14)	Jon Deeble
OVERALL 200I MINOR LEAGUE RECORD			373	319	.539	7th (30)	

*Finish in overall standings (No. of teams in league)

ORGANIZATION LEADERS

BATTING
*AVG	**Ramon Castro**, Calgary	.336
R	Jesus Medrano, Brevard County	93
H	Kevin Hooper, Portland/Kane County	163
TB	Mike Gulan, Calgary	271
2B	Mike Gulan, Calgary	44
3B	Abraham Nunez, Portland	9
HR	**Ramon Castro**, Calgary	27
RBI	Adrian Gonzalez, Kane County	103
BB	Abraham Nunez, Portland	83
SO	Abraham Nunez, Portland	155
SB	Jesus Medrano, Brevard County	61

PITCHING
W	Hansel Izquierdo, Portland/Brevard/K.C.	16
L	**Mike Drumright**, Calgary/Portland	13
#ERA	Josh Beckett, Portland/Brevard	1.54
G	Tim McClaskey, Portland/Brevard	63
CG	Three tied at	2
SV	Johnny Ruffin, Calgary	22
IP	Joe Roa, Calgary/Portland	160
BB	Claudio Vargas, Portland	67
SO	Josh Beckett, Portland/Brevard	203

*Minimum 250 At-Bats   #Minimum 75 Innings

TOP PROSPECTS OF THE DECADE

1993	Nigel Wilson, of
1994	Charles Johnson, c
1995	Charles Johnson, c
1996	Edgar Renteria, ss
1997	Felix Heredia, lhp
1998	Mark Kotsay, of
1999	A.J. Burnett, rhp
2000	A.J. Burnett, rhp
2001	Josh Beckett, rhp

TOP DRAFT PICKS OF THE DECADE

1992	Charles Johnson, c
1993	Marc Valdes, rhp
1994	Josh Booty, ss
1995	Jaime Jones, of
1996	Mark Kotsay, of
1997	Aaron Akin, rhp
1998	Chip Ambres, of
1999	Josh Beckett, rhp
2000	Adrian Gonzalez, 1b
2001	Garrett Berger, rhp (2)

Castro   **Drumright**

RICH ABEL

BEST TOOLS

Best Hitter for Average	Adrian Gonzalez
Best Power Hitter	Jason Stokes
Fastest Baserunner	Jesus Medrano
Best Fastball	Josh Beckett
Best Breaking Ball	Josh Beckett
Best Changeup	Kevin Olsen
Best Control	Kevin Olsen
Best Defensive Catcher	Brandon Harper
Best Defensive Infielder	Derek Wathan
Best Infield Arm	Miguel Cabrera
Best Defensive Outfielder	Abraham Nunez
Best Outfield Arm	Abraham Nunez

PROJECTED 2005 LINEUP

Catcher	Charles Johnson
First Base	Adrian Gonzalez
Second Base	Luis Castillo
Third Base	Mike Lowell
Shortstop	Miguel Cabrera
Left Field	Cliff Floyd
Center Field	Preston Wilson
Right Field	Abraham Nunez
No. 1 Starter	Josh Beckett
No. 2 Starter	Brad Penny
No. 3 Starter	Ryan Dempster
No. 4 Starter	Denny Bautista
No. 5 Starter	A.J. Burnett
Closer	Blaine Neal

ALL-TIME LARGEST BONUSES

Josh Beckett, 1999	$3,625,000
Adrian Gonzalez, 2000	$3,000,000
Livan Hernandez, 1996	$2,500,000
Jason Stokes, 2000	$2,027,000
Miguel Cabrera, 1999	$1,900,000

DraftAnalysis

2001 Draft

Best Pro Debut: RHP Nic Ungs (12) has an 89-94 mph fastball, but what stands out is his command. He didn't walk a batter in 61 innings in the short-season New York-Penn League, going 3-1, 1.62.

Best Athlete: Had OF/RHP **Chris Resop** (4) made it to Miami, he would have been one of college baseball's top two-way players. As a position player he features four tools, with his speed the only thing that doesn't stand out. If the Marlins ever put him back on the mound, he has an 88-91 mph fastball and a plus breaking ball. Resop also started at quarterback for his high school before taking his senior year off to focus on baseball.

Best Hitter: Resop. SS Rex Rundgren (11) also has a projectable bat.

Best Raw Power: During a predraft workout, Resop hit a dozen balls into the club section of Pro Player Stadium.

Fastest Runner: The Marlins signed just two hitters out of the first 13 rounds, so they didn't add much speed. Rundgren has average quickness, which is as good as it gets with this group.

Best Defensive Player: Rundgren has good hands, arm strength and actions at shortstop.

Best Fastball: The good news is that RHP Garrett Berger (2), Florida's top pick, threw as hard as 97 mph. The bad news is that he got hurt in instructional league and required Tommy John surgery. RHPs Allen Baxter (3), Lincoln Holdzkom (7) and Kevin Cave (15) all have reached 95. RHP/OF Jon Asahina, a 31st-round draft-and-follow from

2000, also has done the same.

Most Intriguing Background: Rundgren is the son of pop singer/songwriter Todd. LHP Adam Bostick (6), who works in the low 90s, was more accomplished as a high school quarterback than as a pitcher.

Resop

Closest To The Majors: Florida went young with this draft, so it won't offer much help in the near future. Ungs' control could help him move quickly. The highest-drafted college player was RHP Jeff Fulchino (8), who has a live arm and has made progress in cleaning up his delivery.

Best Late-Round Pick: Not many teams realized that Cave was eligible for the draft as a Xavier sophomore.

The One Who Got Away: The Marlins were disappointed they couldn't finish a deal with projectable 6-foot-4 LHP Tyler Lumsden (5), who opted to go to Clemson.

Assessment: Most teams believed the 2001 draft offered depth in high school pitching, and that's the way Florida went. The Marlins, who had the second and first picks in the previous two drafts, were the last team to pick in 2001. They lost their first-round pick after signing Charles Johnson, then went after young pitchers. Though their system needs bats more than arms, they opted for the best players available on their draft board.

2000 Draft

Florida loaded up on offense with 1B Adrian Gonzalez, the No. 1 overall pick, and OFs Jason Stokes (2), Will Smith (6) and Jim Kavourias (5). LHP Rob Henkel (3) and RHP Jon Asahina (31, draft-and-follow) are also keepers. **Grade: B+**

1999 Draft

RHP Josh Beckett (1), BA's 2001 Minor League Player of the Year, rates a top grade all by himself. SS Josh Wilson (3) has a chance, too. **Grade: A**

1998 Draft

Sleeper RHP Kevin Olsen (26) already has reached the majors. He ultimately may prove to be a better pick than either OF Chip Ambres (1) or SS Derek Wathan (2), the only other prospects. **Grade: C**

1997 Draft

RHP Wes Anderson (14) had the potential to rescue this draft by himself and was mentioned just after Beckett until he imploded in 2001. RHP Aaron Akin (1) came out of nowhere and headed back there quickly. **Grade: D**

Note: Draft analysis prepared by Jim Callis. Numbers in parentheses indicate draft rounds.

. . . He's good, knows he's good and would never think of shrinking from his apparent destiny.

Beckett
Josh
rhp

Born: May 15, 1980.
Ht.: 6-4. **Wt.:** 190.
Bats: R. **Throws:** R.
School: Spring (Texas) HS.
Career Transactions: Selected by Marlins in first round (second overall) of 1999 draft; signed Sept. 1, 1999.

Beckett was the first high school righthander drafted as high as second overall since Bill Gullickson 20 years earlier. He opened 2001 at Class A Brevard County just hoping to stay healthy all season. He had a serious scare after two tours on the disabled list with shoulder tendinitis in 2000. Offseason tests diagnosed a small tear in his labrum, fraying in his rotator cuff, biceps tendinitis and an impingement. Dr. James Andrews advised against surgery. Beckett worked hard to rehabilitate his shoulder in the winter, then came out firing. He dominated both the Florida State League and the Double-A Eastern League. His big league debut against the Cubs was one of the most anticipated Marlins games of the year. He delivered with six innings of one-hit ball, including a couple of epic showdowns with Sammy Sosa. Beckett capped his season with Baseball America's Minor League Player of the Year award.

Beckett has a prototypical power pitcher's build and a true No. 1 starter's repertoire and makeup. His four-seam fastball can touch 97 mph, but he'd rather pitch at 93-94 and get easy outs with his sinker. He has a dazzling 12-to-6 curveball and a plus changeup with excellent arm speed and deception. Beckett's delivery is smooth, making the ball get on top of hitters in a hurry. He has a maturity beyond his years, easily trading barbs with older players, writers and club officials and always looking people in the eye. He's good, knows he's good and would never think of shrinking from his apparent destiny. At the same time, he can be stubborn and too hard on himself. He's still learning to channel his emotions. He needs to get better at holding runners but won't sacrifice too much of his stuff toward that aim. Beckett is athletic but just an adequate fielder. He continues to mature physically and improve his conditioning.

Barring a health setback, Beckett will open 2002 in the Marlins rotation. Club officials were ecstatic with his poise and performance during the callup. It won't be long before he fulfills the promise scouts have long predicted for him. In fact, that could happen in 2002.

Year	Club (League)	Class	W	L	ERA	G	GS	CG	SV	IP	H	R	ER	BB	SO
2000	Kane County (Mid)	A	2	3	2.12	13	12	0	0	59	45	18	14	15	61
2001	Brevard County (FSL)	A	6	0	1.23	13	12	0	0	66	32	13	9	15	101
	Portland (EL)	AA	8	1	1.82	13	13	0	0	74	50	16	15	19	102
	Florida (NL)	MAJ	2	2	1.50	4	4	0	0	24	14	9	4	11	24
MAJOR LEAGUE TOTALS			2	2	1.50	4	4	0	0	24	14	9	4	11	24
MINOR LEAGUE TOTALS			16	4	1.72	39	37	0	0	199	127	47	38	49	264

MORRIS FOSTOFF

2. Miguel Cabrera, ss

Born: April 18, 1983. **Ht:** 6-2. **Wt:** 185. **Bats:** R. **Throws:** R. **Career Transactions:** Signed out of Venezuela by Marlins, July 2, 1999.

Signed for a Venezuelan-record $1.9 million, Cabrera grew up with a diamond just beyond his back yard, and his instincts show as much. Last July in Seattle, he became the youngest player in the short history of the Futures Game. Cabrera plays with an all-around smoothness that makes him stand out, even on a Class A Kane County club that also included Adrian Gonzalez. Cabrera does everything with apparent ease, including driving the ball with authority into both gaps and producing runs in RBI situations. He has a good idea of the strike zone for such a young player. He has plus range and arm strength. Cabrera shed baby fat and became much lighter on his feet with a well-defined physique. Despite the increased quickness, Cabrera's speed is below-average due to his thick legs. He hasn't shown much home run power, but that should come. He missed time in 2001 with a lower back problem, the only thing that could slow what figures to be a rapid rise. Cabrera could make the jump to Double-A to start 2002, and he'll continue to play shortstop primarily. An eventual move to third base no longer is considered essential.

Year	Club (League)	Class	AVG	G	AB	R	H	2B	3B	HR	RBI	BB	SO	SB
2000	Marlins (GCL)	R	.260	57	219	38	57	10	2	2	22	23	46	1
	Utica (NY-P)	A	.250	8	32	3	8	2	0	0	6	2	6	0
2001	Kane County (Mid)	A	.268	110	422	61	113	19	4	7	66	37	76	3
MINOR LEAGUE TOTALS			.265	175	673	102	178	31	6	9	94	62	128	4

3. Denny Bautista, rhp

Born: Oct. 23, 1982. **Ht.:** 6-5. **Wt.:** 170. **Bats:** R. **Throws:** R. **Career Transactions:** Signed out of Dominican Republic by Marlins, April 11, 2000.

Bautista's family is close with the Martinez family in the Dominican Republic, which means Pedro and Ramon have provided guidance to a player they consider their nephew. Largely on Pedro's advice, Bautista signed with the Marlins for about $350,000 after an agreement with the Braves fell through in light of Atlanta's Wilson Betemit transgression. Bautista has added 10-15 pounds of muscle to his tall, wiry frame and his velocity has climbed from the mid-80s to 94-96 mph. He pitches at 90-92 and shows a plus curve that comes in over the top, and an improving changeup. He's in tremendous condition and in offseason workouts actually outpaces Pedro Martinez, who taught him how to throw all three pitches. Bautista still tends to overthrow at times and has a bad habit of spinning off toward first base on his delivery, like Pedro. He still needs to add maturity and consistency with his mechanics. Considering Bautista's youth and inexperience, he likely will begin 2002 at Class A Brevard County.

Year	Club (League)	Class	W	L	ERA	G	GS	CG	SV	IP	H	R	ER	BB	SO
2000	Marlins (GCL)	R	6	2	2.43	11	11	2	0	63	49	24	17	17	58
	Utica (NY-P)	A	0	0	3.60	1	1	0	0	5	4	3	2	3	5
2001	Utica (NY-P)	A	3	1	2.08	7	7	0	0	39	25	16	9	6	31
	Kane County (Mid)	A	3	1	4.35	8	7	0	0	39	43	21	19	14	20
MINOR LEAGUE TOTALS			12	4	2.90	27	26	2	0	146	121	64	47	40	114

4. Adrian Gonzalez, 1b

Born: May 8, 1982. **Ht.:** 6-2. **Wt.:** 190. **Bats:** L. **Throws:** L. **School:** Eastlake HS, Chula Vista, Calif. **Career Transactions:** Selected by Marlins in first round (first overall) of 2000 draft; signed June 6, 2000.

A classic late bloomer, Gonzalez was considered a signability choice atop the 2000 draft. He agreed before the draft to a $3 million bonus and wasted little time validating the pick or the money. His older brother Edgar is a third baseman in the Devil Rays system. Their father David was a top first baseman in the Mexican semipro leagues into his early 40s. Gonzalez isn't intimidated by any pitcher or situation. Intelligent and confident, he publicly set a goal of hitting .420 in 2001 but was far from a disappointment. He knows his swing and the strike zone better than anyone else in the system and makes quick adjustments. He has an encyclopedic knowledge of pitchers, which should serve him well down the road. He has soft hands, decent range and saves plenty of errors with his glove. Gonzalez has gap power but doesn't project as more than a 20-homer threat. He has a tendency to drift with his hips, allowing pitchers to jam him with hard stuff inside. He wore down under the grind of his first full pro season, and his speed is well below-average. Gonzalez could jump to Double-A with a good spring. His makeup and willingness to take instruction portend a rapid rise.

Year	Club (League)	Class	AVG	G	AB	R	H	2B	3B	HR	RBI	BB	SO	SB
2000	Marlins (GCL)	R	.295	53	193 ·	24	57	10	1	0	30	32	35	0
	Utica (NY-P)	A	.310	8	29	7	9	3	0	0	3	7	6	0
2001	Kane County (Mid)	A	.312	127	516	86	161	37	1	17	103	57	83	5
MINOR LEAGUE TOTALS			.308	188	738	117	227	50	2	17	136	96	124	5

5. Allen Baxter, rhp

Born: July 6, 1983. **Ht.:** 6-4. **Wt.:** 215. **Bats:** R. **Throws:** R. **School:** Varina HS, Sandston, Va. **Career Transactions:** Selected by Marlins in third round of 2001 draft; signed June 14, 2001.

Baxter emerged from a pack of high school righthanders the Marlins were considering in the early rounds of the 2001 draft. He signed quickly for $450,000, then wasted little time establishing himself. Baxter pitches at 90-91 mph and has hit 95, a couple of ticks higher than his peak before signing. Marlins officials say he has Kevin Brown-style movement on both his two- and four-seam fastballs, explosive weapons he's still learning to harness. His curve is a plus pitch, and his changeup and command are advanced for a first-year pro. Baxter's makeup is solid, he accepts instruction well and he's quietly intimidating on the mound. He has a prototypical pitcher's frame. He has no weaknesses that are obvious other than a lack of professional experience. He has junked a slider at the Marlins' request and still can improve his changeup. Baxter got a taste of short-season ball and figures to open the year in extended spring training, but his rapid progress could entice the Marlins to send him to Kane County.

Year	Club (League)	Class	W	L	ERA	G	GS	CG	SV	IP	H	R	ER	BB	SO
2001	Marlins (GCL)	R	2	3	2.38	9	7	0	0	34	25	13	9	8	40
	Utica (NY-P)	A	0	0	3.60	1	1	0	0	5	3	2	2	3	5
MINOR LEAGUE TOTALS			2	3	2.54	10	8	0	0	39	28	15	11	11	45

6. Abraham Nunez, of

Born: Feb. 5, 1980. **Ht.:** 6-2. **Wt.:** 186. **Bats:** B. **Throws:** R. **Career Transactions:** Signed out of Dominican Republic by Diamondbacks, Aug. 22, 1996 . . . Traded by Diamondbacks to Marlins, Dec. 14, 1999, completing trade in which Diamondbacks sent RHP Vladimir Nunez, RHP Brad Penny and a player to be named to Marlins for RHP Matt Mantei (July 9, 1999).

Nunez came to the Marlins in December 1999 as the player to be named in the Matt Mantei trade. The Diamondbacks contested his inclusion, but the commissioner's office let the deal stand. His presence was one of the reasons the Marlins dealt 1996 first-rounder Mark Kotsay to the Padres just before Opening Day 2001. Nunez is a five-tool player with plus power from both sides of the plate. His throwing shoulder was back to full strength after a nagging injury limited him mostly to DH in 2000. He has the arm and range to play either center or right field. He has consistently shown the ability to draw walks. Nunez still strikes out too much and overswings most of the time. He has a hard time staying back on pitches, and his swing tends to get too long. His speed is just average. He sometimes makes strange decisions that cause scouts to doubt his instincts. Considering the Marlins' conservative philosophy in promotions, Nunez figures to return to Portland for another crack at Double-A pitching. Much of his game still requires assembly, but once the pieces start to click into place, he could make the majors in a hurry.

Year	Club (League)	Class	AVG	G	AB	R	H	2B	3B	HR	RBI	BB	SO	SB
1997	Diamondbacks (AZL)	R	.305	54	213	52	65	17	4	0	21	26	40	3
	Lethbridge (Pio)	R	.167	2	6	2	1	0	0	0	1	1	0	0
1998	South Bend (Mid)	A	.255	110	364	44	93	14	2	9	47	67	81	12
1999	High Desert (Cal)	A	.273	130	488	106	133	29	6	22	93	86	122	40
2000	Brevard County (FSL)	A	.194	31	103	17	20	4	0	1	9	28	34	11
	Portland (EL)	AA	.276	74	221	39	61	17	3	6	42	44	64	8
2001	Portland (EL)	AA	.240	136	467	75	112	14	9	17	53	83	155	26
MINOR LEAGUE TOTALS			.261	537	1862	335	485	95	24	55	266	335	496	100

7. Claudio Vargas, rhp

Born: May 19, 1979. **Ht.:** 6-3. **Wt.:** 210. **Bats:** R. **Throws:** R. **Career Transactions:** Signed out of Dominican Republic by Marlins, Aug. 25, 1995.

Vargas' star took off in 1999 when he came back from a bout of shoulder tendinitis to throw 96 mph in a playoff game for Kane County. Vargas pitches at 92-93 mph and has touched 97 with his lively fastball. He has a smooth delivery and a live, loose arm to go with a solid pitcher's frame. He spent much of 2001 working on a three-quarters arm slot and showed a better, late-breaking curveball toward the end of the season. He has a bulldog mentality on the mound and loves to pitch up and in. He tends to leave pitches up, and his changeup still needs work. He also must maintain a consistent arm slot and finish his pitches. While other Marlins righthanders have struggled to stay healthy, Vargas has shown the durability of a future middle-of-the-rotation starter. He should get his first taste of Triple-A in 2002, with a big league callup possible in September.

Year	Club (League)	Class	W	L	ERA	G	GS	CG	SV	IP	H	R	ER	BB	SO
1996	Marlins (DSL)	R	2	3	3.09	15	4	0	0	47	41	25	16	26	37
1997	Marlins (DSL)	R	6	2	2.50	13	10	3	0	72	62	32	20	31	81
1998	Marlins (GCL)	R	0	4	4.08	5	4	0	0	29	24	15	13	7	27
	Brevard County (FSL)	A	0	1	4.66	2	2	0	0	10	15	5	5	4	9
1999	Kane County (Mid)	A	5	5	3.88	19	19	1	0	100	97	47	43	41	88
2000	Brevard County (FSL)	A	10	5	3.28	24	23	0	0	145	126	64	53	44	143
	Portland (EL)	AA	1	1	3.60	3	2	0	0	15	16	9	6	6	13
2001	Portland (EL)	AA	8	9	4.19	27	27	0	0	159	122	77	74	67	151
MINOR LEAGUE TOTALS			32	30	4.27	108	91	4	0	577	503	274	230	226	549

8. Blaine Neal, rhp

Born: April 6, 1978. **Ht.:** 6-5. **Wt.:** 205. **Bats:** L. **Throws:** R. **School:** Bishop Eustace HS, Pennsauken, N.J. **Career Transactions:** Selected by Marlins in fourth round of 1996 draft; signed July 13, 1996.

Neal was hampered by mysterious elbow problems his first two pro seasons. The Marlins tried him at first base, and he flopped there as well. Nearly released after the 1998 season, he had arthroscopic surgery to remove several bone spurs and shave down part of a bone to relieve pressure on a nerve. That led to his re-emergence as a pitcher. Neal comes right at hitters with a fastball that has touched 98 mph and sits at 93-95 mph with late movement. He has a short, quick curveball and a strong pitcher's frame with wide back muscles reminiscent of Goose Gossage. He has a smooth, easy delivery and a ferocious competitive streak. His demeanor hints at success as a future big league closer. Neal's fastball can get too straight, and some wonder if he has anything nasty enough to close games. He sometimes doesn't use his lower half, elevating his pitches and giving hitters a clear look. Neal struggled during his first September callup, but he'll be given every opportunity to make the back end of the bullpen in spring training.

Year	Club (League)	Class	W	L	ERA	G	GS	CG	SV	IP	H	R	ER	BB	SO
1996	Marlins (GCL)	R	1	1	4.60	7	5	0	1	29	32	18	15	6	15
1997	Marlins (GCL)	R	4	1	3.63	10	0	0	1	22	24	11	9	11	19
1999	Kane County (Mid)	A	4	2	2.32	26	0	0	6	31	21	8	8	10	31
2000	Brevard County (FSL)	A	2	2	2.15	41	0	0	11	54	40	27	13	24	65
2001	Portland (EL)	AA	2	3	2.36	54	0	0	21	53	43	17	14	21	45
	Florida (NL)	MAJ	0	0	6.75	4	0	0	0	5	7	4	4	5	3
MAJOR LEAGUE TOTALS			0	0	6.75	4	0	0	0	5	7	4	4	5	3
MINOR LEAGUE TOTALS			13	9	2.81	138	5	0	40	189	160	81	59	72	175

9. Josh Wilson, 2b/ss

Born: March 26, 1981. **Ht.:** 6-1. **Wt.:** 165. **Bats:** R. **Throws:** R. **School:** Mount Lebanon (Pa.) HS. **Career Transactions:** Selected by Marlins in third round of 1999 draft; signed June 5, 1999.

Son of the head baseball coach at Duquesne, Wilson developed quickly thanks to his lineage as well as his time with the U.S. junior national team. His instincts are advanced as a result. Wilson has shown marked improvement each year at the plate. He has shortened his swing considerably, allowing him not only to handle inside pitches but also to drive them into the gaps. He has a strong arm and improved his range after dropping some weight. He has quick feet, good agility and has shown the ability to play either middle-infield position as well as third base. His makeup is first-rate, and he carries himself with the confidence of a future big leaguer. Though he has good gap power, Wilson may never hit many home runs, likely ruling out a permanent move to third. His speed is just average, and he needs to get stronger. Wilson figures to start the year at Brevard County, where he again could team with shortstop Miguel Cabrera. If Cabrera is bumped up to Double-A, Wilson could move back to shortstop full-time. His versatility only increases his value.

Year	Club (League)	Class	AVG	G	AB	R	H	2B	3B	HR	RBI	BB	SO	SB
1999	Marlins (GCL)	R	.266	53	203	29	54	9	4	0	27	24	36	14
2000	Kane County (Mid)	A	.269	13	52	2	14	3	1	1	6	3	14	0
	Utica (NY-P)	A	.344	66	259	43	89	13	6	3	43	29	47	9
2001	Kane County (Mid)	A	.285	123	506	65	144	28	5	4	61	28	60	17
MINOR LEAGUE TOTALS			.295	255	1020	139	301	53	16	8	137	84	157	40

10. Rob Henkel, lhp

Born: Aug. 3, 1978. **Ht.:** 6-2. **Wt.:** 210. **Bats:** R. **Throws:** L. **School:** UCLA. **Career Transactions:** Selected by Marlins in third round of 2000 draft; signed Sept. 19, 2000.

Henkel turned down $700,000 from the Mets, who took him in the 20th round of the 1999 draft. After signing for $650,000 in September 2000, the former UCLA star spent nearly a year fighting a balky shoulder that caused his velocity to drop to the low 80s. Henkel worked hard to strengthen his shoulder and saw his velocity climb back up to 89-92 mph. He got six weeks in low Class A, then a brief taste of the Arizona Fall League, where he showed a much-improved changeup to go with his signature pitch, a devastating knuckle-curve with late, quick break. Already a survivor of Tommy John surgery, Henkel showed uncommon hunger and a willingness to attack his rehab with vigor. Henkel tends to overanalyze his performance, though that may be a byproduct of his frustration with the long recovery time. He needs innings after missing the past two summers. Henkel will open 2002 in Class A, but his maturity, intelligence, left-handedness and college time could allow him to move fast.

Year	Club (League)	Class	W	L	ERA	G	GS	CG	SV	IP	H	R	ER	BB	SO
2001	Marlins (GCL)	R	1	3	1.52	9	8	0	0	30	17	9	5	11	38
	Utica (NY-P)	A	0	0	4.32	3	3	0	0	8	7	4	4	6	11
	Kane County (Mid)	A	0	0	4.50	1	1	0	0	4	6	3	2	1	2
MINOR LEAGUE TOTALS			1	3	2.36	13	12	0	0	42	30	16	11	18	51

11. Jason Stokes, of

Born: Jan. 23, 1982. **Ht.:** 6-4. **Wt.:** 225. **Bats:** R. **Throws:** R. **School:** Coppell (Texas) HS. **Career Transactions:** Selected by Marlins in second round of 2000 draft; signed Aug. 29, 2000.

Ranked the top high school power hitter in the 2000 draft, Stokes dropped out of the top 10 only because of signability concerns. He was ready to attend Texas until the Marlins forked over a $2.027 million bonus. He was the leading hitter in extended spring training, launching several tape-measure shots. Stokes homered onto the roof of the Expos complex in Jupiter and another time sent a broken-bat shot over the left-field wall. His stay at short-season Utica, however, was sabotaged from the start by injuries. He went 3-for-5 in his professional debut, then landed on the disabled list with a sore lower back. The cause of the injury was unclear, with theories ranging from the torque of Stokes' swing to the poor quality of his mattress. Stokes missed a month, then pulled a hamstring after his return. After making progress in his routes and jumps back during extended spring, the converted first baseman played just five games in left field at Utica, serving mainly as a DH. Despite his raw power he tends to get too pull-conscious, missing badly on breaking balls and piling up strikeouts. He runs well for a big man but would run better if he lost 10-15 pounds.

Year	Club (League)	Class	AVG	G	AB	R	H	2B	3B	HR	RBI	BB	SO	SB
2001	Utica (NY-P)	A	.231	35	130	12	30	2	1	6	19	11	48	0
MINOR LEAGUE TOTALS			.231	35	130	12	30	2	1	6	19	11	48	0

12. Pablo Ozuna, 2b

Born: Aug. 25, 1978. **Ht.:** 6-0. **Wt.:** 160. **Bats:** R. **Throws:** R. **Career Transactions:** Signed out of the Dominican Republic by Cardinals, April 8, 1996 . . . Traded by Cardinals with RHP Braden Looper and LHP Armando Almanza to Marlins for SS Edgar Renteria, Dec. 14, 1998.

Ozuna was the key player in the deal that sent Edgar Renteria to the Cardinals. Some thought by now Ozuna would have taken over at second base for Luis Castillo, but it hasn't happened. He broke his left wrist playing last winter in the Dominican, then aggravated the injury during spring training. That led to surgery to correct the problem. He missed the whole summer but was back to full strength by instructional league, though he still had some tenderness. He again showed plus makeup as he attacked his rehab program and maintained his upbeat personality throughout the ordeal. He hoped to make up for lost time with another crack at winter ball, where he continued to swing at everything, as per his reputation. A classic bad-ball hitter, Ozuna has the hand-eye coordination and aggressiveness to put all manner of pitches into play. Though he projects as a top-of-the-order hitter, he shows little inclination to work counts. He's a legitimate basestealing threat and a decent bunter but could get better. His average and erratic arm caused the Marlins to switch Ozuna from shortstop to second base, where his defense remains shaky. A move to center field remains possible.

Year	Club (League)	Class	AVG	G	AB	R	H	2B	3B	HR	RBI	BB	SO	SB
1996	Cardinals (DSL)	R	.363	74	295	57	107	12	4	6	60	23	19	18
1997	Johnson City (Appy)	R	.323	56	232	40	75	13	1	5	24	10	24	23
1998	Peoria (Mid)	A	.357	133	538	122	192	27	10	9	62	29	56	62
1999	Portland (EL)	AA	.281	117	502	62	141	25	7	7	46	13	50	31
2000	Portland (EL)	AA	.308	118	464	74	143	25	6	7	59	40	55	35
	Florida (NL)	MAJ	.333	14	24	2	8	1	0	0	0	0	2	1
2001								Did Not Play—Injured						
MAJOR LEAGUE TOTALS			.333	14	24	2	8	1	0	0	0	0	2	1
MINOR LEAGUE TOTALS			.324	498	2031	355	658	102	28	34	251	115	204	169

13. Chip Ambres, of

Born: Dec. 19, 1979. **Ht.:** 6-1. **Wt.:** 190. **Bats:** R. **Throws:** R. **School:** West Brook HS, Beaumont, Texas. **Career Transactions:** Selected by Marlins in first round (27th overall) of 1998 draft; signed Aug. 3, 1998.

Bad luck has shadowed Ambres since the Marlins signed him for $1.5 million, wooing him away from a scholarship to play quarterback for Texas A&M. Concerns over prior knee and hamstring injuries caused him to slip from a projected top 10 pick to No. 27 overall in the 1998 draft. A nagging injury to his right hamstring hindered his 2000 season. Just before the end of his second season at Kane County in 2001, Ambres broke his right fibula when his cleat caught as he slid into second base. He had surgery to install a metal plate and several screws to set the bone. Until the injury, Ambres was supposed to play in the new Panamanian winter league, where it was hoped he could continue to build on adjustments he had made in his stance, swing and plate approach. When healthy he has outstanding speed, but he has yet to apply it fully on the basepaths. No one questions his makeup, intelligence and leadership. He rarely gets overpowered but still struggles with good breaking balls. He has gap power and could lead off or bat third. His arm is accurate but just average.

Year	Club (League)	Class	AVG	G	AB	R	H	2B	3B	HR	RBI	BB	SO	SB
1999	Marlins (GCL)	R	.353	37	139	29	49	13	3	1	15	25	19	22
	Utica (NY-P)	A	.267	28	105	24	28	3	6	5	15	21	25	11
2000	Kane County (Mid)	A	.231	84	320	46	74	16	3	7	28	52	72	26
2001	Kane County (Mid)	A	.265	96	377	79	100	26	8	5	41	53	81	19
MINOR LEAGUE TOTALS			.267	245	941	178	251	58	20	18	99	151	197	78

14. Kevin Olsen, rhp

Born: July 26, 1976. **Ht.:** 6-2. **Wt.:** 200. **Bats:** R. **Throws:** R. **School:** University of Oklahoma. **Career Transactions:** Selected by Marlins in 26th round of 1998 draft; signed June 6, 1998.

Granted a pair of late-season starts after a September callup from Double-A, Olsen impressed the Marlins brass with 13 straight scoreless innings before reporting to the Arizona Fall League. At 25, Olsen was older than Ryan Dempster, A.J. Burnett, Brad Penny and Josh Beckett—and wiser in some ways as well. While those four brandish fastballs that hum into the mid-90s, Olsen relies on an 89-91 mph sinker. He shows no fear and locates his fastball on both sides of the plate with pinpoint accuracy. Olsen posted a 144-21 strikeout-walk ratio at Portland, where he credited pitching coach Jeff Andrews with revamping his changeup, which now features more down action, and giving him a backdoor slider as yet another weapon against lefthanders. A 26th-round pick out of the University of Oklahoma in 1998, Olsen was signed for $1,000 on the recommendation of former crosschecker David Chadd, now the club's scouting director. If the cost-conscious Marlins deal a starter this winter, Olsen could move into the rotation. If nothing else, he has forced his way into the spring mix.

Year	Club (League)	Class	W	L	ERA	G	GS	CG	SV	IP	H	R	ER	BB	SO
1998	Utica (NY-P)	A	4	3	2.60	21	4	0	2	45	37	21	13	10	56
1999	Brevard County (FSL)	A	2	5	5.05	11	11	0	0	57	70	37	32	13	45

Year	Club (League)	Class	W	L	ERA	G	GS	CG	SV	IP	H	R	ER	BB	SO
	Kane County (Mid)	A	5	2	3.38	10	9	0	0	61	65	25	23	16	52
2000	Brevard County (FSL)	A	4	8	2.86	18	18	1	0	110	93	40	35	25	77
	Portland (EL)	AA	3	4	4.83	9	9	0	0	54	54	30	29	21	47
2001	Portland (EL)	AA	10	3	2.68	26	26	2	0	155	123	56	46	21	144
	Florida (NL)	MAJ	0	0	1.20	4	2	0	0	15	11	2	2	2	13
MAJOR LEAGUE TOTALS			0	0	1.20	4	2	0	0	15	11	2	2	2	13
MINOR LEAGUE TOTALS			28	25	3.32	95	77	3	2	482	442	209	178	106	421

15. Hansel Izquierdo, rhp

Born: Jan. 2, 1977. **Ht.:** 6-2. **Wt.:** 205. **Bats:** R. **Throws:** R. **School:** Southwest HS, Miami. **Career Transactions:** Selected by Marlins in seventh round of 1995 draft; signed June 14, 1995 . . . Released by Marlins, June 3, 1997 . . . Signed by White Sox, June 20, 1997 . . . Granted free agency, Oct. 17, 1997; re-signed by White Sox, Nov. 4, 1997 . . . Released by White Sox, May 4, 2000 . . . Signed by Indians, May 30, 2000 . . . Released by Indians, July 21, 2000 . . . Signed by independent Sonoma County (Western), August 2000 . . . Signed by Marlins, Nov. 10, 2000.

Marlins Latin American scouting director Louie Eljaua likes Izquierdo so much that he signed him twice. The first time was in 1995, after the Marlins drafted the former Cuban defector out of a Miami high school. He signed for $60,000 but poor work habits and imma-turity led to his release. Four years and two more releases later, Izquierdo returned to the Marlins for less than $3,000 after scout Keith Snider spotted him pitching in the independ-ent Western League. Despite beginning 2001 in the bullpen at Kane County, Izquierdo wound up 16-3, 2.68 at three stops. He came right at hitters with a 90-92 mph sinker and a plus slider. He needs to do a better job maintaining a consistent arm slot, but his meteoric rise took the organization by surprise. When Gary Knotts went down with a shoulder injury, Izquierdo took his place in the Arizona Fall League. He could contend for a job in the Marlins bullpen but probably will start at Triple-A Calgary.

Year	Club (League)	Class	W	L	ERA	G	GS	CG	SV	IP	H	R	ER	BB	SO
1995	Marlins (GCL)	R	0	0	0.00	1	0	0	0	2	3	3	0	2	0
1996	Marlins (GCL)	R	0	1	2.70	12	0	0	3	13	7	4	4	5	17
1997	White Sox (GCL)	R	0	0	3.48	5	0	0	0	10	9	4	4	8	15
	Bristol (Appy)	R	2	2	4.30	9	2	0	0	23	25	14	11	8	24
1998	Hickory (SAL)	A	9	11	4.37	28	27	2	0	175	159	104	85	76	186
	Winston-Salem (Car)	A	0	0	0.00	1	0	0	1	2	1	0	0	1	2
1999	Winston-Salem (Car)	A	3	5	4.14	18	13	0	0	83	76	46	38	46	72
2000	Birmingham (SL)	AA	1	2	7.50	8	0	0	0	12	12	11	10	5	5
	Kinston (Car)	A	1	3	4.79	10	5	0	1	41	39	29	22	13	34
	Sonoma County (West)	IND	0	1	9.69	4	3	0	0	13	16	14	14	17	10
2001	Kane County (Mid)	A	7	1	1.32	24	2	0	2	48	27	8	7	13	42
	Brevard County (FSL)	A	2	0	2.70	4	4	0	0	27	15	8	8	6	22
	Portland (EL)	AA	7	2	3.81	10	9	1	0	57	47	24	24	10	45
MINOR LEAGUE TOTALS			32	27	3.89	130	62	3	7	493	420	255	213	193	464

16. Will Smith, of

Born: Oct. 23, 1981. **Ht.:** 6-1. **Wt.:** 185. **Bats:** L. **Throws:** R. **School:** Palo Verde HS, Tucson. **Career Transactions:** Selected by Marlins in sixth round of 2000 draft; signed June 9, 2000.

Smith set the Arizona high school record for career home runs but projects as more of a gap-power run producer. Despite an unorthodox stance that has been described as Yaz Lite, he shows a knack for putting the fat part of the bat on the ball. He wore down late in the season, his first full year in pro ball, but rebounded nicely in instructional league. He dropped his back elbow at the club's urging during instructional league and started hitting more balls with authority to left-center. Smith was given a look in center field but lacks the speed for that position. He has played both corner outfield spots and worked hard to improve his routes and jumps, but his arm is a little short for anything but left field. He's no threat on the bases and needs to work on his upper body as well as his strike-zone judg-ment, but overall has taken club officials by surprise with his success to this point.

Year	Club (League)	Class	AVG	G	AB	R	H	2B	3B	HR	RBI	BB	SO	SB
2000	Marlins (GCL)	R	.368	54	204	37	75	21	2	2	34	26	24	7
2001	Kane County (Mid)	A	.280	125	535	92	150	26	2	16	91	32	74	4
MINOR LEAGUE TOTALS			.305	179	739	129	225	47	4	18	125	58	98	11

17. Ramon Castillo, rhp

Born: Dec. 24, 1978. **Ht.:** 6-1. **Wt.:** 155. **Bats:** R. **Throws:** R. **Career Transactions:** Signed out of Dominican Republic by Marlins, Sept. 28, 1995.

Signed as a teenager for $3,000, Castillo slowly has blossomed into a prospect. Sent home for violating team rules midway through the 2000 season, he bounced back with his best year yet, leading Kane County in wins, starts, innings and strikeouts. He pitches at 90-92 mph with good life, topping out at 94, and gets lots of ground balls with his sinker. He shows a plus curve with good depth and late break. His changeup is solid for this stage. Castillo has allowed more hits than innings in all six of his pro seasons, but his supporters say that's because he's around the plate so much. Castillo has a tall, lean frame and a low-effort delivery. His makeup remains a question, as he gets moody at times and can be hard to read, but most believe he is a good person at heart. He might be higher on this list if he were a year or two younger.

Year	Club (League)	Class	W	L	ERA	G	GS	CG	SV	IP	H	R	ER	BB	SO
1996	Marlins (DSL)	R	0	1	13.50	12	0	0	0	14	31	25	21	10	6
1997	Marlins (DSL)	R	4	3	5.10	12	1	0	0	42	49	31	24	15	34
1998	Marlins (DSL)	R	5	4	4.27	13	13	1	0	71	80	52	34	21	55
1999	Marlins (GCL)	R	1	2	3.46	11	10	0	0	52	56	21	20	12	34
2000	Utica (NY-P)	A	4	4	4.75	13	13	0	0	66	80	44	35	31	47
2001	Kane County (Mid)	A	11	2	3.80	28	28	0	0	159	178	79	67	31	108
MINOR LEAGUE TOTALS			25	16	4.48	89	65	1	0	404	474	252	201	120	284

18. Ronald Belizario, rhp

Born: Dec. 31, 1982. **Ht.:** 6-2. **Wt.:** 148. **Bats:** R. **Throws:** R. **Career Transactions:** Signed out of Venezuela by Marlins, Aug. 2, 1999.

Signed the same week as fellow Venezuelan Miguel Cabrera, Belizario came to the Marlins with less fanfare and far cheaper, signing for less than $60,000. Of course, back then Belizario weighed 148 pounds and was topping out at 80 mph. He has grown another inch and packed 30 pounds onto his frame and now pitches at 90-92 mph and touches 95. He has a nasty sinker with hard boring action. He also has a solid curveball and changeup. Belizario has a good personality and loves to compete, though he remains somewhat immature, taking bad results and constructive criticism too personally. He has a flair on the mound that sometimes borders on Perezesque. He also likes to experiment, dropping down to the side at times in a needless effort to trick hitters. He figures to start the year at Kane County.

Year	Club (League)	Class	W	L	ERA	G	GS	CG	SV	IP	H	R	ER	BB	SO
2000	Universidad (VSL)	R	2	3	7.39	17	5	0	6	35	37	34	29	18	27
2001	Marlins (GCL)	R	4	6	2.34	13	10	1	0	73	62	29	19	20	54
MINOR LEAGUE TOTALS			6	9	3.99	30	15	1	6	108	99	63	48	38	81

19. Wes Anderson, rhp

Born: Sept. 10, 1979. **Ht.:** 6-4. **Wt.:** 175. **Bats:** R. **Throws:** R. **School:** Pine Bluff (Ark.) HS. **Career Transactions:** Selected by Marlins in 14th round of 1997 draft; signed Aug. 18, 1997.

If not for Josh Beckett, Anderson would have topped this list last winter. Now he faces a long rehabilitation after undergoing arthroscopic surgery at season's end to repair an 85 percent tear in his labrum and minor fraying in his rotator cuff. Anderson was told not to throw for six months and most likely is looking at a midseason return at the earliest. The mannerly kid from rural Arkansas missed all but one inning over the final 3½ months with a combination of back spasms and shoulder pain. Shoulder problems had landed Anderson on the disabled list for a month in each of the previous two seasons, but he traced the severe pain to late in the 2000 season. He underwent an MRI then that showed a minor labrum tear, and was shut down after one instructional league start. Dr. James Andrews recommended a course of rest and strengthening exercises in hopes that Anderson could avoid surgery. The shoulder was fine for his first trip to major league spring training but he began experiencing pain just before Opening Day. When Anderson's velocity dropped from its usual 91-94 mph range to as low as 84 mph, he knew something was wrong but thought he could pitch through what he believed to be a dead-arm period. The Marlins will be extremely patient with Anderson, who previously showed a plus slider and decent changeup.

Year	Club (League)	Class	W	L	ERA	G	GS	CG	SV	IP	H	R	ER	BB	SO
1998	Marlins (GCL)	R	5	2	1.39	11	11	1	0	65	44	25	10	18	66
1999	Kane County (Mid)	A	9	5	3.21	23	23	2	0	137	111	55	49	51	134
2000	Brevard County (FSL)	A	6	9	3.42	22	21	0	0	116	108	55	44	66	91
2001	Marlins (GCL)	R	0	1	27.00	1	1	0	0	0	3	2	1	1	0
	Brevard County (FSL)	A	1	6	5.63	8	8	0	0	32	48	26	20	21	17
MINOR LEAGUE TOTALS			21	23	3.19	65	64	3	0	350	314	163	124	157	308

20. Geoff Goetz, lhp

Born: April 3, 1979. **Ht.:** 5-11. **Wt.:** 163. **Bats:** L. **Throws:** L. **School:** Jesuit HS, Tampa. **Career Transactions:** Selected by Mets in first round (sixth overall) of 1997 draft; signed July 1, 1997 . . . Traded by Mets to Marlins, July 3, 1998, completing trade in which Marlins sent C Mike Piazza to Mets for OF Preston Wilson, LHP Ed Yarnall and a player to be named (May 22, 1998).

Goetz isn't the only one frustrated by his slow development. Despite an organizational commitment to baby his shoulder, he has not been able to stay healthy. He missed 11 weeks in 2001 with shoulder tendinitis. Goetz was effective in a long-relief role in his first full season at Portland but can't pitch on consecutive days without concern. He mixes a 90-93 mph fastball with a plus knuckle-curve and a developing changeup. He could use more consistency with his curve, which has a big hump and rarely gets hit hard. He needs to learn to control his emotions on the mound, where he tends to show his frustrations, sometimes lapsing into the violent delivery of his past. Once considered a future starter, he now projects as a situational lefthander, and even then there are doubts about his durability.

Year	Club (League)	Class	W	L	ERA	G	GS	CG	SV	IP	H	R	ER	BB	SO
1997	Mets (GCL)	R	0	2	2.73	8	6	0	1	26	23	11	8	18	28
1998	Capital City (SAL)	A	5	4	3.96	15	15	0	0	77	68	45	34	37	68
	Kane County (Mid)	A	1	4	4.64	9	9	0	0	43	44	22	22	24	36
1999	Kane County (Mid)	A	5	3	4.26	16	12	0	0	51	52	28	24	24	43
2000	Brevard County (FSL)	A	6	2	1.75	27	0	0	5	67	43	19	13	36	61
	Portland (EL)	AA	1	2	5.96	17	0	0	1	23	27	15	15	11	21
2001	Portland (EL)	AA	2	2	1.53	25	0	0	0	29	22	10	5	12	24
MINOR LEAGUE TOTALS			20	19	3.45	117	42	0	7	316	279	150	121	162	281

21. Jose Soto, of

Born: June 20, 1980. **Ht.:** 6-0. **Wt.:** 160. **Bats:** B. **Throws:** R. **Career Transactions:** Signed out of Dominican Republic by Marlins, Nov. 5, 1996.

Soto retains his status as a potential five-tool player but has not been able to translate those gifts into production. A switch-hitter with plus power, he has yet to make it out of short-season ball. Still painfully raw, Soto strikes out too frequently and shows little inclination to make adjustments. He has above-average speed and arm strength and is solid defensively, though he still must improve his jumps and routes. He has perhaps the quickest hands in the organization but tends to jump at pitches and make easy outs. He has power to all fields and uses the same swing from both sides. He showed his best improvement as a basestealer, getting caught just twice in 17 attempts. Soto is shy and tends to lose confidence easily. He was healthy again after an injury to his throwing shoulder limited him to pinch-hitting and DH in 2000. He should get his first exposure to full-season ball this year.

Year	Club (League)	Class	AVG	G	AB	R	H	2B	3B	HR	RBI	BB	SO	SB
1997	Marlins (DSL)	R	.247	40	77	13	19	2	0	2	5	14	33	5
1998	Marlins (DSL)	R	.250	66	232	46	58	10	1	6	36	33	64	17
1999	Marlins (GCL)	R	.229	49	175	17	40	8	0	4	20	14	56	10
2000	Marlins (GCL)	R	.218	42	165	24	36	9	2	3	19	12	62	8
2001	Utica (NY-P)	A	.229	48	192	22	44	7	3	2	17	13	52	15
	Brevard County (FSL)	A	.200	2	5	1	1	0	0	0	0	1	2	0
MINOR LEAGUE TOTALS			247	846	123	198	36	6	17	97	87	269	55	

22. Jim Kavourias, of

Born: Oct. 4, 1979. **Ht.:** 6-4. **Wt.:** 230. **Bats:** R. **Throws:** R. **School:** University of Tampa. **Career Transactions:** Selected by Marlins in fifth round of 2000 draft; signed June 12, 2000.

Kavourias hit more home runs than anyone in the system who didn't play in the Pacific Coast League. A hulking figure, he has big-time power. Kavourias has a tendency to pull off pitches and seems reluctant to use the opposite field, even though he has more than enough pop to hit balls out that way. His bat is quick enough to make it difficult to pitch him inside. Some question Kavourias' commitment to the non-hitting aspects of the game, though he did show improved intensity over the final two months. He must work on his outfield play, which right now is below-average. His routes have gotten better but he still has a ways to go. His arm is strong enough but erratic. With improvement he projects as a right fielder in the big leagues.

Year	Club (League)	Class	AVG	G	AB	R	H	2B	3B	HR	RBI	BB	SO	SB
2000	Utica (NY-P)	A	.320	15	50	7	16	4	0	2	7	10	6	1
2001	Kane County (Mid)	A	.261	120	460	77	120	30	4	23	88	48	126	11
MINOR LEAGUE TOTALS			.267	135	510	84	136	34	4	25	95	58	132	12

23. Nate Rolison, 1b

Born: March 27, 1977. **Ht.:** 6-6. **Wt.:** 240. **Bats:** L. **Throws:** R. **School:** Petal (Miss.) HS. **Career Transactions:** Selected by Marlins in second round of 1995 draft; signed June 30, 1995.

Just when Rolison's career was taking off, a freak injury ruined his 2001 season. Rolison fractured the hamate bone in his right wrist while taking batting practice during the winter. He had surgery and a screw was placed in his hand. He rushed back for spring training, but suffered the first of several setbacks. He struggled mightily in the Arizona Fall League, where he took tentative swings and appeared overmatched. Nothing was structurally wrong with his wrist, but Rolison admitted his confidence needed to be rebuilt. The Marlins' minor league player of the year in 2000, Rolison has some of the best power in the organization. It took him awhile, but he learned to turn on pitches on the inner half and drive them out of the park. His strike-zone recognition is good. His defense and speed are below-average, but if he is healthy and productive he should be able to make the final step to the majors.

Year	Club (League)	Class	AVG	G	AB	R	H	2B	3B	HR	RBI	BB	SO	SB
1995	Marlins (GCL)	R	.276	37	134	22	37	10	2	1	19	15	34	0
1996	Kane County (Mid)	A	.243	131	474	63	115	28	1	14	75	66	170	3
1997	Brevard County (FSL)	A	.256	122	473	59	121	22	0	16	65	38	143	3
1998	Portland (EL)	AA	.277	131	484	80	134	35	2	16	83	64	150	5
1999	Portland (EL)	AA	.299	124	438	71	131	20	1	17	69	68	112	0
2000	Calgary (PCL)	AAA	.330	123	443	88	146	37	3	23	88	70	117	3
	Florida (NL)	MAJ	.077	8	13	0	1	0	0	0	2	1	4	0
2001	Marlins (GCL)	R	.500	2	4	1	2	0	0	0	1	3	1	0
	Brevard County (FSL)	A	.378	14	45	7	17	3	0	1	6	10	7	0
	Portland (EL)	AA	.211	5	19	1	4	1	0	0	2	1	7	0
	Calgary (PCL)	AAA	.167	3	12	1	2	0	0	0	1	1	3	0
MAJOR LEAGUE TOTALS			.077	8	13	0	1	0	0	0	2	1	4	0
MINOR LEAGUE TOTALS			.281	692	2526	393	709	156	9	88	409	336	744	14

24. Gary Knotts, rhp

Born: Feb. 12, 1977. **Ht.:** 6-4. **Wt.:** 200. **Bats:** R. **Throws:** R. **School:** Northwest Alabama CC. **Career Transactions:** Selected by Marlins in 11th round of 1995 draft; signed May 11, 1996 . . . Granted free agency, Dec. 21, 1999; re-signed by Marlins, Dec. 21, 1999.

Knotts' first major league callup led to the first health scare of his career. Not wanting to say anything after he felt shoulder discomfort in his big league debut in late August, Knotts aggravated it during his first major league start five days later. He had a small tear in his rotator cuff and was shut down for the winter, though surgery wasn't required. Signed for $35,000 as a draft-and-follow, Knotts adjusted well to the high altitude of the Pacific Coast League. He learned to mix in more changeups to go with a power curve and a fastball that tops out at 95 mph. When he's on, his two-seamer produces plenty of groundballs. His strong pitcher's body should make him a future workhorse. Knotts has the upside of a No. 3 or 4 starter but initially could work his way into the Marlins' plans through long relief.

Year	Club (League)	Class	W	L	ERA	G	GS	CG	SV	IP	H	R	ER	BB	SO
1996	Marlins (GCL)	R	4	2	2.04	12	9	1	0	57	35	16	13	17	46
1997	Kane County (Mid)	A	1	5	13.05	7	7	0	0	20	33	34	29	17	19
	Utica (NY-P)	A	3	5	3.62	12	12	1	0	70	70	34	28	27	65
1998	Kane County (Mid)	A	8	8	3.87	27	27	3	0	158	144	84	68	66	148
1999	Brevard County (FSL)	A	9	6	4.60	16	16	3	0	94	101	52	48	29	65
	Portland (EL)	AA	6	3	3.75	12	12	1	0	82	79	39	34	33	63
2000	Portland (EL)	AA	9	8	4.66	27	27	2	0	156	161	102	81	63	113
2001	Calgary (PCL)	AAA	6	7	5.46	21	21	1	0	119	136	77	72	43	104
	Florida (NL)	MAJ	0	1	6.00	2	1	0	0	6	7	4	4	1	9
MAJOR LEAGUE TOTALS			0	1	6.00	2	1	0	0	6	7	4	4	1	9
MINOR LEAGUE TOTALS			46	44	4.44	134	131	12	0	756	759	438	373	295	623

25. Jason Grilli, rhp

Born: Nov. 11, 1976. **Ht.:** 6-4. **Wt.:** 185. **Bats:** R. **Throws:** R. **School:** Seton Hall University. **Career Transactions:** Selected by Giants in first round (fourth overall) of 1997 draft; signed July 24, 1997 . . . Traded by Giants with RHP Nate Bump to Marlins for RHP Livan Hernandez, July 24, 1999.

Grilli shocked everyone except perhaps himself when he won a spot in the Marlins rotation out of spring training last year. Just months removed from arthroscopic elbow surgery to repair a stress fracture, he showed a smooth delivery, good feel for his curveball and changeup and a 90-92 mph sinker that produced easy groundballs. He also displayed the self-confidence and moxie one might expect from the son of a former big league pitcher

(Steve Grilli, now a Cardinals scout). Upon his demotion to Triple-A in early May, Grilli was inconsistent but had by far his best career success at that level. He suffered a setback with forearm tightness, and nerve and disc problems in his upper back ended a September callup and wiped out a trip to the Arizona Fall League. His availability for the start of spring training was in question. It's uncertain whether Grilli's health ever will allow him to live up to the $1.875 million signing bonus the Giants gave him back in 1997.

Year	Club (League)	Class	W	L	ERA	G	GS	CG	SV	IP	H	R	ER	BB	SO
1998	Shreveport (TL)	AA	7	10	3.79	21	21	3	0	123	113	60	52	37	100
	Fresno (PCL)	AAA	2	3	5.14	8	8	0	0	42	49	30	24	18	37
1999	Fresno (PCL)	AAA	7	5	5.54	19	19	1	0	101	124	69	62	39	76
	Calgary (PCL)	AAA	1	5	7.68	8	8	0	0	41	56	48	35	23	27
2000	Calgary (PCL)	AAA	1	4	7.19	8	8	0	0	41	58	37	33	23	21
	Florida (NL)	MAJ	1	0	5.40	1	1	0	0	7	11	4	4	2	3
2001	Marlins (GCL)	R	0	0	0.00	2	2	0	0	4	2	0	0	0	6
	Brevard County (FSL)	A	2	0	1.98	3	3	0	0	14	12	4	3	5	14
	Portland (EL)	AA	0	1	2.25	1	1	0	0	4	3	1	1	0	3
	Calgary (PCL)	AAA	1	2	4.02	8	8	0	0	47	46	26	21	20	35
MAJOR LEAGUE TOTALS			1	0	5.40	1	1	0	0	7	11	4	4	2	3
MINOR LEAGUE TOTALS			21	30	5.02	78	78	4	0	414	463	275	231	165	319

26. Jon Asahina, rhp/dh

Born: Dec. 31, 1980. **Ht.:** 6-1. **Wt.:** 190. **Bats:** R. **Throws:** R. **School:** Fresno CC. **Career Transactions:** Selected by Marlins in 31st round of 2000 draft; signed May 29, 2001.

Left without a first-round pick in 2001 for the first time in club history, Florida signed Asahina as a $512,000 draft-and-follow. The Northern California junior college player of the year, Asahina is intriguing as a two-way prospect. A switch-hitter in college, he abandoned the left side as a DH at Utica, showing gap power. Though not imposing, he has a 91-95 mph fastball with good movement. He also throws a knee-buckling curve with a late break, a pitch the Marlins emphasized over his slider. His changeup can be a plus pitch when he maintains his arm speed, but he struggles with that at times. He clearly was tired by instructional league after throwing more than 200 innings in 2001, and his velocity dropped as a result. While some see him as a pitcher only, others want to see more of his bat. He's a good enough athlete to merit a look at third base or catcher, depending on his success on the mound.

Year	Club (League)	Class	W	L	ERA	G	GS	CG	SV	IP	H	R	ER	BB	SO
2001	Utica (NY-P)	A	4	6	2.58	15	13	0	0	70	56	27	20	19	55
MINOR LEAGUE TOTALS			4	6	2.58	15	13	0	0	70	56	27	20	19	55

Year	Club (League)	Class	AVG	G	AB	R	H	2B	3B	HR	RBI	BB	SO	SB
2001	Utica (NY-P)	A	.217	30	60	5	13	1	0	0	4	6	14	0
MINOR LEAGUE TOTALS			.217	30	60	5	13	1	0	0	4	6	14	0

27. Jesus Medrano, 2b/ss

Born: Sept. 11, 1978. **Ht.:** 6-0. **Wt.:** 185. **Bats:** R. **Throws:** R. **School:** Bishop Amat HS, La Puente, Calif. **Career Transactions:** Selected by Marlins in 11th round of 1997 draft; signed June 19, 1997.

Few players in the system utilize their speed better than Medrano. He's a proficient bunter with a line-drive stroke who finally learned to avoid hitting fly balls. He's good on the hit-and-run and knows how to move runners over. He shows a solid grasp of the strike zone, which maximizes his gift on the bases. For his career Medrano has been successful on nearly 83 percent of his stolen-base attempts. He exudes confidence on the basepaths, displaying an aggressiveness the Marlins would like to see him take to the plate. He gets excellent jumps and reads. In the field he made the most of a 21-game audition at shortstop, opening eyes with his range and arm, but the organizational backlog at the position probably rules out a permanent move. He was improved at second base as well, slicing his errors from 29 to 17. He needs to improve his body language, which tends to betray his frustrations.

Year	Club (League)	Class	AVG	G	AB	R	H	2B	3B	HR	RBI	BB	SO	SB
1997	Marlins (GCL)	R	.279	40	111	20	31	4	0	0	16	19	18	16
1998	Marlins (GCL)	R	.286	48	175	42	50	11	1	2	15	21	30	26
1999	Kane County (Mid)	A	.274	118	445	64	122	26	5	5	46	36	92	42
2000	Brevard County (FSL)	A	.219	117	466	56	102	18	3	3	46	48	98	32
2001	Brevard County (FSL)	A	.251	124	454	93	114	15	2	1	32	51	81	61
MINOR LEAGUE TOTALS			.254	447	1651	275	419	74	11	11	155	175	319	177

28. Brett Roneberg, of

Born: Feb. 5, 1979. **Ht.:** 6-2. **Wt.:** 205. **Bats:** L. **Throws:** L. **Career Transactions:** Signed out of Australia by Marlins, Feb. 1, 1996.

Roneberg has received valuable experience with the Australian national team, joining the team for the Sydney Olympics as well as the World Cup in Taiwan. Those assignments added more polish to a swing that is among the more advanced in the system. Roneberg is a late developer with deceptive power and an excellent grasp of the strike zone. He hangs in well against lefthanders and uses the whole field. He is learning to turn on inside pitches. He reminds some of Jim Eisenreich, another unimposing lefty hitter with below-average speed who made solid contact. Roneberg gets in trouble sometimes by taking too many pitches. He's a good two-strike hitter and enjoys working counts but could stand to show more aggressiveness on get-ahead fastballs. He has a right fielder's arm and has proven competent in left and at first base. He projects as a valuable fourth outfielder in the majors.

Year	Club (League)	Class	AVG	G	AB	R	H	2B	3B	HR	RBI	BB	SO	SB
1996	Marlins (GCL)	R	.213	50	174	23	37	8	0	1	15	11	39	0
1997	Marlins (GCL)	R	.265	53	185	25	49	11	2	0	13	28	35	6
1998	Kane County (Mid)	A	.271	68	240	35	65	7	0	3	35	25	50	2
1999	Kane County (Mid)	A	.288	132	511	88	147	32	4	8	68	79	82	3
2000	Brevard County (FSL)	A	.261	125	445	51	116	18	2	2	45	77	60	4
2001	Brevard County (FSL)	A	.299	88	331	49	99	20	4	11	63	50	54	5
	Portland (EL)	AA	.262	49	164	17	43	11	0	5	19	17	25	1
MINOR LEAGUE TOTALS			.271	565	2050	288	556	107	12	30	258	287	345	21

29. Kevin Hooper, 2b

Born: Dec. 7, 1976. **Ht.:** 5-10. **Wt.:** 160. **Bats:** R. **Throws:** R. **School:** Wichita State University. **Career Transactions:** Selected by Marlins in eighth round of 1999 draft; signed June 3, 1999.

In a system filled with tools guys and power arms, Hooper stands out for makeup. He draws comparisons to Anaheim's David Eckstein for his grit, intelligence, speed and instincts. Others see a young Casey Candaele. As with both of those gamers, you underestimate Hooper at your own risk. His body is undefined and unimpressive, yet he's an exceptionally fast runner who has a good feel for stealing bases. At the plate he's weak and gets jammed frequently, but he leads the system in flares to all fields. "Second serves," his supporters call them. Hooper has a good grasp of the strike zone and knows how to work counts. What makes him intriguing are his plus arm strength and range, both of which are good enough for the left side of the infield. While he played second base last year, he could make the move to a utility role, including some center field, in preparation for the majors.

Year	Club (League)	Class	AVG	G	AB	R	H	2B	3B	HR	RBI	BB	SO	SB
1999	Utica (NY-P)	A	.280	73	289	52	81	18	6	0	22	39	35	14
2000	Kane County (Mid)	A	.249	123	457	73	114	25	6	3	38	73	83	17
2001	Kane County (Mid)	A	.292	17	65	11	19	2	0	0	4	11	13	3
	Portland (EL)	AA	.308	117	468	70	144	19	6	2	39	59	78	24
MINOR LEAGUE TOTALS			.280	330	1279	206	358	64	18	5	103	182	209	58

30. Derek Wathan, ss

Born: Dec. 13, 1976. **Ht.:** 6-3. **Wt.:** 190. **Bats:** B. **Throws:** R. **School:** University of Oklahoma. **Career Transactions:** Selected by Marlins in second round of 1998 draft; signed June 8, 1998.

Wathan's makeup, instincts and leadership skills are unquestioned. Like his father, former Royals player and manager John Wathan, Derek is a take-charge type who commands the respect of teammates and opponents alike. It's the rest of his game that's open to debate. While some scouts think he could play defensively in the majors now, others say his agility and range are a little short. His arm is just average, but he compensates with a quick release. His lack of offense is troubling. He seemed to improve last year after his older brother Dusty, a catcher, was released off the Portland roster. Wathan's bat tends to drag through the zone and he doesn't have much pop. A switch-hitter, he had made strides from the left side in 2000 but was largely unimpressive last year. He figures to open 2002 in Calgary.

Year	Club (League)	Class	AVG	G	AB	R	H	2B	3B	HR	RBI	BB	SO	SB
1998	Utica (NY-P)	A	.268	60	224	32	60	8	2	0	23	21	35	10
1999	Kane County (Mid)	A	.254	125	469	71	119	18	4	1	49	53	54	33
2000	Brevard County (FSL)	A	.258	91	364	53	94	18	6	6	49	45	54	19
	Portland (EL)	AA	.220	41	141	13	31	3	2	0	17	13	20	3
2001	Portland (EL)	AA	.252	127	469	65	118	12	8	4	35	45	83	25
MINOR LEAGUE TOTALS			.253	444	1667	234	422	59	22	11	173	177	246	90

HOUSTON
Astros

By Jim Callis

I n many ways, the Astros are a model franchise. They've never had more than a midsized payroll, and until Enron Field their revenues were just ordinary. Yet they keep winning and adding prospects, year after year after year.

Houston hit bottom in 2000, going 72-90 to end streaks of three consecutive National League Central titles and eight straight non-losing seasons. Yet the Astros bounced right back in 2001, improving by 21 wins to post the best record in the NL and capture another division crown. Righthander Roy Oswalt was the best rookie pitcher in baseball.

Houston was impressive in the minor leagues as well, leading all organizations with a .598 winning percentage. Class A Lexington won the South Atlantic League and had the best record in the minors at 92-48 (.657). All four full-season affiliates made the playoffs, with Triple-A New Orleans sharing the Pacific Coast League title. The Astros were honored as Baseball America's Organization of the Year for the first time in the 20-year history of the award, while Double-A Round Rock's Jackie Moore was named BA's Minor League Manager of the Year. Even the Astros' Latin American program had success in 2001, as their Dominican Summer League team post-ed the best regular-season record of 33 teams and their Venezuelan Summer League squad won the title in that league.

The Astros don't spend lavishly to acquire amateurs, but they spend wisely. They pay below market value for their first-round picks, yet their choices over the past decade stack up well. Phil Nevin (1992), Billy Wagner (1993) and Lance Berkman (1997) have become stars. Chris Burke (2001) looks like he'll do the same, as could Brad Lidge (1998) and Robert Stiehl (2000) if they stay healthy.

Houston also has excelled at identifying talented but less expensive college seniors (Jason Lane, Morgan Ensberg, Chad Qualls), using the draft-and-follow process (Oswalt and Tim Redding) and working Venezuela (Richard Hidalgo and Carlos Hernandez, plus the departed Bob Abreu and Freddy Garcia). The result is a system deep at almost every position.

The organization has just two obvious weaknesses. It lacks a high Class A club, which alters the normal development path of prospects. That should be addressed after 2002. The other has been a failure to advance past the Division Series, where the Astros have gone 2-12. They're simply too talented for those stumbles to continue.

OrganizationOverview

General manager: Gerry Hunsicker. Farm director: Tim Purpura. Scouting director: David Lakey.

2001 PERFORMANCE

Class	Team	League	W	L	Pct.	Finish*	Manager
Majors	Houston	National	93	69	.574	t-1 (16)	Larry Dierker
Triple-A	New Orleans Zephyrs	Pacific Coast	82	57	.590	2nd (16)	Tony Pena
Double-A	Round Rock Express	Texas	86	54	.614	1st (8)	Jackie Moore
Low A	Michigan Battle Cats	Midwest	82	55	.599	3rd (14)	John Massarelli
Low A	Lexington Legends	South Atlantic	92	48	.657	1st (16)	J.J. Cannon
Short-season	† Pittsfield Astros	New York-Penn	45	30	.600	4th (14)	Ivan DeJesus
Rookie	Martinsville Astros	Appalachian	31	37	.456	t-7th (10)	Jorge Orta
OVERALL 2001 MINOR LEAGUE RECORD			418	281	.598	1st (30)	

*Finish in overall standings (No. of teams in league). †Affiliate will be in Troy, N.Y., in 2002.

ORGANIZATION LEADERS

BATTING

*AVG	**Jason Maule**, Michigan	.347
R	Jason Lane, Round Rock	103
H	Jason Lane, Round Rock	166
TB	Jason Lane, Round Rock	320
2B	Felix Escalona, Lexington	42
3B	Henry Stanley, Michigan	12
HR	Jason Lane, Round Rock	38
RBI	Jason Lane, Round Rock	124
BB	Jon Topolski, Lexington	75
SO	Keith Ginter, New Orleans	147
SB	**Jason Maule**, Michigan	56

PITCHING

W	Three tied at	15
L	Darwin Peguero, Lexington	10
#ERA	D.J. Houlton, Martinsville	2.69
G	Travis Wade, Round Rock	60
CG	**Mike Nannini**, Lexington	4
SV	Jim Mann, New Orleans	27
IP	**Mike Nannini**, Lexington	190
BB	Anthony Pluta, Lexington	86
SO	Carlos Hernandez, Round Rock	167

*Minimum 250 At-Bats #Minimum 75 Innings

TOP PROSPECTS OF THE DECADE

1992	Brian Williams, rhp
1993	Todd Jones, rhp
1994	Phil Nevin, 3b
1995	Brian Hunter, of
1996	Billy Wagner, lhp
1997	Richard Hidalgo, of
1998	Richard Hidalgo, of
1999	Lance Berkman, of
2000	Wilfredo Rodriguez, lhp
2001	Roy Oswalt, rhp

TOP DRAFT PICKS OF THE DECADE

1992	Phil Nevin, 3b
1993	Billy Wagner, lhp
1994	Ramon Castro, c
1995	Tony McKnight, rhp
1996	Mark Johnson, rhp
1997	Lance Berkman, 1b
1998	Brad Lidge, rhp
1999	Mike Rosamond, of
2000	Robert Stiehl, rhp
2001	Chris Burke, ss

Maule   **Nannini**

BEST TOOLS

Best Hitter for Average	Chris Burke
Best Power Hitter	Jason Lane
Fastest Baserunner	Modesto de Aza
Best Fastball	Brad Lidge
Best Breaking Ball	Brad Lidge
Best Changeup	Kirk Saarloos
Best Control	Mike Nannini
Best Defensive Catcher	John Buck
Best Defensive Infielder	Adam Everett
Best Infield Arm	Adam Everett
Best Defensive Outfielder	Mike Rosamond
Best Outfield Arm	Mike Rosamond

PROJECTED 2005 LINEUP

Catcher	John Buck
First Base	Jeff Bagwell
Second Base	Tommy Whiteman
Third Base	Morgan Ensberg
Shortstop	Chris Burke
Left Field	Daryle Ward
Center Field	Richard Hidalgo
Right Field	Lance Berkman
No. 1 Starter	Roy Oswalt
No. 2 Starter	Tim Redding
No. 3 Starter	Wade Miller
No. 4 Starter	Carlos Hernandez
No. 5 Starter	Brad Lidge
Closer	Billy Wagner

ALL-TIME LARGEST BONUSES

Chris Burke, 2001	$2,125,000
Robert Stiehl, 2000	$1,250,000
Brad Lidge, 1998	$1,070,000
Lance Berkman, 1997	$1,000,000
Mark Johnson, 1996	$775,000

DraftAnalysis

2001 Draft

Best Pro Debut: SS Chris Burke (1) and RHP **Kirk Saarloos** (3), All-Americans in the spring, had no problem adjusting to Class A ball. Burke hit .300-3-17 at Michigan, and Saarloos went 1-1, 1.17 with 11 saves and a 40-7 strikeout-walk ratio at Lexington.

Best Athlete: OF Charlton Jimerson (5) was an unknown when the Astros drafted him in the 25th round in 1997 and tried to persuade him to go to junior college. Instead he wound up at Miami on an academic scholarship. He raised his profile considerably as the outstanding player at last year's College World Series as he led the Hurricanes to the title. He has tremendous tools, though he's raw after playing sparingly at Miami.

Best Hitter: Burke and OF Mike Rodriguez (2) should both hit for average at the top of a batting order.

Best Raw Power: Jimerson resembles a young Eric Davis with his power and speed. Pittsfield is a tough home run park, but Jimerson hit nine homers in 197 at-bats.

Fastest Runner: Burke, Rodriguez and Jimerson all have above-average speed. In a 60-yard dash, Rodriguez probably would win in 6.3-6.4 seconds.

Best Defensive Player: The only question with Burke was whether he had the arm to stay at shortstop. After watching him last summer, both the Astros and Midwest League managers were convinced that he does. Jimerson and Rodriguez are plus defenders in the outfield, and Brooks

Conrad (8) is a solid second baseman.

Best Fastball: RHP Joey DeLeon (18), one of two prep players signed by Houston, throws 95 mph. The Astros also found two lefthanders who can reach 92-93 mph in Russ Rohlicek (6) and Chris Little (12).

Most Intriguing Background: Jimerson's inspring story is chronicled on Page 201. 3B/RHP Osvaldo Diaz (40) is a Cuban defector whom Houston is trying to get into a junior college to evaluate him as a draft-and-follow.

Closest To The Majors: Burke could open 2002 in Double-A. Saarloos has less of a shot, as he could be a starter this season after breaking into pro ball as a closer.

Saarloos

Best Late-Round Pick: DeLeon didn't go higher in the draft because he's 5-foot-11. That wasn't a problem for the Astros, who have had success with undersized righthanders such as Roy Oswalt.

The One Who Got Away: RHP Lance Cormier (10) returned to Alabama as the only one of Houston's 20 top picks who didn't sign.

Assessment: Houston took its usual approach, making wise picks with an eye on its budget. The Astros grabbed a fine collection of athletes, and Saarloos has made a habit of exceeding expectations.

2000 Draft

Houston found frontline arms with its first three picks in RHPs Robert Stiehl (1), Chad Qualls (2) and Anthony Pluta (3), though Stiehl needed rotator-cuff surgery last summer. SS Tommy Whiteman (6) had a breakthrough year in 2001.   **Grade: B+**

1999 Draft

One of the secrets to the Astros' success has been making wise middle-round picks. They did that this time with OF Jason Lane (6), RHP Ryan Jamison (17) and since-traded C Garett Gentry (13).   **Grade: B**

1998 Draft

If RHP Brad Lidge (1) ever stays healthy, he could be an ace starter or closer. If he doesn't, Houston still has C John Buck (7), 3B Morgan Ensberg (9), RHP Mike Nannini (1) and 2B Keith Ginter (10).   **Grade: B+**

1997 Draft

OF Lance Berkman (1) is part of the big league team's foundation, and RHP Tim Redding (20, draft-and-follow) could achieve that status as well. The Astros couldn't sign OF Charlton Jimerson (25) this time but got him four years later.   **Grade: A**

Note: Draft analysis prepared by Jim Callis. Numbers in parentheses indicate draft rounds.

. . . Hernandez' best pitch has always been a curveball that makes him unhittable when he throws it for strikes.

Carlos
Hernandez lhp

Born: April 22, 1980.
Ht.: 5-10. **Wt.:** 145.
Bats: L. **Throws:** L.
Career Transactions: Signed out of Venezuela by Astros, April 15, 1997.

For all their success mining Venezuela for talent, the Astros didn't get a major league win from those efforts until last Aug. 18. The first Houston pitcher to jump from Double-A to the majors in a decade, Hernandez blanked the Pirates on two hits over seven innings. He followed up with six score-less innings against the Phillies, and extended his shutout streak to 17 innings in his next start before giving up a two-run homer to the Reds' Adam Dunn. But in that game Hernandez dove headfirst back into second base, slightly tearing his rotator cuff and ending his season. He had shown brilliance in flashes before, with an 18-strikeout game in 1999 and a no-hitter in 2000, but hadn't been consistent. Hernandez set the tone for 2001 before the season even began, as he was the most impressive prospect in Houston's big league camp and threw five perfect innings against the Astros in the exhibition finale.

Hernandez' best pitch has always been a curveball that made him unhittable when he could throw it for strikes. It has a true 12-to-6 break, but he was inconsistent with it and sometimes relied on it too much. At the beginning of the year at Double-A Round Rock, he started using his fastball and changeup more often, which cost him command of his curve. By midseason he had all three pitches working. Hernandez has learned to trust all three pitches. His curve is still his bread and butter, though his fastball is also a quality pitch at 90-95 mph with late life. He'll be encouraged to remove the headfirst slide from his repertoire. Fortunately he didn't need shoulder surgery because rest should heal the tear, but he didn't pitch again until January. Once healthy, he just needs to hone his control, both in terms of throwing strikes and locating his pitches within the zone.

Roy Oswalt, Wade Miller and Shane Reynolds are guaranteed jobs in the Houston rotation, and the Astros are leaning toward keeping Dave Mlicki in the fourth slot. Hernandez and Tim Redding should battle to be the No. 5 starter, and Hernandez may have an advantage because he's a lefty.

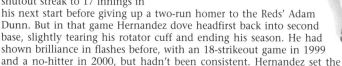

Year	Club (League)	Class	W	L	ERA	G	GS	CG	SV	IP	H	R	ER	BB	SO
1997	San Joaquin 1 (VSL)	R	5	1	2.54	22	0	0	3	46	47	20	13	21	53
1998	Astros (DSL)	R	2	0	1.33	17	0	0	9	27	16	4	4	12	33
1999	Martinsville (Appy)	R	5	1	1.79	13	9	0	0	55	36	21	11	23	82
2000	Michigan (Mid)	A	6	6	3.82	22	22	2	0	111	92	57	47	63	115
2001	Round Rock (TL)	AA	12	3	3.69	24	23	0	0	139	115	60	57	69	167
	Houston (NL)	MAJ	1	0	1.02	3	3	0	0	18	11	2	2	7	17
MAJOR LEAGUE TOTALS			1	0	1.02	3	3	0	0	18	11	2	2	7	17
MINOR LEAGUE TOTALS			30	11	3.14	98	54	2	12	378	306	162	132	188	450

ROBERT GURGANUS

2. John Buck, c

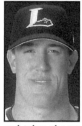

Born: July 7, 1980. **Ht.:** 6-3. **Wt.:** 200. **Bats:** R. **Throws:** R. **School:** Taylorsville (Utah) HS. **Career Transactions:** Selected by Astros in seventh round of 1998 draft; signed June 11, 1998.

Though he hasn't gotten the attention to go with it, Buck may be the best all-around catching prospect in the minors. His continuing development allowed the Astros to include slugging backstop Garett Gentry in the Pedro Astacio trade with the Rockies. In 2001, Buck more than doubled his previous career high of 10 homers as he began to extend his arms more often and turn on fastballs. He also improved at recognizing breaking balls and making adjustments. Behind the plate, he has a strong arm and takes charge of a pitching staff. He's a student of the game, and the Astros love his makeup. Buck's release is a bit lengthy, though he gets rid of throws quickly and nailed 37 percent of basestealers in 2001. He's still getting better as a receiver and needs more exposure to quality pitchers. He has improved significantly since coming out of a Utah high school. His walk rate dipped as he started hitting for more power. After spending two years in low Class A because Houston didn't have a high Class A club, Buck is ready for Double-A. He should be the Astros' starter on Opening Day 2004.

Year	Club (League)	Class	AVG	G	AB	R	H	2B	3B	HR	RBI	BB	SO	SB
1998	Astros (GCL)	R	.286	36	126	24	36	9	0	3	15	13	22	2
1999	Auburn (NY-P)	A	.245	63	233	36	57	17	0	3	29	25	48	7
	Michigan (Mid)	A	.100	4	10	1	1	1	0	0	0	2	3	0
2000	Michigan (Mid)	A	.282	109	390	57	110	33	0	10	71	55	81	2
2001	Lexington (SAL)	A	.275	122	443	72	122	24	1	22	73	37	84	4
MINOR LEAGUE TOTALS			.271	334	1202	190	326	84	1	38	188	132	238	15

3. Chris Burke, ss

Born: March 11, 1980. **Ht.:** 5-11. **Wt.:** 180. **Bats:** R. **Throws:** R. **School:** University of Tennessee. **Career Transactions:** Selected by Astros in first round (10th overall) of 2001 draft; signed June 22, 2001.

Burke broke several of Todd Helton's records at Tennessee, and he's one of six players in Southeastern Conference history to hit .400 in his career. The 2001 SEC player of the year, he signed for $2.125 million, breaking the club bonus record by $875,000. Houston scouting director David Lakey compared Burke to Craig Biggio on draft day. Burke has plenty of leadoff skills, gap power and stolen-base speed and aptitude. The Astros now downplay Biggio comparisons because they believe Burke can play shortstop, which some scouts had questioned. His arm is strong and accurate, and his instincts, hands and feet are all fine. Burke has no glaring flaws. He could walk a little more if he's going to bat at the top of the order, but he really had no difficulty jumping right into pro ball at low Class A Michigan. Burke has a good chance of going to Double-A for his first full season. He may play second base, but only to give Tommy Whiteman some time at shortstop. The only way Burke won't be Houston's shortstop of the future is if defensive whiz Adam Everett jump-starts his bat and pushes Burke to second.

Year	Club (League)	Class	AVG	G	AB	R	H	2B	3B	HR	RBI	BB	SO	SB
2001	Michigan (Mid)	A	.300	56	233	47	70	11	6	3	17	26	31	21
MINOR LEAGUE TOTALS			.300	56	233	47	70	11	6	3	17	26	31	21

4. Jason Lane, of

Born: Dec. 22, 1976. **Ht.:** 6-2. **Wt.:** 220. **Bats:** R. **Throws:** L. **School:** University of Southern California. **Career Transactions:** Selected by Astros in sixth round of 1999 draft; signed June 7, 1999.

Lane is nothing if not productive. He hit a grand slam and picked up the victory in the 1998 College World Series championship game. As a pro, he has won three RBI titles in three seasons, and has earned back-to-back MVP awards in the Class A Midwest League and Texas League. He topped the minors in RBIs and total bases (320) in 2001. In addition to being productive, Lane's tools are better than the Astros thought they were when they drafted him as a senior. Possessing the best power in the system, he drives balls to all fields. Good fastballs don't give him a problem. He has worked diligently to improve his running, throwing and outfield skills. Lane needs to adjust to breaking balls a little better, as he compensates now by looking for them more often than he should. He has some trouble going back on balls in the outfield but should become at least an average corner outfielder. The Astros see parallels between Lane and Lance Berkman. They both broke in as first basemen, and they're similar hitters, athletes and personalities. Triple-A New Orleans is Lane's likely destination in 2001, but he's next in line if Daryle Ward can't handle left field.

Year	Club (League)	Class	AVG	G	AB	R	H	2B	3B	HR	RBI	BB	SO	SB
1999	Auburn (NY-P)	A	.279	74	283	46	79	18	5	13	59	38	46	6
2000	Michigan (Mid)	A	.299	133	511	98	153	38	0	23	104	62	91	20
2001	Round Rock (TL)	AA	.316	137	526	103	166	36	2	38	124	61	98	14
MINOR LEAGUE TOTALS			.302	344	1320	247	398	92	7	74	287	161	235	40

5. Brad Lidge, rhp

Born: Dec. 23, 1976. **Ht.:** 6-5. **Wt.:** 200. **Bats:** R. **Throws:** R. **School:** University of Notre Dame. **Career Transactions:** Selected by Astros in first round (17th overall) of 1998 draft; signed July 2, 1998.

At the start of 2001, Lidge was as dominant as any pitcher on a Round Rock staff that included Carlos Hernandez and Tim Redding. But as too often has been the case, he had to be shut down because of injury. What was thought to be shoulder tendinitis turned out to be fraying that required arthroscopic surgery in July. Lidge has the best power stuff of any Astros pitcher, including the major league staff. He regularly turns bats into kindling. He has a 94-95 mph fastball that rides and sinks and can touch 98, and a slider that's so unhittable it wouldn't matter if he told batters it was coming. Though his pitches are so lively, he can throw them for strikes. Lidge has three surgeries and four victories as a pro. In 2000, he had operations to repair a broken forearm and to clean out his elbow. He hasn't had enough time to refine a changeup. The Astros may have to move Lidge to the bullpen in an effort to preserve him. His story is similar to that of Robb Nen, who has a similar arsenal and was hurt for six straight years in the minors. Houston farm director Tim Purpura copied Nen's bio out of the Giants media guide and gave it to Lidge for inspiration.

Year	Club (League)	Class	W	L	ERA	G	GS	CG	SV	IP	H	R	ER	BB	SO
1998	Quad City (Mid)	A	0	0	3.27	4	4	0	0	11	10	5	4	5	6
1999	Kissimmee (FSL)	A	0	2	3.38	6	6	0	0	21	13	8	8	11	19
2000	Kissimmee (FSL)	A	2	1	2.81	8	8	0	0	42	28	14	13	15	46
2001	Round Rock (TL)	AA	2	0	1.73	5	5	0	0	26	21	5	5	7	42
MINOR LEAGUE TOTALS			4	4	2.70	23	23	0	0	100	72	32	30	38	113

6. Anthony Pluta, rhp

Born: Oct. 28, 1982. **Ht.:** 6-2. **Wt.:** 190. **Bats:** R. **Throws:** R. **School:** Las Vegas HS. **Career Transactions:** Selected by Astros in third round of 2000 draft; signed Aug. 22, 2000.

Pluta didn't start pitching full-time until he was a high school sophomore, and even as a senior he was more successful as a hitter. He was so impressive in instructional league after signing late in 2000, the Astros decided to challenge him by letting him make his pro debut in full-season ball at age 18. Pluta wasn't fazed. Though Pluta's fastball can push triple digits on the radar gun, he's not obsessed with throwing hard. He throws an easy 92-94 mph with plenty of life. He has a hard curveball with a sharp downward break, and it's a big league average pitch when he really snaps it off. Early returns on his changeup have been positive. He's a tough competitor and a quick learner. Pluta has some effort in his delivery and doesn't always stay under control. Once he smooths out and repeats his mechanics more consistently, he'll throw more strikes. He led the low Class A South Atlantic League in walks last season. The Astros don't have a high Class A team, and they aren't going to send Pluta to Double-A as a teenager. He'll either return to Lexington or make a lateral move to Michigan in 2002.

Year	Club (League)	Class	W	L	ERA	G	GS	CG	SV	IP	H	R	ER	BB	SO
2001	Lexington (SAL)	A	12	4	3.20	26	26	0	0	132	107	52	47	86	138
MINOR LEAGUE TOTALS			12	4	3.20	26	26	0	0	132	107	52	47	86	138

7. Morgan Ensberg, 3b

Born: Aug. 26, 1975. **Ht.:** 6-2. **Wt.:** 210. **Bats:** R. **Throws:** R. **School:** University of Southern California. **Career Transactions:** Selected by Astros in ninth round of 1998 draft; signed June 18, 1998.

A teammate of Jason Lane on Southern California's 1998 championship club, Ensberg ranks fourth on the Trojans' career home run list behind Mark McGwire, Geoff Jenkins and Eric Munson. Ensberg struggled in his first two years as a pro, broke out at Round Rock in 2000 and continued at New Orleans in 2001. Like Lane, Ensberg has made himself into a prospect. He played in both Venezuela and the Dominican Republic, refusing to rest after a huge Double-A season. He continues to get more polished at the plate each year, and his power couldn't be muted even after he broke the hamate bone in his left wrist. He has a strong, accurate arm and the chance to be an average third baseman. Ensberg's range is just OK, and his reactions leave something to be desired. His throwing mechanics aren't the prettiest, though he generally gets the job done. He's also not much of a runner. Though Vinny Castilla enjoyed a renaissance in Houston, Ensberg's presence made him expendable. Ensberg is the favorite to win the Astros' third-base job in spring training. He has more offensive upside than Chris Truby, who's a better defender.

Year	Club (League)	Class	AVG	G	AB	R	H	2B	3B	HR	RBI	BB	SO	SB
1998	Auburn (NY-P)	A	.230	59	196	39	45	10	1	5	31	46	51	15
1999	Kissimmee (FSL)	A	.239	123	427	72	102	25	2	15	69	68	90	17
2000	Round Rock (TL)	AA	.300	137	483	95	145	34	0	28	90	92	107	9
	Houston (NL)	MAJ	.286	4	7	0	2	0	0	0	0	0	1	0
2001	New Orleans (PCL)	AAA	.310	87	316	65	98	20	0	23	61	45	60	6
MAJOR LEAGUE TOTALS			.286	4	7	0	2	0	0	0	0	0	1	0
MINOR LEAGUE TOTALS			.274	406	1422	271	390	89	3	71	251	251	308	47

8. Rodrigo Rosario, rhp

Born: Dec. 14, 1979. **Ht.:** 6-2. **Wt.:** 170. **Bats:** R. **Throws:** R. **Career Transactions:** Signed out of Dominican Republic by Astros July 6, 1996.

Because he hadn't distinguished himself beyond owning a good fastball, Rosario began 2001 in the bullpen at Lexington. Moved into the rotation when Ryan Jamison strained his biceps, Rosario responded by not allowing an earned run in his first three outings and went 12-3, 1.97 as a starter. Rosario still has his nasty 91-94 mph fastball with late life. The difference is now he has learned he needs more than one pitch. His slurve has become an out pitch that buckles the knees of righthanders, and he shows good arm action on his changeup. He's all arms and legs in his delivery, making it difficult to pick up his pitches, and he has fine command. He likes to vary his arm angle to further confuse batters, though Rosario needs to recognize that doing so flattens out his breaking ball. His slurve and changeup can get better and should do so as he gains experience. High Class A would be the logical progression for Rosario, but the Astros don't have that option. If he doesn't make Double-A out of spring training, he could by the end of the season.

Year	Club (League)	Class	W	L	ERA	G	GS	CG	SV	IP	H	R	ER	BB	SO
1997	Astros (DSL)	R	6	4	2.46	15	14	0	0	91	63	30	25	24	81
1998	Astros (GCL)	R	2	2	4.12	13	12	0	0	68	61	36	31	30	65
	Auburn (NY-P)	A	0	0	0.00	2	0	0	0	2	0	0	0	3	2
1999	Martinsville (Appy)	R	5	5	4.69	14	14	0	0	79	78	46	41	32	86
2000	Auburn (NY-P)	A	5	6	3.45	14	14	0	0	76	67	36	29	32	67
2001	Lexington (SAL)	A	13	4	2.14	30	21	1	2	147	105	46	35	36	131
MINOR LEAGUE TOTALS			31	21	3.13	88	75	1	2	462	374	194	161	157	432

9. Chad Qualls, rhp

Born: Aug. 17, 1978. **Ht.:** 6-5. **Wt.:** 205. **Bats:** R. **Throws:** R. **School:** University of Nevada. **Career Transactions:** Selected by Astros in second round of 2000 draft; signed Aug. 16, 2000.

The third player drafted as a college senior to make the top 10, Qualls signed late in 2000 and didn't debut until last season. He probably would have been promoted at midseason if the Astros had a high Class A team or weren't loaded at Double-A, but he settled for tying for the Midwest League lead in victories. Qualls gets loads of ground balls with his low-90s sinker and a slider MWL managers considered the best in their league. Pitching from a three-quarters arm angle, he's brutal on righthanders. He challenges hitters while walking the fine line between throwing strikes and making mistakes. Qualls needs to throw his changeup more, something he'll realize when he reaches the upper minors. His mechanics could be smoother, though they don't hamper his control. He sometimes drops down to a low-three-quarters slot, which flattens out his slider. Qualls will go to Double-A in 2002 and could advance very quickly. Houston has a deep stock of starters, which could mean that he settles into Enron Field in middle relief. He has the stuff, mentality and resilience to succeed in that role.

Year	Club (League)	Class	W	L	ERA	G	GS	CG	SV	IP	H	R	ER	BB	SO
2001	Michigan (Mid)	A	15	6	3.72	26	26	3	0	162	149	77	67	31	125
MINOR LEAGUE TOTALS			15	6	3.72	26	26	3	0	162	149	77	67	31	125

10. Tommy Whiteman, ss

Born: July 14, 1979. **Ht.:** 6-3. **Wt.:** 175. **Bats:** R. **Throws:** R. **School:** University of Oklahoma. **Career Transactions:** Selected by Astros in sixth round of 2000 draft; signed June 16, 2000.

Whiteman was as pleasant a surprise as anyone in the system last season. He hit .250 with one homer at short-season Auburn in his pro debut, then led the South Atlantic League in slugging and Class A shortstops in batting in 2001. He isn't Alex Rodriguez, but Whiteman shows all five tools at shortstop. He hits the ball where it's pitched, has gap power and average speed. He should fill out and get stronger. Built like a young Cal Ripken Jr., Whiteman resembles him defensively. Tall and rangy, he's fluid at shortstop, gets to the balls he should and has enough arm strength. Whiteman tends to flip the ball sidearm, which makes some routine plays closer than they should be. He'll have to improve his plate discipline at the upper levels of the minors. Both Chris Burke and Whiteman stand a good chance of playing in Double-A this year, which means they'll have to work out a timeshare at shortstop. It's possible they could share that position, with Whiteman also getting time at second or third base. Long term, he could be the second-base half of a double-play combination with Burke.

Year	Club (League)	Class	AVG	G	AB	R	H	2B	3B	HR	RBI	BB	SO	SB
2000	Auburn (NY-P)	A	.250	70	232	33	58	10	3	1	22	22	52	7
2001	Lexington (SAL)	A	.319	114	389	58	124	26	8	18	57	34	106	17
	Round Rock (TL)	AA	.250	4	16	1	4	0	0	1	1	0	5	0
MINOR LEAGUE TOTALS			.292	188	637	92	186	36	11	20	80	56	163	24

11. Charlton Jimerson, of

Born: Sept. 22, 1979. **Ht.:** 6-3. **Wt.:** 205. **Bats:** R. **Throws:** R. **School:** University of Miami. **Career Transactions:** Selected by Astros in fifth round of 2001 draft; signed June 23, 2001.

Jimerson was a raw unknown when the Astros drafted him in the 25th round out of an Oakland high school in 1997. They thought they had persuaded him to attend Chabot (Calif.) JC as a draft-and-follow, but that plan fell through when he received an academic scholarship from Miami, where he walked on the baseball team. Jimerson played sparingly during his first 3½ years with the Hurricanes, and it looked like his college highlight would be the completion of his computer-science degree. That in itself would have represented a significant triumph for Jimerson, whose mother was a crack addict who often abandoned him and his younger brother, and whose father physically abused his mother and now is homeless. Jimerson got into the lineup, hit three homers in six games against Florida State and became the Hurricanes' hottest postseason player. He was named MVP of the College World Series after spearheading Miami's second championship in three years. Jimerson's ceiling may be higher than any player in the system. Scouts compare his body to a young Eric Davis' and say he has more power than Davis did. Jimerson is a supreme athlete whose power, speed and outfield defense each rank among the best in the organization. His arm strength is another plus, and there are no doubts about his intelligence or desire. Jimerson's one need is to control the strike zone so he can hit consistently enough to be a threat. A wrist injury hampered him in his pro debut but couldn't lessen Houston's excitement over him. Jimerson will spend 2002 with one of Houston's two low Class A teams.

Year	Club (League)	Class	AVG	G	AB	R	H	2B	3B	HR	RBI	BB	SO	SB
2001	Pittsfield (NY-P)	A	.234	51	197	35	46	12	1	9	31	18	79	15
MINOR LEAGUE TOTALS			.234	51	197	35	46	12	1	9	31	18	79	15

12. Adam Everett, ss

Born: Feb. 6, 1977. **Ht.:** 6-0. **Wt.:** 156. **Bats:** R. **Throws:** R. **School:** University of South Carolina. **Career Transactions:** Selected by Red Sox in first round (12th overall) of 1998 draft; signed Aug. 4, 1998 . . . Traded by Red Sox with LHP Greg Miller to Astros for OF Carl Everett, Dec. 15, 1999.

The key player for the Astros when they traded Carl Everett to the Red Sox, Adam (no relation) has a good chance to win Houston's job in spring training. New manager Jimy Williams is expected to want defense from his shortstop, and incumbent Julio Lugo's glove isn't his strong suit. Everett, by contrast, might be the best defensive shortstop in the minors. His range, arm, hands and instincts are all assets and could lead to Gold Gloves in his future. He's also reliable and doesn't make careless errors. Everett's bat remains very much in question, however. He has yet to top .250 in two tries at Triple-A, and after batting .292 in the final two months of 2000 he regressed last year. Everett has some bat control and has begun using the opposite field more often, but he can be overpowered by good fastballs and chases sliders off the plate. One of his strengths had been drawing walks, but he did so much less frequently in 2001. He's also hard on himself, which just compounds his difficulties. Everett, the starting shortstop on the 2000 U.S. Olympic team, made an effort to get stronger over the winter and hit well during a brief stint in Venezuela. He also knows he needs to hit fewer fly balls and bunt more often to take advantage of his good speed.

Year	Club (League)	Class	AVG	G	AB	R	H	2B	3B	HR	RBI	BB	SO	SB
1998	Lowell (NY-P)	A	.296	21	71	11	21	6	2	0	9	11	13	2
1999	Trenton (EL)	AA	.263	98	338	56	89	11	0	10	44	41	64	21
2000	New Orleans (PCL)	AAA	.245	126	453	82	111	25	2	5	37	75	100	13
2001	New Orleans (PCL)	AAA	.249	114	441	69	110	20	8	5	40	39	74	24
	Houston (NL)	MAJ	.000	9	3	1	0	0	0	0	0	0	1	1
MAJOR LEAGUE TOTALS			.000	9	3	1	0	0	0	0	0	0	1	1
MINOR LEAGUE TOTALS			.254	359	1303	218	331	62	12	20	130	166	251	60

13. Wilfredo Rodriguez, lhp

Born: March 20, 1979. **Ht.:** 6-3. **Wt.:** 180. **Bats:** L. **Throws:** L. **Career Transactions:** Signed out of Venezuela by Astros, July 20, 1995.

Two years ago, Rodriguez beat out Lance Berkman, Carlos Hernandez, Wade Miller, Roy Oswalt and Tim Redding for the No. 1 spot on this list. But he hasn't progressed much since then, and his most noteworthy accomplishment has been surrendering Barry Bonds' 70th home run last September. Rodriguez looked good working out of the bullpen in his native Venezuela after the 2000 season, and the Astros thought that role might be a nice fit. But he didn't enjoy pitching middle relief in Double-A and was starting again by the end of 2001. He has a lively 93-95 mph fastball, which is both a positive (it's an out pitch) and a negative (he wants to throw it by everyone). He can buckle hitters with his hard curveball but can't always throw it for strikes. Rodriguez has a better understanding of the importance of throwing his changeup, but the pitch still requires more work. His biggest need is consistent mechanics because his release point varies so much that he doesn't have reliable command. He'll be a Triple-A starter in 2002, which will be a big year for him because he has been passed by several pitchers in the system and several more are poised to do the same.

Year	Club (League)	Class	W	L	ERA	G	GS	CG	SV	IP	H	R	ER	BB	SO
1996	Astros/Red Sox (DSL)	R	1	2	2.97	18	0	0	0	33	28	17	11	21	29
1997	Astros (GCL)	R	8	2	3.04	12	12	1	0	68	54	30	23	32	71
1998	Quad City (Mid)	A	11	5	3.05	28	27	1	0	165	122	70	56	62	170
1999	Kissimmee (FSL)	A	15	7	2.88	25	24	0	0	153	108	55	49	62	148
2000	Kissimmee (FSL)	A	3	5	4.75	9	9	1	0	53	43	29	28	30	52
	Round Rock (TL)	AA	2	4	5.77	11	11	0	0	58	54	42	37	52	55
2001	Round Rock (TL)	AA	5	9	4.78	42	10	0	0	92	94	61	49	56	94
	Houston (NL)	MAJ	0	0	15.00	2	0	0	0	3	6	5	5	1	3
MAJOR LEAGUE TOTALS			0	0	15.00	2	0	0	0	3	6	5	5	1	3
MINOR LEAGUE TOTALS			45	34	3.66	145	93	3	0	622	503	304	253	315	619

14. Ramon German, 3b

Born: Jan. 15, 1980. **Ht.:** 5-11. **Wt.:** 205. **Bats:** B. **Throws:** R. **Career Transactions:** Signed out of Dominican Republic by Astros, Jan. 19, 1997.

After spending three years in the Rookie-level Dominican Summer League, German has made up for lost time with a pair of strong seasons in the United States. He boosted his stock as much as any player in the organization in 2001. Built along the lines of Manny Ramirez, he has toned down his extremely open stance but it's still unorthodox. One scout describes

German's approach as "bail and whale," but he can drive the ball great distances and has a decent idea of the strike zone. He probably would benefit from closing his stance some more and definitely needs to use the opposite field more frequently. As a third baseman, he has an above-average arm and soft hands. He moves fairly well for his size, though he must improve his reactions and footwork. That said, he made just 16 errors last season. Some members of the organization believe German can remain at the hot corner, while others see him as a future first baseman or left fielder. He'd be an obvious candidate for high Class A if the Astros had an affiliate at that level.

Year	Club (League)	Class	AVG	G	AB	R	H	2B	3B	HR	RBI	BB	SO	SB
1997	Astros (DSL)	R	.255	33	98	16	25	7	0	0	8	18	15	3
1998	Astros (DSL)	R	.276	51	181	28	50	16	1	3	27	21	25	3
1999	Astros (DSL)	R	.289	69	249	48	72	23	1	9	47	41	44	19
2000	Martinsville (Appy)	R	.320	59	225	42	72	24	1	7	44	23	64	16
2001	Lexington (SAL)	A	.265	129	461	72	122	37	3	13	93	55	107	21
MINOR LEAGUE TOTALS			.281	341	1214	206	341	107	6	32	219	158	255	62

15. Ryan Jamison, rhp

Born: Jan. 5, 1978. **Ht.:** 6-3. **Wt.:** 185. **Bats:** R. **Throws:** R. **School:** University of Missouri. **Career Transactions:** Selected by Astros in 17th round of 1999 draft; signed June 4, 1999.

The lack of a high Class A team in the Astros system and a logjam of pitching in Double-A meant Jamison had to repeat low Class A in 2001 after overmatching Midwest League hitters the year before. Predictably, he got off to a hot start, posting a 0.98 ERA and a 45-2 strikeout-walk ratio in his first 37 innings before a biceps strain knocked him out for a month. He reached Round Rock in mid-June, only to strain his biceps again a month later. Jamison is a ground-ball machine. His sinking fastball can touch 93-94 mph but usually arrives at 89-91 and runs in on righthanders. He has tremendous command of his slider, which he can throw for strikes or get hitters to chase off the plate. He also can get the slider in on the hands of lefthanders, though he sometimes relies on the pitch too much at the expense of his fastball. That was the case in the Arizona Fall League, where he had a 2.73 ERA as he kept going to the slider when hitters couldn't do much with it. Jamison's change-up drops at the plate and he should use it more against lefties. He'll be a Double-A starter in 2002, though the wealth of pitching in the organization could push him to middle relief.

Year	Club (League)	Class	W	L	ERA	G	GS	CG	SV	IP	H	R	ER	BB	SO
1999	Auburn (NY-P)	A	5	3	4.11	15	15	0	0	88	83	45	40	36	83
2000	Michigan (Mid)	A	8	3	2.10	41	7	0	7	99	66	32	23	38	95
2001	Lexington (SAL)	A	4	2	2.28	9	8	0	0	55	40	17	14	9	63
	Round Rock (TL)	AA	5	2	3.50	10	9	0	0	46	49	25	18	23	32
MINOR LEAGUE TOTALS			22	10	2.97	75	39	0	7	288	238	119	95	106	273

16. Greg Miller, lhp

Born: Sept. 30, 1979. **Ht.:** 6-5. **Wt.:** 215. **Bats:** L. **Throws:** L. **School:** Aurora (Ill.) West HS. **Career Transactions:** Selected by Red Sox in fifth round of 1997 draft; signed July 2, 1997 . . . Traded by Red Sox with SS Adam Everett to Astros for OF Carl Everett, Dec. 15, 1999.

The Astros scouting department deserves credit for getting Miller from the Red Sox as the second player in the Carl Everett trade. He was steaming through the Houston system before nagging injuries sidelined him for much of 2001. Mild shoulder tendinitis kept him out until mid-April, and a strained lower-back muscle in early May cost him 10 weeks. His shoulder flared up again in the Arizona Fall League, requiring arthroscopic surgery to remove a bone spur under his labrum. Miller doesn't have a dominant pitch, but he can throw strikes with an 89-93 mph fastball, curveball, slider and changeup. He aggressively works inside with his fastball and also can paint the outside corner with it. He gets righthanders out by pounding them with breaking balls down and in. He has better command then he showed last year, when he tried to pitch through his physical problems. Miller should be fully healthy in 2002, when he'll return to the Double-A rotation.

Year	Club (League)	Class	W	L	ERA	G	GS	CG	SV	IP	H	R	ER	BB	SO
1997	Red Sox (GCL)	R	0	2	3.72	4	4	0	0	10	8	6	4	6	6
1998	Red Sox (GCL)	R	6	0	2.49	11	7	0	0	43	33	18	12	18	47
1999	Augusta (SAL)	A	10	6	3.10	25	25	1	0	137	109	54	47	56	146
2000	Kissimmee (FSL)	A	10	8	3.70	24	24	1	0	146	131	63	60	46	109
	Round Rock (TL)	AA	0	0	0.00	2	0	0	0	2	0	0	0	1	2
2001	Round Rock (TL)	AA	5	3	3.25	14	14	0	0	55	38	22	20	35	37
MINOR LEAGUE TOTALS			31	19	3.27	80	74	2	0	393	319	163	143	162	347

17. Mike Nannini, rhp

Born: Aug. 9, 1980. **Ht.:** 5-11. **Wt.:** 170. **Bats:** R. **Throws:** R. **School:** Green Valley HS, Henderson, Nev. **Career Transactions:** Selected by Astros in first round (37th overall) of 1998 draft; signed July 1, 1998.

Nannini was hurt more than any other player by Houston's lack of a high Class A club in 2001. He had spent parts of two seasons in the Midwest League and had pitched well in 12 high Class A Florida State League starts in 2000. But when the Astros parted ways with their Kissimmee affiliate and were loaded in Double-A, Nannini had to go to the South Atlantic League, which he led in innings. He had thrown in the low 90s in the past, but last year he operated mainly at 88-89 mph. While his velocity dipped, he did a fine job of improving his secondary pitches. His curveball is the better of his two breaking balls, and his changeup is now trustworthy. Nannini has no trouble throwing strikes but may have to stop pitching up in the zone with his four-seam fastball against better hitters. He was left off the 40-man roster mainly because of the depth of the organization, a decision that will stoke his considerable competitive fire. If Nannini's velocity bounces back in Double-A, he could be special.

Year	Club (League)	Class	W	L	ERA	G	GS	CG	SV	IP	H	R	ER	BB	SO
1998	Astros (GCL)	R	1	1	1.49	8	6	1	0	36	23	6	6	13	39
1999	Michigan (Mid)	A	4	10	4.43	15	15	0	0	87	107	56	43	31	68
	Auburn (NY-P)	A	5	3	1.90	11	11	2	0	76	55	19	16	17	86
2000	Michigan (Mid)	A	7	4	3.55	15	15	3	0	101	85	45	40	33	86
	Kissimmee (FSL)	A	7	3	3.33	12	12	2	0	78	83	34	29	14	56
2001	Lexington (SAL)	A	15	5	2.70	28	27	4	0	190	176	70	57	36	151
MINOR LEAGUE TOTALS			39	26	3.02	89	86	12	0	569	529	230	191	144	486

18. Robert Stiehl, rhp

Born: Dec. 9, 1980. **Ht.:** 6-3. **Wt.:** 205. **Bats:** R. **Throws:** R. **School:** El Camino (Calif.) JC. **Career Transactions:** Selected by Astros in first round (27th overall) of 2000 draft; signed July 21, 2000.

The Astros envisioned him as another Troy Percival. Like Percival, Stiehl was a college catcher with a strong arm and questionable bat. He hit 97 mph in his first start at El Camino (Calif.) JC, cementing his future role as a pro. Though he projected as Billy Wagner's eventual successor as the Houston closer, Stiehl was used as a starter last season to give him some needed innings. Kept on tight pitch limits, he blew away South Atlantic League hitters for two months before his shoulder began acting up. After taking a month off, Stiehl tried to pitch again in July before being shut down and having rotator-cuff surgery. Before he got hurt, Stiehl threw an easy 93-94 mph and topped out at 97. At times, his curveball and changeups were plus pitches as well. He'll miss all of 2002 and it remains to be seen how his stuff will be affected, but a healthy Stiehl has an extremely high ceiling.

Year	Club (League)	Class	W	L	ERA	G	GS	CG	SV	IP	H	R	ER	BB	SO
2000	Auburn (NY-P)	A	1	0	0.93	5	0	0	1	10	4	1	1	4	19
	Michigan (Mid)	A	0	0	9.00	1	0	0	0	1	1	1	1	1	1
2001	Lexington (SAL)	A	2	3	1.98	14	12	0	0	50	28	17	11	34	59
MINOR LEAGUE TOTALS			3	3	1.92	20	12	0	1	61	33	19	13	39	79

19. Keith Ginter, 2b/of

Born: May 5, 1976. **Ht.:** 5-10. **Wt.:** 190. **Bats:** R. **Throws:** R. **School:** Texas Tech. **Career Transactions:** Selected by Astros in 10th round of 1998 draft; signed June 7, 1998.

Ginter was one of the surprise breakthrough players in any organization in 2000, leading all minor leaguers with a .457 on-base percentage while winning the Texas League batting title and MVP award. He led the Astros with five homers and 11 RBIs while batting .340 in spring training last year, but his lack of versatility hurt his chances of making the team. In Triple-A, he worked on learning the outfield. He's too bulky and stiff at second base, and his arm plays better in the outfield. Ginter had resisted a move to third base, which is probably his best position, but he has softened. He also played first base in Venezuela this winter. Though he's an offensive player, he needs to find a defensive home. Ginter has a short stroke and he enhances his on-base ability by walking and getting hit by pitches. He has power but sometimes get homer-happy, pulling too many pitches and hooking them foul. That approach also leads to too many strikeouts. Houston will give a long look again this spring, and Ginter could win a job as a reserve.

Year	Club (League)	Class	AVG	G	AB	R	H	2B	3B	HR	RBI	BB	SO	SB
1998	Auburn (NY-P)	A	.315	71	241	55	76	22	1	8	41	60	68	10
1999	Kissimmee (FSL)	A	.263	103	376	66	99	15	4	13	46	61	90	9
	Jackson (TL)	AA	.382	9	34	9	13	1	0	1	6	4	6	0

2000	Round Rock (TL)	AA	.333	125	462	108	154	30	3	26	92	82	127	24
	Houston (NL)	MAJ	.250	5	8	3	2	0	0	1	3	1	3	0
2001	New Orleans (PCL)	AAA	.269	132	457	76	123	31	5	16	70	61	147	8
	Houston (NL)	MAJ	.000	1	1	0	0	0	0	0	0	0	0	0
MAJOR LEAGUE TOTALS			.222	6	9	3	2	0	0	1	3	1	3	0
MINOR LEAGUE TOTALS			.296	440	1570	314	465	99	13	64	255	268	438	51

20. Nick Roberts, rhp

Born: Nov. 6, 1976. **Ht.:** 6-2. **Wt.:** 185. **Bats:** R. **Throws:** R. **School:** Southern Utah University. **Career Transactions:** Selected by Astros in seventh round of 1999 draft; signed June 4, 1999.

Roberts stood out in his two seasons at Southern Utah and set the school single-season strikeout record twice. He has stood out as a pro as well, shining in the Arizona Fall League this offseason. The Astros thought they might lose him in the major league Rule 5 draft and were elated when they didn't. He uses both two- and four-seam fastballs, usually working from 89-92 mph and getting late movement. He also throws a slider, curveball and change-up and doesn't beat himself with walks. He's another Astros pitching prospect who would have benefited from a high Class A affiliate but had to repeat low Class A at age 24. When he moved up to Double-A he struggled, though he recovered with a strong AFL. Roberts projects as a middle reliever, and he might have to move into that role this year at Round Rock. Chad Qualls, Ryan Jamison, Greg Miller and Mike Nannini figure to open 2002 in the Double-A rotation, and Brad Lidge (if healthy) or Rodrigo Rosario might claim the final spot.

Year	Club (League)	Class	W	L	ERA	G	GS	CG	SV	IP	H	R	ER	BB	SO
1999	Martinsville (Appy)	R	4	2	1.90	10	7	1	1	47	43	11	10	6	56
2000	Michigan (Mid)	A	13	6	3.10	22	20	2	0	139	121	53	48	61	107
2001	Lexington (SAL)	A	10	1	2.95	20	20	3	0	137	118	49	45	21	128
	Round Rock (TL)	AA	2	4	5.16	8	7	0	0	45	52	27	26	10	26
MINOR LEAGUE TOTALS			29	13	3.15	60	54	6	1	369	334	140	129	98	317

21. Kirk Saarloos, rhp

Born: May 23, 1979. **Ht.:** 6-0. **Wt.:** 185. **Bats:** R. **Throws:** R. **School:** Cal State Fullerton. **Career Transactions:** Selected by Astros in third round of 2001 draft; signed June 24, 2001.

Saarloos never should be underestimated. He was a standout reliever in his first three seasons at Cal State Fullerton and wanted to sign as a junior, but he wasn't drafted in 2000. He responded by fashioning a 0.34 ERA as the closer on Team USA's college team that summer, then became a starter as a senior and finished among the NCAA Division I leaders in wins (15-2), ERA (2.18), innings (153) and strikeouts (153). He has an extremely resilient arm, and often would close games on Friday before starting on Sunday. Though Saarloos isn't the most physical pitcher—he's 6 feet tall and throws 86-88 mph—he gets outs. His fastball has plenty of sink, his slider is a plus pitch and his changeup is simply outstanding. He made a seamless transition from college to full-season ball, posting a 40-7 strikeout-walk ratio and holding hitters to a .165 average with one homer. Batters have a tough time picking up pitches from his low three-quarters delivery. Saarloos could go to Double-A as a reliever this year. If he gets a look as a starter, he'll return to low Class A.

Year	Club (League)	Class	W	L	ERA	G	GS	CG	SV	IP	H	R	ER	BB	SO
2001	Lexington (SAL)	A	1	1	1.17	22	0	0	11	31	18	5	4	7	40
MINOR LEAGUE TOTALS			1	1	1.17	22	0	0	11	31	18	5	4	7	40

22. Tom Shearn, rhp

Born: Aug. 28, 1977. **Ht.:** 6-4. **Wt.:** 200. **Bats:** R. **Throws:** R. **School:** Briggs HS, Columbus, Ohio. **Career Transactions:** Selected by Astros in 29th round of 1996 draft; signed June 16, 1996.

Shearn was a Texas League all-star in 2000 but that wasn't enough to earn him a spot on the 40-man roster or a promotion to Triple-A. Returning to Round Rock and getting crowded out of the rotation turned out to be the best thing for his career. Moved to middle relief, Shearn gained 3-4 mph in velocity and stopped putting pressure on himself. He throws 92 mph coming out of the bullpen, and mixes in curveballs, sliders and changeups. His deceptive delivery also helps his cause. Shearn still must refine his command, both in terms of cutting down on his walks and pitching up in the strike zone less often. He had a strong offseason, first in the Arizona Fall League and then at the World Cup, where he pitched 7 1/3 hitless innings before taking the loss in the gold-medal game. He's a longshot to make the Astros out of spring training and more likely will move to Triple-A.

Year	Club (League)	Class	W	L	ERA	G	GS	CG	SV	IP	H	R	ER	BB	SO
1996	Astros (GCL)	R	5	2	1.73	17	3	0	0	42	34	13	8	10	43
1997	Auburn (NY-P)	A	4	6	3.50	14	14	2	0	82	79	42	32	26	59
1998	Quad City (Mid)	A	7	7	2.25	21	21	2	0	120	88	38	30	52	93
1999	Kissimmee (FSL)	A	10	6	3.90	24	24	0	0	145	144	75	63	53	107
2000	Round Rock (TL)	AA	9	6	4.69	25	23	0	0	136	134	79	71	67	102
2001	Round Rock (TL)	AA	5	6	3.85	43	8	0	1	110	94	54	47	51	136
MINOR LEAGUE TOTALS			40	33	3.55	144	93	4	1	636	573	301	251	259	440

23. Gavin Wright, of

Born: May 6, 1979. **Ht.:** 6-2. **Wt.:** 175. **Bats:** R. **Throws:** R. **School:** Blinn (Texas) JC. **Career Transactions:** Selected by Astros in 33rd round of 1998 draft; signed May 21, 1999.

Wright entered 2001 as the Astros' best center-field prospect, but he continued to display a penchant for getting hurt and the club drafted Charlton Jimerson. Wright has played just 204 games in three pro seasons since signing as a draft-and-follow, and he has yet to progress past the Midwest League. He injured his shoulder and wrist in 2000, and his hamstring last year, when he wasn't as impressive in his MWL encore as he had been in his debut. Speed remains his best tool, though he wasn't as quick last year after adding some weight. The upside potential remains for a .275 hitter with 20 homers and 40 steals, but Wright has to synchronize his upper half and lower half when he swings. He also needs much improved plate discipline after regressing in that regard last season. Some scouts thought he lost his enthusiasm and didn't play hard on a regular basis in 2001. He's not ready for Double-A so he'll have to spend a third year in low Class A, though he'll probably get a change of scenery and be assigned to Lexington.

Year	Club (League)	Class	AVG	G	AB	R	H	2B	3B	HR	RBI	BB	SO	SB
1999	Martinsville (Appy)	R	.309	61	236	37	73	17	3	2	29	25	46	31
2000	Michigan (Mid)	A	.288	43	163	22	47	10	5	2	19	18	37	10
2001	Michigan (Mid)	A	.273	100	392	68	107	17	6	8	52	28	76	26
MINOR LEAGUE TOTALS			.287	204	791	127	227	44	14	12	100	71	159	67

24. Jimmy Barrett, rhp

Born: June 7, 1981. **Ht.:** 6-2. **Wt.:** 190. **Bats:** R. **Throws:** R. **School:** Fort Hill HS, Cumberland, Md. **Career Transactions:** Selected by Astros in third round of 1999 draft; signed June 25, 1999.

While Barrett is going to need time to develop, he has an arm that the Astros are willing to wait for. He spent two years in the Rookie-level Appalachian League before moving up to low Class A in 2001, when he went 4-4, 5.61 though June. He was much better in the final two months, going 6-1, 3.21. After reaching 95 mph in the Appy League, he topped out at 92 and pitched at 89-90 last season. His curveball has its moments, and he also throws a slider (which he calls a cutter) and a changeup (which he needs to use more). Barrett stands too upright in his delivery, leading him to work up in the strike zone too often. He's tough to hit when he gets ahead in the count but that didn't happen frequently enough in 2001. He'll try to regroup with one of Houston's low Class A affiliates this year.

Year	Club (League)	Class	W	L	ERA	G	GS	CG	SV	IP	H	R	ER	BB	SO
1999	Martinsville (Appy)	R	0	1	4.42	6	3	0	0	18	15	9	9	10	12
2000	Martinsville (Appy)	R	6	2	4.73	13	13	0	0	67	60	37	35	32	72
2001	Michigan (Mid)	A	10	5	4.48	27	25	1	0	131	122	76	65	62	98
MINOR LEAGUE TOTALS			16	8	4.55	46	41	1	0	216	197	122	109	104	182

25. Dave Matranga, 2b

Born: Jan. 8, 1977. **Ht.:** 6-0. **Wt.:** 196. **Bats:** R. **Throws:** R. **School:** Pepperdine University. **Career Transactions:** Selected by Astros in sixth round of 1998 draft; signed June 12, 1998.

Like Tom Shearn, Matranga blossomed after a change in roles during a return to Round Rock last year. He had been inconsistent at shortstop and let his fielding woes affect his offense, batting .232 in two years of full-season ball. Recast as a second baseman, he was much more aggressive defensively. Managers rated him the best defensive second baseman in the Texas League—he made just six errors in 100 games—and he earned all-star recognition as well. Less tense at the plate, he improved his average 70 points and more than doubled his extra-base hit production from 2000. Matranga still strikes out too much and can get overly pull-conscious. He has average speed. He projects more as a utilityman than as a regular second baseman in the major leagues, and has enhanced his chances of getting there after remaking himself.

Year	Club (League)	Class	AVG	G	AB	R	H	2B	3B	HR	RBI	BB	SO	SB
1998	Auburn (NY-P)	A	.306	40	144	34	44	13	1	4	24	25	38	16
1999	Kissimmee (FSL)	A	.231	124	472	70	109	20	4	6	48	68	118	17
2000	Round Rock (TL)	AA	.233	120	373	50	87	14	3	6	44	48	99	5
2001	Round Rock (TL)	AA	.302	103	387	78	117	34	2	10	60	45	91	17
	New Orleans (PCL)	AAA	.313	4	16	3	5	1	0	1	3	0	5	1
MINOR LEAGUE TOTALS			.260	391	1392	235	362	82	10	27	179	186	351	56

26. Mike Rosamond, of

Born: April 18, 1978. **Ht.:** 6-5. **Wt.:** 225. **Bats:** R. **Throws:** R. **School:** University of Mississippi. **Career Transactions:** Selected by Astros in first round (42nd overall) of 1999 draft; signed June 27, 1999.

In 1996, the Astros drafted Rosamond in the 71st round out of Madison (Miss.) Central High, where his dad Mike was his coach. Houston couldn't sign him then but since has landed both Rosamonds—the son as a supplemental first-round pick in 1999 and the father as an area scout who was hired in 2001. Rosamond always has attracted scouts with his Dale Murphy body and all-around tools, but he never hit much, batting .292 at Mississippi and just .224 in his first two years as a pro. He wasn't happy about returning to low Class A last season and responded by having his best offensive season, though he tailed off after a promotion to Double-A. While he did improve, he still does most of his damage on fastballs left out over the plate. He struggles with offspeed stuff and is a streaky hitter who misses too many pitches. He's the best defensive outfielder and has the best outfield arm in the system, but he also added weight last year and slowed down a step. His center-field play also slipped once he reached Round Rock. He'll go back to Double-A in 2002.

Year	Club (League)	Class	AVG	G	AB	R	H	2B	3B	HR	RBI	BB	SO	SB
1999	Auburn (NY-P)	A	.265	61	230	34	61	9	4	6	24	23	63	22
	Michigan (Mid)	A	.100	4	10	0	1	0	0	0	2	2	3	0
2000	Kissimmee (FSL)	A	.206	129	446	60	92	14	7	16	60	60	151	17
2001	Lexington (SAL)	A	.266	101	394	62	105	19	3	16	55	37	112	32
	Round Rock (TL)	AA	.290	31	107	14	31	5	2	1	12	12	27	3
MINOR LEAGUE TOTALS			.244	326	1187	170	290	47	16	39	153	134	356	73

27. Mike Hill, of

Born: Sept. 30, 1976. **Ht.:** 6-4. **Wt.:** 210. **Bats:** R. **Throws:** R. **School:** Oral Roberts University. **Career Transactions:** Selected by Astros in 18th round of 1999 draft; signed June 6, 1999.

Because they didn't have a high Class A affiliate, the Astros had several outfielders who had productive seasons while trapped in low Class A last year. Jon Topolski and Henry Stanley had slightly better numbers, but Hill is a slightly better prospect. Another astute college senior sign by Houston, Hill ranked among the NCAA Division I leaders with 23 homers and 88 RBIs in his final season at Oral Roberts. In three pro seasons, he has hit for average and gap power. His body, leverage, extension and bat speed all portend more homers in the future. He showed more patience at the plate in 2001. He runs well for his size and has a solid right-field arm, though he needs more work going back on fly balls. Hill is ready for Double-A, where the Astros hope he finally can put together a completely healthy season. He missed much of 2000 with ribcage and knee injuries, and he played through shoulder and ankle problems last year.

Year	Club (League)	Class	AVG	G	AB	R	H	2B	3B	HR	RBI	BB	SO	SB
1999	Auburn (NY-P)	A	.297	69	269	44	80	11	2	6	39	29	65	22
2000	Michigan (Mid)	A	.313	56	198	38	62	18	4	6	35	11	43	6
2001	Lexington (SAL)	A	.305	119	465	82	142	31	6	12	65	48	102	27
MINOR LEAGUE TOTALS			.305	244	932	164	284	60	12	24	139	88	210	55

28. Joey DeLeon, rhp

Born: Oct. 21, 1982. **Ht.:** 5-11. **Wt.:** 180. **Bats:** R. **Throws:** R. **School:** Nixon-Smiley HS, Nixon, Texas. **Career Transactions:** Selected by Astros in 18th round of 2001 draft; signed June 12, 2001.

DeLeon touched 95 mph as a high school senior and still lasted until the 18th round of the 2001 draft, mainly because his lack of size scared teams off. The Astros have had a lot of success with righthanders who aren't much more than 6 feet tall, including Octavio Dotel, Roy Oswalt and Tim Redding. As a result, they may have gotten a steal in DeLeon. Besides his fastball, he also has an 80-mph curveball with an 11-to-5 break. He's very raw and will need his mechanics smoothed out, because the velocity on his fastball and the consistency of his curveball fluctuate dramatically, but he already does a good job of throwing strikes. His changeup is nonexistent at this point. DeLeon already has shown considerable mental toughness, putting together a fine pro debut after his girlfriend, the mother of his child, was killed in an automobile accident last May. Houston will bring him along slowly, so he'll probably begin 2002 in extended spring training before going to the short-season New York-Penn league in June.

Year	Club (League)	Class	W	L	ERA	G	GS	CG	SV	IP	H	R	ER	BB	SO
2001	Martinsville (Appy)	R	1	2	2.32	13	7	0	0	43	27	12	11	11	44
MINOR LEAGUE TOTALS			1	2	2.32	13	7	0	0	43	27	12	11	11	44

29. Brandon Puffer, rhp

Born: Oct. 5, 1975. **Ht.:** 6-3. **Wt.:** 190. **Bats:** R. **Throws:** R. **School:** Capistrano Valley HS, Mission Viejo, Calif. **Career Transactions:** Selected by Twins in 27th round of 1994 draft; signed June 10, 1994 . . . Released by Twins, May 6, 1996 . . . Signed by Angels, May 28, 1996 . . . Released by Angels, Dec. 15, 1997 . . . Signed by Reds, Jan. 14, 1998 . . . Granted free agency, Oct. 16, 1998; re-signed by Reds, Nov. 17, 1998 . . . Granted free agency, Oct. 15, 1999 . . . Signed by Rockies, Nov. 18, 1999 . . . Released by Rockies, May 18, 2000 . . . Signed by independent Somerset (Atlantic), May 2000 . . . Contract purchased by Astros from Somerset, July 17, 2000.

The Astros have a collection of older relievers who performed well in the upper minors and earned spots on the 40-man roster last year. Jim Mann tied for the Triple-A Pacific Coast League saves lead, while Ricky Stone was a solid swingman in Double-A. Both pitched well in brief September stints with Houston as well. Though Puffer didn't reach the majors, he has a bit more upside. After the Twins, Angels, Reds and Rockies let him go earlier in his career, he went to the independent Atlantic League before signing with the Astros in July 2000. In his first full year in the organization, he held opponents to a .181 average, the lowest among Texas League relievers. A sidearmer who hitters can't get comfortable against, Puffer picked up 3-4 mph on his fastball last year and topped out at 93 mph. He throws both two-seamers and four-seamers, so he can make the pitch sink or ride, and he enjoys working inside. He also has a sweeping slider that works versus both righthanders (they chase it out of the zone) and lefthanders (he back-doors it on them for strikes). He'll also changes speeds on his fastball versus lefties, and they give him little trouble. Puffer needs to throw more strikes and prove he can get hitters out in Triple-A. He certainly has the stuff to do so.

Year	Club (League)	Class	W	L	ERA	G	GS	CG	SV	IP	H	R	ER	BB	SO
1994	Twins (GCL)	R	2	2	3.06	18	0	0	2	35	33	18	12	19	40
1995	Twins (GCL)	R	0	3	2.88	14	5	0	1	41	29	21	13	21	35
1996	Angels (AZL)	R	0	1	3.60	1	1	0	0	5	7	2	2	1	3
	Boise (NWL)	A	2	0	4.45	16	0	0	1	30	27	19	15	11	22
1997	Boise (NWL)	A	0	0	2.35	6	0	0	1	15	10	5	4	2	15
	Cedar Rapids (Mid)	A	0	0	2.60	10	0	0	0	17	8	6	5	10	11
1998	Charleston, WV (SAL)	A	2	7	6.93	29	0	0	1	51	68	45	39	23	36
	Chattanooga (SL)	AA	0	0	3.12	7	0	0	0	9	2	3	3	3	6
1999	Clinton (Mid)	A	1	2	1.99	59	0	0	34	63	53	20	14	24	60
2000	Asheville (SAL)	A	0	0	8.16	14	0	0	5	14	19	16	13	11	15
	Somerset (Atl)	IND	2	2	3.52	15	0	0	1	23	25	12	9	9	21
	Kissimmee (FSL)	A	2	3	1.27	18	0	0	9	21	18	6	3	11	26
2001	Round Rock (TL)	AA	6	1	2.07	56	0	0	8	83	52	19	19	35	91
MINOR LEAGUE TOTALS			15	19	3.32	248	6	0	62	385	326	180	142	171	360

30. Monte Mansfield, rhp

Born: March 22, 1981. **Ht.:** 6-4. **Wt.:** 215. **Bats:** R. **Throws:** R. **School:** Riverside (Calif.) CC. **Career Transactions:** Selected by Astros in 16th round of 2000 draft; signed June 27, 2000.

Mansfield teamed with Mariners prospect Derrick Van Dusen in a formidable lefty-righty starting combo that propelled Riverside to the California junior college title in 2000. Mansfield pitched three complete-game victories in three tournament starts before signing with the Astros as a 16th-round pick. While Van Dusen has made a smooth transition to pro ball, Mansfield struggled for most of 2001 in the Midwest League. He had a 7.82 ERA in the first three months before posting a 4.40 mark in July and August. His velocity increased all season long and he was throwing up to 93 mph at the end. He already owned a big league curveball, and Houston hopes he can pick up a changeup so they can try him as a starter. Mansfield has a projectable body and his size and arm angle make him tough on righthanders. He still needs a lot more polish and command, and he'll get the chance to develop both. He'll probably spend 2002 in Lexington.

Year	Club (League)	Class	W	L	ERA	G	GS	CG	SV	IP	H	R	ER	BB	SO
2000	Martinsville (Appy)	R	2	1	2.22	18	0	0	3	24	16	7	6	14	32
2001	Michigan (Mid)	A	5	4	5.60	40	3	0	2	72	72	52	45	42	81
MINOR LEAGUE TOTALS			7	5	4.75	58	3	0	5	97	88	59	51	56	113

KANSAS CITY
Royals

By Jim Callis

Just a year ago, the Royals had a strategy to return to contention. They had an offense that finished fifth in the American League in scoring in 2000. Kansas City's pitching staff may have ranked 13th in ERA, but the club had spent nine first-round picks on arms in the previous four drafts, providing them with more than enough fodder for a solid rotation of the future. The Royals just had to keep the lineup intact while waiting for the young arms to develop.

Now it's apparent that's won't happen. Johnny Damon, the catalyst of the 2000 offense, was sent to Oakland in a three-team deal in January 2001. Kansas City did receive Angel Berroa, a much-needed shortstop prospect, so the plan still had a chance. But by the time Jermaine Dye was traded to the Athletics in another three-team swap that netted the Royals overrated Neifi Perez, the offense had imploded. If Mike Sweeney departs via free agency following this season, Carlos Beltran may be the only above-average major league hitter left in Kansas City until Berroa hits his stride.

Some of those first-round pitchers took a step back last year as well. Chris George still projects as the club's future ace, but he had a rough indoctrination in the majors. Dan Reichert continued to get strafed in Kansas City. Mike MacDougal struggled to harness his stuff, while Mike Stodolka was never 100 percent physically in his first full pro season. There wasn't much cause for optimism as the Royals failed to top .500 or finish within 16 games of first place for the seventh straight year.

They tried to add some juice to the system in Deric Ladnier's first draft as scouting director. Righthander Colt Griffin and outfielder Roscoe Crosby, Kansas City's first two choices, have nearly limitless potential. But they're also high-risk/high-reward players, and the risk can't be ignored. Furthermore, they alone can't cover up the fact that the talent cupboard is fairly bare. Royals affiliates combined for a .469 winning percentage that ranked 24th among baseball's 30 teams in 2001.

Contending in the AL Central in the near future may be an unrealistic goal. The Twins and White Sox have more young talent than most clubs, while the Tigers are improving and the Indians generate more than twice the revenue that the Royals do.

Organization Overview

General manager: Allard Baird. **Farm director:** Bob Hegman. **Scouting director:** Deric Ladnier.

2001 PERFORMANCE

Class	Team	League	W	L	Pct.	Finish*	Manager
Majors	Kansas City	American	65	97	.401	12th (14)	Tony Muser
Triple-A	Omaha Royals	Pacific Coast	70	74	.486	10th (16)	John Mizerock
Double-A	Wichita Wranglers	Texas	79	58	.577	2nd (8)	Keith Bodie
High A	Wilmington Blue Rocks	Carolina	78	62	.557	2nd (8)	Jeff Garber
Low A	Burlington Bees	Midwest	55	79	.410	14th (16)	Joe Szekely
Short-season	Spokane Indians	Northwest	22	54	.289	8th (8)	Tom Poquette
Rookie	GCL Royals	Gulf Coast	20	40	.333	t-13th (14)	Lino Diaz
OVERALL 2001 MINOR LEAGUE RECORD			324	367	.469	24th (30)	

*Finish in overall standings (No. of teams in league)

ORGANIZATION LEAGUERS

BATTING

*AVG	Ken Harvey, Wichita/Wilmington	.350
R	Angel Berroa, Wichita/Wilmington	106
H	Ken Harvey, Wichita/Wilmington	158
TB	**Brandon Berger**, Wichita	294
2B	Angel Berroa, Wichita/Wilmington	38
3B	Jon Guzman, Burlington	12
HR	**Brandon Berger**, Wichita	40
RBI	**Brandon Berger**, Wichita	118
BB	Marco Cunningham, Wilmington	95
SO	Don Ross, Wilmington	159
SB	Jon Guzman, Burlington	34

PITCHING

W	**Kiko Calero**, Wichita	14
L	Shawn Sedlacek, Omaha/Wichita	15
#ERA	Micah Mangrum, Wilmington/Burlington	2.63
G	Nathan Field, Wichita	52
	Micah Mangrum, Wilmington/Burlington	52
CG	Ryan Baerlocher, Wichita	2
SV	Nathan Field, Wichita	19
IP	Ryan Baerlocher, Wichita	181
BB	Mike MacDougal, Omaha	76
SO	Jimmy Gobble, Wilmington	154

*Minimum 250 At-Bats #Minimum 75 Innings

TOP PROSPECTS OF THE DECADE

1992	Joel Johnston, rhp
1993	Johnny Damon, of
1994	Jeff Granger, lhp
1995	Johnny Damon, of
1996	Jim Pittsley, rhp
1997	Glendon Rusch, lhp
1998	Dee Brown, of
1999	Carlos Beltran, of
2000	Dee Brown, of
2001	Chris George, lhp

TOP DRAFT PICKS OF THE DECADE

1992	Michael Tucker, ss
1993	Jeff Granger, lhp
1994	Matt Smith, lhp/1b
1995	Juan LeBron, of
1996	Dee Brown, of
1997	Dan Reichert, rhp
1998	Jeff Austin, rhp
1999	Kyle Snyder, rhp
2000	Mike Stodolka, lhp
2001	Colt Griffin, rhp

 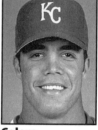

Berger   **Calero**

BEST TOOLS

Best Hitter for Average	Ken Harvey
Best Power Hitter	Brandon Berger
Fastest Baserunner	Jonathan Guzman
Best Fastball	Colt Griffin
Best Breaking Ball	Mike MacDougal
Best Changeup	Miguel Ascencio
Best Control	Jimmy Gobble
Best Defensive Catcher	Mike Tonis
Best Defensive Infielder	Angel Berroa
Best Infield Arm	Angel Berroa
Best Defensive Outfielder	Jeremy Dodson
Best Outfield Arm	Jeremy Dodson

PROJECTED 2005 LINEUP

Catcher	Mike Tonis
First Base	Mike Sweeney
Second Base	Carlos Febles
Third Base	Matt Ferrara
Shortstop	Angel Berroa
Left Field	Dee Brown
Center Field	Carlos Beltran
Right Field	Roscoe Crosby
Designated Hitter	Ken Harvey
No. 1 Starter	Chris George
No. 2 Starter	Jimmy Gobble
No. 3 Starter	Colt Griffin
No. 4 Starter	Miguel Ascencio
No. 5 Starter	Mike MacDougal
Closer	Brad Voyles

ALL-TIME LARGEST BONUSES

Jeff Austin, 1998	$2,700,000
Mike Stodolka, 2000	$2,500,000
Colt Griffin, 2001	$2,400,000
Kyle Snyder, 1999	$2,100,000
Roscoe Crosby, 2001	$1,750,000

DraftAnalysis

2001 Draft

Best Pro Debut: Royals draftees didn't have a lot of initial success, shown by a combined 42-94 record and last-place finishes by the organization's two short-season clubs. Catchers stood out, as short-season Spokane's John Draper (4) and J.D. Alleva (24) hit .261-6-31 and .283-2-38.

Best Athlete: Kansas City talent evaluator Art Stewart, who has been scouting for 48 years, says OF **Roscoe Crosby** (2) reminds him of Ken Griffey. The catch is that Crosby was the top wide receiver recruit in college football as well, and he's going to juggle baseball with playing football at Clemson. The Royals invested a $1.75 million bonus in hopes of keeping him on the diamond.

Best Hitter: Crosby, who had four more touchdown receptions last fall than he had at-bats during the summer. 3B Matt Ferrara (3), who like Crosby has yet to make his pro debut, has a nice approach at the plate and gap power.

Best Raw Power: Crosby.

Fastest Runner: Both Crosby and OF Victor Rosario (12) get from the left side to first base in 4.0 seconds.

Best Defensive Player: A high school shortstop, Ferrara should be a solid average defender at the hot corner. Crosby has the tools to be a standout center fielder.

Best Fastball: The first high schooler known to have broken the 100 mph barrier, RHP Colt Griffin (1) throws harder than anyone in the 2001 draft. He was all over the place in two short outings at Spokane

but the Royals weren't concerned, and his command returned in instructional league. RHP Clint Frost (6) is raw but projectable at 6-foot-7 and already reaches 97 mph.

Most Intriguing Background: Alleva's father Joe is the athletic director at Duke. OF Mervin Williams (19) was better known for his track exploits in high school, while unsigned 3B Bret Berglund (46) received more acclaim for his tennis skills.

Closest To The Majors: RHP Danny Tamayo (10) formed a tough senior tandem with Mets first-rounder Aaron Heilman at Notre Dame. Tamayo has an 88-92 mph fastball and a good changeup, though he needs to refine his overhand curveball.

Crosby

Best Late-Round Pick: SS Angel Sanchez (11) has good speed and a projectable bat.

The One Who Got Away: LHP Daniel Zell (15), who is at Houston, tops out at 90-91 mph but is inconsistent. LHP Taylor Tankersley (39), who is at Alabama, is less physical but more polished, and he can throw 88 mph.

Assessment: Running his first draft for the Royals after scouting for a decade with the Braves, Deric Ladnier used the Atlanta approach of looking for speed, athleticism and power arms. If not for football, the Royals might have taken Crosby over Griffin in the first round. Instead, they got them both.

2000 Draft

C Mike Tonis (2) and RHP Ryan Bukvich (11) could contribute in Kansas City in the near future. LHP Mike Stodolka (1) and C Scott Walter (3) are on a slower track. **Grade: C**

1999 Draft

LHP Jimmy Gobble (1) and RHPs Mike MacDougal and Kyle Snyder (1) all could be members of the Royals' future rotation, with Snyder bouncing back from Tommy John surgery. 1B Ken Harvey (5) is one of the most advanced hitters in the minors, while 2B Mark Ellis (9) could start for Oakland this year. RHP Jay Gehrke (1) has disappointed. **Grade: B+**

1998 Draft

Kansas City went 1-for-3 with first-round picks, scoring with LHP Chris George, possibly finding a useful reliever in RHP Jeff Austin and missing on RHP Matt Burch. Two trades later, RHP Scott Chiasson (5) is now one of the Cubs' better prospects. **Grade: B+**

1997 Draft

RHPs Dan Reichert (1), a signability pick, and Kris Wilson (9) were in the big league rotation last year, while LHP Jeremy Affeldt (3) is an organization favorite. Unsigned Dane Sardinha (2) could have been the catcher the Royals have been seeking. **Grade: C+**

Note: Draft analysis prepared by Jim Callis. Numbers in parentheses indicate draft rounds.

. . . Berroa has Gold Glove potential at shortstop and unlike most standout middle infielders, he can hit.

Berroa **Angel**
ss

Born: Jan. 27, 1980.
Ht.: 6-0. **Wt.:** 175.
Bats: R. **Throws:** R.
Career Transactions: Signed out of Dominican Republic by Athletics, Aug. 14, 1997 . . . Traded by Athletics with C A.J. Hinch and cash to Royals, as part of three-way trade in which Athletics acquired OF Johnny Damon, SS Mark Ellis and a player to be named from Royals and RHP Cory Lidle from Devil Rays, Royals acquired RHP Roberto Hernandez from Devil Rays, and Devil Rays acquired OF Ben Grieve and a player to be named or cash from Athletics, Jan. 8, 2001.

Berroa is the exception to the rule that the Athletics take advantage of the Royals whenever the two clubs swing a trade. In recent years, Oakland has plucked Scott Chiasson (for Jay Witasick), Kevin Appier (for Jeff D'Amico, Brad Rigby and Blake Stein) and Jermaine Dye (in a three-team deal that left Kansas City with Neifi Perez). Kansas City did make out well in January 2001, when it gave up free-agent-to-be Johnny Damon and infield prospect Mark Ellis in another three-team transaction. Berroa gave the Royals the shortstop prospect they coveted. He was as advertised, setting career highs in most offensive categories while improving defensively. Called to the majors in September, Berroa started for the final two weeks of the season and held his own.

Berroa has Gold Glove potential at shortstop, where there's nothing he can't do. He has plenty of range and arm. He can get outs by making the long throw from deep in the hole as well as charging slow rollers. He got steadier in 2001, cutting his errors to 33 after making 54 the prior season. Unlike most standout middle-infield defenders, Berroa can hit. With his speed and pop, Berroa could be a 20-20 player in the majors. He led all minor league shortstops with 60 extra-base hits last season. In order to hit at the top of a lineup, however, Berroa will need to draw more walks. He puts the ball in play early in the count rather than working pitchers. He has become much less nonchalant in the field, though some high Class A Carolina League managers thought he showed off his arm too often. He can become more proficient as a basestealer after getting caught 12 times in 39 attempts last year.

Royals scouts thought Berroa was two years away from being ready for the majors at the time of the trade, but he has developed much more quickly than expected. Even if Berroa begins the year at Triple-A Omaha, he shouldn't stay there long.

Year	Club (League)	Class	AVG	G	AB	R	H	2B	3B	HR	RBI	BB	SO	SB
1998	Athletics West (DSL)	R	.245	58	196	51	48	7	4	8	37	25	37	4
1999	Athletics (AZL)	R	.290	46	169	42	49	11	4	2	24	16	26	11
	Midland (TL)	AA	.059	4	17	3	1	1	0	0	0	0	2	0
2000	Visalia (Cal)	A	.277	129	429	61	119	25	6	10	63	30	70	11
2001	Wilmington (Car)	A	.317	51	199	43	63	18	4	6	25	9	41	10
	Wichita (TL)	AA	.296	80	304	63	90	20	4	8	42	17	55	15
	Kansas City (AL)	MAJ	.302	15	53	8	16	2	0	0	4	3	10	2
MAJOR LEAGUE TOTALS			.302	15	53	8	16	2	0	0	4	3	10	2
MINOR LEAGUE TOTALS			.282	368	1314	263	370	82	22	34	191	97	231	51

HAROLD WEST

2. Jimmy Gobble, lhp

Born: July 19, 1981. **Ht.:** 6-3. **Wt.:** 175. **Bats:** L. **Throws:** L. **School:** John S. Battle HS, Bristol, Va. **Career Transactions:** Selected by Royals in first round (43rd overall) of 1999 draft; signed June 21, 1999.

One of four Royals first-round picks in 1999—and one of three credited to area scout Paul Faulk—Gobble has excelled in Class A the last two seasons. He's built like Chris George, Kansas City's future ace, and has slightly better stuff. He also had more success in the Carolina League at the same age. Gobble has command of three quality pitches. He works with a low-90s fastball, the best curveball in the system and an advanced changeup. There was some concern he'd have trouble keeping his big-breaking curve in the strike zone, but it hasn't been a problem. He does a nice job of keeping the ball down, surrendering just 18 homers in 314 pro innings. He's unflappable on the mound, which he showed when he shut out the Royals for six innings in an exhibition game. Gobble could tweak his changeup and use it more often. But all he really needs is experience because his stuff should play at higher levels. Besides letting him skip short-season Spokane, the Royals have moved him one level at a time. They may not be able to stay so patient if he pitches well at Double-A Wichita to start 2002.

Year	Club (League)	Class	W	L	ERA	G	GS	CG	SV	IP	H	R	ER	BB	SO
1999	Royals (GCL)	R	0	0	2.70	4	1	0	0	7	6	3	2	5	8
2000	Charleston, WV (SAL)	A	12	10	3.66	25	25	3	0	145	144	75	59	34	115
2001	Wilmington (Car)	A	10	6	2.55	27	27	0	0	162	134	58	46	33	154
MINOR LEAGUE TOTALS			22	16	3.07	56	53	3	0	314	284	136	107	72	277

3. Colt Griffin, rhp

Born: Sept. 29, 1982. **Ht.:** 6-4. **Wt.:** 198. **Bats:** R. **Throws:** R. **School:** Marshall (Texas) HS. **Career Transactions:** Selected by Royals in first round (ninth overall) of 2001 draft; signed Aug. 8, 2001.

Until scouts went to see Natchitoches (La.) High righthander Calvin Carpenter pitch against Marshall (Texas) High last spring, Griffin wasn't even on the prospect radar screen. Then he threw 98 mph and attracted a huge following. After becoming the first documented high schooler to hit 100 mph, Griffin went ninth overall in the draft and signed for $2.4 million. Not only can he light up radar guns like few other pitchers, but the ball also comes out of his hand easily. He has a classic pitcher's body that still has room for projection, so he could throw even harder. The Royals expect his slider and changeup eventually will become major league average pitches. Griffin is raw and inexperienced. While everyone coveted his arm strength, some scouts worry that he prizes velocity more than movement. They also wonder how much aptitude he has for a breaking ball. He had no command when he reported to Spokane, though his summer-long layoff for negotiations was at least partly to blame. Griffin needs a lot of polish, so a return trip to Spokane may be in order. The Royals are willing to wait on an arm as special as his.

Year	Club (League)	Class	W	L	ERA	G	GS	CG	SV	IP	H	R	ER	BB	SO
2001	Spokane (NWL)	A	0	1	27.00	3	2	0	0	2	4	7	7	7	0
MINOR LEAGUE TOTALS			0	1	27.00	3	2	0	0	2	4	7	7	7	0

4. Mike MacDougal, rhp

Born: March 5, 1977. **Ht.:** 6-4. **Wt.:** 195. **Bats:** R. **Throws:** R. **School:** Wake Forest University. **Career Transactions:** Selected by Royals in first round (25th overall) of 1999 draft; signed July 1, 1999.

Though MacDougal had just two starts above high Class A entering 2001, Kansas City rushed him to Triple-A. He wasn't ready, as evidenced by his 1-6, 7.02 record through mid-June. He rebounded in the second half, going 7-2, 3.43 to earn his first big league callup. That stint ended when he was struck by a bat in the dugout during a game, fracturing his skull. MacDougal's stuff is better than any pitcher the Royals have, including the major leaguers and Colt Griffin. He throws in the mid-90s with ease, and his fastball dives so much that he can't always throw it for strikes. His slider is the nastiest breaking pitch in the system. His changeup was much improved in the latter half of last season. His pitches are so electric that MacDougal has had difficulty directing them over the plate. He gets behind in counts and gives up more hits and walks than someone with his arsenal should. MacDougal started putting everything together late last summer, so it wouldn't be any surprise if he opened 2002 in Kansas City's rotation. He has no lingering effects from the skull fracture.

Year	Club (League)	Class	W	L	ERA	G	GS	CG	SV	IP	H	R	ER	BB	SO
1999	Spokane (NWL)	A	2	2	4.47	11	11	0	0	46	43	25	23	17	57
2000	Wilmington (Car)	A	9	7	3.92	26	25	0	1	145	115	79	63	76	129
	Wichita (TL)	AA	0	1	7.71	2	2	0	0	12	16	10	10	7	9
2001	Omaha (PCL)	AAA	8	8	4.68	28	27	1	0	144	144	90	75	76	110
	Kansas City (AL)	MAJ	1	1	4.70	3	3	0	0	15	18	10	8	4	7
MAJOR LEAGUE TOTALS			1	1	4.70	3	3	0	0	15	18	10	8	4	7
MINOR LEAGUE TOTALS			19	18	4.44	67	65	1	1	347	318	204	171	176	305

5. Roscoe Crosby, of

Born: Feb. 6, 1983. **Ht.:** 6-2. **Wt.:** 205. **Bats:** L. **Throws:** R. **School:** Union (S.C.) HS. **Career Transactions:** Selected by Royals in second round of 2001 draft; signed July 25, 2001.

The Royals like to go after big-time football recruits, from Willie Wilson and Bo Jackson to 1990s first-round picks Matt Smith and Dee Brown. They considered Crosby before taking Colt Griffin ninth over-all last June, and got Crosby in the second round because he wanted to play wide receiver at Clemson. Signed for $1.75 million, he caught 27 passes and scored four touchdowns for the Tigers as a freshman. Longtime Royals scout Art Stewart says the only high school player comparable to Crosby over the last two decades is Ken Griffey. Crosby has a quick bat and feet to match, and his power-speed combination was the best available in the 2001 draft. He covers a lot of ground in center field, where his arm is average. No matter how athletic prospects may be, though, they almost never develop unless they concentrate on baseball. Crosby isn't close to doing that. His competition in high school wasn't particularly strong, intensifying his need for pro at-bats. Some scouts question his swing. Crosby won't rejoin the organization until mid-May. He likely will make his pro debut in Spokane before returning to Clemson in August. He has NFL first-round potential, which further clouds his future.

Year	Club (League)	Class	AVG	G	AB	R	H	2B	3B	HR	RBI	BB	SO	SB
						Has Not Played								

6. Miguel Ascencio, rhp

Born: Sept. 29, 1980. **Ht.:** 6-2. **Wt.:** 160. **Bats:** R. **Throws:** R. **Career Transactions:** Signed out of Dominican Republic by Phillies, March 2, 1998 . . . Selected by Royals from Phillies in major league Rule 5 draft, Dec. 13, 2001.

Kansas City lost righthanders Corey Thurman and Ryan Baerlocher in December's major league Rule 5 draft, but came out ahead by taking Ascencio from the Phillies with the fifth overall pick. The Royals compare the move to getting an extra first-round pick. Ascencio led the high Class A Florida State League in ERA last season. Unless the Royals want to expose him to waivers and offer him back to Philadelphia for half his $50,000 draft price, he has to stick on the major league roster in 2002. He has two pitches that are ready for that level: a 90-94 mph fastball that chews up bats and the best change-up in the system. Ascencio occasionally will flash a plus curveball but is far from doing so on a consistent basis. His mechanics and his command also need refinement. His status as a Rule 5 pick could hinder his development in 2002. Kansas City general manager Allard Baird says the club won't just carry Ascencio on the 25-man roster to retain him. He'll be given every chance to earn a job as a starter or reliever in spring training.

Year	Club (League)	Class	W	L	ERA	G	GS	CG	SV	IP	H	R	ER	BB	SO
1998	Phillies (DSL)	R	0	2	6.55	11	4	0	0	22	39	29	16	12	7
1999	Phillies (GCL)	R	1	4	5.97	9	5	0	0	29	35	24	19	16	14
2000	Clearwater (FSL)	A	2	1	2.73	5	5	0	0	33	22	10	10	17	24
	Batavia (NY-P)	A	2	2	4.99	7	7	1	0	40	32	23	22	17	28
2001	Clearwater (FSL)	A	12	5	2.84	28	21	2	0	155	124	62	49	70	123
MINOR LEAGUE TOTALS			17	14	3.75	60	42	3	0	279	252	148	116	132	196

7. Ken Harvey, 1b

Born: March 1, 1978. **Ht.:** 6-2. **Wt.:** 240. **Bats:** R. **Throws:** R. **School:** University of Nebraska. **Career Transactions:** Selected by Royals in fifth round of 1999 draft; signed June 4, 1999.

Few hitters can match Harvey's résumé. He won batting titles in NCAA Division I (.478) and the short-season Northwest League (.397) in 1999. He might have done the same in the Carolina League if he hadn't been injured in 2000 or promoted in 2001. His overall .350 average ranked fourth in the minors last year. Harvey's bat caught George Brett's eye—or rather his ears—with the sound the ball makes coming off it. He uses a wide-open stance and laces line drives and gappers to the opposite field. Though he has just 27 homers in 220 pro games, the Royals believe he has the strength to hit with plus power. Though he runs OK for his size, Harvey doesn't offer much besides his bat. He has stiff hands at first base and may move to left field, where he'd do less damage. His ability to put the bat on the ball actually works against him in terms of drawing walks. While Harvey made his major league debut last September, he'll probably spend most of 2002 in Triple-A. Mike Sweeney is a free agent after this season, so the first-base job could be his in 2003.

Year	Club (League)	Class	AVG	G	AB	R	H	2B	3B	HR	RBI	BB	SO	SB
1999	Spokane (NWL)	A	.397	56	204	49	81	17	0	8	41	23	30	7
2000	Wilmington (Car)	A	.335	46	164	20	55	10	0	4	25	14	29	0
2001	Wilmington (Car)	A	.380	35	137	22	52	9	1	6	27	13	21	3
	Wichita (TL)	AA	.338	79	314	54	106	20	3	9	63	18	60	3
	Kansas City (AL)	MAJ	.250	4	12	1	3	1	0	0	2	0	4	0
MAJOR LEAGUE TOTALS			.250	4	12	1	3	1	0	0	2	0	4	0
MINOR LEAGUE TOTALS			.359	216	819	145	294	56	4	27	156	68	140	13

8. Kyle Snyder, rhp

Born: Sept. 9, 1977. **Ht.:** 6-8. **Wt.:** 220. **Bats:** R. **Throws:** R. **School:** University of North Carolina. **Career Transactions:** Selected by Royals in first round (seventh overall); signed June 8, 1999.

The seventh overall pick in the 1999 draft, Snyder was the Northwest League's No. 1 prospect in his pro debut. But he has worked just two regular season innings in the two years since, thanks to two elbow operations, which included Tommy John surgery in September 2000. He started to regain his stuff last fall in instructional league and looked good in a five-inning Arizona Fall League cameo. If Snyder's velocity comes back better than ever, as it has with many Tommy John survivors, look out. He threw 95-96 mph before he got hurt and 90-94 in the AFL. Far from a one-pitch guy, he also had a devastating changeup and a plus curveball. He has worked diligently during his rehabilitation, reinforcing Kansas City's belief that he has the best makeup among its pitching prospects. Snyder's comeback is far from complete. He has just 26 pro innings of experience and more elbow surgeries than victories (one). If he hadn't gotten hurt, Snyder might already have reached the majors. The Royals say they'll evaluate him in spring training before deciding where to send him for 2002. He'll be monitored carefully wherever he lands.

Year	Club (League)	Class	W	L	ERA	G	GS	CG	SV	IP	H	R	ER	BB	SO
1999	Spokane (NWL)	A	1	0	4.13	7	7	0	0	24	20	13	11	7	25
2000	Royals (GCL)	R	0	0	0.00	1	1	0	0	2	1	0	0	0	4
	Wilmington (Car)	A	0	0	0.00	1	1	0	0	0	0	1	0	1	0
2002							Did Not Play—Injured								
MINOR LEAGUE TOTALS			1	0	3.81	9	9	0	0	26	21	14	11	8	29

9. Mike Tonis, c

Born: Feb. 9, 1979. **Ht.:** 6-3. **Wt.:** 215. **Bats:** R. **Throws:** R. **School:** University of California. **Career Transactions:** Selected by Royals in second round of 2000 draft; signed July 12, 2000.

The Royals never have been strong at catcher, with Ellie Rodriguez (1969) and Darrell Porter (1980) the only All-Star Game selections in the franchise's 33 seasons. They tried to bolster the position in 2000, when they took Tonis and Scott Walter with second- and third-round picks. He reached Double-A last year in his first full pro season despite a right knee injury that required arthroscopic surgery. He has lived up to his billing as an advanced defensive catcher. He threw out 39 percent of basestealers in 2001 and is athletic. He once played all nine positions in the same college game, when he was clocked at 90 mph from the mound. Tonis has some power and exhibits more patience than the rest of the Royals' better position prospects. He might never hit for much of an average. He has worked on shortening his swing but it still gets a bit long at times. Journeyman Brent Mayne is the best Kansas City has behind the plate right now, and he won't stand in Tonis' way when he's ready. That should be in 2003 after he gets another year of seasoning in the upper minors.

Year	Club (League)	Class	AVG	G	AB	R	H	2B	3B	HR	RBI	BB	SO	SB
2000	Charleston, WV (SAL)	A	.200	28	100	10	20	8	0	0	17	9	22	1
	Omaha (PCL)	AAA	.500	2	8	1	4	0	0	0	3	0	3	0
2001	Wilmington (Car)	A	.252	33	123	15	31	8	0	3	18	15	34	0
	Wichita (TL)	AA	.270	63	226	36	61	11	1	9	43	22	41	1
MINOR LEAGUE TOTALS			.254	126	457	62	116	27	1	12	81	46	100	2

10. Brad Voyles, rhp

Born: Dec. 30, 1976. **Ht.:** 6-1. **Wt.:** 195. **Bats:** R. **Throws:** R. **School:** Lincoln Memorial (Tenn.) University. **Career Transactions:** Selected by Braves in 45th round of 1998 draft; signed June 7, 1998 . . . Traded by Braves with SS Alejandro Machado to Royals for SS Rey Sanchez, July 31, 2001.

When the Braves went looking for shortstop defense at the 2001 trading deadline, the Royals sent Rey Sanchez to Atlanta for Voyles and infield prospect Alejandro Machado. After falling and breaking his ankle in February, Voyles had been sidelined until June. He recovered to soar from high Class A to the majors, allowing just seven runs in 35 overall appearances. Voyles' two best pitches are his hard curveball and his changeup. His fastball is solid at 88-93 mph, and his career began to take off in 2000 when he started using it more often. He does a good job of keeping the ball in the ballpark and has the tough mindset required to close games. Voyles will overthrow and lose the strike zone, a flaw minor league hitters let him get away with. Those in the majors and Arizona Fall League (where he had a 6.19 ERA) did not. If he can command his fastball during spring training, he stands a good chance of making the Royals. When fading Roberto Hernandez relinquishes the closer role, Voyles might be first in line.

Year	Club (League)	Class	W	L	ERA	G	GS	CG	SV	IP	H	R	ER	BB	SO
1998	Eugene (NWL)	A	0	2	3.09	7	0	0	0	12	9	5	4	10	22
1999	Macon (SAL)	A	3	3	2.98	38	0	0	14	51	27	21	17	39	65
	Myrtle Beach (Car)	A	1	1	2.25	5	0	0	0	12	7	3	3	9	13
2000	Myrtle Beach (Car)	A	5	2	1.11	39	0	0	19	57	21	8	7	25	70
2001	Myrtle Beach (Car)	A	0	0	0.00	2	0	0	1	2	0	0	0	1	3
	Greenville (SL)	AA	0	0	1.08	15	0	0	6	17	11	3	2	10	25
	Wichita (TL)	AA	1	0	0.00	11	0	0	4	15	8	0	0	10	19
	Kansas City (AL)	MAJ	0	0	3.86	7	0	0	0	9	5	4	4	8	6
MAJOR LEAGUE TOTALS			0	0	3.86	7	0	0	0	9	5	4	4	8	6
MINOR LEAGUE TOTALS			10	6	1.80	117	0	0	44	165	83	40	33	104	217

11. Runelvys Hernandez, rhp

Born: Sept. 27, 1980. **Ht.:** 6-3. **Wt.:** 185. **Bats:** R. **Throws:** R. **Career Transactions:** Signed out of Dominican Republic by Royals, Dec. 16, 1997.

Kansas City hasn't signed a major leaguer out of the Dominican Republic since it got Carlos Febles in 1993. Hernandez is poised to break that string within a couple of years. After spending three seasons in the Rookie-level Dominican Summer League, he made a successful U.S. debut last year. He spent the first two months in extended spring, impressing the Royals with how quickly he picked up English, before fitting right in at low Class A Burlington. All three of his pitches show potential. He has an 89-93 mph fastball, a curveball he can spin for strikes and a useful changeup. His command belies his youth, and he has a strong frame that should make him durable. Hernandez will move a step up to high Class A Wilmington in 2002.

Year	Club (League)	Class	W	L	ERA	G	GS	CG	SV	IP	H	R	ER	BB	SO
1998	Royals (DSL)	R	0	2	5.29	19	2	0	0	32	31	26	19	29	27
1999	Royals (DSL)	R	2	2	3.06	16	2	0	5	32	23	19	11	17	36
2000	Royals (DSL)	R	7	3	2.25	14	10	0	1	72	57	25	18	18	70
2001	Burlington (Mid)	A	7	5	3.40	17	17	0	0	101	94	46	38	29	100
MINOR LEAGUE TOTALS			16	12	3.26	66	31	0	6	237	205	116	86	93	233

12. Ryan Bukvich, rhp

Born: May 13, 1978. **Ht.:** 6-3. **Wt.:** 237. **Bats:** R. **Throws:** R. **School:** University of Mississippi. **Career Transactions:** Selected by Royals in 11th round of 2000 draft; signed June 9, 2000.

Area scout Mark Willoughby, who urged the Royals to take Miguel Ascencio in the Rule 5 draft, also deserves the credit for Bukvich, who easily could have slipped through the cracks. Bukvich began his college career at NCAA Division II Delta State (Miss.), then transferred to Mississippi and got lit up for two years before being declared academically ineligible as a senior. Willoughby remembered Bukvich's live arm and persuaded Kansas City to take him in the 11th round of the 2000 draft. All he has done in the last 1 1/2 years is reach Double-A while holding opponents to a .180 average and three homers in 100 innings. Bukvich throws in the mid-90s, and he pleased the Royals by turning his hard slurve into a true slider in 2001. It's an average big league pitch now. To finish his climb toward Kauffman Stadium, he just has to throw more strikes. Another possible closer of the future, he likely will return to Wichita at the outset of this season.

Year	Club (League)	Class	W	L	ERA	G	GS	CG	SV	IP	H	R	ER	BB	SO
2000	Spokane (NWL)	A	2	0	0.64	10	0	0	2	14	5	1	1	9	15
	Charleston, WV (SAL)	A	0	0	1.88	11	0	0	4	14	6	3	3	7	17
	Wilmington (Car)	A	0	1	18.00	2	0	0	0	2	3	4	4	5	3
2001	Wilmington (Car)	A	0	1	1.72	37	0	0	13	58	41	16	11	31	80
	Wichita (TL)	AA	0	0	3.75	7	0	0	0	12	9	6	5	2	14
MINOR LEAGUE TOTALS			2	2	2.16	67	0	0	19	100	64	30	24	54	129

13. Jeremy Affeldt, lhp

Born: June 6, 1979. **Ht.:** 6-4. **Wt.:** 185. **Bats:** L. **Throws:** L. **School:** Northwest Christian HS, Spokane, Wash. **Career Transactions:** Selected by Royals in third round of 1997 draft; signed June 21, 1997.

Long an organization favorite, Affeldt had his best pro season and earned Double-A Texas League all-star honors in 2001. He's a poor man's version of Jimmy Gobble, which means he still has pretty good stuff for a lefthander. Affeldt can reach the low 90s with his fastball, which has nice life. His curveball and changeup improved in 2001, though he must use the latter pitch more often, especially against righthanders. If he has an advantage over Gobble, it's that he has a sturdier frame. Despite his solid arsenal, Affeldt doesn't consistently throw quality strikes and gets hit more than he should. Though there are no plans to take him out of the rotation as he moves to Triple-A in 2002, some scouts outside the organization wonder if he'll top out as a lefty reliever.

Year	Club (League)	Class	W	L	ERA	G	GS	CG	SV	IP	H	R	ER	BB	SO
1997	Royals (GCL)	R	2	0	4.50	10	9	0	0	40	34	24	20	21	36
1998	Lansing (Mid)	A	0	3	9.53	6	3	0	0	17	27	21	18	12	8
	Royals (GCL)	R	4	3	2.89	12	9	0	0	56	50	24	18	24	67
1999	Charleston, WV (SAL)	A	7	7	3.83	27	24	2	0	143	140	78	61	80	111
2000	Wilmington (Car)	A	5	15	4.09	27	26	0	0	147	158	87	67	59	92
2001	Wichita (TL)	AA	10	6	3.90	25	25	0	0	145	153	74	63	46	128
MINOR LEAGUE TOTALS			28	34	4.05	107	96	2	0	549	562	308	247	242	442

14. Mike Stodolka, lhp

Born: Sept. 24, 1981. **Ht.:** 6-2. **Wt.:** 210. **Bats:** L. **Throws:** L. **School:** Centennial HS, Corona, Calif. **Career Transactions:** Selected by Royals in first round (fourth overall) of 2000 draft; signed June 7, 2000.

Though Stodolka's willingness to accept a predraft deal worth $2.5 million led to him being taken fourth overall in the 2000 draft, he had plenty of ability to go with his signability. As a high school junior, in fact, he was more attractive to some teams as a hitter. He rarely was at his best in 2001 after he got mononucleosis and was weak when he arrived in camp. Kept in extended spring in April, he had a 2.21 ERA in his first two months in low Class A before shoulder tendinitis got him. He missed three weeks and got shelled upon his return. Stodolka lost a couple of miles an hour off his usual 90-93 mph last summer but should get the velocity back. He'll show a sharp curveball at times but doesn't consistently finish it off or command it. His changeup is getting better but isn't a finished product. Stodolka could shoot up this list if he's 100 percent in 2002, which he may start back at Burlington.

Year	Club (League)	Class	W	L	ERA	G	GS	CG	SV	IP	H	R	ER	BB	SO
2000	Royals (GCL)	R	0	3	2.68	9	6	0	0	37	31	18	11	16	32
	Charleston, WV (SAL)	A	0	0	7.71	1	1	0	0	5	3	4	4	4	0
2001	Burlington (Mid)	A	3	8	4.67	20	20	0	0	94	105	67	49	30	49
MINOR LEAGUE TOTALS			3	11	4.24	30	27	0	0	136	139	89	64	50	81

15. Jeremy Hill, rhp

Born: Aug. 8, 1977. **Ht.:** 5-10. **Wt.:** 185. **Bats:** R. **Throws:** R. **School:** W.T. White HS, Dallas. **Career Transactions:** Selected by Royals in fifth round of 1996 draft; signed June 4, 1996.

A fifth-round pick as a high school catcher, Hill couldn't solve professional pitchers. He batted .229 with 14 homers in five years before moving to the mound in instructional league after the 2000 season. Hill touched 92 mph in high school and 95 in instructional league, then threw explosive 94-96 heaters throughout last year, when managers rated his fastball the best in the low Class A Midwest League. Opponents hit just .158 against him in his first season on the mound. Hill is working on a hard curveball, though it looks better in the bullpen than in games, when he gets overexcited and tries to power rather than finesse it. He fiddles around with a changeup but for the most part attacks hitters low in the zone with his fastball. If he can refine a second pitch and improve his command, he'll give the Royals another potential closer.

Year	Club (League)	Class	AVG	G	AB	R	H	2B	3B	HR	RBI	BB	SO	SB
1996	Royals (GCL)	R	.178	31	90	4	16	6	0	0	4	12	17	0
1997	Spokane (NWL)	A	.283	60	187	35	53	12	1	3	29	25	53	1
1998	Lansing (Mid)	A	.240	86	288	25	69	12	1	4	37	15	75	4
1999	Wilmington (Car)	A	.234	92	304	37	71	12	1	4	27	38	75	2
2000	Wilmington (Car)	A	.197	99	299	33	59	12	2	3	26	33	84	1
MINOR LEAGUE TOTALS			.229	368	1168	134	268	54	5	14	123	123	304	8

Year	Club (League)	Class	W	L	ERA	G	GS	CG	SV	IP	H	R	ER	BB	SO
2001	Burlington (Mid)	A	0	2	1.51	40	0	0	12	48	22	11	8	25	66
	Wilmington (Car)	A	4	0	0.73	9	0	0	2	12	10	2	1	8	13
MINOR LEAGUE TOTALS			4	2	1.35	49	0	0	14	60	32	13	9	33	79

16. Alexis Gomez, of

Born: Aug. 6, 1980. **Ht.:** 6-2. **Wt.:** 160. **Bats:** L. **Throws:** L. **Career Transactions:** Signed out of Dominican Republic by Royals, Feb. 21, 1997.

Sometimes compared to Willie Wilson and Carlos Beltran, Gomez is the best of a group of young Royals outfield prospects straining to translate their physical tools into baseball skills. A former member of the Dominican junior national volleyball team, Gomez is unquestionably loaded with athleticism. He can run the 60-yard dash in 6.5-6.6 seconds, put on a power display in batting practice and has arm strength. He started to hit for average in 2001, which was a positive sign, but he still has plenty of work to do. He must get stronger so he can produce more extra-base hits. He also must tighten his strike zone so he won't be exploited by better pitchers and must learn the art of basestealing to make better use of his speed. He must get better jumps in center field. Gomez will work on those areas of his game in the upper minors this year.

Year	Club (League)	Class	AVG	G	AB	R	H	2B	3B	HR	RBI	BB	SO	SB
1997	Royals (DSL)	R	.351	64	248	51	87	12	9	0	42	33	52	9
1998	Royals (DSL)	R	.283	67	233	51	66	11	3	1	34	50	46	17
1999	Royals (GCL)	R	.276	56	214	44	59	12	1	5	31	32	48	13
2000	Wilmington (Car)	A	.254	121	461	63	117	13	4	1	33	45	121	21
2001	Wilmington (Car)	A	.302	48	169	29	51	8	2	1	9	11	43	7
	Wichita (TL)	AA	.281	83	342	55	96	15	6	4	34	27	70	16
MINOR LEAGUE TOTALS			.286	439	1667	293	476	71	25	12	183	198	380	83

17. Orber Moreno, rhp

Born: April 27, 1977. **Ht.:** 6-3. **Wt.:** 200. **Bats:** R. **Throws:** R. **Career Transactions:** Signed out of Venezuela by Royals, Nov. 10, 1993 . . . On disabled list, March 24-Oct. 12, 2000.

Moreno used to be Kansas City's closer of the future—back when the future meant 2000. Now the Royals will settle for just getting him healthy and going from there. Promoted to the majors in 1999, Moreno overthrew and wrecked his arm. He went down, first with biceps tendinitis and then with an elbow injury that required Tommy John surgery. He made it back to Triple-A by the end of last year, but he came down with a sore shoulder this winter while pitching in his native Venezuela. Moreno once topped out at 98 mph, and while he doesn't throw quite that hard any longer, he's now a better pitcher. His slider has improved since his surgery, and his changeup is coming along. If he's healthy he still could solve Kansas City's closer problem. But if there's one thing the system is deep in, it's relief prospects, and Moreno must re-establish himself.

Year	Club (League)	Class	W	L	ERA	G	GS	CG	SV	IP	H	R	ER	BB	SO
1994	Royals/Rockies (DSL)	R	3	3	3.19	16	11	0	1	68	51	33	24	27	44
1995	Royals (GCL)	R	1	1	2.45	8	3	0	0	22	15	9	6	7	21
1996	Royals (GCL)	R	5	1	1.36	12	7	0	1	46	37	15	7	10	50
1997	Lansing (Mid)	A	4	8	4.81	27	25	0	0	138	150	83	74	45	128
1998	Wilmington (Car)	A	3	2	0.82	23	0	0	7	33	8	3	3	10	50
	Wichita (TL)	AA	0	1	2.88	24	0	0	7	34	28	13	11	12	40
1999	Omaha (PCL)	AAA	3	1	2.10	16	0	0	4	26	17	6	6	4	30
	Kansas City (AL)	MAJ	0	0	5.63	7	0	0	0	8	4	5	5	6	7
	Royals (GCL)	R	0	0	0.00	1	1	0	0	1	0	0	0	0	1
2000						Did Not Play—Injured									
2001	Wilmington (Car)	A	1	1	2.53	8	1	0	0	11	12	5	3	1	16
	Wichita (TL)	AA	0	0	0.00	5	0	0	1	9	3	0	0	2	10
	Omaha (PCL)	AAA	1	1	4.71	17	0	0	3	21	19	11	11	8	25
MAJOR LEAGUE TOTALS			0	0	5.63	7	0	0	0	8	4	5	5	6	7
MINOR LEAGUE TOTALS			21	19	3.19	157	48	0	24	409	340	178	145	126	415

18. Jeff Austin, rhp

Born: Oct. 19, 1976. **Ht.:** 6-0. **Wt.:** 185. **Bats:** R. **Throws:** R. **School:** Stanford University. **Career Transactions:** Selected by Royals in first round (fourth overall) of 1998 draft; signed Feb. 20, 1999.

The $2.7 million bonus Austin received as the fourth overall pick in the 1998 draft remains a club record, and it looked like a prudent investment until he got to Omaha. Baseball America's 1998 College Player of the Year hit the wall as a Triple-A starter, going 1-7, 9.45 to open last season. Austin's curveball always has been his meal ticket, but he and the Royals both learned that it wasn't enough. His fastball never had notable velocity or movement and his changeup was merely average. But once Austin moved to the bullpen last May, his fastball jumped to 94-96 mph and his curve got a little sharper. He even made it to Kansas City for 21 appearances. Austin lost his effectiveness toward the end of the season, perhaps because he wasn't used to the rigors of relieving. He'll get a chance to make the Royals in spring training.

Year	Club (League)	Class	W	L	ERA	G	GS	CG	SV	IP	H	R	ER	BB	SO
1999	Wilmington (Car)	A	7	2	3.77	18	18	0	0	112	108	52	47	39	97
	Wichita (TL)	AA	3	1	4.46	6	6	0	0	34	40	19	17	11	21
2000	Wichita (TL)	AA	2	2	2.93	6	6	1	0	43	33	16	14	4	31
	Omaha (PCL)	AAA	7	9	4.48	23	19	1	0	127	150	85	63	35	57
2001	Omaha (PCL)	AAA	3	7	6.88	28	8	0	2	71	89	56	54	27	55
	Kansas City (AL)	MAJ	0	0	5.54	21	0	0	0	26	27	17	16	14	27
MAJOR LEAGUE TOTALS			0	0	5.54	21	0	0	0	26	27	17	16	14	27
MINOR LEAGUE TOTALS			22	21	4.53	81	57	2	2	387	420	228	195	116	261

19. Brandon Berger, of

Born: Feb. 21, 1975. **Ht.:** 5-11. **Wt.:** 200. **Bats:** R. **Throws:** R. **School:** Eastern Kentucky University. **Career Transactions:** Selected by Royals in 14th round of 1996 draft; signed June 4, 1996.

Berger spent most of the previous three years in high Class A before coming out of nowhere to lead the Texas League in homers and slugging percentage (.648) in 2001. His 40 longballs ranked second in the minors and more than doubled his previous career high of 18. Did his advanced age of 26 and Wichita's bandbox Lawrence-Dumont Stadium contribute to his power exploding? Certainly. But he also altered his stance and stopped diving into pitches. While he's going to have to prove he can do it again, he did homer twice in five big league starts and went deep four times in the Arizona Fall League. He offers some speed and athleticism, too, though he's a tentative left fielder with a below-average arm. Kansas City has plenty of outfield and DH candidates, so Berger probably faces a year in Triple-A. The ball flies out of Omaha's Rosenblatt Stadium, so he could keep mashing.

Year	Club (League)	Class	AVG	G	AB	R	H	2B	3B	HR	RBI	BB	SO	SB
1996	Spokane (NWL)	A	.307	71	283	46	87	12	1	13	58	31	64	17
1997	Lansing (Mid)	A	.293	107	393	64	115	22	6	12	73	42	79	13
1998	Wilmington (Car)	A	.222	110	338	53	75	18	3	8	50	53	94	13
1999	Wilmington (Car)	A	.293	119	450	73	132	27	4	16	73	45	93	29
2000	Wichita (TL)	AA	.163	27	86	9	14	2	0	3	8	7	27	6
	Wilmington (Car)	A	.285	102	379	63	108	18	4	15	71	40	71	12
2001	Wichita (TL)	AA	.308	120	454	98	140	28	3	40	118	43	91	14
	Kansas City (AL)	MAJ	.313	6	16	4	5	1	1	2	2	2	2	0
MAJOR LEAGUE TOTALS			.313	6	16	4	5	1	1	2	2	2	2	0
MINOR LEAGUE TOTALS			.282	656	2383	406	671	127	21	107	451	261	519	104

20. Tony Cogan, lhp

Born: Dec. 21, 1976. **Ht.:** 6-2. **Wt.:** 195. **Bats:** L. **Throws:** L. **School:** Stanford University. **Career Transactions:** Selected by Royals in 12th round of 1999 draft; signed June 21, 1999.

Pardon Cogan if he has gotten a little confused by how Kansas City has handled him. He began his pro career in relief, the same role he had at Stanford. After he was mediocre in high Class A in 2000, he was demoted and converted to a starter. He posted a 1.83 ERA in 13 starts, then rocketed onto the Royals' Opening Day roster in 2001—as a lefthanded specialist. He gave up a homer to the first big league hitter he faced, Jorge Posada, and rode the Kansas City-Omaha shuttle three times during the year as his considerable mental toughness was put to the test. If Cogan doesn't make the Royals out of spring training, the latest plan calls for him to resume starting. He's probably better off doing that because he doesn't have an out pitch. He's more effective mixing his three average pitches (fastball, curveball, changeup) to keep hitters off balance. Cogan generally throws strikes and keeps the ball in the park, though those traits weren't evident during his major league trials last year.

Year	Club (League)	Class	W	L	ERA	G	GS	CG	SV	IP	H	R	ER	BB	SO
1999	Spokane (NWL)	A	1	3	1.36	27	0	0	4	40	26	10	6	14	37
2000	Wilmington (Car)	A	2	4	4.35	16	3	0	1	39	39	22	19	18	31
	Charleston, WV (SAL)	A	6	2	1.83	13	13	0	0	79	65	19	16	14	51
	Wichita (TL)	AA	1	1	11.57	2	0	0	0	2	6	4	3	2	1
2001	Kansas City (AL)	MAJ	0	4	5.84	39	0	0	0	25	32	17	16	13	17
	Wichita (TL)	AA	1	1	2.08	8	0	0	1	17	13	6	4	4	12
	Omaha (PCL)	AAA	1	1	2.79	9	0	0	2	10	14	3	3	3	8
MAJOR LEAGUE TOTALS			0	4	5.84	39	0	0	0	25	32	17	16	13	17
MINOR LEAGUE TOTALS			12	12	2.45	75	16	0	8	187	163	64	51	55	140

21. Chad Santos, 1b

Born: April 28, 1981. **Ht.:** 6-1. **Wt.:** 215. **Bats:** L. **Throws:** L. **School:** St. Louis School, Honolulu. **Career Transactions:** Selected by Royals in 22nd round of 1999 draft; signed June 8, 1999.

If Ken Harvey can't handle the defensive responsibilities of first base, Santos could be Mike Sweeney's eventual successor in Kansas City. He has the most raw power in the organization, though he hasn't tapped into it as well as Brandon Berger has with his. Santos can drive the ball out of any part of any ballpark, but he needs to realize that sometimes singles can be useful as well. He did make some adjustments last year, shortening his swing and using more of the field, but he still hit just .252 and struck out too much. Santos has soft hands and is a very good defender. He'll be challenged this year in high Class A, where Wilmington's Frawley Stadium is extremely pitcher-friendly.

Year	Club (League)	Class	AVG	G	AB	R	H	2B	3B	HR	RBI	BB	SO	SB
1999	Royals (GCL)	R	.271	48	177	20	48	9	0	4	35	12	54	1
2000	Charleston, WV (SAL)	A	.209	59	187	16	39	9	2	4	18	27	62	0
	Spokane (NWL)	A	.251	73	267	40	67	18	0	14	47	36	103	1
2001	Burlington (Mid)	A	.252	121	444	58	112	32	0	16	83	52	101	0
MINOR LEAGUE TOTALS			.247	301	1075	134	266	68	2	38	183	127	320	2

22. Scott Walter, c

Born: Dec. 28, 1978. **Ht.:** 6-2. **Wt.:** 200. **Bats:** R. **Throws:** R. **School:** Loyola Marymount University. **Career Transactions:** Selected by Royals in third round of 2000 draft; signed June 26, 2000.

Taken one round after Mike Tonis in the 2000 draft, Walter is his opposite. Where Tonis' defense is ahead of his offense, the reverse is true with Walter. He's still adjusting his swing from aluminum to wood, but Walter should hit for more average and power than Tonis. He just needs to show more patience at the plate, staying back and trusting his swing. Walter did make progress with his throwing, blocking and game-calling skills last season. He has a ways to go, however, after erasing just 28 percent of basestealers and permitting 124 swipes in 93 games in 2001. He has been hindered by injuries in both his years a pro, losing time to a broken left thumb in 2000 and a broken left wrist last year. The Royals value defense more than offense from their catchers, so Walter will open 2002 a level behind Tonis, either in high Class A or Double-A.

Year	Club (League)	Class	AVG	G	AB	R	H	2B	3B	HR	RBI	BB	SO	SB
2000	Spokane (NWL)	A	.114	13	35	2	4	1	0	0	2	1	10	1
2001	Burlington (Mid)	A	.274	33	124	24	34	12	1	6	22	6	16	0
	Wilmington (Car)	A	.249	60	201	19	50	9	0	7	33	18	36	1
MINOR LEAGUE TOTALS			.244	106	360	45	88	22	1	13	57	25	62	2

23. Matt Ferrara, 3b

Born: Sept. 27, 1982. **Ht.:** 6-1. **Wt.:** 200. **Bats:** R. **Throws:** R. **School:** Westminster Academy, Fort Lauderdale. **Career Transactions:** Selected by Royals in third round of 2001 draft; signed Aug. 24, 2001.

Ferrara has an interesting pedigree. He played shortstop in high school under coach Rich Hofman—who mentored Alex Rodriguez a decade earlier. After drafting him in the third round last June, the Royals nearly lost Ferrara to defending College World Series champion Miami. He showed up on the Coral Gables campus last fall, but delayed attending classes for three days before signing when Kansas City bumped its offer from $425,000 to $450,000. Converted to third base in instructional league, he labored diligently on his footwork and took to the hot corner. He has a nice approach and gap power at the plate. Ferrara has a solid array of tools and is the most well-rounded player from Kansas City's latest draft crop. The Royals also praise his makeup. He'll begin 2002 in extended spring training.

Year	Club (League)	Class	AVG	G	AB	R	H	2B	3B	HR	RBI	BB	SO	SB
			Has Not Played—Signed 2002 Contract											

24. Shawn Sonnier, rhp

Born: July 5, 1976. **Ht.:** 6-5. **Wt.:** 210. **Bats:** R. **Throws:** R. **School:** Louisiana Tech. **Career Transactions:** Signed as nondrafted free agent by Royals, Aug. 18, 1998.

The Royals got bad news in January, when they learned that Sonnier's shoulder needed more extensive surgery than originally thought. He had his labrum and rotator cuff repaired and his shoulder tightened. He probably won't start throwing until May at the earliest. Before he ran into shoulder problems in 2001, Sonnier had breezed through the minors after signing as a nondrafted free agent. He spent time at two junior colleges and Louisiana Tech before finally attracting attention at the 1998 National Baseball Congress World Series. When healthy, Sonnier can challenge hitters with a 90-94 mph fastball, a slider and a splitter. He doesn't always get a lot of life on his fastball or throw strikes, two shortcomings he'll try to address when he gets back on the mound.

Year	Club (League)	Class	W	L	ERA	G	GS	CG	SV	IP	H	R	ER	BB	SO
1998	Spokane (NWL)	A	0	0	1.35	7	0	0	1	7	7	1	1	1	10
1999	Wilmington (Car)	A	1	2	2.88	44	0	0	13	59	46	20	19	19	73
2000	Wichita (TL)	AA	0	3	2.25	48	0	0	21	64	41	22	16	26	90
2001	Omaha (PCL)	AAA	5	5	4.82	47	2	0	6	71	69	41	38	33	63
MINOR LEAGUE TOTALS			6	10	3.31	146	2	0	41	201	163	84	74	79	236

25. Ira Brown, rhp

Born: Aug. 3, 1982. **Ht.:** 6-4. **Wt.:** 215. **Bats:** R. **Throws:** R. **School:** Willis (Texas) HS. **Career Transactions:** Selected by Royals in eighth round of 2001 draft; signed June 8, 2001.

Until his senior year at Willis (Texas) High, Brown was known mainly for his basketball exploits. In baseball, he had peaked as a junior-varsity outfielder. Last spring, he moved into the varsity rotation and repeatedly showed a 90-93 mph fastball, which got him drafted in the eighth round. Outside of Roscoe Crosby, Brown was the best athlete signed by the Royals in 2001. That athleticism gives him an excellent chance to repeat his delivery, which will allow him to refine his secondary pitches (a curveball and rudimentary changeup) and his command. With his size and heat, Brown resembles a young Lee Smith. He still has a lot to learn about the art of pitching, but his ceiling is extremely high. He may start 2002 in extended spring training before going to Spokane in June.

Year	Club (League)	Class	W	L	ERA	G	GS	CG	SV	IP	H	R	ER	BB	SO
2001	Royals (GCL)	R	2	5	4.99	11	10	0	0	40	40	27	22	25	42
MINOR LEAGUE TOTALS			2	5	4.99	11	10	0	0	40	40	27	22	25	42

26. Chris Tierney, lhp

Born: Sept. 1, 1983. **Ht.:** 6-6. **Wt.:** 205. **Bats:** L. **Throws:** L. **School:** Lockport (Ill.) HS. **Career Transactions:** Selected by Royals in seventh round of 2001 draft; signed July 10, 2001.

Tierney helped his draft status last spring when he faced future White Sox first-round pick Kris Honel in a high school playoff game. Showing a 90-mph fastball and a sharp breaking ball, Tierney got within four outs of a no-hitter before losing 1-0 on two singles and a wild pitch. Tall and lanky, he's ultraprojectable and has an easy arm action, so he should develop plus velocity. His fastball has nice, late life. Tierney made some progress with his changeup after turning pro, though his breaking ball was very inconsistent.

While he did get rocked in the Rookie-level Gulf Coast League, he kept throwing strikes to both sides of the plate. Like Ira Brown, Tierney likely will be kept on the slow track for now.

Year	Club (League)	Class	AVG	G	AB	R	H	2B	3B	HR	RBI	BB	SO	SB
2001	Yakima (NWL)	A	.186	30	86	6	16	6	0	0	5	7	30	0
MINOR LEAGUE TOTALS			.186	30	86	6	16	6	0	0	5	7	30	0

27. Mike Natale, rhp

Born: Sept. 2, 1979. **Ht.:** 6-2. **Wt.:** 195. **Bats:** R. **Throws:** R. **School:** Lewis-Clark State (Idaho) University. **Career Transactions:** Selected by Royals in 22nd round of 2000 draft; signed June 12, 2000.

The cousin of former big league pitcher Greg Harris, Natale spent two years at Santa Ana (Calif.) JC before winning the NAIA World Series with Lewis-Clark State (Idaho) in 2000. While the Royals admit they didn't have huge expectations for him when they drafted him in the 22nd round that June, he has been an extremely pleasant surprise. They knew he had a good splitter. Natale's fastball has sat at 90 mph, which is enough velocity because it sinks and he can spot it where he wants. After he excelled as a reliever in his first taste of pro ball, Kansas City shifted him to the rotation in high Class A last year to see if his stuff would hold up. It did, as his changeup proved to be an effective third pitch. Natale will try to keep beating the odds this year in Double-A.

Year	Club (League)	Class	W	L	ERA	G	GS	CG	SV	IP	H	R	ER	BB	SO
2000	Spokane (NWL)	A	2	1	1.32	23	0	0	8	41	30	7	6	13	43
2001	Wilmington (Car)	A	9	8	3.28	28	27	0	0	159	152	75	58	33	134
MINOR LEAGUE TOTALS			11	9	2.88	51	27	0	8	200	182	82	64	46	177

28. Byron Gettis, of

Born: March 13, 1980. **Ht.:** 6-2. **Wt.:** 220. **Bats:** R. **Throws:** R. **School:** Cahokia (Ill.) HS. **Career Transactions:** Signed as nondrafted free agent by Royals, June 29, 1998.

Among their outfielders, the Royals have a starter kit of football skill-position players. Big leaguer Dee Brown was a prized tailback recruit by Maryland, and 2001 second-rounder Roscoe Crosby spent last fall as a Clemson wide receiver. The quarterback would be Gettis, who was set to throw passes for Minnesota before changing his mind and signing with the Royals in a bowling alley as a nondrafted free agent. He's the cousin of former NFL linebacker Dana Howard. Gettis has the power and arm scouts like to see in a right fielder, but he has yet to get the most out of his tools. It's not for want of trying—Kansas City loves his makeup—but rather it's because he's so raw. His ability to make contact, instincts and weight all have been negatives thus far. Gettis has yet to rise higher than Class A after four years as a pro and might return to Wilmington after struggling there in 2000 and 2001.

Year	Club (League)	Class	AVG	G	AB	R	H	2B	3B	HR	RBI	BB	SO	SB
1998	Royals (GCL)	R	.216	27	88	11	19	2	0	0	4	4	20	0
1999	Royals (GCL)	R	.316	28	95	20	30	6	2	5	21	17	21	3
	Charleston, WV (SAL)	A	.295	43	149	19	44	7	2	2	13	10	36	10
2000	Wilmington (Car)	A	.155	30	97	13	15	2	0	0	10	13	33	2
	Charleston, WV (SAL)	A	.215	94	344	43	74	18	3	5	50	31	95	11
2001	Burlington (Mid)	A	.314	37	140	26	44	9	2	5	26	14	25	4
	Wilmington (Car)	A	.251	82	303	34	76	21	2	6	51	20	70	4
MINOR LEAGUE TOTALS			.248	341	1216	166	302	65	11	23	175	109	300	34

29. Alejandro Machado, 2b/ss

Born: April 26, 1982. **Ht.:** 6-0. **Wt.:** 160. **Bats:** R. **Throws:** R. **Career Transactions:** Signed out of Venezuela by Braves, July 2, 1998 . . . Traded by Braves with RHP Brad Voyles to Royals for SS Rey Sanchez, July 31, 2001.

Machado had moved from shortstop to second base with the Braves, then shifted back after coming to the Royals in the Rey Sanchez trade last summer. His arm is just average for shortstop, but his range, soft hands and instincts may allow him to remain there. He made just eight errors in 110 games between second and short in 2001. As good as he is defensively, Machado is going to have to show a lot more offensively to reach the majors. He has good speed but doesn't get on base enough or know how to use it well once he does. He's a slap hitter who needs to get stronger and improve his bunting ability. He's not adverse to drawing a walk, though he could make more consistent contact. Machado will play in high Class A in 2002.

Year	Club (League)	Class	AVG	G	AB	R	H	2B	3B	HR	RBI	BB	SO	SB
1999	Braves (GCL)	R	.278	56	223	45	62	11	0	0	14	20	22	19
2000	Danville (Appy)	R	.341	61	217	45	74	6	2	0	16	53	29	30
2001	Macon (SAL)	A	.271	82	306	43	83	6	3	1	24	34	56	20
	Burlington (Mid)	A	.239	28	109	17	26	5	0	0	11	10	16	5
MINOR LEAGUE TOTALS			.287	227	855	150	245	28	5	1	65	117	123	74

30. Angel Sanchez, ss

Born: Sept. 20, 1983. **Ht.:** 6-1. **Wt.:** 170. **Bats:** R. **Throws:** R. **School:** Florencia Garcia HS, Las Piedras, P.R. **Career Transactions:** Selected by Royals in 11th round of 2001 draft; signed June 8, 2001.

Sanchez could be the sleeper of the Royals' 2001 draft after they took him out of Puerto Rico in the 11th round. Like Ira Brown and Chris Tierney, Sanchez didn't light up the Gulf Coast League but that couldn't diminish Kansas City's enthusiasm. He's a toolsy shortstop whose arm and speed are plus tools. He's wiry strong and the ball carries off his bat when he centers the ball. For all his upside, Sanchez is going to need plenty of time in the minors. He'll have to develop his body and tighten his strike zone in order to provide much offense. He must get more aggressive on the bases and more steady in the field. Sanchez doesn't figure to make his full-season debut until 2003 at the earliest.

Year	Club (League)	Class	AVG	G	AB	R	H	2B	3B	HR	RBI	BB	SO	SB
2001	Royals (GCL)	R	.242	30	95	10	23	4	0	0	6	6	28	3
MINOR LEAGUE TOTALS			.242	30	95	10	23	4	0	0	6	6	28	3

LOS ANGELES
Dodgers

TOP 30 PROSPECTS

1. Ricardo Rodriguez, rhp
2. Chin-Feng Chen, of
3. Joel Guzman, ss
4. Ben Diggins, rhp
5. Joe Thurston, ss
6. Hong-Chih Kuo, lhp
7. Willy Aybar, 3b
8. Jose Rojas, rhp
9. Joel Hanrahan, rhp
10. Jorge Nunez, ss
11. Koyie Hill, c
12. Jason Repko, ss
13. Brennan King, 3b
14. Luke Allen, of
15. Brian Pilkington, rhp
16. Reggie Abercrombie, of
17. Shane Victorino, of
18. Candido Martinez, of
19. Shane Nance, lhp
20. Kole Strayhorn, rhp
21. Michael Keirstead, rhp
22. Sean Pierce, of
23. Steve Colyer, lhp
24. Bubba Crosby, of
25. Carlos Garcia, rhp
26. Victor Diaz, 2b
27. Jose Diaz, c
28. Will McCrotty, rhp
29. Jose Garcia, of
30. Lamont Matthews, of

By Bill Ballew

After several years as the most dysfunctional family in the major leagues, the Dodgers have stabilized their organization and appear headed in the right direction.

Manager Davey Johnson was fired following the 2000 season and replaced by the unproven Jim Tracy. Gary Sheffield created controversy in spring training by demanding a trade because he didn't like his contract. General manager Kevin Malone argued initially with Sheffield when he wasn't sticking his foot in his mouth, and he was forced to resign in April after a confrontation with a fan.

Dave Wallace took over as interim GM in May before former White Sox assistant GM Dan Evans, who had been hired as a senior adviser, was named GM in October. Wallace remains on board as the senior vice president for baseball operations as Los Angeles put together a strong team of talent evaluators. Former Angels GM Bill Bavasi is the new farm director, ex-Marlins farm director and manager John Boles is a senior adviser and former Astros and Angels skipper Terry Collins is minor league field coordinator.

The new regime has been busy undoing much of the work of Malone, who assembled the major leagues' highest payroll but not a playoff club. The upper levels of the farm system have little to offer, so Evans busily worked the trade market, cutting deals for lefthander Omar Daal and shortstop Cesar Izturis, then following with a blockbuster to send Sheffield to the Braves after he shot his mouth off again. He got Brian Jordan and Odalis Perez in return.

Another big move preceded the Sheffield trade in January, as the Dodgers won the bidding rights to Japanese lefthander Kazuhisa Ishii for $11.25 million. If he signs as expected, he'll give Los Angeles another quality big league starter right away.

Malone does deserve credit for bringing athletes and power arms into an organization that was crippled by terrible drafts in the mid-1990s. Most of the Dodgers' best minor leaguers have been signed since 1999. Of their top 15 prospects, the lone exceptions are righthander Ricardo Rodriguez and outfielder Luke Allen. The efforts of former assistant GM Ed Creech and scouting director Matt Slater, who both joined the organization under Malone in the fall of 1998, have been evident. Creech, however, left to become the Pirates' scouting director in November.

Organization Overview

General manager: Dan Evans. **Farm director:** Bill Bavasi. **Scouting director:** Logan White.

2001 PERFORMANCE

Class	Farm Team	League	W	L	Pct.	Finish*	Manager
Majors	Los Angeles	National	86	76	.531	t-7th (16)	Jim Tracy
Triple-A	Las Vegas 51s	Pacific Coast	68	76	.472	11th (16)	Rick Sofield
Double-A	Jacksonville Suns	Southern	83	56	.597	1st (10)	John Shoemaker
High A	Vero Beach Dodgers	Florida State	67	66	.504	4th (12)	Bob Mariano
Low A	Wilmington Waves	South Atlantic	73	63	.537	6th (16)	Dino Ebel
Rookie	Great Falls Dodgers	Pioneer	37	39	.487	t-4th (8)	Dave Silvestri
Rookie	GCL Dodgers	Gulf Coast	41	19	.683	1st (14)	Juan Bustabad
OVERALL 2001 MINOR LEAGUE RECORD			371	319	.538	8th (30)	

*Finish in overall standings (No. of teams in league)

ORGANIZATION LEADERS

BATTING
*AVG	Phil Hiatt, Las Vegas	.330
R	Phil Hiatt, Las Vegas	107
H	Koyie Hill, Wilmington	150
TB	Phil Hiatt, Las Vegas	315
2B	**Luke Allen**, Las Vegas/Jacksonville	33
3B	Shane Victorino, Vero Beach/Wilmington	9
HR	Phil Hiatt, Las Vegas	44
RBI	Phil Hiatt, Las Vegas	99
BB	Lamont Matthews, Jacksonville/Vero Beach	107
SO	Reggie Abercrombie, Wilmington	154
SB	Candido Martinez, Wilmington	54

PITCHING
W	Ricardo Rodriguez, Vero Beach	14
L	Ben Simon, Las Vegas/Jacksonville	12
#ERA	Shane Nance, Jacksonville/Vero Beach	2.12
G	Pedro Feliciano, Las Vegas/Jacksonville	60
CG	Three tied at	3
SV	**Kris Foster**, Las Vegas/Jacksonville	25
IP	Eric Junge, Jacksonville	164
BB	Steve Colyer, Vero Beach	77
SO	Mark Kiefer, Las Vegas	174

*Minimum 250 At-Bats #Minimum 75 Innings

TOP PROSPECTS OF THE DECADE

1992	Pedro Martinez, rhp
1993	Mike Piazza, c
1994	Darren Dreifort, rhp
1995	Todd Hollandsworth, of
1996	Karim Garcia, of
1997	Paul Konerko, 3b
1998	Paul Konerko, 1b
1999	Angel Pena, c
2000	Chin-Feng Chen, of
2001	Ben Diggins, rhp

TOP DRAFT PICKS OF THE DECADE

1992	Ryan Luzinski, c
1993	Darren Dreifort, rhp
1994	Paul Konerko, c
1995	David Yocum, lhp
1996	Damian Rolls, 3b
1997	Glenn Davis, 1b
1998	Bubba Crosby, of
1999	Jason Repko, ss/of
2000	Ben Diggins, rhp
2001	Brian Pilkington, rhp (2)

Allen   **Foster**

BEST TOOLS

Best Hitter for Average	Koyie Hill
Best Power Hitter	Chin-Feng Chen
Fastest Baserunner	Travis Ezi
Best Fastball	Ben Diggins
Best Breaking Ball	Ricardo Rodriguez
Best Changeup	Shane Nance
Best Control	Steve Langone
Best Defensive Catcher	Jose Diaz
Best Defensive Infielder	Brennan King
Best Infield Arm	Jorge Nunez
Best Defensive Outfielder	Shane Victorino
Best Outfield Arm	Luke Allen

PROJECTED 2005 LINEUP

Catcher	Koyie Hill
First Base	Paul LoDuca
Second Base	Joe Thurston
Third Base	Adrian Beltre
Shortstop	Cesar Izturis
Left Field	Chin-Feng Chen
Center Field	Shawn Green
Right Field	Brian Jordan
No. 1 Starter	Kevin Brown
No. 2 Starter	Ricardo Rodriguez
No. 3 Starter	Hideo Nomo
No. 4 Starter	Odalis Perez
No. 5 Starter	Hong-Chih Kuo
Closer	Ben Diggins

ALL-TIME LARGEST BONUSES

Joel Guzman, 2001	$2,250,000
Ben Diggins, 2000	$2,200,000
Hideo Nomo, 1995	$2,000,000
Willy Aybar, 2000	$1,400,000
Darren Dreifort, 1993	$1,300,000

DraftAnalysis

2001 Draft

Best Pro Debut: OF Sean Pierce (9) hit .311-6-43 with 29 stolen bases for Rookie-level Great Falls. LHP David Cuen (7) went 4-0, 1.42 with 49 strikeouts in the Rookie-level Gulf Coast League.

Best Athlete: OF Cedric Benson (12) was the best athlete in the draft. Both his power and speed earn the maximum 8 on the 2-to-8 scouting scale. He's still raw as a baseball player, and there's no question football is his best sport. He was the starting tailback as a freshman for Texas, where he gained 1,053 yards and rushed for 12 touchdowns. Pierce was a wide receiver at San Diego State.

Best Hitter: Pierce has a mature approach and can handle breaking pitches. For the long term, OFs Ryan Carter (14) and David Cardona (8) also have promise.

Best Raw Power: Benson, by far. The Dodgers didn't go after much power, though Cardona showed pop as a Puerto Rican high schooler.

Fastest Runner: Benson. Pierce also has plenty of quickness, rating a 7 for his speed.

Best Defensive Player: SS Josh Canales (16) made just nine errors in 52 games in full-season Class A.

Best Fastball: RHP **Kole Strayhorn** (4) opened eyes when he threw 96 mph at the 2000 Area Code Games, and the Dodgers saw him hit 97 last spring.

Most Intriguing Background: The Dodgers loaded up on two-sport stars beyond Benson and Pierce. Troy State recruited RHP David Taylor (3) as a quarterback. Canadian RHP

Steve Nelson (5) would have been a 2001 NHL draft pick had he not given up hockey for baseball. For the second straight year, Los Angeles drafted 3B Brooks Bollinger (50), better known as a quarterback at Wisconsin—which doesn't have a baseball team. Bollinger was interested in signing the previous year before Badgers coaches discouraged it. RHP Brian Pilkington (2) is a nephew of Bert Blyleven.

Strayhorn

Closest To The Majors: Pierce or RHP Thom Ott (10), a reliever with a nifty slider.

Best Late-Round Pick: Benson has the highest upside and the Dodgers gambled $250,000 on him, though unclear he'll ever commit to baseball. LHP Luis Gonzalez (11), who showed potential as an outfielder in high school, has a heavy fastball that already reaches 90-91 mph.

The One Who Got Away: SS Michael Hollimon (32), who's also at Texas, might have been a first-round pick if not for his $2 million pricetag. Clint Sammons (43) was one of the best catchers available. He's at Georgia.

Assessment: Pilkington, the Dodgers' first choice, required arthroscopic shoulder surgery after just 16 pro innings. Their first six selections were high school pitchers, always a risky commodity but also the strength of the 2001 draft.

2000 Draft

RHP Ben Diggins (1) has struggled somewhat, though RHP Joel Hanrahan (2) and C Koyie Hill (4) have picked up his slack. 2B Victor Diaz (37, draft-and-follow) won the Rookie-level Gulf Coast League batting title in his pro debut. **Grade: C**

1999 Draft

2B Joe Thurston (4) is the most advanced prospect from this group. Los Angeles looked for some sorely needed athletes, but SS Jason Repko (1), 3B Brennan King (2) and OF Reggie Abercrombie (23, draft-and-follow) have been slow to develop. **Grade: C**

1998 Draft

OF Bubba Crosby (1) took a small step forward in 2001. He's the only player with a chance to reach the majors from one of the worst drafts ever. **Grade: F**

1997 Draft

The Dodgers organization is shallow today because of its drafts in 1997 and '98. LHP Steve Colyer (2) is the only remaining prospect, and that's using the term loosely. LHP Pete Zamora (20) could make the Philadelphia staff this spring. **Grade: F**

Note: Draft analysis prepared by Jim Callis. Numbers in parentheses indicate draft rounds.

. . . Rodriguez has a loose arm, above-average command and is willing to pitch inside.

Ricardo Rodriguez rhp

Born: May 21, 1979.
Ht.: 6-3. **Wt.:** 195.
Bats: R. **Throws:** R.
Career Transactions: Signed out of Dominican Republic by Dodgers, Sept. 2, 1996.

Rodriguez won a total of five games in three years in the Rookie-level Dominican Summer League before making his U.S. debut in 2000. It was a smashing success, as he won the pitching triple crown in the Rookie-level Pioneer League. Tested by skipping two levels to the high Class A Florida State League last year, he responded with another strong performance. Rodriguez topped the FSL in strikeouts and ranked among the leaders in wins, ERA and innings. Both the FSL and the Dodgers named him their pitcher of the year, and he was picked for the Futures Game at midseason.

Rodriguez has all the ingredients to be a solid No. 2 or 3 starter in the big leagues. He has a good two-seam fastball that registers consistently in the 91-93 mph range and as high as 95. He mixes his heater well with a plus curveball that has a hard break and acts like a slider. He added a changeup during instructional league in 2000 and used it extensively last year. What made Rodriguez most effective last season was that he was willing to throw all three of his pitches at any time in the count. He has a loose arm and above-average command, moves the ball around in the strike zone and is willing to pitch inside. Rodriguez also impresses with his maturity and the way he battles on the mound. He shows the ability to be an innings-eater at higher levels. The Dodgers say he needs to refine his mechanics. While some observers said he dominated the Pioneer League the year before because of his age, he had no problems jumping all the way to high Class A. If he can prove himself again at Double-A Jacksonville this year, that should erase all doubts.

The Dodgers have shown plenty of patience with Rodriguez and hope he'll move more rapidly through Double-A and Triple-A. He's developing into a complete pitcher, and his competitive streak should continue to take him up the ladder. Los Angeles has milked the international market for plenty of starters through the years, and Rodriguez has put himself next in line. He could get his chance in Los Angeles at some point in 2003.

WAGNER PHOTOGRAPHY

Year	Club (League)	Class	W	L	ERA	G	GS	CG	SV	IP	H	R	ER	BB	SO
1997	Dodgers (DSL)	R	1	2	6.40	12	10	0	0	32	42	39	23	26	20
1998	Dodgers (DSL)	R	1	1	3.55	13	9	1	0	33	28	19	13	34	36
1999	Dodgers (DSL)	R	3	2	3.43	9	9	0	0	42	34	22	16	18	51
2000	Great Falls (Pio)	R	10	3	1.88	15	15	2	0	96	66	32	20	23	129
2001	Vero Beach (FSL)	A	14	6	3.21	26	26	2	0	154	133	67	55	60	154
MINOR LEAGUE TOTALS			29	14	3.20	75	69	5	0	357	303	179	127	161	390

2. Chin-Feng Chen, of

Born: Oct. 28, 1977. **Ht.:** 6-1. **Wt.:** 189. **Bats:** R. **Throws:** R. **Career Transactions:** Signed out of Taiwan by Dodgers, Jan. 4, 1999.

The Dodgers' top prospect after the 1999 season before falling a notch following 2000, Chen overcame offseason surgery on his right shoulder to reestablish himself as a top prospect. He regained his stroke in the first half as a DH at high Class A Vero Beach before crushing the ball in Double-A. He also displayed his power for host Taiwan in the World Cup in November. Chen has middle-of-the-lineup power and makes quick adjustments. He kills fastballs and is adept at hitting breaking pitches. While his speed is below-average, Chen is an effective baserunner because of his solid instincts. The Dodgers want to see Chen have continued success against better competition. He needs to stay healthy and keep making adjustments against veteran pitchers. Even for a left fielder, his arm is average at best. Chen is back on track toward becoming the first Taiwanese player to reach the major leagues. He has proven to be resilient and has the tools of a run producer. His next stop should be Triple-A, with a September callup to Los Angeles a possibility.

Year	Club (League)	Class	AVG	G	AB	R	H	2B	3B	HR	RBI	BB	SO	SB
1999	San Bernardino (Cal)	A	.316	131	510	98	161	22	10	31	123	75	129	31
2000	San Antonio (TL)	AA	.277	133	516	66	143	27	3	6	67	61	131	23
2001	Vero Beach (FSL)	A	.268	62	235	38	63	15	3	5	41	28	56	2
	Jacksonville (SL)	AA	.313	66	224	47	70	16	2	17	50	41	65	5
MINOR LEAGUE TOTALS			.294	392	1485	249	437	80	18	59	281	205	381	61

3. Joel Guzman, ss

Born: Nov. 24, 1984. **Ht.:** 6-4. **Wt.:** 195. **Bats:** R. **Throws:** R. **Career Transactions:** Signed out of Dominican Republic by Dodgers, July 2, 2001.

The Dodgers wasted little time returning to the Dominican Republic after being barred for a full year as punishment for their illegal signing of Adrian Beltre. Los Angeles outbid 20 teams and inked Guzman last July 2 to a $2.25 million bonus, the largest ever given to a Dominican player. Guzman is a potential five-tool talent whom the Dodgers compare to Alex Rodriguez. An outstanding athlete, he has a projectable body and plus power from the right side of the plate. For his age, he has an advanced knowledge of the strike zone. Guzman speaks fluent English and shows a tremendous aptitude and thirst to improve his game. He has yet to make his pro debut and is several years away from the majors. It remains to be seen how he'll adjust to professional pitchers who are significantly older than he is, though the Dodgers aren't worried. Guzman will be moved slowly during the early stages of his development. He's expected to begin 2002 in extended spring training before moving to the Rookie-level Gulf Coast League in June. He's probably at least five years away from the majors.

Year	Club (League)	Class	AVG	G	AB	R	H	2B	3B	HR	RBI	BB	SO	SB
	Has Not Played—Signed 2002 Contract													

4. Ben Diggins, rhp

Born: June 13, 1979. **Ht.:** 6-7. **Wt.:** 230. **Bats:** R. **Throws:** R. **School:** University of Arizona. **Career Transactions:** Selected by Dodgers in first round (17th overall) of 2000 draft; signed Aug. 23, 2000.

After a strong college career at Arizona that made him the 17th overall pick, Diggins ranked as the top prospect in the organization last winter. But he had an uneven pro debut last season at low Class A Wilmington. He struggled with his velocity at midseason and battled a hamstring problem early in the campaign. He did end on a high note, going 5-0, 1.57 in his final eight starts. After reaching 98 mph with his fastball and consistently hitting the mid-90s in college, Diggins was in the 87-89 mph range at Wilmington. He finally returned to the low 90s with good movement in August, while showing improvements with his curveball. He impressed the Dodgers with his competitiveness and ability to pitch. Diggins played both ways at Arizona and offers plenty of power at the plate. Like many tall pitchers, Diggins struggles with the consistency of his mechanics. He has been working on a changeup since he signed but the pitch still needs a good deal of refinement. Diggins' ceiling remains as high as anyone in the organization.

Some scouts say he's a better prospect as a power hitter, but the Dodgers see him as a pitcher, possibly as a closer. His development will continue this year in high Class A.

Year	Club (League)	Class	W	L	ERA	G	GS	CG	SV	IP	H	R	ER	BB	SO
2001	Wilmington (SAL)	A	7	6	3.58	21	21	0	0	106	88	49	42	48	79
MINOR LEAGUE TOTALS			7	6	3.58	21	21	0	0	106	88	49	42	48	79

5. Joe Thurston, ss

Born: Sept. 29, 1979. **Ht.:** 5-11. **Wt.:** 175. **Bats:** L. **Throws:** R. **School:** Sacramento CC. **Career Transactions:** Selected by Dodgers in fourth round of 1999 draft; signed June 6, 1999.

Los Angeles' minor league player of the year in 2000, Thurston experienced adversity last season but worked his way through it. He struggled at the plate in Double-A before adapting in the second half. Thurston capped his year by finishing third in the Arizona Fall League batting race at .369. He succeeds with his tremendous heart, along with his good speed and quickness. He takes the extra base and possesses enough speed to steal 25 bases annually in the major leagues. He does the little things well with the bat, such as sacrificing, moving guys over and hitting to the opposite field. Defensively, he has excellent range at second base. Thurston likes to jump on the first pitch in an at-bat, but he could stand some more patience and work the count to give him more advantages. Moved from shortstop to second base last year, he's just an adequate defender because his hands aren't particularly soft. Known as Joey Ballgame, Thurston was added to the 40-man roster in November. He'll move up to Triple-A in 2002.

Year	Club (League)	Class	AVG	G	AB	R	H	2B	3B	HR	RBI	BB	SO	SB
1999	Yakima (NWL)	A	.285	71	277	48	79	10	3	0	32	27	34	27
	San Bernardino (Cal)	A	.000	2	3	0	0	0	0	0	0	0	1	0
2000	San Bernardino (Cal)	A	.303	138	551	97	167	31	8	4	70	56	61	43
2001	Jacksonville (SL)	AA	.267	134	544	80	145	25	7	7	46	48	65	20
MINOR LEAGUE TOTALS			.284	345	1375	225	391	66	18	11	148	121	161	90

6. Hong-Chih Kuo, lhp

Born: July 23, 1981. **Ht.:** 6-0. **Wt.:** 200. **Bats:** L. **Throws:** L. **Career Transactions:** Signed out of Taiwan by Dodgers, June 19, 1999.

Kuo continued his battle back from Tommy John surgery last year by rehabbing in extended spring training and making limited appearances in the Gulf Coast League. The Dodgers believe the Taiwan native, who signed for $1.25 million in June 1999, is nearly back to where he was before blowing out his left elbow during his first professional start. Kuo has all the makings of a power pitcher. He features a 95-97 mph fastball, a flexible upper body and thick legs that allow him to drive off the mound, like Tom Seaver. The Dodgers also love his aggressiveness. Surgery retarded the development of his curveball and changeup, but Kuo has shown the desire and talent to improve those pitches. They should become at least average major league offerings. The biggest concern centers on Kuo remaining healthy. He was tentative in 2001 and experienced some tenderness in his elbow during instructional league. The Dodgers believe he'll be significantly stronger and more confident in high Class A this year.

Year	Club (League)	Class	W	L	ERA	G	GS	CG	SV	IP	H	R	ER	BB	SO
2000	San Bernardino (Cal)	A	0	0	0.00	1	1	0	0	3	0	0	0	0	7
2001	Dodgers (GCL)	R	0	0	2.33	7	6	0	0	19	13	5	5	4	21
MINOR LEAGUE TOTALS			0	0	2.01	8	7	0	0	22	13	5	5	4	28

7. Willy Aybar, 3b

Born: March 9, 1983. **Ht.:** 6-0. **Wt.:** 175. **Bats:** B. **Throws:** R. **Career Transactions:** Signed out of Dominican Republic by Dodgers, Jan. 31, 2000.

Before signing Joel Guzman, the Dodgers had the previous record for a Dominican bonus when they gave Aybar $1.4 million. Though his power output in low Class A was nearly identical to his production in Rookie ball, Los Angeles wasn't disappointed with his performance in his first full year as a pro. The Dodgers believe Aybar will be a power-hitting machine. He has a sweet swing and the potential to drive balls from both sides of the plate. His quick, strong wrists keep him from being fooled often. At third base, Aybar shows outstanding hands and a good arm. He needs to add strength to his growing body, in order to get more pop as well as endurance. He has a good eye, but improvement with his pitch recognition will increase his average. Los Angeles may have pushed Aybar last year, though his numbers at Great Falls in 2000 merited a promotion. The Dodgers are in no hurry to get Aybar to the big leagues, preferring instead to see him develop a strong foundation of success. He'll head to high Class A this spring.

Year	Club (League)	Class	AVG	G	AB	R	H	2B	3B	HR	RBI	BB	SO	SB
2000	Great Falls (Pio)	R	.263	70	266	39	70	15	1	4	49	36	45	5
2001	Wilmington (SAL)	A	.237	120	431	45	102	25	2	4	48	43	64	7
	Vero Beach (FSL)	A	.286	2	7	0	2	0	0	0	0	1	2	0
MINOR LEAGUE TOTALS			.247	192	704	84	174	40	3	8	97	80	111	12

8. Jose Rojas, rhp

Born: March 20, 1982. **Ht.:** 5-10. **Wt.:** 160. **Bats:** R. **Throws:** R. **Career Transactions:** Signed out of Dominican Republic by Dodgers, June 13, 1999.

Rojas matured to the point last season that more than one instructor in the Dodgers system described him as "a little Pedro Martinez." Pitching in his first full season in the United States, the righthander led the low Class A South Atlantic League in ERA. Rojas reached the mid-90s early in 2001 and settled in the 92-94 mph range. His fastball is enhanced because he can throw his changeup for strikes and at any point in the count. He also has exceptional control and doesn't make many mistakes in the strike zone. Rojas flashed a plus slider last season but never got it consistent enough to use in crucial situations. If he can add a third pitch to his repertoire, the Dodgers say he'll be unhittable. His stature will lead to continual questions about his durability, though he hasn't had any problems to this point. While his rapid progress last year was a surprise to some, Rojas showed enough that the Dodgers had to restrain themselves from promoting him to high Class A until the end of August. He'll return there in 2002.

Year	Club (League)	Class	W	L	ERA	G	GS	CG	SV	IP	H	R	ER	BB	SO
1999	Dodgers (DSL)	R	5	1	3.15	19	5	0	1	60	39	25	21	16	70
2000	Yakima (NWL)	A	4	4	3.25	13	9	0	1	53	45	26	19	19	47
2001	Wilmington (SAL)	A	10	3	2.12	24	23	1	0	136	107	42	32	42	116
	Vero Beach (FSL)	A	0	0	6.00	1	0	0	0	3	3	2	2	1	3
MINOR LEAGUE TOTALS			19	8	2.64	57	37	1	2	252	194	95	74	88	236

9. Joel Hanrahan, rhp

Born: Oct. 6, 1981. **Ht.:** 6-3. **Wt.:** 215. **Bats:** R. **Throws:** R. **School:** Norwalk (Iowa) Community HS. **Career Transactions:** Selected by Dodgers in second round of 2000 draft; signed June 22, 2000.

Promoted to low Class A as a teenager in his first full year, Hanrahan held up well. He led Wilmington in starts and innings while ranking second in strikeouts. He had success against older competition while making strides with the command of all three of his pitches. Hanrahan throws a 91-92 mph fastball, which alone didn't make him stand out on a Wilmington staff with several quality arms. What did separate him from the pack was his wicked slider and deceptive changeup. He isn't afraid to throw his change, which keeps hitters off balance. His projectable frame makes him a potential workhorse. Despite getting off to a 1-4, 6.33 start last year, Hanrahan didn't panic and instead made steady progress. Hanrahan can refine his mechanics and command, and his willingness to accept instruction should make those tasks easier. The Dodgers say Hanrahan simply needs time to continue working his way up the ladder. Hanrahan is advanced for a high school pitcher out of Iowa, which doesn't have a spring high school baseball season. The Dodgers hope he'll build on his success this year in high Class A.

Year	Club (League)	Class	W	L	ERA	G	GS	CG	SV	IP	H	R	ER	BB	SO
2000	Great Falls (Pio)	R	3	1	4.75	12	11	0	0	55	49	32	29	23	40
2001	Wilmington (SAL)	A	9	11	3.38	27	26	0	0	144	136	71	54	55	116
MINOR LEAGUE TOTALS			12	12	3.75	39	37	0	0	199	185	103	83	78	156

10. Jorge Nunez, ss

Born: March 3, 1978. **Ht.:** 5-10. **Wt.:** 158. **Bats:** R. **Throws:** R. **Career Transactions:** Signed out of Dominican Republic by Blue Jays, April 17, 1995 . . . Traded by Blue Jays with OF Shawn Green to Dodgers for OF Raul Mondesi and LHP Pedro Borbon, Nov. 8, 1999 . . . Granted free agency, Dec. 20, 2000; re-signed by Dodgers, Dec. 21, 2000.

Acquired in the Shawn Green-Raul Mondesi trade with the Blue Jays prior to the 2000 season, Nunez led the Southern League in stolen bases last year. His performance enabled Nunez to return to the Dodgers' 40-man roster in the offseason after he was left off the year before. Nunez is a tools player who can do several things well. He has plus speed and outstanding quickness that he uses on the basepaths and in the field. His arm was rated as the strongest among SL infielders last year. Nunez hit 14 homers in his last year in the Blue Jays system but hasn't shown the same kind of power since the trade. He needs to make more contact instead of trying to hit home runs. His offense will improve if he can tighten his strike zone. If he can't, then he'll have to be relegated to the bottom of the batting order. The Dodgers say Nunez is just beginning to mature physically and get comfortable with his body. He'll open 2002 in Triple-A. Los Angeles' trade for Cesar Izturis has at least temporarily taken away Nunez' status as the shortstop of the future.

Year	Club (League)	Class	AVG	G	AB	R	H	2B	3B	HR	RBI	BB	SO	SB
1995	Blue Jays (DSL)	R	.133	13	15	1	2	0	0	1	4	1	5	0
1996	Blue Jays (DSL)	R	.295	69	258	51	76	10	2	7	40	19	36	19
1997	Blue Jays (DSL)	R	.252	71	262	46	66	5	5	4	33	29	48	44
1998	Hagerstown (SAL)	A	.250	4	16	0	4	0	0	0	1	0	1	1
	Medicine Hat (Pio)	R	.319	74	317	74	101	9	11	6	52	28	45	31
1999	Hagerstown (SAL)	A	.268	133	564	116	151	28	11	14	61	40	103	51
2000	Vero Beach (FSL)	A	.288	128	534	86	154	17	8	4	39	38	104	54
	Albuquerque (PCL)	AAA	.000	1	3	0	0	0	0	0	0	0	0	0
2001	Jacksonville (SL)	AA	.260	123	473	63	123	15	2	4	28	33	88	44
MINOR LEAGUE TOTALS			.277	616	2442	437	677	84	39	40	258	188	430	244

11. Koyie Hill, c

Born: March 9, 1979. **Ht.:** 6-0. **Wt.:** 190. **Bats:** B. **Throws:** R. **School:** Wichita State University. **Career Transactions:** Selected by Dodgers in fourth round of 2000 draft; signed June 22, 2000.

A third baseman who led the Missouri Valley Conference in batting average as a junior at Wichita State, Hill started catching at short-season Yakima after being drafted by the Dodgers in the fourth round in 2000. He made significant strides last year in low Class A to emerge as the organization's top catching prospect. Hill has the potential to be an offensive catcher with power from both sides of the plate. While his arm strength is average, he has excellent footwork and makes easy transfers from his glove to his hand, averaging 1.9 seconds on his throws to second. Hill also has shown a knack for calling a game, and he has attracted raves from his pitchers on the way he handles game situations. Hill didn't become a full-time catcher until spring training in 2001. His overall awareness behind the plate could use some improvement. His next stop will be high Class A.

Year	Club (League)	Class	AVG	G	AB	R	H	2B	3B	HR	RBI	BB	SO	SB
2000	Yakima (NWL)	A	.259	64	251	26	65	13	1	2	29	25	47	0
2001	Wilmington (SAL)	A	.301	134	498	65	150	20	2	8	79	49	82	21
MINOR LEAGUE TOTALS			.287	198	749	91	215	33	3	10	108	74	129	21

12. Jason Repko, ss

Born: Dec. 27, 1980. **Ht.:** 5-11. **Wt.:** 175. **Bats:** R. **Throws:** R. **School:** Hanford HS, Richland, Wash. **Career Transactions:** Selected by Dodgers in first round (37th overall) of 1999 draft; signed June 3, 1999.

Repko was inconsistent with the bat last year in low Class A and missed three weeks with lingering back problems. But when he's at full strength, he rates no worse than average with all five tools. He has above-average speed and the overall talent to be a sparkplug at the top of the lineup. The Dodgers compare him to Paul Molitor, though he won't ever approach that type of production until he gets stronger and learns the strike zone. There also are concerns about Repko's defense and health. Some scouts wonder if his future will be in the infield—he made 26 errors in 77 games at shortstop in 2001—with many believing he'd be better served to concentrate on his hitting while manning left field or possibly center. Repko has played the outfield before and doesn't have the arm strength for right field. His back limited him to 17 at-bats in 2000 before flaring up again last year, but numerous tests haven't revealed anything physically that doctors are able to correct. Repko sorely needs to remain on the field in order to improve all phases of his game. Spring training will determine whether he returns to Wilmington or receives a promotion to high Class A to get a full year's worth of at-bats.

Year	Club (League)	Class	AVG	G	AB	R	H	2B	3B	HR	RBI	BB	SO	SB
1999	Great Falls (Pio)	R	.304	49	207	51	63	9	9	8	32	21	43	12
2000	Yakima (NWL)	A	.294	8	17	3	5	2	0	0	1	1	7	0
2001	Wilmington (SAL)	A	.220	88	337	36	74	17	4	4	32	15	68	17
MINOR LEAGUE TOTALS			.253	145	561	90	142	28	13	12	65	37	118	29

13. Brennan King, 3b

Born: Jan. 20, 1981. **Ht.:** 6-3. **Wt.:** 190. **Bats:** R. **Throws:** R. **School:** Oakland HS, Murfreesboro, Tenn. **Career Transactions:** Selected by Dodgers in second round of 1999 draft; signed June 11, 1999.

King had an outstanding spring training in 2001 and the Dodgers had a bevy of infield prospects set for Wilmington, so he jumped past low Class A to the Florida State League. Skipping a level may have been too challenging for King, who also battled a hamate problem in his wrist. While he struggled at the plate, he did show the solid all-around ability that put him on a fast track in the first place. While he played shortstop in high school, he's an excellent defender with a strong arm and good mobility at third base. He also impressed the Dodgers last year with his ability to remain resilient and maintain his confidence in the face of adversity. With just five home runs in 749 pro at-bats, he has yet to display the power potential Los Angeles officials project him to develop, but they remain confident he'll blossom as he continues to mature physically. King also needs to improve his plate discipline and make more consistent contact. He's expected to climb to Double-A in 2002.

Year	Club (League)	Class	AVG	G	AB	R	H	2B	3B	HR	RBI	BB	SO	SB
1999	Great Falls (Pio)	R	.291	61	247	37	72	13	1	2	30	24	45	9
2000	Yakima (NWL)	A	.239	61	238	27	57	10	1	1	30	29	49	14
2001	Vero Beach (FSL)	A	.243	73	255	24	62	10	0	1	28	13	48	0
	Dodgers (GCL)	R	.556	3	9	3	5	2	0	1	4	0	0	0
MINOR LEAGUE TOTALS			.262	198	749	91	196	35	2	5	92	66	142	23

14. Luke Allen, of

Born: Aug. 4, 1978. **Ht.:** 6-2. **Wt.:** 208. **Bats:** L. **Throws:** R. **School:** Newton County HS, Covington, Ga. **Career Transactions:** Signed as nondrafted free agent by Dodgers, Aug. 4, 1996.

Allen finally showed signs of mastering Double-A in 2001 after spending the previous two full seasons stuck there. A former third baseman who moved to right field last year, he took his offensive game to a higher level while showing signs of being more comfortable on defense. Allen's best tool is his arm, which managers rated as the strongest among outfielders last year in the Southern League after he earned similar praise among Texas League infielders in 2000. What excited the Dodgers most about Allen was the way he hit the ball as hard as he ever has as a professional, resulting in a career-high 16 homers. He made better adjustments against all type of pitches, yet he also struck out 111 times, the highest total of his career. While he has good speed and quick wrists, Allen needs to improve his strikezone judgment and continue to prove he can handle the demands of right field. An energetic player who obviously loves to take the field, he drew praise for his veteran leadership at Jacksonville. He'll finally make it to Triple-A on a full-time basis in 2002.

Year	Club (League)	Class	AVG	G	AB	R	H	2B	3B	HR	RBI	BB	SO	SB
1997	Great Falls (Pio)	R	.345	67	258	50	89	12	6	7	40	19	53	12
1998	San Bernardino (Cal)	A	.298	105	399	51	119	25	6	4	46	30	93	18
	San Antonio (TL)	AA	.333	23	78	9	26	3	1	3	10	6	16	1
1999	San Antonio (TL)	AA	.281	137	533	90	150	16	12	14	82	44	102	14
2000	San Antonio (TL)	AA	.265	90	339	55	90	15	5	7	60	40	71	14
2001	Jacksonville (SL)	AA	.290	125	486	74	141	32	6	16	73	42	111	13
	Las Vegas (PCL)	AAA	.222	2	9	1	2	1	0	0	0	0	0	0
MINOR LEAGUE TOTALS			.294	549	2102	330	617	104	36	51	311	181	446	72

15. Brian Pilkington, rhp

Born: Sep. 17, 1982. **Ht.:** 6-5. **Wt.:** 210. **Bats:** R. **Throws:** R. **School:** Santiago HS, Garden Grove, Calif. **Career Transactions:** Selected by Dodgers in second round of 2001 draft; signed June 14, 2001.

The Dodgers drafted Pilkington with their first pick (second round) in the 2001 draft and signed him quickly. He worked just 16 innings before being shut down with a sore shoulder that required arthroscopic surgery. He's expected to be back at full strength by spring training. A nephew of former major leaguer Bert Blyleven, Pilkington possesses picture-perfect mechanics, a 92-93 mph fastball and command of three pitches. He walked just seven batters as a high school senior and had an impressive 17-2 strikeout-walk ratio in Rookie ball. The Dodgers believe the rest required by the surgery will be beneficial for Pilkington, who pitched nearly year-round in Southern California for two years. He has a projectable body that should allow him to become a true power pitcher. He also has great composure on the mound and could move rapidly with his impressive combination of talent and desire. The Dodgers believe all Pilkington needs is experience and a clean bill of health to start making a name for himself.

Year	Club (League)	Class	W	L	ERA	G	GS	CG	SV	IP	H	R	ER	BB	SO
2001	Great Falls (Pio)	R	0	1	5.63	5	2	0	0	16	19	11	10	2	17
MINOR LEAGUE TOTALS			0	1	5.63	5	2	0	0	16	19	11	10	2	17

16. Reggie Abercrombie, of

Born: July 15, 1981. **Ht.:** 6-3. **Wt.:** 210. **Bats:** R. **Throws:** R. **School:** Lake City (Fla.) CC. **Career Transactions:** Selected by Dodgers in 23rd round of 1999 draft; signed May 24, 2000.

A potential five-tool player, Abercrombie focused most of his attention on football and basketball while he was in high school. Now that he's dedicating himself to baseball after signing as a draft-and-follow in 2000, he's showing the raw ability the Dodgers knew he had. Abercrombie's arm and speed both rate above average, and his instincts are helping him make up for lost time. He has good defensive skills and takes the right routes to fly balls in the outfield. His power improved last year, when he tripled his extra-base output compared to the previous season. He's an efficient basestealer as well. Abercrombie's strike-zone knowledge is atrocious at this point, and his pitch recognition also needs a lot of work. He's still learning how to harness his skills and understand the mental aspects of the game. Los Angeles hopes he'll have a coming-out party this year in high Class A.

Year	Club (League)	Class	AVG	G	AB	R	H	2B	3B	HR	RBI	BB	SO	SB
2000	Great Falls (Pio)	R	.273	54	220	40	60	7	1	2	29	22	66	32
2001	Wilmington (SAL)	A	.226	125	486	63	110	17	3	10	41	19	154	44
MINOR LEAGUE TOTALS			.241	179	706	103	170	24	4	12	70	41	220	76

17. Shane Victorino, of

Born: Nov. 30, 1980. **Ht.:** 5-9. **Wt.:** 160. **Bats:** R. **Throws:** R. **School:** St. Anthony HS, Wailuku, Hawaii. **Career Transactions:** Selected by Dodgers in sixth round of 1999 draft; signed June 8, 1999.

Victorino moved to center field in low Class A last year after two seasons of modest success at second base, and he blossomed into the type of prospect the Dodgers always thought he was. The move enabled him to be much more consistent on offense and develop into one of the best defensive outfielders in the South Atlantic League. Victorino's speed rates as a 7 on the 2-to-8 scouting scale, and several SAL managers commented about how few fly balls dropped in center. After attempting to switch-hit in 2000, he returned to batting from the right side only and did an excellent job of turning on fastballs. He also showed significant improvement in taking pitches the opposite way with some power. Though his strikeout total dropped last year, Victorino needs a better grasp of the strike zone. He swings too aggressively at times when he could be more effective if he simply made contact. His arm strength is just average for center field. Few position players in the system improved more last year than Victorino. A promotion to high Class A will be his next challenge.

Year	Club (League)	Class	AVG	G	AB	R	H	2B	3B	HR	RBI	BB	SO	SB
1999	Great Falls (Pio)	R	.280	55	225	53	63	7	6	2	25	20	31	20
2000	Yakima (NWL)	A	.246	61	236	32	58	7	2	2	20	20	44	21
2001	Wilmington (SAL)	A	.283	112	435	71	123	21	9	4	32	36	61	47
	Vero Beach (FSL)	A	.167	2	6	2	1	0	0	0	0	3	1	0
MINOR LEAGUE TOTALS			.272	230	902	158	245	35	17	8	77	79	137	88

18. Candido Martinez, of

Born: Oct. 26, 1980. **Ht.:** 6-4. **Wt.:** 210. **Bats:** R. **Throws:** R. **Career Transactions:** Signed out of Dominican Republic by Dodgers, Oct. 28, 1996.

Like many Dominican players, Martinez took some time to develop after signing as a teenager. Dedicated work in the weight room and an improved diet strengthened his once-skinny body into an impressive 6-foot-4, 210-pound build. He now has good power and some of the best speed in the organization. He joined Willy Aybar and Reggie Abercrombie in putting on some spectacular shows during Wilmington's batting practices in 2001. Despite his size, Martinez runs the 60-yard dash in 6.4 seconds, enabling him to steal 54 bases in low Class A last year. But even with his quickness, he's no better than adequate as an outfielder and is limited to left field by his arm. He also needs to tighten his strike zone significantly so more advanced pitchers don't exploit his aggressiveness. The Dodgers believe Martinez is just beginning to tap into his abilities. He'll try to continue his progress in high Class A this year.

Year	Club (League)	Class	AVG	G	AB	R	H	2B	3B	HR	RBI	BB	SO	SB
1997	Dodgers (DSL)	R	.333	39	69	22	23	5	0	3	14	7	19	3
1998	Dodgers (DSL)	R	.228	67	228	45	52	5	7	4	28	21	51	14
1999	Great Falls (Pio)	R	.234	69	265	43	62	8	3	4	42	22	87	11
2000	Yakima (NWL)	A	.270	39	137	20	37	7	2	3	14	9	53	6
2001	Wilmington (SAL)	A	.260	120	443	69	115	27	4	7	66	29	138	54
MINOR LEAGUE TOTALS			.253	334	1142	199	289	52	16	21	164	88	348	88

19. Shane Nance, lhp

Born: Sept. 7, 1977. **Ht.:** 5-8. **Wt.:** 180. **Bats:** L. **Throws:** L. **School:** University of Houston. **Career Transactions:** Selected by Dodgers in 11th round of 2000 draft; signed June 12, 2000.

After a successful college career, Nance was nevertheless not a premium draft pick because of his size. But he breezed through high Class A en route to Double-A in his first full pro season. He also pitched well in the Arizona Fall League and was even better at the World Cup, pitching 6 1/3 scoreless innings with 12 strikeouts and no walks for Team USA. Short and stocky, Nance isn't overly impressive except for his ability to get hitters out. His fastball, curveball and changeup aren't overwhelming but are effective. His command of all three pitches is inconsistent from game to game, but he has shown encouraging signs that the pieces are starting to come together. The Dodgers say they're more interested in a player's heart than his size, and they love the way Nance wants the ball in any situation. He'll probably get promoted to Triple-A this spring and could get a look in Chavez Ravine at some point during the 2002 campaign.

Year	Club (League)	Class	W	L	ERA	G	GS	CG	SV	IP	H	R	ER	BB	SO
2000	Yakima (NWL)	A	2	4	2.48	12	9	0	0	58	41	19	16	22	66
2001	Vero Beach (FSL)	A	6	3	2.63	21	0	0	4	48	28	15	14	21	63
	Jacksonville (SL)	AA	7	0	1.59	28	0	0	1	45	31	11	8	17	44
MINOR LEAGUE TOTALS			15	7	2.26	61	9	0	5	151	100	45	38	60	173

20. Kole Strayhorn, rhp

Born: Oct. 1, 1982. **Ht.:** 6-0. **Wt.:** 185. **Bats:** R. **Throws:** R. **School:** Shawnee (Okla.) HS. **Career Transactions:** Selected by Dodgers in fourth round of 2001 draft; signed June 9, 2001.

Few pitchers have the arm speed and the overall velocity Strayhorn possesses. His fastball sat on 93-94 mph during his pro debut and overpowered many Gulf Coast League hitters. Some scouts had worried about the health of Strayhorn's arm prior to the draft. He touched 96 mph during the 2000 Area Code Games but threw in the low 90s for most of last spring. The Dodgers were impressed with the strides he made in the GCL. He also showed a plus breaking ball and outstanding makeup. He's very aggressive and isn't afraid to use both sides of the plate. He doesn't have a very projectable body, and it's possible his maximum-effort delivery could lead to injuries down the road. Los Angeles will continue to monitor him closely this year in low Class A.

Year	Club (League)	Class	W	L	ERA	G	GS	CG	SV	IP	H	R	ER	BB	SO
2001	Dodgers (GCL)	R	5	3	2.19	12	6	0	0	53	41	15	13	17	47
	Great Falls (Pio)	R	0	0	15.43	2	0	0	0	2	4	4	4	1	1
MINOR LEAGUE TOTALS			5	3	2.78	14	6	0	0	55	45	19	17	18	48

21. Michael Keirstead, rhp

Born: Jan. 26, 1981. **Ht.:** 6-3. **Wt.:** 210. **Bats:** R. **Throws:** R. **School:** Eastern Oklahoma State JC. **Career Transactions:** Selected by Dodgers in 28th round of 1999 draft; signed May 23, 2000.

A draft-and-follow who signed in 2000, Keirstead started putting things together last year. He finished the season in low Class A, and pitched well in three appearances for Canada at the World Cup in Taiwan in November. Keirstead struggled somewhat with his command in the South Atlantic League, yet proved to be overpowering at times with a 93-95 mph fastball. He has good size and excellent strength. He has learned to throw a splitter that makes him much tougher to hit. A native of New Brunswick, Keirstead lacks extensive amateur experience. That's obvious at times, particularly with the slow development of his change-up. His fastball also loses movement on occasion, which leaves him vulnerable. Even so, he's making solid progress and would surprise no one in the organization if he made another significant leap in 2002.

Year	Club (League)	Class	W	L	ERA	G	GS	CG	SV	IP	H	R	ER	BB	SO
2000	Great Falls (Pio)	R	4	3	4.81	18	7	0	0	58	68	38	31	23	36
2001	Wilmington (SAL)	A	0	1	4.82	7	1	0	0	9	9	7	5	5	12
	Great Falls (Pio)	R	1	1	2.34	25	3	0	5	35	35	14	9	12	52
MINOR LEAGUE TOTALS			5	5	3.97	50	11	0	5	102	112	59	45	40	100

22. Sean Pierce, of

Born: Nov. 26, 1978. **Ht.:** 5-9. **Wt.:** 190. **Bats:** R. **Throws:** R. **School:** San Diego State University. **Career Transactions:** Selected by Dodgers in ninth round of 2001 draft; signed June 11, 2001.

Drafted last year as a college senior, Pierce impressed the organization with the plus speed and outstanding toughness. He developed those skills while returning kickoffs and catching passes for San Diego State's football team. Voted the MVP at Rookie-level Great Falls after leading the club in on-base percentage (.414) and triples while ranking second in steals and RBIs, Pierce earned a promotion to low Class A at season's end. He showed signs of being a mature hitter at the plate and handled breaking pitches with little difficulty. He also gets the job done in center field. The Dodgers believe that if he can continue to make consistent contact, Pierce's excellent speed and quickness will make him a dangerous offensive player. Though he's just now living up to his potential as he devotes himself entirely to baseball for the first time, Pierce was old for the Pioneer League and must prove he can produce against more advanced pitchers. He may get the chance in high Class A this year.

Year	Club (League)	Class	AVG	G	AB	R	H	2B	3B	HR	RBI	BB	SO	SB
2001	Great Falls (Pio)	R	.311	72	273	59	85	11	7	6	43	43	54	29
	Wilmington (SAL)	A	.250	3	12	0	3	0	0	0	0	0	2	1
MINOR LEAGUE TOTALS			.309	75	285	59	88	11	7	6	43	43	56	30

23. Steve Colyer, lhp

Born: Feb. 22, 1979. **Ht.:** 6-4. **Wt.:** 205. **Bats:** L. **Throws:** L. **School:** Meramec (Mo.) JC. **Career Transactions:** Selected by Dodgers in second round of 1997 draft; signed May 23, 1998.

The Dodgers' 1997 draft was one of the worst in recent memory—not just for them but for any team. Of the players they've signed and solely developed, only Colyer has a legitimate chance to reach the majors. And for the second straight year, he experienced an inconsistent season as a starter in high Class A. Colyer would blow hitters away with his 95-mph fastball one game, only to come back five days later and have trouble finding the strike zone. Despite his difficulties, the Dodgers still view Colyer as a potential lefty set-up man in the majors. His overhand curveball gives him a second plus pitch, but he has had trouble throwing a changeup. Besides his command and changeup, he's also inconsistent with his mental approach and maturity. Colyer will try to make the necessary refinements in Double-A in 2002.

Year	Club (League)	Class	W	L	ERA	G	GS	CG	SV	IP	H	R	ER	BB	SO
1998	Yakima (NWL)	A	2	2	4.96	15	12	0	0	65	72	46	36	36	75
1999	San Bernardino (Cal)	A	7	9	4.70	27	25	1	0	146	145	82	76	86	131
2000	Vero Beach (FSL)	A	5	7	5.76	26	18	1	0	95	97	74	61	68	80
2001	Vero Beach (FSL)	A	4	8	3.96	24	24	0	0	120	101	62	53	77	118
MINOR LEAGUE TOTALS			18	26	4.77	92	79	2	0	427	415	264	226	267	404

24. Bubba Crosby, of

Born: Aug. 11, 1976. **Ht.:** 5-11. **Wt.:** 185. **Bats:** L. **Throws:** L. **School:** Rice University. **Career Transactions:** Selected by Dodgers in first round (23rd overall) of 1998 draft; signed June 19, 1998.

As bad as Los Angeles' 1997 draft was, its 1998 effort might have been even worse. The only reasonable hope to make it to the big leagues from that crop is first-rounder Crosby. After three disappointing seasons in Class A, he reinvented himself last year in Double-A. A slugger during his days at Rice, he abandoned his college slugging approach and focused on hitting line drives and dropping down bunts from the No. 2 spot. Crosby had difficulties adjusting to wood bats, then lost confidence in his ability while battling injuries.

He regained his poise last year and stayed healthy for his first extended period as a pro. Crosby finally has discovered how to get on base in a variety of ways, and his batting eye has improved. He has above-average speed and is a decent outfielder, albeit with a marginal arm. If he can maintain consistency, he could have a major league career as a fourth outfielder.

Year	Club (League)	Class	AVG	G	AB	R	H	2B	3B	HR	RBI	BB	SO	SB
1998	San Bernardino (Cal)	A	.216	56	199	25	43	9	2	0	14	17	38	3
1999	San Bernardino (Cal)	A	.296	96	371	53	110	21	3	1	37	42	71	19
2000	Vero Beach (FSL)	A	.266	73	274	50	73	13	8	8	51	31	41	27
	San Bernardino (Cal)	A	.250	3	12	2	3	0	0	0	2	0	4	1
2001	Jacksonville (SL)	AA	.302	107	384	68	116	22	5	6	47	37	60	22
	Las Vegas (PCL)	AAA	.214	13	42	5	9	2	1	0	5	1	8	1
MINOR LEAGUE TOTALS			.276	348	1282	203	354	67	19	15	156	128	222	73

25. Carlos Garcia, rhp

Born: Sept. 23, 1978. **Ht.:** 6-3. **Wt.:** 232. **Bats:** R. **Throws:** R. **Career Transactions:** Signed out of Mexico by Dodgers, July 14, 1996 . . . Loaned by Dodgers to Mexico City Red Devils (Mexican), March 18-Oct. 28, 1998 . . . Loaned to Mexico City, June 18-Sept. 20, 1999.

The Dodgers didn't bring Garcia to the United States to play until 2000, after he spent two seasons pitching for Mexico City. He looked good in his debut and led the high Class A California League in victories and ERA in 2000, when he was named pitcher of the year by both the league and the organization. He opened 2001 in extended spring training because of shoulder tendinitis and was expected to head to Double-A in May. However, the pain didn't decrease until the end of the year and he never pitched an inning. When healthy, Garcia dominates with a sinking 92-93 mph fastball and an unmatched desire to take the mound. He also throws a plus changeup, possesses excellent command and does a good job of mixing his pitches to keep hitters off balance. The Dodgers' lone concern about Garcia prior to his tendinitis was his reluctance to pitch inside. His work ethic is unquestioned, and Los Angeles officials know he would have pitched through the pain last season if capable. They hope an offseason of additional rest will allow Garcia to report to Double-A in 2002.

Year	Club (League)	Class	W	L	ERA	G	GS	CG	SV	IP	H	R	ER	BB	SO
1997	Dodgers (DSL)	R	8	1	1.70	12	12	0	0	69	57	17	13	19	58
1998	M.C. Reds (Mex)	AAA	2	1	5.74	17	0	0	0	31	37	21	20	15	11
1999	M.C. Reds (Mex)	AAA	12	4	4.05	25	25	2	0	153	170	78	69	78	58
2000	San Bernardino (Cal)	A	14	7	2.57	27	27	2	0	182	162	61	52	49	106
2001					Did Not Play—Injured										
MINOR LEAGUE TOTALS			36	13	3.18	81	64	4	0	436	426	177	154	161	233

26. Victor Diaz, 2b

Born: Dec. 10, 1981. **Ht.:** 6-0. **Wt.:** 200. **Bats:** R. **Throws:** R. **School:** Grayson County (Texas) CC. **Career Transactions:** Selected by Dodgers in 37th round of 2000 draft; signed May 19, 2001.

Diaz couldn't have been much more impressive in his pro debut after signing last May as a draft-and-follow. He won the Gulf Coast League batting title and also led the circuit in hits, doubles, extra-base hits (27), total bases (104) and slugging percentage (.533). He also helped guide the Dodgers' GCL entry to a league-best 41-19 record. Diaz attracted comparisons to Carlos Baerga with his fundamentally sound approach at the plate and his uncanny pop for a middle infielder. Also like Baerga, however, Diaz isn't a standout defender at second base. His hands aren't soft, and neither his arm nor his glove is really steady enough for the infield. Diaz could add some more strength to produce enough power for left field. His bat should enable him to make the climb to low Class A while he continues to search for a position.

Year	Club (League)	Class	AVG	G	AB	R	H	2B	3B	HR	RBI	BB	SO	SB
2001	Dodgers (GCL)	R	.354	53	195	36	69	22	2	3	31	16	23	6
MINOR LEAGUE TOTALS			.354	53	195	36	69	22	2	3	31	16	23	6

27. Jose Diaz, c

Born: April 13, 1980. **Ht.:** 6-0. **Wt.:** 205. **Bats:** R. **Throws:** R. **Career Transactions:** Signed out of Dominican Republic by Dodgers, Aug. 24, 1996.

Managers in both the Pioneer and South Atlantic leagues raved about how Diaz' defensive abilities were no worse than major league average last year. He's one of the best catch-

and-throw guys in the minors. His throws were timed consistently in the 1.85-second range at Wilmington and as low as 1.75 at Great Falls, where he gunned down 45 percent of basestealers. Opposing skippers admitted that Diaz completely shut down their running games. Several scouts who saw Ivan Rodriguez at the same point in his development compare Diaz favorably to him, and people in the Dodgers organization compare him to Steve Yeager, one of the organization's best defensive catchers ever. The missing element is Diaz' inability to put the bat on the ball. He hit a combined .184 last year and has not batted higher than .219 in four minor league seasons. Given his arm strength and his impotent bat, there's the possibility that Diaz could move to the mound. Los Angeles successfully converted Felix Rodriguez from catcher to pitcher and is trying to do the same with Will McCrotty. For now, however, the Dodgers will hope Diaz' bat will come around when he begins 2002 in low Class A.

Year	Club (League)	Class	AVG	G	AB	R	H	2B	3B	HR	RBI	BB	SO	SB
1997	Dodgers (DSL)	R	.147	30	95	12	14	1	0	1	5	6	30	3
1998	Dodgers (DSL)	R	.209	51	163	24	34	6	0	1	27	15	34	4
1999			Did Not Play—Injured											
2000	Great Falls (Pio)	R	.219	57	210	29	46	9	1	7	31	18	52	2
2001	Wilmington (SAL)	A	.175	23	80	7	14	4	0	2	5	4	31	1
	Great Falls (Pio)	R	.189	48	159	18	30	8	0	3	17	15	38	2
MINOR LEAGUE TOTALS			.195	209	707	90	138	28	1	14	85	58	185	12

28. Will McCrotty, rhp

Born: June 22, 1979. **Ht.:** 6-2. **Wt.:** 195. **Bats:** R. **Throws:** R. **School:** Russellville (Ark.) HS. **Career Transactions:** Selected by Dodgers in sixth round of 1997 draft; signed June 20, 1997.

McCrotty toiled as a defensive-oriented catcher for four years before moving to the mound during instructional league in 2000. He responded with aplomb and ranked among the hardest throwers in the South Atlantic League last year. McCrotty's 94-95 mph fastball possesses excellent movement. He also has made impressive improvement with his curveball, making it a solid complementary pitch. Unlike most former catchers who tend to short-arm their throws, he has excellent arm action for a converted player. McCrotty pitched well enough to earn a promotion to high Class A during the second half of 2001, then stood out during instructional league while displaying progress with his developing changeup. He has developed quickly over a short period of time. His biggest needs are improved command and better consistency with his changeup. McCrotty has the necessary ingredients to blossom into a dominating reliever at higher levels. He'll probably begin this year back in the Florida State League.

Year	Club (League)	Class	AVG	G	AB	R	H	2B	3B	HR	RBI	BB	SO	SB
1997	Yakima (NWL)	A	.200	43	135	12	27	2	0	1	10	9	19	2
1998	San Bernardino (Cal)	A	.221	103	344	20	76	18	0	3	29	11	69	1
1999	San Bernardino (Cal)	A	.254	93	319	43	81	12	3	4	43	27	49	0
2000	Vero Beach (FSL)	A	.215	76	256	19	55	10	0	3	34	31	53	0
MINOR LEAGUE TOTALS			.227	315	1054	94	239	42	3	11	116	78	190	3

Year	Club (League)	Class	W	L	ERA	G	GS	CG	SV	IP	H	R	ER	BB	SO
2001	Wilmington (SAL)	A	2	1	1.96	21	0	0	4	37	24	9	8	10	46
	Vero Beach (FSL)	A	0	2	4.37	20	0	0	5	23	22	11	11	14	17
MINOR LEAGUE TOTALS			2	3	2.88	41	0	0	9	59	46	20	19	24	63

29. Jose Garcia, of

Born: Aug. 22, 1980. **Ht.:** 6-1. **Wt.:** 195. **Bats:** R. **Throws:** R. **Career Transactions:** Signed out of Dominican Republic by Dodgers, Aug. 24, 1996.

Garcia turned 21 late in the 2001 season, which coincided with several Pioneer League managers noting how much the potential five-tool outfielder matured physically over the course of the summer. He has added close to 50 pounds of muscle since signing in 1996, and he's starting to incorporate the added strength into his game. He reached career highs in virtually every category last season and led Great Falls in hits, doubles, home runs and RBIs. Several Pioneer League skippers compared him to Raul Mondesi. Garcia impresses scouts with his loose body, obvious athleticism and budding power. He's a decent defender with good speed and enough arm to play right field. His powerful wrists enable him to whip the bat through the strike zone, resulting in hard-hit line drives to all fields. Garcia is somewhat of a late bloomer, but the Dodgers believe he's ready to start making up for lost time. His next stop will be low Class A.

Year	Club (League)	Class	AVG	G	AB	R	H	2B	3B	HR	RBI	BB	SO	SB
1997	Dodgers (DSL)	R	.296	29	54	10	16	0	0	2	8	6	11	3
1998	Dodgers (DSL)	R	.294	61	204	39	60	11	1	2	31	18	29	15
1999	Dodgers (DSL)	R	.287	65	251	46	72	13	3	0	43	26	41	12
2000	Great Falls (Pio)	R	.211	6	19	2	4	0	0	0	3	1	4	2
2001	Great Falls (Pio)	R	.291	74	306	46	89	23	4	8	50	13	49	15
MINOR LEAGUE TOTALS			.289	235	834	143	241	47	8	12	135	64	134	47

30. Lamont Matthews, of

Born: June 15, 1978. **Ht.:** 6-2. **Wt.:** 210. **Bats:** L. **Throws:** L. **School:** Oklahoma State University. **Career Transactions:** Selected by Dodgers in 10th round of 1999 draft; signed June 22, 1999.

Matthews was named the Dodgers' minor league player of the month last May, at the same time his wife gave birth to their first child, a tribute to his resiliency. He showed signs of becoming a better all-around player last year in high Class A prior to struggling at the plate following a promotion to Double-A. Earlier in his career, the free-swinging Matthews was a feast-or-famine type of hitter who produced either extra-base hits or strikeouts. After the 2000 season, the Dodgers sat down with him and suggested he start focusing his efforts on plate discipline. He took the advice to heart and ranked fifth among all minor leaguers with a .436 on-base percentage last year. Matthews possesses a somewhat stiff stroke and his actions aren't always fluid. Even so, he hit a career-high .285 last year and possesses above-average power. If he puts everything together, he could be a dangerous player. He has plenty of arm for right field, totaling 37 assists over the last two years, though he also has made 20 errors during that time. He'll start 2002 in Double-A.

Year	Club (League)	Class	AVG	G	AB	R	H	2B	3B	HR	RBI	BB	SO	SB
1999	Yakima (NWL)	A	.225	66	249	46	56	11	2	17	52	34	87	4
	San Bernardino (Cal)	A	.267	4	15	2	4	1	0	1	3	2	7	0
2000	San Bernardino (Cal)	A	.245	131	473	79	116	28	9	24	90	88	170	12
2001	Vero Beach (FSL)	A	.307	107	349	61	107	26	3	10	57	95	106	1
	Jacksonville (SL)	AA	.145	18	55	4	8	4	0	0	7	12	25	0
MINOR LEAGUE TOTALS			.255	326	1141	192	291	70	14	52	209	231	395	17

MILWAUKEE
Brewers

By Tom Haudricourt

You don't build a farm system overnight. Or in two years, for that matter. The lesson has been driven home for Dean Taylor since he took over as Brewers general manager in September 1999. The previous regime left behind a couple of pitching prospects (Ben Sheets and Nick Neugebauer) and little else.

A look at this year's prospect list reveals the rebuilding project Taylor and his staff faced. Just four members of the top 10 are position players, and two—shortstop Bill Hall and outfielder Cristian Guerrero—were in the system when the Taylor administration took over.

The dearth of quality position prospects has taken its toll at the major league level. The Brewers suffered their traditional string of injuries in 2001, and when they looked for help in the minors they didn't find much. The result was a 94-loss season that left everyone involved disappointed.

As Milwaukee attempts to rebuild its system, it has identified another goal: keeping prospects healthy. Sheets, No. 1 on last year's list, made the National League all-star ream as a rookie but barely pitched in the second half because of shoulder prob-

lems. Neugebauer hurt his shoulder in September and had surgery, so his status at the beginning of 2002 is clouded.

Yet another top pitching prospect, righthander Jose Mieses, missed most of the second half of 2001 with back and shoulder injuries, and he also had surgery. This has to stop if the Brewers are to end their string of nine losing seasons and become competitive again.

Taylor and his staff remain committed to player development, and the good news is that their first two drafts look good. Their top picks in 2000 (outfielder David Krynzel) and 2001 (righthander Mike Jones) were the Rookie-level Pioneer League's No. 1 prospects in their pro debuts.

"We have some quality players we feel we've injected into the system," Taylor said. "Are they going to be playing in Milwaukee next year? No. Are they going to be playing here in 2003? Probably not.

"But if you ask any of us about the strength of the minor leagues compared to where we were two years ago, I don't think there's any question that we have definitely improved."

Like we said: A turnaround doesn't happen overnight.

OrganizationOverview

General manager: Dean Taylor. **Farm director:** Greg Riddoch. **Scouting director:** Jack Zduriencik.

2001 PERFORMANCE

Class	Farm Team	League	W	L	Pct.	Finish*	Manager
Majors	Milwaukee	National	68	94	.420	t-13th (16)	Davey Lopes
Triple-A	Indianapolis Indians	International	66	78	.458	11th (14)	Wendell Kim
Double-A	Huntsville Stars	Southern	75	63	.543	4th (10)	Ed Romero
High A	High Desert Mavericks	California	71	69	.507	5th (10)	Frank Kremblas
Low A	Beloit Snappers	Midwest	67	71	.486	7th (14)	Don Money
Rookie	Ogden Raptors	Pioneer	36	38	.486	6th (8)	Ed Sedar
Rookie	AZL Brewers	Arizona	27	29	.482	4th (7)	Carlos Lezcano
OVERALL 2001 MINOR LEAGUE RECORD			342	348	.496	15th (30)	

*Finish in overall standings (No. of teams in league)

ORGANIZATION LEADERS

BATTING
*AVG **Jim Rushford**, Huntsville/High Desert .354
  R **Jim Rushford**, Huntsville/High Desert .. 103
  H **Jim Rushford**, Huntsville/High Desert .. 158
 TB **Jim Rushford**, Huntsville/High Desert .. 265
 2B Bill Scott, High Desert 42
 3B Bobby Darula, Huntsville/High Desert 7
    Bill Hall, Huntsville/High Desert 7
 HR Lance Burkhart, Huntsville/High Desert 32
RBI Bill Scott, High Desert 102
 BB Steve Scarborough, High Desert.............. 65
    Lance Burkhart, Huntsville/High Desert 65
 SO Dave Krynzel, High Desert/Beloit 150
 SB Dave Krynzel, High Desert/Beloit 45
    Ryan Knox, Huntsville/High Desert 45

PITCHING
  W Matt Parker, High Desert 13
  L Matt Childers, Huntsville/High Desert........ 11
#ERA Rocky Coppinger, Indianapolis/Huntsville 1.97
  G Brian Mallette, Indianapolis/Huntsville 56
 CG Six tied at 1
 SV Brian Mallette, Indianapolis/Huntsville 19
 IP Tim Harikkala, Indianapolis...................... 172
 BB **Carlos Chantres**, Indianapolis 93
 SO Nick Neugebauer, Indianapolis/Huntsville 175

*Minimum 250 At-Bats #Minimum 75 Innings

TOP PROSPECTS OF THE DECADE

1992 .... Tyrone Hill, lhp
1993 .... Tyrone Hill, lhp
1994 .... Jeff D'Amico, rhp
1995 .... Antone Williamson, 3b
1996 .... Jeff D'Amico, rhp
1997 .... Todd Dunn, of
1998 .... Valerio de los Santos, lhp
1999 .... Ron Belliard, 2b
2000 .... Nick Neugebauer, rhp
2001.. Ben Sheets, rhp

TOP DRAFT PICKS OF THE DECADE

1992 .... Kenny Felder, of
1993 .... Jeff D'Amico, rhp
1994 .... Antone Williamson, 3b
1995 .... Geoff Jenkins, of
1996... Chad Green, of
1997.. Kyle Peterson, rhp
1998.. J.M. Gold, rhp
1999... Ben Sheets, rhp
2000 .... David Krynzel, of
2001... Mike Jones, rhp

Rushford   **Chantres**

BEST TOOLS

Best Hitter for Average...................... David Krynzel
Best Power Hitter................................. Kade Johnson
Fastest Baserunner............................ David Krynzel
Best Fastball.................................. Nick Neugebauer
Best Breaking Ball .... Ben Hendrickson
Best Changeup .... Jose Mieses
Best Control .... Jose Mieses
Best Defensive Catcher .... Brian Moon
Best Defensive Infielder .... Bill Hall
Best Infield Arm .... J.J. Hardy
Best Defensive Outfielder.................. David Krynzel
Best Outfield Arm......................... Cristian Guerrero

PROJECTED 2005 LINEUP

Catcher .... Kade Johnson
First Base .... Richie Sexson
Second Base .... J.J. Hardy
Third Base .... Daryl Clark
Shortstop .... Bill Hall
Left Field.. Geoff Jenkins
Center Field.. David Krynzel
Right Field .... Christian Guerrero
No. 1 Starter .... Ben Sheets
No. 2 Starter .... Nick Neugebauer
No. 3 Starter .... Mike Jones
No. 4 Starter................................. Ben Hendrickson
No. 5 Starter .... Glendon Rusch
Closer .... Chad Fox

ALL-TIME LARGEST BONUSES

Ben Sheets, 1999 .... $2,450,000
Mike Jones, 2001 .... $2,075,000
David Krynzel, 2000 .... $1,950,000
J.M. Gold, 1998 .... $1,675,000
Kyle Peterson, 1997 .... $1,400,000

DraftAnalysis

2001 Draft

Best Pro Debut: RHP **Mike Jones** (1) held his own as a high schooler facing college hitters in the Rookie-level Pioneer League. He went 4-1, 3.74 with 32 strikeouts in 34 innings, and was the league's top prospect. 2B Ralph Santana (42) batted .337 and finished second in the league with 30 steals.

Best Athlete: SS J.J. Hardy (2) has good genes, as his father Mark played pro tennis and his mother Susan golfed on the LPGA tour. All of his tools are average or better, and he also threw 88-92 mph as a high school closer. Jones, who also excelled in the outfield, and RHP Calvin Carpenter (6) are very athletic for pitchers.

Best Hitter: The Brewers compare 1B Brad Nelson (4) to Sean Casey.

Best Raw Power: Nelson was one of the best high school sluggers available in the draft. He also has power in his arm, reaching the low 90s when he pitched.

Fastest Runner: Santana can run the 60-yard dash in 6.5 seconds, a tick faster than Hardy and SS Chris Barnwell (25).

Best Defensive Player: Hardy. Some teams liked Hardy's upside as a pitcher, but the Brewers took him with the intention of making him their shortstop of the future. Nothing thus far has changed their minds.

Best Fastball: Jones throws 93-94 mph with ease and still was throwing as hard as 97 mph in instructional league. RHPs Jon Steitz (3), Dennis Sarfate (9) and Aaron Sheffield (14) all can register 95s on a radar gun.

Most Intriguing Background: The son of two Yale professors, Steitz returned there last fall to complete his degree in molecular biophysics and biochemistry. 3B Taylor McCormack's (7) father Don played in the majors, as did unsigned C Tim Dillard's (15) father Steve. RHP David Nolasco (23) and C Matt Serafini (43) have brothers who were drafted by the Cubs and Twins. 1B Brandon Gemoll's (8) brother Justin plays in the Royals system.

MEL BAILEY

Jones

Closest To The Majors: Steitz, despite his 6.68 ERA in the Pioneer League. His fastball and slider are plus pitches, and he was rusty after not pitching for two months.

Best Late-Round Pick: Sheffield entered 2001 as the top junior college prospect in the nation, then left Young Harris (Ga.) JC and returned home to be with his father, who was dying of cancer.

The One Who Got Away: LHP Ray Liotta (12) is 6-foot-4 and touches 90 mph. Tulane beat out the Brewers for his services.

Assessment: The Brewers need pitching, and Jones has the best arm in the system now that Ben Sheets and Nick Neugebauer have reached Milwaukee. Hardy, Steitz and Nelson debut high on the organization's prospect list. The Brewers took a liking to players from Arizona in this draft as their first two picks were from the state, as well as six of their top 20.

2000 Draft

A solid if not spectacular effort. OF David Krynzel (1) is off to a good start, while 3B Daryl Clark (17), RHP Matt Yeatman (13) and 1B Corey Hart (11) are among the organization's top 15 prospects. C Jason Belcher (4) and OF Bill Scott (8) aren't there yet but may have the best bats of the bunch. **Grade: C+**

1999 Draft

RHP Ben Sheets (1) fell into the Brewers' lap with the 10th overall pick, the best thing that has happened to the franchise in a while. RHP Ben Hendrickson (10) and C Kade Johnson (2) also have nice ceilings. **Grade: B+**

1998 Draft

RHP Nick Neugebauer (2) and SS Bill Hall (6) are the organization's top prospects. RHP J.M. Gold (1) has an arm in the same class as Neugebauer's but is still coming back from Tommy John surgery. **Grade: B+**

1997 Draft

RHP Kyle Peterson (1) reached the majors quickly before injuries derailed his career. Now hopes ride on RHP Matt Childers (9), who has a career ERA of 5.06. **Grade: C**

Note: Draft analysis prepared by Jim Callis. Numbers in parentheses indicate draft rounds.

. . . On days when he gets his slurve over, Neugebauer is nearly unhittable.

Nick
Neugebauer rhp

Born: July 15, 1980.
Ht.: 6-3. **Wt.:** 225.
Bats: R. **Throws:** R.
School: Arlington HS, Riverside, Calif.
Career Transactions: Selected by Brewers in second round of 1998 draft; signed Aug. 27, 1998.

The Brewers hoped to get Neugebauer to the big leagues in 2001, and that mission was accomplished with a September callup. A wonderful debut was overshadowed, however, by shoulder problems that were diagnosed as slight tears of his labrum and rotator cuff. The injuries were repaired with arthroscopic surgery. Doctors saw no reason Neugebauer would lose his chief asset—the ability to throw very hard—but whether he'll be back to 100 percent by spring training is in question. Because Neugebauer is a horse with a solid work ethic, there's every reason to believe he'll work to regain the form that made him one of the most feared pitchers in the minors. Neugebauer spun his wheels for a while at Double-A in 2001 but was dominating at Triple-A when the Brewers summoned him.

The ability to throw hard can't be taught, and that's what sets Neugebauer apart. He once threw consistently in the high 90s but didn't always know where the ball was going. Instructors taught him the value of throwing 95 mph in the strike zone as opposed to 98 mph to the backstop. He made big strides in that department in 2001, more than doubling his strikeout-walk ratio from the year before. On days when he gets his slurve over the plate, Neugebauer is nearly unhittable. He has the frame of a power pitcher and can be an intimidating presence on the mound. He doesn't overthrow as often as he once did, but when he does his mechanics get out of whack and leave him prone to injury. Now he'll have to prove he can stay healthy and consistent enough to warrant a spot in the Brewers rotation. Health is the only real roadblock to a solid major league career. He's working to become more consistent with his changeup.

If Neugebauer is healthy in spring training, look for him to win a spot in Milwaukee's rotation. If not, he'll have to regroup. One way or the other, Neugebauer should spend most of 2002 in a Brewers uniform. Ben Sheets and Neugebauer would give them a legitimate 1-2 pitching punch.

BOB LIBBY

Year	Club (League)	Class	W	L	ERA	G	GS	CG	SV	IP	H	R	ER	BB	SO
1999	Beloit (Mid)	A	7	5	3.90	18	18	0	0	81	50	41	35	80	125
2000	Mudville (Cal)	A	4	4	4.19	18	18	0	0	77	43	40	36	87	117
	Huntsville (SL)	AA	1	3	3.73	10	10	0	0	51	35	28	21	47	57
2001	Huntsville (SL)	AA	5	6	3.46	21	21	1	0	107	94	46	41	52	149
	Indianapolis (IL)	AAA	2	1	1.50	4	4	0	0	24	10	5	4	9	26
	Milwaukee (NL)	MAJ	1	1	7.50	2	2	0	0	6	6	5	5	6	11
MAJOR LEAGUE TOTALS			1	1	7.50	2	2	0	0	6	6	5	5	6	11
MINOR LEAGUE TOTALS			19	19	3.63	71	71	1	0	339	232	160	137	275	474

2. Bill Hall, ss

Born: Dec. 28, 1979. **Ht.:** 6-0. **Wt.:** 175. **Bats:** R. **Throws:** R. **School:** Nettleton (Miss.) HS. **Career Transactions:** Selected by Brewers in sixth round of 1998 draft; signed June 7, 1998.

No player in the organization moved up more than Hall did in 2001. Ranked as the club's No. 21 prospect a year ago, he was named the Brewers' minor league player of the year. He showed the offensive capabilities to be something special at shortstop, though he found the going a lot tougher at Double-A Huntsville. Few shortstops can hit like Hall. Not only did he hit for average at high Class A High Desert, but he also showed previously untapped power. Hall also runs well and has great range in the field. He often gets too cute on defense, resulting in needless errors. Hall had a combined 45 errors in 2001, a career high. He gets to balls other shortstops don't, but he has to learn when to eat the ball and when to attempt a fabulous play. He also must work on plate discipline, as shown by his .279 on-base percentage in Double-A. If Hall's defense catches up to his offense, look out. One member of the organization compares him to Miguel Tejada at the same stage of their careers. Tejada's defense once was considered a possible roadblock to the majors as well.

Year	Club (League)	Class	AVG	G	AB	R	H	2B	3B	HR	RBI	BB	SO	SB
1998	Helena (Pio)	R	.176	29	85	11	15	3	0	0	5	9	27	5
1999	Ogden (Pio)	R	.289	69	280	41	81	15	2	6	31	15	61	19
2000	Beloit (Mid)	A	.262	130	470	57	123	30	6	3	41	18	127	10
2001	High Desert (Cal)	A	.303	89	346	61	105	21	6	15	51	22	78	18
	Huntsville (SL)	AA	.256	41	160	14	41	8	1	3	14	5	46	5
MINOR LEAGUE TOTALS			.272	358	1341	184	365	77	15	27	142	69	339	57

3. David Krynzel, of

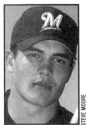

Born: Nov. 7, 1981. **Ht.:** 6-1. **Wt.:** 180. **Bats:** L. **Throws:** L. **School:** Green Valley HS, Henderson, Nev. **Career Transactions:** Selected by Brewers in first round (11th overall) of 2000 draft; signed June 12, 2000.

The Brewers challenged Krynzel in 2001 and liked the way he responded. After he got off to a nice start at Beloit, they bumped him up to High Desert, realizing he would be the youngest player in the California League and would struggle. That's what happened at first, but by season's end Krynzel held his own as the second-youngest player in the Cal League. Speed is what will get Krynzel to the big leagues. Because he can make things happen on the bases and go get the ball in the outfield, he's a prototype leadoff hitter in the mold of Kenny Lofton. The Brewers also expect him to get stronger and drive the ball more, which he began doing at High Desert. He has passed the mental toughness test. Krynzel must make contact more consistently than he did in 2001. On-base percentage is critical for a leadoff hitter, and he also has to do better in that department. Bunting more often for hits would be a good start. At High Desert at the end of 2001 Krynzel was playing so well that he'll probably get the chance to play at Huntsville this spring. That would be quite a leap for a 20-year-old.

Year	Club (League)	Class	AVG	G	AB	R	H	2B	3B	HR	RBI	BB	SO	SB
2000	Ogden (Pio)	R	.359	34	131	25	47	8	3	1	29	16	23	8
2001	Beloit (Mid)	A	.305	35	141	22	43	1	1	1	19	9	28	11
	High Desert (Cal)	A	.277	89	383	65	106	19	5	5	33	27	122	34
MINOR LEAGUE TOTALS			.299	158	655	112	196	28	9	7	81	52	173	53

4. Mike Jones, rhp

Born: April 23, 1983. **Ht.:** 6-4. **Wt.:** 200. **Bats:** R. **Throws:** R. **School:** Thunderbird HS, Phoenix. **Career Transactions:** Selected by Brewers in first round (12th overall) of 2001 draft; signed June 27, 2001.

The Brewers were thrilled when Jones was still on the board when the 12th overall pick came around in the 2001 draft. He was expected to go higher, but concerns about shoulder problems and diminished velocity in his senior year made some teams back off. Milwaukee didn't hesitate and projects him as a bona fide No. 1 starter. The Brewers love three things above all else about Jones: his large frame, his blazing fastball and his smooth delivery. It isn't easy to find high school pitchers so mechanically sound, or who can throw 93-94 mph with ease. Beyond that, he has demonstrated considerable poise and focus on the mound. Jones was a multisport athlete and talented basketball player who played shortstop when he didn't pitch in high school. Because Jones can blow away hitters with his fastball, he hasn't always concentrated on improving his curveball and changeup. If he continues to work on his breaking ball, there's every reason to think he could move quickly through the system. He was ranked as the top prospect in the Rookie-level Pioneer League and is probably ready to take on Class A in 2002. He's still a teenager but is mature for his age.

Year	Club (League)	Class	W	L	ERA	G	GS	CG	SV	IP	H	R	ER	BB	SO
2001	Ogden (Pio)	R	4	1	3.74	9	7	0	0	34	29	17	14	10	32
MINOR LEAGUE TOTALS			4	1	3.74	9	7	0	0	34	29	17	14	10	32

5. Cristian Guerrero, of

Born: April 12, 1980. **Ht.:** 6-5. **Wt.:** 200. **Bats:** R. **Throws:** R. **Career Transactions:** Signed out of Dominican Republic by Brewers, Aug. 28, 1997.

The Brewers are still waiting for Vladimir Guerrero's cousin to approach his potential. Because Cristian is just 21 they're far from panicking, even though he has shown little evidence of Guerreroesque performance so far. He missed six weeks at High Desert with a broken foot last season, so he didn't make as much progress as club officials had hoped. Guerrero still has the tools to become a star player. He hits for average, shows flashes of power and has a solid arm in the outfield. Guerrero isn't a great runner but gets the job done in the field. With four tools, he can be an impact player in the majors if he gets the most out of all of them. He must continue to work on his defense and also needs to add strength, which should increase his power numbers. He's a free swinger who doesn't draw many walks. "He has so much ability," one member of the organization said. "We're just waiting for it all to come together." Guerrero is still young, so the Brewers won't rush him. If they can get him to the Double-A level at some point in 2002, they'll be pleased.

Year	Club (League)	Class	AVG	G	AB	R	H	2B	3B	HR	RBI	BB	SO	SB
1998	Brewers (DSL)	R	.268	64	213	45	57	9	3	5	37	43	54	5
1999	Ogden (Pio)	R	.310	65	226	51	70	7	3	5	28	23	59	26
2000	Ogden (Pio)	R	.341	66	255	56	87	14	4	12	54	37	42	24
	Beloit (Mid)	A	.164	15	55	5	9	4	0	2	8	1	18	1
2001	High Desert (Cal)	A	.312	85	327	50	102	18	2	7	41	18	79	22
MINOR LEAGUE TOTALS			.302	295	1076	207	325	52	12	31	168	122	252	78

6. Ben Hendrickson, rhp

Born: Feb. 4, 1981. **Ht.:** 6-3. **Wt.:** 185. **Bats:** R. **Throws:** R. **School:** Jefferson HS, Bloomington, Minn. **Career Transactions:** Selected by Brewers in 10th round of 1999 draft; signed Sept. 1, 1999.

After a so-so year in Rookie ball in 2000, Hendrickson had a superb season at Beloit. He took a regular turn in the rotation and pitched well more often than not, and suddenly the Brewers think they're on to something. They didn't have much luck in the middle to late rounds of the draft in the 1990s, so perhaps Hendrickson will be an exception. Hendrickson can get his fastball into the 93-94 mph range at times, but he more regularly pitches at 90-91. What sets him apart is a killer curveball. That combination allowed him to average a strikeout per inning at Beloit, and Hendrickson also kept the ball down and in the ballpark. With only 50 innings of pro experience prior to 2001, Hendrickson simply needs to pitch. And it wouldn't hurt to add muscle to his lanky frame, which should provide more strength and the ability to go deeper into games. The Brewers were careful with his pitch counts in 2001. Hendrickson handled himself so well that he might be able to jump right past High Desert and go directly to Huntsville in 2002. Either way, he figures to be in Double-A before the year is out.

Year	Club (League)	Class	W	L	ERA	G	GS	CG	SV	IP	H	R	ER	BB	SO
2000	Ogden (Pio)	R	4	3	5.68	13	7	0	1	51	50	37	32	29	48
2001	Beloit (Mid)	A	8	9	2.84	25	25	1	0	133	122	58	42	72	133
MINOR LEAGUE TOTALS			12	12	3.62	38	32	1	1	184	172	95	74	101	181

7. J.J. Hardy, ss

Born: Aug. 19, 1982. **Ht.:** 6-1. **Wt.:** 170. **Bats:** R. **Throws:** R. **School:** Sabino HS, Tucson. **Career Transactions:** Selected by Brewers in second round of 2001 draft; signed July 16, 2001.

Hardy has such a good arm that some teams considered drafting him as a pitcher out of high school. The Brewers believe he can be a short-stop, however, with the skills of a Robin Yount. Though they got him in the second round, they consider Hardy a first-round talent. He has good genes, as his father Mark played professional tennis and his mother Susan golfed on the LPGA tour. Hardy has superior instincts and skills on defense, including a great arm and range. He has soft hands and is fundamentally sound beyond his years. The Brewers also believe he'll develop into a good hitter one day, and he walked more than he struck out in his first pro summer. His defense is far ahead of his offense at this point, but many believe he merely needs more experience with a wood bat. He doesn't have much foot speed to speak of but gets good jumps on the ball and makes plays other shortstops don't. Hardy's career is just starting, but the Brewers see a big league shortstop in the making. The next step for him is Beloit in 2002.

Year	Club (League)	Class	AVG	G	AB	R	H	2B	3B	HR	RBI	BB	SO	SB
2001	Brewers (AZL)	R	.250	5	20	6	5	2	1	0	1	1	2	0
	Ogden (Pio)	R	.248	35	125	20	31	5	0	2	15	15	12	1
MINOR LEAGUE TOTALS			.248	40	145	26	36	7	1	2	16	16	14	1

8. Jose Mieses, rhp

Born: Oct. 14, 1979. **Ht.:** 6-1. **Wt.:** 180. **Bats:** R. **Throws:** R. **Career Transactions:** Signed out of Dominican Republic by Brewers, Dec. 11, 1996.

The Brewers had every reason to believe Mieses would pitch in the major leagues in 2001. And he would have, if not for a back problem midway through the season, followed by a shoulder injury near the end that required surgery. Doctors expect him to make a full recovery by spring training or shortly thereafter. Mieses has a nasty palmball that befuddles hitters and poise on the mound. Those advantages, and the ability to put his pitches where he wants them, allow him to get away with an average fastball and curveball. When you're not an overpowering pitcher, you have to hit your spots. Hitters who lay off Mieses' palmball cause him problems. This year, doctors discovered he has a back condition that will have to be monitored regularly. If Mieses comes back from his injury, there's no reason to think he can't pitch for the Brewers in 2002. Whether he'll ever be more than an end-of-the-rotation pitcher is debatable.

Year	Club (League)	Class	W	L	ERA	G	GS	CG	SV	IP	H	R	ER	BB	SO
1997	Brewers (DSL)	R	3	2	2.40	20	5	0	1	56	34	22	15	36	49
1998	Brewers (DSL)	R	4	5	3.00	14	13	3	0	84	70	39	28	38	77
1999	Helena (Pio)	R	10	2	2.67	15	15	3	0	108	79	36	32	28	87
2000	Beloit (Mid)	A	13	6	2.53	21	21	2	0	135	107	43	38	37	132
	Mudville (Cal)	A	4	1	2.65	6	6	0	0	34	25	11	10	18	40
2001	Brewers (AZL)	R	0	1	0.00	2	2	0	0	4	3	1	0	1	5
	Ogden (Pio)	R	0	1	27.00	1	1	0	0	1	3	3	3	1	2
	Huntsville (SL)	AA	0	0	2.22	5	4	0	0	24	21	7	6	3	35
	Indianapolis (IL)	AAA	0	3	6.08	3	3	0	0	13	23	12	9	7	13
MINOR LEAGUE TOTALS			34	21	2.76	87	70	8	1	460	365	174	141	169	440

9. J.M. Gold, rhp

Born: April 18, 1980. **Ht.:** 6-5. **Wt.:** 220. **Bats:** R. **Throws:** R. **School:** Toms River (N.J.) North HS. **Career Transactions:** Selected by Brewers in first round (13th overall) of 1998 draft; signed June 24, 1998.

After a fast ascent in the organization, Gold fell completely off the Brewers' radar screen after having Tommy John surgery in 2000. Scouts were anxious to see if he would regain the stuff that made him a first-round draft pick, and after the long recovery he showed his arm was sound again. Gold was taken a round ahead of Nick Neugebauer in 1998, which tells you how highly the Brewers regarded him. He could throw 95 mph consistently with a sharp-breaking curve, and showed flashes of that after returning in 2001. He's learned a lot about conditioning and dedication along the way, and is hungrier after losing a season. Because he had mechanical flaws in his delivery, Gold was a prime candidate to break down. Having gone through the grueling recovery from Tommy John surgery, he now understands the importance of staying fundamentally sound. It was a big wakeup call. Barring any recurrences of elbow problems, Gold should get back on the fast track. Assuming he can stay healthy, he has the upside of a No. 2 or 3 starter in the majors.

Year	Club (League)	Class	W	L	ERA	G	GS	CG	SV	IP	H	R	ER	BB	SO
1998	Ogden (Pio)	R	1	0	2.61	5	5	0	0	21	21	13	6	7	15
1999	Beloit (Mid)	A	6	10	5.40	21	21	2	0	112	120	82	67	54	93
2000	Beloit (Mid)	A	3	1	2.91	7	7	0	0	34	27	13	11	16	33
2001	Brewers (AZL)	R	0	1	7.56	4	4	0	0	8	17	7	7	2	7
	Ogden (Pio)	R	1	1	2.17	7	7	0	0	29	20	12	7	9	42
MINOR LEAGUE TOTALS			11	13	4.33	44	44	2	0	204	205	127	98	88	190

10. Matt Childers, rhp

Born: Dec. 3, 1978. **Ht.:** 6-5. **Wt.:** 215. **Bats:** R. **Throws:** R. **School:** Westside HS, Augusta, Ga. **Career Transactions:** Selected by Brewers in ninth round of 1997 draft; signed June 6, 1997.

His older brother Jason has a career 30-31, 2.92 record in the Brewers system, while Matt has gone 27-45, 5.06 and got lit up at High Desert for much of 2001. Yet Matt is considered a far better prospect because of his potential as a power pitcher. He made a lot of progress in 2001, pitching better after he moved up to Huntsville. Childers is a big, strong guy who can get his fastball into the 95 mph neighborhood. He doesn't lose his cool often and bounces back from tough outings better than most pitchers. It's mainly a matter of trusting his stuff and not giving in to hitters. Childers is inconsistent with his curveball and gets the ball up too much, resulting in too many home runs. He also gets mechanically out of whack at times. He spent most of four years in Class A but appears finally ready to make a move. The Brewers showed Childers what they thought of him by sending him to the Arizona Fall League for more seasoning. If he pitches as well in Triple-A as he did in Double-A, he could be in the majors before 2002 is over. But the underachieving must end.

Year	Club (League)	Class	W	L	ERA	G	GS	CG	SV	IP	H	R	ER	BB	SO
1997	Helena (Pio)	R	1	4	6.20	14	10	0	1	61	81	49	42	24	19
1998	Helena (Pio)	R	1	0	0.64	2	2	1	0	14	9	1	1	4	4
	Beloit (Mid)	A	3	7	5.10	14	12	3	0	67	89	55	38	20	49
1999	Beloit (Mid)	A	3	10	5.94	20	19	0	0	100	129	72	66	30	52
2000	Beloit (Mid)	A	8	2	2.71	12	12	1	0	73	64	33	22	17	47
	Mudville (Cal)	A	3	9	4.75	15	15	0	0	85	103	59	45	32	43
2001	High Desert (Cal)	A	6	11	6.44	20	20	0	0	117	155	95	84	29	76
	Huntsville (SL)	AA	2	2	3.43	7	7	0	0	39	41	19	15	12	21
MINOR LEAGUE TOTALS			27	45	5.06	104	97	5	1	557	671	383	313	168	311

11. Matt Yeatman, rhp

Born: Aug. 2, 1982. **Ht.:** 6-4. **Wt.:** 200. **Bats:** R. **Throws:** R. **School:** Tomball (Texas) HS. **Career Transactions:** Selected by Brewers in 13th round of 2000 draft, signed on Aug. 4, 2000.

After signing too late to pitch in 2000, Yeatman really opened some eyes in Rookie ball last season with a fastball in the mid-90s and a sharp-breaking curveball. His numbers weren't great but his stuff was electric at times. Used as both a starter and short reliever, he has the stuff to excel in either role. With his two plus pitches and his good frame, he's definitely somebody to watch. "He can be a Kevin Millwood type with better stuff," one Brewers official said. "He has a natural curveball." Yeatman needs to work on his concentration and command, which will come with more experience. He also doesn't have much of a changeup at this point, which won't matter as much if he's used to finish games rather than start them. He should be able to make the jump to full-season ball in 2002 and will open the season in low Class A.

Year	Club (League)	Class	W	L	ERA	G	GS	CG	SV	IP	H	R	ER	BB	SO
2001	Ogden (Pio)	R	2	4	4.95	13	8	0	1	60	72	40	33	27	61
MINOR LEAGUE TOTALS			2	4	4.95	13	8	0	1	60	72	40	33	27	61

12. Kade Johnson, c/of

Born: Sept. 28, 1978. **Ht.:** 6-1. **Wt.:** 195. **Bats:** R. **Throws:** R. **School:** Seminole State (Okla.) JC. **Career Transactions:** Selected by Brewers in second round of 1999 draft; signed Sept. 3, 1999.

Rated seventh on this list a year ago, Johnson fell because he simply didn't catch enough in 2001. In 101 games at High Desert, he went behind the plate just 62 times while playing 16 games in the outfield and DHing the rest of the time. Nagging injuries and a low pain threshold cost him time as a catcher, and Johnson still must prove he can be counted on defensively. Besides health concerns, he also makes too many errors, though he still shows good arm strength despite shoulder surgery in 2000. Not many catchers can hit with the power that Johnson has displayed, so his best path to the big leagues is at that position. If he can't play behind the plate, his value is significantly diminished. Johnson could be a 20-25 home run hitter in the majors, but he'll probably always strike out a lot. Catching depth is a problem in the organization, so he'll move up quickly if he gets his game together and stays healthy.

Year	Club (League)	Class	AVG	G	AB	R	H	2B	3B	HR	RBI	BB	SO	SB
2000	Ogden (Pio)	R	.316	28	98	16	31	7	0	10	35	14	20	2
2001	High Desert (Cal)	A	.254	101	370	57	94	21	1	21	67	35	118	9
MINOR LEAGUE TOTALS			.267	129	468	73	125	28	1	31	102	49	138	11

13. Luis Martinez, lhp

Born: Jan. 20, 1980. **Ht.:** 6-4. **Wt.:** 185. **Bats:** R. **Throws:** L. **Career Transactions:** Signed out of Dominican Republic by Brewers, Oct. 15, 1996.

Martinez has split time between starting and relieving in the minor leagues, and he has been hit harder than he should have been, considering his stuff. He throws his fastball in the 92-93 mph range and has a good breaking ball. He has the body frame to get bigger and stronger, and therefore he could pick up even more velocity. Martinez needs to challenge hitters more and make them hit his pitch. He gets a little stubborn at times but has the ability to strike out hitters and has shown fairly good command to this point. Martinez' future in the big leagues could be as a situational lefty, much the way Valerio de los Santos developed for the Brewers before he was injured last season.

Year	Club (League)	Class	W	L	ERA	G	GS	CG	SV	IP	H	R	ER	BB	SO
1997	Brewers (DSL)	R	0	2	12.96	11	2	0	0	17	21	27	24	24	17
1998	Helena (Pio)	R	0	9	10.13	17	10	0	0	48	64	73	54	66	47
1999	Ogden (Pio)	R	0	7	6.97	15	7	0	1	50	66	65	39	34	43
2000	Beloit (Mid)	A	5	7	3.79	28	13	0	0	93	71	49	39	61	77
2001	High Desert (Cal)	A	8	9	5.19	22	22	0	0	113	112	67	65	64	121
MINOR LEAGUE TOTALS			13	34	6.20	93	54	0	1	321	334	281	221	249	305

14. Daryl Clark, 3b

Born: Sept. 25, 1979. **Ht.:** 6-2. **Wt.:** 205. **Bats:** L. **Throws:** R. **School:** UNC Charlotte. **Career Transactions:** Selected by Brewers in 17th round of 2000 draft; signed June 15, 2000.

Nobody questions Clark's ability to hit and drive in runs. After batting .339 and finishing second in the Pioneer League in homers in his pro debut, he came through again last year as the top run producer at Beloit. It's in the field where Clark leaves himself open to question. He committed a whopping 47 errors in 2001, though Beloit's Pohlman Field is hardly fielder-friendly. The Brewers already have Richie Sexson in the big leagues and enough first-base types in the system, so it would behoove Clark to prove he can handle the hot corner. He strikes out a lot, though he also draws walks and his lack of contact won't be a huge concern unless he stops hitting. He's expected to move to high Class A in 2002, with the chance to reach Double-A by the end of the year.

Year	Club (League)	Class	AVG	G	AB	R	H	2B	3B	HR	RBI	BB	SO	SB
2000	Ogden (Pio)	R	.339	64	218	54	74	12	4	15	64	67	53	5
2001	Beloit (Mid)	A	.283	133	501	76	142	24	2	21	92	61	135	4
MINOR LEAGUE TOTALS			.300	197	719	130	216	36	6	36	156	128	188	9

15. Corey Hart, 1b

Born: March 24, 1982. **Ht.:** 6-1. **Wt.:** 180. **Bats:** S. **Throws:** R. **School:** Greenwood HS, Bowling Green, Ky. **Career Transactions:** Selected by Brewers in 11th round of 2000 draft; signed June 6, 2000.

Milwaukee officials refer to Hart as a miniature Richie Sexson, which is no small praise in this organization. After all, Sexson tied the franchise record with 45 homers last year and his 125 RBIs fell one short of equaling another. Hart has a similar offensive ceiling, plus the potential to hit for more average, though he also is several steps away from the majors. He had a monster year in his second tour of duty at Ogden and is definitely ready for his shot at Class A this season. Hart runs well enough and has enough athleticism to try the outfield, valuable assets considering the wealth of first basemen in the organization. He has a decent eye at the plate and doesn't strike out excessively, one thing that separates him from Sexson. The Brewers believe Hart has tremendous upside and will move up quickly because of his bat.

Year	Club (League)	Class	AVG	G	AB	R	H	2B	3B	HR	RBI	BB	SO	SB
2000	Ogden (Pio)	R	.287	57	216	32	62	9	1	2	30	13	27	6
2001	Ogden (Pio)	R	.340	69	262	53	89	18	1	11	62	26	47	14
MINOR LEAGUE TOTALS			.316	126	478	85	151	27	2	13	92	39	74	20

16. Brad Nelson, 1b

Born: Dec. 23, 1982. **Ht.:** 6-2. **Wt.:** 225. **Bats:** L. **Throws:** R. **School:** Bishop Garrigan HS, Algona, Iowa. **Career Transactions:** Selected by Brewers in fourth round of 2001 draft; signed July 25, 2001.

The Brewers compare Nelson to a young Sean Casey, and Casey doesn't have the pop that Nelson is expected to display once he gets more experience with a wood bat. His raw power sets him apart from most hitters his age, though he didn't homer in 105 at-bats in Rookie ball. Nelson pitched extensively in high school and showed a low-90s fastball, which gives him a better arm than most players at his position. He has soft hands, but his lack of speed prompted his move from third base to first once he turned pro. Milwaukee is stockpiling first basemen, and Nelson will have to hit his way out of the pack there because he doesn't seem able to handle another position. A good spring training could land him a job in low Class A rather than a return to Rookie ball.

Year	Club (League)	Class	AVG	G	AB	R	H	2B	3B	HR	RBI	BB	SO	SB
2001	Brewers (AZL)	R	.302	17	63	10	19	6	1	0	13	8	18	0
	Ogden (Pio)	R	.262	13	42	5	11	4	0	0	10	3	9	0
MINOR LEAGUE TOTALS			.286	30	105	15	30	10	1	0	23	11	27	0

17. Jon Steitz, rhp

Born: Sept. 5, 1980. **Ht.:** 6-3. **Wt.:** 197. **Bats:** R. **Throws:** R. **School:** Yale University. **Career Transactions:** Selected by Brewers in third round of 2001 draft; signed June 22, 2001.

Steitz projected as the first Ivy League first-rounder since Doug Glanville came out of Penn in 1991, but the Brewers were able to grab him in the third round after he didn't show all scouts were looking for in his junior season at Yale. As he matures and grows stronger, scouts believe he'll pick up velocity on his sinking fastball, which already stands at 91-95 mph. He also has a sharp slider but lacks consistency in the strike zone with it. Steitz' numbers weren't impressive in Rookie ball, which the Brewers wrote off to the two-month layoff between the end of his college season and his pro debut. The Brewers wanted him to go to instructional league for further seasoning but he opted to return to Yale to finish his studies. He must commit to baseball to realize his full potential. Not every player has parents who are professors of molecular biophysics and biochemistry at Yale, but not every pitcher has Steitz' upside either.

Year	Club (League)	Class	W	L	ERA	G	GS	CG	SV	IP	H	R	ER	BB	SO
2001	Ogden (Pio)	R	2	4	6.68	11	10	0	0	34	44	32	25	25	28
MINOR LEAGUE TOTALS			2	4	6.68	11	10	0	0	34	44	32	25	25	28

18. Jason Belcher, c

Born: Jan. 13, 1982. **Ht.:** 6-1. **Wt.:** 190. **Bats:** L. **Throws:** R. **School:** Walnut Ridge (Ark.) HS. **Career Transactions:** Selected by Brewers in fifth round of 2000 draft; signed June 30, 2000.

Belcher ranked 11th on this list after his pro debut, mostly because of the prowess he showed with the bat in Rookie ball. He again topped .300 in 2001, but it was in extremely limited action and he made absolutely no progress behind the plate. There are doubts about his ability to be an everyday catcher at higher levels, and he must prove he can handle that duty. Like Kade Johnson, his value will dip if he can't play catcher. He stayed in extended spring to work on his defense and didn't join Beloit until June. With the Snappers, he appeared in just 38 games before he broke his hand. In his 17 games behind the plate, he permitted 42 steals in 47 attempts (90 percent). Belcher is strong and has a good work ethic, and it will be up to him to get better defensively. A lefthanded-hitting catcher with pop would be welcomed in an organization hurting at that position. He has to fit that description in more than name only.

Year	Club (League)	Class	AVG	G	AB	R	H	2B	3B	HR	RBI	BB	SO	SB
2000	Helena (Pio)	R	.333	46	162	30	54	18	2	4	36	20	25	3
2001	Beloit (Mid)	A	.326	38	144	23	47	6	0	2	23	15	16	0
MINOR LEAGUE TOTALS			.330	84	306	53	101	24	2	6	59	35	41	3

19. Jorge Sosa, rhp

Born: April 28, 1978. **Ht.:** 6-3. **Wt.:** 198. **Bats:** B. **Throws:** R. **Career Transactions:** Signed out of Dominican Republic by Rockies, June 23, 1995 . . . Selected by Mariners from Rockies in Rule 5 minor league draft, Dec. 11, 2000 . . . Selected by Brewers from Mariners in Rule 5 major league draft, Dec. 13, 2001.

Sosa spent six seasons in the Rockies system without reaching full-season ball, hitting .222 as an outfielder. His best tool by far was his arm, which intrigued the Mariners when they saw him play in the short-season Northwest League. They took him in the 2000 Triple-A Rule 5 draft for $12,000 and immediately converted him into a pitcher. The move was an instant success, as Sosa threw 95-96 mph on a consistent basis and had little trouble throwing strikes. He still needs work on his secondary pitches and wasn't considered close to being ready for the major leagues, so Seattle gambled and left him off its 40-man roster this winter. The Brewers swooped in and claimed Sosa in the major league Rule 5 draft in December, which means they'll have to keep him on their 25-man roster throughout 2002, or expose him to waivers before offering him back to the Mariners for half his $50,000 purchase price. It may be difficult to hold onto Sosa, but his arm makes it worth taking the chance.

Year	Club (League)	Class	AVG	G	AB	R	H	2B	3B	HR	RBI	BB	SO	SB
1995	Royals/Rockies (DSL)	R	.253	32	91	10	23	3	0	0	1	8	26	1
1996	Royals/Rockies (DSL)	R	.241	51	162	29	39	13	2	3	25	25	54	2
1997	Rockies (AZL)	R	.140	29	93	13	13	1	2	0	6	13	36	6
1998	Rockies (AZL)	R	.237	45	152	23	36	6	1	2	11	12	57	4
1999	Portland (NWL)	A	.204	35	113	15	23	3	0	2	8	13	57	2
2000	Portland (NWL)	A	.230	62	200	24	46	7	5	4	26	37	102	4
MINOR LEAGUE TOTALS			.222	254	811	114	180	33	10	11	77	108	332	19

Year	Club (League)	Class	W	L	ERA	G	GS	CG	SV	IP	H	R	ER	BB	SO
2001	Everett (NWL)	A	3	1	1.69	21	7	0	7	59	45	22	11	19	57
	Wisconsin (Mid)	A	0	0	9.00	2	0	0	0	2	3	2	2	0	4
MINOR LEAGUE TOTALS			3	1	1.92	23	7	0	7	61	48	24	13	19	61

20. Ozzie Chavez, ss

Born: July 13, 1983. **Ht.:** 6-1. **Wt.:** 155. **Bats:** S. **Throws:** R. **Career Transactions:** Signed out of Dominican Republic by the Brewers, Aug. 1, 1999.

His parents must have known something when they named their child Ozzie Smith Chavez. That's a high standard to shoot for, but the Brewers believe the sky's the limit for the slightly built shortstop. Chavez has outstanding tools and natural shortstop actions, including soft hands and good range in the field. Though he has yet to fill out, the ball jumped off his bat when he made his U.S. debut in the Rookie-level Arizona League last year. As he moves to higher levels, he'll need to tighten his strike zone and learn how to use his speed better on the basepaths. Like most young shortstops, he also must get more consistent in the field. Noted scout Epy Guerrero has signed some spiffy infielders out of the Dominican, and Chavez appears to be another one to add to his list. He'll get the chance to jump to full-season ball at Beloit with a good spring.

Year	Club (League)	Class	AVG	G	AB	R	H	2B	3B	HR	RBI	BB	SO	SB
2000	Brewers (DSL)	R	.273	64	187	44	51	5	1	1	29	41	33	14
2001	Brewers (AZL)	R	.305	52	210	38	64	12	6	0	27	13	36	9
MINOR LEAGUE TOTALS			.290	116	397	82	115	17	7	1	56	54	69	23

21. Jeff Deardorff, of

Born: Aug. 14, 1978. **Ht.:** 6-3. **Wt.:** 220. **Bats:** R. **Throws:** R. **School:** South Lake HS, Clermont, Fla. **Career Transactions:** Selected by Brewers in third round of 1997 draft; signed June 21, 1997.

Entering 2001, Deardorff had spun his wheels for three seasons at the Class A level, failing to live up to offensive expectations and playing himself off his original position of third base. The switch to the outfield finally allowed him to relax at the plate and develop as a hitter. He turned on the power switch and finally got to Double-A with a midseason promotion. Finally, he's a prospect again, though not a particularly young one. Deardorff continued to hit in the Arizona Fall League and was leading Maryvale with five homers in 18 games when he was selected to play for the silver-medal U.S. team in the World Cup tournament in Taiwan. That experience was a fitting end to a long-awaited breakthrough year. Deardorff's development has been slower than expected but perhaps it's not too late.

Year	Club (League)	Class	AVG	G	AB	R	H	2B	3B	HR	RBI	BB	SO	SB
1997	Ogden (Pio)	R	.275	63	222	33	61	17	3	2	27	24	74	2
1998	Beloit (Mid)	A	.255	88	326	41	83	17	1	11	45	27	125	3
1999	Stockton (Cal)	A	.266	126	436	59	116	22	2	10	47	40	150	2
2000	Mudville (Cal)	A	.245	111	421	48	103	20	7	10	54	32	120	7
2001	High Desert (Cal)	A	.304	69	260	40	79	18	1	15	57	22	70	5
	Huntsville (SL)	AA	.279	58	201	30	56	11	1	14	43	13	66	1
MINOR LEAGUE TOTALS			.267	515	1866	251	498	105	15	62	273	158	605	20

22. Brian Mallette, rhp

Born: Jan. 19, 1975. **Ht.:** 6-0. **Wt.:** 185. **Bats:** R. **Throws:** R. **School:** Columbus (Ga.) College. **Career Transactions:** Selected by Brewers in 27th round on 1997 draft; signed June 9, 1997.

Like Jeff Deardorff, Mallette was stuck at the Class A level for three years before finally making the jump to Double-A in 2001. After pitching brilliantly in short relief at Huntsville, he was promoted to Triple-A Indianapolis and fared even better. Suddenly Mallette is in the Brewers' picture in 2002, projecting as a middle reliever or setup man. For whatever reason, his velocity improved into the low 90s and his command also sharpened. He quit trying to pick at the corners so much and began challenging hitters, getting ahead in the count. It was the proverbial light bulb going off in a pitcher's head. Mallette caught the notice of club officials, who assigned him to the Arizona Fall League, where he built on his regular-season success. He's hardly flashy but gets the job done.

Year	Club (League)	Class	W	L	ERA	G	GS	CG	SV	IP	H	R	ER	BB	SO
1997	Helena (Pio)	R	6	2	4.33	23	0	0	5	35	33	19	17	20	58
1998	Beloit (Mid)	A	2	1	3.09	50	0	0	23	55	40	23	19	29	76
1999	Stockton (Cal)	A	2	0	1.50	28	0	0	4	36	38	16	6	16	34
2000	Mudville (Cal)	A	4	4	3.30	50	0	0	2	71	52	35	26	52	94
2001	Huntsville (SL)	AA	7	2	1.96	44	0	0	17	55	43	13	12	23	71
	Indianapolis (IL)	AAA	0	1	1.06	12	0	0	2	17	10	4	2	8	23
MINOR LEAGUE TOTALS			21	10	2.74	207	0	0	53	269	216	110	82	148	356

23. Bill Scott, 1b/of

Born: April 8, 1979. **Ht.:** 6-1. **Wt.:** 210. **Bats:** R. **Throws:** R. **School:** UCLA. **Career Transactions:** Selected by Brewers in the eighth round of the 2000 draft; signed Sept. 27, 2000.

Scott is yet another Brewers first-base prospect who can hit. In order to advance him to Milwaukee, the club has tried him in the outfield, where he played in college. But he's marginal at best as a left fielder, in part because he has bad throwing mechanics and doesn't cover much ground. He needs a lot of work to be able to handle outfield duties. His bat is far more polished. Scott can hit for average with plenty of gap power, though he needs to be more selective and make more contact. Nevertheless, he led the system with 102 RBIs in his first pro season. A wrist injury in his final season at UCLA—where he set a school record with a career .389 average—had prevented him from playing in 2000. Scott will move up to Double-A this year, and his defense may dictate his future more than his bat.

Year	Club (League)	Class	AVG	G	AB	R	H	2B	3B	HR	RBI	BB	SO	SB
2001	High Desert (Cal)	A	.283	132	513	73	145	42	1	16	102	50	135	9
MINOR LEAGUE TOTALS			.283	132	513	73	145	42	1	16	102	50	135	9

24. Mike Penney, rhp

Born: March 29, 1977. **Ht.:** 6-1. **Wt.:** 190. **Bats:** R. **Throws:** R. **School:** University of Southern California. **Career Transactions:** Selected by Brewers in eighth round of 1998 draft; signed July 3, 1998.

No Milwaukee farmhand took a bigger step in the wrong direction in 2001 than Penney, who was in the organization top 10 a year ago but proved not able to take the final step in his development. The Brewers expected him to be ready to make the jump from Triple-A to the big leagues if needed. Instead, he pitched poorly and was demoted to Double-A. The club hoped Penney would recover in the Arizona Fall League, but he experienced some shoulder stiffness and was shut down almost immediately. Before the year was done, he was dropped from the 40-man roster. The low-90s fastball and plus curveball that he had shown in 2000 weren't apparent last year. He should be moving forward, not backward, which makes 2002 a make-or-break year.

Year	Club (League)	Class	W	L	ERA	G	GS	CG	SV	IP	H	R	ER	BB	SO
1998	Helena (Pio)	R	1	5	7.38	10	10	0	0	46	63	47	38	20	36
1999	Beloit (Mid)	A	9	12	4.24	27	27	4	0	170	171	94	80	70	109
2000	Mudville (Cal)	A	2	4	3.24	13	13	0	0	67	63	31	24	28	45
	Huntsville (SL)	AA	0	1	2.66	20	0	0	7	20	19	7	6	6	22
	Indianapolis (IL)	AAA	1	1	3.44	17	0	0	1	18	16	9	7	10	13
2001	Huntsville (SL)	AA	4	3	3.31	21	5	0	7	49	50	24	18	22	30
	Indianapolis (IL)	AAA	4	3	5.37	22	5	0	1	57	70	38	34	23	35
MINOR LEAGUE TOTALS			21	29	4.36	130	60	4	16	427	452	250	207	179	290

25. Florian Villanueva, c/3b

Born: Oct. 5, 1980. **Ht.:** 6-2. **Wt.:** 160. **Bats:** R. **Throws:** R. **Career Transactions:** Signed out of Dominican Republic by Brewers, Sept. 13, 1997.

After three years in the Rookie-level Dominican Summer League, Villanueva was brought to the United States in 2001. He made a big splash at Ogden with his ability to hit for average and power and to drive in runs. Even more impressive was the versatility he showed while starting games at catcher, second base, third base and the outfield. The Brewers believe his future is behind the plate, where he shows nice instincts and skills for a young player, though he saw more action at the hot corner. He has an infielder's hands and feet and really moves around well. Villanueva threw out 13 of 24 (54 percent) basestealers last year, and the Brewers consider him potentially the best all-around catcher in their system. He likely will get the opportunity to play in low Class A in 2002, though fellow backstop prospect Jason Belcher may also be sent there to work on his defense.

Year	Club (League)	Class	AVG	G	AB	R	H	2B	3B	HR	RBI	BB	SO	SB
1998	Brewers (DSL)	R	.212	21	33	10	7	1	1	0	2	9	6	1
1999	Brewers (DSL)	R	.239	50	155	31	37	12	0	4	31	22	19	6
2000	Brewers (DSL)	R	.322	70	261	56	84	24	4	10	51	32	29	8
2001	Ogden (Pio)	R	.308	68	273	52	84	21	2	6	53	18	27	5
MINOR LEAGUE TOTALS			.294	209	722	149	212	58	7	20	137	81	81	20

26. Todd West, ss

Born: March 2, 1979. **Ht.:** 5-11. **Wt.:** 165. **Bats:** R. **Throws:** R. **School:** University of Texas. **Career Transactions:** Selected by Brewers in 14th round of 2000 draft; signed June 23, 2000.

Managers rated West the best defensive shortstop in the low Class A Midwest League last season, as he led the league in putouts (214), assists (374), double plays (72) and fielding percentage (.983). That .983 mark was the best among Class A shortstops, and anyone who has visited Beloit's Pohlman Field understands what an accomplishment that was. Besides his sure hands and accurate arm, he also has above-average range. West's offense is not anywhere close to his defense, however. He gets the bat knocked out of his hands and needs to gain some strength to be considered more of a threat at the plate. On defense alone, he projects as a big leaguer. How far he comes with the bat will determine whether he's an everyday player or utilityman.

Year	Club (League)	Class	AVG	G	AB	R	H	2B	3B	HR	RBI	BB	SO	SB
2000	Helena (Pio)	R	.271	57	207	44	56	6	0	0	12	28	29	7
	Ogden (Pio)	R	.500	5	20	5	10	3	0	0	4	2	0	1
2001	Beloit (Mid)	A	.235	132	408	62	96	14	0	0	40	60	62	16
MINOR LEAGUE TOTALS			.255	194	635	111	162	23	0	0	56	90	91	24

27. Roberto Maysonet, rhp

Born: Jan. 16, 1980. **Ht.:** 6-0. **Wt.:** 175. **Bats:** R. **Throws:** R. **School:** Vega Baja (P.R.) HS. **Career Transactions:** Selected by Brewers in 32nd round of 1998 draft; signed June 9, 1998.

Maysonet is part of the corps of young pitchers at the lower levels of the system that give the Brewers hope they can develop a significant number of arms in the future. Following three years in Rookie ball, Maysonet moved up to low Class A last season, when he showed the best raw arm on the Beloit staff. His fastball registers in the mid-90s, but he's still very raw. He needs more consistency with his breaking ball and changeup. His command is also iffy, as he hit 11 batters and uncorked 12 wild pitches in addition to walking 61 batters in 111 innings. Developing a consistent release point would be a good start. While he throws hard, he's not very tall and thus not very projectable. He's going to have to show something more than velocity, though the Brewers are encouraged by what they have to work with.

Year	Club (League)	Class	W	L	ERA	G	GS	CG	SV	IP	H	R	ER	BB	SO
1998	Ogden (Pio)	R	3	2	5.70	14	6	0	0	43	47	35	27	30	33
1999	Brewers (DSL)	R	0	0	2.70	3	2	0	0	10	9	3	3	2	12
2000	Helena (Pio)	R	3	6	4.23	15	13	0	0	79	78	52	37	39	84
	Beloit (Mid)	A	0	0	15.00	1	1	0	0	3	5	5	5	4	5
2001	Beloit (Mid)	A	5	10	4.22	28	17	0	0	111	99	64	52	61	109
MINOR LEAGUE TOTALS			11	18	4.54	61	39	0	0	246	238	159	124	136	243

28. Francisco Plasencia, of

Born: June 19, 1994. **Ht.:** 6-2. **Wt.:** 160. **Bats:** L. **Throws:** L. **Career Transactions:** Signed out of Venezuela by Brewers, July 4, 2000.

Reflecting the organization's renewed commitment to scouting Latin America, Plasencia is the only player from Venezuela in the top 30. The Brewers like to dream about what Plasencia might become. He's only 17 and thin as a reed, but he also moves with fluid grace in center field, reminding some of a very young Cesar Geronimo. Plasencia has great instincts and can chase down balls in the gaps with the best of them. He's also fundamentally sound, particularly for a player his age, and made just one error in 49 games in the field last year. As he fills out and becomes stronger, Milwaukee believes he'll be a .300 hitter and a threat on the basepaths. He draws plenty of walks, though he'll have to do a better job of making contact and learn to add at least a little power. Scouts who watched him in the Arizona League loved his tools and upside. He probably won't be ready for full-season ball until 2003 at the earliest.

Year	Club (League)	Class	AVG	G	AB	R	H	2B	3B	HR	RBI	BB	SO	SB
2001	Brewers (AZL)	R	.270	49	200	38	54	7	1	0	19	31	46	10
MINOR LEAGUE TOTALS			.270	49	200	38	54	7	1	0	19	31	46	10

29. Derry Hammond, of

Born: Oct. 19, 1979. **Ht.:** 6-2. **Wt.:** 205. **Bats:** R. **Throws:** R. **School:** West Point (Miss.) HS. **Career Transactions:** Selected by Brewers in third round of 1998 draft; signed June 13, 1998.

In his first three years in the organization, Hammond was a flop. He didn't hit for average and he struck out way too often, and some wondered how the Brewers could make such a mistake with a third-round pick. Returning to Class A level for a third year in 2001, Hammond finally began approaching his potential, though his numbers still weren't gaudy. Power is his best tool, though he still has plenty of work to do, as his plate discipline and ability to make consistent contract remain problems. He has little speed to speak of and doesn't offer much defensively, though his arm is average. If he can continue to build on what he showed in 2001, he'll have a chance to reach the majors. He may even get out of Class A ball in 2002.

Year	Club (League)	Class	AVG	G	AB	R	H	2B	3B	HR	RBI	BB	SO	SB
1998	Helena (Pio)	R	.216	62	232	31	50	13	1	13	45	12	98	4
1999	Beloit (Mid)	A	.229	107	380	65	87	17	2	17	50	43	141	1
2000	Mudville (Cal)	A	.167	66	210	23	35	6	0	5	23	15	87	2
2001	Beloit (Mid)	A	.269	96	360	57	97	23	0	19	73	32	109	2
MINOR LEAGUE TOTALS			.228	331	1182	176	269	59	3	54	191	102	435	9

30. Jim Rushford, of

Born: March 24, 1974. **Ht.:** 6-1. **Wt.:** 190. **Bats:** L. **Throws:** L. **School:** San Diego State University.
Career Transactions: Signed by independent Dubois County (Heartland), June 1996 . . . Signed by independent Schaumburg (Northern), May 1999 . . . Signed by independent Duluth-Superior (Northern), May 2000 . . . Signed by Brewers, Nov. 22, 2000.

One of the most unlikely players ever to lead the minors in batting, Rushford hit .354 to edge out better-known prospects Hank Blalock (Rangers) and Lyle Overbay (Diamondbacks) by two points last year. Undrafted after completing his college career as a two-way player at San Diego State in 1995, Rushford hooked on with independent teams, mainly as a pitcher, in 1996 and 1997. He came down with a sore arm, though, and left the game for the better part of two years. He spent much of the time working as a pizza delivery man, a job he still works in the baseball offseason. He might have stayed out of baseball if the independent Northern League hadn't expanded to Schaumburg, Ill., near where Rushford grew up. He made the club as a right fielder in 1999, and hit .314 in two years in the league. Brewers minor league pitching coach R.C. Lichtenstein, who had signed him to his first independent contract in 1996, urged Milwaukee to acquire Rushford. Though at 27 he was going to be old for whatever leagues he played in during his Organized Baseball debut, Rushford hit for average and power while walking more than he struck out. His bat is going to be his ticket to the majors because he's not going to offer much in the way of speed or defense. He made himself into a better hitter by working out and getting much stronger. He also learned to turn on the ball after going through life as an inside-out slap hitter. Rushford said when he came back from his baseball sabbatical, something just clicked and he's been hitting ever since. He'll to have to prove himself all over again this year in Triple-A, but he's a good story no matter where he ends up.

Year	Club (League)	Class	AVG	G	AB	R	H	2B	3B	HR	RBI	BB	SO	SB
1996	Dubois County (Heart)	IND	.341	40	44	9	15	2	0	2	6	6	10	6
1997	Mission Viejo (West)	IND	—	8	0	0	0	0	0	0	0	0	0	0
1998					Did Not Play									
1999	Schaumburg (Nor)	IND	.289	47	166	26	48	12	2	2	28	23	27	7
2000	Duluth-Superior (Nor)	IND	.329	75	289	53	95	16	3	12	53	25	32	13
2001	High Desert (Cal)	A	.363	65	259	68	94	22	2	14	61	38	35	3
	Huntsville (SL)	AA	.342	57	187	35	64	16	1	7	30	23	22	3
MINOR LEAGUE TOTALS			.354	122	446	103	158	38	3	21	91	61	57	6

MINNESOTA Twins

TOP 30 PROSPECTS

1. Joe Mauer, c
2. Justin Morneau, 1b
3. Michael Cuddyer, of/3b
4. Michael Restovich, of
5. Adam Johnson, rhp
6. Brad Thomas, lhp
7. Juan Rincon, rhp
8. Rob Bowen, c
9. Matt Kinney, rhp
10. Sandy Tejada, rhp
11. Grant Balfour, rhp
12. J.D. Durbin, rhp
13. Jon McDonald, rhp
14. Kevin Frederick, rhp
15. Angel Garcia, rhp
16. Bobby Kielty, of
17. B.J. Garbe, of
18. Jeff Randazzo, lhp
19. Kevin Cameron, rhp
20. Brian Wolfe, rhp
21. Ronnie Corona, rhp
22. Dusty Gomon, 1b
23. Jon Pridie, rhp
24. Scott Tyler, rhp
25. Colby Miller, rhp
26. Trent Oeltjen, of
27. J.C. Contreras, lhp
28. Dustan Mohr, of
29. Terry Tiffee, 3b
30. Ryan Mills, lhp

By Josh Boyd

erhaps the only thing that could have spoiled the Twins' optimism following their breakthrough 2001 season was commissioner Bud Selig's announcement that Major League Baseball planned to contract two teams. The clubs weren't identified, but it was obvious that Minnesota owner Carl Pohlad expected his would be one of them.

In the midst of a winter of uncertainty, the Twins have tried to maintain a positive vibe, though it was a chore. General manager Terry Ryan pledged his allegiance by declining to interview for the Blue Jays' GM position, but his managerial search was in limbo for months. Paul Molitor was expected to be Tom Kelly's successor, but his concerns about contraction caused him to decline the opportunity. He also chose not to be on new manager Ron Gardenhire's staff.

Alabama millionaire Donald Watkins has expressed interest in purchasing the franchise and paying for a stadium to save the Twins from extinction. But whether Watkins would be willing to match or Pohlad would accept less than the rumored $150 million contraction buyout fee—Forbes places the value of the team at $99 million—remains to be seen.

All this speculation pushes Minnesota's resurgence deeper into the background. After a 69-93 last place finish in 2000, the Twins went into the all-star break last July with a five-game lead in the American League Central. Though Minnesota went just 30-45 in the second half and finished seven games behind the Indians, it managed to contend despite the second-lowest payroll in the game.

Improved pitching and defense were key factors in the turnaround. So was the jelling of a young, primarily homegrown lineup. After Matt Lawton was traded in July, 28-year-old Corey Koskie was the lineup's senior citizen with just over three years of service. Doug Mientkiewicz and Torii Hunter finally became full-time starters and won Gold Gloves. The rotation's top three pitchers—Brad Radke, Eric Milton and Joe Mays—all won at least 15 games and none of them has turned 30.

If Major League Baseball doesn't make them go away, the Twins are in position to contend. Their biggest need on the field is power, and they've got plenty coming up through the farm system in catcher Joe Mauer (the No. 1 pick in the 2001 draft), first baseman Justin Morneau and outfielders Michael Cuddyer and Michael Restovich.

Organization Overview

General manager: Terry Ryan. **Farm director:** Jim Rantz. **Scouting director:** Mike Radcliff.

2001 PERFORMANCE

Class	Team	League	W	L	Pct.	Finish*	Manager
Majors	Minnesota	American	85	77	.525	5th (14)	Tom Kelly
Triple-A	Edmonton Trappers	Pacific Coast	60	83	.420	16th (16)	John Russell
Double-A	New Britain Rock Cats	Eastern	87	55	.613	1st (12)	Stan Cliburn
High A	Fort Myers Miracle	Florida State	68	69	.496	t-7th (12)	Jose Marzan
Low A	Quad City River Bandits	Midwest	80	57	.584	5th (14)	Jeff Carter
Rookie	Elizabethton Twins	Appalachian	41	22	.651	1st (10)	Rudy Hernandez
Rookie	GCL Twins	Gulf Coast	32	26	.552	6th (14)	Al Newman
OVERAL 2001 MINOR LEAGUE RECORD			368	312	.541	6th (30)	

*Finish in overall standings (No. of teams in league)

ORGANIZATION LEADERS

BATTING
*AVG	Quinton McCracken, Edmonton	.338
R	Michael Cuddyer, New Britain	95
H	**Dustan Mohr**, New Britain	174
TB	**Dustan Mohr**, New Britain	293
2B	**Dustan Mohr**, New Britain	41
3B	Nestor Smith, New Britain	8
HR	Michael Cuddyer, New Britain	30
RBI	Justin Morneau, N.B./Ft.Myers/Q.C.	97
BB	Luis Rodriguez, Fort Myers	82
SO	Michael Restovich, New Britain	125
SB	Rafael Boitel, Quad City	36

PITCHING
W	Juan Rincon, New Britain	14
L	Brent Schoening, New Britain/Fort Myers	15
#ERA	**Kevin Frederick**, N.B./Fort Myers	1.52
G	Juan Padilla, Fort Myers	56
CG	Six tied at	2
SV	Henry Bonilla, Quad City	25
IP	Matt Kinney, Edmonton	162
BB	Matt Kinney, Edmonton	74
SO	Matt Kinney, Edmonton	146

*Minimum 250 At-Bats #Minimum 75 Innings

TOP PROSPECTS OF THE DECADE
1992	David McCarty, of
1993	David McCarty, of
1994	Rich Becker, of
1995	LaTroy Hawkins, rhp
1996	Todd Walker, 2b
1997	Todd Walker, 2b
1998	Luis Rivas, ss
1999	Michael Cuddyer, 3b
2000	Michael Cuddyer, 3b
2001	Adam Johnson, rhp

TOP DRAFT PICKS OF THE DECADE
1992	Dan Serafini, lhp
1993	Torii Hunter, of
1994	Todd Walker, 2b
1995	Mark Redman, lhp
1996	*Travis Lee, 1b
1997	Michael Cuddyer, ss
1998	Ryan Mills, lhp
1999	B.J. Garbe, of
2000	Adam Johnson, rhp
2001	Joe Mauer, c

*Did not sign.

Mohr

Frederick

BEST TOOLS
Best Hitter for Average	Justin Morneau
Best Power Hitter	Michael Cuddyer
Fastest Baserunner	Inocencio Hiraldo
Best Fastball	Matt Kinney
Best Breaking Ball	Grant Balfour
Best Changeup	Jon McDonald
Best Control	Jon McDonald
Best Defensive Catcher	Rob Bowen
Best Defensive Infielder	Luis Rodriguez
Best Infield Arm	Luis Maza
Best Defensive Outfielder	Bobby Kielty
Best Outfield Arm	B.J. Garbe

PROJECTED 2005 LINEUP
Catcher	Joe Mauer
First Base	Doug Mientkiewicz
Second Base	Luis Rivas
Third Base	Corey Koskie
Shortstop	Cristian Guzman
Left Field	Michael Restovich
Center Field	Torii Hunter
Right Field	Michael Cuddyer
Designated Hitter	Justin Morneau
No. 1 Starter	Eric Milton
No. 2 Starter	Joe Mays
No. 3 Starter	Brad Radke
No. 4 Starter	Brad Thomas
No. 5 Starter	Juan Rincon
Closer	Adam Johnson

ALL-TIME LARGEST BONUSES
Joe Mauer, 2001	$5,150,000
B.J. Garbe, 1999	$2,750,000
Adam Johnson, 2000	$2,500,000
Ryan Mills, 1998	$2,000,000
Michael Cuddyer, 1997	$1,850,000

DraftAnalysis

2001 Draft

Best Pro Debut: C **Joe Mauer** (1) handled all the pressure of being the No. 1 overall pick by his hometown team, hitting .400-0-14 in the Rookie-level Appalachian League. RHP Matt Vorwald (7) and LHP Jared Hemus (8) tied for the Appy wins lead with six each, and both posted sub-2.00 ERAs.

Best Athlete: Mauer was Baseball America's High School Player of the Year and won the same award in football from several publications. He starred at the same high school that produced Chris Weinke, and planned to be Florida State's quarterback until he signed with the Twins. He averaged nearly 20 points a game in basketball.

Best Hitter: Mauer. Another hitter to watch is OF Garrett Guzman (10), who doesn't have the speed for center field or the power for a corner. But he can hit, batting .355 in the Rookie-level Gulf Coast League.

Best Raw Power: Mauer will hit for power, but 1B Dusty Gomon (9) has more pop and a true home run swing.

Fastest Runner: 2B Kaulana Kahaulua (12) and OFs Scott Whitrock (19) and Ryan Spataro (41) all have 6.65-second speed in the 60-yard dash, with Kahaulua getting the best jump out of the batter's box.

Best Defensive Player: 2B Jose Morales (3) didn't have the speed to stick at shortstop, but he has the tools to excel at his new position. Mauer is agile behind the plate and threw out 32 percent of Appy basestealers.

Best Fastball: RHP Kevin Cameron (13) hit 95 mph while compiling a 1.57 ERA and 13 saves in the Appy League. RHP Scott Tyler (2) touched 95 in high school.

Most Intriguing Background: RHP Erik Lohse's (40) brother Kyle pitched for the Twins last year. 2B Josh Renick's (11) father Rick played in the majors and was Montreal's interim manager last summer. Mauer's older brother Jake was taken in the 23rd round by the Twins. Kuhaulua's dad Fred once pitched for the Angels, for whom C Bryan Kennedy's (24) brother Adam starts at second base. LHP Vince Serafini's (6) twin brother Matt signed with Milwaukee.

Mauer

Closest To The Majors: Mauer. He should reach high Class A this season.

Best Late-Round Pick: Cameron. He was overshadowed as Georgia Tech's No. 3 starter, and his velocity jumped once he moved to the bullpen after signing.

The One Who Got Away: SS/RHP Matt Macri (17) would have been a sure first-round pick had he not told teams he was intent on attending Notre Dame.

Assessment: The Twins didn't let money completely dictate the No. 1 pick, and they were rewarded with Mauer, already the best catching prospect in baseball. A year earlier, they did a prearranged deal with the No. 2 pick (Adam Johnson) and failed to sign RHP Aaron Heilman or 3B/1B Taggert Bozied.

2000 Draft

RHP Adam Johnson (1) was the first pitcher from the 2000 draft to reach the majors. RHPs J.D. Durbin (2), Ronnie Corona (6) and Colby Miller (3) could follow him. Not signing RHP Aaron Heilman (1) and 3B/1B Taggert Bozied (3) really hurt, however. **Grade: C+**

1999 Draft

OF B.J. Garbe (1) hasn't played anywhere near his tools. But that doesn't matter because 1B Justin Morneau (3) is a true masher and C Rob Bowen (2) has all-around talents. LHP Mike Randazzo (4) and RHP Brian Wolfe (6) are sleepers. **Grade: B+**

1998 Draft

LHP Ryan Mills (1) got hurt almost immediately and hasn't found the plate since, and Minnesota would have been better off signing LHP Mike Gosling (14), a 2001 second-rounder. RHP Kevin Frederick (34) is this crop's best hope. **Grade: F**

1997 Draft

The Twins found the heart of their future order with their first three picks: OF/3B Michael Cuddyer (1), C Matt LeCroy (1) and OF Michael Restovich (2). They also drafted Johnson (25) and Bozied (50) for the first time. **Grade: A**

Note: Draft analysis prepared by Jim Callis. Numbers in parentheses indicate draft rounds.

. . . Behind the plate, he has a rocket arm and unusual quickness for someone his size.

Joe
Mauer c

Born: April 19, 1983.
Ht.: 6-4. **Wt.:** 215.
Bats: L. **Throws:** R.
School: Cretin-Derham Hall, St. Paul, Minn.
Career Transactions: Selected by Twins in first round (first overall) of 2001 draft; signed July 17, 2001.

General manager Terry Ryan graded Mauer higher than any high school prospect he had ever seen, with three exceptions: Alex Rodriguez, Dwight Gooden and Darryl Strawberry. The No. 1 overall pick in the 2001 draft, Mauer capped his amateur career by leading Cretin-Derham Hall to the Minnesota state title and winning Baseball America's High School Player of the Year award. He was a three-sport star in high school, winning national football player of the year awards and tying a state record with 41 touchdown passes as a senior. He also averaged nearly 20 points a game on the basketball court. Mauer signed a letter of intent to follow Cretin-Derham alum Chris Weinke to play quarterback at Florida State, but the Twins put any doubts about Mauer's athletic future to rest by signing the local product to a $5.15 million bonus, the second-highest ever for a player signing with the team that drafted him. Mauer hit .400 in his first pro summer and was an easy choice as the Rookie-level Appalachian League's No. 1 prospect. Mauer played at Elizabethton with his brother Jake, an infielder drafted in the 23rd round last year.

Though he didn't homer in his pro debut, Mauer has excellent bat speed and gets good extension. The ball carries off his bat to all fields. He tied a national mark by homering in seven consecutive games in high school. He struck out only once in four years at Cretin-Derham Hall, a testament to his natural hitting ability. Mauer is so athletically gifted that one scout said he could be a top-of-the-line defender at first base or third base, if not catcher. Behind the plate, he has a rocket arm and unusual quickness for someone his size. He has a quick release and the ball comes out of his hand with ease. Mauer's makeup matches his talent. He is remarkably polished for a high school player and needs experience more than anything. If he fine-tunes his mechanics, he'll become a top-notch catcher.

Mauer was the first high school backstop drafted No. 1 overall since Danny Goodwin in 1971 and the track record of prep catchers taken in the top five picks isn't promising. Of the 14, only Darrell Porter and Mike Lieberthal have stayed at the position and fulfilled their potential (reserving judgment on Ben Davis). The Twins are confident he'll buck those odds. Mauer will make his full-season debut at low Class A Quad City in 2002 and could reach Minnesota by 2004.

Year	Club (League)	Class	AVG	G	AB	R	H	2B	3B	HR	RBI	BB	SO	SB
2001	Elizabethton (Appy)	R	.400	32	110	14	44	6	2	0	14	19	10	4
MINOR LEAGUE TOTALS			.400	32	110	14	44	6	2	0	14	19	10	4

2. Justin Morneau, 1b

Born: May 15, 1981. **Ht.:** 6-4. **Wt.:** 205. **Bats:** L. **Throws:** R. **School:** New Westminster (B.C.) Secondary School. **Career Transactions:** Selected by Twins in third round of 1999 draft; signed June 17, 1999.

Morneau put on a power display for Twins brass in a batting-practice session at the Metrodome shortly after he was drafted. Nagging injuries held him back in each of his first two pro seasons, but after he had surgery to remove bone chips from his right elbow, he earned two promotions in 2001. Morneau's offensive ceiling rivals Joe Mauer's. His classic lefthanded stroke draws comparisons to John Olerud, but Morneau projects to hit for more power than Olerud. Morneau shows the aptitude to make adjustments at the plate and is starting to figure out which pitches he can turn on. Drafted as a catcher, he will be limited to first base by his growing body. He's not mobile and will be an average defender at best. He saw time in right field during instructional league. One scout guaranteed Morneau will hit 35-40 home runs in the big leagues. He's on the fast track, reaching Double-A New Britain last year two months after turning 20. He'll return there to start 2002.

Year	Club (League)	Class	AVG	G	AB	R	H	2B	3B	HR	RBI	BB	SO	SB
1999	Twins (GCL)	R	.302	17	53	3	16	5	0	0	9	2	6	0
2000	Twins (GCL)	R	.402	52	194	47	78	21	0	10	58	30	18	3
	Elizabethton (Appy)	R	.217	6	23	4	5	0	0	1	3	1	6	0
2001	Quad City (Mid)	A	.356	64	236	50	84	17	2	12	53	26	38	0
	Fort Myers (FSL)	A	.294	53	197	25	58	10	3	4	40	24	41	0
	New Britain (EL)	AA	.158	10	38	3	6	1	0	0	4	3	8	0
MINOR LEAGUE TOTALS			.333	202	741	132	247	54	5	27	167	86	117	3

3. Michael Cuddyer, of/3b

Born: March 27, 1979. **Ht.:** 6-2. **Wt.:** 202. **Bats:** R. **Throws:** R. **School:** Great Bridge HS, Chesapeake, Va. **Career Transactions:** Selected by Twins in first round (ninth overall) of 1997 draft; signed Aug. 19, 1997.

After a disappointing 2000 season, Cuddyer returned to New Britain and reestablished himself as an important part of the Twins' future. The system's top prospect entering 1999 and 2000, he was the organization's minor league player of the year last year. He followed that up by hitting .336-4-29 in the Arizona Fall League. After his power disappeared in 2000, Cuddyer launched a career-best 30 homers last year. He's a disciplined, professional hitter. He has the bat speed to crush fastballs and the patience to stay back on offspeed stuff. He has a short, compact stroke and has gotten better at driving the ball to right field, though most of his power is to left. A high school All-American as a shortstop, Cuddyer has learned to harness his arm strength, which was the main culprit for his high error totals early in his career. He split time between third base, first base and right field during 2001. Sent to the AFL to work on his routes on fly balls, he played just five games in the outfield. Cuddyer will compete for Minnesota's right-field job in spring training with Bobby Kielty, Brian Buchanan and Dustan Mohr. The Twins lack righthanded power and think Cuddyer is the answer.

Year	Club (League)	Class	AVG	G	AB	R	H	2B	3B	HR	RBI	BB	SO	SB
1998	Fort Wayne (Mid)	A	.276	129	497	82	137	37	7	12	81	61	107	16
1999	Fort Myers (FSL)	A	.298	130	466	87	139	24	4	16	82	76	91	14
2000	New Britain (EL)	AA	.263	138	490	72	129	30	8	6	61	55	93	5
2001	New Britain (EL)	AA	.301	141	509	95	153	36	3	30	87	75	106	5
	Minnesota (AL)	MAJ	.222	8	18	1	4	2	0	0	1	2	6	1
MAJOR LEAGUE TOTALS			.222	8	18	1	4	2	0	0	1	2	6	1
MINOR LEAGUE TOTALS			.284	538	1962	336	558	127	22	64	311	267	397	40

4. Michael Restovich, of

Born: Jan. 3, 1979. **Ht.:** 6-4. **Wt.:** 233. **Bats:** R. **Throws:** R. **School:** Mayo HS, Rochester, Minn. **Career Transactions:** Selected by Twins in second round of 1997 draft; signed Aug. 15, 1997.

As with Michael Cuddyer, Restovich rebounded after a 2000 season below his previous standards. He also had a successful stint in the Arizona Fall League, batting .289-6-28. Like Joe Mauer, he was a multi-sport star at a Minnesota high school. Restovich set the Mayo High record for career points in basketball. Even at a burly 6-foot-4 and 233 pounds, Restovich is one of the system's best all-around athletes. He generates light-tower power with the natural loft in his swing. He can crush the ball to right-center and is learning to pull the ball with authority. His arm is average, and he has the agility and range to cover the spacious left-field territory in the Metrodome. High strikeout totals are going to be a tradeoff for Restovich's power. He's a step behind Mauer, Justin Morneau and Cuddyer with his hitting approach. His ceiling is as high as anyone's in the organization. It's just a matter of maturing at the plate and recognizing counts and situations. After a full year at Triple-A Edmonton, he should be ready to join Cuddyer and Torii Hunter in Minnesota's outfield.

Year	Club (League)	Class	AVG	G	AB	R	H	2B	3B	HR	RBI	BB	SO	SB
1998	Elizabethton (Appy)	R	.355	65	242	68	86	20	1	13	64	54	58	5
	Fort Wayne (Mid)	A	.444	11	45	9	20	5	2	0	6	4	12	0
1999	Quad City (Mid)	A	.312	131	493	91	154	30	6	19	107	74	100	7
2000	Fort Myers (FSL)	A	.263	135	475	73	125	27	9	8	64	61	100	19
2001	New Britain (EL)	AA	.269	140	501	69	135	33	4	23	84	54	125	15
MINOR LEAGUE TOTALS			.296	482	1756	310	520	115	22	63	325	247	395	46

5. Adam Johnson, rhp

Born: July 12, 1979. **Ht.:** 6-2. **Wt.:** 210. **Bats:** R. **Throws:** R. **School:** Cal State Fullerton. **Career Transactions:** Selected by Twins in first round (second overall) of 2000 draft; signed June 19, 2000.

Johnson made an immediate impact in the organization after the Twins drafted him with the second overall choice in 2000. He agreed to a predraft deal worth $2.5 million, overpowered the high Class A Florida State League and ranked No. 1 on this list a year ago. His outstanding spring performance caught former manager Tom Kelly's eye and nearly earned Johnson a spot on the Opening Day roster in 2001. He made his major league debut in July. He has one of the livest arms in the system and is capable of touching 94-95 mph. As a starter, his fastball regularly sits in the 90-92 range. Though he has refined and compacted his delivery since college, his intense makeup and aggressive arm action point to a future as a closer. By the time he reached Minnesota last year, Johnson didn't have the same sharpness on his slider and curveball that he'd shown previously. He's still learning the finer points of pitching, including setting up hitters and changing speeds. The Twins didn't want to rush Johnson but couldn't help themselves. His long-term role has yet to be defined, but he'll continue to build up innings and experience in the minors before returning to Minnesota.

Year	Club (League)	Class	W	L	ERA	G	GS	CG	SV	IP	H	R	ER	BB	SO
2000	Fort Myers (FSL)	A	5	4	2.47	13	12	1	0	69	45	21	19	20	92
2001	New Britain (EL)	AA	5	6	3.82	18	18	0	0	113	105	53	48	39	110
	Minnesota (AL)	MAJ	1	2	8.28	7	4	0	0	25	32	25	23	13	17
	Edmonton (PCL)	AAA	1	1	5.70	4	4	0	0	24	19	15	15	10	25
MAJOR LEAGUE TOTALS			1	2	8.28	7	4	0	0	25	32	25	23	13	17
MINOR LEAGUE TOTALS			11	11	3.58	35	34	1	0	206	169	89	82	69	227

6. Brad Thomas, lhp

Born: Oct. 22, 1977. **Ht.:** 6-3. **Wt.:** 204. **Bats:** L. **Throws:** L. **Career Transactions:** Signed out of Australia by Dodgers, July 2, 1995 . . . Released by Dodgers, May 9, 1997 . . . Signed by Twins, May 12, 1997.

The Twins lost out to the Dodgers in 1995 for Thomas' services, but believe they struck it rich two years later when he was cut. The State Department had ordered Los Angeles to release a number of players because of visa troubles, and the Dodgers didn't consider Thomas a prospect after his velocity had dipped into the low 80s. Minnesota scooped him up three days after Los Angeles let him go. Thomas now can run his fastball up to 95-96 mph. What makes him effective, though, is the movement he gets when he cuts or sinks the pitch and throws at 90-92. His curveball and changeup project as major league average. He's tough on lefthanders, and he has the stamina and diverse arsenal to remain effective late into a game. Thomas ran into trouble against major leaguers when he struggled to locate his fastball. He has good control but sometimes catches too much of the strike zone, which is how he surrendered six homers in 16 big league innings. As with Adam Johnson, injuries forced Thomas to Minnesota well ahead of schedule. He needs another full year of innings in Triple-A, but might be called upon for major league bullpen duty this year.

Year	Club (League)	Class	W	L	ERA	G	GS	CG	SV	IP	H	R	ER	BB	SO
1996	Great Falls (Pio)	R	3	2	6.31	11	5	0	0	36	48	27	25	11	28
1997	Elizabethton (Appy)	R	3	4	4.48	14	13	0	0	70	78	43	35	21	53
1998	Fort Wayne (Mid)	A	11	8	2.95	27	26	1	0	152	146	68	50	45	126
1999	Fort Myers (FSL)	A	8	11	4.78	27	27	1	0	153	182	99	81	46	108
2000	Fort Myers (FSL)	A	6	2	1.66	12	12	0	0	65	62	33	12	16	57
	New Britain (EL)	AA	6	6	4.06	14	13	1	0	75	80	47	34	46	66
2001	Minnesota (AL)	MAJ	0	2	9.37	5	5	0	0	16	20	17	17	14	6
	New Britain (EL)	AA	10	3	1.96	19	19	1	0	119	91	37	26	26	97
MAJOR LEAGUE TOTALS			0	2	9.37	5	5	0	0	16	20	17	17	14	6
MINOR LEAGUE TOTALS			47	36	3.53	124	15	4	0	670	687	354	263	211	535

7. Juan Rincon, rhp

Born: Jan. 23, 1979. **Ht.:** 5-11. **Wt.:** 190. **Bats:** R. **Throws:** R. **Career Transactions:** Signed out of Venezuela by Twins, Nov. 4, 1996.

RICH ABEL

Rincon has always tended to be advanced for his age, though he repeated the low Class A Midwest League after an uninspiring 1998 season. His first trip to Double-A also produced undesirable results, but he returned in 2001 and finished among the Eastern League leaders in wins, ERA and strikeouts. After his rough half-season in New Britain in 2000, the Twins were unsure Rincon would last as a starter. Then he bolstered his three-pitch attack last year by pumping his fastball up to 94 mph and honing his nasty slider and changeup. He can throw strikes with all three pitches and is durable. He became too dependent on his slider before learning to mix up his pitch sequence last season and needs to avoid falling into that trap again. He doesn't have prototypical size for a starter. There always will be concerns about the stamina of undersized starters. There are exceptions such as Pedro Martinez and Roy Oswalt, and others like Octavio Dotel and Ugueth Urbina who became successful relievers. Rincon will remain a starter for now and move up to Triple-A.

Year	Club (League)	Class	W	L	ERA	G	GS	CG	SV	IP	H	R	ER	BB	SO
1997	Twins (GCL)	R	3	3	2.95	11	10	1	0	58	55	21	19	24	46
	Elizabethton (Appy)	R	0	1	3.86	2	1	0	0	9	11	4	4	3	7
1998	Fort Wayne (Mid)	A	6	4	3.83	37	13	0	6	96	84	51	41	54	74
1999	Quad City (Mid)	A	14	8	2.92	28	28	0	0	163	146	67	53	66	153
2000	Fort Myers (FSL)	A	5	3	2.12	13	13	0	0	76	67	26	18	23	55
	New Britain (EL)	AA	3	9	4.65	15	15	2	0	89	96	55	46	39	79
2001	New Britain (EL)	AA	14	6	2.88	29	23	2	0	153	130	60	49	57	133
	Minnesota (AL)	MAJ	0	0	6.35	4	0	0	0	6	7	5	4	5	4
MAJOR LEAGUE TOTALS			0	0	6.35	4	0	0	0	6	7	5	4	5	4
MINOR LEAGUE TOTALS			45	34	3.21	135	103	5	6	646	589	284	230	266	547

8. Rob Bowen, c

Born: Feb. 24, 1981. **Ht.:** 6-2. **Wt.:** 206. **Bats:** B. **Throws:** R. **School:** Homestead HS, Fort Wayne, Ind. **Career Transactions:** Selected by Twins in second round of 1999 draft; signed July 10, 1999.

STEVE MOORE

The Twins have ignored the pitfalls of drafting high school catchers in the early rounds, and they could have two potential impact players in Joe Mauer and Bowen. Some scouts compare Bowen to Ben Davis, the No. 2 overall pick in 1995, at the same stage of development. Bowen's power is developing in a hurry. After hitting four home runs in 150 at-bats over his first two pro seasons, he erupted for 18 in his first exposure to full-season ball. A switch-hitter, he has a better swing lefthanded but most of his power comes from the right side. Bowen is one of the best defensive players in the organization and has advanced receiving skills, plus the arm and quick release to deter basestealers. He still has limited exposure to professional pitching, as cracking his collarbone cost him much of 2000. He needs to tighten his strike zone and put himself in better hitter's counts. He tired down the stretch last season and homered just once in his final 131 at-bats. He'll be challenged this year in high Class A. Fort Myers' Hammond Stadium is a pitcher's park in a pitcher's league.

Year	Club (League)	Class	AVG	G	AB	R	H	2B	3B	HR	RBI	BB	SO	SB
1999	Twins (GCL)	R	.260	29	77	10	20	4	0	0	11	20	15	2
2000	Elizabethton (Appy)	R	.288	21	73	17	21	3	0	4	19	11	18	0
2001	Quad City (Mid)	A	.255	106	385	47	98	18	2	18	70	37	112	4
MINOR LEAGUE TOTALS			.260	156	535	74	139	25	2	22	100	68	145	6

9. Matt Kinney, rhp

Born: Dec. 16, 1976. **Ht.:** 6-5. **Wt.:** 220. **Bats:** R. **Throws:** R. **School:** Bangor (Maine) HS. **Career Transactions:** Selected by Red Sox in sixth round of 1995 draft; signed June 30, 1995 . . . Traded by Red Sox with LHP Joe Thomas and OF John Barnes to Twins for LHP Greg Swindell and 1B Orlando Merced, July 31, 1998.

Kinney entered last spring as the favorite to fill a vacancy in the Twins rotation, but a miserable spring snowballed into a poor season. After finishing 2000 in Minnesota, he allowed his disappointment at not making the big club in the spring to affect his performance in Triple-A. He won his first decision, dropped the next nine and didn't regain his focus until August, when he won his final four starts. There never was any question about Kinney's stuff. He's armed with one of the best fastballs in the system, regularly hitting 93-94 mph with heavy sink and run. He touched 96 every time out last year. He mixes in a plus slurve and usable change. He has the broad shoulders of a workhorse. Kinney needs to throw more strikes and keep his emotions in check. Though he has an easy motion and delivery, he has encountered elbow tenderness more than once in his career. He showed flashes of big league-caliber stuff during his stint in Minnesota two years ago. The Twins once again are counting on him to fill the fifth slot in their rotation. He could strengthen what already is one of baseball's brightest young rotations.

Year	Club (League)	Class	W	L	ERA	G	GS	CG	SV	IP	H	R	ER	BB	SO
1995	Red Sox (GCL)	R	1	3	2.93	8	2	0	2	28	29	13	9	10	11
1996	Lowell (NY-P)	A	3	9	2.68	15	15	0	0	87	68	51	26	44	72
1997	Michigan (Mid)	A	8	5	3.53	22	22	2	0	117	93	59	46	78	123
1998	Sarasota (FSL)	A	9	6	4.01	22	20	2	1	121	109	70	54	75	96
	Fort Myers (FSL)	A	3	2	3.13	7	7	0	0	37	31	18	13	18	39
1999	New Britain (EL)	AA	4	7	7.12	14	13	0	0	61	69	54	48	36	50
	Twins (GCL)	R	0	1	4.76	3	3	0	0	6	6	4	3	3	8
2000	New Britain (EL)	AA	6	1	2.71	15	15	0	0	86	74	31	26	35	93
	Salt Lake (PCL)	AAA	5	2	4.25	9	9	0	0	55	42	26	26	26	59
	Minnesota (AL)	MAJ	2	2	5.10	8	8	0	0	42	41	26	24	25	24
2001	Edmonton (PCL)	AAA	6	11	5.07	29	29	2	0	162	178	101	91	74	146
MAJOR LEAGUE TOTALS			2	2	5.10	8	8	0	0	42	41	26	24	25	24
MINOR LEAGUE TOTALS			45	47	4.05	144	135	6	3	760	699	427	342	399	697

10. Sandy Tejada, rhp

Born: April 16, 1982. **Ht.:** 6-2. **Wt.:** 188. **Bats:** R. **Throws:** R. **Career Transactions:** Signed out of Dominican Republic by Twins, Sept. 17, 1998.

Tejada is one of the most promising graduates of the Twins' academy in the Dominican Republic. Known as Manny prior to last season, he signed for a $10,000 bonus in 1998. He electrified the Appalachian League last summer, averaging more than eight strikeouts a start despite never working past the sixth inning. Tejada threw 86 mph when he signed, but regularly registers 90-94 now. He has always been able to throw strikes, which puts him ahead of a lot of pitchers his age. He has a projectable frame with a loose arm action, and he works on an effective downhill plane. He already shows a good feel for changing speeds. Tejada needs to refine his breaking ball and become more consistent with his changeup. Both pitches have the potential to be average by big league standards. At the beginning of 2001, Tejada was in over his head as a teenager in the Midwest League. Now he's ready for another shot at full-season ball with Quad City. All the ingredients are there for a rapid ascent.

Year	Club (League)	Class	W	L	ERA	G	GS	CG	SV	IP	H	R	ER	BB	SO
1999	Twins (DSL)	R	2	3	4.77	20	11	0	3	77	93	58	41	27	86
2000	Twins (GCL)	R	6	2	4.53	15	10	1	0	58	57	30	29	20	49
2001	Quad City (Mid)	A	0	1	4.50	4	2	0	0	10	7	8	5	9	13
	Elizabethton (Appy)	R	5	3	3.20	11	10	0	0	56	43	26	20	20	87
MINOR LEAGUE TOTALS			13	9	4.25	50	33	1	3	201	200	122	95	76	235

11. Grant Balfour, rhp

Born: Dec. 30, 1977. **Ht.:** 6-2. **Wt.:** 170. **Bats:** R. **Throws:** R. **Career Transactions:** Signed out of Australia by Twins, Jan. 19, 1997.

The first time the Twins scouted Balfour, he was a skinny 5-foot-10 catcher at an under-16 tournament in Australia. Glenn Williams and Damian Moss were the most coveted prospects being scouted—both would sign with the Braves—but Brad Thomas was playing first base and Luke Prokopec, who would sign and reach the big leagues as a pitcher with the Dodgers, was in right field. When Balfour moved to the mound, he showed little more than an easy arm action to go with his 78-82 mph fastball. He was up to 86 mph by the time he signed, and his stuff steadily has improved as he's evolved into a smoke-throwing reliever. Balfour's fastball regularly travels 93-95 mph and his hard 87-mph slider is the best breaking pitch in the system. His devastating two-pitch arsenal held batters to a .149 average last season in the Eastern League, where he allowed runs in just three of 35 appearances. Balfour's command wavered after a premature promotion to Minnesota and he walked 23 in 31 innings between the majors, Triple-A and the Arizona Fall League. Balfour is a fitness nut with 6 percent body fat, but his slender frame raises questions about his durability over the course of a season. His stuff is good enough to close if he shows improved location and resiliency.

Year	Club (League)	Class	W	L	ERA	G	GS	CG	SV	IP	H	R	ER	BB	SO
1997	Twins (GCL)	R	2	4	3.76	13	12	0	0	67	73	31	28	20	43
1998	Elizabethton (Appy)	R	7	2	3.36	13	13	0	0	78	70	36	29	27	75
1999	Quad City (Mid)	A	8	5	3.53	19	14	0	1	92	66	39	36	37	95
2000	Fort Myers (FSL)	A	8	5	4.25	35	10	0	6	89	91	46	42	34	90
2001	New Britain (EL)	AA	2	1	1.08	35	0	0	13	50	26	6	6	22	72
	Minnesota (AL)	MAJ	0	0	13.50	2	0	0	0	3	3	4	4	3	2
	Edmonton (PCL)	AAA	2	2	5.51	11	0	0	0	16	18	11	10	10	17
MAJOR LEAGUE TOTALS			0	0	13.50	2	0	0	0	3	3	4	4	3	2
MINOR LEAGUE TOTALS			29	19	3.47	126	49	0	20	392	344	169	151	150	392

12. J.D. Durbin, rhp

Born: Feb. 24, 1982. **Ht.:** 6-0. **Wt.:** 177. **Bats:** R. **Throws:** R. **School:** Coronado HS, Scottsdale, Ariz. **Career Transactions:** Selected by Twins in second round of 2000 draft; signed July 18, 2000.

Durbin was named Arizona's high school player of the year in 2000 after he went 10-2, 0.84 with 135 strikeouts in 85 innings on the mound and hit .475-12-53 as an outfielder. He also earned all-state recognition as a wide receiver. The Twins swayed him away from an Arizona State baseball scholarship with a $722,500 bonus. Durbin's pro career began inauspiciously with a tender elbow limiting him to two innings in 2000. His coming-out party was stalled by a soreness again last season, but he provided an exciting glimpse of the future in his eight appearances. Durbin touched 97 mph, sat at 91-92 and showed a filthy slider compared to the best in the organization. Minnesota scouting director Mike Radcliff likens Durbin's aggressiveness to Adam Johnson's. After shouldering a heavy workload in high school, Durbin just needs to get healthy and learn to repeat his delivery before stepping forward into the upper echelon of Twins prospects.

Year	Club (League)	Class	W	L	ERA	G	GS	CG	SV	IP	H	R	ER	BB	SO
2000	Twins (GCL)	R	0	0	0.00	2	0	0	0	2	2	0	0	0	4
2001	Elizabethton (Appy)	R	3	2	1.87	8	7	0	0	34	23	13	7	17	39
MINOR LEAGUE TOTALS			3	2	1.77	10	7	0	0	36	25	13	7	17	43

13. Jon McDonald, rhp

Born: Oct. 16, 1977. **Ht.:** 6-3. **Wt.:** 195. **Bats:** R. **Throws:** R. **School:** Florida State University. **Career Transactions:** Signed as nondrafted free agent by Twins, July 12, 2000.

Despite compiling a 31-9, 3.94 record at Florida State, McDonald was overlooked in the draft after his junior season in 2000. Two outings in the Cape Cod League with a new arm slot and increased velocity was all the Twins needed to see before signing him as a free agent for $50,000. Like many Seminoles pitchers, he threw from a low three-quarters arm slot in college, which generated more movement at the cost of velocity. He jumped from 85-87 mph to 89-92 in the Cape when he went to a high three-quarters delivery. Control never has been an issue for McDonald, and he complements his fastball with a polished curveball and deceptive changeup. He had Tommy John surgery as a freshman but has been healthy ever since. McDonald led the Puerto Rican League in ERA this winter, enhancing his chances to move into the Edmonton rotation this year.

Year	Club (League)	Class	W	L	ERA	G	GS	CG	SV	IP	H	R	ER	BB	SO
2000	Fort Myers (FSL)	A	3	3	3.99	10	10	0	0	50	42	24	22	16	33
2001	Fort Myers (FSL)	A	4	2	1.98	9	9	0	0	50	44	15	11	15	44
	New Britain (EL)	AA	8	3	3.44	17	17	0	0	97	88	47	37	34	68
MINOR LEAGUE TOTALS			15	8	3.21	36	36	0	0	196	174	86	70	65	145

14. Kevin Frederick, rhp

Born: Nov. 4, 1976. **Ht.:** 6-1. **Wt.:** 208. **Bats:** L. **Throws:** R. **School:** Creighton University. **Career Transactions:** Selected by Twins in 34th round of 1998 draft; signed June 3, 1998.

The Twins failed to sign Frederick in the 17th round in 1997 after his junior season at Creighton. Their interest didn't fade, though, and they signed him a year later for a $1,000 bonus in the 34th round. A corner infielder/righthander in college, he had shoulder surgery to repair a detached labrum after he was drafted, preventing him from getting significant innings until 2000. Frederick showed signs of coming on that year, then really blossomed into a prospect last season in Double-A. When Saul Rivera got hurt and Grant Balfour was promoted, Frederick dominated as the closer. His mound presence is befitting of the role, and he has a 91-93 mph fastball that touched 94 along with a nasty slider. He has held hitters to a .205 average as a pro. After working a career-high 100 innings in 2001, Frederick went to the Arizona Fall League and struck out 20 in 21 frames. He was added to the 40-man roster in November. While he's slated for Triple-A, an early-season call to Minnesota could be just an injury away.

Year	Club (League)	Class	W	L	ERA	G	GS	CG	SV	IP	H	R	ER	BB	SO
1998	Elizabethton (Appy)	R	1	4	4.25	17	0	0	1	30	28	21	14	10	46
1999	Twins (GCL)	R	0	0	15.43	2	0	0	0	2	6	5	4	1	3
2000	Quad City (Mid)	A	5	0	2.35	27	0	0	4	46	34	17	12	23	51
	Fort Myers (FSL)	A	2	1	2.70	19	0	0	3	30	20	11	9	14	37
2001	Fort Myers (FSL)	A	2	0	1.00	9	0	0	1	18	9	2	2	3	19
	New Britain (EL)	AA	6	2	1.63	44	0	0	7	83	56	17	15	28	109
MINOR LEAGUE TOTALS			16	7	2.42	118	0	0	16	209	153	73	56	79	265

15. Angel Garcia, rhp

Born: Oct. 28, 1983. **Ht.:** 6-6. **Wt.:** 200. **Bats:** R. **Throws:** R. **School:** Nicolas Sevilla HS, Dorado, P.R. **Career Transactions:** Selected by Twins in fourth round of 2001 draft; signed June 19, 2001.

Garcia was regarded as the top pitching prospect in Puerto Rico for last year's draft. The Twins got him in the fourth round, one pick after taking Puerto Rican shortstop Jose Morales. A converted catcher, Garcia didn't begin pitching full time until two months before the draft. He took to the mound rapidly and watched his velocity steadily climb from the upper 80s to the low 90s with explosive, late life. Though his delivery is in the rudimentary stages, he touched 95 after the draft. He took immediately to a deceptive three-finger changeup with good tumbling action, taught to him in Puerto Rico by former big leaguer Edwin Correa. He needs to tighten the rotation on his slurvy breaking ball. Garcia is raw and untested, so the Twins will proceed with caution and bring him along slowly.

Year	Club (League)	Class	W	L	ERA	G	GS	CG	SV	IP	H	R	ER	BB	SO
2001	Twins (GCL)	R	0	3	5.60	9	6	0	0	18	20	15	11	12	22
MINOR LEAGUE TOTALS			0	3	5.60	9	6	0	0	18	20	15	11	12	22

16. Bobby Kielty, of

Born: Aug. 5, 1976. **Ht.:** 6-1. **Wt.:** 215. **Bats:** B. **Throws:** R. **School:** University of Mississippi. **Career Transactions:** Signed as nondrafted free agent by Twins, Feb. 16, 1999.

Like Jon McDonald, Kielty went to the Cape Cod League after not being drafted as a junior. He won the league's MVP award and was Baseball America's Summer Player of the Year in 1998, and suddenly commanded much more attention on the open market. Kielty signed for $500,000 and blitzed through the system to make his major league debut last summer. He doesn't profile as a prototypical everyday corner outfielder, but he offers versatile tools. Among them are the ability to drive the ball into the gaps from both sides of the plate with average power. Kielty's biggest asset is his discipline. He's also capable of playing all three outfield spots. A sore left elbow prevented Kielty from swinging from the left side early last season. He's the favorite to be Minnesota's Opening Day right fielder, though the position ultimately will belong to Michael Cuddyer.

Year	Club (League)	Class	AVG	G	AB	R	H	2B	3B	HR	RBI	BB	SO	SB
1999	Quad City (Mid)	A	.294	69	245	52	72	13	1	13	43	43	56	12
2000	New Britain (EL)	AA	.262	129	451	79	118	30	3	14	65	98	109	6
	Salt Lake (PCL)	AAA	.242	9	33	8	8	4	0	0	2	7	10	0
2001	Edmonton (PCL)	AAA	.287	94	341	58	98	25	2	12	50	53	76	5
	Minnesota (AL)	MAJ	.250	37	104	8	26	8	0	2	14	8	25	3
MAJOR LEAGUE TOTALS			.250	37	104	8	26	8	0	2	14	8	25	3
MINOR LEAGUE TOTALS			.277	301	1070	197	296	72	6	39	160	201	251	23

17. B.J. Garbe, of

Born: Feb. 3, 1981. **Ht.:** 6-2. **Wt.:** 195. **Bats:** R. **Throws:** R. **School:** Moses Lake (Wash.) HS. **Career Transactions:** Selected by Twins in first round (fifth overall) of 1999 draft; signed July 7, 1999.

Based on tools alone, Garbe belongs in the Top 10. But the fifth overall pick in 1999 has shown little progress to justify the hype that surrounded him as a highly coveted amateur. He was regarded as the best high school athlete and a better pure hitter than No. 1 overall pick Josh Hamilton. As a high school quarterback, Garbe both rushed and passed for 1,000 yards as a senior. While he has proven to be a natural athlete, he has had a difficult time making adjustments at the plate. He threw 94 mph off the mound in high school and has the strongest outfield arm in the system. He's an above-average defender, but that's not going to carry him to the big leagues. Based on his career .331 slugging percentage, it's hard to envision Garbe becoming a power hitter, but the Twins remain hopeful. He flashes plus tools, including pull power with the snap of his bat. He's somewhat stiff and has been stubborn to improve at the mental aspects of hitting. Garbe will have to dedicate himself to improve his recognition of breaking stuff. Minnesota might let him repeat high Class A this year in hopes he'll start to hit.

Year	Club (League)	Class	AVG	G	AB	R	H	2B	3B	HR	RBI	BB	SO	SB
1999	Elizabethton (Appy)	R	.316	41	171	33	54	8	0	3	32	20	34	4
2000	Quad City (Mid)	A	.233	133	476	62	111	12	3	5	51	63	91	14
2001	Fort Myers (FSL)	A	.242	127	463	55	112	14	4	6	61	51	86	13
MINOR LEAGUE TOTALS			.250	301	1110	150	277	34	7	14	144	134	211	31

18. Jeff Randazzo, lhp

Born: Aug. 12, 1981. **Ht.:** 6-7. **Wt.:** 200. **Bats:** R. **Throws:** L. **School:** Cardinal O'Hara HS, Springfield, Pa. **Career Transactions:** Selected by Twins in fourth round of 1999 draft; signed Aug. 18, 1999.

Though he finished the 2000 season in low Class A, the Twins weren't convinced Randazzo was ready to start last year there. But he went on to exceed their expectations while earning a spot on the Midwest League's midseason all-star team. He went 6-2, 3.53 in the first two months before posting a 6.27 ERA over the remainder of the season. A raw and projectable southpaw, Randazzo wore down in the second half and battled a dead arm. His velocity has increased each year, though he ended 2001 with 83-mph fastballs, down from 88-90 earlier in the year. A high school basketball player, Randazzo is a natural athlete with a free and easy arm action. While he has a chance to throw in the low 90s, he won't be overpowering. He should be able to rely on command of a quality downer curveball and a changeup, however. Randazzo is ticketed for a return to Quad City before advancing to high Class A.

Year	Club (League)	Class	W	L	ERA	G	GS	CG	SV	IP	H	R	ER	BB	SO
2000	Twins (GCL)	R	7	2	3.15	13	12	3	0	69	70	35	24	19	58
	Quad City (Mid)	A	1	1	3.97	2	2	0	0	11	10	5	5	8	12
2001	Quad City (Mid)	A	9	3	4.62	20	18	0	0	103	116	58	53	31	69
MINOR LEAGUE TOTALS			17	6	4.03	35	32	3	0	183	196	98	82	58	139

19. Kevin Cameron, rhp

Born: Dec. 15, 1979. **Ht.:** 6-1. **Wt.:** 175. **Bats:** R. **Throws:** R. **School:** Georgia Tech. **Career Transactions:** Selected by Twins in 13th round of 2001 draft; signed June 9, 2001.

Cameron spent the majority of his career at Georgia Tech coming out of the bullpen and probably wouldn't have cracked the weekend rotation as a junior last spring if preseason All-American Brian Sager hadn't gotten hurt. The Twins recognized Cameron's raw arm strength and think he could be a mid-round gem. After some minor mechanical tinkering, he moved back to the pen as a pro and started blowing 94-95 fastballs by hitters. He also showed an above-average 82-85 mph curveball and limited opponents to a .186 average in his debut. Cameron kept on impressing during instructional league, where he touched 96-97 with his fastball. With his maturity and control, Cameron could jump right onto the fast track.

Year	Club (League)	Class	W	L	ERA	G	GS	CG	SV	IP	H	R	ER	BB	SO
2001	Elizabethton (Appy)	R	1	1	1.57	22	0	0	13	23	16	4	4	5	30
MINOR LEAGUE TOTALS			1	1	1.57	22	0	0	13	23	16	4	4	5	30

20. Brian Wolfe, rhp

Born: Nov. 29, 1980. **Ht.:** 6-2. **Wt.:** 200. **Bats:** R. **Throws:** R. **School:** Servite HS, Anaheim. **Career Transactions:** Selected by Twins in sixth round of 1999 draft; signed June 15, 1999.

Wolfe was just 19 when he spent his first full season in Quad City in 2000, so his return to the Midwest League last year wasn't considered a setback. He operates with average stuff across the board and started to master the command and control of his three-pitch repertoire in the second half. In August, he tossed a nine-inning no-hitter. Wolfe was more effective after the Twins urged him to be more aggressive with his 88-92 mph fastball. He understands how to locate his fastball, slider and solid changeup. His feel for pitching is advanced for his age. He shouldn't be confused with 29-year-old Bryan Wolff, who pitched for the Twins in Triple-A last year. This Wolfe will move to high Class A this year and advance one level at a time.

Year	Club (League)	Class	W	L	ERA	G	GS	CG	SV	IP	H	R	ER	BB	SO
1999	Twins (GCL)	R	4	0	2.84	9	5	2	0	38	33	14	12	9	40
2000	Quad City (Mid)	A	5	9	4.74	31	18	0	0	123	148	73	65	34	91
2001	Quad City (Mid)	A	13	8	2.81	28	23	2	0	160	128	64	50	32	128
MINOR LEAGUE TOTALS			22	17	3.56	68	46	4	0	321	309	151	127	75	259

21. Ronnie Corona, rhp

Born: Jan. 27, 1979. **Ht.:** 6-0. **Wt.:** 180. **Bats:** R. **Throws:** R. **School:** Cal State Fullerton. **Career Transactions:** Selected by Twins in sixth round of 2000 draft; signed June 22, 2000.

After two years at a California junior college, Corona transferred to Cal State Fullerton in 2000. He started the season in the rotation with Adam Johnson, but was demoted to the bullpen to set up Kirk Saarloos (now an Astros prospect). The Twins kept Corona in the bullpen for his first two seasons, but injuries have limited his work. A Florida State League all-star in 2001, he was shut down in the second half and had surgery to repair a slightly torn labrum. When he's healthy, the slightly built 6-footer deals a nasty four-pitch repertoire. His 92-94 mph fastball has plus movement with sink and run. He's expected to be healthy this year and the Twins plan to move him into the Double-A rotation. Though he has yet to show the stamina for the role, he has the command and stuff to succeed.

Year	Club (League)	Class	W	L	ERA	G	GS	CG	SV	IP	H	R	ER	BB	SO
2000	Elizabethton (Appy)	R	0	0	3.52	3	1	0	0	8	8	4	3	2	8
	Quad City (Mid)	A	2	1	2.66	18	0	0	8	24	17	8	7	8	36
	New Britain (EL)	AA	0	0	6.35	3	0	0	0	6	6	4	4	2	9
2001	Fort Myers (FSL)	A	3	1	2.19	16	7	0	0	49	45	15	12	16	47
MINOR LEAGUE TOTALS			5	2	2.71	40	8	0	8	86	76	31	26	28	100

22. Dusty Gomon, 1b

Born: Sept. 3, 1982. **Ht.:** 6-3. **Wt.:** 220. **Bats:** R. **Throws:** R. **School:** Terry Parker HS, Jacksonville. **Career Transactions:** Selected by Twins in ninth round of 2001 draft; signed June 7, 2001.

While the Twins are thin around the infield—especially lacking up the middle—Gomon gives the organization a second power bat at first base to go with Justin Morneau's. Gomon probably has more raw power than fellow 2001 draftee Joe Mauer. He showcased his pop in instructional league, crushing balls to all fields. Gomon's bat is undeniably his best tool, but he's agile for his size and can handle the glove at first base. He may need to tighten his strike zone. After debuting in the Rookie-level Gulf Coast League, he jumped all the way to high Class A Fort Myers for six games. The move speaks volumes about the confidence the Twins have in him—and he wasn't overmatched. Gomon should spend 2002 in low Class A.

Year	Club (League)	Class	AVG	G	AB	R	H	2B	3B	HR	RBI	BB	SO	SB
2001	Twins (GCL)	R	.324	19	74	13	24	6	0	2	10	5	15	1
	Fort Myers (FSL)	A	.278	6	18	2	5	0	0	1	3	0	6	0
MINOR LEAGUE TOTALS			.315	25	92	15	29	6	0	3	13	5	21	1

23. Jon Pridie, rhp

Born: Dec. 7, 1979. **Ht.:** 6-4. **Wt.:** 205. **Bats:** R. **Throws:** R. **School:** Prescott (Ariz.) HS. **Career Transactions:** Selected by Twins in 11th round of 1998 draft; signed July 13, 1998.

Pridie's career began as a corner infielder, but he has taken to the mound and made nice progress. His younger brother Jason is also a rising two-way prospect at Prescott (Ariz.) High and should be selected early in the 2002 draft. The Twins couldn't find room for Jon on their 40-man roster this offseason and worried that another team would take a chance on him in the major league Rule 5 draft. Pridie features a 91-92 mph fastball and has touched 95. He works with four pitches, with his slider being the most advanced of his secondary offerings. Pridie has bounced between the bullpen and rotation, and he must hone his offspeed stuff for starting to remain an option. His command also needs refinement, and he might return to high Class A for the start of this season.

Year	Club (League)	Class	AVG	G	AB	R	H	2B	3B	HR	RBI	BB	SO	SB
1998	Twins (GCL)	R	.217	31	106	10	23	6	0	1	15	6	24	0
MINOR LEAGUE TOTALS			.217	31	106	10	23	6	0	1	15	6	24	0

Year	Club (League)	Class	W	L	ERA	G	GS	CG	SV	IP	H	R	ER	BB	SO
1998	Twins (GCL)	R	0	0	6.75	1	0	0	0	1	2	1	1	2	1
1999	Elizabethton (Appy)	R	5	6	4.48	14	14	0	0	76	93	44	38	33	64
2000	Quad City (Mid)	A	7	7	3.43	45	8	0	2	97	89	47	37	42	91
2001	Quad City (Mid)	A	6	3	3.40	12	11	1	0	56	40	26	21	24	48
	Fort Myers (FSL)	A	1	3	4.58	14	9	0	0	57	54	31	29	37	42
MINOR LEAGUE TOTALS			19	19	3.95	86	42	1	2	287	278	149	126	138	246

24. Scott Tyler, rhp

Born: Aug. 20, 1982. **Ht.:** 6-6. **Wt.:** 215. **Bats:** R. **Throws:** R. **School:** Downingtown (Pa.) HS. **Career Transactions:** Selected by Twins in second round of 2001 draft; signed July 8, 2001.

Tyler and Jeff Randazzo were high school rivals in Pennsylvania, and they're also two of the tallest pitchers in the system. But unlike the rangy lefthander, Tyler is all about power. Like many pitchers from the Northeast, Tyler didn't get an extended opportunity to showcase his stuff in high school because of the climate. He needs to compact his delivery, which requires a lot of effort and a high leg kick, but he's capable of generating plus-plus velocity. He touched 95 mph in high school, though he pitched at 90-91 in instructional league, where he struggled and didn't demonstrate a good feel for his arm action. His flashes plus potential with the spin on his hard slider and needs to learn a changeup. Tyler is considered a work in progress and could return to the Gulf Coast League this year.

Year	Club (League)	Class	W	L	ERA	G	GS	CG	SV	IP	H	R	ER	BB	SO
2001	Twins (GCL)	R	0	1	6.75	5	3	0	0	11	11	8	8	2	14
MINOR LEAGUE TOTALS			0	1	6.75	5	3	0	0	11	11	8	8	2	14

25. Colby Miller, rhp

Born: March 19, 1982. **Ht.:** 6-2. **Wt.:** 185. **Bats:** R. **Throws:** R. **School:** Weatherford (Olka.) HS. **Career Transactions:** Selected by Twins in third round of 2000 draft; signed June 19, 2000.

While it isn't the Twins' philosophy to go after raw tools in the draft, they do have an affinity for quarterbacks. Miller, who quarterbacked Weatherford High to the Oklahoma state championship in 1999, fits right in with Joe Mauer, B.J. Garbe and former University of Minnesota passer Andy Persby. After winning the football title, Miller led his baseball team to a perfect 41-0 record and another state crown. Miller is athletic and also played shortstop in high school, but his durability has been a concern as a pro. After throwing 92-94 mph in 2000, Miller sat in the 86-90 range with his fastball last season. He didn't lose his plus movement, however, and continued to show the makings of an above-average breaking ball. Miller could benefit from some added weight on his slender frame to help him hold up in the Midwest League this season.

Year	Club (League)	Class	W	L	ERA	G	GS	CG	SV	IP	H	R	ER	BB	SO
2000	Twins (GCL)	R	3	2	3.09	14	10	0	0	55	44	26	19	21	55
	Quad City (Mid)	A	0	1	6.75	2	2	0	0	7	10	6	5	7	6
2001	Elizabethton (Appy)	R	5	1	2.44	15	6	0	0	48	39	15	13	12	61
MINOR LEAGUE TOTALS			8	4	3.03	31	18	0	0	110	93	47	37	40	122

26. Trent Oeltjen, of

Born: Feb. 28, 1983. **Ht.:** 6-0. **Wt.:** 180. **Bats:** L. **Throws:** L. **Career Transactions:** Signed out of Australia by Twins, Feb. 7, 2001.

Considering their tight budget, it's a testament to Twins scouts that the organization has been successful internationally. Oeltjen leads a group of promising young Australians—which also included hard-throwing righthander Joshua Hill and Paul Mutch—who made their pro debuts in 2001. Oeltjen is a lean, athletic player who already has added more than 20 pounds since signing. He has a fluid, line-drive swing, good bunting skills and above-average speed. He had Tommy John surgery at the age of 16, so his arm is below average, but he makes up for it with solid defensive skills. Despite their efforts, the Twins have yet to produce a top position prospect from Australia. Oeltjen has the tools to be the first.

Year	Club (League)	Class	AVG	G	AB	R	H	2B	3B	HR	RBI	BB	SO	SB
2001	Twins (GCL)	R	.321	45	134	21	43	7	3	0	18	14	16	10
	Elizabethton (Appy)	R	.233	9	30	4	7	1	0	0	4	0	6	2
MINOR LEAGUE TOTALS			.305	54	164	25	50	8	3	0	22	14	22	12

27. J.C. Contreras, lhp

Born: April 24, 1982. **Ht.:** 6-0. **Wt.:** 140. **Bats:** L. **Throws:** L. **Career Transactions:** Signed out of Venezuela by Twins, Nov. 6, 1998.

The Twins' Venezuelan baseball academy is slowly starting to develop and produce promising prospects. Signed by Enrique Brito, the same scout who found Luis Rivas and Juan Rincon, Contreras made his U.S. debut last June after two outstanding seasons in the Venezuelan Summer League. Despite an underdeveloped frame, Contreras can generate above-average velocity and life on his fastball. He also has the makings of a plus curveball. Contreras baffled lefthanders, who managed a .174 average against him without an extra-base hit. His command can be spotty, and he's most effective when he keeps the ball down. He's probably headed for high Class A in 2002.

Year	Club (League)	Class	W	L	ERA	G	GS	CG	SV	IP	H	R	ER	BB	SO
1999	Ciudad Alianza (VSL)	R	0	1	0.95	3	3	0	0	19	15	8	2	8	22
2000	San Joaquin (VSL)	R	0	1	1.93	5	2	0	0	14	11	3	3	6	18
2001	Fort Myers (FSL)	A	0	0	3.38	6	0	0	1	8	6	3	3	6	4
	Quad City (Mid)	A	2	0	2.67	26	0	0	2	34	28	14	10	11	38
MINOR LEAGUE TOTALS			2	2	2.17	40	5	0	3	75	60	28	18	·31	82

28. Dustan Mohr, of

Born: June 19, 1976. **Ht.:** 6-2. **Wt.:** 210. **Bats:** R. **Throws:** R. **School:** University of Alabama. **Career Transactions:** Selected by Indians in ninth round of 1997 draft; signed June 15, 1997 . . . Released by Indians, March 31, 2000 . . . Signed by Twins, April 1, 2000.

A hard worker with outstanding makeup, Mohr is a self-made prospect. Released by the Indians after three marginal seasons, he's now coming off a dream season in which he led the organization in hits, doubles and total bases (293). Prior to 2001 he wasn't even on the map, but he won the Eastern League batting crown and the Twins couldn't resist calling him up in late August. Mohr is strong with power to the gaps and occasional over-the-fence pop. He has an average, accurate arm and is an aggressive runner. Mohr profiles as a reserve outfielder but will compete for Minnesota's right-field job in spring training.

Year	Club (League)	Class	AVG	G	AB	R	H	2B	3B	HR	RBI	BB	SO	SB
1997	Watertown (NY-P)	A	.291	74	275	52	80	20	2	7	53	31	76	3
1998	Kinston (Car)	A	.242	134	491	60	119	23	9	19	65	39	146	8
1999	Akron (EL)	AA	.167	12	42	3	7	2	1	0	2	5	7	0
	Kinston (Car)	A	.280	112	429	46	120	29	3	8	60	26	104	6
2000	Fort Myers (FSL)	A	.265	101	370	58	98	19	2	11	75	35	65	7
2001	New Britain (EL)	AA	.336	135	518	90	174	41	3	24	91	49	111	9
	Minnesota (AL)	MAJ	.235	20	51	6	12	2	0	0	4	5	17	1
MAJOR LEAGUE TOTALS			.235	20	51	6	12	2	0	0	4	5	17	1
MINOR LEAGUE TOTALS			.281	568	2125	309	598	134	20	69	346	185	509	33

29. Terry Tiffee, 3b

Born: April 21, 1979. **Ht.:** 6-3. **Wt.:** 225. **Bats:** B. **Throws:** R. **School:** Pratt (Kan.) CC. **Career Transactions:** Selected by Twins in 26th round of 1999 draft; signed Aug. 17, 1999.

Tiffee was an out-of-shape 260-pounder in high school. He weighed in at 230 when the Twins signed him out of junior college, just before he was to enroll at Louisiana State. Thanks to a strict conditioning program and hard work, he's down to a solid 210 pounds. Tiffee has natural hitting ability with a smooth, adjustable swing from both sides of the plate. Drafted as a first baseman, he's playing third base because of his arm strength. Due to limited agility, though, he's ideally a first baseman, which isn't where the organization needs him. Tiffee makes solid contact and drives the ball into the gaps. He's starting to figure out his power stroke. He's a smart hitter with a good idea at the plate. His lack of a defensive home could hinder his ascent, but he'll move to high Class A next season.

Year	Club (League)	Class	AVG	G	AB	R	H	2B	3B	HR	RBI	BB	SO	SB
2000	Quad City (Mid)	A	.254	129	493	59	125	25	0	7	60	29	73	2
2001	Quad City (Mid)	A	.309	128	495	65	153	32	1	11	86	32	48	3
MINOR LEAGUE TOTALS			.281	257	988	124	278	57	1	18	146	61	121	5

30. Ryan Mills, lhp

Born: July 21, 1977. **Ht.:** 6-5. **Wt.:** 205. **Bats:** R. **Throws:** L. **School:** Arizona State University. **Career Transactions:** Selected by Twins in first round (sixth overall) of 1998 draft; signed June 30, 1998.

Drafted in the 13th round by the Yankees after an All-America high school career, Mills turned down $500,000 to attend Arizona State. He emerged as one of the best pitching prospects in the 1998 draft, going sixth overall. His father Dick reached the majors for two appearances in 1970, but he's better known as his son's pitching coach. Ryan became the poster boy for his father's business of selling pitching instruction and the focus of the company's videotapes. Ironically, his mechanics, which were considered textbook, have become the culprit for his demise since signing for $2 million. When Mills pitched the Sun Devils to the 1998 College World Series, he had a 92-95 fastball and a plus curveball. He has thrown 88-90 as a pro, and that was before he was shut down early in 2001 for surgery to remove bone chips in his elbow. His command and confidence have dwindled, but the organization hasn't lost all hope for him. Perhaps the layoff will allow him to clear all of the mechanical concerns cluttering his head. Provided he's healthy, Mills will return to the Double-A rotation in 2002.

Year	Club (League)	Class	W	L	ERA	G	GS	CG	SV	IP	H	R	ER	BB	SO
1998	Fort Myers (FSL)	A	0	0	1.80	2	2	0	0	5	2	3	1	1	3
1999	Fort Myers (FSL)	A	3	10	8.87	27	21	0	0	95	121	107	94	87	70
2000	Quad City (Mid)	A	3	6	3.53	20	20	0	0	120	101	54	47	64	110
	New Britain (EL)	AA	0	7	9.28	8	8	0	0	32	47	49	33	34	21
2001	New Britain (EL)	AA	2	5	6.42	8	8	0	0	41	45	31	29	14	29
MINOR LEAGUE TOTALS			8	28	6.27	65	59	0	0	293	316	244	204	200	233

MONTREAL
Expos

TOP 30 PROSPECTS

1. Brandon Phillips, ss
2. Brad Wilkerson, of
3. Grady Sizemore, of
4. Donnie Bridges, rhp
5. Josh Karp, rhp
6. Justin Wayne, rhp
7. Rich Rundles, lhp
8. Zach Day, rhp
9. Luke Lockwood, lhp
10. Eric Good, lhp
11. Cliff Lee, lhp
12. Don Levinski, rhp
13. Wilkin Ruan, of
14. Josh Girdley, lhp
15. Ignacio Puello, rhp
16. Scott Hodges, 3b
17. T.J. Tucker, rhp
18. Ron Chiavacci, rhp
19. Shawn Hill, rhp
20. Val Pascucci, of/1b
21. Ron Calloway, of
22. Terrmel Sledge, of/1b
23. Juan Lima, rhp
24. Wilson Valdez, ss
25. Brandon Watson, of
26. Mike Hinckley, lhp
27. Phil Seibel, lhp
28. Henry Mateo, 2b
29. Matt Watson, of
30. Anthony Ferrari, lhp

By Michael Levesque

The Expos continued their downward spiral, as 2001 marked their fifth straight losing season. When the game shut down in 1994, Montreal had the best record in baseball and one of the game's deepest minor league systems. A foundation remains for the Expos to develop into a contender, but sagging attendance, rumors of contraction or a possible move continue to place a dark cloud over the organization.

Two prominent figures departed in 2001. Manager Felipe Alou, who played an essential role in the organization for three decades, was fired in late May. General manager Jim Beattie, who had served since 1995, resigned in September. Jeff Torborg replaced Alou, and Beattie's assistant Larry Beinfest stepped in as GM.

The club's big offseason trade with the Cardinals also failed to pay dividends. Fernando Tatis missed a good chunk of the season because of knee problems.

Finally, owner Jeffrey Loria gave up on his efforts in Montreal, with plans to buy the Marlins and presumably leave Major League Baseball to run the Expos for a year, after which they'll be moved or folded.

Despite all the doom and gloom, the organization has cause for optimism on the field, with an improving core of homegrown players and a rotation on the verge of becoming one of the best in the league. Righthander Javier Vazquez won 16 games and emerged as one of baseball's top young pitchers. Outfielder Vladimir Guerrero had the franchise's first 30-30 season. Orlando Cabrera won a Gold Glove at shortstop while driving in 96 runs, and his double-play partner, second baseman Jose Vidro, continued to hit.

The farm system had a disappointing year, with three clubs finishing last and only one posting a winning record. That doesn't reflect the talent level in the organization because Montreal ran young, inexperienced teams out on the field. The system also absorbed several injuries, most notably to key pitching prospects Donnie Bridges and Josh Girdley and third baseman Scott Hodges.

Though the system isn't as loaded as it was in the early 1990s, interesting prospects are on the way, especially on the mound. Scouting director Jim Fleming's focus on pitching has restored the system's depth. Trade-deadline additions of Zach Day from the Indians and Rich Rundles from the Red Sox further added to an abundance of arms.

Organization Overview

General manager: Larry Beinfest. **Farm director:** Vacant. **Scouting director:** Jim Fleming.

2001 PERFORMANCE

Class	Team	League	W	L	Pct.	Finish*	Manager(s)
Majors	Montreal	National	68	94	.420	t-13th (16)	F. Alou/J. Torborg
Triple-A	Ottawa Lynx	International	68	76	.472	t-7th (14)	Stan Hough
Double-A	Harrisburg Senators	Eastern	66	76	.465	9th (12)	Luis Dorante
High A	Jupiter Hammerheads	Florida State	70	69	.504	t-4th (12)	Tim Leiper
Low A	Clinton Lumber Kings	Midwest	51	85	.375	14th (14)	Steve Phillips
Short-season	Vermont Expos	New York-Penn	28	47	.373	12th (14)	Steve Balboni
Rookie	GCL Expos	Gulf Coast	20	40	.333	t-14th (14)	Dave Dangler
OVERALL 2001 MINOR LEAGUE RECORD			303	393	.435	29th (30)	

*Finish in overall standings (No. of teams in league)

ORGANIZATION LEADERS

BATTING
*AVG	Matt Watson, Jupiter	.330
R	**Val Pascucci**, Harrisburg	79
	Jason Bay, Jupiter/Clinton	79
H	Brandon Watson, Clinton	160
TB	Ron Calloway, Ottawa/Harrisburg	254
2B	Ron Calloway, Ottawa/Harrisburg	34
3B	Henry Mateo, Ottawa	12
HR	**Val Pascucci**, Harrisburg	21
RBI	Ron Calloway, Ottawa/Harrisburg	82
BB	Grady Sizemore, Clinton	81
SO	Tootie Myers, Harrisburg	118
	Rich Lane, Jupiter	118
SB	Henry Mateo, Ottawa	47

PITCHING
W	Justin Wayne, Harrisburg/Jupiter	16
L	Pat Collins, Jupiter	12
	Ben Washburn, Clinton	12
#ERA	Luke Lockwood, Clinton	2.70
G	Jim Serrano, Ottawa/Harrisburg	56
CG	Luke Lockwood, Clinton	3
SV	Bob Scanlan, Ottawa	23
IP	**T.J. Tucker**, Ottawa	166
BB	Ron Chiavacci, Harrisburg	81
SO	Ron Chiavacci, Harrisburg	161

*Minimum 250 At-Bats #Minimum 75 Innings

TOP PROSPECTS OF THE DECADE

TOP DRAFT PICKS OF THE DECADE

*Did not sign

Pascucci   **Tucker**

BEST TOOLS

Best Hitter for Average	Brad Wilkerson
Best Power Hitter	Val Pascucci
Fastest Baserunner	Wilkin Ruan
Best Fastball	Donnie Bridges
Best Breaking Ball	Don Levinski
Best Changeup	Luke Lockwood
Best Control	Rich Rundles
Best Defensive Catcher	Drew McMillan
Best Defensive Infielder	Brandon Phillips
Best Infield Arm	Brandon Phillips
Best Defensive Outfielder	Wilkin Ruan
Best Outfield Arm	Wilkin Ruan

PROJECTED 2005 LINEUP

Catcher	Michael Barrett
First Base	Fernando Tatis
Second Base	Jose Vidro
Third Base	Brandon Phillips
Shortstop	Orlando Cabrera
Left Field	Brad Wilkerson
Center Field	Grady Sizemore
Right Field	Vladimir Guerrero
No. 1 Starter	Javier Vazquez
No. 2 Starter	Tony Armas
No. 3 Starter	Carl Pavano
No. 4 Starter	Donnie Bridges
No. 5 Starter	Josh Karp
Closer	Scott Strickland

ALL-TIME LARGEST BONUSES

Justin Wayne, 2000	$2,950,000
Josh Karp, 2001	$2,650,000
Grady Sizemore, 2000	$2,000,000
Josh Girdley, 1999	$1,700,000
Josh McKinley, 1998	$1,250,000

DraftAnalysis

2001 Draft

Best Pro Debut: There's nothing flashy about LHP David Maust (17)—except for his 0.72 ERA at short-season Vermont. Using command and deception, he went 4-2 with a 45-6 strikeout-walk ratio and a .173 opponent average in 50 innings.

Best Athlete: OF Reggie Fitzpatrick (5) struggled as a high school senior, but he can fly and has bat speed. Rival Southeastern Conference coaches weren't looking forward to him running wild on the artificial turf at Arkansas, which had recruited him.

Best Hitter: Fitzpatrick and 3B Greg Thissen (8) have good swings, quick bats and solid approaches at the plate. They're both works in progress, because Fitzpatrick needs more at-bats to add polish and Thissen must get stronger.

Best Raw Power: Thissen projects to have average power.

Fastest Runner: Fitzpatrick can run the 60-yard dash in 6.5 seconds, plus he has a quick first step.

Best Defensive Player: C Danny Kahr (12) excels behind the plate, but he didn't dispel worries about his bat when he hit .169 in the Rookie-level Gulf Coast League.

Best Fastball: RHP **Josh Karp** (1) threw 91-94 mph every time the Expos scouted him at UCLA. His changeup and curveball are plus pitches, and his stuff compares well to that of Mark Prior, the No. 2 overall pick. But Prior had much more success in the Pacific-10 Conference.

Most Intriguing Background: LHP Chad Bentz (7) was born without a complete right hand, similar to former major leaguer Jim Abbott. RHP Chad Scarbery (50) is the son of two-time first-round pick Randy. RHP Nick Long (4) and his older brother Brandon were part of the same Georgia recruiting class, though only Brandon made it to Athens.

Karp

Closest To The Majors: Karp goes to big league camp and will make his pro debut with one of Montreal's Class A affiliates. The Expos vow not to rush him, though if he puts everything together it will be difficult to hold him back.

Best Late-Round Pick: RHP Rob Caputo (18) and LHPs Tyler Kirkman (13) and Tory Imotichy (15) all have potential. Imotichy, who's from scouting director Jim Fleming's hometown of Purcell, Okla., can reach 91-92 mph.

The One Who Got Away: The Expos did not lose anyone they wanted to sign. They came to terms with 19 of their top 20 picks and still control the rights to 27 of the 30 players who didn't turn pro.

Assessment: Karp has the stuff to be a frontline starter, and the Expos are ecstatic about the high school pitchers led by RHPs Don Levinski (2) and Long, and LHP Mike Hinckley (3). All have quality arms. On the other hand, they didn't add much in the way of position players.

2000 Draft

OF Grady Sizemore (3) and RHP Justin Wayne (1) cost $4.95 million between them and have lived up to their hefty price tags so far. LHP Cliff Lee (4) is coming on, while OF Jason Bay (22) won the low Class A Midwest League batting title last year.　　　**Grade: B+**

1999 Draft

Brandon Phillips (2) emerged last year as one of the game's best shortstop prospects. Luke Lockwood (8) and Josh Girdley (1) add to Montreal's depth in lefthanders.　　　**Grade: B+**

1998 Draft

The Expos blew a signability pick on SS Josh McKinley (1). They recovered with their next two choices, OF/LHP Brad Wilkerson (1) and LHP Eric Good (2).　　　**Grade: C+**

1997 Draft

With eight first-round picks, Montreal should consider C a failing grade for this draft, which should have stocked the system but still hasn't produced anyone who can get past Double-A. RHP Scott Strickland (10) has done better than any of the first-rounders so far, though RHPs Donnie Bridges and T.J. Tucker have been beset by injuries.　　　**Grade: C**

Note: Draft analysis prepared by Jim Callis. Numbers in parentheses indicate draft rounds.

. . . Phillips is a potential five-tool player at a premium position. He has a live, athletic body and rare natural ability.

Brandon
Phillips ss

Born: June 28, 1981.
Ht.: 5-10. **Wt.:** 170.
Bats: R. **Throws:** R.
School: Redan HS, Stone Mountain, Ga.
Career Transactions: Selected by Expos in second round of 1999 draft; signed June 21, 1999.

The Expos have raved about Phillips' ability since they selected him in the second round of the 1999 draft. Their enthusiasm remained strong after he hit .242-11-72 at low Class A Cape Fear in 2000, and he justified it in 2001, when he made impressive strides with his strike-zone judgment. Phillips needed just 55 games at high Class A Jupiter to equal his walk total from the previous season and was rated the Florida State League's third-best prospect. He joined Double-A Harrisburg in midseason, becoming the Senators' first teenage player since Ugueth Urbina in 1993. Phillips headed to the Arizona Fall League after the season and batted .344 while playing second base, shortstop and third base on a Scottsdale team that also featured top infield prospects Angel Berroa (Royals) and Orlando Hudson (Blue Jays).

Phillips is a potential five-tool player at a premium position. He has a live, athletic body and rare natural ability. He's an above-average defender at shortstop with soft hands, solid range, superior lateral movement, excellent first-step quickness and a cannon for an arm. He has enough power on his throws to go into the hole and nail runners from short left field. At the plate, he has a line-drive swing and impressive bat speed that projects to produce more power in the future. Phillips uses the whole field, gets deep into counts and has an advanced awareness of the strike zone. He is an average runner with astute baserunning skills. Despite Phillips' ability to beat teams with his glove, bat or speed, he's still rough around the edges. He made 18 errors in 55 FSL games. Though he cut his errors down to 12 in 67 Double-A contests and was much steadier after his promotion, he still needs to show more consistency with routine plays.

The Expos have an abundance of slick-fielding shortstops, but Phillips' offense separates him from the rest of the pack. Expos officials say he rises to the occasion, so they'll challenge him with a promotion to Triple-A Ottawa, where he'll start the 2002 season at age 20. With Orlando Cabrera entrenched in Montreal, Phillips will be given time to develop his skills.

RICK BATTLE

Year	Club (League)	Class	AVG	G	AB	R	H	2B	3B	HR	RBI	BB	SO	SB
1999	Expos (GCL)	R	.290	47	169	23	49	11	3	1	21	15	35	12
2000	Cape Fear (SAL)	A	.242	126	484	74	117	17	8	11	72	38	97	23
2001	Jupiter (FSL)	A	.284	55	194	36	55	12	2	4	23	38	45	17
	Harrisburg (EL)	AA	.298	67	265	35	79	19	0	7	36	12	42	13
MINOR LEAGUE TOTALS			.270	295	1112	168	300	59	13	23	152	103	219	65

2. Brad Wilkerson, of

Born: June 1, 1977. **Ht.:** 6-0. **Wt.:** 200. **Bats:** L. **Throws:** L. **School:** University of Florida. **Career Transactions:** Selected by Expos in first round (33rd overall) of 1998 draft; signed Aug. 29, 1998.

The organization's 2000 minor league player of the year and starting center fielder on the U.S. Olympic team, Wilkerson missed the first month of the 2001 season after surgery on his left shoulder the previous December. Promoted to Montreal in early July, he struggled mightily and was sent back to Triple-A six weeks later. Wilkerson is the best pure hitter in the system. He has a fluid swing with good extension, impressive plate coverage, opposite-field power and an advanced understanding of the strike zone. He makes adjustments and uses the entire field. He's a relentless defensive player with an average but accurate arm. He has average speed and keen baserunning skills. Wilkerson's difficulties in the majors persuaded the Expos to let him go back to using the high leg kick he employed in college. He's beginning to cover up holes on the inner half of the plate. Wilkerson was used sparingly in September after his return from Ottawa. With a good spring, he should be the Expos' everyday left fielder in 2002.

Year	Club (League)	Class	AVG	G	AB	R	H	2B	3B	HR	RBI	BB	SO	SB
1999	Harrisburg (EL)	AA	.235	138	422	66	99	21	3	8	49	88	100	3
2000	Harrisburg (EL)	AA	.336	66	229	53	77	36	2	6	44	42	38	8
	Ottawa (IL)	AAA	.250	63	212	40	53	11	1	12	35	45	60	5
2001	Jupiter (FSL)	A	.231	6	26	3	6	3	0	0	1	3	10	0
	Ottawa (IL)	AAA	.270	69	233	43	63	10	0	12	48	60	68	12
	Montreal (NL)	MAJ	.205	47	117	11	24	7	2	1	5	17	41	2
MAJOR LEAGUE TOTALS			.205	47	117	11	24	7	2	1	5	17	41	2
MINOR LEAGUE TOTALS			.266	342	1122	205	298	81	6	38	177	238	276	28

3. Grady Sizemore, of

Born: Aug. 2, 1982. **Ht.:** 6-2. **Wt.:** 195. **Bats:** L. **Throws:** L. **School:** Cascade HS, Everett, Wash. **Career Transactions:** Selected by Expos in third round of 2000 draft; signed June 16, 2000.

Sizemore was a standout football player who had committed to play both baseball and football at Washington before the Expos lured him with a $2 million bonus. He made considerable progress during his first full season, batting .327 over the final two months of the season. Sizemore has a lean, athletic body with loose, flexible actions. He has above-average center fielder range, speed and instinctive flychasing skills. At the plate he has an uncanny understanding of the strike zone and shows advanced pitch recognition. He has a smooth, easy swing with impressive bat speed. He does a good job of staying back with his swing, so he isn't fooled by breaking pitches and changeups. Once Sizemore learns to incorporate his lower half into his swing, he projects to hit with plus power to all fields. He has below-average arm strength and needs to improve his throwing mechanics by keeping his front shoulder closed. Expos officials are giddy with excitement when they talk about Sizemore. He'll open 2002 with Jupiter and could find himself in Harrisburg by season's end.

Year	Club (League)	Class	AVG	G	AB	R	H	2B	3B	HR	RBI	BB	SO	SB
2000	Expos (GCL)	R	.293	55	205	31	60	8	3	1	14	23	24	16
2001	Clinton (Mid)	A	.268	123	451	64	121	16	4	2	61	81	92	32
MINOR LEAGUE TOTALS			.276	178	656	95	181	24	7	3	75	104	116	48

4. Donnie Bridges, rhp

Born: Dec. 10, 1978. **Ht.:** 6-4. **Wt.:** 220. **Bats:** R. **Throws:** R. **School:** Oak Grove HS, Hattiesburg, Miss. **Career Transactions:** Selected by Expos in first round (23rd overall) of 1997 draft; signed July 21, 1997.

The organization's top prospect last year, Bridges logged just 81 innings in 2001 as he tried to regain his stuff. Bridges began the season in Triple-A before being shut down with a sore shoulder—possibly the result of working 201 innings in 2000. After he missed two months, he worked his way back to Triple-A in August. When Bridges is right, he's a power starter who locates a 92-94 mph fastball on both sides of the plate. His heater has good sink and tails to the right. He complements it with a biting curveball with late, two-plane break that's a plus pitch at times, as is his changeup. Like his fastball, it sinks and tails. Bridges had erratic command in 2001 because his delivery got out of sync. His front side kept flying open, leaving his pitches up and off the plate. He rarely looked comfortable on the mound. Bridges will return to Ottawa, where the Expos would like to see him healthy and successful before he vies for a rotation spot.

Year	Club (League)	Class	W	L	ERA	G	GS	CG	SV	IP	H	R	ER	BB	SO
1997	Expos (GCL)	R	0	2	6.30	5	2	0	0	10	14	9	7	5	6
1998	Vermont (NY-P)	A	5	6	4.90	13	13	0	0	68	71	42	37	37	43
1999	Cape Fear (SAL)	A	6	1	2.28	8	8	1	0	47	37	12	12	17	44
	Jupiter (FSL)	A	4	6	4.09	18	18	1	0	99	116	53	45	36	63
2000	Jupiter (FSL)	A	5	5	3.19	11	11	0	0	73	58	29	26	20	66
	Harrisburg (EL)	AA	11	7	2.39	19	19	6	0	128	104	39	34	49	84
2001	Expos (GCL)	R	0	1	8.44	2	2	0	0	5	2	6	5	5	9
	Jupiter (FSL)	A	0	1	6.75	1	1	0	0	4	7	6	3	3	2
	Harrisburg (EL)	AA	1	2	3.24	3	3	0	0	17	14	10	6	13	14
	Ottawa (IL)	AAA	3	5	7.48	13	13	0	0	55	60	50	46	43	49
MINOR LEAGUE TOTALS			35	36	3.92	93	90	8	0	507	483	256	221	228	380

5. Josh Karp, rhp

Born: Sept. 21, 1979. **Ht.:** 6-5. **Wt.:** 210. **Bats:** R. **Throws:** R. **School:** UCLA **Career Transactions:** Selected by Expos in first round (6th overall) of 2001 draft; signed Sept. 29, 2001.

Drafted in the eighth round out of high school by the Braves, Karp passed on a seven-figure bonus to attend UCLA. He went 23-7 over three seasons for the Bruins but rarely showed signs of dominance. After a summer-long holdout as the sixth overall pick in the 2001 draft, he signed in late September for $2.65 million. Karp has the potential to be a front-of-the-rotation starter if everything comes together. He has a prototype pitcher's body to go with a clean, easy arm action, sound mechanics and, at times, three above-average pitches. His arsenal includes a 90-94 mph fastball with exceptional late action at the plate, a tight-breaking curveball with good spin and bite, and an outstanding circle change with late sink. Karp relied on his changeup in college, and the Expos would like to see him establish his fastball more in the pro ranks. He needs to improve the command and consistency of his pitches. Karp never experienced a lot of success in college but will be put on the fast track. He'll go to big league camp before making his pro debut with one of Montreal's Class A affiliates.

Year	Club (League)	Class	W	L	ERA	G	GS	CG	SV	IP	H	R	ER	BB	SO
					Has Not Played—Signed 2002 Contract										

6. Justin Wayne, rhp

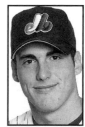

Born: April 16, 1979. **Ht.:** 6-3. **Wt.:** 200. **Bats:** R. **Throws:** R. **School:** Stanford University. **Career Transactions:** Selected by Expos in first round (fifth overall) of 2000 draft; signed July 20, 2000.

Wayne pitched well enough at Jupiter to earn a promotion to Double-A after seven starts. The fifth overall selection in the 2000 draft then reeled off eight wins in his final nine decisions. Wayne has good command of four pitches. His two main weapons are an 88-91 mph two-seam fastball that sinks down and in on righthanders, and a deceptive change that does an outstanding job of decelerating bats. He has an average slider with fair tilt and break. Wayne does a good job of using both sides of the plate and getting in on hitters with his fastball. Wayne has a 71-75 mph curveball that he seldom uses. It still needs work because it lacks bite and depth, and he has a tendency to drift and cut it off at times. His four-seam fastball generates fringe-average velocity without much effort but lacks movement. The Expos planned for Wayne to pitch in the Arizona Fall league, but they decided against it after he came down with a tired arm. Though he doesn't have overwhelming stuff, he has won everywhere he has pitched. That should continue at Triple-A Ottawa in 2002.

Year	Club (League)	Class	W	L	ERA	G	GS	CG	SV	IP	H	R	ER	BB	SO
2000	Jupiter (FSL)	A	0	3	5.81	5	5	0	0	26	26	22	17	11	24
2001	Jupiter (FSL)	A	2	3	3.02	8	7	0	0	42	31	16	14	9	35
	Harrisburg (EL)	AA	9	2	2.62	14	14	2	0	93	87	28	27	34	70
MINOR LEAGUE TOTALS			11	8	3.24	27	26	2	0	161	144	66	58	54	129

7. Rich Rundles, lhp

Born: June 3, 1981. **Ht.:** 6-5. **Wt.:** 180. **Bats:** L. **Throws:** L. **School:** Jefferson County HS, Dandridge, Tenn. **Career Transactions:** Selected by Red Sox in third round of 1999 draft; signed July 9, 1999 . . . Traded by Red Sox with RHP Tomo Ohka to Expos for RHP Ugueth Urbina, July 31, 2001.

Though Tomo Ohka also was included in the deal and wound up pitching for Montreal last season, Rundles was the key player in the July deadline deal that saw closer Ugueth Urbina shipped to Boston. After spending two seasons in complex leagues, he ranked third in ERA in the South Atlantic League in 2001. Rundles is a strike-throwing machine. He has the ability to throw with command and purpose to both sides of the plate, inducing grounder after grounder. He has an 86-90 mph two-seam fastball that runs and sinks. It breaks late, as does his curveball. Rundles also owns a plus changeup, a fine feel for pitching and plenty of composure. Rundles doesn't have overpowering velocity with his fastball, but he projects to throw harder because of his smooth compact delivery, loose easy arm stroke and projectable body. At times his curve can be consistent. Rundles will follow the natural progression and start 2002 with Jupiter. The Expos view him as a potential No. 2 or 3 starter in the majors.

Year	Club (League)	Class	W	L	ERA	G	GS	CG	SV	IP	H	R	ER	BB	SO
1999	Red Sox (GCL)	R	1	0	2.13	5	1	0	0	13	13	3	3	1	11
2000	Red Sox (GCL)	R	3	1	2.45	9	6	0	0	40	31	15	11	10	32
2001	Augusta (SAL)	A	7	6	2.43	19	19	0	0	115	109	46	31	10	94
	Clinton (Mid)	A	1	1	2.33	4	4	0	0	27	26	10	7	3	20
MINOR LEAGUE TOTALS			12	8	2.40	37	30	0	0	195	179	74	52	24	157

8. Zach Day, rhp

Born: June 15, 1978. **Ht.:** 6-4. **Wt.:** 185. **Bats:** R. **Throws:** R. **School:** LaSalle HS, Cincinnati. **Career Transactions:** Selected by Yankees in fifth round of 1996 draft; signed July 14, 1996 . . . Traded by Yankees with RHP Jake Westbrook to Indians, July 24, 2000, completing trade in which Indians sent OF David Justice to Yankees for OF Ricky Ledee and two players to be named (June 29, 2000) . . . Traded by Indians to Expos for OF Milton Bradley, July 31, 2001.

Originally drafted by the Yankees, Day is with his third organization in just over a year after coming over to the Expos in a swap with the Indians for outfield prospect Milton Bradley. The Yankees had sent him to Cleveland in 2000 in a package for David Justice. Day has made a complete recovery from 1999 rotator-cuff surgery. He has a three-pitch mix that consists of a 90-94 mph fastball with sink, an 81-83 mph curve with good bite and two-plane break, and a 78-84 mph change with nice arm speed and sink. He has a sound delivery with good rhythm, mixes his pitches well, works ahead in the count and tries to induce early contact. The ball comes out of his hand with ease. Day will drift through his balance point and throw across his body from time to time. He sometimes flies open in his delivery, making his control inconsistent. Day, who got his first taste of Triple-A after coming to the Expos, will return to Ottawa to polish his game before making a run at a spot in the rotation in 2003.

Year	Club (League)	Class	W	L	ERA	G	GS	CG	SV	IP	H	R	ER	BB	SO
1996	Yankees (GCL)	R	5	2	5.61	7	5	0	0	34	41	26	21	3	23
1997	Oneonta (NY-P)	A	7	2	2.15	14	14	0	0	92	82	26	22	23	92
1998	Tampa (FSL)	A	5	8	5.49	18	17	0	0	100	142	89	61	32	69
	Greensboro (SAL)	A	1	2	2.75	7	6	1	0	36	35	22	11	6	37
1999	Yankees (GCL)	R	1	1	3.78	5	4	0	0	17	20	10	7	4	17
	Greensboro (SAL)	A	0	1	2.25	2	2	0	0	8	14	11	2	1	4
2000	Greensboro (SAL)	A	9	3	1.90	13	13	1	0	85	72	29	18	31	101
	Tampa (FSL)	A	2	4	4.19	7	7	0	0	34	33	22	16	15	36
	Akron (EL)	AA	4	2	3.52	8	8	0	0	46	38	20	18	21	43
2001	Akron (EL)	AA	9	10	3.10	22	22	2	0	137	123	57	47	45	94
	Ottawa (IL)	AAA	3	2	6.34	7	6	0	0	33	41	24	23	9	19
MINOR LEAGUE TOTALS			46	37	3.56	110	104	4	0	622	641	336	246	190	535

9. Luke Lockwood, lhp

Born: July 21, 1981. **Ht.:** 6-2. **Wt.:** 165. **Bats:** L. **Throws:** L. **School:** Silverado HS, Victorville, Calif. **Career Transactions:** Selected by Expos in eighth round of 1999 draft; signed June 3, 1999.

Lockwood was the organization's most consistent pitcher in 2001 despite a 5-10 record with low Class A Clinton. He led the Midwest League in complete games and placed second in ERA and innings. He was shut down late in the year, not because of injury but because the Expos didn't want to pile any more innings on him. Lockwood has a lean, wiry, strong body with a whip-like arm action. He does an outstanding job of repeating his delivery, throwing first-pitch strikes and mixing his pitches well to keep hitters off balance. Lockwood pitches inside and commands both sides of the plate with his 86-88 mph two-seamer, which has good downward movement. He has a solid 75-77 mph curveball. His changeup is also an above-average major league pitch. Lockwood would rate higher if he threw harder, though he's still young and projectable. He sometimes tips off his changeup by slowing down his arm speed. Lockwood is a few years away from getting serious consideration for a big league spot. He'll head to Jupiter in 2002 to continue his climb.

Year	Club (League)	Class	W	L	ERA	G	GS	CG	SV	IP	H	R	ER	BB	SO
1999	Expos (GCL)	R	1	2	4.57	11	7	0	0	41	46	21	21	13	32
2000	Jupiter (FSL)	A	0	1	10.93	3	3	0	0	14	24	17	17	5	2
	Vermont (NY-P)	A	1	0	2.25	2	2	0	0	12	12	3	3	1	8
	Cape Fear (SAL)	A	2	4	4.50	9	9	0	0	48	49	32	24	20	33
2001	Clinton (Mid)	A	5	10	2.70	26	26	3	0	163	152	78	49	49	114
MINOR LEAGUE TOTALS			10	17	3.69	51	47	3	0	278	283	151	114	88	189

10. Eric Good, lhp

Born: April 10, 1980. **Ht.:** 6-3. **Wt.:** 180. **Bats:** R. **Throws:** L. **School:** Mishawaka (Ind.) HS. **Career Transactions:** Selected by Expos in second round of 1998 draft; signed June 15, 1998.

The Expos love lefthanders and have been infatuated with Good since drafting him. After missing the majority of 2000 with a sprained nerve in his elbow, he pitched pain-free in 2001 and would have led the Florida State League in ERA had he not fallen four innings short of qualifying. Good has an effortless arm action, a compact delivery and three plus pitches. His best is a 79-81 mph changeup that he keeps down in the zone with tail and sink. He complements it with an 88-91 mph two-seam fastball and a hard-biting 78-81 mph curveball. Good has a tendency to get his fastball up in the zone at times because he'll spin off in his delivery and get poor extension on his pitches, something that's correctable. He also needs to show more consistency with his curve. He doesn't stay on top of it, causing it to flatten out and become loopy. He also does a poor job of holding runners. In 2002, Good is scheduled to anchor a prospect-laden Harrisburg rotation that also will include prospects Cliff Lee and Phil Seibel.

Year	Club (League)	Class	W	L	ERA	G	GS	CG	SV	IP	H	R	ER	BB	SO
1998	Expos (GCL)	R	1	2	2.08	6	3	0	0	17	11	4	4	8	20
1999	Vermont (NY-P)	A	5	5	5.79	15	15	0	0	70	77	49	45	30	59
2000	Cape Fear (SAL)	A	1	2	2.75	8	8	0	0	36	31	15	11	12	32
2001	Jupiter (FSL)	A	5	5	2.82	21	20	1	0	108	104	42	34	26	70
MINOR LEAGUE TOTALS			12	14	3.66	50	46	1	0	231	223	110	94	76	181

11. Cliff Lee, lhp

Born: August 30, 1978. **Ht.:** 6-3. **Wt.:** 190. **Bats:** L. **Throws:** L. **School:** University of Arkansas. **Career Transactions:** Selected by Expos in fourth round of 2000 draft; signed July 6, 2000.

The Expos thought Lee was one of the top three college lefthanders available in the 2000 draft, and at times he shows the pure stuff to justify that ranking. He entered a Florida State League game last August in the second inning and promptly pitched eight no-hit innings with one walk and 10 strikeouts. He just missed winning the Florida State League ERA title, falling 2⅓ innings short of qualifying because he was out for a month with a stiff shoulder. When everything is clicking, Lee has two varieties of an 88-93 mph fastball, a two-seamer that sinks and runs to the left, and a four-seamer that he's aggressive with up in the zone. He has an impressive 78-79 mph changeup that also runs to the left, an 80-82 mph slider with late break and depth, and a 69-73 mph curveball with tight spin and bite. At times he shows four above-average pitches, but his main stumbling block has been lack of consistency with his command. Lee must do a better job of concentrating and improve his ability to hold runners, but the Expos think he'll evolve into a middle-of-the-rotation starter.

Year	Club (League)	Class	W	L	ERA	G	GS	CG	SV	IP	H	R	ER	BB	SO
2000	Cape Fear (SAL)	A	1	4	5.24	11	11	0	0	45	50	39	26	36	63
2001	Jupiter (FSL)	A	6	7	2.79	21	20	0	0	110	78	43	34	46	129
MINOR LEAGUE TOTALS			7	11	3.48	32	31	0	0	155	128	82	60	82	192

12. Don Levinski, rhp

Born: October 20, 1982. **Ht.:** 6-4. **Wt.:** 205. **Bats:** R. **Throws:** R. **School:** Weimar (Texas) HS. **Career Transactions:** Selected by Expos in second round of 2001 draft; signed August 4, 2001.

There were rumors that the Expos might make Levinski the sixth overall selection last June in what would have been a signability decision, but they waited until the second round and landed him for $825,000. He has an athletic body with broad shoulders, and he should get bigger and stronger. He has a sound, balanced delivery and loose arm action that produces a heavy 88-94 mph fastball with outstanding sink. He also throws a 78-81 mph power curve, one of the best breaking pitches in the 2001 draft. It has a tight, fast rotation with good depth and late, sharp break, though he needs to gain better consistency with it. He sometimes drops his arm slot, causing his curve to flatten out. His circle change also has a chance to be a plus pitch, as he throws it with fastball type trajectory and arm speed. The Expos like the way Levinski handles himself on the mound, showing a controlled presence with confidence. They were pleased with the progress he made during the pitching minicamp they held after the season and believe he may have a chance to start 2002 at Clinton if he has a good spring.

Year	Club (League)	Class	W	L	ERA	G	GS	CG	SV	IP	H	R	ER	BB	SO
2001	Jupiter (GCL)	R	0	0	3.46	3	3	0	0	13	15	5	5	7	15
MINOR LEAGUE TOTALS			0	0	3.46	3	3	0	0	13	15	5	5	7	15

13. Wilkin Ruan, of

Born: Nov. 18, 1979. **Ht.:** 6-0. **Wt.:** 170. **Bats:** R. **Throws:** R. **Career Transactions:** Signed out of Dominican Republic by Expos, Nov. 15, 1996.

Ruan has been one of the best athletes in the system for a while. In a midseason survey of Florida State League managers, he was named the circuit's fastest baserunner, best defensive outfielder and best outfield arm. He also earned a spot in the Futures Game, though he missed 31 games after a needless headfirst slide into second base fractured one of his fingers. He's the fastest runner in the system, with outstanding range, flychasing skills and basestealing potential. Ruan has a lean body that has gotten noticeably stronger in the past year. With his compact, line-drive swing and good bat speed, Expos officials see plenty of power potential in Ruan. Now he needs to start refining his tools. He's a free swinger who needs to be more selective at the plate, and his basestealing skills also could stand some improvement. He did begin to take some pitches in 2001, though the results didn't show up in his walk totals. Ruan will start 2002 in Double-A. If he progresses with the bat, he could be the long-term answer in center field for Montreal.

Year	Club (League)	Class	AVG	G	AB	R	H	2B	3B	HR	RBI	BB	SO	SB
1997	Expos (DSL)	R	.348	69	293	53	102	16	5	4	46	31	34	33
1998	Expos (GCL)	R	.239	54	201	22	48	9	3	1	19	5	43	13
	Jupiter (FSL)	A	.167	5	18	2	3	0	0	0	0	1	3	2
1999	Cape Fear (SAL)	A	.224	112	397	43	89	16	4	1	47	18	79	29
2000	Cape Fear (SAL)	A	.287	134	574	95	165	29	10	0	51	24	75	64
2001	Jupiter (FSL)	A	.283	72	293	41	83	8	2	2	26	10	35	25
	Harrisburg (EL)	AA	.248	30	117	14	29	7	0	0	6	3	18	6
MINOR LEAGUE TOTALS			.274	476	1893	270	519	85	24	8	195	92	287	172

14. Josh Girdley, lhp

Born: Aug. 29, 1980. **Ht.:** 6-3. **Wt.:** 185. **Bats:** L. **Throws:** L. **School:** Jasper (Texas) HS. **Career Transactions:** Selected by Expos in first round (sixth overall) of 1999 draft; signed June 2, 1999.

Montreal drafted Girdley sixth overall in 1999, signing him for a below-market $1.7 million, which was the second-lowest bonus in the top 15 picks. He dominated the short-season New York-Penn League in 2000 and the Expos were excited about seeing him in full-season ball. But an offseason motorcycle accident derailed him. After missing all of April, Girdley managed to start just six games with Clinton before a sore elbow shut him down for the year. He has received a clean bill of health and will be ready for the start of 2002. Girdley is a projectable lefthander with the potential for three plus pitches: a low-90s fastball with late life, a curveball with excellent two-plane break and a developing changeup. He has a smooth easy arm action and does an outstanding job of repeating his delivery. Lee should start the season with Clinton, and a good start could put him in Jupiter by midseason.

Year	Club (League)	Class	W	L	ERA	G	GS	CG	SV	IP	H	R	ER	BB	SO
1999	Expos (GCL)	R	0	2	3.32	12	11	0	1	43	41	19	16	16	49
2000	Vermont (NY-P)	A	5	0	2.95	14	14	0	0	79	60	32	26	28	70
2001	Clinton (Mid)	A	0	2	3.68	6	6	0	0	29	28	15	12	18	21
MINOR LEAGUE TOTALS			5	4	3.22	32	31	0	1	151	129	66	54	62	140

15. Ignacio Puello, rhp

Born: Oct. 16, 1980. **Ht.:** 6-1. **Wt.:** 170. **Bats:** R. **Throws:** R. **Career Transactions:** Signed out of Dominican Republic by Expos, May 14, 1998.

Puello produced three lackluster seasons in the Dominican Summer League before making his U.S. late in 2000. At the suggestion of Expos minor league coach Salomon Torres, Puello lowered his arm slot to three-quarters in the offseason and immediately showed improved velocity. Puello has one of the best arms in the Expos system. His fastball is consistently in the 92-94 mph range with good sinking movement and tops out at 96 mph. He complements his heat with a 78-80 mph curveball that has a late power break. A plus changeup rounds out his repertoire. He tends to drop down a bit on his curveball, pushing the ball, so sometimes it flattens out. After moving from the Gulf Coast League to Clinton, Puello became tentative and it showed in his command. He may have the highest ceiling of any pitcher in the organization but will take some time to develop.

Year	Club (League)	Class	W	L	ERA	G	GS	CG	SV	IP	H	R	ER	BB	SO
1998	Expos (DSL)	R	0	3	5.59	13	9	0	0	37	34	31	23	47	20
1999	Expos (DSL)	R	1	2	3.75	11	5	0	0	24	17	15	10	31	21
2000	Expos (DSL)	R	2	4	5.02	11	11	0	0	43	37	38	24	44	55
	Expos (GCL)	R	1	1	6.06	4	3	0	0	16	20	13	11	12	13
2001	Expos (GCL)	R	1	3	2.06	8	8	0	0	35	28	11	8	10	37
	Clinton (Mid)	A	3	3	5.57	7	7	0	0	32	29	21	20	26	21
MINOR LEAGUE TOTALS			8	16	4.62	54	43	0	0	187	165	129	96	170	167

16. Scott Hodges, 3b

Born: Dec. 26, 1978. **Ht.:** 6-0. **Wt.:** 190. **Bats:** L. **Throws:** R. **School:** Henry Clay HS, Lexington, Ky. **Career Transactions:** Selected by Expos in first round (38th overall) of 1997 draft; signed June 5, 1997.

Hodges lost considerable weight and missed the last 51 games of last season after it was discovered that he had colitis. That came on the heels of a breakout 2000 campaign that saw him earn a spot on Baseball America's Class A all-star team. Hodges is one of the best pure hitters in the system. He has a smooth lefthanded stroke with above-average bat speed and good top-hand extension. Hodges is an aggressive hitter but makes decent contact, driving the ball hard from gap to gap. He projects to be a legitimate middle-of-the-order threat with plus power. A shortstop in high school, he immediately was switched to third base upon signing. Defensively, he has an above-average arm, solid hands and adequate range. Hodges should be healthy and ready to go for the start of this season. He'll make a return visit to Harrisburg, with Fernando Tatis eventually standing between him and a big league job.

Year	Club (League)	Class	AVG	G	AB	R	H	2B	3B	HR	RBI	BB	SO	SB
1997	Expos (GCL)	R	.235	57	196	26	46	13	2	2	23	23	47	2
1998	Vermont (NY-P)	A	.278	67	266	35	74	13	3	3	35	11	59	8
1999	Cape Fear (SAL)	A	.258	127	449	62	116	31	2	8	59	45	105	8
2000	Jupiter (FSL)	A	.306	111	422	75	129	32	1	14	83	49	66	8
	Harrisburg (EL)	AA	.176	6	17	2	3	0	0	1	5	2	4	1
2001	Harrisburg (EL)	AA	.275	85	305	30	84	11	2	5	32	25	56	3
MINOR LEAGUE TOTALS			.273	453	1655	230	452	100	10	33	237	155	337	30

17. T.J. Tucker, rhp

Born: Aug. 20, 1978. **Ht.:** 6-3. **Wt.:** 245. **Bats:** R. **Throws:** R. **School:** River Ridge HS, New Port Richey, Fla. **Career Transactions:** Selected by Expos in first round (47th overall) of 1997 draft; signed June 9, 1997.

Tucker made his major league debut in 2000, when he made two starts with the Expos in

June. He left the second game with forearm pain and ended up missing the second half of the season after having arthroscopic elbow surgery. He returned last season and was able to remain healthy, pitching 166 innings between Harrisburg and Ottawa. Tucker is a moose on the mound with four major league average pitches. He has a 90-92 mph fastball with very good boring and sinking action. He throws it to both sides of the plate and keeps it down in the strike zone. A 77-78 mph curveball, 81-85 mph slider and 80-83 mph changeup with good sink round out his repertoire. His command can be a little off at times, and his stuff isn't so dominant that he can get away with mistakes. The Expos have an opening at the end of their rotation and Tucker will be in the running to fill the void.

Year	Club (League)	Class	W	L	ERA	G	GS	CG	SV	IP	H	R	ER	BB	SO
1997	Expos (GCL)	R	1	0	1.93	3	2	0	0	5	5	1	1	1	11
1998	Expos (GCL)	R	1	0	0.75	7	7	0	0	36	23	5	3	5	40
	Vermont (NY-P)	A	3	1	2.18	6	6	0	0	33	24	9	8	15	34
	Jupiter (FSL)	A	1	1	1.00	2	1	0	0	9	5	1	1	0	10
1999	Jupiter (FSL)	A	5	1	1.23	7	7	0	0	44	24	7	6	16	35
	Harrisburg (EL)	AA	8	5	4.10	19	19	1	0	116	110	55	53	38	85
2000	Harrisburg (EL)	AA	2	1	3.60	8	8	0	0	45	33	19	18	17	24
	Montreal (NL)	MAJ	0	1	11.57	2	2	0	0	7	11	9	9	3	2
2001	Harrisburg (EL)	AA	5	5	3.73	13	13	0	0	82	77	38	34	37	57
	Ottawa (IL)	AAA	3	5	3.11	14	14	1	0	84	68	42	29	33	63
MAJOR LEAGUE TOTALS			0	1	11.57	2	2	0	0	7	11	9	9	3	2
MINOR LEAGUE TOTALS			29	19	3.39	78	76	2	0	454	369	195	171	162	359

18. Ron Chiavacci, rhp

Born: Sept. 5, 1977. **Ht.:** 6-1. **Wt.:** 230. **Bats:** R. **Throws:** R. **School:** Kutztown (Pa.) University. **Career Transactions:** Selected by Expos in 44th round of 1998 draft; signed June 9, 1998.

Chiavacci doesn't have the typical prospect background, coming out of NCAA Division II Kutztown (Pa.) University as a 44th-round pick. But he's making a name for himself, leading the Double-A Eastern League and setting a Harrisburg franchise record with 161 strikeouts last year. His 3-11, 3.97 record hardly was reflective of his performance, as his teammates supplied him with three or fewer runs in 20 of his 25 starts. Chiavacci comes right after batters with a four-pitch mix. His best pitch is an overpowering 91-95 mph fastball than runs in on righthanders. He complements it with a 77-78 mph curve, an 82-83 mph slider and a deceptive changeup. His slider is still developing, as he occasionally will drop his arm slot and cause it to flatten out, and he needs to improve his command. He'll work on those things in Triple-A this year.

Year	Club (League)	Class	W	L	ERA	G	GS	CG	SV	IP	H	R	ER	BB	SO
1998	Expos (GCL)	R	6	3	2.13	13	6	0	0	55	43	17	13	13	42
	Jupiter (FSL)	A	0	1	2.35	4	0	0	1	7	5	2	2	2	5
1999	Cape Fear (SAL)	A	5	3	3.59	20	8	0	1	62	60	39	25	34	67
	Jupiter (FSL)	A	4	4	2.23	8	8	0	0	48	36	15	12	17	32
2000	Jupiter (FSL)	A	11	11	3.65	28	26	1	0	158	145	80	64	59	131
2001	Harrisburg (EL)	AA	3	11	3.97	25	25	2	0	147	137	77	65	76	161
MINOR LEAGUE TOTALS			29	33	3.42	98	73	3	2	477	426	230	181	201	438

19. Shawn Hill, rhp

Born: April 28, 1981. **Ht.:** 6-2. **Wt.:** 185. **Bats:** R. **Throws:** R. **School:** Bishop Reding HS, Georgetown, Ontario. **Career Transactions:** Selected by Expos in sixth round of 2000 draft; signed June 16, 2000.

Hill was a shortstop for his Ontario Connie Mack team before converting to the mound four years ago. For a raw Canadian with very little pitching experience, he's a very polished pitcher. He has a balanced delivery with a long, loose arm action and very good extension. He has a projectable body with big, wide shoulders. Hill uses an 89-92 mph two-seam fastball to get ground balls. He pitches to both sides of the plate and his fastball command is outstanding. He also has a sharp curveball and good feel for a changeup, both of which he throws at 73-76 mph. Limited to seven starts at short-season Vermont last year before getting shut down with a tired arm, Hill will make his full-season debut with Clinton in 2002.

Year	Club (League)	Class	W	L	ERA	G	GS	CG	SV	IP	H	R	ER	BB	SO
2000	Expos (GCL)	R	1	3	4.81	7	7	0	0	24	25	17	13	10	20
2001	Vermont (NY-P)	A	2	2	2.27	7	7	0	0	36	22	12	9	8	23
MINOR LEAGUE TOTALS			3	5	3.30	14	14	0	0	60	47	29	22	18	43

20. Val Pascucci, of/1b

Born: Nov. 17, 1978. **Ht.:** 6-6. **Wt.:** 225. **Bats:** R. **Throws:** R. **School:** University of Oklahoma. **Career Transactions:** Selected by Expos in 15th round of 1999 draft; signed June 2, 1999.

In an effort to increase his versatility, the Expos had Pascucci play exclusively at first base in the Arizona Fall League. He had been primarily a corner outfielder, but with Vladimir Guerrero and Brad Wilkerson ticketed for those spots in the majors, the team is looking at ways to get Pascucci's bat in the lineup. He's a good athlete who can hit the ball a long ways. He has good plate coverage and discipline, and a short stroke with nice extension for someone his size. With all those tools, he must produce more than he did in 2001, when he hit .244 (and .228 against righthanders) with just 39 extra-base hits. A former pitcher, Pascucci has an above-average arm with good carry and pinpoint accuracy. Three of his throws where clocked at 94 mph from the outfield in spring training. He has average speed and is intelligent on the bases, though he has a choppy stride when he runs. Pascucci could be in line to replace incumbent Lee Stevens at first base in 2003.

Year	Club (League)	Class	AVG	G	AB	R	H	2B	3B	HR	RBI	BB	SO	SB
1999	Vermont (NY-P)	A	.351	72	259	62	91	26	1	7	48	53	46	17
2000	Cape Fear (SAL)	A	.319	20	69	17	22	4	0	3	10	16	15	5
	Jupiter (FSL)	A	.284	113	405	70	115	30	2	14	66	66	98	14
2001	Harrisburg (EL)	AA	.244	138	476	79	116	17	1	21	67	65	114	8
MINOR LEAGUE TOTALS			.285	343	1209	228	344	77	4	45	191	200	273	44

21. Ron Calloway, of

Born: Sept. 6, 1976. **Ht.:** 6-0. **Wt.:** 190. **Bats:** L. **Throws:** L. **School:** Canada (Calif.) JC. **Career Transactions:** Selected by Diamondbacks in eighth round of 1997 draft; signed June 3, 1997 . . . Traded by Diamondbacks to Expos, July 5, 1999, completing trade in which Expos sent C John Pachot to Diamondbacks for future considerations (May 21, 1999).

Calloway opened the 2001 season in a reserve capacity with Harrisburg, yet by the time he departed in late June he was leading the Eastern League in batting and had established himself as a bona fide prospect. He finished the season by hitting eight homers in Triple-A in August. He's athletic and has solid tools across the board. Calloway is a competent center fielder with an above-average arm, good range and the ability to track down balls. He's an aggressive hitter with a quiet, line-drive swing and emerging power, but he needs to improve his discipline at the plate. Calloway is an above-average runner with a long, looping stride. He further enhances his speed with his accomplished bunting skills. Calloway profiles as a fourth outfielder in the majors, and some Montreal officials believe he should be given a shot in center field if Peter Bergeron continues to struggle.

Year	Club (League)	Class	AVG	G	AB	R	H	2B	3B	HR	RBI	BB	SO	SB
1997	Lethbridge (Pio)	R	.250	43	148	23	37	5	0	0	9	14	29	5
	South Bend (Mid)	A	.280	9	25	3	7	1	0	0	1	2	8	1
1998	South Bend (Mid)	A	.263	69	251	29	66	12	2	3	33	25	50	6
	High Desert (Cal)	A	.282	44	156	30	44	8	2	3	27	12	38	2
1999	High Desert (Cal)	A	.316	60	196	41	62	14	1	3	23	30	34	22
	El Paso (TL)	AA	.219	11	32	4	7	0	0	0	1	7	7	1
	Jupiter (FSL)	A	.270	54	211	30	57	8	4	3	25	15	45	5
2000	Jupiter (FSL)	A	.277	135	530	78	147	24	6	6	65	55	89	34
2001	Harrisburg (EL)	AA	.330	74	279	48	92	22	4	9	47	24	46	25
	Ottawa (IL)	AAA	.264	61	239	27	63	12	0	10	35	16	64	11
MINOR LEAGUE TOTALS			.282	560	2067	313	582	106	19	37	266	200	410	112

22. Terrmel Sledge, of/1b

Born: March 18, 1977. **Ht.:** 6-0. **Wt.:** 185. **Bats:** L. **Throws:** L. **School:** Long Beach State University. **Career Transactions:** Selected by Mariners in eighth round of 1999 draft; signed June 18, 1999 . . . Traded by Mariners to Expos, Sept. 27, 2000, completing trade in which Expos sent C Chris Widger to Mariners for two players to be named (Aug. 8, 2000); Expos also acquired LHP Sean Spencer (Aug. 10, 2000).

One of the players to be named in the trade that sent Chris Widger to Seattle in 2000, Sledge won the high Class A California League batting title that year before his season ended in August because he strained his right shoulder. The injury left Sledge at first base for Harrisburg for the majority of 2001. He has an unorthodox trigger mechanism when starting his swing, yet generally gets the job done. He'll have to hit for more power to earn a big league job, however. He's an above average runner and is a threat to steal 30 bases annually in the majors. The Expos are taking every precaution with Sledge's shoulder and hope to have him playing the outfield on a full-time basis in 2002.

Year	Club (League)	Class	AVG	G	AB	R	H	2B	3B	HR	RBI	BB	SO	SB
1999	Everett (NWL)	A	.318	62	233	43	74	8	3	5	32	27	35	9
2000	Wisconsin (Mid)	A	.217	7	23	5	5	2	2	0	3	3	3	1
	Lancaster (Cal)	A	.339	103	384	90	130	22	7	11	75	72	49	35
2001	Harrisburg (EL)	AA	.277	129	448	66	124	22	6	9	48	51	72	30
MINOR LEAGUE TOTALS			.306	301	1088	204	333	54	18	25	158	153	159	75

23. Juan Lima, rhp

Born: April 10, 1982. **Ht.:** 6-0. **Wt.:** 160. **Bats:** R. **Throws:** R. **Career Transactions:** Signed out of Dominican Republic by Expos, May 14, 1999.

Lima has an electric arm, though he didn't get to show it as often as hoped in 2001 because he had a strained elbow. As he gains experience and learns to separate speeds, he'll be tough to hit. He has good control of an explosive 92-94 mph fastball with late life. He also has an 84-86 mph slider that already has major league break and velocity. It has the potential to be a big league strikeout pitch with better command and consistency. Lima has a balanced delivery with an easy arm action, though he gets very little extension after release. His changeup, which is in the developmental stage, can be too hard at times. Montreal hopes to get a full season out of Lima at Clinton in 2002, which could significantly boost him on the prospect charts.

Year	Club (League)	Class	W	L	ERA	G	GS	CG	SV	IP	H	R	ER	BB	SO
1999	Expos (DSL)	R	2	4	4.36	14	9	0	0	54	52	34	26	20	27
2000	Expos (DSL)	R	4	0	2.06	8	5	0	1	39	30	12	9	16	39
	Expos (GCL)	R	2	1	2.60	8	3	0	0	28	21	13	8	9	15
2001	Vermont (NY-P)	A	2	6	4.68	12	9	0	0	50	55	34	26	17	34
	Jupiter (FSL)	A	0	0	0.00	1	0	0	0	2	0	0	0	0	1
MINOR LEAGUE TOTALS			10	11	3.59	43	26	0	1	173	158	93	69	62	116

24. Wilson Valdez, ss

Born: May 20, 1980. **Ht.:** 5-11. **Wt.:** 150. **Bats:** R. **Throws:** R. **Career Transactions:** Signed out of Dominican Republic by Expos, Feb. 4, 1997.

Valdez scaled two levels in his fifth professional season and made significant improvement that never showed up in the stats. The Expos say the more you watch him, the more you end up liking him. Valdez is a superb defensive shortstop with outstanding range to both sides and good hands. He has excellent lateral movement and a plus arm with accuracy. Valdez has a simple line-drive stroke at the plate, uses the whole field and is a proficient bunter. When he gets in a rut, he'll start his trigger late and drop his bat head towards the catcher. He tends to swing at balls out of the strike zone. The Expos praise his intelligence and ability to anticipate both on defense and on the bases. Valdez is an average runner who gets down the line. With Orlando Cabrera and Brandon Phillips in front of him, Valdez will be given plenty of time to develop and may have a position change in his future. He'll do so this year at Harrisburg.

Year	Club (League)	Class	AVG	G	AB	R	H	2B	3B	HR	RBI	BB	SO	SB
1997	Expos (DSL)	R	.303	62	244	39	74	13	1	2	29	25	19	19
1998	Expos (DSL)	R	.300	64	247	42	74	9	0	3	30	19	12	15
1999	Expos (GCL)	R	.293	22	82	12	24	2	0	0	7	5	7	10
	Vermont (NY-P)	A	.246	36	130	19	32	7	0	1	10	7	21	4
2000	Cape Fear (SAL)	A	.245	15	49	6	12	2	0	0	3	2	9	3
	Vermont (NY-P)	A	.266	65	248	32	66	8	1	1	30	17	32	16
2001	Clinton (Mid)	A	.252	59	214	31	54	8	1	0	11	9	22	6
	Jupiter (FSL)	A	.249	64	233	34	58	13	2	2	19	10	33	7
MINOR LEAGUE TOTALS			.272	387	1447	215	394	62	5	9	139	94	155	80

25. Brandon Watson, of

Born: Sept. 30, 1981. **Ht.:** 6-1. **Wt.:** 170. **Bats:** L. **Throws:** R. **School:** Westchester HS, Los Angeles. **Career Transactions:** Selected by Expos in ninth round of 1999 draft; signed June 7, 1999.

Montreal drafted Watson as a second baseman and immediately switched him to the outfield, where he's showing some promise. He started in the Midwest League all-star game as a teenager before battling a heel injury and a slump in the second half. He's a leadoff prospect with most of the skills necessary to succeed in that role. He has outstanding speed, though he still gets caught far too often as a basestealer. He has a line-drive stroke, uses the whole field and is considered the best bunter in the Expos minor league system. Watson is a contact hitter but needs to do a better job of drawing walks and working the count. He's an efficient center fielder who makes good reads and has a playable arm. He'll step up to Jupiter this year.

Year	Club (League)	Class	AVG	G	AB	R	H	2B	3B	HR	RBI	BB	SO	SB
1999	Expos (GCL)	R	.303	33	119	15	36	2	0	0	12	11	11	4
2000	Vermont (NY-P)	A	.291	69	278	53	81	9	1	0	30	25	38	26
2001	Clinton (Mid)	A	.327	117	489	74	160	16	9	2	38	29	65	33
MINOR LEAGUE TOTALS			.313	219	886	142	277	27	10	2	80	65	114	63

26. Mike Hinckley, lhp

Born: October 5, 1982. **Ht.:** 6-3. **Wt.:** 170. **Bats:** R. **Throws:** L. **School:** Moore (Okla.) HS. **Career Transactions:** Selected by Expos in third round of 2001 draft; signed July 5, 2001.

Hinckley was a lefthander with middling velocity before he reinvented his arm action prior to his senior season. The result helped jump his fastball into the low 90s and made him a third-round pick in last June's draft. Hinckley has a lean rail-thin but projectable body with wide shoulders. In the Gulf Coast League, he routinely threw his sinker in the 88-91 mph range. His command was erratic because he's such a competitor that he got too pumped up at times and couldn't settle into a consistent rhythm. Another flaw is that he sometimes opens his front foot too soon, causing his arm to drag and come across his body. Hinckley has good feel for a 79-81 mph straight changeup and a 72-74 mph curveball with downward spin. If he develops as expected, the Expos may have something special.

Year	Club (League)	Class	W	L	ERA	G	GS	CG	SV	IP	H	R	ER	BB	SO
2001	Expos (GCL)	R	2	2	5.24	8	5	0	0	34	46	23	20	12	28
MINOR LEAGUE TOTALS			2	2	5.24	8	5	0	0	34	46	23	20	12	28

27. Phil Seibel, lhp

Born: Jan. 28, 1979. **Ht.:** 6-1. **Wt.:** 185. **Bats:** L. **Throws:** L. **School:** University of Texas. **Career Transactions:** Selected by Expos in eighth round of 2000 draft; signed Aug. 7, 2000.

Seibel boosted his stock as a member of Team USA's college squad in 1999, posting a 2.12 ERA that ranked second behind eventual Dodgers first-round pick Ben Diggins. Then he strained a tendon in his elbow at the University of Texas, causing him to slide to the eighth round in the 2000 draft, where the Expos scooped him up. He didn't make his pro debut until last season—in high Class A, no less—when he worked exclusively as a starter after also seeing time in the bullpen as a Longhorn. Seibel is a crafty lefthander with three solid pitches. He has an 87-89 mph two-seam fastball that produces ground balls, a 78-80 mph slider and a plus 79-80 mph changeup. Seibel needs to maintain a consistent delivery because he'll fly open in his delivery and lose command of his pitches. Montreal officials compare him to a young Mike Hampton, a comparison he'll try to justify in Double-A this year.

Year	Club (League)	Class	W	L	ERA	G	GS	CG	SV	IP	H	R	ER	BB	SO
2001	Jupiter (FSL)	A	10	7	3.95	29	21	0	0	134	144	70	59	28	88
MINOR LEAGUE TOTALS			10	7	3.95	29	21	0	0	134	144	70	59	28	88

28. Henry Mateo, 2b

Born: Oct. 14, 1976. **Ht.:** 5-11. **Wt.:** 180. **Bats:** B. **Throws:** R. **School:** Centro Estudios Libres, Santurce, P.R. **Career Transactions:** Selected by Expos in second round of 1995 draft; signed June 11, 1995.

After leading the Eastern League with 48 stolen bases in 2000, Mateo led the International League with 47 thefts last season. The sparkplug also used his above-average speed to accumulate 12 triples, also tops in the league. Mateo is an athletic middle infielder with solid tools across the board. He has a line-drive stroke but needs to temper his aggressive nature and improve his strike-zone judgment. Defensively he has smooth actions, plus range and plenty of arm strength. Mateo, who made his major league debut last July and went 3-for-9, will return for a second stint at Triple-A in 2002. Unfortunately for him, the Expos are awash in top-notch middle infielders with Orlando Cabrera, Jose Vidro and No. 1 prospect Brandon Phillips.

Year	Club (League)	Class	AVG	G	AB	R	H	2B	3B	HR	RBI	BB	SO	SB
1995	Expos (GCL)	R	.148	38	122	11	18	0	0	0	6	14	47	2
1996	Expos (GCL)	R	.250	14	44	8	11	3	0	0	3	5	11	5
1997	Vermont (NY-P)	A	.246	67	228	32	56	9	3	1	31	30	44	21
1998	Cape Fear (SAL)	A	.276	114	416	72	115	20	5	4	41	40	111	22
	Jupiter (FSL)	A	.279	12	43	11	12	3	1	0	6	2	6	3
1999	Jupiter (FSL)	A	.260	118	447	69	116	27	7	4	58	44	112	32
2000	Harrisburg (EL)	AA	.287	140	530	91	152	25	11	5	63	58	97	48

2001	Ottawa (IL)	AAA	.268	118	500	71	134	14	12	5	43	33	89 47
	Expos (NL)	MAJ	.333	5	9	1	3	1	0	0	0	0	1 0
MAJOR LEAGUE TOTALS			.33	5	9	1	3	1	0	0	0	0	1 0
MINOR LEAGUE TOTALS			.264	621	2330	365	614	101	39	19	251	226	517 180

29. Matt Watson, of

Born: Sept. 5, 1978. **Ht.:** 5-11. **Wt.:** 190. **Bats:** L. **Throws:** R. **School:** Xavier University. **Career Transactions:** Selected by Expos in 16th round of 1999 draft; signed June 5, 1999.

Watson (no relation to Brandon) missed much of 2000 because of rotator-cuff surgery and entered last season as an afterthought. Healthy again, he won the Florida State League batting crown and Expos minor league player of the year honors. He also had an impressive .417 on-base percentage, walked more than he struck out and contributed his share of doubles and steals. A pure hitter, Watson has a short stroke and gap power. He's a solid left fielder with a playable arm and good range. He's an intelligent base runner with average speed, and the Expos rave about his makeup and determination. Watson will have a chance to go for his third batting title in four years—he hit .380 to lead the New York-Penn League in 1999—when he heads close to home to play for Harrisburg.

Year	Club (League)	Class	AVG	G	AB	R	H	2B	3B	HR	RBI	BB	SO	SB
1999	Vermont (NY-P)	A	.380	70	284	55	108	12	3	7	47	30	27	17
2000	Jupiter (FSL)	A	.175	40	137	10	24	5	2	0	8	18	23	4
2001	Jupiter (FSL)	A	.330	124	446	70	147	33	4	5	74	63	45	17
MINOR LEAGUE TOTALS			.322	234	867	135	279	50	9	12	129	111	95	38

30. Anthony Ferrari, lhp

Born: June 22, 1978. **Ht.:** 5-9. **Wt.:** 165. **Bats:** L. **Throws:** L. **School:** Lewis-Clark State (Idaho) College. **Career Transactions:** Selected by Expos in 44th round of 2000 draft; signed June 16, 2000.

A year after finding Ron Chiavacci in the 44th round, the Expos scored there again with Ferrari. Montreal crosschecker Scott Goldby was impressed with him after watching him win the championship game in the 2000 NAIA World Series. Ferrari has had plenty of success as a pro, earning postseason all-star recognition in the Florida State League in 2001. He throws much harder than the typical 5-foot-9 lefthander, pitching down in the zone with a 92-94 mph two-seam fastball. He also has an 81-83 mph slider and an 80-81 mph changeup. Ferrari has a jerky, unconventional delivery, which causes his release point to be inconsistent at times. He'll try to keep defying the odds at Harrisburg in 2002.

Year	Club (League)	Class	W	L	ERA	G	GS	CG	SV	IP	H	R	ER	BB	SO
2000	Vermont (NY-P)	A	2	2	1.71	25	0	0	5	47	31	14	9	15	37
2001	Jupiter (FSL)	A	2	3	0.79	51	0	0	21	57	36	11	5	17	45
MINOR LEAGUE TOTALS			4	5	1.21	76	0	0	26	104	67	25	14	32	82

NEW YORK
Mets

TOP 30 PROSPECTS

1. Aaron Heilman, rhp
2. Jose Reyes, ss
3. Pat Strange, rhp
4. Jae Weong Seo, rhp
5. David Wright, 3b
6. Satoru Komiyama, rhp
7. Grant Roberts, rhp
8. Tyler Yates, rhp
9. Jaime Cerda, lhp
10. Neal Musser, lhp
11. Mark Corey, rhp
12. Eric Cammack, rhp
13. Enrique Cruz, 3b
14. Ken Chenard, rhp
15. Nick Maness, rhp
16. Tyler Walker, rhp
17. Jason Phillips, c
18. Bob Keppel, rhp
19. Chris Basak, ss
20. Lenny DiNardo, lhp
21. Craig House, rhp
22. Adam Walker, lhp
23. Angel Pagan, of
24. Justin Huber, c
25. Luz Portobanco, rhp
26. Craig Brazell, 1b
27. Jeremy Griffiths, rhp
28. Jake Joseph, rhp
29. Robert Stratton, of
30. Prentice Redman, of

By Bill Ballew

With little or no help from the farm system on the immediate horizon, the Mets became one of the most active teams in the game in the offseason. They jettisoned two of their five best prospects (outfielder Alex Escobar and lefthander Billy Traber) and minor league player of the year (first baseman Earl Snyder) to the Indians for Roberto Alomar. They acquired Mo Vaughn, Jeromy Burnitz, Roger Cedeno, David Weathers and Shawn Estes, all at no cost to the farm system. They also dealt third baseman Robin Ventura to the Yankees for David Justice, who was later dealt to Oakland for lefthander Mark Guthrie and righthander Tyler Yates—the only net gain for a system that had its ups and downs in 2001.

Tragedy hit New York long before Sept. 11. The Mets lost outfield prospect Brian Cole, who died in an automobile accident at the end of spring training. Cole was one of the most popular and well-liked players in the organization, and his passing had an adverse effect.

While the Mets may not be loaded at the upper levels of the minor leagues after several years of trades and signing free agents cost them draft picks, the organization had made improvements in the past year or two.

New York also has depth at a few positions, particularly behind the plate. The Mets traded veteran Todd Pratt and gave longtime minor leaguer Vance Wilson a shot at the reserve role behind Mike Piazza. Prospects Jason Phillips, Mike Jacobs and Justin Huber made solid progress during 2001. The draft class also featured three receivers in the first 16 rounds, including Tyler Beuerlein and Brett Kay.

The team's international efforts also continue to pay dividends, though outfielder Tsuyoshi Shinjo went to the Giants for Estes and Escobar went to the Indians. Puerto Rican Dicky Gonzalez pitched well at times in New York while Dominican shortstop Jose Reyes blossomed in his first full season. Korean righthander Jae Weong Seo earned a place in the Futures Game. Huber, an Australian, showed promise behind plate. Japanese righthander Satoru Komiyama, 36, signed and the Mets had their eyes on more foreign recruits.

Mets minor league teams also had some success, and the biggest was in nearby Coney Island. The Brooklyn Cyclones shattered the New York-Penn League attendance record with 289,381 fans, went a league-best 52-24 and were co-champions along with Williamsport.

Organization**Overview**

General manager: Steve Phillips. **Farm director:** Jim Duquette. **Scouting director:** Gary LaRocque.

2001 PERFORMANCE

Class	Team	League	W	L	Pct.	Finish*	Manager
Majors	New York	National	82	80	.506	9th(16)	Bobby Valentine
Triple-A	Norfolk Tides	International	85	57	.599	2nd (14)	John Gibbons
Double-A	Binghamton Mets	Eastern	73	68	.518	6th (12)	Howie Freiling
High A	St. Lucie Mets	Florida State	63	76	.453	13th (14)	Tony Tijerina
Low A	Capital City Bombers	South Atlantic	62	73	.459	11th (16)	Ken Oberkfell
Short-season	Brooklyn Cyclones	New York-Penn	52	24	.684	1st (14)	Edgar Alfonzo
Rookie	Kingsport Mets	Appalachian	31	35	.470	t-5th (10)	Joey Cora
OVERALL 2001 MINOR LEAGUE RECORD			366	333	.524	10th(30)	

*Finish in overall standings (No. of teams in league)

ORGANIZATION LEADERS

BATTING

*AVG	Angel Pagan, Capital City/Brooklyn	.312
R	Chris Basak, Binghamton/St. Lucie	82
H	Ron Acuna, St. Lucie/Capital City	136
TB	**Rob Stratton**, Norfolk/Binghamton	243
2B	Earl Snyder, Norfolk/Binghamton	38
3B	Jose Reyes, Capital City	15
HR	**Rob Stratton**, Norfolk/Binghamton	30
RBI	**Rob Stratton**, Norfolk/Binghamton	86
BB	Marvin Seale, St. Lucie	61
	Earl Snyder, Norfolk/Binghamton	61
SO	**Rob Stratton**, Norfolk/Binghamton	203
SB	Jeff Duncan, Capital City	41

PITCHING

W	Pete Walker, Norfolk	13
L	**Jason Saenz**, Binghamton	15
#ERA	Jaime Cerda, Norfolk/Bing./St. Lucie	1.67
G	Corey Brittan, Norfolk	58
CG	Jeremy Griffiths, Binghamton/St. Lucie	3
SV	Mark Corey, Norfolk/Binghamton	27
IP	Pete Walker, Norfolk	168
BB	Jason Saenz, Binghamton	80
SO	Neal Musser, St. Lucie/Capital City	138

*Minimum 250 At-Bats #Minimum 75 Innings

TOP PROSPECTS OF THE DECADE

1992	Todd Hundley, c
1993	Bobby Jones, rhp
1994	Bill Pulsipher, lhp
1995	Bill Pulsipher, lhp
1996	Paul Wilson, rhp
1997	Jay Payton, of
1998	Grant Roberts, rhp
1999	Alex Escobar, of
2000	Alex Escobar, of
2001	Alex Escobar, of

TOP DRAFT PICKS OF THE DECADE

1992	Preston Wilson, ss
1993	Kirk Presley, rhp
1994	Paul Wilson, rhp
1995	Ryan Jaroncyk, ss
1996	Robert Stratton, of
1997	Geoff Goetz, lhp
1998	Jason Tyner, of
1999	Neal Musser, lhp (2)
2000	Billy Traber, lhp
2001	Aaron Heilman, rhp

Stratton   **Saenz**

BEST TOOLS

Best Hitter for Average	David Wright
Best Power Hitter	Robert Stratton
Fastest Baserunner	Angel Pagan
Best Fastball	Craig House
Best Breaking Ball	Neal Musser
Best Changeup	Pat Strange
Best Control	Jae Weong Seo
Best Defensive Catcher	Jason Phillips
Best Defensive Infielder	Jose Reyes
Best Infield Arm	Jose Reyes
Best Defensive Outfielder	Prentice Redman
Best Outfield Arm	Robert Stratton

PROJECTED 2005 LINEUP

Catcher	Mike Piazza
First Base	Mo Vaughn
Second Base	Roberto Alomar
Third Base	Edgardo Alfonzo
Shortstop	Jose Reyes
Left Field	David Wright
Center Field	Roger Cedeno
Right Field	Jeromy Burnitz
No. 1 Starter	Aaron Heilman
No. 2 Starter	Al Leiter
No. 3 Starter	Pedro Astacio
No. 4 Starter	Shawn Estes
No. 5 Starter	Bruce Chen
Closer	Armando Benitez

ALL-TIME LARGEST BONUSES

Geoff Goetz, 1997	$1,700,000
Paul Wilson, 1994	$1,550,000
Aaron Heilman, 2001	$1,508,750
Jason Tyner, 1998	$1,070,000
Robert Stratton, 1996	$975,000

DraftAnalysis

2001 Draft

Best Pro Debut: OF Frank Corr (17) batted .302-13-46 and led the short-season New York-Penn League in homers, slugging percentage (.594) and extra-base hits (35) with Brooklyn. 2B Danny Garcia (5) hit .321 for the Cyclones and then .301 for Class A Capital City. RHP **Aaron Heilman** (1), sent to high Class A, responded by going 0-1, 2.35 with 39 strikeouts in 38 innings.

Best Athlete: SS Corey Ragsdale (2) and OF Darren Watts (12) are loaded with tools. Ragsdale was an all-state performer for his Arkansas high school basketball team. LHP Jayson Weir (9) draws comparisons to Mike Hampton because both are short, aggressive southpaws from central Florida with potential as outfielders. The Mets will keep Weir on the mound to take advantage of his 88-91 mph fastball and solid breaking ball.

Best Hitter: 3B David Wright (1), one of the top high school bats available, hit .300-4-17 at Rookie-level Kingsport. He should develop true corner-infield power to go with his ability to hit for average.

Best Raw Power: OF Alhaji Turay (2) has plenty of power but needs more discipline at the plate. He has solid all-around tools, with average speed and a strong arm.

Fastest Runner: Watts is a little quicker than Ragsdale, running an effortless 6.6-second 60-yard dash.

Best Defensive Player: The Mets are high on the glovework of Garcia at second base, Ragsdale at shortstop and Wright at third.

Best Fastball: Heilman throws an easy 91-94 mph, maintaining consistent velocity and boring action.

Most Intriguing Background: Unsigned RHP Trevor Hutchinson's (20) brother Chad reached the majors in 2001 with the Cardinals. Unsigned LHP John Sawatski (40) is related to former big league catcher and Texas League president Carl Sawatski.

Heilman

Closest To The Majors: Heilman will begin 2002 in Double-A. He's polished and won't require much time in the minors. LHP Lenny DiNardo (3) also has savvy and command of three pitches.

Best Late-Round Pick: Watts or Corr. 1B Jay Caligiuri (13) hit .328-5-34 and was Brooklyn's MVP.

The One Who Got Away: The Mets signed their first 15 picks, and 18 of 19. Hutchinson was considered a potential first-round pick before he tailed off at the University of California. The Mets didn't sign him after he had a strong summer in the Cape Cod League.

Assessment: The Mets had a balanced draft, mixing hitters and pitchers, high schoolers and collegians. Heilman and possibly DiNardo could help restock the big league rotation in a hurry, while the position players will take longer to develop.

2000 Draft
LHP Billy Traber (1) helped land Roberto Alomar in a trade with Cleveland this winter. No other member of this draft cracks New York's top 15, though the club likes RHPs Bob Keppel (1) and Luz Portobanco (38) and SS Chris Basak (6). **Grade: C**

1999 Draft
LHP Neal Musser (2), the top pick, is the only shining light from this group. OF Angel Pagan (4, draft-and-follow) and RHP Jeremy Griffiths (3) still have a shot. **Grade: D**

1998 Draft
OF Brian Cole (18) was arguably the system's best prospect when he was killed in an auto accident at the end of spring training last year. Jason Tyner (1), traded to Tampa Bay, is no more than a fourth outfielder. Pat Strange (2) and draft-and-follows Jaime Cedra (23) and Ken Chenard (46) rank among the system's better pitchers. **Grade: C**

1997 Draft
This draft's contribution was trade fodder, as LHP Geoff Goetz (1) and 2B/OF Cesar Crespo (3) went to Florida in deals for Mike Piazza and Al Leiter. RHPs Eric Cammack (13), Nick Maness (12) and Tyler Walker (2) are middling prospects. **Grade: C**

Note: Draft analysis prepared by Jim Callis. Numbers in parentheses indicate draft rounds.

. . . His 91-94 mph fastball has incredible movement and bores in on righthanders.

Heilman **Aaron** rhp

Born: Nov. 12, 1978.
Ht.: 6-5. **Wt.:** 220.
Bats: R. **Throws:** R.
School: University of Notre Dame.
Career Transactions: Selected by Mets in first round (18th overall) of 2001 draft; signed July 17, 2001.

After turning down the Twins' overtures as the 31st overall selection in the 2000 draft, Heilman returned to Notre Dame for his senior season. He helped the Fighting Irish to their first-ever No. 1 rank and the Big East Conference regular-season title by going 15-0, 1.74 with 12 complete games and three shutouts. He also completed his degree. Heilman signed six weeks after the Mets made him the 18th overall pick in June and lived up to his billing at Class A St. Lucie, posting a 3-1 strikeout-walk ratio while holding opponents to a .190 average. He would have ranked high on Baseball America's Florida State League Top 10 Prospects list had he pitched enough innings to qualify.

Heilman is a polished pitcher. Mature and focused, he works off his 91-94 mph fastball, which has incredible movement and bores in on righthanders. He also features a plus slider with excellent downward action, along with a decent changeup and splitter. His command is another positive, and he maintains control of all four of his offerings throughout the game with his improved stamina. Scouts love his 6-foot-5, 225-pound frame and his feisty approach with runners in scoring position. His three-quarters delivery is easy and fluid, reducing the stress on his arm, a key trait for a pitcher who will be counted upon to eat innings at higher levels. Heilman has all the makings of a potential workhorse who could be a solid No. 2 or No. 3 starter in the New York rotation. Despite his maturity, he has just seven starts and less than 40 professional innings. His secondary offerings, particularly his changeup, need more consistency. Most scouts don't believe his fastball will add any more velocity, so his 83-84 mph splitter must stay consistent in order for him to get experienced lefthanders out. He made strides with the pitch in college last spring.

Heilman is ready to jump on the fast track to the big leagues. His desire to learn and improve impressed the Mets at St. Lucie and during instructional league. He's slated to open 2002 at Double-A Binghamton and could be a candidate for the New York rotation as soon as 2003.

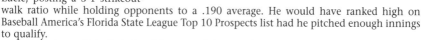

Year	Club (League)	Class	W	L	ERA	G	GS	CG	SV	IP	H	R	ER	BB	SO
2001	St. Lucie (FSL)	A	0	1	2.35	7	7	0	0	38	26	11	10	13	39
MINOR LEAGUE TOTALS			0	1	2.35	7	7	0	0	38	26	11	10	13	39

2. Jose Reyes, ss

Born: June 11, 1983. **Ht.:** 6-0. **Wt.:** 160. **Bats:** B. **Throws:** R. **Career Transactions:** Signed out of Dominican Republic by Mets, Aug. 16, 1999.

DAVID SCHOFIELD

No player made greater strides in the organization than Reyes, the youngest player in a full-season league last year. After hitting .250 at Rookie-level Kingsport in 2000, Reyes placed fifth in the South Atlantic League in hitting, ranked second in the minors in triples and emerged as the league's best defensive shortstop. Managers rated him the second-best prospect in the league. A good contact hitter from both sides of the plate, Reyes can drive the ball and make things happen with his above-average speed. His glove is his forte, as he has outstanding range, a plus arm and soft hands. He committed just 18 errors at Capital City and led Sally League shortstops with a .964 fielding percentage. Reyes has strong legs but needs to add strength to his upper body. He also lacks patience at the plate, but should improve as he gains experience. Some Sally League managers suggested Reyes could jump to the big leagues without much difficulty. The Mets will be patient, but he could open the season in Double-A. With Rey Ordonez out of favor, Reyes will get a shot as soon as he is deemed ready.

Year	Club (League)	Class	AVG	G	AB	R	H	2B	3B	HR	RBI	BB	SO	SB
2000	Kingsport (Appy)	R	.250	49	132	22	33	3	3	0	8	20	37	10
2001	Capital City (SAL)	A	.307	108	407	71	125	22	15	5	48	18	71	30
MINOR LEAGUE TOTALS			.293	157	539	93	158	25	18	5	56	38	108	40

3. Pat Strange, rhp

Born: Aug. 23, 1980. **Ht.:** 6-5. **Wt.:** 243. **Bats:** R. **Throws:** R. **School:** Springfield (Mass.) Central HS. **Career Transactions:** Selected by Mets in second round of 1998 draft; signed July 29, 1998.

RODGER WOOD

The Mets' 2000 minor league pitcher of the year, Strange was more hittable in his second stint in Double-A. He made progress after raising his arm angle to a three-quarters slot. Strange is a sinkerball pitcher who succeeds when he keeps his pitches down in the strike zone. His fastball is clocked consistently at 91-94 mph, and he has impressive command of his changeup. At 6-foot-5 and 245 pounds, he is a potential workhorse. Comparisons to former Mets prospect Bill Pulsipher continue for Strange, in part because of his inconsistent mechanics. Though his violent arm action hasn't led to any injuries to date, some scouts fear he could get hurt unless he makes adjustments. His breaking ball isn't as good as his other two pitches. It's easy to forget Strange didn't celebrate his 21st birthday until the end of the 2001 season. He broke his ankle in the Arizona Fall League, but he'll be invited to big league spring training and is expected to make his major league debut at some point in 2002.

Year	Club (League)	Class	W	L	ERA	G	GS	CG	SV	IP	H	R	ER	BB	SO
1998	Mets (GCL)	R	1	1	1.42	4	4	0	0	19	18	3	3	7	19
1999	Capital City (SAL)	A	12	5	2.63	28	21	2	1	154	138	57	45	29	113
2000	St. Lucie (FSL)	A	10	1	3.58	19	13	2	0	88	78	48	35	32	77
	Binghamton (EL)	AA	4	3	4.55	10	10	0	0	55	62	30	28	30	36
2001	Binghamton (EL)	AA	11	6	4.87	26	24	1	0	153	171	94	83	52	106
	Norfolk (IL)	AAA	1	0	0.00	1	1	0	0	6	4	0	0	1	6
MINOR LEAGUE TOTALS			39	16	3.68	88	73	5	1	475	471	232	194	151	357

4. Jae Weong Seo, rhp

Born: May 24, 1977. **Ht.:** 6-1. **Wt.:** 215. **Bats:** R. **Throws:** R. **Career Transactions:** Signed out of Korea by Mets, Jan. 6, 1998.

RODGER WOOD

After missing nearly two full years following Tommy John surgery in May 1999, Seo emerged as a strong prospect again. He worked his way from Class A to Triple-A and posted a 2.77 ERA, the best of any Mets minor leaguer with more than 100 innings. Seo works off a fastball that reached 90 mph in 2001. His heater was 3-5 mph quicker prior to his surgery, and his velocity should continue to come back. Seo also had success with his splitter and changeup, giving every indication that he will be a solid three-pitch pitcher in the years to come. He has amazing control. The Mets weren't pleased with Seo's conditioning last spring. He gained weight after visiting his native Korea and needed six weeks to get into shape. He went to the Arizona Fall League to work on his conditioning and arm strength, though he pitched just three innings. Manager Bobby Valentine was the driving force behind the signing of Seo in 1997. He impressed Valentine again in 2001 and is on the verge of earning consideration for the Mets rotation.

Year	Club (League)	Class	W	L	ERA	G	GS	CG	SV	IP	H	R	ER	BB	SO
1998	Mets (GCL)	R	0	0	0.00	2	0	0	0	5	4	0	0	0	5
	St. Lucie (FSL)	A	3	1	2.31	8	7	0	0	35	26	13	9	10	37
1999	St. Lucie (FSL)	A	2	0	1.84	3	3	0	0	15	8	3	3	2	14
2000						Did Not Play—Injured									
2001	St. Lucie (FSL)	A	2	3	3.55	6	5	0	0	25	21	11	10	6	19
	Binghamton (EL)	AA	5	1	1.94	12	10	0	0	60	44	14	13	11	47
	Norfolk (IL)	AAA	2	2	3.42	9	9	0	0	47	53	18	18	6	25
MINOR LEAGUE TOTALS			14	7	2.55	40	34	0	0	187	156	59	53	35	147

5. David Wright, 3b

Born: Dec. 20, 1982. **Ht.:** 6-0. **Wt.:** 195. **Bats:** R. **Throws:** R. **School:** Hickory HS, Chesapeake, Va. **Career Transactions:** Selected by Mets in first round (38th overall) of 2001 draft; signed July 12, 2001.

Wright was considered one of the best high school hitters available in the 2001 draft. He adjusted to wood bats easily, with consistent line drives to the gaps. Wright has a strong body, quick wrists and improving swing extension that should allow him to hit for both power and average as his body matures. Many scouts say he has the ability and approach to hit .300 with 30 home runs in the major leagues. He's aggressive and has good mobility at third base. He also runs well for a player his size, and Appalachian League observers raved about his work ethic. Wright simply needs to face better pitching to continue his maturation as a hitter. While some wonder if he can stay at third base, he has the instincts and athleticism to move to a corner outfield position if necessary. Few teams are more conservative with young players than the Mets. With a solid debut under his belt, Wright is expected to move to Capital City in 2002 and should move up this list soon.

Year	Club (League)	Class	AVG	G	AB	R	H	2B	3B	HR	RBI	BB	SO	SB
2001	Kingsport (Appy)	R	.300	36	120	27	36	7	0	4	17	16	30	9
MINOR LEAGUE TOTALS			.300	36	120	27	36	7	0	4	17	16	30	9

6. Satoru Komiyama, rhp

Born: Sept. 15, 1965. **Ht.:** 6-2. **Wt.:** 195. **Bats:** R. **Throws:** R. **Career Transactions:** Signed out of Japan by Mets, Dec. 1, 2001.

After getting more than they expected from outfielder Tsuyoshi Shinjo last season, the Mets returned to the Far East and signed Komiyama to a one-year deal worth $500,000. He had his best season in Japan in 1995, when current Mets manager Bobby Valentine was his skipper with the Chiba Lotte Marines. Komiyama had another strong campaign in 2001, going 12-9, 3.03 in 24 games with the Yokohama Bay Stars. He has been billed as the "Japanese Greg Maddux," which is more hyperbole than anything else. Komiyama does have tremendous control and mixes his five pitches well. He works both sides of the plate, including a liberal use of the black, and rarely falls behind hitters. His fastball resides in the 87-89 mph range but has good movement. He also throws a curveball, changeup, cutter and forkball. Like Maddux, Komiyama gives up singles but is frugal with home runs and walks. A starter for most of his career, his role on the Mets staff will be determined by the team's needs come spring training.

Year	Club (League)	Class	W	L	ERA	G	GS	CG	SV	IP	H	R	ER	BB	SO
1990	Lotte (PL)	JAP	6	10	3.27	30	—	6	2	171	159	70	62	—	126
1991	Lotte (PL)	JAP	10	16	3.95	29	—	15	0	212	219	104	93	—	130
1992	Chiba (PL)	JAP	8	15	3.96	29	—	9	0	173	187	86	76	—	124
1993	Chiba (PL)	JAP	12	14	3.44	27	—	14	0	204	193	90	78	—	160
1994	Chiba (PL)	JAP	3	9	4.24	14	—	3	0	85	81	48	40	—	67
1995	Chiba (PL)	JAP	11	4	2.60	25	—	6	0	187	150	60	54	—	169
1996	Chiba (PL)	JAP	8	13	4.54	25	—	2	0	155	192	86	78	—	90
1997	Chiba (PL)	JAP	11	9	2.49	27	—	3	0	188	186	62	52	—	130
1998	Chiba (PL)	JAP	11	12	3.57	27	—	10	0	202	224	101	80	—	126
1999	Chiba (PL)	JAP	7	10	4.07	21	—	4	0	142	158	74	64	—	96
2000	Yokohama (CL)	JAP	8	11	3.96	26	—	5	0	161	166	72	71	—	108
2001	Yokohama (CL)	JAP	12	9	3.03	24	18	6	0	149	150	55	50	30	74
JAPANESE LEAGUE TOTALS			107	132	3.54	304		83	2	2027	2065	908	798	537	1400

7. Grant Roberts, rhp

Born: Sept. 13, 1977. **Ht.:** 6-3. **Wt.:** 205. **Bats:** R. **Throws:** R. **School:** Grossmont HS, La Mesa, Calif. **Career Transactions:** Selected by Mets in 11th round of 1995 draft; signed June 11, 1995.

The organization's former top prospect, Roberts is approaching a career crossroads. A starter for most of his pro career, Roberts went 0-3, 8.54 in his first five outings at Norfolk in 2001. Not only did it keep him from getting a promotion when injuries struck New York's rotation in May, but it also prompted a move to the bullpen. He showed promise in his new role before tiring at the end of the year. Roberts has a 93-94 mph fastball with excellent movement. It can be overpowering, particularly against righthanders. When he's throwing his curveball and slider for strikes, Roberts does a good job of keeping hitters off balance. Due to an inconsistent release point on his breaking pitches, Roberts struggles with his command. When the going gets tough he becomes a one-pitch pitcher, allowing hitters to sit on his fastball. Roberts also tends to leave his pitches up in the strike zone, making him vulnerable to homers. The Mets were encouraged with the maturity Roberts showed, compared with his brief stint in the majors in 2000. Based on the adjustments he makes in spring training, Roberts could be their fifth starter, part of their bullpen or a member of the Norfolk staff.

Year	Club (League)	Class	W	L	ERA	G	GS	CG	SV	IP	H	R	ER	BB	SO
1995	Mets (GCL)	R	2	1	2.15	11	3	0	0	29	19	13	7	14	24
1996	Kingsport (Appy)	R	9	1	2.10	13	13	2	0	69	43	18	16	37	92
1997	Capital City (SAL)	A	11	3	2.36	22	22	2	0	130	98	37	34	44	122
1998	St. Lucie (FSL)	A	4	5	4.23	17	17	0	0	72	72	37	34	37	70
1999	Binghamton (EL)	AA	7	6	4.87	23	23	0	0	131	135	81	71	49	94
	Norfolk (IL)	AAA	2	1	4.50	5	5	0	0	28	32	15	14	11	30
2000	Norfolk (IL)	AAA	7	8	3.38	25	25	5	0	157	154	67	59	63	115
	New York (NL)	MAJ	0	0	11.57	4	1	0	0	7	11	10	9	4	6
2001	Norfolk (IL)	AAA	3	5	4.52	30	6	0	2	68	80	38	34	19	54
	New York (NL)	MAJ	1	0	3.81	16	0	0	0	26	24	11	11	8	29
MAJOR LEAGUE TOTALS			1	0	5.45	20	1	0	0	33	35	21	20	12	35
MINOR LEAGUE TOTALS			45	30	3.53	146	114	9	2	685	633	306	269	274	601

8. Tyler Yates, rhp

Born: Aug. 7, 1977. **Ht.:** 6-4. **Wt.:** 225. **Bats:** R. **Throws:** R. **School:** University of Hawaii-Hilo. **Career Transactions:** Selected by Athletics in 23rd round of 1998 draft; signed June 10, 1998 . . . Traded by Athletics with LHP Mark Guthrie to Mets for OF David Justice and cash, December 14, 2001.

After three years of working on his mechanics and pitching style, Yates emerged as a candidate for a bullpen job in Oakland. Then the Athletics sent him to the Mets in December as part of the David Justice trade, and he now appears ticketed for a year in Triple-A. A native Hawaiian who pitched for Hawaii-Hilo, Yates was a starter with a mid-80s fastball when he signed. Thanks to development and improved mechanics, he has increased his fastball to the mid-90s. He complements his heater with a plus slider in the mid-80s, giving him a two-pitch repertoire sufficient for relief work. Yates spent his first two full seasons as a middle reliever, then became a closer last season at Double-A Midland and proved highly impressive. He still needs to improve his command, both in terms of throwing strikes and locating his pitches within the strike zone. He has been more hittable than a pitcher with his stuff should be.

Year	Club (League)	Class	W	L	ERA	G	GS	CG	SV	IP	H	R	ER	BB	SO
1998	Athletics (AZL)	R	0	0	3.91	15	0	0	2	23	28	12	10	14	20
	S. Oregon (NWL)	A	0	0	0.00	2	0	0	1	2	2	0	0	0	1
1999	Visalia (Cal)	A	2	5	5.47	47	1	0	4	82	98	64	50	35	74
2000	Modesto (Cal)	A	4	2	2.86	30	0	0	1	57	50	23	18	23	61
	Midland (TL)	AA	1	1	6.15	22	0	0	0	26	28	20	18	15	24
2001	Midland (TL)	AA	4	6	4.31	56	0	0	17	63	66	39	30	27	61
	Sacramento (PCL)	AAA	1	0	0.00	4	0	0	1	5	3	0	0	1	3
MINOR LEAGUE TOTALS			12	14	4.40	176	1	0	26	258	275	158	126	115	244

9. Jaime Cerda, lhp

Born: Oct. 26, 1978. **Ht.:** 6-0. **Wt.:** 175. **Bats:** L. **Throws:** L. **School:** Fresno CC.
Career Transactions: Selected by Mets in 23rd round of 1998 draft; signed May 25,
1999 . . . Placed on disabled list, June 18, 1999 . . . Contract voided, July 20, 1999 . . .
Signed by Mets, July 25, 1999.

Cerda signed as a draft-and-follow in 1999, only to have his original
contract voided because of an injury. He re-signed with the Mets and did-
n't make his pro debut until 2000, posting a 1.27 career ERA and reaching Triple-A. He succeeds with a deceptive delivery and consistency in
throwing strikes. Fearless on the mound, he goes right after hitters and
uses both sides of the plate. The lefty has an average fastball in the 90 mph range with good
movement, along with a decent repertoire of secondary pitches. After rising as rapidly as he
did, Cerda must continue to be consistent at higher levels against more experienced hitters.
Because his game is more finesse than overpowering, he needs to upgrade his changeup and
breaking ball. While Cerda is being penciled in for the Norfolk bullpen in 2002, he could
make his major league debut should the need arise in New York. John Franco is the only
lefty reliever guaranteed to have a job with the Mets.

Year	Club (League)	Class	W	L	ERA	G	GS	CG	SV	IP	H	R	ER	BB	SO
1999					Did Not Play—Injured										
2000	Pittsfield (NY-P)	A	4	1	0.57	20	1	0	5	47	33	6	3	6	51
2001	St. Lucie (FSL)	A	2	1	0.97	28	0	0	6	56	40	8	6	12	56
	Binghamton (EL)	AA	1	0	3.10	12	0	0	3	20	17	7	7	6	22
	Norfolk (IL)	AAA	0	0	3.86	3	0	0	0	5	2	2	2	2	4
MINOR LEAGUE TOTALS			7	2	1.27	63	1	0	14	128	92	23	18	26	133

10. Neal Musser, lhp

Born: Aug. 25, 1980 **Ht.:** 6-2. **Wt.:** 185. **Bats:** L. **Throws:** L. **School:** Oxford (Ind.)
HS. **Career Transactions:** Selected by Mets in second round of 1999 draft; signed June
23, 1999.

Musser boosted his stock as much as any pitcher in the Mets system in
2001. After working just 66 innings in two years, in part because his
weightlifting routine left him stiff and tight, he worked a solid 141
innings between Capital City and St. Lucie. Musser throws an average
fastball and a good changeup, and he has started to show more consistency with his curveball. He has made impressive strides with his command and works ahead of hitters on a regular basis. Some still wonder about Musser's durability. He's not particularly big or strong, and he barely averaged five innings a start after his
promotion to high Class A. It may have just been an anomaly, but Musser started slowly in
2001. His ERA was 5.96 in the first inning of his starts. Musser probably will return to St.
Lucie to begin 2002, with a promotion to Binghamton a strong possibility later in the season. He'll shoot up the prospect list if he continues to progress as rapidly as he did in 2001.

Year	Club (League)	Class	W	L	ERA	G	GS	CG	SV	IP	H	R	ER	BB	SO
1999	Mets (GCL)	R	2	1	2.01	8	7	0	0	31	26	13	7	18	22
2000	Capital City (SAL)	R	3	2	2.10	7	7	0	0	34	33	10	8	6	21
2001	St. Lucie (FSL)	A	3	4	3.55	9	9	0	0	46	45	24	18	19	40
	Capital City (SAL)	A	7	4	2.84	17	17	1	0	95	86	38	30	18	98
MINOR LEAGUE TOTALS			15	11	2.75	41	40	1	0	206	190	85	63	61	181

11. Mark Corey, rhp

Born: Nov. 16, 1974. **Ht.:** 6-3. **Wt.:** 210. **Bats:** R. **Throws:** R. **School:** Edinboro (Pa.) University. **Career**
Transactions: Selected by Reds in fourth round of 1995 draft; signed June 3, 1995 . . . Traded by Reds to
Mets for 2B Ralph Milliard, Feb. 4, 1999.

Corey spent most of his five previous seasons as a starter before becoming one of the top
closers in the minors in 2001. After succeeding in 17 of 19 save situations in Double-A, he
was even more effective following his promotion to Triple-A. That effort earned Corey a cup
of coffee in New York during September and the Mets' minor league pitcher of the year
award. He underwent labrum surgery in 1997, but has shown no ill effects since. His fastball, which remains on the same plane without any natural drop, improved 3-4 mph last
season and clocked as high as 96 mph. Corey is a versatile hurler who can handle a variety
of roles on a pitching staff, but he'll also be 27 this season and only recently has shown the
ingredients necessary to pitch in the major leagues. He must continue to prove that his

recent success wasn't a fluke. The Mets would like for Corey to put together another strong half-season in Triple-A before he joins their bullpen.

Year	Club (League)	Class	W	L	ERA	G	GS	CG	SV	IP	H	R	ER	BB	SO
1995	Princeton (Appy)	R	1	1	3.68	4	3	0	0	15	12	7	6	6	8
1996	Did Not Play—Injured														
1997	Charleston, WV (SAL)	A	8	13	4.57	26	26	1	0	136	169	87	69	42	97
1998	Burlington (Mid)	A	12	6	2.44	20	20	6	0	140	125	55	38	36	109
	Chattanooga (SL)	AA	0	4	8.20	6	6	0	0	26	32	25	24	16	6
	Indianapolis (IL)	AAA	0	1	4.50	1	1	1	0	6	4	3	3	3	2
1999	Binghamton (EL)	AA	7	13	5.40	29	27	0	0	155	175	108	93	64	111
2000	Binghamton (EL)	AA	0	0	1.05	14	2	0	0	26	15	5	3	11	19
	Norfolk (IL)	AAA	3	7	6.79	20	11	0	1	64	80	52	48	29	43
2001	Binghamton (EL)	AA	1	2	1.80	25	0	0	17	35	23	10	7	12	50
	Norfolk (IL)	AAA	8	2	1.47	28	0	0	10	37	24	7	6	22	42
	New York (NL)	MAJ	0	0	16.20	2	0	0	0	2	5	3	3	3	3
MAJOR LEAGUE TOTALS			0	0	16.20	2	0	0	0	2	5	3	3	3	3
MINOR LEAGUE TOTALS			40	49	4.18	173	96	8	28	639	659	359	297	241	487

12. Eric Cammack, rhp

Born: Aug. 14, 1975. **Ht.:** 6-1. **Wt.:** 185. **Bats:** R. **Throws:** R. **School:** Lamar University. **Career Transactions:** Selected by Mets in 13th round of 1997 draft; signed June 9, 1997.

Cammack underwent surgery to remove a bone spur from his right elbow last April, costing him a chance at making an impact in the major leagues during 2001. He missed the entire regular season before making a rehab appearance in instructional league and pitching in winter ball in order to rebuild his arm strength. Despite the setback, the Mets remain confident that Cammack is on the verge of making the jump to Shea Stadium. Surgery took little away from his repertoire, which features a low-90s fastball, curveball, slider and changeup. His offerings become tougher to hit due to his sneaky delivery and his overall feel for pitching, which may be his forte. The Mets are most concerned about Cammack's occasionally erratic control. If he can throw strikes in spring training, he'll be a strong candidate for the New York bullpen.

Year	Club (League)	Class	W	L	ERA	G	GS	CG	SV	IP	H	R	ER	BB	SO
1997	Pittsfield (NY-P)	A	0	1	0.86	23	0	0	8	31	9	4	3	14	32
1998	Capital City (SAL)	A	4	0	2.81	25	0	0	8	32	17	13	10	13	49
	St. Lucie (FSL)	A	3	2	2.02	29	0	0	11	36	22	12	8	14	53
1999	Binghamton (EL)	AA	4	2	2.38	45	0	0	15	57	28	17	15	38	83
	Norfolk (IL)	AAA	0	0	3.12	9	0	0	4	9	7	3	3	1	17
2000	Norfolk (IL)	AAA	6	2	1.70	47	0	0	9	64	38	14	12	31	67
	New York (NL)	MAJ	0	0	6.30	8	0	0	0	10	7	7	7	10	9
2001	Did Not Play—Injured														
MAJOR LEAGUE TOTALS			0	0	6.30	8	0	0	0	10	7	7	7	10	9
MINOR LEAGUE TOTALS			17	7	2.01	178	0	0	55	228	121	63	51	111	301

13. Enrique Cruz, 3b

Born: Nov. 21, 1981. **Ht.:** 6-1. **Wt.:** 175. **Bats:** R. **Throws:** R. **Career Transactions:** Signed out of Dominican Republic by Mets, Aug. 5, 1998.

The Mets no longer are sure what they have in Cruz. Signed for a lofty $400,000, he has been slow to make adjustments. He struggled mightily at Capital City during the early stages of 2000 before being sent to Kingsport, where managers rated him the Appalachian League's second-best prospect. Cruz returned to the South Atlantic League last year and again had difficulty finding his rhythm at the plate and in the field. He got off to a slow start and hit a soft .251. The former shortstop also didn't look smooth in the field while committing 30 errors at the hot corner. The Mets are remaining patient with Cruz, realizing that he's still quite young and has impressive raw tools. He has an excellent arm, above-average speed and promising power potential, though his maturing body has yet to produce extra-base hits on a consistent basis. That may come, however, once Cruz gains a better grasp of the strike zone and gets stronger. His performance in spring training will determine whether he moves up to St. Lucie or reports to Capital City for the third straight season.

Year	Club (League)	Class	AVG	G	AB	R	H	2B	3B	HR	RBI	BB	SO	SB
1999	Mets (GCL)	R	.306	54	183	34	56	14	2	4	24	28	41	0
2000	Capital City (SAL)	A	.185	49	157	19	29	12	0	1	12	25	44	1
	Kingsport (Appy)	R	.251	63	223	35	56	14	0	9	39	26	56	19
2001	Capital City (SAL)	A	.251	124	438	60	110	20	2	9	59	59	106	33
MINOR LEAGUE TOTALS			.251	290	1001	148	251	60	4	23	134	138	247	53

14. Ken Chenard, rhp

Born: Aug. 30, 1978. **Ht.:** 6-3. **Wt.:** 185. **Bats:** R. **Throws:** R. **School:** Fullerton (Calif.) JC. **Career Transactions:** Selected by Mets in 46th round of 1998 draft; signed May 12, 1999.

Like Eric Cammack, Chenard is coming off surgery that all but ruined his 2001 season. He saw some action in instructional league, and the Mets believe he'll be back to full strength in March. He has outstanding potential and will shoot up this list once he proves he's healthy. That has been a challenge to date, for Chenard was shut down twice during the 2000 season with shoulder soreness associated with a lesion attached to his labrum. Now that the situation appears to be resolved, Chenard could return to the fast track. He has a low-90s fastball with outstanding movement, an above-average curveball and a changeup. Since signing as a draft-and-follow, he has averaged more than a strikeout per inning. Command remains his biggest obstacle, which he'll try to address this year in high Class A.

Year	Club (League)	Class	W	L	ERA	G	GS	CG	SV	IP	H	R	ER	BB	SO
1999	Kingsport (Appy)	R	6	3	3.07	14	13	1	0	76	64	32	26	25	80
2000	Capital City (SAL)	A	4	5	2.86	21	21	0	0	94	75	39	30	48	112
2001	Capital City (SAL)	A	0	1	4.50	4	4	0	0	16	14	8	8	8	12
	St. Lucie (FSL)	A	0	2	37.80	2	2	0	0	2	3	7	7	4	2
MINOR LEAGUE TOTALS			10	11	3.39	41	40	1	0	188	156	86	71	85	206

15. Nick Maness, rhp

Born: Oct. 17, 1978. **Ht.:** 6-4. **Wt.:** 210. **Bats:** R. **Throws:** R. **School:** North Moore HS, Robbins, N.C. **Career Transactions:** Selected by Mets in 12th round of 1997 draft; signed June 12, 1997.

No player in the organization was more affected by Brian Cole's death than Maness, his best friend. After an impressive showing in spring training which earned praise from Mets manager Bobby Valentine, Maness battled through a trying Double-A season. His fastball, which had been in the low 90s in the past, dropped to the high 80s. He did impress New York's brass by pitching well over his final five starts. Maness always has been considered an emotional pitcher with inconsistent mechanics who can be unhittable when everything is in sync. In addition to his fastball, he throws an above-average changeup and a modest curveball. Following his difficult season, the Mets hope Maness can regain his 2000 form this year.

Year	Club (League)	Class	W	L	ERA	G	GS	CG	SV	IP	H	R	ER	BB	SO
1997	Mets (GCL)	R	3	2	3.02	11	6	0	0	45	52	25	15	20	54
1998	Kingsport (Appy)	R	5	3	4.48	13	13	0	0	64	68	41	32	30	76
1999	Capital City (SAL)	A	5	6	4.95	23	22	0	0	107	92	74	59	57	99
2000	St. Lucie (FSL)	A	11	7	3.22	26	25	0	0	145	116	58	52	68	124
	Binghamton (EL)	AA	1	0	1.93	2	1	0	0	9	8	2	2	4	3
2001	Binghamton (EL)	AA	6	12	4.97	28	26	1	0	143	168	94	79	65	107
MINOR LEAGUE TOTALS			31	30	4.19	103	93	1	0	514	504	294	239	244	463

16. Tyler Walker, rhp

Born: May 15, 1976. **Ht.:** 6-3. **Wt.:** 225. **Bats:** R. **Throws:** R. **School:** University of California. **Career Transactions:** Selected by Mets in second round of 1997 draft; signed July 29, 1997.

Walker earned a spot on the Mets' 40-man roster after a breakthrough season in 2000. A torn labrum in his right shoulder, however, kept him sidelined for six months. He returned to the mound in Double-A last June, having shed more than 30 pounds after undergoing an intense conditioning regimen. The weight loss and surgery did nothing to reduce Walker's velocity, as he consistently threw in the low 90s. As a college closer, he touched 96 mph. His fastball makes his sweeping curveball and above-average changeup even more effective. He's intelligent and has a good feel for pitching. He'll open 2002 season in Triple-A, where the overall consistency of his pitches will determine whether his future lies as a starter or reliever.

Year	Club (League)	Class	W	L	ERA	G	GS	CG	SV	IP	H	R	ER	BB	SO
1997	Mets (GCL)	R	0	0	1.00	5	0	0	3	9	8	1	1	2	9
	Pittsfield (NY-P)	A	0	0	13.50	1	0	0	0	1	2	2	1	1	1
1998	Capital City (SAL)	A	5	5	4.12	34	13	0	1	116	122	63	53	38	110
1999	St. Lucie (FSL)	A	6	5	2.94	13	13	2	0	80	64	31	26	29	64
	Binghamton (EL)	AA	6	4	6.22	13	13	0	0	68	78	49	47	32	59
2000	Binghamton (EL)	AA	7	6	2.75	22	22	0	0	121	82	43	37	55	111
	Norfolk (IL)	AAA	1	3	2.39	5	5	0	0	26	29	7	7	9	17
2001	St. Lucie (FSL)	A	0	2	8.04	4	4	0	0	16	19	14	14	3	11
	Binghamton (EL)	AA	1	0	0.40	4	3	0	0	22	9	2	1	13	13
	Norfolk (IL)	AAA	3	2	4.02	8	8	0	0	40	34	19	18	8	35
MINOR LEAGUE TOTALS			29	27	3.71	109	81	2	4	498	447	231	205	190	430

17. Jason Phillips, c

Born: Sept. 27, 1976. **Ht.:** 6-1. **Wt.:** 180. **Bats:** R. **Throws:** R. **School:** San Diego State University. **Career Transactions:** Selected by Mets in 24th round of 1997 draft; signed June 11, 1997.

Phillips continued to show last year that he's the top catching prospect in the organization. A classic catch-and-throw receiver who was named the Double-A Eastern League's best defensive catcher, Phillips earned a late-season callup to New York after hitting a combined .295 with 14 home runs between Norfolk and Binghamton. The Mets are extremely pleased with the way Phillips has become more of an offensive threat over the past couple of seasons. He should continue to have some pop in the big leagues, and is expected to be a tough out in the bottom half of the batting order. His strength centers on his ability to call games and work with pitchers. With the way he has made steady progress in all phases of his game, Phillips just needs to put together a full season of similar success in Triple-A this year. Should he meet that challenge, Phillips could be the catcher who pushes Mike Piazza to first base.

Year	Club (League)	Class	AVG	G	AB	R	H	2B	3B	HR	RBI	BB	SO	SB
1997	Pittsfield (NY-P)	A	.206	48	155	15	32	9	0	2	17	13	24	4
1998	Capital City (SAL)	A	.271	69	251	36	68	15	1	5	37	23	35	5
	St. Lucie (FSL)	A	.464	8	28	4	13	2	0	0	2	2	1	0
1999	St. Lucie (FSL)	A	.258	81	283	36	73	12	1	9	48	23	28	0
	Binghamton (EL)	AA	.227	39	141	13	32	5	0	7	23	13	20	0
2000	St. Lucie (FSL)	A	.276	80	297	53	82	21	0	6	41	23	19	1
	Binghamton (EL)	AA	.388	27	98	16	38	4	0	0	13	7	9	0
2001	Binghamton (EL)	AA	.293	93	317	42	93	21	0	11	55	31	25	0
	Norfolk (IL)	AAA	.303	19	66	8	20	2	0	2	14	7	8	0
	New York (NL)	MAJ	.143	6	7	2	1	1	0	0	0	0	1	0
MAJOR LEAGUE TOTALS			.143	6	7	2	1	1	0	0	0	0	1	0
MINOR LEAGUE TOTALS			.276	464	1636	223	451	91	2	42	250	142	169	10

18. Bob Keppel, rhp

Born: June 11, 1982. **Ht.:** 6-5. **Wt.:** 185. **Bats:** R. **Throws:** R. **School:** DeSmet HS, St. Louis. **Career Transactions:** Selected by Mets in first round (36th overall) of 2000 draft; signed July 7, 2000.

Keppel showed good poise, outstanding command and the ability to work both sides of the plate in his first full season in the pro ranks to emerge as the steadiest starter at Capital City last year. He gained more consistency with his low-90s fastball, which features excellent sinking action. He also threw his changeup for strikes and made encouraging progress with his developing curveball. The lone negative was his slider, which had been his best pitch the year before. He started gripping the pitch too hard, thereby making it more of a flat cutter than a slider, though he appeared to have regained his feel for the pitch during instructional league. The 36th overall pick in the 2000 draft, Keppel has done an impressive job of putting together a solid repertoire and could be on the verge of a breakout season this year in high Class A.

Year	Club (League)	Class	W	L	ERA	G	GS	CG	SV	IP	H	R	ER	BB	SO
2000	Kingsport (Appy)	R	1	2	6.83	8	6	0	0	29	31	22	22	13	29
2001	Capital City (SAL)	A	6	7	3.11	26	20	1	0	124	118	58	43	25	87
MINOR LEAGUE TOTALS			7	9	3.82	34	26	1	0	153	149	80	65	38	116

19. Chris Basak, ss

Born: Dec. 6, 1978. **Ht.:** 6-2. **Wt.:** 185. **Bats:** R. **Throws:** R. **School:** University of Illinois. **Career Transactions:** Selected by Mets in sixth round of 2000 draft; signed June 20, 2000.

The Mets rarely allow a drafted player to bypass low Class A, but the team made an exception with Basak last year. After he led the short-season New York-Penn League with a .349 batting average and hit .412 during a short stint at St. Lucie in 2000, Basak returned to the Florida State League at the beginning of last season. He again finished strong, hitting .372 after a late-August promotion to Double-A. Basak is a tough and aggressive player whose game is better than the sum of his tools. With his strike-zone judgment and willingness to play within himself, he has the ability to bat at the top of the lineup. His hands and footwork are outstanding at shortstop, his range is good and his arm is average yet strong enough for throws from the hole. Basak is also an intelligent player who comes to the ballpark ready to play every day. While the Mets would have liked him to hit higher than .233 at St. Lucie, he should stay in Double-A in 2002 and continue his ascent as a steady infielder and potential utilityman.

Year	Club (League)	Class	AVG	G	AB	R	H	2B	3B	HR	RBI	BB	SO	SB
2000	Pittsfield (NY-P)	A	.349	63	249	46	87	18	4	0	15	26	36	32
	St. Lucie (FSL)	A	.412	4	17	2	7	1	0	0	3	4	2	3
2001	St. Lucie (FSL)	A	.233	126	472	71	110	19	4	4	46	47	125	30
	Binghamton (EL)	AA	.372	13	43	11	16	6	1	1	7	3	10	2
MINOR LEAGUE TOTALS			.282	206	781	130	220	44	9	5	71	80	173	67

20. Lenny DiNardo, lhp

Born: Sept. 19, 1979. **Ht.:** 6-4. **Wt.:** 190. **Bats:** L. **Throws:** L. **School:** Stetson University. **Career Transactions:** Selected by Mets in third round of 2001 draft; signed July 14, 2001.

Based on his performance in 2000, when he went 21-1 between Stetson and Team USA, DiNardo looked like a first-round pick in the 2001 draft. Then his stock slipped as a junior, when his velocity dropped from the low 90s to the mid-80s. After the Mets took him in the third round, he showed an increase in arm strength during his stay in the New York-Penn League. His fastball has above-average movement, and he also throws a solid changeup and decent slider. DiNardo has a thorough understanding of how to pitch and sets up hitters by using all of his pitches, which should allow him to adapt to pro ball without too much difficulty. The Mets also like DiNardo's competitiveness and his desire to go deep into games. Some scouts wonder if his stuff is good enough to succeed at higher levels, and he needs to use his height to pitch on a downward plane and keep the ball down in the strike zone. When his pitches stay up, he doesn't have enough pure stuff to avoid getting clobbered. New York officials are confident DiNardo has the overall package to reach the majors.

Year	Club (League)	Class	W	L	ERA	G	GS	CG	SV	IP	H	R	ER	BB	SO
2001	Brooklyn (NY-P)	A	1	2	2.00	9	5	0	0	36	26	10	8	17	40
MINOR LEAGUE TOTALS			1	2	2.00	9	5	0	0	36	26	10	8	17	40

21. Craig House, rhp

Born: July 8, 1977. **Ht.:** 6-2. **Wt.:** 210. **Bats:** R. **Throws:** R. **School:** University of Memphis. **Career Transactions:** Selected by Rockies in 12th round of 1999 draft; signed June 18, 1999 . . . Traded by Rockies with OF Ross Gload to Mets, as part of three-way trade in which Rockies acquired OF Benny Agbayani, 3B Todd Zeile and cash from Mets, Brewers acquired IF Lenny Harris and LHP Glendon Rusch from Mets, Mets acquired OF Jeromy Burnitz, IF Lou Collier, RHP Jeff D'Amico, OF Mark Sweeney and cash from Brewers, and Brewers acquired OF Alex Ochoa from Rockies, Jan. 21, 2001.

House made a rapid climb, getting to the big leagues slightly more than a year after he was drafted. But big leaguers weren't intimidated by his wild mechanics and he wound up spending the entire 2001 season in Triple-A. House has a deceptive delivery with his body parts seeming to go in totally different directions, and he hops towards the plate when he lets go of the ball. Converted to a reliever once he turned pro, House has a fastball that reaches the upper 90s, a mid-80s slider and a changeup that freezes hitters. The problem is he can't throw his pitches for strikes. He was exposed by major leaguer hitters, who took pitches and let House put himself behind in the count. He has been asked to iron out his herky-jerky mechanics but the adjustments have been difficult. House shows flashes of progress, then reverts to the style he says is more comfortable. If he masters the strike zone, he has the stuff to be a dominant closer. The Mets acquired House in a three-team, 11-player trade with the Brewers and Rockies in January. He most likely will return to Triple-A for a second full season in 2002.

Yr	Club (League)	Class	W	L	ERA	G	GS	CG	SV	IP	H	R	ER	BB	SO
1999	Portland (NWL)	A	2	1	2.08	26	0	0	11	35	28	14	8	14	58
2000	Salem (Car)	A	2	0	2.25	13	0	0	8	16	7	4	4	10	24
	Carolina (SL)	AA	0	2	3.80	18	0	0	9	21	14	11	9	15	28
	Colo. Spr. (PCL)	AAA	0	0	3.24	8	0	0	4	8	6	4	3	2	8
	Colorado (NL)	MAJ	1	1	7.24	16	0	0	0	14	13	11	11	17	8
2001	Colo. Spr. (PCL)	AAA	2	2	4.45	54	0	0	6	59	50	32	29	31	62
MAJOR LEAGUE TOTALS			1	1	7.24	16	0	0	0	14	13	11	11	17	8
MINOR LEAGUE TOTALS			6	5	3.43	119	0	0	38	139	105	65	53	72	180

22. Adam Walker, lhp

Born: May 28, 1976. **Ht.:** 6-7. **Wt.:** 210. **Bats:** L. **Throws:** L. **School:** University of Mississippi. **Career Transactions:** Selected by Phillies in 27th round of 1997 draft; signed June 9, 1997 . . . Traded by Phillies with LHP Bruce Chen to Mets for LHP Dennis Cook and RHP Turk Wendell, July 27, 2001.

The Mets acquired Walker along with Bruce Chen from Philadelphia in exchange for veteran relievers Dennis Cook and Turk Wendell just prior to the July 31 trading deadline.

Walker, who was on the disabled list with an elbow strain earlier in the year, experienced elbow soreness shortly after switching organizations and missed the season's final month. When healthy, Walker dominated the Eastern League. He posted a 1.88 ERA and threw a one-hitter and a no-hitter (the first nine-inning no-no in Reading history) in consecutive June starts. While he has impressive size at 6-foot-7, Walker is far from overpowering. He retires hitters by changing speeds, locating his pitches and making adjustments as the game progresses. Walker throws a sneaky fastball in the 86-88 mph range that sets up his solid changeup. His breaking ball could use some work, especially if he hopes to remain a starter. He'll spend 2002 in the Norfolk rotation.

Year	Club (League)	Class	W	L	ERA	G	GS	CG	SV	IP	H	R	ER	BB	SO
1997	Martinsville (Appy)	R	0	5	6.28	21	2	0	2	29	32	28	20	11	30
1998	Piedmont (SAL)	A	9	0	2.04	15	15	0	0	84	60	21	19	21	114
1999	Clearwater (FSL)	A	9	7	3.93	26	25	3	0	149	156	80	65	52	100
2000	Piedmont (SAL)	A	6	1	2.05	8	8	0	0	48	37	11	11	14	50
	Clearwater (FSL)	A	9	8	3.08	18	17	1	0	114	116	50	39	39	87
2001	Reading (EL)	AA	7	4	1.88	15	15	3	0	91	50	22	19	28	81
	Binghamton (EL)	AA	0	0	0.00	2	2	0	0	4	3	0	0	2	7
MINOR LEAGUE TOTALS			40	25	3.00	105	84	7	2	519	454	212	173	167	469

23. Angel Pagan, of

Born: July 2, 1981. **Ht.:** 6-1. **Wt.:** 175. **Bats:** B. **Throws:** R. **School:** Indian River (Fla.) CC. **Career Transactions:** Selected by Mets in fourth round of 1999 draft; signed May 28, 2000.

Pagan showed some tremendous promise in his first full year as a pro. A fourth-round pick in 1999 who signed as a draft-and-follow a week prior to the 2000 draft, Pagan had his debut season limited by a forearm injury after 19 games at Kingsport. He opened last year in extended spring training before getting a brief taste of the South Atlantic League and then reporting to short-season Brooklyn. He tied for the New York-Penn League lead in stolen bases and ranked eighth in batting. Pagan is a speed-oriented player who puts constant pressure on the defense with his ability to drop down a bunt or drive the ball in the gaps. His defensive skills are outstanding in center field, and his arm rates slightly above average. The Mets believe Pagan could develop power from both sides of the plate, though he has yet to hit a home run in 367 pro at-bats. He needs to add strength to his upper body, become more patient at the plate and make more solid contact instead of slapping at every pitch. Nevertheless, Pagan is a top-of-the-order hitter who should be the starting center fielder at Capital City in 2002.

Year	Club (League)	Class	AVG	G	AB	R	H	2B	3B	HR	RBI	BB	SO	SB
2000	Kingsport (Appy)	R	.361	19	72	13	26	5	1	0	8	6	8	6
2001	Brooklyn (NY-P)	A	.315	62	238	46	75	10	2	0	15	22	30	30
	Capital City (SAL)	A	.298	15	57	4	17	1	1	0	5	6	5	3
MINOR LEAGUE TOTALS			.322	96	367	63	118	16	4	0	28	34	43	39

24. Justin Huber, c

Born: July 1, 1982. **Ht.:** 6-2. **Wt.:** 190. **Bats:** R. **Throws:** R. **Career Transactions:** Signed out of Australia by Mets, July 26, 2000.

The 19-year-old Huber exceeded most expectations in 2001, the first professional season in the U.S. for the Australia native discovered by Mets assistant GM Omar Minaya. Huber led Kingsport in home runs and RBIs and ranked sixth in the Appalachian League batting race. The Mets were pleasantly surprised with the polish Huber showed, particularly with his efforts behind the plate. He does a good job of calling a game and working with pitchers. He also stands out for his mobility and ability to block balls in the dirt. He has an above-average arm and remained strong throughout the course of the humid Southern summer. Scouts like Huber's gritty, hard-nosed style and believe he has the ideal makeup to succeed as a catcher. Huber will move to full-season ball in 2002 at Capital City.

Year	Club (League)	Class	AVG	G	AB	R	H	2B	3B	HR	RBI	BB	SO	SB
2001	Kingsport (Appy)	R	.314	47	159	24	50	11	1	7	31	17	42	4
	Brooklyn (NY-P)	A	.000	3	9	0	0	0	0	0	0	0	4	0
	St. Lucie (FSL)	A	.000	2	6	0	0	0	0	0	0	0	2	0
MINOR LEAGUE TOTALS			.287	52	174	24	50	11	1	7	31	17	48	4

25. Luz Portobanco, rhp

Born: Sept. 15, 1979. **Ht.:** 6-3. **Wt.:** 205. **Bats:** R. **Throws:** R. **School:** Miami-Dade CC. **Career Transactions:** Selected by Mets in 36th round of 2000 draft; signed June 15, 2000.

After opening last season in extended spring training, Portobanco made steady progress in the New York-Penn League, where he finished seventh in ERA. He throws three potentially above-average pitches, including a lively fastball in the low 90s, a changeup and a curveball. Both his command and control are solid, and he has excellent size on the mound that should enable him to work longer into his starts as he gains size and strength. The worst aspect of Portobanco's game is his approach. He isn't aggressive and tends to pitch backwards, working off his offspeed pitches instead of his fastball. He struck out only 52 batters in 71 innings, which can be attributed to his unwillingness to go after hitters. Portobanco has the necessary pitches to succeed at higher levels and should continue his progress in low Class A this year.

Year	Club (League)	Class	W	L	ERA	G	GS	CG	SV	IP	H	R	ER	BB	SO
2000	Kingsport (Appy)	R	3	3	4.89	16	9	0	0	57	62	43	31	18	38
2001	Brooklyn (NY-P)	A	5	3	2.04	13	12	0	0	71	51	20	16	29	52
MINOR LEAGUE TOTALS			8	6	3.31	29	21	0	0	128	113	63	47	47	90

26. Craig Brazell, 1b

Born: May 10, 1980. **Ht.:** 6-3. **Wt.:** 195. **Bats:** L. **Throws:** R. **School:** Jefferson Davis HS, Montgomery, Ala. **Career Transactions:** Selected by Mets in fifth round of 1998 draft; signed June 4, 1998.

Brazell blossomed into a dangerous offensive player in 2001, leading Capital City in home runs and RBIs during his second season in the South Atlantic League. The son of Ted Brazell, who played and coached 14 years in the Tigers system, Craig drove the ball consistently from the left side of the plate, learned to go to the opposite field when necessary, and improved his defense at first base. The lone negative came when he dislocated his knee July 19 and missed the remainder of the season. At the time of his injury, Brazell ranked among the SAL leaders in several offensive categories. He had been unstoppable with the bases loaded, going 5-for-5 with a home run and 14 RBIs. An aggressive hitter who did a better job with his pitch selection last year, Brazell must continue to be selective. He's slated to move up to high Class A this season.

Year	Club (League)	Class	AVG	G	AB	R	H	2B	3B	HR	RBI	BB	SO	SB
1998	Mets (GCL)	R	.298	13	47	6	14	3	1	1	6	2	13	0
1999	Kingsport (Appy)	R	.385	59	221	27	85	16	1	6	39	7	34	6
2000	Capital City (SAL)	A	.241	112	406	35	98	28	0	8	57	15	82	3
2001	Capital City (SAL)	A	.308	83	331	51	102	25	5	19	72	15	74	0
MINOR LEAGUE TOTALS			.298	267	1005	119	299	72	7	34	174	39	203	9

27. Jeremy Griffiths, rhp

Born: March 22, 1978. **Ht.:** 6-6. **Wt.:** 230. **Bats:** R. **Throws:** R. **School:** University of Toledo. **Career Transactions:** Selected by Mets in third round of 1999 draft; signed June 9, 1999.

For the third time in as many pro seasons, Griffiths' won-lost record didn't reflect how well he pitched. He formed an impressive one-two punch with Billy Traber (since traded to the Indians in the Roberto Alomar deal) in the St. Lucie rotation. Standing 6-foot-7 and weighing 230 pounds, Griffiths showed more consistency with his mechanics, resulting in better control of his low-90s fastball, which he throws on a nice downward plane. He also displayed improvement with his changeup and slider. Before the Australian winter league canceled its season, New York had hoped to send Griffiths there so he could continue working on the command of his secondary offerings. With his improving production and impressive maturity, it wouldn't be a surprise to scouts if he puts together a big year in 2002. He'll begin in Double-A, where he pitched very well in two late-season starts.

Year	Club (League)	Class	W	L	ERA	G	GS	CG	SV	IP	H	R	ER	BB	SO
1999	Kingsport (Appy)	R	3	5	3.30	14	14	1	0	76	68	40	28	36	74
2000	Capital City (SAL)	A	7	12	4.34	26	26	0	0	129	120	78	62	39	138
2001	St. Lucie (FSL)	A	7	8	3.75	23	20	2	0	132	126	63	55	35	95
	Binghamton (EL)	AA	2	0	0.69	2	2	1	0	13	8	3	1	4	12
MINOR LEAGUE TOTALS			19	25	3.75	65	62	4	0	350	322	184	146	114	319

28. Jake Joseph, rhp

Born: Jan. 24, 1978. **Ht.:** 6-1. **Wt.:** 210. **Bats:** R. **Throws:** R. **School:** Cosumnes River (Calif.) JC. **Career Transactions:** Selected by Mets in second round of 1999 draft; signed July 7, 1999.

The Mets were a little disappointed by Joseph's performance during 2001. He had a down year in the Florida State League, winning just four of 16 decisions with a 5.34 ERA in a pitcher's league. His biggest problem was that the movement on his pitches wasn't as impressive as it had been previously, making him more hittable. New York was pleased with Joseph's efforts during instructional league and believes his pitches improved considerably. Joseph uses his low-90s fastball and slider almost exclusively, and he needs to develop an offspeed pitch if he hopes to remain a starter. He also must improve his control. Joseph will have to show in spring training that he's ready to make the jump to Double-A.

Year	Club (League)	Class	W	L	ERA	G	GS	CG	SV	IP	H	R	ER	BB	SO
1999	Pittsfield (NY-P)	A	3	2	2.91	11	6	0	1	43	35	19	14	27	26
2000	Capital City (SAL)	A	4	3	2.85	15	15	0	0	85	81	45	27	29	59
2001	St. Lucie (FSL)	A	4	12	5.34	25	24	0	0	128	162	93	76	52	69
MINOR LEAGUE TOTALS			11	17	4.10	51	45	0	1	257	278	157	117	108	154

29. Robert Stratton, of

Born: Oct. 7, 1977. **Ht.:** 6-2. **Wt.:** 251. **Bats:** R. **Throws:** R. **School:** San Marcos HS, Santa Barbara, Calif. **Career Transactions:** Selected by Mets in first round (13th overall) of 1996 draft; signed July 12, 1996 . . . Traded by Mets with LHP Jesus Sanchez and RHP A.J. Burnett to Marlins for LHP Al Leiter and 2B Ralph Milliard, Feb. 6, 1998 . . . Traded by Marlins to Mets for RHP Brandon Villafuerte and a player to be named, March 20, 1998; Marlins acquired 2B Cesar Crespo to complete trade (Sept. 14, 1998).

Stratton stands out in an organization that isn't deep with power. The 13th overall pick in the 1996 draft, he's one of the most feared home run hitters in the minors, having gone deep 29 times in each of the past two seasons. That power comes with a price, as he set an Eastern League record with 201 strikeouts last year after whiffing 180 times in 2000. For his career, Stratton has averaged one strikeout every 2.4 trips to the plate while batting .247. He has trouble with most types of breaking balls, and his strike-zone judgment has improved little since he was drafted. Stratton is an average outfielder with a strong, accurate arm that's suitable for right field. He also possesses good mobility for a big player. Stratton has advanced one step at a time in the organization over the past four years, and is line for a promotion to Triple-A this season. If he can reduce his strikeouts while maintaining his power, Stratton soon could get a look in New York.

Year	Club (League)	Class	AVG	G	AB	R	H	2B	3B	HR	RBI	BB	SO	SB
1996	Mets (GCL)	R	.254	17	59	5	15	2	0	2	9	2	22	3
1997	Kingsport (Appy)	R	.249	63	245	51	61	11	5	15	50	19	94	11
1998	Mets (GCL)	R	.261	12	46	4	12	1	0	3	13	2	15	1
	Pittsfield (NY-P)	A	.226	34	124	18	28	5	4	6	18	11	55	3
1999	Capital City (SAL)	A	.274	95	318	58	87	17	3	21	60	48	112	7
2000	St. Lucie (FSL)	A	.228	108	381	61	87	18	4	29	87	60	180	3
2001	Binghamton (EL)	AA	.248	133	483	70	120	30	1	29	83	53	201	9
	Norfolk (IL)	AAA	.143	2	7	1	1	0	0	1	3	0	2	0
MINOR LEAGUE TOTALS			.247	464	1663	268	411	84	17	106	323	195	681	37

30. Prentice Redman, of

Born: Aug. 23, 1979. **Ht.:** 6-3. **Wt.:** 185. **Bats:** R. **Throws:** R. **School:** Bevill State (Ala.) CC. **Career Transactions:** Selected by Mets in 10th round of 1999 draft; signed June 4, 1999.

Last year, Redman started to show some aggressiveness that the Mets had been longing to see since drafting him in 1999. Pushed to the Florida State League to open the season, Redman overcame a slow start to earn a trip to the FSL all-star game, where he was named MVP. Redman gained confidence from the recognition and developed into one of the organization's most pleasant surprises. His quickness and baserunning ability are his biggest assets. Redman must continue to try to make things happen in all phases of the game. He needs to make better contact and add some strength so he can drive balls better. He also can improve his defense by upgrading his below-average arm strength and his routes on fly balls and hits in the gaps. Redman will have the opportunity to hone those aspects of his game in Double-A this year.

Year	Club (League)	Class	AVG	G	AB	R	H	2B	3B	HR	RBI	BB	SO	SB
1999	Kingsport (Appy)	R	.295	58	200	40	59	14	1	6	29	24	42	16
2000	Capital City (SAL)	A	.260	131	497	60	129	19	1	3	46	52	90	26
2001	St. Lucie (FSL)	A	.261	132	495	70	129	18	1	9	65	42	91	29
MINOR LEAGUE TOTALS			.266	321	1192	170	317	51	3	18	140	118	223	71

NEW YORK Yankees

TOP 30 PROSPECTS

1. Drew Henson, 3b
2. Nick Johnson, 1b
3. Brandon Claussen, lhp
4. John-Ford Griffin, of
5. Juan Rivera, of
6. Sean Henn, lhp
7. Marcus Thames, of
8. Erick Almonte, ss
9. Jason Arnold, rhp
10. Bronson Sardinha, ss
11. David Martinez, lhp
12. Alex Graman, lhp
13. Adrian Hernandez, rhp
14. Deivi Mendez, ss
15. Matt Smith, lhp
16. Jon Skaggs, rhp
17. Manny Acosta, rhp
18. Edison Reynoso, rhp
19. Dioner Navarro, c
20. Julio DePaula, rhp
21. Adam Roller, rhp
22. Danny Borrell, lhp
23. Yhency Brazoban, of
24. Chase Wright, lhp
25. John Rodriguez, of
26. Aaron Rifkin, 1b
27. Jason Grove, of
28. Elvis Corporan, 3b
29. Jason Anderson, rhp
30. Richard Brown, of

By Josh Boyd

D espite reaching their fifth World Series in six years, the Yankees began remodeling their aging lineup shortly after Jay Bell crossed home plate with the Diamond-backs' first championship.

Third baseman Scott Brosius (35) and right fielder Paul O'Neill (38) retired, left fielder Chuck Knoblauch (33) and first baseman Tino Martinez (34) weren't re-signed, and DH David Justice (35) was traded. Hitting coach Gary Denbo was fired and replaced with Rick Down. General manager Brian Cashman, fresh off signing a three-year extension, struck quickly to sign free agents Jason Giambi, Steve Karsay and Rondell White and trade for Robin Ventura.

Martinez' departure from the Bronx was supposed to signal the arrival of three-time No. 1 prospect Nick Johnson at first base. Then Giambi came aboard—though his presence doesn't preclude the potential for a fully homegrown infield in the future. While Johnson is expected to start off as DH, he's clearly the superior first baseman and should get more time there as the 2002 season goes on.

Ventura fills the void left by Brosius, and more important, provides another crucial year of development for Drew Henson in Triple-A. Henson ranks as the organization's top prospect based on his ceiling, but he's not ready for the majors quite yet.

Despite all their activity on the open market, a large part of the Yankees' success came from the farm system, and keeping it well stocked allowed them to acquire several key players in their championship run. The two deadline deals Cashman made last summer backfired, however, when he turned shortstop D'Angelo Jimenez and righthander Ricardo Aramboles into disappointing relievers Jay Witasick and Mark Wohlers. Jimenez will be a middle-infield starter for the Padres, and Aramboles ranks as Cincinnati's No. 4 prospect.

While some say Johnson, Henson and outfielders Juan Rivera and Marcus Thames could be sufficient replacements for the departed veterans, the Yankees rarely hand such heavy responsibilities to rookies. Second baseman Alfonso Soriano was an exception. He finished third in the American League rookie of the year balloting and delivered clutch home runs in both the AL Championship Series and the World Series.

OrganizationOverview

General manager: Brian Cashman. **Farm Director:** Mark Newman. **Scouting director:** Lin Garrett.

2001 PERFORMANCE

Class	Team	League	W	L	Pct.	Finish*	Manager
Majors	New York	American	95	65	.594	3rd (14)	Joe Torre
Triple-A	Columbus Clippers	International	67	76	.469	9th (14)	Trey Hillman
Double-A	Norwich Navigators	Eastern	83	59	.585	3rd (12)	Stump Merrill
High A	Tampa Yankees	Florida State	77	62	.554	2nd (12)	Brian Butterfield
Low A	Greensboro Bats	South Atlantic	70	70	.500	8th (16)	Mitch Seoane
Short-season	Staten Island Yankees	New York-Penn	48	28	.632	3rd (14)	Dave Jorn
Rookie	GCL Yankees	Gulf Coast	35	25	.583	4th (14)	Derek Shelton
OVERALL 2001 MINOR LEAGUE RECORD			380	320	.543	t-4th (30)	

*Finish in overall standings (No. of teams in league)

ORGANIZATION LEADERS

BATTING
*AVG	Juan Rivera, Columbus/Norwich	.322
R	Marcus Thames, Norwich	114
H	Marcus Thames, Norwich	167
TB	Marcus Thames, Norwich	311
2B	Marcus Thames, Norwich	43
3B	Mike Vento, Tampa	10
HR	Marcus Thames, Norwich	31
RBI	Juan Rivera, Columbus/Norwich	98
BB	Nick Johnson, Columbus	81
	Mitch Jones, Tampa	81
SO	**Mitch Jones**, Tampa	135
SB	Bernabel Castro, G'boro/Staten Island	37

PITCHING
W	Julio DePaula, Tampa/Greensboro	16
L	Jason Anderson, G'boro/Staten Island	10
#ERA	**Dave Martinez**, Tampa/Greensboro	2.10
G	Kevin Lovingier, Columbus/Norwich	62
	Jason Faigin, Greensboro	62
CG	Sam Marsonek, Tampa	5
SV	Alex Pacheco, Norwich	26
IP	Brandon Claussen, Norwich/Tampa	187
BB	Julio DePaula, Tampa/Greensboro	76
SO	Brandon Claussen, Norwich/Tampa	220

*Minimum 250 At-Bats #Minimum 75 Innings

TOP PROSPECTS OF THE DECADE
1992	Brien Taylor, lhp
1993	Brien Taylor, lhp
1994	Derek Jeter, ss
1995	Ruben Rivera, of
1996	Ruben Rivera, of
1997	Ruben Rivera, of
1998	Eric Milton, lhp
1999	Nick Johnson, 1b
2000	Nick Johnson, 1b
2001	Nick Johnson, 1b

TOP DRAFT PICKS OF THE DECADE
1992	Derek Jeter, ss
1993	Matt Drews, rhp
1994	Brian Buchanan, of
1995	Shea Morenz, of
1996	Eric Milton, lhp
1997	*Tyrell Godwin, of
1998	Andy Brown, of
1999	David Walling, rhp
2000	David Parrish, c
2001	John-Ford Griffin, of

*Did not sign.

Jones   **Martinez**

PROJECTED 2005 LINEUP
Catcher	Jorge Posada
First Base	Nick Johnson
Second Base	Alfonso Soriano
Third Base	Drew Henson
Shortstop	Derek Jeter
Left Field	John-Ford Griffin
Center Field	Bernie Williams
Right Field	Juan Rivera
Designated Hitter	Jason Giambi
No. 1 Starter	Mike Mussina
No. 2 Starter	Brandon Claussen
No. 3 Starter	Sean Henn
No. 4 Starter	Andy Pettitte
No. 5 Starter	Jason Arnold
Closer	Mariano Rivera

BEST TOOLS
Best Hitter for Average	Nick Johnson
Best Power Hitter	Drew Henson
Fastest Baserunner	Kaazim Summerville
Best Fastball	Sean Henn
Best Breaking Ball	Brandon Claussen
Best Changeup	Danny Borrell
Best Control	Matt Smith
Best Defensive Catcher	Dioner Navarro
Best Defensive Infielder	Deivi Mendez
Best Infield Arm	Elvis Corporan
Best Defensive Outfielder	Juan Rivera
Best Outfield Arm	Yhency Brazoban

ALL-TIME LARGEST BONUSES
Hideki Irabu, 1997	$8,500,000
Wily Mo Pena, 1999	$2,440,000
Drew Henson, 1998	$2,000,000
Chien-Ming Wang, 2000	$1,900,000
Sean Henn, 2001	$1,700,000

DraftAnalysis

2001 Draft

Best Pro Debut: RHP Jason Arnold (2) threw a no-hitter and went 7-2, 1.50 in the short-season New York-Penn League, with a 74-15 strikeout-walk ratio and a .158 opponent average in 66 innings. OF **John-Ford Griffin** (1) and SS Bronson Sardinha (1) both hit better than .300 with some power and double-digit steal totals in the NY-P and the Rookie-level Gulf Coast League.

Best Athlete: The Yankees believe Sardinha will be able to stay at shortstop, but he has the arm strength and bat to play anywhere he might eventually move. LHP Chase Wright (3) has average velocity and showed power and speed as a high school outfielder.

Best Hitter: Griffin hit .400 or better in each of his three years in college. He walked (40) nearly as much as he struck out (41) in his pro debut.

Best Raw Power: OF Shelley Duncan (2), who holds every University of Arizona home run record imaginable, can hit the ball out of the park to all fields.

Fastest Runner: OF Kaazim Summerville (23) is a 7 runner on the 2-to-8 scouting scale. He hit .186 and reached base just 22 times in 35 NY-P games.

Best Defensive Player: Once Sardinha improves the accuracy of his throws, he'll be a strong defender in the middle infield.

Best Fastball: Arnold threw a consistent 93-95 mph and topped out at 97. RHP Jon Skaggs (1) works at 92-94 mph. The most electric arm signed in 2001 by New York was LHP Sean Henn, a 26th-round draft-and-fol-

low from 2000 who tops out at 99 mph but had Tommy John surgery after the season.

Most Intriguing Background: Sardinha's brother Dane signed with the Reds as a 2000 second-round pick, while another brother, Duke, turned down the Rockies as a 41st-rounder in 2001. Duncan's brother Chris was a Cardinals first-rounder in 1999, while their father Dave was a former big league catcher and is St. Louis' pitching coach.

RICH ABEL

Griffin

Closest To The Majors: Ticketed for Double-A in 2002, Arnold is at the head of the pack.

Best Late-Round Pick: RHPs Adam Wheeler (13), who threw as hard as 94 mph in the GCL, and Bobby Wood (24), who has an 88-92 mph fastball.

The One Who Got Away: RHP Adam Peterson (8), with a 92-94 mph fastball, would have gone higher in the draft had he not been curtailed by a pulled muscle in his back. He returned to Wichita State.

Assessment: Signing Henn was a coup, even if it cost New York $1.7 million, a record for a draft-and-follow. That took a sizable chunk out of the Yankees' signing budget—yes, they have a budget—in a year in which they had a rare run of extra picks. They were forced to take eight college seniors in the first 10 rounds.

2000 Draft

The best prospect, LHP Sean Henn (26), didn't sign until 2001 as a draft-and-follow and had Tommy John surgery shortly afterward. Such players as LHPs Matt Smith (4) and Danny Borrell (2), OF Jason Grove (3) and RHP Jason Anderson (10) have attracted notice in a deep system. C David Parrish was a surprise first-rounder and didn't have a good 2001 . **Grade: B**

1999 Draft

RHP David Walling (1) left the organization temporarily last summer because he became obsessed with delivering the ball to first base rather than to the plate. That leaves LHP Alex Graman (3) as the best hope for this draft. **Grade: C**

1998 Draft

3B Drew Henson (3) could be a star and LHP Brandon Claussen (34, draft-and-follow) has a lot of upside as well. OF Andy Brown (1) has stagnated, while New York still kicks itself for not signing its other first-rounder, RHP Mark Prior, the No. 2 overall pick in 2001. **Grade: A**

1997 Draft

RHP Ryan Bradley (1) ascended quickly and fizzled just as fast, leaving LHP Randy Choate (5) to carry the flag. The Yankees failed to sign four future first-rounders in OF Tyrell Godwin (1), Parrish (10) and RHPs Beau Hale (22) and Aaron Heilman (55). **Grade: D**

Note: Draft analysis prepared by Jim Callis. Numbers in parentheses indicate draft rounds.

. . . He's a unique physical specimen, with unusual athleticism for his size.

Drew Henson 3b

Born: Feb. 13, 1980.
Ht.: 6-5. **Wt.:** 222.
Bats: R. **Throws:** R.
School: Brighton (Mich.) HS.
Career Transactions: Selected by Yankees in third round of 1998 draft; signed July 24, 1998 . . . Traded by Yankees with OF Jackson Melian, LHP Ed Yarnall and RHP Brian Reith to Reds for LHP Denny Neagle and OF Mike Frank, July 12, 2000 . . . Traded by Reds with OF Michael Coleman to Yankees for OF Wily Mo Pena, March 20, 2001.

Henson was unhappy after the Yankees traded him to the Reds in a package for Denny Neagle in July 2000, shortly after he wouldn't commit full-time to baseball. He appeared to be leaning closer to football, where his future was just as bright as it is in baseball. After he passed for 2,146 yards and 18 touchdowns at Michigan in 2000, football experts projected him as No. 1 pick material for the 2002 NFL draft. Henson favored baseball but wanted to be a Yankee, so the Reds dealt him back to New York for outfielder Wily Mo Pena and $1.9 million. Henson signed a six-year, $17 million major league contract and left the gridiron for good after the trade. Five games into last season, a pitch broke his left wrist and sidelined him for two months.

Henson has special power potential. His raw power rates near 80 on the 20-to-80 scouting scale, and he has launched mammoth, 500-foot blasts since he was a high school freshman. He established the national high school record for home runs. He's a unique physical specimen, with unusual athleticism for his size. He's not ready to play third base in the majors yet but has the tools to be an above-average defender. He has plus-plus arm strength and soft hands. He lost valuable experience by splitting his time between two sports, and it shows most in his pitch recognition and plate discipline. The Yankees rushed Henson to Triple-A last year, and he would have been better served by a full year in Double-A. The holes in his swing were exposed as he struck out once every three at-bats during the regular season and in the Arizona Fall League. Henson's .314-6-33 performance there spurred speculation he was ready for New York. The Yankees put an end to that by trading for Robin Ventura, but Henson remains the third baseman of the future. Henson has a chance to be a franchise player because his work ethic and intelligence are as outstanding as his talent.

Year	Club (League)	Class	AVG	G	AB	R	H	2B	3B	HR	RBI	BB	SO	SB
1998	Yankees (GCL)	R	.316	10	38	5	12	3	0	1	2	3	9	0
1999	Tampa (FSL)	A	.280	69	254	37	71	12	0	13	37	26	71	3
2000	Tampa (FSL)	A	.333	5	21	4	7	2	0	1	1	1	7	0
	Norwich (EL)	AA	.287	59	223	39	64	9	2	7	39	20	75	0
	Chattanooga (SL)	AA	.172	16	64	7	11	8	0	1	9	4	25	2
2001	Tampa (FSL)	A	.143	5	14	2	2	0	0	1	3	2	7	1
	Norwich (EL)	AA	.368	5	19	2	7	1	0	0	2	1	4	0
	Columbus (IL)	AAA	.222	71	270	29	60	6	0	11	38	10	85	2
MINOR LEAGUE TOTALS			.259	240	903	125	234	41	2	35	131	67	283	8

2. Nick Johnson, 1b

Born: Sept. 19, 1978. **Ht.:** 6-3. **Wt.:** 224. **Bats:** L. **Throws:** L. **School:** McClatchy HS, Sacramento. **Career Transactions:** Selected by Yankees in third round of 1996 draft; signed June 14, 1996.

Johnson missed the entire 2000 season with a mysterious wrist injury that originated with a checked swing in spring training. Healthy again, he made his second trip to the Futures Game last summer. His game is reminiscent of Don Mattingly, whom Johnson has worked with in recent spring trainings. He is a nephew of Larry Bowa. Johnson retained his uncanny knack for getting on base in 2001. He's an ultra-patient hitter who uses the whole field, waits for a pitch in his zone and isn't afraid to hit deep in the count. He has been more conscious of turning on pitches and lifting balls. Johnson is a slick fielder with natural actions and good footwork around first base. Johnson doesn't clog the bases, but he's a below-average runner. He'll have to adapt to DH after the Yankees invested $120 million in Jason Giambi, who prefers to play first base. Johnson will have to break in as a DH until it's apparent he's a better defender than Giambi. He could see time in the outfield, and he'll be a rookie of the year candidate if he gets enough at-bats.

Year	Club (League)	Class	AVG	G	AB	R	H	2B	3B	HR	RBI	BB	SO	SB
1996	Yankees (GCL)	R	.287	47	157	31	45	11	1	2	33	30	35	0
1997	Greensboro (SAL)	A	.273	127	433	77	118	23	1	16	75	76	99	16
1998	Tampa (FSL)	A	.317	92	303	69	96	14	1	17	58	68	76	1
1999	Norwich (EL)	AA	.345	132	420	114	145	33	5	14	87	123	88	8
2000					Did Not Play—Injured									
2001	Columbus (IL)	AAA	.256	110	359	68	92	20	0	18	49	81	105	9
	New York (AL)	MAJ	.194	23	67	6	13	2	0	2	8	7	15	0
MAJOR LEAGUE TOTALS			.194	23	67	6	13	2	0	2	8	7	15	0
MINOR LEAGUE TOTALS			.297	508	1672	359	496	101	8	67	302	378	403	34

3. Brandon Claussen, lhp

Born: May 1, 1979. **Ht.:** 6-2. **Wt.:** 175. **Bats:** L. **Throws:** L. **School:** Howard (Texas) JC. **Career Transactions:** Selected by Yankees in 34th round of 1998 draft; signed May 20, 1999.

The Yankees have a strong track record with draft-and-follows out of Texas. They went back for more after signing Andy Pettitte out of San Jacinto Junior College in 1991. Area scout Mark Batchko tabbed Claussen in 1998 and Sean Henn last year. Claussen's 220 strikeouts led the minors in 2001. Claussen has increased his velocity during his ascent through the minors. He works his 89-94 mph fastball to both sides of the plate, and he had more success locating it last year than in the past. His knockout pitch is a quality slider with excellent two-plane depth. Claussen's changeup came on last season but still needs improvement to become more than a show-me pitch. He issued a few too many walks once he reached Double-A. Claussen was one of the few top pitching prospects in the organization to avoid injury last year, when he proved durable over 187 innings. Though they received several trade inquiries about him, the Yankees' refusal to part with him speaks volumes. He'll begin 2002 in Triple-A and is in line for a promotion later in the year.

Year	Club (League)	Class	W	L	ERA	G	GS	CG	SV	IP	H	R	ER	BB	SO
1999	Yankees (GCL)	R	0	1	3.18	2	2	0	0	11	7	4	4	2	16
	Staten Island (NY-P)	A	6	4	3.38	12	12	1	0	72	70	30	27	12	89
	Greensboro (SAL)	A	0	1	10.50	1	1	1	0	6	8	7	7	2	5
2000	Greensboro (SAL)	A	8	5	4.05	17	17	1	0	98	91	49	44	44	98
	Tampa (FSL)	A	2	5	3.10	9	9	1	0	52	49	24	18	17	44
2001	Tampa (FSL)	A	5	2	2.73	8	8	0	0	56	47	21	17	13	69
	Norwich (EL)	AA	9	2	2.13	21	21	1	0	131	101	42	31	55	151
MINOR LEAGUE TOTALS			30	20	3.12	70	70	5	0	426	373	177	148	145	472

4. John-Ford Griffin, of

Born: Nov. 19, 1979. **Ht.:** 6-2. **Wt.:** 215. **Bats:** L. **Throws:** L. **School:** Florida State University. **Career Transactions:** Selected by Yankees in first round (23rd overall) of 2001 draft; signed June 14, 2001.

Griffin finished fourth in NCAA Division I with a .450 average last year, wrapping up a career in which he hit better than .400 in each of his three seasons at Florida State. Seminoles coach Mike Martin called him the best hitter in the program's history, which also includes all-time college greats such as J.D. Drew. Not surprisingly, Griffin was considered one of the best pure hitters in the draft. Griffin personifies the Yankees' philosophy with his professional approach to hitting. He generates tremendous bat speed and sprays line drives all over the ballpark. He makes excellent adjustments from pitch to pitch and is a dangerous two-strike hitter. Griffin had shoulder surgery after his sophomore season, leaving him with a below-average arm that will relegate him to left field. Having average power prevented him from going higher in the draft, though he has the bat speed and leverage to hit more home runs. Griffin's understanding of the strike zone will help him make adjustments. His bat is ready for Double-A, though he'll head to high Class A Tampa first.

Year	Club (League)	Class	AVG	G	AB	R	H	2B	3B	HR	RBI	BB	SO	SB
2001	Staten Island (NY-P)	A	.311	66	238	46	74	17	1	5	43	40	41	10
MINOR LEAGUE TOTALS			.311	66	238	46	74	17	1	5	43	40	41	10

5. Juan Rivera, of

Born: July 3, 1978. **Ht.:** 6-2. **Wt.:** 170. **Bats:** R. **Throws:** R. **Career Transactions:** Signed out of Venezuela by Yankees, April 12, 1996.

Rivera's ascent is similar to that of former Yankees prospect Ricky Ledee, who spent seven seasons in the minors before making his major league debut. Rivera made his debut after his best offensive season since he emerged as the top prospect in the Rookie-level Gulf Coast League in 1998. Rivera's tools far surpass Ledee's and he's a better all-around athlete. Hard work with Norwich hitting coach Dan Radison paid off. Rivera got bigger and stronger before last season, and more important he did a better job staying back and recognizing breaking balls. He is a prototypical right fielder with an above-average arm. Rivera's strength allows him to hammer mistakes on the inner half, but he has holes in his swing that experienced pitchers can exploit. His walk rate declined and he'll have to be more patient. Rivera continued to play well this winter in Venezuela. The acquisition of Rondell White and John Vander Wal clouds his immediate future, so he'll likely return to Triple-A.

Year	Club (League)	Class	AVG	G	AB	R	H	2B	3B	HR	RBI	BB	SO	SB
1996	Yankees (DSL)	R	.167	10	18	0	3	0	0	0	2	0	1	0
1997	Maracay 2 (VSL)	R	.282	52	142	25	40	9	0	0	14	12	16	12
1998	Yankees (GCL)	R	.333	57	210	43	70	9	1	12	45	26	27	8
	Oneonta (NY-P)	A	.278	6	18	2	5	0	0	1	3	1	4	1
1999	Tampa (FSL)	A	.263	109	426	50	112	20	2	14	77	26	67	5
	Yankees (GCL)	R	.333	5	18	7	6	0	0	1	4	4	1	0
2000	Norwich (EL)	AA	.226	17	62	9	14	5	0	2	12	6	15	0
	Tampa (FSL)	A	.276	115	409	62	113	26	1	14	69	33	56	11
2001	Norwich (EL)	AA	.320	77	316	50	101	18	3	14	58	15	50	5
	Columbus (IL)	AAA	.327	55	199	39	65	11	1	14	40	15	31	4
	New York (AL)	MAJ	.000	3	4	0	0	0	0	0	0	0	0	0
MAJOR LEAGUE TOTALS			.000	3	4	0	0	0	0	0	0	0	0	0
MINOR LEAGUE TOTALS			.291	503	1818	287	529	98	8	72	324	138	268	46

6. Sean Henn, lhp

Born: April 23, 1981. **Ht.:** 6-5. **Wt.:** 205. **Bats:** R. **Throws:** L. **School:** McLennan (Texas) JC. **Career Transactions:** Selected by Yankees in 26th round of 2000 draft; signed May 25, 2001.

The Yankees took a significant chunk out of their draft budget by signing Henn to a draft-and-follow record $1.7 million bonus a week before the 2001 draft. They had coveted him since drafting him out of high school in 1999's 30th round. But his pro debut came to a halt when elbow pain led to Tommy John surgery. Once word spread of Henn's explosive velocity, it was clear the Yankees were going to have to give him first-round money. He touched 98-99 mph and dialed it up to 95-97 after signing. He sits at 91-95 mph and maintains quick arm action on his changeup, which should become a plus pitch. Henn has imposing size and works on a tough downward plane. He has made progress with his breaking ball. Henn needs to improve his location. He tends to break his hands too late in his delivery, causing his fastball to stay up. His four-seamer lacks movement and he's learning to work it to both sides of the plate. The surgery will set Henn back a year, and the rehabilitation will require a lot of dedication. The Yankees say he'll return to full strength, and not many lefthanders can match his power arsenal.

Year	Club (League)	Class	W	L	ERA	G	GS	CG	SV	IP	H	R	ER	BB	SO
2001	Staten Island (NY-P)	A	3	1	3.00	9	8	0	1	42	26	15	14	15	49
MINOR LEAGUE TOTALS			3	1	3.00	9	8	0	1	42	26	15	14	15	49

7. Marcus Thames, of

RICH ABEL

Born: March 6, 1977. **Ht.:** 6-2. **Wt.:** 205. **Bats:** R. **Throws:** R. **School:** East Central (Miss.) CC. **Career Transactions:** Selected by Yankees in 30th round of 1996 draft; signed May 16, 1997.

Another draft-and-follow project, Thames has been highly regarded for his tools, but his breakthrough last season was a pleasant surprise. In his third season at Norwich, Thames made a run at the Eastern League triple crown. His 78 extra-base hits tied journeyman Phil Hiatt for most in the minors. Like Juan Rivera, Thames worked with hitting coach Dan Radison and his game took off. It was just a matter of translating his tools into baseball skills. He was able to do so by improving his plan from at-bat to at-bat. Thames has above-average power to all parts of the park. He's an instinctive outfielder with the range for center and an above-average arm for right. After hitting .236 in his first 656 at-bats in Norwich, Thames will have to prove his season wasn't a fluke. He's a borderline five-tool prospect and needs to avoid falling back into the bad habits that plagued him prior to 2001. Thames continued to rake in the Arizona Fall League, hitting .346-4-20, and would have challenged for a job in New York if the club hadn't acquired Rondell White and John Vander Wal. Thames will spend the 2001 season in Triple-A or wait for a trade.

Year	Club (League)	Class	AVG	G	AB	R	H	2B	3B	HR	RBI	BB	SO	SB
1997	Yankees (GCL)	R	.344	57	195	51	67	17	4	7	36	16	26	6
	Greensboro (SAL)	A	.313	4	16	2	5	1	0	0	2	0	3	1
1998	Tampa (FSL)	A	.284	122	457	62	130	18	3	11	59	24	78	13
1999	Norwich (EL)	AA	.225	51	182	25	41	6	2	4	26	22	40	0
	Tampa (FSL)	A	.244	69	266	47	65	12	4	11	38	33	58	3
2000	Norwich (EL)	AA	.241	131	474	72	114	30	2	15	79	50	89	1
2001	Norwich (EL)	AA	.321	139	520	114	167	43	4	31	79	73	101	10
MINOR LEAGUE TOTALS			.279	573	2110	373	589	127	19	79	337	218	395	34

8. Erick Almonte, ss

STEVE MOORE

Born: Feb. 1, 1978. **Ht.:** 6-2. **Wt.:** 180. **Bats:** R. **Throws:** R. **Career Transactions:** Signed out of Dominican Republic by Yankees, Feb. 12, 1996.

Almonte is a chiseled athlete who has added 20 pounds of muscle since signing as a wiry third baseman in 1996. After breaking in as the Gulf Coast League's No. 4 prospect in 1998, he stalled until blossoming in the Arizona Fall League in 2000. He made his major league debut last September and singled in his first at-bat. The Yankees rave about Almonte's combination of size and tools, which are similar to Derek Jeter's. He hits for power, and his bat speed and strength suggest more could be on the way. He displays deft actions at shortstop and gets good carry from a cannon arm and quick release. Almonte struggles with breaking stuff and gets off-balance by lunging at pitches. He has toned down his swing, however. He has the tools to be a solid defender but makes careless errors. Shortstop could be a dead end, but the athleticism and versatility of Almonte and Alfonso Soriano give the Yankees options. Almonte could handle a move to second base or the outfield.

Year	Club (League)	Class	AVG	G	AB	R	H	2B	3B	HR	RBI	BB	SO	SB
1996	Yankees (DSL)	R	.282	58	216	37	61	7	0	8	36	15	30	3
1997	Yankees (GCL)	R	.283	52	180	32	51	4	4	3	31	21	27	8
1998	Greensboro (SAL)	A	.209	120	450	53	94	13	0	6	33	29	121	6
1999	Tampa (FSL)	A	.257	61	230	36	59	8	2	5	25	18	49	3
	Yankees (GCL)	R	.300	9	30	5	9	2	0	2	9	3	10	1

Year	Club (League)	Class	AVG	G	AB	R	H	2B	3B	HR	RBI	BB	SO	SB
2000	Norwich (EL)	AA	.271	131	454	56	123	18	4	15	77	35	129	12
2001	Columbus (IL)	AAA	.287	97	345	55	99	19	3	12	55	44	90	4
	Norwich (EL)	AA	.250	3	12	2	3	0	0	0	0	1	6	1
	New York (AL)	MAJ	.500	8	4	0	2	1	0	0	0	0	1	2
MAJOR LEAGUE TOTALS			.500	8	4	0	2	1	0	0	0	0	1	2
MINOR LEAGUE TOTALS			.260	531	1917	276	499	71	13	51	266	166	462	38

9. Jason Arnold, rhp

Born: May 2, 1979. **Ht.:** 6-3. **Wt.:** 210. **Bats:** R. **Throws:** R. **School:** University of Central Florida. **Career Transactions:** Selected by Yankees in second round of 2001 draft; signed June 15, 2001.

The Reds drafted Arnold in the 16th round in 2000 but wouldn't give him the $60,000 he wanted to forgo his senior season of college. After three all-TransAmerica Athletic Conference seasons as a reliever, he went 14-3, 1.97 as a starter last spring and earned second-team All-America honors. He signed for $400,000, then threw a no-hitter and finished third in the short-season New York-Penn League in ERA. Arnold blew away hitters as a closer in college with pure arm strength and a mid-90s fastball. He worked comfortably between 90-97 mph at Staten Island, but had more tailing action when he threw 90-91. His slider and changeup have improved markedly and both are potential out pitches. Arnold was shut down during the summer with elbow tendinitis. While he's expected to be fine, he did have a heavy workload in his first year as a starter. He throws across his body with a bit of a herky-jerky delivery, another cause for concern. The Yankees have put Arnold on the fast track following his inspiring pro debut. He should jump to high Class A this year, with a promotion to Double-A not out of the question.

Year	Club (League)	Class	W	L	ERA	G	GS	CG	SV	IP	H	R	ER	BB	SO
2001	Staten Island (NY-P)	A	7	2	1.50	10	10	2	0	66	35	13	11	15	74
MINOR LEAGUE TOTALS			7	2	1.50	10	10	2	0	66	35	13	11	15	74

10. Bronson Sardinha, ss

Born: April 6, 1983. **Ht.:** 6-1. **Wt.:** 195. **Bats:** L. **Throws:** R. **School:** Kamehameha HS, Honolulu. **Career Transactions:** Selected by Yankees in first round (34th overall) of 2001 draft; signed June 13, 2001.

Named after actor Charles Bronson, Sardinha comes from excellent Hawaiian bloodlines. His brother Dane is the Reds' No. 9 prospect after an All-America career at Pepperdine, where brother Duke currently plays. Managers rated Bronson the No. 3 prospect in the Gulf Coast League and he was regarded as the league's best pure hitter. Sardinha owns a sweet lefthanded stroke and sprays the ball to all fields. He can mash fastballs and projects to hit for slightly above-average power as he fills out. Though he likes to hit early in the count, he doesn't chase bad pitches and he does draw his fair share of walks. His instincts are excellent, and he has a plus arm and soft hands. It's not clear Sardinha will maintain the quickness to stay at shortstop as he adds muscle. He has correctable flaws in his swing, such as committing too early. The system is loaded with bright young shortstops, but the Yankees will keep Sardinha there for now. Though his advanced approach should help him make the adjustments to full-season ball, he's several years away from New York.

Year	Club (League)	Class	AVG	G	AB	R	H	2B	3B	HR	RBI	BB	SO	SB
2001	Yankees (GCL)	R	.303	55	188	42	57	14	3	4	27	28	51	11
MINOR LEAGUE TOTALS			.303	55	188	42	57	14	3	4	27	28	51	11

11. David Martinez, lhp

Born: June 7, 1980. **Ht.:** 6-1. **Wt.:** 165. **Bats:** L. **Throws:** L. **Career Transactions:** Signed out of Venezuela by Yankees, Dec. 23, 1996.

Martinez overmatched the low Class A South Atlantic League for the first two months of last season. He led the league in ERA and was coming off back-to-back shutouts when he was promoted to high Class A. Shortly after he was shut down for the remainder of the season with a sore shoulder, possibly a result of high pitch counts accrued with Greensboro. Martinez isn't physically imposing, but he can carve up hitters with a sneaky moving fastball that consistently sits around 89-92 mph, a sharp-breaking curveball that's clocked at 73 mph and a changeup he can throw for strikes. His curve is outstanding, though it suffered early in 2001 when he was dropping his elbow. Martinez eventually found a consistent arm slot and then began repeating his delivery. His shoulder required only arthroscopic surgery and no further setbacks are anticipated. Yet Martinez never has worked more than 81 innings in a season, so durability is a question. He'll return to Tampa and move one level at a time.

Year	Club (League)	Class	W	L	ERA	G	GS	CG	SV	IP	H	R	ER	BB	SO
1997	Maracay 2 (VSL)	R	2	1	1.66	6	0	0	0	22	19	7	4	9	15
1998	La Pradera (VSL)	R	2	4	4.27	15	13	0	0	72	75	42	34	25	67
1999	Yankees (GCL)	R	5	3	2.97	12	11	2	0	67	52	29	22	22	67
2000	Staten Island (NY-P)	A	2	2	2.51	6	4	0	0	32	20	12	9	11	33
	Greensboro (SAL)	A	2	5	2.92	8	8	1	0	49	33	24	16	27	44
2001	Greensboro (SAL)	A	6	0	1.13	11	11	3	0	79	54	17	10	28	67
	Tampa (FSL)	A	0	3	6.05	4	3	1	0	19	20	15	13	9	19
MINOR LEAGUE TOTALS			19	18	2.86	62	50	7	0	340	273	146	108	131	312

12. Alex Graman, lhp

Born: Nov. 17, 1977. **Ht.:** 6-4. **Wt.:** 200. **Bats:** L. **Throws:** L. **School:** Indiana State University. **Career Transactions:** Selected by Yankees in third round of 1999 draft; signed June 5, 1999.

Graman's name often is bantered about in the trade rumors that constantly swirl around the Yankees. In 2000, he reportedly was to be included in a package for Sammy Sosa, and more recently was involved in talks for Darin Erstad. In 2001, Graman didn't find his groove until July. After going 6-6, 5.30 in his first 15 starts, he went 7-3, 2.12 over the final two months. His surge can be attributed to locating his fastball. Graman goes after hitters' weaknesses with a diverse four-pitch repertoire consisting of a 90-94 mph fastball, a tough splitter, a slider and a changeup. Graman enjoyed pitching in Norwich's spacious Dodd Memorial Stadium last year, where his ERA (2.73) was nearly two runs lower than on the road (4.58). Improving his changeup would help him against righthanders, who batted .276 against him in 2001. Graman will head to Triple-A and could be ready to help New York in a pinch. However, he'll require extra effort to stand out in a crowded group of lefthanders including Brandon Claussen, Randy Keisler and Ted Lilly at the upper levels of the system.

Year	Club (League)	Class	W	L	ERA	G	GS	CG	SV	IP	H	R	ER	BB	SO
1999	Staten Island (NY-P)	A	6	3	2.99	14	14	0	0	81	74	30	27	16	85
2000	Tampa (FSL)	A	8	9	3.65	28	28	3	0	143	120	64	58	58	111
	Norwich (EL)	AA	0	1	11.81	1	1	0	0	5	6	7	7	4	3
2001	Norwich (EL)	AA	12	9	3.52	28	28	1	0	166	174	83	65	60	138
MINOR LEAGUE TOTALS			26	22	3.57	71	71	4	0	396	374	184	157	138	337

13. Adrian Hernandez, rhp

Born: Aug. 30, 1974. **Ht.:** 6-2. **Wt.:** 185. **Bats:** R. **Throws:** R. **Career Transactions:** Signed out of Cuba by Yankees, June 2, 2000.

The Yankees signed Hernandez to a four-year, $4 million contract in 2000 after the Cuban defector sneaked on a flight to Costa Rica and trained for scouts in Guatemala. Two years into his career, El Duquecito has attracted more attention for his likeness to his mentor Orlando "El Duque" Hernandez (no relation), than for his performance. Adrian made his big league debut last year, but drew the ire of Roger Clemens when he missed a start due to illness. Like El Duque, Hernandez can be effective when his fastball is in the mid-80s or the low 90s because he alters his delivery and comes at hitters from all arm angles. All of his stuff has good movement and he throws a variety of breaking pitches, making it difficult for batters to get locked in. Hernandez needs to improve his changeup, especially to combat lefthanders, who hit .300 off him last year. He lacks a true out pitch, which might limit him to the bullpen or a swingman role. He could start 2002 in the big leagues or in Triple-A depending on how he performs in spring training.

Year	Club (League)	Class	W	L	ERA	G	GS	CG	SV	IP	H	R	ER	BB	SO
2000	Tampa (FSL)	A	1	0	1.35	1	1	0	0	7	3	1	1	1	13
	Norwich (EL)	AA	5	1	4.04	6	6	1	0	36	34	17	16	18	44
	Columbus (IL)	AAA	2	1	4.40	5	5	2	0	31	24	18	15	18	29
2001	Columbus (IL)	AAA	8	7	5.51	21	21	0	0	118	116	75	72	60	97
	New York (AL)	MAJ	0	3	3.68	6	3	0	0	22	15	10	9	10	10
MAJOR LEAGUE TOTALS			0	3	3.68	6	3	0	0	22	15	10	9	10	10
MINOR LEAGUE TOTALS			16	9	4.91	33	33	3	0	191	177	111	104	97	183

14. Deivi Mendez, ss

Born: June 24, 1983. **Ht.:** 6-1. **Wt.:** 165. **Bats:** R. **Throws:** R. **Career Transactions:** Signed out of Dominican Republic by Yankees, July 2, 1999.

The system is stocked with shortstops, but Mendez is nearly five years younger than Erick Almonte, and he's nine months younger than Ferdin Tejada, who will make his U.S. debut this year after finishing first and second in hitting in the Rookie-level Dominican Summer League in the last two years. Expectations were sky-high for Mendez after he hit .300 and ranked as the Gulf Coast League's No. 3 prospect in 2000. But a leap to a full-season league at age 18 proved to be unrealistic last year, as he struggled before a demotion to Staten Island in the second half. He pulled his hamstring in August and didn't return until the postseason. Though he didn't display it last season, Mendez can drive the ball into the gaps and his power should improve as he matures physically. He's blessed with a well above-average arm and natural shortstop actions in the field. He has good range up the middle and in the hole, but he runs a tick below average. The Yankees rushed Mendez last season and he should return to low Class A Greensboro for a full season.

Year	Club (League)	Class	AVG	G	AB	R	H	2B	3B	HR	RBI	BB	SO	SB
2000	Yankees (GCL)	R	.300	56	210	37	63	20	1	2	25	26	39	4
2001	Greensboro (SAL)	A	.215	49	172	25	37	6	0	2	15	14	35	5
	Staten Island (NY-P)	A	.231	53	186	23	43	10	2	1	21	9	31	2
MINOR LEAGUE TOTALS			.252	158	568	85	143	36	3	5	61	49	105	11

15. Matt Smith, lhp

Born: June 15, 1979. **Ht.:** 6-5. **Wt.:** 225. **Bats:** L. **Throws:** L. **School:** Oklahoma State University. **Career Transactions:** Selected by Yankees in fourth round of 2000 draft; signed June 21, 2000.

Despite a disappointing junior season in 2000, Smith established Oklahoma State's career strikeout record and went in the fourth round based on the stuff he showcased throughout his freshman and sophomore season. His velocity faded from 90 mph to 85-87 as a junior, and he stayed at that plateau during his pro debut. The Yankees were pleasantly surprised when his fastball returned to the 88-92 mph range last season. He gets effective sink on his two-seamer, and uses a curve with slurvy action that rivals Brandon Claussen's breaking ball. Smith also has a developing changeup to keep hitters guessing. He throws strikes and doesn't beat himself. After a strong second half of 2001 in high Class A, Smith should be ready to handle a move to Norwich.

Year	Club (League)	Class	W	L	ERA	G	GS	CG	SV	IP	H	R	ER	BB	SO
2000	Staten Island (NY-P)	A	5	4	2.38	14	14	0	0	76	74	32	20	20	59
2001	Greensboro (SAL)	A	5	3	2.59	16	16	1	0	97	69	37	28	32	116
	Tampa (FSL)	A	6	2	2.24	11	11	0	0	68	54	21	17	22	71
MINOR LEAGUE TOTALS			16	9	2.42	41	41	1	0	241	197	90	65	74	246

16. Jon Skaggs, rhp

Born: March 27, 1978. **Ht.:** 6-5. **Wt.:** 225. **Bats:** R. **Throws:** R. **School:** Rice University. **Career Transactions:** Selected by Yankees in first round (42nd overall) of 2001 draft; signed June 13, 2001.

The Orioles selected Skaggs in the fourth round in 2001, but he elected to return to Rice to give the Owls a talented senior tandem along with Kenny Baugh, now a top prospect in the Tigers system. A ribcage injury last spring probably prevented Skaggs from joining Baugh as a true first-round pick—his maximum-effort delivery and sporadic command also were concerns—though the Yankees used their second supplemental first-rounder on him. Skaggs strained his elbow in his first pro start and didn't pitch again during the summer. When he's healthy, Skaggs' fastball sits between 88-94 mph and runs to the right when he keeps it down in the strike zone. His 80-mph curveball has tight downward rotation, and he shows the makings of a well above-average changeup with late fade. Skaggs should be healthy this spring and could jump on the fast track, probably starting in low Class A.

Year	Club (League)	Class	W	L	ERA	G	GS	CG	SV	IP	H	R	ER	BB	SO
2001	Staten Island (NY-P)	A	0	0	1.93	1	1	0	0	5	4	1	1	1	4
MINOR LEAGUE TOTALS			0	0	1.93	1	1	0	0	5	4	1	1	1	4

17. Manny Acosta, rhp

Born: May 1, 1981. **Ht.:** 6-4. **Wt.:** 170. **Bats:** R. **Throws:** R. **Career Transactions:** Signed out of Panama by Yankees, Jan. 6, 1998.

The Yankees have Panamanian righthanders Ramiro Mendoza and Mariano Rivera in their current bullpen, and Acosta gives them another in their pipeline. After spending three years in Rookie ball, he made the transition into full-season look easy in 2001 following a stint in extended spring training. Acosta's fastball already reaches 93-95 and projects to add even more when he fills out his classic projectable frame. Rather than just throwing his heat by batters, he shows pitchability. His 80-82 mph power curveball is a second weapon, while his changeup is still remedial. Acosta limited South Atlantic League hitters to a .166 average, with the only negative being two trips to the disabled list with a shoulder strain. Acosta pitched in the new Panama League in the winter, proving his arm was sound. He should return to high Class A, where he struggled to throw strikes last season.

Year	Club (League)	Class	W	L	ERA	G	GS	CG	SV	IP	H	R	ER	BB	SO
1998	Yankees (DSL)	R	0	1	16.43	9	0	0	1	8	20	15	14	10	5
1999	Yankees (DSL)	R	4	2	3.16	8	4	0	0	31	27	13	11	18	38
2000	Yankees (GCL)	R	4	2	3.47	12	10	0	0	62	64	28	24	21	46
2001	Tampa (FSL)	A	0	1	7.71	2	2	0	0	7	7	7	6	6	8
	Greensboro (SAL)	A	5	2	1.51	10	10	1	0	66	37	14	11	37	67
MINOR LEAGUE TOTALS			13	8	3.41	41	26	1	1	174	155	77	66	92	164

18. Edison Reynoso, rhp

Born: Nov. 10, 1975. **Ht.:** 6-1. **Wt.:** 170. **Bats:** R. **Throws:** R. **Career Transactions:** Signed out of Dominican Republic by Astros, July 24, 1992 . . . Released by Astros, June 8, 1994 . . . Signed by Tigers, June 18, 1997 . . . Granted free agency, Oct. 17, 1997 . . . Signed by Hiroshima (Japan) 1999 . . . Signed by Yankees, Feb. 1, 2001.

A product of the Hiroshima Carp's baseball academy in the Dominican Republic, Reynoso signed with the Yankees for $900,000 last year. The Astros originally signed Reynoso as a 16-year-old in 1992 before releasing him in 1994. Out of baseball for three years, he signed with the Tigers and spent one season pitching in the Dominican Summer League before winding up in Japan for two years. Reynoso's fastball has been clocked as high as 98 mph, which spurred speculation he would blitz through the minors and help the Yankees bridge the gap between the starters and Mariano Rivera. But a 2001 season that began with visa problems and a groin injury in spring training also included a sore arm and a seriously sprained knee incurred while covering first base. Despite all the distractions, Reynoso displayed an electric arsenal featuring three potential big league pitches: a 94-98 mph fastball, a splitter and a slider. His knee problem will delay the start to his 2002 season, and he appears to be a long way from making an impact in the Yankees bullpen.

Year	Club (League)	Class	W	L	ERA	G	GS	CG	SV	IP	H	R	ER	BB	SO
1993	Astros (DSL)	R	2	1	5.47	18	0	0	0	26	31	21	16	24	15
1994								Did Not Play							
1995								Did Not Play							
1996								Did Not Play							
1997	Tigers (DSL)	R	6	4	3.50	11	11	4	0	75	73	39	29	38	59
1998								Did Not Play							
1999	Hiroshima (WL)	JPN	2	5	6.59	26	3	0	1	42	54	33	31	23	29
	Hiroshima (CL)	JPN	0	2	9.00	9	1	0	0	13	13	14	13	13	4
2000	Hiroshima (WL)	JPN	3	4	4.70	12	6	1	2	44	52	29	23	19	40
	Hiroshima (CL)	JPN	0	0	27.00	1	0	0	0	2	6	6	6	3	3
2001	Tampa (FSL)	A	0	0	0.00	1	1	0	0	4	1	0	0	0	5
	Staten Island (NY-P)	A	1	0	0.00	1	1	0	0	5	3	1	0	2	9
	Norwich (EL)	AA	1	0	3.93	5	3	0	0	18	19	12	8	5	17
MINOR LEAGUE TOTALS			10	5	3.73	36	16	4	0	128	127	73	53	69	105

19. Dioner Navarro, c

Born: Feb. 9, 1984. **Ht.:** 5-10. **Wt.:** 189. **Bats:** B. **Throws:** R. **Career Transactions:** Signed out of Venezuela by Yankees, Aug. 21, 2000.

Signed for $260,000 out of Venezuela, Navarro made his pro debut at age 17 and earned all-star recognition in the Gulf Coast League. He also earned the nickname "Pudgito" for his defensive prowess and his physical resemblance to Ivan Rodriguez. Navarro used his plus arm strength, soft hands and quick feet to throw out 35 percent of basestealers. At the plate, the young switch-hitter appeared more comfortable from his natural right side but showed the ability to use the whole field from both sides. He's also a slightly above-average runner. Navarro needs to get stronger and drive the ball more, which should happen in time. He'll probably begin this year in extended spring training before going to Staten Island in June.

Year	Club (League)	Class	AVG	G	AB	R	H	2B	3B	HR	RBI	BB	SO	SB
2001	Yankees (GCL)	R	.280	43	143	27	40	10	1	2	22	17	23	6
MINOR LEAGUE TOTALS			.280	43	143	27	40	10	1	2	22	17	23	6

20. Julio DePaula, rhp

Born: July 27, 1979. **Ht.:** 6-1. **Wt.:** 160. **Bats:** R. **Throws:** R. **Career Transactions:** Signed out of Dominican Republic by Rockies, Jan. 13, 1997 . . . Traded by Rockies to Yankees, April 20, 2001, completing trade in which Yankees sent RHP Craig Dingman to Rockies for a player to be named (March 29, 2001).

The Yankees obtained DePaula as the player to be named in the trade that sent reliever Craig Dingman to Colorado last spring. DePaula finished second in the South Atlantic League in strikeouts in 2000, and returned to dominate at that level during the first half last season. He rang up 10 or more strikeouts in a game four times before earning a promotion to high Class A in June. His delivery is deceptive and he has a fast arm that generates 90-95 mph fastballs. His plus changeup is among the best in the system and is a strikeout pitch, and he has shown the ability to spin his slider. DePaula works fast with an energetic demeanor bordering on arrogance. The Yankees believe he has his emotions under control because he doesn't lose his composure. DePaula's command wavered in Tampa, and becoming more consistent with his breaking ball will be the key for him handling Double-A. His fastball-changeup knockout punch gives him a chance to move rapidly, and at worst he should develop into an effective big league reliever.

Year	Club (League)	Class	W	L	ERA	G	GS	CG	SV	IP	H	R	ER	BB	SO
1997	Rockies (DSL)	R	3	6	4.75	15	11	1	0	66	77	46	35	28	59
1998	Rockies (AZL)	R	5	5	3.81	17	9	0	2	54	54	30	23	18	62
1999	Portland (NWL)	A	6	6	6.01	16	16	0	0	85	97	67	57	43	77
2000	Asheville (SAL)	A	8	13	4.70	28	27	1	0	155	151	90	81	62	187
2001	Asheville (SAL)	A	1	1	3.78	3	3	0	0	17	19	13	7	2	26
	Greensboro (SAL)	A	6	1	2.75	8	8	0	0	56	35	19	17	21	67
	Tampa (FSL)	A	9	5	3.58	16	13	0	0	83	65	43	33	53	77
MINOR LEAGUE TOTALS			38	37	4.41	103	87	2	2	516	498	308	253	227	555

21. Adam Roller, rhp

Born: June 27, 1978. **Ht.:** 6-3. **Wt.:** 208. **Bats:** R. **Throws:** R. **School:** Hillsborough (Fla.) CC. **Career Transactions:** Selected by Red Sox in 33rd round of 1996 draft; signed May 25, 1997 . . . Released by Red Sox, March 31, 2000 . . . Signed by Yankees, April 17, 2000.

The Red Sox released Roller in 2000 after he surfaced above Rookie ball for just one game in three pro seasons. He opened the 2001 season with 31 consecutive innings without permitting an earned run, and he only allowed an earned run in just three of his 51 appearances. Roller overpowered opponents to the tune of a stingy .174 average against and didn't allow a home run. His command was the main culprit behind his struggles in the lowest levels of the Boston chain, but he has drastically improved his control since joining the Yankees organization. Though he has a high-maintenance delivery that doesn't look very natural, it works for him and he unloads pure power. Roller's fastball is consistently clocked between 93-95 mph, complemented by a knee-buckling breaking ball. His changeup is below average. Roller followed up his coming-out party with a stint in the Arizona Fall League. He was exposed to the major league Rule 5 draft but no one took him from New York. He'll open 2002 as a Double-A closer and could reach Triple-A this season.

Year	Club (League)	Class	W	L	ERA	G	GS	CG	SV	IP	H	R	ER	BB	SO
1997	Red Sox (GCL)	R	1	1	3.18	10	0	0	0	17	7	9	6	14	21
1998	Red Sox (GCL)	R	0	2	4.85	15	2	0	1	39	51	31	21	22	27
1999	Sarasota (FSL)	A	0	0	16.88	1	0	0	0	3	5	5	5	2	2
	Lowell (NY-P)	A	4	5	2.54	23	0	0	2	39	30	16	11	29	41
2000	Tampa (FSL)	A	1	4	4.21	19	0	0	1	26	29	17	12	9	26
	Greensboro (SAL)	A	0	1	1.31	13	0	0	1	21	15	6	3	5	22
2001	Tampa (FSL)	A	2	3	1.20	51	0	0	23	68	42	14	9	15	76
	Norwich (EL)	AA	0	0	0.00	2	0	0	0	3	3	0	0	0	2
MINOR LEAGUE TOTALS			8	16	2.81	134	2	0	28	215	182	98	67	96	217

22. Danny Borrell, lhp

Born: Jan. 24, 1979. **Ht.:** 6-3. **Wt.:** 190. **Bats:** L. **Throws:** L. **School:** Wake Forest University. **Career Transactions:** Selected by Yankees in second round of 2000 draft; signed June 19, 2000.

Borrell had more success as a first baseman/outfielder at Wake Forest, slugging 37 homers while compiling a 6.21 ERA as a starter, but his free and easy arm action on the mound was too enticing to pass up. The Yankees immediately made him a pitcher after signing him as a 2000 second-round pick, and he has been much more effective in the minors. He mixes up an average 87-91 mph fastball, a curveball and a changeup. He works from a balanced, clean delivery and exhibits advanced pitchability. He needs to sharpen his consistency with his curveball and is toying with a slider. Borrell was shut down in the second half last year with shoulder pain, but he returned for the Florida State League postseason. He'll pitch in Double-A in 2002.

Year	Club (League)	Class	W	L	ERA	G	GS	CG	SV	IP	H	R	ER	BB	SO
2000	Yankees (GCL)	R	0	1	0.00	1	1	0	0	3	2	1	0	0	2
	Staten Island (NY-P)	A	4	2	3.20	10	10	0	0	56	39	21	20	19	44
2001	Tampa (FSL)	A	7	9	3.97	22	20	0	0	111	109	58	49	38	84
MINOR LEAGUE TOTALS			11	12	3.65	33	31	0	0	170	150	80	69	57	130

23. Yhency Brazoban, of

Born: June 11, 1980. **Ht.:** 6-1. **Wt.:** 170. **Bats:** R. **Throws:** R. **Career Transactions:** Signed out of Dominican Republic by Yankees, July 10, 1997.

Brazoban patterns his game after Vladimir Guerrero's. He shares the No. 27, doesn't wear batting gloves and tries to imitate the Expos superstar's actions at the plate and in the field. While Brazoban has rare five-tool potential and one of the highest ceilings in the system, he has a long way to go before approaching his countryman's MVP credentials. Like Guerrero, he has outstanding bat speed and a maximum-effort swing, but Brazoban doesn't have command of the strike zone and needs to tone down his furious hacks. Because he's a free swinger, his power has yet to blossom. He crushes fastballs in his zone. His most advanced tools—range and a cannon arm—are on display in right field. Brazoban faces a tough challenge developing his offense in the pitching-friendly Florida State League this year, where his main focus should be developing a patient eye.

Year	Club (League)	Class	AVG	G	AB	R	H	2B	3B	HR	RBI	BB	SO	SB
1998	Yankees (DSL)	R	.319	68	251	51	80	19	2	9	46	31	75	10
1999	Yankees (GCL)	R	.320	56	200	33	64	14	5	1	26	12	47	7
2000	Greensboro (SAL)	A	.188	12	48	6	9	3	0	0	8	3	15	1
	Yankees (GCL)	R	.303	54	201	36	61	14	4	5	28	11	28	2
2001	Greensboro (SAL)	A	.273	124	469	51	128	23	3	6	52	19	98	6
	Columbus (IL)	AAA	.200	1	5	2	1	1	0	0	0	0	2	0
MINOR LEAGUE TOTALS			.292	315	1174	179	343	74	14	21	160	76	265	26

24. Chase Wright, lhp

Born: Feb. 8, 1983. **Ht.:** 6-2. **Wt.:** 190. **Bats:** L. **Throws:** L. **School:** Iowa Park (Texas) HS. **Career Transactions:** Selected by Yankees in third round of 2001 draft; signed June 10, 2001.

Coveted for both his live arm and live bat, Wright was considered one of the top two-way Texas high school talents last spring. His velocity jumped from 86-87 mph to 90-93 in a workout following the draft. Physically, he reminds the Yankees of Eric Milton, their 1996 first-round pick. After Wright's pro debut, New York believes his stuff might not be far behind Milton's at the same stage of development. Wright maintained his increased velocity, sitting in the 90-91 range during his stay in the Gulf Coast League. His control plagued him in the GCL, though. Because he's an excellent athlete—he ran the 60-yard dash in 6.6 seconds in high school and had intriguing power potential—he should be able to repeat his delivery and throw more strikes in the future. The Yankees will be patient with him until he does.

Year	Club (League)	Class	W	L	ERA	G	GS	CG	SV	IP	H	R	ER	BB	SO
2001	Yankees (GCL)	R	2	3	7.92	10	7	0	0	25	33	28	22	21	33
MINOR LEAGUE TOTALS			2	3	7.92	10	7	0	0	25	33	28	22	21	33

25. John Rodriguez, of

Born: Jan. 20, 1978. **Ht.:** 6-0. **Wt.:** 185. **Bats:** L. **Throws:** L. **School:** Louis Brandeis HS, New York. **Career Transactions:** Signed as nondrafted free agent by Yankees, Nov. 17, 1996.

The Yankees' big budget didn't have anything to do with landing Rodriguez. It was more a credit to Bronx area scout Cesar Presbott, who got a tip and signed the nondrafted free agent for $1,000 after a tryout at Yankee Stadium. Rodriguez attracted little attention outside the organization until last season, when he emerged as a legitimate power-hitting prospect. He has outstanding bat speed and hit 22 homers last year despite playing his home games at Norwich's cavernous Dodd Memorial Stadium. Rodriguez is an aggressive hitter who needs to gain a better understanding of the strike zone and learn to lay off bad pitches. He made progress on cutting down his swing last year and showed much improved defensive skills. With Juan Rivera and Marcus Thames ahead of him on the depth chart, plus the Yankees' preference for veterans, Rodriguez' future in the organization is uncertain. He'll spend 2002 in Triple-A and could serve as a lefthanded option off the bench in New York if needed.

Year	Club (League)	Class	AVG	G	AB	R	H	2B	3B	HR	RBI	BB	SO	SB
1997	Yankees (GCL)	R	.299	46	157	31	47	10	2	3	23	30	32	7
1998	Greensboro (SAL)	A	.252	119	408	64	103	18	4	10	49	64	93	14
1999	Tampa (FSL)	A	.305	71	269	37	82	14	3	8	43	41	52	2
	Yankees (GCL)	R	.286	3	7	1	2	0	1	0	1	3	0	0
2000	Norwich (EL)	AA	.196	17	56	4	11	4	0	1	10	8	22	0
	Tampa (FSL)	A	.268	105	362	59	97	14	2	16	44	40	81	3
2001	Norwich (EL)	AA	.285	103	393	64	112	31	1	22	66	26	117	2
	Yankees (GCL)	R	.833	2	6	2	5	0	0	0	2	0	0	0
MINOR LEAGUE TOTALS			.277	466	1658	262	459	91	13	60	238	212	397	28

26. Aaron Rifkin, 1b

Born: March 12, 1979. **Ht.:** 6-3. **Wt.:** 220. **Bats:** L. **Throws:** L. **School:** Cal State Fullerton. **Career Transactions:** Selected by Yankees in fourth round of 2001 draft; signed June 15, 2001.

Rifkin was the fourth of eight college seniors drafted in the first 10 rounds by the Yankees last June. The Diamondbacks took him in the 54th round out of high school in 1997, but he opted for NCAA Division III Chapman (Calif.) before transferring to Cal State Fullerton. Rifkin went undrafted after hitting .322-8-27 in his junior season, and batted .300-16-60 as a senior. Many draft experts were surprised to see Rifkin go in the top 10 rounds last year, but he went on to win the MVP in the New York-Penn League. Rifkin has a picturesque swing, and he attracted the Yankees with his advanced hitting approach. He has good plate coverage, uses the whole field and attacks pitches in his zone. Despite his large frame, Rifkin is a polished defensive first baseman. At 23, Rifkin could afford to skip a level and jump to high Class A. The Yankees believe they may have uncovered a sleeper.

Year	Club (League)	Class	AVG	G	AB	R	H	2B	3B	HR	RBI	BB	SO	SB
2001	Staten Island (NY-P)	A	.318	69	245	41	78	19	5	10	49	31	47	3
MINOR LEAGUE TOTALS			.318	69	245	41	78	19	5	10	49	31	47	3

27. Jason Grove, of

Born: Aug. 15, 1978. **Ht.:** 6-2. **Wt.:** 200. **Bats:** L. **Throws:** L. **School:** Washington State University. **Career Transactions:** Selected by Yankees in third round of 2000 draft; signed June 10, 2000.

Grove broke the hamate bone in his right wrist during batting practice before his junior season at Washington State. After he returned, the wrist hampered his performance and knocked him out of the top two rounds. Upon signing, Grove broke a foot in a postdraft minicamp, which delayed his pro debut until 2001. After a slow start last season, the sweet-swinging lefty hit .339 over the final three months. His didn't show enough patience at the plate in his debut, but Yankees brass raves about his makeup and aptitude. Grove strokes the ball to all fields and can drive the ball into the alleys with some authority. He's a below-average runner with a left-field arm. Grove improved his defense over the course of the season by spending extra time reading balls off the bat in batting practice. Grove's season should start in high Class A, where he ended 2001 in the Florida State League postseason.

Year	Club (League)	Class	AVG	G	AB	R	H	2B	3B	HR	RBI	BB	SO	SB
2000			Did Not Play—Injured											
2001	Greensboro (SAL)	A	.296	115	446	68	132	21	8	15	68	36	108	0
	Tampa (FSL)	A	.400	1	5	1	2	2	0	0	2	0	2	0
MINOR LEAGUE TOTALS			.297	116	451	69	134	23	8	15	70	36	110	0

28. Elvis Corporan, 3b

Born: June 9, 1980. **Ht.:** 6-3. **Wt.:** 200. **Bats:** B. **Throws:** R. **School:** Lake City (Fla.) CC. **Career Transactions:** Selected by Yankees in 31st round of 1998 draft; signed May 19, 1999.

Drafted out of high school in Puerto Rico, Corporan attended Lake City (Fla.) CC to hone his skills for a year before signing as a draft-and-follow. He was named after Elvis Presley. In each of the last two seasons, Corporan has struggled in low Class A. He has a long swing and is working on developing his plate discipline, which the Yankees stress. He grew up playing other sports in Puerto Rico and is still raw on a baseball field. He has power potential from both sides of the plate. Defensively, he's athletic with quick, smooth actions and a strong arm. Juan Camacho could push Corporan if he doesn't show improvement at the plate this year in high Class A.

Year	Club (League)	Class	AVG	G	AB	R	H	2B	3B	HR	RBI	BB	SO	SB
1999	Yankees (GCL)	R	.278	56	212	29	59	13	3	4	30	19	41	3
2000	Greensboro (SAL)	A	.247	63	255	37	63	10	1	4	31	28	66	10
	Staten Island (NY-P)	A	.260	73	281	37	73	14	2	8	36	23	61	7
2001	Greensboro (SAL)	A	.225	135	484	65	109	25	6	15	53	35	124	15
MINOR LEAGUE TOTALS			.247	327	1232	168	304	62	12	31	150	105	292	35

29. Jason Anderson, rhp

Born: June 9, 1979. **Ht.:** 6-0. **Wt.:** 170. **Bats:** L. **Throws:** R. **School:** University of Illinois. **Career Transactions:** Selected by Yankees in 10th round of 2000 draft; signed June 13, 2000.

As a junior in 2000, Anderson was named Big Ten Conference pitcher of the year and MVP of the league tournament. His 14 wins that year set Illinois' single-season record and boosted his career mark to 29-5. Still relatively unheralded, he began his pro career as a starter. Shifted to the bullpen in favor of David Martinez during the 2000 New York-Penn League postseason, Anderson caught everyone's attention with 96 mph gas. As a starter, he regularly sits in the 90-91 range and shows potential to have four slightly above-average pitches. He demonstrates a good feel for setting up hitters with his curveball. He uses a sweeping slider against righthanders and also has a deceptive changeup. With workhorse stamina and command of four pitches, Anderson will remain a starter. Though he got off to a promising start in low Class A last year, a rash of injuries in Staten Island's rotation forced him to take a step back. He could move faster in a short-relief role.

Year	Club (League)	Class	W	L	ERA	G	GS	CG	SV	IP	H	R	ER	BB	SO
2000	Staten Island (NY-P)	A	6	5	4.03	15	15	0	0	80	84	41	36	25	73
2001	Greensboro (SAL)	A	7	9	3.76	23	19	1	1	124	127	68	52	40	101
	Staten Island (NY-P)	A	5	1	1.70	7	7	0	0	48	32	9	9	12	56
MINOR LEAGUE TOTALS			18	15	3.46	45	41	1	1	252	243	118	97	77	230

30. Richard Brown, of

Born: April 28, 1977. **Ht.:** 6-1. **Wt.:** 196. **Bats:** L. **Throws:** L. **School:** Nova HS, Fort Lauderdale. **Career Transactions:** Selected by Yankees in second round of 1995 draft; signed July 28, 1995 . . . Released by Yankees, Nov. 7, 2001; re-signed by Yankees, Nov. 21, 2001.

The Yankees always have loved football players and drafted several in 1995. They took a pair of college quarterbacks in Texas' Shea Morenz (first round) and Florida State's Danny Kanell (25th), as well as two Florida high school outfielders with football scholarships in Brown (second, Florida State) and Daunte Culpepper (26th, Central Florida). Brown was considered one of the best athletes in the draft but also a gamble because of his football prowess. Though he's been slow to develop, New York still thinks highly of him and re-signed him to a minor league deal in December after removing him from the 40-man roster a month earlier. Injuries have hampered him throughout his career, yet his tools remain evident. A broken foot stalled him in 2000 and a torn rotator cuff limited him to 14 games last season. Brown's blazing speed grades out as a 70 on the 20-80 scouting scale. His bat speed gives him power potential. He still needs to learn the nuances of the game, and his throwing arm limits him to left field. The Yankees hope Brown's athleticism will take over when he returns to action in Double-A.

Year	Club (League)	Class	AVG	G	AB	R	H	2B	3B	HR	RBI	BB	SO	SB
1996	Yankees (GCL)	R	.287	47	164	33	47	8	3	0	23	23	32	2
1997	Yankees (GCL)	R	.367	10	30	7	11	3	0	0	3	5	6	0
1998	Tampa (FSL)	A	.298	80	282	46	84	13	3	11	38	45	54	8
	Yankees (GCL)	R	.429	6	14	6	6	0	0	2	2	1	3	2
1999	Norwich (EL)	AA	.261	104	383	46	100	18	8	6	54	34	81	5
2000	Columbus (IL)	AAA	.216	10	37	1	8	2	0	0	2	1	7	0
	Norwich (EL)	AA	.238	82	319	52	76	15	3	4	30	25	34	15
2001	Norwich (EL)	AA	.349	11	43	7	15	2	0	3	7	5	9	1
	Yankees (GCL)	R	.167	2	6	1	1	1	0	0	2	2	4	0
	Tampa (FSL)	A	.600	1	5	0	3	1	0	0	2	0	0	0
MINOR LEAGUE TOTALS			.274	353	1283	199	351	63	17	26	163	141	230	33

OAKLAND
Athletics

TM

TOP 30 PROSPECTS

1. Carlos Pena, 1b
2. Eric Byrnes, of
3. Chad Harville, rhp
4. Esteban German, 2b
5. Bobby Crosby, ss
6. Mark Ellis, ss
7. Jeremy Bonderman, rhp
8. Freddie Bynum, 2b/ss
9. Franklyn German, rhp
10. Chris Tritle, of
11. Mike Wood, rhp
12. John Rheinecker, lhp
13. Matt Allegra, of
14. Neal Cotts, lhp
15. Chris Enochs, rhp
16. Aaron Harang, rhp
17. Juan Pena, lhp
18. Bert Snow, rhp
19. Marcus McBeth, of
20. Matt Bowser, of
21. Rich Harden, rhp
22. Mike Frick, rhp
23. Jon Adkins, rhp
24. Marshall McDougall, 3b/2b
25. Francis Gomez Alfonseca, ss
26. Daylan Holt, of
27. Claudio Galva, lhp
28. Oscar Salazar, 2b/ss
29. Mike Lockwood, of
30. Keith Surkont, rhp

By Casey Tefertiller

The Athletics have been a model of success, drafting and developing their own talent to build a winner, then trading away prospects to bring in players who could make instant contributions. That formula brought Oakland an American League West title in 2000 and a wild-card berth in 2001. Both playoff adventures ended at the hands of the Yankees.

After the 2001 postseason ended, the A's began a new era—again, thanks to the Yankees. Jason Giambi accepted a seven-year, $120 million contract to wear pinstripes, while Oakland also lost Johnny Damon and Jason Isringhausen to free agency. General manager Billy Beane scrambled to fill the holes, using prospects Eric Hinske, Justin Miller and Tyler Yates in deals that returned Billy Koch and David Justice.

Beane's biggest trade came in mid-January and addressed Giambi's departure. Oakland landed Carlos Pena, the best first-base prospect in baseball, and Mike Venafro at the cost of four prospects: lefthander Mario Ramos, whom some in the organization expect to become a frontline starter, along with outfielder Ryan Ludwick, first baseman Jason Hart and catcher Gerald Laird. While

such moves have strengthened the big league team, they have left the farm system weakened. Last year was the first since 1992 that A's affiliates combined for a losing record. Oakland hardly is bereft of talent, but the system isn't as stocked as it has been.

Big changes also took place off the field this offseason. Director of player personnel J.P. Ricciardi was named Blue Jays GM, while scouting director Grady Fuson became assistant GM for the Rangers. Ricciardi excelled at evaluating talent. Fuson had been innovative and creative, amassing a record of success by both hitting big in the first round and by finding surprises later in the draft. Longtime administrator Karl Kuehl, most recently a minor league adviser, left for a job with the Indians.

National crosschecker Ron Hopkins and former Devil Rays advance scout Matt Keough were named special assistants to Beane, filling the duties performed by Ricciardi and the late Bill Rigney. Eric Kubota was promoted from supervisor of international scouting to replace Fuson.

The A's have become very different very quickly. Oakland hopes it can make another run at contention as baseball's anomaly: a small-revenue team with consistent success.

Organization Overview

General manager: Billy Beane. **Farm director:** Keith Lieppman. **Scouting director:** Eric Kubota.

2001 PERFORMANCE

Class	Farm Team	League	W	L	Pct.	Finish*	Manager
Majors	Oakland	American	102	60	.630	2nd (14)	Art Howe
Triple-A	Sacramento RiverCats	Pacific Coast	75	69	.521	5th (16)	Bob Geren
Double-A	Midland RockHounds	Texas	71	69	.507	4th (8)	Tony DeFrancesco
High A	Modesto A's	California	55	85	.393	10th (10)	Greg Sparks
High A	Visalia Oaks	California	61	79	.436	8th (10)	Juan Navarrete
Short-season	Vancouver Canadians	Northwest	37	39	.487	4th (8)	Webster Garrison
Rookie	AZL Athletics	Arizona	35	21	.625	1st (7)	Ricky Nelson
OVERALL 2001 MINOR LEAGUE RECORD			334	362	.480	18th (30)	

*Finish in overall standings (No. of teams in league)

ORGANIZATION LEADERS

BATTING
*AVG	Eddy Furniss, Midland/Visalia	.317
R	Esteban German, Sacra./Midland	119
H	Esteban German, Sacra./Midland	151
TB	Jacques Landry, Midland	252
2B	Marshall McDougall, Visalia	43
3B	Austin Nagle, AZL Athletics	9
HR	Jacques Landry, Midland	36
RBI	Ryan Ludwick, Sacra./Midland	103
BB	Esteban German, Sacra./Midland	81
SO	Jacques Landry, Midland	184
SB	**Carlos Rosario**, Visalia	54

PITCHING
W	Mario Ramos, Sacramento/Midland	16
L	Mark Gwyn, Modesto	13
#ERA	Mike Wood, Modesto/Vancouver	2.59
G	Tyler Yates, Sacramento/Midland	60
CG	Erik Hiljus, Sacramento	3
SV	Frank German, Visalia	19
IP	Mario Ramos, Sacramento/Midland	174
BB	**Justin Miller**, Sacramento	64
SO	Wayne Nix, Midland/Visalia	179

*Minimum 250 At-Bats #Minimum 75 Innings

TOP PROSPECTS OF THE DECADE

1992	Todd Van Poppel, rhp
1993	Todd Van Poppel, rhp
1994	Steve Karsay, rhp
1995	Ben Grieve, of
1996	Ben Grieve, of
1997	Miguel Tejada, ss
1998	Ben Grieve, of
1999	Eric Chavez, 3b
2000	Mark Mulder, lhp
2001	Jose Ortiz, 2b

TOP DRAFT PICKS OF THE DECADE

1992	Benji Grigsby, rhp
1993	John Wasdin, rhp
1994	Ben Grieve, of
1995	Ariel Prieto, rhp
1996	Eric Chavez, 3b
1997	Chris Enochs, rhp
1998	Mark Mulder, lhp
1999	Barry Zito, lhp
2000	Freddie Bynum, ss (2)
2001	Bobby Crosby, ss

Rosario

Miller

BEST TOOLS

Best Hitter for Average	Carlos Pena
Best Power Hitter	Carlos Pena
Fastest Baserunner	Marcus McBeth
Best Fastball	Franklyn German
Best Breaking Ball	Jeremy Bonderman
Best Changeup	Juan Pena
Best Control	Aaron Harang
Best Defensive Catcher	Casey Myers
Best Defensive Infielder	Mark Ellis
Best Infield Arm	Bobby Crosby
Best Defensive Outfielder	Marcus McBeth
Best Outfield Arm	Marcus McBeth

PROJECTED 2005 LINEUP

Catcher	Ramon Hernandez
First Base	Carlos Pena
Second Base	Esteban German
Third Base	Eric Chavez
Shortstop	Miguel Tejada
Left Field	Terrence Long
Center Field	Eric Byrnes
Right Field	Jermaine Dye
Designated Hitter	Adam Piatt
No. 1 Starter	Tim Hudson
No. 2 Starter	Mark Mulder
No. 3 Starter	Barry Zito
No. 4 Starter	Jeremy Bonderman
No. 5 Starter	Cory Lidle
Closer	Chad Harville

ALL-TIME LARGEST BONUSES

Mark Mulder, 1998	$3,200,000
Barry Zito, 1999	$1,625,000
Bobby Crosby, 2001	$1,350,000
Jeremy Bonderman, 2001	$1,350,000
Chris Enochs, 1997	$1,204,000

DraftAnalysis

2001 Draft

Best Pro Debut: LHP Neal Cotts (2) and RHP Mike Wood (10) don't usually top 90 mph, but they get hitters out. Cotts went 3-2, 2.32 with 34 strikeouts in 31 innings at Class A Visalia after pitching well at short-season Vancouver. Wood also had success at Vancouver before moving up to Class A Modesto, where he went 4-3, 3.09 with a 52-10 strikeout-walk ratio in 58 innings.

Best Athlete: OF Marcus McBeth (4) does a lot of things well. He had one of the best outfield arms in the draft and chases down everything in center field. SSs **Bobby Crosby** (1) and J.T. Stotts (3) and OF Austin Nagle (6) also are fine athletes.

Best Hitter: For now, C Casey Myers (9). He earned short-season Northwest League all-star honors by hitting .278-7-35. Long term, Crosby should pass him.

Best Raw Power: Using his quick hands and loft swing, lefthanded-hitting 1B Dan Johnson (7) crushes tape-measure shots. He broke Nebraska's single-season homer mark with 25 last spring.

Fastest Runner: Stotts takes just 4.15-4.2 seconds to get from the right side of the plate to first base.

Best Defensive Player: At 6-foot-3 and 195 pounds, Crosby doesn't fit the usual shortstop profile. He has sure hands, a strong, accurate arm and plenty of range.

Best Fastball: RHP Jeremy Bonderman's (1) velocity was inconsistent this spring, though he threw as hard as 96 mph and was at 92-93 in instructional league.

Most Intriguing Background: 3B Mark Hilde (32) died in a car accident that also killed top Padres prospect Gerik Baxter. After getting his GED diploma, Bonderman became the first high school junior to be drafted. Crosby's father Ed played in the majors and signed Jason Giambi.

Crosby

Closest To The Majors: Crosby is on the fast track despite the presence of Miguel Tejada in Oakland. LHP John Rheinecker (1) has average velocity and plus life on his fastball. RHP Jeff Bruksch (5) has a tough slider and big-game experience as Stanford's closer.

Best Late-Round Pick: Wood, who began his career at North Florida as an infielder. Area scout John Poloni, who signed Tim Hudson, also pushed hard for Wood because he has similar sink on his pitches.

The One Who Got Away: 1B/RHP Jason Dixon (18) has Richie Sexson power potential and an 88-89 mph fastball. He turned down Oakland for North Florida.

Assessment: The A's value skills over raw tools, which leads them to college players, with Bonderman the lone exception in the first 10 rounds last year. They got Bonderman and Rheinecker with compensation picks for free agent Kevin Appier, a trade they'll make every time.

2000 Draft

The Athletics surprised everyone by taking 2B/SS Freddie Bynum (2) with their top pick. OF Daylan Holt (3) has struggled, so the best players might be OF Chris Tritle (19) and RHP Rich Harden (17, draft-and-follow). **Grade: C**

1999 Draft

Oakland got a pair of LHPs, Barry Zito (1) and Mario Ramos (6), who made a quick impact. Ramos and OF Ryan Ludwick (2), another good choice, were packaged to get first-base prospect Carlos Pena. OF Matt Allegra (16, draft-and-follow) bears watching. **Grade: A**

1998 Draft

LHP Mark Mulder (1) was a nice start, and C Gerald Laird (2, draft-and-follow) and 1B Jason Hart (5) were in the Pena deal. OF Eric Byrnes (8) is on the verge of starting for Oakland, and RHP Tyler Yates (23) was traded for Dave Justice this offseason. **Grade: B+**

1997 Draft

The Athletics spent three of their four first-round picks looking for an ace, but didn't find one in Chris Enochs, Eric DuBose or Denny Wagner. They did with RHP Tim Hudson (6). OF Nathan Haynes (1) was traded and is a promising Angels prospect. OF Adam Piatt (8) got to the majors quickly, while RHP Chad Harville (2) is the A's best pitching prospect. **Grade: A**

Note: Draft analysis prepared by Jim Callis. Numbers in parentheses indicate draft rounds.

... He has a silky smooth lefthanded stroke and always has maintained solid strike-zone judgment.

Carlos Pena 1b

Born: May 17, 1978.
Ht.: 6-2. **Wt.:** 210.
Bats: L. **Throws:** L.
School: Northeastern University.
Career Transactions: Selected by Rangers in first round (10th overall) of 1998 draft; signed July 24, 1998 . . . Traded by Rangers with LHP Mike Venafro to Athletics for 1B Jason Hart, C Gerald Laird, OF Ryan Ludwick and LHP Mario Ramos, January 14, 2002.

Pena established himself as the top first-base prospect in the game last year. After driving in more than 100 runs in each of his first two full pro seasons, he slumped at the start of 2001. Hamstring and ribcage problems contributed to him hitting just .229 in his first 50 games. He got healthy and batted .326-15-50 in the second half and was impressive during his September callup with the Rangers, which included a two-homer game against Oakland. Because Rafael Palmeiro is still at first in Texas, Pena worked out in right field in the Dominican Republic this winter. He was born in the Dominican before moving to Boston with his family in 1992, later becoming a local star at Northeastern and in the Cape Cod League. Any chance that Pena might switch positions ended in mid-January, when the Athletics acquired him and Mike Venafro for four of their top prospects.

Pena showed opposite-field power in the majors that was better than advertised. He had gotten into trouble in the past by trying to pull too many pitches. He has a silky smooth lefthanded stroke and always has maintained solid strike-zone judgment. Pena is a good athlete who runs well enough to leg out doubles and steal an occasional base. He's smart and has the character to be a clubhouse leader. He must stay back on breaking pitches to handle them better. He looks for fastballs too often, contributing to his average of 129 strikeouts the last three seasons. Big league lefthanders noticed and held him to one hit and five whiffs in 11 at-bats. Pena sometimes tries to be too flashy at first base, and he got caught in between hops on too many balls while in the majors.

The Athletics are giving the daunting assignment of replacing Jason Giambi to Pena, who has the tools and makeup to handle it well. He's a leading candidate for American League rookie of the year and has the potential to be a perennial all-star.

Year	Club (League)	Class	AVG	G	AB	R	H	2B	3B	HR	RBI	BB	SO	SB
1998	Rangers (GCL)	R	.400	2	5	1	2	0	0	0	0	3	1	1
	Savannah (SAL)	A	.325	30	117	22	38	14	0	6	20	8	26	3
	Charlotte (FSL)	A	.273	7	22	1	6	1	0	0	3	2	8	0
1999	Charlotte (FSL)	A	.255	136	501	85	128	31	8	18	103	74	135	2
2000	Tulsa (TL)	AA	.299	138	529	117	158	36	2	28	105	101	108	12
2001	Oklahoma (PCL)	AAA	.288	119	431	71	124	38	3	23	74	80	127	11
	Texas (AL)	MAJ	.258	22	62	6	16	4	1	3	12	10	17	0
MAJOR LEAGUE TOTALS			.258	22	62	6	16	4	1	3	12	10	17	0
MINOR LEAGUE TOTALS			.284	432	1605	297	456	120	13	75	305	268	405	29

2. Eric Byrnes, of

Born: Feb. 16, 1976. **Ht.:** 6-2. **Wt.:** 210. **Bats:** R. **Throws:** R. **School:** UCLA. **Career Transactions:** Selected by Athletics in eighth round of 1998 draft; signed June 12, 1998.

Byrnes played his high school ball near Oakland in Mountain View, Calif., and has been impressive since turning pro. He batted .357 in his debut, was a California League all-star in 1999 and earned playing time in the majors the last two years. After earning a spot on the Athletics' 2001 playoff roster, he was MVP of the Dominican League in the offseason. Byrnes has hit at every stop, and the A's believe he has solid power potential that he'll unlock as he continues to develop his game. His speed is another asset. He also has an intense work ethic that has led to continual improvement, and he always exhibits all-out hustle. While Byrnes has improved greatly on defense the last two years, he has work remaining to become a top-level outfielder. Some still question whether he has the tools to become an everyday major leaguer or is just a supreme overachiever. The trade of Ryan Ludwick and Byrnes' huge winter have raised his standing in the organization, though. He'll come to spring training fighting for a big league job. Oakland hopes he'll become a leadoff man who can set the table for the rest of the order.

Year	Club (League)	Class	AVG	G	AB	R	H	2B	3B	HR	RBI	BB	SO	SB
1998	S. Oregon (NWL)	A	.314	42	169	36	53	10	2	7	31	16	16	6
	Visalia (Cal)	A	.426	29	108	26	46	9	2	4	21	18	15	11
1999	Modesto (Cal)	A	.337	96	365	86	123	28	1	6	66	58	37	28
	Midland (TL)	AA	.238	43	164	25	39	14	0	1	22	17	32	6
2000	Midland (TL)	AA	.301	67	259	49	78	25	2	5	37	43	38	21
	Sacramento (PCL)	AAA	.333	67	243	55	81	23	1	9	47	31	30	12
	Oakland (AL)	MAJ	.300	10	10	5	3	0	0	0	0	0	1	2
2001	Sacramento (PCL)	AAA	.289	100	415	81	120	23	2	20	51	33	66	25
	Oakland (AL)	MAJ	.237	19	38	9	9	1	0	3	5	4	6	1
MAJOR LEAGUE TOTALS			.250	29	48	14	12	1	0	3	5	4	7	3
MINOR LEAGUE TOTALS			.313	444	1723	358	540	132	10	52	275	216	234	109

3. Chad Harville, rhp

Born: Sept. 16, 1976. **Ht.:** 5-9. **Wt.:** 186. **Bats:** R. **Throws:** R. **School:** University of Memphis. **Career Transactions:** Selected by Athletics in second round of 1997 draft; signed June 19, 1997.

Harville tasted the majors barely two years after signing, then went through a bit of a lull. He came to spring training last year shooting for a job on the big league roster, only to land on the 60-day disabled list instead with a strained rotator cuff. He used the down time to develop a smoother delivery to reduce the strain on his shoulder. Harville threw 98 mph when he signed, but the injury and refined motion have dropped him to 95, albeit with better movement on his four-seam fastball. He also has a plus slider, giving him two hard pitches that could make him a major league closer. Last year he added both a low-90s two-seamer and a slow curveball, making it more difficult for hitters to sit on his hard stuff. He had a problem throwing his four-seam fastball at the knees, as it often would arrive thigh-high, but the difficulty was less pronounced after he expanded his repertoire. He's still learning to use all four pitches together. Oakland has been waiting three years for Harville to refine his skills and bring his heat to the majors on a full-time basis. He'll compete for a set-up job this spring.

Year	Club (League)	Class	W	L	ERA	G	GS	CG	SV	IP	H	R	ER	BB	SO
1997	S. Oregon (NWL)	A	1	0	0.00	3	0	0	0	5	3	0	0	3	6
	Visalia (Cal)	A	0	0	5.79	14	0	0	0	19	25	14	12	13	24
1998	Visalia (Cal)	A	4	3	3.00	24	7	0	4	69	59	25	23	31	76
	Huntsville (SL)	AA	0	0	2.45	12	0	0	8	15	6	4	4	13	24
1999	Midland (TL)	AA	2	0	2.01	17	0	0	7	22	13	6	5	9	35
	Vancouver (PCL)	AAA	1	0	1.75	22	0	0	11	26	24	5	5	11	36
	Oakland (AL)	MAJ	0	2	6.91	15	0	0	0	14	18	11	11	10	15
2000	Sacramento (PCL)	AAA	5	3	4.50	53	0	0	9	64	53	35	32	35	77
2001	Modesto (Cal)	A	0	0	3.00	2	1	0	0	3	2	2	1	0	3
	Visalia (Cal)	A	0	0	0.00	1	1	0	0	3	3	0	0	0	3
	Sacramento (PCL)	AAA	5	2	3.98	33	0	0	8	41	35	20	18	12	55
	Oakland (AL)	MAJ	0	0	0.00	3	0	0	0	3	2	0	0	0	2
MAJOR LEAGUE TOTALS			0	2	5.71	18	0	0	0	17	20	11	11	10	17
MINOR LEAGUE TOTALS			18	8	3.38	181	9	0	47	266	223	111	100	127	339

4. Esteban German, 2b

Born: Dec. 26, 1978. **Ht.:** 5-10. **Wt.:** 180. **Bats:** R. **Throws:** R. **Career Transactions:** Signed out of Dominican Republic by Athletics, July 4, 1996.

German put up quality numbers during his first four seasons in the system, but there were reservations about his long-term ability. His long swing and propensity to hit pop-ups to the right side made the Athletics wonder if he'd adjust at higher levels. But in 2001, he concentrated on playing the little man's game and was Oakland's minor league player of the year. Speed is his game, and when he uses it he becomes an offensive force. He stole 83 bases in 2000, then 48 in 61 attempts last season. He has a knack for reading pitchers and getting jumps that make for a prolific basestealer. A prototypical leadoff man, he works pitchers well, can hit late in the count and has developed a propensity to reach base. After making more contact and hitting more balls on the ground, German needs to grow more comfortable with that approach. He also must become more consistent on defense, where he's limited to second base and isn't exceptional there. He has an outside chance at Oakland's second-base job this spring. More likely, he'll open the year at Triple-A Sacramento. He could be a better long-term fit in the leadoff role than Eric Byrnes.

Year	Club (League)	Class	AVG	G	AB	R	H	2B	3B	HR	RBI	BB	SO	SB
1997	Athletics East (DSL)	R	.317	69	249	69	79	17	1	2	29	73	30	58
1998	Athletics West (DSL)	R	.313	10	32	9	10	1	1	0	4	7	2	1
	Athletics (AZL)	R	.307	55	202	52	62	3	10	2	28	33	43	40
1999	Modesto (Cal)	A	.311	128	501	107	156	16	12	4	52	102	128	40
2000	Visalia (Cal)	A	.264	109	428	82	113	14	10	2	35	61	86	78
	Midland (TL)	AA	.213	24	75	13	16	1	0	1	6	18	21	5
2001	Midland (TL)	AA	.284	92	335	79	95	20	3	6	30	63	66	31
	Sacramento (PCL)	AAA	.373	38	150	40	56	8	0	4	14	18	20	17
MINOR LEAGUE TOTALS			.298	525	1972	451	587	80	37	21	198	375	396	270

5. Bobby Crosby, ss

Born: Jan. 12, 1980. **Ht.:** 6-3. **Wt.:** 195. **Bats:** R. **Throws:** R. **School:** Long Beach State University. **Career Transactions:** Selected by Athletics in first round (25th overall) of 2001 draft; signed July 3, 2001.

As the son of Ed Crosby, the former A's scout who signed Jason Giambi and is now with the Diamondbacks, Bobby has a baseball pedigree. The 2001 Big West Conference player of the year, he played only briefly after signing because of a hip flexor injury. He reported to instructional league, but the organization decided he would be best off going home to recover. Crosby has the potential to become a big-time hitter for a middle infielder. He was arguably the top defensive player in the 2001 draft. The A's rave about his baseball instincts. He's a field general whose head is always in the game. Despite his reputation, Crosby will need more flexibility to become a fluid big league shortstop. At 6-foot-3, he's tall for the position and doesn't bend well to snare grounders. Nevertheless, he seemed to make all the plays during his brief stop in the California League. Crosby will return to high Class A to hone his skills during his first full year as a pro. The A's want to see him as a shortstop for a full season before deciding if he might be better suited for third base.

Year	Club (League)	Class	AVG	G	AB	R	H	2B	3B	HR	RBI	BB	SO	SB
2001	Modesto (Cal)	A	.395	11	38	7	15	5	0	1	3	3	8	0
MINOR LEAGUE TOTALS			.395	11	38	7	15	5	0	1	3	3	8	0

6. Mark Ellis, ss

Born: June 6, 1977. **Ht.:** 5-11. **Wt.:** 180. **Bats:** R. **Throws:** R. **School:** University of Florida. **Career Transactions:** Selected by Royals in ninth round of 1999 draft; signed June 3, 1999 . . . Traded by Royals with OF Johnny Damon and a player to be named to Athletics, as part of three-way trade in which Royals acquired C A.J. Hinch, SS Angel Berroa and cash from Athletics and RHP Roberto Hernandez from Devil Rays, Devil Rays acquired OF Ben Grieve and a player to be named or cash from Athletics and Athletics acquired RHP Cory Lidle from Devil Rays, Jan. 8, 2001.

Oakland netted three players in a three-team deal with the Devil Rays and Royals in January 2001: Johnny Damon and Cory Lidle, who contributed to the club's wild-card run, and the lesser-known Ellis. Though he had played just seven games in Double-A, the A's sent him to Triple-A last season. He was impressive at Sacramento and again in the Arizona Fall League, where he hit .308 with nine steals. A consistent, effective middle infielder, Ellis is a heady player who rarely makes mistakes. Offensively, he uses the whole field, hits for average and draws his share of walks. Despite only average speed, he has the skill to steal bases and is an outstanding baserunner. The big question is whether he has the arm to play shortstop at the big league level. He helps his cause with a quick first step and release. He has ample arm to play second base, and that may be his position of the future if he's to become a regular. The presence of Miguel Tejada is another factor that will push Ellis toward second. He will compete with Esteban German, Randy Velarde and incumbent Frank Menechino at second base this spring.

Year	Club (League)	Class	AVG	G	AB	R	H	2B	3B	HR	RBI	BB	SO	SB
1999	Spokane (NWL)	A	.327	71	281	67	92	14	0	7	47	47	40	21
2000	Wilmington (Car)	A	.302	132	484	83	146	27	4	6	62	78	72	25
	Wichita (TL)	AA	.318	7	22	4	7	1	0	0	4	5	5	1
2001	Sacramento (PCL)	AAA	.273	132	472	71	129	38	0	10	53	54	78	21
MINOR LEAGUE TOTALS			.297	342	1259	225	374	80	4	23	166	184	195	68

7. Jeremy Bonderman, rhp

Born: Oct. 28, 1982. **Ht.:** 6-1. **Wt.:** 210. **Bats:** R. **Throws:** R. **School:** Pacso (Wash.) HS. **Career Transactions:** Selected by Athletics in first round (26th overall) of 2001 draft; signed Aug. 22, 2001.

Because he was 18 and received his GED diploma, Bonderman was able to enter the 2001 draft and became the first high school junior ever selected. He drew scouts' attention the previous summer, when he was the ace of the U.S. team that finished second at the World Junior Championship. Hamstring problems and high expectations kept him at less than his best last spring. Negotiations with Oakland stalled before he signed for $1.35 million and went to instructional league. The A's have prospered by drafting college pitches, but Bonderman was too enticing to resist. With a fastball that ranges from 93-96 mph and a hard breaking ball that's a cross between a curveball and slider, his ceiling is in orbit. Bonderman pitched just three innings in instructional league and he's as raw as the wind off the Columbia River. His ability to throw strikes and come up with a changeup are unproven, and the A's haven't seen enough of him to know what else might need to be done. Oakland probably will start Bonderman in high Class A (their lowest level with a full-season affiliate) on a tight pitch count, then send him to short-season Vancouver in June. They don't want to overwhelm him early in his career.

Year	Club (League)	Class	W	L	ERA	G	GS	CG	SV	IP	H	R	ER	BB	SO
			Has Not Played—Signed 2002 Contract												

8. Freddie Bynum, 2b/ss

Born: March 15, 1980. **Ht.:** 6-1. **Wt.:** 180. **Bats:** L. **Throws:** R. **School:** Pitt County (N.C.) CC. **Career Transactions:** Selected by Athletics in second round of 2000 draft; signed June 19, 2000.

Bynum hit .521 and went 27-for-27 in steals at Pitt (N.C.) Community College in 2000, leading to his somewhat surprising selection as Oakland's top draft pick (second round). Managers rated him the No. 1 prospect in the short-season Northwest League during his pro debut, but continuing problems with his right ankle limited his progress in 2001. The A's moved him from shortstop to second base last year, and second may be a better fit because he has extra time to make plays. Bynum has the raw tools to make for an outstanding top-of-the-order hitter and middle infielder. He has a plus arm, plus speed, outstanding hand-eye coordination and remarkable range. He plays with an enthusiasm that becomes contagious to those around him. The recurring injuries robbed Bynum of needed experience against pro pitching to refine his stroke. He also needs to show more patience to bat early in a lineup. He struggled at shortstop, fumbling grounders, but at second base he was able to recover in time more often to get the out. Bynum will return to the California League in 2002 to make up for lost time. He needs to start converting his raw tools into skills.

Year	Club (League)	Class	AVG	G	AB	R	H	2B	3B	HR	RBI	BB	SO	SB
2000	Vancouver (NWL)	A	.256	72	281	52	72	10	1	1	26	31	58	22
2001	Modesto (Cal)	A	.261	120	440	59	115	19	7	2	46	41	95	28
MINOR LEAGUE TOTALS			.259	192	721	111	187	29	8	3	72	72	153	50

9. Franklyn German, rhp

Born: Jan. 20, 1980. **Ht.:** 6-6. **Wt.:** 245. **Bats:** R. **Throws:** R. **Career Transactions:** Signed out of Dominican Republic by Athletics, July 2, 1996.

German, who's not related to Esteban German, has gone through a metamorphosis from a slender teenager into a Lee Smith lookalike and throwalike. The A's added him to the 40-man roster in November, anticipating he could go in the major league Rule 5 draft despite never having pitched above Class A. Considering how well he pitched in his native Dominican this winter—he didn't allow a run and held opponents to a .075 average in his first 14 appearances—German likely would have been taken. A power arm with huge potential, German hit 97 mph during the regular season and 99 in the Dominican. His velocity has increased each year since he signed. He uses both a splitter and a changeup to complement his heat. His biggest weaknesses are his command and maturity, neither of which is consistent. But he made strides in both areas this winter thanks to working with Sacramento manager Bob Geren, the skipper of a rival Dominican club. Oakland will send German to Double-A this season and see how he develops. Though Billy Koch and Chad Harville are ahead of him for now, German could give the A's another closer option in two years or so.

Year	Club (League)	Class	W	L	ERA	G	GS	CG	SV	IP	H	R	ER	BB	SO
1997	Athletics West (DSL)	R	8	3	2.33	13	13	5	0	89	66	33	23	31	80
1998	Athletics (AZL)	R	2	1	6.13	14	12	0	0	54	69	43	37	18	46
1999	S. Oregon (NWL)	A	3	5	5.99	15	15	0	0	74	89	52	49	45	58
2000	Modesto (Cal)	A	5	5	5.50	17	14	0	0	72	88	55	44	37	52
	Vancouver (NWL)	A	1	0	1.77	9	2	0	0	20	13	4	4	10	20
2001	Visalia (Cal)	A	2	4	3.98	53	0	0	19	63	67	34	28	31	93
MINOR LEAGUE TOTALS			21	18	4.47	121	56	5	19	372	392	221	185	172	349

10. Chris Tritle, of

Born: June 22, 1982. **Ht.:** 6-3. **Wt.:** 195. **Bats:** R. **Throws:** R. **School:** Center Point-Urbana HS, Center Point, Iowa. **Career Transactions:** Selected by Athletics in 19th round of 2000 draft; signed June 28, 2000.

A multisport star at his Iowa high school, Tritle ran in the state track meet and earned all-conference honors in basketball. He had several football scholarship offers as a wide receiver, which caused him to slide in the 2000 draft, but he signed with Oakland. He returned to the Rookie-level Arizona League last summer and was named the league's MVP and No. 1 prospect. Tritle is a five-tool player with a high ceiling. He led the AZL in homers and steals and has the potential to be a 30-30 player in time. He has the speed and ability to play center field, getting outstanding jumps on balls and showing fine instincts. Still a long way from the majors, Tritle will need time to develop. He has to make more contact, as breaking balls currently give him problems. More of a pull hitter at this point, he could use right field more effectively. Oakland hopes he proves ready for the California League in spring training. He's a player who really would benefit if the A's had a low Class A affiliate as opposed to two in high Class A.

Year	Club (League)	Class	AVG	G	AB	R	H	2B	3B	HR	RBI	BB	SO	SB
2000	Athletics (AZL)	R	.233	44	150	30	35	10	1	3	21	20	39	8
2001	Athletics (AZL)	R	.336	52	214	47	72	6	8	9	42	22	55	26
MINOR LEAGUE TOTALS			.294	96	364	77	107	16	9	12	63	42	94	34

11. Mike Wood, rhp

Born: April 26, 1980. **Ht.:** 6-3. **Wt.:** 175. **Bats:** R. **Throws:** R. **School:** University of North Florida. **Career Transactions:** Selected by Athletics in 10th round of 2001 draft; signed June 10, 2001.

Wood emerged as one of the big surprises of the 2001 draft, exhibiting a sinking two-seam fastball that drops from hitters' thighs to their ankles, the same sort of pitch that has lifted Tim Hudson to prominence. Wood was signed by John Poloni, the same area scout who tabbed Hudson as a sixth-round selection in 1997, so the comparisons are inevitable. Wood also throws a slider, splitter and changeup, giving him an effective four-pitch repertoire. After just five appearances in short-season ball, he was moved on to high Class A, where he continued to prove effective. During most of his pro debut, Wood pitched with a tired arm and worked in the mid-80s with his sinker. He threw in the low 90s in college, and the A's expect a return to that velocity after an offseason of rest and weight work. Wood walked on at North Florida an infielder before moving to the mound as a sophomore. He set a school record with 16 saves last spring as the Ospreys finished third in the Division II College World Series. He could reach Double-A Midland at some point in 2002.

Year	Club (League)	Class	W	L	ERA	G	GS	CG	SV	IP	H	R	ER	BB	SO
2001	Vancouver (NWL)	A	2	0	1.25	5	2	0	0	22	17	4	3	4	24
	Modesto (Cal)	A	4	3	3.09	10	9	0	0	58	46	22	20	10	52
MINOR LEAGUE TOTALS			6	3	2.59	15	11	0	0	80	63	26	23	14	76

12. John Rheinecker, lhp

Born: May 29, 1979. **Ht.:** 6-2. **Wt.:** 215. **Bats:** L. **Throws:** L. **School:** Southwest Missouri State University. **Career Transactions:** Selected by Athletics in first round (37th overall) of 2001 draft; signed June 30, 2001.

Rheinecker would have been a high pick in the 2000 draft, but he tore the anterior cruciate ligament in his right knee while playing the outfield for Southwest Missouri State. He returned for his senior season and improved to the point where the A's probably wouldn't have gotten him with a supplemental first-rounder last June if he hadn't had some forearm tenderness late in the college season. Former scouting director Grady Fuson said Rheinecker was a priority pick for the A's, who had monitored him closely during his college career. He has very good stuff for a lefthander, with a lively 90-mph fastball and quality breaking pitches (both curveball and slider) that he can throw to both sides of the plate. He's a tough competitor who battles for every out, and his main need is to improve his command. He'll spend this year in high Class A.

Year	Club (League)	Class	W	L	ERA	G	GS	CG	SV	IP	H	R	ER	BB	SO
2001	Vancouver (NWL)	A	0	1	1.59	6	5	0	0	23	13	5	4	4	17
	Modesto (Cal)	A	0	1	6.30	2	2	0	0	10	10	7	7	5	5
MINOR LEAGUE TOTALS			0	2	3.03	8	7	0	0	33	23	12	11	9	22

13. Matt Allegra, of

Born: July 10, 1981. **Ht.:** 6-3. **Wt.:** 195. **Bats:** R. **Throws:** R. **School:** Manatee (Fla.) CC. **Career Transactions:** Selected by Athletics in 16th round of 1999 draft; signed June 2, 2000.

Selected in the 16th round out of high school in 1999, Allegra signed as a draft-and-follow the next year after a stint at Manatee (Fla.) CC. He was named Oakland's most improved position player in the 2000 instructional league camp, where he altered his batting approach. When he proved unable to handle high Class A as a teenager last season, the A's moved Allegra to Vancouver, where he began to display the power potential they believe he has. He wows opponents during batting practice, showing thunder in the cage and excellent arm strength in the outfield. However, he's very raw and has trouble hitting inside pitches. He's going to have to severely upgrade his ability to make contact after fanning 165 times in 2001. Allegra is ready for another shot at the California League.

Year	Club (League)	Class	AVG	G	AB	R	H	2B	3B	HR	RBI	BB	SO	SB
2000	Athletics (AZL)	R	.270	42	141	26	38	7	3	0	13	25	44	15
2001	Modesto (Cal)	A	.209	51	153	19	32	3	2	2	17	21	61	3
	Vancouver (NWL)	A	.220	71	273	36	60	16	2	11	39	30	104	5
MINOR LEAGUE TOTALS			.229	164	567	81	130	26	7	13	69	76	209	23

14. Neal Cotts, lhp

Born: March 25, 1980. **Ht.:** 6-2. **Wt.:** 200. **Bats:** L. **Throws:** L. **School:** Illinois State University. **Career Transactions:** Selected by Athletics in second round of 2001 draft; signed June 13, 2001.

Cotts became the highest draft pick ever from Illinois State when the A's called his name in the second round last June. An all-Missouri Valley Conference selection as both a pitcher and a scholar-athlete, he outdueled John Rheinecker 2-0 in a conference matchup last spring that attracted droves of scouts. Cotts uses movement more than velocity, getting his high 80s fastball to run and sink toward the left side of the plate. He also throws a curveball and a changeup, decent pitches that need to get better. Cotts knows how to pitch and delivers strikes to both sides of the plate. Unfazed by the California League in his pro debut, he'll return there this season with the potential to advance quickly.

Year	Club (League)	Class	W	L	ERA	G	GS	CG	SV	IP	H	R	ER	BB	SO
2001	Vancouver (NWL)	A	1	0	3.09	9	7	0	0	35	28	14	12	13	44
	Visalia (Cal)	A	3	2	2.32	7	7	0	0	31	27	14	8	15	34
MINOR LEAGUE TOTALS			4	2	2.73	16	14	0	0	66	55	28	20	28	78

15. Chris Enochs, rhp

Born: Oct. 11, 1975. **Ht.:** 6-3. **Wt.:** 225. **Bats:** R. **Throws:** R. **School:** West Virginia University. **Career Transactions:** Selected by Athletics in first round (11th overall) of 1997 draft; signed June 12, 1997.

The first of three first-round picks Oakland spent on college pitchers in the 1997 draft, Enochs was revitalized by a move to the bullpen last year. A hip injury and tendinitis had hampered him for three consecutive seasons before he began regaining his form in 2001. His velocity returned to the point where he again was hitting the low 90s. With a better fastball came improved confidence. The A's now believe a relief role is most conducive to keeping him healthy. Enochs' delivery has been altered somewhat so he's no longer a drop-and-drive pitcher, and his arm angles have been changed. As a result, his curveball has regained its nasty bite and Oakland thinks he'll stay healthier. Enochs will move to Triple-A this year and may not be far from a big league opportunity.

Year	Club (League)	Class	W	L	ERA	G	GS	CG	SV	IP	H	R	ER	BB	SO
1997	S. Oregon (NWL)	A	0	0	3.48	3	3	0	0	10	12	4	4	2	10
	Modesto (Cal)	A	3	0	2.78	10	9	0	0	45	51	20	14	12	45
1998	Huntsville (SL)	AA	9	10	4.74	26	26	0	0	148	159	101	78	64	100
1999	Midland (TL)	AA	3	5	10.00	13	11	0	0	45	69	57	50	34	33
	Visalia (Cal)	A	0	0	4.91	4	4	0	0	18	24	10	10	10	19
2000	Visalia (Cal)	A	2	5	4.64	18	18	0	0	97	116	61	50	38	75
2001	Midland (TL)	AA	5	4	4.33	39	10	0	1	100	102	57	48	39	67
MINOR LEAGUE TOTALS			22	24	4.93	113	81	0	1	464	533	310	254	199	349

16. Aaron Harang, rhp

Born: May 9, 1978. **Ht.:** 6-7. **Wt.:** 240. **Bats:** R. **Throws:** R. **School:** San Diego State University. **Career Transactions:** Selected by Rangers in sixth round of 1999 draft; signed June 7, 1999 . . . Traded by Rangers with LHP Ryan Cullen to Athletics for 2B Randy Velarde, Dec. 12, 2000.

With the Rangers looking for a second baseman and the A's trying to create an opening for Jose Ortiz, Oakland traded Randy Velarde to Texas in November 2000 for Harang and lefthander Ryan Cullen. Harang had gone 22-7 in 1½ years in the Rangers organization, making a major step forward when Texas roving pitching instructor Al Nipper taught him a changeup. It's probably Harang's most effective pitch. He also throws a fastball in the low 90s and a good slider, plus he has the best command in the A's system. His poise and feel for pitching have impressed Oakland, as has his continuing maturation with his mechanics as well as the mental game. He has a strong and durable body. After surviving a year pitching his home games in a bandbox in an overall hitter's league, Harang is ready for Triple-A.

Year	Club (League)	Class	W	L	ERA	G	GS	CG	SV	IP	H	R	ER	BB	SO
1999	Pulaski (Appy)	R	9	2	2.30	16	10	1	1	78	64	22	20	17	87
2000	Charlotte (FSL)	A	13	5	3.32	28	27	3	0	157	128	68	58	50	136
2001	Midland (TL)	AA	10	8	4.14	27	27	0	0	150	173	81	69	37	112
MINOR LEAGUE TOTALS			32	15	3.43	71	64	4	1	385	365	171	147	104	335

17. Juan Pena, lhp

Born: June 4, 1979. **Ht.:** 6-3. **Wt.:** 195. **Bats:** L. **Throws:** L. **Career Transactions:** Signed out of Dominican Republic by Athletics, Nov. 1, 1995.

The brother of the oft-injured Red Sox righthander of the same name, this Juan Pena has great potential and a background of success. The California League strikeout leader in 2000, he learned to work the outside corner against righthanders in 2001, adding to his effectiveness. He has a low-90s fastball, plus a devastating changeup that he can throw as much as 20 percent of the time to keep hitters off balance. He still needs to develop his command as more advanced hitters are less likely to chase his pitches out of the strike zone. Improving his breaking ball is also on his agenda as he returns to Double-A in 2002.

Year	Club (League)	Class	W	L	ERA	G	GS	CG	SV	IP	H	R	ER	BB	SO
1996	Athletics (DSL)	R	8	2	3.21	12	12	0	0	70	75	34	25	15	59
1997	Athletics (AZL)	R	6	2	2.91	14	13	0	0	65	54	38	21	33	67
1998	S. Oregon (NWL)	A	1	2	2.15	8	8	0	0	46	46	21	11	10	38
	Modesto (Cal)	A	3	2	5.18	6	6	0	0	33	50	25	19	7	32
1999	Visalia (Cal)	A	9	5	5.76	33	18	0	1	131	168	106	84	61	107
2000	Modesto (Cal)	A	6	9	3.86	29	27	0	0	154	132	85	66	75	177
2001	Midland (TL)	AA	11	9	4.07	27	27	0	0	148	164	88	67	46	106
MINOR LEAGUE TOTALS			44	31	4.07	129	111	0	1	648	689	397	293	247	586

18. Bert Snow, rhp

Born: March 23, 1977. **Ht.:** 6-1. **Wt.:** 200. **Bats:** R. **Throws:** R. **School:** Vanderbilt University. **Career Transactions:** Selected by Athletics in 10th round of 1998 draft; signed June 20, 1998.

The native of Brooksville, Fla., seemed headed for a job in the A's bullpen when his arm went bad last season. In April he had elbow reconstruction—Tommy John surgery—that shut him down for the year. The A's are hopeful he will be ready to report for limited duty, and the plan will be to spend the season working more on rehabilitation than development. There will be no timetable, just a plan to get him ready for future seasons. In 2000, he led all minor league relievers with an average of 13.05 strikeouts per nine innings. He lives by an exceptional slider, which he mixes with a sinking fastball to keep hitters off balance. He had been working on adding a splitter when the elbow injury took him down. He has the ability to enter a game and immediately throw strikes, a talent some in the organization believe make him best suited for those emergency situations in the 7th or 8th when a rally must be squelched. He graduated from Hernando High in 1995 before moving on to Vanderbilt, where he posted a 5-7, 4.78 his junior year, before getting drafted.

Year	Club (League)	Class	W	L	ERA	G	GS	CG	SV	IP	H	R	ER	BB	SO
1998	S. Oregon (NWL)	A	1	3	5.64	11	8	0	0	45	52	38	28	18	35
	Modesto (Cal)	A	1	1	3.12	2	2	0	0	9	12	8	3	6	12
1999	Visalia (Cal)	A	3	2	5.15	31	3	0	5	65	55	43	37	40	90
	Midland (TL)	AA	1	1	1.71	21	0	0	13	21	14	4	4	9	32
	Vancouver (PCL)	AAA	1	0	3.86	2	0	0	0	2	3	1	1	1	3
2000	Midland (TL)	AA	1	7	3.59	59	0	0	27	68	58	33	27	36	98
	Sacramento (PCL)	AAA	0	0	4.50	3	0	0	0	2	1	1	1	3	3
2001						Did Not Play—Injured									
MINOR LEAGUE TOTALS			8	14	4.31	129	13	0	45	211	195	128	101	113	273

19. Marcus McBeth, of

Born: Aug. 23, 1980. **Ht.:** 6-1. **Wt.:** 185. **Bats:** R. **Throws:** R. **School:** University of South Carolina. **Career Transactions:** Selected by Athletics in fourth round of 2001 draft; signed Aug. 16, 2001.

A former return specialist for the South Carolina football team, McBeth might have been the best defensive outfielder in college baseball last spring. He almost returned to the Gamecocks for his senior season, then signed just before classes began and reported to instructional league. After wowing the organization with his plus speed, arm and defensive instincts, not to mention his power potential, McBeth found out he had a separation in his non-throwing shoulder. The injury kept him out of hitting workouts the rest of the fall. The A's hope weight work will strengthen the shoulder and allow full extension on his swing. McBeth's drawback in college was that he didn't hit for average and stuck out too much, faults Oakland blames partly on his shoulder ailment. A lack of plate discipline and pitch recognition also were factors. Nicknamed "Shakespeare" for obvious reasons, he's considered intelligent. The A's would like him to develop at the plate so they could use his speed and baserunning skills in the leadoff spot. He should surface in high Class A in 2002.

Year	Club (League)	Class	AVG	G	AB	R	H	2B	3B	HR	RBI	BB	SO	SB
			Has Not Played—Signed 2002 Contract											

20. Matt Bowser, of

Born: March 8, 1979. **Ht.:** 6-3. **Wt.:** 205. **Bats:** L. **Throws:** L. **School:** University of Central Florida. **Career Transactions:** Selected by Athletics in 11th round of 2000 draft; signed June 22, 2000.

After a miserable first year in the organization, Bowser arrived at spring training in 2001 with a new plate approach and became the talk of camp. He got off to a big start, hitting .357 in April and twice was named the organization's player of the month. He wasn't nearly as productive afterward, hitting .234 in the final three months as he stopped making consistent contact. He did enough overall to impress the A's with his power, then went to instructional league and began making the same adjustments that turned Jason Giambi into a top hitter; he learned to drive the ball to all fields. Bowser plays competent defense at the corner outfield positions, grading out with average speed and arm strength. He may just be beginning to come into his own and could have a huge year in Double-A, thanks in part to Midland's cozy Christensen Stadium.

Year	Club (League)	Class	AVG	G	AB	R	H	2B	3B	HR	RBI	BB	SO	SB
2000	Vancouver (NWL)	A	.228	68	237	29	54	11	2	4	39	32	61	1
2001	Visalia (Cal)	A	.273	131	479	92	131	32	7	21	83	70	92	10
MINOR LEAGUE TOTALS			.258	199	716	121	185	43	9	25	122	102	153	11

21. Rich Harden, rhp

Born: Nov. 30, 1981. **Ht.:** 6-1. **Wt.:** 180. **Bats:** L. **Throws:** R. **School:** Central Arizona JC. **Career Transactions:** Selected by Athletics in 17th round of 2000 draft; signed May 18, 2001.

After attending high school in British Columbia, Harden went to junior college in Arizona and caught the eye of A's scout John Kuehl. A 17th-round pick in 2000, Harden returned for his sophomore season and led national juco pitchers in strikeouts last spring before signing as a draft-and-follow. He's a power pitcher with a mid-90s fastball and a curveball that's outstanding when he can get it over the plate. After an impressive debut in the Northwest League, he spent instructional league developing a changeup. The A's say he has the raw ability to start in the major leagues one day, and they like his mound presence. He still needs much work, because his curveball and changeup are highly inconsistent. He also tends to challenge hitters by just throwing heat over the middle of the plate. Headed to high Class A, Harden will have to learn to pitch down in the strike zone against more refined hitters.

Year	Club (League)	Class	W	L	ERA	G	GS	CG	SV	IP	H	R	ER	BB	SO
2001	Vancouver (NWL)	A	2	4	3.39	18	14	0	0	74	47	29	28	38	100
MINOR LEAGUE TOTALS			2	4	3.39	18	14	0	0	74	47	29	28	38	100

22. Mike Frick, rhp

Born: March 18, 1980. **Ht.:** 6-3. **Wt.:** 230. **Bats:** R. **Throws:** R. **School:** Cal State Northridge. **Career Transactions:** Selected by Athletics in eighth round of 2001 draft; signed June 21, 2001.

Frick is an Athletics kind of player. He enjoys working out and building his body. He goes right after hitters and shows no fear. He also knows how to use the strike zone, getting outs by pitching to all quadrants. In his pro debut last summer, the A's used him primarily as a reliever, the role in which he starred as a junior at Cal State Northridge. Frick's two-pitch mix of a low-90s fastball and a tough slider is effective out of the bullpen. He did so well in instructional league that when the Phoenix club in the Arizona Fall League needed another reliever, Oakland sent Frick. He allowed only one earned run in three appearances. He'll spend 2002 in high Class A, and the A's have yet to decide whether they want to test him as a starter.

Year	Club (League)	Class	W	L	ERA	G	GS	CG	SV	IP	H	R	ER	BB	SO
2001	Vancouver (NWL)	A	7	2	2.70	21	1	0	3	40	38	15	12	15	54
MINOR LEAGUE TOTALS			7	2	2.70	21	1	0	3	40	38	15	12	15	54

23. Jon Adkins, rhp

Born: Aug. 30, 1977. **Ht.:** 6-0. **Wt.:** 200. **Bats:** L. **Throws:** R. **School:** Oklahoma State University. **Career Transactions:** Selected by Athletics in ninth round of 1998 draft; signed June 27, 1998.

After a highly impressive 2000 season, Adkins posted a 2.33 ERA in his first eight starts before Double-A Texas League hitters solved him. He wasn't able to adjust because his changeup didn't develop, which kept him as a two-pitch pitcher. He made too many mistakes, leaving hittable pitches in the strike zone. Drafted out of Oklahoma State in 1998 despite sitting out that spring to rest a partially torn elbow ligament, he had Tommy John surgery the following year. After rehabilitation, he had an improved fastball and slider. His fastball arrives in the low-90s and has good two-seam sink. His slider is also effective. The A's have been beseeching him to work on his changeup, without which he's destined to become a middle reliever. Oakland believes he needs to rededicate himself to the weight room like he did during his comeback. Demoted to the California League at the end of 2001, he still has something to prove in Double-A.

Year	Club (League)	Class	W	L	ERA	G	GS	CG	SV	IP	H	R	ER	BB	SO
1998									Did Not Play—Injured						
1999	Modesto (Cal)	A	9	5	4.76	26	15	0	1	102	113	65	54	30	93
2000	Athletics (AZL)	R	1	1	3.00	4	2	0	0	15	15	6	5	3	17
	Sacramento (PCL)	AAA	0	1	9.00	1	1	0	0	4	6	4	4	1	2
	Modesto (Cal)	A	5	2	1.81	9	7	1	0	50	41	17	10	17	38
2001	Midland (TL)	AA	8	8	4.46	24	24	1	0	137	147	71	68	36	74
	Sacramento (PCL)	AAA	1	0	4.26	3	2	0	0	13	17	9	6	8	7
MINOR LEAGUE TOTALS			24	17	4.13	67	51	2	1	321	339	172	147	95	231

24. Marshall McDougall, 3b/2b

Born: Dec. 19, 1978. **Ht.:** 6-1. **Wt.:** 200. **Bats:** R. **Throws:** R. **School:** Florida State University. **Career Transactions:** Selected by Athletics in ninth round of 2000 draft; signed June 28, 2000.

McDougall owns one of the great home run records in college baseball history, hitting six in one game against Maryland on May 9, 1999. He hit .419-28-106 and was the College World Series MVP that year, but still didn't get drafted until the Red Sox took him in the 26th round. The perception among scouts was that he lacked athleticism and owed a lot of his power to the aluminum bat. McDougall returned to Florida State for his senior year, then signed with Oakland as a ninth-round pick. A back injury limited him in his first pro summer, but last year he showed gap power and versatility in high Class A. The A's believe he has home run potential, especially after he shortened his swing and made better use of the opposite field in instructional league. He still needs to show more plate discipline. He's defensively sound at third base, plus he played all four infield positions last year. He tried the outfield during instructional league and may work out some at catcher in the future.

Year	Club (League)	Class	AVG	G	AB	R	H	2B	3B	HR	RBI	BB	SO	SB
2000	Vancouver (NWL)	A	.275	27	102	17	28	4	2	0	11	18	19	5
2001	Visalia (Cal)	A	.257	134	534	79	137	43	7	12	84	46	110	14
MINOR LEAGUE TOTALS			.259	161	636	96	165	47	9	12	95	64	129	19

25. Francis Gomez Alfonseca, ss

Born: Sept. 2, 1981. **Ht.:** 6-1. **Wt.:** 165. **Bats:** R. **Throws:** R. **Career Transactions:** Signed out of Dominican Republic by Athletics, Dec. 5, 1998.

Known alternately during his career as Francis Gomez and Francis Alfonseca, the half-brother of Antonio Alfonseca has yet to settle on the name he wishes to use. Even more difficult was his attempt to jump from Rookie ball to high Class A as a teenager last year. Alfonseca has exceptional tools, with excellent hands and range on defense and quick hands with the bat. A's officials repeatedly compare him to Miguel Tejada because of his defensive skills and power potential. Alfonseca is very aggressive, both with the bat and in the field, which is both a positive and a negative. He lacks plate discipline, makes too many errors and is very streaky. He's athletic and has shown the ability to play second and third base as well as shortstop. He'll get some more seasoning in the California League this year.

Year	Club (League)	Class	AVG	G	AB	R	H	2B	3B	HR	RBI	BB	SO	SB
1999	Athletics West (DSL)	R	.233	66	257	50	60	14	2	4	43	50	52	10
2000	Athletics (AZL)	R	.355	17	62	17	22	3	1	3	28	11	10	8
2001	Visalia (Cal)	A	.234	120	384	43	90	15	2	5	45	28	100	9
MINOR LEAGUE TOTALS			.245	203	703	110	172	32	5	12	116	89	162	27

26. Daylan Holt, of

Born: Oct. 4, 1978. **Ht.:** 6-1. **Wt.:** 200. **Bats:** R. **Throws:** R. **School:** Texas A&M University. **Career Transactions:** Selected by Athletics in third round of 2000 draft; signed Aug. 2, 2000.

Not much has gone right for Holt since he positioned himself as an early first-round pick entering the 2000 season at Texas A&M. He slumped as a junior, dropped to the third round and had just about everything possible go wrong in 2001, his first full year as a pro. His statistics last year speak for themselves, as he hit for neither power nor average. He had difficulty dealing with failure, taking out his frustrations by yelling at umpires, then didn't get borderline calls the rest of the season. Holt rebounded by putting together an outstanding instructional league, improving his stroke and readjusting his mindset. The A's expect him to return to the California League improved in all areas. With an above-average arm and surprising speed for his size, he has the potential to become a fine right fielder.

Year	Club (League)	Class	AVG	G	AB	R	H	2B	3B	HR	RBI	BB	SO	SB
2000	Vancouver (NWL)	A	.271	32	118	17	32	6	0	2	17	10	26	1
2001	Modesto (Cal)	A	.179	101	341	31	61	15	1	2	39	40	90	5
MINOR LEAGUE TOTALS			.203	133	459	48	93	21	1	4	56	50	116	6

27. Claudio Galva, lhp

Born: Nov. 28, 1979. **Ht.:** 6-2. **Wt.:** 205. **Bats:** L. **Throws:** L. **Career Transactions:** Signed out of Dominican Republic by Athletics, July 19, 1996.

Since moving into the bullpen in 2000, Galva has been both impressive and frustrating.

He constantly pitches behind in the count and gets himself into trouble before finding ways to extricate himself. Despite his proclivity for putting himself in jams, he consistently gets results. He was effective last year as a secondary closer behind Tyler Yates, who was traded to the Mets for David Justice this offseason. Galva's biggest improvement in 2001 was his increased use of his changeup. His fastball, which has life and low-90s velocity, and his slider are both solid pitches. His arm is extremely resilient and allows him to pitch several days in a row. The A's expect he'll eventually become a setup man or lefty specialist because he lacks a dominant pitch to close. They hope that a year in Triple-A will help Galva develop the consistency to make the next step to the majors.

Year	Club (League)	Class	W	L	ERA	G	GS	CG	SV	IP	H	R	ER	BB	SO
1997	Athletics West (DSL)	R	2	1	1.30	18	0	0	5	28	18	4	4	8	21
1998	Athletics West (DSL)	R	11	0	1.00	13	12	4	0	90	39	15	10	14	97
1999	Athletics (AZL)	R	6	2	2.38	14	11	0	0	68	64	23	18	16	59
2000	Visalia (Cal)	A	7	4	3.61	48	7	0	15	97	103	54	39	29	98
2001	Midland (TL)	AA	1	2	2.82	55	0	0	11	61	56	24	19	27	44
	Sacramento (PCL)	AAA	1	0	3.60	4	0	0	0	5	7	2	2	5	6
MINOR LEAGUE TOTALS			28	9	2.37	152	30	4	31	349	287	122	92	99	325

28. Oscar Salazar, 2b/ss

Born: June 27, 1978. **Ht.:** 5-11. **Wt.:** 178. **Bats:** R. **Throws:** R. **Career Transactions:** Signed out of Venezuela by Athletics, July 2, 1994.

A free-spirited, happy-go-lucky player, Salazar is a favorite among teammates and coaches despite being an atypical A's player. He's a free-swinging, undisciplined hitter who doesn't walk often enough to suit the organization. Despite chasing pitches out of the strike zone, he has hit for some average and power during his tenure in the system. But in his second year in Double-A, his average dropped 33 points. Both Esteban German and Mark Ellis moved ahead of Salazar on the middle-infield depth chart last season. He can play second base, shortstop and third base, but has proven most adept at second. With his decent hands and a good arm, he can be a competent defender. If German or Ellis makes the majors, Salazar could get a shot at Triple-A this year. If not, he will most likely return for his third season at Midland.

Year	Club (League)	Class	AVG	G	AB	R	H	2B	3B	HR	RBI	BB	SO	SB
1995	Athletics (DSL)	R	.271	53	166	29	45	10	1	0	23	22	23	5
1996	Athletics (DSL)	R	.256	69	219	49	56	9	4	3	29	47	37	9
1997	Athletics West (DSL)	R	.299	66	268	65	80	20	4	12	48	34	39	3
1998	Athletics (AZL)	R	.324	26	102	29	33	7	5	2	18	12	15	4
	S. Oregon (NWL)	A	.317	28	101	19	32	4	1	5	28	16	22	5
1999	Modesto (Cal)	A	.295	130	525	100	155	26	18	18	105	39	106	14
2000	Midland (TL)	AA	.300	111	427	70	128	27	1	13	57	39	71	4
	Sacramento (PCL)	AAA	.154	4	13	0	2	1	0	0	1	1	1	1
2001	Midland (TL)	AA	.267	130	521	75	139	31	4	18	95	49	100	10
	Sacramento (PCL)	AAA	.063	5	16	0	1	0	0	0	1	1	5	0
MINOR LEAGUE TOTALS			.285	622	2358	436	671	135	38	71	405	260	419	55

29. Mike Lockwood, of

Born: Dec. 27, 1976. **Ht.:** 6-0. **Wt.:** 190. **Bats:** L. **Throws:** L. **School:** Ohio State University. **Career Transactions:** Selected by Athletics in 23rd round of 1999 draft; signed June 13, 1999.

After hitting .343 at his first two stops in the organization, Lockwood has hit a wall since leaving high Class A. He started 2001 in a 7-for-48 slump in Double-A and never quite got himself righted. When he's going well, Lockwood is a pure hitter who uses the entire field. To advance to the majors, he must regain his high-average swing and produce more power. He's a solid defensive left fielder who can play center if needed. His arm is fair but lacks the strength typical of a right fielder. His drive has been impressive, and the A's expect his tenacity will help him rebound in 2002.

Year	Club (League)	Class	AVG	G	AB	R	H	2B	3B	HR	RBI	BB	SO	SB
1999	S. Oregon (NWL)	A	.361	69	255	48	92	18	5	7	51	39	49	6
2000	Modesto (Cal)	A	.314	47	159	42	50	12	0	6	35	46	25	9
	Midland (TL)	AA	.309	56	236	45	73	16	1	4	31	21	33	1
	Sacramento (PCL)	AAA	.254	36	126	14	32	3	0	1	13	17	14	0
2001	Midland (TL)	AA	.260	131	493	71	128	36	3	6	69	49	80	9
MINOR LEAGUE TOTALS			.296	339	1269	220	375	85	9	24	199	172	201	25

30. Keith Surkont, rhp

Born: April 4, 1977. **Ht.:** 6-2. **Wt.:** 200. **Bats:** R. **Throws:** R. **School:** Williams (Mass.) College. **Career Transactions:** Selected by Athletics in fourth round of 1999 draft; signed June 12, 1999.

After dazzling the organization in his first full pro season in 2001, Surkont hit a rough spot last year. A sore shoulder robbed him of his velocity, and he lost the sink and explosion on his fastball. The A's hope an offseason of rest will allow him to recover. The grandson of former big league pitcher Max Surkont, he has an excellent changeup and a fine breaking ball, though he needs to develop more consistency. As with most New Englanders, he hasn't had the mound time that players from warmer-weather areas have. He'll need more time to develop and build endurance. He didn't seriously consider a baseball career out of high school, choosing to attend academically oriented Williams (Mass.), an NCAA Division III school that's the alma mater of George Steinbrenner and Fay Vincent. Surkont even spent his junior year in Denmark rather than concentrating on baseball. He tore the anterior cruciate ligament in his right knee while abroad, and came back throwing harder after the surgery.

Year	Club (League)	Class	W	L	ERA	G	GS	CG	SV	IP	H	R	ER	BB	SO
1999	S. Oregon (NWL)	A	5	3	4.48	17	13	0	1	74	85	45	37	35	39
2000	Visalia (Cal)	A	8	7	2.72	27	22	0	1	126	104	60	38	54	122
2001	Modesto (Cal)	A	8	9	5.31	24	24	0	0	124	152	90	73	42	93
MINOR LEAGUE TOTALS			21	19	4.12	68	59	0	2	324	341	195	148	131	254

PHILADELPHIA
Phillies

TOP 30 PROSPECTS

1. Marlon Byrd, of
2. Brett Myers, rhp
3. Gavin Floyd, rhp
4. Taylor Buchholz, rhp
5. Anderson Machado, ss
6. Jorge Padilla, of
7. Chase Utley, 2b
8. Eric Valent, of
9. Carlos Silva, rhp
10. Yoel Hernandez, rhp
11. Franklin Nunez, rhp
12. Ryan Madson, rhp
13. Brad Baisley, rhp
14. Carlos Rodriguez, ss
15. Ryan Howard, 1b
16. Doug Nickle, rhp
17. Keith Bucktrot, rhp
18. Terry Jones, 3b
19. Ezequiel Astacio, rhp
20. Vinny DeChristofaro, lhp
21. Robinson Tejada, rhp
22. Juan Richardson, 3b
23. Elio Serrano, rhp
24. Jesus Cordero, rhp
25. G.G. Sato, c
26. Pete Zamora, lhp
27. Jason Michaels, of
28. Eric Junge, rhp
29. Cary Hiles, rhp
30. Reggie Taylor, of

By Josh Boyd

A pair of fiery short-stops—manager Larry Bowa and rookie sensation Jimmy Rollins—spurred the Phillies to a 21-game improvement over their last-place finish in 2000. They battled the Braves for the National League East title into the final week of the 2001 season, but fell two games short of earning worst-to-first distinction. Still, it marked the club's first winning season since the 1993 World Series trip.

The Phillies had an eight-game lead in the division after a 35-18 start and everything was clicking. Though Bowa's intensity wasn't always in favor with players, the overall recipe seemed to work. Rollins sparked the young nucleus on both sides of the ball. The organization's top prospect heading into the season showed poise and confidence surpassing his 22 years. He set the tone atop the order, tying for the league lead in steals and earning a spot on the NL all-star team.

The Phillies didn't panic and trade away a big chunk of their future when they needed help in their rotation. Dave Coggin, Brandon Duckworth and Nelson Figueroa occupied crucial rotation spots with the pennant on the line, and posted better ERAs than emerging staff ace Robert Person. Earlier, the farm system provided catcher Johnny Estrada when all-star Mike Lieberthal injured his right knee 24 games into the season, though Estrada didn't have as much success as the rookie starters.

The breakthrough season raised expectations in Philadelphia. Fortunately for the Phillies, they have a foundation of youth capable of living up to it. General manager Ed Wade faces a difficult decision with third baseman Scott Rolen's pending free agency following the 2002 season. But the farm system is as strong as it has been in years, with a mix of athletes, productive hitters and live arms.

When Mike Arbuckle took over as scouting director in 1992, the farm system had an embarrassing lack of Latin American players. The organization's commitment to scouting and player development has turned things around, as ownership equipped Arbuckle's scouts with the resources to aggressively sign and develop international talent. Arbuckle's overhaul of the system resulted in his promotion to assistant GM in charge of scouting and player development after the 2001 season.

Organization Overview

General manager: Ed Wade. **Farm director:** Mike Arbuckle. **Scouting director:** Marti Wolever.

2001 PERFORMANCE

Class	Team	League	W	L	Pct.	Finish*	Manager(s)
Majors	Philadelphia	National	86	76	.531	t-7th (16)	Larry Bowa
Triple-A	Scranton/W-B Red Barons	International	78	65	.545	4th (14)	M. Bombard/J. Martin
Double-A	Reading Phillies	Eastern	77	65	.542	4th (12)	Gary Varsho
High A	Clearwater Phillies	Florida State	68	69	.496	t-7th (12)	Ramon Aviles
Low A	Lakewood Blue Claws	South Atlantic	60	79	.432	14th (16)	Greg Legg
Short-season	Batavia Muckdogs	New York-Penn	37	39	.487	8th (14)	Frank Klebe
Rookie	GCL Phillies	Gulf Coast	31	29	.517	7th (14)	Roly de Armas
OVERALL 2001 MINOR LEAGUE RECORD			351	346	.504	13th (30)	

*Finish in overall standings (No. of teams in league)

ORGANIZATION LEADERS

BATTING
*AVG	Gary Burnham, Reading	.318
R	Marlon Byrd, Reading	108
H	Marlon Byrd, Reading	161
TB	Marlon Byrd, Reading	283
2B	Scott Youngbauer, Lakewood	35
3B	**Reggie Taylor**, Scranton	9
HR	Marlon Byrd, Reading	28
RBI	Marlon Byrd, Reading	89
BB	Nate Espy, Clearwater	88
SO	Juan Richardson, Lakewood	147
SB	Nick Punto, Scranton	33

PITCHING
W	Carlos Silva, Reading	15
L	Taylor Buchholz, Lakewood	14
#ERA	Adam Walker, Reading	1.88
G	Jason Boyd, Scranton	52
CG	Taylor Buchholz, Lakewood	5
SV	Trevor Bullock, Lakewood	16
	Brad Pautz, Reading/Clearwater	16
IP	Carlos Silva, Reading	180
BB	Miguel Ascencio, Clearwater	70
	Ryan Carter, Clearwater/Lakewood	70
SO	**Robinson Tejeda**, Lakewood	152

*Minimum 250 At-Bats #Minimum 75 Innings

TOP PROSPECTS OF THE DECADE

1992	Tyler Green, rhp
1993	Tyler Green, rhp
1994	Tyler Green, rhp
1995	Scott Rolen, 3b
1996	Scott Rolen, 3b
1997	Scott Rolen, 3b
1998	Ryan Brannan, rhp
1999	Pat Burrell, 1b
2000	Pat Burrell, 1b/of
2001	Jimmy Rollins, ss

TOP DRAFT PICKS OF THE DECADE

1992	Chad McConnell, of
1993	Wayne Gomes, rhp
1994	Carlton Loewer, rhp
1995	Reggie Taylor, of
1996	Adam Eaton, rhp
1997	*J.D. Drew, of
1998	Pat Burrell, 1b
1999	Brett Myers, rhp
2000	Chase Utley, 2b
2001	Gavin Floyd, rhp

*Did not sign.

Taylor   Tejeda

BEST TOOLS

Best Hitter for Average	Marlon Byrd
Best Power Hitter	Ryan Howard
Fastest Baserunner	Jay Sitzman
Best Fastball	Franklin Nunez
Best Breaking Ball	Gavin Floyd
Best Changeup	Pete Zamora
Best Control	Carlos Silva
Best Defensive Catcher	Russ Jacobson
Best Defensive Infielder	Anderson Machado
Best Infield Arm	Anderson Machado
Best Defensive Outfielder	Reggie Taylor
Best Outfield Arm	Jorge Padilla

PROJECTED 2005 LINEUP

Catcher	Mike Lieberthal
First Base	Travis Lee
Second Base	Chase Utley
Third Base	Scott Rolen
Shortstop	Jimmy Rollins
Left Field	Pat Burrell
Center Field	Marlon Byrd
Right Field	Bobby Abreu
No. 1 Starter	Brett Myers
No. 2 Starter	Gavin Floyd
No. 3 Starter	Robert Person
No. 4 Starter	Brandon Duckworth
No. 5 Starter	Randy Wolf
Closer	Franklin Perez

ALL-TIME LARGEST BONUSES

Gavin Floyd, 2001	$4,200,000
Pat Burrell, 1998	$3,150,000
Brett Myers, 1999	$2,050,000
Chase Utley, 2000	$1,780,000
Seung Lee, 2001	$1,200,000

DraftAnalysis

2001 Draft

Best Pro Debut: Sidearming RHP Ryan Hutchinson (17) had nine saves and a 0.55 ERA at short-season Batavia. Among prospects, LHP Vinny DeChristofaro (7) saw his velocity rebound into the high 80s and went 1-2, 2.17 with 33 strikeouts in 37 innings in the Rookie-level Gulf Coast League.

Best Athlete: OF Andre Marshall (13) got just 63 at-bats and hit .222 as a Washington junior in 2001, but the Phillies love his physical tools. He's a 6-foot-4, 205-pound switch-hitter with 6.5-second speed in the 60-yard dash. OF Rod Perry (12) played wide receiver for Southern California and Penn State.

Best Hitter: 1B Ryan Howard (5) entered 2001 viewed as a first- or second-round pick. Then he caught a bad case of draftitis and slogged through a mediocre spring. He got straightened out after signing, batting .272-5-35 at Batavia.

Best Raw Power: Howard. 3B Terry Jones (4) has notable pop as well, though Philadelphia hasn't seen much of it because he signed late and then came down with a hernia in instructional league.

Fastest Runner: Marshall and OF Chris Roberson (9).

Best Defensive Player: Departing from the norm, the Phillies tout a pair of corner infielders. 1B Brian Hansen (6) has exceptional hands, and the team compares him to Rico Brogna and Travis Lee. Jones is agile and has a plus arm to go with soft hands.

Best Fastball: Gavin Floyd (1) was the head of a special class of high school righthanders.

He has thrown 95-96 mph and touched 97. He also has a hard 78-80 mph curveball, and at times it gives him a second well above-average pitch. He has a feel for a changeup that at worst will be an average third offering.

Most Intriguing Background: Philadelphia got a package deal with Floyd, also signing his brother, OF Mike (22). OF Vince Vukovich's (20) father John once played for the Phillies and serves as their third-base coach. Perry's father Rod Sr. spent a decade in the NFL as a defensive back.

Floyd

Closest To The Majors: Lee will start hearing Howard's footsteps soon.

Best Late-Round Pick: Marshall. His .287-1-13 debut in the GCL was a strong first step.

The One Who Got Away: It was almost Gavin Floyd; the Phillies announced he had turned down their final offer only to sign him a day later. They landed all but three of their picks in the first 37 rounds. C Jason Jaramillo (39), a switch-hitter with defensive skills who's now at Oklahoma State, was the biggest loss.

Assessment: Philadelphia stuck to its guns and signed Gavin Floyd for the price ($4.2 million) it wanted. The Phillies forfeited their second- and third-round picks in exchange for free-agent relievers Rheal Cormier and Jose Mesa, but recovered by getting Howard in the fifth round.

2000 Draft

RHP Taylor Buchholz (6) has been the best performer to this point. 2B Chase Utley (1) and RHP Keith Bucktrot (3) have promise and are among the organization's top prospects but need to kick it up a gear.   **Grade: C**

1999 Draft

OF Marlon Byrd (10) and RHP Brett Myers (1) are the system's top two prospects. Unsigned OF Jason Cooper (2) and LHP Joe Saunders (5) are likely to be early picks in the 2002 draft.   **Grade: B+**

1998 Draft

3B Pat Burrell (1), the No. 1 overall pick, is going to be a star. OFs Jorge Padilla (3) and Eric Valent (1) and RHPs Ryan Madson (9) and Brad Baisley (2) all have upside.   **Grade: B+**

1997 Draft

Philadelphia got into a philosophical battle with OF J.D. Drew (1) and didn't sign him. At least the club salvaged LHP Randy Wolf (2). RHP Derrick Turnbow (5), another promising arm, was lost to Anaheim in the 1999 major league Rule 5 draft.   **Grade: B**

Note: Draft analysis prepared by Jim Callis. Numbers in parentheses indicate draft rounds.

. . . He resembles a young Kirby Puckett and is a fitness freak with a rock-solid physique.

Byrd **Marlon**
of

Born: Aug. 30, 1977.
Ht: 6-0. **Wt.:** 225.
Bats: R. **Throws:** R.
School: Georgia Perimeter JC
Career Transactions: Selected by Phillies in 10th round of 1999 draft; signed June 4, 1999.

Though most Phillies officials expected Byrd to spend the 2001 season at high Class A Clearwater, he fell two home runs shy of becoming the second player in Double-A Eastern League history to record a 30-30 season. A careless accident as a Georgia Tech freshman nearly cost him his athletic future. He karate-kicked a door in jest and sustained muscular damage to his right leg. He came down with an infection that cut off the circulation to the nerves in his leg and required three operations. Byrd ballooned to 315 pounds, a far cry from the days when he was a sought-after high school running back. After transferring to Georgia Perimeter Junior College, he rededicated himself and has been on a mission since. In case there were any doubts about Byrd's breakthrough, he was among the top hitters in the Arizona Fall League.

Byrd removed all of his limitations in 2001 and now offers average to above-average tools across the board. He resembles a young Kirby Puckett, but don't be fooled by his stocky frame. Byrd is a fitness freak with a rock-solid physique. He has a quiet, compact stroke, and the ball jumps off his bat to all fields. He stays back on offspeed stuff and is an intelligent hitter with a decent idea of the strike zone. Like Puckett, Byrd uses his instincts well in center field and gets good jumps in all directions. The Phillies call him a manager's dream because he never stops striving for improvement. A year ago, his below-average speed and below-average arm relegated him to left field. He got himself on a long-toss program and improved his throwing. He also worked on his running, resulting in 30 steals. His power was in question, so he built up his upper-body strength and slugged a career-best .555. He doesn't have as much baseball experience as the typical 24-year-old prospect because he lost two years to his leg injury, but he's quickly making up for lost time.

Byrd has rapidly emerged as the Phillies' center fielder of the future. He has already caught manager Larry Bowa's attention with his work ethic. Adding him to an outfield with Pat Burrell and Bob Abreu would give Philadelphia two potential 30-30 men in the lineup.

Year	Club (League)	Class	AVG	G	AB	R	H	2B	3B	HR	RBI	BB	SO	SB
1999	Batavia (NY-P)	A	.296	65	243	40	72	7	6	13	50	28	70	8
2000	Piedmont (SAL)	A	.309	133	515	104	159	29	13	17	93	51	110	41
2001	Reading (EL)	AA	.316	137	510	108	161	22	8	28	89	52	93	32
MINOR LEAGUE TOTALS			.309	335	1268	252	392	58	27	58	232	131	273	81

DAVID SCHOFIELD

2. Brett Myers, rhp

Born: Aug. 17, 1980. **Ht.:** 6-4. **Wt.:** 215. **Bats:** R. **Throws:** R. **School:** Edgewood HS, Jacksonville, Fla. **Career Transactions:** Selected in first round (12th overall) of 1999 draft; signed July 9, 1999.

Myers was challenged by jumping past Clearwater into Reading's rotation as one of the youngest players in Double-A in 2001. The fiery righthander answered the call. Myers showcased his overpowering arsenal in two scoreless innings at Safeco Field in the Futures Game. For the second year, Myers got better as the season went on, proving his durability. He added a darting two-seam fastball to a dominant 92-94 mph fourseamer that touches 95-96. He also throws a plus-plus curveball with late, sharp bite, and he has an average changeup. Myers didn't make the Eastern League Top 20 Prospect list because he didn't consistently show his outstanding stuff. Some think his future is in the bullpen because of his intensity and delivery, but he has smoothed out his mechanics and built up his endurance. His emotions sometimes get the best of him. Like he was a year ago behind Jimmy Rollins, Myers is the organization's No. 1A prospect. He'll anchor the staff someday like his idol Curt Schilling, and he shares the same big league swagger. Myers went 6-0, 3.26 after a pep talk from Schilling in Seattle, and he was generally more in control of himself in the second half.

Year	Club (League)	Class	W	L	ERA	G	GS	CG	SV	IP	H	R	ER	BB	SO
1999	Phillies (GCL)	R	2	1	2.33	7	5	0	0	27	17	8	7	7	30
2000	Piedmont (SAL)	A	13	7	3.18	27	27	2	0	175	165	78	62	69	140
2001	Reading (EL)	AA	13	4	3.87	26	23	1	0	156	156	71	67	43	130
MINOR LEAGUE TOTALS			28	11	3.42	60	55	3	0	358	338	157	136	119	300

3. Gavin Floyd, rhp

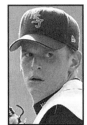

Born: Jan. 27, 1983. **Ht.:** 6-6. **Wt.:** 210. **Bats:** R. **Throws:** R. **School:** Mount St. Joseph HS, Severna Park, Md. **Career Transactions:** Selected in the first round (fourth overall) of the 2001 draft; signed Aug. 22, 2001.

With consecutive picks the Phillies and Rangers selected a pair of Severna Park, Md., neighbors, Floyd and Georgia Tech third baseman Mark Teixeira. Floyd's brother Mike, an outfielder, was selected by the Phillies in the 22nd round. The Floyd brothers were enrolled at South Carolina and on campus before Gavin agreed to a club-record $4.2 million bonus. Floyd's arm draws comparisons to Darryl Kile, Wade Miller and Brett Myers. He signed too late to pitch during the 2001 season, but he made a strong first impression in instructional league. Floyd showed his best stuff for Phillies brass, including an explosive 95-96 mph fastball that bores in on righthanders. Roving pitching instructor Gary Ruby, now with the Pirates, called Floyd's punchout curveball the best he's seen in 16 years of coaching in the minors. Floyd hasn't had to use his changeup much, though it could be a plus pitch. He's refined for his age but needs mechanical fine-tuning. He finished his delivery too straight up in instructional league. Spring training will dictate where Floyd debuts. His ceiling is comparable to that of Myers, who spent his first full season in the low Class A South Atlantic League.

Year	Club (League)	Class	W	L	ERA	G	GS	CG	SV	IP	H	R	ER	BB	SO
					Has Not Played—Signed 2002 Contract										

4. Taylor Buchholz, rhp

Born: Oct. 13, 1981. **Ht.:** 6-3. **Wt.:** 220. **Bats:** R. **Throws:** R. **School:** Springfield (Pa.) HS. **Career Transactions:** Selected by Phillies in sixth round of 2000 draft; signed June 19, 2000.

After starting his first full season with a 1-10 record, Buchholz kept his composure and reeled off six straight victories, including four complete games and three shutouts. Buchholz slid to the sixth round in the 2000 draft because most teams expected him to attend North Carolina. It took third-round money to sign him, but it looks like a wise investment. Buchholz is an exceptional athlete with a major league body, and the Phillies love his aggressiveness. He goes after hitters with a lively 92 mph fastball that tops out at 94. His curveball and changeup improved throughout the 2001 season as he became more consistent with his delivery. He showed his strong makeup by bouncing back from his ugly start. Buchholz was one of the most consistent starters in a young rotation at low Class A Lakewood, and the Phillies believe that he just needs to improve his situational pitching. The biggest culprit behind his 1-10 start was an offense that averaged 3.7 runs a game. Philadelphia has been willing to move pitchers quickly, but Buchholz will follow a more normal ascent for now. He'll head to Clearwater as one of the youngest starters in the Florida State League.

Year	Club (League)	Class	W	L	ERA	G	GS	CG	SV	IP	H	R	ER	BB	SO
2000	Phillies (GCL)	R	2	3	2.25	12	7	0	0	44	46	22	11	14	41
2001	Lakewood (SAL)	A	9	14	3.36	28	26	5	0	177	165	83	66	57	136
MINOR LEAGUE TOTALS			11	17	3.14	40	33	5	0	221	211	105	77	71	177

5. Anderson Machado, ss

Born: Jan. 25, 1981. **Ht.:** 5-11. **Wt.:** 165. **Bats:** B. **Throws:** R. **Career Transactions:** Signed out of Venezuela by Phillies, Jan. 14, 1998.

Machado returned to Clearwater in 2001 and still was one of the youngest everyday players in the Florida State League. He was named the circuit's top defensive shortstop for the second straight year. Machado's slick glovework has landed him in the Double-A playoffs in the last two seasons as a teenager. Machado cut his errors from 43 in 2000 to 25 in 2001. He has a knack for making tough plays in the hole and is close to major league-ready on defense with a strong arm, quick feet, soft hands and body control. He has excellent speed, running the 60-yard dash in 6.6 seconds. Machado can drive the ball to the opposite field from the left side, but he doesn't have any power in his frail frame. He strikes out much too often. He also suffers through momentary concentration lapses in the field, a product of his youth. After looking overmatched in Reading, Machado headed to Venezuela for the winter. With Jimmy Rollins at shortstop, the Phillies don't need to rush Machado. They have depth at the position but plan to keep him at short for now.

Year	Club (League)	Class	AVG	G	AB	R	H	2B	3B	HR	RBI	BB	SO	SB
1998	Phillies (DSL)	R	.201	68	219	26	44	7	0	0	17	30	44	4
1999	Phillies (GCL)	R	.259	43	143	26	37	6	3	2	12	15	38	6
	Clearwater (FSL)	A	.000	1	2	0	0	0	0	0	0	0	1	0
	Piedmont (SAL)	A	.233	20	60	7	14	4	2	0	7	7	20	2
2000	Clearwater (FSL)	A	.245	117	417	55	102	19	7	1	35	54	103	32
	Reading (EL)	AA	.364	3	11	2	4	1	0	1	2	0	4	0
2001	Clearwater (FSL)	A	.261	82	272	49	71	5	8	5	36	31	66	23
	Reading (EL)	AA	.149	31	101	13	15	2	0	1	8	12	25	5
MINOR LEAGUE TOTALS			.234	365	1225	178	287	44	20	10	117	149	301	72

6. Jorge Padilla, of

Born: Aug. 11, 1979. **Ht.:** 6-2. **Wt.:** 200. **Bats:** R. **Throws:** R. **School:** Florida Air Academy, Melbourne, Fla. **Career Transactions:** Selected by Phillies in third round of 1998 draft; signed July 19, 1998.

Padilla, a Puerto Rican who attended high school in Florida, has the size and tools that make scouts jump. Inconsistent performance has prevented him from getting the most of his ability since being drafted. A foot injury kept him out for a month in 2000, while a hamstring robbed him of 40 games in 2001. Padilla has tremendous untapped power, which began to surface in 2001. He uses a strong lower half to drive pitches, and he does a good job of staying inside the ball with his swing. He's a solid fielder with an above-average arm and good speed. Padilla nearly doubled his previous career total by stealing 23 bases in 2001. There were some concerns about Padilla's approach prior to 2000, but he has responded well to the criticism and now it's just a matter of staying healthy. His plate discipline also is lacking, but he has made strides there as well. The Phillies compare Padilla's upside to that of White Sox all-star Magglio Ordonez. While Padilla needs to prove his durability, he hasn't allowed injuries to hinder his ascent. Double-A will present a good measuring stick for him in 2002.

Year	Club (League)	Class	AVG	G	AB	R	H	2B	3B	HR	RBI	BB	SO	SB
1998	Martinsville (Appy)	R	.356	23	90	10	32	3	0	5	25	4	24	2
1999	Piedmont (SAL)	A	.208	44	168	13	35	10	1	3	17	5	44	0
	Batavia (NY-P)	A	.252	65	238	28	60	10	1	3	30	22	79	2
2000	Piedmont (SAL)	A	.305	108	413	62	126	24	8	11	67	26	89	8
2001	Clearwater (FSL)	A	.260	100	358	62	93	13	2	16	66	40	73	23
MINOR LEAGUE TOTALS			.273	340	1267	175	346	60	12	38	205	97	309	35

7. Chase Utley, 2b

Born: Dec. 17, 1978. **Ht.:** 6-1. **Wt.:** 185. **Bats:** L. **Throws:** R. **School:** UCLA. **Career Transactions:** Selected by Phillies in first round (15th overall) of 2000 draft; signed July 29, 2000.

Utley was drafted out of Long Beach Poly High, the same school that produced Tony Gwynn and Milton Bradley, before spurning the Dodgers to attend UCLA. A Little League teammate of Padres prospect Sean Burroughs, Utley was reunited with him at the 2001 Futures Game. After Marlon Anderson hit .228 in 2000, the Philadelphia press hailed Utley as his successor. While Anderson had a career year in 2001, Utley was challenged by the Florida State League. Utley profiles as a productive hitter for average and generates good power with a quick bat. He has become more conscious of using the entire field. He will never be a Gold Glover, but the Phillies are thrilled with the progress he made with his range and double-play pivot. He has enough arm to play second base but lacks natural actions around the bag. Utley hit .203 against southpaws and his swing can get long through the strike zone. Utley could have debuted at Lakewood and posted better offensive numbers, but the Phillies wanted to test him. He'll make the jump to Reading with double-play partner Anderson Machado.

Year	Club (League)	Class	AVG	G	AB	R	H	2B	3B	HR	RBI	BB	SO	SB
2000	Batavia (NY-P)	A	.307	40	153	21	47	13	1	2	22	18	23	5
2001	Clearwater (FSL)	A	.257	122	467	65	120	25	2	16	59	37	88	19
MINOR LEAGUE TOTALS			.269	162	620	86	167	38	3	18	81	55	111	24

8. Eric Valent, of

Born: April 4, 1977. **Ht.:** 6-0. **Wt.:** 191. **Bats:** L. **Throws:** L. **School:** UCLA. **Career Transactions:** Selected by Phillies in first round (42nd overall) of 1998 draft; signed July 1, 1998.

Valent, who broke Troy Glaus' career home run record at UCLA, got his first opportunity in Philadelphia in 2001. After collecting hits in four of his first five games, he went hitless for the rest of the season. He was leading the International League in RBIs when he was called up. Valent is a solid major league corner outfielder with right-field arm strength and accuracy. He generates above-average pull power with quick hands and hips. Valent hits hard line drives from alley to alley against both lefties and righties. Prior to his big league callup, Valent was able to avoid the peaks and valleys that had led to his label as a streak hitter. After spending time on the Phillies' bench, he took a while to get back into gear in Triple-A. His swing tends to get long when he's trying to do too much at the plate. Valent could be a victim of the organization's outfield depth. He played 27 games at first base and has the potential to be a potent bat off the bench if he isn't dangled in a trade.

Year	Club (League)	Class	AVG	G	AB	R	H	2B	3B	HR	RBI	BB	SO	SB
1998	Piedmont (SAL)	A	.427	22	89	24	38	12	0	8	28	14	19	0
	Clearwater (FSL)	A	.264	34	125	24	33	8	1	5	25	16	29	1
1999	Clearwater (FSL)	A	.288	134	520	91	150	31	9	20	106	58	110	5
2000	Reading (EL)	AA	.258	128	469	81	121	22	5	22	90	70	89	2
2001	Scranton/W-B (IL)	AAA	.272	117	448	65	122	30	2	21	78	49	105	0
	Philadelphia (NL)	MAJ	.098	22	41	3	4	2	0	0	1	4	11	0
MAJOR LEAGUE TOTALS			.098	22	41	3	4	2	0	0	1	4	11	0
MINOR LEAGUE TOTALS			.281	435	1651	285	464	103	17	76	327	207	352	8

9. Carlos Silva, rhp

Born: April 23, 1979. **Ht.:** 6-4. **Wt.:** 225. **Bats:** R. **Throws:** R. **Career Transactions:** Signed out of Venezuela by Phillies, March 22, 1996.

The story remains the same on Silva. He has had one of the organization's best arms since signing at age 16, yet has never dominated hitters. He has established himself as a workhorse and finished second in the Eastern League in 2001 with 180 innings. Silva throws a heavy 93-94 mph sinker from a three-quarters angle, and the pitch moves on a tough downward plane. He'll touch 95-96 on occasion and offers a fringe-average changeup that helps him get tons of groundouts. He's around the plate too much with his fastball. He lacks confidence in his secondary pitches and allowed opponents to settle in and hit him at a .284 clip with 20 home runs in 2001. There had been some discussion of moving Silva into the bullpen due to his lack of a consistent breaking pitch, but that was shelved after he made encouraging progress with his slider in instructional league. The Phillies once again are encouraged that Silva will be a 200-inning starter in the majors. He'll have to use his 84-mph slider and his changeup well in the Triple-A Scranton/Wilkes-Barre rotation in 2002 to avoid being banished to the bullpen.

Year	Club (League)	Class	W	L	ERA	G	GS	CG	SV	IP	H	R	ER	BB	SO
1996	Martinsville (Appy)	R	0	0	4.00	7	1	0	0	18	20	11	8	5	16
1997	Martinsville (Appy)	R	2	2	5.15	11	11	0	0	58	66	46	33	14	31
1998	Martinsville (Appy)	R	1	4	5.05	7	7	1	0	41	48	24	23	4	21
	Batavia (NY-P)	A	2	3	6.35	9	7	0	0	45	61	37	32	9	27
1999	Piedmont (SAL)	A	11	8	3.12	26	26	3	0	164	176	79	57	41	99
2000	Clearwater (FSL)	A	8	13	3.57	26	24	4	0	176	229	99	70	26	82
2001	Reading (EL)	AA	15	8	3.90	28	28	4	0	180	197	85	78	27	100
MINOR LEAGUE TOTALS			39	38	3.97	114	104	12	0	683	797	381	301	126	376

10. Yoel Hernandez, rhp

Born: April 15, 1982. **Ht.:** 6-2. **Wt.:** 170. **Bats:** R. **Throws:** R. **Career Transactions:** Signed out of Venezuela by Phillies, Nov. 5, 1998.

It's silly to read too much into Rookie-level Gulf Coast League statistics, but the Phillies were eager to see Hernandez face full-season league competition after he claimed the GCL's ERA title in 2000. Pitching with savvy beyond his youth, he took advantage of the comfortable pitching conditions at Lakewood's new GPU Energy Park. Hernandez displays an advanced feel for changing speeds and commands three pitches for strikes. He locates his 90-92 mph sinker efficiently and mixes in a late-breaking curveball and good changeup. He'll throw any of his offerings in any situation. He's aggressive with his fastball on the inner half of the plate. Hernandez hit 18 batters last year, a number the Phillies like to see. He doesn't own overpowering velocity, so he'll have to continue to be fine with his command and control. He could afford to add some weight, but he proved his stamina by logging 160 innings after spending the winter pitching in Venezuela. Hernandez will spend another winter pitching in his homeland and then start the 2002 season in high Class A. He projects as a middle-of-the-rotation starter.

Year	Club (League)	Class	W	L	ERA	G	GS	CG	SV	IP	H	R	ER	BB	SO
1999	La Victoria (VSL)	R	2	2	3.32	14	11	0	1	60	48	27	22	29	57
2000	Phillies (GCL)	R	4	1	1.35	10	9	2	0	60	39	10	9	17	46
2001	Lakewood (SAL)	A	6	9	3.47	25	25	1	0	161	153	94	62	42	111
MINOR LEAGUE TOTALS			12	12	2.99	49	45	3	1	280	240	131	93	88	214

11. Franklin Nunez, rhp

Born: Jan. 18, 1977. **Ht.:** 6-0. **Wt.:** 175. **Bats:** R. **Throws:** R. **Career Transactions:** Signed out of Dominican Republic by Dodgers, Sept. 1, 1994 . . . Released by Dodgers, Jan. 12, 1996 . . . Signed by Phillies, June 20, 1998.

The Dodgers released Nunez after one season in the Rookie-level Dominican Summer League at the age of 18. They soon may regret giving up on him so quickly. To be fair, Nunez never showed the electric stuff for the Dodgers that the Phillies have discovered since. In four years in the Philadelphia organization, Nunez has worked his way up the ladder on the strength of a fastball that reaches 99 mph. He has the best arm in the system but still is trying to corral his command. He has drawn comparisons to Mariano Rivera for his slight build and free and easy arm action, but he lacks Rivera's resilient demeanor and tends to lose his concentration and composure too easily. Nunez' overpowering stuff is best suited for the bullpen, as he never has surpassed 112 innings in a season. But the Phillies have kept him in the rotation to build stamina and provide an opportunity for Nunez to learn to repeat his delivery. At times he loses his rhythm and his mechanics break down. He worked toward improving his slurvy curveball in the Arizona Fall League. With his outstanding fastball, Nunez could jump to the big leagues in a hurry. If everything clicks for him, he could be a dynamic reliever.

Year	Club (League)	Class	W	L	ERA	G	GS	CG	SV	IP	H	R	ER	BB	SO
1995	Dodgers (DSL)	R	1	0	7.36	12	1	0	0	22	27	25	18	20	17
1996						Did Not Play									
1997						Did Not Play									
1998	Phillies (DSL)	R	0	2	2.18	5	5	1	0	33	23	14	8	14	37
	Martinsville (Appy)	R	2	2	2.49	6	4	0	0	25	23	10	7	8	19
1999	Piedmont (SAL)	A	4	8	3.39	13	13	1	0	77	69	39	29	25	88
2000	Clearwater (FSL)	A	10	4	3.62	23	14	1	2	112	112	54	45	57	81
2001	Reading (EL)	AA	8	7	4.42	39	14	0	3	110	107	68	54	51	112
MINOR LEAGUE TOTALS			25	23	3.82	98	51	3	5	379	361	210	161	175	354

12. Ryan Madson, rhp

Born: Aug. 28, 1980. **Ht.:** 6-6. **Wt.:** 180. **Bats:** L. **Throws:** R. **School:** Valley View HS, Moreno Valley, Calif. **Career Transactions:** Selected by Phillies in ninth round of 1998 draft; signed June 10, 1998.

Coming off a breakthrough season in the South Atlantic League, Madson got off to a slow start in Clearwater last year. He didn't find his groove until July, when he returned from a month-long DL stint to rest his shoulder. He answered any doubts about his health by going 3-1, 0.98 in August. Long and wiry, Madson has an ideal, projectable frame, making his slightly above-average 90-92 mph velocity more intriguing. More important, his stuff runs and sinks, causing hitters to pound the ball into the ground. He induces groundouts in bunches and was victimized for just four homers in 2001. Madson has made strides with his changeup. After fiddling with both a curveball and slider, he finally settled on an overhand curveball in instructional league. He's always demonstrated solid command of his stuff and he has a clean delivery, but he tries to get too fine at times. He was pitching behind in the count too often during the first half, taking his breaking stuff out of the equation. He lacks an out pitch, though he's better than the .290 average FSL opponents managed against him. He'll be ahead of schedule by spending 2002 in Double-A as a 21-year-old, and he figures to be a middle-of-the-rotation starter in the future.

Year	Club (League)	Class	W	L	ERA	G	GS	CG	SV	IP	H	R	ER	BB	SO
1998	Martinsville (Appy)	R	3	3	4.83	12	10	0	0	54	57	38	29	20	52
1999	Batavia (NY-P)	A	5	5	4.72	15	15	0	0	88	80	51	46	43	75
2000	Piedmont (SAL)	A	14	5	2.59	21	21	2	0	136	113	50	39	45	123
2001	Clearwater (FSL)	A	9	9	3.90	22	21	1	0	118	137	68	51	49	101
MINOR LEAGUE TOTALS			31	22	3.76	70	67	3	0	395	387	207	165	157	351

13. Brad Baisley, rhp

Born: Aug. 24, 1979. **Ht.:** 6-9. **Wt.:** 205. **Bats:** R. **Throws:** R. **School:** Land O' Lakes (Fla.) HS. **Career Transactions:** Selected by Phillies in second round of 1998 draft; signed July 16, 1998.

Baisley ranked third on this list entering 2001, trailing only Jimmy Rollins and Brett Myers. Elbow tenderness restricted Baisley to 89 innings in 2000, and the repercussions of the injury carried over into last year, when he was at his worst in Double-A. After missing most of spring training, he didn't join Reading until May. He began rushing his delivery, causing him to lose his leverage on his pitches. High hopes remain for the athletic and lanky Baisley, whose velocity didn't return to 91-93 mph until the final month of the season. His curveball is still a potential knockout pitch, and his changeup should be reliable enough to keep hitters off balance. After battling injuries for two years, Baisley desperately needs a healthy season to learn his body and mechanics. With all of the righthanded pitching prospects brewing in the system, he can't afford further setbacks.

Year	Club (League)	Class	W	L	ERA	G	GS	CG	SV	IP	H	R	ER	BB	SO
1998	Martinsville (Appy)	R	3	2	3.58	7	7	0	0	28	27	12	11	4	14
1999	Piedmont (SAL)	A	10	7	2.26	23	23	3	0	148	116	56	37	55	110
2000	Clearwater (FSL)	A	3	9	3.74	16	15	2	1	89	95	47	37	34	60
2001	Clearwater (FSL)	A	2	4	3.78	11	9	0	0	64	59	31	27	18	43
	Reading (EL)	AA	5	4	6.50	12	10	0	0	62	82	50	45	14	37
MINOR LEAGUE TOTALS			23	26	3.61	69	64	5	1	391	379	196	157	125	264

14. Carlos Rodriguez, ss

Born: Oct. 4, 1983. **Ht.:** 6-0. **Wt.:** 170. **Bats:** B. **Throws:** R. **Career Transactions:** Signed out of Dominican Republic by Phillies, Oct. 13, 2000.

Rodriguez debuted on this list last year at No. 11 before ever playing a pro game. He surfaced as one of the top prospects in the 2000 Area Code Games in Long Beach. At the time he was known as Carlos Rosario, and signed shortly after for $700,000. He made a promising pro debut in the Gulf Coast League. At 5-foot-8 and 160 pounds, Rodriguez doesn't command attention with his size but he possesses thrilling shortstop skills. He's a plus-plus runner with a strong arm and soft hands. He won't ever win a home run derby, but he can drive the ball and generates excellent bat speed, especially from the left side of the plate. He faces competition at shortstop with Jimmy Rollins in Philadelphia and Anderson Machado, Danny Gonzalez and Esteban de los Santos on the way. Rodriguez will compete for a job in Lakewood in 2002, but Gonzalez likely will relegate him to short-season Batavia.

Year	Club (League)	Class	AVG	G	AB	R	H	2B	3B	HR	RBI	BB	SO	SB
2001	Phillies (GCL)	R	.297	35	128	22	38	10	1	3	23	11	25	6
MINOR LEAGUE TOTALS			.297	35	128	22	38	10	1	3	23	11	25	6

15. Ryan Howard, 1b

Born: Nov. 19, 1979. **Ht.:** 6-4. **Wt.:** 220. **Bats:** L. **Throws:** L. **School:** Southwest Missouri State University.
Career Transactions: Selected by Phillies in fifth round of 2001 draft; signed July 2, 2001.

Howard hit .379 with a Missouri Valley Conference-leading 18 home runs as a sophomore and projected as a first-round pick for 2001. Then he suffered through a miserable junior campaign, batting .271-13-54 while setting Southwest Missouri State's single-season strikeout record. Coupled with his .231 performance with Team USA the previous summer, Howard endured questions about his bat. But his raw power and physical strength remind the Phillies of John Mayberry, a lefthanded slugger who hit 255 home runs in a 15-year career. Howard got untracked in his pro debut, displaying tape-measure power and good strike-zone knowledge. He's a low-ball hitter with power to drive the ball out of any part of the park. Scouts felt he had trouble pulling pitches with authority during the spring, but the Phillies believe it was just a case of draftitis. Despite his size, Howard moves well around first base and should be a solid average defender. Howard is considered the best raw power hitter in the system and the Phillies expect him to handle Class A in 2002 without problems.

Year	Club (League)	Class	AVG	G	AB	R	H	2B	3B	HR	RBI	BB	SO	SB
2001	Batavia (NY-P)	A	.272	48	169	26	46	7	3	6	35	30	55	0
MINOR LEAGUE TOTALS			.272	48	169	26	46	7	3	6	35	30	55	0

16. Doug Nickle, rhp

Born: Oct. 2, 1974. **Ht.:** 6-4. **Wt.:** 210. **Bats:** R. **Throws:** R. **School:** University of California. **Career Transactions:** Selected by Angels in 13th round of 1997 draft; signed June 9, 1997 . . . Traded by Angels to Phillies, Sept. 10, 1998, completing trade in which Phillies sent OF Gregg Jefferies to Angels for a player to be named (Aug. 28, 1998).

The Phillies have groomed Nickle as a closer for three years since stealing him from the Angels for Gregg Jefferies. Nickle has compiled 51 saves over that period after being converted from the rotation to the bullpen. His velocity jumped from 88-89 mph as a starter to 93-94 in relief. He has posted a 2.12 ERA since shifting to the bullpen and limited Triple-A hitters to a .206 average last year. Nickle relies on his above-average fastball and a hard, downward-biting knuckle-curve. He worked on a short, tight slider in instructional league. He has demonstrated a closer's mentality and the stamina to handle multiple-inning appearances. Command in the strike zone is the key for Nickle. He hasn't consistently demonstrated the control and mechanics to handle a closer role in the majors. But Nickle could replace disgruntled Turk Wendell and join Ricky Bottalico in Jose Mesa's setup tandem in Philadelphia.

Year	Club (League)	Class	W	L	ERA	G	GS	CG	SV	IP	H	R	ER	BB	SO
1997	Boise (NWL)	A	0	1	6.41	17	2	0	0	20	27	17	14	8	22
1998	Cedar Rapids (Mid)	A	8	4	3.78	20	7	1	0	69	66	30	29	20	59
	Lake Elsinore (Cal)	A	3	4	4.48	11	10	1	0	66	68	40	33	25	69
1999	Clearwater (FSL)	A	2	4	2.29	60	0	0	28	71	60	25	18	23	70
2000	Reading (EL)	AA	8	3	2.44	49	0	0	16	77	55	25	21	22	58
	Philadelphia (NL)	MAJ	0	0	13.50	4	0	0	0	3	5	4	4	2	0
2001	Scranton/W-B (IL)	AAA	9	3	1.68	47	1	0	7	86	62	19	16	37	60
	Philadelphia (NL)	MAJ	0	0	0.00	2	0	0	0	2	1	0	0	0	1
MAJOR LEAGUE TOTALS			0	0	7.20	6	0	0	0	−5	6	4	4	2	1
MINOR LEAGUE TOTALS			30	19	3.03	204	20	2	51	389	338	156	131	135	338

17. Keith Bucktrot, rhp

Born: Nov. 27, 1980. **Ht.:** 6-3. **Wt.:** 190. **Bats:** L. **Throws:** R. **School:** Claremore (Okla.) HS. **Career Transactions:** Selected by Phillies in third round of 2000 draft; signed June 26, 2000.

In the 2000 draft, some teams sought Bucktrot for his potent lefthanded bat rather than his live right arm. He was considered a raw, athletic talent coming out of high school, though his draft stock was hurt by off-the-field concerns. The Phillies have seen only positive results since signing Bucktrot, including a seven-inning no-hitter he threw in his second start of last season. He flashed overpowering potential again three starts later, when he carried a no-hitter into the ninth inning before settling for a two-hit complete game. His first full season was full of ups and downs. He followed his two nine-inning complete games with his worst outings of the season. While his 90-94 mph fastball and curveball are both plus pitches, Bucktrot didn't show the ability to repeat his mechanics from start to start. He also flashed the makings of a solid changeup, but lacked mound presence and a consistent feel for pitching. Bucktrot should continue to move up one level at a time, though he'll need to develop command and a better feel for pitching to avoid stalling along the way.

Year	Club (League)	Class	W	L	ERA	G	GS	CG	SV	IP	H	R	ER	BB	SO
2000	Phillies (GCL)	R	3	2	4.78	11	7	0	0	38	39	21	20	19	40
2001	Lakewood (SAL)	A	6	11	5.28	24	24	3	0	135	139	93	79	58	97
MINOR LEAGUE TOTALS			9	13	5.17	35	31	3	0	172	178	114	99	77	137

18. Terry Jones, 3b

Born: March 20, 1983. **Ht.:** 6-2. **Wt.:** 195. **Bats:** R. **Throws:** R. **School:** Upland (Calif.) HS. **Career Transactions:** Selected by Phillies in fourth round of 2001 draft; signed July 26, 2001.

Jones slipped in the 2001 draft because of his commitment to the University of California. After losing their second- and third-round picks as compensation for signing free agents, Philadelphia gambled its fourth-rounder on Jones and landed him for third-round money. A high school shortstop, he shifted to third base in the Gulf Coast League. He continued to work on the transition in instructional league before requiring hernia surgery. His athleticism draws comparisons to that of Chipper Jones, and the Phillies believe he could remain at short, though they expect him to outgrow the position. His swing should allow him to hit for average and he has raw power. Jones has the lateral mobility, quick hands and strong arm to play the hot corner, and the projectable bat to justify the move. He's just an average runner. The hernia surgery is considered a minor setback and he's ticketed for Batavia in 2002.

Year	Club (League)	Class	AVG	G	AB	R	H	2B	3B	HR	RBI	BB	SO	SB
2001	Phillies (GCL)	R	.194	9	36	3	7	0	0	0	4	2	5	0
MINOR LEAGUE TOTALS			.194	9	36	3	7	0	0	0	4	2	5	0

19. Ezequiel Astacio, rhp

Born: Nov. 4, 1980. **Ht.:** 6-3. **Wt.:** 156. **Bats:** R. **Throws:** R. **Career Transactions:** Signed out of Dominican Republic by Phillies, Feb. 22, 1998.

Astacio made his U.S. debut last year after tuning up his live, young arm in the Dominican Summer League. His impressive performance earned him recognition as the Gulf Coast League's No. 8 prospect. Astacio flirts with mid-90s velocity already, sitting at 93 mph, and he has a sharp curveball to boot. He has a projectable 6-foot-3, 156-pound frame with long, loose actions and an understanding of how to pitch. The Phillies' underrated Dominican program just keeps producing quality arms. They already are raving about 18-year-old righthander Elizardo Ramirez, who went 10-1, 1.26 in the DSL last summer. Astacio could make the leap to Lakewood this year, like Yoel Hernandez did from the GCL in 2001.

Year	Club (League)	Class	W	L	ERA	G	GS	CG	SV	IP	H	R	ER	BB	SO
1998	Phillies (DSL)	R	0	3	7.71	15	4	0	0	21	26	29	18	22	16
1999	Phillies (DSL)	R	5	2	2.67	12	12	0	0	64	50	24	19	27	42
2000	Phillies (DSL)	R	7	5	2.20	15	15	0	0	90	70	40	22	20	97
2001	Phillies (GCL)	R	4	2	2.30	9	9	0	0	47	48	16	12	10	42
MINOR LEAGUE TOTALS			16	12	2.88	51	40	0	0	222	194	109	71	79	197

20. Vinny DeChristofaro, lhp

Born: April 2, 1982. **Ht.:** 6-2. **Wt.:** 168. **Bats:** L. **Throws:** L. **School:** Richmond Hill (Ga.) HS. **Career Transactions:** Selected by Phillies in seventh round of 2001 draft; signed June 6, 2001.

The Phillies may have found a mid-round gem in DeChristofaro, who was considered potential first-round material early in the spring. His velocity fluctuated and was down from 91-92 mph to 86 by the time scouting directors flocked to see him. A late bloomer, DeChristofaro was a soft-tossing lefty who had a 7.42 ERA as a sophomore. He emerged as one of the top hurlers in a well-stocked region as a senior and engaged in a notable duel with crosstown rival Macay McBride, who became a Braves first-rounder. DeChristofaro matched McBride and nationally ranked Screven County High, but suffered a tough loss despite fanning 15. Phillies brass likens DeChristofaro to a young Tom Glavine. He did a fine job of commanding his 86-90 mph fastball to both sides of the plate after signing. He displays outstanding mound presence and owns a clean delivery. His changeup is above average and he shows the makings of a good curveball. In a system stockpiled with righthanders, DeChristofaro projects as the top lefty and could move fast as he fills out his physically immature frame.

Year	Club (League)	Class	W	L	ERA	G	GS	CG	SV	IP	H	R	ER	BB	SO
2001	Phillies (GCL)	R	1	2	2.17	9	9	0	0	37	32	12	9	14	33
MINOR LEAGUE TOTALS			1	2	2.17	9	9	0	0	37	32	12	9	14	33

21. Robinson Tejada, rhp

Born: March 24, 1982. **Ht.:** 6-3. **Wt.:** 188. **Bats:** R. **Throws:** R. **Career Transactions:** Signed out of Dominican Republic by Phillies, Nov. 24, 1998.

Tejada already had an average major league fastball when he signed at age 16 in November 1998. After two years in the Gulf Coast League, he came out of spring training last year throwing harder and landed his first spot in a full-season rotation. He was among the South Atlantic League leaders in strikeouts and dominated at times, including a 14-strikeout performance in July. Tejada pitches comfortably between 92-94. He has cleaned up his delivery, though his offspeed pitches still have a lot of room to improve. He tends to fall in love with his fastball and will complement it with an average changeup, but he lacks confidence in his curveball. He'll spend 2002 in high Class A at age 20.

Year	Club (League)	Class	W	L	ERA	G	GS	CG	SV	IP	H	R	ER	BB	SO
1999	Phillies (GCL)	R	1	3	4.27	12	9	0	0	46	47	27	22	27	39
2000	Phillies (GCL)	R	2	5	5.54	10	6	1	0	39	44	30	24	12	22
2001	Lakewood (SAL)	A	8	9	3.40	26	24	1	0	151	128	74	57	58	152
MINOR LEAGUE TOTALS			11	17	3.93	48	39	2	0	236	219	131	103	97	213

22. Juan Richardson, 3b

Born: Jan. 10, 1981. **Ht.:** 6-1. **Wt.:** 175. **Bats:** R. **Throws:** R. **Career Transactions:** Signed out of Dominican Republic by Phillies, July 1, 1998.

The Phillies had high hopes for Richardson when he signed out of the Dominican as a 17-year-old in 1998. Then he hit .216 with just eight homers in 388 at-bats over his first two seasons. Though still considered a raw prospect, he made major strides in 2001 under the guidance of Lakewood hitting coach Jeff Manto. Despite striking out 147 times, Richardson showed progress in handling offspeed stuff, tracking pitches better and using the whole field. He also improved in the field, exhibiting a strong arm and improved range at third. Richardson must cut down on his strikeouts, though he owns as much raw power as any prospect in the system. The pitching-friendly Florida State League will provide him a formidable test in 2002.

Year	Club (League)	Class	AVG	G	AB	R	H	2B	3B	HR	RBI	BB	SO	SB
1999	Phillies (GCL)	R	.226	46	164	27	37	14	0	5	23	11	46	7
	Batavia (NY-P)	A	.125	7	24	1	3	0	0	1	2	2	8	0
	Piedmont (SAL)	A	.167	4	12	0	2	1	0	0	2	1	5	0
2000	Batavia (NY-P)	A	.154	10	39	0	6	2	0	0	2	3	15	0
	Piedmont (SAL)	A	.242	43	149	19	36	11	0	2	15	17	43	0
2001	Lakewood (SAL)	A	.240	137	505	68	121	31	2	22	83	51	147	7
MINOR LEAGUE TOTALS			.230	247	893	115	205	59	2	30	127	85	264	14

23. Elio Serrano, rhp

Born: Dec. 4, 1978. **Ht.:** 6-3. **Wt.:** 215. **Bats:** R. **Throws:** R. **Career Transactions:** Signed out of Venezuela by Phillies, Jan. 17, 1996.

Serrano's career started slowly after he signed out of Venezuela at age 17. He spent four seasons in short-season ball before reaching Double-A in 2001. He has been used primarily as a reliever, and his future lies as a short man out of the pen. Serrano consistently pumps 92-94 mph fastballs with late, heavy sink. He throws a fringe-average slider with occasional sharp bite, and is trying to develop an effective changeup from a high three-quarters release. Serrano will drop down and vary his arm slot, but being consistent with his delivery has been the key to his turnaround. He has a Jose Mesa-type body and his weight is a concern.

Serrano is one of several relief prospect the Phillies are monitoring closely, along with righthanders Franklin Nunez, Doug Nickle, Jesus Cordero, Cary Hiles and Geoff Geary, and lefthander Pete Zamora.

Year	Club (League)	Class	W	L	ERA	G	GS	CG	SV	IP	H	R	ER	BB	SO
1996	Phillies (DSL)	R	5	4	4.01	15	14	1	0	85	76	63	38	49	71
1997	Martinsville (Appy)	R	1	5	5.93	21	0	0	1	41	46	34	27	16	40
1998	Batavia (NY-P)	A	3	2	2.55	13	3	0	1	35	28	13	10	10	26
1999	Batavia (NY-P)	A	0	4	4.12	19	3	0	1	39	38	22	18	20	29
2000	Piedmont (SAL)	A	4	2	2.27	38	0	0	5	67	67	26	17	15	56
2001	Clearwater (FSL)	A	2	2	3.31	17	1	0	1	35	34	14	13	7	22
	Reading (EL)	AA	1	1	2.89	30	0	0	2	37	22	12	12	9	30
MINOR LEAGUE TOTALS			16	20	3.57	153	21	1	11	340	311	184	135	126	274

24. Jesus Cordero, rhp

Born: May 5, 1979. **Ht.:** 6-2. **Wt.:** 195. **Bats:** R. **Throws:** R. **Career Transactions:** Signed out of Dominican Republic by Indians, July 8, 1996 . . . Released by Indians, May 23, 1997 . . . Signed by Marlins, July 2, 1997 . . . Granted free agency, Oct. 16, 1998 . . . Signed by Dodgers, Jan. 7, 1999 . . . Traded by Dodgers with RHP Eric Junge to Phillies for LHP Omar Daal, Nov. 9, 2001.

When the Phillies decided to excise Omar Daal's salary, they picked up Cordero and Eric Junge from the Dodgers in November. Philadelphia became Cordero's fourth organization in his young career. Originally signed as an outfielder by the Indians, he was released after playing in the Dominican Summer League. The Marlins signed him to a one-year deal, though they could have locked him up for as many as five years. Cordero's stuff improved so much by the end of his contract that he was highly sought after before the Dodgers signed him for $643,000. Working out of the pen, Cordero has showcased a live arm. He can run his fastball up into the 95-96 mph range with an effortless delivery. He also developed an effective hard slider last year. Because Cordero lacks anything offspeed, he's limited to relief. He finished 2001 on a positive note after a promotion to high Class A Vero Beach.

Year	Club (League)	Class	W	L	ERA	G	GS	CG	SV	IP	H	R	ER	BB	SO
1998	Marlins (DSL)	R	3	1	3.04	17	6	0	2	47	50	24	16	16	40
1999	Great Falls (Pio)	R	0	5	10.43	11	6	0	0	29	51	43	34	24	20
2000	Great Falls (Pio)	R	1	1	2.37	18	1	0	1	30	30	15	8	21	27
2001	Vero Beach (FSL)	A	0	1	4.32	4	1	0	0	8	7	5	4	3	10
	Wilmington (SAL)	A	8	4	2.47	33	1	0	9	69	49	20	19	25	56
MINOR LEAGUE TOTALS			12	12	3.95	83	15	0	12	185	187	107	81	89	153

25. G.G. Sato, c

Born: Aug. 9, 1978.. **Ht.:** 6-2. **Wt.:** 220. **Bats:** R. **Throws:** R. **Career Transactions:** Signed out of Japan by Phillies, Dec. 12, 2000.

The Phillies' Latin American program has provided a significant boost to the system's depth under the direction of international supervisor Sal Agostinelli, and the organization hasn't been content to stop there. The signings of Korean righthanders Seung Lee and Il Kim last year represented Philadelphia's first foray into the Pacific Rim, and Sato became its first Japanese player. Pacific Rim supervisor Doug Takargawa discovered Sato playing shortstop in college. Though he lacked the quickness to remain in the middle infield, he has the size and hands to move behind the plate. He has average major league arm strength and threw out 30 percent of basestealers in his pro debut. While learning a new position along with a new culture, Sato was forced to make quick adjustments. He held his own defensively while displaying above-average raw power. Sato, who projects as a .250-.260 hitter, should move to low Class A this year.

Year	Club (League)	Class	AVG	G	AB	R	H	2B	3B	HR	RBI	BB	SO	SB
2001	Batavia (NY-P)	A	.261	37	138	22	36	10	3	4	21	6	33	2
MINOR LEAGUE TOTALS			.261	37	138	22	36	10	3	4	21	6	33	2

26. Pete Zamora, lhp

Born: Aug. 13, 1975. **Ht.:** 6-3. **Wt.:** 185. **Bats:** L. **Throws:** L. **School:** UCLA. **Career Transactions:** Selected by Dodgers in 20th round of 1997 draft; signed June 16, 1997 . . . Selected by Phillies from Dodgers in Rule 5 minor league draft, Dec. 13, 1999.

A two-way standout at UCLA, Zamora has focused on pitching as a pro. He joined the Phillies as a Triple-A Rule 5 draft pick in 1999 and pitched a seven-inning perfect game in his first start for the organization in June 2000. Working out with college teammates Troy Glaus and Eric Valent in a rigorous plyometrics program gave Zamora improved velocity and stamina in 2001. He generates sink on his 88-90 mph fastball and his aggressiveness always has been a strong suit. He's not afraid to come inside, which is why he hasn't been limited to a situational lefthander's role. He brushed back Pawtucket's Izzy Alcantara last summer, resulting in Alcantara's infamous dropkicking escapade. Zamora will enter spring training vying for the lefthander's job in the bullpen vacated by free agent Dennis Cook.

Year	Club (League)	Class	W	L	ERA	G	GS	CG	SV	IP	H	R	ER	BB	SO
1997	Great Falls (Pio)	R	2	5	2.58	13	10	1	2	70	59	27	20	30	73
1998	San Bernardino (Cal)	A	4	1	2.09	25	5	0	6	82	43	21	19	33	77
	San Antonio (TL)	AA	3	8	4.46	12	12	0	0	67	71	52	33	27	47
1999	San Antonio (TL)	AA	2	1	6.08	35	0	0	3	64	79	48	43	30	41
2000	Reading (EL)	AA	2	3	4.09	43	7	1	6	101	105	50	46	45	94
2001	Scranton/W-B (IL)	AAA	8	4	2.93	45	6	0	3	89	64	29	29	41	79
MINOR LEAGUE TOTALS			21	22	3.62	173	40	2	20	472	421	227	190	206	411

27. Jason Michaels, of

Born: May 4, 1976. **Ht.:** 6-0. **Wt.:** 204. **Bats:** R. **Throws:** R. **School:** University of Miami. **Career Transactions:** Selected by Phillies in fourth round of 1998 draft; signed June 19, 1998.

Michaels has enjoyed a steady climb through the system. He hit a career-low .261 in 2001, though he did bat .313 against lefthanders and overall blasted a career-best 17 home runs in his first year at Triple-A. Michaels followed up by hitting .300-4-21 in the Arizona Fall League. He offers fringe-to-solid average tools across the board and can play all three outfield positions. The Phillies thought of moving him to third base to add versatility was scrapped in spring training, however. Michaels played 104 games in the outfield for Scranton without making an error. His strike-zone judgment has worsened with each promotion. He projects more as a fourth outfielder than as a regular in the big leagues. Philadelphia manager Larry Bowa likes his competitive streak, and he'll compete for a reserve job this spring.

Year	Club (League)	Class	AVG	G	AB	R	H	2B	3B	HR	RBI	BB	SO	SB
1998	Batavia (NY-P)	A	.268	67	235	45	63	14	3	11	49	40	69	4
1999	Clearwater (FSL)	A	.306	122	451	91	138	31	6	14	65	68	103	10
2000	Reading (EL)	AA	.295	113	437	71	129	30	4	10	74	28	87	7
2001	Scranton/W-B (IL)	AAA	.261	109	418	58	109	19	3	17	69	37	126	11
	Philadelphia (NL)	MAJ	.167	6	6	0	1	0	0	0	1	0	2	0
MAJOR LEAGUE TOTALS			.167	6	6	0	1	0	0	0	1	0	2	0
MINOR LEAGUE TOTALS			.285	411	1541	265	439	94	16	52	257	173	385	32

28. Eric Junge, rhp

Born: Jan. 5, 1977. **Ht.:** 6-5. **Wt.:** 215. **Bats:** R. **Throws:** R. **School:** Bucknell University. **Career Transactions:** Selected by Dodgers in 11th round of 1999 draft; signed June 5, 1999 . . . Traded by Dodgers with RHP Jesus Cordero to Phillies for LHP Omar Daal, Nov. 9, 2001.

The second of two prospects acquired from the Dodgers for Omar Daal, Junge was a starter for championship teams in the high Class A California League and Double-A Southern League the past two years. He's attractive because of his 91-94 mph fastball. His command wavers at times, and his hard slider and changeup are average at best. He has a big, durable frame and went at least six innings in 20 of his 27 starts in 2001. At times, he doesn't finish off his delivery and loses some of the leverage his size affords him. Phillies general manager Ed Wade envisions Junge as a potential No. 3 or 4 starter. At 25, he's ticketed for a full year at Triple-A.

Year	Club (League)	Class	W	L	ERA	G	GS	CG	SV	IP	H	R	ER	BB	SO
1999	Yakima (NWL)	A	5	7	5.82	15	15	0	0	82	98	60	53	31	55
2000	San Bernardino (Cal)	A	8	1	3.36	29	24	0	1	158	159	69	59	53	116
2001	Jacksonville (SL)	AA	10	11	3.46	27	27	1	0	164	143	72	63	56	116
MINOR LEAGUE TOTALS			23	19	3.90	71	66	1	1	404	400	201	175	140	287

29. Cary Hiles, rhp

Born: Nov. 29, 1975. **Ht.:** 5-10. **Wt.:** 173. **Bats:** R. **Throws:** R. **School:** University of Memphis. **Career Transactions:** Selected by Phillies in 23rd round of 1998 draft; signed June 7, 1998.

Though Hiles isn't young for a prospect, he only began pitching in college. He set the Jackson State (Tenn.) CC record for steals as a speedy outfielder before transferring to Memphis as a junior. Despite his small stature, Hiles attacks hitters with a powerful repertoire and pitches with a fearless attitude. His main weapons are a lively 90-94 mph fastball and a nasty slider. He added a splitter to combat lefties and had his best season in Double-

A in 2001. Both his slider and splitter need improvement but show signs of becoming aver-age major league pitches. His control got better last year, though he needs to do a better job of locating his pitches in the strike zone. He pitches with a fearless attitude that belies his size. Hiles will move up to Triple-A this year and could compete for a big league bullpen job before long.

Year	Club (League)	Class	W	L	ERA	G	GS	CG	SV	IP	H	R	ER	BB	SO
1998	Batavia (NY-P)	A	2	2	2.97	25	0	0	10	30	27	11	10	13	45
1999	Piedmont (SAL)	A	3	2	2.21	44	0	0	26	61	52	20	15	12	84
2000	Clearwater (FSL)	A	8	3	3.16	46	0	0	20	63	76	27	22	22	41
2001	Reading (EL)	AA	2	3	2.42	51	0	0	11	82	60	24	22	21	62
MINOR LEAGUE TOTALS			15	10	2.64	166	0	0	67	236	215	82	69	68	232

30. Reggie Taylor, of

Born: Jan. 12, 1977. **Ht.:** 6-1. **Wt.:** 178. **Bats:** L. **Throws:** R. **School:** Newberry (S.C.) HS. **Career Transactions:** Selected by Phillies in first round (14th overall) of 1995 draft; signed June 13, 1995.

Taylor's tools kept him on the club's Top 10 Prospects list for six straight seasons, but his performance rarely matched the hype. Injuries have hampered his progress in three of the last four seasons. He entered 2001 with a chance to put pressure on incumbent center field-er Doug Glanville, but he severely sprained an ankle two games into the season and wasn't healthy until May. His batting average didn't climb above .200 until mid-June. Taylor is the most athletic player in the organization. His strong arm and excellent range give him above-average major league defensive skills. His lack of plate discipline and his inability to make adjustments at the plate have prevented him from reaching his potential. Entering his eighth season in the organization, he still isn't ready for Philadelphia. Taylor's name keeps surfacing in trade rumors, and a change of scenery could be beneficial. He may never be more than an extra outfielder in the majors.

Year	Club (League)	Class	AVG	G	AB	R	H	2B	3B	HR	RBI	BB	SO	SB
1995	Martinsville (Appy)	R	.222	64	239	36	53	4	6	2	32	23	58	18
1996	Piedmont (SAL)	A	.263	128	499	68	131	20	6	0	31	29	136	36
1997	Clearwater (FSL)	A	.244	134	545	73	133	18	6	12	47	30	130	40
1998	Reading (EL)	AA	.273	79	337	49	92	14	6	5	22	12	73	22
1999	Reading (EL)	AA	.266	127	526	75	140	17	10	15	61	18	79	38
2000	Scranton/W-B (IL)	AAA	.275	98	422	60	116	10	8	15	43	21	87	23
	Philadelphia (NL)	MAJ	.091	9	11	1	1	0	0	0	0	0	8	1
2001	Scranton/W-B (IL)	AAA	.263	111	464	56	122	20	9	7	50	24	94	31
	Philadelphia (NL)	MAJ	.000	5	7	1	0	0	0	0	0	1	1	0
MAJOR LEAGUE TOTALS			.056	14	18	2	1	0	0	0	0	1	9	1
MINOR LEAGUE TOTALS			.260	741	3032	417	787	103	51	56	286	157	657	208

PITTSBURGH
Pirates

TOP 30 PROSPECTS
1. J.R. House, c
2. John VanBenschoten, rhp
3. Sean Burnett, lhp
4. Bobby Bradley, rhp
5. Jose Castillo, ss
6. Tony Alvarez, of
7. Ryan Vogelsong, rhp
8. Adrian Burnside, lhp
9. Humberto Cota, c
10. Chris Young, rhp
11. Justin Reid, rhp
12. Nate McLouth, of
13. Aron Weston, of
14. Jose Bautista, 3b
15. Domingo Cuello, 2b
16. Ryan Doumit, c
17. Josh Fogg, rhp
18. Ian Oquendo, rhp
19. John Grabow, lhp
20. J.J. Davis, of
21. Yurendell DeCaster, 3b
22. Chris Duffy, of
23. B.J. Barns, of
24. Jason Sharber, rhp
25. Roberto Novoa, rhp
26. Edwin Yan, 2b/ss
27. Jeff Miller, rhp
28. Ben Shaffar, rhp
29. Rico Washington, 3b/2b
30. Mike Gonzalez, lhp

By John Perrotto

When the Pirates had a worse season in the fifth year of their five-year plan than they did in the first year, owner Kevin McClatchy knew it was time to make changes. McClatchy started revamping the organization last June 11 when he fired general manager Cam Bonifay, who never had a winning season during a nearly eight-year run.

McClatchy and Bonifay hatched the five-year plan prior to the 1997 season. Baseball America ranked the Pirates' minor league talent as the best in baseball, and Pittsburgh finished a surprising 79-83 that year, good for second in a weak National League Central. A return to championship form seemed only a matter of time.

That was the high-water mark of their five-year plan, though. Pittsburgh bottomed out in 2001, finishing 62-100 and matching the Devil Rays for the worst record in the major leagues. That wasn't the way the franchise envisioned breaking in PNC Park.

Dave Littlefield, who had been assistant GM of the Marlins, is now entrusted with bringing the Pirates back to respectability after a ninth straight losing season and their first 100-loss season since 1985.

Injuries at the major league level in 2001—a total of 17 players went on the disabled list—forced the Pirates to rush many of their prospects, and injures struck the minors as well. Eight of the system's top 10 prospects going into 2001 either spent time on the disabled list or had surgery after the season.

Littlefield began reshaping the player development and scouting departments late in the season. Farm director Paul Tinnell was fired. Scouting director Mickey White, the architect of strong drafts from 1999-2001, was reassigned and assistant GM John Sirignano left the organization. Minor league field coordinator Steve Demeter, who spent 30 seasons in the organization, also left after instructional league ended.

Dodgers assistant GM Ed Creech was hired as scouting director, and Marlins field coordinator Brian Graham joined Littlefield as farm director.

In January, Pittsburgh added three more former Florida employees as special assistants to Littlefield: scouts Jax Robertson and Bill Singer, and Al Avila, the former scouting director who had been part of the Marlins' GM by committee and had been mentioned as a possible GM candidate in Boston.

OrganizationOverview

General manager: Dave Littlefield. **Farm director:** Brian Graham. **Scouting director:** Ed Creech.

2001 PERFORMANCE

Class	Team	League	W	L	Pct.	Finish*	Manager
Majors	Pittsburgh	National	62	100	.383	16th (16)	Lloyd McClendon
Triple-A	Nashville Sounds	Pacific Coast	64	77	.454	13th (16)	Marty Brown
Double-A	Altoona Curve	Eastern	63	79	.444	10th (12)	Dale Sveum
High A	Lynchburg Hillcats	Carolina	58	79	.423	7th (8)	Curtis Wilkerson
Low A	Hickory Crawdads	South Atlantic	67	73	.479	10th (16)	Pete Mackanin
Short-season	Williamsport Crosscutters	New York-Penn	48	26	.649	2nd (14)	Tony Beasley
Rookie	GCL Pirates	Gulf Coast	22	34	.393	t-11th (14)	Woody Huyke
OVERALL 2001 MINOR LEAGUE RECORD			322	368	.467	26th (30)	

*Finish in overall standings (No. of teams in league)

ORGANIZATION LEADERS

BATTING
*AVG	Tony Alvarez, Altoona/Lynchburg	.326
R	Chad Hermansen, Nashville	75
H	Shaun Skrehot, Nashville/Altoona	138
TB	**Jeremy Cotten**, Hickory	211
2B	Shaun Skrehot, Nashville/Altoona	33
	James Langston, Altoona/Lynchburg	33
3B	Tike Redman, Nashville	10
HR	**Jeremy Cotten**, Hickory	25
RBI	**Jeremy Cotten**, Hickory	78
	Yurendell DeCaster, Lynch./Hickory	78
BB	Chris Combs, Lynchburg	66
SO	Chad Hermansen, Nashville	154
SB	Manny Ravelo, Lynchburg/Hickory	70

PITCHING
W	Three tied at	11
L	Ryan Ledden, Lynchburg	13
#ERA	Ian Oquendo, Williamsport/GCL Pirates	1.18
G	Clint Chrysler, Nashville/Altoona	58
CG	Ryan Ledden, Lynchburg	3
	Brady Borner, Hickory/Williamsport	3
SV	**Tony Pavlovich**, Altoona/Lynchburg	25
IP	Jeff Bennett, Altoona/Lynchburg	173
BB	Steve Sparks, Nashville/Altoona	89
SO	Sean Burnett, Hickory	134

*Minimum 250 At-Bats #Minimum 75 Innings

TOP PROSPECTS OF THE DECADE

1992	Steve Cooke, lhp
1993	Kevin Young, 1b
1994	Midre Cummings, of
1995	Trey Beamon, of
1996	Jason Kendall, c
1997	Kris Benson, rhp
1998	Kris Benson, rhp
1999	Chad Hermansen, of
2000	Chad Hermansen, of
2001	J.R. House, c

TOP DRAFT PICKS OF THE DECADE

1992	Jason Kendall, c
1993	Charles Peterson, of
1994	Mark Farris, ss
1995	Chad Hermansen, ss
1996	Kris Benson, rhp
1997	J.J. Davis, of
1998	Clint Johnston, lhp/of
1999	Bobby Bradley, rhp
2000	Sean Burnett, lhp
2001	John VanBenschoten, rhp/of

Cotten   **Pavlovich**

BEST TOOLS

Best Hitter for Average	Nate McLouth
Best Power Hitter	J.J. Davis
Fastest Baserunner	Manny Ravelo
Best Fastball	John VanBenschoten
Best Breaking Ball	Bobby Bradley
Best Changeup	Sean Burnett
Best Control	Justin Reid
Best Defensive Catcher	Ryan Doumit
Best Defensive Infielder	Jose Castillo
Best Infield Arm	Jose Castillo
Best Defensive Outfielder	B.J. Barns
Best Outfield Arm	Jeremy Harts

PROJECTED 2005 LINEUP

Catcher	J.R. House
First Base	Craig Wilson
Second Base	Jose Castillo
Third Base	Aramis Ramirez
Shortstop	Jack Wilson
Left Field	Brian Giles
Center Field	Tony Alvarez
Right Field	Jason Kendall
No. 1 Starter	Kris Benson
No. 2 Starter	John VanBenschoten
No. 3 starter	Kip Wells
No. 4 starter	Sean Burnett
No. 5 starter	Bobby Bradley
Closer	Mike Williams

ALL-TIME LARGEST BONUSES

John VanBenschoten, 2001	$2,400,000
Bobby Bradley, 1999	$2,250,000
Kris Benson, 1996	$2,000,000
J.J. Davis, 1997	$1,675,000
Sean Burnett, 2000	$1,650,000
Chris Young, 2000	$1,650,000

DraftAnalysis

2001 Draft

Best Pro Debut: RHP **John VanBenschoten** (1) was named the top prospect in the short-season New York-Penn League, though he had pedestrian numbers at 0-2, 3.51 with 19 strikeouts in 25 innings. OF Chris Duffy (8) batted .317-1-24 and topped the NY-P with 30 steals, while RHP Jeff Miller (15) had a 1.13 ERA and led the league with 15 saves. LHP Brady Borner (31) had a 0.71 ERA in 13 NY-P innings before gong 5-1, 2.43 with 59 strikeouts in 58 innings in full-season Class A.

Best Athlete: Most clubs envisioned VanBenschoten, who led NCAA Division I with 31 homers, as a prototype right fielder because of his power, arm strength and speed. He also was used as a reliever at Kent State, and the Pirates decided to keep him on the mound. OF Rajai Davis (38) played basketball at Connecticut-Avery Point.

Best Hitter: 3B Jose Bautista, a 20th-round draft-and-follow from 2000, has the best bat of the players signed last year. From the draft, it would be either Duffy or C Chris Shelton (33), who batted .305-2-33 in the NY-P.

Best Raw Power: VanBenschoten's power graded out as 75 on the 20-to-80 scouting scale. Of the draftees who will focus on hitting, 1B Tim Brown (12) has the most, though Bautista has more.

Fastest Runner: Duffy and Davis can run sub-6.5-second 60-yard dashes. Both switch-hitters can get from the left side of the plate to first base in 3.6 seconds on bunts.

Best Defensive Player: Duffy is an above-average center fielder who makes up for lackluster arm strength with his quickness and accuracy.

Best Fastball: VanBenschoten. Miller, a two-way player himself at New Orleans, can touch 94 mph. He has good life on his fastball and late-breaking slider.

VanBenschoten

Most Intriguing Background: Unsigned SS Stephen Drew's (11) brothers J.D. and Tim were 1997 first-round picks. They played in the majors last year, as did unsigned RHP Robert Coomer's (25) brother Ron.

Closest To The Majors: VanBenschoten's ETA at PNC Park should be quicker as a pitcher than it would have been as an outfielder.

Best Late-Round Pick: Miller or RHP Casey Shumaker (23), a projected early-round pick who fell because of signability. Shumaker used a low-90s sinker and nasty slider to lead Division I with 14.0 strikeout per nine innings before dominating the Cape Cod League during the summer.

The One Who Got Away: Sophomore-eligible RHP Jeremy Guthrie (3) decided to return to Stanford for his junior season. He could be a first-rounder in 2002.

Assessment: Scouting director Mickey White turned in three straight solid drafts for the Pirates before being reassigned in October. The pressure will be on White's successor Ed Creech; the Pirates have the first pick in 2002.

2000 Draft

LHP Sean Burnett (1) and RHPs Chris Young (3) and Jason Sharber (5) bolstered the system's pitching depth, while OF Nate McLouth (25) is an underrated bat. The outlook got brighter with last summer's draft-and-follow addition of 3B Jose Bautista (20).   **Grade: B**

1999 Draft

After several poor drafts, Pittsburgh got back on track with C J.R. House (5) and LHP Bobby Bradley (1), even if they lost a little of their luster in 2001. RHP Justin Reid (4), OF Aron Weston (3) and C Ryan Doumit (2) all could pan out.   **Grade: B**

1998 Draft

The Pirates missed out on future first-rounders in LHP Chris Smith (11) and RHP Wyatt Allen (32) while blowing theirs on LHP/OF Clinton Johnston (1). At least LHP Joe Biemel (18) made the majors last year.   **Grade: F**

1997 Draft

OF J.J. Davis (1) isn't getting it done, setting the tone for this group. LHP John Grabow (3) is the only player who figures to help Pittsburgh, and he had a lost year after arthroscopic elbow surgery.   **Grade: D**

Note: Draft analysis prepared by Jim Callis. Numbers in parentheses indicate draft rounds.

. . . House has the potential to hit for both power and average. He has good power to the opposite field.

J.R. House c

Born: Nov. 11, 1979.
Ht.: 6-1. **Wt.:** 202.
Bats: R. **Throws:** R.
School: Seabreeze HS, Daytona Beach, Fla.
Career Transactions: Selected by Pirates in fifth round of 1999 draft; signed June 12, 1999.

House made more headlines for what he didn't do last summer than for what he did. He flirted with the idea of becoming a two-sport athlete through the first three months of the season, giving heavy consideration to playing quarterback for West Virginia. House finally decided on baseball as a full-time vocation and said he wouldn't change his mind. House is the nation's all-time leading prep passer, throwing for 14,457 yards at Nitro (W. Va.) High from 1995-98. Because he had dual residency, House played baseball at Seabreeze High in Daytona Beach, Fla. The Pirates lured House away from football with a $266,000 signing bonus as their fifth-round pick in 1999. He rankled veterans in the major league clubhouse when he received an audience with owner Kevin McClatchy before making his decision to stick with baseball.

House has the potential to hit for both power and average, and he showed it in 2000 when he was co-MVP of the South Atlantic League despite missing a month with mononucleosis. He has particularly good power to the opposite field. House made strides defensively last season, particularly with his handling of pitchers. He also has a confident aura about him, something that becomes obvious when you are around him. His strike-zone judgement regressed as he jumped from low Class A to Double-A Altoona in 2001, though that's not unusual for a young player making that kind of leap. He also still has work to do defensively as his throwing is average at best. House has seen action at first base, but his bat is much more valuable at catcher. Typical of a backstop, House doesn't run well. He had injury problems early in 2001 as he was hampered by hamstring and ribcage strains.

House struggled to adjust against advanced pitching in 2001 and seemed lost at times. With catcher Jason Kendall staying behind the plate for now, House doesn't need to be rushed. He seemed to be on the fast track prior to 2001. Now it's not out of the question that House could go back to Altoona, at least to start the season, to give him a better chance of dominating the competition before moving up to Triple-A Nashville.

Year	Club (League)	Class	AVG	G	AB	R	H	2B	3B	HR	RBI	BB	SO	SB
1999	Pirates (GCL)	R	.327	33	113	13	37	9	3	5	23	11	23	1
	Williamsport (NY-P)	A	.300	26	100	11	30	6	0	1	13	9	21	0
	Hickory (SAL)	A	.273	4	11	1	3	0	0	0	0	0	3	0
2000	Hickory (SAL)	A	.348	110	420	78	146	29	1	23	90	46	91	1
2001	Altoona (EL)	AA	.258	112	426	51	110	25	1	11	56	37	103	1
MINOR LEAGUE TOTALS			.305	285	1070	154	326	69	5	40	182	103	241	3

RODGER WOOD

2. John VanBenschoten, rhp

Born: April 14, 1980. **Ht.:** 6-4. **Wt.:** 215. **Bats:** R. **Throws:** R. **School:** Kent State University. **Career Transactions:** Selected by Pirates in first round (8th overall) of 2001 draft; signed July 3, 2001.

VanBenschoten led NCAA Division I with 31 home runs while also serving as Kent State's closer in 2001. The Pirates, unlike most teams, liked VanBenschoten better for his arm and drafted him eighth overall as a pitcher. He was the No. 1 prospect in the short-season New York-Penn League, where he also got 75 at-bats as a DH. Tall with broad shoulders, VanBenschoten has a good pitcher's frame. He's a hard thrower, running his fastball up to 94 mph with the chance to add more velocity as he builds up regular innings and arm strength. His curveball has a chance to be a good pitch with its tight rotation. He lacks experience against top-flight competition, as he was primarily a reliever at a mid-major college program. He was a star pitcher in high school but needs time to settle in as a full-time pitcher. He also must develop a changeup. The Pirates believe they made the right choice in drafting VanBenschoten as a pitcher. He's a work in progress and likely will start this season at low Class A Hickory. If he bombs as a pitcher, the Pirates always have the option of making him a hitter.

Year	Club (League)	Class	AVG	G	AB	R	H	2B	3B	HR	RBI	BB	SO	SB
2001	Williamsport (NY-P)	A	.227	32	75	9	17	5	0	0	8	7	23	3
MINOR LEAGUE TOTALS			.227	32	75	9	17	5	0	0	8	7	23	3

Year	Club (League)	Class	W	L	ERA	G	GS	CG	SV	IP	H	R	ER	BB	SO
2001	Williamsport (NY-P)	A	0	2	3.51	9	9	0	0	25	23	11	10	10	19
MINOR LEAGUE TOTALS			0	2	3.51	9	9	0	0	25	23	11	10	10	19

3. Sean Burnett

Born: Sept. 17, 1982. **Ht.:** 6-1. **Wt.:** 172. **Bats:** L. **Throws:** L. **School:** Wellington (Fla.) Community HS. **Career Transactions:** Selected by Pirates in first round (19th overall) of 2000 draft; signed July 7, 2000.

Burnett has followed Bobby Bradley over the past two years. Burnett was a junior and the No. 2 starter and Bradley was a senior and the No. 1 starter when they pitched Wellington Community High to the Florida Class 6-A state title in 1999. Bradley was the Pirates' first-round pick in 1999 and Burnett went in the first round to Pittsburgh the following year. He was the Pirates' minor league pitcher of the year in 2001. Like Bradley, Burnett has a good feel for pitching and outstanding mound presence. His best pitch is a changeup that he disguises well. It also has late tumbling action. His fastball generally reaches 88 mph, but he can get it as high as 91 mph after adding 15 pounds of muscle. Burnett wore down at the end of the 2001 season and pitched sparingly in instructional league. That was only natural for an 18-year-old in his first full season of pro ball. He has the beginnings of a good curveball but needs to tighten its rotation. Burnett has made a seamless adjustment into pro ball and his next step is to show he can get more advanced hitters out on a regular basis. He'll get that chance in 2002 at high Class A Lynchburg.

Year	Club (League)	Class	W	L	ERA	G	GS	CG	SV	IP	H	R	ER	BB	SO
2000	Pirates (GCL)	R	2	1	4.06	8	6	0	0	31	31	17	14	3	24
2001	Hickory (SAL)	A	11	8	2.62	26	26	1	0	161	164	63	47	33	134
MINOR LEAGUE TOTALS			13	9	2.85	34	32	1	0	192	195	80	61	36	158

4. Bobby Bradley, rhp

Born: Dec. 15, 1980. **Ht.:** 6-1. **Wt.:** 170. **Bats:** R. **Throws:** R. **School:** Wellington (Fla.) Community HS. **Career Transactions:** Selected by Pirates in first round (eighth overall) of 1999 draft; signed July 7, 1999.

Both of Bradley's full seasons have been cut short by elbow problems. He sat out two months at Hickory in 2000 and was limited to nine starts with Lynchburg a year later before exploratory arthroscopic surgery in July. He continued to feel pain during instructional league and had Tommy John surgery in mid-October. Bradley has a great feel for pitching and is an outstanding competitor. His best pitch is a curveball and he throws two different kinds, a big bender and one with a shorter break. His fastball can touch 95 mph but usually sits around 88-89 mph. He's able to sink and cut the fastball while moving it in the strike zone. His changeup is an adequate pitch. Bradley won't be able to pitch until 2003 after having surgery so late in the year. He has been throwing curves since early childhood and no one knows if the pitch will have the same bite once he returns. He also has to adjust against advanced hitters who aren't so apt to chase curveballs in the dirt and fastballs off the plate. Bradley once was on a fast track to the major leagues. While pitchers now routinely return from major elbow surgery, it's far too early to determine when Bradley might get to PNC Park.

Year	Club (League)	Class	W	L	ERA	G	GS	CG	SV	IP	H	R	ER	BB	SO
1999	Pirates (GCL)	R	1	1	2.90	6	6	0	0	31	31	13	10	4	31
2000	Hickory (SAL)	A	8	2	2.29	14	14	3	0	83	62	31	21	21	118
2001	Lynchburg (Car)	A	1	2	3.12	9	9	0	0	49	44	23	17	20	46
MINOR LEAGUE TOTALS			10	5	2.66	29	29	3	0	163	137	67	48	45	195

5. Jose Castillo, ss

Born: March 19, 1981. **Ht.:** 5-11. **Wt.:** 185. **Bats:** R. **Throws:** R. **Career Transactions:** Signed out of Venezuela by Pirates, July 2, 1997.

Castillo burst into prospect status in 2000 but struggled in the first half of the 2001 season at Lynchburg, hitting .200 in the first two months as he played with a torn wrist ligament. He finished strong before having arthroscopic surgery in early September. Castillo has plenty of tools, chief among them a quick bat with good pop. He also continues to make improvement on the defensive side. He has above-average range, soft hands and a strong arm that enables him to make throws from deep in the hole at shortstop. Castillo is a plus runner who can steal a base. Wrist injuries can linger and the hope is Castillo can regain the power in his bat. He also needs to show more consistency on defense, though he did cut his errors from 60 in 2000 to 37. Castillo showed enough in the second half of the 2001 season, despite playing hurt, to make the Pirates believe he still has a bright future. That could wind up being at second base, especially because Pittsburgh liked rookie shortstop Jack Wilson's defense last year. Castillo probably will go back to Lynchburg to start 2002, with a promotion to Altoona likely once he proves he's healthy.

Year	Club (League)	Class	AVG	G	AB	R	H	2B	3B	HR	RBI	BB	SO	SB
1998	Montalban (VSL)	R	.291	55	179	31	52	9	1	1	13	20	30	23
1999	Pirates (GCL)	R	.266	47	173	27	46	9	0	4	30	11	23	8
2000	Hickory (SAL)	A	.299	125	529	95	158	32	8	16	72	29	107	16
2001	Lynchburg (Car)	A	.245	125	485	57	119	20	7	7	49	21	94	23
MINOR LEAGUE TOTALS			.275	352	1366	210	375	70	16	28	164	81	254	70

6. Tony Alvarez, of

Born: May 10, 1979. **Ht.:** 6-1. **Wt.:** 202. **Bats:** R. **Throws:** R. **Career Transactions:** Signed out of Venezuela by Pirates, Sept. 27, 1995.

Alvarez first came into prominence in 1999, when he was named New York-Penn League MVP. He has continued to progress up the ladder and was promoted to Double-A last June. Alvarez missed the final month of the 2001 season to return home to Venezuela, where his father was fighting cancer. He has settled in as an outfielder after also playing third and second base earlier in his career. Alvarez has the potential to be a power/speed player. He has good pop in his bat and it should improve as his body fills out. Alvarez also runs well and is aggressive on the bases. He has the speed to play center field but seems more comfortable in left, where he's adept at turning doubles into singles by moving quickly to the foul line. Alvarez is known to have mental lapses. He tends to run in situations where he should play it safe and swings at too many bad pitches. He almost certainly will begin the 2002 season back at Altoona after missing time at the end of last season. However, he's moving quickly and could reach Triple-A later in the year.

Year	Club (League)	Class	AVG	G	AB	R	H	2B	3B	HR	RBI	BB	SO	SB
1996	Pirates (DSL)	R	.138	39	109	12	15	2	0	1	9	8	12	6
1997	Guacara-1 (VSL)	R	.220	38	91	15	20	3	0	0	6	9	10	3
1998	Pirates (GCL)	R	.247	50	190	27	47	13	1	4	29	13	24	19
1999	Williamsport (NY-P)	A	.321	58	196	44	63	14	1	7	45	21	36	38
2000	Hickory (SAL)	A	.285	118	442	75	126	25	4	15	77	39	93	52
2001	Lynchburg (Car)	A	.344	25	93	10	32	4	0	2	11	7	11	7
	Altoona (EL)	AA	.319	67	254	34	81	16	1	6	25	9	30	17
MINOR LEAGUE TOTALS			.279	395	1375	217	384	77	7	35	202	106	216	142

7. Ryan Vogelsong, rhp

Born: July 22, 1977. **Ht.:** 6-3. **Wt.:** 195. **Bats:** R. **Throws:** R. **School:** Kutztown (Pa.) University. **Career Transactions:** Selected by Giants in fifth round of 1998 draft; signed June 7, 1998 . . . Traded by Giants with OF Armando Rios to Pirates for RHP Jason Schmidt and OF John Vander Wal, July 30, 2001.

San Francisco traded Vogelsong and Armando Rios to the Pirates for veterans Jason Schmidt and John Vander Wal prior to the 2001 trade deadline. Vogelsong was sent to Nashville to build up arm strength as a starter after serving as a reliever for the Giants. He was part of Pittsburgh's late-season callups and tore an elbow ligament in his second start, necessitating Tommy John surgery in mid-September. Vogelsong doesn't have one dominant pitch but has command of four good ones. His fastball reaches 94 mph and he throws it to both sides of the plate. He also has a fine curveball, a late-breaking slider and an improving changeup. Vogelsong has outstanding makeup, as he's intelligent and noted for his competitiveness. Vogelsong's future is cloudy after surgery. He'll miss all of 2002, which figured to be his first full season in the major leagues. The Pirates hope Vogelsong eventually can slot into the middle of their rotation, maybe even as a No. 2 starter.

Year	Club (League)	Class	W	L	ERA	G	GS	CG	SV	IP	H	R	ER	BB	SO
1998	Salem-Keizer (NWL)	A	6	1	1.77	10	10	0	0	56	37	15	11	16	66
	San Jose (Cal)	A	0	0	7.58	4	4	0	0	19	23	16	16	4	26
1999	San Jose (Cal)	A	4	4	2.45	13	13	0	0	70	37	26	19	27	86
	Shreveport (TL)	AA	0	2	7.31	6	6	0	0	28	40	25	23	15	23
2000	Shreveport (TL)	AA	6	10	4.23	27	27	1	0	155	153	82	73	69	147
	San Francisco (NL)	MAJ	0	0	0.00	4	0	0	0	6	4	0	0	2	6
2001	Fresno (PCL)	AAA	3	3	2.79	10	10	0	0	58	35	18	18	18	53
	Nashville (PCL)	AAA	2	3	3.98	6	6	0	0	32	26	15	14	15	33
	San Francisco (NL)	MAJ	0	3	5.65	13	0	0	0	29	29	21	18	14	17
	Pittsburgh (NL)	MAJ	0	2	12.00	2	2	0	0	6	10	10	8	6	7
MAJOR LEAGUE TOTALS			0	5	4.98	19	2	0	0	41	43	31	26	22	30
MINOR LEAGUE TOTALS			21	23	3.75	76	76	1	0	418	351	197	174	164	434

8. Adrian Burnside, lhp

Born: March 15, 1977. **Ht.:** 6-4. **Wt.:** 190. **Bats:** R. **Throws:** L. **Career Transactions:** Signed out of Australia by Dodgers, July 12, 1995 . . . Selected by Reds from Dodgers in Rule 5 major league draft, Dec. 13, 1999 . . . Returned to Dodgers, March 14, 2000 . . . Traded by Dodgers with RHP Mike Fetters to Pirates for LHP Terry Mulholland, July 31, 2001.

Burnside may have looked like a throw-in in the 2001 deadline deal that saw the Pirates ship Terry Mulholland to the Dodgers for Mike Fetters. But the Pirates coveted Burnside, and he was the primary reason they made the deal. He made six starts with Altoona after the trade, and the Pirates were pleased with what they saw there and in the Arizona Fall League. Burnside is a rare lefthander in that his fastball reaches 93 mph and he isn't afraid to throw inside. He also has a hard slider with a sharp break. He proved he was healthy in 2001 after arthroscopic elbow surgery that cost him the chance to pitch for his native Australia in the Sydney Olympics. Burnside has yet to develop his changeup, which could prevent him from becoming a major league starter. He also didn't take up baseball until his late teens and is still learning the game. He's a happy-go-lucky guy, causing some to question his intensity. Burnside figures to begin the 2002 season in the Nashville rotation. Whether he winds up a starter or reliever remains to be seen, but he has a decent chance to reach Pittsburgh in 2002.

Year	Club (League)	Class	W	L	ERA	G	GS	CG	SV	IP	H	R	ER	BB	SO
1996	Great Falls (Pio)	R	1	3	6.80	14	5	0	0	41	44	35	31	38	33
1997	Yakima (NWL)	A	6	3	4.93	15	13	0	0	66	67	53	36	49	66
1998	San Bernardino (Cal)	A	1	10	7.81	21	12	0	0	78	97	79	68	48	65
	Yakima (NWL)	A	1	4	4.05	8	6	0	0	33	27	21	15	30	34
1999	San Bernardino (Cal)	A	10	9	4.17	26	22	0	0	132	124	69	61	55	129
2000	San Antonio (TL)	AA	6	5	2.90	17	17	0	0	93	73	40	30	55	82
2001	Jacksonville (SL)	AA	4	3	2.66	13	12	0	0	68	44	21	20	30	67
	Altoona (EL)	AA	0	2	3.62	6	6	0	0	32	28	15	13	14	32
MINOR LEAGUE TOTALS			29	39	4.54	120	93	0	0	543	504	333	274	319	508

9. Humberto Cota, c

Born: Feb. 7, 1979. **Ht.:** 6-0. **Wt.:** 175. **Bats:** R. **Throws:** R. **Career Transactions:** Signed out of Mexico by Braves, Dec. 22, 1995 . . . Loaned by Braves to Mexico City Tigers (Mexican), June 23-Sept. 23, 1996 . . . Released by Braves, Jan. 27, 1997 . . . Signed by Devil Rays, May 22, 1997 . . . Traded by Devil Rays with C Joe Oliver to Pirates for OF Jose Guillen and RHP Jeff Sparks, July 23, 1999.

Acquired from the Devil Rays in a trade for Jose Guillen in midseason 1999, Cota has risen rapidly through the Pirates system. He was their minor league player of the year in 2001, when he also appeared in the Futures Game. Cota is becoming a good offensive catcher. He's showing the ability to hit for average while adding more power to his game each season. Cota also is developing the reputation of being a good clutch hitter. He's mobile behind the plate and very good at blocking balls. Like so many hitters in the Pirates system, Cota has weak strike-zone judgment. He's impatient and can be made to swing at bad pitchers. While Cota has made strides as a catcher, he has a below-average arm and can be scattershot with his throws to second base. Cota is in a tough spot as a catcher, with Jason Kendall and Keith Osik ahead of him in Pittsburgh and highly regarded J.R. House behind him in the minors. Cota almost certainly will go back to Triple-A in 2002 and have to wait until 2003 to get his crack at the majors.

Year	Club (League)	Class	AVG	G	AB	R	H	2B	3B	HR	RBI	BB	SO	SB
1997	Devil Rays (GCL)	R	.241	44	133	14	32	6	1	2	20	17	27	3
	Hudson Valley (NY-P)	A	.222	3	9	0	2	0	0	0	2	0	1	0
1998	Princeton (Appy)	R	.310	67	245	48	76	13	4	15	61	32	59	4
1999	Charleston, SC (SAL)	A	.280	85	336	42	94	21	1	9	61	20	51	1
	Hickory (SAL)	A	.271	37	133	28	36	11	2	2	20	21	20	3
2000	Altoona (EL)	AA	.261	112	429	49	112	20	1	8	44	21	80	6
2001	Nashville (PCL)	AAA	.297	111	377	61	112	22	2	14	72	25	74	7
	Pittsburgh (NL)	MAJ	.222	7	9	0	2	0	0	0	1	0	5	0
MAJOR LEAGUE TOTALS			.222	7	9	0	2	0	0	0	1	0	5	0
MINOR LEAGUE TOTALS			.279	459	1662	242	464	93	11	50	280	136	312	24

10. Chris Young, rhp

Born: May 25, 1979. **Ht.:** 6-10. **Wt.:** 255. **Bats:** R. **Throws:** R. **School:** Princeton University. **Career Transactions:** Selected by Pirates in third round of 2000 draft; signed Sept. 6, 2000.

The Pirates signed Young away from a potential career as an NBA center by giving him a $1.65 million bonus. He had been an all-Ivy League basketball player at Princeton. Young signed too late to play in 2000 and made his pro debut at Hickory last June after finishing the spring semester at Princeton. Young has an intriguing body as he stands 6-foot-10, drawing inevitable comparisons to Randy Johnson. He's also a bright guy, as expected from an Ivy Leaguer, and throws a heavy ball with boring action that breaks bats when he's healthy. His command is surprisingly good for a tall pitcher who had been torn between two sports. Young is raw, as he pitched sparingly in college. His velocity was a concern in 2001 as his fastball topped out at 86 mph, though arthroscopic elbow surgery to remove a bone spur should solve that problem. His breaking pitches and changeup need work. Young probably will rejoin the Hickory rotation to start 2002, though a good spring could push him to Lynchburg. Needing just one semester to graduate, Young will spend the entire 2002 season concentrating on baseball and should make up for lost time.

Year	Club (League)	Class	W	L	ERA	G	GS	CG	SV	IP	H	R	ER	BB	SO
2001	Hickory (SAL)	A	5	3	4.12	12	12	2	0	74	79	39	34	20	72
MINOR LEAGUE TOTALS			5	3	4.12	12	12	2	0	74	79	39	34	20	72

11. Justin Reid, rhp

Born: June 30, 1977. **Ht.:** 6-6. **Wt.:** 205. **Bats:** R. **Throws:** R. **School:** UC Davis. **Career Transactions:** Selected by Pirates in fourth round of 1999 draft; signed June 6, 1999.

Reid was drafted by the Pirates without fanfare following a fine career at UC Davis, an NCAA Division II school. Also without fanfare, he quickly has moved up the ladder in the minors while posting fine numbers. Reid won't dazzle scouts with his stuff or blow out any radar guns. However, he does have exceptional pitching savvy and uses that to his advantage. Despite his 6-foot-6 frame, Reid rarely touches 90 mph with his fastball, but he spots his heater well while mixing it up with a slider and changeup. His deceptive delivery makes it tough for hitters to pick up his pitches. Reid has to be fine with his pitches because he doesn't have a power arm to overmatch hitters or a great breaking pitch to fool them. He also tired after pitching 166 innings last season, causing Pittsburgh to scratch him from the Arizona Fall League. Reid will go to Triple-A this season, and his performance likely will determine if he eventually can be a starter in the major leagues.

Year	Club (League)	Class	W	L	ERA	G	GS	CG	SV	IP	H	R	ER	BB	SO
1999	Williamsport (NY-P)	A	2	6	4.62	16	11	0	1	62	71	41	32	23	68
2000	Hickory (SAL)	A	9	8	3.02	27	22	5	3	170	146	82	57	30	176
2001	Lynchburg (Car)	A	2	4	2.25	8	8	1	0	56	50	15	14	6	48
	Altoona (EL)	AA	5	5	2.54	17	16	1	0	110	104	38	31	14	70
MINOR LEAGUE TOTALS			18	23	3.03	68	57	7	4	398	371	176	134	73	362

12. Nate McLouth, of

Born: Oct. 28, 1981. **Ht.:** 5-11. **Wt.:** 170. **Bats:** L. **Throws:** R. **School:** Whitehall (Mich.) HS. **Career Transactions:** Selected by Pirates in 25th round of 2000 draft; signed Aug. 29, 2000.

Most clubs shied away from McLouth in the 2000 draft because he had planned on attending Michigan after being named the state's high school player of the year. The Pirates took a shot on him and after they failed to sign fourth-rounder Patrick Boyd, they found the money to sign McLouth and righthander Jason Sharber. Seemingly everyone who has seen McLouth play has the same impression, that he's a gamer and fun to watch. McLouth is a somewhat stocky leadoff hitter who draws comparisons to a young Lenny Dykstra, right down to his lisp. He works counts and knows how to get on base, making him an ideal candidate to stay in the No. 1 hole. He also shows good power potential and could wind up hitting lower in the order. McLouth signed as a second baseman but the Pirates feel he lacks the range needed from a pro infielder. He made his pro debut and played center field in low Class A last season. He may not cover quite enough ground to handle that position in the major leagues, which would force a move to one of the corner spots. McLouth went from extended spring training to full-season ball last May and made a rather seamless transition. He'll probably get a shot at high Class A this season and could move fast.

Year	Club (League)	Class	AVG	G	AB	R	H	2B	3B	HR	RBI	BB	SO	SB
2001	Hickory (SAL)	A	.285	96	351	59	100	17	5	12	54	43	54	21
MINOR LEAGUE TOTALS			.285	96	351	59	100	17	5	12	54	43	54	21

13. Aron Weston, of

Born: Nov. 5, 1980. **Ht.:** 6-6. **Wt.:** 172. **Bats:** L. **Throws:** L. **School:** Solon (Ohio) HS. **Career Transactions:** Selected by Pirates in third round of 1999 draft; signed June 13, 1999.

Smitten with Weston's athletic ability as a high school player, the Pirates took Weston in the third round pick of the 1999 draft, which also yielded high-profile prospects J.R. House and Bobby Bradley. Weston's development was slowed greatly last season, when he was limited to 20 games by a severely strained hamstring. He has great tools. He has the build of a power hitter, with long arms and legs, while also possessing above-average speed. Former Gold Glove center fielder Andy Van Slyke worked with Weston last spring training and came away impressed with his outfield instincts. Weston has had problems turning his potential into production during his three pro seasons. He needs a lot of polish, especially with the bat as he gets tied up by inside fastballs and chases breaking pitches low and away. Weston most likely will return to Hickory for a third season in hopes of getting his career on track. While he has had setbacks, he certainly is still young enough to blossom.

Year	Club (League)	Class	AVG	G	AB	R	H	2B	3B	HR	RBI	BB	SO	SB
1999	Pirates (GCL)	R	.218	33	119	26	26	2	1	0	5	20	36	14
2000	Hickory (SAL)	A	.267	82	315	52	84	13	2	2	21	36	89	28
2001	Hickory (SAL)	A	.122	20	74	8	9	2	1	0	2	3	25	5
MINOR LEAGUE TOTALS			.234	135	508	86	119	17	4	2	28	59	150	47

14. Jose Bautista, 3b

Born: Oct. 19, 1980. **Ht.:** 6-0. **Wt.:** 190. **Bats:** R. **Throws:** R. **School:** Chipola (Fla.) JC. **Career Transactions:** Selected by Pirates in 20th round of 2000 draft; signed May 19, 2001.

The Pirates drafted Bautista in 2000 but weren't able to sign him that summer. He returned to Chipola, was named Florida's 2001 juco player of the year and projected to go in the first two or three rounds if Pittsburgh hadn't signed him as a draft-and-follow. Bautista made a big impression with the bat in his pro debut. His quick hands and ability to make adjustments particularly impressed the Pirates. He has good power and can turn on a ball while also hitting for average. Bautista has quick reflexes at third base, a strong arm and good speed. Like many youngsters, he can be made to chase some bad pitches but that problem can be corrected with time. He sometimes shows a hitch in his swing that will have to be eliminated. Bautista occasionally rushes throws from third base and makes some errors on plays where he has no chance to get the runner. He'll be challenged in 2002 by starting in low Class A. With Aramis Ramirez seemingly entrenched at third base in Pittsburgh, the Pirates will start taking occasional looks at Bautista as a corner outfielder.

Year	Club (League)	Class	AVG	G	AB	R	H	2B	3B	HR	RBI	BB	SO	SB
2001	Williamsport (NY-P)	A	.286	62	220	43	63	10	3	5	30	21	41	8
MINOR LEAGUE TOTALS			.286	62	220	43	63	10	3	5	30	21	41	8

15. Domingo Cuello, 2b

Born: April 12, 1983. **Ht.:** 5-11. **Wt.:** 160. **Bats:** R. **Throws:** R. **Career Transactions:** Signed out of Dominican Republic by Pirates, Nov. 5, 1999.

Cuello was one of the last of a multitude players from the Dominican Republic signed by scout Pablo Cruz before he cut his longstanding ties with the Pirates and moved to the Padres. Cuello had a so-so debut in the Rookie-level Dominican Summer League in 2000 then was a major surprise in his first taste of the United States last season. He's an exciting player with outstanding speed who always seems to be in the middle of the action. Though he seems best suited to hit No. 2 in the batting order, he has some gap power. He has good range, particularly to his left, and is very adept at turning double plays. Cuello has a tendency to try to make the spectacular play when it isn't there. He needs to get under control and not take so many needless risks. He also tends to swing at bad pitches and needs to develop more patience if he is to hit high in the order. Cuello is still a ways from the major leagues. He'll get a chance to prove himself over a full season this year as Hickory's second baseman.

Year	Club (League)	Class	AVG	G	AB	R	H	2B	3B	HR	RBI	BB	SO	SB
2000	Pirates (DSL)	R	.269	70	268	59	72	15	7	3	23	42	45	49
2001	Hickory (SAL)	A	.220	18	59	6	13	0	1	0	2	2	11	6
	Williamsport (NY-P)	A	.278	62	230	35	64	9	2	6	30	16	40	28
MINOR LEAGUE TOTALS			.268	150	557	100	149	24	10	9	55	60	96	83

16. Ryan Doumit, c

Born: April 3, 1981. **Ht.:** 6-0. **Wt.:** 180. **Bats:** B. **Throws:** R. **School:** Moses Lake (Wash.) HS. **Career Transactions:** Selected by Pirates in second round of 1999 draft; signed June 16, 1999.

Doumit was one of three players taken out of Moses Lake (Wash.) High in the top two rounds of the 1999 draft, a first for any high school in any draft. His career has progressed better than those of outfielders B.J. Garbe, who went fifth overall to the Twins, and Jason Cooper, who turned down the Phillies to attend Stanford. However, Doumit hit a bit of a wall last season. He had a strained back that kept him out nearly two full months and limited his effectiveness. He's a good receiver with soft hands, handles pitchers well and has a strong and accurate arm. Doumit also has shown the ability to hit for average in the lower levels of the minors. Back injuries are nothing to mess with, especially for a catcher, and Doumit's time on the disabled list raises a red flag. He isn't the biggest catcher around, which leads to more doubts about his durability. He also needs to learn how to turn on more balls and show more power. His attitude tends to flag when he's struggling. The Pirates are loaded with catchers, so there's no need to rush Doumit. They will likely send him back to low Class A to start the season and watch him closely to ensure he has no further back trouble.

Year	Club (League)	Class	AVG	G	AB	R	H	2B	3B	HR	RBI	BB	SO	SB
1999	Pirates (GCL)	R	.282	29	85	17	24	5	0	1	7	15	14	4
2000	Williamsport (NY-P)	A	.313	66	246	25	77	15	5	2	40	23	33	2
2001	Pirates (GCL)	R	.235	7	17	2	4	2	0	0	3	2	0	0
	Hickory (SAL)	A	.270	39	148	14	40	6	0	2	14	10	32	2
	Altoona (EL)	AA	.250	2	4	0	1	0	0	0	2	1	1	0
MINOR LEAGUE TOTALS			.292	143	500	58	146	28	5	5	66	51	80	8

17. Josh Fogg, rhp

Born: Dec. 13, 1976. **Ht.:** 6-2. **Wt.:** 205. **Bats:** R. **Throws:** R. **School:** University of Florida. **Career Transactions:** Selected by White Sox in third round of 1998 draft; signed July 3, 1998 . . . Traded by White Sox with RHP Kip Wells and RHP Sean Lowe to Pirates for RHP Todd Ritchie and C Lee Evans, Dec. 13, 2001.

In a White Sox organization that likes to hype its pitching prospects, Fogg operated just off the radar screen. However, the Pirates noticed the former University of Florida All-

American and got him in the five-player Todd Ritchie trade at the 2001 Winter Meetings. Fogg relies on intelligence, finesse and command. His statistics predictably suffered when he made a move from pitcher-friendly Double-A Birmingham to Triple-A Charlotte's bandbox, though he continued to throw strikes because he just won't panic. Fogg remained poised when promoted to Chicago in September, putting together a strikeout-walk ratio far superior to any of the organization's power pitchers. His fastball averages 88-89 mph but he makes it work with an outstanding slider and an excellent changeup. He's durable, too, having led the Southern League in innings in 2000. The Pirates initially will look at Fogg as a starter, but he also could settle into a middle-relief role in the majors this season.

Year	Club (League)	Class	W	L	ERA	G	GS	CG	SV	IP	H	R	ER	BB	SO
1998	White Sox (AZL)	R	1	0	0.00	2	0	0	0	4	0	0	0	1	5
	Hickory (SAL)	A	1	3	2.18	8	8	0	0	41	36	17	10	13	29
	Winston-Salem (Car)	A	0	1	0.00	1	0	0	0	1	2	2	0	0	2
1999	Winston-Salem (Car)	A	10	5	2.96	17	17	1	0	103	93	44	34	33	109
	Birmingham (SL)	AA	3	2	5.89	10	10	0	0	55	66	37	36	18	40
2000	Birmingham (SL)	AA	11	7	2.57	27	27	2	0	192	190	68	55	44	136
2001	Charlotte (IL)	AAA	4	7	4.79	40	16	0	4	115	129	68	61	30	89
	Chicago (AL)	MAJ	0	0	2.03	11	0	0	0	13	10	3	3	3	17
MAJOR LEAGUE TOTALS			0	0	2.03	11	0	0	0	13	10	3	3	3	17
MINOR LEAGUE TOTALS			30	25	3.45	105	78	3	4	512	516	236	196	139	410

18. Ian Oquendo, rhp

Born: Oct. 30, 1981. **Ht.:** 5-11. **Wt.:** 160. **Bats:** R. **Throws:** R. **School:** Caesar Rodney HS, Camden, Del. **Career Transactions:** Selected by Pirates in 26th round of 2000 draft; signed June 21, 2000.

Oquendo has been unbeatable as a pro, going 11-0 in 17 games since signing as a 26th-round pick in 2000. Oquendo was known as Ian Snell when he was drafted, then married after his first pro season and decided to take his wife's last name. He was a teammate of Pirates lefty Dave Williams at Caesar Rodney High in Camden, Del. Oquendo has very good stuff. His fastball regularly reaches 93 mph and has good movement. He also has command of a sharp slider that he uses as an out pitch. He's perhaps the best-conditioned athlete in the organization and an excellent fielder. Oquendo is on the smallish side, which raises durability issues. His mind also tends to wander on the mound at times and there are some questions about how seriously he takes the game. Oquendo will get another chance to prove himself this year when he takes his first crack at full-season ball with Hickory.

Year	Club (League)	Class	W	L	ERA	G	GS	CG	SV	IP	H	R	ER	BB	SO
2000	Pirates (GCL)	R	1	0	2.35	4	0	0	0	8	5	2	2	1	8
2001	Pirates (GCL)	R	3	0	0.47	3	3	0	0	19	12	2	1	5	13
	Williamsport (NY-P)	A	7	0	1.39	10	9	1	0	65	55	16	10	10	56
MINOR LEAGUE TOTALS			11	0	1.27	17	12	1	0	92	72	20	13	16	77

19. John Grabow, lhp

Born: Nov. 4, 1978. **Ht.:** 6-2. **Wt.:** 189. **Bats:** L. **Throws:** L. **School:** San Gabriel (Calif.) HS. **Career Transactions:** Selected by Pirates in third round of 1997 draft; signed June 12, 1997.

Grabow had a lost season in 2001 after being placed on the Pirates' 40-man roster the previous winter. He struggled to return from the arthroscopic elbow surgery he had following the 2000 season and his command, which had been one of his strong points, deserted him when he reached Double-A. Grabow throws relatively hard for a lefty at 92 mph, but his best pitch is a changeup that regularly fools hitters. He's also a bright guy with a good understanding of pitching, though he tends to think too much at times. Grabow developed a mental block last season, becoming hesitant to cut loose with his fastball and losing the strike zone. He appeared to bounce back during a productive six weeks in instructional league, and Pittsburgh hopes his control will be fine now that he's another year removed from surgery. He likely will begin the year back in Double-A before he proves his arm and command are sound. Once he does, he'll move up to Triple-A.

Year	Club (League)	Class	W	L	ERA	G	GS	CG	SV	IP	H	R	ER	BB	SO
1997	Pirates (GCL)	R	2	7	4.57	11	8	0	0	45	57	32	23	14	28
1998	Augusta (SAL)	A	6	3	5.78	17	16	0	0	72	84	59	46	34	67
1999	Hickory (SAL)	A	9	10	3.80	26	26	0	0	156	152	82	66	32	164
2000	Altoona (EL)	AA	8	7	4.33	24	24	1	0	145	145	81	70	65	109
2001	Pirates (GCL)	R	0	1	3.75	6	6	0	0	12	11	6	5	4	9
	Lynchburg (Car)	A	1	3	6.38	7	7	0	0	37	42	30	26	26	35
	Altoona (EL)	AA	2	5	3.38	10	10	0	0	51	30	23	19	39	42
MINOR LEAGUE TOTALS			28	36	4.43	101	97	1	0	518	521	313	255	214	454

20. J.J. Davis, of

Born: Oct. 25, 1978. **Ht.:** 6-4. **Wt.:** 250. **Bats:** R. **Throws:** R. **School:** Baldwin Park (Calif.) HS. **Career Transactions:** Selected by Pirates in first round (eighth overall) of 1997 draft; signed June 3, 1997.

The Pirates have waited a long time for Davis to blossom into a power hitter since making him their first-round draft pick in 1997. However, he hit just four homers in Double-A as a fifth-year pro last season, when he was hobbled by a strained hamstring. Davis threw 96 mph in high school but the Pirates drafted him as a hitter. He wanted to go to instructional league at the end of last season to be converted into a pitcher, but the Pittsburgh didn't go for the idea. Davis looks the part of a cleanup hitter. He's tall with long arms and a thick trunk. He also still shows a good arm in the outfield despite having elbow surgery in 1999. Davis never has learned to use the whole field as a hitter. He tries to pull everything and therefore can be worked away by pitchers. He also struggles to make consistent contact. He has a tendency to put on weight and needs to work on his conditioning. Davis will go back to Double-A this year, when his goal once again will be to turn his tools into production. The Pirates are losing patience with him, and perhaps the time has come to grant Davis his wish and try him on the mound.

Year	Club (League)	Class	AVG	G	AB	R	H	2B	3B	HR	RBI	BB	SO	SB
1997	Pirates (GCL)	R	.255	45	165	19	42	10	2	1	18	14	44	0
	Erie (NY-P)	A	.077	4	13	1	1	0	0	0	0	0	4	0
1998	Augusta (SAL)	A	.198	30	106	11	21	6	0	4	11	3	24	1
	Erie (NY-P)	A	.270	52	196	25	53	12	2	8	39	20	54	4
1999	Hickory (SAL)	A	.265	86	317	58	84	26	1	19	65	44	99	2
2000	Lynchburg (Car)	A	.243	130	485	77	118	36	1	20	80	52	171	9
2001	Pirates (GCL)	R	.471	4	17	3	8	1	0	2	6	1	2	0
	Altoona (EL)	AA	.250	67	228	21	57	13	3	4	26	21	79	2
MINOR LEAGUE TOTALS			.251	418	1527	215	384	104	9	58	245	155	477	18

21. Yurendell DeCaster, 3b

Born: Sept. 26, 1979. **Ht.:** 6-1. **Wt.:** 202. **Bats:** R. **Throws:** R. **Career Transactions:** Signed out of Curacao, Netherlands Antilles by Devil Rays, Aug. 2, 1996 . . . Selected by Pirates from Devil Rays in Rule 5 minor league draft, Dec. 11, 2000.

The Pirates spent just $12,000 to select DeCaster from the Devil Rays in the Triple-A phase of the Rule 5 draft following his injury-plagued 2000 season. It turned out to be a wise investment, as DeCaster performed well last year in low Class A after struggling initially in high Class A. He has good bat speed and developing power, and it's possible he could blossom into a home run threat. DeCaster also has the makings of a good defensive third baseman with fine range and a strong arm. He's a decent runner, though he doesn't steal many bases. After four years in the minors, DeCaster must prove he can play well against higher competition. He also needs to develop better patience at the plate. DeCaster has had shoulder and toe problems that have kept him out of the lineup in the past. His arm is erratic and sometimes he'll make errors in bunches. This will be a pivotal year for DeCaster, who will go back to Lynchburg to show he can handle advanced pitching. DeCaster eventually may need to move to the outfield because of the presence of Aramis Ramirez in Pittsburgh.

Year	Club (League)	Class	AVG	G	AB	R	H	2B	3B	HR	RBI	BB	SO	SB
1997	Devil Rays (DSL)	R	.239	68	243	27	58	8	1	5	31	29	44	4
1998	Devil Rays (GCL)	R	.236	56	174	25	41	4	3	2	17	19	48	10
1999	Princeton (Appy)	R	.257	48	183	37	47	12	0	11	36	20	65	4
2000	Charleston, SC (SAL)	A	.240	69	242	34	58	21	0	7	28	16	89	4
2001	Lynchburg (Car)	A	.104	13	48	1	5	2	0	0	4	3	16	0
	Hickory (SAL)	A	.290	97	341	56	99	17	4	19	74	35	83	4
MINOR LEAGUE TOTALS			.250	351	1231	180	308	64	8	44	190	122	345	26

22. Chris Duffy, of

Born: April 20, 1980. **Ht.:** 5-10. **Wt.:** 185. **Bats:** B. **Throws:** L. **School:** Arizona State University. **Career Transactions:** Selected by Pirates in eighth round of 2001 draft; signed June 8, 2001.

The Pirates leaned toward college players in last year's draft and grabbed Duffy in the eighth round from Arizona State. His leadoff skills are attractive in an organization that lacks table setters. He tied for the New York-Penn League in stolen bases, finished third in runs and walked as often as he struck out. Duffy has an advanced knowledge of hitting, making contact and showing a good eye. He also crowds the plate and dares pitchers to drill him—which they did 15 times in 64 games last summer. He has above-average speed and reads pickoff moves particularly well. Duffy's instincts in center field are outstanding and he tracks down balls in both gaps. He doesn't hit with much power and there's some fear he could be overmatched as he sees more advanced pitching. His arm is only ordinary but he makes up for it by hitting the cutoff man and throwing to the right base. Duffy could jump right to high Class A in 2002.

Year	Club (League)	Class	AVG	G	AB	R	H	2B	3B	HR	RBI	BB	SO	SB
2001	Williamsport (NY-P)	A	.317	64	221	50	70	12	4	1	24	33	33	30
MINOR LEAGUE TOTALS			.317	64	221	50	70	12	4	1	24	33	33	30

23. B.J. Barns, of

Born: July 21, 1977. **Ht.:** 6-4. **Wt.:** 195. **Bats:** L. **Throws:** L. **School:** Duquesne University. **Career Transactions:** Selected by Pirates in sixth round of 1999 draft; signed June 8, 1999.

The Pirates only needed to look in their backyard to find Barns. He set several school records at Duquesne University in Pittsburgh, where he was a teammate of Pirates lefthander Joe Beimel. Barns stepped up to the challenge of playing at a higher level in 2001, hitting with more power than he had previously shown while spending the final month in Double-A. He's an above-average defensive outfielder who's better suited for the corners but can handle center with his instincts and good speed. Before the end of last season, he continually had trouble adjusting to inside fastballs throughout his career, and will have to show he has solved the problem in 2002. He also must become more patient because he tends to get himself out by swinging at everything. Barns will go back to Double-A this year to build on his late-season success. The Pirates feel Barns is ready for a breakthrough season that could propel him toward the major leagues.

Year	Club (League)	Class	AVG	G	AB	R	H	2B	3B	HR	RBI	BB	SO	SB
1999	Williamsport (NY-P)	A	.400	14	50	10	20	4	0	1	11	12	11	0
	Hickory (SAL)	A	.230	52	174	16	40	8	4	6	25	25	47	5
2000	Lynchburg (Car)	A	.244	120	398	46	97	20	1	8	48	44	95	8
2001	Lynchburg (Car)	A	.246	103	386	60	95	18	4	6	57	31	87	5
	Altoona (EL)	AA	.220	30	109	12	24	6	2	6	15	7	37	3
MINOR LEAGUE TOTALS			.247	319	1117	144	276	56	11	27	156	119	277	21

24. Jason Sharber, rhp

Born: Feb. 24, 1982. **Ht.:** 6-3. **Wt.:** 215. **Bats:** R. **Throws:** R. **School:** Oakland HS, Murfreesboro, Tenn. **Career Transactions:** Selected by Pirates in fifth round of 2000 draft; signed Aug. 29, 2000.

The Pirates were able to land many draft picks considered tough signs during Mickey White's three years as scouting director. Count Sharber among them, as the Pirates steered him away from a scholarship to Vanderbilt late in the summer of 2000. He started off last year in extended spring training, overmatched hitters in three starts in the Rookie-level Gulf Coast League and continued to pitch well after being promoted to low Class A. Sharber has relied primarily on a 92-mph fastball to get hitters out at the lower levels. He also has a good slider. Like many novice pro pitchers, he still is learning how to change speeds off his fastball. He also needs to refine his changeup. Sharber has a stocky build and there's concern that his conditioning could hinder his development. He has had little trouble making the jump into pro ball to this point. The Pirates will consider challenging this season, starting him in high Class A if he has a good spring training.

Year	Club (League)	Class	W	L	ERA	G	GS	CG	SV	IP	H	R	ER	BB	SO
2001	Pirates (GCL)	R	1	0	0.50	3	3	0	0	18	5	1	1	4	19
	Hickory (SAL)	A	2	2	1.99	7	7	0	0	45	34	13	10	19	57
MINOR LEAGUE TOTALS			3	2	1.57	10	10	0	0	63	39	14	11	23	76

25. Roberto Novoa, rhp

Born: Aug. 16, 1981. **Ht.:** 6-5. **Wt.:** 200. **Bats:** R. **Throws:** R. **Career Transactions:** Signed out of Dominican Republic by Pirates, July 3, 1999.

Though Novoa was mediocre in the Dominican Summer League in 2000, the Pirates decided to bring him to the United States last season. He made a seamless transition, going from extended spring training to the New York-Penn League, where he helped Williamsport win a share of the championship. Novoa has a projetable frame at 6-foot-5 and 200 pounds. He already has an explosive fastball that tops out at 94 mph, and as he fills out he eventually could reach 98. The heater moves so much that Williamsport's catchers had trouble corralling it. Despite the life on his heater, Novoa can throw it for strikes. His other pitches are in the rudimentary stages at this point. He doesn't have a consistent breaking ball and is still developing a feel for a changeup. Like many young pitchers, he needs to work on little things like his pickoff move and fielding. Novoa will join the Hickory rotation this season, though his long-term role might be in relief if he can't develop a complement for his fastball.

Year	Club (League)	Class	W	L	ERA	G	GS	CG	SV	IP	H	R	ER	BB	SO
2000	DSL Pirates (DSL)	R	4	6	4.15	13	13	1	0	82	99	65	38	29	44
2001	Williamsport (NY-P)	A	5	5	3.39	14	13	1	0	80	76	40	30	20	55
MINOR LEAGUE TOTALS			9	11	3.78	27	26	2	0	162	175	105	68	49	99

26. Edwin Yan, 2b/ss

Born: Feb. 18, 1982. **Ht.:** 6-0. **Wt.:** 165. **Bats:** B. **Throws:** R. **Career Transactions:** Signed out of Dominican Republic by Pirates, Jan. 4, 1999.

Yan's U.S. debut was limited to just 12 games in the Gulf Coast League in 2000 because of a bad hamstring. He made a strong impression in a limited time and followed that up with a solid performance in low Class A last year. He's a quality defender who can handle both shortstop and second base. He's athletic and has above-average range, good hands and a fine arm. Yan also has very good speed and instincts on the bases. He understands how to play the little man's game and will take a pitch or drop down a bunt. He draws high marks for his enthusiasm and attitude. Yan needs to be more consistent defensively, as he tends to make silly mistakes when he loses his concentration. He's quite thin and needs to get stronger, because pitchers with good fastballs can knock the bat out of his hands. Yan will move up to high Class A this season, which will be a big step to see if he can handle more advanced competition.

Year	Club (League)	Class	AVG	G	AB	R	H	2B	3B	HR	RBI	BB	SO	SB
1999	Pirates (DSL)	R	.300	69	250	61	75	6	1	3	21	49	49	48
2000	Pirates (GCL)	R	.357	12	42	10	15	0	1	0	1	12	8	5
2001	Hickory (SAL)	A	.283	128	446	58	126	8	4	2	24	42	62	56
MINOR LEAGUE TOTALS			.293	209	738	129	216	14	6	5	46	103	119	109

27. Jeff Miller, rhp

Born: Feb. 1, 1980. **Ht.:** 6-4. **Wt.:** 215. **Bats:** R. **Throws:** R. **School:** University of New Orleans. **Career Transactions:** Selected by Pirates in 15th round of 2001 draft; signed June 13, 2001.

Miller's grand plan was to get to the major leagues as an outfielder. Instead, he's now on a path to make it as a closer. Miller began his college career as a Seton Hall outfielder before transferring to New Orleans, where he was converted into a pitcher. In his pro debut, he led the New York-Penn League with 15 saves in as many opportunities. Miller has a live arm that's still fresh because of all the years he spent as an outfielder. He already reaches 94 mph with a fastball that has movement and has the chance to add velocity as he gains experience. He also has a closer's mentality, as he's fearless and attacks hitters. The fastball is Miller's only consistently reliable pitch at this point. He has the makings of a good slider but needs to be more consistent with it. The Pirates haven't developed a closer since Stan Belinda in the late 1980s. Miller is still a long way from the majors, but he's off to a nice start and will continue his development with one of Pittsburgh's Class A affiliates this season.

Year	Club (League)	Class	W	L	ERA	G	GS	CG	SV	IP	H	R	ER	BB	SO
2001	Williamsport (NY-P)	A	0	0	1.13	21	0	0	15	24	17	3	3	5	28
MINOR LEAGUE TOTALS			0	0	1.13	21	0	0	15	24	17	3	3	5	28

28. Ben Shaffar, rhp

Born: Sept. 28, 1977. **Ht.:** 6-3. **Wt.:** 185. **Bats:** B. **Throws:** R. **School:** University of Kentucky. **Career Transactions:** Selected by Cubs in sixth round of 1999 draft; signed June 14, 1999 . . . Traded by Cubs with RHP Chris Booker to Reds for OF Michael Tucker, July 20, 2001 . . . Traded by Reds to Pirates for RHP Jose Silva, December 21, 2001.

The Pirates acquired Shaffar from the Reds for injury-plagued pitcher Jose Silva just before Christmas. It was the second time Shaffar was traded in 2001, as the Cubs shipped him and fellow minor league righthander Chris Booker to Cincinnati for Michael Tucker in July. Shaffar took a big step forward in 2001 after going 10-14, 5.27 in his first two pro seasons. His fastball usually tops out at 92-93 mph and is more notable for its exceptional movement. He also has a darting splitter that has enabled him to strike out more than a batter an inning in his three professional seasons. Shaffar likely will begin 2002 in Double-A and projects as a possible No. 3 or 4 starter in the major leagues.

Year	Club (League)	Class	W	L	ERA	G	GS	CG	SV	IP	H	R	ER	BB	SO
1999	Eugene (NWL)	A	4	5	5.79	14	13	0	0	65	79	54	42	27	76
2000	Lansing (Mid)	A	6	9	4.94	19	18	1	0	102	127	70	56	30	72
2001	Daytona (FSL)	A	6	4	3.12	19	19	2	0	107	83	42	37	45	118
	Mudville (Cal)	A	3	2	3.52	6	6	0	0	31	29	15	12	12	24
MINOR LEAGUE TOTALS			19	20	4.34	58	56	3	0	305	318	181	147	114	290

29. Rico Washington, 3b/2b

Born: May 30, 1978. **Ht.:** 5-10. **Wt.:** 182. **Bats:** L. **Throws:** R. **School:** Jones County HS, Gray, Ga. **Career Transactions:** Selected by Pirates in 10th round of 1997 draft; signed June 12, 1997.

Washington hails from Gray, a small rural Georgia town that already has produced a pair of big leaguers in Willie Greene (Washington's cousin) and Rondell White. Washington missed nearly half of 2001 with tendinitis in his right hand, an ailment that also cut short his stay in the Arizona Fall League. He has a short, line-drive stroke that has enabled him to hit for a high average at each stop in the minors. He also offers versatility. Primarily a third baseman, he also can catch and play second base and he was learning the outfield in the AFL. He's a standout defender at third thanks to his quick reactions. Washington once projected to have average power but has hit just 12 homers in two years at Double-A. His hand injury was partially responsible for his power outage last season, though more advanced pitchers have been able to get him to chase pitches off the plate. Washington will get a chance to prove himself at Triple-A in 2002. If he does well, he likely will land in Pittsburgh as a utilityman the following year.

Year	Club (League)	Class	AVG	G	AB	R	H	2B	3B	HR	RBI	BB	SO	SB
1997	Pirates (GCL)	R	.245	28	98	12	24	6	0	1	11	4	13	1
1998	Erie (NY-P)	A	.330	51	197	31	65	14	2	6	31	17	33	1
	Augusta (SAL)	A	.300	12	50	12	15	2	1	2	12	7	9	2
1999	Hickory (SAL)	A	.355	76	287	70	102	15	1	13	50	48	45	5
	Lynchburg (Car)	A	.283	57	205	31	58	7	0	7	32	30	45	4
2000	Altoona (EL)	AA	.258	135	503	74	130	22	7	8	59	55	74	4
2001	Altoona (EL)	AA	.302	75	291	31	88	17	0	4	29	21	49	5
MINOR LEAGUE TOTALS			.296	434	1631	261	482	83	11	41	224	182	268	22

30. Mike Gonzalez, lhp

Born: May 23, 1978. **Ht.:** 6-2. **Wt.:** 217. **Bats:** R. **Throws:** L. **School:** San Jacinto (Texas) JC. **Career Transactions:** Selected by Pirates in 30th round of 1997 draft; signed June 24, 1997.

Gonzalez went to the Arizona Fall League at the end of last season only after righthander Justin Reid was scratched because of a tired arm. He made the most of his stint, ranking second in the AFL with a 1.99 ERA. He was so impressive that the Pirates placed him on their 40-man roster so they wouldn't lose him in the Rule 5 draft. Gonzalez throws a fastball that routinely reaches 90-92 mph and a sharp slider. He has yet to totally get the feel for throwing a changeup, which makes his future more likely as a reliever than starter. The Pirates always have liked him, though his stock slipped when he struggled in Class A in 2000. He had arthroscopic shoulder surgery that October and quickly rebounded. The Pirates aren't scared to rush pitchers, particularly lefties, so Gonzalez will compete for a spot in their bullpen this spring.

Year	Club (League)	Class	W	L	ERA	G	GS	CG	SV	IP	H	R	ER	BB	SO
1997	Pirates (GCL)	R	2	0	2.48	7	3	0	0	29	21	9	8	8	33
	Augusta (SAL)	A	1	1	1.86	4	3	0	0	19	11	5	4	8	22
1998	Augusta (SAL)	A	4	2	2.84	11	9	0	0	51	43	24	16	26	72
	Lynchburg (Car)	A	0	3	6.67	7	7	0	0	28	40	21	21	13	22
1999	Lynchburg (Car)	A	10	4	4.02	20	20	0	0	112	98	55	50	63	119
	Altoona (EL)	AA	2	3	8.10	7	5	0	0	27	34	25	24	19	31
2000	Pirates (GCL)	R	1	0	4.50	2	1	0	0	6	8	6	3	4	7
	Lynchburg (Car)	A	4	3	4.66	12	10	0	0	56	57	34	29	34	53
2001	Lynchburg (Car)	A	2	2	2.93	14	2	0	0	31	28	14	10	7	32
	Altoona (EL)	AA	5	4	3.71	14	14	1	0	87	81	38	36	36	66
MINOR LEAGUE TOTALS			31	22	4.06	98	74	1	0	446	421	231	201	218	457

ST. LOUIS Cardinals

By Will Lingo

It's the best of times and worst of times for the Cardinals. The major league team tied for the best record in the National League in 2001 before losing a tight Division Series to the Diamondbacks. St. Louis worked rookies Bud Smith and Albert Pujols, its Nos. 1 and 2 prospects entering the year, into the big league picture. Smith threw a no-hitter in his 11th major league start, and Pujols had one of the best offensive seasons of any rookie in baseball history.

At the same time, pitching phenoms Rick Ankiel and Chad Hutchinson, who opened the season with St. Louis, ended it in the minors. Ankiel continued to struggle with wildness that cropped up in the 2000 playoffs after a strong rookie season. He fell all the way to Rookie-level Johnson City but performed well there, raising hopes that he can get back on track. Hutchinson, on the other hand, apparently grew so frustrated with his struggles in baseball that he began a serious flirtation with football.

Those four players represent an increasingly rare commodity in the organization: premium talents with clear major league potential. Years of prospect trades and a rash of injuries have left the organization with a lot of question marks. It has shown in the results of the Cardinals' farm teams. The six affiliates produced the worst overall record in baseball in 2001—the third-worst record for St. Louis clubs since Branch Rickey developed the farm system concept in the 1920s.

The system has no surefire major league players among its position players. Prospects such as Jack Wilson, who had a solid rookie season with the Pirates, frequently have been used in trades. The Cardinals have some intriguing pitchers, but many of them are dealing with serious injuries. Journell is one of six of the organization's top arms with a Tommy John operation on his resume.

Yet the major league team continues to win, which remains the ultimate measure of a franchise.

Bruce Manno takes over as farm director from Mike Jorgensen, who accepted a special-assignment scouting position, but the future of the franchise will depend on the scouts, who will need to continue bringing in talent because most of it at the upper levels of the system has been exhausted.

Organization Overview

General manager: Walt Jocketty. **Farm director:** Bruce Manno. **Scouting director:** Marty Maier.

2001 PERFORMANCE

Class	Team	League	W	L	Pct.	Finish*	Manager
Majors	St. Louis	National	93	69	.574	t-1st (16)	Tony La Russa
Triple-A	Memphis Redbirds	Pacific Coast	62	81	.434	15th (16)	Gaylen Pitts
Double-A	New Haven Ravens	Eastern	47	95	.331	12th (12)	Danny Sheaffer
High A	Potomac Cannons	Carolina	66	74	.471	6th (8)	Joe Cunningham
Low A	Peoria Chiefs	Midwest	57	81	.413	11th (14)	Joe Hall
Short-season	New Jersey Cardinals	New York-Penn	35	41	.461	9th (14)	Brian Rupp
Rookie	Johnson City Cardinals	Appalachian	31	35	.470	t-5th (10)	Chris Maloney
OVERALL 2001 MINOR LEAGUE RECORD			298	407	.423	30th (30)	

*Finish in overall standings (No. of teams in league)

ORGANIZATION LEADERS

BATTING
*AVG	**John Gall**, Potomac/Peoria	.311
R	Chris Morris, Peoria	89
H	**John Gall**, Potomac/Peoria	163
TB	**John Gall**, Potomac/Peoria	235
2B	**John Gall**, Potomac/Peoria	48
3B	Chris Morris, Peoria	9
HR	Andy Bevins, Memphis/New Haven	20
RBI	**John Gall**, Potomac/Peoria	77
BB	Chris Morris, Peoria	83
SO	Tim Lemon, Peoria	165
SB	Chris Morris, Peoria	111

PITCHING
W	Jimmy Journell, New Haven/Potomac	15
L	Frank Tejada, Potomac	14
	Dave Zancanaro, Memphis/New Haven	14
#ERA	**Rick Ankiel**, Memphis/Johnson City	2.25
G	Mike Crudale, New Haven	62
CG	Three tied at	2
SV	Scotty Layfield, Potomac	31
IP	Josh Pearce, Memphis/New Haven	185
BB	Chad Hutchinson, Memphis	104
SO	**Rick Ankiel**, Memphis/Johnson City	162
	Jimmy Journell, New Haven/Potomac	162

*Minimum 250 At-Bats #Minimum 75 Innings

Gall   **Ankiel**

BEST TOOLS

Best Hitter for Average	Luis Garcia
Best Power Hitter	Chris Duncan
Fastest Baserunner	Chris Morris
Best Fastball	Jimmy Journell
Best Breaking Ball	Chad Hutchinson
Best Changeup	Chris Narveson
Best Control	Chris Narveson
Best Defensive Catcher	Yadier Molina
Best Defensive Infielder	Ramon Carvajal
Best Infield Arm	Chase Voshell
Best Defensive Outfielder	Luis Saturria
Best Outfield Arm	John Nelson

TOP PROSPECTS OF THE DECADE

1992	Donovan Osborne, lhp
1993	Allen Watson, lhp
1994	Brian Barber, rhp
1995	Alan Benes, rhp
1996	Alan Benes, rhp
1997	Matt Morris, rhp
1998	Rick Ankiel, lhp
1999	J.D. Drew, of
2000	Rick Ankiel, lhp
2001	Bud Smith, lhp

PROJECTED 2005 LINEUP

Catcher	Eli Marrero
First Base	Luis Garcia
Second Base	Fernando Vina
Third Base	Albert Pujols
Shortstop	Edgar Renteria
Left Field	So Taguchi
Center Field	Jim Edmonds
Right Field	J.D. Drew
No. 1 Starter	Matt Morris
No. 2 Starter	Rick Ankiel
No. 3 Starter	Jimmy Journell
No. 4 Starter	Bud Smith
No. 5 Starter	Chris Narveson
Closer	Jason Isringhausen

TOP DRAFT PICKS OF THE DECADE

1992	Sean Lowe, rhp
1993	Alan Benes, rhp
1994	Bret Wagner, lhp
1995	Matt Morris, rhp
1996	Braden Looper, rhp
1997	Adam Kennedy, ss
1998	J.D. Drew, of
1999	Chance Caple, rhp
2000	Shaun Boyd, of
2001	Justin Pope, rhp

ALL-TIME LARGEST BONUSES

J.D. Drew, 1998	$3,000,000
Rick Ankiel, 1997	$2,500,000
Chad Hutchinson, 1998	$2,300,000
Shaun Boyd, 2000	$1,750,000
Braden Looper, 1996	$1,675,000

DraftAnalysis

2001 Draft

Best Pro Debut: The Cardinals' top two picks, RHPs **Justin Pope** (1) and Dan Haren (2), were as polished as advertised. Pope went 2-4, 2.60 with 66 strikeouts in 69 innings at short-season New Jersey. Haren went 3-3, 3.10 with 57 whiffs in 52 innings. RHP Jared Blasdell (38) had a 1.26 ERA and 11 saves for New Jersey, while LHP Anthony Rawson (42) posted a 0.60 ERA and 10 saves at Rookie-level Johnson City.

Best Athlete: John Nelson (8), a college shortstop, had little trouble making a transition to center field. He's an above-average runner with a solid arm and some pop.

Best Hitter: Down the road, 3B Joe Mather (3) should hit for average and power. For now, 1B Jesse Roman (11) and 3B Matt Williams (15) are more advanced.

Best Raw Power: 1B John Davie (32) is raw and batted .221-2-22 at Johnson City. He's 6-foot-5 and 230 pounds, so it's not difficult to envision him becoming a slugger.

Fastest Runner: Nelson is a 4.1-second runner from the right side to first base. He holds the Big 12 Conference record for career stolen bases.

Best Defensive Player: Cody Gunn (21) could develop into a frontline catcher. SS Seth Davidson (10) has terrific hands and good actions, though his arm isn't as strong as desired for his position.

Best Fastball: Haren topped out at 95-96 mph during the college season and was showing close to that velocity at the end of the summer. Josh Brey (4), a 5-foot-10 left-

hander, has a 94 mph fastball. Pope works at 92-93 mph and gets nifty life on his fastball.

Most Intriguing Background: Pope threw 38 consecutive scoreless innings last spring for Central Florida. Unsigned OF Michael Cust's (35) brother Jack made his big league debut in September, while a third brother, Kevin, plays in the Braves system.

RICH ABEL

Pope

Closest To The Majors: Pope and Haren could reach Double-A in their first full pro season.

Best Late-Round Pick: RHP Mike Wodnicki (16) went 13-1 in limited duty at Stanford. Both his low-90s fastball and his breaking ball are plus pitches.

The One Who Got Away: RHP Blake Hawksworth (28), who touches 92-93 mph, was lost to Cal State Fullerton before he transferred to Bellevue (Wash.) CC, so the Cardinals still control his rights. OF/RHP Billy Paganetti (45) should get a chance to be a two-way player for Stanford.

Assessment: St. Louis is trying to improve its stock of position players, yet most of the quality in its draft appears to lie on the mound. In addition to Brey, Harn and Pope, LHP John Killalea (6) and RHP Tyler Adamczyk (7) are nice high school arms. The Cardinals paid out the smallest bonus for a first-rounder, Pope, but made up for it with a $700,000 payout to Adamczyk.

2000 Draft

The jury is out on both first-round picks, as RHP Blake Williams had Tommy John surgery and 2B Shaun Boyd has had mixed results. LHP Chris Narveson (2) was the real find, though he too had Tommy John surgery. **Grade: B**

1999 Draft

3B Albert Pujols (13) had one of the best rookie seasons ever. RHPs Jimmy Journell (4) and Josh Pearce (2) are two of the club's top prospects. Who cares the three first-round picks, 1B Chris Duncan and RHPs Chance Caple and Nick Stocks, haven't done much? **Grade: A**

1998 Draft

OF J.D. Drew (1) and LHP Bud Smith (4) are two players St. Louis is building around. Following a trade, SS Jack Wilson (9) started for Pittsburgh last year. That takes the sting out of RHP/OF Ben Diggins (1), who didn't sign and became a 2000 first-rounder, and RHP Chad Hutchinson (2), who has flamed out and seems headed to the NFL. **Grade: A**

1997 Draft

This effort is tough to evaluate because of the uncertain future of LHP Rick Ankiel (2). 2B Adam Kennedy (1) was dealt to Anaheim to get Jim Edmonds. Signing Padres slugging prospect Xavier Nady (4) out of high school would have been nice. **Grade: B**

Note: Draft analysis prepared by Jim Callis. Numbers in parentheses indicate draft rounds.

. . . Journell has an electric fastball and isn't afraid to go after hitters.

Jimmy Journell rhp

Born: Dec. 29, 1977.
Ht.: 6-4. **Wt.:** 205.
Bats: R. **Throws:** R.
School: University of Ilinois.
Career Transactions: Selected by Cardinals in fourth round of 1999 draft; signed Aug. 12, 1999.

Like a lot of organizations before the 1999 draft, the Cardinals loved Journell's arm but didn't know what to make of the Tommy John surgery he had a week before the draft. Before that, he had been a dominant closer at Illinois and projected him as a first-round pick. They took him in the fourth round, signed him for $250,000 and tried to be patient. He didn't pitch at all in 1999 and worked out of the bullpen in 2000, in what has become an organization practice for pitchers in Tommy John recovery. His breakout came in 2001, as his stuff was back and he lit up the high Class A Carolina League before earning a promotion to Double-A New Haven, where he threw a seven-inning no-hitter in his only start. He ended up as the CL player of the year, the organization's minor league pitcher of the year, and Baseball America's Class A Player of the Year.

Journell has everything you could ask for in a big league pitcher. He throws an electric fastball that can touch 97 mph and sits at 93-94. He has good command of it and works it inside and out on hitters. He has a hard slider that's sharp when he stays on top of it, and he made great strides with his changeup in 2001. His arm problems actually helped his development of those two pitches and helped him become more of a pitcher, rather than just trying to blow hitters away with his fastball. Journell has big league makeup, and he's not afraid to go after hitters. The Cardinals raised his arm slot from low three-quarters to keep him on top of his breaking ball and reduce the stress on his elbow. He went back to a lower slot, where he's more comfortable, during the season. The hope is that Journell and the Cardinals have found a happy medium. Beyond that, he needs to continue his evolution from thrower to pitcher. He can be stubborn at times.

It's possible Journell could show up in St. Louis in 2002, but the organization really just wants to see another healthy, successful year. The larger question is whether he's a starter or closer. The signing of free agent Jason Isringhausen may push Journell closer to the rotation.

Year	Club (League)	Class	W	L	ERA	G	GS	CG	SV	IP	H	R	ER	BB	SO
2000	New Jersey (NY-P)	A	1	0	1.97	13	1	0	0	32	12	12	7	24	39
2001	Potomac (Car)	A	14	6	2.50	26	26	0	0	151	121	54	42	42	156
	New Haven (EL)	AA	1	0	0.00	1	1	1	0	7	0	0	0	3	6
MINOR LEAGUE TOTALS			16	6	2.32	40	28	1	0	190	133	66	49	69	201

MICHAEL WALBY

2. Chris Narveson, lhp

Born: Dec. 20, 1981. **Ht.:** 6-3. **Wt.:** 180. **Bats:** L. **Throws:** L. **School:** T.C. Roberson HS, Skyland, N.C. **Career Transactions:** Selected by Cardinals in second round of 2000 draft; signed June 27, 2000.

Narveson was in the midst of a breakthrough year when the affliction that has hit so many Cardinals pitchers hit him—he needed Tommy John surgery in August. He won a state championship in his senior year of high school in 2000, and he won a promotion to high Class A in 2001 after just eight starts in low Class A. Before his injury, Narveson earned comparisons to both Rick Ankiel and Bud Smith. He throws his fastball at 89-91 mph, and his changeup can be devastating. His best pitch is a big-breaking slider, but his best quality is his maturity and mound presence. He has good command of all of his pitches. Narveson's injury was a surprise because he's not a hard thrower and has solid mechanics and an effortless motion. The prognosis for Tommy John surgery is good now, but it still costs him a year of development and creates big questions about his future. The Cardinals are optimistic Narveson can return to game action by July. When he does he'll follow the organization's path of working in relief until his arm is judged completely sound.

Year	Club (League)	Class	W	L	ERA	G	GS	CG	SV	IP	H	R	ER	BB	SO
2000	Johnson City (Appy)	R	2	4	3.27	12	12	0	0	55	57	33	20	25	63
2001	Peoria (Mid)	A	3	3	1.98	8	8	0	0	50	32	14	11	11	53
	Potomac (Car)	A	4	3	2.57	11	11	1	0	67	52	22	19	13	53
MINOR LEAGUE TOTALS			9	10	2.62	31	31	1	0	172	141	69	50	49	169

3. Luis Garcia, 1b

RICK BATTLE

Born: Nov. 5, 1978. **Ht.:** 6-4. **Wt.:** 184. **Bats:** R. **Throws:** R. **Career Transactions:** Signed out of Mexico by Red Sox, March 14, 1996 . . . Loaned by Red Sox to Monterrey (Mexican), April 30-Sept. 20, 1999 . . . Traded by Red Sox with 1B Dustin Brisson and OF Rick Asadoorian to Cardinals for RHP Dustin Hermanson, Dec. 15, 2001.

Garcia was the key player for the Cardinals in the trade that sent Dustin Hermanson to the Red Sox in December. In a deal between teams with precious few legitimate prospects, Garcia provided a solid bat to a St. Louis system particularly weak in hitters. He signed with Boston as a pitcher and threw in the low 90s, but an arm injury ended his career on the mound. He emerged as a hitter in the Rookie-level Arizona League in 1999, playing for a co-op team of Mexican League players after the Red Sox loaned him to the Monterrey Sultans. He jumped to Double-A at midseason in 2001 and performed so well that he was named Boston's Double-A player of the year. He has a loose, balanced swing with good leverage and can drive the ball to all fields. He's wiry strong with a body like Richie Sexson's, and he's more athletic than might be expected. He showed good pitch recognition and is a potential No. 5 hitter. Garcia is a good defensive first baseman with smooth actions, though at times he's awkward going to his left. He played 10 games in the outfield last season and could move there if needed. Garcia could win a Triple-A job this spring and has few bats in the system ahead of him.

Year	Club (League)	Class	W	L	ERA	G	GS	CG	SV	IP	H	R	ER	BB	SO
1996	Astros/Red Sox (DSL)	R	2	0	3.75	14	0	0	0	24	13	12	10	23	17
1997	Red Sox (DSL)	R	0	3	5.91	4	3	0	0	11	10	10	7	7	12
	Red Sox (GCL)	R	1	2	2.87	8	1	0	1	16	12	10	5	10	18
1998	Red Sox (DSL)	R	0	0	0.00	3	0	0	0	8	3	0	0	4	7
MINOR LEAGUE TOTALS			3	5	3.38	29	4	0	1	59	38	32	22	44	54

Year	Club (League)	Class	AVG	G	AB	R	H	2B	3B	HR	RBI	BB	SO	SB
1998	Red Sox (DSL)	R	.212	54	189	31	40	6	2	8	32	27	33	3
1999	Mexico (AZL)	R	.330	50	188	35	62	9	6	13	40	22	31	1
2000	Augusta (SAL)	A	.260	128	493	72	128	27	5	20	77	51	112	8
2001	Sarasota (FSL)	A	.303	65	267	38	81	14	1	12	44	18	61	2
	Trenton (EL)	AA	.310	63	229	35	71	20	1	14	45	28	68	0
MINOR LEAGUE TOTALS			.280	360	1366	211	382	76	15	67	238	146	305	14

4. Josh Pearce, rhp

Born: Aug. 20, 1977. **Ht.:** 6-3. **Wt.:** 215. **Bats:** R. **Throws:** R. **School:** University of Arizona. **Career Transactions:** Selected by Cardinals in second round of 1999 draft; signed June 18, 1999.

If nothing else, Pearce has proven he's a workhorse. The Cardinals determined he threw nearly 300 innings from college fall ball in 1998 to instructional league in 1999. In spite of that and an organizational epidemic of arm injuries, Pearce threw 185 innings in 28 minor league starts in 2001. As Pearce has shown, he's a bulldog who's always ready to take the ball. He hasn't missed a professional turn and gives his team confidence he'll go six or seven innings every time out. His fastball is in the 88-91 mph range with good sink, and he has good command of it. His slurve and changeup are also effective pitches. Pearce's stuff is just average. He succeeds with superior makeup and knowing how to make the pitches he needs. He has to keep the ball down to be effective. The Cardinals say because he's not a hard thrower, they don't think his arm has been overworked. He'll likely start the 2002 season at Triple-A Memphis, but don't be surprised if Pearce shows up in St. Louis at some point. He projects as a middle-of-the-rotation innings-eater.

Year	Club (League)	Class	W	L	ERA	G	GS	CG	SV	IP	H	R	ER	BB	SO
1999	New Jersey (NY-P)	A	3	7	4.98	14	14	1	0	78	78	45	43	20	78
2000	Potomac (Car)	A	5	3	3.45	10	10	1	0	63	70	25	24	10	42
	Arkansas (TL)	AA	5	6	5.46	17	17	0	0	97	117	68	59	35	63
2001	New Haven (EL)	AA	6	8	3.75	18	18	0	0	115	111	55	48	34	96
	Memphis (PCL)	AAA	4	4	4.26	10	10	0	0	70	72	43	33	12	36
MINOR LEAGUE TOTALS			23	28	4.41	69	69	2	0	423	448	236	207	111	315

5. Justin Pope, rhp

Born: Nov. 8, 1979. **Ht.:** 6-0. **Wt.:** 185. **Bats:** B. **Throws:** R. **School:** University of Central Florida. **Career Transactions:** Selected by Cardinals in first round (28th overall) of 2001 draft; signed June 8, 2001.

Pope comes out of the Wellington (Fla.) High program that produced Pirates pitching prospects Bobby Bradley and Sean Burnett, and employs his father Walt as pitching coach. Pope threw 38 straight scoreless innings at Central Florida last spring and was named TransAmerica Athletic Conference player of the year. He signed for $900,000, the lowest bonus in the first round. Befitting the son of a pitching coach, Pope has moxie and a great idea of how to attack hitters. He works inside with an 88-92 mph fastball that has good movement. His slider and changeup are also advanced. Pope was considered a fringe first-rounder because of his size and lack of overpowering stuff. He succeeds by spotting the ball around the strike zone. After 123 innings at Central Florida, he worked another 69 innings at short-season New Jersey because he signed so quickly, raising more workload questions. Pope will try to build on an impressive pro debut by getting more advanced hitters out at the Class A level. He was clearly tired by the end of last summer, so his stuff could improve in 2002.

Year	Club (League)	Class	W	L	ERA	G	GS	CG	SV	IP	H	R	ER	BB	SO
2001	New Jersey (NY-P)	A	2	4	2.60	15	15	0	0	69	64	32	20	14	66
MINOR LEAGUE TOTALS			2	4	2.60	15	15	0	0	69	64	32	20	14	66

6. So Taguchi, of

Born: July 2, 1969. **Ht.:** 5-10. **Wt.:** 163. **Bats:** R. **Throws:** R. **Career Transactions:** Signed out of Japan by Cardinals, Jan. 9, 2002.

The Cardinals made their first foray into the Far East in January, signing Taguchi to a three-year deal with a base salary of $1 million per year and the chance to double it with incentives. A 10-year veteran of Japan's Pacific League, he became a free agent after spending his entire career with the Orix BlueWave. Taguchi is a defensive specialist who won five Golden Glove awards in Japan, and he has good speed and an above-average arm. He has the skills to play any of the outfield positions. Though he was a longtime teammate of Ichiro Suzuki in Japan, the Cardinals aren't looking for that much offensive production from Taguchi. As a .277 lifetime hitter in Japan with little power, he would be considered a success with a season like Tsuyoshi Shinjo's with the

Mets in 2001. He'll wear No. 99 with the Cardinals and will compete with Eli Marrero, Placido Polanco and Kerry Robinson for the big league left-field job in spring training.

Year	Club (League)	Class	AVG	G	AB	R	H	2B	3B	HR	RBI	BB	SO	SB
1992	Orix (PL)	JPN	.268	47	123	12	33	10	0	1	7	8	26	5
1993	Orix (PL)	JPN	.277	31	83	12	23	7	1	0	5	3	12	3
1994	Orix (PL)	JPN	.307	108	329	55	101	17	1	6	43	23	62	10
1995	Orix (PL)	JPN	.246	130	495	76	122	24	2	9	61	43	80	14
1996	Orix (PL)	JPN	.279	128	509	74	142	24	1	7	44	29	61	10
1997	Orix (PL)	JPN	.294	135	572	92	168	32	4	10	56	49	74	7
1998	Orix (PL)	JPN	.272	132	497	85	135	26	2	9	41	48	68	8
1999	Orix (PL)	JPN	.269	133	524	77	141	21	1	9	56	29	91	11
2000	Orix (PL)	JPN	.279	129	509	77	142	26	3	8	49	55	80	9
2000	Orix (PL)	JPN	.280	134	453	70	127	21	6	8	42	43	88	6
JAPANESE LEAGUE TOTALS			.277	1107	4094	630	1134	208	21	67	404	330	642	83

7. Yadier Molina, c

Born: July 13, 1982. **Ht.:** 5-11. **Wt.:** 187. **Bats:** R. **Throws:** R. **School:** Maestro Ladi HS, Vega Alta, P.R. **Career Transactions:** Selected by Cardinals in fourth round of 2000 draft; signed Sept. 6, 2000.

Not many Rookie-level Appalachian League catchers earn a mention in ESPN Magazine, but not many Appy catchers work with Rick Ankiel either. Molina is the younger brother of catchers Ben and Jose Molina, both of whom are with the Angels. He made his pro debut last year after signing late in 2000. Ankiel raved about Molina's work behind the plate, and defense is his calling card. He has a good frame and will be strong enough to catch every day. He has a plus-plus arm and recalls the defensive skills of Eli Marrero, though he blocks balls better at the same point of development. Molina has some pop but he has work to do with the bat. He has a good swing but it tends to get long, and he needs to work on finer points like his stance. When he's short and quick to the ball he shows power potential. He doesn't run well. The Cardinals already project Molina as a big league catcher based solely on his defense. If his offense develops, he could be a standout. He'll face a significant test with his first full season, likely at low Class A Peoria.

Year	Club (League)	Class	AVG	G	AB	R	H	2B	3B	HR	RBI	BB	SO	SB
2001	Johnson City (Appy)	R	.259	44	158	18	41	11	0	4	18	12	23	1
MINOR LEAGUE TOTALS			.259	44	158	18	41	11	0	4	18	12	23	1

8. Scotty Layfield, rhp

Born: Sept. 13, 1976. **Ht.:** 6-2. **Wt.:** 205. **Bats:** R. **Throws:** R. **School:** Valdosta State (Ga.) University. **Career Transactions:** Selected by Cardinals in 20th round of 1999 draft; signed June 4, 1999.

Layfield came to pitching late, going to Valdosta State as a corner infielder. After a couple of unimpressive seasons in the organization, Layfield broke out as a closer at high Class A Potomac in 2001. He missed time during the season with elbow tendinitis, but he was fine by the end of the year and was added to the 40-man roster. Layfield is a physical specimen who actually spent too much time in the weight room before 2001. He loosened up and went from throwing 86-88 mph in 2000 to 91-93 in 2001. It's a power fastball with sinker movement. With his hard slider, which is a swing-and-miss pitch, he has top-quality stuff for the bullpen. At 25, Layfield still hasn't proven he can get hitters out above Class A. He has a changeup but doesn't need it out of the bullpen, and the Cardinals are satisfied with that as his role. The Cardinals now say they probably should have promoted Layfield from Potomac, but he'll benefit from his first big league spring training and could skip Double-A. If his sinker-slider combination remains potent, he could move fast.

Year	Club (League)	Class	W	L	ERA	G	GS	CG	SV	IP	H	R	ER	BB	SO
1999	New Jersey (NY-P)	A	2	2	3.15	23	3	0	8	34	27	16	12	21	26
2000	Peoria (Mid)	A	2	4	5.13	53	0	0	15	54	65	46	31	40	50
2001	Potomac (Car)	A	1	2	1.84	47	0	0	31	54	36	13	11	18	66
MINOR LEAGUE TOTALS			5	8	3.41	123	3	0	54	142	128	75	54	79	142

9. Dan Haren, rhp

Born: Sept. 17, 1980. **Ht.:** 6-5. **Wt.:** 220. **Bats:** R. **Throws:** R. **School:** Pepperdine University. **Career Transactions:** Selected by Cardinals in second round of 2001 draft; signed June 20, 2001.

Haren teamed with lefthander Noah Lowry, a first-round pick of the Giants, to give Pepperdine one of the best pitching tandems in college baseball in 2001. Haren also DHed for the Waves, hitting .308-5-47 in 224 at-bats, and was named West Coast Conference player of the year. Haren has a big body and a quick arm, and he could get bigger, giving him the potential to be a special pitcher. He threw at 89-93 mph after signing but touched 96 at Pepperdine. He has a good feel for a changeup and maintains consistent arm speed with it, and he works inside effectively with outstanding command. The long college and pro season wore Haren down, and he was at 195 pounds by the end of the summer with New Jersey, meaning he lost about 15-20 pounds. The Cardinals want to see him hold his weight so he can stay strong and durable for a full pro season. His curveball and splitter still need work. Though Haren was tired, the Cardinals still loved what they saw and are excited about his potential. He'll move into a Class A league in 2002 and should become a middle-of-the-rotation starter.

Year	Club (League)	Class	W	L	ERA	G	GS	CG	SV	IP	H	R	ER	BB	SO
2001	New Jersey (NY-P)	A	3	3	3.10	12	8	0	1	52	47	22	18	8	57
MINOR LEAGUE TOTALS			3	3	3.10	12	8	0	1	52	47	22	18	8	57

10. Chris Duncan, 1b

Born: May 5, 1981. **Ht.:** 6-5. **Wt.:** 210. **Bats:** L. **Throws:** R. **School:** Canyon del Oro HS, Tucson. **Career Transactions:** Selected by Cardinals in first round (46th overall) of 1999 draft; signed June 23, 1999.

Duncan's father Dave is St. Louis' pitching coach, and his older brother Shelley was a second-round pick of the Yankees in 2001 after setting numerous home run records at the University of Arizona. Chris committed to the Wildcats out of high school but ended up signing with the Cardinals for $900,000. Duncan has exceptional power potential. He hasn't learned to harness it yet but should get stronger and pull the ball more as he gets older. He was regarded as a better talent than his brother coming out of high school, when he showed flashes of athleticism. So far Duncan hasn't offered much besides his power potential. His hands and arm are decent, but he's rigid on defense and made 30 errors at first base. He also needs to control the strike zone better. He's a below-average runner. Duncan will get another shot at Potomac in 2002 after washing out there in 2001. He has worked to get a looser, more athletic body and even has worked out in the outfield in an effort to be more than a one-dimensional player.

Year	Club (League)	Class	AVG	G	AB	R	H	2B	3B	HR	RBI	BB	SO	SB
1999	Johnson City (Appy)	R	.214	55	201	23	43	8	1	6	34	25	62	3
2000	Peoria (Mid)	A	.256	122	450	52	115	34	0	8	57	36	111	1
2001	Potomac (Car)	A	.179	49	168	12	30	6	0	3	16	10	47	4
	Peoria (Mid)	A	.306	80	297	44	91	23	2	13	59	36	55	13
MINOR LEAGUE TOTALS			.250	306	1116	131	279	71	3	30	166	107	275	21

11. Bill Ortega, of

Born: July 24, 1975. **Ht.:** 6-4. **Wt.:** 205. **Bats:** R. **Throws:** R. **Career Transactions:** Signed out of Cuba by Cardinals, March 11, 1997.

Ortega is one of the many position players frustrating the Cardinals with his stalled development. A Cuban defector, he finally broke through in 2000 but hurt his wrist, an injury that seemed to affect his play most of the 2001 season. He was at his best again in the Arizona Fall League, hitting .387-2-20 in 93 at-bats to raise optimism in the organization again. Ortega is one of the best hitters in the organization. He uses the whole field, though Cardinals officials would like him to show more power. He's big and strong, and he should add power if he gets more lift in his swing. Defense is Ortega's biggest bugaboo and it was dreadful at times in 2001. He needs to get better jumps, play smarter and show more motivation to improve in the outfield. Even with all that, he doesn't project to be anything more than an average left fielder at best. Ortega made his major league debut in 2001 and could see time in St. Louis again in 2002, though he'll be hard-pressed to find any regular work there. The Cardinals will be pleased if he puts together a big year at Memphis.

Year	Club (League)	Class	AVG	G	AB	R	H	2B	3B	HR	RBI	BB	SO	SB
1997	Prince William (Car)	A	.229	73	249	23	57	14	0	0	15	21	42	1
1998	Peoria (Mid)	A	.276	105	398	57	110	23	2	2	60	39	69	4
1999	Potomac (Car)	A	.306	110	421	66	129	27	4	9	74	38	69	7
	Arkansas (TL)	AA	.377	20	69	10	26	9	0	2	10	10	9	0
2000	Arkansas (TL)	AA	.325	86	332	51	108	18	5	12	62	28	42	1
2001	Memphis (PCL)	AAA	.287	134	495	55	142	26	4	6	62	40	74	6
	St. Louis (NL)	MAJ	.200	5	5	0	1	0	0	0	0	0	1	0
MAJOR LEAGUE TOTALS			.200	5	5	0	1	0	0	0	0	0	1	0
MINOR LEAGUE TOTALS			.291	528	1964	262	572	117	15	31	283	176	305	19

12. Chad Hutchinson, rhp

Born: Feb. 21, 1977. **Ht.:** 6-5. **Wt.:** 230. **Bats:** R. **Throws:** R. **School:** Stanford University. **Career Transactions:** Selected by Cardinals in second round of 1998 draft; signed June 30, 1998.

After starting the year as a surprise inclusion on the big league roster, Hutchinson finished it by trying out with NFL teams as a quarterback. He was considered a potential football first-round pick at Stanford before St. Louis signed him to a major league deal with a $2.3 million bonus in 1998. Hutchinson is the kind of spectacular athlete who makes scouts ga-ga. He can reach the mid-90s with his fastball. His out pitch is an 84-85 mph slider that looks like a curveball. He's intelligent and intense, and he has been the Cardinals' best pitcher in spring training the last couple of years. The Cardinals have always wondered when Hutchinson would figure it all out, and the football dalliance raises new questions. He lacks consistent command of all of his pitches, though it comes and goes, and he hasn't handled adversity on the mound well. Hutchinson is a bigger wild card than ever, but his arm still demands attention. It might be to the Cardinals' advantage if he pursues football in the off-season so he can get it out of his system.

Year	Club (League)	Class	W	L	ERA	G	GS	CG	SV	IP	H	R	ER	BB	SO
1998	New Jersey (NY-P)	A	0	1	3.52	3	3	0	0	15	15	7	6	4	20
	Prince William (Car)	A	2	0	2.79	5	5	0	0	29	20	12	9	11	31
1999	Arkansas (TL)	AA	7	11	4.72	25	25	0	0	141	127	79	74	85	150
	Memphis (PCL)	AAA	2	0	2.19	2	2	0	0	12	4	3	3	8	16
2000	Memphis (PCL)	AAA	0	1	25.92	5	4	0	0	8	10	24	24	27	9
	Arkansas (TL)	AA	2	3	3.38	11	11	1	0	48	40	21	18	27	54
2001	St. Louis (NL)	MAJ	0	0	24.75	3	0	0	0	4	9	11	11	6	2
	Memphis (PCL)	AAA	4	9	7.92	27	20	0	0	98	99	91	86	104	111
MAJOR LEAGUE TOTALS			0	0	24.75	3	0	0	0	4	9	11	11	6	2
MINOR LEAGUE TOTALS			17	25	5.63	78	70	1	0	352	315	237	220	266	391

13. Blake Williams, rhp

Born: Feb. 22, 1979. **Ht.:** 6-5. **Wt.:** 210. **Bats:** R. **Throws:** R. **School:** Southwest Texas State University. **Career Transactions:** Selected by Cardinals in first round (24th overall) of 2000 draft; signed July 19, 2000.

After an encouraging pro debut in 2000 and a strong start in 2001, Williams followed the unfortunate path of other Cardinals pitching prospects and was felled by an elbow injury that required Tommy John surgery. He went under the knife in June, so the Cardinals hope he can get back on a mound by the end of 2002. Before the injury, Williams was on the fast track to St. Louis, having begun his first full season in high Class A. He has an average fastball that can touch the mid-90s at times, and his best pitch is a curveball with slider action. He has great command and also has good mechanics, so he's not expected to have chronic arm problems. Williams' changeup needs improvement, but that should come with experience. That's his biggest need at this point: to come back healthy and log innings. Williams projects as a solid middle-of-the-rotation starter who could get better if his arm bounces back. The Cardinals are anxious for him to return.

Year	Club (League)	Class	W	L	ERA	G	GS	CG	SV	IP	H	R	ER	BB	SO
2000	New Jersey (NY-P)	A	3	1	1.59	6	6	0	0	28	20	7	5	9	25
2001	Potomac (Car)	A	4	10	2.43	17	17	2	0	107	82	43	29	30	92
MINOR LEAGUE TOTALS			7	11	2.27	23	23	2	0	135	102	50	34	39	117

14. Chance Caple, rhp

Born: Aug. 9, 1978. **Ht.:** 6-6. **Wt.:** 215. **Bats:** R. **Throws:** R. **School:** Texas A&M University. **Career Transactions:** Selected by Cardinals in first round (30th overall) of 1999 draft; signed July 15, 1999.

Caple has all the tools to be a standout pitcher, but so far he hasn't shown much as a pro. He has been either ineffective or injured since signing. The latest setback came last spring, when he went down and required—stop us if you've heard this one before—Tommy John surgery in April. Doctors found that scar tissue had already built up in his elbow, so Caple had been pitching in pain for some time. When healthy, he has good sink on a fastball that ranges from 89-93 mph. His slider could be an above-average pitch and his changeup shows potential but still needs a lot of work. He's most effective when he keeps the ball down and uses the movement on his pitches to get guys out. The Cardinals hope he'll be back on the mound in spring training and could see game action out of the bullpen by the middle of the summer. Caple has the potential to be a No. 2 or 3 starter, but St. Louis wants to see how he does in a bullpen role in 2002.

Year	Club (League)	Class	W	L	ERA	G	GS	CG	SV	IP	H	R	ER	BB	SO
1999	New Jersey (NY-P)	A	0	4	4.38	7	7	0	0	37	35	24	18	18	36
2000	Potomac (Car)	A	7	9	4.39	22	22	0	0	125	128	68	61	34	97
2001	Did Not Play—Injured														
MINOR LEAGUE TOTALS			7	13	4.39	29	29	0	0	162	163	92	79	52	133

15. Cristobal Correa, rhp

Born: Dec. 27, 1979. **Ht.:** 6-1. **Wt.:** 175. **Bats:** R. **Throws:** R. **Career Transactions:** Signed out of Venezuela by Cardinals, May 20, 1998.

No, the Cardinals don't get a group rate on Tommy John surgery. Correa had his operation in 2000, and he went through his bullpen year in 2001 as part of the Cardinals' rehabilitation program—a program that should be perfected by now. He'll be expected to log a full, healthy season in 2002, his fifth with the organization since signing out of Venezuela. Correa has a small frame but a quick, potentially electric arm. His fastball ranges from 90-95 mph and has nice sink. He throws a good curveball that leads to a lot of grounders when it's working. Before the injury, Correa's changeup and command needed work, and they remain weaknesses. Innings would likely resolve most of those questions, and he'll try to prove he's sound and ready to get back on the fast track in 2002. He'll open in the high Class A rotation.

Year	Club (League)	Class	W	L	ERA	G	GS	CG	SV	IP	H	R	ER	BB	SO
1998	San Joaquin 2 (VSL)	R	1	1	3.15	23	2	0	5	34	28	14	12	28	27
1999	New Jersey (NY-P)	A	3	3	2.94	9	9	0	0	52	41	20	17	26	59
	Peoria (Mid)	A	0	2	10.35	5	5	0	0	20	26	24	23	14	15
2000	Potomac (Car)	A	6	6	3.24	18	18	0	0	100	82	41	36	49	76
2001	New Jersey (NY-P)	A	1	3	5.40	15	1	0	3	40	48	34	24	17	32
MINOR LEAGUE TOTALS			11	15	4.09	70	35	0	8	246	225	133	112	134	209

16. Nick Stocks, rhp

Born: Aug. 27, 1978. **Ht.:** 6-2. **Wt.:** 185. **Bats:** R. **Throws:** R. **School:** Florida State University. **Career Transactions:** Selected by Cardinals in first round (36th overall) of 1999 draft; signed Aug. 29, 1999.

Stocks got his Tommy John surgery out of the way before he came to the organization, as a freshman at Florida State. He bounced back to become a supplemental first-round pick, but he has continued to be bothered by injuries as a pro and hasn't put up performances to match his considerable tools. He missed time in 2000 with back problems and was bothered by shoulder, back and hamstring woes in 2001. He went to the Arizona Fall League to make up innings but was shut down with shoulder soreness. When healthy, Stocks has a quick arm and a plus fastball that consistently reaches 94-95 mph. His hammer curveball is one of the best breaking pitches in the organization, though he tends to rely on it too much. Stocks has no changeup to speak of but the Cardinals believe he has the potential to develop a good one. His biggest obstacle is learning to pitch, which is hard to do if he can't stay healthy. He has a closer's mentality, so the Cardinals might try him in that role if his changeup doesn't come along and he can't handle a starter's workload. Stocks should be healthy for spring training and could jump to Triple-A if he pitches well.

Year	Club (League)	Class	W	L	ERA	G	GS	CG	SV	IP	H	R	ER	BB	SO
2000	Peoria (Mid)	A	10	10	3.78	25	24	1	0	150	133	88	63	52	118
2001	New Haven (EL)	AA	2	12	5.16	16	15	1	0	82	89	52	47	33	63
MINOR LEAGUE TOTALS			12	22	4.27	41	39	2	0	232	222	140	110	85	181

17. B.R. Cook, rhp

Born: March 2, 1978. **Ht.:** 6-4. **Wt.:** 200. **Bats:** R. **Throws:** R. **School:** Oregon State University. **Career Transactions:** Selected by Cardinals in third round of 1999 draft; signed June 18, 1999.

In 2001, when good performances were hard to find in the organization, Cook put together a solid season. His stuff is coming along as he grows into his good pitcher's frame, though his fastball is on the low end of average. It sits at 89-90 mph and reaches 92 at times. His best pitch is his slider, which has a hard downward break almost like a curveball. His changeup should be an average major league pitch. Cook's control is improving, and when he's making all his pitches and putting the ball where he wants, he's capable of cruising through innings. He was more successful last year because he was more aggressive in throwing strikes and going after hitters. The Cardinals see him as an innings-eater in the mold of Josh Pearce, and about a year behind him in his path through the organization. Cook went back to high Class A in 2001 after finishing the previous year there, and he'll return to Double-A this season.

Year	Club (League)	Class	W	L	ERA	G	GS	CG	SV	IP	H	R	ER	BB	SO
1999	New Jersey (NY-P)	A	5	1	2.84	9	8	0	0	44	42	19	14	16	42
2000	Peoria (Mid)	A	5	7	3.69	18	18	0	0	98	90	66	40	52	83
	Potomac (Car)	A	0	4	5.53	8	8	0	0	42	48	31	26	27	23
2001	Potomac (Car)	A	4	2	2.86	8	8	0	0	50	35	20	16	12	36
	New Haven (EL)	AA	5	8	3.99	20	20	0	0	122	115	68	54	37	84
MINOR LEAGUE TOTALS			19	22	3.79	63	62	0	0	356	330	204	150	144	268

18. Covelli Crisp, of

Born: Nov. 1, 1979. **Ht.:** 6-0. **Wt.:** 185. **Bats:** B. **Throws:** R. **School:** Los Angeles Pierce JC. **Career Transactions:** Selected by Cardinals in seventh round of 1999 draft; signed June 7, 1999.

Crisp comes from a family with a rich athletic background. His father was a boxer, his mother was a world-class sprinter and his sister is an ice skater. His grandfather invented a type of track starting block and trained track athletes. After a couple of nondescript seasons in the organization, Crisp spent the offseason after 2000 getting stronger and refining his swing from the right side of the plate. It showed in 2001, as he led the Carolina League in games, at-bats, hits and total bases (224) while finishing third in batting. His speed and bat make him a prospect. Crisp now has a good approach to hitting from both sides of the plate. He has a quick bat and has shown a little pop as well, though he understands his role and doesn't try to crush the ball. Crisp likes to play and has a good attitude. To become a major leaguer he'll have to improve his defense, though. He has the legs to play center field but probably not the arm, so he'll have to get comfortable in left. He'll move up to Double-A to open 2002.

Year	Club (League)	Class	AVG	G	AB	R	H	2B	3B	HR	RBI	BB	SO	SB
1999	Johnson City (Appy)	R	.258	65	229	55	59	5	4	3	22	44	41	27
2000	New Jersey (NY-P)	A	.239	36	134	18	32	5	0	0	14	11	22	25
	Peoria (Mid)	A	.276	27	98	14	27	9	0	0	7	16	15	7
2001	Potomac (Car)	A	.306	139	530	80	162	23	3	11	47	52	64	39
MINOR LEAGUE TOTALS			.283	267	991	167	280	42	7	14	90	123	142	98

19. Chris Morris, of

Born: July 1, 1979. **Ht.:** 5-8. **Wt.:** 180. **Bats:** B. **Throws:** R. **School:** The Citadel. **Career Transactions:** Selected by Cardinals in 15th round of 2000 draft; signed June 16, 2000.

The Cardinals drafted Morris out of The Citadel because of his speed. He led NCAA Division I with 84 steals in 94 attempts in 2000, and finished one off the New York-Penn League lead with 42 after signing, despite batting a paltry .170. That made him look like the second coming of Esix Snead, who stole 109 bases in 2000 and was lost on waivers to the Mets after the 2001 season because he never developed a good approach to hitting. But Morris showed potential with the bat in 2001, raising his overall average 60 points after ending May with a .234 average. In addition to leading the Midwest League with 111 steals (and 24 failed attempts), he also topped the low Class A league with 83 walks. He's a 75 runner on the 20-to-80 scouting scale even though he's short and stocky. Morris is a go-getter and developed into a strong bunter when he hurt his thumb in instructional league after the 2000 season and had to bunt nearly every time at bat. He was able to get on base then though everyone knew what was coming. Morris has no power to speak of and still needs to hone his swing and put the ball in play more. He has the speed to play anywhere in the outfield, but he needs work on other aspects of his defense, such as his routes to balls. He'll move up to high Class A and could move faster if he can handle better pitching.

Year	Club (League)	Class	AVG	G	AB	R	H	2B	3B	HR	RBI	BB	SO	SB
2000	New Jersey (NY-P)	A	.170	63	182	34	31	2	1	0	15	50	48	42
2001	Peoria (Mid)	A	.294	134	480	89	141	11	9	2	39	83	101	111
MINOR LEAGUE TOTALS			.260	197	662	123	172	13	10	2	54	133	149	153

20. Shaun Boyd, 2b

Born: Aug. 15, 1981. **Ht.:** 5-10. **Wt.:** 175. **Bats:** R. **Throws:** R. **School:** Vista HS, Oceanside, Calif. **Career Transactions:** Selected by Cardinals in first round (13th overall) of 2000 draft; signed June 26, 2000.

Primarily a shortstop in high school, Boyd passed on a scholarship to UCLA and signed as a first-round pick with the Cardinals, who moved him to the outfield for his 2000 debut. He told the organization he wanted to move back to shortstop, and they compromised on second base last year. His bat got the Cardinals excited, as he raised his average steadily after a slow start, but his season ended in August when a fastball hit him in the face and broke his jaw. Boyd is a potential .300 hitter with gap power now. He has the bat speed to hit home runs eventually. Boyd has a good approach to hitting for his level of experience, but he needs to learn the strike zone. He's athletic and has the tools to play second base, though he still requires a lot of refinement. He has quick feet and his arm still needs work. Boyd is young and hasn't played a lot of baseball, so the Cardinals will send him one step up to high Class A and see what develops.

Year	Club (League)	Class	AVG	G	AB	R	H	2B	3B	HR	RBI	BB	SO	SB
2000	Johnson City (Appy)	R	.263	43	152	15	40	9	0	2	15	10	22	6
2001	Peoria (Mid)	A	.282	81	277	42	78	12	2	5	27	33	42	20
MINOR LEAGUE TOTALS			.275	124	429	57	118	21	2	7	42	43	64	26

21. Jeremy Lambert, rhp

Born: Jan. 10, 1979. **Ht.:** 6-1. **Wt.:** 195. **Bats:** R. **Throws:** R. **School:** Kearns (Utah) HS. **Career Transactions:** Selected by Cardinals in 16th round of 1997 draft; signed June 7, 1997.

Not being a premium draft pick actually helped Lambert in his progress through the Cardinals system. The organization saw his potential but took a patient approach with him because of his youth and inexperience. He blossomed in 2001 as a Double-A closer and earned a promotion to Triple-A. He started to put it all together in 2000, as he figured out how to attack hitters and made significant strides with his command. He's not overpowering, as his fastball touches 90 mph but is more consistently in the high 80s. His slider is his best pitch, and he has become adept at moving the ball around in the strike zone. Lambert also has deception and a good mentality for the bullpen. He needs to develop a better weapon to get lefthanded hitters out, as they hit .304 against him last year (compared to .200 by righthanders). Because he isn't overpowering, he must be precise with his location. Lambert should open 2002 as the closer in Triple-A.

Year	Club (League)	Class	W	L	ERA	G	GS	CG	SV	IP	H	R	ER	BB	SO
1997	Johnson City (Appy)	R	1	1	9.19	27	0	0	1	32	46	42	33	37	29
1998	Johnson City (Appy)	R	4	4	4.92	13	11	0	0	64	73	44	35	37	30
1999	Peoria (Mid)	A	2	1	8.91	21	0	0	0	34	48	36	34	27	27
2000	Potomac (Car)	A	0	0	4.40	16	3	0	0	29	30	17	14	7	28
	Arkansas (TL)	AA	0	2	3.83	39	0	0	3	47	41	27	20	28	63
2001	New Haven (EL)	AA	2	2	2.97	31	0	0	14	33	32	17	11	17	48
	Memphis (PCL)	AAA	5	1	3.23	28	0	0	3	31	23	14	11	8	39
MINOR LEAGUE TOTALS			14	11	5.26	175	14	0	21	270	293	197	158	161	264

22. Tyler Adamczyk, rhp

Born: Nov. 9, 1982. **Ht.:** 6-6. **Wt.:** 190. **Bats:** R. **Throws:** R. **School:** Westlake HS, Westlake Village, Calif. **Career Transactions:** Selected by Cardinals in seventh round of 2001 draft; signed Aug. 17, 2001.

Adamczyk was a two-way standout in high school, but scouts viewed him strictly as a pitcher. His talent dictated getting picked in the first two rounds, but he fell to the seventh because of an inconsistent high school season, a commitment to the University of California (he is a good student) and a reported price tag of as much as $1.5 million. The Cardinals signed him at the end of the summer for $700,000 and he didn't pitch until instructional league. Adamczyk has a tall, thin body with plenty of room for projection and a quick arm. He's athletic and played basketball in high school. He already throws his fastball 88-92 mph with good sink, and he should add velocity. His slider has the potential to be a plus pitch, but it will need a lot of refinement, and he never has worked much with a changeup. Command and other fine points of pitching will come as he gets innings. Unless he pitches lights-out in spring training, Adamczyk will start the season in extended spring and move to a short-season affiliate in June.

Year	Club (League)	Class	W	L	ERA	G	GS	CG	SV	IP	H	R	ER	BB	SO
	Has Not Played—Signed 2002 Contract														

23. Justin Woodrow, of

Born: March 26, 1982. **Ht.:** 6-1. **Wt.:** 185. **Bats:** L. **Throws:** R. **School:** Knoch HS, Saxonburg, Pa. **Career Transactions:** Selected by Cardinals in sixth round of 2000 draft; signed July 13, 2000.

Woodrow spent his second season in the Appalachian League in 2001, and it paid dividends as he made significant improvement in just about every aspect of his game. He worked hard in the Cardinals' offseason training program to get stronger, and added experience improved his approach at the plate. Woodrow has the tools that excite scouts, and he's just a pup with plenty of room to get better. If he reaches his ceiling as a hitter, he projects as a Dave Justice type, with a quick bat, a knack for making contact and legitimate power potential. Woodrow worked hard to get better at the plate and now needs to apply the same focus to his defense. He has center-field skills and a right-field arm, and he should settle in right if he works on his jumps and shows enough power for the position. The Cardinals are interested to see what he can do in his first try at full-season ball this year.

Year	Club (League)	Class	AVG	G	AB	R	H	2B	3B	HR	RBI	BB	SO	SB
2000	Johnson City (Appy)	R	.281	40	135	22	38	3	0	0	14	22	29	7
2001	Johnson City (Appy)	R	.313	60	211	32	66	11	3	2	21	38	27	4
MINOR LEAGUE TOTALS			.301	100	346	54	104	14	3	2	35	60	56	11

24. Rhett Parrott, rhp

Born: Nov. 12, 1979. **Ht.:** 6-2. **Wt.:** 190. **Bats:** R. **Throws:** R. **School:** Georgia Tech. **Career Transactions:** Selected by Cardinals in ninth round of 2001 draft; signed July 11, 2001.

Parrott was drafted off his performance in the Cape Cod League in 2000 and his potential, as he never put up the numbers at Georgia Tech to match expectations for him. That trend continued in his pro debut, as he posted mediocre statistics but showed enough to make the Cardinals optimistic about his future. He already has drawn comparisons to Matt Morris and Brad Radke, but that's a bit premature. Parrott has a nice frame and a fastball that reaches 92-94 mph with good life. He threw a slider through most of his college career but abandoned it last year in favor of a curveball that St. Louis officials say is one of the better ones in the organization. The slider is also a potentially above-average pitch if he goes back to it. Parrott needs to work on his approach to pitching and his command, which did improve after Cardinals coaches tweaked his mechanics. He gave up just four walks while striking out 25 in his last three starts, covering 15 innings. He'll begin this year at one of the organization's Class A affiliates.

Year	Club (League)	Class	W	L	ERA	G	GS	CG	SV	IP	H	R	ER	BB	SO
2001	New Jersey (NY-P)	A	1	3	4.93	11	11	0	0	46	45	27	25	28	58
MINOR LEAGUE TOTALS			1	3	4.93	11	11	0	0	46	45	27	25	28	58

25. John Gall, 1b/3b

Born: April 2, 1978. **Ht.:** 6-0. **Wt.:** 195. **Bats:** R. **Throws:** R. **School:** Stanford University. **Career Transactions:** Selected by Cardinals in 11th round of 2000 draft; signed June 22, 2000.

Gall left his name all over the Stanford record books after a four-year career there. He's the Cardinal's career leader in at-bats (1,027), hits (368), doubles (80) and RBIs (263), and also set Pacific-10 Conference standards in the first three categories. He was an all-conference selection three times. So it's no surprise Gall has continued hitting with the Cardinals. He's an intelligent player with a great approach and a love for the game. He puts the ball in play and is rarely caught off-balance by pitchers. Gall consistently plays above his tools, which is a blessing and a curse. He's a defensive liability at third base, so he spent most of last season at first. He's fine there defensively, but he hasn't shown enough power for the position and isn't expected to add much more. He's also a below-average runner. Guys who can hit like Gall always are able to find work, but unless he adds power he's not likely to be more than a role player in the major leagues.

Year	Club (League)	Class	AVG	G	AB	R	H	2B	3B	HR	RBI	BB	SO	SB
2000	New Jersey (NY-P)	A	.239	71	259	28	62	10	0	2	27	25	37	16
2001	Peoria (Mid)	A	.302	57	205	27	62	23	0	4	44	16	18	0
	Potomac (Car)	A	.317	84	319	44	101	25	0	4	33	24	40	5
MINOR LEAGUE TOTALS			.287	212	783	99	225	58	0	10	104	65	95	21

26. John Novinsky, rhp

Born: April 25, 1979. **Ht.:** 6-3. **Wt.:** 190. **Bats:** R. **Throws:** R. **School:** Iona College. **Career Transactions:** Selected by Cardinals in ninth round of 2000 draft; signed Sept. 7, 2000.

When signing with the Cardinals proved a bit stickier than he expected, Novinsky went to the Cape Cod League for the summer of 2000 and posted a 3.11 ERA in 38 innings with Yarmouth-Dennis before finally signing. He made his pro debut in 2001 and held his own with a bad Peoria team that was, by several accounts, not a positive development situation. Novinsky has a good arm and can touch 94 mph with his fastball. He throws an array of pitches, including two fastballs, a slider, a changeup and a knuckle-curve. He's confident to the point of brashness, and the organization considers him a tad stubborn. Novinsky needs to refine all his pitches and develop a better feel for pitching. He has dumped the knuckle-curve for now and probably will be better off without it at this point in his career. He'll move up to high Class A for 2002 and show whether he's a face in the crowd or a legitimate prospect.

Year	Club (League)	Class	W	L	ERA	G	GS	CG	SV	IP	H	R	ER	BB	SO
2001	Peoria (Mid)	A	9	11	5.52	25	25	1	0	139	165	95	85	43	115
MINOR LEAGUE TOTALS			9	11	5.52	25	25	1	0	139	165	95	85	43	115

27. Rick Asadoorian, of

Born: July 23, 1980. **Ht.:** 6-2. **Wt.:** 185. **Bats:** R. **Throws:** R. **School:** Northbridge HS, Whitinsville, Mass. **Career Transactions:** Selected by Red Sox in first round (17th overall) of 1999 draft; signed Aug. 16, 1999 . . . Traded by Red Sox with 1B Dustin Brisson and 1B Luis Garcia to Cardinals for RHP Dustin Hermanson, Dec. 15, 2001.

Asadoorian seemed to be a perfect fit for the Red Sox, a New England product whose dream was to play in Boston. Signed for a club-record $1.7255 million bonus as a 1999 first-round pick, he was included in a package of three players used to obtain Dustin Hermanson in December. Asadoorian was the best defensive outfielder in the Boston system, with a plus arm sometimes compared to Dwight Evans' and the range to play center field. Asadoorian has good instincts in center and can go and get the ball. His offense is a huge question mark, however. He chases bad pitches and doesn't even read fastballs well, and he's aggressive at the plate without a real concept of what he's doing. He also needs to get stronger. Scouts have compared him to a young Bob Dernier because he's lean and rangy, runs well and has a long swing. Dernier hit .255 and played in parts of 10 big league seasons, but Asadoorian has a long way to go to reach the majors. The Cardinals might return him to low Class A to see if he can have some success and build confidence in his bat.

Year	Club (League)	Class	AVG	G	AB	R	H	2B	3B	HR	RBI	BB	SO	SB
2000	Red Sox (GCL)	R	.264	54	197	43	52	9	3	5	31	26	56	22
2001	Augusta (SAL)	A	.212	116	406	50	86	13	6	6	40	47	139	13
MINOR LEAGUE TOTALS			.229	170	603	93	138	22	9	11	71	73	195	35

28. Matt Williams, 3b

Born: March 24, 1979. **Ht.:** 6-1. **Wt.:** 215. **Bats:** R. **Throws:** R. **School:** Baylor University. **Career Transactions:** Selected by Cardinals in 15th round of 2001 draft; signed June 8, 2001.

A 34th-round pick out of high school by the Royals in 1997, Williams got off to a strong start in his first two seasons at Baylor, but disappointing junior and senior years hurt his draft status. The Cardinals took him based on his power potential, and he showed promise after signing last summer. A shoulder injury limited him at New Jersey, but he showed his tools in a postdraft minicamp and again in instructional league. Williams could be an above-average offensive player, with power clearly his best tool. He already has a good approach at the plate, illustrated by his .416 on-base percentage at New Jersey. If all goes well, he could develop into a decent third baseman, as he has good hands and an average arm. His speed is below average, and he may have to move to first base if he can't handle third. Williams will advance to full-season ball in 2002, and the Cardinals hope he shows he's ready for high Class A.

Year	Club (League)	Class	AVG	G	AB	R	H	2B	3B	HR	RBI	BB	SO	SB
2001	New Jersey (NYP)	A	.294	41	136	25	40	11	2	2	17	25	43	1
MINOR LEAGUE TOTALS			.294	41	136	25	40	11	2	2	17	25	43	1

29. Robinson Mojica, of

Born: May 31, 1982. **Ht.:** 6-2. **Wt.:** 170. **Bats:** R. **Throws:** R. **Career Transactions:** Signed out of Dominican Republic by Cardinals, April 1, 2000.

Mojica got the Cardinals' attention with a solid season in the Rookie-level Dominican Summer League in 2000, so they brought him in to make his U.S. debut last year. His season ended early, however, when he was hit in the face by a fastball. Mojica is a tools player who quickly gets the attention of scouts. His physical attributes are similar to Justin Woodrow's, and Mojica still is filling out his frame. He has the range and arm to play center field, but at the plate he's trying to figure things out. His swing got long last year and he lost control of the strike zone, but the Cardinals say his problems are correctable. He has power potential as his body matures. Some in the organization thought Mojica was rushed a bit to the Appalachian League last year, so he'll return there in 2002. The hope is that second stint there will be as successful as Woodrow's.

Year	Club (League)	Class	AVG	G	AB	R	H	2B	3B	HR	RBI	BB	SO	SB
2000	Cardinals (DSL)	R	.282	60	227	33	64	8	9	6	43	19	40	13
2001	Johnson City (Appy)	R	.220	36	118	7	26	5	1	0	8	3	25	0
MINOR LEAGUE TOTALS			.261	96	345	40	90	13	10	6	51	22	65	13

30. Bo Hart, 2b

Born: Sept. 27, 1976. **Ht.:** 5-11. **Wt.:** 175. **Bats:** R. **Throws:** R. **School:** Gonzaga University. **Career Transactions:** Selected by Cardinals in 33rd round of 1999 draft; signed June 6, 1999.

The Cardinals have a knack for developing gritty utilitymen who play above their tools, and Hart is the latest to follow in the footsteps of Joe McEwing and Stubby Clapp. Hart has made his mark on the organization in spite of repeated nagging injuries. He broke his right hand when he was plunked by a fastball at midseason last year, knocking him out for eight weeks. He wasn't even a standout in college, so he approaches the game as a scrapper who's looking to prove himself every time he takes the field. Hart is a manager's dream who plays to win. He has no above-average tool but usually finds a way to get the job done. He has gap power, makes consistent contact and serves as a sparkplug for a lineup. He's best suited to play second base on defense but is versatile and willing to play anywhere to get himself in the lineup. He'll move up to Double-A in 2002.

Year	Club (League)	Class	AVG	G	AB	R	H	2B	3B	HR	RBI	BB	SO	SB
1999	New Jersey (NY-P)	A	.184	50	163	23	30	3	3	3	15	10	38	4
2000	Potomac (Car)	A	.256	75	273	42	70	25	4	0	20	23	42	9
2001	Potomac (Car)	A	.305	81	279	48	85	23	3	5	34	17	69	16
MINOR LEAGUE TOTALS			.259	206	715	113	185	51	10	8	69	50	149	29

SAN DIEGO
Padres

By Jim Callis

Since making their World Series run in 1998, the Padres have had to be patient. With a franchise value and a payroll that are roughly 50 percent or less of each of their National League West rivals, they haven't had a winning record or finished better than fourth in the last three seasons.

San Diego planned to complete its rebuilding in 2002, when its new ballpark also figured to be finished. But money for the project ran out in October 2000 in the midst of a federal investigation into city councilwoman Valerie Stallings' stock dealings with a company run by Padres owner John Moores. Stallings pleaded guilty to a pair of misdemeanors and resigned from the city council in January 2001. Finally, after several lawsuits continued to stall the project, the city council voted in late November to issue $166 million in bonds. The opening of the new ballpark is now set for 2004.

While the Padres have two seasons before getting a big revenue boost, they won't have to wait that long to contend. They gathered a stockpile of pitchers in 1999 and 2000, then addressed an organizational shortfall of hitters by getting more offense than any other club out of the 2001 draft.

San Diego has amassed talent in a variety of ways. Besides drafting well, the Padres have strengthened their commitment to finding talent all over the globe in the last two years. They hired international scouting supervisor Bill Clark in 2000 and doubled their foreign scouting budget in 2001. In December, San Diego entered into a five-year working agreement with the Mexico City Red Devils, who funneled players such as Francisco Cordova and Ricardo Rincon to the Pirates during their 14-year affiliation. The Padres set up a similar arrangement with Japan's Chiba Lotte Marines in 1997.

General manager Kevin Towers, in charge since November 1995, also has made several astute trades. Ryan Klesko and Phil Nevin, San Diego's two best hitters, arrived in lopsided deals, as did promising young righthanders Adam Eaton and Dennis Tankersley. In 2001, Towers kept at it by picking up Cesar Crespo and Mark Kotsay from the Marlins, D'Angelo Jimenez from the Yankees, and most recently Brett Tomko and Ramon Vazquez from the Mariners during the 2001 Winter Meetings.

Organization Overview

General manager: Kevin Towers. **Farm director:** Tye Waller. **Scouting director:** Bill Gayton.

2001 PERFORMANCE

Class	Team	League	W	L	Pct.	Finish*	Manager(s)
Majors	San Diego	National	79	83	.488	10th (16)	Bruce Bochy
Triple-A	Portland Beavers	Pacific Coast	71	73	.493	8th (16)	Rick Sweet
Double-A	Mobile BayBears	Southern	65	73	.471	6th (10)	Tracy Woodson
High A	Lake Elsinore Storm	California	91	49	.650	1st (10)	Craig Colbert
Low A	Fort Wayne Wizards	Midwest	54	83	.394	13th (14)	Tom Lawless
Short-season	Eugene Emeralds	Northwest	32	44	.421	7th (8)	Jeff Gardner
Rookie	Idaho Falls Braves	Pioneer	21	54	.280	7th (8)	Jake Molina
OVERALL 2001 MINOR LEAGUE RECORD			334	376	.470	23rd (30)	

*Finish in overall standings (No. of teams in league)

ORGANIZATION LEADERS

BATTING
*AVG	Abner Arroyo, Fort Wayne	.338
R	Xavier Nady, Lake Elsinore	96
H	Xavier Nady, Lake Elsinore	158
TB	Xavier Nady, Lake Elsinore	276
2B	Xavier Nady, Lake Elsinore	38
3B	Shawn Garrett, Lake Elsinore	8
HR	Kevin Witt, Portland	27
RBI	Xavier Nady, Lake Elsinore	100
BB	Graham Koonce, Portland/Mobile	94
SO	**Jeremy Owens**, Mobile/Lake Elsinore	188
SB	**Jeremy Owens**, Mobile/Lake Elsinore	37

PITCHING
W	Jimmy Osting, Portland/Mobile	11
L	**Rick Guttormson**, Portland/Mobile	17
#ERA	Eric Cyr, Lake Elsinore	1.61
G	Clay Condrey, Portland/Mobile	66
	J.J. Trujillo, Portland/Mobile	66
CG	Justin Germano, Ft. Wayne/Eugene	2
SV	J.J. Trujillo, Portland/Mobile	19
IP	Chris Rojas, Lake Elsinore	160
BB	Chris Rojas, Lake Elsinore	71
SO	Jacob Peavy, Mobile/Lake Elsinore	188

*Minimum 250 At-Bats #Minimum 75 Innings

TOP PROSPECTS OF THE DECADE

1992	Joey Hamilton, rhp
1993	Ray McDavid, of
1994	Joey Hamilton, rhp
1995	Dustin Hermanson, rhp
1996	Ben Davis, c
1997	Derrek Lee, 1b
1998	Matt Clement, rhp
1999	Matt Clement, rhp
2000	Sean Burroughs, 3b
2001	Sean Burroughs, 3b

TOP DRAFT PICKS OF THE DECADE

1992	*Todd Helton, 1b (2)
1993	Derrek Lee, 1b
1994	Dustin Hermanson, rhp
1995	Ben Davis, c
1996	Matt Halloran, ss
1997	Kevin Nicholson, ss
1998	Sean Burroughs, 3b
1999	Vince Faison, of
2000	Mark Phillips, lhp
2001	Jake Gautreau, 3b

*Did not sign.

Owens

Guttormson

TYLER BOLEN

BEST TOOLS

Best Hitter for Average	Sean Burroughs
Best Power Hitter	Xavier Nady
Fastest Baserunner	Marcus Nettles
Best Fastball	Ben Howard
Best Breaking Ball	Dennis Tankersley
Best Changeup	Jeremy Fikac
Best Control	Jacob Peavy
Best Defensive Catcher	Andres Pagan
Best Defensive Infielder	Julius Matos
Best Infield Arm	Jackson Aquino
Best Defensive Outfielder	Jeremy Owens
Best Outfield Arm	Jeremy Owens

PROJECTED 2005 LINEUP

Catcher	Wiki Gonzalez
First Base	Xavier Nady
Second Base	Jake Gautreau
Third Base	Sean Burroughs
Shortstop	Ramon Vazquez
Left Field	Ryan Klesko
Center Field	Mark Kotsay
Right Field	Phil Nevin
No. 1 Starter	Dennis Tankersley
No. 2 Starter	Jacob Peavy
No. 3 Starter	Mark Phillips
No. 4 Starter	Ben Howard
No. 5 Starter	Eric Cyr
Closer	Trevor Hoffman

ALL-TIME LARGEST BONUSES

Mark Phillips, 2000	$2,200,000
Sean Burroughs, 1998	$2,100,000
Jake Gautreau, 2001	$1,875,000
Vince Faison, 1999	$1,415,000
Ben Davis, 1995	$1,300,000

DraftAnalysis

2001 Draft

Best Pro Debut: 2B/3B **Jake Gautreau** (1) hit .309-6-36 in the short-season Northwest League and homered in his first Triple-A game. 2B Josh Barfield (4) batted .310-4-53 in Rookie ball. 1B/3B Greg Sain (5) hit .293-16-40 and led the NWL in homers, while OF Marcus Nettles (11) topped the league with 35 steals.

Best Athlete: The Padres considered Nettles the fastest player in the draft. They were elated to get such a fluid athlete in the 11th round, and they think he'll hit and play a sterling center field.

Best Hitter: Gautreau and Barfield are two premium hitters who should produce for average with plus power.

Best Raw Power: San Diego got more legitimate power hitters than any other club. OF Doc Brooks (7) has the most sock in a group that includes Gautreau, 3B/OF Taggert Bozied (3), Barfield, Sain and 1B Jon Benick (9).

Fastest Runner: Nettles runs the 60-yard dash in 6.2-6.3 seconds.

Best Defensive Player: SS Jason Bartlett (13) has good hands, quick feet and a loose arm.

Best Fastball: RHP Matt Harrington (2) threw 94-96 mph as a high school senior in 2000, when he was considered the top prospect in the draft and was taken by the Rockies. He still hadn't signed, so the best fastball belongs to RHP Zach Wykoff (34), who dropped out of Kennesaw State (Ga.) and threw 94-95 mph at a tryout camp.

Most Intriguing Background: Barfield's father Jesse was the 1986 American League home run champion. Unsigned OF Nick Walters (39) is attending Princeton, where his father Gary is athletic director.

Closest To The Majors: Gautreau and OF Matt Hellman (26) were two of four players from the 2001 draft to reach Triple-A, though Hellman was promoted only to fill a sudden hole. Gautreau will start 2002 in high Class A, and Double-A is a realistic goal. His defense at third base has been a question, but the Padres like the skills he showed at second base in instructional league.

Gautreau

Best Late-Round Pick: Bartlett, a four-tool shortstop who was a Northwest League all-star. He shined defensively and hit .300-3-37 with 12 steals. The only thing he lacks is power, though it's fine for his position.

The One Who Got Away: Harrington, who's recovering from shoulder tendinitis, played in the independent Northern League and still was negotiating with the Padres. The best player who definitely won't sign is RHP Scott Shapiro (18), who has a 92-94 mph fastball that peaks at 96. He's at Vanderbilt.

Assessment: San Diego had plenty of pitching, so it focused on position players in the draft. No organization signed as many intriguing hitters, and the Padres could get a bonus if Harrington signs and regains his 2000 form.

2000 Draft

1B Xavier Nady (2) and LHP Mark Phillips (1) have all-star potential. OF Kevin Reese (27) was traded to the Yankees this offseason for promising 2B Bernabel Castro. RHP Justin Germano (13) is a precocious strike thrower. **Grade: B+**

1999 Draft

This group, which includes six first-round picks, looked better a year ago before RHP Gerik Baxter (1) died in an auto accident and LHP Mike Bynum (1) had an injury-plagued season. RHP Jacob Peavy (15) continues to excel, even if the other first-rounders—OF Vince Faison, RHPs Omar Ortiz (since traded) and Casey Burns, C Nick Trzesniak—have not. **Grade: B**

1998 Draft

3B Sean Burroughs (1) alone makes this a terrific draft. The emergence last season of LHP Eric Cyr (30, draft-and-follow), and RHPs Brian Lawrence (17) and Jeremy Fikac (19) makes it all the better. **Grade: A**

1997 Draft

Kevin Nicholson (1) wasn't the shortstop San Diego has sought. But RHP Ben Howard (2) is interesting, and RHP Junior Herndon (9) reached the majors last year. **Grade: C**

Note: Draft analysis prepared by Jim Callis. Numbers in parentheses indicate draft rounds.

. . . He has a picture-perfect swing, a quick bat and an uncanny sense of the strike zone.

Sean Burroughs 3b

STEVE MOORE

Born: Sept. 12, 1980.
Ht.: 6-2. **Wt.:** 200.
Bats: L. **Throws:** R.
School: Wilson HS, Long Beach.
Career Transactions: Selected by Padres in first round (ninth overall) of 1998 draft; signed Sept. 2, 1998.

Burroughs entered 2001 with the reputation as the best pure hitter in the minor leagues. He led Long Beach to consecutive Little League World Series titles in 1992-93 and in 2000, his second pro season, he was named MVP of the Futures Game and won a gold medal with the U.S. Olympic team. The only thing missing from his résumé was adversity, but he got his first dose last April. Burroughs was batting .328 at Triple-A Portland despite a sore right knee, which proved to be a torn meniscus that required surgery. Sidelined for a month, Burroughs returned and hit like he always had. Managers rated him the best prospect in the Pacific Coast League.

Burroughs is a career .327 hitter in the minors despite being young for his league each year. The Padres are excited about 2001 first-round pick Jake Gautreau, another gifted offensive player—and Gautreau is 10 months older than Burroughs, who's on the verge of the major leagues. He has a picture-perfect swing, a quick bat and an uncanny sense of the strike zone, with more walks than whiffs as a pro. He isn't troubled by lefthanders, against whom he batted .349 last year. He works hard and makes adjustments easily when needed. His instincts are another asset, no surprise considering he's the son of former No. 1 overall pick and American League MVP Jeff Burroughs. Sean has soft hands and a strong, accurate arm at third base. His power potential has yet to manifest itself. He has just 17 homers in 340 pro games. He has started to look for specific pitches to drive, depending on the situation, and projects to hit 25-30 homers annually once he gets acclimated to the major leagues. His speed is his worst tool, though he runs the bases well and makes the plays at third base.

San Diego has an impressive array of talent at third base, and there's still some thought that Burroughs could play second. The Padres would rather just get his bat in the lineup, so all-star Phil Nevin will move to first base and Ryan Klesko will shift to the outfield in order to open third for Burroughs. He is a prime 2002 Rookie of the Year candidate and a batting champion waiting to happen.

Year	Club (League)	Class	AVG	G	AB	R	H	2B	3B	HR	RBI	BB	SO	SB
1999	Fort Wayne (Mid)	A	.359	122	426	65	153	30	3	5	80	74	59	17
	Rancho Cuca. (Cal)	A	.435	6	23	3	10	3	0	1	5	3	3	0
2000	Mobile (SL)	AA	.291	108	392	46	114	29	4	2	42	58	45	6
2001	Portland (PCL)	AAA	.322	104	394	60	127	28	1	9	55	37	54	9
MINOR LEAGUE TOTALS			.327	340	1235	174	404	90	8	17	182	172	161	32

2. Dennis Tankersley. rhp

Born: Feb. 24, 1979. **Ht.:** 6-2. **Wt.:** 185. **Bats:** R. **Throws:** R. **School:** Meramec (Mo.) JC. **Career Transactions:** Selected by Red Sox in 38th round of 1998 draft; signed May 18, 1999 . . . Traded by Red Sox with SS Cesar Saba to Padres for 3B Ed Sprague, June 30, 2000.

Tankersley was an unknown when the Padres stole him from the Red Sox in a June 2000 trade for fading veteran Ed Sprague. He immediately blossomed into one of the game's top pitching prospects. Managers rated him the No. 1 prospect in the high Class A California League last year; he reached Triple-A before his arm tired in August. Tankersley can throw four pitches for strikes, and most of them are nasty. He can reach the mid-90s with his four-seam fastball, and his sinking two-seamer arrives in the low 90s. Hitters can't sit on his fastball because he has a mid-80s slider that was rated the best breaking ball in the Cal League. Tankersley's changeup lags behind his other three pitches, though it's getting better as he starts to use it more often. He may need to add strength after fading in Triple-A. Tankersley could get a long look for the big league rotation in spring training. It's more likely that he'll get work at Portland before joining San Diego during the season.

Year	Club (League)	Class	W	L	ERA	G	GS	CG	SV	IP	H	R	ER	BB	SO
1999	Red Sox (GCL)	R	1	0	0.76	11	6	0	1	36	14	7	3	9	57
2000	Augusta (SAL)	A	5	3	4.06	15	15	1	0	75	73	41	34	32	74
	Fort Wayne (Mid)	A	5	2	2.85	12	12	0	0	66	48	25	21	25	87
2001	Lake Elsinore (Cal)	A	5	1	0.52	9	8	0	0	52	29	5	3	12	68
	Mobile (SL)	AA	4	1	2.07	13	13	0	0	70	44	23	16	24	89
	Portland (PCL)	AAA	1	2	6.91	3	3	0	0	14	16	13	11	4	10
MINOR LEAGUE TOTALS			21	9	2.53	63	57	1	1	313	224	114	88	106	385

3. Jacob Peavy, rhp

Born: May 31, 1981. **Ht.:** 6-1. **Wt.:** 180. **Bats:** R. **Throws:** R. **School:** St. Paul's HS, Mobile, Ala. **Career Transactions:** Selected by Padres in 15th round of 1999 draft; signed June 9, 1999.

Peavy was running neck and neck with Gerik Baxter and Mike Bynum as the best prospect from San Diego's 1999 draft class, but last year Baxter was killed in an auto accident and Bynum regressed. The only minor league starter who topped Peavy's 12.7 strikeouts per nine innings last year was Minor League Player of the Year Josh Beckett. One veteran Padres scout says Peavy is the closest thing to Greg Maddux he has seen, and Double-A Southern League managers seconded that comparison. Peavy puts the ball wherever he wants, whenever he wants. He uses a lively low-90s fastball, a slider and a changeup. Peavy sometimes falls into a finesse mode but has enough on his fastball to beat hitters with it. He began to understand this last year. Of his three pitches, his slider needs the most work. Peavy has a chance to be the rare high school player who makes the major leagues before he has to be added to the 40-man roster. He'll probably open 2002 in Triple-A and could reach Qualcomm Stadium by the end of the year.

Year	Club (League)	Class	W	L	ERA	G	GS	CG	SV	IP	H	R	ER	BB	SO
1999	Padres (AZL)	R	7	1	1.34	13	11	1	0	74	52	16	11	23	90
	Idaho Falls (Pio)	R	2	0	0.00	2	2	0	0	11	5	0	0	1	13
2000	Fort Wayne (Mid)	A	13	8	2.90	26	25	0	0	134	107	61	43	53	164
2001	Lake Elsinore (Cal)	A	7	5	3.08	19	19	0	0	105	76	41	36	33	144
	Mobile (SL)	AA	2	1	2.57	5	5	0	0	28	19	8	8	12	44
MINOR LEAGUE TOTALS			31	15	2.51	65	62	1	0	352	259	126	98	122	455

4. Xavier Nady, 1b

Born: Nov. 14, 1978. **Ht.:** 6-1. **Wt.:** 185. **Bats:** R. **Throws:** R. **School:** University of California. **Career Transactions:** Selected by Padres in second round of 2000 draft; signed Sept. 17, 2000.

Once projected as the No. 1 overall pick in the 2000 draft, Nady lasted until the second round because of a disappointing junior season and signability concerns. Despite just one at-bat of pro experience, he led the California League in homers, extra-base hits (65) and total bases (276) while winning MVP honors in his first full pro season. A classic run producer, Nady has an advanced concept of hitting and will produce for both power and average. He drives the ball to all fields and adjusted easily to pro ball.

Moved around the infield in college, he was named the Cal League's best defensive first baseman in 2001. Nady tore ligaments in his elbow in the Arizona Fall League in 2000. The injury kept him from trying second base or the outfield last year, and he stayed in high Class A so he could DH when needed. He doesn't run well. Nady required Tommy John surgery in the offseason and won't be able to throw before mid-2002, so he'll spend most of the year as a DH at Double-A Mobile. His elbow is the only thing holding him back, and it's preventing him from settling into a position.

Year	Club (League)	Class	AVG	G	AB	R	H	2B	3B	HR	RBI	BB	SO	SB
2000	San Diego (NL)	MAJ	1.000	1	1	1	1	0	0	0	0	0	0	0
2001	Lake Elsinore (Cal)	A	.302	137	524	96	158	38	1	26	100	62	109	6
MAJOR LEAGUE TOTALS			1.000	1	1	1	1	0	0	0	0	0	0	0
MINOR LEAGUE TOTALS			.302	137	524	96	158	38	1	26	100	62	109	6

5. Mark Phillips, lhp

Born: Dec. 30, 1981. **Ht.:** 6-3. **Wt.:** 205. **Bats:** L. **Throws:** L. **School:** Hanover (Pa.) HS. **Career Transactions:** Selected by Padres in first round (ninth overall) of 2000 draft; signed July 6, 2000.

Phillips' willingness to agree to a club-record $2.2 million bonus before the 2000 draft played a role in the Padres picking him ninth overall, but his ability outstrips his signability. Sentenced to extended spring at the start of 2001 because he arrived out of shape in spring training, he ended the year in high Class A. Phillips' arm is rare among lefties. He throws 92-94 mph with little effort, and the pitch seems to jump when it gets to the plate. Phillips also has a plus curveball he can throw for strikes or get hitters to chase out of the zone. Mechanics are the key for Phillips. His velocity was down in spring training because his delivery was off, and staying in sync will improve his command. His changeup lags behind his other pitches at this point. Phillips could begin this year in Double-A at age 20, or the Padres could play it safe and give him a few more starts in the Cal League. Either way, it's going to be hard to keep him in the minors for long once he learns to repeat his delivery.

Year	Club (League)	Class	W	L	ERA	G	GS	CG	SV	IP	H	R	ER	BB	SO
2000	Idaho Falls (Pio)	R	1	1	5.35	10	10	0	0	37	35	30	22	24	37
2001	Eugene (NWL)	A	3	1	3.74	4	4	0	0	22	16	10	9	9	19
	Fort Wayne (Mid)	A	4	1	2.64	5	5	0	0	31	19	11	9	14	27
	Lake Elsinore (Cal)	A	2	1	2.57	5	5	0	0	28	19	8	8	14	34
MINOR LEAGUE TOTALS			10	4	3.68	24	24	0	0	117	89	59	48	61	117

6. Ben Howard, rhp

Born: Jan. 15, 1979. **Ht.:** 6-2. **Wt.:** 190. **Bats:** R. **Throws:** R. **School:** Central Merry HS, Jackson, Tenn. **Career Transactions:** Selected by Padres in second round of 1997 draft; signed June 25, 1997.

Despite a lightning arm, Howard went 16-30, 5.90 in his first four seasons, leading his league in walks each year. After Padres minor league pitching coach Darren Balsley worked with him following the 2000 season, Howard arrived in spring training with a lower arm slot and was an entirely different pitcher. Howard's fastball is the best in the system. Consistently arriving in the mid-90s and peaking at 99 mph, it always had been unhittable but now he throws it for strikes. His hard slider gives him a second plus pitch, and he has made strides with his changeup. Howard cut his walk rate by nearly two-thirds in 2001, though it climbed to 4.5 per nine innings once he reached Double-A. If he can maintain his control, he shouldn't have any problems. His changeup still needs refinement. Balsley worked with Howard at high Class A Lake Elsinore last year, and they'll be reunited in Double-A to start 2002. Tankersley, Peavy and Howard overmatched the Cal League last year and could be together in the San Diego rotation by the end of 2003.

Year	Club (League)	Class	W	L	ERA	G	GS	CG	SV	IP	H	R	ER	BB	SO
1997	Padres (AZL)	R	1	4	7.45	13	12	0	0	54	54	53	45	63	59
1998	Idaho Falls (Pio)	R	4	5	6.03	15	15	0	0	69	67	61	46	87	79
1999	Fort Wayne (Mid)	A	6	10	4.73	28	28	0	0	145	123	100	76	110	131
2000	Rancho Cuca. (Cal)	A	5	11	6.37	32	19	0	0	107	88	87	76	111	150
2001	Lake Elsinore (Cal)	A	8	2	2.83	18	18	0	0	102	86	37	32	32	107
	Mobile (SL)	AA	2	0	2.40	7	5	0	0	30	17	9	8	15	29
MINOR LEAGUE TOTALS			26	32	5.03	113	97	0	0	507	435	347	283	418	555

7. Eric Cyr, lhp

Born: Feb. 11, 1979. **Ht.:** 6-4. **Wt.:** 200. **Bats:** R. **Throws:** L. **School:** Seminole State (Okla.) JC. **Career Transactions:** Selected by Padres in 30th round of 1998 draft; signed May 31, 1999.

A Canadian who signed as a draft-and-follow in 1999, Cyr worked a total of just 76 innings in his first two pro seasons. He missed much of 2000 after having bone chips removed from his elbow and began 2001 in the Lake Elsinore bullpen. Cyr's breakthrough year was interrupted in April when the FBI arrested him on charges that he had sex with a 15-year-old girl during his return flight from playing in Australia the previous winter. Cyr was sentenced to 30 days in jail (which he has already served) and a year's probation. He's the cousin of former NHL winger Paul Cyr. Cyr's combination of a 91-92 mph fastball and knuckle-curve allowed him to limit California League hitters to a .184 average and one homer in 369 at-bats. His fastball tops out at 94 and explodes at the plate with heavy life. His command is yet another positive. Cyr is still developing his slider and changeup. When his offspeed pitches are working, he's untouchable. Showing his regular season performance was no fluke, Cyr starred in the Arizona Fall League. He'll start 2002 in Double-A and has the stuff to advance quickly.

Year	Club (League)	Class	W	L	ERA	G	GS	CG	SV	IP	H	R	ER	BB	SO
1999	Padres (AZL)	R	2	1	3.26	11	5	0	0	39	34	19	14	15	39
	Idaho Falls (Pio)	R	1	0	1.80	1	1	0	0	5	5	1	1	1	3
2000	Fort Wayne (Mid)	A	2	2	4.68	9	6	0	0	33	28	18	17	15	31
	Padres (AZL)	R	0	0	3.00	2	1	0	0	3	4	1	1	2	4
2001	Lake Elsinore (Cal)	A	7	4	1.61	21	16	0	0	101	68	28	18	24	131
MINOR LEAGUE TOTALS			12	7	2.55	44	29	0	0	180	139	67	51	57	208

8. Jake Gautreau, 2b/3b

Born: Nov. 14, 1979. **Ht.:** 6-0. **Wt.:** 185. **Bats:** L. **Throws:** R. **School:** Tulane University. **Career Transactions:** Selected by Padres in first round (14th overall) of 2001 draft; signed June 21, 2001.

A two-time Conference USA player of the year, "Jake the Rake" led NCAA Division I with 96 RBIs and carried Tulane to its first College World Series appearance in 2001. Gautreau showed he was proficient with wood bats while with Team USA the previous summer, so his initial success at the plate was no surprise. Like Burroughs and Nady, Gautreau should hit for power and average; no system has three pure hitters as good as San Diego's. Moved to second base in instructional league because of the organizational glut at third, Gautreau was a revelation. He showed agility, hands and arm strength, and he even was fine on the double-play pivot. Gautreau doesn't have great first-step quickness, though he gets to balls and make plays. He struck out a bit too much in his debut. The Padres knew they were getting a premium bat in Gautreau, and now they're envisioning a lefthanded Jeff Kent. He's ticketed for Lake Elsinore and could reach Double-A this year.

Year	Club (League)	Class	AVG	G	AB	R	H	2B	3B	HR	RBI	BB	SO	SB
2001	Eugene (NWL)	A	.309	48	178	28	55	19	0	6	36	22	47	1
	Portland (PCL)	AAA	.286	2	7	2	2	0	0	1	2	2	2	0
MINOR LEAGUE TOTALS			.308	50	185	30	57	19	0	7	38	24	49	1

9. Ramon Vazquez, ss

Born: Aug. 21, 1976. **Ht.:** 5-11. **Wt.:** 170. **Bats:** L. **Throws:** R. **School:** Indian Hills (Iowa) JC. **Career Transactions:** Selected by Mariners in 27th round of 1995 draft; signed June 26, 1995 . . . Traded by Mariners with RHP Brett Tomko and C Tom Lampkin to Padres for C Ben Davis, RHP Wascar Serrano, and IF Alex Arias, Dec. 12, 2001.

After realizing D'Angelo Jimenez was better suited for second base, the Padres swung a six-player trade with the Mariners in December, getting Vazquez and righthander Brett Tomko. Vazquez was a Pacific Coast League all-star, and managers named him the league's most exciting player. Vazquez does a little of everything at shortstop. He hits for a solid average, occasionally stings the ball into the gaps and draws plenty of walks. Defensively, he offers range and soft hands, and he made just 12 errors last year. Vazquez doesn't have the speed or the arm strength normally associated with shortstops, though he has a quick first step that allows him to make plays. It took him seven years to move through the minors, so he may not have much room for improvement. The MVP and batting champion in Puerto Rico this winter, Vazquez is the frontrunner to start at shortstop for San Diego this year. Donaldo Mendez, a 2000 major league Rule 5 draft pick, could compete for the job in the future. He has more defensive upside than Vazquez but provides less offense.

Year	Club (League)	Class	AVG	G	AB	R	H	2B	3B	HR	RBI	BB	SO	SB
1995	Mariners (AZL)	R	.206	39	141	20	29	3	1	0	11	19	27	4
1996	Everett (NWL)	A	.278	33	126	25	35	5	2	1	18	26	26	7
	Tacoma (PCL)	AAA	.224	18	49	7	11	2	1	0	4	4	12	0
	Wisconsin (Mid)	A	.300	3	10	1	3	1	0	0	1	2	2	0
1997	Wisconsin (Mid)	A	.269	131	479	79	129	25	5	8	49	78	93	16
1998	Lancaster (Cal)	A	.276	121	468	77	129	26	4	2	72	81	66	15
1999	New Haven (EL)	AA	.258	127	438	58	113	27	3	5	45	62	77	8
2000	New Haven (EL)	AA	.286	124	405	58	116	25	4	8	59	52	76	1
MINOR LEAGUE TOTALS			.267	596	2116	325	565	114	20	24	259	324	379	51

10. Oliver Perez, lhp

Born: Aug. 15, 1981. **Ht.:** 6-3. **Wt.:** 160. **Bats:** L. **Throws:** L. **Career Transactions:** Signed out of Mexico by Padres, March 4, 1999 . . . Loaned by Padres to Yucatan (Mexican), June 2-22, 2000 . . . Loaned to Yucatan, July 18-Sept. 6, 2000.

Before signing an agreement with the Mexico City Red Devils, the Padres were affiliated with the Mexican League's Yucatan Lions, to whom they loaned Perez for most of 2000. He made his U.S. full-season debut last year and was the only regular member of low Class A Fort Wayne's rotation to post a winning record. Perez already has average velocity on his fastball and can run it up to 94 mph, but his best pitch is his slider. He moves his pitches in and out, changes speeds and shows no fear. He was the toughest pitcher to run on in the Midwest League, as only five of 15 basestealers succeeded against him. Perez sometimes relies on his fastball too much. When he's willing to throw his slider in any count, he's tough. His changeup and command can use improvement. He has made progress adding weight to his skinny frame, but he still can get stronger. He's just 20, so Perez probably will return to high Class A despite pitching well in nine starts for Lake Elsinore last year. It will be difficult to hold him back if he continues his rapid development.

Year	Club (League)	Class	W	L	ERA	G	GS	CG	SV	IP	H	R	ER	BB	SO
1999	Padres (AZL)	R	1	2	5.08	15	2	0	3	28	28	20	16	16	37
2000	Yucatan (Mex)	AAA	3	2	4.36	11	6	0	1	43	39	24	21	17	37
	Idaho Falls (Pio)	R	3	1	4.07	5	5	0	0	24	24	14	11	9	27
2001	Fort Wayne (Mid)	A	8	5	3.46	19	19	0	0	101	84	46	39	43	98
	Lake Elsinore (Cal)	A	2	4	2.72	9	9	0	0	53	45	22	16	25	62
MINOR LEAGUE TOTALS			17	14	3.70	59	41	0	4	250	220	126	103	110	261

11. Ben Johnson, of

Born: June 18, 1981. **Ht.:** 6-1. **Wt.:** 200. **Bats:** R. **Throws:** R. **School:** Germantown (Tenn.) HS. **Career Transactions:** Selected by Cardinals in fourth round of 1999 draft; signed June 24, 1999 . . . Traded by Cardinals with RHP Heathcliff Slocumb to Padres for C Carlos Hernandez and SS Nate Tebbs, July 31, 2000.

Padres general manager Kevin Towers has a gift for making trades, and one of his best was the July 2000 deal that sent overpriced backup catcher Carlos Hernandez to St. Louis for Johnson. While Hernandez missed all of last season with back problems, Johnson would be one of the Cardinals' two best position-player prospects if he hadn't left. He has made slow but steady progress since switching organizations. His numbers last year were boosted by The Diamond at Lake Elsinore, where he hit .332 as opposed to .221 on the road, but he had a solid high Class A season for a 20-year-old. While he still needs to make more contact, comparisons to a young Brian Jordan are still valid. Johnson has the potential to be at least a 20-20 player, and he has started to make adjustments and use the whole field. He saw some time in center field in 2001 but projects more as a right fielder with the range and arm to be an above-average defender. He's still young, so he might return to the California League for a month or two if San Diego deems him not ready for Double-A.

Year	Club (League)	Class	AVG	G	AB	R	H	2B	3B	HR	RBI	BB	SO	SB
1999	Johnson City (Appy)	R	.330	57	203	38	67	9	1	10	51	29	57	14
2000	Peoria (Mid)	A	.242	93	330	58	80	22	1	13	46	53	78	17
	Fort Wayne (Mid)	A	.193	29	109	11	21	6	2	3	13	7	25	0
2001	Lake Elsinore (Cal)	A	.276	136	503	79	139	35	6	12	63	54	141	22
MINOR LEAGUE TOTALS			.268	315	1145	186	307	72	10	38	173	143	301	53

12. Josh Barfield, 2b

Born: Dec. 17, 1982. **Ht.:** 6-0. **Wt.:** 185. **Bats:** R. **Throws:** R. **School:** Klein HS, Spring, Texas. **Career Transactions:** Selected by Padres in fourth round of 2001 draft; signed June 15, 2001.

The Padres entered 2001 with a deep store of pitching but not nearly as much hitting in their system. They rectified that situation in Bill Gayton's first draft as scouting director, getting more quality bats last June than any other organization. Barfield wasn't the most heralded Texas high school prospect and lasted until the fourth round, then opened a lot of eyes with a strong pro debut against Rookie-level Pioneer League pitchers who generally were 2-3 years older than he was. The son of former American League home run champ Jesse Barfield, Josh already has an advanced understanding of the game. He recognizes pitches, makes adjustments and is fundamentally sound. He's athletic and getting stronger, so his ceiling with the bat is very high. He hit two monster blasts over the center-field batting eye during instructional league, a sign of his power potential. While he played some shortstop last summer, Barfield spent most of his time at second base. He runs well and has soft hands and average range. If he gets as big as his father, he'll probably move to third base or perhaps a corner-outfield spot. San Diego is looking forward to seeing how he handles low Class A this year.

Year	Club (League)	Class	AVG	G	AB	R	H	2B	3B	HR	RBI	BB	SO	SB
2001	Idaho Falls (Pio)	R	.310	66	277	51	86	15	4	4	53	16	54	12
MINOR LEAGUE TOTALS			.310	66	277	51	86	15	4	4	53	16	54	12

13. Jason Middlebrook, rhp

Born: June 26, 1975. **Ht.:** 6-3. **Wt.:** 215. **Bats:** R. **Throws:** R. **School:** Stanford University. **Career Transactions:** Selected by Padres in ninth round of 1996 draft; signed Sept. 20, 1996 . . . Claimed on waivers by Mets from Padres, Oct. 5, 2000 . . . Claimed on waivers by Padres from Mets, Nov. 22, 2000.

When Middlebrook was a freshman at Stanford, he was the frontrunner to be the No. 1 overall pick in the 1996 draft. Then elbow problems limited him to a total of 11 appearances as a sophomore and junior, and he lasted until the ninth round. The Padres signed him for $750,000, still a record bonus for a player selected that low. Middlebrook had more physical problems after turning pro, with a strained elbow in 1999 and a shoulder impingement in 2000. San Diego removed him from its 40-man roster in October 2000 and lost him to the Mets, only to reclaim him off waivers a month later. Healthy in 2001, he looked better than he had in years. He consistently threw 91-94 mph and reached 96 with his fastball. At times he gets a lot of movement on the pitch, though it straightens out when he overthrows. The key for Middlebrook is pitching, rather than just throwing his fastball. He tried to blow the ball by Barry Bonds last September, and gave up three homers to him in the span of five days. When Middlebrook moves the fastball in and out, and mixes it with his plus curveball and his changeup, he's very successful. Getting married before last season seemed to agree with him, as he was more mature and stopped, as one Padres official put it, "finding a way to lose." He'll get a chance to make San Diego's rotation in spring training.

Year	Club (League)	Class	W	L	ERA	G	GS	CG	SV	IP	H	R	ER	BB	SO
1997	Rancho Cuca. (Cal)	A	0	2	4.03	6	6	0	0	22	29	15	10	12	18
	Clinton (Mid)	A	6	4	3.98	14	14	2	0	81	76	46	36	39	86
1998	Rancho Cuca. (Cal)	A	10	12	4.92	28	28	0	0	150	162	99	82	63	132
1999	Padres (AZL)	R	1	0	7.20	1	1	0	0	5	9	5	4	1	3
	Mobile (SL)	AA	4	6	8.06	13	13	0	0	64	78	59	57	30	38
2000	Mobile (SL)	AA	5	13	6.15	24	24	0	0	120	133	89	82	52	75
	Las Vegas (PCL)	AAA	0	1	216.00	1	1	0	0	0	8	8	8	0	0
2001	Mobile (SL)	AA	3	0	1.20	10	9	0	0	53	36	10	7	9	51
	Portland (PCL)	AAA	7	4	3.29	15	15	0	0	90	86	34	33	23	66
	San Diego (NL)	MAJ	2	1	5.12	4	3	0	0	19	18	11	11	10	10
MAJOR LEAGUE TOTALS			2	1	5.12	4	3	0	0	19	18	11	11	10	10
MINOR LEAGUE TOTALS			36	42	4.90	112	111	2	0	586	617	365	319	229	469

14. Mike Bynum, lhp

Born: March 20, 1978. **Ht.:** 6-4. **Wt.:** 200. **Bats:** L. **Throws:** L. **School:** University of North Carolina. **Career Transactions:** Selected by Padres in first round (19th overall) of 1999 draft; signed July 1, 1999.

Bynum injured a knee during spring-training drills last year, and compounded the problem by trying to pitch through it instead of telling the Padres. He never looked like the pitcher who rocketed to Double-A by the end of his first full season. He spent all of June on the disabled list, returned and got shelled in July, then had season-ending arthroscopic surgery. Previously, Bynum had carved up hitters with a slider that drew comparisons to that of Hall of Famer Steve Carlton. His fastball was very average at 89-90 mph, and commanding it on a consistent basis was all that stood between Bynum and the major leagues. He also has a changeup that he should use more often. Bynum is expected to be 100 percent by spring training and will return to Double-A in 2002.

Year	Club (League)	Class	W	L	ERA	G	GS	CG	SV	IP	H	R	ER	BB	SO
1999	Idaho Falls (Pio)	R	1	0	0.00	5	3	0	0	17	7	0	0	4	21
	Rancho Cuca. (Cal)	A	3	1	3.29	7	7	0	0	38	35	17	14	8	44
2000	Rancho Cuca. (Cal)	A	9	6	3.00	21	21	0	0	126	101	55	42	51	129
	Mobile (SL)	AA	3	1	2.91	6	6	0	0	34	31	12	11	16	27
2001	Mobile (SL)	AA	2	7	5.02	16	15	0	0	84	90	53	47	35	69
MINOR LEAGUE TOTALS			18	15	3.42	55	52	0	0	300	264	137	114	114	290

15. Taggert Bozied, 3b/of

Born: July 24, 1979. **Ht.:** 6-3. **Wt.:** 210. **Bats:** R. **Throws:** R. **School:** University of San Francisco. **Career Transactions:** Signed by independent Sioux Falls (Northern), June 2001 . . . Selected by Padres in third round of 2001 draft; signed Nov. 9, 2001.

Bozied topped NCAA Division I with a .936 slugging percentage and was among the leaders in all three triple-crown categories when he hit .412-30-82 as a San Francisco sophomore in 1999, but he failed to approach that production in his final two seasons with the Dons. Getting him signed wasn't the easiest task, as he turned down the Twins as a 2000 second-rounder and went to the independent Northern League rather than immediately signing with the Padres last summer. He finally joined the organization for a $725,000 bonus in November. Like many of San Diego's early picks in the 2001 draft, Bozied's forte is his bat and, in particular, his power. He also runs well for his size and has some arm strength, but most scouts remain unconvinced that he can play third base at the upper levels. He doesn't have a body suited for catching, so if he can't cut it at the hot corner he'll move to left field. Bozied hit well in the Northern League, so the Padres don't have any qualms about starting him at high Class A this year.

Year	Club (League)	Class	AVG	G	AB	R	H	2B	3B	HR	RBI	BB	SO	SB
2001	Sioux Falls (Nor)	IND	.307	58	228	35	70	17	0	6	31	13	34	3

16. Kevin Eberwein, 3b/1b

Born: March 30, 1977. **Ht.:** 6-4. **Wt.:** 200. **Bats:** R. **Throws:** R. **School:** University of Nevada-Las Vegas. **Career Transactions:** Selected by Padres in fifth round of 1998 draft; signed June 4, 1998.

Eberwein is a solid third-base prospect but his chances of starting at the hot corner for the Padres have been remote ever since the club drafted Sean Burroughs four rounds ahead of him in 1998. Since then, San Diego has stockpiled several more hitters in the majors and minors who can play the positions Eberwein can, including Xavier Nady, Jake Gautreau and Taggert Bozied. Getting hurt isn't the best way to keep from slipping down the depth chart, but Eberwein injured his ankle in 2000 and missed the first three weeks last season following arthroscopic surgery. Upon returning, he played just 36 games before being lost for the year with a cracked bone in his right hand. Eberwein has plenty of power and the upside of a Richie Sexson. He needs to make more contact and remember to use the entire field. He's agile and athletic for his size, and he's might be the best defender of all the potential third basemen. Because he moves well and has a strong arm, the Padres may try him in the outfield when he returns to Triple-A in 2002.

Year	Club (League)	Class	AVG	G	AB	R	H	2B	3B	HR	RBI	BB	SO	SB
1998	Clinton (Mid)	A	.296	65	247	42	73	20	3	10	38	26	66	4
1999	Rancho Cuca. (Cal)	A	.259	110	417	69	108	30	4	18	69	42	139	7
	Mobile (SL)	AA	.171	10	35	5	6	1	0	1	2	3	16	0
2000	Mobile (SL)	AA	.263	100	372	57	98	16	2	18	71	45	77	2
2001	Lake Elsinore (Cal)	A	.333	9	30	6	10	4	0	2	6	6	6	0
	Portland (PCL)	AAA	.266	27	94	16	25	8	1	3	11	10	22	0
MINOR LEAGUE TOTALS			.268	321	1195	195	320	79	10	52	195	132	326	13

17. Jeremy Fikac, rhp

Born: April 8, 1975. **Ht.:** 6-2. **Wt.:** 195. **Bats:** R. **Throws:** R. **School:** Southwest Texas State University. **Career Transactions:** Selected by Padres in 19th round of 1998 draft; signed June 5, 1998.

Organizations love guys like Fikac, low-round picks who work hard and get better every year, surprising everyone but themselves when they reach the majors. And Fikac, who was more accomplished as a hitter than as a pitcher at Southwest Texas State, didn't just reach the majors last August. He struck out the side against the Mets in his debut and didn't allow a run in his first 12 appearances as he cemented a role for himself in the 2002 bullpen. Like Padres closer Trevor Hoffman, Fikac's best pitch is his changeup. His fastball isn't notable for its velocity or life, while his slider is average. He succeeds because he can throw any of his three pitches in any count and put them wherever he wants. Big league lefthanders were hitless in 27 at-bats against him. While Fikac has the fearlessness but not the stuff to close, he can be an extremely effective setup man for San Diego. He learned in January that he needs to have a cyst removed from his right index finger, surgery that will sideline hime until at least Opening Day.

Year	Club (League)	Class	W	L	ERA	G	GS	CG	SV	IP	H	R	ER	BB	SO
1998	Idaho Falls (Pio)	R	2	0	2.25	12	0	0	1	20	11	6	5	8	19
1999	Rancho Cuca. (Cal)	A	8	3	5.08	40	6	0	0	85	94	50	48	43	75
2000	Rancho Cuca. (Cal)	A	5	3	1.80	61	0	0	20	75	46	19	15	24	101
2001	Mobile (SL)	AA	6	0	1.97	53	0	0	18	69	54	16	15	20	75
	Portland (PCL)	AAA	0	0	3.00	1	0	0	0	3	3	1	1	0	3
	San Diego (NL)	MAJ	2	0	1.37	23	0	0	0	26	15	6	4	5	19
MAJOR LEAGUE TOTALS			2	0	1.37	23	0	0	0	26	15	6	4	5	19
MINOR LEAGUE TOTALS			21	6	3.00	167	6	0	39	252	208	92	84	95	273

18. Nobuaki Yoshida, lhp

Born: Aug. 10, 1981. **Ht.:** 6-1. **Wt.:** 170. **Bats:** L. **Throws:** L. **Career Transactions:** Signed out of Japan by Padres, Jan. 10, 2000.

Yoshida was just the third Japanese high school player to sign with a U.S. team, following Mets lefthander Juei Ushiromatsu and Red Sox outfielder Kenichiro Kawabata. Those two didn't pan out, while Yoshida seemed on the fast track after a strong debut in 2000. But he never was completely healthy last season. A dental problem cost him two weeks in minor league camp, so he was sent to extended spring training to build up his arm. A sore shoulder knocked him out after five starts at Fort Wayne, and a pectoral injury limited him at short-season Eugene. Yoshida pitches right around 90 mph with his fastball, but enhances the pitch by moving it in and out and hitting his spots. He also throws a curveball, a semi-screwball that runs away from righthanders, and a changeup. He'll get a second shot at low Class A this year.

Yr	Club (League)	Class	W	L	ERA	G	GS	CG	SV	IP	H	R	ER	BB	SO
2000	Padres (AZL)	R	0	2	2.32	7	7	0	0	31	23	11	8	7	32
	Idaho Falls (Pio)	R	1	0	3.00	4	4	0	0	18	16	8	6	3	21
2001	Fort Wayne (Mid)	A	1	2	3.86	5	5	1	0	23	23	13	10	13	12
	Eugene (NWL)	A	0	0	1.19	8	3	0	0	23	23	7	3	4	17
MINOR LEAGUE TOTALS			2	4	2.56	24	19	1	0	95	85	39	27	27	72

19. Andy Shibilo, rhp

Born: Sept. 16, 1976. **Ht.:** 6-7. **Wt.:** 220. **Bats:** R. **Throws:** R. **School:** Pepperdine University. **Career Transactions:** Selected by Cardinals in 23rd round of 1998 draft; signed June 5, 1998 . . . Released by Cardinals, March 30, 2000 . . . Signed by independent Lehigh Valley (Atlantic), April 2000 . . . Signed by Padres, March 4, 2001.

The Padres have uncovered several relief prospects in independent leagues. Last year, David Lundquist reached the majors and J.J. Trujillo tied for the minor league lead with 66 appearances. San Diego also is excited about fall signee Matt Hampton. But the best of the crop is Shibilo, an Atlantic League refugee who previously spent two years in the Cardinals system. He was signed out of a tryout camp last March because he demonstrated considerable arm strength, and it never waned. Shibilo's fastball remained at 91-94 mph throughout 2001 and he topped out at 93-96 mph game in and game out. He also has a nasty slider with average to plus velocity and two-plane break, and if he masters the splitter he's working on he could be closer material. Shibilo led the California League in appearances and won its joint all-star game against the Carolina League. After earning a spot on the 40-man roster, he'll probably start 2002 in Double-A but could advance quickly.

Yr	Club (League)	Class	W	L	ERA	G	GS	CG	SV	IP	H	R	ER	BB	SO
1998	New Jersey (NY-P)	A	4	4	3.45	9	9	0	0	47	51	21	18	8	54
	Peoria (Mid)	A	1	3	8.51	7	7	0	0	31	42	30	29	11	22
1999	Peoria (Mid)	A	4	13	5.11	27	24	2	0	136	157	105	77	41	96
2000	Lehigh Valley (Atl)	IND	11	13	4.02	27	26	11	0	179	173	99	80	61	128
2001	Lake Elsinore (Cal)	A	10	2	1.96	60	0	0	15	83	66	24	18	27	105
MINOR LEAGUE TOTALS			19	22	4.32	103	40	2	15	296	316	180	142	87	277

20. Mike Nicolas, rhp

Born: Nov. 5, 1981. **Ht.:** 6-3. **Wt.:** 207. **Bats:** R. **Throws:** R. **Career Transactions:** Signed out of Dominican Republic by Padres, March 21, 2000.

Though Nicolas never had pitched in the United States before 2001, he was determined to start the year at low Class A. So each day during minor league camp, he'd arrive at the ballpark at 6:30 a.m., get into his uniform and sit in the lunch area outside while withstanding low-50s temperatures. He'd be out there in his short sleeves, drinking coffee and—Padres officials still chuckle over this—"practicing cold." It must have worked, because Nicolas went to Fort Wayne and ended the season in high Class A. He has one of the best raw arms in the system, throwing 96-97 mph and threatening triple digits. His velocity is an asset and a detriment, because he overthrows too much and loses his command. His slider is coming along though he also has trouble throwing it for strikes. Nicolas' resolve has made him an organization favorite. He'll begin this year back at Lake Elsinore.

Year	Club (League)	Class	W	L	ERA	G	GS	CG	SV	IP	H	R	ER	BB	SO
2000	Padres (DSL)	R	4	5	2.89	17	6	0	2	56	42	27	18	27	65
2001	Fort Wayne (Mid)	A	1	5	3.45	54	0	0	7	63	44	30	24	34	70
	Lake Elsinore (Cal)	A	0	1	5.25	8	0	0	0	12	11	7	7	5	15
MINOR LEAGUE TOTALS			5	11	3.38	79	6	0	9	131	97	64	49	66	150

21. Justin Germano, rhp

Born: Aug. 6, 1982. **Ht.:** 6-2. **Wt.:** 190. **Bats:** R. **Throws:** R. **School:** Claremont (Calif.) HS. **Career Transactions:** Selected by Padres in 13th round of 2000 draft; signed June 13, 2000.

Germano opened 2001, his first full year as a pro, in low Class A at age 18. Though he gave up three earned runs or less in nine of his 13 starts, he had just a 2-2 record in those games and was 2-6 overall. The Padres sent him down to Eugene in mid-June, more to boost his confidence than as a result of his performance. Germano has an uncanny ability to throw strikes for a teenager. In his two professional seasons, his 5.4 strikeout-walk ratio is the fourth-best among minor leaguers with 200 innings, trailing San Francisco's Jeff Clark (7.0), Pittsburgh's Justin Reid (5.9) and Houston's Roy Oswalt (5.7). Germano relies on an 86-91 mph fastball, a curveball that has 12-to-6 break at times and slurvy action at others, plus a changeup. While his command and willingness to challenge hitters are positives, he needs to learn not to be around the plate as much in order to avoid giving up hits. Getting stronger also would help after he wore down by instructional league last year. He'll return to what should be an improved Fort Wayne club in 2002.

Year	Club (League)	Class	W	L	ERA	G	GS	CG	SV	IP	H	R	ER	BB	SO
2000	Padres (AZL)	R	5	5	4.59	17	8	0	1	67	65	36	34	9	67
2001	Fort Wayne (Mid)	A	2	6	4.98	13	13	0	0	65	80	47	36	16	55
	Eugene (NWL)	A	6	5	3.49	13	13	2	0	80	77	35	31	11	74
MINOR LEAGUE TOTALS			13	16	4.29	43	34	2	1	212	222	118	101	36	196

22. Vince Faison, of

Born: Jan. 22, 1981. **Ht.:** 6-0. **Wt.:** 180. **Bats:** L. **Throws:** R. **School:** Toombs County HS, Lyons, Ga. **Career Transactions:** Selected by Padres in first round (20th overall) of 1999 draft; signed June 4, 1999.

The first of San Diego's six first-round picks in 1999, Faison accepted a $1.415 million bonus to give up a scholarship to play defensive back at Georgia. He was named the No. 1 prospect in the Arizona League that summer but has hit just .220 since leaving Rookie ball. Faison reminds the Padres of a young Ray Lankford, and the club still sees him as an impact player if he can produce at the plate. He has power potential that remains mostly untapped because he's still learning his swing and the importance of plate discipline. His raw speed makes him a terror on the bases but he doesn't get on often enough. Faison covers lots of ground in center field, and his arm is adequate for the position. He was promoted to high Class A last year to ease Ben Johnson's burden by shifting him to right field, and Faison hit a little better at that level. Then he turned in a lukewarm performance in instructional league. He's not ready for Double-A yet, and he needs to start making progress this year.

Year	Club (League)	Class	AVG	G	AB	R	H	2B	3B	HR	RBI	BB	SO	SB
1999	Padres (AZL)	R	.309	44	178	40	55	6	6	4	28	18	45	30
	Fort Wayne (Mid)	A	.208	11	48	10	10	2	0	0	1	6	18	7
2000	Fort Wayne (Mid)	A	.219	117	457	65	100	20	2	12	39	26	159	21
2001	Fort Wayne (Mid)	A	.200	41	140	14	28	5	0	1	8	18	35	10
	Lake Elsinore (Cal)	A	.233	73	275	27	64	11	3	7	36	24	94	12
MINOR LEAGUE TOTALS			.234	286	1098	156	257	44	11	24	112	92	351	80

23. Jason Bartlett, ss

Born: Oct. 30, 1979. **Ht.:** 6-0. **Wt.:** 175. **Bats:** R. **Throws:** R. **School:** University of Oklahoma. **Career Transactions:** Selected by Padres in 13th round of 2001 draft; signed June 14, 2001.

Catcher and shortstop are the weakest positions in the system, so Bartlett was a very welcome surprise last summer after signing as a 13th-round pick. He hit just .282-6-31 with aluminum as an Oklahoma senior before batting .300 with wood and making the Northwest League all-star team. Now the Padres believe they have a four-tool shortstop on their hands. Bartlett won't hit for power, but he should hit for average and draw walks. Once he reaches base, he's a threat because he has average speed and excellent instincts. Defensively, he has fine actions to go with the arm, hands and feet for shortstop. Because of his success and his age, Bartlett has a chance to open 2002 in high Class A.

Year	Club (League)	Class	AVG	G	AB	R	H	2B	3B	HR	RBI	BB	SO	SB
2001	Eugene (NWL)	A	.300	68	267	49	80	12	4	3	37	28	47	12
MINOR LEAGUE TOTALS			.300	68	267	49	80	12	4	3	37	28	47	12

24. Greg Sain, 1b/3b

Born: Dec. 26, 1979. **Ht.:** 6-2. **Wt.:** 205. **Bats:** R. **Throws:** R. **School:** University of San Diego. **Career Transactions:** Selected by Padres in fifth round of 2001 draft; signed June 14, 2001.

Another offensive-minded member of the Padres' 2001 draft class, Sain won two home run crowns in 2001. He led the West Coast Conference with 16 longballs during the spring, then topped the Northwest League with 16 more in his pro debut. He also tied for the NWL lead in extra-base hits (36) and earned all-star honors as a DH. Power is Sain's best tool, but what really makes him intriguing is the possibility that he could catch. Sain spent a good deal of time behind the plate at the University of San Diego, where he worked with former big league catcher Chris Cannizzaro. He showed a 55 arm on the 20-to-80 scouting scale during the spring, and it can be a plus tool if he learns to set his feet properly when he throws. Sain, whose father Tommy reached Triple-A in the Twins system, came down with a tender shoulder, so he didn't catch much at Eugene. The Padres hope to get a better idea of what he can do this year in high Class A.

Yr	Club (League)	Class	AVG	G	AB	R	H	2B	3B	HR	RBI	BB	SO	SB
2001	Eugene (NWL)	A	.293	67	256	48	75	19	1	16	40	21	68	1
MINOR LEAGUE TOTALS			.293	67	256	48	75	19	1	16	40	21	68	1

25. Ryan Baerlocher, rhp

Born: Aug. 6, 1977. **Ht.:** 6-5. **Wt.:** 220. **Bats:** R. **Throws:** R. **School:** Lewis-Clark State (Idaho) College. **Career Transactions:** Selected by Royals in sixth round of 1999 draft; signed June 3, 1999 . . . Selected by Padres from Royals in Rule 5 major league draft, Dec. 13, 2001.

Baerlocher won two NAIA World Series at Lewis-Clark State (Idaho), where he began his career as a third baseman, before signing as a sixth-round pick in 1999. In his first full season, he led the low Class A South Atlantic League in ERA and ranked second in the minors in strikeouts, and last year he pitched effectively at Double-A Wichita in a home ballpark and league that favors hitters. Nevertheless, the Royals didn't protect him on their 40-man roster and the Padres selected him in the major league Rule 5 draft in December. He'll have to stick in San Diego all season or clear waivers and be offered back to Kansas City for half the $50,000 draft price. Baerlocher doesn't throw as hard as his size might indicate. His best pitch is an outstanding changeup. In an effort to build velocity, the Royals had him go away from his changeup and throw his fastball more often in 2001, and he consistently worked at 88-91 mph. His third pitch, a slider, showed improvement as well. Baerlocher throws strikes and is durable, having led the Texas League in innings last year. He also topped the TL with 26 homers allowed, an indication that he has a small margin for error with his stuff.

Year	Club (League)	Class	W	L	ERA	G	GS	CG	SV	IP	H	R	ER	BB	SO
1999	Spokane (NWL)	A	7	2	4.70	15	15	0	0	75	78	43	39	32	68
2000	Charleston, WV (SAL)	A	5	6	2.14	19	19	0	0	114	88	43	27	33	139
	Wilmington (Car)	A	5	1	2.98	8	8	0	0	51	35	18	17	17	54
2001	Wichita (TL)	AA	13	8	3.99	28	28	2	0	181	180	94	80	55	124
MINOR LEAGUE TOTALS			30	17	3.49	70	70	2	0	420	381	198	163	137	385

26. Bernie Castro, 2b

Born: July 14, 1981. **Ht.:** 5-10. **Wt.:** 165. **Bats:** B. **Throws:** R. **Career Transactions:** Signed out of Dominican Republiv by Yankees, Sept. 25, 1997 . . . Traded by Yankees to Padres for OF Kevin Reese, Dec. 14, 2001.

Straight prospect-for-prospect trades are rare, but the Padres pulled one off in September, sending outfielder Kevin Reese to the Yankees for Castro. While Reese was old for the Midwest League, he showed some offensive promise. So too has Castro, who's three years younger and led the South Atlantic League in stolen bases last year. He also adds to the middle-infield depth that San Diego has been trying to build. Clocked from the left side of the plate to first base in 3.6 seconds on a drag bunt, Castro has plus-plus speed. He's a potential leadoff man because he's a switch-hitter who has shown a willingness to draw walks. To bat atop a lineup, he'll need to stop chasing high fastballs and take the first pitch more often. His best defensive tool is his arm, while his hands and range are average. In time, he should be an asset at second base. Castro won the batting title in his native Dominican Republic this winter, and the Padres hope he can carry the momentum to high Class A this year.

Year	Club (League)	Class	AVG	G	AB	R	H	2B	3B	HR	RBI	BB	SO	SB
1998	Yankees (DSL)	R	.330	61	224	78	74	6	4	0	17	37	40	63
1999					Did Not Play—Injured									
2000	Yankees (DSL)	R	.348	55	210	69	73	9	2	2	13	36	24	56
	Yankees (GCL)	R	.441	9	34	7	15	4	1	0	6	6	4	3
2001	Greensboro (SAL)	A	.260	101	389	71	101	15	7	1	36	54	67	67
	Staten Island (NY-P)	A	.351	15	57	6	20	1	0	0	7	11	12	8
MINOR LEAGUE TOTALS			.310	241	914	231	283	35	14	3	79	144	147	197

27. Pedro de los Santos, 2b

Born: Aug. 8, 1983. **Ht.:** 5-10. **Wt.:** 165. **Bats:** B. **Throws:** R. **Career Transactions:** Signed out of Dominican Republic by Padres, March 21, 2000.

Though de los Santos batted just .210 as a 16-year-old in the Rookie-level Dominican Summer League in 2000, the Padres thought highly enough of him to bring him here last year for his U.S. debut. He proved up to the challenge, hitting safely in 11 of his 12 games against more advanced Pioneer League pitchers, but his season ended when he broke a bone in his leg sliding into second base. De los Santos has a nice swing from both sides of the plate and he's one of the fastest players in the system. He's a legitimate basestealing threat who just needs to get stronger and more disciplined at the plate. He's still a work in progress as a second baseman and eventually could move the outfield, but San Diego plans on keeping him in the infield for the next few season. The club is waiting anxiously to see if de los Santos' injury will take away any of his trademark speed. He'll probably return to Idaho Falls this year.

Year	Club (League)	Class	AVG	G	AB	R	H	2B	3B	HR	RBI	BB	SO	SB
2000	Padres (DSL)	R	.210	49	167	38	35	6	1	1	10	46	38	24
2001	Idaho Falls (Pio)	R	.348	12	46	11	16	4	1	0	5	2	10	5
MINOR LEAGUE TOTALS			.239	61	213	49	51	10	2	1	15	48	48	29

28. Kory DeHaan, of

Born: July 16, 1976. **Ht.:** 6-2. **Wt.:** 187. **Bats:** L. **Throws:** R. **School:** Morningside (Iowa) College. **Career Transactions:** Selected by Pirates in seventh round of 1997 draft; signed June 5, 1997 . . . Selected by Padres from Pirates in Rule 5 major league draft, Dec. 13, 1999.

It's much more difficult to keep a position player than a pitcher as a major league Rule 5 draft pick. While pitchers can get semiregular work in a mopup role, hitters often are limited to pinch-hitting and pinch-running duty. And even if a position player sticks the entire year, he essentially has wasted a year of development. That's the situation that faced DeHaan after he got just 158 at-bats in 2000. He wasn't ready for Triple-A at the start of last season, but he rebounded in Double-A and made the all-prospect team in the Arizona Fall League, which he led with 13 doubles and 39 RBIs. He hit a mammoth homer over the batting eye at Peoria in one AFL game. DeHaan has made significant adjustments and improved his plate discipline. The Padres believe he has some pull power, and his speed allows him to steal bases and cover plenty of ground in center field. His arm is average. DeHaan will start 2002 in Triple-A to get some more badly needed at-bats. If he continues to blossom like he did in the latter part of 2001, he'll rocket up this list and to San Diego.

Year	Club (League)	Class	AVG	G	AB	R	H	2B	3B	HR	RBI	BB	SO	SB
1997	Erie (NY-P)	A	.239	58	205	43	49	8	6	1	18	38	43	14
1998	Augusta (SAL)	A	.314	132	475	85	149	39	8	8	75	69	114	33
1999	Lynchburg (Car)	A	.325	78	295	55	96	19	5	7	42	36	63	32
	Altoona (EL)	AA	.268	47	190	26	51	13	2	3	24	11	46	14
2000	Rancho Cuca. (Cal)	A	.214	4	14	2	3	1	0	1	1	1	4	0
	Las Vegas (PCL)	AAA	.293	10	41	7	12	4	0	0	3	2	11	3
	San Diego (NL)	MAJ	.204	90	103	19	21	7	0	2	13	5	39	4
2001	Portland (PCL)	AAA	.253	87	304	35	77	9	5	7	28	20	71	12
	Mobile (SL)	AA	.296	42	159	29	47	8	2	4	23	22	27	12
MAJOR LEAGUE TOTALS			.204	90	103	19	21	7	0	2	13	5	39	4
MINOR LEAGUE TOTALS			.288	458	1683	282	484	101	28	31	214	199	379	120

29. Henry Perez, rhp

Born: Oct. 27, 1982. **Ht.:** 6-3. **Wt.:** 210. **Bats:** R. **Throws:** R. **Career Transactions:** Signed out of Dominican Republic by Padres, July 25, 1999.

The downside of the Padres giving up their former Arizona League affiliate for a Northwest League club is that their Pioneer League team became the lowest rung on their system's latter. Thus their youngest pitchers had to face more experienced hitters. Though righthanders Javier Martinez, David Pauley and Perez all got pounded for 6.00-plus ERAs, San Diego still values them as prospects. The best of the group is Perez, whose fastball already tops out at 95 mph. He just lacks consistency in all phases of the game. He generally throws from 88-90 mph, and his curveball, changeup and command all need work. He's just a raw arm at this point, but he's worth watching. He'll start 2002 in extended spring training and likely will head to Eugene at midseason.

Year	Club (League)	Class	W	L	ERA	G	GS	CG	SV	IP	H	R	ER	BB	SO
2000	Padres (AZL)	R	2	5	4.53	13	10	0	0	48	40	32	24	36	39
2001	Idaho Falls (Pio)	R	4	8	6.28	15	15	0	0	72	79	60	50	39	82
MINOR LEAGUE TOTALS			6	13	5.58	28	25	0	0	119	119	92	74	75	121

30. Todd Donovan, of

Born: Aug. 12, 1978. **Ht.:** 6-1. **Wt.:** 175. **Bats:** R. **Throws:** R. **School:** Siena College. **Career Transactions:** Selected by Padres in eighth round of 1999 draft; signed June 13, 1999.

Added to the 40-man roster in November, Donovan has been an organization favorite since stealing 40 bases in 45 attempts in his pro debut in 1999. The Padres would like him even more if he could stay healthy. He has played in just 94 games over the last two seasons. In 2000, he tore a ligament in his right elbow and required arthroscopic surgery. Last year he missed a month after tearing a ligament in his left thumb in mid-April, then hurt the thumb again in his second game back and was out for two more months. Fellow San Diego outfield prospects Marcus Nettles and Jeremy Owens have similar top-of-the-line speed, but for now Donovan has a better chance to hit. He's not going to hit for power but he accepts that and focuses on getting on base. He knows how to swipe bases, succeeding on 84 percent of his attempts as a pro and going 23-for-25 in 2001. Donovan can go gap to gap in center field, though his arm is merely adequate. San Diego will jump him to Double-A this year and would love to get a full season out of him.

Year	Club (League)	Class	AVG	G	AB	R	H	2B	3B	HR	RBI	BB	SO	SB
1999	Idaho Falls (Pio)	R	.298	53	198	57	59	11	3	1	22	25	39	40
2000	Fort Wayne (Mid)	A	.284	53	204	39	58	12	4	0	23	25	45	18
2001	Lake Elsinore (Cal)	A	.304	41	168	37	51	7	0	1	12	19	25	23
MINOR LEAGUE TOTALS			.295	147	570	133	168	30	7	2	57	69	109	81

SAN FRANCISCO Giants

By John Manuel

Barry Bonds was the story in San Francisco last season. The Giants figure to have a much different plotline in 2002. "This year will probably be as big a challenge in turning the club around as we've faced since '97," GM Brian Sabean said. "We've got a track record of doing it and we're confident we can do it."

Bonds' return (he signed for $90 million over five years) solves one problem. But the club also faces questions at third base, in the outfield and on the mound. Rookie Pedro Feliz didn't fit the bill at the hot corner, center fielder Calvin Murray has proven to be just a role player, and the pitching staff needed free agent Jason Schmidt back because it was not clear a minor leaguer was ready to immediately step into the rotation.

That will change soon, though. San Francisco has done an excellent job of acquiring power arms through the draft and in Latin America the last three years, stocking the system with hard throwers both righthanded and lefthanded.

While this is the high mark in recent years for the Giants in terms of prominent prospects, it's not a new phenomenon. The organization's philosophy under Sabean and farm/scouting director Dick Tidrow has involved drafting and developing power arms to use in trades. The Giants have traded first-round picks such as Nate Bump, Joe Fontenot and Jason Grilli, as well as less heralded arms such as Lorenzo Barcelo, Keith Foulke and Bobby Howry.

Sabean smartly held onto rotation stalwarts such as Russ Ortiz. Now the Giants must decide whom to keep and whom to trade among their current stable of pitchers. If San Francisco seeks help at the plate, it won't come from the farm system. The need for hitters, especially up the middle of the field, worsened in 2001.

The system was aided by last year's addition of a low Class A affiliate, Hagerstown of the South Atlantic League. After four seasons with two affiliates in the high Class A California League, the Giants chose the SAL for its weather and relatively easy travel. The young Suns responded with a 45-25 effort in the second half to make the playoffs, and some of the organization's top prospects, such as Boof Bonser, Felix Diaz, Erick Threets and John Thomas, were able to experience success and pitch in games that mattered.

OrganizationOverview

General manager: Brian Sabean. **Farm/scouting director:** Dick Tidrow.

2001 PERFORMANCE

Class	Team	League	W	L	Pct.	Finish*	Manager
Majors	San Francisco	National	90	72	.556	4th (16)	Dusty Baker
Triple-A	Fresno Grizzlies	Pacific Coast	68	71	.489	9th (16)	Shane Turner
Double-A	Shreveport Swamp Dragons	Texas	54	81	.400	8th (8)	Bill Russell
High A	San Jose Giants	California	77	63	.550	2nd (10)	Lenn Sakata
Low A	Hagerstown Suns	South Atlantic	83	57	.593	2nd (16)	Bill Hayes
Short-season	Salem-Keizer Volcanoes	Northwest	51	25	.671	2nd (8)	Fred Stanley
Rookie	AZL Giants	Arizona	29	27	.518	3rd (7)	Keih Comstock
OVERALL 2001 MINOR LEAGUE RECORD			362	324	.528	9th (30)	

*Finish in overall standings (No. of teams in league)

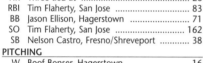

ORGANIZATION LEADERS

BATTING
*AVG	Tony Torcato, Fresno/Shreveport/San Jose	.323
R	Jason Ellison, Hagerstown	95
H	Tony Torcato, Fresno/Shreveport/San Jose	179
TB	**Sean McGowan**, Fresno/Shreveport	241
2B	Jason Ellison, Hagerstown	38
	Tony Torcato, Fresno/Shreveport/San Jose	38
3B	Arturo McDowell, San Jose	11
HR	Three tied at	26
RBI	Tim Flaherty, San Jose	83
BB	Jason Ellison, Hagerstown	71
SO	Tim Flaherty, San Jose	162
SB	Nelson Castro, Fresno/Shreveport	38

PITCHING
W	Boof Bonser, Hagerstown	16
L	Jeff Andra, Fresno/Shreveport	12
#ERA	Jon Cannon, Shreveport/San Jose	3.22
G	Robbie Crabtree, Fresno	63
CG	Jerome Williams, Shreveport	2
	Mike Riley, Fresno/Shreveport	2
SV	**Jackson Markert**, Hagerstown	39
IP	Vance Cozier, San Jose	170
BB	Joe Nathan, Fresno/Shreveport	70
SO	Boof Bonser, Hagerstown	178

*Minimum 250 At-Bats #Minimum 75 Innings

TOP PROSPECTS OF THE DECADE
1992	Royce Clayton, ss
1993	Calvin Murray, of
1994	Salomon Torres, rhp
1995	J.R. Phillips, 1b
1996	Shawn Estes, lhp
1997	Joe Fontenot, rhp
1998	Jason Grilli, rhp
1999	Jason Grilli, rhp
2000	Kurt Ainsworth, rhp
2001	Jerome Williams, rhp

TOP DRAFT PICKS OF THE DECADE
1992	Calvin Murray, of
1993	Steve Soderstrom, rhp
1994	Dante Powell, of
1995	Joe Fontenot, rhp
1996	*Matt White, rhp
1997	Jason Grilli, rhp
1998	Tony Torcato, 3b
1999	Kurt Ainsworth, rhp
2000	Boof Bonser, rhp
2001	Brad Hennessey, rhp

*Did not sign.

McGowan   **Markert**

BEST TOOLS
Best Hitter for Average	Tony Torcato
Best Power Hitter	Todd Linden
Fastest Baserunner	Arturo McDowell
Best Fastball	Erick Threets
Best Breaking Ball	Brad Hennessey
Best Changeup	Felix Diaz
Best Control	Jerome Williams
Best Defensive Catcher	Yorvit Torrealba
Best Defensive Infielder	Cody Ransom
Best Infield Arm	Nelson Castro
Best Defensive Outfielder	Arturo McDowell
Best Outfield Arm	Jason Ellison

PROJCTED 2005 LINEUP
Catcher	Yorvit Torrealba
First Base	Lance Niekro
Second Base	Jeff Kent
Third Base	Rich Aurilia
Shortstop	Cody Ransom
Left Field	Barry Bonds
Center Field	Carlos Valderrama
Right Field	Tony Torcato
No. 1 Starter	Jerome Williams
No. 2 Starter	Boof Bonser
No. 3 Starter	Russ Ortiz
No. 4 Starter	Jason Schmidt
No. 5 Starter	Kurt Ainsworth
Closer	Robb Nen

ALL-TIME LARGEST BONUSES
Jason Grilli, 1997	$1,875,000
Brad Hennessey, 2001	$1,380,000
Osvaldo Fernandez, 1996	$1,300,000
Kurt Ainsworth, 1999	$1,300,000
Boof Bonser, 2000	$1,245,000

DraftAnalysis

2001 Draft

Best Pro Debut: RHP Jesse Foppert (2) was the top pitching prospect in the short-season Northwest League after he went 8-1 with a league-best 1.93 ERA and 88 strikeouts in 70 innings. RHP Wesley Hutchison (10) went 6-2, 1.64 with 45 whiffs in 33 innings, leading the NWL with 10 saves.

Best Athlete: SS Jamie Athas (7) and 2B Derin McMains (11) are acrobatic middle infielders. Athas is quicker and has a stronger arm, and he handled Class A ball, batting .274-2-28 with 17 steals.

Best Hitter: 3B Julian Benavidez (3) was unheralded out of Diablo Valley (Calif.) CC, but he batted .319-9-39 in the NWL and drew comparisons to Edgar Martinez.

Best Raw Power: OF Todd Linden (1), the talk of the Cape Cod League in 2000, can go deep from both sides of the plate. That gives him an edge over Benavidez and 1B Tyler Von Schell (15).

Fastest Runner: Athas isn't a burner, but he has above-average speed and a nose for stealing bases.

Best Defensive Player: Athas and McMains. C Keith Anderson (27) has a cannon arm and led the NWL by erasing 46 percent of basestealers.

Best Fastball: RHP Justin Knoedler (5), a converted catcher, tops out at 93-96 mph. RHP **Brad Hennessey** (1) and Foppert both touch 95 mph, though Hennessey did that less often last summer because he was worn down. All three were primarily position players before the 2001 college season.

Most Intriguing Background: The Giants drafted two Bulger brothers, SS Kevin (43) and RHP Brian (49), and might have taken a third if the Diamondbacks hadn't beaten them to RHP Jason in the first round. Knoedler's twin brother Jason signed with the Tigers as a sixth-round pick. Hutchison was MVP of the 2000 NAIA World Series, earning two saves to help Lewis-Clark State win the championship.

MEL BAILEY

Hennessey

Closest To The Majors: Foppert is ticketed for Double-A at the outset of the 2002 season. Also keep an eye on LHP Noah Lowry (1), who has three solid pitches and seems to get better every year.

Best Late-Round Pick: Hutchison or RHP R.D. Spiehs (33),who spent the summer in Alaska and helped the Anchorage Glacier Pilots win the National Baseball Congress World Series. He can hit 93 mph with his fastball and also has a tough slider.

The One Who Got Away: The Giants signed or have under control every player from the first 19 rounds. OF Richard Giannotti (20) is a tools player who could blossom at Miami.

Assessment: San Francisco signed only one high school player—and that selection was voided. Its first nine picks adapted quickly and impressively to pro ball and will restock a farm system that has been thinned out by trades over the last few years.

2000 Draft

RHP Boof Bonser, a surprise first-rounder, justified his selection in a dominating 2001. 3B Lance Niekro and LHPs Erick Threets (7) and Ryan Hannaman (4) give this draft plenty of upside. RHP Jackson Markert (11) led the minors in saves last summer.   **Grade: B+**

1999 Draft

RHPs Jerome Williams (1) and Kurt Ainsworth (1) could pitch at the front of San Francisco's rotation for years to come, and RHP Jeff Verplancke (11) could finish games for them.   **Grade: B+**

1998 Draft

Of five first-rounders, only OF Tony Torcato is a likely big leaguer. RHP Nate Bump, OF Arturo McDowell and LHPs Chris Jones and Jeff Urban have stalled in the minors. Bump was used in a trade for Livan Hernandez, while promising RHP Ryan Vogelsong (5) helped get Jason Schmidt last summer. SS Cody Ransom (9) could crack the 2003 infield.   **Grade: B**

1997 Draft

RHP Jason Grilli (1) was pawned off on the Marlins for Hernandez. The other first-rounder, OF Dan McKinley, has fared worse. RHPs Scott Linebrink (2) and Kevin Joseph (6) also were used in trades, the only way this draft benefited the Giants.   **Grade: D**

Note: Draft analysis prepared by Jim Callis. Numbers in parentheses indicate draft rounds.

Jerome Williams rhp

Born: Dec. 4, 1981.
Ht.: 6-3. **Wt.:** 190.
Bats: R. **Throws:** R.
School: Waipahu HS, Honolulu.
Career Transactions: Selected by Giants in first round (39th overall) of 1999 draft; signed July 10, 1999.

Williams has worn the label of No. 1 prospect in the organization for a year, and he has worn it well through what he and the Giants hope were the worst of times. He pitched the entire season at age 19 at Double-A Shreveport as the youngest player in the Texas League, all while overcoming the death of his mother Deborah. Williams left for spring training in early March, only to return two weeks later to Hawaii for her funeral. His father Glenn, who hasn't been able to work for six years due to neck injuries, urged Williams to stay in Arizona for spring training, but he returned and took time out during the trip to help give pitching lessons to players at Waipahu High, his alma mater. The missed time in the spring meant Williams was working his way into shape during the early part of the season, and it showed. In his first 65 innings, he had a 5.26 ERA, .256 opponent batting average, 10 home runs allowed and a 42-22 strikeout-walk ratio. In his final 65, he had a 2.63 ERA, a .213 opponent average, four homers and a 42-12 strikeout-walk ratio.

The Giants love Williams' maturity, physically and emotionally. Athletic and coordinated, he pitches at 90-92 mph with a fastball that features good life. When he wants to, he can run his fastball up to 95 mph. Late in the season, he showed the kind of command the Giants were used to. He has tightened the rotation on his slider and improved his curve and changeup. Overcoming his mother's death and finishing the year strong were two more indications of Williams' mental toughness, which combined with his stuff makes him a potential No. 1 starter. He has yet to become a workhorse in pro ball, averaging 128 innings in his two full seasons, and missing spring training forced the Giants to keep him on strict pitch counts early in the 2001 season. But he threw a pair of complete games and pitched fewer than six innings just twice in the last three months of the year.

Williams remains one of the best pitching prospects in baseball. The Giants' major league staff is deep enough that Williams need not be rushed. When ready, he figures to be the ace the Giants now lack. He'll begin 2002 at Triple-A Fresno.

Year	Club (League)	Class	W	L	ERA	G	GS	CG	SV	IP	H	R	ER	BB	SO
1999	Salem-Keizer (NWL)	A	1	1	2.19	7	7	1	0	37	29	13	9	11	34
2000	San Jose (Cal)	A	7	6	2.94	23	19	0	0	126	89	53	41	48	115
2001	Shreveport (TL)	AA	9	7	3.95	23	23	2	0	130	116	69	57	34	84
MINOR LEAGUE TOTALS			17	14	3.29	53	49	3	0	293	234	135	107	93	233

2. Boof Bonser, rhp

Born: Oct. 14, 1981. **Ht.:** 6-4. **Wt.:** 230. **Bats:** R. **Throws:** R. **School:** Gibbs HS, St. Petersburg, Fla. **Career Transactions:** Selected by Giants in first round (21st overall) of 2000 draft; signed July 3, 2000.

Bonser officially changed his name from John to Boof, a childhood nickname that stuck, last offseason. Don't let that fool you, though—the Giants point to increased maturity as the biggest reason Bonser was named the low Class A South Atlantic League's No. 1 prospect in 2001. Maturity and talent are his strengths. Bonser maintained a 92-95 mph fastball throughout his first full pro season. He can run two-seamers that sink or pitch up in the zone with a four-seamer. The other improvement Bonser made was throwing his curveball more consistently, which came with improved, smooth mechanics. He ate up righthanders, who batted just .179 against him. Bonser will have to take care of his big, strong body, but his work ethic has eased any weight concerns. He has the makings of a good changeup, though he didn't need to use it much while he overpowered Sally League hitters with two plus pitches. Because the Giants have the likes of Williams and Kurt Ainsworth ahead of him, Bonser won't have to be rushed through the system. The poster child for the organization's successful move to low Class A, Bonser will step up to high Class A San Jose in 2002.

Year	Club (League)	Class	W	L	ERA	G	GS	CG	SV	IP	H	R	ER	BB	SO
2000	Salem-Keizer (NWL)	A	1	4	6.00	10	9	0	0	33	21	23	22	29	41
2001	Hagerstown (SAL)	A	16	4	2.49	27	27	0	0	134	91	40	37	61	178
MINOR LEAGUE TOTALS			17	8	3.18	37	36	0	0	167	112	63	59	90	219

3. Kurt Ainsworth, rhp

Born: Sept. 9, 1978. **Ht.:** 6-3. **Wt.:** 185. **Bats:** R. **Throws:** R. **School:** Louisiana State University. **Career Transactions:** Selected by Giants in first round (24th overall) of 1999 draft; signed June 17, 1999.

Ainsworth had Hall of Fame manager Tommy Lasorda at his wedding in January 2001, and Lasorda called to boost Ainsworth's confidence when he struggled out of the gate in Triple-A. Ainsworth pitched for Lasorda on the 2000 U.S. Olympic team, winning both his starts. He throws a 92-93 mph two-seam fastball, circle changeup, curve and slider. He keeps the ball down and lets his defense work for him. After struggling early in the season, he learned to trust his breaking stuff more and adjusted well to his first adversity as a pro. Ainsworth nibbled too much for his own good, putting himself in hitter's counts and leading to his early struggles. After recovering with a strong August (3-0, 2.73), he fell into the same trap in his brief big league debut. He also had some blister problems from throwing his curveball. Ainsworth won't have a spot in the rotation handed to him. But his fast finish in Fresno encouraged the Giants, who will give Ainsworth and Ryan Jensen a chance to take over as the No. 5 starter after Shawn Estes was traded.

Year	Club (League)	Class	W	L	ERA	G	GS	CG	SV	IP	H	R	ER	BB	SO
1999	Salem-Keizer (NWL)	A	3	3	1.61	10	10	1	0	45	34	18	8	18	64
2000	Shreveport (TL)	AA	10	9	3.30	28	28	0	0	158	138	67	58	63	130
2001	Fresno (PCL)	AAA	10	9	5.07	27	26	0	0	149	139	91	84	54	157
	San Francisco (NL)	MAJ	0	0	13.50	2	0	0	0	2	3	3	3	2	3
MAJOR LEAGUE TOTALS			0	0	13.50	2	0	0	0	2	3	3	3	2	3
MINOR LEAGUE TOTALS			23	21	3.84	65	64	1	0	352	311	176	150	135	351

4. Tony Torcato, of

Born: Oct. 25, 1979. **Ht.:** 6-1. **Wt.:** 195. **Bats:** L. **Throws:** R. **School:** Woodland (Calif.) HS. **Career Transactions:** Selected by Giants in first round (19th overall) of 1998 draft; signed June 3, 1998.

Giants trainers have called Torcato a freak for his ability to come back from injury. He has had three operations on his right shoulder, the latest last March 8 after he got hurt in spring training. His problems prompted his move from third base to the outfield. With a gifted natural stroke that produces consistent line drives, Torcato is easily the best hitter in the system. The Giants project more than just gap power once he stays healthy enough to get in a groove. He still has good arm strength despite his shoulder woes, and he takes good routes in the outfield, a sign of his excellent baseball instincts. The Giants hope the move off third base will minimize further entries on his medical chart. He'll hit for more power once he learns the patience to work into hitter's counts. Torcato was the leading in-house candidate if a corner spot had opened in San Francisco's outfield, but the club signed Barry Bonds to a long-term deal, signed Reggie Sanders and traded for Tsuyoshi Shinjo. The extra Triple-A time Torcato will get should benefit him.

Year	Club (League)	Class	AVG	G	AB	R	H	2B	3B	HR	RBI	BB	SO	SB
1998	Salem-Keizer (NWL)	A	.291	59	220	31	64	15	2	3	43	14	38	4
1999	Bakersfield (Cal)	A	.291	110	422	50	123	25	0	4	58	30	67	2
2000	San Jose (Cal)	A	.324	119	490	77	159	37	2	7	88	41	62	19
	Shreveport (TL)	AA	.500	2	8	1	4	0	0	0	2	0	1	0
2001	San Jose (Cal)	A	.341	67	258	38	88	21	2	2	47	17	40	9
	Shreveport (TL)	AA	.293	36	147	13	43	9	1	1	23	9	15	0
	Fresno (PCL)	AAA	.320	35	150	20	48	8	1	2	8	2	20	0
MINOR LEAGUE TOTALS			.312	428	1695	230	529	115	8	19	269	113	243	34

5. Felix Diaz, rhp

Born: July 27, 1981. **Ht.:** 6-1. **Wt.:** 165. **Bats:** R. **Throws:** R. **Career Transactions:** Signed out of Dominican Republic by Giants, March 20, 1998.

The Giants have redoubled their Latin American efforts the last four years, and Diaz is the crown jewel of their work. He missed 2½ months with a tender arm as a precaution in 2001, his first full season, but came back with a dominant effort in the Arizona Fall League. Diaz' fastball regularly reaches 95-96 mph, and he showed good command of it before his temporary layoff. Diaz throws three complementary pitches for strikes: a hard slider in the mid-80s, a plus changeup with good sink and a decent curveball. All his pitches have life down in the zone. Diaz has become more consistent and slower with his delivery, leading to better command of his changeup and curve. He takes his craft seriously. The Giants want to be careful with Diaz. He could use more pro innings but also must show his small frame can hold up under a heavier workload. Sometimes he's too hard on himself, though that has improved with maturity. Diaz' power potential is exciting. He's the latest slight Dominican with an electric arm to earn comparisons to Pedro Martinez. He'll pitch in high Class A this year.

Year	Club (League)	Class	W	L	ERA	G	GS	CG	SV	IP	H	R	ER	BB	SO
1998	Giants (DSL)	R	0	4	7.55	14	5	0	0	39	52	44	33	26	34
1999	Giants (DSL)	R	0	0	0.75	3	3	0	0	12	6	2	1	7	19
2000	Giants (AZL)	R	3	4	4.16	11	11	0	0	63	56	35	29	16	58
	Salem-Keizer (NWL)	A	0	1	8.10	3	0	0	0	3	6	6	3	1	2
2001	Hagerstown (SAL)	A	1	4	3.66	15	12	0	0	52	49	27	21	16	56
MINOR LEAGUE TOTALS			4	13	4.63	46	31	0	0	169	169	114	87	66	169

6. Jesse Foppert, rhp

Born: July 10, 1980. **Ht.:** 6-6. **Wt.:** 210. **Bats:** R. **Throws:** R. **School:** University of San Francisco. **Career Transactions:** Selected by Giants in second round of 2001 draft; signed June 8, 2001.

After starting his college career as primarily a first baseman, Foppert emerged as a pitching prospect in the wood-bat Shenandoah Valley League in 2000, posting a 2.11 ERA and allowing just 44 hits in 64 innings. He led the Northwest League in ERA in his pro debut. Foppert has an athletic pitcher's body and a smooth, easy delivery right out of the textbook. Short-season Salem-Keizer manager Fred Stanley compared Foppert's smooth motion to Jim Palmer's. His no-effort mechanics produce pinpoint command, and the Giants expect him to be a workhorse. He has a low-90s fastball that touches 95 mph, a plus slider with late action, and a solid changeup and curveball. Foppert really just needs innings. He has yet to experience much failure on the mound and needs to pick up the nuances of the position, such as holding runners. The Giants say he has the aptitude to learn quickly. Foppert gives the Giants five righthanders among their top six prospects. He's on the fast track and should start 2002 at Class A San Jose.

Year	Club (League)	Class	W	L	ERA	G	GS	CG	SV	IP	H	R	ER	BB	SO
2001	Salem-Keizer (NWL)	A	8	1	1.93	14	14	0	0	70	35	18	15	23	88
MINOR LEAGUE TOTALS			8	1	1.93	14	14	0	0	70	35	18	15	23	88

7. Lance Niekro, 3b

Born: Jan. 29, 1979. **Ht.:** 6-3. **Wt.:** 210. **Bats:** R. **Throws:** R. **School:** Florida Southern College. **Career Transactions:** Selected by Giants in second round of 2000 draft; signed July 3, 2000.

Niekro's father Joe and his uncle Phil, a Hall of Famer, were accomplished knuckleball pitchers in the majors, and Lance can throw the floater as well. He nearly won the Cape Cod League's triple crown in 1999, but a shoulder injury and diminished power caused him to fall to the second round of the draft a year later. Niekro plays with passion and grit like a big leaguer. He reminds the Giants of Jeff Kent offensively: a good fastball hitter who crushes mistake breaking balls and has power to all fields. He has soft, sure hands and an accurate if not overwhelming arm at third base. He's athletic enough for the position as well. Niekro has had health problems since his Cape coming-out party. He went to spring training last year with a tender right shoulder and injured the same shoulder May 15 when he landed wrong after catching a popup. He must show he can remain healthy to be considered an elite prospect. He also can improve his plate discipline. Niekro allayed fears about his recurring shoulder problems by hitting .306-2-13 in 62 instructional league at-bats. He'll move up to Double-A in 2002 and get back on the express route to the majors.

Year	Club (League)	Class	AVG	G	AB	R	H	2B	3B	HR	RBI	BB	SO	SB
2000	Salem-Keizer (NWL)	A	.362	49	196	27	71	14	4	5	44	11	25	2
2001	San Jose (Cal)	A	.288	42	163	18	47	11	0	3	34	4	14	4
MINOR LEAGUE TOTALS			.329	91	359	45	118	25	4	8	78	15	39	6

8. Erick Threets, lhp

Born: Nov. 4, 1981. **Ht.:** 6-5. **Wt.:** 220. **Bats:** L. **Throws:** L. **School:** Modesto (Calif.) JC. **Career Transactions:** Selected by Giants in seventh round of 2000 draft; signed Aug. 1, 2000.

A sore arm thanks to poor high school mechanics limited Threets to the bullpen and just 38 innings in 2000 between the juco ranks and the Cape Cod League, where the Giants signed him. He hails from Randy Johnson's hometown of Livermore, Calif., and if instructional league radar guns are to be believed, Threets has staked his claim as Livermore's hardest thrower. He could have the hardest fastball in the minors as club officials insist he threw four pitches in the 102-103 mph range. Threets' wide-shouldered, powerful build and narrow hips provide a perfect pitcher's frame. His slider is a work in progress but can be nasty when he stays on top of the pitch. Still raw, he doesn't have an offspeed pitch. His delivery tends to get stiff if he doesn't relax and let it go. Threets reacted well to the situation he was put at high Class A last year, where an 85-pitch limit and his lack of polish contributed to him going winless. He shook it off by dominating instructional league. A return to San Jose as a starter is in the offing, but a move to the bullpen could come eventually.

Year	Club (League)	Class	W	L	ERA	G	GS	CG	SV	IP	H	R	ER	BB	SO
2001	Hagerstown (SAL)	A	2	0	0.75	12	0	0	1	24	13	3	2	9	32
	San Jose (Cal)	A	0	10	4.25	14	14	0	0	59	49	34	28	40	60
MINOR LEAGUE TOTALS			2	10	3.25	26	14	0	1	83	62	37	30	49	92

9. Todd Linden, of

Born: June 30, 1980. **Ht.:** 6-2. **Wt.:** 215. **Bats:** B. **Throws:** R. **School:** Louisiana State University. **Career Transactions:** Selected by Giants in first round (41st overall) of 2001 draft; signed Sept. 4, 2001.

Linden hit .390 as a sophomore at Washington and was named the No. 1 prospect in the Cape Cod League in 2000. He had a stormy breakup with the Huskies, transferred to Louisiana State and had an inconsistent junior season. He returned to Baton Rouge in August but changed his mind and signed, negotiating the contract sans agent Tommy Tanzer. Linden reminds the Giants of Will Clark with his sweet swing and absolute confidence in his ability. He immediately became the system's top power prospect with an impressive instructional league effort, showing pop from both sides of the plate. He recognizes breaking balls well and is a good runner for his size. Linden shows at least average arm strength and projects as a right fielder. His swagger rubbed people the wrong way at Washington, and his makeup was questioned in the Cape League. The Giants would like to see him 15-20 pounds under his fall weight. The organization is barren in the outfield in the minor leagues, and Linden has a chance to move very quickly. If he's in shape, he could advance to Double-A with a good spring.

Year	Club (League)	Class	AVG	G	AB	R	H	2B	3B	HR	RBI	BB	SO	SB
	Has Not Played—Signed 2002 Contract													

10. Cody Ransom, ss

Born: Feb. 17, 1976. **Ht.:** 6-2. **Wt.:** 190. **Bats:** R. **Throws:** R. **School:** Grand Canyon (Ariz.) University. **Career Transactions:** Selected by Giants in ninth round of 1998 draft; signed June 4, 1998.

MEL BAILEY

The Giants drafted Ransom's brother Troy in the 29th round in 1999 as an outfielder, but moved him to the mound in 2001. Arm strength must run in the family, because Cody's arm rates a 7 on the 2 to 8 scouting scale. Named the best defensive shortstop in the Triple-A Pacific Coast League, Ransom rates as the best defender in the organization. He gets to balls average shortstops wouldn't dream of. Despite that range and huge arm, he made just 12 errors in 588 chances at Fresno. He made strides offensively, showing above-average power for his size and position. Ransom's glove remains ahead of his bat. He has too many holes in his swing, though he made progress making more consistent contact. He needs to improve his pitch recognition. He tends to jump to his front foot during his swing, cheating to catch up to fastballs. Ransom needs more minor league at-bats before his defense can become a factor in the big leagues. If he improves after another season in Triple-A, he could push Rich Aurilia to third base and take over at short in 2003.

Year	Club (League)	Class	AVG	G	AB	R	H	2B	3B	HR	RBI	BB	SO	SB
1998	Salem-Keizer (NWL)	A	.233	71	236	52	55	12	7	6	27	43	56	19
1999	Bakersfield (Cal)	A	.275	99	356	69	98	12	6	11	47	54	108	15
	Shreveport (TL)	AA	.122	14	41	6	5	0	0	2	4	4	22	0
2000	Shreveport (TL)	AA	.200	130	459	58	92	21	2	7	47	40	141	9
2001	Fresno (CAL)	AAA	.241	134	469	77	113	21	6	23	78	44	137	17
	San Francisco (NL)	MAJ	.000	9	7	1	0	0	0	0	0	0	5	0
MAJOR LEAGUE TOTALS			.000	9	7	1	0	0	0	0	0	0	5	0
MINOR LEAGUE TOTALS			.233	448	1561	262	363	66	21	49	203	185	464	60

11. Ryan Jensen, rhp

Born: Sept. 17, 1975. **Ht.:** 6-0. **Wt.:** 205. **Bats:** R. **Throws:** R. **School:** Southern Utah University. **Career Transactions:** Selected by Giants in eighth round of 1996 draft; signed June 6, 1996.

Jensen seemed to be stuck in neutral after consecutive seasons at Fresno with ERAs higher than 5.00, and he was removed from the 40-man roster in February 2001. He never has pitched in Double-A, and he finally adjusted to Triple-A. He earned three promotions to San Francisco, joining the rotation when first Shawn Estes and then Mark Gardner went on the disabled list. Surgery before the 2001 season on both of Jensen's knees helped his conditioning and endurance, and he was able to sustain the average velocity on his fastball deeper into games and for the duration of the season. He also added a knuckle-curve as an out pitch to his varied arsenal. While none are considered above-average offerings, he also throws a curveball, slider and changeup. Jensen will battle Ainsworth, whose ceiling is much higher, and Joe Nathan for the No. 5 spot in the rotation in spring training.

Year	Club (League)	Class	W	L	ERA	G	GS	CG	SV	IP	H	R	ER	BB	SO
1996	Bellingham (NWL)	A	2	4	4.98	13	11	0	0	47	35	30	26	38	31
1997	Bakersfield (Cal)	A	0	0	13.50	1	1	0	0	1	3	2	2	0	2
	Salem-Keizer (NWL)	A	7	3	5.15	16	16	0	0	80	87	55	46	32	67
1998	Bakersfield (Cal)	A	11	12	3.37	29	27	0	0	168	162	89	63	61	164
	Fresno (PCL)	AAA	0	0	4.76	2	1	0	0	6	4	5	3	4	6
1999	Fresno (PCL)	AAA	11	10	5.12	27	27	0	0	156	160	96	89	68	150
2000	Fresno (PCL)	AAA	5	8	5.79	26	26	1	0	135	167	106	87	63	114
2001	Fresno (PCL)	AAA	11	2	3.48	20	17	1	0	106	97	43	41	34	95
	San Francisco (NL)	MAJ	1	2	4.25	10	7	0	0	42	44	21	20	25	26
MAJOR LEAGUE TOTALS			1	2	4.25	10	7	0	0	42	44	21	20	25	26
MINOR LEAGUE TOTALS			47	39	4.59	134	126	2	0	700	715	426	357	300	629

12. Jeff Verplancke, rhp

Born: Nov. 18, 1977. **Ht.:** 6-3. **Wt.:** 200. **Bats:** R. **Throws:** R. **School:** Cal State Los Angeles. **Career Transactions:** Selected by Giants in 11th round of 1999 draft; signed Aug. 27, 1999.

Though he spells his name differently, Verplancke is the cousin of professional golfer Scott Verplank. Jeff's older brother Joe is a former Diamondbacks farmhand. Jeff chose baseball over soccer, which he played on a partial scholarship at Cal State Los Angeles. The Mariners drafted him in the second round in 1998, but didn't sign him after he was diagnosed with a torn elbow ligament and needed Tommy John surgery. Verplancke had the operation, didn't pitch in 1999 and was set to transfer to Long Beach State that fall before the Giants signed him just before classes were to start for a $600,000 bonus. San Francisco used him as a starter in his first pro season to build up his endurance and get him more innings. He since has blossomed with a move to the bullpen, becoming the club's top closer prospect ahead of the likes of Luke Anderson, Jackson Markert and Wesley Hutchison. Verplancke has two plus pitches: a 94-mph fastball with heavy bite down in the strike zone, and a plus slider. He still struggles with command and wore down in the Arizona Fall League. A strong spring, though, could catapult him into the bullpen mix to setup Felix Rodriguez and Robb Nen.

Year	Club (League)	Class	W	L	ERA	G	GS	CG	SV	IP	H	R	ER	BB	SO
2000	San Jose (Cal)	A	6	14	5.86	26	25	1	0	140	159	111	91	67	129
	Fresno (PCL)	AAA	0	0	1.80	1	0	0	0	5	3	1	1	2	6
2001	Shreveport (TL)	AA	1	8	4.44	43	0	0	22	49	50	27	24	20	46
	Fresno (PCL)	AAA	2	1	2.92	8	0	0	1	12	9	4	4	6	13
MINOR LEAGUE TOTALS			9	23	5.24	78	25	1	23	206	221	143	120	95	194

13. Ryan Hannaman, lhp

Born: Aug. 28, 1981. **Ht.:** 6-3. **Wt.:** 190. **Bats:** L. **Throws:** L. **School:** Murphy HS, Mobile, Ala. **Career Transactions:** Selected by Giants in fourth round of 2000 draft; signed June 11, 2000.

The Giants' collection of power lefthanders should be the envy of most organizations. In addition to Erick Threets, Hannaman and No. 14 prospect Francisco Liriano have electric fastballs that are well above average for southpaws. Hannaman was as raw as they come out of high school. Tales of his inexperience include not knowing which foot to put on the rubber while pitching from the stretch. The Giants have brought him along slowly, teaching him the nuances of the game in small doses. The results are starting to show. Hannaman alternately dazzled and digressed in instructional league, but when he was on he threw a fastball in the high 90s with an easy arm action. He also showed flashes of a slider with tight rotation and a good bite, which allows him to pitch inside to righthanders. Inconsistent mechanics and command, plus his own inexperience, remain Hannaman's biggest obstacles to moving faster through the system. He shined in his late callup to the short-season Northwest League and is ticketed for a full year at low Class A Hagerstown in 2001. The Giants are willing to be patient.

Year	Club (League)	Class	W	L	ERA	G	GS	CG	SV	IP	H	R	ER	BB	SO
2000	Giants (AZL)	R	0	1	21.60	5	0	0	0	3	4	8	8	11	6
	Salem-Keizer (NWL)	A	0	0	0.00	1	0	0	0	1	1	0	0	1	1
2001	Giants (AZL)	R	4	1	2.00	11	11	0	0	54	34	14	12	31	67
	Salem-Keizer (NWL)	A	1	1	2.08	3	3	0	0	13	8	5	3	8	19
MINOR LEAGUE TOTALS			5	3	2.90	20	14	0	0	71	47	27	23	51	93

14. Francisco Liriano, lhp

Born: Oct. 26, 1983. **Ht.:** 6-2. **Wt.:** 185. **Bats:** L. **Throws:** L. **Career Transactions:** Signed out of Dominican Republic by Giants, Sept. 9, 2000.

The Giants have put a greater emphasis (read: more money) into Latin America since 1998, and the results are starting to percolate up through the system. Felix Diaz is the best example, but Liriano could surpass him with a strong performance in a full-season league in 2002. Several club officials describe his arm as special, which must have been obvious when the Giants first worked him out. They immediately moved him to the mound after he showed up as an outfielder. Liriano has added two inches and 25 pounds to his athletic, lithe frame and has touched 96 mph with his fastball. He pitched regularly at 91-92 in Rookie ball and in a brief stint with short-season Salem-Keizer. His curveball is a plus pitch and he has shown a good feel for pitching. Liriano has a sound delivery and may move faster than Hannaman, though both will start this year in low Class A.

Year	Club (League)	Class	W	L	ERA	G	GS	CG	SV	IP	H	R	ER	BB	SO
2001	Giants (AZL)	R	5	4	3.63	13	12	0	0	62	51	26	25	24	67
	Salem-Keizer (NWL)	A	0	0	5.00	2	2	0	0	9	7	5	5	1	12
MINOR LEAGUE TOTALS			5	4	3.80	15	14	0	0	71	58	31	30	25	79

15. Julian Benavidez, 3b

Born: April 14, 1982. **Ht.:** 6-2. **Wt.:** 215. **Bats:** R. **Throws:** R. **School:** Diablo Valley (Calif.) CC. **Career Transactions:** Selected by Giants in third round of 2001 draft; signed July 12, 2001.

Signed away from a scholarship offer to Arizona State, Benavidez impressed managers enough to be rated the No. 3 prospect in the Northwest League in his pro debut last summer. Salem skipper Fred Stanley, who played in the majors and used to run the Brewers system, compared him to a young Edgar Martinez because of his ability to drive the ball to all fields at a young age. Benavidez has more raw power than anyone in the system save fellow 2001 draftee Todd Linden, and the Giants expect some adjustments in his approach and swing will help bring it out soon. His swing tends to get long and Benavidez has had trouble identifying breaking balls. But he has no trouble hitting fastballs with authority and isn't afraid to work deep into a count. He's a streaky hitter, another indication of his youth. Defensively, his hands and range are average. He has an accurate arm with adequate strength when he doesn't short-arm his throws. A full season in low Class A will determine how fast a track his development will take.

Year	Club (League)	Class	AVG	G	AB	R	H	2B	3B	HR	RBI	BB	SO	SB
2001	Salem-Keizer (NWL)	A	.319	50	188	36	60	12	1	9	39	24	54	2
MINOR LEAGUE TOTALS			.319	50	188	36	60	12	1	9	39	24	54	2

16. Felix Escalona, 2b/ss

Born: March 12, 1979. **Ht.:** 6-0. **Wt.:** 185. **Bats:** R. **Throws:** R. **Career Transactions:** Signed out of Venezuela by Astros, Sept. 20, 1995 . . . Selected by Giants from Astros in Rule 5 major league draft, Dec. 13, 2001.

The Giants acknowledge one of their organization's biggest weaknesses is up the middle of the field. They hope that major league Rule 5 pick Escalona, drafted away from the Astros, will help them now and in the future. Primarily a second baseman, he led the South Atlantic League in doubles and extra-base hits last year, an indication that he has plenty of bat for his position. Stocky to the point where Houston thought he might need to lose some weight, Escalona has just average speed. He does have better range than one would think, and he turns the double play well. Scouts praised his instincts and poise, traits that attracted San Francisco in the Rule 5 draft as well. Interestingly, the Giants announced Escalona as a third baseman at the draft. Though he didn't play there in 2001, the hot corner has been a weak spot at the major league level. With the acquisition of Desi Relaford in the Shawn Estes trade, the Giants should be able to carry Escalona through 2002. Then they can figure out where to use him in the future.

Year	Club (League)	Class	AVG	G	AB	R	H	2B	3B	HR	RBI	BB	SO	SB
1996	Astros (GCL)	R	.147	28	75	8	11	2	0	1	9	8	31	1
1997	Astros (GCL)	R	.206	51	189	27	39	9	0	1	9	20	49	11
	Kissimmee (FSL)	A	.222	3	9	6	2	0	0	0	0	1	2	0
1998	Kissimmee (FSL)	A	.000	3	4	0	0	0	0	0	0	0	1	0
	Auburn (NY-P)	A	.208	51	149	22	31	5	0	1	17	11	33	4
1999	Michigan (Mid)	A	.288	116	396	78	114	29	4	6	47	29	60	7
2000	Michigan (Mid)	A	.259	64	251	42	65	14	1	6	35	22	49	7
	Kissimmee (FSL)	A	.252	42	143	19	36	5	1	0	8	9	21	5
2001	Lexington (SAL)	A	.289	130	536	92	155	42	2	16	64	30	85	46
MINOR LEAGUE TOTALS			.259	488	1752	294	453	106	8	31	189	130	331	81

17. Carlos Valderrama, of

Born: Nov. 30, 1977. **Ht.:** 5-11. **Wt.:** 175. **Bats:** R. **Throws:** R. **Career Transactions:** Signed out of Venezuela by Giants, Feb. 23, 1995.

While he shares a name with the flamboyant Colombian soccer player, this Valderrama has more to his game than his legs. He entered 2001 as the Giants' only bona fide outfield prospect. He was coming off the first full healthy season of his career and had shown elements of all five tools, with the best being baserunning and hitting. Valderrama made a strong showing in spring training and got off to a good start last year in Double-A, where he exhibited better plate discipline and improved defensive play in center field. Then he tore his left rotator cuff trying to make a sliding catch on wet turf May 19. Valderrama had surgery and didn't return during the regular season, but encouraged the Giants by taking Tony Torcato's place late in the Arizona Fall League season and going 6-for-21. A healthy Valderrama will try to regain his form in 2002, most likely starting back in Shreveport.

Year	Club (League)	Class	AVG	G	AB	R	H	2B	3B	HR	RBI	BB	SO	SB
1995	Giants (DSL)	R	.228	22	57	7	13	1	0	0	4	6	10	1
1996	Giants (DSL)	R	.223	46	166	29	37	4	1	0	11	29	24	26
1997	Salem-Keizer (NWL)	A	.319	41	138	21	44	7	3	3	28	12	29	22
1998	Salem-Keizer (NWL)	A	.345	7	29	5	10	1	0	0	4	1	7	4
1999	San Jose (Cal)	A	.256	26	90	12	23	2	0	0	12	4	19	8
	Salem-Keizer (NWL)	A	.291	40	134	27	39	3	1	2	18	12	34	17
2000	Bakersfield (Cal)	A	.315	121	435	78	137	21	5	13	81	39	96	54
2001	Shreveport (TL)	AA	.308	41	159	29	49	12	2	1	8	18	29	11
MINOR LEAGUE TOTALS			.291	344	1208	208	352	51	12	19	166	121	248	143

18. Brad Hennessey, rhp

Born: Feb. 7, 1980. **Ht.:** 6-1. **Wt.:** 180. **Bats:** R. **Throws:** R. **School:** Youngstown State University. **Career Transactions:** Selected by Giants in first round (21st overall) of 2001 draft; signed June 30, 2001.

Hennessey went from obscurity to the first round of the 2001 draft on the strength of his slider, which Giants scouts alternately rated as a 75 or 80 on the 20-to-80 scale during the spring. He also possesses plenty of athleticism and a fresh arm, the result of his intriguing college career. Hennessey was a No. 3 starter on his Toledo high school team and went to Youngstown State as a two-way player. He was the club's shortstop for most of 2000, earning a few innings as a reliever and posting a 7.75 ERA. He convinced coach Mike Florak to make him a starter last spring, and his stuff took off as he shared the Mid-Continent Conference pitcher of the year award with Oral Roberts' Michael Rogers. In addition to his wicked slider, which has a tight rotation and sharp, late break, Hennessey throws a 91-92 mph fastball that touched 95 in the spring, plus a quick arm. He still has much to learn about pitching, such as an offspeed pitch, and was worn out in instructional league, so the Giants will bring him along slowly.

Year	Club (League)	Class	W	L	ERA	G	GS	CG	SV	IP	H	R	ER	BB	SO
2001	Salem-Keizer (NWL)	A	1	0	2.38	9	9	0	0	34	28	9	9	11	22
MINOR LEAGUE TOTALS			1	0	2.38	9	9	0	0	34	28	9	9	11	22

19. Noah Lowry, lhp

Born: Oct. 10, 1980. **Ht.:** 6-3. **Wt.:** 210. **Bats:** L. **Throws:** L. **School:** Pepperdine University. **Career Transactions:** Selected by Giants in first round (30th overall) of 2001 draft; signed June 20, 2001.

Of the three pitchers the Giants took in the first two rounds of the 2001 draft, Lowry has the most experience and polish, even if he ranks behind Jesse Foppert and Brad Hennessey on this list. A first-team All-American at Pepperdine last spring, Lowry and righthander Dan Haren (a Cardinals second-round pick) gave the Waves one of college baseball's top pitching duos. The 2001 West Coast Conference pitcher of the year, Lowry emerged after a bad back and broken left hand sidelined him for most of his senior year in high school, diverting him for a year to Ventura (Calif.) Junior College and another year in the Waves bullpen. His 142 strikeouts last spring were the second-most in school history, and were the result of an 87-91 mph fastball with good life, a consistent overhand curve and a plus changeup. San Francisco still sees some projection left in his fastball. Lowry throws all three pitches for strikes and holds runners well. He looks like a future innings-eater, though the Giants took it easy with him last year after he pitched 121 innings at Pepperdine. He should join Hennessey in the Hagerstown rotation in 2002.

Year	Club (League)	Class	W	L	ERA	G	GS	CG	SV	IP	H	R	ER	BB	SO
2001	Salem-Keizer (NWL)	A	1	1	3.60	8	7	0	0	25	26	15	10	8	28
MINOR LEAGUE TOTALS			1	1	3.60	8	7	0	0	25	26	15	10	8	28

20. Jamie Athas, ss

Born: Oct. 14, 1979. **Ht.:** 6-2. **Wt.:** 190. **Bats:** L. **Throws:** R. **School:** Wake Forest University. **Career Transactions:** Selected by Giants in seventh round of 2001 draft; signed June 16, 2001.

Athas was an impact player in two college programs. First he was the starting shortstop for the last team in Providence College history in 1999, helping the Friars to 47 wins and an NCAA regional berth. When the program was dissolved, Athas transferred to Wake Forest, where he played every infield position as a sophomore and became the everyday shortstop as a junior. He signed quickly, immediately becoming one of the top middle-infield prospects in an organization lacking in that area. He showed good all-around athleticism and leadership skills at Hagerstown, helping lead the Suns down the stretch to the playoffs. He surprised the Giants with gap power and above-average speed and baserunning ability, though he's no burner. Defensively, his range is average or a tick above. He has fluid actions, soft hands and an accurate, more-than-adequate arm. He solidified his standing with a strong effort in instructional league and could be pushed to Double-A in 2002, as the system is woefully short on athletic shortstops. Athas' younger brother Mike is following his brother's footsteps, transferring after one season from Connecticut to Massachusetts to continue his own baseball career.

Year	Club (League)	Class	AVG	G	AB	R	H	2B	3B	HR	RBI	BB	SO	SB
2001	Hagerstown (SAL)	A	.274	65	234	44	64	10	3	2	28	31	55	17
MINOR LEAGUE TOTALS			.274	65	234	44	64	10	3	2	28	31	55	17

21. Deivis Santos, 1b

Born: Feb. 9, 1980. **Ht.:** 6-2. **Wt.:** 175. **Bats:** L. **Throws:** L. **Career Transactions:** Signed out of Dominican Republic by Giants, May 30, 1997.

Though he signed in 1997, Santos had just 50 at-bats outside of the Rookie-level Dominican Summer League coming into 2001. He held his own in his first full season last year, leading Hagerstown in RBIs. The Giants signed him because he showed good swing mechanics at an early age, and that stroke continues to make Santos an above-average hitter. As he has added strength with time and American training methods, he has started to hit for more and more power, though he remains more of a gap hitter than a classic slugger. He's agile, runs well for his position and is smooth and polished around the bag at first, which hasn't been true of past San Francisco first-base prospects like Damon Minor and Sean McGowan. The organization likes Santos' work ethic but believes he'll hit for more power with a more patient approach at the plate. He finished strong, hitting .322 in his final 30 games last year and smacking two hits in each of his final five games. He's ready for high Class A.

Year	Club (League)	Class	AVG	G	AB	R	H	2B	3B	HR	RBI	BB	SO	SB
1997	Giants (DSL)	R	.271	70	258	29	70	13	2	4	24	23	40	5
1998	Giants (DSL)	R	.281	60	221	26	62	17	0	1	22	24	22	5
1999	Giants (DSL)	R	.236	67	237	27	56	10	2	3	40	44	31	7
2000	Giants (AZL)	R	.372	12	43	13	16	2	1	2	10	7	6	4
	Salem-Keizer (NWL)	A	.000	2	7	0	0	0	0	0	0	0	0	0
2001	Hagerstown (SAL)	A	.290	131	520	64	151	27	3	12	80	25	91	16
MINOR LEAGUE TOTALS			.276	342	1286	159	355	69	8	22	176	123	190	37

22. Sean McGowan, 1b/of

Born: May 15, 1977. **Ht.:** 6-6. **Wt.:** 240. **Bats:** R. **Throws:** R. **School:** Boston College. **Career Transactions:** Selected by Giants in third round of 1999 draft; signed June 7, 1999.

On the surface, McGowan had a solid 2001 season. He hit more home runs than he had the previous year, wasn't overmatched by Triple-A pitching despite just 69 previous at-bats above Class A, and he played some left field in addition to first base. But McGowan fell hard in the eyes of the organization, which seems to have lost patience waiting for him to develop home run power befitting his large frame. His swing is compact but he hasn't learned to pull the ball with authority, and he continues to have problems with good inside fastballs. In Triple-A, he hit just .251 with five home runs away from Fresno's cozy Beiden Field, and he continued to strike out four times as often as he walked. The Giants also had high hopes that McGowan's athletic ability would allow a smooth move to the outfield, but instead he didn't take to the experiment, prompting a pair of demotions to Double-A. McGowan could put the pieces back together, but he must put in more work defensively at first base and hit for more power to supplant J.T. Snow in San Francisco.

Year	Club (League)	Class	AVG	G	AB	R	H	2B	3B	HR	RBI	BB	SO	SB
1999	Salem-Keizer (NWL)	A	.335	63	257	40	86	12	1	15	62	20	56	3
	San Jose (Cal)	A	.375	2	8	1	3	1	0	0	1	0	3	0
2000	San Jose (Cal)	A	.327	114	456	58	149	32	2	12	106	43	71	4
	Shreveport (TL)	AA	.348	18	69	5	24	4	0	0	12	1	8	0
2001	Shreveport (TL)	AA	.304	31	125	11	38	6	0	3	17	5	19	0
	Fresno (PCL)	AAA	.286	104	391	59	112	30	2	14	65	23	95	1
MINOR LEAGUE TOTALS			.315	332	1306	174	412	85	5	44	263	92	252	8

23. John Thomas, lhp

Born: July 24, 1981. **Ht.:** 6-2. **Wt.:** 190. **Bats:** L. **Throws:** L. **School:** Righetti HS, Orcutt, Calif. **Career Transactions:** Selected by Giants in second round of 1999 draft; signed Sept. 27, 1999.

Thomas had a difficult beginning with the organization, but the Giants are glad they stuck with him because he's another hard-throwing lefthander in a system deep in them. He could have had his contract voided after he signed late in 1999 for a $565,000 bonus when the club discovered he needed Tommy John surgery. Because he already had spent time at Salem-Keizer in 1999, though he didn't pitch, San Francisco decided to keep him through 2000, when he rehabilitated but didn't take the mound. The Giants were rewarded by Thomas' encouraging effort when he finally made his pro debut last year. He regained the velocity on his fastball after his rehab, topping out at 93 mph. Thomas also has a hard over-hand curveball, but his best pitch is a changeup with good arm speed and late sink. He was rolling in June when he was shut down again with a tender arm. He's another good example of how the presence of a low Class A club helped the farm system immensely. Thomas will move up a step to high Class A this year if healthy.

Year	Club (League)	Class	W	L	ERA	G	GS	CG	SV	IP	H	R	ER	BB	SO
2000					Did Not Play—Injured										
2001	Hagerstown (SAL)	A	3	3	4.16	15	15	0	0	71	70	40	33	22	65
MINOR LEAGUE TOTALS			3	3	4.16	15	15	0	0	71	70	40	33	22	65

24. David Cash, rhp

Born: July 25, 1979. **Ht.:** 6-1. **Wt.:** 185. **Bats:** R. **Throws:** R. **School:** University of California. **Career Transactions:** Selected by Giants in sixth round of 2001 draft; signed June 19, 2001.

The Devil Rays drafted Cash out of high school in 1997 in the 40th round, but Cash attended Modesto (Calif.) Junior College—where Erick Threets later pitched—as a draft-and-follow. He didn't sign the following spring and moved on to California after one season, working primarily in middle relief. Undrafted as a junior despite leading the Bears with eight wins, he had a much better season in 2001 while increasing the velocity on his fastball from 87-90 to 92-93 mph. Cash complements it with a plus slider, improved curveball and a changeup that he has shown decent feel for. His maturity and polish convinced the Giants to put him on the fast track, and he responded by averaging 10.6 strikeouts per nine innings while debuting in high Class A. He has good arm strength and profiles as a middle reliever. He should start this year in Double-A.

Year	Club (League)	Class	W	L	ERA	G	GS	CG	SV	IP	H	R	ER	BB	SO
2001	San Jose (Cal)	A	4	0	2.08	20	0	0	1	39	23	9	9	17	46
MINOR LEAGUE TOTALS			4	0	2.08	20	0	0	1	39	23	9	9	17	46

25. Luke Anderson, rhp

Born: April 9, 1978. **Ht.:** 6-5. **Wt.:** 210. **Bats:** R. **Throws:** R. **School:** University of Nevada-Las Vegas. **Career Transactions:** Selected by Giants in 18th round of 2000 draft; signed June 11, 2000.

In a system with several hard-throwing closers, Anderson stands out because he is different. His fastball, which has reached the high 80s in the past and touched 90-91 mph, more often was in the mid-80s last year. Despite his drop in velocity, he continued to rack up impressive strikeout numbers thanks to a hard splitter that he can throw for strikes or send tumbling out of the zone. Because he has plus command of both pitches and aggressively goes after hitters, Anderson stays ahead in the count and doesn't give in. He'll have to develop a better breaking ball to offset lefthanded hitters, who batted .281 against him. The Giants would like to see his old velocity or more movement on his fastball. He hasn't had to go deep into games and will need to prove he can be more than a one-inning pitcher. Still, his splitter is good enough that Anderson soon could work his way into a big league setup role.

Year	Club (League)	Class	W	L	ERA	G	GS	CG	SV	IP	H	R	ER	BB	SO
2000	Salem-Keizer (NWL)	A	1	0	1.45	25	0	0	12	31	19	5	5	10	55
2001	San Jose (Cal)	A	2	2	2.59	59	0	0	30	66	56	22	19	13	76
MINOR LEAGUE TOTALS			3	2	2.23	84	0	0	42	97	75	27	24	23	131

26. Jackson Markert, rhp

Born: Feb. 9, 1979. **Ht.:** 6-6. **Wt.:** 215. **Bats:** R. **Throws:** R. **School:** Oral Roberts University. **Career Transactions:** Selected by Giants in 11th round of 2000 draft; signed June 11, 2000.

Markert's 39 saves last year represented the ninth-highest total in minor league history, and he won the minor league edition of the Rolaids Relief Man award. However, of the closers who have surpassed his total in the minors, only Mike Perez and Steve Reed had significant big league careers. The saves don't get the Giants excited, though Markert's stuff does. He has a hard sinker that regularly reaches 93 mph, and San Francisco's think he'll throw harder with weight training. He gets good leverage on the sinker, though he could do more in that regard. Markert's out pitch is a splitter, which he uses to induce plenty of ground balls. He must keep the ball down to be effective. His strikeout numbers were better in his short-season debut, and the organization wants to see if he can develop a third pitch to help him miss more bats. A third pitch also could lead to a move to the rotation, though Markert is likely to close in high Class A in 2002.

Year	Club (League)	Class	W	L	ERA	G	GS	CG	SV	IP	H	R	ER	BB	SO
2000	Salem-Keizer (NWL)	A	3	1	2.27	21	0	0	6	36	28	9	9	15	38
2001	Hagerstown (SAL)	A	3	3	2.82	58	0	0	39	61	57	26	19	18	45
MINOR LEAGUE TOTALS			6	4	2.62	79	0	0	45	96	85	35	28	33	83

27. Leonel Cabrera, 2b/ss

Born: Jan. 10, 1981. **Ht.:** 6-1. **Wt.:** 177. **Bats:** R. **Throws:** R. **Career Transactions:** Signed out of Dominican Republic by Giants, May 20, 1998.

The Giants have brought Cabrera along slowly, giving him two years in the Dominican Summer League and two more in the Rookie-level Arizona League. Though he played primarily second base last summer, he spent the fall working at shortstop and has played seven positions overall, giving San Francisco a versatile young athlete. Cabrera has offensive potential, showing the ability to play the small game and use his speed. He also has improved his ability to stay inside the ball and drive pitches. Cabrera has gotten stronger since signing and needs to keep doing so. The Giants consider him the most dedicated Latin American player in the system and a role model for other youngsters following him from the Dominican. He should get a chance to show his skills in full-season ball this year at Hagerstown.

Year	Club (League)	Class	AVG	G	AB	R	H	2B	3B	HR	RBI	BB	SO	SB
1998	Giants (DSL)	R	.226	37	106	8	24	4	1	0	4	8	20	1
1999	Giants (DSL)	R	.309	65	246	34	76	10	1	0	37	13	36	18
2000	Giants (AZL)	R	.295	39	112	14	33	6	2	0	9	5	17	6
2001	Giants (AZL)	R	.322	46	205	45	66	14	2	1	31	6	22	12
	Hagerstown (SAL)	A	.300	10	30	8	9	1	0	0	1	1	7	3
MINOR LEAGUE TOTALS			.298	197	699	109	208	35	6	1	82	33	102	40

28. Justin Knoedler, rhp

Born: July 17, 1980. **Ht.:** 6-2. **Wt.:** 210. **Bats:** R. **Throws:** R. **School:** Miami (Ohio) University. **Career Transactions:** Selected by Giants in fifth round of 2001 draft; signed June 20, 2001.

The Giants have built their pitching depth by finding hard throwers in less-than-obvious places, often with later draft picks or converted players. They found Knoedler, who played alongside his twin brother Jason in college, behind the plate. Drafted in the 41st round in 1998 out of high school and again in the 13th round out of junior college in 1999, Knoedler was the National Junior College Athletic Association Division II player of the year for Lincoln Land (Ill.) Community College in 2000. Justin was the more highly touted Knoedler before they transferred to Miami (Ohio), but Jason had the bigger year for the RedHawks, hitting .402, earning second-team All-America honors and getting drafted in the sixth round by the Tigers. Justin hit .283-9-25 as a catcher for Miami and also made 14 appearances as a reliever, compiling a 7.02 ERA. The Giants preferred his strong arm and immediately moved him to the mound full-time. Knoedler has one of the system's better fastballs in terms of velocity, 93-96 mph, and his athleticism helps him throw strikes. He'll need to flesh out the rest of his repertoire, which he'll work on this year in low Class A.

Year	Club (League)	Class	W	L	ERA	G	GS	CG	SV	IP	H	R	ER	BB	SO
2001	Salem-Keizer (NWL)	A	1	1	1.26	13	0	0	1	29	22	4	4	9	38
MINOR LEAGUE TOTALS			1	1	1.26	13	0	0	1	29	22	4	4	9	38

29. Wesley Hutchison, rhp

Born: May 31, 1979. **Ht.:** 6-3. **Wt.:** 200. **Bats:** R. **Throws:** R. **School:** Lewis Clark-State (Idaho) College. **Career Transactions:** Selected by Giants in 10th round of 2001 draft; signed June 9, 2001.

Hutchison continues the Giants' long association with Idaho's NAIA powerhouse, Lewis-Clark State. Longtime Warriors coach Ed Cheff and area scout John Shafer, who has worked the region for the Giants for more than 20 years, have an excellent relationship. Five Giants big leaguers have had ties to Cheff's program, including current outfielder Marvin Benard. Hutchison and Giants outfield prospect Jason Ellison are the best bets to join that fraternity in the future. Hutchison was the MVP of the 2000 NAIA World Series as the Warriors' closer, and he acquitted himself well in that role in his pro debut last year as Salem-Keizer won the Northwest League title. Hutchison has three pitches—a low-90s fastball, plus slider (his best pitch) and developing changeup—so he may not be limited to the bullpen. He worked in both roles in college and Hutchison could move into the low Class A rotation with a good spring. His versatility figures to be an asset as his career moves along.

Year	Club (League)	Class	W	L	ERA	G	GS	CG	SV	IP	H	R	ER	BB	SO
2001	Salem-Keizer (NWL)	A	6	2	1.64	25	0	0	10	33	21	8	6	14	45
MINOR LEAGUE TOTALS			6	2	1.64	25	0	0	10	33	21	8	6	14	45

30. Nelson Castro, ss/2b

Born: June 4, 1976. **Ht.:** 5-10. **Wt.:** 190. **Bats:** B. **Throws:** R. **Career Transactions:** Signed out of Dominican Republic by Angels, Jan. 14, 1994 . . . Claimed on waivers by Giants from Angels, Oct. 13, 1999.

Castro reminds the Giants in part of where they've been as an organization, and also where they need improvement. Picked up off waivers from the Angels, he has become one of the organization's most effective middle infielders, spending 2001 as the everyday shortstop in Double-A before getting a short trial at second base in Triple-A. Castro's best tools are his arm, which the organization grades as a 75 on the 20-to-80 scouting scale, and his speed. He showed offensive improvement at Shreveport, hitting for more power than in the past, but he strikes out too much to expect that power to play at higher levels. Castro's play is erratic at the plate and in the field, which makes him unlikely to be a big league starter. He makes careless mistakes that drive managers crazy. His tools are too much to ignore, though, and the Giants hope to turn him into a utilityman extraordinaire, adding center field to his repertoire. Down the line, they think he can fill the role Shawon Dunston has played for them in recent years.

Year	Club (League)	Class	AVG	G	AB	R	H	2B	3B	HR	RBI	BB	SO	SB
1994	Angels (DSL)	R	.254	59	205	44	52	6	1	1	33	38	28	15
1995	Angels (AZL)	R	.195	55	190	34	37	1	2	0	22	27	50	15
1996	Boise (NWL)	A	.000	1	1	0	0	0	0	0	0	0	0	0
	Angels (AZL)	R	.204	53	186	31	38	4	3	3	14	32	42	25
1997	Boise (NWL)	A	.294	69	293	74	86	16	1	7	37	38	53	26
1998	Lake Elsinore (Cal)	A	.234	131	470	73	110	16	7	4	41	40	101	36
1999	Lake Elsinore (Cal)	A	.250	125	444	68	111	16	12	1	50	36	75	53
2000	Bakersfield (Cal)	A	.284	53	218	38	62	14	3	5	41	20	40	27
	Fresno (PCL)	AAA	.254	67	244	27	62	7	2	5	20	14	51	10
2001	Shreveport (TL)	AA	.296	122	479	76	142	27	6	11	60	42	122	38
	Fresno (PCL)	AAA	.130	6	23	3	3	1	0	0	1	1	5	0
MINOR LEAGUE TOTALS			.255	741	2753	468	703	108	37	37	319	288	567	245

Year	Club (League)	Class	W	L	ERA	G	GS	CG	SV	IP	H	R	ER	BB	SO
1994	Angels (DSL)	R	3	5	2.27	15	12	2	1	83	82	34	21	21	56
1995	Angels (DSL)	R	1	0	1.80	3	0	0	1	5	3	1	1	2	2
MINOR LEAGUE TOTALS			4	5	2.24	18	12	2	2	88	85	35	22	23	58

SEATTLE
Mariners

TOP 30 PROSPECTS

1. Ryan Anderson, lhp
2. Rafael Soriano, rhp
3. Antonio Perez, ss
4. Chris Snelling, of
5. Clint Nageotte, rhp
6. Jeff Heaverlo, rhp
7. Shin-Soo Choo, of
8. Ryan Christianson, c
9. Jamal Strong, of
10. Matt Thornton, lhp
11. Kenny Kelly, of
12. Rett Johnson, rhp
13. Aaron Taylor, rhp
14. Derrick Van Dusen, lhp
15. Craig Anderson, lhp
16. J.J. Putz, rhp
17. Michael Wilson, of
18. Michael Garciaparra, ss
19. Allan Simpson, rhp
20. Gustavo Martinez, rhp
21. Rene Rivera, c
22. Tim Merritt, 2b/ss
23. Jose Lopez, ss
24. Wascar Serrano, rhp
25. Pedro Liriano, 2b
26. Willie Bloomquist, ss/2b
27. Travis Blackley, lhp
28. Cha Seung Baek, rhp
29. Justin Kaye, rhp
30. Julio Mateo, rhp

By Jim Callis

Even without winning the World Series, the Mariners had just about a perfect season in 2001. After Alex Rodriguez followed Randy Johnson and Ken Griffey out of Seattle, the club tied a big league record with 116 victories. Leading the charge was Ichiro Suzuki, the first Japanese position player in the majors—and the second man to be American League MVP and rookie of the year in the same season.

Not only did Ichiro personify the organization's major league success, but he also symbolized its resourcefulness in acquiring talent. Seattle paid $13.125 million for his negotiating rights, and another $14.088 million to sign him. The Mariners have spanned the globe and made other prudent (and less expensive) investments to build one of the game's best farm systems. They also combine winning and development in the minors as well as any organization.

Seattle's affiliates led baseball with a .577 combined winning percentage in 2000 and ranked third at .560 last year. Five of its six clubs made their league playoffs in 2001, with Tacoma sharing the Triple-A Pacific Coast League championship. Meanwhile, the Mariners joined the Braves as the only organizations with 10 players on Baseball America's minor league Top 10 Prospects lists.

Seattle also continued to add to its vast base of talent. The club took some gambles in the draft but believes players such as first-round pick Michael Garciaparra will pay off. The Mariners also signed pitchers out of China and Russia, and witnessed the U.S. debuts of prospects from Australia (Travis Blackley), Colombia (Emiliano Fruto), Korea (Shin-Soo Choo) and Venezuela (Roman Cordova and Jose Lopez). They're stacked at every position except corner infielders.

Not quite everything went right for the Mariners in 2001. Lefthander Ryan Anderson and shortstop Antonio Perez were the game's top prospects at their positions before they missed virtually the entire year to injuries. Korean righthander Cha Seung Baek had Tommy John surgery during the summer, while Blackley broke his pitching elbow in instructional league. Seattle also lost four players in December's major league Rule 5 draft.

The Mariners may never approach 116 victories again, because that kind of magic can't be bottled. But with everything they have in place, it will be a bigger upset if they don't contend for years in the AL West.

Organization Overview

General manager: Pat Gillick. Farm director: Benny Looper. Scouting director: Frank Mattox.

2001 PERFORMANCE

Class	Team	League	W	L	Pct.	Finish*	Manager
Majors	Seattle	American	116	46	.716	1st (30)	Lou Piniella
Triple-A	Tacoma Rainiers	Pacific Coast	85	59	.590	1st (16)	Dan Rohn
Double-A	San Antonio Missions	Texas	70	67	.511	3rd (8)	Dave Brundage
High A	San Bernardino Stampede	California	76	64	.543	3rd (10)	Daren Brown
Low A	Wisconsin Timber Rattlers	Midwest	84	52	.618	2nd (14)	Gary Thurman
Short-season	Everett AquaSox	Northwest	36	39	.480	5th (8)	Terry Pollreisz
Rookie	AZL Mariners	Arizona	34	22	.607	2nd (7)	Omer Munoz
OVERALL 2001 MINOR LEAGUE RECORD			385	303	.560	3rd (30)	

*Finish in overall standings (No. of teams in league)

ORGANIZATION LEADERS

BATTING
*AVG	Chris Snelling, San Bernardino	.336
R	Jamal Strong, San Bern./Wisconsin	115
H	Jamal Strong, San Bern./Wisconsin	168
TB	Juan Thomas, Tacoma	263
2B	Chad Alexander, Tacoma	45
3B	**Jaime Bubela**, Wisconsin	12
HR	Juan Thomas, Tacoma	23
RBI	Juan Thomas, Tacoma	95
BB	Jamal Strong, San Bern./Wisconsin	91
SO	Justin Leone, San Bernardino	158
SB	Jamal Strong, San Bern./Wisconsin	82

PITCHING
W	Denny Stark, Tacoma/San Antonio	15
L	Rob Ramsay, Tacoma	11
	Aaron Looper, San Bernardino	11
#ERA	Jared Hoerman, San Bern./Wisconsin	1.89
G	Kevin Gryboski, Tacoma	58
CG	Greg Wooten, Tacoma	5
SV	Julio Mateo, San Bernardino	26
IP	**Craig Anderson**, San Bernardino	179
BB	Rett Johnson, San Bern./Wisconsin	63
SO	Matt Thornton, San Bernardino	192

*Minimum 250 At-Bats #Minimum 75 Innings

TOP PROSPECTS OF THE DECADE
1992	Roger Salkeld, rhp
1993	Marc Newfield, of
1994	Alex Rodriguez, ss
1995	Alex Rodriguez, ss
1996	Jose Cruz Jr., of
1997	Jose Cruz Jr., of
1998	Ryan Anderson, lhp
1999	Ryan Anderson, lhp
2000	Ryan Anderson, lhp
2001	Ryan Anderson, lhp

TOP DRAFT PICKS OF THE DECADE
1992	Ron Villone, lhp
1993	Alex Rodriguez, ss
1994	Jason Varitek, c
1995	Jose Cruz Jr., of
1996	Gil Meche, rhp
1997	Ryan Anderson, lhp
1998	Matt Thornton, lhp
1999	Ryan Christianson, c
2000	Sam Hays, lhp (4)
2001	Michael Garciaparra, ss

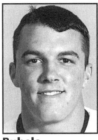 

Bubela   **Anderson**

BEST TOOLS
Best Hitter for Average	Chris Snelling
Best Power Hitter	Shin-Soo Choo
Fastest Baserunner	Jamal Strong
Best Fastball	Ryan Anderson
Best Breaking Ball	Clint Nageotte
Best Changeup	Craig Anderson
Best Control	Craig Anderson
Best Defensive Catcher	Ryan Christianson
Best Defensive Infielder	Antonio Perez
Best Infield Arm	Antonio Perez
Best Defensive Outfielder	Chris Snelling
Best Outfield Arm	Shin-Soo Choo

PROJECTED 2005 LINEUP
Catcher	Ryan Christianson
First Base	John Olerud
Second Base	Bret Boone
Third Base	Jeff Cirillo
Shortstop	Antonio Perez
Left Field	Chris Snelling
Center Field	Mike Cameron
Right Field	Ichiro Suzuki
Designated Hitter	Shin-Soo Choo
No. 1 Starter	Freddy Garcia
No. 2 Starter	Ryan Anderson
No. 3 Starter	Rafael Soriano
No. 4 Starter	Joel Pineiro
No. 5 Starter	Clint Nageotte
Closer	Kazuhiro Sasaki

ALL-TIME LARGEST BONUSES
Ichiro Suzuki, 2000	$5,000,000
Ryan Anderson, 1997	$2,175,000
Ryan Christianson, 1999	$2,100,000
Kazuhiro Sasaki, 2000	$2,000,000
Michael Garciaparra, 2001	$2,000,000

DraftAnalysis

2001 Draft

Best Pro Debut: 2B Tim Merritt (3) was a short-season Northwest League all-star, batting .306-5-30 with 11 steals while making a smooth transition from shortstop.

Best Athlete: Seattle signed two of the best athletes and football players in the draft in OFs Matthew Ware (21) and Michael Wilson (2). Ware ran track as a high school junior and senior, and his best sport is football, as he started at cornerback for UCLA as a freshman. Wilson could have been a first-round pick had he not been a linebacker thought to be on the way to Oklahoma. Wilson, who gave up the gridiron, is more refined than Ware. SS **Michael Garciaparra** (1), Nomar's brother, excelled in baseball, football and soccer in high school. He was the biggest surprise in the first round, as several teams didn't have him on their draft board because they hadn't seen him. Seattle raves about his tools and his desire.

Best Hitter: 2B John Cole (5) hit .418 for Nebraska's College World Series team but sustained a stress fracture in his knee to shorten his pro debut. He later blew out his elbow and is expected to miss the entire 2002 season after Tommy John surgery. Merritt also is a gifted hitter.

Best Raw Power: Wilson or 3B Jonathan Nelson (26), who was on a Mormon mission and like Ware he hasn't played in two years.

Fastest Runner: Ware can blaze through a 60-yard dash in 6.38 seconds.

Best Defensive Player: SS Jeff Ellena (8) is a scrapper with soft hands and plus range. His arm might be a little short, but he'll get every chance to prove otherwise.

Best Fastball: Seattle signed just six pitchers, and LHP Bobby Livingston (4) has the best velocity at 91-92 mph. If 6-foot-10 RHP Justin Ockerman (6) ever improves his mechanics, he could blow by Livingston.

Most Intriguing Background: Garciaparra isn't the only draftee with a baseball relative. Unsigned OF Trevor Heid's (34) father Ted supervises Pacific Rim operations for

Garciaparra

the Mariners. Unsigned OF Marquis Pettis (40) is the son of Seattle scout Stacey and the nephew of ex-big leaguer Gary.

Closest To The Majors: Merritt is ahead of Cole because of his injuries.

Best Late-Round Pick: Nelson and Ware, though it may be difficult to keep the latter away from the NFL.

The One Who Got Away: The Mariners were close to signing Canada's top prospect, RHP John Axford (7), but he ultimately decided to join Notre Dame's banner recruiting class.

Assessment: In a draft heavy on pitching, Seattle targeted position players and athletes. While many teams considered Garciaparra a reach, the Mariners got a first-round talent in Wilson and bolstered their catching depth with Rene Rivera (2) and Lazaro Abreu (3).

2000 Draft

Even without picks in the first three rounds and LHP Sam Hays (4), getting off to a slow start as a pro, Seattle found talent. OF Jamal Strong (6), RHP Rett Johnson (8) and LHP Derrick Van Dusen (5) all are advanced prospects.   **Grade: B+**

1999 Draft

RHPs Clint Nageotte (5) and Jeff Heaverlo (1) have a good chance to be in a future rotation, throwing to C Ryan Christianson (1). RHP J.J. Putz (6) and SS/2B Willie Bloomquist (3) are organization favorites.   **Grade: B+**

1998 Draft

LHP Matt Thornton was a shocking first-round pick but finally began to justify the selection in 2001. Another promising southpaw, Andy Van Hekken (3), went to Detroit in an ill-advised trade for Brian Hunter. And yet another southpaw, John Rheinecker (30), didn't sign and became a first-rounder three years later.   **Grade: C**

1997 Draft

Ryan Anderson (1) remains the minors' best lefty prospect despite missing all of 2001 after shoulder surgery. RHP Joel Pineiro (12) was a revelation last season.   **Grade: A**

Note: Draft analysis prepared by Jim Callis. Numbers in parentheses indicate draft rounds.

. . . With his stuff, there's no question Anderson can become a legitimate No. 1 starter.

Ryan
Anderson lhp

Born: July 12, 1979.
Ht.: 6-10. **Wt.:** 215.
Bats: L. **Throws:** L.
School: Divine Child HS, Dearborn, Mich.
Career Transactions: Selected by Mariners in first round (19th overall) of 1997 draft; signed Sept. 10, 1997.

Anderson has ranked No. 1 on this list for five consecutive seasons. He didn't figure to be eligible again because he was expected to lose his rookie status in 2001. But while the game's other great left-hander prospect, C.C. Sabathia, was winning 17 games for Cleveland, Anderson didn't take the mound during the regular season. He couldn't get loose during a spring workout and was diagnosed with a torn labrum, requiring shoulder surgery that kept him out until instructional league. It was a blow to an organization that had just lost another rotation candidate, Gil Meche, to a similar injury the month before.

Few players can match Anderson's ceiling. The only left-hander in baseball who's more intimidating is Randy Johnson, to whom he's often compared. Anderson isn't nicknamed "Little Unit" for nothing. He has a 94-97 mph fastball that he has used to average 11.9 strikeouts per nine innings as a pro. He was refining his slider into a plus pitch and developing his changeup before he got hurt. He also had improved his command each season. With his stuff, there's no question Anderson can become a legitimate No. 1 starter. He should be stronger than ever once his rehabilitation is complete.

Anderson's latest step was to throw in the bullpen in instructional league, so he still hasn't come all the way back. He also came down with shoulder tendinitis at the end of 2000, costing him any chance of making the U.S. Olympic team. His career record is just 20-26 because he's never put together an extended run of dominance. Anderson still has to improve his secondary pitches and control, though he did hold his own in Triple-A before he reached the legal drinking age. Lefthanders shouldn't stand a chance against him, but they've hit .329 since he reached Double-A.

The Mariners aren't going to take any chances with Anderson. He'll report early to spring training. He won't be in the running for a rotation spot and may open the year in Double-A San Antonio, where the climate is warmer than in Triple-A Tacoma. He'll be kept on tight pitch counts wherever he goes. His future is still bright, though he won't have much if any major league impact before 2003.

Year	Club (League)	Class	W	L	ERA	G	GS	CG	SV	IP	H	R	ER	BB	SO
1998	Wisconsin (Mid)	A	6	5	3.23	22	22	0	0	111	86	47	40	67	152
1999	New Haven (EL)	AA	9	13	4.50	24	24	0	0	134	131	77	67	86	162
2000	Tacoma (PCL)	AAA	5	8	3.98	20	20	1	0	104	83	51	46	55	146
2001							Did Not Play—Injured								
MINOR LEAGUE TOTALS			20	26	3.94	66	66	1	0	349	300	175	153	208	460

2. Rafael Soriano, rhp

Born: Dec. 19, 1979. **Ht.:** 6-1. **Wt.:** 175. **Bats:** R. **Throws:** R. **Career Transactions:** Signed out of Dominican Republic by Mariners, Aug. 30, 1996.

Soriano spent two years in the Rookie-level Arizona League as an out-fielder, hitting .220 while his best tool clearly was his arm. Converted to the mound in 1999, he has been a quick learner. Last year he held hitters to a .174 average, second behind only Josh Beckett among minor league starters. Soriano's arm is nearly as live as Ryan Anderson's. His mid-90s fastball and hard slider give him two plus pitches. He's not a finished product by any means, but he has good polish considering his experi-ence. That's especially true of his mechanics. He's still refining his changeup, but Soriano has made strides toward adding the third pitch he'll need as a starter. His control also needs tweaking. He missed the final three weeks of 2001 with a shoulder impingement after pitch-ing a career-high 137 innings, so his durability is slightly in question. Based on his stuff, Soriano could go to Triple-A, but the Mariners may start him in Double-A this year so he can focus on his approach to pitching. He could be competing for a big league job in 2003.

Year	Club (League)	Class	AVG	G	AB	R	H	2B	3B	HR	RBI	BB	SO	SB
1997	Mariners (AZL)	R	.269	38	119	19	32	3	2	0	12	14	31	7
1998	Mariners (AZL)	R	.167	32	108	17	18	4	0	0	6	11	34	5
MINOR LEAGUE TOTALS			.220	70	227	36	50	7	2	0	18	25	65	12

Year	Club (League)	Class	W	L	ERA	G	GS	CG	SV	IP	H	R	ER	BB	SO
1999	Everett (NWL)	A	5	4	3.11	14	14	0	0	75	56	34	26	49	83
2000	Wisconsin (Mid)	A	8	4	2.87	21	21	1	0	122	97	41	39	50	90
2001	San Bernardino (Cal)	A	6	3	2.53	15	15	2	0	89	49	28	25	39	98
	San Antonio (TL)	AA	2	2	3.35	8	8	0	0	48	34	18	18	14	53
MINOR LEAGUE TOTALS			21	13	2.90	58	58	3	0	335	236	121	108	152	324

3. Antonio Perez, ss

Born: July 26, 1981. **Ht.:** 5-11. **Wt.:** 175. **Bats:** R. **Throws:** R. **Career Transactions:** Signed out of Dominican Republic by Reds, March 21, 1998 . . . Traded by Reds with RHP Jake Meyer, OF Mike Cameron and RHP Brett Tomko to Mariners for OF Ken Griffey, Feb. 10, 2000.

When the Mariners traded Ken Griffey, they wanted an infielder as part of the package. Cincinnati refused to give up Pokey Reese (who was not offered a contract this winter) or Gookie Dawkins (who hit .226 in Double-A this year), so Seattle wound up with Perez. He blossomed into a blue-chip prospect in 2000, but played just five games last year because he had a broken navicular bone in his right wrist. Perez is a rare five-tool shortstop. He can hit for average and power—he led the high Class A California League in slugging as a teenager—and has basestealing speed. His strong arm, soft hands and range to both sides make him the best defensive shortstop in the organization, including the majors. Perez let success get to his head and arrived out of shape for spring training last year. He still has to work on little things, such as making more contact, getting better reads and jumps as a basestealer and improving his defensive footwork. Though he lost 2001 to an injury sustained in winter ball, Perez is still well ahead of the development curve. He'll spend this year in Double-A at age 20.

Year	Club (League)	Class	AVG	G	AB	R	H	2B	3B	HR	RBI	BB	SO	SB
1998	Reds (DSL)	R	.255	63	212	57	54	11	0	2	24	53	33	58
1999	Rockford (Mid)	A	.288	119	385	69	111	20	3	7	41	43	80	35
2000	Lancaster (Cal)	A	.276	98	395	90	109	36	6	17	63	58	99	28
2001	San Antonio (TL)	AA	.143	5	21	3	3	0	0	0	0	0	7	0
MINOR LEAGUE TOTALS			.273	285	1013	219	277	67	9	26	128	154	219	121

4. Chris Snelling, of

Born: Dec. 3, 1981. **Ht.:** 5-10. **Wt.:** 165. **Bats:** L. **Throws:** L. **Career Transactions:** Signed out of Australia by Mariners, March 2, 1999.

Some Mariners officials thought Snelling was undersized when they signed him, but he has played big since arriving in the United States. A member of Australia's 2000 Olympic team, he was rated the best position prospect in the low Class A Midwest League that year. Last season he won the California League batting title while playing through a stress fracture in his right ankle. Hitters don't come much more pure than Snelling, but his best attributes might be his confidence and instincts. He has no trouble making hard contact or handling lefthanders. Despite just average speed, he's a terrific center fielder because he gets tremendous jumps and takes direct routes to balls. He has enough arm to play in right. Snelling often gets compared to Lenny Dykstra, and like Dykstra he plays so aggressively that he beats himself up. He broke his hand and injured his wrist diving into a wall in 2000, then hurt his ankle last year. While he has good gap power, he may not hit more than 15-20 homers a season in the majors. Though Seattle has promoted Snelling aggressively, he hasn't been fazed. Don't bet against him reaching Triple-A this year or challenging for a big league job in 2003.

Year	Club (League)	Class	AVG	G	AB	R	H	2B	3B	HR	RBI	BB	SO	SB
1999	Everett (NWL)	A	.306	69	265	46	81	15	3	10	50	33	24	8
2000	Wisconsin (Mid)	A	.305	72	259	44	79	9	5	9	56	34	34	7
2001	San Bernardino (Cal)	A	.336	114	450	90	151	29	10	7	73	45	63	12
MINOR LEAGUE TOTALS			.319	255	974	180	311	53	18	26	179	112	121	27

5. Clint Nageotte, rhp

Born: Oct. 25, 1980. **Ht.:** 6-4. **Wt.:** 200. **Bats:** R. **Throws:** R. **School:** Brooklyn HS, Cleveland. **Career Transactions:** Selected by Mariners in fifth round of 1999 draft; signed Aug. 18, 1999.

A basketball star in high school, Nageotte signed too late in 1999 to play that summer. He has made up for lost time, winning the one-game playoff in the Arizona League in 2000 and ranking as the top pitching prospect in the Midwest League last year. He led the MWL in strikeouts and strikeouts per nine innings (11.0). Nageotte had the best stuff in a prospect-laden Wisconsin rotation that also featured Rett Johnson and Derrick Van Dusen. Nageotte's lively low-90s fastball and his wicked slider give him two above-average pitches. Last year he did a nice job of tightening his slider, which had been more slurvy in 2000, and improving his command. Nageotte needs to develop a better changeup so he can combat lefthanders, who hit .263 against him in 2001. He also can refine his control within the strike zone. He must get stronger so he can pitch deeper into games. He had a 2.04 ERA through the first four innings last year, but a 5.33 mark afterward. While some organizations might want to expedite an arm like Nageotte's, the Mariners can be patient because of all the pitching they have. He's ticketed for high Class A in 2002.

Year	Club (League)	Class	W	L	ERA	G	GS	CG	SV	IP	H	R	ER	BB	SO
2000	Mariners (AZL)	R	4	1	2.16	12	7	0	1	50	29	15	12	28	59
2001	Wisconsin (Mid)	A	11	8	3.13	28	26	0	0	152	141	65	53	50	187
MINOR LEAGUE TOTALS			15	9	2.89	40	33	0	1	202	170	80	65	78	246

6. Jeff Heaverlo, rhp

Born: Jan. 13, 1978. **Ht.:** 6-1. **Wt.:** 185. **Bats:** R. **Throws:** R. **School:** University of Washington. **Career Transactions:** Selected by Mariners in first round (33rd overall) of 1999 draft; signed July 25, 1999.

Of all the players in Seattle's top 10, Heaverlo easily has the least imposing physical gifts. But the son of former big leaguer Dave Heaverlo exudes pitching savvy and is a winner. He led the Double-A Texas League in complete games, shutouts (a minor league-best four) and strikeouts in 2001. Heaverlo just knows how to get batters out. His best pitch is a slider that isn't quite in the same league as Clint Nageotte's. His changeup has improved dramatically since he has signed and will give him a second plus pitch. His fastball has life and average velocity, topping out at 92 mph. With his command and ability to mix his pitches and speeds, his fastball is good enough. Heaverlo's lone weakness last year was lefthanders, who hit .303 against him (compared to .202 by righties). His changeup is the key to doing better in that regard. He probably won't be more than a middle-of-the-rotation starter, though he could be a good one. Once he proves himself in Triple-A, Heaverlo will get a look in Seattle. He's probably first on the list if the Mariners need to pluck a starter out of the minors this season.

Year	Club (League)	Class	W	L	ERA	G	GS	CG	SV	IP	H	R	ER	BB	SO
1999	Everett (NWL)	A	1	0	2.08	3	0	0	0	9	5	5	2	2	9
	Wisconsin (Mid)	A	1	0	2.55	3	3	1	0	18	15	6	5	7	24
2000	Lancaster (Cal)	A	14	6	4.22	27	27	0	0	156	170	84	73	52	159
	Tacoma (PCL)	AAA	0	1	4.85	2	2	0	0	13	14	7	7	6	4
2001	San Antonio (TL)	AA	11	6	3.12	27	27	4	0	179	164	75	62	40	173
MINOR LEAGUE TOTALS			27	13	3.59	62	59	5	0	374	368	177	149	107	369

7. Shin-Soo Choo, of

Born: July 30, 1982. **Ht.:** 5-11. **Wt.:** 175. **Bats:** L. **Throws:** L. **Career Transactions:** Signed out of Korea by Mariners, Aug. 14, 2000.

The second player signed by the Mariners out of Korea, Choo attended the same high school as the first, righthander Cha Seung Baek. Seattle didn't have a first-round pick in 2000 and compensated by pouring $1.335 million into signing Choo. He was MVP of the World Junior Championship that summer, beating Team USA twice as Korea won the gold medal. In his pro debut last year, he topped the Arizona League in runs, triples and walks. Though Choo threw in the mid-90s as a left-hander, the Mariners decided he offers even more upside as a center fielder. He's a disciplined hitter with huge power potential. His good speed serves him well as a basestealer and a defender. He's poised, works hard and adapted to the United States very quickly. Choo showed some holes in his swing in the AZL, however. Pitchers started pounding him inside and he struggled to adjust. He needs to work on his jumps and instincts in the outfield. The Mariners promoted Choo for the Midwest League playoffs last year, and he'll return to low Class A in 2002. The system is loaded with center fielders, so he'll probably remain in Wisconsin all year.

Year	Club (League)	Class	AVG	G	AB	R	H	2B	3B	HR	RBI	BB	SO	SB
2001	Mariners (AZL)	R	.302	51	199	51	60	10	10	4	35	34	49	12
	Wisconsin (Mid)	A	.462	3	13	1	6	0	0	0	3	1	3	2
MINOR LEAGUE TOTALS			.311	54	212	52	66	10	10	4	38	35	52	14

8. Ryan Christianson, c

Born: April 21, 1981. **Ht.:** 6-2. **Wt.:** 210. **Bats:** R. **Throws:** R. **School:** Arlington HS, Riverside, Calif. **Career Transactions:** Selected by Mariners in first round (11th overall) of 1999 draft; signed July 18, 1999.

Many high school catchers drafted in the first round turn out to be busts. Christianson is proving to be an exception. He made the best of a difficult situation last year at high Class A San Bernardino, which centered a marketing campaign on him because he grew up 10 miles away in Riverside, Calif. His brother Robby pitched in the Seattle system in 1996-97. Shoulder tendinitis robbed Christianson of arm strength in 2000, but he was healthy again and ranked third in the California League by nailing 38 percent of basestealers last year. Cal League pitcher of the year Matt Thornton credited Christianson with showing him how to break down hitters. Offensively, Christianson has burgeoning power. Some of his doubles will turn into homers as he gets stronger and more experienced, and seven of his 12 longballs came in August. Christianson tends to get pull-conscious. He won't hit for average until he uses the whole field more often and tightens his strike zone. He runs like a catcher. Seattle's offseason trade for Ben Davis doesn't have to pose a roadblock for Christensen if he can make adjustments at the plate. He'll work on that in Double-A this year.

Year	Club (League)	Class	AVG	G	AB	R	H	2B	3B	HR	RBI	BB	SO	SB
1999	Mariners (AZL)	R	.263	11	38	3	10	8	0	0	7	2	12	2
	Everett (NWL)	A	.280	30	107	19	30	7	0	8	17	14	31	3
2000	Wisconsin (Mid)	A	.249	119	418	60	104	20	0	13	59	50	98	1
2001	San Bernardino (Cal)	A	.248	134	528	65	131	42	5	12	85	53	112	3
MINOR LEAGUE TOTALS			.252	294	1091	147	275	77	5	33	168	119	253	9

9. Jamal Strong, of

Born: Aug. 5, 1978. **Ht.:** 5-10. **Wt.:** 180. **Bats:** R. **Throws:** R. **School:** University of Nebraska. **Career Transactions:** Selected by Mariners in sixth round of 2000 draft; signed June 14, 2000.

Named MVP of the short-season Northwest League in his pro debut, Strong proved he was no fluke last year. He was a postseason all-star and a Top 10 Prospect in both the Midwest and California Leagues. He also was host Seattle's representative in the Futures Game and was named the organization's minor league player of the year. Strong is the best leadoff prospect in the game. He ranked second in the minors in runs and steals and fourth in on-base percentage (.436) in 2001. He plays to his strengths, which start with top-of-the-line speed. He hits the ball on the ground, draws walks and is both a prolific and proficient basestealer. His center-field range is also impressive. Strong doesn't have much juice in his bat or in his arm. It's not a huge handicap for his style of offense, though it would be nice if he could sting the ball in the gaps more often. He hasn't thrown well since dislocating his shoulder in college, but compensates by getting to balls quickly and unloading in a hurry. He's ready for Double-A. Strong will have to break through Seattle's glut of outfield talent to earn big league playing time down the road.

Year	Club (League)	Class	AVG	G	AB	R	H	2B	3B	HR	RBI	BB	SO	SB
2000	Everett (NWL)	A	.314	75	296	63	93	7	3	1	28	52	29	60
2001	Wisconsin (Mid)	A	.353	51	184	41	65	12	1	0	19	40	27	35
	San Bernardino (Cal)	A	.311	81	331	74	103	11	2	0	32	51	60	47
MINOR LEAGUE TOTALS			.322	207	811	178	261	30	6	1	79	143	116	142

10. Matt Thornton, lhp

Born: Sept. 15, 1976. **Ht.:** 6-6. **Wt.:** 220. **Bats:** L. **Throws:** L. **School:** Grand Valley State (Mich.) University. **Career Transactions:** Selected by Mariners in first round (22nd overall) of 1998 draft; signed July 3, 1998.

Thornton was a surprise first-round pick in 1998 out of NCAA Division II Grand Valley State, where he was better known as a basketball player. He never won a game in college or in his first two years as a pro, when he was beset by a sore elbow and tricep tendinitis. He finally justified his selection in 2001, when he led the California League in strikeouts and was both the organization's and the circuit's pitcher of the year. Thornton always had a live arm but until last year he lacked the confidence to succeed. His fastball sits at 90-92 mph and has plenty of life, and he can get it by righthanders when he throws it down and in. His slider got a lot better in 2001, making him death on lefties, who batted .208 with no homers in 77 at-bats. The next steps for Thornton are to improve his changeup and his command. There were questions about his durability, but he put those to rest by holding up for 27 starts last year. If he can't master a third pitch, Thornton's fastball and slider alone would make him an intriguing reliever. He'll pitch out of the Double-A rotation in 2002.

Year	Club (League)	Class	W	L	ERA	G	GS	CG	SV	IP	H	R	ER	BB	SO
1998	Everett (NWL)	A	0	0	27.00	2	0	0	0	1	1	4	4	3	0
1999	Wisconsin (Mid)	A	0	0	4.91	25	1	0	1	29	39	19	16	25	34
2000	Wisconsin (Mid)	A	6	9	4.01	26	17	0	0	103	94	59	46	72	88
2001	San Bernardino (Cal)	A	14	7	2.52	27	27	0	0	157	126	56	44	60	192
MINOR LEAGUE TOTALS			20	16	3.40	80	45	0	1	291	260	138	110	160	314

11. Kenny Kelly, of

Born: Jan. 26, 1979. **Ht.:** 6-3. **Wt.:** 180. **Bats:** R. **Throws:** R. **School:** Tampa Catholic HS. **Career Transactions:** Selected by Devil Rays in second round of 1997 draft; signed June 12, 1997 . . . Traded by Devil Rays to Mariners for a player to be named, April 4, 2001.

The Devil Rays' financial difficulties were the Mariners' gain last April. Ken Dorsey's predecessor as the University of Miami's starting quarterback, Kelly gave up football to sign a four-year major league contract worth $2.2 million in February 2000. He followed with a mediocre season in Double-A, and last spring Tampa Bay was looking for ways to save money. The Rays sold Kelly to Seattle for $350,000 and saved another $1.25 million by shedding his contract. He continued to struggle in Double-A, hitting just .223 through July. Then he finished with a flourish, batting .298-7-27 over the final two months and earning all-prospect honors in the Arizona Fall League, where he hit .351-7-21. The Mariners think Kelly's improvement is for real, that all he needed was time to get acclimated to baseball and some subtle adjustments to his swing. He has all the raw tools, including power that has begun to show, exciting speed and a strong arm. He's yet another quality center fielder in an organization loaded with them. Kelly still needs some time in Triple-A to hone his strike-zone judgment and his instincts, but he's not far from being able to contribute in the major leagues.

Year	Club (League)	Class	AVG	G	AB	R	H	2B	3B	HR	RBI	BB	SO	SB
1997	Devil Rays (GCL)	R	.212	27	99	21	21	2	1	2	7	11	24	6
1998	Charleston, SC (SAL)	A	.280	54	218	46	61	7	5	3	17	19	52	19
1999	St. Petersburg (FSL)	A	.277	51	206	39	57	10	4	3	21	18	46	14
2000	Orlando (SL)	AA	.252	124	489	73	123	17	8	3	29	59	119	31
	Tampa Bay (AL)	MAJ	.000	2	1	0	0	0	0	0	0	0	0	0
2001	San Antonio (TL)	AA	.262	121	478	72	125	20	5	11	46	45	111	18
MAJOR LEAGUE TOTALS			.000	2	1	0	0	0	0	0	0	0	0	0
MINOR LEAGUE TOTALS			.260	377	1490	251	387	56	23	22	120	152	352	88

12. Rett Johnson, rhp

Born: July 6, 1979. **Ht.:** 6-2. **Wt.:** 211. **Bats:** L. **Throws:** R. **School:** Coastal Carolina University. **Career Transactions:** Selected by Mariners in eighth round of 2000 draft; signed June 13, 2000.

Johnson set a Coastal Carolina record with 151 strikeouts as a junior in 2000. His 133 innings established another Chanticleers mark, and the workload took a toll on his fastball. When his velocity began to slide before the draft, so did his stock, and the Mariners stole him in the eighth round. Seattle eased him into pro ball as a reliever and put him back in the rotation once his arm bounced back. Johnson held up throughout his first full pro season, during which he pitched well at both Class A levels. He has a 90-93 mph fastball with good life and a quality slider, both of which seem to get better when he has to pitch out of a jam. Teams already are asking for him in trades. Johnson just needs some more innings to work on his changeup and command. If his changeup doesn't come around, his fastball-slider combination will make him an effective reliever. He should reach Double-A in 2002.

Year	Club (League)	Class	W	L	ERA	G	GS	CG	SV	IP	H	R	ER	BB	SO
2000	Everett (NWL)	A	5	4	2.07	17	8	0	0	70	51	26	16	21	88
2001	Wisconsin (Mid)	A	5	5	2.27	16	16	2	0	99	92	33	25	30	96
	San Bernardino (Cal)	A	6	2	4.09	12	12	0	0	66	56	36	30	33	70
MINOR LEAGUE TOTALS			16	11	2.72	45	36	2	0	235	199	95	71	84	254

13. Aaron Taylor, rhp

Born: Aug. 20, 1977. **Ht.:** 6-7. **Wt.:** 230. **Bats:** R. **Throws:** R. **School:** Lowndes HS, Valdosta, Ga. **Career Transactions:** Selected by Braves in 11th round of 1996 draft; signed June 5, 1996 . . . Selected by Mariners from Braves in Rule 5 minor league draft, Dec. 13, 1999 . . . On voluntarily retired list, March 30-June 4, 2001.

Taylor was the organization's biggest surprise in 2001, though that seemed unlikely in spring training. Frustrated at the direction his career was going after posting a 6.26 ERA in five pro seasons, he quit and went home. The Mariners had told him he'd be welcomed back if he changed his mind, which he did a week later. The only problem was that he had been placed on the voluntary retired list, which meant he had to sit out the first 60 days of the season. Taylor returned with a vengeance in the Midwest League, dealing 93-98 mph heat every time out. He intimidated hitters with his size and his fastball, and they didn't exactly relish facing his splitter or newly developed slider. All of a sudden he made the $4,000 Seattle spent to get him from Atlanta in the 1999 Double-A Rule 5 draft look like a bargain. Taylor's control still isn't perfect and at 23 he was old for low Class A. The Mariners love his makeup and are ready to move him quickly. He'll probably begin 2002 in Double-A and could reach Seattle by the end of the season.

Year	Club (League)	Class	W	L	ERA	G	GS	CG	SV	IP	H	R	ER	BB	SO
1996	Braves (GCL)	R	0	9	7.74	13	9	0	0	52	68	54	45	28	33
1997	Danville (Appy)	R	1	8	5.53	15	7	0	0	55	65	49	34	31	38
1998	Danville (Appy)	R	3	6	6.25	14	14	1	0	72	87	60	50	36	55
1999	Macon (SAL)	A	6	7	4.88	27	8	0	1	79	86	56	43	27	78
2000	Everett (NWL)	A	1	4	7.43	15	14	0	0	63	76	54	52	37	57
2001	Wisconsin (Mid)	A	3	1	2.45	28	0	0	9	29	19	9	8	11	50
MINOR LEAGUE TOTALS			14	35	5.94	112	52	1	10	351	401	282	232	170	311

14. Derrick Van Dusen, lhp

Born: June 6, 1981. **Ht.:** 6-2. **Wt.:** 175. **Bats:** L. **Throws:** L. **School:** Riverside (Calif.) CC. **Career Transactions:** Selected by Mariners in fifth round of 2000 draft; signed June 19, 2000.

After pitching Riverside CC to the California community college championship and having a wildly successful pro debut in 2000, baseball wasn't Van Dusen's primary focus at the start of last season. Assigned to Wisconsin, he pitched twice before going home to California to be with his mother, who was dying of cancer. He worked out with San Bernardino, pitching just once more before returning to the Midwest League in mid-June. The highlight of his season came in August, when he threw a 12-strikeout no-hitter against a Cedar Rapids lineup stacked with righthanders. He gets righties out with his slider, his lone plus pitch. His fastball sits in the high 80s and tops out at 92 mph, and his changeup is coming along. He competes very well and aggressively pitches inside. He reminds the Mariners of Andy Van Hekken, a lefty they drafted in the third round in 1998 and traded to the Tigers a year later. Van Dusen has been very stingy with baserunners, holding hitters to a .233 average and posting a 5.3-1 strikeout-walk ratio since turning pro. He just needs to build more confidence in his changeup. He'll return to high Class A under happier circumstances in 2002.

Year	Club (League)	Class	W	L	ERA	G	GS	CG	SV	IP	H	R	ER	BB	SO
2000	Mariners (AZL)	R	6	0	2.63	10	2	0	0	41	38	14	12	6	58
	Everett (NWL)	A	1	1	3.60	4	2	0	0	15	17	13	6	5	24
2001	Wisconsin (Mid)	A	5	4	3.19	18	18	1	0	96	82	40	34	24	103
	San Bernardino (Cal)	A	0	1	5.40	1	1	0	0	3	3	2	2	1	3
MINOR LEAGUE TOTALS			12	6	3.13	33	23	1	0	155	140	69	54	36	188

15. Craig Anderson, lhp

Born: Oct. 30, 1980. **Ht.:** 6-3. **Wt.:** 182. **Bats:** L. **Throws:** L. **Career Transactions:** Signed out of Australia by Mariners, March 2, 1999.

When Mariners vice president Roger Jongewaard and then-Pacific Rim coordinator Jim Colborn made a scouting trip to Australia in 1999, they spotted Anderson and Chris Snelling. Jongewaard liked Snelling, whom Colborn thought was undersized. Colborn preferred Anderson, whom Jongewaard didn't think threw hard enough. Colborn and Jongewaard cut a deal with each other to sign both players, who have had nothing but success in the minors. Anderson earned one of Australia's two victories at the 2000 Olympics. He still has his doubters because he still operates in the mid-80s with his fastball, though he may be starting to satisfy them after his 2001 performance. He turned in his third straight year with double-digit victories while leading the California League in innings and strikeouts. He ripped off 19 consecutive quality starts to finish the regular season. Anderson does it with a great changeup, a good curveball and exquisite command that managers rated as the best in the Cal League. His style earns him comparisons to crafty lefthanders Jimmy Key and Jamie Moyer. Anderson will have to keep proving himself each year but has the moxie to pull it off. He'll be tested in Double-A this season.

Year	Club (League)	Class	W	L	ERA	G	GS	CG	SV	IP	H	R	ER	BB	SO
1999	Everett (NWL)	A	10	2	3.20	15	15	2	0	90	81	42	32	13	82
2000	Wisconsin (Mid)	A	11	8	3.71	26	26	1	0	158	161	81	65	40	131
2001	San Bernardino (Cal)	A	11	4	2.26	28	28	0	0	179	142	65	45	39	178
MINOR LEAGUE TOTALS			32	14	3.00	69	69	3	0	427	384	188	142	92	391

16. J.J. Putz, rhp

Born: Feb. 22, 1977. **Ht.:** 6-5. **Wt.:** 220. **Bats:** R. **Throws:** R. **School:** University of Michigan. **Career Transactions:** Selected by Mariners in sixth round of 1999 draft; signed June 17, 1999.

A White Sox third-round pick out of high school in 1995, Putz chose the University of Michigan over signing. He underachieved for the Wolverines for three years before rebounding late in his senior year to go in the sixth round of the 1999 draft, and signing for only $10,000. Putz pitched a seven-inning no-hitter in low Class A in 2000, then really made an impression last year in spring training. He reported early and got into some split-squad games, and some scouts thought he could have made the big club. The Mariners settled for skipping him a level and sending him to Double-A, and the move rattled his confidence early on. Putz got himself together down the stretch, going 6-3, 2.71 in his final 13 outings to earn a spot on the Mariners 40-man roster. His two best pitches are a low-90s fastball and an average slider. He has a terrific pitcher's body and is strong and durable. Putz still needs some minor league innings to improve his changeup and command, and he'll get them this year in Triple-A.

Year	Club (League)	Class	W	L	ERA	G	GS	CG	SV	IP	H	R	ER	BB	SO
1999	Everett (NWL)	A	0	0	4.84	10	0	0	2	22	23	13	12	11	17
2000	Wisconsin (Mid)	A	12	6	3.15	26	25	3	0	143	130	71	50	63	105
2001	San Antonio (TL)	AA	7	9	3.83	27	26	0	0	148	145	80	63	59	135
MINOR LEAGUE TOTALS			19	15	3.59	63	51	3	2	313	298	164	125	133	257

17. Michael Wilson, of

Born: Sept. 29, 1978. **Ht.:** 6-1. **Wt.:** 205. **Bats:** R. **Throws:** R. **School:** University of Kentucky. **Career Transactions:** Selected by Mets in 11th round of 2000 draft; signed June 19, 2000.

The Mariners signed two football prospects out of the 2001 draft, Wilson in the second round and fellow outfielder Matthew Ware in the 21st. While Ware starred as a UCLA freshman defensive back last fall and seems destined for the NFL, Seattle will hold onto Wilson, who gave up a scholarship to play linebacker for Oklahoma. Signability concerns caused Wilson to slide out of the first round, and he did take most of the summer to negotiate a $900,000 bonus. He's yet another multitooled center-field prospect in an organization already loaded with them. He offers a rare combination of power and speed and was clocked throwing 90 mph as a high school sophomore. He's still very raw because he hasn't concentrated on baseball until now. Wilson will need some time to develop a sound approach at the plate and to get the football stiffness out of his body. He pulled a hamstring in instructional league, so Seattle hasn't been able to work with him much to this point. He'll probably go to extended spring training before making his pro debut in 2002.

Year	Club (League)	Class	AVG	G	AB	R	H	2B	3B	HR	RBI	BB	SO	SB
				Has Not Played—Signed 2002 Contract										

18. Michael Garciaparra, ss

Born: April 2, 1983. **Ht.:** 6-1. **Wt.:** 165. **Bats:** R. **Throws:** R. **School:** Don Bosco Tech HS, Rosemead, Calif. **Career Transactions:** Selected by Mariners in first round (36th overall) of 2001 draft; signed Aug. 20, 2001.

Garciaparra's older brother Nomar already has won two American League batting titles, while Michael was selected with a supplemental first-round pick Seattle received for the loss of free agent Alex Rodriguez. As if that wasn't pressure enough, Garciaparra was the biggest surprise in the 2001 draft, as some teams didn't even list him on their draft boards. A baseball/football/soccer star in high school, he played little baseball as a senior after tearing the anterior cruciate ligament in his knee while making a tackle during the previous fall. The Mariners knew Garciaparra because he had played on their scout team in California since he was a freshman, and area scout Derek Valenzuela (who since has joined the Red Sox) is very close to Nomar. Getting word that Boston might take Michael with the 48th pick, Seattle decided to pop him with the 36th selection. It cost $2 million to steer him away from the University of Tennessee, and the Mariners are confident he'll justify the investment. Michael is bigger and more athletic than Nomar was at the same age. He has gap power and could fit into a lineup as a No. 2 or No. 7 hitter. He'll have to get stronger and already has toyed with switch-hitting. Garciaparra also has the tools and instincts to stay at shortstop as he moves up the ladder. He likely won't make his pro debut until this summer, getting some time in extended spring training beforehand.

Year	Club (League)	Class	AVG	G	AB	R	H	2B	3B	HR	RBI	BB	SO	SB
				Has Not Played—Signed 2002 Contract										

19. Allan Simpson, rhp

Born: Aug. 26, 1977. **Ht.:** 6-4. **Wt.:** 185. **Bats:** R. **Throws:** R. **School:** Taft (Calif.) JC. **Career Transactions:** Selected by Mariners in eighth round of 1997 draft; signed June 3, 1997.

Simpson has blossomed from project to prospect since signing as an eighth-round pick out of Taft (Calif.) CC in 1997. He was just a tall, skinny kid with a projectable fastball and little else when he entered pro ball, and he didn't really find his niche until he repeated high Class A and became a full-time reliever in 2000. Simpson usually pitches at 92-94 mph and hit 96 in the Arizona Fall League, which prompted the Mariners to include him on their 40-man roster last November. His slider gives him a solid second pitch and hitters don't get a good luck at his stuff. They batted just .180 with two homers against him in 2001. The Mariners will give him a look in big league camp, but he's most likely headed for Triple-A.

Year	Club (League)	Class	W	L	ERA	G	GS	CG	SV	IP	H	R	ER	BB	SO
1997	Everett (NWL)	A	0	3	6.84	16	0	0	0	26	26	23	20	24	26
1998	Wisconsin (Mid)	A	3	5	4.44	19	19	0	0	93	89	52	46	61	86
	Mariners (AZL)	R	1	0	0.96	3	0	0	1	9	8	2	1	3	12
1999	Wisconsin (Mid)	A	2	9	4.38	24	13	1	0	90	83	56	44	48	88
	Lancaster (Cal)	A	0	0	6.33	9	0	0	0	21	17	16	15	14	25
2000	Lancaster (Cal)	A	3	2	2.08	46	0	0	6	52	34	17	12	27	67
2001	San Bernardino (Cal)	A	1	0	1.80	16	0	0	1	30	19	7	6	12	40
	San Antonio (TL)	AA	2	1	1.86	22	0	0	9	39	25	8	8	15	37
MINOR LEAGUE TOTALS			12	20	3.79	155	32	1	17	361	301	181	152	204	381

20. Gustavo Martinez, rhp

Born: Nov. 9, 1980. **Ht.:** 6-0. **Wt.:** 175. **Bats:** R. **Throws:** R. **Career Transactions:** Signed out of Dominican Republic by Mariners, June 23, 1998.

Martinez joins Clint Nageotte, Jeff Heaverlo and Matt Thornton as Seattle farmhands who led their leagues in strikeouts last season. He's not a big guy but generates surprising power for his size. His fastball tops out at 93 mph, but his out pitch is a plus-plus slider that ranks right behind Nageotte's and Heaverlo's as the best in the organization.

Martinez has a bulldog mentality, which contributed to him drilling a Northwest League-high 18 batters in 2001. He's not close to being a finished product, because his changeup and command aren't strong and his maximum-effort delivery needs some cleaning up. The Mariners will see how he fares in full-season ball this year before they get truly excited about him.

Year	Club (League)	Class	W	L	ERA	G	GS	CG	SV	IP	H	R	ER	BB	SO
1998	Mariners (DSL)	R	4	4	3.47	12	7	3	1	49	38	26	19	21	57
1999	Mariners (DSL)	R	5	0	0.74	29	1	1	8	73	29	14	6	38	122
2000	Mariners (AZL)	R	6	3	3.59	17	1	0	1	43	42	27	17	25	53
2001	San Antonio (TL)	AA	0	0	1.93	3	0	0	0	9	5	2	2	2	6
	Tacoma (PCL)	AAA	1	0	1.50	1	1	0	0	6	2	1	1	4	7
	Everett (NWL)	A	5	3	2.67	15	15	0	0	84	62	30	25	34	100
MINOR LEAGUE TOTALS			21	10	2.38	77	25	4	10	264	178	100	70	124	345

21. Rene Rivera, c

Born: July 31, 1983. **Ht.:** 5-10. **Wt.:** 190. **Bats:** R. **Throws:** R. **School:** Pope John XXIII HS, Bayamon, P.R. **Career Transactions:** Selected by Mariners in second round of 2001 draft; signed June 14, 2001.

Rivera boosted his stock immensely at a predraft showcase for Puerto Rican prospects last May. Scouts had questioned his bat before he put on a power display, which caused the Mariners to take him with a second-round pick they had gotten from the Rangers as compensation for Alex Rodriguez. Rivera struggled when he was initially sent to the Northwest League, then hit much better once he was demoted to the Rookie-level Arizona League. He'll have to make major improvements to his plate discipline, however. Built along the lines of Pudge Rodriguez, Rivera always has impressed scouts with his solid catch-and-throw skills. He threw out 39 percent of basestealers in his pro debut, showing nimble feet, a quick release and a strong arm. Like most of Seattle's early-round picks from the 2001 draft, he's not quite ready for full-season ball yet.

Year	Club (League)	Class	AVG	G	AB	R	H	2B	3B	HR	RBI	BB	SO	SB
2001	Everett (NWL)	A	.089	15	45	3	4	1	0	2	3	1	19	0
	Mariners (AZL)	R	.338	21	71	13	24	4	0	2	12	2	11	0
MINOR LEAGUE TOTALS			.241	36	116	16	28	5	0	4	15	3	30	0

22. Tim Merritt, 2b/ss

Born: Feb. 7, 1980. **Ht.:** 6-0. **Wt.:** 180. **Bats:** R. **Throws:** R. **School:** University of South Alabama. **Career Transactions:** Selected by Mariners in third round of 2001 draft; signed June 29, 2001.

A third-round pick last June, Merritt is extremely versatile both in terms of his tools and the positions he can play. He has good offensive potential for a middle infielder, and he bounced back from a lackluster junior season at South Alabama by raising his average 24 points once he switched from aluminum bats to wood. He has gap power and runs well enough to steal some bases. However, he could stand to be a little less aggressive at the plate. He played second base at short-season Everett because Jose Lopez was the primary shortstop. Merritt also saw time at shortstop and third base, and he played the outfield in college and with Team USA's college squad. Scouts are divided on whether he can play shortstop at higher levels. With Antonio Perez, Lopez and major league Rule 5 draft acquistion Luis Ugueto on hand, Merritt probably is destined for second base. Nevertheless, the Mariners will try to keep him at shortstop in 2002, which means he'll go to high Class A if Lopez makes the low Class A roster.

Year	Club (League)	Class	AVG	G	AB	R	H	2B	3B	HR	RBI	BB	SO	SB
2001	Everett (NWL)	A	.306	51	196	33	60	13	3	5	30	9	35	11
	Wisconsin (Mid)	A	.308	3	13	1	4	0	0	0	1	0	2	0
MINOR LEAGUE TOTALS			.306	54	209	34	64	13	3	5	31	9	37	11

23. Jose Lopez, ss

Born: Nov. 24, 1983. **Ht.:** 6-2. **Wt.:** 170. **Bats:** R. **Throws:** R. **Career Transactions:** Signed out of Venezuela by Mariners, July 2, 2000.

The Mariners thought so highly of Lopez that they sent him to the Northwest League for his pro debut in 2001. The youngest player in the league, he was also its best defensive shortstop. Lopez has pure actions, great hands, plenty of range and a solid-to-plus arm. Though he wasn't nearly as advanced as most of the pitchers he faced, he held his own at the plate. He showed some gap power and speed, and hitting .256 in his situation must be considered a success. He'll have to get stronger and tighten his strike zone, but the foundation is clearly there. Seattle will continue to be aggressive with his development and may send him to low Class A at age 18 in 2002.

Year	Club (League)	Class	AVG	G	AB	R	H	2B	3B	HR	RBI	BB	SO	SB
2001	Everett (NWL)	A	.256	70	289	42	74	15	0	2	20	13	44	13
MINOR LEAGUE TOTALS			.256	70	289	42	74	15	0	2	20	13	44	13

24. Wascar Serrano, rhp

Born: June 2, 1978. **Ht.:** 6-2. **Wt.:** 180. **Bats:** R. **Throws:** R. **Career Transactions:** Signed out of Dominican Republic by Padres, May 31, 1995 . . . Traded by Padres with C Ben Davis and 3B Alex Arias to Mariners for C Tom Lampkin, RHP Brett Tomko, SS Ramon Vazquez and cash, Dec. 11, 2001.

Serrano entered 2001 ranked as San Diego's No. 3 prospect. He ended it having been traded to the Mariners after hitting the wall in Triple-A for the second straight year. The Padres once figured he'd be in their rotation by now, but decided that his best use would be to help bring them the shortstop (prospect Ramon Vazquez) they've been seeking for a while. Serrano tried to focus on throwing strikes last year, but only had modest success. Worse, the velocity on his fastball dropped from the low to mid-90s down to the high 80s. He didn't make much progress with his slider and changeup. Called up to the majors on three occasions, he got rocked as a starter and hammered even harder as a reliever. San Diego concluded that his best role was in the bullpen, and Seattle concurs. He'll probably get another dose of Triple-A, where he'll try to avoid becoming just another live arm who never rounds out his repertoire.

Year	Club (League)	Class	W	L	ERA	G	GS	CG	SV	IP	H	R	ER	BB	SO
1995	Cubs/Padres (DSL)	R	3	3	3.11	12	7	0	0	46	63	24	16	15	23
1996	Cubs/Padres (DSL)	R	3	7	7.88	22	2	0	1	54	77	58	47	24	44
1997	Idaho Falls (Pio)	R	0	1	11.88	2	2	0	0	8	13	12	11	4	13
	Padres (AZL)	R	6	3	3.18	12	11	0	1	71	60	43	25	22	75
	Clinton (Mid)	A	0	1	6.00	1	1	1	0	6	6	5	4	2	2
1998	Clinton (Mid)	A	9	7	3.22	26	26	0	0	157	150	74	56	54	143
1999	Rancho Cuca. (Cal)	A	9	8	3.33	21	21	1	0	132	110	58	49	43	129
	Mobile (SL)	AA	2	3	5.53	7	7	0	0	42	48	27	26	17	29
2000	Mobile (SL)	AA	9	4	2.80	20	20	1	0	112	93	42	35	42	112
	Las Vegas (PCL)	AAA	0	1	14.18	4	4	0	0	13	24	23	21	10	19
2001	Portland (PCL)	AAA	6	5	4.53	27	13	0	0	93	98	50	47	35	73
	San Diego (NL)	MAJ	3	3	6.56	20	5	0	0	47	60	37	34	21	39
MAJOR LEAGUE TOTALS			3	3	6.56	20	5	0	0	47	60	37	34	21	39
MINOR LEAGUE TOTALS			47	43	4.12	154	114	3	2	735	742	416	337	268	662

25. Pedro Liriano, 2b

Born: Feb. 20, 1982. **Ht.:** 5-11. **Wt.:** 165. **Bats:** R. **Throws:** R. **Career Transactions:** Signed out of Dominican Republic by Mariners, May 30, 1999.

Liriano's performance has far outstripped his tools during his two pro seasons, but his performance simply can't be ignored. In 2000, he became the third player in Arizona League history to bat .400 while leading the Mariners to a championship. He encored by leading all minor league second basemen with a .326 average in 2001, and adding 65 steals in 85 attempts before breaking a bone in his hand on a slide in late August. From a physical standpoint, he's not as impressive. He's not very strong or even very fast, despite his basestealing prowess. He's a slap hitter who excels at making contact but doesn't have outstanding onbase ability. His defense is a concern, as he has stiff hands and has trouble backhanding grounders. He makes too many careless errors. Liriano has made the effort to improve, and it showed this winter when he played in his native Dominican. The Mariners will see how he fares in high Class A in 2002.

Year	Club (League)	Class	AVG	G	AB	R	H	2B	3B	HR	RBI	BB	SO	SB
1999	Mariners (DSL)	R	.367	58	199	63	73	10	3	13	47	55	26	25
2000	Mariners (AZL)	R	.400	43	170	46	68	15	2	1	30	21	11	18
	Everett (NWL)	A	.200	4	15	2	3	0	0	0	2	4	4	4
2001	Wisconsin (Mid)	A	.326	113	442	76	144	28	3	4	47	30	50	65
MINOR LEAGUE TOTALS			.349	218	826	187	288	53	8	18	126	110	91	112

26. Willie Bloomquist, ss/2b

Born: Nov. 27, 1977. **Ht.:** 5-11. **Wt.:** 185. **Bats:** R. **Throws:** R. **School:** Arizona State University. **Career Transactions:** Selected by Mariners in third round of 1999 draft; signed June 10, 1999.

The Mariners couldn't sign Bloomquist as an eighth-round pick out of a Washington high school in 1996, but they got him as a third-rounder three years later after he capped his Arizona State career by being named Pacific-10 Conference player of the year. He was leading the California League with a .379 average in his first full pro season when the Mariners had a hole at Triple-A and promoted him to fill it. His bat tailed off and hasn't recovered, though injuries to both hands over the last two years have been a contributing factor. The best thing about Bloomquist is his makeup, and there isn't a Seattle official who doesn't appreciate him. He's a contact hitter with very little power, and he's not quite as fast as his steals totals would indicate. He doesn't walk very much, so his batting average makes up most of his offensive contribution. He's a steady defender who really belongs at second base, though he played shortstop in Double-A last year because Antonio Perez was hurt. He also played the outfield for the Sun Devils and projects as a utilityman. Slated for Triple-A this year, Bloomquist could have a Rex Hudler-type career.

Year	Club (League)	Class	AVG	G	AB	R	H	2B	3B	HR	RBI	BB	SO	SB
1999	Everett (NWL)	A	.287	42	178	35	51	10	3	2	27	22	25	17
2000	Lancaster (Cal)	A	.379	64	256	63	97	19	6	2	51	37	27	22
	Tacoma (PCL)	AAA	.225	51	191	17	43	5	1	1	23	7	28	5
2001	San Antonio (TL)	AA	.255	123	491	59	125	23	2	0	28	28	55	34
MINOR LEAGUE TOTALS			.283	280	1116	174	316	57	12	5	129	94	135	78

27. Travis Blackley, lhp

Born: Nov. 4, 1982. **Ht.:** 6-3. **Wt.:** 190. **Bats:** L. **Throws:** L. **Career Transactions:** Signed out of Australia by Mariners, Oct. 29, 2000.

While they were scouting Shin-Soo Choo at the 2000 World Junior Championships in Edmonton, the Mariners also saw Blackley. He took the loss against Choo's Korean team, the eventual champions, in the semifinals. Blackley tasted defeat just once last summer in his pro debut despite being one of the youngest pitchers in the Northwest League. He's similar to Australian countryman Craig Anderson, though he's bigger and eventually will throw harder. The bad news is that Blackley fractured his elbow while pitching in instructional league last fall. He had a pin removed from the elbow and won't take the mound until June. Before he got hurt, he had a nice three-pitch mix with a mid-80s fastball, a plus curveball and an average changeup. Like Anderson, he has an advanced feel for pitching. Blackley would have been placed on a similar fast track if he hadn't been injured.

Year	Club (League)	Class	W	L	ERA	G	GS	CG	SV	IP	H	R	ER	BB	SO
2001	Everett (NWL)	A	6	1	3.32	14	14	0	0	79	60	34	29	29	90
MINOR LEAGUE TOTALS			6	1	3.32	14	14	0	0	79	60	34	29	29	90

28. Cha Seung Baek, rhp

Born: May 29, 1980. **Ht.:** 6-4. **Wt.:** 190. **Bats:** R. **Throws:** R. **Career Transactions:** Signed out of Korea by Mariners, Sept. 25, 1998.

Two years before Kazuhiro Sasaki, Shin-Soo Choo and Ichiro Suzuki came aboard, Baek was Seattle's first big-ticket international signing. He accepted a $1.3 million bonus in 1998, when he was considered the top pitching prospect in Korea. He had visa problems in 1999 and a tender elbow in each of his first two pro seasons, limiting his time on the mound. Baek made two starts in 2001 before his elbow began bothering him again. After being shut down for a month, he pitched three more times before tearing a ligament and needing Tommy John surgery. He won't return to the mound until late 2002 at the earliest. Baek had pretty good stuff, including a low-90s fastball and a late-breaking slider, and he was able to throw it for strikes. The Mariners only can hope that he joins the growing number of pitchers who have come back better than ever after Tommy John surgery.

Year	Club (League)	Class	W	L	ERA	G	GS	CG	SV	IP	H	R	ER	BB	SO
1999	Mariners (AZL)	R	3	0	3.67	8	4	0	0	27	30	13	11	6	25
2000	Wisconsin (Mid)	A	8	5	3.95	24	24	0	0	128	137	71	56	36	99
2001	San Bernardino (Cal)	A	1	0	3.43	5	4	0	0	21	17	10	8	2	16
MINOR LEAGUE TOTALS			12	5	3.84	37	32	0	0	176	184	94	75	44	140

29. Justin Kaye, rhp

Born: June 9, 1976. **Ht.:** 6-4. **Wt.:** 195. **Bats:** R. **Throws:** R. **School:** Bishop Gorman HS, Las Vegas. **Career Transactions:** Selected by Mariners in 19th round of 1995 draft; signed June 7, 1995.

The Mariners were able to include Jose Paniagua and Brian Fuentes in the Jeff Cirillo trade with the Rockies because they have several relief prospects knocking on the door of the majors. Kaye is in that group after leading Triple-A Pacific Coast League relievers in hits (6.0) and strikeouts (12.5) per nine innings in 2001. He made little progress in his first four years in the system, which included an ill-fated stint as a starter, before breaking through in Double-A in 2000. His hard slider is an out pitch that he easily throws for strikes. He has less control of his average fastball, which has some sink. He occasionally mixes in a changeup to keep hitters off balance. If Kaye can command his fastball in big league camp, he could open the season in Seattle.

Year	Club (League)	Class	W	L	ERA	G	GS	CG	SV	IP	H	R	ER	BB	SO
1995	Mariners (AZL)	R	0	1	10.71	12	0	0	0	19	33	28	23	19	13
1996	Mariners (AZL)	R	1	0	3.62	20	0	0	3	32	34	23	13	19	36
1997	Wisconsin (Mid)	A	8	12	7.30	28	26	0	0	127	129	113	103	104	115
1998	Wisconsin (Mid)	A	6	2	1.71	28	0	0	9	47	25	11	9	30	79
	Lancaster (Cal)	A	1	2	6.82	16	0	0	0	30	37	24	23	13	34
1999	Lancaster (Cal)	A	3	5	5.75	53	0	0	14	61	68	42	39	40	66
2000	New Haven (EL)	AA	2	5	2.67	50	0	0	8	84	80	32	25	36	109
2001	Tacoma (PCL)	AAA	3	2	2.92	56	0	0	4	77	51	27	25	46	107
MINOR LEAGUE TOTALS			24	29	4.89	263	26	0	38	479	457	300	260	307	559

30. Julio Mateo, rhp

Born: Aug. 22, 1979. **Ht.:** 6-0. **Wt.:** 180. **Bats:** R. **Throws:** R. **Career Transactions:** Signed out of Dominican Republic by Mariners, May 15, 1996.

Mateo is the best prospect among the Mariners' second tier of minor league relievers, which also includes Aquilino Lopez and Roy Wells. Mateo led the system in saves last year, his first season as a closer. After mixed success in his first four years as a pro, he made improvements across the board in 2001. His fastball jumped to the mid-90s at times and he was more consistent with his slider. He also threw strikes more often and limited lefthanders to a .209 average and no homers in 67 at-bats. Mateo isn't very tall, so his pitches arrive on a fairly flat plane. If he makes similar strides in Double-A this year, he might be able to help Seattle at some point in 2003.

Year	Club (League)	Class	W	L	ERA	G	GS	CG	SV	IP	H	R	ER	BB	SO
1996	Mariners (DSL)	R	4	2	1.74	14	5	2	1	52	42	14	10	19	23
1997	Mariners (AZL)	R	3	1	3.30	13	6	0	1	60	45	32	22	23	54
1998	Lancaster (Cal)	A	0	0	6.75	1	0	0	0	1	1	1	1	1	1
	Everett (NWL)	A	3	3	4.70	28	0	0	4	38	40	25	20	17	37
1999	Wisconsin (Mid)	A	1	3	4.34	20	0	0	4	29	31	18	14	8	27
2000	Wisconsin (Mid)	A	4	8	4.19	36	1	0	4	69	63	38	32	23	73
2001	San Bernardino (Cal)	A	5	4	2.86	56	0	0	26	66	58	28	21	16	79
MINOR LEAGUE TOTALS			20	21	3.43	168	12	2	40	315	280	156	120	107	294

TAMPA BAY
Devil Rays

By Bill Ballew

Devil Rays general manager Chuck LaMar won't get fooled again by the get-rich-quick approach. Burned two years ago after owner Vince Naimoli urged the signings of Vinny Castilla, Greg Vaughn and Gerald Williams, LaMar has returned to his roots by trying to build Tampa Bay through the farm system. The returns have been anything but rapid, but the plan does provide the best chance for long-term success in a market that has yet to embrace major league baseball.

The Devil Rays were encouraged with unexpected success from youngsters in 2001. Lefthander Joe Kennedy made the jump from Class A to Tropicana Field in less than a year. Relievers Jesus Colome, Travis Phelps and Victor Zambrano did well in steady activity out of the bullpen. Catcher Toby Hall earned International League MVP honors before playing well in the majors, while second baseman Brent Abernathy looked like a keeper following a midseason promotion. At one point the Devil Rays fielded 12 rookies on their 25-man roster and gave opportunities to 14 in all during the 2001 season.

Not unexpectedly, the influx of rookies didn't coincide with improvement on the field. Tampa Bay lost 100 games for the first time in its four seasons of existence, though the team went an encouraging 35-39 over the second half. Manager Larry Rothschild was fired early in the season and batting coach Hal McRae replaced him. LaMar got a new boss as well when commissioner Bud Selig persuaded John McHale Jr. to move from Detroit and become Tampa Bay's new chief executive. The front office was bolstered further when former Pirates GM Cam Bonifay was named farm director.

While the Rays struggled at the major league level, they have formed one of the American League's deepest farm systems behind scouting director Dan Jennings. Tampa Bay is building with athletes and strong-armed pitchers, and could field a big league starting lineup of homegrown products within the next three seasons. Such a lineup not only has the potential of being both talented and young, but it also will fit the team's budget, at least until the players reach arbitration eligibility. By then, everyone in the organization hopes the long-term future of the Devil Rays is more certain than it is heading into 2002.

OrganizationOverview

General manager: Chuck LaMar. **Farm director:** Cam Bonifay. **Scouting Director:** Dan Jennings.

2001 PERFORMANCE

Class	Team	League	W	L	Pct.	Finish*	Manager(s)
Majors	Tampa Bay	American	62	100	.383	14th (14)	L. Rothschild, H. McRae
Triple-A	Durham Bulls	International	74	70	.514	5th (14)	Bill Evers
Double-A	Orlando Rays	Southern	59	81	.421	10th (10)	Mike Ramsey
High A	Bakersfield Blaze	California	71	69	.507	t-5th (10)	Charlie Montoyo
Low A	Charleston RiverDogs	South Atlantic	64	76	.457	12th (16)	Buddy Biancalana
Short-season	Hudson Valley Renegades	New York-Penn	39	37	.513	6th (14)	Dave Howard
Rookie	Princeton Devil Rays	Appalachian	28	39	.418	10th (10)	Edwin Rodriguez
OVERALL 2001 MINOR LEAGUE RECORD			335	372	.474	22nd (30)	

*Finish in overall standings (No. of teams in league)

ORGANIZATION LEADERS

BATTING
*AVG	Toby Hall, Durham	.335
R	**Matt Diaz**, Bakersfield	79
H	**Matt Diaz**, Bakersfield	172
TB	**Matt Diaz**, Bakersfield	267
2B	**Matt Diaz**, Bakersfield	40
3B	Dan Dement, Bakersfield/Charleston	11
HR	Justin Schuda, Charleston	25
RBI	**Matt Diaz**, Bakersfield	81
BB	Justin Schuda, Charleston	65
SO	Justin Schuda, Charleston	166
SB	Irwin Centeno, Charleston	48

PITCHING
W	**Travis Harper**, Durham	12
L	Mark Malaska, Bakersfield/Charleston	13
#ERA	Tim Coward, Bakersfield/Charleston	1.86
G	Talley Haines, Durham/Orlando	59
CG	Three tied at	2
SV	Hans Smith, Bakersfield	17
IP	Jim Magrane, Orlando	182
BB	Brian Stokes, Bakersfield	64
SO	Seth McClung, Charleston	165

*Minimum 250 At-Bats #Minimum 75 Innings

TOP PROSPECTS OF THE DECADE

1997	Matt White, rhp
1998	Matt White, rhp
1999	Matt White, rhp
2000	Josh Hamilton, of
2001	Josh Hamilton, of

TOP DRAFT PICKS OF THE DECADE

1996	Paul Wilder, of
1997	Jason Standridge, rhp
1998	Josh Pressley, 1b (4)
1999	Josh Hamilton, of
2000	Rocco Baldelli, of
2001	Dewon Brazelton, rhp

BEST TOOLS

Best Hitter for Average	Carl Crawford
Best Power Hitter	Josh Hamilton
Fastest Baserunner	Carl Crawford
Best Fastball	Dewon Brazelton

Diaz   **Harper**

Best Breaking Ball	Chris Flinn
Best Changeup	Dewon Brazelton
Best Control	Jim Magrane
Best Defensive Catcher	Shawn Riggans
Best Defensive Infielder	Ramon Soler
Best Infield Arm	Juan Salas
Best Defensive Outfielder	Rocco Baldelli
Best Outfield Arm	Josh Hamilton

PROJECTED 2005 LINEUP

Catcher	Toby Hall
First Base	Aubrey Huff
Second Base	Brent Abernathy
Third Base	Jared Sandberg
Shortstop	Jorge Cantu
Left Field	Carl Crawford
Center Field	Rocco Baldelli
Right Field	Josh Hamilton
Designated Hitter	Ben Grieve
No. 1 Starter	Dewon Brazelton
No. 2 Starter	Seth McClung
No. 3 Starter	Joe Kennedy
No. 4 Starter	Matt White
No. 5 Starter	Jason Standridge
Closer	Jesus Colome

ALL-TIME LARGEST BONUSES

Matt White, 1996	$10,200,000
Rolando Arrojo, 1997	$7,000,000
Dewon Brazelton, 2001	$4,200,000
Josh Hamilton, 1999	$3,960,000
Bobby Seay, 1996	$3,000,000

DraftAnalysis

2001 Draft

Best Pro Debut: OF Jonny Gomes (18) was named MVP of the Rookie-level Appalachian League after hitting .291-16-44 with 15 steals. RHP Jake Carney (20) posted matching 0.64 ERAs at short-season Hudson Valley and Class A Charleston.

Best Athlete: The Devil Rays received a lot of attention for signing Toe Nash out of the semipro Sugar Cane League in 2000, and they went back there to find OF Joey Gathright (32) a year later. He has more experience with football than with baseball, but his physical gifts are undeniable, particularly his speed. Tampa Bay also likes his offensive potential.

Best Hitter: 2B Fernando Cortez (9) batted .278-1-25 at Hudson Valley. Drafted out of Grossmont (Calif.) CC, Cortez moved from shortstop to third base, then to second during instructional league.

Best Raw Power: OF Aaron Clark (8) has lefthanded power, though he may have to tone down his swing after hitting .201-6-35 with 66 strikeouts at Hudson Valley.

Fastest Runner: The Devil Rays have clocked Gathright at 6.18 seconds in the 60-yard dash.

Best Defensive Player: 2B/SS Jason St. Clair (10) is solid at both middle-infield positions.

Best Fastball: RHP **Dewon Brazelton** (1) didn't pitch in a game between the end of Middle Tennessee State's season in May and instructional league in September. But he was as good as ever when he took the mound, easily throwing 93-94 mph and reaching 97.

Tampa Bay got several power arms, including three LHPs—Jon Switzer (2), Chris Seddon (5) and Tim King (7)—who have topped out at 93 mph. RHP Chris Flinn (3) can hit 94 mph and also has a nasty knuckle-curve.

Brazelton

Most Intriguing Background: Brazelton and Switzer were roommates on Team USA in 2000. Unsigned C Daron Roberts (25) is the son of 1972 No. 1 overall pick Dave Roberts. Unsigned 2B Matt Lukevics' (45) father Mitch works for the Devil Rays in player development.

Closest To The Majors: Giving Brazelton an immediate September callup was the inducement that got him to agree to a $4.2 million big league contract. He didn't pitch in a game, but it wouldn't be an upset if he did in 2002.

Best Late-Round Pick: Gomes. Carney has a good arm, and RHP Joshua Parker (29) has a hard sinker that bears watching.

The One Who Got Away: RHP David Bush (4) would have fit with what the Devil Rays were trying to accomplish. He threw 96 mph during the Cape Cod League all-star game and returned to Wake Forest.

Assessment: Even without Bush, Tampa Bay can't help but be pleased with its pitching haul. They stole Seddon in the fifth round after shoulder tendinitis kept his velocity down as a high school senior.

2000 Draft

With no second-, third- or fourth-round picks, Tampa Bay must hope athletic OF Rocco Baldelli (1) can turn his tools into skills. SS Jace Brewer (5) got a major league contract but has been hampered by shoulder problems. **Grade: C**

1999 Draft

OFs Josh Hamilton (the No. 1 overall pick) and Carl Crawford (2) are the system's two best prospects. RHP Seth McClung (5) isn't that far behind. **Grade: A**

1998 Draft

The Devil Rays didn't have picks in the first three rounds and missed on 1B Josh Pressley in the fourth. They recovered quickly, however, landing big leaguers in 3B Aubrey Huff (5), RHP Ryan Rupe (6) and LHP Joe Kennedy (8). **Grade: B**

1997 Draft

Toby Hall (9) is one of the game's brightest young catchers. RHP Jason Standridge (1) and OF Kenny Kelly (2) have reached the majors, though Kelly didn't start to blossom until he was sold to Seattle. Tampa Bay could have used RHPs Chris Bootcheck (17), Kenny Baugh (70) and Blake Williams (83), who all became future first-round picks. **Grade: B**

Note: Draft analysis prepared by Jim Callis. Numbers in parentheses indicate draft rounds.

. . . Despite his large frame, Hamilton has good speed and is graceful in the outfield.

Hamilton **Josh** of

Born: May 21, 1981.
Ht.: 6-4. **Wt.:** 209.
Bats: L. **Throws:** L.
School: Athens Drive HS, Raleigh, N.C.
Career Transactions: Selected by Devil Rays in first round (first overall) of 1999 draft; signed June 3, 1999.

The No. 1 overall pick in 1999 and the South Atlantic League co-MVP in 2000, Hamilton had a lost season in 2001. A series of injuries that began with a car accident during spring training and continued with ailments to his back and legs cost him most of the campaign. After jumping past high Class A Bakersfield, Hamilton hit just .180 at Double-A Orlando in April before being sidelined. He tried to make up for lost time in the Arizona Fall League, only to have a sore shoulder slow him down during the first week. Then a recurring lower back strain shelved him for the remainder of the winter. In a rare bit of good news, he didn't require surgery.

A five-tool player, Hamilton is expected to excel in all phases of the game. He has outstanding power potential with great leverage, a quick swing and an ideal body at 6-foot-4 and 210 pounds. Despite his large frame and size 19 feet, Hamilton has good speed and is graceful in the outfield. A pitcher in high school who attracted interest from several teams for his 94 mph fastball, he has a plus arm that will enable him to play either right or center. All the potential in the world doesn't mean anything if a player can't remain on the field, though. Before last year's injury woes, Hamilton hurt his right knee in June 2000 and missed most of that season's second half. Despite his unquestioned ability, he needs to fine-tune all aspects of his game. That was obvious last April, when Hamilton failed to show patience while Southern League hurlers fed him a steady diet of offspeed pitches. He needs to work deeper into counts and stay back on pitches in order to maximize his power.

Tampa Bay was guilty of pushing Hamilton too fast last spring. The team flirted with the thought of having Hamilton jump all the way from low Class A to the big leagues, only to watch him fall victim to a lack of activity in between his various ailments. The Rays learned their lesson and want nothing more in 2002 than to see Hamilton stay healthy. While he should reach the majors in the not-too-distant future, he should spend most of this year sharpening his skills in Double-A.

Year	Club (League)	Class	AVG	G	AB	R	H	2B	3B	HR	RBI	BB	SO	SB
1999	Princeton (Appy)	R	.347	56	236	49	82	20	4	10	48	13	43	17
	Hudson Valley (NY-P)	A	.194	16	72	7	14	3	0	0	7	1	14	1
2000	Charleston, SC (SAL)	A	.302	96	391	62	118	23	3	13	61	27	71	14
2001	Orlando (SL)	AA	.180	23	89	5	16	5	0	0	4	5	22	2
	Charleston, SC (SAL)	A	.364	4	11	3	4	1	0	1	2	2	3	0
MINOR LEAGUE TOTALS			.293	195	799	126	234	52	7	24	122	48	153	34

2. Carl Crawford, of

Born: Aug. 5, 1981. **Ht.:** 6-2. **Wt.:** 203. **Bats:** L. **Throws:** L. **School:** Jefferson Davis HS, Houston. **Career Transactions:** Selected by Devil Rays in second round of 1999 draft; signed June 14, 1999.

Crawford was one of the youngest players in Double-A last year. After leading the South Atlantic League in hits and stolen bases in 2000, Crawford skipped high Class A and overcame initial struggles to rank third in the Southern League in steals and fifth in hits. He continued to blossom with a fast start in the Arizona Fall League before joining Team USA in World Cup competition in Taiwan in November. A potential four-tool player, Crawford is a pure athlete who had basketball and football scholarship offers from big-time colleges. He has great speed, quick wrists and a good idea of how to hit. His superior work ethic rivals that of any player in the system, and he's considered the Devil Rays' most coachable prospect. Crawford's arm is his lone below-average tool. His baseball instincts, such as taking the correct routes on fly balls, should get better with experience. His pitch recognition and ability to work counts need improvement, and his swing could use some refinement. The temptation for a player developing as quickly as Crawford would be to give him a taste of the big leagues. Tampa Bay, however, is scheduled to send Crawford to Triple-A Durham in 2002.

Year	Club (League)	Class	AVG	G	AB	R	H	2B	3B	HR	RBI	BB	SO	SB
1999	Princeton (Appy)	R	.319	60	260	62	83	14	4	0	25	13	47	17
2000	Charleston, SC (SAL)	A	.301	135	564	99	170	21	11	6	57	32	102	55
2001	Orlando (SL)	AA	.274	132	537	64	147	24	3	4	51	36	90	36
MINOR LEAGUE TOTALS			.294	327	1361	225	400	59	18	10	133	81	239	108

3. Dewon Brazelton, rhp

Born: June 16, 1980. **Ht.:** 6-4. **Wt.:** 205. **Bats:** R. **Throws:** R. **School:** Middle Tennessee State University. **Career Transactions:** Selected by Devil Rays in first round (third overall) of 2001 draft; signed August 25, 2001.

The No. 3 overall pick in the 2001 draft, Brazelton spent most of the summer haggling over his signing bonus. He agreed to a $4.2 million deal in late August that included a September callup, though he didn't pitch. Brazelton set a Team USA record with a 0.65 ERA in 2000 and finished third in NCAA Division I with a 1.42 ERA last spring. Brazelton's fastball sat on 95 mph during instructional league. He had the best changeup in the 2001 draft crop, and he added depth to his breaking ball during his one-month apprenticeship in Tampa. He also showed a good feel for mixing his pitches. He has a long and loose body, isn't afraid to challenge hitters and works both sides of the plate. Brazelton simply needs experience against top-notch hitters. His curveball could use some more fine-tuning before he'll be a legitimate three-pitch pitcher. The Rays believe Brazelton has the ability and maturity to reach the big leagues quickly. His showing in spring training will determine whether he makes his debut in Double-A or Triple-A, and he could climb the mound at Tropicana Field at some point in 2002.

Year	Club (League)	Class	W	L	ERA	G	GS	CG	SV	IP	H	R	ER	BB	SO
			Has Not Played—Signed 2002 Contract												

4. Jesus Colome, rhp

Born: June 2, 1980. **Ht.:** 6-2. **Wt.:** 170. **Bats:** R. **Throws:** R. **Career Transactions:** Signed out of Dominican Republic by Athletics, Sept. 29, 1996 . . . Traded by Athletics with cash to Devil Rays for RHP Jim Mecir and LHP Todd Belitz, July 28, 2000.

Acquired from the Athletics in a July 2000 trade for two relievers, Colome bounced between Triple-A Durham and the major leagues last year. While he struggled in 13 International League outings, he was one of Tampa Bay's more consistent relievers, limiting hitters to a .208 average. Colome's fastball touches triple digits and has above-average movement. He has an easy throwing motion that reminds scouts of Mariano Rivera. His slider is effective against righthanders, and big league lefties batted just .186 against him. The Rays were impressed with the way Colome increased his intensity with runners in scoring position. Colome needs more consistency with his pitches and better overall command. His changeup comes and goes, causing him to lose confidence in it and allowing hitters to sit on his hard stuff. Colome could become an overpowering closer, though either Esteban Yan or Travis Phelps is expected to finish games for Tampa Bay in 2002. Just 21, Colome needs to establish himself as a situational reliever before he can be trusted in save situations.

Year	Club (League)	Class	W	L	ERA	G	GS	CG	SV	IP	H	R	ER	BB	SO
1997	Athletics West (DSL)	R	9	3	2.71	18	7	3	0	90	73	33	27	22	55
1998	Athletics (AZL)	R	2	5	3.18	12	11	0	0	57	47	27	20	16	62
1999	Modesto (Cal)	A	8	4	3.36	31	22	0	1	129	125	63	48	60	127
2000	Midland (TL)	AA	9	4	3.59	20	20	0	0	110	99	62	44	50	95
	Orlando (SL)	AA	1	2	6.75	3	3	0	0	15	18	12	11	7	9
2001	Durham (IL)	AAA	0	3	6.23	13	0	0	0	17	22	13	12	6	18
	Tampa Bay (AL)	MAJ	2	3	3.33	30	0	0	0	49	37	22	18	25	31
MAJOR LEAGUE TOTALS			2	3	3.33	30	0	0	0	49	37	22	18	25	31
MINOR LEAGUE TOTALS			29	21	3.49	97	63	3	1	417	384	210	162	161	366

5. Rocco Baldelli, of

Born: Sept. 25, 1981. **Ht.:** 6-4. **Wt.:** 183. **Bats:** R. **Throws:** R. **School:** Bishop Hendricken HS, Warwick, R.I. **Career Transactions:** Selected by Devil Rays in first round (sixth overall) of 2000 draft; signed June 19, 2000.

Drafted sixth overall in 2000, Baldelli was recruited in three different sports before signing for $2.25 million. Despite battling minor back and hand injuries last year at low Class A Charleston, Baldelli ranked second on the team in triples, home runs and stolen bases. Baldelli impresses scouts with his instincts for the game. He has great quickness and runs the 60-yard dash in 6.38 seconds. His maturing body is starting to add strength, and he could develop above-average power. The Rays envision Baldelli as a pure center fielder capable of hitting in the middle of the lineup. The biggest hurdle Baldelli faces is making adjustments with his bat. He gets himself out more often than pitchers do, and he must tighten his strike zone. His arm is his lone tool that isn't considered above-average. Added strength will keep him from wearing down over the season, a problem in 2001 The Rays say Baldelli is making steady progress. Tampa Bay's center fielder of the future (he'll push Carl Crawford to left field), he'll open 2002 at Bakersfield.

Year	Club (League)	Class	AVG	G	AB	R	H	2B	3B	HR	RBI	BB	SO	SB
2000	Princeton (Appy)	R	.216	60	232	33	50	9	2	3	25	12	56	11
2001	Charleston, SC (SAL)	A	.249	113	406	58	101	23	6	8	55	23	89	25
MINOR LEAGUE TOTALS			.237	173	638	91	151	32	8	11	80	35	145	36

6. Seth McClung, rhp

Born: Feb. 7, 1981. **Ht.:** 6-6. **Wt.:** 235. **Bats:** R. **Throws:** R. **School:** Greenbrier East HS, Lewisburg, W.Va. **Career Transactions:** Selected by Devil Rays in fifth round of 1999 draft; signed June 21, 1999.

A seven-sport athlete in high school who signed for $350,000, McClung saw his second tour of duty in the South Atlantic League last season. He ranked third in the league in strikeouts and held hitters to a .231 average. McClung throws bullets, with a fastball clocked as high as 99 mph. The pitch consistently sat in the 93-95 mph range, and managers rated it as the SAL's best heater. He has the makings of a plus curveball. McClung has a power pitcher's body, with thick thighs and excellent size. He has given up six home runs during the past two years and is a good all-around athlete. McClung needs to improve his secondary offerings to succeed at higher levels. He worked on a circle changeup during instructional league, learning that it was more effective when he toned it down from 86-90 mph to 82-83. While his command has improved the last two years, he still can do a better job of hitting his spots. McClung is still discovering the nuances of pitching. He's expected to move one spot up the ladder this spring to Bakersfield, though a promotion to Orlando might not be far away.

Year	Club (League)	Class	W	L	ERA	G	GS	CG	SV	IP	H	R	ER	BB	SO
1999	Princeton (Appy)	R	2	4	7.69	13	10	0	0	46	53	47	39	48	46
2000	Hudson Valley (NY-P)	A	2	2	1.85	8	8	0	0	44	37	18	9	17	38
	Charleston, SC (SAL)	A	2	1	3.19	6	6	0	0	31	30	14	11	19	26
2001	Charleston, SC (SAL)	A	10	11	2.79	28	28	2	0	164	142	72	51	53	165
MINOR LEAGUE TOTALS			16	18	3.48	55	52	2	0	285	262	151	110	137	275

7. Matt White, rhp

Born: Aug. 13, 1978. **Ht.:** 6-5. **Wt.:** 230. **Bats:** R. **Throws:** R. **School:** Waynesboro Area (Pa.) HS. **Career Transactions:** Selected by Giants in first round (seventh overall) of 1996 draft; granted free agency . . . Signed by Devil Rays, Nov. 25, 1996.

Tampa Bay entered the 2001 season expecting White to make a strong push for the rotation. Instead, he faltered in spring training and lost his five decisions in Triple-A because of poor mechanics. His altered delivery was the result of shoulder pain that required arthroscopic surgery on May 31. He didn't pitch again in 2001. White has the tools to be an effective pitcher in the big leagues. He throws a mid-90s fastball with average movement, along with a plus overhand power curve. He's an intelligent pitcher who has matured in all phases of his game. Inconsistent mechanics have been White's downfall throughout his career. When his delivery gets off track, his entire game can suffer. He also tends to fall in love with his curveball instead of using his fastball to set it up. White has yet to provide much of a return on the $10.2 million Tampa Bay invested in him when he was a draft free agent in 1996. The Devil Rays are confident, however, that won't be the case much longer. He's expected to be close to full strength by Opening Day and could finally reach the big leagues in 2002.

Year	Club (League)	Class	W	L	ERA	G	GS	CG	SV	IP	H	R	ER	BB	SO
1997	Hudson Valley (NY-P)	A	4	6	4.07	15	15	0	0	84	78	44	38	29	82
1998	Charleston, SC (SAL)	A	4	3	3.82	12	12	0	0	75	72	41	32	21	59
	St. Petersburg (FSL)	A	4	8	5.55	17	17	1	0	96	107	70	59	41	64
1999	St. Petersburg (FSL)	A	9	7	5.18	21	20	2	0	113	125	75	65	33	92
2000	Orlando (SL)	AA	7	6	3.75	20	20	2	0	120	94	56	50	58	98
	Durham (IL)	AAA	3	2	2.83	6	6	0	0	35	36	14	11	16	28
2001	Durham (IL)	AAA	0	5	7.80	7	7	0	0	30	33	28	26	25	16
MINOR LEAGUE TOTALS			31	37	4.57	98	97	5	0	553	545	328	281	223	439

8. Jorge Cantu, ss

Born: Jan. 30, 1982. **Ht.:** 6-1. **Wt.:** 178. **Bats:** R. **Throws:** R. **Career Transactions:** Signed out of Mexico by Devil Rays, July 2, 1998.

At 19 Cantu was the youngest regular in the Southern League last year, when he reached Double-A in just his third pro season. Content to just survive early in the year, he earned a starting job in the SL all-star game and finished the season on an upswing. Cantu is a steady defender who has a chance to become an offensive shortstop. His tall, lean body, as well as his quick wrists and excellent bat speed, could make him a poor man's Nomar Garciaparra, though he has yet to even approach Garciaparra's production. Cantu possesses some of the best hand-eye coordination in the organization. Cantu needs to refine his approach at the plate. He's enamored of his occasional power and tries to drive every pitch rather than settling for making solid contact. His range is no better than average, and his footwork and throwing mechanics need significant improvement if he hopes to remain at short. Cantu was slated to play in the Arizona Fall League before a sprained left ankle sidelined him for nearly two months. A promotion to Triple-A is on his immediate agenda.

Year	Club (League)	Class	AVG	G	AB	R	H	2B	3B	HR	RBI	BB	SO	SB
1999	Hudson Valley (NY-P)	A	.260	72	281	33	73	17	2	1	33	20	59	3
2000	Charleston, SC (SAL)	A	.301	46	186	25	56	13	2	2	24	10	39	3
	St. Petersburg (FSL)	A	.292	36	130	18	38	5	2	1	14	3	13	4
2001	Orlando (SL)	AA	.256	130	512	58	131	26	3	4	45	17	93	4
MINOR LEAGUE TOTALS			.269	284	1109	134	298	61	9	8	116	50	204	14

9. Jason Standridge, rhp

Born: Nov. 9, 1978. **Ht.:** 6-4. **Wt.:** 217. **Bats:** R. **Throws:** R. **School:** Hewitt-Trussville HS, Trussville, Ala. **Career Transactions:** Selected by Devil Rays in first round (31st overall) of 1997 draft; signed June 6, 1997.

Standridge had a disappointing 2001 season in Triple-A yet still reached the major leagues in July. After a stellar showing during spring training, the former Auburn quarterback recruit became tentative after hitting Toledo's Tom Evans with a pitch, which led to a bench-clearing brawl that left Standridge with a swollen eye and sore hand. Standridge has a combination of above-average stuff and impeccable makeup as one of the organization's hardest workers. He has a 92-94 mph fastball and a hard, sharp-breaking curveball. He showed amazing confidence and ease in dueling Roger Clemens and the Yankees late last season. To succeed in the majors, Standridge must use both sides of the plate and pitch inside. His curveball got much better last year, but he still needs to fine-tune his changeup. He is trying to add a cut fastball to his repertoire. The Rays say Standridge is on the verge of success. His game came together late in the regular season and during the Arizona Fall League, and he could win a job in the Opening Day rotation.

Year	Club (League)	Class	W	L	ERA	G	GS	CG	SV	IP	H	R	ER	BB	SO
1997	Devil Rays (GCL)	R	0	6	3.59	13	13	0	0	58	56	30	23	13	55
1998	Princeton (Appy)	R	4	4	7.00	12	12	0	0	63	82	61	49	28	47
1999	Charleston, SC (SAL)	A	9	1	2.02	18	18	3	0	116	80	35	26	31	84
	St. Petersburg (FSL)	A	4	4	3.91	8	8	0	0	48	49	21	21	20	26
2000	St. Petersburg (FSL)	A	2	4	3.38	10	10	1	0	56	45	28	21	31	41
	Orlando (SL)	AA	6	8	3.62	17	17	2	0	97	85	46	39	43	55
2001	Durham (IL)	AAA	5	10	5.28	20	20	0	0	102	130	73	60	50	48
	Tampa Bay (AL)	MAJ	0	0	4.66	9	1	0	0	19	19	10	10	14	9
	Orlando (SL)	AA	0	2	5.59	2	2	0	0	10	12	6	6	4	7
MAJOR LEAGUE TOTALS			0	0	4.66	9	1	0	0	19	19	10	10	14	9
MINOR LEAGUE TOTALS			30	39	4.01	100	100	6	0	550	539	300	245	220	363

10. Delvin James, rhp

Born: Jan. 3, 1978. **Ht.:** 6-4. **Wt.:** 222. **Bats:** R. **Throws:** R. **School:** Nacogdoches (Texas) HS. **Career Transactions:** Selected by Devil Rays in 14th round of 1996 draft; signed June 11, 1996.

A former linebacker who maintains his football aggressiveness on the mound, James had an up-and-down season in 2001 while he moved between starting and relieving. He was practically unhittable as a Double-A starter before struggling to find his rhythm in Triple-A. James has one of the strongest arms in the organization. His fastball has been clocked as high as 97 mph and resides in the 93-95 range. He throws a decent changeup with stellar control of all his pitches. James has developed from a raw hurler thanks to his attitude and impeccable work ethic. The Rays would like to see James add a breaking ball, particularly a slider, to his repertoire. The extra pitch would give him another weapon to mix, keeping hitters more off balance. The Rays haven't determined which role James will play in the major leagues. His overpowering fastball, good command and tenacity could make him an ideal closer. His future responsibilities will depend on the needs of the Tampa Bay staff, which is where he could find himself with a solid showing in spring training.

Year	Club (League)	Class	W	L	ERA	G	GS	CG	SV	IP	H	R	ER	BB	SO
1996	Devil Rays (GCL)	R	2	8	8.87	11	11	1	0	48	64	52	47	21	40
1997	Princeton (Appy)	R	4	4	4.94	20	5	0	0	58	71	57	32	24	46
1998	St. Petersburg (FSL)	A	0	0	10.80	1	0	0	0	2	2	2	2	0	0
	Charleston, SC (SAL)	A	2	0	5.40	7	0	0	0	8	12	5	5	2	8
	Hudson Valley (NY-P)	A	7	4	2.98	15	15	0	0	82	71	39	27	32	64
1999	Charleston, SC (SAL)	A	8	8	3.64	25	25	1	0	158	142	76	64	33	106
	St. Petersburg (FSL)	A	3	0	3.18	3	2	0	0	17	18	6	6	4	6
2000	St. Petersburg (FSL)	A	7	9	4.26	22	22	3	0	137	142	74	65	27	74
	Orlando (SL)	AA	1	3	2.92	6	6	1	0	37	31	15	12	7	26
2001	Orlando (SL)	AA	2	0	1.65	7	7	0	0	44	25	8	8	9	31
	Durham (IL)	AAA	3	7	4.80	31	9	1	0	84	99	51	45	27	51
MINOR LEAGUE TOTALS			39	43	4.17	148	102	7	0	675	677	385	313	186	452

11. Bobby Seay, lhp

Born: June 20, 1978. **Ht.:** 6-2. **Wt.:** 221. **Bats:** L. **Throws:** L. **School:** Sarasota (Fla.) HS. **Career Transactions:** Selected by White Sox in first round (12th overall) of 1996 draft; granted free agency . . . Signed by Devil Rays, Nov. 8, 1996.

Seay landed on the disabled list for the sixth time in five professional seasons during 2001, thereby limiting his progress while pitching in Double-A. A draft loophole free agent who signed with much fanfare for $3 million in 1996, he missed a month early in the season with a finger injury before picking up his first win in nearly a year in late July. Despite his difficult campaign, he continues to possess the potential to be a significant contributor in the major leagues. Seay has a low-90s fastball with plus movement, along with an above-average curveball. He also uses both sides of the plate and has a bulldog-type tenacity that could lead to success as a late-innings reliever. A lack of overall maturity and a mediocre changeup remain his primary weaknesses. He also must refine his command. A member of the 2000 U.S. Olympic team, Seay needs to stay healthy and learn from his mistakes. He should move up to Triple-A to start this season.

Year	Club (League)	Class	W	L	ERA	G	GS	CG	SV	IP	H	R	ER	BB	SO
1997	Charleston, SC (SAL)	A	3	4	4.55	13	13	0	0	61	56	35	31	37	64
1998	Charleston, SC (SAL)	A	1	7	4.30	15	15	0	0	69	59	40	33	29	74
1999	St. Petersburg (FSL)	A	2	6	3.00	12	11	0	0	57	56	25	19	23	45
	Orlando (SL)	AA	1	2	7.94	6	6	0	0	17	22	15	15	15	16
2000	Orlando (SL)	AA	8	7	3.88	24	24	0	0	132	132	64	57	53	106
2001	Orlando (SL)	AA	2	5	5.98	15	13	0	0	65	81	48	43	26	49
	Tampa Bay (AL)	MAJ	1	1	6.23	12	0	0	0	13	13	11	9	5	12
MAJOR LEAGUE TOTALS			1	1	6.23	12	0	0	0	13	13	11	9	5	12
MINOR LEAGUE TOTALS			17	31	4.44	85	82	0	0	401	406	227	198	183	354

12. Jon Switzer, lhp

Born: Aug. 13, 1979. **Ht.:** 6-3. **Wt.:** 190. **Bats:** L. **Throws:** L. **School:** Arizona State University. **Career Transactions:** Selected by Devil Rays in second round of 2001 draft; signed Aug. 13, 2001.

The Devil Rays believe they drafted two future members of their starting rotation when they plucked Dewon Brazelton and Switzer with their first two picks in the 2001 draft. They were roommates on Team USA's college squad in 2000 and will be given every opportunity to reach Tropicana Field as quickly as possible. Switzer entered his junior year at Arizona State as a potential first-round pick before enduring a midseason slump. He rebounded in his brief pro debut. Switzer has a low-90s fastball and a good changeup. He added a splitter and a slider during his last season in college and displayed fine location with all of his offerings during instructional league. While he must continue to improve his consistency with his new pitches, Switzer appears ready to jump on the fast track. A solid showing in spring training could lead to a spot in the Double-A Orlando in April.

Year	Club (League)	Class	W	L	ERA	G	GS	CG	SV	IP	H	R	ER	BB	SO
2001	Hudson Valley (NY-P)	A	2	0	0.63	5	0	0	0	14	9	3	1	2	20
MINOR LEAGUE TOTALS			2	0	0.63	5	0	0	0	14	9	3	1	2	20

13. Jonny Gomes, of

Born: Nov. 22, 1980. **Ht.:** 6-1. **Wt.:** 205. **Bats:** R. **Throws:** R. **School:** Santa Rosa (Calif.) CC. **Career Transactions:** Selected by Devil Rays in 18th round of 2001 draft; signed June 13, 2001.

No one from the Rays' 2001 draft class made a bigger splash last summer than Gomes. The 18th-round pick has a non-stop motor and showed an impressive blend of power, speed and hitting ability as he was named MVP in the Rookie-level Appalachian League. He topped the Appy League in homers, on-base percentage (.442) and slugging percentage (.597) and ranked second in runs, RBIs and extra-base hits (29). Undrafted out of high school and after his first junior college season, Gomes has excellent raw power and a quick bat. He generates most of his power from his thick lower body. He uses the entire field and should have the ability to hit just about anywhere in the lineup provided he closes some of the holes in his swing. A catcher in high school, Gomes has adjusted to the outfield over the past two years thanks to his above-average athleticism, but he still needs to get better jumps on fly balls. He appears to be a late bloomer who could continue to surprise scouts this year in Class A.

Year	Club (League)	Class	AVG	G	AB	R	H	2B	3B	HR	RBI	BB	SO	SB
2001	Princeton (Appy)	R	.291	62	206	58	60	11	2	16	44	33	73	15
MINOR LEAGUE TOTALS			.291	62	206	58	60	11	2	16	44	33	73	15

14. Steve Kent, lhp

Born: Oct. 3, 1978. **Ht:** 5-11. **Wt.:** 170. **Bats:** B. **Throws:** L. **School:** Florida International University. **Career Transactions:** Selected by Mariners in ninth round of 1999 draft; signed June 3, 1999 . . . Selected by Angels from Mariners in Rule 5 major league draft, Dec. 13, 2001.

After two years in the short-season Northwest League, Kent blossomed in high Class A in 2001 yet couldn't make the Mariners' crowded 40-man roster. The Angels purchased him for $50,000 in the major league Rule 5 draft in December, then immediately sold him to the Devil Rays for $75,000. He has to stick on Tampa Bay's 25-man roster throughout this season, or else he has to clear waivers and be offered back to Seattle for $25,000, but the Rays think he can be a situational lefty for them. They're enticed by Kent's sharp slider and his ability to get lefthanded hitters out. Lefties managed just a .130 batting average and .167 slugging percentage against him last year. Kent also has a live arm that delivers fastballs that Tampa Bay scouts clocked as high as 93 mph, as well as an improving changeup. Not unlike most developing southpaws, Kent must work on his control. He was impressive this winter in Panama as a starter, but he'll remain in relief if the Devil Rays can hold onto him.

Year	Club (League)	Class	W	L	ERA	G	GS	CG	SV	IP	H	R	ER	BB	SO
1999	Everett (NWL)	A	3	2	5.35	21	0	0	4	37	31	24	22	26	43
2000	Everett (NWL)	A	4	1	2.56	24	3	0	0	53	38	16	15	23	61
2001	San Bernardino (Cal)	A	0	3	2.20	51	0	0	1	65	50	21	16	34	73
MINOR LEAGUE TOTALS			7	6	3.08	96	3	0	5	155	119	61	53	83	177

15. Shawn Riggans, c

Born: July 25, 1980. **Ht.:** 6-2. **Wt.:** 195. **Bats:** R. **Throws:** R. **School:** Indian River (Fla.) CC. **Career Transactions:** Selected by Devil Rays in 24th round of 2000 draft; signed May 7, 2001.

A draft-and-follow pick from the 2000 draft, Riggans showed tremendous thunder in his bat in his pro debut last summer before elbow problems sidelined him. He required Tommy John surgery, and the Devil Rays hope he'll be ready to report to short-season Hudson Valley in June. Riggans generates outstanding bat speed with his compact swing. He drilled a 440-foot homer to center field off a 94-mph fastball at Rookie-level Princeton. In addition to his stick, Riggans also has impressive defensive skills. He had a plus arm prior to surgery, and he also earned high marks for his ability to block balls and his overall movement behind the plate. He has impressive natural strength and mental toughness. Riggans' ability to call a game isn't refined, and he's just beginning to learn how to work with pitchers. But the tools are definitely there for him to be an all-around catcher if he returns to health.

Year	Club (League)	Class	AVG	G	AB	R	H	2B	3B	HR	RBI	BB	SO	SB
2001	Princeton (Appy)	R	.345	15	58	15	20	4	0	8	17	9	18	1
MINOR LEAGUE TOTALS			.345	15	58	15	20	4	0	8	17	9	18	1

16. Chris Flinn, rhp

Born: Aug. 18, 1980. **Ht.:** 6-2. **Wt.:** 185. **Bats:** R. **Throws:** R. **School:** Stony Brook University. **Career Transactions:** Selected by Devil Rays in third round of 2001 draft; signed June 13, 2001.

The only thing that kept Flinn out of the first two rounds of the 2001 draft was his height. There's a scouting bias against righthanders around 6 feet tall, but if first impressions mean anything, Flinn will rise above such prejudices. After rewriting the record books at Stony Brook and ranking as the top college pitcher in the Northeast last spring, he opened some eyes with equally impressive showings in the short-season New York-Penn League and instructional league. Though not overpowering, Flinn throws a lot of strikes by spotting his 89-93 mph fastball. His out pitch is a knuckle-curve with great life and above-average depth. The pitch has been compared to Mike Mussina's. Flinn's mechanics are also polished, and his delivery reminds some scouts of David Cone. Yet during instructional league, he impressed the Rays the most with his intelligence and overall maturity. While some observers believe his overall package might fit best in the bullpen down the road, Flinn needs to be challenged with innings against more experienced hitters at higher levels. He'll continue starting this year either at one of Tampa Bay's Class A affiliates.

Year	Club (League)	Class	W	L	ERA	G	GS	CG	SV	IP	H	R	ER	BB	SO
2001	Hudson Valley (NY-P)	A	3	4	2.36	15	10	0	2	69	54	33	18	21	72
MINOR LEAGUE TOTALS			3	4	2.36	15	10	0	2	69	54	33	18	21	72

17. Chris Seddon, lhp

Born: Oct. 13, 1983. **Ht.:** 6-3. **Wt.:** 170. **Bats:** L. **Throws:** L. **School:** Canyon HS, Santa Clarita, Calif. **Career Transactions:** Selected by Devil Rays in fifth round of 2001 draft; signed July 31, 2001.

Another product of Tampa Bay's 2001 draft, Seddon is a potential lefthanded power pitcher. His fastball has been clocked as high as 93 mph, though it resided between 86-90 last summer. The Rays believe his inconsistent velocity was a product of a sore shoulder and the stress of moving from high school to pro ball. They think an offseason of rest and a new conditioning program will bring his velocity back. Tampa Bay was ecstatic when Seddon's name was still on the board after four rounds, knowing that a minor battle with shoulder tendinitis as a high school senior had scared some teams. He showed a loose arm and few lingering effects from the ailment in Rookie ball. In addition to his solid fastball, Seddon has a decent curveball and a serviceable changeup that will require more consistency on the outside edges of the plate. His greatest need at this point is becoming bigger and stronger, which should occur naturally as his body matures. The Rays are hoping that Seddon will show he's ready to make the jump to low Class A in spring training.

Year	Club (League)	Class	W	L	ERA	G	GS	CG	SV	IP	H	R	ER	BB	SO
2001	Princeton (Appy)	R	1	2	5.11	4	2	0	0	12	15	7	7	6	18
MINOR LEAGUE TOTALS			1	2	5.11	4	2	0	0	12	15	7	7	6	18

18. Jace Brewer, ss

Born: June 6, 1979. **Ht.:** 6-0. **Wt.:** 170. **Bats:** R. **Throws:** R. **School:** Baylor University. **Career Transactions:** Selected by Devil Rays in fifth round of 2000 draft; signed June 16, 2000.

A draft-eligible sophomore in 2000, Brewer sent a letter to major league teams to explain he was intent on returning to Baylor for a third season. The Devil Rays changed his mind after taking him in the fifth round, signing him to a $1.5 million major league contract. Brewer underwent surgery after the 2000 season to repair a small tear in his throwing shoulder and continued to battle soreness in his rotator cuff last year. He injured his thumb early in the season, missing most of May and not getting untracked offensively until August. Brewer rebounded to hit .298 with gap power in the final month, concluding 2001 on a positive note. He has natural athleticism that results in fluid actions with above-average range at shortstop. He also has a plus arm when healthy, and possesses above-average speed and baserunning ability. Brewer is a line-drive hitter who needs to add strength in order to drive the ball more consistently. His plate discipline showed some improvement last year but still needs work. The Rays believe Brewer could develop quickly provided he remains on the field. He's expected to start 2002 in high Class A.

Year	Club (League)	Class	AVG	G	AB	R	H	2B	3B	HR	RBI	BB	SO	SB
2000	Charleston, SC (SAL)	A	.219	37	137	10	30	7	2	0	15	6	28	3
2001	Charleston, SC (SAL)	A	.217	108	414	50	90	12	4	3	35	18	74	6
MINOR LEAGUE TOTALS			.218	145	551	60	120	19	6	3	50	24	102	9

19. Travis Harper, rhp

Born: May 21, 1976. **Ht.:** 6-4. **Wt.:** 193. **Bats:** L. **Throws:** R. **School:** James Madison University. **Career Transactions:** Selected by Red Sox in third round of 1997 draft; signed July 14, 1997 . . . Contract voided, Oct. 29, 1997 . . . Signed by Devil Rays, June 29, 1998.

After making his major league debut in September 2000, Harper was a candidate for the Tampa Bay rotation last spring but was bypassed during 2001 by such rookies as Joe Kennedy and newly acquired Nick Bierbrodt. Harper spent all of the season in Triple-A, leading Durham in wins, starts, innings and strikeouts. He finished strong and the Devil Rays were pleased with his overall performance, believing he added strength and improved the consistency of his changeup and curveball. Harper continues to have tremendous control of his low-90s fastball and he shows intelligence and competitiveness every time he takes the mound. What's more, he continued to prove that he's healthy after having his first professional contract voided by the Red Sox in 1997 because he had elbow tendinitis. With a full year of Triple-A seasoning under his belt, Harper will compete for a major league job once again this spring.

Year	Club (League)	Class	W	L	ERA	G	GS	CG	SV	IP	H	R	ER	BB	SO
1998	Hudson Valley (NY-P)	A	6	2	1.92	13	10	0	0	56	38	14	12	20	81
1999	St. Petersburg (FSL)	A	5	4	3.43	14	14	0	0	81	82	36	31	23	79
	Orlando (SL)	AA	6	3	5.38	14	14	1	0	72	73	45	43	26	68
2000	Orlando (SL)	AA	3	1	2.63	9	9	0	0	51	49	19	15	11	33
	Durham (IL)	AAA	7	4	4.24	17	17	0	0	104	98	53	49	26	48
	Tampa Bay (AL)	MAJ	1	2	4.78	6	5	1	0	32	30	17	17	15	14
2001	Tampa Bay (AL)	MAJ	0	2	7.71	2	2	0	0	7	15	11	6	3	2
	Durham (IL)	AAA	12	6	3.70	25	25	1	0	156	140	70	64	38	115
MAJOR LEAGUE TOTALS			1	4	5.31	8	7	1	0	39	45	28	23	18	16
MINOR LEAGUE TOTALS			39	20	3.70	92	89	2	0	521	480	237	214	144	424

20. Jim Magrane, rhp

Born: July 23, 1978. **Ht.:** 6-2. **Wt.:** 208. **Bats:** R. **Throws:** R. **School:** University of Iowa. **Career Transactions:** Signed as nondrafted free agent by Devil Rays, Aug. 21, 1999.

After being named the Rays' minor league pitcher of the year and leading the system in wins and ERA in 2000, Magrane made a successful jump from low Class A to Double-A last season. He topped Orlando in wins, ERA, starts, innings and strikeouts. Signed as a nondrafted free agent, the nephew of former major league pitcher and Rays television broadcaster Joe Magrane succeeds by throwing strikes and moving his pitches around in the strike zone. None of his pitches is overpowering, but Magrane knows how to mix his offerings effectively to keep hitters off balance. He throws two- and four-seam fastballs at 87-89 mph, a changeup, a slider and a curveball. He also possesses outstanding poise and impressive maturity both on the field and off. A classic overachiever, Magrane will continue his ascent in Triple-A this year.

Year	Club (League)	Class	W	L	ERA	G	GS	CG	SV	IP	H	R	ER	BB	SO
2000	Charleston, SC (SAL)	A	12	5	2.76	27	27	1	0	173	158	64	53	43	162
2001	Orlando (SL)	AA	8	12	2.97	29	28	1	0	182	166	87	60	56	126
MINOR LEAGUE TOTALS			20	17	2.86	56	55	2	0	355	324	151	113	99	288

21. Hans Smith, lhp

Born: Aug. 3, 1978. **Ht.:** 6-9. **Wt.:** 265. **Bats:** L. **Throws:** L. **School:** Fresno State University. **Career Transactions:** Selected by Devil Rays in 11th round of 2000 draft; signed June 15, 2000.

Managers rated Smith the best reliever in the high Class A California League last year despite minor elbow problems that all but shut him down after mid-June. He's a strike machine who creates an intimidating presence with his 6-foot-9 frame and lefthanded delivery. He's a sinker-slider pitcher who touches 92 mph with his fastball. His hard slider is particularly effective against lefthanders because it jams them with its boring movement. Smith prefers to work inside and down in the strike zone, and possesses a good splitter that makes his regular fastball even more effective. The Rays are impressed with the way he's able to repeat his delivery for a pitcher of his size. Provided he maintains his consistency with his mechanics, he has a chance to move quickly. Smith didn't need offseason surgery and will be promoted to Double-A for 2002.

Year	Club (League)	Class	W	L	ERA	G	GS	CG	SV	IP	H	R	ER	BB	SO
2000	Princeton (Appy)	R	1	1	8.59	7	0	0	3	7	6	7	7	4	9
	Charleston, SC (SAL)	A	1	2	1.74	17	0	0	7	31	33	8	6	6	23
2001	Bakersfield (Cal)	A	1	0	1.45	31	0	0	17	37	36	10	6	15	42
MINOR LEAGUE TOTALS			3	3	2.26	55	0	0	27	76	75	25	19	25	74

22. Ramon Soler, 2b

Born: July 6, 1981. **Ht.:** 6-0. **Wt.:** 174. **Bats:** B. **Throws:** R. **Career Transactions:** Signed out of Dominican Republic by Devil Rays, July 23, 1997.

After missing the entire 2000 season with a separated right shoulder that required surgery, Soler battled more arm problems last year before showing signs of returning to full strength during instructional league. Converted from shortstop to second base in 2001, he has the tools to be outstanding at his new position. He has soft hands, excellent range and the ability to make plays to both sides. The Rays also believe Soler has made solid strides with his hitting ability. A switch-hitter, he continues to add strength that allows him to spray the ball to all fields. His plate discipline is good, and he tries to draw walks in order to employ his plus speed on the bases. He ranked third in the system in stolen bases last year. Because of his shoulder injury and his youth, Soler doesn't have extensive professional experience. But he might be ready for a breakthrough season in Double-A.

Year	Club (League)	Class	AVG	G	AB	R	H	2B	3B	HR	RBI	BB	SO	SB
1998	Devil Rays (GCL)	R	.252	58	226	47	57	7	7	1	19	27	48	23
1999	Charleston, SC (SAL)	A	.237	108	389	74	92	17	2	1	28	56	93	46
2000						Did Not Play—Injured								
2001	Bakersfield (Cal)	A	.263	103	418	72	110	14	4	2	27	46	75	25
MINOR LEAGUE TOTALS			.251	269	1033	193	259	38	13	4	74	129	216	94

23. Jason Smith, ss

Born: July 24, 1977. **Ht.:** 6-3. **Wt.:** 195. **Bats:** L. **Throws:** R. **School:** Meridian (Miss.) CC. **Career Transactions:** Selected by Cubs in 23rd round of 1996 draft; signed May 25, 1997 . . . Traded by Cubs to Devil Rays, Aug. 6, 2001, completing trade in which Devil Rays sent 1B Fred McGriff to Cubs for RHP Manny Aybar and a player to be named (July 27, 2001).

Tampa Bay acquired Smith as the player to be named later in the Fred McGriff deal trade with the Cubs. Smith missed almost all of 1999 with hamstring problems, which struck him again last year during the regular season and the Arizona Fall League. The Rays' medical staff has taken steps that they hope will improve the situation and allow him to contribute in Tampa Bay in the near future. A tools player, Smith has good athleticism and plus speed. He also provides some solid lefthanded pop for a middle infielder, though he has struggled throughout his career with his plate discipline. Defensively, Smith is inconsistent with the glove and has an average arm. If the Devil Rays hadn't re-signed Chris Gomez, they had planned on giving Smith a chance to earn their starting job during spring training. Now he'll go to Triple-A instead.

Year	Club (League)	Class	AVG	G	AB	R	H	2B	3B	HR	RBI	BB	SO	SB
1997	Williamsport (NY-P)	A	.288	51	205	25	59	5	2	0	11	10	44	9
	Rockford (Mid)	A	.182	9	33	4	6	0	1	0	3	2	11	1
1998	Rockford (Mid)	A	.239	126	464	67	111	15	9	7	60	31	122	23
1999	Daytona (FSL)	A	.261	39	142	22	37	5	2	5	26	12	29	9
2000	West Tenn (SL)	AA	.237	119	481	55	114	22	7	12	61	22	130	16
2001	Iowa (PCL)	AAA	.233	70	240	31	56	8	6	4	15	12	71	6
	Chicago (NL)	MAJ	.000	2	1	0	0	0	0	0	0	0	1	0
	Durham (IL)	AAA	.194	8	31	2	6	1	0	0	3	0	11	0
MAJOR LEAGUE TOTALS			.000	2	1	0	0	0	0	0	0	0	1	0
MINOR LEAGUE TOTALS			.244	422	1596	206	389	56	27	28	179	89	418	64

24. Brandon Backe, rhp

Born: April 5, 1978. **Ht.:** 6-0. **Wt.:** 182. **Bats:** R. **Throws:** R. **School:** Galveston (Texas) JC. **Career Transactions:** Selected by Devil Rays in 18th round of 1998 draft; signed June 5, 1998.

Backe made impressive progress during 2001, his first season as a pitcher after converting from the outfield. He blazed his way through two levels with a moving fastball that touches 93 mph. A career .235 hitter in three minor league seasons, Backe was moved to the mound because of his live arm. The Rays were pleasantly surprised when he displayed a solid feel for pitching. Despite his inexperience, Backe throws four pitches, complementing his fastball with a curveball, slider and changeup. He spent much of his time in the Arizona Fall League trying to refine his hard 82-mph slider in hopes that it could become his out pitch at higher levels. At 6 feet Backe doesn't have the size that leaves scouts salivating, but he could have the total package that enables him to develop into a short reliever in the majors. Spring training will determine whether he opens the 2002 season in Double-A or Triple-A.

Year	Club (League)	Class	AVG	G	AB	R	H	2B	3B	HR	RBI	BB	SO	SB
1998	Princeton (Appy)	R	.250	27	92	14	23	5	1	0	7	12	31	1
	Hudson Valley (NY-P)	A	.231	11	26	3	6	2	0	0	1	2	7	0
1999	Charleston, SC (SAL)	A	.232	84	272	43	63	11	2	9	40	35	81	3
	St. Petersburg (FSL)	A	.197	41	132	21	26	6	1	1	11	21	34	0
2000	St. Petersburg (FSL)	A	.247	112	376	38	93	25	6	1	34	31	99	3
	Orlando (SL)	AA	.250	4	8	1	2	0	0	0	0	2	1	0
MINOR LEAGUE TOTALS			.235	279	906	120	213	49	10	11	93	103	253	7

Yr	Club (League)	Class	W	L	ERA	G	GS	CG	SV	IP	H	R	ER	BB	SO
1998	Princeton (Appy)	R	0	0	0.00	1	0	0	0	2	0	0	0	2	3
2001	Charleston, SC (SAL)	A	2	1	2.92	16	0	0	7	25	17	8	8	7	20
	Bakersfield (Cal)	A	1	0	1.09	17	0	0	3	25	13	7	3	8	33
	Orlando (SL)	AA	1	0	5.73	14	0	0	0	22	20	14	14	11	20
MINOR LEAGUE TOTALS			4	1	3.07	48	0	0	10	73	50	29	25	28	76

25. Enger Veras, rhp

Born: July 9, 1981. **Ht.:** 6-5. **Wt.:** 218. **Bats:** R. **Throws:** R. **Career Transactions:** Signed out of Dominican Republic by Devil Rays, Jan. 19, 1998.

Veras put together a great first half in high Class A last year before experiencing difficulties after the all-star break. He was 9-3, 2.53 entering July, yet failed to post a victory in his last 11 starts while his overall ERA climbed two full runs. Veras' fastball will touch as high as 97 mph and has a comfort zone at 93-95. But he has no consistency with his secondary pitches. His breaking ball comes and goes, and he becomes much more hittable when he starts relying primarily on his heater. The Rays believe that once he gains confidence in all of his pitches and learns how to mix them instead of falling back on his fastball every time the going gets tough, he'll start to make significant progress. Tampa Bay plans for him to spend this year in Double-A.

Year	Club (League)	Class	W	L	ERA	G	GS	CG	SV	IP	H	R	ER	BB	SO
1998	Devil Rays (GCL)	R	1	1	6.75	5	4	0	0	16	19	14	12	12	19
1999	Princeton (Appy)	R	3	5	7.12	14	14	0	0	61	74	57	48	50	48
2000	Charleston, SC (SAL)	A	8	8	4.81	20	20	1	0	107	125	74	57	41	102
2001	Bakersfield (Cal)	A	9	8	4.53	27	27	0	0	153	163	104	77	55	138
MINOR LEAGUE TOTALS			21	22	5.20	66	65	1	0	336	381	249	194	158	307

26. Doug Waechter, rhp

Born: Jan. 28, 1981. **Ht.:** 6-4. **Wt.:** 210. **Bats:** R. **Throws:** R. **School:** Northeast HS, St. Petersburg, Fla.
Career Transactions: Selected by Devil Rays in third round of 1999 draft; signed June 27, 1999.

Waechter underwent a learning experience in low Class A last year while pitching for the first time in a full-season league. As he has throughout his professional career, the former South Florida quarterback recruit battled inconsistency with all of his pitches. He has a low-90s fastball, and his curveball and changeup showed some improvement. He upgraded his control sharply from his first two years. Waechter still has work to do, as he was too hittable in 2001 and his mechanics require refinement. He has good size and the Devil Rays hope he can develop into a workhorse. A promotion to high Class A is in his immediate future.

Year	Club (League)	Class	W	L	ERA	G	GS	CG	SV	IP	H	R	ER	BB	SO
1999	Princeton (Appy)	R	0	5	9.77	11	7	0	0	35	46	45	38	35	38
2000	Hudson Valley (NY-P)	A	4	4	2.35	14	14	2	0	73	53	23	19	37	58
2001	Charleston (SAL)	A	8	11	4.34	26	26	1	0	153	179	97	74	38	107
MINOR LEAGUE TOTALS			12	20	4.52	51	47	3	0	261	278	163	131	110	203

27. Jamie Shields, rhp

Born: Dec. 20, 1981. **Ht.:** 6-3. **Wt.:** 195. **Bats:** R. **Throws:** R. **School:** Hart HS, Newhall, Calif. **Career Transactions:** Selected by Devil Rays in 16th round of 2000 draft; signed Aug. 17, 2000.

After signing late as a 16th-round draft pick in 2000, Shields put together an impressive debut last year. He overcame a mild shoulder injury and opened the season in extended spring training. He had no difficulty in low Class A as a teenager. Shields has good command of his fastball, which was clocked as high as 91 mph last summer. He also has a plus curveball that features sharp, late-breaking action, making it particularly troublesome for righthanders. Shields has impressive determination and excellent endurance, as evidenced by his two complete games in the South Atlantic League. His changeup is no better than average, but the Rays believe that once he makes it more consistent, he could move rapidly. Shields made the most of his opportunities last year. His next step is expected to come in high Class A this season.

Year	Club (League)	Class	W	L	ERA	G	GS	CG	SV	IP	H	R	ER	BB	SO
2001	Hudson Valley (NY-P)	A	2	1	2.30	5	5	0	0	27	27	8	7	5	25
	Charleston, SC (SAL)	A	4	5	2.65	10	10	2	0	71	63	24	21	10	60
MINOR LEAGUE TOTALS			6	6	2.55	15	15	2	0	99	90	32	28	15	85

28. Ramon Mercedes, ss

Born: July 9, 1981. **Ht.:** 5-11. **Wt.:** 160. **Bats:** R. **Throws:** R. **Career Transactions:** Signed out of Dominican Republic by Devil Rays, Jan. 4, 1999.

After spending two seasons in the Rookie-level Dominican Summer League, where he hit .301, Mercedes continued his development in the United States last year. One of the best defensive shortstops in the Appalachian League, he has soft hands and a strong arm. He also has above-average range and is capable of making the routine plays as well as the occasional spectacular one. Mercedes' greatest weakness is a lack of overall strength. He has a smooth swing and makes consistent contact with a good knowledge of the strike zone, but power pitchers can knock the bat out of his hands. The Rays believe his hitting ability will be fine once he adds some muscle to his 160-pound frame. Still making adjustments, he could start to blossom in low Class A this year.

Year	Club (League)	Class	AVG	G	AB	R	H	2B	3B	HR	RBI	BB	SO	SB
1999	Devil Rays (DSL)	R	.310	67	242	39	75	15	3	0	34	33	22	7
2000	Devil Rays (DSL)	R	.292	66	253	41	74	8	1	1	39	40	19	13
2001	Princeton (Appy)	R	.252	48	163	22	41	5	0	1	19	11	26	5
MINOR LEAGUE TOTALS			.289	181	658	102	190	28	4	2	92	84	67	25

29. Mark Malaska, lhp

Born: Jan. 17, 1978. **Ht.:** 6-3. **Wt.:** 191. **Bats:** L. **Throws:** L. **School:** University of Akron. **Career Transactions:** Selected by Devil Rays in eighth round of 2000 draft; signed June 19, 2000.

Primarily an outfielder in college, Malaska reached high Class A as a starter in his first full pro season. His overall stuff, which includes a low-90s fastball with fine sinking action, reminds some observers of Jim Abbott. Malaska also does a good job of keeping his pitches low in the strike zone and maintaining the inside part of the plate. While his feel for pitching has been impressive considering his lack of experience on the mound, Malaska needs to fine-tune most aspects of his game. He's currently starting in order to give him innings, provide him time to work on his entire repertoire and build his arm strength. His eventual role may come as a reliever who can retire lefthanders late in games, but the plan for 2002 has Malaska beginning back in the Bakersfield rotation.

Year	Club (League)	Class	W	L	ERA	G	GS	CG	SV	IP	H	R	ER	BB	SO
2000	Charleston, SC (SAL)	A	0	0	9.00	2	0	0	0	2	3	2	2	0	3
	Hudson Valley (NY-P)	A	0	2	4.91	10	5	0	0	40	44	27	22	14	36
2001	Charleston, SC (SAL)	A	7	12	2.92	25	25	1	0	157	153	71	51	35	152
	Bakersfield (Cal)	A	2	1	4.08	3	3	0	0	18	14	8	8	5	13
MINOR LEAGUE TOTALS			9	15	3.44	40	33	1	0	217	214	108	83	54	204

30. Cedrick Bowers, lhp

Born: Feb. 10, 1978. **Ht.:** 6-2. **Wt.:** 223. **Bats:** R. **Throws:** L. **School:** Chiefland (Fla.) HS. **Career Transactions:** Selected by Devil Rays in fourth round of 1996 draft; signed June 5, 1996.

Bowers bounced back with a solid effort as a swingman in Triple-A last year. Used primarily as a starter early in his career, he did a good job of pitching extensively out of the bullpen for the first time and reestablished himself as a potential situational lefty for the Devil Rays. Bowers has always piled up strikeouts in the minor leagues by employing one of the best curveballs in the organization. He prevents hitters from making solid contact by mixing the curve with an average fastball and a modest changeup. His albatross has been his control, which is what stands between him and a big league job. He could get a callup this year if he can throw strikes on a regular basis.

Year	Club (League)	Class	W	L	ERA	G	GS	CG	SV	IP	H	R	ER	BB	SO
1996	Devil Rays (GCL)	R	3	5	5.37	13	13	0	0	60	50	39	36	39	85
1997	Charleston, SC (SAL)	A	8	10	3.21	28	28	0	0	157	119	74	56	78	164
1998	St. Petersburg (FSL)	A	5	9	4.38	28	26	0	0	150	144	89	73	80	156
1999	Orlando (SL)	AA	6	9	5.98	27	27	1	0	125	125	94	83	76	138
2000	Orlando (SL)	AA	5	8	2.78	20	19	1	0	107	85	45	33	44	92
	Durham (IL)	AAA	3	1	5.49	4	4	0	0	20	21	13	12	13	20
2001	Durham (IL)	AAA	6	5	3.06	42	11	0	0	94	83	38	32	56	67
MINOR LEAGUE TOTALS			36	47	4.10	162	128	2	0	713	627	392	325	386	722

TEXAS
Rangers

TOP 30 PROSPECTS
1. Hank Blalock, 3b
2. Mark Teixeira, 3b
3. Mario Ramos, lhp
4. Colby Lewis, rhp
5. Ryan Ludwick, of
6. Ryan Dittfurth, rhp
7. Joaquin Benoit, rhp
8. Jovanny Cedeno, rhp
9. Kevin Mench, of
10. Jason Hart, 1b
11. Jason Bourgeois, 2b
12. Omar Beltre, rhp
13. Andy Pratt, lhp
14. Jose Dominguez, rhp
15. Jason Romano, of/2b
16. Travis Hafner, 1b
17. Laynce Nix, of
18. Patrick Boyd, of
19. Gerald Laird, c
20. Kelvin Jimenez, rhp
21. Justin Duchscherer, rhp
22. Nick Regilio, rhp
23. Jason Botts, of/1b
24. Scott Heard, c
25. Travis Hughes, rhp
26. Jose Morban, ss
27. Chris Russ, lhp
28. Reynaldo Garcia, rhp
29. C.J. Wilson, lhp
30. Greg Runser, rhp

By Gerry Fraley

In seven seasons as Rangers general manager, Doug Melvin did many good things. He brought a sense of order to a rudderless franchise. He was creative in the maneuvers that resulted in three American League West titles, the first championships in Rangers history.

But in the end, none of that could offset Texas' most pressing problem: a lack of pitching throughout the organization. The Rangers never made up for their 1995-96 drafts, when they had four first-round picks and spent them all on pitchers who flopped.

Owner Tom Hicks, with others whispering in his ear, fired Melvin in October after a disappointing 73-89 season. The situation looked worse, Hicks said, because of all the talented young arms on their AL West rivals. "Our organization needs a fresh look," Hicks said. "I was afraid we'd be in the same place two years from now."

Hicks helped create the problem. He gave Melvin concurrent mandates of winning in the majors and stocking the farm system. After two consecutive last-place finishes, Hicks may now have the stomach to take a step backward in hopes of having a stronger team for the future.

He brought in a new management team of GM John Hart, who got out of Cleveland before the Indians began cutting payroll, and assistant GM Grady Fuson, a key player as scouting director in Oakland's dynamic player-development operation.

Hart wasted little time making big moves, signing Chan Ho Park (five years, $65 million) and Juan Gonzalez (two years, $24 million) as free agents and acquiring the volatile Carl Everett and John Rocker in trades that cost Texas next to nothing. The most shocking transaction might have come in mid-January. Slugging first baseman Carlos Pena, who had been the pride of the farm system, was shipped to Athletics (along with Mike Venafro) for four of Oakland's best prospects: lefthander Mario Ramos, outfielder Ryan Ludwick, first baseman Jason Hart and catcher Gerald Laird.

Fuson, who drafted all four of those players for the A's, acknowledged the trade could determine his legacy in Texas.

"There's risk involved, but if you don't like that part of the kitchen, you probably shouldn't be there," he said. "It's flattering that somebody trusts your judgment enough to allow you to do this. What we're trying to do is make the club better for now and the future. If it fails, and we need a gardener in the future, I'm the guy."

OrganizationOverview

General Manager: John Hart. **Farm director:** Trey Hillman. **Scouting director:** Grady Fuson.

2001 PERFORMANCE

Class	Team	League	W	L	Pct.	Finish*	Manager(s)
Majors	Texas	American	73	89	.451	10th (14)	J. Oates/J. Narron
Triple-A	Oklahoma RedHawks	Pacific Coast	74	69	.517	6th (16)	DeMarlo Hale
Double-A	Tulsa Drillers	Texas	69	70	.496	5th (8)	Paul Carey
High A	Charlotte Rangers	Florida State	67	70	.489	10th (12)	Darryl Kennedy
Low A	Savannah Sand Gnats	South Atlantic	54	80	.403	14th (16)	B. Slack/P. Lopez
Rookie	Pulaski Rangers	Appalachian	38	30	.559	3rd (10)	Bruce Crabbe
Rookie	GCL Rangers	Gulf Coast	24	35	.407	10th (14)	Carlos Subero
OVERALL 2001 MINOR LEAGUE RECORD			326	356	.478	t-19th (30)	

*Finish in overall standings (No. of teams in league)

ORGANIZATION LEADERS

BATTING
*AVG	Hank Blalock, Tulsa/Charlotte	.352
R	Hank Blalock, Tulsa/Charlotte	96
H	Hank Blalock, Tulsa/Charlotte	179
TB	Hank Blalock, Tulsa/Charlotte	280
2B	Carlos Pena, Oklahoma	38
3B	**Jose Morban**, Savannah	11
HR	Kevin Mench, Tulsa	26
RBI	Hank Blalock, Tulsa/Charlotte	108
BB	Carlos Pena, Oklahoma	80
SO	Carlos Pena, Oklahoma	127
SB	**Jose Morban**, Savannah	46

PITCHING
W	**R.A. Dickey**, Oklahoma	11
	Colby Lewis, Tulsa/Charlotte	11
L	Corey Lee, Oklahoma/Tulsa	12
#ERA	Keith Stamler, Charlotte/Savannah	2.43
	Hayden Gardner, Charlotte/Pulaski	2.43
G	Greg Runner, Charlotte	50
CG	Three tied at	3
SV	Greg Runner, Charlotte	30
IP	Andy Pratt, Tulsa	168
BB	Dave Elder, Oklahoma/Tulsa	86
SO	Colby Lewis, Tulsa/Charlotte	170

*Minimum 250 At-Bats #Minimum 75 Innings

TOP PROSPECTS OF THE DECADE

1992	Kurt Miller, rhp
1993	Benji Gil, ss
1994	Benji Gil, ss
1995	Julio Santana, rhp
1996	Andrew Vessel, of
1997	Danny Kolb, rhp
1998	Ruben Mateo, of
1999	Ruben Mateo, of
2000	Ruben Mateo, of
2001	Carlos Pena, 1b

TOP DRAFT PICKS OF THE DECADE

1992	Rick Helling, rhp
1993	Mike Bell, 3b
1994	Kevin Brown, c (2)
1995	Jonathan Johnson, rhp
1996	R.A. Dickey, rhp
1997	Jason Romano, 3b
1998	Carlos Pena, 1b
1999	Colby Lewis, rhp
2000	Scott Heard, c
2001	Mark Teixeira, 3b

Morban   **Dickey**

BEST TOOLS

Best Hitter for Average	Hank Blalock
Best Power Hitter	Mark Teixeira
Fastest Baserunner	Masjid Khairy
Best Fastball	Colby Lewis
Best Breaking Ball	Colby Lewis
Best Changeup	Mario Ramos
Best Control	Mario Ramos
Best Defensive Catcher	Scott Heard
Best Defensive Infielder	Brandon Warriax
Best Infield Arm	Jose Morban
Best Defensive Outfielder	Patrick Boyd
Best Outfield Arm	Julin Charles

PROJECTED 2005 LINEUP

Catcher	Ivan Rodriguez
First Base	Mark Teixeira
Second Base	Mike Young
Third Base	Hank Blalock
Shortstop	Alex Rodriguez
Left Field	Juan Gonzalez
Center Field	Carl Everett
Right Field	Ryan Ludwick
Designated Hitter	Kevin Mench
No. 1 Starter	Chan Ho Park
No. 2 Starter	Mario Ramos
No. 3 Starter	Colby Lewis
No. 4 Starter	Ryan Dittfurth
No. 5 Starter	Joaquin Benoit
Closer	John Rocker

ALL-TIME LARGEST BONUSES

Mark Teixeira, 2001	$4,500,000
Carlos Pena, 1998	$1,850,000
Scott Heard, 2000	$1,475,000
Jonathan Johnson, 1995	$1,100,000
Colby Lewis, 1999	$862,500

DraftAnalysis

2001 Draft

Best Pro Debut: A two-way player at Loyola Marymount, LHP C.J. Wilson (5) went 3-9, 6.95 last spring. Allowed to focus on pitching as a pro, he went 2-2, 2.01 with a 75-18 strikeout-walk ration in 72 innings.

Best Athlete: OF Masjid Khairy (8) has good speed and body control. He's figuring out how to hit, though he did steal 26 bases in the Rookie-level Gulf Coast League. RHP Gerald Smiley (9), a guard for his high school basketball team, is athletic for a pitcher.

Best Hitter: 3B **Mark Teixeira** (1) is the best all-around hitter to come out of college in recent memory. The best comparison is to Pat Burrell, the No. 1 overall pick in 1998, though Teixeira is a switch-hitter, makes better contact and is more athletic.

Best Raw Power: Not only was Teixeira the best pure hitter in the 2001 draft, he also was the best power hitter. Still recovering from a broken ankle in February 2001, he should be 100 percent by spring training.

Fastest Runner: Khairy can run a 6.4-second 60-yard dash.

Best Defensive Player: OF Patrick Boyd (7) has Shawn Green tools and plays a fine center field. After missing most of 2001 with a back injury, he signed in January.

Best Fastball: Smiley and RHP Paul Abraham (12) both touched 94 mph in Rookie ball. RHP Chris Bradshaw (14) has hit 93.

Most Intriguing Background: Unsigned RHP Andy Myette's (44) brother Aaron won four games for Texas this season; as a junior college player, the younger Myette remains under Rangers control. Unsigned RHP Josh Baker's (4) father Johnny was an NFL linebacker, his uncle Frank was a major league infielder and his brother Jacob played in the Royals system before retiring last spring. And his sister married Lance Berkman.

Closest To The Majors: Teixeira, who signed a $9.5 million major league contract, could debut in Double-A. He won't need much time in the minors.

Best Late-Round Pick: Bradshaw pitched in the Rangers' backyard at Texas Christian and could prove to be a bargain senior sign for $5,000. OF Brad Stockton (22), another college senior, has pop.

Teixeira

The One Who Got Away: Baker, who opted to go to Alabama, is a 6-foot-4, 205-pounder with average velocity and a plus splitter. The Rangers were disappointed RHP Ryan Dixon (15) didn't attend junior college. They lost his rights when he headed to Miami instead.

Assessment: The Rangers signed 16 players, including one in the first four rounds—it gave up its second- and third-rounders to sign free agents Alex Rodriguez and Mark Petkovsek—but Teixeira could make this draft by himself. The Rangers have an obvious need for pitching, but astutely grabbed Teixeira with the fifth pick. If Boyd is healthy and regains the stroke he had in 1999, he could also be something special.

2000 Draft

C Scott Heard (1) may never hit, and a deal with OF Tyrell Godwin (1) broke down when doctors found a knee injury during his physical. A third first-rounder, RHP Chad Hawkins, has had elbow trouble. There's still hope for 2B Jason Bourgeois (2), OF Laynce Nix (4), LHP Chris Russ (3) and RHPs Greg Runser (5) and Nick Masset (8, draft-and-follow).   **Grade: C**

1999 Draft

3B Hank Blalock (3) is baseball's best offensive prospect. RHP Colby Lewis (1) and OF Kevin Mench (4) are two more of the organization's top prospects. RHPs Nick Regilio (2) and David Mead (1) and OF/1B Jason Botts (46, draft-and-follow) add more depth.   **Grade: A**

1998 Draft

1B Carlos Pena (1) makes this a tremendous draft all by himself. Just imagine if Texas had signed LHP Barry Zito (3). RHP Ryan Dittfurth (5) and LHP Andy Pratt (9) are two of the system's few upper-level pitching prospects who have stayed healthy.   **Grade: A**

1997 Draft

2B/OF Jason Romano's (1) stock is slipping along with his slugging percentage. 3B Mike Lamb (7) is keeping the hot corner warm in Texas for Blalock. RHP David Elder (4) was all it cost to get John Rocker from Cleveland this winter.   **Grade: C+**

Note: Draft analysis prepared by Jim Callis. Numbers in parentheses indicate draft rounds.

. . . He knows how to play the game the right way and has an advanced grasp of using the entire field.

Blalock Hank 3b

Born: Nov. 21, 1980.
Ht.: 6-1. **Wt.:** 192.
Bats: L. **Throws:** R.
School: Rancho Bernardo HS, San Diego.
Career Transactions: Selected by Rangers in third round of 1999 draft; signed June 4, 1999.

Blalock is another in the long line of players to come out of the San Diego talent hotbed and powerful Rancho Bernardo High, which also produced Scott Heard, the Rangers' 2000 first-round pick. Blalock's father Dana and uncle Sam are prominent influences in the baseball community—Sam coaches Rancho Bernardo—and his younger brother Jake is expected to go in the first three rounds of the 2002 draft. While scouts said Blalock was limited offensively in high school, he turned down Cal State Fullerton after being drafted as a shortstop. His stock has soared since. He won the Rookie-level Gulf Coast League batting title in 1999 and ranked second in the minors with a .352 average in 2001. Blalock was the No. 2 prospect in the high Class A Florida State League, and was second to none in the Double-A Texas League and the Arizona Fall League.

Blalock's strong amateur background shows. He knows how to play the game the right way and has an advanced grasp of using the entire field. He makes solid contact and sprays the ball from foul line to foul line. He has power to the alleys and some scouts project him to hit 30 or more homers a season because of his bat speed and the natural lift in his swing. He has a short, compact swing and handles lefthanders and righthanders equally well. He also has the discipline to sit back on offspeed stuff. Despite below-average wheels, Blalock lets his instincts take over on the bases and can be an occasional basestealing threat. He has improved his defense, committing just 15 errors last season. He can become too selective at times, and the Rangers would like to see him expand his hitting zone and trade a few strikeouts for a few extra-base hits. Like most young infielders, he needs to devote more time to his footwork on defense.

Blalock is six months younger than Mark Teixeira, and two years ahead of him in professional experience. The Rangers plan to start the season with both playing third base at different levels. Blalock is more athletic and more capable of handling a position change, if necessary. He could be a second baseman in the mold of Jeff Kent or handle a move to left field. The platoon of Herb Perry and Mike Lamb buys Blalock a year in Triple-A Oklahoma.

Year	Club (League)	Class	AVG	G	AB	R	H	2B	3B	HR	RBI	BB	SO	SB
1999	Rangers (GCL)	R	.361	51	191	34	69	17	6	3	38	25	23	3
	Savannah (SAL)	A	.240	7	25	3	6	1	0	1	2	1	3	0
2000	Savannah (SAL)	A	.299	139	512	66	153	32	2	10	77	62	53	31
2001	Charlotte (FSL)	A	.380	63	237	46	90	19	1	7	47	26	31	7
	Tulsa (TL)	AA	.327	68	272	50	89	18	4	11	61	39	38	3
MINOR LEAGUE TOTALS			.329	328	1237	199	407	87	13	32	225	153	148	44

RON CUNI

2. Mark Teixeira, 3b

Born: April 11, 1980. **Ht.:** 6-3. **Wt.:** 225. **Bats:** B. **Throws:** R. **School:** Georgia Tech. **Career Transactions:** Selected by Rangers in first round (fifth overall) of 2001 draft; signed Aug. 24, 2001.

Teixeira turned down the Red Sox' seven-figure bonus offer out of high school as a ninth-rounder in 1998. He was the top prospect in the Cape Cod League in 1999 and Baseball America's College Player of the Year in 2000. Despite missing most of his junior season with a fractured right ankle, he went fifth overall in the 2001 draft and signed for a major league contract worth $9.5 million. Teixeira was both the best pure hitter and the best power hitter available in the 2001 draft, and the most advanced college bat since Pat Burrell went No. 1 overall in the 1998 draft. A switch-hitter, he is proficient from both sides of the plate. Before he got hurt, he had made strides with his running and defense. He didn't play the field after returning from the injury, so there will be questions about his defense until he does. He still has to show he can play third base in the majors, though Hank Blalock's presence and Carlos Pena's trade will make it easier to move Teixeira to first base. The injury and protracted contract negotiations left Teixeira rusty in instructional league, where he hit .246 with one homer in 57 at-bats. He'll stay at the hot corner for now and could debut as high as Double-A Tulsa.

Year	Club (League)	Class	AVG	G	AB	R	H	2B	3B	HR	RBI	BB	SO	SB
			Has Not Played—Signed 2002 Contract											

3. Mario Ramos, lhp

Born: Oct. 19, 1977. **Ht.:** 6-0. **Wt.:** 180. **Bats:** L. **Throws:** L. **School:** Rice University. **Career Transactions:** Selected by Athletics in sixth round of 1999 draft; signed Aug. 23, 1999 . . . Traded by Athletics with 1B Jason Hart, C Gerald Laird and OF Ryan Ludwick to Rangers for 1B Carlos Pena and LHP Mike Venafro, Jan. 14, 2002.

Ramos was the key to the Carlos Pena trade for the Rangers, who lacked a major league-ready pitching prospect with his upside. The Athletics considered him the cream of their minor league crop and compared his ability to learn and make adjustments to Mark Mulder and Barry Zito, two other college lefties who zoomed through their system. After Ramos' first year as a pro, the A's told him to develop a breaking ball to compete at higher levels. So he went to work and came up with a plus curveball that some consider his best pitch. More than anything, he knows how to pitch. He lives by changing speeds off his 88 mph fastball, and both his changeup and command are outstanding. Doubters wonder whether a pitcher who doesn't break 90 can quickly become a force in the major leagues, though Ramos has a knack for putting the ball by hitters. His only real flaw is a tendency to pound righthanders inside. Ramos will compete with Rob Bell, Hideki Irabu and Aaron Myette for the fifth spot in the Texas rotation this spring. If he doesn't win out, he still figures to surface with the Rangers at some point in 2002.

Year	Club (League)	Class	W	L	ERA	G	GS	CG	SV	IP	H	R	ER	BB	SO
2000	Modesto (Cal)	A	12	5	2.90	26	24	1	0	152	131	63	49	50	134
	Midland (TL)	AA	2	0	1.32	4	4	0	0	27	24	6	4	6	19
2001	Midland (TL)	AA	8	1	3.07	15	15	0	0	94	71	37	32	28	68
	Sacramento (PCL)	AAA	8	3	3.14	13	13	1	0	80	74	32	28	27	82
MINOR LEAGUE TOTALS			**30**	**9**	**2.88**	**58**	**56**	**2**	**0**	**353**	**300**	**138**	**113**	**111**	**303**

4. Colby Lewis, rhp

Born: Aug. 2, 1979. **Ht.:** 6-4. **Wt.:** 215. **Bats:** R. **Throws:** R. **School:** Bakersfield (Calif.) JC. **Career Transactions:** Selected by Rangers in first round (38th overall) of 1999 draft; signed June 15, 1999.

Texas' belated attempt to add more power arms began when it took Lewis with its first choice in the 1999 draft. He had Tommy John surgery after high school but has held up well since. He led the system in strikeouts last season and held hitters in the offense-crazed Texas League to a .252 average. Everything Lewis throws is hard. He has the velocity to be effective with a high, riding four-seamer that clocks in the mid-90s and has late movement. He also utilizes a hard curveball. When his power doesn't work, Lewis has trouble surviving. He didn't make it past the fifth inning in eight of his 24 Double-A starts, and he allowed five homers in a game in which he had a 97 mph fastball. He could avoid the inconsistency by getting a better offspeed pitch. Lewis lost valuable development time when a sore shoulder forced him out of the Arizona Fall League. The Rangers believe the soreness is related to pitching at least 160 innings in consecutive seasons after his elbow injury. They'll monitor him closely this year in Triple-A.

Year	Club (League)	Class	W	L	ERA	G	GS	CG	SV	IP	H	R	ER	BB	SO
1999	Pulaski (Appy)	R	7	3	1.95	14	11	1	0	65	46	24	14	27	84
2000	Charlotte (FSL)	A	11	10	4.07	28	27	3	0	164	169	83	74	45	153
2001	Charlotte (FSL)	A	1	0	0.00	1	0	0	0	4	0	0	0	0	8
	Tulsa (TL)	AA	10	10	4.50	25	25	1	0	156	150	85	78	62	162
MINOR LEAGUE TOTALS			29	23	3.84	68	63	5	0	389	365	192	166	134	407

5. Ryan Ludwick, of

JOHN SPEAR

Born: July 13, 1978. **Ht.:** 6-3. **Wt.:** 203. **Bats:** R. **Throws:** L. **School:** University of Nevada-Las Vegas. **Career Transactions:** Selected by Athletics in second round of 1999 draft; signed July 17, 1999 . . . Traded by Athletics with 1B Jason Hart, C Gerald Laird and LHP Mario Ramos to Rangers for 1B Carlos Pena and LHP Mike Venafro, Jan. 14, 2002.

Once projected as a first-round pick in the 1999 draft, Ludwick slid after a shaky junior season at Nevada-Las Vegas. He regained his stroke with the Athletics before being included in the Carlos Pena trade. He's the brother of ex-big league pitcher Eric Ludwick. Ryan has the tools to become a legitimate major league slugger. He's also an above-average out-fielder with a plus arm in right field. He lacks the burning speed of most center fielders, but he's faster than most corner outfielders. As he has advanced, though, he has been slow to make adjustments. He doesn't incorporate his lower half well into his swing. He needs to mature as a hitter rather than letting one bad at-bat affect his next trip to the plate. The question remains whether he can develop into a major league center fielder or if he's better suited to right. Ludwick is similar to Gabe Kapler, whom he may have to battle for a big league starting job in the near future. For now, Ludwick will go to Triple-A.

Year	Club (League)	Class	AVG	G	AB	R	H	2B	3B	HR	RBI	BB	SO	SB
1999	Modesto (Cal)	A	.275	43	171	28	47	11	3	4	34	19	45	2
2000	Modesto (Cal)	A	.264	129	493	86	130	26	3	29	102	68	128	10
2001	Midland (TL)	AA	.269	119	443	82	119	23	3	25	96	56	113	9
	Sacramento (PCL)	AAA	.228	17	57	10	13	3	0	1	7	2	16	2
MINOR LEAGUE TOTALS			.265	308	1164	206	309	63	9	59	239	145	302	23

6. Ryan Dittfurth, rhp

RODGER WOOD

Born: Oct. 18, 1979. **Ht.:** 6-6. **Wt.:** 180. **Bats:** R. **Throws:** R. **School:** Tulsa Union HS. **Career Transactions:** Selected by Rangers in fifth round of 1998 draft; signed June 29, 1998.

To sway Dittfurth to turn pro rather than attending Texas A&M, the Rangers arranged for him to meet Nolan Ryan. Three years later, Dittfurth won the organization's Nolan Ryan award as its minor league pitcher of the year. He has spent one season at each of the four lowest levels of the system, flourishing at that pace. Dittfurth uses four pitches, the best of which is a 93 mph running fastball. It has heavy sink that makes it diffi-cult for hitters to lift. He also throws a sweeping curveball that's effective against left-handers, plus a slider and changeup. The key for him in 2001 was much improved com-mand. He gained better control of his body and focused on attacking the strike zone. He uses his gangly body to hide the ball well in his delivery. Dittfurth's mound composure has improved but still needs work. He had shown a tendency to come undone in the face of adversity. He can be difficult to catch, as evidenced by his 15 wild pitches last season. The combination of four good pitches and growing maturity could allow Dittfurth to come on in a hurry. He'll start this season in Double-A but could finish in Triple-A.

Year	Club (League)	Class	W	L	ERA	G	GS	CG	SV	IP	H	R	ER	BB	SO
1998	Rangers (GCL)	R	3	2	1.34	8	6	0	0	34	25	8	5	11	33
1999	Pulaski (Appy)	R	7	2	2.60	14	14	1	0	83	66	35	24	42	85
2000	Savannah (SAL)	A	8	13	4.25	29	29	2	0	159	127	83	75	99	158
2001	Charlotte (FSL)	A	9	6	3.48	27	24	2	0	147	123	66	57	66	134
MINOR LEAGUE TOTALS			27	23	3.43	78	73	5	0	423	341	192	161	218	410

7. Joaquin Benoit, rhp

Born: July 26, 1979. **Ht.:** 6-3. **Wt.:** 205. **Bats:** R. **Throws:** R. **Career Transactions:** Signed out of Dominican Republic by Rangers, May 20, 1996.

The Rangers keep waiting for Benoit's breakthrough year, but so far it has been in vain. After turning in a strong Arizona Fall League performance in 2000, he failed to build on it. He did set a career high for innings in 2001, which wasn't hard considering he was sidelined by nagging injuries through his first three full seasons in the United States. When Benoit throws strikes with his plus fastball and slider, he can be overpowering. He devours righthanded hitters with the slider, holding them to a .216 average in 2001. He also has an above-average changeup. Benoit likes to work high in the strike zone, sometimes too high. He still walks too many batters, and he has a bad habit of showing up umpires when he's displeased by their calls. He tends to shut himself down at the first sign of soreness, which makes it difficult for him to maintain his consistency. There have been some concerns that his delivery could lead to more serious arm problems. Benoit will be just 22 on Opening Day, but it's time for him to step forward after six years in the organization. Slated to open 2002 in Triple-A, he could crack the Texas rotation later in the year if he pitches to his potential.

Year	Club (League)	Class	W	L	ERA	G	GS	CG	SV	IP	H	R	ER	BB	SO
1996	Rangers (DSL)	R	6	5	2.28	14	13	2	0	75	63	26	19	23	63
1997	Rangers (GCL)	R	3	3	2.05	10	10	1	0	44	40	14	10	11	38
1998	Savannah (SAL)	A	4	3	3.83	15	15	1	0	80	79	41	34	18	68
1999	Charlotte (FSL)	A	7	4	5.31	22	22	0	0	105	117	67	62	50	83
2000	Tulsa (TL)	AA	4	4	3.83	16	16	0	0	82	73	40	35	30	72
2001	Tulsa (TL)	AA	1	0	3.32	4	4	0	0	22	23	8	8	6	23
	Oklahoma (PCL)	AAA	9	5	4.19	24	24	1	0	131	113	63	61	73	142
	Texas (AL)	MAJ	0	0	10.80	1	1	0	0	5	8	6	6	3	4
MAJOR LEAGUE TOTALS			0	0	10.80	1	1	0	0	5	8	6	6	3	4
MINOR LEAGUE TOTALS			34	24	3.82	105	104	5	0	539	508	259	229	211	489

8. Jovanny Cedeno, rhp

Born: Oct. 25, 1979. **Ht.:** 6-0. **Wt.:** 170. **Bats:** R. **Throws:** R. **Career Transactions:** Signed out of Dominican Republic by Rangers, Feb. 2, 1997.

Injuries struck several of Texas' better pitching prospects in 2001, and no news was more devastating than that surrounding Cedeno. The Rangers had nagging concerns about his slender frame for a while, and had to shut him down after three starts at high Class A Charlotte. Doctors diagnosed a torn labrum in his shoulder that required season-ending surgery. When healthy, Cedeno dazzles with his fastball/changeup combination. Like his idol and fellow Dominican Pedro Martinez, he gets exceptional movement on his changeup because of his large hands and fingers. Cedeno's fastball is explosive and travels into the mid-90s. He has the same love for the game that Martinez has. Still, Cedeno has pitched just 276 innings in five years as a pro. With only two options remaining, he may have to be kept in the majors before he accumulates the minor league experience he needs. He hasn't been healthy enough to develop a consistent breaking ball. Cedeno threw off a mound during instructional league and could have pitched in winter ball, but the Rangers decided to err on the side of caution. They hope he'll be ready for big league camp, though he might start this season in extended spring training. If he's healthy, Cedeno's ceiling is as high as high as any pitcher in the system.

Year	Club (League)	Class	W	L	ERA	G	GS	CG	SV	IP	H	R	ER	BB	SO
1997	Rangers (DSL)	R	10	2	2.56	14	14	1	0	84	70	29	24	23	73
1998	Rangers (DSL)	R	1	0	1.42	5	2	0	1	19	14	5	3	5	22
1999	Rangers (GCL)	R	3	0	0.33	6	6	1	0	27	13	3	1	4	32
	Charlotte (FSL)	A	1	0	5.40	1	1	0	0	5	7	3	3	1	5
2000	Savannah (SAL)	A	11	4	2.42	24	22	0	0	130	95	40	35	40	153
2001	Charlotte (FSL)	A	0	0	1.86	3	3	0	0	10	3	2	2	5	12
MINOR LEAGUE TOTALS			26	6	2.22	53	48	2	1	276	202	82	68	91	297

9. Kevin Mench, of

Born: Jan. 7, 1978. **Ht.:** 6-0. **Wt.:** 215. **Bats:** R. **Throws:** R. **School:** University of Delaware. **Career Transactions:** Selected by Rangers in fourth round of 1999 draft; signed June 16, 1999.

Mench won the NCAA Division I home run title in 1998 with 33 as a Delaware sophomore. He slipped as a junior, hurting his draft status, but has been a power hitter in the pros. He led the Appalachian League in home runs in 1999 and has 71 in 323 pro games. Mench has been com- pared to a Pete Incaviglia with better outfield skills. He has become more and more of a dead-pull hitter with exceptional power. He crushed left- handers in the Texas League last season, hitting .352 with 10 homers in 128 at-bats against them. He has shown slightly above-average speed, but lingering hamstring problems kept him from running last season. He also bulked up last season, which may have been the cause of his leg problems. If he sticks with the pull-everything approach, he'll never hit for average. He hit just .233 against righthanders in 2001 and his patience at the plate slipped. His arm limits him to left field. Mench must keep his body under control. He's in danger of getting too stiff across the shoulders, a development that could tie up his swing. The Rangers hope he'll make some improvements in Triple-A this year.

Year	Club (League)	Class	AVG	G	AB	R	H	2B	3B	HR	RBI	BB	SO	SB
1999	Pulaski (Appy)	R	.362	65	260	63	94	22	1	16	60	28	48	12
	Savannah (SAL)	A	.304	6	23	4	7	1	1	2	8	2	4	0
2000	Charlotte (FSL)	A	.334	132	491	118	164	39	9	27	121	78	72	19
2001	Tulsa (TL)	AA	.265	120	475	78	126	34	2	26	83	34	76	4
MINOR LEAGUE TOTALS			.313	323	1249	263	391	96	13	71	272	142	200	35

10. Jason Hart, 1b

Born: Sept. 5, 1977. **Ht.:** 6-4. **Wt.:** 237. **Bats:** R. **Throws:** R. **School:** Southwest Missouri State University. **Career Transactions:** Selected by Athletics in fifth round of 1998 draft; signed June 5, 1998 . . . Traded by Athletics with C Gerald Laird, OF Ryan Ludwick and LHP Mario Ramos to Rangers for 1B Carlos Pena and LHP Mike Venafro, Jan. 14, 2002.

Another component of the Carlos Pena trade, Hart sped through the Oakland system with .303-70-317 totals in his first 350 pro games. Then everything fell apart for him last year in Triple-A. The Athletics think he may have put too much pressure on himself because of Jason Giambi's pending free agency. Before he got to Triple-A, Hart showed he could hit for both power and average. He used the whole field and was an offensive force. After spend- ing many hours honing his skills, he has made himself into a good defensive first baseman. Hart has to readjust his approach and return to the form that allowed him to terrorize pitch- ers at lower levels. Getting a bit more selective would help. He doesn't fit at another posi- tion, and he could have problems winning a starting job with the Rangers because they have a number of candidates for first base and DH, both in the present and in the future. Had he produced in 2001, Hart might have been Giambi's successor in Oakland. Instead he'll return to Triple-A, where he'll try to rebound and await a big league opening.

Year	Club (League)	Class	AVG	G	AB	R	H	2B	3B	HR	RBI	BB	SO	SB
1998	S. Oregon (NWL)	A	.258	75	295	58	76	19	1	20	69	36	67	0
1999	Modesto (Cal)	A	.305	135	550	96	168	48	2	19	123	56	105	2
2000	Midland (TL)	AA	.326	135	546	98	178	44	3	30	121	67	112	4
	Sacramento (PCL)	AAA	.278	5	18	4	5	1	0	1	4	3	7	0
2001	Sacramento (PCL)	AAA	.247	134	494	71	122	26	1	19	75	57	102	3
MINOR LEAGUE TOTALS			.288	484	1903	327	549	138	7	89	392	219	393	9

11. Jason Bourgeois, 2b

Born: Jan. 4, 1982. **Ht.:** 5-9. **Wt.:** 170. **Bats:** B. **Throws:** R. **School:** Forest Brook HS, Houston. **Career Transactions:** Selected by Rangers in second round of 2000 draft; signed June 19, 2000.

Texas ignored Bourgeois' size and took him with the 64th pick overall in the 2000 draft because of his energy. He's an electric player who has had to learn to harness his enthusi- asm. Managers ranked him as the Rookie-level Appalachian League's No. 3 prospect last year, when he increased his batting average 72 points from his pro debut. Bourgeois is more than just a pesky middle infielder. He stopped lunging at pitches and showed unexpected power. His motor and instincts prompted Appy League skippers to compare him to Charlie

Hustle himself. Bourgeois is an above-average runner with excellent first-step quickness. He gets in trouble when he becomes too power-conscious and forgets to be selective. He has below-average arm strength and his overall defense can be erratic. Playing on rough infields, he led Pulaski with 18 errors. Bourgeois will face his biggest test yet this year when he advances to full-season ball. If he doesn't improve his glovework, he's athletic enough to handle a move to center field.

Year	Club (League)	Class	AVG	G	AB	R	H	2B	3B	HR	RBI	BB	SO	SB
2000	Rangers (GCL)	R	.239	24	88	18	21	4	0	0	6	14	15	9
2001	Pulaski (Appy)	R	.311	62	251	60	78	12	2	7	34	26	47	21
MINOR LEAGUE TOTALS			.292	86	339	78	99	16	2	7	40	40	62	30

12. Omar Beltre, rhp

Born: Aug. 24, 1982. **Ht.:** 6-3. **Wt.:** 192. **Bats:** R. **Throws:** R. **Career Transactions:** Signed out of Dominican Republic by Rangers, March 1, 2000.

Former scouting director Chuck McMichael concentrated on big-ticket signings in the Dominican Republic. The Rangers snatched Beltre away from the Reds for a $650,000 bonus at age 17. He has handled the trying move of coming to the United States at such a young age. Beltre has a live arm and can throw his plus four-seam fastball past hitters. He has the frame that should allow him to grow into a power pitcher. Beltre needs an off-speed pitch to complement his fastball and slider. He uses a changeup but isn't fully comfortable with it. He had some control problems last season. A dose of humility also would be helpful. Beltre can be headstrong and reluctant to take coaching. He'll need to develop physically and mentally into a pitcher to continue his success as he jumps to full-season ball in 2002.

Year	Club (League)	Class	W	L	ERA	G	GS	CG	SV	IP	H	R	ER	BB	SO
2000	Rangers (GCL)	R	5	4	3.54	13	13	0	0	61	54	30	24	15	44
2001	Pulaski (Appy)	R	6	3	3.38	13	12	0	0	69	56	28	26	23	83
MINOR LEAGUE TOTALS			11	7	3.45	26	25	0	0	130	110	58	50	38	127

13. Andy Pratt, lhp

Born: Aug. 27, 1979. **Ht.:** 5-11. **Wt.:** 160. **Bats:** L. **Throws:** L. **School:** Chino Valley (Ariz.) HS. **Career Transactions:** Selected by Rangers in ninth round of 1998 draft; signed June 8, 1998.

Pratt was destined to be a pitcher. His father Tom pitched in the Royals organization and worked as a college pitching coach and major league scout before moving into his current role of minor league pitching coach in the Cubs system. Pratt performs like the son of a pitching coach. He's smart and has a fundamentally sound delivery. He's a classic finesse lefty who's at his best when changing speeds and tempting hitters. Pratt has been able to work the outside corner while still throwing strikes. He can touch 90-91 mph with his fastball, but he fell in love with his cutter last season and suffered for it. He lost command of his curveball and two changeups, and posted a 5.58 ERA in the final two months last season. He did get back on track in the Arizona Fall League. Pratt's pitchability may be unmatched in the system, but he'll need to miss more bats as he heads to Triple-A. He could be an end-of-the-rotation starter in a couple of years.

Year	Club (League)	Class	W	L	ERA	G	GS	CG	SV	IP	H	R	ER	BB	SO
1998	Rangers (GCL)	R	4	3	3.86	12	8	0	0	56	49	25	24	14	49
1999	Savannah (SAL)	A	4	4	2.89	13	13	1	0	72	66	30	23	16	100
2000	Charlotte (FSL)	A	7	4	2.72	16	16	2	0	93	68	37	28	26	95
	Tulsa (TL)	AA	1	6	7.22	11	11	0	0	52	66	48	42	33	42
2001	Tulsa (TL)	AA	8	10	4.61	27	26	3	0	168	175	99	86	57	132
MINOR LEAGUE TOTALS			24	27	4.15	79	74	6	0	441	424	239	203	146	418

14. Jose Dominguez, rhp

Born: Aug. 7, 1982. **Ht.:** 6-2. **Wt.:** 180. **Bats:** R. **Throws:** R. **Career Transactions:** Signed out of Dominican Republic by Rangers, Dec. 26, 1999.

The new regime of general manager John Hart and assistant GM Grady Fuson reaffirmed that the Rangers will invest heavily in the international market. After allowing their foothold to slip in the Dominican Republic, Texas has re-established its interests there. The club's best Dominican newcomer last year was Jose Dominguez, who made his U.S. debut at age 18. He led the Gulf Coast League club in innings and strikeouts. His live arm and projectable, lean frame have the Rangers eagerly anticipating his future. He throws a plus-plus fastball that touched 96 mph last year. Like Jovanny Cedeno,

Dominguez displays a feel for a deceptive changeup. He also has the makings of an above-average curveball. Dominguez is raw but filled with promise and is expected to make the leap to low Class A Savannah.

Year	Club (League)	Class	W	L	ERA	G	GS	CG	SV	IP	H	R	ER	BB	SO
2000	Rangers (DSL)	R	1	6	4.52	14	14	0	0	68	69	49	34	38	56
2001	Rangers (GCL)	R	4	2	4.01	11	9	1	0	58	56	29	26	12	55
	Charlotte (FSL)	A	1	0	3.60	2	0	0	0	5	4	2	2	1	5
MINOR LEAGUE TOTALS			6	8	4.26	27	23	1	0	131	129	80	62	51	116

15. Jason Romano, of/2b

Born: June 24, 1979. **Ht.:** 6-0. **Wt.:** 185. **Bats:** R. **Throws:** R. **School:** Hillsborough HS, Tampa. **Career Transactions:** Selected by Rangers in first round (39th overall) of 1997 draft; signed July 11, 1997.

Michael Young shot past Romano in the Rangers' second-base plans last season, forcing Romano to change positions. With Young quickly establishing himself at second base in Texas, Romano was sent all the way back to the Gulf Coast League to learn center field. With his natural athletic ability and zeal for down-in-the-dirt work, he took to the position. He's an above-average runner with good baseball instincts. The drawbacks about making him a center fielder are his limited arm strength and pop. Romano went into an offensive funk when he began 2001 in Double-A. His average rose after the position switch and a promotion to Oklahoma, but he didn't show the line-drive, gap power that was prominent early in his career. His slugging percentage has dropped from .516 in high Class A in 1999 to .389 and .369 the last two years. With the Rangers trading for Carl Everett, Romano will have a hard time making the jump from Triple-A this year.

Year	Club (League)	Class	AVG	G	AB	R	H	2B	3B	HR	RBI	BB	SO	SB
1997	Rangers (GCL)	R	.257	34	109	27	28	5	3	2	11	13	19	13
1998	Savannah (SAL)	A	.271	134	524	72	142	19	4	7	52	46	94	40
	Charlotte (FSL)	A	.208	7	24	3	5	1	0	0	1	2	2	1
1999	Charlotte (FSL)	A	.312	120	459	84	143	27	14	13	71	39	72	34
2000	Tulsa (TL)	AA	.271	131	535	87	145	35	2	8	70	56	84	25
2001	Tulsa (TL)	AA	.242	46	186	19	45	9	1	1	19	16	31	8
	Oklahoma (PCL)	AAA	.315	41	149	32	47	6	1	4	13	20	28	3
	Rangers (GCL)	R	.143	5	21	2	3	0	0	0	0	1	8	1
	Charlotte (FSL)	A	.400	3	10	3	4	2	0	0	1	4	1	1
MINOR LEAGUE TOTALS			.279	521	2017	329	562	104	25	35	238	197	339	126

16. Travis Hafner, 1b

Born: June 3, 1977. **Ht.:** 6-3. **Wt.:** 240. **Bats:** L. **Throws:** R. **School:** Cowley County (Kan.) CC. **Career Transactions:** Selected by Rangers in 31st round of 1996 draft; signed June 2, 1997.

Problems with his right wrist have dogged Hafner for more than a year. He left the Puerto Rican winter league early in 2000 because of wrist soreness and had spring-training surgery to repair a broken hamate bone. Limited during the 2001 season at Tulsa, Hafner had only a brief stay in the Arizona Fall League because of more wrist problems that required a second operation. The Rangers name an offseason of rest will cure the problem. When he did play last year, he showed his trademark farmboy power. The strongest player in the organization, he can drive the ball a great distance to any part of the ballpark. Lefthanders don't give him any trouble, as he has hit .358 with a .575 slugging percentage against them over the last two years. Hafner is a poor defensive first baseman and his slow feet aren't suited for any other position. There are questions as to whether he'll be able to catch up to a major league fastball, but at this pace he'll get a chance to find out. The offseason acquisition of Jason Hart may force Hafner to repeat Double-A at the beginning of 2002.

Year	Club (League)	Class	AVG	G	AB	R	H	2B	3B	HR	RBI	BB	SO	SB
1997	Rangers (GCL)	R	.286	55	189	38	54	14	0	5	24	24	45	7
1998	Savannah (SAL)	A	.237	123	405	62	96	15	4	16	84	68	139	7
1999	Savannah (SAL)	A	.292	134	480	94	140	30	4	28	111	67	151	5
2000	Charlotte (FSL)	A	.346	122	436	90	151	34	1	22	109	67	86	0
2001	Tulsa (TL)	AA	.282	88	323	59	91	25	0	20	74	59	82	3
MINOR LEAGUE TOTALS			.290	522	1833	343	532	118	9	91	402	285	503	22

17. Laynce Nix, of

Born: Oct. 30, 1980. **Ht.:** 6-0. **Wt.:** 190. **Bats:** L. **Throws:** L. **School:** Midland (Texas) HS. **Career Transactions:** Selected by Rangers in fourth round of 2000 draft; signed June 21, 2000.

Nix plays the game with the same toughness that made him an outstanding quarterback at Midland (Texas) High. His brother Jayson made his pro debut last season after the Rockies drafted him in the supplemental first round. Laynce is probably the most intense player in the Rangers organization, a trait that leads to favorable comparisons to Rusty Greer. His mental toughness allowed him to handle a big jump to low Class A in 2001 after he struggled in his pro debut in the Gulf Coast League. Nix, who overcame a spring-training wrist injury, concentrated on hitting the ball up the middle last season, which served him well. However, he'll need to add more power and patience as he advances. He currently projects as a platoon corner outfielder, but Nix has the drive to accomplish more than that. This year he'll go to high Class A, where he ended last season.

Year	Club (League)	Class	AVG	G	AB	R	H	2B	3B	HR	RBI	BB	SO	SB
2000	Rangers (GCL)	R	.226	51	199	34	45	7	1	2	25	23	37	4
2001	Savannah (SAL)	A	.278	104	407	50	113	26	8	8	59	37	94	9
	Charlotte (FSL)	A	.297	9	37	4	11	3	1	0	2	1	13	0
MINOR LEAGUE TOTALS			.263	164	643	88	169	36	10	10	86	61	144	13

18. Patrick Boyd, of

Born: Sept. 7, 1978. **Ht.:** 6-3. **Wt.:** 205. **Bats:** B. **Throws:** R. **School:** Clemson University. **Career Transactions:** Selected by Rangers in seventh round of 2001 draft; signed Jan. 15, 2002.

Coming off an All-America sophomore season at Clemson, Boyd looked like a lock to be one of the first players taken in the 2000 draft. But he hit just .293 with three homers as a junior, went in the fourth round to the Pirates and didn't sign. His senior year went even worse, as he had a stress fracture in his back and played in just one game. After getting a medical redshirt he could have returned to the Tigers in 2002, but he signed with the Rangers for $600,000 in mid-January. That's the second-largest bonus ever given to a seventh-round pick, trailing only the $775,000 Matt Holliday got from the Rockies in 1998. Boyd is a tremendously gifted player who has drawn comparisons to Shawn Green. As a sophomore, he showed a sweet stroke that should allow him to hit for power and average. His willingness to accept a walk is commendable, but he's too passive at the plate and allows pitchers to dictate the action. He's an above-average runner and a fine center fielder. It's mainly a matter of whether he can stay healthy and get more aggressive.

Year	Club (League)	Class	AVG	G	AB	R	H	2B	3B	HR	RBI	BB	SO	SB
	Has Not Played—Signed 2002 Contract													

19. Gerald Laird, c

Born: Nov. 13, 1979. **Ht.:** 6-2. **Wt.:** 195. **Bats:** R. **Throws:** R. **School:** Cypress (Calif.) JC. **Career Transactions:** Selected by Athletics in second round of 1998 draft; signed June 1, 1999 . . . Traded by Athletics with 1B Jason Hart, OF Ryan Ludwick and LHP Mario Ramos to Rangers for 1B Carlos Pena and LHP Mike Venafro, Jan. 14, 2002.

The least advanced player among the four the Rangers acquired in the Carlos Pena trade, Laird still has plenty of tools. The problem is that a series of injuries have limited him during his first two full years as a pro. He played just 47 games in 2000 because of hamstring and arm troubles. After he appeared in 119 regular-season games in 2001, the Athletics thought a stint in the Arizona Fall League would be good for his development. But Laird took a foul ball off his throwing hand, leaving a hairline fracture, and exited Arizona after eight games. When he's healthy, Laird he has a strong arm, good hands behind the plate and surprising speed for a catcher—enough that he has visions of becoming a leadoff hitter. Though he hasn't hit much in the minors, the A's believed he had significant offensive potential. An offseason weight program has helped Laird build upper-body strength, which should help him to produce at the plate and to stay in the lineup. He's slated for Double-A in 2002.

Year	Club (League)	Class	AVG	G	AB	R	H	2B	3B	HR	RBI	BB	SO	SB
1999	S. Oregon (NWL)	A	.285	60	228	45	65	7	2	2	39	28	43	10
2000	Visalia (Cal)	A	.243	33	103	14	25	3	0	0	13	14	27	7
	Athletics (AZL)	R	.300	14	50	10	15	2	1	0	9	6	7	2
2001	Modesto (Cal)	A	.255	119	443	71	113	13	5	5	46	48	101	10
MINOR LEAGUE TOTALS			.265	226	824	140	218	25	8	7	107	96	178	29

20. Kelvin Jimenez, rhp

Born: Oct. 27, 1982. **Ht.:** 6-2. **Wt.:** 153. **Bats:** R. **Throws:** R. **Career Transactions:** Signed out of Dominican Republic by Rangers, May 7, 2000.

Another young and promising Dominican find, Jimenez also came to the United States as an 18-year-old last summer and flashed impressive stuff. He held opponents to a .214 average with an electric arsenal similar to Jose Dominguez'. Jimenez has a plus fastball that can reach the mid-90s, and he already is more than a thrower. He displays a mature grasp of pitching, with the ability to change speeds and work both sides of the plate. He needs to fill out his lithe body to avoid the troubles that have plagued the wiry Jovanny Cedeno. Jimenez will pitch in low Class A this year with Dominguez.

Year	Club (League)	Class	W	L	ERA	G	GS	CG	SV	IP	H	R	ER	BB	SO
2000	Rangers (DSL)	R	3	6	4.62	17	9	0	0	64	70	47	33	32	60
2001	Pulaski (Appy)	R	0	3	6.28	4	4	0	0	14	24	14	10	4	10
	Rangers (GCL)	R	3	3	2.56	9	6	1	1	46	36	19	13	9	51
MINOR LEAGUE TOTALS			6	12	4.05	30	19	1	1	124	130	80	56	45	121

21. Justin Duchscherer, rhp

Born: Nov. 19, 1977. **Ht.:** 6-3. **Wt.:** 164. **Bats:** R. **Throws:** R. **School:** Coronado HS, Lubbock, Texas. **Career Transactions:** Selected by Red Sox in eighth round of 1996 draft; signed June 14, 1996 . . . Traded by Red Sox to Rangers for C Doug Mirabelli, June 12, 2001.

Former GM Doug Melvin specialized in the small trade. He sent backup catcher Doug Mirabelli to Boston for Duchscherer last June and Duchscherer went from being buried in the Red Sox system to the big leagues for the Rangers. He operates with fringe-average velocity but is willing to use his fastball. Helped by a sound delivery, he has good command of a tight curveball that acts like a slider, plus a changeup. Duchscherer has to maintain his fine control because his limited fastball leaves a small margin of error. He won his major league debut as a starter in July, then gave up 16 runs in eight innings after a September callup. All of the Rangers' activity in the free-agent market doesn't bode well for him, but he'll be on call in Triple-A.

Year	Club (League)	Class	W	L	ERA	G	GS	CG	SV	IP	H	R	ER	BB	SO
1996	Red Sox (GCL)	R	0	2	3.13	13	8	0	1	55	52	26	19	14	45
1997	Red Sox (GCL)	R	2	3	1.81	10	8	0	0	45	34	18	9	17	59
	Michigan (Mid)	A	1	1	5.63	4	4	0	0	24	26	17	15	10	19
1998	Michigan (Mid)	A	7	12	4.79	30	26	0	0	143	166	87	76	47	106
1999	Augusta (SAL)	A	4	0	0.22	6	6	0	0	41	21	1	1	8	39
	Sarasota (FSL)	A	7	7	4.49	20	18	0	0	112	101	62	56	30	105
2000	Trenton (EL)	AA	7	9	3.39	24	24	2	0	143	134	59	54	35	126
2001	Trenton (EL)	AA	6	3	2.44	12	12	1	0	74	49	25	20	14	69
	Tulsa (TL)	AA	4	0	2.08	6	6	1	0	43	39	14	10	10	55
	Texas (AL)	MAJ	1	1	12.27	5	2	0	0	15	24	20	20	4	11
	Oklahoma (PCL)	AAA	3	3	2.84	7	7	1	0	51	48	20	16	10	52
MAJOR LEAGUE TOTALS			1	1	12.27	5	2	0	0	15	24	20	20	4	11
MINOR LEAGUE TOTALS			41	40	3.40	132	119	5	1	730	670	329	276	195	675

22. Nick Regilio, rhp

Born: Sept. 4, 1978. **Ht.:** 6-2. **Wt.:** 185. **Bats:** R. **Throws:** R. **School:** Jacksonville University. **Career Transactions:** Selected by Rangers in second round of 1999 draft; signed June 11, 1999.

Like Justin Duchscerer, Regilio won't knock the bats out of hitter's hands with his average velocity but he understands there's more to pitching than high gun readings. He gets late sink on his 88-91 mph fastball and can throw strikes with his slider. His changeup is an out pitch. He held Florida State League hitters to a .200 average and tossed a perfect game before earning a promotion to Double-A. Lefthanders at that level didn't chase his splitter and teed off on Regilio, hitting .390 against him. Shoulder problems shelved him late last season, and there's some concern within the organization that they could recur. He'll return to the Texas League in 2002 with something to prove.

Year	Club (League)	Class	W	L	ERA	G	GS	CG	SV	IP	H	R	ER	BB	SO
1999	Pulaski (Appy)	R	4	2	1.63	11	8	1	0	50	30	12	9	16	58
2000	Charlotte (FSL)	A	4	3	4.52	20	20	0	0	86	94	54	43	29	63
2001	Charlotte (FSL)	A	6	2	1.55	11	11	1	0	64	47	16	11	16	60
	Tulsa (TL)	AA	1	3	5.54	10	10	0	0	52	62	34	32	20	40
MINOR LEAGUE TOTALS			15	10	3.40	52	49	2	0	251	233	116	95	81	221

23. Jason Botts, of/1b

Born: July 26, 1980. **Ht.:** 6-6. **Wt.:** 245. **Bats:** B. **Throws:** R. **School:** Glendale (Calif.) JC. **Career Transactions:** Selected by Rangers in 46th round of 1999 draft; signed May 15, 2000.

Based on early results, Botts could become one of the few Rangers draft-and-follows to make a significant impact. A close friend of Laynce Nix, Botts shares the same off-the-charts makeup. He didn't start switch-hitting until turning pro and now displays power from both sides. He showed a bit more power as a righthander but is effective either way. The next step is for Botts to become comfortable at turning the bat loose and slugging more homers. He has a slight uppercut to his swing, but his raw power potential has yielded only 15 homers in 567 career at-bats. Botts runs surprisingly well and ran an organization-best 6.55 seconds in the 60-yard dash last spring. His athleticism prompted a move from first base to the outfield. He's still learning the nuances of the position. A full-time move to high Class A in 2002 will be an important step in Botts' development.

Year	Club (League)	Class	AVG	G	AB	R	H	2B	3B	HR	RBI	BB	SO	SB
2000	Rangers (GCL)	R	.319	48	163	36	52	12	0	6	34	26	29	4
2001	Savannah (SAL)	A	.309	114	392	63	121	24	2	9	50	53	88	13
	Charlotte (FSL)	A	.167	4	12	1	2	1	0	0	0	4	4	0
MINOR LEAGUE TOTALS			.309	166	567	100	175	37	2	15	84	83	121	17

24. Scott Heard, c

Born: Sept. 2, 1981. **Ht.:** 6-2. **Wt.:** 190. **Bats:** L. **Throws:** R. **School:** Rancho Bernardo HS, San Diego. **Career Transactions:** Selected by Rangers in first round (25th overall) of 2000 draft; signed July 8, 2000.

Shortly before the 2000 draft, Heard was a candidate to be the No. 1 overall choice by the Marlins. Concerns about how he'd hit with pro pitching with wood bats caused him to slide all the way to the 25th pick, and the Rangers have learned the hard truth about why Heard fell. He's slow and has the body of "a 40-year-old backup catcher," according to one National League scout. Heard must increase his commitment to conditioning. His lack of offense earned him a demotion last summer, though he returned to low Class A in August with a somewhat shorter swing and hit .257 with three homers in his final 20 games. Heard's defensive skills never have come into question, and he's equipped with plus arm strength. He'll get every chance because he can catch and throw, but he's years away from being considered even a major league backup.

Year	Club (League)	Class	AVG	G	AB	R	H	2B	3B	HR	RBI	BB	SO	SB
2000	Rangers (GCL)	R	.351	31	111	21	39	16	0	2	16	20	17	1
	Savannah (SAL)	A	.250	2	8	0	2	0	0	0	0	0	3	0
2001	Savannah (SAL)	A	.228	77	268	25	61	13	1	5	36	30	71	1
	Pulaski (Appy)	R	.298	32	114	24	34	6	1	5	20	12	31	3
MINOR LEAGUE TOTALS			.271	142	501	70	136	35	2	12	72	62	122	5

25. Travis Hughes, rhp

Born: May 25, 1978. **Ht.:** 6-5. **Wt.:** 215. **Bats:** R. **Throws:** R. **School:** Cowley County (Kan.) CC. **Career Transactions:** Selected by Rangers in 19th round of 1997 draft; signed June 1, 1998.

One of the biggest challenges to the Texas player-development staff, Hughes signed as a draft-and-follow in 1998 after leading Cowley County (Kan.) CC to the Junior College World Series title. He has a legitimate mid-90s sinker but lacks consistency with it. The problems start with Hughes' lack of coordination. He can be ungainly on the mound, and that causes his delivery to often go haywire—which leads to control difficulties. He also throws a slider and a changeup, but both pitches need more refinement. Hughes made five starts last year to amass innings, but his future is in the bullpen. His quirk in that role, according to scouts, is a tendency to pitch better after inheriting runners than with the bases empty. Hughes lacks a deep pitching background because his high school didn't field a baseball team. The Rangers saw enough hopeful signs from him last season in Double-A to place him in the Arizona Fall League and on their 40-man roster. He won't be ready for spring training because of an offseason knee injury.

Year	Club (League)	Class	W	L	ERA	G	GS	CG	SV	IP	H	R	ER	BB	SO
1998	Pulaski (Appy)	R	2	6	3.89	22	3	0	2	42	30	25	18	25	48
1999	Savannah (SAL)	A	11	7	2.81	30	23	1	2	157	127	60	49	54	150
2000	Charlotte (FSL)	A	9	9	4.42	39	14	1	9	126	122	76	62	54	96
2001	Tulsa (TL)	AA	5	7	4.64	47	5	0	8	87	91	52	45	45	86
MINOR LEAGUE TOTALS			27	29	3.80	138	45	2	21	412	370	213	174	178	380

26. Jose Morban, ss

Born: Dec. 2, 1979. **Ht.:** 6-1. **Wt.:** 170. **Bats:** R. **Throws:** R. **Career Transactions:** Signed out of Dominican Republic by Rangers, Dec. 15, 1996.

All the tools are there. Morban runs well, has a plus arm and range for a shortstop and hits with above-average power for a middle infielder. He's a fluid, gifted athlete and represents one of the few five-tool prospects in the organization. But he frustrates the Rangers by showing flashes of those raw skills, only to suffer through long stretches of inconsistency. Last year was his second consecutive season with more than 100 strikeouts, an indication of his unwillingness to make adjustments at the plate. He also gets caught stealing too much and makes too many errors for someone with his skills. After nearly two years in low Class A, Morban probably will move to high Class A for what could be a make-or-break season.

Year	Club (League)	Class	AVG	G	AB	R	H	2B	3B	HR	RBI	BB	SO	SB
1997	Rangers (DSL)	R	.313	13	16	5	5	0	0	0	2	4	7	3
1998	Rangers (DSL)	R	.232	54	168	31	39	10	5	4	25	24	35	13
1999	Rangers (GCL)	R	.283	54	205	45	58	10	5	4	18	31	70	19
2000	Savannah (SAL)	A	.220	80	273	44	60	8	4	4	28	41	79	27
	Pulaski (Appy)	R	.225	30	120	21	27	3	2	3	17	12	35	6
2001	Savannah (SAL)	A	.251	122	474	71	119	20	11	8	47	42	119	46
MINOR LEAGUE TOTALS			.245	353	1256	217	308	51	27	23	137	154	345	114

27. Chris Russ, lhp

Born: Oct. 26, 1979. **Ht.:** 6-3. **Wt.:** 185. **Bats:** L. **Throws:** L. **School:** Towson University. **Career Transactions:** Selected by Rangers in third round of 2000 draft; signed June 21, 2000.

Back problems limited Russ to 70 innings in 2001, his first full pro season. It was another setback for the pitching-starved Rangers, because he was building on a solid debut when he got sidelined. He gets groundball outs with a late-sinking fastball that has ordinary velocity. He has a quality curveball to complement his fastball. He tends to pitch backward, possessing the confidence to throw his curveball in fastball counts, taking away an advantage from hitters. Russ uses the angles of his slender body to hide the ball well in his delivery. He's polished and pitches with a plan. Texas expects him to be limited at the start of spring training, and he'll need at least another half-season in high Class A.

Year	Club (League)	Class	W	L	ERA	G	GS	CG	SV	IP	H	R	ER	BB	SO
2000	Pulaski (Appy)	R	2	0	0.83	6	2	0	0	22	14	4	2	4	26
	Savannah (SAL)	A	3	1	2.43	7	7	0	0	41	38	14	11	14	34
2001	Charlotte (FSL)	A	5	2	3.47	13	12	0	0	70	67	36	27	19	56
MINOR LEAGUE TOTALS			10	3	2.72	26	21	0	0	132	119	54	40	37	116

28. Reynaldo Garcia, rhp

Born: April 15, 1978. **Ht.:** 6-3. **Wt.:** 170. **Bats:** R. **Throws:** R. **Career Transactions:** Signed out of Dominican Republic by Rangers, Dec. 16, 1996.

Garcia might be the biggest sleeper in the system. He began to make progress in 2001, his fifth year as a pro, despite his 5-10 record. He already had a promising fastball and slider, then added a splitter to give him strikeout potential. He has yet to show much in the way of an offspeed pitch, but hitters still didn't have much success against him last year. Garcia moved to the bullpen in 2001 but shifted back to the rotation at midseason and posted a 3.86 ERA as a starter. He continued to pitch well in the Panamanian winter league this offseason and still has a good deal of projectability. The Rangers are considering moving him back to the bullpen this year in Double-A, where he'll try to further refine his splitter.

Year	Club (League)	Class	W	L	ERA	G	GS	CG	SV	IP	H	R	ER	BB	SO
1997	Rangers (DSL)	R	1	3	6.75	16	1	0	5	37	39	34	28	22	27
1998	Rangers (DSL)	R	3	8	4.58	13	13	1	0	73	88	50	37	27	36
1999	Rangers (GCL)	R	4	4	3.23	12	11	0	0	64	55	30	23	26	42
2000	Savannah (SAL)	A	6	7	2.69	49	2	1	14	97	87	37	29	33	82
2001	Charlotte (FSL)	A	5	10	3.56	35	16	0	4	116	107	62	46	45	111
MINOR LEAGUE TOTALS			19	32	3.79	125	43	2	23	387	376	213	163	153	298

29. C. J. Wilson, lhp

Born: Nov. 18, 1980. **Ht.:** 6-2. **Wt.:** 195. **Bats:** L. **Throws:** L. **School:** Loyola Marymount University. **Career Transactions:** Selected by Rangers in fifth round of 2001 draft; signed June 12, 2001.

Scout Tim Fortugno, a former big league lefthander, relied on the power of projection in convincing the Rangers to draft Wilson with their second pick (fifth round) last June. Wilson's stock suffered after he went 3-9, 6.95 as a junior at Loyola Marymount. He was a two-way player for the Lions, which Fortugno believes hindered his pitching. After signing, Wilson had the best debut of any member of Texas' 2001 draft class, dominating the Appy

League before holding his own in low Class A. He threw 91 mph as a pro after sitting at 89 for Loyola Marymount. He also has tight rotation on his curveball, feel for a changeup and the ability to throw strikes. He's a superb athlete who's extremely coachable. Wilson is smart enough to incorporate what he learns in side work into games. He may return to Savannah at the start of this season but could advance in a hurry.

Year	Club (League)	Class	W	L	ERA	G	GS	CG	SV	IP	H	R	ER	BB	SO
2001	Pulaski (Appy)	R	1	0	0.96	8	8	0	0	38	24	6	4	9	49
	Savannah (SAL)	A	1	2	3.18	5	5	2	0	34	30	13	12	9	26
MINOR LEAGUE TOTALS			2	2	2.01	13	13	2	0	72	54	19	16	18	75

30. Greg Runser, rhp

Born: April 5, 1979. **Ht.:** 6-1. **Wt.:** 200. **Bats:** R. **Throws:** R. **School:** University of Houston. **Career Transactions:** Selected by Rangers in fifth round of 2000 draft; signed June 16, 2000.

Converted to relief after transferring from San Jacinto (Texas) JC to Houston, Runser hasn't looked back. He had a 1.12 ERA in his pro debut in 2000, then saved 30 games and was a Florida State League all-star in his first full pro season. He's a workhorse who throws a 90-95 mph fastball, a hard slider and a useful changeup. He pounds the strike zone and has the mentality to handle closing. Runser suffered through a dead-arm period in the middle of the Florida heat last summer, but rebounded in the second half. He earned saves in his first eight appearances in Panama this winter, an assignment that could help him advance more rapidly. He's ticketed for Double-A in 2002.

Year	Club (League)	Class	W	L	ERA	G	GS	CG	SV	IP	H	R	ER	BB	SO
2000	Pulaski (Appy)	R	3	3	1.12	21	0	0	6	48	35	18	6	14	47
2001	Charlotte (FSL)	A	3	4	2.93	50	0	0	30	68	66	26	22	28	66
MINOR LEAGUE TOTALS			6	7	2.17	71	0	0	36	116	101	44	28	42	113

TORONTO
Blue Jays

BLUE JAYS

TOP 30 PROSPECTS

1. Josh Phelps, c
2. Gabe Gross, of
3. Jayson Werth, c/1b
4. Dustin McGowan, rhp
5. Orlando Hudson, 2b/3b
6. Eric Hinske, 3b/1b
7. Brandon League, rhp
8. Alexis Rios, of
9. Kevin Cash, c
10. Tyrell Godwin, of
11. Joe Lawrence, c
12. Justin Miller, rhp
13. Mike Smith, rhp
14. Miguel Negron, of
15. Eric Stephenson, lhp
16. Chris Baker, rhp
17. Peter Bauer, rhp
18. Vinny Chulk, rhp
19. Jim Deschaine, 3b
20. Matt Ford, lhp
21. Cameron Reimers, rhp
22. Franklyn Gracesqui, lhp
23. Charles Kegley, rhp
24. Scott Cassidy, rhp
25. Mike Rouse, 2b/ss
26. Ron Davenport, of
27. Manuel Mayorson, ss
28. Corey Thurman, rhp
29. Diegomar Markwell, lhp
30. Guillermo Quiroz, c

By John Manuel

It was never more evident than in 2001 that something—anything—had to change for the Blue Jays. After one year of ownership, during which the club claims to have lost more than $50 million, the Rogers Communications group and club president Paul Godfrey fired veteran general manager Gord Ash. Godfrey passed over assistant GM Dave Stewart and former Rangers GM Doug Melvin, a native Canadian, and instead brought in J.P. Ricciardi, who was the Athletics' director of player personnel.

Industry observers give Ricciardi a large share of the credit for Oakland's ability to win on a budget, and he'll be asked to do much the same with Toronto. "At some point," Ricciardi said, "we have to let the kids play."

Ricciardi got started even before the Winter Meetings, shipping Alex Gonzalez and his hefty contract to the Cubs for Felix Heredia and minor league infielder Jim Deschaine. He then pried two prized prospects away from his old organization, getting corner infielder Eric Hinske and righthander Justin Miller for Billy Koch. He continued to deal from Toronto's strengths in the middle infield and bullpen, getting righthanders Luke Prokopec and Chad Ricketts from the Dodgers for Cesar Izturis and Paul Quantrill.

The result is a big league payroll south of $80 million and plenty of opportunity for young players. Shortstop Felipe Lopez, who played well while out of position at third base last year, moves into Gonzalez' old spot, while Hinske will get every chance to win the job at the hot corner. Orlando Hudson will push incumbent Homer Bush at second base and could play at third as well. A trade still has to happen for two-time top prospect Vernon Wells to take over in center field, but Wells (who no longer qualifies for our list) probably won't go back to Triple-A again. The bullpen also gets a makeover, with Kelvim Escobar moving into the closer's job as youngsters Bob File, Ricketts and Vinny Chulk get a chance at set-up roles.

The Blue Jays started this process last year, when seven rookies made their big league debuts. The top talent coming through the farm system looks too far away to help in 2002. Then again, righthander Brandon Lyon zoomed to the big leagues after pitching in the New York-Penn League in 2000. The decisions on whom to zoom now belong to Ricciardi.

OrganizationOverview

General manager: J.P. Ricciardi. **Farm Director:** Dick Scott. **Scouting director:** Chris Buckley.

2001 PERFORMANCE

Class	Team	League	W	L	Pct.	Finish*	Manager
Majors	Toronto	American	80	82	.509	8th (14)	Buck Martinez
Triple-A	Syracuse SkyChiefs	International	71	73	.493	6th (14)	Omar Malave
Double-A	Tennessee Smokies	Southern	80	60	.571	2nd (10)	Rocket Wheeler
High A	Dunedin Blue Jays	Florida State	71	64	.526	3rd (14)	Marty Pevey
Low A	Charleston Alley Cats	South Atlantic	51	87	.370	16th (16)	Rolando Pino
Short-season	Auburn Doubledays	New York-Penn	32	42	.432	11th (14)	Paul Elliott
Rookie	Medicine Hat Blue Jays	Pioneer	20	56	.263	8th (8)	Tom Bradley
OVERALL 2001 MINOR LEAGUE RECORD			325	382	.460	27th (30)	

*Finish in overall standings (No. of teams in league)

ORGANIZATION LEADERS

BATTING

*AVG	Aaron McEachran, Medicine Hat	.336
R	**Reed Johnson**, Tennessee	104
H	**Reed Johnson**, Tennessee	174
TB	Josh Phelps, Tennessee	273
2B	Josh Phelps, Tennessee	36
	Orlando Hudson, Syr./Tennessee	36
3B	Orlando Hudson, Syr./Tennessee	11
HR	Josh Phelps, Tennessee	31
RBI	Josh Phelps, Tennessee	97
BB	Shawn Fagan, Dunedin	86
SO	Justin Singleton, Tenn./Charleston	164
SB	Rich Thompson, Syracuse/Dunedin	44

PITCHING

W	Chris Baker, Tennessee	15
L	Tracy Thorpe, Charleston	13
#ERA	Mike Smith, Tennessee /Charleston	2.26
G	Brian Bowles, Syracuse	66
CG	Chris Baker, Tennessee	4
	Scott Cassidy, Syracuse/Tennessee	4
SV	Matt Dewitt, Syracuse	27
	Jarrod Kingrey, Tennessee	27
IP	Mike Smith, Tennessee /Charleston	187
BB	Charles Kegley, Dunedin	76
SO	Mike Smith, Tennessee /Charleston	129

*Minimum 250 At-Bats #Minimum 75 Innings

TOP PROSPECTS OF THE DECADE

TOP DRAFT PICKS OF THE DECADE

Johnson   **Cassidy**

BEST TOOLS

Best Hitter for Average	Gabe Gross
Best Power Hitter	Josh Phelps
Fastest Baserunner	Tyrell Godwin
Best Fastball	Dustin McGowan
Best Breaking Ball	Peter Bauer
Best Changeup	Chris Baker
Best Control	Scott Cassidy
Best Defensive Catcher	Kevin Cash
Best Defensive Infielder	Manuel Mayorson
Best Infield Arm	Nom Siriveaw
Best Defensive Outfielder	Miguel Negron
Best Outfield Arm	Morrin Davis

PROJECTED 2005 LINEUP

Catcher	Jayson Werth
First Base	Carlos Delgado
Second Base	Orlando Hudson
Third Base	Eric Hinske
Shortstop	Felipe Lopez
Left Field	Shannon Stewart
Center Field	Jose Cruz
Right Field	Gabe Gross
Designated Hitter	Josh Phelps
No. 1 Starter	Roy Halladay
No. 2 Starter	Dustin McGowan
No. 3 Starter	Chris Carpenter
No. 4 Starter	Brandon Lyon
No. 5 Starter	Luke Prokopec
Closer	Kelvim Escobar

ALL-TIME LARGEST BONUSES

Felipe Lopez, 1998	$2,000,000
Gabe Gross, 2001	$1,865,000
Vernon Wells, 1997	$1,600,000
Billy Koch, 1996	$1,450,000
Guillermo Quiroz, 1998	$1,200,000

DraftAnalysis

2001 Draft

Best Pro Debut: OF **Gabe Gross** (1) batted .302-4-15 at high Class A Dunedin, then drilled three homers in 11 Double-A games. OF Tyrell Godwin (3) didn't play as a North Carolina senior but hit .368-2-15 in the short-season New York-Penn League.

Best Athlete: Godwin's tools made him a two-time first-round pick, by the Yankees in 1997 and the Rangers in 2000. A deal with the Rangers fell apart after a physical revealed that he was missing a ligament in his right knee. Godwin had surgery and is running as well as ever, and his instincts seem to have improved. Gross started six games at quarterback for Auburn as a freshman and was a standout high school basketball player. OF Luke Hetherington (9) was a state champion wrestler and star wide receiver in high school.

Best Hitter: Gross was one of the top three or four college hitters available. Godwin opened eyes with his performance.

Best Raw Power: It's Gross and Godwin in a 1-2 finish again. 2B/SS Mike Rouse (5) has good pop for a middle infielder.

Fastest Runner: Godwin can take a full swing and still get from the left side of home plate to first base in 4.0 seconds.

Best Defensive Player: Rouse and Canadian SS Lee Delfino (6) are quality middle infielders.

Best Fastball: The Blue Jays have seen RHP Brandon League (2) throw 99 mph. RHP Chris Sheffield (4) couldn't hold a regular job in Miami's rotation, but he throws 90-95 mph and has a mid-80s slider.

Most Intriguing Background: The Blue Jays

Gross

believe in bloodlines. 1B Ernie Durazo's (12) brother Erubiel hit a key National League Championship Series homer for the Diamondbacks. Unsigned OF Sean Gamble (11, Oscar), SS Isaac Iorg (18, Garth) and OF Jon Ashford (20, Tucker) all have fathers who played in the big leagues. Isaac's father is Toronto's first-base coach, and the Blue Jays employ unsigned 2B Kenny Holmberg's (49) dad Dennis as Dunedin's hitting coach. Toronto also drafted twins, RHPs Mark (29) and P.J. McDonald (43), but didn't sign them.

Closest To The Majors: Toronto soon will have to trade Raul Mondesi or Shannon Stewart in order to make room for Gross, who will start 2002 in Double-A.

Best Late-Round Pick: RHP Brendan Fuller (13) or Iorg, who's the same kind of player his father was.

The One Who Got Away: Gamble is a legitimate center fielder with a sweet lefthanded swing and power potential. He's playing at Auburn.

Assessment: New ownership expanded the draft budget after the club spent first-round picks in recent years on players it could sign for well below market value. First-year scouting director Chris Buckley reaped the benefits, scoring with Gross, League and Godwin.

2000 Draft

They still have much to prove, but RHPs Dustin McGowan (1) and Mike Smith (5), OF Miguel Negron (1) and LHP Eric Stephenson (15) all rank among the club's top 15 prospects. RHPs Peter Bauer (2) and Mark Perkins (18, draft-and-follow) aren't far behind.   **Grade: C**

1999 Draft

RHP Brandon Lyon (14) was pitching in Toronto's rotation 15 months after signing as a draft-and-follow. OF Alexis Rios (1) was a pure signability pick but is starting to emerge in the minors.   **Grade: C**

1998 Draft

SS Felipe Lopez (1) is the best of a wave of middle infielders the Blue Jays have signed over the last few years. OF Jay Gibbons is another promising hitter but was lost to Baltimore in the 2000 major league Rule 5 draft.   **Grade: B**

1997 Draft

Toronto's trade of Brad Fullmer clears a spot in the lineup for multitooled OF Vernon Wells (1). 2B/3B Orlando Hudson (43) could be Lopez' future double-play partner, a role that might have been 2B Michael Young's (4) if he hadn't been traded to Texas.   **Grade: B+**

Note: Draft analysis prepared by Jim Callis. Numbers in parentheses indicate draft rounds.

. . . He's strong enough to overpower pitches that catch too much of the plate.

Josh
Phelps c

Born: Born: May 12, 1978
Ht.: 6-3. **Wt.:** 215.
Bats: R. **Throws:** R.
School: Lakeland HS, Rathdrum, Idaho.
Career Transactions: Selected by Blue Jays in 10th round of 1996 draft; signed June 6, 1996.

Born in Anchorage and signed out of a rural Idaho high school, Phelps has the history and look of a raw, physical prospect from the Pacific Northwest. He has had to make up for his lack of experience by repeating levels, but in each case he has answered the challenge. His lack of plate discipline caught up with him in his first year at Double-A Tennessee, where he hit .228-9-28 with 66 strikeouts in 184 at-bats in 2000, earning a demotion. In his second try, Phelps won the Southern League's MVP award, leading the league in home runs and doubles, ranking second in RBIs and slugging percentage (.562), and third in on-base percentage (.406).

Phelps isn't the biggest Blue Jay, but he's the strongest, with a body the organization compares to former all-star catchers such as Jody Davis and Carlton Fisk. His raw power is the best in the system, and he's an intelligent hitter who has learned how to use it. He projects to hit 30-35 homers a season in the big leagues. Phelps has worked hard to shorten a swing than can get long, and he's strong enough to overpower pitches that catch too much of the plate. Defensively, the Blue Jays say his receiving and throwing rate with his power potential. With his swing, Phelps will never be a contact hitter and has struck out more than 100 times in each of his last three seasons. Injuries have slowed his development, especially defensively, and he threw out just 18 percent of basestealers last year. In 2000, an inflamed elbow limited him to DH much of the season, and last season he labored with a torn meniscus in his right knee that required offseason surgery. Club officials say Phelps' footwork is the root of his problem and hope health and a full year behind the plate will be the remedy.

Phelps is expected to be healthy for spring training, and a lights-out spring could help him land a platoon job with veteran Darrin Fletcher in Toronto. Considering the defensive work Phelps needs, a full year in Triple-A Syracuse seems more reasonable. With Toronto's catching glut, his future could be as a DH/first baseman if his defense doesn't improve.

DANNY PARKER

Year	Club (League)	Class	AVG	G	AB	R	H	2B	3B	HR	RBI	BB	SO	SB
1996	Medicine Hat (Pio)	R	.241	59	191	28	46	3	0	5	29	27	65	5
1997	Hagerstown (SAL)	A	.210	68	233	26	49	9	1	7	24	15	72	3
1998	Hagerstown (SAL)	A	.265	117	385	48	102	24	1	8	44	40	80	2
1999	Dunedin (FSL)	A	.328	110	406	72	133	27	4	20	88	28	104	6
2000	Tennessee (SL)	AA	.228	56	184	23	42	9	1	9	28	15	66	1
	Toronto (AL)	MAJ	.000	1	1	0	0	0	0	0	0	0	1	0
	Dunedin (FSL)	A	.319	30	113	26	36	7	0	12	34	12	34	0
2001	Tennessee (SL)	AA	.292	136	486	95	142	36	1	31	97	80	127	3
	Toronto (AL)	MAJ	.000	8	12	3	0	0	0	0	1	2	5	1
MAJOR LEAGUE TOTALS			.000	9	13	3	0	0	0	0	1	2	6	1
MINOR LEAGUE TOTALS			.275	576	1998	318	550	115	8	92	344	217	548	20

2. Gabe Gross, of

Born: Oct. 21, 1979. **Ht.:** 6-3. **Wt.:** 205. **Bats:** L. **Throws:** R. **School:** Auburn University. **Career Transactions:** Selected by Blue Jays in first round (15th overall) of 2001 draft; signed July 1, 2001.

Gross began his college career following his father's footsteps as an Auburn football player. After passing for 1,222 yards and seven touchdowns as a freshman, Gross left quarterbacking behind to focus on baseball. A first-team All-American as a sophomore, his numbers dived in a depleted Auburn lineup in 2001. While Gross slumped as a junior, the Blue Jays believed in him and he looked strong during the summer and in the Arizona Fall League. A natural hitter, he has good balance, an easy stroke and good power in a package that reminds the organization of Shawn Green. Gross' athleticism and plus arm make him a prototypical right fielder. Gross showed good patience in his pro debut but chased too many pitches off the plate in college. His speed is just OK and he needs to improve his baserunning skills. Gross is on the fast track to join a crowded Blue Jays outfield. He played some first and third base in college, which could help him move faster if the Blue Jays are forced to move Carlos Delgado's large contract. He'll start 2002 in Double-A.

Year	Club (League)	Class	AVG	G	AB	R	H	2B	3B	HR	RBI	BB	SO	SB
2001	Dunedin (FSL)	A	.302	35	126	23	38	9	2	4	15	26	29	4
	Tennessee (SL)	AA	.244	11	41	8	10	1	0	3	11	6	12	0
MINOR LEAGUE TOTALS			.287	46	167	31	48	10	2	7	26	32	41	4

3. Jayson Werth, c/1b

Born: May 20, 1979. **Ht.:** 6-5. **Wt.:** 191. **Bats:** R. **Throws:** R. **School:** Glenwood HS, Chatham, Ill. **Career Transactions:** Selected by Orioles in first round (22nd overall) of 1997 draft; signed June 13, 1997 . . . Traded by Orioles to Blue Jays for LHP John Bale, Dec. 11, 2000.

Werth's athletic bloodlines include a grandfather (Ducky Schofield), uncle (Dick Schofield) and stepfather (Dennis Werth) who played in the big leagues. His mother Kim competed in the U.S. Olympic trials in the long jump and 100 meters. The Blue Jays stole him from the Orioles in a winter 2000 trade for situational lefthander John Bale. Werth's athletic ability surpasses the average catcher. He's as close to a five-tool player as the position produces. He's a plus runner and has the bat speed and leverage to hit for power, which he finally provided in 2001. His soft hands, steady receiving and strong arm make him an above-average defender. Werth's work ethic slipped with the Orioles, and the Blue Jays credit Tennessee coach Hector Torres with whipping him into shape. His swing can get long, leading to strikeouts. Because he's more athletic than Josh Phelps, Werth is a more natural candidate to switch positions. But he's also a better defender. He could compete for a platoon spot this year, but likely will move to Triple-A for another time-sharing arrangement with Phelps.

Year	Club (League)	Class	AVG	G	AB	R	H	2B	3B	HR	RBI	BB	SO	SB
1997	Orioles (GCL)	R	.295	32	88	16	26	6	0	1	8	22	22	7
1998	Delmarva (SAL)	A	.265	120	408	71	108	20	3	8	53	50	92	21
	Bowie (EL)	AA	.158	5	19	2	3	2	0	0	1	2	6	1
1999	Frederick (Car)	A	.305	66	236	41	72	10	1	3	30	37	37	16
	Bowie (EL)	AA	.273	35	121	18	33	5	1	1	11	17	26	7
2000	Bowie (EL)	AA	.228	85	276	47	63	16	2	5	26	54	50	9
	Frederick (Car)	A	.277	24	83	16	23	3	0	2	18	10	15	5
2001	Dunedin (FSL)	A	.200	21	70	9	14	3	0	2	14	17	19	1
	Tennessee (SL)	AA	.285	104	369	51	105	23	1	18	69	63	93	12
MINOR LEAGUE TOTALS			.268	492	1670	271	447	88	8	40	230	272	360	79

4. Dustin McGowan, rhp

Born: March 24, 1982. **Ht.:** 6-3. **Wt.:** 190. **Bats:** R. **Throws:** R. **School:** Long County HS, Ludowici, Ga. **Career Transactions:** Selected by Blue Jays in first round (33rd overall) of 2000 draft; signed June 20, 2000.

A bout with tendinitis as a high school senior dropped McGowan out of the first round, allowing the Blue Jays to nab him with a supplemental pick for the loss of Graeme Lloyd. Also a star basketball player in high school, McGowan had an invitation to big league camp in his contract, then stayed in extended spring as Toronto brought him along slowly. McGowan has a fluid, easy arm action and a good pitcher's body, giving him the most electric stuff in the system. His athleticism and arm speed help generate 92-96 mph velocity on his fastball and command of his 78-80 mph power curveball. He also has improved his level of concentration. While McGowan finished third in the New-York Penn League in strikeouts, he also led the league in walks. He'll have to improve his command and changeup as he faces tougher competition. The Blue Jays believe his main need is just getting more pro experience. McGowan and 2001 draftee Brandon League should front an intriguing rotation at Class A Charleston. Then Toronto will learn which of their power arms is the best in the organization.

Year	Club (League)	Class	W	L	ERA	G	GS	CG	SV	IP	H	R	ER	BB	SO
2000	Medicine Hat (Pio)	R	0	3	6.48	8	8	0	0	25	26	21	18	25	19
2001	Auburn (NY-P)	A	3	6	3.76	15	14	0	0	67	57	33	28	49	80
MINOR LEAGUE TOTALS			3	9	4.50	23	22	0	0	92	83	54	46	74	99

5. Orlando Hudson, 2b/3b

Born: Dec. 12, 1977. **Ht.:** 6-0. **Wt.:** 175. **Bats:** B. **Throws:** R. **School:** Spartanburg Methodist (S.C.) JC. **Career Transactions:** Selected by Blue Jays in 43rd round of 1997 draft; signed May 20, 1998.

Left off the 40-man roster after the 2000 season, Hudson moved from third base to second last year and blossomed. He was leading the Arizona Fall League in slugging and on-base percentage when he left to play for Team USA in the World Cup in Taiwan, where he hit .429 and led the Americans with 12 runs and seven steals in 10 games. Hudson sprays line drives to all parts of the park and has tremendous instincts and aptitude. Though he has below-average speed, he anticipates ground balls, reads pitchers well and is the best baserunner in the system. An outgoing personality and born leader, Hudson plays with passion. Except for his bat, Hudson's tools grade out as average or a tick below across the board. He gets the most out of what he has, but sometimes those players just aren't talented enough. No one in the system doubts Hudson will continue to achieve. If the Blue Jays find a taker for Homer Bush, Hudson will be their starting second baseman. He also could figure into the third-base picture if Eric Hinske can't handle the job defensively.

Year	Club (League)	Class	AVG	G	AB	R	H	2B	3B	HR	RBI	BB	SO	SB
1998	Medicine Hat (Pio)	R	.293	65	242	50	71	18	1	8	42	22	36	6
1999	Hagerstown (SAL)	A	.267	132	513	66	137	36	6	7	74	42	85	8
2000	Dunedin (FSL)	A	.285	96	358	54	102	16	2	7	48	37	42	9
	Tennessee (SL)	AA	.239	39	134	17	32	4	3	2	15	15	18	3
2001	Tennessee (SL)	AA	.307	84	306	51	94	22	8	4	52	37	42	8
	Syracuse (IL)	AAA	.304	55	194	31	59	14	3	4	27	23	34	11
MINOR LEAGUE TOTALS			.283	471	1747	269	495	110	23	32	258	176	257	45

6. Eric Hinske, 3b/1b

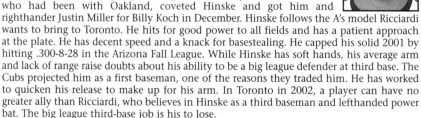

Born: Aug. 5, 1977. **Ht.:** 6-2. **Wt.:** 225. **Bats:** L. **Throws:** R. **School:** University of Arkansas. **Career Transactions:** Selected by Cubs in 17th round of 1998 draft; signed June 17, 1998 . . . Traded by Cubs to Athletics for 2B Miguel Cairo and right to retain RHP Scott Chiasson, March 28, 2001 . . . Traded by Athletics with RHP Justin Miller to Blue Jays for RHP Billy Koch, Dec. 7, 2001.

Hinske was traded for closers twice within a year. The Cubs sent him to the Athletics for Miguel Cairo and the rights to major league Rule 5 pick Scott Chiasson during spring training. New Blue Jays GM J.P. Ricciardi, who had been with Oakland, coveted Hinske and got him and righthander Justin Miller for Billy Koch in December. Hinske follows the A's model Ricciardi wants to bring to Toronto. He hits for good power to all fields and has a patient approach at the plate. He has decent speed and a knack for basestealing. He capped his solid 2001 by hitting .300-8-28 in the Arizona Fall League. While Hinske has soft hands, his average arm and lack of range raise doubts about his ability to be a big league defender at third base. The Cubs projected him as a first baseman, one of the reasons they traded him. He has worked to quicken his release to make up for his arm. In Toronto in 2002, a player can have no greater ally than Ricciardi, who believes in Hinske as a third baseman and lefthanded power bat. The big league third-base job is his to lose.

Year	Club (League)	Class	AVG	G	AB	R	H	2B	3B	HR	RBI	BB	SO	SB
1998	Williamsport (NY-P)	A	.298	68	248	46	74	20	0	9	57	35	61	19
	Rockford (Mid)	A	.450	6	20	8	9	4	0	1	4	5	6	1
1999	Daytona (FSL)	A	.297	130	445	76	132	28	6	19	79	62	90	16

	Iowa (PCL)	AAA	.267	4	15	3	4	0	1	1	2	1	4	0
2000	West Tenn (SL)	AA	.259	131	436	76	113	21	9	20	73	78	133	14
2001	Sacramento (PCL)	AAA	.282	121	436	71	123	27	1	25	79	54	113	20
MINOR LEAGUE TOTALS			.284	460	1600	280	455	100	17	75	294	235	407	70

7. Brandon League, rhp

Born: March 16, 1983. **Ht.:** 6-2. **Wt.:** 180. **Bats:** R. **Throws:** R. **School:** St. Louis HS, Honolulu. **Career Transactions:** Selected by Blue Jays in second round of 2001 draft; signed July 3, 2001.

League, who helped Team USA to a silver medal at the 2000 World Junior Championship, planned on becoming part of Pepperdine's Hawaii pipeline before the Blue Jays signed him for $660,000. His high school pitching coach was former big leaguer Carlos Diaz. League challenges Dustin McGowan as the best arm in the system. He generates excellent sinking and running movement on his fastball from a three-quarters arm slot, as well as above-average velocity. League touched 96 mph in high school and as high as 99 in instructional league. League has shown the ability to throw his curveball, circle change-up and slider for strikes. League's release point keeps him from staying on top of his breaking stuff consistently, so he doesn't always find the strike zone. While he has a good feel for his changeup, he'll need to throw it more for it to be effective. His curve and slider sometimes blend together into a rolling slurve. Departed assistant GM Dave Stewart liked League as a future No. 1 starter. He has plenty of time to develop and should start his first full season pitching with McGowan in low Class A.

Year	Club (League)	Class	W	L	ERA	G	GS	CG	SV	IP	H	R	ER	BB	SO
2001	Medicine Hat (Pio)	R	2	2	4.66	9	9	0	0	39	36	23	20	11	38
MINOR LEAGUE TOTALS			2	2	4.66	9	9	0	0	39	36	23	20	11	38

8. Alexis Rios, of

Born: Feb. 18, 1981. **Ht.:** 6-5. **Wt.:** 185. **Bats:** R. **Throws:** R. **School:** San Pedro Martir HS, Guaynabo, P.R. **Career Transactions:** Selected by Blue Jays in first round (19th overall) of 1999 draft; signed June 4, 1999.

The Blue Jays took criticism in 1999 for drafting Rios in the first round. He signed for a below-market $845,000 as Toronto bypassed college talents such as Larry Bigbie, Matt Ginter and Ryan Ludwick. While money had much to do with the pick, so did projection, and Rios is starting to make the Jays look good. What attracted scouts Tim Wilken and Chris Buckley to Rios was his swing, an easy, short stroke that comes naturally. He also makes consistent contact and is tough to strike out. He has an athletic body and plus speed. He has gone from scrawny to slender, and he has big hands and broad shoulders to grow into. He has the range and ballhawking abilities for center field and the arm for right. Rios still needs more experience and strength. His strike-zone judgment needs to start including some walks. Eventually, he'll grow out of center field and move to a corner. The Jays consider Rios' ceiling among the highest in the organization. He and Tyrell Godwin have the best chance among Toronto farmhands to be five-tool talents down the line. Rios will keep growing at Dunedin this year.

Year	Club (League)	Class	AVG	G	AB	R	H	2B	3B	HR	RBI	BB	SO	SB
1999	Medicine Hat (Pio)	R	.269	67	234	35	63	7	3	0	13	17	31	8
2000	Hagerstown (SAL)	A	.230	22	74	5	17	3	1	0	5	2	14	2
	Queens (NY-P)	A	.267	50	206	22	55	9	2	1	25	11	22	5
2001	Charleston, WV (SAL)	A	.263	130	480	40	126	20	9	2	58	25	59	22
MINOR LEAGUE TOTALS			.263	269	994	102	261	39	15	3	101	55	126	37

9. Kevin Cash, c

Born: Dec. 6, 1977. **Ht.:** 6-0. **Wt.:** 185. **Bats:** R. **Throws:** R. **School:** Florida State University. **Career Transactions:** Signed as nondrafted free agent by Blue Jays, Aug. 7, 1999.

Former scouting director Tim Wilken was in the Cape Cod League watching the Falmouth Commodores when the club ran out of catchers. A corner infielder at Florida State, Cash volunteered to go behind the plate and was a natural. He had never caught but threw out two basestealers, and Wilken signed him shortly thereafter. In a system bursting with catching prospects, Cash has the best catch-and-throw skills despite having the least experience. With a plus arm, excellent footwork and a quick release, Cash shuts down running games. He led the Florida State League by nailing 56 percent of basestealers in 2001. He also has power, leading Dunedin in home runs and slugging (.453), and uses the whole field offensively. Cash doesn't have the offensive ceiling of either Werth or Phelps because he doesn't have as much over-the-fence power. He's learning the nuances of calling a game and handling a staff. His inexperience showed, with 12 errors and 18 passed balls. The Blue Jays are overloaded with catchers, and Ricciardi has shown he's not afraid to make moves. If he remains with the organization, Cash will start 2002 in Double-A.

Year	Club (League)	Class	AVG	G	AB	R	H	2B	3B	HR	RBI	BB	SO	SB
2000	Hagerstown (SAL)	A	.245	59	196	28	48	10	1	10	27	22	54	5
2001	Dunedin (FSL)	A	.283	105	371	55	105	27	0	12	66	43	80	4
MINOR LEAGUE TOTALS			.270	164	567	83	153	37	1	22	93	65	134	9

10. Tyrell Godwin, of

Born: July 10, 1979. **Ht.:** 6-0. **Wt.:** 200. **Bats:** L. **Throws:** R. **School:** University of North Carolina. **Career Transactions:** Selected by Blue Jays in third round of 2001 draft; signed July 2, 2001.

The Yankees drafted Godwin 24th overall in 1997, but he turned down a $1.9 million bonus to attend North Carolina to play baseball and football. The Rangers picked him 35th overall in 2000 and withdrew their $1.2 million bonus offer when they discovered a torn anterior cruciate ligament in his right knee. He signed with the Blue Jays for $480,000 a year ago. Godwin has blazing speed (3.9 seconds to first base) and a quick bat that lashes line drives to all fields. He improved significantly in a short time, cutting down what was a violent swing. The Jays project him as a center fielder, though he worked out in right in instructional league and could wind up there. Some scouts soured on Godwin's desire after he twice didn't sign as a first-round pick and didn't play baseball as a senior, instead working on rehabbing his knee. The Blue Jays say Godwin is hungry to prove 29 other teams wrong. His knee held up well in his debut, though he had lingering hamstring problem. Godwin's ceiling isn't much lower than that of Gross, but his lesser power potential is the difference. He'll start the year at Dunedin and could move quickly.

Year	Club (League)	Class	AVG	G	AB	R	H	2B	3B	HR	RBI	BB	SO	SB
2001	Auburn (NY-P)	A	.368	33	117	26	43	8	2	2	15	19	27	9
MINOR LEAGUE TOTALS			.368	33	117	26	43	8	2	2	15	19	27	9

11. Joe Lawrence, c

Born: Feb. 13, 1977. **Ht.:** 6-2. **Wt.:** 190. **Bats:** R. **Throws:** R. **School:** Barbe HS, Lake Charles, La. **Career Transactions:** Selected by Blue Jays in first round (16th overall) of 1996 draft; signed July 1, 1996.

Lawrence has had a long trip in the organization, but if he doesn't have a good spring training that road will end. Drafted in the first round in 1996 as a shortstop, he moved to third base early in his career and dutifully shifted to catcher after 1999, taking a step back to high Class A to learn the new position. He seemed to take to it well but saw his progress stall in 2001, thanks in part to a mysterious left hand injury that lingered for much of the season. Two trips to the University of Virginia to visit a hand specialist determined Lawrence didn't need surgery, but the injury sapped his power at the plate. As he struggled, he expanded his strike zone, negating the plate discipline that had been one of his bigger strengths. Defensively, Lawrence led the International League with 15 passed balls and threw out just 23 percent of basestealers. His athletic ability and past offensive performances have convinced the Blue Jays that he has the tools to be a big leaguer. He has only one option left and will have to have a healthy spring to win a job as the big league backup to Darrin Fletcher. The Jays have plenty other catching options if Lawrence struggles again.

Year	Club (League)	Class	AVG	G	AB	R	H	2B	3B	HR	RBI	BB	SO	SB
1996	St. Catharines (NY-P)	A	.224	29	98	23	22	7	2	0	11	14	17	1
1997	Hagerstown (SAL)	A	.229	116	446	63	102	24	1	8	38	49	107	10
1998	Dunedin (FSL)	A	.308	125	454	102	140	31	6	11	44	105	88	15
1999	Knoxville (SL)	AA	.264	70	250	52	66	16	2	7	24	56	48	7
2000	Dunedin (FSL)	A	.301	101	375	69	113	32	1	13	67	69	74	21
	Tennessee (SL)	AA	.263	39	133	22	35	9	0	0	9	30	27	7
2001	Syracuse (IL)	AAA	.220	93	318	27	70	11	4	1	26	36	62	6
MINOR LEAGUE TOTALS			.264	573	2074	358	548	130	16	40	219	359	423	67

12. Justin Miller, rhp

Born: Aug. 27, 1977. **Ht.:** 6-2. **Wt.:** 209. **Bats:** R. **Throws:** R. **School:** Los Angeles Harbor JC. **Career Transactions:** Selected by Rockies in fifth round of 1997 draft; signed June 17, 1997 . . . Traded by Rockies with cash to Athletics as part of three-way trade in which Rockies sent RHP Jamey Wright and C Henry Blaco to Brewers, Brewers sent 3B Jeff Cirillo, LHP Scott Karl and cash to Rockies and Athletics sent RHP Jimmy Haynes to Brewers, Dec. 13, 1999 . . . Traded by Athletics with 3B Eric Hinske to Blue Jays for RHP Billy Koch, Dec. 7, 2001.

Miller came to the Blue Jays in the Billy Koch trade after being a favorite of new Jays GM J.P. Ricciardi when both were in the Athletics organization. After an impressive 2000 campaign, Miller endured a difficult 2001 season, constantly falling behind hitters and struggling for consistency with his big slider. He also lost command of his fastball. He was more impressive in his first half dozen games in the Dominican Winter League than he had been during the regular season. When the pieces come together, Miller is a power pitcher with a 96-mph four-seam fastball, a two-seam sinker, the slider and a hard splitter. He needs an off-speed pitch to contrast with his hard stuff, and his power pitches make him a candidate to be a setup man in Toronto's reconstructed bullpen. Originally drafted by the Rockies, Miller missed most of 1999 with elbow tendinitis but has been an innings-eater since. That durability means he probably will get another chance as a Triple-A starter to rediscover his command and develop his changeup.

Year	Club (League)	Class	W	L	ERA	G	GS	CG	SV	IP	H	R	ER	BB	SO
1997	Portland (NWL)	A	4	2	2.14	14	11	0	0	67	68	26	16	20	54
1998	Asheville (SAL)	A	13	8	3.69	27	27	3	0	163	177	89	67	40	142
1999	Salem (Car)	A	1	2	4.14	8	8	0	0	37	35	18	17	11	35
2000	Midland (TL)	AA	5	4	4.55	18	18	0	0	87	74	49	44	41	82
	Sacramento (PCL)	AAA	4	1	2.47	9	9	0	0	55	42	18	15	13	34
2001	Sacramento (PCL)	AAA	7	10	4.75	29	28	1	0	165	174	94	87	64	134
MINOR LEAGUE TOTALS			34	27	3.85	105	101	4	0	574	570	294	246	189	481

13. Mike Smith, rhp

Born: Sept. 19, 1977. **Ht.:** 5-11. **Wt.:** 195. **Bats:** R. **Throws:** R. **School:** University of Richmond. **Career Transactions:** Selected by Blue Jays in fifth round of 2000 draft; signed June 15, 2000.

In 2001, Brandon Lyon defied the Blue Jays' model. The organization favors tall, athletic, projectable righthanders like Roy Halladay and Chris Carpenter, but Lyon spent only a year in the minors before pitching his way into the Toronto rotation. Smith, Lyon's teammate at short-season Queens in 2000, is on a slower track but not by much. Like Lyon, Smith is small by Blue Jays standards for a pitcher and has good command of his fastball. Unlike Lyon, he has power stuff, working in the 92-94 mph range and touching 96 with his fastball. Smith gets his velocity from a quick arm action and strong legs, which he uses to drive to the plate and which help him maintain his velocity. His second pitch is a hard slider that needs more consistency. His changeup remains a work in progress, but when he stays on top of his breaking ball and keeps his fastball down in the zone, he can dominate for long stretches, as he did after his promotion to Double-A. A return to Double-A to start the year is in the offing, as the organization wants to see Smith work on an offspeed pitch.

Year	Club (League)	Class	W	L	ERA	G	GS	CG	SV	IP	H	R	ER	BB	SO
2000	Queens (NY-P)	A	2	2	2.29	14	12	0	0	51	41	18	13	17	55
2001	Charleston, WV (SAL)	A	5	5	2.10	14	14	2	0	94	78	32	22	21	85
	Tennessee (SL)	AA	6	2	2.42	14	14	1	0	93	80	32	25	26	77
MINOR LEAGUE TOTALS			13	9	2.27	42	40	3	0	238	199	82	60	64	217

14. Miguel Negron, of

Born: Aug. 22, 1982. **Ht.:** 6-2. **Wt.:** 170. **Bats:** L. **Throws:** L. **School:** Manuela Toro HS, Caguas, P.R. **Career Transactions:** Selected by Blue Jays in first round (18th overall) of 2000 draft; signed June 12, 2000.

Negron is frequently linked with Alexis Rios because they were first-round picks out of Puerto Rico in consecutive years, but they're pretty different in terms of tools. Where Rios is long, lean and has plenty of power potential, Negron's game is predicated much more on speed. He's a plus runner and one of the fastest players in the system, and his range and solid arm make him a true center fielder. While he's more mature physically at a similar stage than Rios was, Negron is a year behind in development and in emotional maturity. He has some power, just enough to make him forget to play within himself and use his speed to his advantage. Negron's ceiling began to show last year after he was demoted to short-season Auburn, where he showed better patience and the ability to steal bases. He'll get a second try in the South Atlantic League in 2002.

Year	Club (League)	Class	AVG	G	AB	R	H	2B	3B	HR	RBI	BB	SO	SB
2000	Medicine Hat (Pio)	R	.232	53	190	26	44	5	0	0	13	23	39	5
2001	Charleston, WV (SAL)	A	.192	25	99	11	19	1	0	0	2	6	21	5
	Auburn (NY-P)	A	.253	50	186	27	47	6	1	1	13	15	22	7
MINOR LEAGUE TOTALS			.232	128	475	64	110	12	1	1	28	44	82	17

15. Eric Stephenson, lhp

Born: Sept. 3, 1982. **Ht.:** 6-4. **Wt.:** 180. **Bats:** R. **Throws:** L. **School:** Triton HS, Erwin, N.C. **Career Transactions:** Selected by Blue Jays in 15th round of 2000 draft; signed June 14, 2000.

The Blue Jays have a burning need for lefthanders, and the only big league remedy would be a healthy return by Mike Sirotka. Stephenson has the highest ceiling among the lefties in the farm system, but Toronto will have to be patient with him. He has added an inch and 10-15 pounds since signing and has continued to grow into his stuff, which already turns heads. Stephenson, whose father Earl pitched in the majors, has a plus fastball for a lefty at 88-92 mph. That's quite a jump from when he signed, when he threw 80-85 mph, but his growing strength and increasingly smoother mechanics turned his fastball into a second plus pitch. His best remains a big breaking pitch one Jays scout termed "the curveball from hell." When he throws both for strikes, he reminds the organization of Andy Pettitte. He'll get his first taste of full-season ball this year, joining Dustin McGowan and Brandon League in a prospect-heavy Charleston rotation.

Year	Club (League)	Class	W	L	ERA	G	GS	CG	SV	IP	H	R	ER	BB	SO
2000	Medicine Hat (Pio)	R	1	1	8.33	19	0	0	0	27	41	28	25	13	21
2001	Auburn (NY-P)	A	3	6	4.04	15	14	0	0	78	80	45	35	44	62
MINOR LEAGUE TOTALS			4	7	5.14	34	14	0	0	105	121	73	60	57	83

16. Chris Baker, rhp

Born: Aug. 24, 1977. **Ht.:** 6-1. **Wt.:** 194. **Bats:** R. **Throws:** R. **School:** Oklahoma City University. **Career Transactions:** Selected by Blue Jays in 29th round of 1999 draft; signed June 10, 1999.

One of the bigger surprises in the organization in 2001, Baker has traveled a lot already in his baseball career, through College of the Canyons (Calif.) to NAIA power Oklahoma City to Toronto. With the Blue Jays, he has made steady progress while changing roles from reliever to starter. The development of a changeup to go with his 88-92 mph fastball, curveball and slider has given Baker four pitches he could throw for strikes. At times, both his slider and curve can be above average. The organization praises his command and competitiveness. He's not afraid to drill hitters who crowd the plate or to retaliate for a teammate. The whole package reminds the organization of Pat Hentgen and they want to see if Baker can maintain it in Triple-A this year If not, Baker has a resilient arm and consistently has reached 95 mph when used out of the bullpen, so relief could be his quickest route to the big leagues.

Year	Club (League)	Class	W	L	ERA	G	GS	CG	SV	IP	H	R	ER	BB	SO
1999	Medicine Hat (Pio)	R	0	1	3.12	3	1	0	0	9	8	4	3	2	9
	St. Catharines (NY-P)	A	2	4	6.20	12	10	0	0	49	61	37	34	14	55
2000	Dunedin (FSL)	A	9	5	3.20	41	6	0	5	104	91	50	37	29	85
2001	Tennessee (SL)	AA	15	6	3.37	28	26	4	1	179	162	73	67	42	121
MINOR LEAGUE TOTALS			26	16	3.72	84	43	4	6	341	322	164	141	87	270

17. Peter Bauer, rhp

Born: Nov. 6, 1978. **Ht.:** 6-7. **Wt.:** 250. **Bats:** L. **Throws:** R. **School:** University of South Carolina. **Career Transactions:** Selected by Blue Jays in second round of 2000 draft; signed July 4, 2000.

One-third of South Carolina's Killer Bs rotation in 2000 along with Scott Barber (Diamondbacks) and Kip Bouknight (Rockies), Bauer was considered the best prospect of the trio. He was worked hard that season and lost some velocity on his fastball, but he regained his prospect status with a fresher arm in 2001. Bauer's heater was back in the 89-93 mph range with a good downhill plane, and the organization thinks there's some projection left in his big body. He always has had a plus slider, and when his fastball is lively and has its good sink he's a groundball machine. He tired down the stretch, though, losing velocity again and leaving his fastball up in the strike zone. The Blue Jays have voiced concerns about Bauer's conditioning and his propensity to work off his slider instead of off his fastball, a pitch that only gets better with practice. While he's a good competitor, that sometimes works against him in jams. He'll try to overpower hitters instead of using his slider or improving changeup. He'll return to Double-A this year.

Year	Club (League)	Class	W	L	ERA	G	GS	CG	SV	IP	H	R	ER	BB	SO
2000	Hagerstown (SAL)	A	1	5	5.06	9	9	0	0	32	37	27	18	8	22
2001	Charleston, WV (SAL)	A	1	2	2.39	6	6	0	0	38	26	15	10	10	47
	Tennessee (SL)	AA	6	8	5.11	21	21	0	0	129	147	84	73	37	71
MINOR LEAGUE TOTALS			8	15	4.58	36	36	0	0	198	210	126	101	55	140

18. Vinny Chulk, rhp

Born: Dec. 19, 1978. **Ht.:** 6-2. **Wt.:** 185. **Bats:** R. **Throws:** R. **School:** St. Thomas (Fla.) University. **Career Transactions:** Selected by Blue Jays in 12th round of 2000 draft; signed June 12, 2000.

Alternately known as Charles or Charlie, Chulk made a name for himself in the organization in 2001 with a breakthrough season. Like Chris Baker, Chulk starred at an NAIA program and can work in either a starting role or out of the bullpen. His role in 2002 will depend on his performance in spring training and the organization's needs. Chulk has power stuff the organization likes out of its relievers. He throws three pitches from three different arm slots: a 90-94 mph fastball, a hard slider and a show-me changeup. Chulk generally uses a low three-quarters slot that gives his fastball nasty sink, and his slider is a plus pitch when he stays on top of it. He has the athleticism and coordination to repeat his many deliveries and also fields his position well. He has the mentality to close eventually and could fill a bullpen opening in Toronto this year. If the Blue Jays decide to keep him as a starter, he'll begin 2002 back in Double-A.

Year	Club (League)	Class	W	L	ERA	G	GS	CG	SV	IP	H	R	ER	BB	SO
2000	Medicine Hat (Pio)	R	2	4	3.80	14	13	0	0	69	75	36	29	20	51
2001	Dunedin (FSL)	A	1	2	3.12	16	1	0	1	35	38	16	12	13	50
	Syracuse (IL)	AAA	1	0	1.50	5	0	0	0	6	5	1	1	4	3
	Tennessee (SL)	AA	2	5	3.14	24	1	0	2	43	34	15	15	8	43
MINOR LEAGUE TOTALS			6	11	3.37	59	15	0	3	152	152	68	57	45	147

19. Jim Deschaine, 3b

Born: Sept. 18, 1977. **Ht.:** 6-0. **Wt.:** 200. **Bats:** R. **Throws:** R. **School:** Brandeis (Mass.) University. **Career Transactions:** Selected by Cubs in 10th round of 1999 draft; signed June 4, 1999 . . . Traded by Cubs to Blue Jays, Dec. 13, 2001, completing trade in which Blue Jays sent SS Alex Gonzalez to Cubs for LHP Felix Heredia and a player to be named (Dec. 10, 2001).

Deschaine would have ranked toward the bottom of the Top 30 in a deep Cubs organization, and he fits the profile of what GM J.P. Ricciardi is trying to do in Toronto. He was acquired for shortstop Alex Gonzalez, who never played up to his tools with the Blue Jays. Not considered overly athletic, Deschaine gets it done with his bat. He has the plate discipline to fit in fine with Ricciardi's old outfit, the Athletics, as well as a short stroke that produces power. A good fastball hitter who adjusts well to breaking stuff, Deschaine tied for the Florida State League lead in home runs and was the league's all-star third baseman. He began the season at shortstop but move to third after third-round pick Ryan Theriot arrived in Dayton. Deschaine has enough arm for either spot but isn't considered an above-average defender anywhere. His fielding percentage was actually higher at shortstop (.932) than at third (.923). The Blue Jays don't think of him as a middle infielder and will use him at the hot corner, an organizational weak spot, in Double-A this year.

Year	Club (League)	Class	AVG	G	AB	R	H	2B	3B	HR	RBI	BB	SO	SB
1999	Eugene (NWL)	A	.298	73	272	49	81	12	0	10	48	29	59	7
2000	Lansing (Mid)	A	.293	130	478	81	140	33	4	16	73	69	91	19
	Iowa (PCL)	AAA	.250	4	8	3	2	0	0	2	5	2	1	0
2001	Daytona (FSL)	A	.289	134	485	68	140	26	2	21	82	62	103	6
MINOR LEAGUE TOTALS			.292	341	1243	201	363	71	6	49	208	162	254	32

20. Matt Ford, lhp

Born: April 8, 1981. **Ht.:** 6-1. **Wt.:** 175. **Bats:** B. **Throws:** L. **School:** Taravella HS, Coral Springs, Fla. **Career Transactions:** Selected by Blue Jays in third round of 1999 draft; signed June 2, 1999.

After ranking ninth on this list a year ago—directly ahead of current No. 1 prospect Josh Phelps—Ford was one of the organization's bigger disappointments in 2001. He can regain his standing if he makes progress changing speeds and throwing strikes. Ford has the stuff to move up. His best pitch is a power curveball that he can throw at any point in a count, and an average 87-90 mph fastball with decent life. Ford used his fastball too much last year and got hammered. A demotion and a talk with former assistant GM Dave Stewart convinced him to use his changeup more, especially against lefthanders, and the pitch improved dramatically. Ford gained physical and mental maturity during the year, thanks to an improved work ethic. As his 2001 workload nearly doubled his career total, he stayed healthy except for some minor elbow soreness. The Jays hope Ford just had to take a step back to take two forward. He'll return to high Class A at the beginning of 2002, and a promotion will come quickly if he makes the necessary adjustments.

Year	Club (League)	Class	W	L	ERA	G	GS	CG	SV	IP	H	R	ER	BB	SO
1999	Medicine Hat (Pio)	R	4	0	2.05	13	7	0	0	48	31	11	11	23	68
2000	Hagerstown (SAL)	A	5	3	3.87	18	14	1	0	84	81	42	36	36	86
2001	Dunedin (FSL)	A	2	7	5.85	13	12	0	0	60	67	41	39	37	48
	Charleston, WV (SAL)	A	4	4	2.42	11	11	1	0	71	62	28	19	22	69
MINOR LEAGUE TOTALS			15	14	3.60	55	44	2	0	263	241	122	105	118	271

21. Cameron Reimers, rhp

Born: Sept. 15, 1978. **Ht.:** 6-5. **Wt.:** 220. **Bats:** R. **Throws:** R. **School:** JC of Southern Idaho. **Career Transactions:** Selected by Blue Jays in 35th round of 1998 draft; signed May 25, 1999.

The Blue Jays signed three draft-and-follows from the 1998 draft—Aaron Dean, Ryan Houston and Reimers—who wound up in the Dunedin rotation last year. None were protected on Toronto's 40-man roster during the offseason, but the club projects Reimers as a middle-of-the-rotation workhorse. A 14th-round pick out of high school who was lured away from a Mississippi State scholarship, he has put on 30 pounds since signing and is now a solid 6-foot-5, 220 pounds. He's still growing into his body and gaining coordination. While his fastball touches 94 mph, he pitches at 89-92 with good sink, though not as consistently as Peter Bauer. Reimers has above-average command and a changeup that can be a plus pitch. His power slider tends to flatten out, and he doesn't have enough power to pitch in the middle of the plate, meaning he has to nibble. The Jays like his maturity and plan to move him to Double-A.

Year	Club (League)	Class	W	L	ERA	G	GS	CG	SV	IP	H	R	ER	BB	SO
1999	Medicine Hat (Pio)	R	1	5	3.25	13	5	0	2	44	39	21	16	12	29
2000	Hagerstown (SAL)	A	7	11	3.73	26	26	2	0	154	158	79	64	45	112
2001	Dunedin (FSL)	A	10	6	4.40	22	22	3	0	141	150	81	69	24	88
	Tennessee (SL)	AA	1	2	6.60	5	4	0	0	30	32	22	22	5	19
MINOR LEAGUE TOTALS			19	24	4.16	66	57	5	2	370	379	203	171	86	248

22. Franklyn Gracesqui, lhp

Born: Aug. 20, 1979. **Ht.:** 6-5. **Wt.:** 230. **Bats:** B. **Throws:** L. **School:** George Washington HS, New York. **Career Transactions:** Selected by Blue Jays in 21st round of 1998 draft; signed June 7, 1998.

A Dominican from New York, Gracesqui earned a spot on the Jays' 40-man roster after an impressive display of power during the 2001 season and in instructional league. His big frame generates velocity and deception, and his three-quarters delivery makes it look like the ball comes out of his sleeve. Because he's still a little wild—though much less so than in his first three seasons—hitters rarely dig in against him. Gracesqui's 89-94 mph fastball and slider help him eat up lefthanded hitters, who rarely get a good swing against him. He still needs to refine his command and his slider, which can get slurvy at times. Because everything he throws is hard, Gracesqui figures to stay in the bullpen when he starts this year in high Class A.

Year	Club (League)	Class	W	L	ERA	G	GS	CG	SV	IP	H	R	ER	BB	SO
1998	St. Catharines (NY-P)	A	1	0	6.61	11	0	0	0	16	16	12	12	12	19
1999	St. Catharines (NY-P)	A	2	3	5.05	15	10	0	1	46	44	30	26	41	45
2000	Medicine Hat (Pio)	R	0	1	2.63	8	4	0	0	24	15	11	7	21	20
	Hagerstown (SAL)	A	0	1	4.91	3	1	0	0	7	4	4	4	9	6
2001	Charleston, WV (SAL)	A	2	8	3.17	35	2	0	1	65	60	40	23	34	66
	Dunedin (FSL)	A	1	0	0.00	4	0	0	0	6	2	0	0	8	6
MINOR LEAGUE TOTALS			6	13	3.93	76	17	0	2	165	141	97	72	125	162

23. Charles Kegley, rhp

Born: Dec. 17, 1979. **Ht.:** 6-3. **Wt.:** 205. **Bats:** R. **Throws:** R. **School:** Okaloosa-Walton (Fla.) CC. **Career Transactions:** Selected by Blue Jays in 11th round of 1999 draft; signed July 20, 1999.

After his pro debut in 2000, Kegley ranked sixth on this list and was considered to have the best arm in the system. But not only did Kegley have to return to the Florida State League for a second year after a poor spring training, he also had an alarming drop in his velocity. His fastball never came close to reaching its previous peak of 97 mph. Kegley pitched at 87-91 during the season and had trouble locating any of his pitches. The Blue Jays say his delivery got out of whack and Kegley had it completely remade after he was pulled from the rotation in August. A medical exam found some shoulder weakness and he worked hard to regain strength. The good news was that he was back to throwing 94 mph in instructional league. Toronto hopes an offseason of hard work and getting acclimated to his new mechanics will allow Kegley to become a power reliever. His 2002 assignment will depend on what kind of spring he has. He can't afford a repeat of 2001.

Year	Club (League)	Class	W	L	ERA	G	GS	CG	SV	IP	H	R	ER	BB	SO
2000	Dunedin (FSL)	A	3	9	3.88	23	23	0	0	111	96	60	48	74	66
2001	Dunedin (FSL)	A	6	9	6.03	26	20	0	0	112	120	94	75	76	76
MINOR LEAGUE TOTALS			9	18	4.96	49	43	0	0	223	216	154	123	150	142

24. Scott Cassidy, rhp

Born: Oct. 3, 1975. **Ht.:** 6-2. **Wt.:** 175. **Bats:** R. **Throws:** R. **School:** LeMoyne College. **Career Transactions:** Signed as nondrafted free agent by Blue Jays, May 21, 1998.

Cassidy has overcome diabetes and not being drafted to become a fringe prospect. He already has accomplished more than seemed likely, pitching effectively in the second half of 2001 at Syracuse, his hometown. Afterward he traveled a little further from home, going to the World Cup in Taiwan as one of Team USA's top three starters. He went 1-0, 2.30 in a team-high 16 innings. Cassidy has displayed durability belying his slight build, answering concerns about whether his diabetes would preclude him from remaining a starter. His 86-89 mph fastball runs in on righthanders, whom he held to a .203 average last year. His curveball has improved but still could use more depth. Cassidy's ability to spot those pitches, as well as a solid changeup and slider, and his maturity make him a candidate for a big league setup role in 2002. If he stays in the rotation, he projects as a No. 4 or 5 starter. A full season in Triple-A may be needed to convince Toronto he should remain a starter.

Year	Club (League)	Class	W	L	ERA	G	GS	CG	SV	IP	H	R	ER	BB	SO
1998	Medicine Hat (Pio)	R	8	1	2.43	15	14	0	0	81	71	31	22	14	82
1999	Hagerstown (SAL)	A	13	7	3.27	27	27	1	0	171	151	78	62	30	178
2000	Dunedin (FSL)	A	9	3	1.33	14	13	1	0	88	53	15	13	34	89
	Tennessee (SL)	AA	2	2	5.91	8	7	0	0	43	48	30	28	15	39
2001	Tennessee (SL)	AA	6	6	3.44	16	15	4	0	97	78	45	37	27	81
	Syracuse (IL)	AAA	3	3	2.71	11	11	0	0	63	60	24	19	26	48
MINOR LEAGUE TOTALS			41	22	3.00	91	87	6	0	542	461	223	181	146	517

25. Mike Rouse, 2b/ss

Born: April 25, 1980. **Ht.:** 5-11. **Wt.:** 185. **Bats:** L. **Throws:** R. **School:** Cal State Fullerton. **Career Transactions:** Selected by Blue Jays in fifth round of 2001 draft; signed July 2, 2001.

Rouse was an unknown commodity coming into 2001. After a standout freshman season at San Jose State, he transferred to Cal State Fullerton, but the Spartans didn't release him from his scholarship and Rouse had to sit out all of 2000. He impressed Titans coaches with his work ethic during his year of inactivity and helped lead Fullerton to the 2001 College World Series, leading the team in RBIs. After signing, he excelled in high Class A. Rouse has a sound swing, getting his whole body into the ball and making adjustments to offspeed stuff. He surprised Toronto's scouting staff by showing power to all fields and better defensive tools than expected. He has adequate hands and range at shortstop, but his arm is better suited for second base, especially as young Latin shortstops Manuel Mayorson, Raul Tablado and Juan Peralta work their way up the system. Rouse will learn the nuances of his new position in Double-A this year.

Year	Club (League)	Class	AVG	G	AB	R	H	2B	3B	HR	RBI	BB	SO	SB
2001	Dunedin (FSL)	A	.272	48	180	27	49	17	2	5	24	13	45	3
MINOR LEAGUE TOTALS			.272	48	180	27	49	17	2	5	24	13	45	3

26. Ron Davenport, of

Born: Oct. 16, 1981. **Ht.:** 6-2. **Wt.:** 190. **Bats:** L. **Throws:** R. **School:** Leesville Road HS, Raleigh, N.C. **Career Transactions:** Selected by Blue Jays in 22nd round of 2000 draft; signed June 14, 2000.

Signed away from a scholarship to Florida State, Davenport has work to do in several phases of the game. His offensive potential, though, means the Blue Jays will be patient. Davenport has a smooth swing and lashes line drives to all fields. His compact stroke should allow him to make more consistent contact as he gains experience and gets to know pitchers better. A studious hitter, he carries a notebook in which he writes up every pitcher he faces. Davenport projects to have plus power if he continues to get stronger, particularly in his upper body. He needed to stay in extended spring training last year to convert from first base to the outfield. He has improved as a left fielder, though his arm strength is modest. He draws comparisons to former Jays farmhand Jay Gibbons, a pure hitter lost to the Orioles in the 2000 major league Rule 5 draft. Davenport likely will return to low Class A in April.

Year	Club (League)	Class	AVG	G	AB	R	H	2B	3B	HR	RBI	BB	SO	SB
2000	Medicine Hat (Pio)	R	.345	59	229	37	79	16	2	4	46	21	28	5
2001	Charleston, WV (SAL)	A	.289	79	298	37	86	18	2	4	54	20	53	11
MINOR LEAGUE TOTALS			.313	138	527	74	165	34	4	8	100	41	81	16

27. Manuel Mayorson, ss

Born: March 10, 1983. **Ht.:** 5-10. **Wt.:** 167. **Bats:** R. **Throws:** R. **Career Transactions:** Signed out of Dominican Republic by Blue Jays, July 5, 1999.

As the Blue Jays have traded away several middle infielders in the last couple of years, Latin American coordinator Tony Arias has created an influx of shortstops at the lower levels. Mayorson has the highest ceiling of those players, starting with his well above-average speed. He still needs to learn the finer points of baserunning, but he has shown evidence of developing enough plate discipline to hit near the top of the order. He has little power to speak of for now and projects for no more than gap power down the road. Mayorson plays shortstop naturally with good instincts and plenty of arm, earning comparisons within the organization to Abraham Nunez, whose career started with the Blue Jays before he was dealt to the Pirates. Mayorson will get his first taste of full-season ball this year at Charleston.

Year	Club (League)	Class	AVG	G	AB	R	H	2B	3B	HR	RBI	BB	SO	SB
2000	Medicine Hat (Pio)	R	.220	56	218	39	48	2	1	0	12	33	27	3
2001	Charleston, WV (SAL)	A	.000	1	2	0	0	0	0	0	0	0	1	0
	Dunedin (FSL)	A	.189	18	37	6	7	0	0	0	2	2	2	0
	Auburn (NY-P)	A	.263	62	247	28	65	5	0	0	18	21	19	25
MINOR LEAGUE TOTALS			.238	137	504	73	120	7	1	0	32	56	49	28

28. Corey Thurman, rhp

Born: Nov. 5, 1978. **Ht.:** 6-1. **Wt.:** 215. **Bats:** R. **Throws:** R. **School:** Texas HS, Texarkana, Texas. **Career Transactions:** Selected by Royals in fourth round of 1996 draft; signed June 7, 1996 . . . Selected by Blue Jays in major league Rule 5 draft, December 13, 2001.

It's somewhat perplexing that Thurman was available to the Blue Jays in the major league Rule 5 draft in December. He was left unprotected by the Royals after winning 27 games in his previous two seasons, including a strong performance in Double-A last year. He finished fourth in the Texas League in ERA and held opponents to a .206 average, all at age 22. But Kansas City opted to protect low-ceiling veterans such as Cory Bailey and Raul Ibanez over Thurman. He has the stuff to stick with Toronto throughout 2002 and the opportunity to do it as a long reliever. He broke through in 2000 when he started working off his 88-90 mph fastball more, making his plus changeup more effective. On occasion, his fastball will touch 93 mph. The Jays also like reports on his good work ethic, his durability and the development of his curveball, which has become an out pitch.

Year	Club (League)	Class	W	L	ERA	G	GS	CG	SV	IP	H	R	ER	BB	SO
1996	Royals (GCL)	R	1	6	6.08	11	11	0	0	47	53	32	32	28	52
1997	Royals (GCL)	R	2	1	2.38	8	8	1	0	34	28	12	9	22	42
	Spokane (NWL)	A	1	2	5.16	5	5	0	0	23	23	19	13	13	24
1998	Lansing (Mid)	A	5	6	3.61	14	11	0	0	62	47	31	25	30	61
	Spokane (NWL)	A	3	3	4.05	12	12	0	0	60	72	35	27	31	49
1999	Wilmington (Car)	A	8	11	4.88	27	27	0	0	149	160	89	81	64	131
2000	Wilmington (Car)	A	10	5	2.26	19	19	1	0	116	97	33	29	46	96
	Wichita (TL)	AA	4	5	4.83	9	9	0	0	50	46	34	27	24	47
2001	Omaha (PCL)	AAA	0	0	5.40	1	1	0	0	5	6	4	3	2	4
	Wichita (TL)	AA	13	5	3.37	25	25	0	0	155	117	66	58	65	148
MINOR LEAGUE TOTALS			47	44	3.90	131	128	2	0	702	649	355	304	325	654

29. Diegomar Markwell, lhp

Born: Aug. 8, 1980. **Ht.:** 6-2. **Wt.:** 197. **Bats:** L. **Throws:** L. **Career Transactions:** Signed as out of Netherlands Antilles by Blue Jays, Aug. 8, 1996.

The Blue Jays have few lefthanded starters in sniffing distance of the major leagues. While Gustavo Chacin has advanced further in his development and will start 2002 in Triple-A, his fastball-changeup repertoire pegs him more as an Omar Daal clone with a limited ceiling. Markwell offers hope for the future. He drew headlines in 1996 when he signed for $750,000, breaking the club's foreign-bonus record held at the time by Brazilian Jose Pett, and finally started to show signs of progress last season in his fourth try at the short-season New York-Penn League. Markwell works off his average 87-91 mph fastball, mixing in two plus pitches in his curveball and changeup. His curve has a tight rotation and he gets good arm speed on his changeup, helping him shut down lefthanders. As his strength has caught up with his poise and feel for pitching, he has started living up to his bonus. Markwell figures to start 2002 in high Class A but soon could catch the more polished Chacin.

Year	Club (League)	Class	W	L	ERA	G	GS	CG	SV	IP	H	R	ER	BB	SO
1997	St. Catharines (NY-P)	A	1	6	4.99	16	11	0	0	49	50	35	27	40	33
1998	St. Catharines (NY-P)	A	3	3	5.54	17	5	0	0	52	61	39	32	35	40
1999	St. Catharines (NY-P)	A	3	4	7.58	14	13	0	0	59	72	55	50	38	54
2000	Hagerstown (SAL)	A	0	1	9.00	2	0	0	0	2	3	2	2	5	2
	Queens (NY-P)	A	4	3	3.05	14	13	0	0	74	59	29	25	31	66
2001	Charleston, WV (SAL)	A	5	7	3.87	22	21	3	0	123	121	58	53	32	99
	Dunedin (FSL)	A	3	1	3.21	5	5	0	0	34	27	12	12	13	26
MINOR LEAGUE TOTALS			19	25	4.61	90	68	3	0	393	393	230	201	194	320

30. Guillermo Quiroz, c

Born: Nov. 29, 1981. **Ht.:** 6-1. **Wt.:** 202. **Bats:** R. **Throws:** R. **Career Transactions:** Signed out of Venezuela by Blue Jays, Sept. 25, 1998.

Signed for $1.2 million, Quiroz now seems like a luxury in an organization full of catchers with all kind of skills: offensive versus catch-and-throw, experienced versus raw. He falls into the raw and catch-and-throw categories, as his statistics would indicate. Offensively, Quiroz has problems with timing and his approach to hitting. He has a fairly short swing with good bat speed. His defensive tools are top-notch. A good arm and athletic build complement Quiroz' receiving skills, and he rapidly has developed into a leader. He speaks good English considering his background and limited time in the United States, and he has a good feel for calling a game and handling a pitching staff. Because of their backlog of catchers, the Blue Jays can and will be patient with Quiroz, who fought nagging injuries and played just 82 games in 2001. He'll likely return to low Class A to handle top arms such as Dustin McGowan, Brandon League and Eric Stephenson.

Year	Club (League)	Class	AVG	G	AB	R	H	2B	3B	HR	RBI	BB	SO	SB
1999	Medicine Hat (Pio)	R	.221	63	208	25	46	7	0	9	28	18	55	0
2000	Hagerstown (SAL)	A	.162	43	136	14	22	4	0	1	12	16	44	0
	Queens (NY-P)	A	.224	55	196	27	44	9	0	5	29	27	48	1
2001	Charleston, WV (SAL)	A	.199	82	261	25	52	12	0	7	25	29	67	5
MINOR LEAGUE TOTALS			.205	243	801	91	164	32	0	22	94	90	214	6

DraftSigning**Bonuses**

EVOLUTION OF THE BONUS RECORD
Domestic Players Only

Pre-Draft Record

Year	Team, Player, Pos., School	Bonus
1964	Angels. Rick Reichart, of, U. of Wisconsin	$205,000

Draft Era Record

Year	Team, Player, Pos., School, Round	Bonus
1965	Athletics. Rick Monday, of, Arizona State U. (1)	$104,000
1966	Phillies. Steve Arlin, rhp, Ohio State U. (1/secondary)	105,000
1973	Rangers. David Clyde, lhp, HS—Houston (1)	125,000
1975	Angels. Danny Goodwin, c, Southern U. (1)	125,000
1978	Braves. Bob Horner, 3b, Arizona State U. (1)	175,000
	Tigers. Kirk Gibson, of, Michigan State U. (1)	200,000
1988	Padres. Andy Benes, rhp, U. of Evansville (1)	235,000
1989	Braves. Tyler Houston, c, HS—Las Vegas (1)	241,000
	Orioles. #Ben McDonald, rhp, Louisiana State U. (1)	350,000
	Blue Jays. John Olerud, 1b, Washington State U. (3)	575,000
1991	Braves. Mike Kelly, of, Arizona State (1)	575,000
	Yankees. Brien Taylor, lhp, HS—Beaufort, N.C. (1)	1,550,000
1994	Mets. Paul Wilson, rhp, Florida State U. (1)	1,550,000
	Marlins. Josh Booty, 3b, HS—Shreveport, La. (1)	1,600,000
1996	Pirates. Kris Benson, rhp, Clemson U. (1)	2,000,000
	*Diamondbacks. Travis Lee, 1b, San Diego State U. (1)	10,000,000
	*Devil Rays. Matt White, rhp, HS—Chambersburg, Pa. (1)	10,200,000

* Declared free agent on contract tendering technicality. # Signed major league contract. Round indicated in parentheses

NOTES: 1. For players signed to major league contracts, the amount is only the stated bonus in the contract. 2. For players signed to standard minor league contracts, the amount is the full compensation to be paid out over the life of the contract.

---

20 LARGEST BONUSES, DRAFT HISTORY
For players signing with the team that drafted them

Rank, Club, Player, Pos., School	Year	Bonus
1. White Sox. Joe Borchard, of, Stanford U.	2000	$5,300,000
2. Twins. Joe Mauer, c, HS—St. Paul	2001	5,150,000
3. Rangers. #Mark Teixeira, 3b, Georgia Tech	2001	4,500,000
4. Devil Rays. #Dewon Brazelton, rhp, Middle Tennessee State U.	2001	4,200,000
Phillies. Gavin Floyd, rhp, HS—Severna Park, Md.	2001	4,200,000
6. Cubs. #Mark Prior, rhp, U. of Southern California	2001	4,000,000
7. Devil Rays. Josh Hamilton, of, HS—Raleigh, N.C.	1999	3,960,000
8. Cubs. Corey Patterson, of, HS—Kennesaw, Ga.	1998	3,700,000
9. Marlins. #Josh Beckett, rhp, HS—Spring, Texas	1999	3,625,000
10. Tigers. #Eric Munson, c, U. of Southern California	1999	3,500,000
11. Athletics. Mark Mulder, lhp, Michigan State U.	1998	3,200,000
12. Phillies. #Pat Burrell, 1b, U. of Miami	1998	3,150,000
13. Cardinals. #J.D. Drew, of, St. Paul/Northern	1998	3,000,000
Marlins. Adrian Gonzalez, 1b, HS—Chula Vista, Calif.	2000	3,000,000
15. Expos. Justin Wayne, rhp, Stanford U.	2000	2,950,000
16. Twins. B.J. Garbe, of, HS—Moses Lake, Wash.	1999	2,750,000
Cubs. Luis Montanez, ss, HS—Miami	2000	2,750,000
Rockies. Jason Young, rhp, Stanford U.	2000	2,750,000
19. Royals. Jeff Austin, rhp, Stanford U.	1998	2,700,000
20. Expos. Josh Karp, rhp, UCLA	2001	2,650,000

Signed major league contract

NOTES: 1. For players signed to major league contracts, the amount is only the stated bonus in the contract. 2. For players signed to standard minor league contracts, the amount is the full compensation to be paid out over the life of the contract.

Signing Bonuses 2001

TOP 100 PICKS, 2001 DRAFT

FIRST ROUND

Order. Player, Pos.	Bonus
1. Twins. Joe Mauer, c	$5,150,000
2. # Cubs. Mark Prior, rhp	4,000,000
3. # Devil Rays. Dewon Brazelton, rhp	4,200,000
4. Phillies. Gavin Floyd, rhp	4,200,000
5. # Rangers. Mark Teixeira, 3b	4,500,000
6. Expos. Josh Karp, rhp	2,650,000
7. Orioles. Chris Smith, lhp	2,175,000
8. Pirates. John VanBenschoten, rhp/1b	2,400,000
9. Royals. Colt Griffin, rhp	2,400,000
10. Astros. Chris Burke, ss	2,125,000
11. Tigers. *Kenny Baugh, rhp	1,800,000
12. Brewers. Mike Jones, rhp	2,075,000
13. Angels. Casey Kotchman, 1b	2,075,000
14. Padres. Jake Gautreau, 3b	1,875,000
15. Blue Jays. Gabe Gross, of	1,865,000
16. White Sox. Kris Honel, rhp	1,500,000
17. Indians. Dan Denham, rhp	1,860,000
18. Mets. *Aaron Heilman, rhp	1,508,750
19. Orioles. Mike Fontenot, 2b	1,300,000
20. Reds. Jeremy Sowers, lhp	Did Not Sign
21. Giants. Brad Hennessey, rhp	1,380,000
22. Diamondbacks. *Jason Bulger, rhp	937,000
23. Yankees. John-Ford Griffin, of	1,200,000
24. Braves. Macay McBride, lhp	1,340,000
25. Athletics. Bobby Crosby, ss	1,350,000
26. Athletics. Jeremy Bonderman, rhp	1,350,000
27. Indians. Alan Horne, rhp	Did Not Sign
28. Cardinals. Justin Pope, rhp	900,000
29. Braves. Josh Burrus, ss	1,250,000
30. Giants. Noah Lowry, lhp	1,175,000

SUPPLEMENTAL FIRST ROUND

31. Orioles. Bryan Bass, ss	1,150,000
32. Tigers. Michael Woods, 2b	1,100,000
33. Angels. Jeff Mathis, c	850,000
34. Yankees. Bronson Sardinha, ss	1,000,000
35. Indians. J.D. Martin, rhp	975,000
36. Mariners. Michael Garciaparra, ss	2,000,000
37. Athletics. *John Rheinecker, lhp	600,000
38. Mets. David Wright, 3b	960,000
39. White Sox. Wyatt Allen, rhp	872,500
40. Braves. Richard Lewis, 2b	850,000
41. Giants. Todd Linden, of	750,000
42. Yankees. *Jon Skaggs, rhp	600,000
43. Indians. Mike Conroy, of	870,000
44. Rockies. Jayson Nix, ss	925,000

SECOND ROUND

45. Twins. Scott Tyler, rhp	875,000
46. Cubs. Andy Sisco, lhp	1,000,000
47. Devil Rays. Jon Switzer, lhp	850,000
48. Red Sox. Kelly Shoppach, c	737,500
49. Mariners. Rene Rivera, c	688,000
50. Expos. Donald Levinski, rhp	825,000
51. Indians. Jake Dittler, rhp	750,000
52. Braves. J.P. Howell, lhp	Did Not Sign
53. Royals. Roscoe Crosby, of	1,750,000
54. Astros. Mike Rodriguez, of	675,000
55. Tigers. Preston Larrison, rhp	685,000
56. Brewers. J.J. Hardy, ss	735,000
57. Angels. Dallas McPherson, 3b	660,000
58. Padres. Matt Harrington, rhp	Unsigned
59. Blue Jays. Brandon League, rhp	660,000
60. Marlins. Garrett Berger, rhp	795,000
61. Red Sox. Matt Chico, lhp	Did Not Sign
62. Yankees. Shelley Duncan, of	655,000
63. Yankees. *Jason Arnold, rhp	400,000
64. Reds. Justin Gillman, rhp	625,000
65. Tigers. Matt Coenen, lhp	620,000
66. Diamondbacks. Mike Gosling, lhp	2,000,000
67. Mariners. Michael Wilson, of	900,000
68. Dodgers. Brian Pilkington, rhp	600,000
69. Athletics. Neal Cotts, lhp	525,000
70. Mets. Alhaji Turay, of	517,000
71. White Sox. Ryan Wing, lhp	575,000
72. Cardinals. Dan Haren, rhp	530,000
73. Braves. Cole Barthel, 3b	475,000
74. Giants. Jesse Foppert, rhp	520,000

SUPPLEMENTAL SECOND ROUND

75. Rockies. Trey Taylor, lhp	Did Not Sign
76. Mets. Corey Ragsdale, ss	550,000

THIRD ROUND

77. Twins. Jose Morales, ss	490,000
78. Cubs. Ryan Theriot, ss	480,000
79. Devil Rays. Chris Flinn, rhp	466,000
80. Mariners. Lazaro Abreu, c	400,000
81. Angels. Steven Shell, rhp	460,000
82. Expos. Mike Hinckley, lhp	425,000
83. Orioles. Dave Crouthers, rhp	425,000
84. Pirates. Jeremy Guthrie, rhp	Did Not Sign
85. Royals. Matt Ferrara, 3b	450,000
86. Astros. *Kirk Saarloos, rhp	300,000
87. Tigers. Jack Hannahan, 3b	435,000
88. Brewers. Jon Steitz, rhp	460,000
89. Angels. Jake Woods, lhp	442,500
90. Padres. *Taggert Bozied, 3b	725,000
91. Blue Jays. *Tyrell Godwin, of	480,000
92. Marlins. Allen Baxter, rhp	450,000
93. Red Sox. Jon DeVries, c	450,000
94. Rockies. Jason Frome, of	420,000
95. Yankees. Chase Wright, lhp	400,000
96. Reds. Alan Moye, of	400,000
97. Indians. Nick Moran, rhp	400,000
98. Diamondbacks. Scott Hairston, 2b	400,000
99. Mariners. Tim Merritt, ss	400,000
100. Dodgers. David Taylor, rhp	385,000

#Signed major league contract. *College senior.

Signing Bonuses 2000

TOP 100 PICKS, 2000 DRAFT

FIRST ROUND

Order. Player, Pos.	Bonus
1. Marlins. Adrian Gonzalez, 1b	$3,000,000
2. Twins. Adam Johnson, rhp	2,500,000
3. Cubs. Luis Montanez, ss	2,750,000
4. Royals. Mike Stodolka, lhp	2,500,000
5. Expos. Justin Wayne, rhp	2,950,000
6. Devil Rays. Rocco Baldelli, of	2,250,000
7. Rockies. Matt Harrington, rhp	Did Not Sign
8. Tigers. Matt Wheatland, rhp	2,150,000
9. Padres. Mark Phillips, lhp	2,200,000
10. Angels. Joe Torres, lhp	2,080,000
11. Brewers. Dave Krynzel, of	1,950,000
12. White Sox. Joe Borchard, of	5,300,000
13. Cardinals. Shaun Boyd, of/2b	1,750,000
14. Orioles. Beau Hale, rhp	2,250,000
15. Phillies. Chase Utley, 2b	1,780,000
16. Mets. Billy Traber, lhp	400,000
17. Dodgers. Ben Diggins, rhp	2,200,000
18. Blue Jays. Miguel Negron, of	950,000
19. Pirates. Sean Burnett, lhp	1,650,000
20. Angels. Chris Bootcheck, rhp	1,800,000
21. Giants. Boof Bonser, rhp	1,245,000
22. Red Sox. Phil Dumatrait, lhp	1,275,000
23. # Reds. David Espinosa, ss	None
24. Cardinals. Blake Williams, rhp	1,375,000
25. Rangers. Scott Heard, c	1,475,000
26. Indians. Corey Smith, ss	1,375,000
27. Astros. Robert Stiehl, rhp	1,250,000
28. Yankees. David Parrish, c	1,425,000
29. Braves. Adam Wainwright, rhp	1,250,000
30. Braves. Scott Thorman, rhp	1,225,000

SUPPLEMENTAL FIRST-ROUND

31. Twins. Aaron Heilman, rhp	Did Not Sign
32. Orioles. Tripper Johnson, 3b	1,050,000
33. Blue Jays. Dustin McGowan, rhp	950,000
34. Reds. Dustin Moseley, rhp	900,000
35. Rangers. Tyrell Godwin, of	Did Not Sign
36. Mets. Bob Keppel, rhp	895,000
37. Indians. Derek Thompson, lhp	850,000
38. Braves. Kelly Johnson, ss	790,000
39. Rangers. *Chad Hawkins, rhp	625,000
40. Braves. Aaron Herr, ss	850,000

SECOND ROUND

41. Marlins. Jason Stokes, 1b	2,027,000
42. Twins. Taggert Bozied, 1b	Did Not Sign
43. Cubs. Bobby Hill, ss	1,425,000
44. Royals. Mike Tonis, c	800,000
45. Blue Jays. Peter Bauer, rhp	800,000
46. # Reds. Dane Sardinha, c	None
47. Rockies. Jason Young, rhp	2,750,000
48. Tigers. Chad Petty, lhp	600,000

49. # Padres. Xavier Nady, 3b	1,100,000
50. Angels. Jared Abruzzo, c	687,500
51. Braves. Bubba Nelson, rhp	675,000
52. White Sox. Tim Hummel, ss	645,000
53. Cardinals. Chris Narveson, lhp	675,000
54. Twins. J.D. Durbin, rhp	722,500
55. Indians. Brian Tallet, lhp	595,000
56. Rangers. Jason Bourgeois, ss	621,000
57. Dodgers. Joel Hanrahan, rhp	615,000
58. Blue Jays. Dominic Rich, 2b	600,000
59. Pirates. David Beigh, rhp	635,000
60. Athletics. Freddie Bynum, ss	495,000
61. Giants. Lance Niekro, 3b	655,000
62. Red Sox. Manny Delcarmen, rhp	700,000
63. Reds. Ryan Snare, lhp	595,000
64. Rangers. Randy Truselo, rhp	600,000
65. Mets. Matt Peterson, rhp	575,000
66. Indians. Mark Folsom, of	700,000
67. Astros. *Chad Qualls, rhp	415,000
68. Yankees. Danny Borrell, lhp	600,000
69. Diamondbacks. Mike Schultz, rhp	500,000
70. Braves. Bryan Digby, rhp	450,000

THIRD ROUND

71. Marlins. Rob Henkel, lhp	650,000
72. Twins. Colby Miller, rhp	480,000
73. Cubs. Aaron Krawiec, lhp	450,000
74. Royals. Scott Walter, c	447,500
75. Expos. Grady Sizemore, of	2,000,000
76. Cubs. Nic Jackson, of	425,000
77. Rockies. Chris Buglovsky, rhp	410,000
78. Tigers. Nook Logan, ss	450,000
79. Padres. Omar Falcon, c	425,000
80. Angels. Tommy Murphy, ss	440,000
81. Brewers. Dane Artman, lhp	475,000
82. White Sox. Mike Morse, ss	365,000
83. Cardinals. Chase Voshell, ss	430,000
84. Orioles. Richard Bartlett, rhp	455,000
85. Phillies. Keith Bucktrot, rhp	435,000
86. Orioles. Tommy Arko, c	400,000
87. Dodgers. Jeff Tibbs, rhp	440,000
88. Blue Jays. Morrin Davis, of	440,000
89. Pirates. Chris Young, rhp	1,650,000
90. Athletics. Daylan Holt, of	450,000
91. Giants. Brion Treadway, rhp	410,000
92. Red Sox. Matt Cooper, 1b	400,000
93. Reds. *David Gil, rhp	160,000
94. Rangers. Chris Russ, lhp	407,500
95. Mets. Josh Reynolds, rhp	400,000
96. Indians. Sean Swedlow, 1b	450,000
97. Astros. Anthony Pluta, rhp	450,000
98. Yankees. Jason Grove, of	400,000
99. Diamondbacks. Bill White, lhp	387,500
100. Braves. Blaine Boyer, rhp	375,000

#Signed major league contract. *College senior.

Signing Bonuses 1999

TOP 100 PICKS, 1999 DRAFT

FIRST ROUND

Order. Player, Pos.	Bonus
1. Devil Rays. Josh Hamilton, of	$3,960,000
2. # Marlins. Josh Beckett, rhp	3,625,000
3. # Tigers. Eric Munson, c	3,500,000
4. Diamondbacks. Corey Myers, ss	2,000,000
5. Twins. B.J. Garbe, of	2,750,000
6. Expos. Josh Girdley, lhp	1,700,000
7. Royals. Kyle Snyder, rhp	2,100,000
8. Pirates. Bobby Bradley, rhp	2,250,000
9. Athletics. Barry Zito, lhp	1,590,000
10. Brewers. Ben Sheets, rhp	2,450,000
11. Mariners. Ryan Christianson, c	2,100,000
12. Phillies. Brett Myers, rhp	2,050,000
13. Orioles. Mike Paradis, rhp	1,700,000
14. Reds. Ty Howington, lhp	1,750,000
15. White Sox. Jason Stumm, rhp	1,750,000
16. Rockies. Jason Jennings, rhp	1,675,000
17. Red Sox. Rick Asadoorian, of	1,725,500
18. Orioles. Richard Stahl, lhp	1,795,000
19. Blue Jays. Alexis Rios, 3b	845,000
20. Padres. Vince Faison, of	1,415,000
21. Orioles. Larry Bigbie, of	1,200,000
22. White Sox. Matt Ginter, rhp	1,275,000
23. Orioles. Keith Reed, of	1,150,000
24. Giants. Kurt Ainsworth, rhp	1,300,000
25. Royals. Mike MacDougal, rhp	1,150,000
26. Cubs. Ben Christensen, rhp	1,062,500
27. Yankees. David Walling, rhp	1,075,000
28. Padres. Gerik Baxter, rhp	1,100,000
29. Padres. Omar Ortiz, rhp	1,050,000
30. Cardinals. Chance Caple, rhp.	1,200,000

FIRST-ROUND SUPPLEMENTAL

31. Diamondbacks. Casey Daigle, rhp	1,300,000
32. Royals. Jay Gehrke, rhp	1,025,000
33. Mariners. Jeff Heaverlo, rhp	987,500
34. Orioles. Josh Cenate, lhp	950,000
35. White Sox. Brian West, rhp	1,000,000
36. Cardinals. Nick Stocks, rhp	1,410,000
37. Dodgers. Jason Repko, ss	660,000
38. Rangers. Colby Lewis, rhp	862,500
39. Giants. Jerome Williams, rhp	832,500
40. Red Sox. Brad Baker, rhp	832,500
41. Padres. Casey Burns, rhp	750,000
42. Astros. Michael Rosamond, of	725,000
43. Royals. Jimmy Gobble, lhp	725,000
44. Orioles. Scott Rice, lhp	737,500
45. White Sox. Rob Purvis, rhp	730,000
46. Cardinals. Chris Duncan, 1b	900,000
47. Rangers. David Mead, rhp	600,000
48. Red Sox. Casey Fossum, lhp	660,000
49. Padres. Mike Bynum, lhp	650,000
50. Orioles. Brian Roberts, ss	650,000
51. Padres. Nick Trzesniak, c	650,000

SECOND ROUND

52. Devil Rays. Carl Crawford, of	1,245,000
53. Marlins. Terence Byron, rhp	350,000
54. Royals. Brian Sanches, rhp	615,000
55. Astros. Jay Perez, c.	605,000
56. Twins. Rob Bowen, c	605,000
57. Expos. Brandon Phillips, ss	607,000
58. Royals. *Wes Obermueller, rhp	400,000
59. Pirates. Ryan Doumit, c	600,000
60. Athletics. Ryan Ludwick, of	567,500
61. Brewers. Kade Johnson, c	650,000
62. Giants. John Thomas, lhp	565,000
63. Phillies. Jason Cooper, of	Did Not Sign
64. White Sox. Danny Wright, rhp	602,500
65. Reds. *Ben Broussard, 1b	380,000
66. White Sox. Bobby Hill, ss	Did Not Sign
67. Rockies. Ryan Kibler, rhp	699,000
68. Angels. John Lackey, rhp	470,000
69. Dodgers. Brennan King, 3b	800,000
70. Blue Jays. Michael Snyder, 3b	495,000
71. Diamondbacks. Jeremy Ward, rhp.	475,000
72. Rangers. Nick Regilio, rhp	510,000
73. Mets. Neal Musser, lhp	725,000
74. Indians. Will Hartley, c	725,000
75. Giants. Jack Taschner, lhp	450,000
76. Red Sox. Mat Thompson, rhp	485,000
77. Cubs. Michael Mallory, of	490,000
78. Yankees. Tommy Winrow, of	525,000
79. Padres. Alberto Concepcion, c	Did Not Sign
80. Astros. Travis Anderson, rhp	365,000
81. Braves. Matt Butler, rhp	800,000

SECOND-ROUND SUPPLEMENTAL

82. Cardinals. Josh Pearce, rhp	410,000
83. Dodgers. Drew Meyer, ss	Did Not Sign
84. Mets. Jake Joseph, rhp	410,000

THIRD ROUND

85. Devil Rays. Doug Waechter, rhp	500,000
86. Marlins. Josh Wilson, ss	450,000
87. Tigers. Neil Jenkins, 3b-of	900,000
88. Red Sox. Rich Rundles, lhp	425,000
89. Twins. Justin Morneau, c	290,000
90. Expos. Drew McMillan, c	400,000
91. Royals. Kiki Bengochea, rhp	Did Not Sign
92. Pirates. Aron Weston, of	500,000
93. Athletics. *Jorge Soto, c	270,000
94. Brewers. Ruddy Lugo, rhp	375,000
95. Mariners. Willie Bloomquist, 2b/ss	425,000
96. Phillies. Russ Jacobson, c	415,000
97. Mariners. Sheldon Fulse, ss	420,000
98. Reds. Brandon Love, rhp	360,000
99. White Sox. Jon Rauch, rhp.	310,000
100. Rockies. Josh Bard, c	387,500

#Signed major league contract. *College senior.

Signing Bonuses 1998

TOP 100 PICKS, 1998 DRAFT

FIRST ROUND

Order. Player, Pos.	Bonus
1. # Phillies. Pat Burrell, 1b	$3,150,000
2. Athletics. Mark Mulder, lhp	3,200,000
3. Cubs. Corey Patterson, of	3,700,000
4. Royals. Jeff Austin, rhp	2,700,000
5. # Cardinals. J.D. Drew, of	3,000,000
6. Twins. Ryan Mills, lhp	2,000,000
7. Reds. Austin Kearns, of.	1,950,000
8. Blue Jays. Felipe Lopez, ss	2,000,000
9. Padres. Sean Burroughs, 3b	2,100,000
10. Rangers. Carlos Pena, 1b	1,850,000
11. Expos. Josh McKinley, ss	1,250,000
12. Red Sox. Adam Everett, ss	1,725,000
13. Brewers. J.M. Gold, rhp	1,675,000
14. Tigers. Jeff Weaver, rhp	1,750,000
15. Pirates. Clint Johnston, lhp/of	1,000,000
16. White Sox. Kip Wells, rhp	1,495,000
17. Astros. Brad Lidge, rhp	1,070,000
18. Angels. *Seth Etherton, rhp	1,075,000
19. Giants. Tony Torcato, 3b	975,000
20. Indians. C.C. Sabathia, lhp	1,300,000
21. Mets. Jason Tyner, of	1,070,000
22. Mariners. Matt Thornton, lhp	925,000
23. Dodgers. Bubba Crosby, of	995,000
24. Yankees. Andy Brown, of	1,050,000
25. Giants. *Nate Bump,rhp.	750,000
26. Orioles. Rick Elder, of/1b	950,000
27. Marlins. Chip Ambres, of	1,500,000
28. Rockies. Matt Roney, rhp	1,012,500
29. Giants. Arturo McDowell, of	937,500
30. Royals. Matt Burch, rhp	975,000

FIRST-ROUND SUPPLEMENTAL

31. Royals. Chris George, lhp	1,162,500
32. Cardinals. Ben Diggins, 1b/rhp	Did Not Sign
33. Expos. Brad Wilkerson, of/lhp	1,000,000
34. Tigers. Nate Cornejo, rhp	865,000
35. White Sox. Aaron Rowand, of	575,000
36. Rockies. Choo Freeman, of	1,400,000
37. Astros. Michael Nannini, rhp	595,000
38. Giants. Chris Jones, lhp	587,500
39. Orioles. Mamon Tucker, of	650,000
40. Rockies. Jeff Winchester, c	537,000
41. Giants. Jeff Urban, lhp	650,000
42. Phillies. Eric Valent, of	615,000
43. Yankees. Mark Prior, rhp	Did Not Sign

SECOND ROUND

44. Phillies. Brad Baisley, rhp	700,000
45. Athletics. Gerard Laird, c	1,000,000
46. Cubs. David Kelton, 3b	400,000
47. Royals. Robbie Morrison, rhp	475,000
48. # Cardinals. Chad Hutchinson, rhp	2,300,000
49. Twins. Marcus Sents, rhp	495,000
50. Reds. Adam Dunn, of	772,000
51. Orioles. Ben Knapp, rhp	575,000
52. Braves. Matt Belisle, rhp	1,750,000
53. Rangers. Cody Nowlin, of	420,000
54. Expos. Eric Good, lhp	431,000
55. Cardinals. Tim Lemon, of	650,000
56. Brewers. Nick Neugebauer, rhp	1,000,000
57. Tigers. Brandon Inge, c/ss	450,000
58. Pirates. Jeremy Cotten, 3b	606,000
59. White Sox. Gary Majewski, rhp	465,000
60. Rockies. Jermaine Van Buren, rhp	375,000
61. Angels. Brandon Emanuel, rhp	390,000
62. Cubs. Jeff Goldbach, c	440,000
63. Indians. Zach Sorensen, ss	450,000
64. Mets. Pat Strange, rhp	500,000
65. Mariners. Jeff Verplancke	Did Not Sign
66. Dodgers. Mike Fischer, rhp	420,000
67. Yankees. Randy Keisler, lhp	525,000
68. Giants. Sammy Serrano, c	390,000
69. Orioles. Alex Hart, rhp	Did Not Sign
70. Marlins. Derek Wathan, ss	360,000
71. Rockies. Jody Gerut, of	450,000
72. Giants. Chris Magruder, of	325,000
73. Tigers. Adam Pettyjohn, lhp	392,500

THIRD ROUND

74. Phillies. Jorge Padilla, of	435,000
75. Athletics. Kevin Miller, ss	255,000
76. Cubs. Kevin Bass, 3b	266,000
77. Royals. Ben Cordova, of	400,000
78. Cardinals. Gabe Johnson, c	220,000
79. Twins. Brent Hoard, lhp	280,000
80. Reds. Greg Porter, ss	Did Not Sign
81. Expos. Clyde Williams, 1b	250,000
82. Padres. Beau Craig, c	Did Not Sign
83. Rangers. Barry Zito, lhp	Did Not Sign
84. Expos. Kevin Kelly, 3b	Did Not Sign
85. Red Sox. Mike Maroth, lhp	225,000
86. Brewers. Derry Hammond, of	280,000
87. Tigers. Tommy Marx, lhp	400,000
88. Pirates. Jeremy Harts, of	300,000
89. White Sox. Josh Fogg, rhp	275,000
90. Rockies. Kevin Gordon, rhp	270,000
91. Angels. Paul French, rhp	Did Not Sign
92. Astros. Brad Busbin, rhp	Did Not Sign
93. Indians. Scott Pratt, 2b	270,000
94. Mets. Jason Saenz, lhp	245,000
95. Mariners. Andy Van Hekken, lhp	270,000
96. Dodgers. Alex Santos, rhp	Did Not Sign
97. Yankees. Drew Henson, 3b	2,000,000
98. Giants. Mike Dean, c	195,000
99. Orioles. Steven Bechler, rhp	225,000
100. Marlins. David Callahan, 1b	275,000

#Signed major league contract. *College senior.

Signing Bonuses 1994-97

FIRST ROUND, 1997

Order. Player, Pos.	Bonus
1. Tigers. Matt Anderson, rhp	$2,500,000
2. Phillies. J.D. Drew, of	Did Not Sign
3. Angels. Troy Glaus, 3b	2,000,000
4. Giants. Jason Grilli, rhp	1,875,000
5. Blue Jays. Vernon Wells, of	1,600,000
6. Mets. Geoff Goetz, lhp	1,700,000
7. Royals. Dan Reichert, rhp	1,450,000
8. Pirates. J.J. Davis, of/rhp	1,675,000
9. Twins. Michael Cuddyer, 3b	1,850,000
10. Cubs. Jon Garland, rhp	1,325,000
11. Athletics. Chris Enochs, rhp	1,204,000
12. Marlins. Aaron Akin, rhp	1,050,000
13. Brewers. Kyle Peterson, rhp	1,400,000
14. Reds. *Brandon Larson, ss	1,220,000
15. White Sox. Jason Dellaero, ss	1,056,000
16. Astros. Lance Berkman, 1b	1,000,000
17. Red Sox. John Curtice, lhp	975,000
18. Rockies. Mark Mangum, rhp	875,000
19. Mariners. Ryan Anderson, lhp	2,175,000
20. Cardinals. Adam Kennedy, ss	650,000
21. Athletics. Eric DuBose, lhp	860,000
22. Orioles. Jayson Werth, c	885,000
23. Expos. Donnie Bridges, rhp	870,000
24. Yankees. Tyrell Godwin, of	Did Not Sign
25. Dodgers. Glenn Davis, 1b	825,000
26. Orioles. Darnell McDonald, of	1,900,000
27. Padres. Kevin Nicholson, ss	830,000
28. Indians. Tim Drew, rhp	1,600,000
29. Braves. Troy Cameron, ss	825,000
30. Diamondbacks. Jack Cust, 1b	825,000

FIRST ROUND, 1995

Order. Player, Pos.	Bonus
1. Angels. Darin Erstad, of	$1,600,000
2. Padres. Ben Davis, c	1,300,000
3. Mariners. Jose Cruz Jr., of	1,285,000
4. Cubs. Kerry Wood, rhp	1,265,000
5. Athletics. Ariel Prieto, rhp	1,200,000
6. Marlins. Jaime Jones, of	1,337,000
7. Rangers. Jonathan Johnson, rhp	1,100,000
8. Rockies. Todd Helton, 1b	892,500
9. Brewers. Geoff Jenkins, of	911,000
10. Pirates. Chad Hermansen, ss	1,150,000
11. Tigers. Mike Drumright, rhp	970,000
12. Cardinals. Matt Morris, rhp	850,000
13. Twins. Mark Redman, lhp	830,000
14. Phillies. Reggie Taylor, of	970,000
15. Red Sox. Andy Yount, rhp	986,000
16. Giants. Joe Fontenot, rhp	900,000
17. Blue Jays. Roy Halladay, rhp	895,000
18. Mets. Ryan Jaroncyk, ss	850,000
19. Royals. Juan LeBron, of	650,000
20. Dodgers. David Yocum, lhp	825,000
21. Orioles. Alvie Shepherd, rhp	650,000
22. Astros. Tony McKnight, rhp	500,000
23. Indians. David Miller, 1b	620,000
24. Red Sox. Corey Jenkins, of	575,000
25. White Sox. Jeff Liefer, 3b	550,000
26. Braves. Chad Hutchinson, rhp	Did Not Sign
27. Yankees. Shea Morenz, of	650,000
28. Expos. Michael Barrett, ss	500,000

FIRST ROUND, 1996

Order. Player, Pos.	Bonus
1. Pirates. Kris Benson, rhp	$2,000,000
2. + Twins. Travis Lee, 1b	10,000,000
3. Cardinals. Braden Looper, rhp	1,675,000
4. Blue Jays. Billy Koch, rhp	1,450,000
5. + Expos. John Patterson, rhp	6,075,000
6. Tigers. Seth Greisinger, rhp	1,415,000
7. • Giants. Matt White, rhp	10,200,000
8. Brewers. Chad Green, of	1,060,000
9. Marlins. Mark Kotsay, of	1,125,000
10. Athletics. Eric Chavez, 3b	1,140,000
11. Phillies. Adam Eaton, rhp	1,100,000
12. • White Sox. Bobby Seay, lhp	3,000,000
13. Mets. Robert Stratton, of	975,000
14. Royals. Dermal Brown, of	1,000,000
15. Padres. Matt Halloran, ss	1,000,000
16. Blue Jays. Joe Lawrence, ss	907,500
17. Cubs. Todd Noel, rhp	900,000
18. Rangers. R.A. Dickey, rhp	75,000
19. Astros. Mark Johnson, rhp	775,000
20. Yankees. Eric Milton, lhp	775,000
21. Rockies. Jake Westbrook, rhp	750,000
22. Mariners. Gil Meche, rhp	820,000
23. Dodgers. Damian Rolls, 3b	695,000
24. Rangers. Sam Marsonek, rhp	834,000
25. Reds. John Oliver, of	672,000
26. Red Sox. Josh Garrett, rhp	665,000
27. Braves. A.J. Zapp, 1b	650,000
28. Indians. Danny Peoples, 1b	400,000
29. Devil Rays. Paul Wilder, of	650,000
30. Diamondbacks. Nick Bierbrodt, lhp	1,046,000

+ Declared free agent; signed with Diamondbacks
• Declared free agent; signed with Devil Rays

FIRST ROUND, 1994

Order. Player, Pos.	Bonus
1. Mets. Paul Wilson, rhp	$1,550,000
2. Athletics. Ben Grieve, of	1,200,000
3. Padres. Dustin Hermanson, rhp	960,000
4. Brewers. Antone Williamson, 3b	895,000
5. Marlins. Josh Booty, ss	1,600,000
6. Angels. McKay Christensen, of	700,000
7. Rockies. Doug Million, lhp	905,000
8. Twins. Todd Walker, 2b	815,000
9. Reds. C.J. Nitkowski, lhp	675,000
10. Indians. Jaret Wright, rhp	1,150,000
11. Pirates. Mark Farris, ss	820,000
12. Red Sox. Nomar Garciaparra, ss	895,000
13. Dodgers. Paul Konerko, c	830,000
14. Mariners. *Jason Varitek, c	650,000
15. Cubs. Jayson Peterson, rhp	712,500
16. Royals. Matt Smith, lhp/1b	1,000,000
17. Astros. Ramon Castro, c	450,000
18. Tigers. Cade Gaspar, rhp	825,000
19. Cardinals. Bret Wagner, lhp	525,000
20. Mets. Terrence Long, 1b/of	500,000
21. Expos. Hiram Bocachica, ss	635,000
22. Giants. Dante Powell, of	507,500
23. Phillies. Carlton Loewer, rhp	590,000
24. Yankees. Brian Buchanan, 1b/of	500,000
25. Astros. Scott Elarton, rhp	750,000
26. White Sox. Mark Johnson, c	520,000
27. Braves. Jacob Shumate, rhp	500,000
28. Blue Jays. Kevin Witt, ss	470,000

Signing Bonuses 1990-93

FIRST ROUND, 1993

Order. Player, Pos.	Bonus
1. # Mariners. Alex Rodriguez, ss	$1,000,000
2. Dodgers. Darren Dreifort, rhp	1,300,000
3. Angels. Brian Anderson, lhp	680,000
4. Phillies. Wayne Gomes, rhp	750,000
5. Royals. Jeff Granger, lhp	695,000
6. Giants. Steve Soderstrom, rhp	750,000
7. Red Sox. Trot Nixon, of	890,000
8. Mets. Kirk Presley, rhp	900,000
9. Tigers. Matt Brunson, ss	800,000
10. Cubs. Brooks Kieschnick, 1b/of	650,000
11. Indians. Daron Kirkreit, rhp	600,000
12. Astros. Billy Wagner, lhp	550,000
13. Yankees. Matt Drews, rhp	620,000
14. Padres. Derrek Lee, 1b	600,000
15. Blue Jays. Chris Carpenter, rhp	580,000
16. Cardinals. Alan Benes, rhp	500,000
17. White Sox. Scott Christman, lhp	450,000
18. Expos. Chris Schwab, of	425,000
19. Orioles. Jay Powell, rhp	492,000
20. Twins. Torii Hunter, of	450,000
21. Twins. Jason Varitek, c	Did Not Sign
22. Pirates. Charles Peterson, of	420,000
23. Brewers. Jeff D'Amico, rhp	525,000
24. Cubs. Jon Ratliff, rhp	355,000
25. Athletics. John Wasdin, rhp	365,000
26. Brewers. Kelly Wunsch, lhp	400,000
27. Marlins. Marc Valdes, rhp	410,000
28. Rockies. Jamey Wright, rhp	395,000

FIRST ROUND, 1992

Order. Player, Pos.	Bonus
1. Astros. Phil Nevin, 3b	$700,000
2. Indians. Paul Shuey, rhp	650,000
3. Expos. B.J. Wallace, lhp	550,000
4. Orioles. Jeffrey Hammonds, of	975,000
5. Reds. Chad Mottola, of	400,000
6. Yankees. Derek Jeter, ss	700,000
7. Giants. Calvin Murray, of	825,000
8. Angels. Pete Janicki, rhp	90,000
9. Mets. Preston Wilson, of	500,000
10. Royals. Michael Tucker, ss	450,000
11. Cubs. Derek Wallace, rhp	550,000
12. Brewers. Kenny Felder, of	525,000
13. Phillies. Chad McConnell, of	475,000
14. Mariners. Ron Villone, lhp	550,000
15. Cardinals. Sean Lowe, rhp	300,000
16. Tigers. Rick Greene, rhp	470,000
17. Royals. Jim Pittsley, rhp	410,000
18. Mets. Chris Roberts, lhp	365,000
19. Blue Jays. Shannon Stewart, of	450,000
20. Athletics. Benji Grigsby, rhp	380,000
21. Braves. Jamie Arnold, rhp	380,000
22. Rangers. Rick Helling, rhp	397,000
23. Pirates. Jason Kendall, c	336,000
24. White Sox. Eddie Pearson, 1b	354,000
25. Blue Jays. Todd Steverson, of	450,000
26. Twins. Dan Serafini, lhp	350,000
27. Rockies. John Burke, rhp	336,000
28. Marlins. Charles Johnson, c	575,000

FIRST ROUND, 1991

Order. Player, Pos.	Bonus
1. Yankees. Brien Taylor, lhp	$1,550,000
2. Braves. Mike Kelly, of	575,000
3. Twins. David McCarty, 1b	395,000
4. Cardinals. Dmitri Young, 3b	385,000
5. Brewers. Kenny Henderson, rhp	Did Not Sign
6. Astros. John Burke, rhp	Did Not Sign
7. Royals. Joe Vitiello, 1b-of	345,000
8. Padres. Joey Hamilton, rhp	385,000
9. Orioles. Mark Smith, of	350,000
10. Phillies. Tyler Green, rhp	325,000
11. Mariners. Shawn Estes, lhp	332,500
12. Cubs. Doug Glanville, of	325,000
13. Indians. Manny Ramirez, of	257,000
14. Expos. Cliff Floyd, 1b	290,000
15. Brewers. Tyrone Hill, lhp	280,000
16. Blue Jays. Shawn Green, of	725,000
17. Angels. Eduardo Perez, 1b	250,000
18. Mets. Al Shirley, of	245,000
19. Rangers. Benji Gil, ss	310,000
20. Reds. Pokey Reese, ss	200,000
21. Cardinals. Allen Watson, lhp	225,000
22. Cardinals. Brian Barber, rhp	200,000
23. Red Sox. Aaron Sele, rhp	210,000
24. Pirates. Jon Farrell, c/of	220,000
25. White Sox. Scott Ruffcorn, rhp	185,000
26. Athletics. Brent Gates, ss	205,000

FIRST ROUND, 1990 DRAFT

Order. Player, Pos.	Bonus
1. Braves. Chipper Jones, ss	$275,000
2. Tigers. Tony Clark, of	500,000
3. Phillies. Mike Lieberthal, c	225,000
4. White Sox. Alex Fernandez, rhp	350,000
5. Pirates. Kurt Miller, rhp	232,000
6. Mariners. Marc Newfield, of	220,000
7. Reds. Dan Wilson, c	220,000
8. Indians. Tim Costo, ss	300,000
9. Dodgers. Ron Walden, lhp	215,000
10. Yankees. Carl Everett, of	250,000
11. Expos. Shane Andrews, 3b	175,000
12. Twins. Todd Ritchie, rhp	252,500
13. Cardinals. Donovan Osborne, lhp	240,000
14. # Athletics. Todd Van Poppel, rhp	500,000
15. Giants. Adam Hyzdu, of	250,000
16. Rangers. Dan Smith, lhp	220,000
17. Mets. Jeromy Burnitz, of	192,500
18. Cardinals. Aaron Holbert, ss	195,000
19. Giants. Eric Christopherson, c	175,000
20. Orioles. Mike Mussina, rhp	225,000
21. Astros. Tom Nevers, ss	250,000
22. Blue Jays. Steve Karsay, rhp	180,000
23. Cubs. Lance Dickson, lhp	180,000
24. Expos. Rondell White, of	175,000
25. Padres. Robbie Beckett, lhp	175,000
26. Athletics. Don Peters, rhp	175,000

Minor League Top 20s

A s a complement to our organizational prospect rankings, Baseball America also ranks prospects in every minor league immediately after the season. Like the organizational lists, they place more weight on potential than present performance and should not be regarded as minor league all-star teams.

The league lists do differ a little bit from the organizational lists, which are taken more from a scouting perspective. The league lists are based on conversations with league managers. It is not strictly a poll, though we do try to talk with every manager. Some players on these lists, such as Adam Dunn and Bud Smith, are not eligible for our organization prospect lists because they are no longer rookie-eligible. Such players are indicated with an asterisk (*). Players who have been traded from the organizations they are listed with are indicated with a pound (#).

Remember that managers and scouts tend to look at players differently. Managers give more weight to what a player does on the field, while scouts look at what a player might eventually do. We think both perspectives are useful, so we give you both even though they don't always jibe with each other.

For a player to qualify for a league prospect list, he must have spent at least one-third of the season in a league. Position players must have one plate appearance per league game. In other words, for a league that plays 140 games, a player is eligible if he has at least 140 plate appearances. Pitchers must pitch ⅓ inning per league game. Relievers must make at least 20 appearances in a full-season league or 10 appearances in a short-season league.

TRIPLE-A

INTERNATIONAL LEAGUE

1. *Adam Dunn, of, Louisville (Reds)
2. *Toby Hall, c, Durham (Devil Rays)
3. *Felipe Lopez, ss/3b, Syracuse (Blue Jays)
4. Nick Johnson, 1b, Columbus (Yankees)
5. *Brandon Duckworth, rhp, Scranton/Wilkes-Barre (Phillies)
6. Tim Spooneybarger, rhp, Richmond (Braves)
7. #Alex Escobar, of, Norfolk (Mets)
8. Erick Almonte, ss, Columbus (Yankees)
9. Juan Rivera, of, Columbus (Yankees)
10. *#Cesar Izturis, ss/2b, Syracuse (Blue Jays)
11. Joe Crede, 3b, Charlotte (White Sox)
12. *Vernon Wells, of, Syracuse (Blue Jays)
13. Aaron Rowand, of, Charlotte (White Sox)
14. Drew Henson, 3b, Columbus (Yankees)
15. *Marcus Giles, 2b, Richmond (Braves)
16. Eric Valent, of, Scranton/Wilkes-Barre (Phillies)
17. *Dave Coggin, rhp, Scranton/Wilkes-Barre (Phillies)
18. *Brian Roberts, ss, Rochester (Orioles)
19. Orlando Hudson, 2b, Syracuse (Blue Jays)
20. Brad Wilkerson, of, Ottawa (Expos)

PACIFIC COAST LEAGUE

1. Sean Burroughs, 3b, Portland (Padres)
2. #Carlos Pena, 1b, Oklahoma (Rangers)
3. *Corey Patterson, of, Iowa (Cubs)
4. *Bud Smith, lhp, Memphis (Cardinals)
5. *Juan Uribe, ss, Colorado Springs (Rockies)
6. *Chris George, lhp, Omaha (Royals)
7. #Ramon Vazquez, ss, Tacoma (Mariners)
8. Kurt Ainsworth, rhp, Fresno (Giants)
9. *#Tony McKnight, rhp, New Orleans (Astros)
10. *Joel Pineiro, rhp, Tacoma (Mariners)
11. Carlos Zambrano, rhp, Iowa (Cubs)
12. Morgan Ensberg, 3b, New Orleans (Astros)
13. #Denny Stark, rhp, Tacoma (Mariners)
14. Hee Seop Choi, 1b, Iowa (Cubs)
15. Joaquin Benoit, rhp, Oklahoma (Rangers)
16. #Ryan Vogelsong, rhp, Fresno (Giants)
17. #Mario Ramos, lhp, Sacramento (Athletics)
18. #Jack Cust, of, Tucson (Diamondbacks)
19. Tony Torcato, of, Fresno (Giants)
20. *Cesar Crespo, util, Portland (Padres)

DOUBLE-A

EASTERN LEAGUE

1. Josh Beckett, rhp, Portland (Marlins)
2. Marlon Byrd, of, Reading (Phillies)
3. Nate Cornejo, rhp, Erie (Tigers)
4. Michael Cuddyer, 3b/1b, New Britain (Twins)
5. Brad Thomas, lhp, New Britain (Tigers)
6. Juan Rivera, of, Norwich (Yankees)
7. Brandon Claussen, lhp, Norwich (Yankees)
8. Marcus Thames, of, Norwich (Yankees)
9. Juan Rincon, rhp, New Britain (Twins)
10. Omar Infante, ss, Erie (Tigers)
11. Michael Restovich, of, New Britain (Twins)
12. Brandon Phillips, ss, Harrisburg (Expos)
13. #Luis Pineda, rhp, Erie (Tigers)
14. Casey Fossum, lhp, Trenton (Red Sox)
15. Mike Rivera, c, Erie (Tigers)
16. Ryan Drese, rhp, Akron (Indians)
17. Carlos Silva, rhp, Reading (Phillies)
18. John Stephens, rhp, Bowie (Orioles)
19. Abraham Nunez, of, Portland (Marlins)
20. Robert Stratton, of, Binghamton (Mets)

SOUTHERN LEAGUE

1. *Adam Dunn, of, Chattanooga (Reds)
2. Nick Neugebauer, rhp, Huntsville (Brewers)
3. Wilson Betemit, ss, Greenville (Braves)
4. *Joe Kennedy, lhp, Orlando (Devil Rays)
5. Joe Borchard, of, Birmingham (White Sox)
6. Dennis Tankersley, rhp, Mobile (Padres)
7. Juan Cruz, rhp, West Tennessee (Cubs)
8. *Danny Wright, rhp, Birmingham (White Sox)
9. Josh Phelps, c, Tennessee (Blue Jays)
10. Carl Crawford, of, Orlando (Devil Rays)
11. Orlando Hudson, 2b, Tennessee (Blue Jays)
12. Dave Kelton, 3b, West Tennessee (Cubs)
13. Matt Guerrier, rhp, Birmingham (White Sox)
14. Jorge Cantu, ss, Orlando (Devil Rays)
15. Ben Broussard, 1b, Chattanooga (Reds)
16. Chin-Feng Chen, of, Jacksonville (Dodgers)
17. Bobby Hill, 2b, West Tennessee (Cubs)
18. Reed Johnson, of, Tennessee (Blue Jays)
19. Scott Chiasson, rhp, West Tennessee (Cubs)
20. Austin Kearns, of, Chattanooga (Reds)

TEXAS LEAGUE

1. Hank Blalock, 3b, Tulsa (Rangers)
2. *Tim Redding, rhp, Round Rock (Astros)
3. Carlos Hernandez, lhp, Round Rock (Astros)
4. Rafael Soriano, rhp, San Antonio (Mariners)
5. Jeff Heaverlo, rhp, San Antonio (Mariners)
6. #Mario Ramos, lhp, Midland (Athletics)
7. Angel Berroa, ss, Wichita (Royals)
8. Lyle Overbay, 1b, El Paso (Diamondbacks)
9. Ken Harvey, 1b, Wichita (Royals)
10. Jason Lane, of, Round Rock (Astros)
11. Nathan Haynes, of, Arkansas (Angels)
12. Jerome Williams, rhp, Shreveport (Giants)
13. #Ryan Ludwick, of, Midland (Athletics)
14. John Lackey, rhp, Arkansas (Angels)
15. Alfredo Amezaga, ss, Arkansas (Angels)
16. Jose Valverde, rhp, El Paso (Diamondbacks)
17. Kenny Kelly, of, San Antonio (Mariners)
18. Wilfredo Rodriguez, lhp, Round Rock (Astros)
19. Mike Tonis, c, Wichita (Royals)
20. Tom Shearn, rhp, Round Rock (Astros)

HIGH CLASS A
CALIFORNIA LEAGUE

1. Dennis Tankersley, rhp, Lake Elsinore (Padres)
2. Xavier Nady, 1b, Lake Elsinore (Padres)
3. Rafael Soriano, rhp, San Bernardino (Mariners)
4. Chris Snelling, of, San Bernardino (Mariners)
5. Jake Peavy, rhp, Lake Elsinore (Padres)
6. Jamal Strong, of, San Bernardino (Mariners)
7. Ryan Christianson, c, San Bernardino (Mariners)
8. Ben Howard, rhp, Lake Elsinore (Padres)
9. Bill Hall, ss, High Desert (Brewers)
10. Chris Bootcheck, rhp, Rancho Cucamonga (Angels)
11. Matt Thornton, lhp, San Bernardino (Mariners)
12. Tony Torcato, of, San Jose (Giants)
13. Rainer Olmedo, ss, Mudville (Reds)
14. Freddie Bynum, ss, Modesto (Athletics)
15. David Krynzel, of, High Desert (Brewers)
16. Ben Johnson, of, Lake Elsinore (Padres)
17. Dane Sardinha, c, Mudville (Reds)
18. Eric Cyr, lhp, Lake Elsinore (Padres)
19. Mike O'Keefe, of, Rancho Cucamonga (Angels)
20. Craig Anderson, lhp, San Bernardino (Mariners)

CAROLINA LEAGUE

1. Wilson Betemit, ss, Myrtle Beach (Braves)
2. Jimmy Journell, rhp, Potomac (Cardinals)
3. Angel Berroa, ss, Wilmington (Royals)
4. Ryan Kibler, rhp, Salem (Rockies)
5. Chris Narveson, lhp, Potomac (Cardinals)
6. Brett Evert, rhp, Myrtle Beach (Braves)
7. Bobby Bradley, rhp, Lynchburg (Pirates)
8. Jimmy Gobble, lhp, Wilmington (Royals)
9. Jason Young, rhp, Salem (Rockies)
10. Victor Martinez, c, Kinston (Indians)
11. Ken Harvey, 1b, Wilmington (Royals)
12. Ed Rogers, ss, Frederick (Orioles)
13. Blake Williams, rhp, Potomac (Cardinals)
14. Alex Herrera, lhp, Kinston (Indians)
15. Jung Bong, lhp, Myrtle Beach (Braves)
16. Erik Bedard, lhp, Frederick (Orioles)
17. Shane Wallace, lhp, Kinston (Indians)
18. Trey Hodges, rhp, Myrtle Beach (Braves)
19. Brian Tallet, lhp, Kinston (Indians)
20. Covelli Crisp, of, Potomac (Cardinals)

FLORIDA STATE LEAGUE

1. Josh Beckett, rhp, Brevard County (Marlins)
2. Hank Blalock, 3b, Charlotte (Rangers)
3. Brandon Phillips, ss, Jupiter (Expos)
4. Nic Jackson, of, Daytona (Cubs)
5. Ricardo Rodriguez, rhp, Vero Beach (Dodgers)
6. Justin Morneau, 1b, Fort Myers (Twins)
7. Brandon Claussen, lhp, Tampa (Yankees)
8. #Billy Traber, lhp, St. Lucie (Mets)
9. Ryan Dittfurth, rhp, Charlotte (Rangers)
10. #Miguel Ascencio, rhp, Clearwater (Phillies)
11. Anderson Machado, ss, Clearwater (Phillies)
12. Seung Song, rhp, Sarasota (Red Sox)
13. Gabe Gross, of, Dunedin (Blue Jays)
14. Wilkin Ruan, of, Jupiter (Expos)
15. Chase Utley, 2b, Clearwater (Phillies)
16. Greg Montalbano, lhp, Sarasota (Red Sox)
17. Freddy Sanchez, ss, Sarasota (Red Sox)
18. Mitch Jones, of, Tampa (Yankees)
19. #Luis Garcia, 1b, Sarasota (Red Sox)
20. Nick Regilio, rhp, Charlotte (Rangers)

LOW CLASS A
MIDWEST LEAGUE

1. Adrian Gonzalez, 1b, Kane County (Marlins)
2. Justin Morneau, 1b, Quad City (Twins)
3. Wily Mo Pena, of, Dayton (Reds)
4. Clint Nageotte, rhp, Wisconsin (Mariners)
5. Chris Narveson, lhp, Peoria (Cardinals)
6. #Garett Gentry, c, Michigan (Astros)
7. Jamal Strong, of, Wisconsin (Mariners)
8. Chris Burke, ss, Michigan (Astros)
9. Miguel Cabrera, ss, Kane County (Marlins)
10. Grady Sizemore, of, Clinton (Expos)
11. David Espinosa, ss, Dayton (Reds)
12. Will Smith, of, Kane County (Marlins)
13. Chad Qualls, rhp, Michigan (Astros)
14. Aaron Taylor, rhp, Wisconsin (Mariners)
15. Ben Hendrickson, rhp, Beloit (Brewers)
16. Beltran Perez, rhp, South Bend (Diamondbacks)
17. Jose Cueto, rhp, Lansing (Cubs)
18. Oliver Perez, lhp, Fort Wayne (Padres)
19. Josh Hall, rhp, Dayton (Reds)
20. Todd Wellemeyer, rhp, Lansing (Cubs)

SOUTH ATLANTIC LEAGUE

1. Boof Bonser, rhp, Hagerstown (Giants)
2. Jose Reyes, ss, Capital City (Mets)
3. Adam Wainwright, rhp, Macon (Braves)
4. Corwin Malone, lhp, Kannapolis (White Sox)
5. Kelly Johnson, ss, Macon (Braves)
6. Corey Smith, 3b, Columbus (Indians)
7. Seung Song, rhp, Augusta (Red Sox)
8. Anthony Pluta, rhp, Lexington (Astros)
9. Tony Blanco, 3b, Augusta (Red Sox)
10. Ben Kozlowski, lhp, Macon (Braves)
11. David Martinez, lhp, Greensboro (Yankees)
12. Guillermo Reyes, ss, Kannapolis (White Sox)
13. Sean Burnett, lhp, Hickory (Pirates)
14. #Rich Rundles, lhp, Augusta (Red Sox)
15. Taylor Buchholz, rhp, Lakewood (Phillies)
16. Mike Nannini, rhp, Lexington (Astros)
17. Ben Diggins, rhp, Wilmington (Dodgers)
18. Seth McClung, rhp, Charleston, S.C. (Devil Rays)
19. Koyie Hill, c, Wilmington (Dodgers)
20. Rocco Baldelli, of, Charleston, S.C. (Devil Rays)

SHORT-SEASON

NEW YORK-PENN LEAGUE

1. John VanBenschoten, rhp/dh, Williamsport (Pirates)
2. Sean Henn, lhp, Staten Island (Yankees)
3. Jason Arnold, rhp, Staten Island (Yankees)
4. Juan Francia, 2b, Oneonta (Tigers)
5. Denny Bautista, rhp, Utica (Marlins)
6. John-Ford Griffin, of, Staten Island (Yankees)
7. Zach Miner, rhp, Jamestown (Braves)
8. Dustin McGowan, rhp, Auburn (Blue Jays)
9. Tyrell Godwin, of, Auburn (Blue Jays)
10. Domingo Cuello, 2b, Williamsport (Pirates)
11. Justin Pope, rhp, New Jersey (Cardinals)
12. Ryan Raburn, 3b, Oneonta (Tigers)
13. Chris Flinn, rhp, Hudson Valley (Devil Rays)
14. Angel Pagan, of, Brooklyn (Mets)
15. Jason Stokes, of, Utica (Marlins)
16. Luz Portobanco, rhp, Brooklyn (Mets)
17. Tony Pena Jr., ss, Jamestown (Braves)
18. Charlton Jimerson, of, Pittsfield (Astros)
19. Aaron Rifkin, 1b, Staten Island (Yankees)
20. Juan Camacho, 3b, Staten Island (Yankees)

NORTHWEST LEAGUE

1. J.J. Johnson, of, Boise (Cubs)
2. Jesse Foppert, rhp, Salem-Keizer (Giants)
3. Julian Benavidez, 3b, Salem-Keizer (Giants)
4. Angel Guzman, rhp, Boise (Cubs)
5. Jake Gautreau, 3b, Eugene (Padres)
6. Dontrelle Willis, lhp, Boise (Cubs)
7. Corey Slavik, 3b, Boise (Cubs)
8. Matt Allegra, of, Vancouver (Athletics)
9. Jason Bartlett, ss, Eugene (Padres)
10. Jose Lopez, ss, Everett (Mariners)
11. #Condor Cash, of, Boise (Cubs)
12. Tim Merritt, 2b/ss, Everett (Mariners)
13. Justin Germano, rhp, Eugene (Padres)
14. Brad Hennessey, rhp, Salem-Keizer (Giants)
15. Gustavo Martinez, rhp, Everett (Mariners)
16. Rich Harden, rhp, Vancouver (Athletics)
17. Jorge Sosa, rhp, Everett (Mariners)
18. Travis Blackley, lhp, Everett (Mariners)
19. Keto Anderson, of, Boise (Cubs)
20. Kip Bouknight, rhp, Tri-City (Rockies)

ROOKIE

APPALACHIAN LEAGUE

1. Joe Mauer, c, Elizabethton (Twins)
2. Dan Denham, rhp, Burlington (Indians)
3. Jason Bourgeois, 2b, Pulaski (Rangers)
4. J.D. Martin, rhp, Burlington (Indians)
5. Bryan Digby, rhp, Danville (Braves)
6. Kris Honel, rhp, Bristol (White Sox)
7. Sandy Tejada, rhp, Elizabethton (Twins)
8. Rashad Eldridge, of, Burlington (Indians)
9. David Wright, 3b, Kingsport (Mets)
10. Jonny Gomes, of, Princeton (Devil Rays)
11. Toe Nash, of, Princeton (Devil Rays)
12. Justin Woodrow, of, Johnson City (Cardinals)
13. Justin Huber, c, Kingsport (Mets)
14. Scott Heard, c, Pulaski (Rangers)
15. Travis Foley, rhp, Burlington (Indians)
16. Yadier Molina, c, Johnson City (Cardinals)
17. Omar Rogers, 2b, Bluefield (Orioles)
18. C.J. Wilson, lhp, Pulaski (Rangers)
19. D.J. Houlton, rhp, Martinsville (Astros)
20. Brayan Pena, c, Danville (Braves)

ARIZONA LEAGUE

1. Chris Tritle, of, Athletics
2. Shin-Soo Choo, of, Mariners
3. Andy Gonzalez, ss, White Sox
4. Ryan Hannaman, lhp, Giants
5. Ronny Cedeno, ss, Cubs
6. Johan Santana, rhp, Angels
7. Anthony Webster, of, White Sox
8. Francisco Liriano, lhp, Giants
9. Leonel Cabrera, 2b, Giants
10. Pedro Esparragoza, c, Brewers
11. Bryan Simmering, rhp, Athletics
12. Alejandro Cadena, dh, Mariners
13. Aaron Kirkland, rhp, White Sox
14. Rene Rivera, c, Mariners
15. Andy Sisco, lhp, Cubs
16. Austin Nagle, of, Athletics
17. Emiliano Fruto, lhp, Mariners
18. Chris Collins, 3b, Mariners
19. Kory Wayment, ss, Athletics
20. Jimbo McAuliff, of, Giants

GULF COAST LEAGUE

1. Chad Petty, lhp, Tigers
2. Anderson Hernandez, ss, Tigers
3. Bronson Sardinha, ss, Yankees
4. Manny Delcarmen, rhp, Red Sox
5. Carlos Duran, of, Braves
6. Josh Thigpen, rhp, Red Sox
7. Victor Diaz, 2b, Dodgers
8. Ezequiel Astacio, rhp, Phillies
9. Gonzalo Lopez, rhp, Braves
10. Alan Moye, of, Reds
11. Carlos Rodriguez, ss, Phillies
12. Matt Cooper, 1b, Red Sox
13. Kole Strayhorn, rhp, Dodgers
14. Bryan Bass, ss, Orioles
15. Juan Gonzalez, 3b, Tigers
16. Jose Dominguez, rhp, Rangers
17. Allen Baxter, rhp, Marlins
18. Josh Burrus, ss, Braves
19. Alex Santa, of, Yankees
20. Elvin Andujar, of, Reds

PIONEER LEAGUE

1. Mike Jones, rhp, Ogden (Brewers)
2. Jesus Cota, 1b, Missoula (Diamondbacks)
3. Josh Barfield, 2b, Idaho Falls (Padres)
4. Brandon League, rhp, Medicine Hat (Blue Jays)
5. Dallas McPherson, 3b, Provo (Angels)
6. Jose Diaz, c, Great Falls (Dodgers)
7. Scott Hairston, 2b, Missoula (Diamondbacks)
8. Jose Garcia, of, Great Falls (Dodgers)
9. Jon Steitz, rhp, Ogden (Brewers)
10. J.J. Hardy, ss, Ogden (Brewers)
11. Corby Medlin, rhp, Missoula (Diamondbacks)
12. William Bergolla, 2b/ss, Billings (Reds)
13. Jeff Mathis, c, Provo (Angels)
14. Jayson Nix, ss, Casper (Rockies)
15. Michael Keirstead, rhp, Great Falls (Dodgers)
16. Gary Varner, of, Billings (Reds)
17. Edwin Encarnacion, 3b, Billings (Reds)
18. Clinton Hosford, rhp, Great Falls (Dodgers)
19. Corey Hart, 1b, Ogden (Brewers)
20. Mark O'Sullivan, rhp, Provo (Angels)

Index

Dawkins, Gookie (Reds) 125
Day, Zach (Expos) 275
Deardorff, Jeff (Brewers) 250
DeCaster, Yurendell (Pirates) 355
DeChristofaro, Vinny (Phillies) 340
DeHaan, Kory (Padres) 387
DeHart, Casey (Reds) 132
De la Rosa, Jorge (Red Sox) 84
Delcarmen, Manny (Red Sox) 78
DeLeon, Joey (Astros) 207
De los Santos, Pedro (Padres) 387
Denham, Dan (Indians) 139
DePaula, Julio (Yankees) 310
Deschaine, Jim (Blue Jays) 459
Devore, Doug (Diamondbacks) 39
Diaz, Alejandro (Reds) 129
Diaz, Felix (Giants) 394
Diaz, Jose (Dodgers) 236
Diaz, Juan (Red Sox) 82
Diaz, Victor (Dodgers) 236
Digby, Bryan (Braves) 52
Diggins, Ben (Dodgers) 228
DiNardo, Lenny (Mets) 295
Dittfurth, Ryan (Rangers) 439
Dominguez, Jose (Rangers) 442
Donovan, Todd (Padres) 388
Douglass, Sean (Orioles) 64
Doumit, Ryan (Pirates) 353
Drese, Ryan (Indians) 138
Drew, Tim (Indians) 142
Duffy, Chris (Pirates) 355
Dumatrait, Phil (Red Sox) 80
Duncan, Chris (Cardinals) 366
Duncan, Courtney (Cubs) 101
Duran, Carlos (Braves) 49
Durbin, J.D. (Twins) 262
Duchscherer, Justin (Rangers) 445

E

Eberwein, Kevin (Padres) 383
Eckenstahler, Eric (Tigers) 177
Ellis, Mark (Athletics) 319
Encarnacion, Edwin (Reds) 127
Encarnacion, Mario (Rockies) 162
Enochs, Chris (Athletics) 323
Ensberg, Morgan (Astros) 200
Escalona, Felix (Giants) 398
Escobar, Alex (Indians) 138
Espinosa, David (Reds) 125
Esslinger, Cam (Rockies) 157
Evans, Kyle (Indians) 147
Everett, Adam (Astros) 202
Evert, Brett (Braves) 48

F

Faison, Vince (Padres) 385
Farnsworth, Jeff (Tigers) 176
Ferrara, Matt (Royals) 221
Ferrari, Anthony (Expos) 283
Fikac, Jeremy (Padres) 383
Fischer, Rich (Angels) 27
Flinn, Chris (Devil Rays) 428
Floyd, Gavin (Phillies) 333
Fogg, Josh (Pirates) 353
Fontenot, Mike (Orioles) 67
Foppert, Jesse (Giants) 394
Ford, Matt (Blue Jays) 459
Fossum, Casey (Red Sox) 79
Foster, Kris (Orioles) 71
Francisco, Franklin (Red Sox) 81
Frederick, Kevin (Twins) 263

Freeman, Choo (Rockies) 158
Frick, Mike (Athletics) 325
Fuentes, Brian (Rockies) 159

G

Gall, John (Cardinals) 371
Galva, Claudio (Athletics) 326
Gamble, Jerome (Red Sox) 88
Garabito, Eddy (Orioles) 73
Garbe, B.J. (Twins) 264
Garcia, Angel (Twins) 263
Garcia, Carlos (Dodgers) 236
Garcia, Jose (Dodgers) 237
Garcia, Lino (Diamondbacks) 35
Garcia, Luis (Cardinals) 363
Garcia, Reynaldo (Rangers) 447
Garciaparra, Michael (Mariners) 414
Gautreau, Jake (Padres) 380
Gentry, Garett (Rockies) 158
George, Trey (Rockies) 160
German, Esteban (Athletics) 319
German, Franklyn (Athletics) 321
German, Ramon (Astros) 202
Germano, Justin (Padres) 385
Gettis, Byron (Royals) 222
Gil, David (Reds) 130
Gil, Jerry (Diamondbacks) 40
Gillman, Justin (Reds) 127
Ginter, Keith (Astros) 204
Ginter, Matt (White Sox) 112
Girdley, Josh (Expos) 277
Gobble, Jimmy (Royals) 213
Godwin, Tyrell (Blue Jays) 456
Goetz, Geoff (Marlins) 190
Gold, J.M. (Brewers) 245
Gomes, Jonny (Devil Rays) 427
Gomez, Alexis (Royals) 218
Gomon, Dusty (Twins) 265
Gonzalez, Andy (White Sox) 114
Gonzalez, Adrian (Marlins) 183
Gonzalez, Mike (Pirates) 358
Good, Eric (Expos) 276
Gosling, Mike (Diamondbacks) 33
Grabow, John (Pirates) 354
Gracesqui, Franklyn (Blue Jays) 460
Graman, Alex (Yankees) 307
Gray, Josh (Angels) 23
Gredvig, Doug (Orioles) 67
Green, Andy (Diamondbacks) 43
Green, Steve (Angels) 24
Griffin, Colt (Royals) 213
Griffin, John-Ford (Yankees) 304
Griffiths, Jeremy (Mets) 297
Grilli, Jason (Marlins) 191
Gripp, Ryan (Cubs) 102
Gross, Gabe (Blue Jays) 453
Grove, Jason (Yankees) 312
Guerrero, Cristian (Brewers) 244
Guerrier, Matt (White Sox) 108
Guzman, Angel (Cubs) 97
Guzman, Elpidio (Angels) 26
Guzman, Joel (Dodgers) 228

H

Hafner, Travis (Rangers) 443
Hairston, Scott (Diamondbacks) 33
Hale, Beau (Orioles) 66
Hall, Bill (Brewers) 243
Hall, Victor (Diamondbacks) 42
Hamilton, Josh (Devil Rays) 422
Hammond, Derry (Brewers) 252

Hancock, Josh (Red Sox) 87
Hannahan, Jack (Tigers) 171
Hannaman, Ryan (Giants) 397
Hanrahan, Joel (Dodgers) 230
Harang, Aaron (Athletics) 323
Harden, Rich (Athletics) 325
Hardy, J.J. (Brewers) 245
Harvey, Ken (Royals) 215
Haren, Dan (Cardinals) 366
Harper, Travis (Devil Rays) 429
Harris, Willie (Orioles) 65
Hart, Bo (Cardinals) 373
Hart, Corey (Brewers) 248
Hart, Jason (Rangers) 441
Harville, Chad (Athletics) 318
Hawpe, Brad (Rockies) 162
Haynes, Nathan (Angels) 20
Heard, Scot (Rangers) 446
Heaverlo, Jeff (Mariners) 409
Heilman, Aaron (Mets) 287
Hendrickson, Ben (Brewers) 244
Henkel, Rob (Marlins) 186
Henn, Sean (Yankees) 304
Hennessey, Brad (Giants) 399
Henson, Drew (Yankees) 302
Hernandez, Adrian (Yankees) 307
Hernandez, Anderson (Tigers) 178
Hernandez, Carlos (Astros) 197
Hernandez, Runelvys (Royals) 216
Hernandez, Yoel (Phillies) 336
Herrera, Alex (Indians) 141
Hiles, Cary (Phillies) 343
Hill, Bobby (Cubs) 94
Hill, Jeremy (Royals) 218
Hill, Koyie (Dodgers) 231
Hill, Mike (Astros) 207
Hill, Shawn (Expos) 279
Hinckley, Mike (Expos) 282
Hinske, Eric (Blue Jays) 454
Hodges, Scott (Expos) 278
Hodges, Trey (Braves) 53
Holliday, Matt (Rockies) 156
Holt, Daylan (Athletics) 326
Honel, Kris (White Sox) 110
Hooper, Kevin (Marlins) 193
House, Craig (Mets) 295
House, J.R. (Pirates) 347
Howard, Ben (Padres) 379
Howard, Ryan (Phillies) 338
Howington, Ty (Reds) 123
Huang, Kevin (Red Sox) 83
Huber, Justin (Mets) 296
Hudson, Luke (Reds) 129
Hudson, Orlando (Blue Jays) 454
Hughes, Travis (Rangers) 446
Hummel, Tim (White Sox) 109
Hutchinson, Chad (Cardinals) 367
Hutchison, Wesley (Giants) 402

I

Infante, Omar (Tigers) 168
Izquierdo, Hansel (Marlins) 188
Izturis, Maicer (Indians) 145

J

Jackson, Nic (Cubs) 95
James, Delvin (Devil Rays) 426
Jamison, Ryan (Astros) 203
Jenkins, Neil (Tigers) 174
Jenks, Bobby (Angels) 18
Jennings, Jason (Rockies) 155

Pagan, Angel (Mets) 296
Paradis, Mike (Orioles) 71
Parker, Zach (Rockies) 161
Parrott, Rhett (Cardinals) 371
Pascucci, Val (Expos) 280
Patterson, John (Diamondbacks) 37
Pearce, Josh (Cardinals) 364
Peavy, Jacob (Padres) 378
Pena, Carlos (Athletics) 317
Pena, Juan (Athletics) 323
Pena, Juan (Red Sox) 85
Pena, Wily Mo (Reds) 123
Penney, Mike (Brewers) 251
Peralta, Joel (Angels) 27
Peralta, John (Indians) 144
Perez, Antonio (Mariners) 408
Perez, Beltran (Diamondbacks) 36
Perez, Henry (Padres) 388
Perez, Luis (Red Sox) 84
Perez, Oliver (Padres) 381
Petty, Chad (Tigers) 173
Phelps, Josh (Blue Jays) 452
Phillips, Brandon (Expos) 272
Phillips, Heath (White Sox) 117
Phillips, Jason (Mets) 294
Phillips, Mark (Padres) 379
Pierce, Sean (Dodgers) 235
Piersoll, Chris (Reds) 130
Pilkington, Brian (Dodgers) 232
Pineda, Luis (Reds) 130
Plasencia, Francisco (Brewers) 252
Pluta, Anthony (Astros) 199
Pope, Justin (Cardinals) 364
Porter, Greg (Angels) 26
Portobanco, Luz (Mets) 296
Pratt, Andy (Rangers) 442
Pridie, Jon (Twins) 265
Prior, Mark (Cubs) 92
Puello, Ignacio (Expos) 278
Puffer, Brandon (Astros) 208
Putz, J.J. (Mariners) 413

Q

Qualls, Chad (Astros) 200
Quintero, Humberto (White Sox) 116
Quiroz, Guillermo (Blue Jays) 463

R

Rabelo, Mike (Tigers) 175
Raburn, Johnny (Angels) 27
Raburn, Ryan (Tigers) 174
Raines Jr., Tim (Orioles) 65
Ramos, Mario (Rangers) 438
Randazzo, Jeff (Twins) 264
Ransom, Cody (Giants) 396
Rauch, Jon (White Sox) 108
Redman, Prentice (Mets) 298
Reed, Keith (Orioles) 63
Regilio, Nick (Rangers) 445
Reid, Justin (Pirates) 351
Reimers, Cameron (Blue Jays) 460
Reith, Brian (Reds) 127
Repko, Jason (Dodgers) 231
Requena, Alex (Indians) 143
Restovich, Michael (Twins) 258
Reyes, Guillermo (White Sox) 116
Reyes, Jose (Mets) 288
Reyes, Rene (Rockies) 155
Reynoso, Edison (Yankees) 309
Rheinecker, John (Athletics) 322
Richardson, Juan (Phillies) 340

Rifkin, Aaron (Yankees) 312
Riggan, Jerrod (Indians) 142
Riggans, Shawn (Devil Rays) 428
Riley, Matt (Orioles) 63
Rincon, Juan (Twins) 260
Rios, Alexis (Blue Jays) 455
Riske, David (Indians) 140
Rivera, Juan (Yankees) 304
Rivera, Luis (Orioles) 69
Rivera, Mike (Tigers) 172
Rivera, Rene (Mariners) 415
Rleal, Sendy (Orioles) 71
Roberts, Grant (Mets) 290
Roberts, Nick (Astros) 205
Rodney, Fernando (Tigers) 173
Rodriguez, Carlos (Phillies) 337
Rodriguez, Francisco (Angels) 20
Rodriguez, John (Yankees) 311
Rodriguez, Rafael (Angels) 22
Rodriguez, Ricardo (Dodgers) 227
Rodriguez, Wilfredo (Astros) 202
Rogers, Ed (Orioles) 64
Rogowski, Casey (White Sox) 113
Rojas, Jose (Dodgers) 230
Rolison, Nate (Marlins) 191
Roller, Adam (Yankees) 310
Romano, Jason (Rangers) 443
Roneberg, Brett (Marlins) 192
Rosamond, Mike (Astros) 207
Rosario, Rodrigo (Astros) 200
Ross, Cody (Tigers) 170
Rouse, Michael (Blue Jays) 461
Rowand, Aaron (White Sox) 111
Ruan, Wilkin (Expos) 277
Rundles, Rich (Expos) 275
Runser, Greg (Rangers) 448
Rushford, Jim (Brewers) 253
Russ, Chris (Rangers) 447
Ryu, Jae-Kuk (Cubs) 97

S

Saarloos, Kirk (Astros) 205
Sager, Brian (White Sox) 118
Sain, Greg (Padres) 386
Salazar, Oscar (Athletics) 327
Sanchez, Angel (Royals) 223
Sanchez, Felix (Cubs) 98
Sanchez, Freddy (Red Sox) 79
Santana, Johan (Angels) 21
Santiago, Ramon (Tigers) 169
Santos, Angel (Red Sox) 87
Santos, Chad (Royals) 220
Santos, Deivis (Royals) 400
Sardinha, Bronson (Yankees) 306
Sardinha, Dane (Reds) 126
Sato, G.G. (Phillies) 341
Scott, Bill (Brewers) 250
Seay, Bobby (Devil Rays) 426
Seddon, Chris (Devil Rays) 428
Seibel, Phil (Expos) 282
Seo, Jae Weong (Mets) 288
Serrano, Elio (Phillies) 340
Serrano, Wascar (Mariners) 416
Shaffar, Ben (Pirates) 357
Sharber, Jason (Pirates) 356
Shearn, Tom (Astros) 205
Shell, Steven (Angels) 23
Shibilo, Andy (Padres) 384
Shields, Jamie (Devil Rays) 432
Shields, Scot (Angels) 25
Shoppach, Kelly (Red Sox) 85
Silva, Carlos (Phillies) 335

Simpson, Allan (Mariners) 414
Simpson, Gerrit (Rockies) 161
Sisco, Andy (Cubs) 101
Sizemore, Grady (Expos) 273
Skaggs, Jon (Yankees) 308
Sledge, Terrmel (Expos) 280
Smith, Chris (Orioles) 67
Smith, Corey (Indians) 137
Smith, Hans (Devil Rays) 430
Smith, Jason (Devil Rays) 430
Smith, Matt (Yankees) 308
Smith, Mike (Blue Jays) 457
Smith, Will (Marlins) 188
Smitherman, Steve (Reds) 132
Smyth, Steve (Cubs) 96
Snare, Ryan (Reds) 126
Snelling, Chris (Mariners) 408
Snow, Bert (Athletics) 324
Snyder, Earl (Indians) 147
Snyder, Kyle (Royals) 215
Soler, Ramon (Devil Rays) 430
Song, Seung (Red Sox) 77
Sonnier, Shawn (Royals) 221
Sorensen, Zach (Indians) 146
Soriano, Rafael (Mariners) 408
Sosa, Jorge (Brewers) 249
Soto, Jose (Marlins) 190
Specht, Brian (Angels) 21
Spooneybarger, Tim (Braves) 51
Stahl, Richard (Orioles) 62
Standridge, Jason (Devil Rays) 425
Stanford, Jason (Indians) 146
Stark, Denny (Rockies) 157
Steitz, Jon (Brewers) 248
Stenson, Dernell (Red Sox) 84
Stephens, John (Orioles) 66
Stephenson, Eric (Blue Jays) 458
Stern, Adam (Braves) 56
Stiehl, Robert (Astros) 204
Stocks, Nick (Cardinals) 368
Stodolka, Mike (Royals) 217
Stokes, Jason (Marlins) 186
Strange, Pat (Mets) 288
Stratton, Robert (Mets) 298
Strayhorn, Kole (Dodgers) 234
Strong, Jamal (Mariners) 410
Stumm, Jason (White Sox) 113
Surkont, Keith (Athletics) 328
Sweeney, James (Rockies) 162
Switzer, Jon (Devil Rays) 427
Sylvester, Billy (Braves) 53

T

Taguchi, So (Cardinals) 364
Tallet, Brian (Indians) 140
Tankersley, Dennis (Padres) 378
Taveras, Willy (Indians) 141
Taylor, Aaron (Mariners) 412
Taylor, Reggie (Phillies) 343
Teixeira, Mark (Rangers) 438
Tejada, Robinson (Phillies) 340
Tejada, Sandy (Twins) 261
Terrero, Luis (Diamondbacks) 32
Thames, Marcus (Yankees) 305
Theriot, Ryan (Cubs) 101
Thigpen, Josh (Red Sox) 80
Thomas, Brad (Twins) 259
Thomas, John (Giants) 400
Thompson, Mat (Red Sox) 81
Thornton, Matt (Mariners) 411
Threets, Erick (Giants) 395
Thurman, Corey (Blue Jays) 462

Thurston, Joe (Dodgers)	229	Veras, Enger (Devil Rays)	431	Wilkerson, Brad (Expos)	273
Tierney, Chris (Royals)	221	Verplancke, Jeff (Giants)	396	Williams, Blake (Cardinals)	367
Tiffee, Terry (Twins)	267	Victorino, Shane (Dodgers)	233	Williams, Jerome (Giants)	392
Tonis, Mike (Royals)	215	Viera, Rolando (Red Sox)	86	Williams, Matt (Cardinals)	372
Torcato, Tony (Giants)	393	Villanueva, Florian (Brewers)	251	Willis, Dontrelle (Cubs)	100
Torres, Andres (Tigers)	169	Villarreal, Oscar (Diamondbacks)	37	Wilson, C.J. (Rangers)	447
Torres, Joe (Angels)	19	Vogelsong, Ryan (Pirates)	350	Wilson, Josh (Marlins)	185
Traber, Billy (Indians)	141	Voyles, Brad (Royals)	216	Wilson, Michael (Mariners)	413
Tracy, Chad (Diamondbacks)	39			Wilson, Phil (Angels)	23
Tritle, Chris (Athletics)	321			Wilson, Travis (Braves)	58
Tsao, Chin-Hui (Rockies)	152	**W**		Wolensky, David (Angels)	24
Tucker, T.J. (Expos)	278	Waechter, Doug (Devil Rays)	432	Wolfe, Brian (Twins)	265
Turnbow, Derrick (Angels)	22	Wainwright, Adam (Braves)	48	Wood, Mike (Athletics)	321
Tyler, Scott (Twins)	266	Walker, Adam (Mets)	295	Woodrow, Justin (Cardinals)	371
		Walker, Tyler (Mets)	293	Woods, Jake (Angels)	28
		Wallace, Shane (Indians)	144	Woods, Michael (Tigers)	172
U		Walter, Scott (Royals)	220	Woodyard, Mark (Tigers)	176
Ulacia, Dennis (White Sox)	111	Ward, Jeremy (Diamondbacks)	38	Wright, Chase (Yankees)	311
Utley, Chase (Phillies)	335	Warden, Jim Ed (Indians)	144	Wright, David (Mets)	289
		Washington, Rico (Pirates)	358	Wright, Gavin (Astros)	206
		Waters, Chris (Braves)	55	Wright, Matt (Braves)	54
V		Wathan, Derek (Marlins)	193	Wuertz, Mike (Cubs)	102
Valderrama, Carlos (Giants)	398	Watson, Brandon (Expos)	281	Wylie, Mitch (White Sox)	115
Valdez, Wilson (Expos)	281	Watson, Matt (Expos)	283		
Valent, Eric (Phillies)	335	Wayne, Justin (Expos)	274	**Y**	
Valentine, Joe (Tigers)	175	Webb, Brandon (Diamondbacks)	42	Yan, Edwin (Pirates)	357
Valenzuela, Mario (White Sox)	117	Webb, John (Cubs)	102	Yates, Tyler (Mets)	290
Valera, Luis (Reds)	131	Webster, Anthony (White Sox)	115	Yeatman, Matt (Brewers)	246
Valverde, Jose (Diamondbacks)	34	Wellemeyer, Todd (Cubs)	99	Yoshida, Nobuaki (Padres)	384
VanBenschoten, John (Pirates)	348	Werth, Jayson (Blue Jays)	453	Youkilis, Kevin (Red Sox)	88
Vance, Cory (Rockies)	158	West, Brian (White Sox)	112	Young, Chris (Pirates)	351
Van Dusen, Derrick (Mariners)	412	West, Todd (Brewers)	251	Young, Jason (Rockies)	154
Van Hekken, Andy (Tigers)	170	Weston, Aron (Pirates)	352		
Vargas, Claudio (Marlins)	185	Wheatland, Matt (Tigers)	171	**Z**	
Vargas, Martin (Indians)	145	White, Bill (Diamondbacks)	40		
Varner, Gary (Reds)	131	White, Matt (Devil Rays)	425	Zambrano, Carlos (Cubs)	94
Vasquez, Jose (Rockies)	159	Whiteman, Tommy (Astros)	201	Zamora, Pete (Phillies)	342
Vazquez, Ramon (Padres)	380	Whiteside, Eli (Orioles)	70		

ALL THROUGH 2002...

We know the Prospect Handbook has a valuable place on your bookshelf as the quintessential guide to baseball's brightest stars of tomorrow.

But what about all the exciting action—on and off the field—that takes place in the new year? From spring training to the World Series, including the most complete draft coverage anywhere (and don't forget statistics for every minor league team), Baseball America magazine is the best source for baseball information. Since 1981, BA has been finding the prospects and tracking them from the bushes to the big leagues. That means you get comprehensive reporting and commentary every step of the way.

Subscribing is easy and you'll save $32⁵⁵ off the cover price!

So join the team now to receive Baseball America every other week, and be the first to know about today's rising stars.

It's baseball news you can't get anywhere else.

you need Baseball America

baseballamerica.com